W9-COM-957

Zondervan

EXPOSITORY DICTIONARY OF BIBLE WORDS

Zondervan

EXPOSITORY DICTIONARY OF BIBLE WORDS

Lawrence O. Richards

ZondervanPublishingHouse
Academic and Professional Books
Grand Rapids, Michigan

A Division of HarperCollinsPublishers

ZONDERVAN EXPOSITORY DICTIONARY OF BIBLE WORDS
Copyright © 1985, 1991 by The Zondervan Corporation

Formerly published under the title *Expository Dictionary of Bible Words*

Requests for information should be addressed to:
Zondervan Publishing House
Academic and Professional Books
1415 Lake Drive S.E.
Grand Rapids, Michigan 49506

Library of Congress Cataloging-in-Publication Data

Richards, Larry, 1931–
    [Expository dictionary of Bible words]
    Zondervan expository dictionary of Bible words / Lawrence O.
Richards.
        p.   cm.
    Reprint. Originally published: Expository dictionary of Bible
words. Grand Rapids, Mich. : Regency Reference Library, c1985.
    Includes indexes.
    ISBN 0-310-57270-3 (alk. paper)
    1. Bible—Dictionaries. 2. Hebrew language—Dictionaries.
3. Greek language, Biblical—Dictionaries. I. Title.
[BS440.R525   1991]
220.3—dc20   91-17045
                                                                    CIP

Edited by Lyman Rand Tucker, Jr., and Gerard H. Terpstra
Interior Design by Louise Bauer
Jacket Design by Art Jacobs

Printed in the United States of America

91 92 93 94 95 / AM / 13 12 11 10 9

This edition is printed on acid-free paper and meets the American
National Standards Institute Z39.48 standard.

To my father

Vivian S. Richards

whose death from cancer
took place during the
writing of this book
and whose life displayed
in simple ways a commitment
to the Word of God, which
this book honors

Contents

Preface .... *ix*

How to Use This Dictionary .... *xiii*

Abbreviations for the Books of the Bible .... *xiv*

Transliterations... *xv*

Dictionary 1

Indexes.. 643

    Index of Hebrew Words 645

    Index of Greek Words 651

    Index of Subjects... 659

    Index of Scripture References................................. 681

Preface

The Bible is and remains God's Word to us, accessible in our own language. The original Hebrew and Greek texts have been translated into hundreds of different languages and into many different English versions. The translators of the Bible have attempted to express as clearly as possible the meaning of the original languages so that contemporary readers may understand the divine message.

It is important that we understand God's message. We live in a society cluttered by many visions of reality. Competing views of truth, of values, and of life's meaning all struggle for our allegiance. But in Scripture we can find an unclouded vision of reality, communicated to us by God Himself. In Scripture we can find the truth, and as we live out the truth we can know freedom. God's Word speaks to transform our perspective on reality, to reshape our attitudes and values, and to create in us a vital, new way of life.

The multiplication of versions has given us excellent translations that accurately capture the original message. But there are still problems for the typical reader of Scripture. Our problems are not with the versions so much as with ourselves. These problems can be summed up in the fact that when we read the Bible, we bring to it our own notions about the words used in Scripture. Rather than letting Scripture reshape our ideas, all too often our ideas are imposed on Scripture. When we read a word like "hope" or "judge" in the Bible, we frequently fail to read it *with the Bible's own meaning*. Instead, we read it with meanings shaped by our society and our personal experiences. Instead of being reshaped by the Bible's message, we ourselves reshape that message by imposing our meanings on it.

It is very important, then, that the Bible student read the Bible with an awareness of *what Bible terms mean, as they are used in the Bible*. This statement crystallizes the purpose of this *Expository Dictionary of Bible Words*. This book explores for the English reader the meaning of many important words as they are used in English versions of the Scriptures.

Two things are particularly important if we are to determine the meaning of Bible words. First, we must go back to the original languages to discover the Hebrew and Greek words that have been translated by certain English terms. This gives us the basic meaning of Bible words. But this is not enough. We must go beyond the usage of these words in the Hebrew and Greek culture and see how these words are used to develop or express a biblical concept. Often the use of a word in Scripture infuses it with new meaning. So in this *Expository Dictionary,* after the Hebrew and Greek words that underlie English terms are discussed, there is a discussion on how the original words are used in Scripture to build a distinctive biblical concept.

Because there are so many different versions of the Bible in English, it is necessary to narrow our focus; we will consider the two versions that are used most frequently in Bible study. These are the NIV and the NASB.

The NIV is especially acceptable to Evangelicals. This translation was undertaken by over a hundred scholars from many countries and various denominations. All of them were conservative in their commitment to the full authority and trustworthiness of Scripture as God's Word. The result of their years of work is an attractive, readable, and clear expression in contemporary English of the thought of the original Hebrew and Greek writings.

Translators face a number of problems. Many of these occur because single words in any language have more than single meanings. It is the task of Bible translators, therefore, to study the way a Hebrew or Greek term is used in particular sentences and to determine the shade of meaning intended in each context. Thus different English words or phrases are used to translate a single original term. Conversely, the same English word may be used to translate several different Hebrew or Greek terms.

None of the English versions provides a word-for-word translation, with the same English word always being used to translate the same Hebrew or Greek word. Instead, in varying degrees translators adopted a principle called dynamic equivalence. That is, they have attempted to ascertain the *meaning* (or connotation) of the word or phrase in the source language and to express that meaning in the receptor language. The more the translators of a given version relied on the use of dynamic equivalence, the more difficulty we can expect in tracing concepts from English back to specific Hebrew or Greek words.

How have the translators of different versions approached their task? The translators of the ASV attempted to translate word for word as much as possible. Ken Taylor's *Living Bible,* on the other hand, is a very loose paraphrase, shaped often by the translator's own interpretations. The NASB tends toward the approach of the ASV. The RSV and NIV fall between these extremes, though the translators of the NIV were more ready to seek dynamic equivalents than were the RSV translators.

The difference in approach to translation between NASB and NIV translators is partly responsible for the different treatment given the two versions in the book. More attention is given to the NIV because its translations are more complex. Also, at this writing there is an exhaustive NASB concordance that traces each English word to the original Hebrew or Greek. This kind of tool is not presently available for the NIV; therefore more data must be provided here for NIV readers.

A common goal, however, infuses the treatment given each word and each version. That goal is to help the Bible student *read the English Bible with an understanding of every significant concept expressed in English Bible words*. We want to clear our minds of meanings shaped—and often distorted—by the ways the words are used in Western culture. We want to read Bible words with a better understanding of their meaning *as that meaning is defined in Scripture itself*.

One final word is appropriate. This *Expository Dictionary of Bible Words* was not written because the author or publisher intended to add to scholarly knowledge in the field of original languages. In fact, the author relied on the knowledge of various scholars (whose writings are found in a number of modern and older works) and on a variety of studies of various concepts (e.g., adoption) in Roman culture. With the data from such sources—not always readily available to most people—was combined a study of the use of the Hebrew and Greek terms within Scripture. The goal was to share not simply raw data on the original languages but also insights into the vital concepts developed from them and expressed within the Scriptures.

This work, which has taken many months to complete, was undertaken because of my personal conviction concerning the significance of Scripture. In the Word of God we meet God himself, and we are called by him to reshape our view of life. God calls us to reshape our values and our attitudes, our relationships with others, our choices, and our actions. In Scripture we come to know the will of God, which, when we respond to it with faith's obedience, proves good and profitable and acceptable to each of us. Thus the Bible uniquely conveys God's good word to us; it is his word of transformation, vitalized by the Spirit himself. There can be nothing more important for any of us than to hear God's word accurately and to respond willingly to his voice.

This volume is offered to the public in the simple hope that it will enable believers to understand God's Word more accurately and thus live more fully in accord with God's revealed will.

LAWRENCE O. RICHARDS

How to Use This Dictionary

Here's how this *Expository Dictionary* can best be used. Suppose you note the word "hope" in the Bible passage you are studying. You know that "hope" has a number of meanings in English—from the expression of a desire to an expression of baseless optimism. But what does "hope" mean in Scripture? Is there some meaning here that communicates a distinctive message to God's people? Paging alphabetically through this dictionary, you can find the article on hope, which discusses the various Hebrew and Greek words that deal with this concept and goes on to explore how these words are used in the Bible to give "hope" a shining meaning, intended to shape our faith and brighten our lives.

Cross references (indicated by an arrow followed by the name of the suggested article, e.g., ◆ *Adultery*) will guide the reader to discussions in which a particular subject is significantly treated and where added insights can be gained. There is also a thorough subject index.

Two additional indexes—a Hebrew-and-Greek index and a Scripture index—are designed to make this work even more useful. The Hebrew-and-Greek index lists Hebrew and Greek words and the pages where they are discussed in the dictionary and the pages on which they are mentioned. This is important because a single Hebrew or Greek term may have a number of meanings, or meanings that are expressed in several English words. So this index makes possible a study of the shades of meaning that a word may have in various Scripture contexts.

The Scripture index is especially helpful. This dictionary discusses terms in general and also their uses in specific contexts. Thus, individual verses are explored when they seem to be (1) particularly significant in the development of a biblical concept or (2) difficult to interpret. Anyone puzzled by a particular verse need not read extended discussions on the meanings of key words; the Scripture index gives the pages on which that verse is dealt with specifically. As a further aid, pages on which a verse is discussed—and not merely referred to—are listed in boldface type.

This dictionary uses the following list of abbreviations of Bible books and transliterations of Hebrew and Greek words.

Abbreviations for Books of the Bible

Genesis	Ge	Nahum	Na
Exodus	Ex	Habbakuk	Hab
Leviticus	Lev	Zephaniah	Zep
Numbers	Nu	Haggai	Hag
Deuteronomy	Dt	Zechariah	Zec
Joshua	Jos	Malachi	Mal
Judges	Jdg	Matthew	Mt
Ruth	Ru	Mark	Mk
1 Samuel	1 Sa	Luke	Lk
2 Samuel	2 Sa	John	Jn
1 Kings	1 Ki	Acts	Ac
2 Kings	2 Ki	Romans	Ro
1 Chronicles	1 Ch	1 Corinthians	1 Co
2 Chronicles	2 Ch	2 Corinthians	2 Co
Ezra	Ezr	Galatians	Gal
Nehemiah	Ne	Ephesians	Eph
Esther	Est	Philippians	Php
Job	Job	Colossians	Col
Psalms	Ps	1 Thessalonians	1 Th
Proverbs	Pr	2 Thessalonians	2 Th
Ecclesiastes	Ecc	1 Timothy	1 Ti
Song of Songs	SS	2 Timothy	2 Ti
Isaiah	Isa	Titus	Tit
Jeremiah	Jer	Philemon	Phm
Lamentations	La	Hebrews	Heb
Ezekiel	Eze	James	Jas
Daniel	Da	1 Peter	1 Pe
Hosea	Hos	2 Peter	2 Pe
Joel	Joel	1 John	1 Jn
Amos	Am	2 John	2 Jn
Obadiah	Ob	3 John	3 Jn
Jonah	Jnh	Jude	Jude
Micah	Mic	Revelation	Rev

Transliterations

Hebrew

א	= '	ד	= $\underline{d}$	י	= y	ס	= s	ר	= r
בּ	= b	ה	= $\underline{h}$	כּ	= k	ע	= '	שׁ	= ś
ב	= $\underline{b}$	ו	= w	ך כ	= $\underline{k}$	פ	= p	שׁ	= š
גּ	= g	ז	= z	ל	= l	ף פ	= $\underline{p}$	ת	= t
ג	= $\underline{g}$	ח	= ḥ	ם מ	= m	ץ צ	= ṣ	ת	= $\underline{t}$
ד	= d	ט	= ṭ	ן נ	= n	ק	= q		

(ה)ָ	= â (h)	ָ	= ā	ַ	= a	ֳ	= ᵃ
יֵ	= ê	ֵ	= ē	ֶ	= e	ֱ	= ᵉ
יִ	= î	ֹ	= ō	ִ	= i	ְ	= ᵉ (if vocal)
וֹ	= ô			ָ	= o	ֳ	= ᵒ
וּ	= û			ֻ	= u		

Greek

α	=	a	ν	=	n	γγ	=	ng	
β	=	b	ξ	=	x	γκ	=	nk	
γ	=	g	ο	=	o	γξ	=	nx	
δ	=	d	π	=	p	γχ	=	nch	
ε	=	e	ρ	=	r				
ζ	=	z	σ,ς	=	s	ᾳ	=	ā	
η	=	ē	τ	=	t	ῃ	=	ē	
θ	=	th	υ	=	y	ῳ	=	ō	
ι	=	i	φ	=	ph				
κ	=	k	χ	=	ch	ʹ	=	h	
λ	=	l	ψ	=	ps	ῥ	=	rh	
μ	=	m	ω	=	ō				

A

ABANDON/ABANDONED

There are times when we feel abandoned. It is a terrible feeling, and when crushed by it, we are likely to wonder if God has forsaken us too. Looking into Scripture, though, we make several encouraging discoveries. The Bible does not speak of "feeling" abandoned: it focuses our attention on the reality of commitment and rejection. While Scripture expresses concern about our human tendency to turn away from God and from godliness, it also assures us that God is faithful to his commitments. Even those OT passages that warn that God will abandon those who turn from him convey, on close examination, a message rich in warmth and encouragement.

OT 1. Abandon
    2. Forsake
    3. The covenant context
NT 4. Forsake
    5. Summary

OT — Usually the word *abandon*, or *forsake*, in the OT is a translation of one of two Hebrew words, one of which is stronger than the other. The milder term is the one normally used in speaking of God's "casting off," or "forsaking," his people.

1. Abandon. The stronger of the two Hebrew words is *'āzaḇ*. It has three common meanings: "to depart," "to abandon," and "to loose." This is the word usually chosen by OT writers when they portray man's willful abandonment of God, as when God warned Moses, "These people will soon prostitute themselves to the foreign gods of the land

they are entering. They will forsake [abandon] me and break the covenant I made with them" (Dt 31:16). Man's willful rejection of God is implied when the OT speaks of our abandoning the Lord. This is not mere drifting away but a clear choice to depart, and so Jeremiah announces God's warning: "I will pronounce my judgments on my people because of their wickedness in forsaking [abandoning] me" (1:16). In most OT cases, abandoning God involved substituting the worship of idols for a relationship with the Lord (e.g., 1 Ki 19:10,14; Jnh 2:8).

The same strong Hebrew word is used by the writers of Proverbs to show their concern that God's people not abandon the wisdom that promotes righteous moral qualities (e.g., 2:13; 4:2,6; 10:17). Surely "stern discipline awaits him who leaves [abandons] the path" (Pr 15:10).
▶ *Wisdom*

When God is the subject of *'āzaḇ*, the dominant message is one of reassurance. "You, LORD," the psalmist says, "have never forsaken [abandoned] those who seek you" (Ps 9:10; see also 37:25,33; Isa 41:17). When tragedy overwhelms believers, it may appear that God has abandoned them (Ps 22:1), but the passing of time will prove conclusively that "he has not despised or disdained the suffering of the afflicted one" (22:24).

There are infrequent occasions in which this stronger term describes God's action in abandoning a sinning generation to an enemy (e.g., 2 Ch 12:5; Jer 12:7). But the OT echoes with strong affirmations that God is faithful to his commitments. God may punish the one who sins by allowing that person to suffer under an enemy, but he declares, "I will not take my love from him, nor will I ever betray my faithfulness" (Ps. 89:33; see vv. 30–37).

2. Forsake. *Nātaš* is the second major Hebrew word translated "abandon" in the NIV and the NASB. This is the word we are most likely to meet when God is the subject of a sentence and is said to abandon or cast off his people (as in Jdg 6:13; 1 Ki 8:57; 2 Ki 21:14; Isa 2:6; Jer 7:29; 12:7; 23:33,39). Yet even here are words of promise: "For the LORD will not reject his people; he will never forsake [abandon] his inheritance" (Ps 94:14) and "for the sake of his great name the LORD will not reject his people, because the LORD was pleased to make you his own" (1 Sa 12:22).

We gain insight into the sense of this milder word by seeing how it is used in other connections. This is the word chosen to describe the action (or inaction) of a farmer who lets his land lie unplowed (Ex 23:11). It is used in describing the custom of giving the land rest every seventh year as required in the law (Ne 10:31). It is also used of a person who leaves a flock of sheep for which he has been caring (1 Sa 17:20,28). These common uses give an impression, not of active, decisive rejection, but of withdrawal of active involvement or leaving something alone.

The word calls to mind Isaiah's famous image of Israel as God's cherished vineyard (Isa 5:1–7). Isaiah tells how God lovingly and actively chose a fertile hillside. He cleared the land, built a watchtower, and planted choice vines. But the fruit was bitter, and the moral product was bloodshed and distress, not justice and righteousness. So, the prophet explains, God broke down the protective wall and stepped back, refusing to prune or cultivate or water. It is this—the withdrawal of care—that *nātaš* seems to connote. When sin leads us away from a close relationship with the Lord, his love may lead him to withdraw his active guardianship.

3. The covenant context. No study of the Hebrew words, however, frees us from the problem posed by apparently conflicting statements. Moses promised, "The LORD . . . will never leave you nor forsake ['*āzab*] you" (Dt 31:8). But a prophet moved by the Spirit of God warned, "If you forsake him, he will forsake ['*āzab*] you" (2 Ch 15:2). And Isaiah laments, "You have abandoned [*nātaš*] your people" (Isa 2:6). The apparent conflict can be resolved only when we remember distinctive characteristics of the covenant relationship between God and his people. ◗ *Covenant*

Two types of covenants defining the relationship between God and his people are found in the OT. The first is the eschatological covenant (Abrahamic, Davidic, new), in which God makes binding promises about his intentions for his people. These eschatological promises are focused on the end of history and are great towering statements about God's plans for the future. When the day of fulfillment comes, God will keep every promise made in these magnificent and unconditional covenants.

The second kind of covenant is also unconditional, God announcing beforehand what he would surely do. But this covenant (the Mosaic, or law covenant) is existential and was made afresh with each new generation of Israelites. Under this covenant, God spelled out how he would react to each generation, based on their obedience or disobedience to his written law. As long as a particular generation was obedient and did not abandon the Lord, He blessed them. But if a given generation turned from him to idols, he abandoned that generation to discipline.

What emerges from our understanding of the covenant context of the OT are some significant truths. (1) God remains totally faithful to his great, historic promises about the future. No generation's sins will cause him to abandon either Israel as a people or the sure future toward which history moves. (2) In the course of history, whether or not a particular generation experiences abandonment will depend on how that generation responds to God. God remains committed to those who are committed to him. (3) When God does abandon or forsake a particular generation, it is always understood that the abandonment is temporary, as God himself reassures, "For a brief moment I abandoned you, but with deep compassion I will bring you back" (Isa 54:7). The temporary discipline involved is never understood to threaten the underlying relationship, which rests on God's assured promises of hope and a future for his people.

NT — The NT references to abandonment reflect the translators' understanding of several different Greek terms. Some elements are in full harmony with OT meanings, but there are significant differences. In both Testaments, the human choice to abandon God is portrayed as a willful, rebellious act. Hebrews describes the cause as a "sinful, unbelieving heart that turns away from [abandons] the living God" (Heb 3:12). But the NT is empty of warnings that God might abandon the believer. Instead there are many instances of this kind of promise for the believer: "God has said, 'Never will I leave you; never will I forsake you' " (Heb 13:5).

4. Forsake. The Greek word *aphistēmi* and closely related words mean "to withdraw [from a place, association, or relationship]." In common speech they might be used to describe leaving the temple or another location (Lk 2:37; 4:13; Ac 5:37; 12:10; 15:38; 19:9). They were also used when Paul spoke of men's abandoning "natural relations with women" because they were "inflamed with lust for one another" (Ro 1:27) and in the exhortation to "turn away from" iniquity (2 Ti 2:19). While Paul warns that in later times "some will abandon the faith and follow deceiving spirits" (1 Ti 4:1), there is no suggestion that God will withdraw from his relationship with believers.

Kataleipō and *enkataleipō* are also translated "abandon." The first word is milder and simply means "to leave." It is used descriptively of physical actions. *Enkataleipō* has stronger moral and emotional overtones. Jesus was not abandoned (*enkataleipō*) to the grave (Ac 2:27), and

the Resurrection proves that he was not left (*kataleipō*) there (Ac 2:31). Paul experienced persecution but was deeply aware that he had not been abandoned (*enkataleipō*) by the Lord (2 Co 4:9). It is this latter word, however, that is used in Jesus' cry from the cross "Why have you forsaken me?" (Mt 27:46; Mk 15:34). The same tone of pain is felt when Paul describes to Timothy how all deserted (abandoned) him when he was on trial in Rome (2 Ti 4:10,16). In these and other NT uses we sense the pain of being deserted—but realize with wonder that God never threatens to desert us! The NT never even suggests that God would take such an action!

5. Summary. We are likely to feel forsaken at times. We may be troubled by a personal failure and wonder if God has abandoned us. We may feel a momentary uncertainty when reading in the OT of God's abandoning some generation that had abandoned him. But such fears come when we forget how this concept is developed in the Bible.

We are helped when we remember that even in OT times, "abandon" and "forsake" include a deliberate, human choice to turn from a relationship with God to the worship of idols. A formal relationship between God and man is in view. The true believer, with a relationship with God won by Christ and accepted by faith, is not in this danger.

We are helped when we remember that in OT times, sins and failures could be forgiven if a people returned to God. God was ever eager to extend forgiveness. As long as God's people clung to him they would never be forsaken, even if they did sin. Today too our trust is placed in a faithful, forgiving God.

We are helped when we remember that God's OT people related to God through the Mosaic covenant. All OT references to God's abandoning his people are directly related to this covenant. But Jesus' death introduced what each Testament calls the new covenant. ♦ **Covenant** It replaces the old covenant. As part of this new covenant, God plants his perfect law in our hearts; and no threat of withdrawal or abandonment is ever directed toward the people who are part of the new covenant.

We are helped when we remember that Jesus was himself forsaken by the Father (Mt 27:46; Mk 15:34). Because the Father did turn away from the Son for that awesome moment on the cross when Jesus bore our sins, we can be confident that God never will turn from us who believe. The sins that alienated us from God are gone now, and, because of Jesus, God is eternally committed to us who believe. May we forsake the sin that made the Father forsake the Son.

ABBA

Abba is an Aramaic word, drawn from the everyday language of Palestine. As the first word a child might learn, it is equivalent to our word *Daddy* and is laden with a warm sense of intimacy. The word is found in our Bibles in a combined form, "Abba, Father," which links the Aramaic word with the Greek word for father (*abba, ho patēr*). It may be that the Greek word is added to explain the unfamiliar *abba* to believers beyond Palestine. But even in Palestine in NT times, the combined formula was used in prayer and as a way family members addressed the head of the household. No slave or servant in the household had the privilege of using this personal formula to address his master.

This fact underlies the argument in Ro 8:15 and Gal 4:6, two of the three NT occurrences of *abba*. Paul wants us to grasp the dramatic change of relationship that comes with being a Christian. We believers no longer address God as would a servant or a slave. We come to the Lord in the full assurance that we are family.

The full intimacy of our relationship is sensed in the only other biblical use of the phrase. "Abba, Father" was the anguished cry of Jesus in Gethsemane, anticipating the agony of Calvary (Mk 14:36). When we hurt, we too can call on a God who welcomes us into his arms as dearly loved children.

ABHOR/ABHORRENT

"Abhorrence" is a distinctly OT concept, closely linked with Israel's life under law. The Hebrew word translated "abhor" in Leviticus is *gāʿal*. It conveys intense aversion and loathing. The loathing motivates a strong reaction, as when a person strikes out in revulsion to crush some loathsome insect. When Israel abhorred God's decrees and ordinances, the nation became abhorrent to the Lord, and they were struck down with punishments (Lev 26:30). The four NIV uses of *abhor* in Jeremiah (15:4; 24:9; 29:18; 34:17) are translations of a word that means "to cause to remove" and are directly linked with the Levitical warnings. Israel had abhorred God's word, and the Lord had reacted, thrusting them out of the Promised Land into captivity.

The other Hebrew word most commonly translated "abhor" is *tāʿab*, which also means "to loathe or detest." In a physical sense, the slumped Job—awash in the stench of his rotting body—was loathsome (*tāʿab* [Job 9:31; 19:19; 30:10]). Israel's abandonment of the moral and ceremonial law of God caused a similar spiritual stench and made her loathsome to God. ▶ *Abominable/Abomination*

When we read "abhor" or "abhorrent" in the Bible, it is intended that we sense the intense emotional reaction caused by the person or thing so identified (e.g., Ps 119:163; Isa 49:7).

ABILITY/ABLE

What is the biblical view of humankind? What are our strengths and limitations? What does the Bible mean when it refers to persons "of ability"? How "able" are we human beings, anyway?

OT 1. Human limitations
NT 2. Divine power

OT — 1. Human limitations. The philosophical questions raised above are not addressed directly in OT passages containing the word "able" or "ability." Yet the underlying picture provided is rich in insights.

Hayil is a Hebrew noun that occurs 235 times in the OT. About 100 times it means "an army" or "a strong force." It is also used to indicate physical strength and the power of wealth. About 85 times it is used as an attribute of people. In the historical books *ḥayil* suggests membership in a class with other able, respected persons. Although the word communicates the idea of ability, it is seldom translated "able" or "ability" (see Ge 47:6; Dt 8:18; 1 Ch 9:13; 26:7,9,30,32; 2 Ch 13:3).

The verb most commonly translated "be able" is *yākōl*. It occurs 196 times in the OT and is linked with physical, ethical, and religious ability. Strikingly, about 85 percent of the OT uses involve the negative: the emphasis rests on what people or pagan gods are *unable* to do! There is probably more than a hint of shame associated with Israel's inability to drive out her enemies (Jos 15:63; 17:12) and with the failure of the magicians of Egypt to match miracles with Moses (Ex 9:11). Certainly Moses' emotional argument that God must not reject rebellious Israel focuses on concern for God's reputation. His power might be discounted and the Egyptians might ridicule God "because the LORD was not able to take them into the land he had promised them" (Dt 9:28; cf. Nu 14:16). Similarly, an Assyrian envoy's ridicule of the Lord as just another powerless local deity (2 Ch 32:13–15) moved God to intervene and deliver Jerusalem (v. 21).

There is no question that the OT reflects a deep awareness of human limitations. We are but creatures in a universe shaped and ruled by a sovereign, all-powerful God. This truth is clearly taught in certain magnificent OT passages such as Job 35–39 and Isa 41. The awed awareness of God's great power colors the way OT writers thought and wrote of human abilities.

NT — 2. Divine power. The NT carries over the OT attitude toward human ability. We are most likely to find NT writers referring to what human beings are not able to do (e.g., Mk 3:20; Lk 1:20; Ac 5:39; Heb 3:19) and emphasizing the fact that God is "able to do immeasurably more than all we ask or imagine" (Eph 3:20).

The word *ischyō* is translated "able" only in some of Luke's usages of it (Lk 13:24; 14:29,30; Ac 15:10) and means "strength" or "power." Luke employs it to warn that a person planning a project must consider whether he is able to complete it. He used it also in speaking of OT law as a "yoke that neither we nor our fathers have been able [have had strength] to bear" (Ac 15:10).

Dynamis (noun) and *dynamai* (verb) account for nearly half of the NT references to "able" and "ability." These words look to the inherent physical, spiritual, or natural strength or power of individuals. The verb raises the issue of one's being "strong enough" and thus able.

It is no surprise to find that when speaking of native human ability, the NT is most likely to speak of limitations. Thus we are reminded that the ancient Israelites were "not able to enter" the Promised Land because of the inherent weakness caused by unbelief (Heb 3:19). And we are told that OT sacrifices had no inherent ability to "clear the conscience of the worshiper" (Heb 9:9).

In contrast, the NT speaks boldly of the overwhelming ability of God. Because of his inherent nature, God is able to help those who come to him (Heb 2:18), to save completely those who trust Jesus (Heb 7:25; Jude 24), and, in short, to make every grace abound toward us (2 Co 9:8). Because God's power is unlimited, he is even capable of providing armor that will make us "able to stand [our] ground" (Eph 6:13) when evil days come.

OT and NT occurrences of the words "able" and "ability" fail to give full answers to our questions about human abilities. ◆ *Strength/Might/Power* But the way both Testaments portray human potential makes it clear that we are not strong enough to build a spiritual life on our own. Thus, the focus should shift dramatically from questions about human ability to an issue Jesus raised when two blind men begged for help. Jesus asked simply, "Do you believe that I am able to do this?" (Mt 9:28).

Our future hinges not on what we are able to do, but on whether or not we place our faith in Jesus, the one who *is* able to act and able to meet our every need.

ABOLISH

The word "abolish" can be understood in its normal English sense of "do away with" or "put an end to." But two different Greek words are used in the theologically important Mt 5:17 and Eph 2:15.

Jesus says in Mt 5:17, "Do not think that I have come to abolish the Law or the Prophets; I have not come to abolish them but to fulfill them." The word here is *katalyō*, "to tear down, to destroy." There are two senses in which Jesus' teaching fulfilled rather than tore down the structure erected by law. First, Jesus' teaching was exposition. His statement placed him in the established tradition of other rabbis whose goal in life was to explain the law's true meaning and thus to "fulfill" it. Second, Jesus' death and resurrection fulfilled the OT in another sense: he himself was the one to whom the older Testament pointed. The meaning of law as a revelation of a righteousness that could be won only by faith, rather than as a way of salvation, is fully established in the Cross.

Eph 2:15 seems to contradict Jesus. There Paul writes of Jesus' death as "abolishing in his flesh the law with its commandments and regulations." The apparent contradiction is resolved when we note the meaning of the Greek word translated "abolishing" (*katargeō*). This word means "to annul," or "to make of no effect." Paul's point is that the old law, which made strict distinctions between Jews and the rest of humanity and thus erected uncrossable barriers, is now irrelevant. The issue of unity in the Christian community focuses on our common reconciliation to God through Jesus' death. We are one with all our brothers and sisters. Every cultural and human difference is now irrelevant, for Jesus brings together all believers into one family of God.

ABOMINABLE/ABOMINATION

Often the KJV uses "abominable" and "abomination" in the OT to translate four different Hebrew words. NIV usage focuses on a single Hebrew concept, *šiqqûṣ*. The NASB focuses on a different concept, *tôʻēḇah*, which the NIV usually translates "detestable."

Šiqqûṣ is a strong word, always linked with idolatry and its immoral practices. It is intended to express the extreme wickedness of religious sins. ◗ *Idol/Image*

Tôʻēḇah likewise expresses strong revulsion caused by some physical, moral, or ethical abomination. It tends to be used with aesthetic and moral, rather than religious, objects.

The Greek term *bdelygma* is translated "abomination(s)" or "abominable" four times in the NT (Mt 24:15; Mk 13:14; Rev 17:4–5). It and two related Greek words (*bdelyktos* and *bdelyssomai*) appear with different renderings another five times (Lk 16:15; Ro 2:22; Tit 1:16; Rev 21:8,27). These reflect the meaning of *šiqqûṣ*, rather than *tôʻēḇah*, and bear a special prophetic significance. Both Daniel (Da 11:31; 12:11; cf. 8:13; 9:27) and Jesus (Mt 24:15; Mk 13:14) speak of "the abomination that causes desolation" at history's end. It is associated with mankind's final rebellion, when the Antichrist will set up an idol to be worshiped in the very Jerusalem temple dedicated to the worship of the one true God. ◗ *Antichrist*

Included in the morally abominable practices to be totally rejected by believers are homosexuality (Lev 18:22; 20:13), engaging in occult practices (Dt 18:9–14), and conducting dishonest business (Dt 25:13–16). Pr 6:16–19 lists seven more abominations that will awaken God's wrath. It is most important to be repulsed by that which is repulsive to God.

ABOUND/ABOUNDING

Both OT and NT occurrences of the word "abound" portray an overflowing abundance. In fact, the Greek term (*perisseuō*) is translated "overflow" in every use in the NT Epistles (Ro 5:15; 15:13; 2 Co 1:5; 4:15; 8:2; 9:12; Col 2:7; Php 1:26; 1 Th 3:12). The OT emphasis is on the character of God. He is "abounding in love" to all who call on him (Ps 86:5). Often God is described as "slow to anger" and "abounding in love" (Ex 34:6; Ne 9:17; Ps 86:15; 103:8; Joel 2:13; Jnh 4:2). The repetition of this formula shows that in building our concept of God it is important for us to grasp God's hesitancy to be angry. We need to realize his eagerness to love.

It is wonderful that as we experience God's overflowing love he will work in us, so that we too will have a growing love for others that abounds more and more (Php 1:9).

ABSTAIN

OT occurrences of this word (Ex 19:15; 31:17; Nu 6:3) do not translate a particular word but rather a variety of constructions (e.g., "do not come at your wives" [KJV] is clearly improved by "abstain from sexual relations" [NIV]). The NT uses "abstain" in translating *apechomai*, which means "keep away from, refrain from." The same word is translated "avoid" in the NIV in 1 Th 4:3; 5:22.

In Acts, early Gentile believers are urged to keep away from practices associated with idolatry. The NT letters call on believers to avoid immorality and evil but not to permit the growth of a new legalism (1 Ti 4:3; cf. 4:1–5).

ABUNDANCE/ABUNDANT

A number of Hebrew words, with meanings that range from "blessing" (and thus the good things with which one is blessed) to "plenty" and "much," are reflected in the use of "abundance" and "abundant" in modern English versions.

The concept is important. Under the Mosaic covenant, God promised that obedience would bring rich material blessings to God's people (Dt 30:9–10).
◗ *Wealth/Riches/Possessions*
But Jesus' warning is an important corrective to those who might use wealth as a measure of one's relationship with God. "Watch out!" Jesus said. "Be on your guard against all kinds of greed; a

man's life does not consist in the abundance of his possessions" (Lk 12:15).

ABYSS

The Greek word *abyssos* is an adjective meaning "bottomless" or "unfathomable." The abyss was identified in Greek thought with the underworld, the realm of the dead.

In the NT this realm of the dead is pictured as a prison, smoldering with subterranean fires, where demons are captive. ◗ *Heaven and Hell* This same word occurs in Ro 10:7, where it is translated "deep" in the NIV. In the next verse Paul states that we have immediate access to the message of salvation. We need to search neither heaven nor the abyss: the gospel's good word is "near you."

ACCEPT

In most cases "accept" is used in its normal English sense, though it may reflect one of several Hebrew or Greek concepts. One Hebrew word pictures the act of picking up, and thus accepting, a gift or an offering. Another indicates that an offering, person, or instruction is favorably received. But implied in each word is a responsive decision by the one accepting.

In the NT, "accept" and "receive" are typically used to translate one of two very common Greek word groups. One of these, the *dechomai* group, indicates acceptance and approval, with the root meaning "to take, receive, accept." The *lambanō* group, which appears some 262 times in the NT, also means to "take" or "receive." Often this latter group is used in a passive sense, as in receiving the Spirit (Jn 7:39), grace (Ro 1:5), and mercy (Heb 4:16). All of these ideas are adequately expressed by our English words "accept" and "receive."

There are, however, three special uses of "accept" that need to be identified.

Accept (receive) the Word. This phrase occurs several times in the NT. It is a formula, or technical expression, that means "believe the gospel" (Lk 8:13; Ac 8:14; 11:1; cf. Ac 17:11; 1 Th 1:6).

Accept one another. The Greek word *proslambanō* (compound of *lambanō*) is a significant relational term. It means to actively accept into one's society or circle of friends. We might well translate it "welcome," for it is used in the NT to communicate the warm sense of welcome to be given to fellow believers by a local community of faith. Thus when Paul writes, "Accept him whose faith is weak, without passing judgment on disputable matters" (Ro 14:1), he chooses *proslambanō*, to call for a full and complete and warm welcome into full fellowship. We sense the power of this call to welcome others when we see that Paul uses the same word in Ro 14:3 to express the total way that God has welcomed us into full membership in his family.

This word, with its exhortation to draw others into full, intimate fellowship, is also found in three other verses (Ro 15:7 and Phm 12,17), where the NIV translates it "welcome."

Make room. The third special case is the NIV and NASB translation of *chōreō* as "accept" in Mt 19:11–12. The NIV reads, "Not everyone can accept this word, but only those to whom it has been given. . . . The one who can accept this should accept it."

The Pharisees, demanding to know his stand on grounds for divorce, were told by Jesus that marriage should be permanent. ♦ *Divorce and Remarriage* Afterward Jesus' disciples reacted. If there is no way out of a marriage that might prove to be a tragic mistake, "it is better not to marry" (v. 10). The words of these verses are Jesus' response to this conclusion reached by the Twelve.

The word *chōreō* literally means "to make room for" and is sometimes used to express the idea of comprehending or grasping. Paul chose it to urge the believers at Corinth, "Make room for us in your hearts" (2 Co 7:2). It is also the word John used in his Gospel when he supposed that the world itself would not have room for all the books that might be written about what Jesus said and did (21:25).

In the context of Jesus' teaching on marriage and divorce, the meaning is clear. Celibacy cannot be accepted by all, for not everyone is able to make room for such a lifestyle. But although the single state is not for everyone, it should be chosen by those who find they do have room in their personalities for this way of life (cf. 1 Co 7:25–35).

ACCEPTABLE/ACCEPTANCE

The prophet Malachi utters God's scornful message to the people of his day. These Israelites offered God crippled and diseased animals on the altar, animals they would never dare to offer a human governor as a tax payment. "I am not pleased with you," the prophet quotes the Lord Almighty, "and I will accept no offering from your hands" (Mal 1:10). The OT and the NT often speak of the acceptability of offerings or of service (e.g., Ex 28:38; Jer 6:20; 2 Co 8:12; Php 4:18). What is involved in making a response to God acceptable?

OT **1. Acceptable worship**
NT **2. Acceptable lives**
     3. Becoming acceptable to God

OT — 1. Acceptable worship. Most OT references to acceptance and acceptability involve use of the Hebrew verb *rāṣâh* and the derivative noun *rāṣôn*. The verb means "to be pleased with" and the noun means "delight," or "favor," and thus expresses God's positive attitude in accepting a gift of sacrifice (Lev 1:3; 22:20–21; Isa 56:7). One major association of these words in the OT is with worship: they express the ritual acceptability of an offering made under OT law (esp. Lev 22:1–33).

It is clear that more than correctness of the ritual is linked with acceptable worship. Worship can be offered to God only in the context of a heart that is committed to the Lord and to his ways. "Do not profane my holy name," God warns in Leviticus, for the Lord "must be acknowledged as holy by the Israelites." In context, this worship implies keeping

God's commandments and thus maintaining a holy lifestyle (Lev 22:31–32).

God scorned the ceremonially correct worship offered in Isaiah's day, because the worshipers had abandoned his moral law. He called their sacrifices "meaningless offerings" and described their approach as a "trampling" of the temple courts. God will hide his eyes from these people, for their "hands are full of blood." Before the worship of that generation could be acceptable to the Lord, the people had to "stop doing wrong, learn to do right! Seek justice, encourage the oppressed. Defend the cause of the fatherless, plead the case of the widow" (Isa 2:10–17).

It is one's heart commitment to God (demonstrated by a life lived by God's values), along with faith (demonstrated by bringing offerings in God's prescribed way), that makes a person and his or her worship acceptable to God.

NT — 2. Acceptable lives. Modern versions usually translate words from the *dechomai* group "accepted" and "acceptable"—though one other word, usually expressed as "well pleasing," needs to be considered. ◆ *Accept* As we look through the NT, however, we note careful development of a thrust emphasized in the prophets. Acceptability is not merely a matter of paying attention to ritual: acceptability calls for close attention to the moral quality of the worshiper's life. In exploring the nature of the moral life, the NT calls us to give ourselves to a life of loving service, through which we actually become sacrificial gifts offered to the Lord.

Dektos and *apodektos* mean "acceptable," "pleasing." *Apodektos*, translated "pleasing" in the NIV and "acceptable" in the NASB, is found only in 1 Ti 2:3; 5:4. Here we see that the life that pleases God is lived quietly and respectably in a hostile world, with religion put into practice by caring for one's own family. *Dektos* is found in Lk 4:18,24; Ac 10:35; 2 Co 6:2; Php 4:18. The context makes it clear that the acceptable life is one of commitment to righteousness and of giving sacrificially to help the brothers and sisters in the faith.

Euprosdektos is a compound that means "acceptable and pleasant." It is found in Ro 15:16,31; 2 Co 6:2; 8:12; 1 Pe 2:5. Acceptability begins with our acceptance of the gospel. Christian giving is acceptable according to our eager willingness to share, not according to the amount given. Believers are to see themselves as a holy priesthood, set aside by God to offer "spiritual sacrifices acceptable to God through Jesus Christ."

Euarestos is from a different Greek root but also means "acceptable," or "pleasing." It is used only to speak of acceptability to God (Ro 12:1,2; 14:18; 2 Co 5:9; Eph 5:10; Php 4:18; Col 3:20; Tit 2:9; Heb 13:21). Where this word is used, we are taught that our whole lives are to be viewed as a sacrifice and lived to God's glory and are thus acceptable to him. Even slaves and children, though limited by their station in life, have opportunities to serve God by doing good.

3. Becoming acceptable to God. The initial stress in the OT was laid on people showing their commitment to God by careful observation of his worship instructions, though a holy lifestyle was also important. The prophets showed that God's concern was not so much with the ritual aspects of worship as with the broad provisions of the law, which showed Israel how to live godly lives. The NT continues this emphasis. We who have come to God through Jesus are ourselves the very sacrifices he cherishes. We can live acceptable, well-pleasing lives when we (1) realize that our reasonable service is to surrender our life to be lived for the Lord and (2) when we follow up our initial commitment by daily choosing those things that are pleasing to him.

Acceptability is thus linked with a willing eagerness to do God's will. And God has not left us in doubt about what his will involves. We are to live quietly, untainted by the warped and twisted values that mar our society. We are to turn our backs on unrighteousness and live godly, caring lives, ever eager to do good.

ACCESS

The Greek word translated "access" occurs only three times in the NT. It is *prosagōgē* and means "entrance," "introduction," or "access." Each occurrence of the word (rendered by NIV as "access" in Ro 5:2 and Eph 2:18 but as "approach God" in Eph 3:12) is theologically significant. Each passage stresses the fact that Jesus Christ is the one through whom all who believe have gained entrance to the unique relationship with God that they now enjoy.

ACCOMPANY

Although the word "accompany" is used to translate a number of different Hebrew and Greek words or phrases, it can be understood in its normal English sense. However, several NT passages are historically or theologically important and deserve special comment.

1. The ending to Mark's Gospel speaks of "signs" (miracles) that accompany (are associated with) accepting the good news about Jesus (Mk 16:17,20). Are such signs to be expected today?

Some note that the earliest and best Greek manuscripts do not include Mk 16:9–20. These verses may be a later addition and thus may not be Scripture.

Others believe that the recorded miracles associated with first-century ministry (e.g., Ac 3:1–10; 4:30; 6:8) fulfill the intent and teaching of the Markan passage. Still others hold that such miracles should be expected today.

2. A Jewish tradition forms the backdrop for Paul's comment in 1 Co 10:3–4. The rabbis believed that a literal well of water miraculously followed Israel on their wilderness wanderings. Paul says that Jesus was the spiritual rock that accompanied Israel. His point is that Jesus was the true unseen source of all miraculous OT blessings.

3. The NT speaks of things that accompany salvation (Heb 6:9) and faith (Jas 2:17). The Greek construction in each case stresses close, intimate, and necessary linkage.

The writer of Hebrews is sure that everything intimately linked with salvation does belong to the wavering recipients of his letter. ◆ *Salvation/Save* This comment is meant to reassure, to let the readers know that his strong warning (6:1–8) is not to be understood as a suggestion that they are lost.

James makes the statement that "faith by itself, if it is not accompanied by action, is dead" (2:17). His point is that anything that one might call "faith" and that exists in isolation from a transformed life of Christlike concern for others is counterfeit. It is not a "faith" that God can accept when he calls us to faith in Christ. ◆ *Belief/Faith*

ACCOUNT/ACCOUNTABLE

Modern English translations of both Testaments use these words with the full flexibility of the language. An "account" may be a written or a verbal report (Ge 2:4; Nu 13:27; Lk 1:1). It can be a business investment, to which interest and deposits are credited (Php 4:17). A person may be called on to give an account of funds in his care (2 Ki 12:15; Lk 16:2). The phrase "on account of" indicates that the cause of an action or event is about to be revealed (Ge 26:9; Nu 9:6; Dt 9:5; Mt 26:33). But both Testaments also consider our personal accountability to God. What are we accountable for? The Bible makes it clear that we need to understand the nature of our accountability, both in personal and social relationships and in our relationship to God.

OT   1. **Capital punishment and the OT legal justice system**
      2. **Ultimate accountability to God**
      3. **Limited accountability for others**
NT   4. **NT emphasis on accountability**
      5. **Special meanings of "account" in the NT**
      6. **Summary**

OT — Two parallel and usually equivalent words, *bāqaš* and *dāraš*, are typically found in NIV passages that speak of being held accountable for or giving account of one's actions. The words may also be translated "seek" and "require." The KJV usually translates these words "require at your hand," and in this context the NASB follows the KJV. When we explore these passages, we are introduced to a concept of accountability that involves us in several important aspects of Israel's lifestyle under law.

1. Capital punishment and the OT legal justice system. The OT strongly emphasizes individual accountability for one's actions. This is seen in early Genesis, where God says to Noah's family after the Flood: "From each man, too, I will demand an accounting for the life of his fellow man. Whoever sheds the blood of man, by man shall his blood be shed; for in the image of God has God made man" (Ge 9:5–6).

This passage does more than establish the death penalty for murder (cf. Lev 24:17–21; Nu 35:6–32). ◆ *Murder/Kill* It likewise establishes individual accountability and makes society responsible for holding the individual accountable. Because of this, Ge 9:5–6 has been recognized as instituting human government. ◆ *Authorities*

Under the Mosaic Law, administration of justice was not centralized in any agency. Instead, administration of the legal code was distributed to the whole community. God's people were to act as God's agents, and the community was to hold individuals accountable for their actions (e.g., Lev 24:10–23). Moses called the entire assembly together to stone a blasphemer (vv. 13–16), and there he announced principles for dealing with those who caused property loss and personal injury (vv. 17–21). The thrust of the passage is that the individual "will be held responsible" and the "entire assembly must" participate in holding the individual accountable.

Much of the angry complaint of the prophets can be traced to Israel's failure to live by God's law or to hold others accountable for their disobedience. Habakkuk laments that when "the wicked hem in the righteous," then "the law is paralyzed, and justice never prevails" (1:4).

OT law did provide for checks and balances—principles by which the community was to administer justice (e.g., Dt 17:2–20; 19:1–20). But no generation of Israelites ever followed these guidelines, which were intended, like the rest of the law system, to shape a just and moral community.

2. Ultimate accountability to God. The "whole assembly" of Israel was to act as God's agent in criminal justice matters. Israel failed. Yet the believer never doubted that each person would be held accountable by God. "You must bear the consequences of your sins," the prophet Ezekiel announced (23:35; cf. v. 49). Consequences were usually thought to come through both natural processes and the sequence of events set in motion by one's actions. A young prophet, ordered stoned by King Joash, cried out in dying, "May the LORD see this and call you to account." A few months later the king was wounded in battle. His officials "conspired against him for murdering the son of Jehoiada the priest [the young prophet], and they killed him in his bed" (2 Ch 24:20–26). The king's evil actions had set in motion a series of events that led to his death.

This understanding of how God works in the world of people is expressed in the psalmist's cry to God not to forget the helpless but to "break the arm of the wicked and evil man; call him to account for his wickedness that would not be found out" (Ps 10:15).

However, there were those in Israel who denied the doctrine of personal accountability. When warned by both Jeremiah and Ezekiel that Jerusalem was about to be destroyed, the population shrugged. If the forefathers had sinned and now their children must pay the penalty, so be it. There was nothing an individual could do.

God's response to this attitude came through Ezekiel and reaffirms the principle of individual accountability (Eze 18). God warned that "the soul [person] who sins is the one who will die" (18:4). The righteous man would not be killed in the coming invasion (18:5–9), but his violent son would die "and his blood will be on his own head" (18:10–13). Likewise, the good son of an evil father would be spared (18:14–20). A wicked man who turned to good would be reprieved, and a good man who turned to the practice of evil would be killed (18:21–29). The whole argument hinges on the fact that each person *is* accountable for his actions and that God would act even in the coming national disaster to make distinctions among individuals.

Although we are used to thinking of accountability in view of eternal reward and punishment, it is important to remember that the OT concentrates attention on what happens in this life. It strongly affirms, with the apostle Paul: "Do not be deceived: God cannot be mocked. A man reaps what he sows" (Gal 6:7).

3. Limited accountability for others. With no just moral community to maintain the law, individuals could not be responsible for punishing the wicked. Realizing this, the later prophets increasingly called on God to punish, through circumstance and war and famine, if not through his people. The godly individual is, however, still accountable to God in a limited way for his neighbor. This limited accountability is also dealt with in Ezekiel, where the figure of a night watchman is used. "If the watchman sees the sword coming and does not blow the trumpet to warn the people and the sword comes and takes the life of one of them, that man will be taken away because of his sin, but I will hold the watchman accountable for his blood" (Eze 33:6). The believer-watchman is responsible to the wicked to "speak out to dissuade him from his ways" (33:8). But the watchman is not responsible for how the person warned responds.

Yet the responsibility to warn remains. The wicked must be given the opportunity to turn to God.

NT — The NT does not develop the theme of accountability in the same way the OT does. The OT held the Jewish community responsible for controlling its members through a criminal justice system that distributed accountability to the whole nation. This is analogous to, but not the same as, the NT's teaching on discipline in the church. ◆ *Discipline*

Both Testaments show a balance between obligation toward others and personal accountability to the Lord. While the OT concentrates on God's working through natural consequences and events to punish sin, the NT concentrates on the eternal consequences of wrongdoing.

4. NT emphasis on accountability. The NT speaks a number of times about giving account to God for words and actions. Each passage locates the time of that accounting as "the day of judgment" (Mt 12:36; cf. Ro 14:12; Heb 4:13; 13:17; 1 Pe 4:5). Twin NT themes are that (1) we are directly responsible to God for our choices and (2) there is a day coming when we will give an account for them.

One basic difference sets NT teaching apart from that of the OT: the OT speaks of accountability for wrong—for criminal or sinful acts; the NT references to accountability focus our attention on God's evaluation of the believer's life, and this is not related to punishment. Christ has paid in full for our sins; so when NT passages speak of the day of our evaluation, the emphasis is on rewards (e.g., 1 Co 3:10–15; 2 Co 5:9–10). ◆ *Reward*

But the common conviction of both Testaments is that ultimately every human being is personally responsible for his or her choices. Both unsaved and redeemed are held accountable by God.

5. Special meanings of "account" in the NT. A few NT passages are understood better when the Greek term translated "account" is known. Some special cases and their meanings follow.

a. Ro 3:19 reads, "Whatever the law says, it says to those who are under the law, so that every mouth may be silenced and the whole world held accountable to God." The word *hypodikos* used only here in the NT) is a legal term that means that a person is answerable to a court and thus liable for punishment or judgment. Paul's point is that all mankind is without excuse or defense, already condemned under the divine jurisdiction.

b. 1 Co 6:4 calls on believers to settle disputes among themselves by appointing judges from the fellowship. Even

using people "of little account in the church" would be better than taking disputes to pagan law courts. The Greek word is from the verb *exoutheneō*, which means "to despise, disdain, or reject with contempt." Paul was not actually suggesting that a council of despised judges be convened; he asked whether anyone among them was "wise enough" to deal with the disputes. Paul used the strong derogatory expression for effect— to stress the great importance of working out differences within the family of faith.
♦ *Judge/Judging*

6. **Summary.** The Bible teaches unequivocally that each human being is personally responsible for his or her actions. We are accountable first to God and also, in a limited way, to each other.

This means, on the one hand, that we can never validly claim that someone else "made" us act as we did or that some tragic childhood experience "made" us make choices against our will. On the other hand, we are called on to influence the free choices of others toward good. How others respond to our influence is up to them. But we are to try.

Most excitingly, we learn in Ezekiel 18 that no one's future is determined by others, nor even by his or her own past choices. It is always possible to make life's most vital choices responsibly. Anyone can turn to God, abandon old ways, and begin to live a life that is pleasing to the Lord.

ACCURSED

Different Hebrew words are translated "accursed" in the few instances that this word is used in modern English versions. Each word indicates a violent emotional reaction; each indicates that the person or thing is despised by all. Peter's exclamation "accursed brood!" (2 Pe 2:14) shows the same revulsion to the lifestyle of false teachers, which Peter describes graphically. ♦ *Curse*

ACCUSE/ACCUSATION

The concept of accusation has important legal, interpersonal, and theological implications. Some principles expressed remain constant through OT and NT teaching, such as the wickedness of making false accusations. But there is one significant theological distinction between OT and NT—a distinction that helps us grasp just how full is the forgiveness we enjoy in Jesus.

Understanding what the Bible teaches on this subject can help us test our attitude toward others, help us guard against hurting our brothers and sisters, and help us find even deeper joy in our relationship with the Lord.

OT 1. OT legal system
2. **In court with God**
3. **Satan as accuser**
NT 4. **Accusation as a legal charge**
5. **Special uses of "accuse"**
6. **Summary**

OT — A number of phrases, such as "speak evil against," and several different Hebrew words communicate the sense of "accuse" and "accusation." The OT warns against making false accusations, sets up safeguards in its legal system, and sees God as involved in every dispute. It also introduces Satan as humanity's great adversary, eager to accuse God's people.

1. **OT legal system.** When disputes arose between members of an OT community, the protagonists were to bring the issue to village elders to be settled according to principles laid down in the Mosaic Law. Similarly, anyone accused of a crime was to be judged by local elders and priests, who represented the community. To protect the individual against malicious enemies, the law stated that "one witness is not enough to convict a man accused of any crime or offense he may have committed. A matter must be established by the testimony of two or three witnesses" (Dt 19:15). The elders were charged with the responsibility of thorough investigation and were told, "If the witness proves to be a liar, giving false testimony against his brother, then do to him as he intended to do to his brother" (Dt 19:18–19).

Full protection was guaranteed the accused, even in the case of homicide

(Nu 35:22–28; Jos 21:13–38), and the burden of proof lay on the accuser. False accusation (the slanderous destruction of reputation) was strongly condemned in the OT (e.g., Ps 35:20; Pr 3:30). The NT also has this principle, as no charge against an elder is to be heeded without multiple witnesses (1 Ti 5:19).

2. In court with God. The OT is infused with the belief that God is party to every human dispute and failure. This is reflected in OT passages using the word *rîb*. The word means "strife" "controversy" and—when used of a person—"opponent" or "adversary." The idea is easily extended to verbal disputes and arguments and slides naturally into the legal realm. *Rîb* is translated in a legal-accusatory sense in nine of the NIV's uses of "accuse" (Ne 5:7; Job 31:35; 40:2; Ps 103:9; Pr 3:30; Isa 50:8; 57:16; Hos 4:4; Mi 6:2).

Perhaps surprisingly, OT uses of *rîb* do not always cast God as prosecutor or unfriendly judge. God may be involved in a dispute as an advocate of the accused. Still, it is clear that the guilty and unrepentant must face an accusing God: "The LORD takes his place in court; he rises to judge [*rîb*] the people. The LORD enters into judgment against the elders and leaders of his people: 'It is you who have ruined my vineyard; the plunder from the poor is in your houses'" (Isa 3:13–14). Yet the godly can call freely on God to intervene and can appeal for mercy. Even stained people can expect to be heard by a God who remains compassionate while just: "He will not always accuse [*rîb*], nor will he harbor his anger forever; he does not treat us as our sins deserve or repay us according to our iniquities" (Ps 103:9–10). The prophets often offered this prospect in words of comfort, as Isaiah does in 57:16: "I will not accuse [*rîb*] forever, nor will I always be angry."

The thrust of the OT, then, affirms that God himself is involved when sins or wrongs are committed. He stands over every human dispute as the great adjudicator who actively enters into the whole process and who ultimately condemns or vindicates. God's role as vindicator is triumphantly affirmed in the NT. ♦ *Justice/Injustice*

3. Satan as accuser. The Hebrew word *śāṭān* means "adversary." Satan is presented in both Testaments as the eager accuser of believers. Two OT books (Job 1:6–12; 2:1–7; Zec 3:1) show Satan active as the accuser.

NT — The Gospels and Acts use "accuse" in a legal sense, with most occurrences related to the trials of Jesus and of Paul. But there are other NT uses that are theologically significant.

4. Accusation as a legal charge. Most often the Greek words used by the Gospel writers are drawn from the *katēgoreō/katēgoria* word group. These words were in everyday use as legal terms, involving criminal charges and accusations. When we read of Jesus or of Paul being accused at their trials, a word from this group is used in the original.

Jesus used such a word when he warned the unbelieving Jewish leaders of his day that Moses through the OT law is the one who was bringing charges against them (Jn 5:45).

Satan will still scream his vindictive charges against the saints at history's end, even though he has been overcome by the blood of the Lamb (Rev 12:11).

Today the conscience of the pagan generates thoughts that charge him with wrongdoing (Ro 2:15), for it is only those who have been reconciled to God and thus made holy who can be pronounced unblemished in God's court (Col 1:22). ♦ *Conscience*

Katēgoreō is also the word used of accusations against NT elders—accusations that are to be rejected unless several witnesses support the charges (1 Ti 5:19; cf. Dt 19:15). It is also used by Paul when he says that those chosen as leaders must not have children who are vulnerable to a charge of wild or rebellious behavior (Tit 1:6).

5. Special uses of "accuse". Two other Greek words translated "accuse" provide special insights. Both 2 Pe 2:11 and Jude 9 say that even angels do not bring "slanderous accusations" against (fallen) angelic beings. In each case the Greek word is *krisis*. The implications of this legal term go beyond simply bringing a charge. It suggests actually pronouncing judgment. Only God is able to take this final legal step.

The word *enkaleō* in Ro 8:33 is particularly exciting. Paul reminds us that now, because of Jesus, God is totally for us. He asks, "Who then will bring any charge [*enkaleō*] against those whom God has chosen? It is God who justifies. Who is he that condemns?" (vv. 33–34).

Enkaleō is also a legal term but is much weaker than *katēgoreō*. It does not indicate a charge filed in court but may mean the mere threat of legal proceedings. Paul's point is that now, with God fully committed to us because of Jesus, no charge against us can even be entered on the docket of the divine court! On the basis of Christ's substitutionary death we have been cleared already of every charge. Danger of condemnation is forever past.

6. Summary. The Bible's teaching on accusation is significant for us in several ways. Both Testaments warn us to guard against giving voice to false charges and to be sure that any accusation is fully supported by sufficient evidence. We are to watch our tongues and protect the reputation of our brothers and sisters.

Both Testaments picture God as involved in disputes. He acts on behalf of the accused innocent. Because of Jesus, God has already acquitted us even of the sins with which we might have been justly charged. This divine acquittal frees us not to keep on sinning but to become truly good. ♦ *Good*

It is possible that as we live the Christian life, some will speak out against us and accuse us (1 Pe 2:12). We are simply to commit ourselves, then, to do good, knowing that ultimately God will be glorified in us as the good works we perform vindicate his decision to forgive us freely. "Blessed are you when people . . . falsely say all kinds of evil against you" (Mt 5:11).

ACKNOWLEDGE

We seldom use this word in casual conversation. When we do, it usually implies reluctant admission of something we have tried to deny or to keep hidden. But in the OT and the NT, "acknowledge" is a powerful term. It has deep moral implications when directed inward and deep religious significance when applied to one's relationship with God. When we grasp what it means to acknowledge God and to acknowledge our sins, we sense much more fully the unique commitment to which faith calls us.

The OT uses the word "acknowledge" in three senses: social, moral, and religious. But the core meaning is expressed in the NIV's first use of this word—in Dt 4:39: "Acknowledge and take to heart this day that the LORD is God."

Only the religious use of "acknowledge" is found in modern translations. The moral concept is expressed in the NT by "confess."

OT 1. Social use of "acknowledge"
2. Moral use of "acknowledge"
3. Religious use of "acknowledge"
NT 4. Religious use of "acknowledge"
5. Other uses of "acknowledge"
6. Summary

OT — 1. Social use of "acknowledge". The Hebrew word *nāḵar* is found where the word "acknowledge" is used in a social sense (e.g., Dt 21:17; 33:9; Isa 61:9; 63:16). The word means "to recognize," or to give individuals the full rights associated with their position. Dt 21:17 illustrates this: A father "must acknowledge the son of his unloved wife as the firstborn by giving him a double share of all he has." *Nāḵar* is often translated "recognize" in both the NIV and the NASB, as when Joseph recognized his brothers in Egypt or when the friends of Job failed to recognize the once-prosperous sufferer, slumped in the ash heap. Of the fifty instances in which this Hebrew word is used in the OT, none has a moral or religious emphasis.

2. Moral use of "acknowledge". The OT speaks several times of acknowledging guilt or wickedness (Ps 32:5; Isa 59:12; Jer 3:13; 14:20; Eze 12:16). The Hebrew word in these cases is *yāda'*. *Yāda'* is a common word, found some 933 times in the OT. It means "to know." In the moral sense, *yāda'* means to recognize the moral quality of one's choices or actions and to take the added step of acknowledging culpability in public confession. ♦ *Confession of Sins*

3. Religious use of "acknowledge". Most OT passages containing "acknowledge" focus on human acknowledgment of God. In some passages, the people of God are called on to remember some trait or characteristic of God, such as his holiness (Lev 22:32; Isa 29:23), his rule (Da 4:25–26), or his sovereign position as the Most High (Da 4:32; 5:21). Most passages, however, seem quite personal. God calls on his dearly loved people to acknowledge him. The personal God who entered into covenant relationship with Israel is eager to be known and loved. Yet over and over, God's complaint is heard through the prophets: "You [or, they] do not [or, refuse to] acknowledge me" (Isa 45:4; Jer 9:3,6).

The Hebrew term translated "acknowledge" in some of these passages comes from the root *yāda'*, "to know," or a word derived from it. It can be and often is used to express the idea of knowledge gained by personal experience, to express acquaintance or more intimate relationships with a person, to identify a capacity to discern or distinguish, as a rich euphemism for sexual intercourse, and to speak of personal relationship with the divine. When it is used of knowing or acknowledging God, at least two aspects seem important.

First, there must be a knowledge of who God is. The OT reports that one purpose of the plagues on Egypt was that the Israelites might know that he is God (Ex 10:2). The rest of the OT often points back to God's mighty acts and to his revelation of his plans to Abraham and through Moses. God's self-revelation in history was the solid foundation on which any concept of God must be based.

But knowledge was never enough. Moses called on Israel to "acknowledge and take to heart that the LORD is God" (Dt 4:39). This is a clear expression of how Israel was to respond to God's self-disclosures. The believer's whole outlook is to be shaped by awareness that God exists and that God can and does act in the world of humans. To "acknowledge" God means to take him seriously, conscious always of his presence and his power.

Second, there must be personal commitment to God. To acknowledge God means more than to recognize his power and presence. It implies a deep personal response. That response is one of moral commitment rather than simply intellectual assent. Thus, where God is not known (acknowledged), "there is no faithfulness, no love. . . . There is only cursing, lying and murder, stealing and adultery; they break all bounds, and bloodshed follows bloodshed" (Hos 4:1–2). In contrast, Jeremiah recalls the reign of a godly king with these words: " 'He did what was right and just, so all went well with him. He defended the cause of the poor and needy, and so all went well. Is that not what it means to know [*yāda'*, acknowledge] me?' declares the LORD" (Jer 22:15–16).

Acknowledging, or knowing, the Lord implies a deep personal commitment to God, expressed in moral and personal transformation. On the basis of God's self-revelation we make a commitment of ourselves to him, acknowledging him as Lord of our lives. Only this full commitment adequately expresses what the OT means in its call for us to acknowledge the Lord (cf. Pr 3:5–6).

NT — 4. Religious use of "acknowledge". The Gospels and the Epistles speak of acknowledging Jesus before other people (Mt 10:32; 2 Jn 7). In such passages the KJV typically speaks of "confessing" him.

The Greek word here is *homologeō* and means "to say the same" and thus to agree in one's statement. The word has strong legal connotations. A person can confess to a charge in court and thus openly acknowledge guilt. Or one may agree with a court order and thus make a legally binding commitment to abide by it.

This last sense is implied in passages that call on us to acknowledge Jesus. We are to express our binding commitment to Jesus publicly and thus acknowledge our relationship to him as our Lord. John puts the importance of this issue succinctly: "No one who denies the Son has the Father; whoever acknowledges the Son has the Father also" (1 Jn 2:23). Commitment to Jesus brings us into full relationship with God.

5. Other uses of "acknowledge". Not every occurrence of "acknowledge" in the NIV and the NASB reflects the presence of *homologeō*. In one place, Paul speaks of persons who are "always learning but never able to acknowledge the truth" (2 Ti 3:7). The phrase means that these persons are incapable of recognizing the truth and thus are unable to acknowledge it.

Forms of the Greek word for "to know" are used in 1 Co 14:37 and Rev 3:9. In each case, an admission of a truth is forced from persons who were previously unwilling to acknowledge it.

6. Summary. What do we learn about our faith and our relationship with God from passages in which the word "acknowledge" is found? The moral implications of acknowledging sin are explored in another article. ◆ *Confession of Sins* The religious implications of acknowledging God, discussed here, are especially significant for us.

We are reminded that God has made himself known through history and Scripture. You and I are called on to take this person, who truly is the Most High God, with utmost seriousness. Meeting God through his revelation requires a response that has two definite aspects: (1) The OT stresses our inner and moral response to the Lord. We commit ourselves to God and to his ways and experience the inner transformation that relationship with God always brings. (2) The NT stresses our public response. We are to openly acknowledge Jesus as God's Son and express faith's binding commitment to him. We take our stand with God on the truth that only through Jesus can any human being approach relationship with the Father.

It is indeed good to know that we who do acknowledge God have his own binding promise: "If anyone acknowledges that Jesus is the Son of God, God lives in him and he in God" (1 Jn 4:15).

ACQUIT

In the OT and NT the thought is the same: acquittal is a judicial act that declares a person to be innocent. The Hebrew word translated "acquit" (*ṣādaq*) is found in 1 Ki 8:32 and 2 Ch 6:23, the latter capturing its full meaning: "Declare the innocent not guilty and so establish his innocence."

Jesus' reference to "careless words" that acquit or condemn (Mt 12:36–37) can be understood in the context of the passage. A good man speaks and acts according to his character. Likewise, the words and actions of an evil person flow spontaneously from his character (heart). Thus, every spontaneous expression ("careless word") reflects the person's character and provides a valid basis for judgment or acquittal.

ACTS/ACTIONS

Both human beings and God are portrayed in the Bible as persons who act freely and responsibly in the material universe. The NIV and the NASB convey this truth in the words they use to translate Hebrew and Greek words that deal with acts and actions.

OT 1. The Hebrew words
    2. The moral framework of human actions
    3. God's mighty acts in history
NT 4. The Greek words
    5. The source of moral actions
    6. Summary

OT — 1. The Hebrew words. In passages where the Hebrew terms have moral or religious significance, the KJV tends to render these terms by either "doings" or "deeds," whereas modern English versions sometimes have "deeds" but more frequently have either "acts" or "actions."

The NASB adds to its use of "acts" a common formula in the historical books, summing up a king's record by the formula "the rest of the acts of." The Hebrew in these instances is *dābār*, which in this formula is translated "events" by the NIV.

The most common Hebrew word that expresses the idea of acts or actions is *'āśâh*, which means "to do," "to fashion," or "to accomplish." It is found almost twenty-six hundred times in the OT. When *'āśâh* is used of God, it emphasizes his acts in history. God is not distant or removed from the physical universe he created. God is fully able to act in the material world.

The noun *ma'ᵃśeh* is translated "actions" or "deeds" and is often applied to the awesome works that God has performed (Ps 66:3; 118:17).

Frequently other Hebrew words related to the verb *'ālal* are also rendered "deeds" or "actions." When used of human actions, these words have a strong negative connotation and emphasize the wicked quality of particular actions. In contrast, when God is the subject, the same words stress the righteous quality of his actions (Ps 66:5; 105:1).

2. The moral framework of human actions. Human actions are not morally neutral. We are responsible for our choices, and responsibility is reflected in many OT descriptive terms. The OT decries the fact that people at times act deceitfully (Ex 8:29), impurely (Lev 20:21), treacherously (Jdg 9:23), irreverently (2 Sa 6:7), wickedly (2 Ch 6:37), corruptly (Jer 6:28; Zep 3:7), and lewdly (Eze 22:9). The prophets Jeremiah and Ezekiel were particularly critical of the immoral "conduct and actions" of the people of Judah just prior to the Babylonian captivity (Jer 4:18; 7:3,5; 18:11; 26:13; 35:15; Eze 14:22,23; 24:14; 36:17,19).

The OT establishes the standard by which human actions can be judged. All Israel was called to act "in accordance with what is written in the Law, in the Book of Moses" (2 Ch 25:4). Therefore, righteous and honest actions can be known, and "every prudent man" can act on this knowledge (Pr 13:16; cf. Jdg 9:16,19; 1 Sa 12:7; 2 Ki 12:15;). By comparing actions of the individual with the moral framework provided in the divine law, "even a child is known by his actions" (Pr 20:11). As Micah (6:8) reminded an indifferent generation: "He has shown you, O man, what is good. And what does the LORD require of you? To act justly and to love mercy and to walk humbly with your God." God hates the vile deeds of the corrupt (Ps 14:1). He has provided a revelation of the moral framework within which human beings are to choose to live.

3. God's mighty acts in history. The descriptive words linked with God's actions tend to stress his greatness and his power. God's deeds are mighty (Ps 71:16; 106:2; 145:4,12), awesome (Ps 65:5; 66:3), wonderful (Ps 26:7; 105:2), and marvelous (Ps 71:17; 72:18; 86:10). They are acts of power (Ps 150:2). His acts are also righteous (Ps 71:24) and praiseworthy (Ps 78:4).

An awed sense of wonder at God's ability to act in history grips the writers of the OT. "Has any god ever tried to take for himself one nation out of another nation," Moses asks, "by testings, by miraculous signs and wonders, by war, by a mighty hand and an outstretched arm, or by great and awesome deeds, like all the things the LORD your God did for you in Egypt before your very eyes?" (Dt 4:34).

The God of the OT is a God with unlimited ability to act in the world of humans beings. Confident of this fact, Jonathan and a single armor-bearer boldly attacked a detachment of Philistines (1 Sa 14:6,13). Similarly, God's OT saints cried out in prayer, "It is time for you to act, O LORD " (Ps 119:126; cf. Da 9:19).

God's acts in creation, in bringing the Genesis flood, and in redeeming Israel from Egypt are to be told and retold by his people (1 Ch 16:9) so that his people will stand in awe of the Lord and of his deeds (Hab 3:2). Our concept of what God is like ought to be shaped by the conviction that he lives and that he is able to act on our behalf.

NT — 4. The Greek words. The NT Greek words usually translated "doings," "deeds," and "works" are sometimes rendered "acts" and "actions." A survey of NT use shows that much stress is laid on doing good deeds and good works.

The most common words so translated are *ergazomai* (verb) and *ergon* (noun), which call attention to an action as something that stands in contrast to inactivity or talk, and *poieō*, which means simply "to do." *Ergon* occurs some 176 times in the NT, and the verb *ergazomai* 39 times. *Poieō* is very common, with 577 occurrences. Because these are common words, the implication of each must be determined by the context.

5. The source of moral actions. The NT makes clear that lawless deeds erupt from man's sinful nature (Gal 5:19–21). But there is no doubt that the NT emphasis is on good deeds and actions—an appropriate emphasis for a believing community "who profess to worship God" (1 Ti 2:10; cf. 5:10; 6:18; Heb 10:24).

While the OT directs our attention to an external standard by which we can assess the good or evil character of our actions, the NT directs our attention within—to the source of goodness. In order to make it possible for human beings to perform truly good actions, God had to take steps to make "alive with Christ" (Eph 2:5) individuals who were spiritually dead. As God's own handiwork in Christ, believers are reshaped within and are enabled to "do good works, which God prepared in advance for [them] to do" (Eph 2:10). God himself exercises supernatural power within the redeemed to accomplish his good purposes (Php 2:13).

The conviction that God does work an inner transformation underlies James's concern over those who claim to have faith but whose lives are not marked by appropriate actions (Jas 2:14). That kind of faith is both useless and dead (vv. 20,26), for the regenerate person will have a new heart that will express itself in what he or she says and does (cf. Mt 12:33–37). ◆ *Works*

6. Summary. God's mighty acts in history—in creation, judgment, redemption, and Jesus' resurrection—testify to his ability to exercise his sovereign power in our world. God's actions thus reveal his existence and much about his nature.

Human actions are similarly revealing. When people act contrary to the moral framework expressed in the divine law, human sinfulness is exposed. This is the primary emphasis in the OT approach to dealing with human actions.

The NT focuses on God's remedy. The death and resurrection of Jesus opened the way for new creative activity. God acts through Christ to transform the believer within, bringing life where there was only spiritual darkness and death. Reshaped and renewed, and empowered by God's presence, believers today are able to live lives that are marked by truly loving acts and by truly good deeds.

ADMINISTER/ADMINISTRATION

What is the spiritual gift of administration (1 Co 12:28)? How do elders administer the grace of God within the church (1 Pe 4:10)? Do the passages in the Bible that speak of administration help us answer questions like these?

OT terminology. A number of different Hebrew words or phrases are translated "administer" in modern English versions. Such phrases in the original as "do justice" and "execute judgment" are so translated in the NIV (1 Ki 3:28; Jer 21:12). At other times, the Hebrew word indicating "administrator" means "one who is over or above" (*'al*). Daniel apparently borrowed a foreign word for use in 6:2–3 to identify the administrators in the Persian bureaucracy; it is a word that tells us little of the administrative system or the administrators' roles and responsibilities. Other OT words and phrases simply serve as general references to governing: they encompass the full range of legislative, executive, and judicial functions without clear definition.

NT terminology. The NT words and their usage are no more precise than those of the OT. Three times the Greek words translated "administer" or "administration" are *oikonomos* or *oikonomia* (Eph 3:2,9; 1 Pe 4:10). An *oikonomos* was a slave who served as manager of a man's property and household.

In most NT occurrences, the Greek word involved refers to such a manager or managerial responsibility (Lk 12:42; 16:1,2,3,4,8; Gal 4:2). In some passages it is applied to the exercise of leadership in the church (1 Co 4:1,2; Tit 1:7).

When Paul in 2 Co 8:19 speaks of an offering, he uses *diakoneō*, which means an act of service or a ministry. When he speaks of a gift of administration in 1 Co 12:28, the word is *kybernēsis* (used only here in the NT). This is a nautical term that signifies the steersman, who holds the ship on the course directed by the captain.

Conclusions. It is clear that leaders of the NT church were called to "administer" the body of Christ. But just how they administered cannot be established from the very general terms used in the original text. As managers, leaders are expected to be faithful (1 Co 4:2) and personally blameless (Tit 1:7). But we must seek from other Bible portions to define how God expects leaders to lead. ◆ *Leadership*

ADMIT

Some occurrences of this word (Job 27:5; 40:14; Hos 5:15; 2 Co 11:21) use it in the sense of acknowledging something to be true. Ac 24:14 and Heb 11:13 use the word in a more powerful religious sense, involving open confession and public commitment to God. ◆ *Acknowledge*

ADMONISH

The NT calls on believers to admonish one another (Col 3:16). What is involved in this term?

In OT passages, the one admonishing is God. In Mal 2:1,4, for example, the "admonition" is a "commandment," in which God's will is set in sharp contrast with the actions of his priests. The "admonition" in Ne 9:26,30 is a "word of warning," a testimony or witness uttered to turn God's wandering people back to him.

In the NT, admonishing is done by believers. The Greek word translated "admonish" is *noutheteō*. It means "to warn or advise" and, in this sense, "to instruct." The verb occurs eight times in the NT (Ac 20:31; Ro 15:14; 1 Co 4:14; Col 1:28; 3:16; 1 Th 5:12,14; 2 Th 3:15), and the noun form, *nouthesia* (admonition), is found three times (1 Co 10:11; Eph 6:4; Tit 3:10). In these passages it is usually translated "warn" or "warning" but may be rendered "instruct" or "train."

When we examine the passages, we sense that "admonishing" is a ministry calling for much warmth and closeness. There is no hint of a distant judgmentalism or of criticism launched from some height of supposed superiority. Paul's admonitions were stimulated by a deep love for young believers. His love was so deep that his admonitions were often accompanied by tears.

Paul does not see admonition as an exclusive prerogative of leaders. The members of the body of Christ at Rome were "competent to instruct [admonish] one another" (Ro 14:15), and all believers are called to exercise this ministry with one another (Col 3:16). When we love our brothers and sisters and have a genuine concern for their well-being, we can hardly hesitate to encourage them to live godly lives and thus bring glory to the Lord.

ADOPT/ADOPTION

This concept is theologically significant, for the Bible tells us that we have been adopted into God's family. The Greek word *huiothesia* is found five times in the NT (Ro 8:15, "sonship"; 8:23; 9:4; Gal 4:5, "full rights of sons"; Eph 1:5).

Adoption was a legal act, in the NT referred to only by Paul. The roots of this metaphor are found in Roman rather than in Jewish or Greek culture. The most significant factor of the Roman legal system is the fundamental place given a father's authority.

In adoption an individual's old relationships were severed. Old debts and obligations were canceled. The person was placed under the authority of the father of the new family. The father was considered owner of all the adoptee's possessions and was believed to have the right to control the adoptee's behavior. The father also had the right of discipline and became liable for the new son or daughter's actions. Each was committed by the act of adoption to support and to help maintain the other.

What does this mean for us who have been adopted by God? It means we owe no allegiance to our old masters (cf. Gal 3:26–4:7). We now owe total allegiance to God the Father, and all that we have is his. On his part, God commits himself to guide us and to discipline us, that we might bring credit to his household.

For his part, God has given us the Holy Spirit to guarantee our release from all that once enslaved us (Gal 4:6–7). The Spirit's presence assures us that at the resurrection we will experience fully every benefit belonging to God's heirs (Ro 8:23).

ADULTERY

The Bible is serious about sex sins. Adultery and its companion, fornication (sometimes translated "prostitution" or "sexual immorality" in the NIV and the NASB), are forbidden to God's people. Our loving God rules out these practices for us. And in Scripture both "adultery" and "prostitution" sometimes represent spiritual unfaithfulness to the Lord.

OT 1. The nature of adultery and prostitution
2. Spiritual adultery or prostitution
3. The timeless message of Hosea

NT 4. Attitudes toward adultery and prostitution
5. The adulterous look
6. Adultery as grounds for divorce
7. Summary

OT — 1. The nature of adultery and prostitution. Two Hebrew words introduce us to God's view of heterosexual relationships outside of marriage. Nā'ap ("adultery") is intercourse with or by a married or engaged woman. The OT prohibition here is unequivocal: the sixth commandment states, "You shall not commit adultery" (Ex 20:14; Dt 5:18). The law instructed Israel to put adulterers and adulteresses to death (Lev 20:10). Both the inclusion of this prohibition among the Ten Commandments and the severity of the penalty underline the importance of sexual faithfulness as a foundation to a healthy marriage and society.

Zānâh is the Hebrew word translated "fornication" in older versions and often "prostitution" or "marital unfaithfulness" in modern versions. It occurs some ninety-three times in the OT and simply means illicit intercourse between a man and a woman. There is a basic difference between zānâh and nā'ap. The former does not involve violation of the marriage vow. But like adultery, zānâh is forbidden by God (Lev 19:29). The OT distinctions are carried over into the NT in two similarly separate Greek words (see accompanying chart).

The biblical commitment to sexual purity, which was so integral a part of God's will for Israel, is striking in view of the role of sexuality in the other religions of the time and area. Those religions stressed fertility, and their rites often called for sexual orgies to stimulate the gods and goddesses and thus ensure bountiful harvests. Ritual prostitution by men and women was also part of these religions, and the role of a religious prostitute was viewed as honorable, to be accepted by the respectable of society.

Pagan attitudes toward sexuality reflected the beliefs of the people about their gods and goddesses. The attitude of the OT toward sexuality reveals the na-

	Adultery	Prostitution (Fornication)
OT	*nā'ap*	*zānâh*
NT	*moicheia*	*porneia*
d i f f e r e n c e s	usually refers to men relations with a married person not spouse not a professional prostitute death penalty appropriate	usually refers to women relations outside of marriage often a professional prostitute death penalty not appropriate
s i m i l a r i t i e s	both are forbidden by God both are used figuratively to represent spiritual and moral unfaithfulness in God's people both merit and will receive divine punishment	

ture of God and the nature of God's relationship with his people. Pagan gods and goddesses were selfish and capricious, ruled by the passions that rule humans. By contrast, the God portrayed in the Bible is not selfish nor untrustworthy: he is ruled by the covenant relationship he committed himself to with Abraham. Because sexual relationships between a man and a woman are intended to reflect the intimate relationship between God and his people, a covenant of faithfulness between marriage partners is essential. Adultery and other sex relations outside of marriage violate something basic to the very nature of God and

to our own nature as beings created in his image. ◊ **Marriage** ◊ **Sex** Marriage, as an exclusive commitment, is the necessary context for sexual expression for God's people. Our faithfulness to that relationship is critical.

2. Spiritual adultery or prostitution. Ancient Israel fell short of God's call to sexual purity. The Israelites found the pagan religions, with their open sensuality, all too attractive. The symbolic linkage of idolatry with the sexual sins that idolatry encouraged is found early—in Lev 17:7. There God warns the people that they "must no longer offer any of their sacrifices to the idols to whom they prostitute themselves."

The later prophets picked up the thought. Over and over the prophets represented Israel's unfaithfulness to God in turning to idolatry as an act of spiritual adultery or prostitution (e.g., Jer 3:1–9; Eze 23:1–45; Hos 4). These terms are used in the same way in Revelation (2:20–22; 17:1–16). The association of *nā'ap* and *zānâh* with idolatry, the most detestable of religious sins, shows how seriously God considers sex sins to be. ♦ *Idol/Image*

3. The timeless message of Hosea. The prophet Hosea preached to Israel in the decades just before that northern kingdom was taken captive by Assyria (722 B.C.). The people in the northern part of that divided land had been unfaithful to God for some 250 years and during that time had been led by eighteen evil kings, many of whom imported pagan religions and morals. In the first three chapters of his book, Hosea tells his own story to Israel. The prophet was commanded by God to marry "an adulterous wife" (1:2). The couple had children, but then the wife, Gomer, left home to live with a series of lovers. Hosea was called to bear the pain of this betrayal and finally was told: "Go, show your love to your wife again, though she is loved by another and is an adulteress. Love her as the Lord loves the Israelites" (3:1). To restore the shattered relationship, Hosea actually purchased his prostitute wife from the one who then owned her.

The rest of the book draws parallels between Hosea and Gomer's relationship and that of God and faithless Israel. Prostitute Israel had abandoned God and hurt him deeply. But God continued to love them. Israel's coming defeat by Assyria and subsequent exile would be a severe discipline for them, but God said, "They will seek my face; in their misery they will earnestly seek me" (5:15). They were told to pray for restoration through forgiveness (14:2). God promised to heal their waywardness (14:4), and they would again become a faithful and fruitful people (14:5–8).

The message of Hosea is a message of pain and of healing. It is a triumphant affirmation of the faithfulness of God. Both sexual unfaithfulness and spiritual unfaithfulness tear at the basis of intimate interpersonal relationships and bring deep suffering. But God remains faithful to his wandering people, and he acts to restore. The forgiveness and the inner transformation God offers all who will respond to him is the key that makes all things possible—even the restoration of a shattered home.

NT — 4. Attitudes toward adultery and prostitution. The NT speaks just as strongly as the OT against adultery and prostitution. However, there is an important shift of rationale. There is a powerful new reason why sex outside of marriage is repugnant to the Lord. But some NT statements on adultery have often been misunderstood.

The NT never suggests that adultery (*moicheia*) or prostitution (*porneia*) is acceptable. But it makes clear how we should deal with individuals who fall short.

a. We must not avoid such persons who are outside the Christian fellowship. Paul told the Corinthians not to associate with "sexually immoral people" (*pornos*). Later he had to write and explain. He did "not at all mean" to suggest withdrawal from "the people of this world" (1 Co 5:10). That would mean isolation from the very people Christians are called to lead to Jesus! Certainly Jesus did not avoid such persons; and as the story of the woman caught in the act of adultery illustrates, Jesus' first concern was to bring forgiveness and then, with it, release from the power of every kind of sin (Jn 8:1–11).

b. There must be discipline for those within. Thus, sexual immorality (*porneia*) in the fellowship is to be dealt with decisively by the Christian community (1 Co 5:1–12). ♦ *Discipline*

The rationale is explained in 1 Co 6:12–20. In a Christian's relationship with Jesus, the believer is actually an organic part of the Lord's body. It is unthinkable that Christ would be involved in immorality. Thus our bodies, linked with Jesus and being the temples of the Holy Spirit, must be kept holy. We are to treat ourselves as holy instruments, to be used in God's service and not involved in sexual sins. Finally, Paul reminds us, "You are not your own: you were bought with a price. Therefore honor God with your body" (6:20).

c. Judgment is coming. Sexual immorality is characteristic of those who reject God and the lifestyle of his kingdom (2 Pe 2:14). Those who practice immorality will be judged and excluded from the eternal kingdom (1 Ti 1:10; Heb 13:4; Rev 21:8; 22:15).

5. The adulterous look. Matthew quotes Jesus as saying, "You have heard that it was said, 'Do not commit adultery.' But I tell you that anyone who looks at a woman lustfully has already committed adultery with her in his heart" (Mt 5:27–28).

What does this mean? Is an appreciative glance at a member of the opposite sex a sin? Even the original words for "longing look" are not decisive in helping us interpret Jesus' meaning.

But the context is decisive. Jesus had just told his listeners that he came to "fulfill" (express the true meaning of) the divine law (Mt 5:17). He warned that to come near heaven's kingdom one must have a righteousness exceeding the righteousness of the Pharisees. Jesus then explained by providing a series of illustrations. The law on which the Pharisees pinned their hope of heaven forbade murder, but Jesus shows that anger is the source of murderous intent (Mt 5:21–22). The law forbade adultery, but Jesus shows that adultery grows out of lust located in the heart (Mt 5:27–28). In his illustrations, Jesus shows that while law is able only to help regulate behavior, God is concerned with the human heart. To live as members of the heavenly kingdom, something must be done about the anger that produces murder and the lust that leads to adultery. Righteousness for Jesus' people is not simply a matter of what a person does or does not do. Righteousness is a matter of what a person is within. God's kingdom can be entered and enjoyed only by those

whose hearts are pure; the Pharisees' legalistic approach stressed actions but ignored the human heart.

In this context, then, Jesus is not speaking of appreciating beauty, nor even of momentary desire. Jesus is teaching us that we need to become the kind of individuals who do not perceive others as objects to be used but see them as persons to be respected and valued. To fix our attention on another person and indulge in sexual fantasies about him or her (other than one's spouse) shows that God must still do much purifying work within our hearts.

6. Adultery as grounds for divorce. It is commonly accepted in the Christian community that adultery provides biblical grounds for divorce and subsequent remarriage. ♦ *Divorce and Remarriage* This interpretation of Mt 5:32 and 19:9 is questionable. The verses state: "Anyone who divorces his wife, except for marital unfaithfulness [*porneia*]," causes her to commit adultery" [*moicheia*], and if he then "marries another woman [he] commits adultery [*moicheia*]."

As seen above, *porneia* is a general term for any kind of illicit sexual intercourse. In later rabbinic thought it included prostitution, forbidden marriages (such as between relatives), incest, and all kinds of unnatural intercourse. The rendering of *porneia* as "marital unfaithfulness" in these passages may suggest adultery to an English reader, but the specific word for adultery was available and not used by Jesus.

Some commentators have concluded that Jesus may have been referring to prostitution rather than to adultery as a ground for divorce. But the term is so inclusive that we cannot be certain what is meant!

There are other reasons why we should hesitate before leaping to the common conclusion that adultery provides automatic grounds for divorce. OT law called for stoning adulterers, not for divorce. Yet there was divorce in the OT. God's own example, provided in Hosea, showed that the way to deal with marital unfaithfulness was to accept the suffering and seek through forgiveness to find reconciliation.

This divine model is supported by the argument of two chapters of Matthew's Gospel (Mt 18–19). The sequence begins with a definition of greatness in God's kingdom. We are to remember that all Christians who fall into sin are, like straying sheep, to be restored with joy. We are to realize that we are like quarreling children, and we must cover hurts with forgiveness. When it is hard to forgive, we are to remember that we ourselves have been forgiven an incalculable debt.

Adultery is a sin that can devastate a marriage, the most intimate of personal relationships. But adultery should not be viewed as grounds for an automatic termination of the relationship.

7. Summary. Sexual intercourse outside of marriage is sin for both the married and the unmarried. God forbids it, for our good. The commandments against adultery and sexual immorality are rooted deep in the character of God as a faithful and loyal person. We are to mirror his faithfulness and show the same kind of loyalty in our relationships.

The serious nature of adultery is seen in references to it in the OT and in Revelation as an illustration of the ultimate unfaithfulness, apostasy, and idolatry. The NT reinforces the serious nature of sex sins for believers by reminding us that we are linked forever with Jesus and indwelt by the Holy Spirit. Jesus has paid the ultimate price for us, and, as His own people now, we are to commit our bodies to the Lord's service, not to serve sinful passions.

As sexual beings we will experience the pull of temptation toward *moicheia* and *porneia*. To surrender is not only wrong but also foolish. Like other sins, adultery erodes our character and brings guilt and suffering. As the biblical proverbs remind us, we need to be guided by the traditions of the godly and the commands of the Scripture, for they are "the way to life, keeping you from the immoral woman, from the smooth tongue of the wayward wife. Do not lust in your heart after her beauty or let her captivate you with her eyes, for the prostitute reduces you to a loaf of bread, and the adulteress preys upon your very life" (6:23–26).

ADVERSARY ♦ *Enemy*

ADVICE ♦ *Counsel/Advice*

AFFECTION

Occurrences of the word "affection" in modern translations usually reflect one of several common OT terms for love. In the NT, such references translate a single, uncommonly powerful Greek word.

The verb form of this Greek word, *splanchnizomai*, is found only in the Gospels. There it is used to communicate the deepest of divine emotions called out by human needs. We can sense best the meaning and power of this emotional term by reading such stories as the one that reveals the lonely agony of the man with leprosy (Mk 1:41) or the confusion of the harassed and hungry crowds (Mt 9:36). In response to both needs, Jesus was "moved with compassion" (KJV). The Lord is portrayed as being so moved also elsewhere in the Gospels: Mt 9:36; 14:14; 15:32; 18:27 (in a parable); 20:34; Mk 1:41; 6:34; 8:2; 9:22–27; Lk 7:13; 10:33.

The noun form of the word *splanchna* is found nine times in the Epistles. We discover that Christ's own affection invades the heart of Paul (Php 1:8). The apostle expects those of us who are now united to Christ to have Jesus' own compassion (*splanchna*) for each other (Php 2:1; Col 3:12). See also 2 Co 7:15; Phm 7,12,20; 1 Jn 3:17.

Originally the word *splanchna* was a physical term, encompassing all vital inner organs. Extended, it became a powerful emotional word, expressing the total involvement of one's being at the deepest possible level. The complete caring and deep love projected by *splanchna* are possible only for God. But God makes it possible for believers to begin to share this quality, for we are being transformed to share Jesus' own likeness (2 Co 3:18).

AFFLICTION

This common OT word is usually a translation of some form of *'ānâh*, "to afflict, oppress, humble." The word expresses a sense of helplessness and distress. It is associated with poverty and may imply that the afflicted person is socially and economically defenseless, subject to the oppression by others.

God not only permits affliction but he also uses it. Although affliction is sometimes a punishment (2 Ki 15:5), it is actually intended as a blessing. When Solomon dedicated the Jerusalem temple, he expressed that thought. He called on God to respond to the people "when they pray toward this place and confess your name and turn from their sin because you have afflicted them" (1 Ki 8:35). Affliction is never pleasant. But the godly will say, "It was good for me to be afflicted so that I might learn your decrees" (Ps 119:71).

We cannot, however, dismiss the devastating impact of the pain suffered by the afflicted in society. We sense something of that helplessness when Isaiah twice uses the word "afflicted" to describe the sufferings of the Messiah as he is crushed for our sins and burdened with the weight of our iniquities (Isa 53:4,7). ◆ *Poor and Oppressed* The psalmists often cry out to God, expressing the despair of the afflicted. Isaiah responds with a promise: "The LORD comforts his people and will have compassion on his afflicted ones" (Isa 49:13).

The NIV renders *thlipsis* "affliction" once (Col 1:24) but uses other words to translate the same term elsewhere (Ac 7:10; 20:23; 2 Co 6:4; 1 Th 3:3; 2 Th 1:4). NASB uses "affliction(s)" in all of these verses. The Greek word *thlipsis* is not linked with social vulnerability. It focuses attention on external conditions as the cause of emotional pressures. Paul's thought in Colossians is that the afflictions and the suffering that have come to him in the course of his ministry should not be viewed as discipline or as punishment. Instead, such suffering is an extension of the suffering experienced by Jesus, for it comes from the same source. Following Jesus, Paul also willingly chose a course of action that would bring him into conflict with human society. We, too, have the privilege of making such choices, knowing that the pain that comes to us is far outweighed by the benefits our suffering will bring to others.

AFRAID ◆ *Fear*

AGE (OLD AGE)

What is the attitude of Scripture toward aging? Is any particular portion of the human life span especially valued?

OT 1. Normal life span
    2. Old age
    3. The age of accountability
    4. Long life before the Flood
NT 5. Age and maturity

OT — 1. Normal life span. Several different words for age and aging occur in Hebrew. According to Ps 90:10, the normal life span was some seventy years. It was unusual for people to live to eighty, and typically the very old were infirm (e.g., 1 Ki 1:1).

The OT seems to distinguish certain ages of demarcation. Twenty was evidently particularly significant as an age of initiation into adulthood (Nu 14:29). At thirty a Levite or priest could begin his ministry (Nu 4:3,23,30,35,39), as did Jesus (Lk 3:23). ◆ *Priests and Levites* Sixty may have been considered the point at which one passed into old age (Lev 27:1–8).

2. Old age. Despite the loss of physical vigor owned by the youth and the mature person (Isa 40:29–31), attaining old age was viewed as a blessing from God (Pr 9:11; Isa 65:20). Older members of the community were to be given special respect (Lev 19:32), and it was unwise to ignore their advice (e.g., 1 Ki 12:6–20). Typically each community in Israel had its own group of local elders to settle disputes and guide daily life. ◆ *Elders* In the vision of the ideal community provided in the Pentateuch, these elders had a most significant role in maintaining the integrity of the community.

3. The age of accountability. Some have raised the question of when a person becomes responsible for his or her actions. Closely linked is the question of how old a person must be to truly understand and respond to the gospel message.

There are no answers to such questions. On the one hand the OT points to twenty as the age when a youth is allowed to serve in the army. The same age was specified when the Israelites rebelled against God and refused to enter Canaan. "Every one . . . twenty years old or more" was considered responsible and was doomed to die during the years of wilderness wandering (Nu 14:29).

On the other hand, the NT reminds us that Timothy knew the Scriptures "from infancy" (probably specifying a span between three and seven years of age). It is these Scriptures that "are able to make [one] wise for salvation through faith in Christ Jesus" (2 Ti 3:15).

Rather than speculate on the age of accountability, it is best to simply share our faith with others, including children, and trust God to work in their lives. ◗ *Children*

4. Long life before the Flood. According to the chronologies of Genesis, the ancients each lived for hundreds of years (Ge 5 and 11). How can we explain this phenomenon?

One good suggestion is linked with these people's closeness to Adam and Eve. The original vigor transmitted from the first pair faded with the debilitating impact of sin on the human physiognomy as the millennia passed. Another possible explanation is linked with vast changes introduced by the Flood. Some believe that early Genesis indicates that heavy masses of water vapor floated in the atmosphere before the Flood. The flood waters remained on the earth, the atmosphere thus providing less protection from cosmic radiation after the Flood. Cosmic rays have been shown to be associated with aging.

NT — 5. Age and maturity. The NT also teaches that older persons are due the respect of others (1 Ti 5:1–2). There is reason to believe that NT church elders were mature not only spiritually but also in age. ◗ *Elders* The existence in the NT church of a special "widows roll" of women over sixty who had been faithful wives and were known for good deeds gives insight into one reason why older persons were considered for leadership. Not only did they have time to mature, but also the quality of their lives would have been observed for years, and their established character would be well known (1 Ti 5:9–10; cf. 3:1–12). The NT reminds us that besides the normal respect due an aged person, a special degree of respect is won by a godly life and spiritual maturity. ◗ *Maturity*

The fact that Paul had to urge Timothy to speak up despite his relative youth— Timothy being probably just under forty at the time—reflects the attitude of the culture that considered older persons wiser than younger ones. Paul urged Timothy to overcome that disadvantage by setting "an example for the believers in speech, in life, in love, in faith and in purity" (1 Ti 4:12). The quality of one's life as a disciple, not one's age, is the ultimate qualification for spiritual influence and is the basis on which any of us can win respect.

AGE/AGES

What do the Gospels mean when they speak of the "end of the age" or of the "age to come"? What is "this present evil age" that is described so graphically in the Epistles? And how do you and I relate to God's "ages"?

NT 1. The Greek word
2. This present evil age
3. The end of this age
4. The age to come

NT — 1. The Greek word. The NT use of *aiōn*, the word translated "age" in the NIV and the NASB—"world" in some NASB occurrences—reflects the OT's use of the Hebrew word *ʿôlām*. That Hebrew word indicates a person's life span. The distant past and far future lie well beyond the limited time allotted a single generation. They cannot be directly experienced by any individual. But the OT is awed by the fact that God has an unlimited "lifetime." He is with us now, he has always existed, and he will always exist. Because human beings can relate to God by faith, each generation can find security, rooted not in present circumstances but in the promises of the One who remains the same "yesterday and today and forever" (lit., to the *aiōnas* [Heb 13:8]).

The NT word *aiōn* retains the flavor of *'ôlām* but has additional import. The noun *aiōn*, found some one hundred and two times in the NT, indicates a time of unspecified duration. With a preposition like "from" it means "from the beginning" or "since the world began" (Ac 3:21; 15:18; Jn 9:32). With the preposition "to" it is understood as "forever" (cf. Lk 1:33,55; Ro 1:25; 2 Co 9:9).

Often *aiōn* indicates an "age," or "epoch." Then it focuses our attention on a time span marked by some distinctive or moral characteristics. According to Scripture, the underlying idea of history is that time and events flow in a series of successive ages toward God's intended culmination (Mt 13:39; 28:20; 1 Co 10:11; Heb 9:26). It is likely that this meaning should also be read in Heb 1:2 and 11:3, which speak of God's creating the "universe" (NIV). Faith shows us a God who not only originates the physical universe but also shapes the course of history.

God, then, distinguishes between succeeding historical epochs and calls on us to be alert to the characteristics of the age in which we live.

2. This present evil age. Descriptions of "this" age focus on characteristics of the human societies within which Christians are called to live. "This age" is not only the undetermined period of time between Christ's first and second comings; it is also the spiritual and psychological state of a humanity that ignores all that God has done in Christ to redeem mankind.

As a spiritual and psychological state, this age is evil (Gal 1:4). Its wise men and

its philosophers are blind to God and ignorant of him, for they scornfully reject the crucified Christ (1 Co 1:20–25). The principles by which this age operates are "foolishness in God's sight" (1 Co 3:19), for lost humanity is blinded by illusions that are sponsored by Satan, the unacknowledged "god of this age" (2 Co 4:4).

The Bible's exciting news about this present age is that God has invaded it and mankind's dark territory (Eph 6:12). Jesus has acted to rescue us (Gal 1:4), not by removing us from the world but by calling us to share in a divine transformation. Believers actually taste "the powers of the coming age" (Heb 6:5), for God is at work now to transform us into Jesus' likeness (2 Co 3:18), and he will do so fully at the resurrection (1 Jn 3:2–3). Our calling is to "live godly lives in this present age" (Tit 2:12), refusing to be "conformed to this world" (*aiōn*, Ro 12:2). Instead of conforming, we are to open our lives to God, permitting him to reshape our attitudes and perspective.

▶ **Mind** We thus learn to live by God's principles rather than by the subtly distorted principles that infuse human society, and we experience God's blessings now and in the age to come (Mk 10:29–30; Lk 18:30; 1 Ti 6:19).

3. The end of this age. The Bible consistently announces that history is on the move—toward a planned culmination. The present age, marred by Satan's evil influence and by the dark passions and twisted values of a lost humanity, will come to an end. God himself will break into history again. He will gather all mankind together for final judgment (Mt 13:40–43; 25:31–46; Mk 13).

For now, the present age with its evil characteristics coexists with a unique expression of God's kingdom, seen in the living church. But when history reaches its intended end, God's decisive intervention will forever separate light from darkness, good from evil, true from false.

4. The age to come. God is unquestionably the "King of the Ages" (*tō basilei tōn aiōnōn*, [1 Ti 1:17]); he not only created the physical universe but also guides the course of history (Heb 1:2;

11:3). Although key elements of God's plan and purpose remained hidden from the ancients (Ro 16:25; Eph 3:9; Col 1:26), God has remained in control. In a real sense, this present age is the "end of the ages," for in it the full meaning of human existence and the answer to man's struggle with sin and death have been revealed. Jesus has come and unveiled God's plan in his sacrifice to take away sin (Heb 9:26–28). From our present perspective we can see the full scope of God's plan to redeem and purify humanity. We look ahead with confidence to our resurrection to an endless life in God's new and purified universe to come.

Whenever we feel dismayed or discouraged about current events or about our present trials, we can find comfort by remembering that God is in control. He works out his purposes in history and in our lives. Today we are aliens, living in a society of the lost. But even in this present age, we have access through Jesus to the blessings of the age to come.

AGONY

"Agony" is a strong word in English. It is seldom used in modern translations, and then only to render a number of equally strong words or phrases in Hebrew and Greek. The "agony" of Ps 42:10 is literally "a sword in [the] bones." Pain overflows as Jeremiah (4:19) cries: "Oh, my anguish, my anguish! I writhe in pain. Oh, the agony of my heart! My heart pounds within me, I cannot keep silent."

Each NT occurrence of "agony" translates one of four different Greek words, each of which goes beyond common words for suffering. ♦ *Pain and Suffering* Lk 16:24–25 expresses the physical anguish and mental pain of the unbelieving dead. ♦ *Heaven and Hell* Ac 2:24 uses a word that means the "sharp pangs" associated with childbirth (cf. Rev 12:2). Another Greek word, *basanismos* ("torture" or "torment"), is used six times in Scripture, all in Revelation (9:5; 14:11; 18:7,10,15), in 14:11 picturing the agony of the damned. Rev 16:10 uses another

word, *masaomai* (found only here in Scripture), which portrays a pain so intolerable that the sufferer gnaws on his own tongue in mindless anguish.

Although there are a number of different words found in the original Hebrew and Greek, we can be sure when we read "agony" in our translations that the most intense of physical and mental suffering is in view.

AGREEMENT

Six of the nine OT occurrences of "agreement" are translations of *berît*, a word denoting a more or less formal treaty in which the rights and obligations of each party are spelled out. ♦ *Covenant* Other passages using "agreement" speak of an appointment (Job 2:11) or a less formal confederacy (Da 11:23). Each of the three NT uses of the noun agreement in the NIV translates a different Greek word.

Acts 15:15 says that the words of the prophets are "in agreement" with the stunning discovery that Gentiles as well as Jews can respond to the gospel message. The word is *symphōneō*, meaning, literally, to be in harmony with (symphony). The same word is found in Mt 18:19. In that verse is this promise of Jesus: "If two of you on earth agree about anything you ask for, it will be done for you by my Father in heaven." A harmonious unity about how we should pray together shows that God is at work in our hearts and is evidence that God intends to answer our prayer. Other NT occurrences of *symphōneō* are found in Mt 20:2,13; Lk 5:36; Ac 5:9. A related word, *symphōnēsis* (used only once in the NT), is found in 2 Co 6:15 ("What harmony is there between Christ and Belial?"), and yet another word, *symphōnos*, occurs only in 1 Co 7:5 ("Do not deprive each other [of sexual relations] except by mutual consent and for a time").

"Agreement" in 2 Co 6:16 is a translation of the word *synkatathesis*, found only here in the NT. The passage warns against being yoked with unbelievers and sets up a number of contrasts: of righteousness with wickedness, of Christ with Belial (the Devil), and of God's temple with idols. There is no way that adherents of such contradictory paths can form a union or reach a consensus on the basic issues of life.

"Agreement" also occurs in 1 Jn 5:8, a difficult passage to interpret. The verse speaks of God's testimony to Jesus by water, blood, and Spirit and says that "the three are in agreement." The original can be literally translated, "These three *are at one*" (*eis to hen eisin*). The problem has to do with the nature of the three witnesses. One acceptable interpretation links water to Jesus' baptism—the occasion at which he was announced to be God's Son (Jn 1:32–34). Blood is linked with Jesus' crucifixion in payment for our sins. The Spirit is seen in his present work as he brings eternal life to mankind through the merits of the sacrificial death of the Son. Thus these three—the deity of Jesus, his sacrificial death, and the transformation that faith in Jesus brings—all witness powerfully to the Son of God.

AID

The thrice-repeated promise "God will surely come to your aid" (Ge 50:24–25; Ex 13:19) are the first appearances of the word "aid" in the NIV. Here, as in Ruth 1:6 and Ps 106:4, the Hebrew word is *pāqad*. This word appears 309 times in the OT. In 57 of these, KJV translates it "visit." A person in charge takes action and, as a result, causes a dramatic change in the situation of a subordinate. Thus the promise "God will come to your aid" implies that God is sovereign, is able to act on our behalf, and surely will do so.

However, *pāqad* itself does not tell us what action God will take. The change in circumstances that the Lord's intervention brings may be for the worse as well as for the better. This same word is found in Lev 18:25, where God says, "Even the land was defiled; so I punished [*pāqad*] it for its sin" (cf. Ex 32:34; Ps 89:32). When you and I suffer oppression, we can call on God to act to change

our situation. On the other hand, when we sin, we cannot expect God to be paralyzed; we must remember that as sovereign Lord, God can and will act to discipline us.

In three uses of "aid" (Ps 35:2; 60:11; 108:12), the noun is *'ezrāh*, which means "to give help, support, or assistance."

Isaiah 38:14 offers us a beautiful picture. The word is *'ārab* and means "to become surety," or "to pledge." The dying Hezekiah cried out to God, "O Lord, I am oppressed, be my security" (NASB). Only a pledge of God's power could offer help to the godly king. In Christ, you and I know a God who does pledge himself to us and thus provides us with security peace, and confidence (cf. Ro 8:31–39).

AIR

The Greek word *aēr* occurs only seven times in the NT. (In the Gospels, "birds of the air" is literally "birds of the heavens" or "birds of the sky.") Three times "air" refers to the space around and above us (Ac 22:23; 1 Th 4:17; Rev 16:17). Twice the word is used in idioms. In one of the passages, Paul says his spiritual warfare is not "like a man beating the air" (1 Co 9:26); i.e., Paul is not shadow boxing but is in the ring with a real and dangerous opponent. In the other instance, exercising the gift of tongues without an interpreter is compared to "speaking into the air" (1 Co 14:9). Only intelligible speech will be understood by human listeners and will build up the church (cf. 14:1–19).

One other use of *aēr* is significant. The air is referred to in Eph 2:2 as ruled by Satan, that "spirit who is now at work in those who are disobedient." The reference is both to the oppressive atmosphere of evil that shrouds human society and to the common belief of the Greeks and of later Judaism that the air is the home of evil spirits and demons. Paul's point is that evil affects every individual, as seen in the cravings of our sinful nature.

ALARM/ALARMED

A number of biblical words are translated "alarm" in modern versions. Although fear is implicit in each of them, the focus is often on an external tumult and clamor that creates overwhelming internal uncertainty. It is good to know that amid the wars and rumors of war that make life in this world so uncertain, we have a quieting word from Jesus. Of all mankind, only Jesus' followers need not be alarmed (Mt 24:6; Mk 13:7). We alone know that God is still in control.

ALERT

The Greek word most commonly translated "alert" is *grēgoreō*, which means "to keep awake," "to be watchful and vigilant." It is variously translated, often appearing in the Gospels and the Epistles in exhortations stressing the importance of the warning or the instruction given (cf. Mt 24:42; 25:13; Mk 13:35,37; 14:38; Ac 20:31; 1 Co 16:13; 1 Pe 5:8; Rev 3:2).

ALIEN/ALIENS

Aliens are normally viewed with some suspicion. They are likely to feel strange and uncomfortable in the unfamiliar land. With this is mind, both OT and NT teachings take on personal significance.

OT 1. The alien in Israel
NT 2. Aliens in a hostile world

OT — 1. The alien in Israel. Three Hebrew words are usually translated "alien" or "foreigner," and sometimes "stranger." *Zār*, used about seventy times, conveys the idea of being unrelated, or not acquainted. *Nokrî* is used forty-five times and implies the unfamiliar or unknown. The most significant term is *gēr*, which occurs eighty-eight times and denotes one who is not a member of the community and thus does not possess the rights or the privileges of a member.

The Mosaic Law protected resident aliens in Israel. The rights of aliens in the nation were guarded (Ex 22:21; 23:9; Lev 19:33–34; Dt 10:18–19; 24:14, 17–18). When aliens were living in Israel, they were required to live by the divine law (Lev 24:22; 25:35; Dt 14:29; 24:19; 26:11–15). The writings of the prophets show that Israelites did not relate to aliens in the thoughtful way the law required (Jer 7:6; 22:3; Eze 22:7,29; Mal 3:5), even though Isaiah promised that one day aliens would gain a relationship with God (Isa 14:1; 61:5). By Jesus' time, aliens were regarded with deep hostility by the Jewish people (Mt 15:21–28; Mk 7:24–30; Jn 4:4–26; Ac 10:28 with 11:2–3; Gal 2:11–14).

NT — 2. Aliens in a hostile world. Three Greek words are commonly translated by a single family of words: *alien, foreigner,* and *stranger. Parepidēmos,* occurring only three times in the NT, refers to one staying for a while in a place he cannot call home (Heb 11:13; 1 Pe 1:1; 2:11). Three other Greek words, occurring a total of eight times in the NT, also visualize an alien living in a place not his home: *paroikeō* (Lk 24:18; Heb 11:9), *paroikia* (Ac 13:17; 1 Pe 1:17), and *paroikos* (Ac 7:6,29; Eph 2:19; 1 Pe 2:11). *Xenos,* used fourteen times in the NT, is a word that emphasizes the alienness of a person, a practice, or a doctrine to the community (Mt 25:35,38, 43–44; 27:7; Ac 17:18,21; Ro 16:23; Eph 2:12,19; Heb 11:13; 13:9; 1 Pe 4:12; 3 Jn 5).

The NT Epistles draw on the legal distinctions between Roman citizens and noncitizens to enrich the metaphor. Paul typically emphasizes the meaning of citizenship in God's kingdom, whereas Peter (who, unlike Paul, was not a Roman citizen) and the writer of Hebrews stress the Christian's position as an alien in this present world.

In NT times, most inhabitants of the Roman world were not citizens and were legally classed as aliens (Latin, *peregrinus*). Although aliens were subjects of Rome and burdened with heavy taxes, they were without rights under Roman law. Instead, they were held to be subject to the laws of their own citizenship. As a result, resident aliens had no right to claim protection in local courts. Yet, although their rights might not be recognized, their duty to Rome could be commanded. Resident aliens thus often banded together to form smaller subcommunities within the cities of the Roman Empire. The alien colonies operated under the laws of their homeland rather than under local law, which did not recognize them.

This situation in the empire helps us to understand implications of Jesus' teachings that his followers are to be in the world but not of it (Jn 15:18–19; 17:6–18). As aliens in this present world, Christians are vulnerable, without a basis to claim protection from, or rights under, an ungodly society. So we band together as Christ's church, God's own colony in man's world, to help each other follow the unique laws of our heavenly homeland (Eph 2:19; Php 3:20; 1 Pe 2:1–11; cf. Heb 11:8–16). ♦ *Foreign*

ALIENATE/ALIENATED

Alienation is a powerful term that has various connotations. The subtle differences are seen in three different Greek words translated "alienation" and "alienated" in modern English versions.

Gal 4:17 unveils the desire of false teachers to alienate the Galatian believers from Paul, who founded their church. The word used is *ekkleiō*, "to shut out, or exclude." This word is found only here and in Ro 3:27, where Paul teaches that the principle of justification by faith excludes boasting because it makes keeping the law clearly irrelevant to obtaining salvation.

Col 1:21 says of the believers in Colosse: "Once you were alienated from God and were enemies in your mind because of your evil behavior." The word here is *apallotrioō*. This is a powerful term, indicating the desperate and settled state of the lost. It is found only here and in two other places. In Eph 2:12 the lost are described as "separate from Christ, excluded from citizenship in Israel," and in 4:18 they are said to be "separated from the life of God." This alienated state is marked by blindness and hostility to God, by a loss of sensitivity that is caused when sensuality and lust dominate the personality, and by hopelessness. Though alienation is the settled state of the lost, Christ is able to reach their deadened personalities and to bring life to them through the gospel. Every believer was once just as far away but is now "brought near [to God] through the blood of Christ" (Eph 2:13).

Gal 5:4 has troubled many. The verse reads: "You who are trying to be justified by law have been alienated from Christ: you have fallen away from grace." The word translated "alienated" here is *katargeō*, which, with the preposition, simply means "to be separated from." The same construction is found in Ro 7:2,6. These verses teach that as death releases a widow from the law of marriage, so Christ's death releases believers (who are united with him) from the Mosaic Law. The word thus means "disconnection": its use in other NT passages shows no special association with the lost state, as does *apallotrioō*.

Paul further defines his thought in Gal 5 by adding the phrase "you are fallen away from grace." The Greek word rendered *fallen away from* is *ekpiptō*, which means "to fall out of" or "to loosen one's grasp of." *Ekpiptō* is used of stars that fall from heaven (Mt 13:25), chains that fall from hands (Ac 12:7), and words that have no effect (Ro 9:6), as well as of love that never fails (1 Co 13:8). Twice *ekpiptō* is used of a flower that withers and falls, no longer sustained by the life of the plant (Jas 1:11; 2 Pe 3:17).

The meaning of the phrases is thus suggested by the words used and is defined in the context. Paul is arguing with believers who, after salvation, abandon faith as the basis for Christian living. They have turned back to seek in the OT law a way to righteousness: they struggle to keep the law and thus to be vindicated by their own efforts. ♦ *Justify/Justification*

Paul argues that faith is as essential to Christian growth as to salvation. Anyone who turns away from the simplicity of faith-response to Jesus and who struggles to live by rules cuts himself off from the benefits found in the faith relationship. He loses his connection with God's transforming and enabling grace, which alone is able to sustain the growth of the new life given us in Christ.

To fall from grace here is not to lose salvation; it is a slipping away from that intimate relationship with Jesus through which God's grace can be claimed by faith to enable us to live godly lives.

ALIVE ▶ Life and Death

ALLY/ALLIANCE

God forbade Israel to make international alliances for defensive or even economic purposes—a practice common among other nations. Israel, as God's peculiar people, was to be distinctly different from the surrounding nations. Israel was warned a number of times against forming alliances (Ex 23:32; Jos 23:12).

The primary reason for this prohibition was religious. Treaty relationships would involve contact with pagan religions and call for toleration of pagan practices. This proved to be exactly what happened when Solomon adopted the strategy of interlinking international alliances. Solomon avoided war during his lifetime; but the alliances were sealed by royal marriages. Through the foreign women Solomon married, his heart was turned from the Lord to idolatry, and pagan worship centers were established in Jerusalem itself (1 Ki 11).

That the principle of nonalliance extended beyond international treaties to trading relationships may be inferred from 2 Ch 20:35–37. Jehoshaphat made a trade alliance with Israel's wicked king Ahaziah. A prophet came to Jehoshaphat and announced, "Because you have made an alliance with Ahaziah, the LORD will destroy what you have made" (v. 37). A subsequent storm wrecked the ships provided for the joint venture.

Perhaps the most significant reason to reject alliances was found in God's promises to Israel. God committed himself to protect his people and to give them victory over their enemies when Israel was obedient and followed his law (Dt 7:12–24; 28:7). In a very basic sense, making an alliance in a search for security was failure to trust God.

This same general principle of nonalliance is restated in the NT (2 Co 6:14–18). Faith and unbelief can never be yoked together. Believers are to be separated (as far as alliances are concerned) from all that is unclean and to live lives characterized by righteousness. Exactly to what relationships this principle of separation should extend must be determined by each individual. But it is clear that all our relationships and associations are to be carefully scrutinized.

ALMIGHTY

God's power is unlimited—he is omnipotent. His sovereignty and authority are unseen but active in our universe. These and other qualities are communicated in those biblical titles of the Lord that are translated "Almighty."

OT 1. God Almighty
    2. LORD Almighty
NT 3. The Almighty
    4. Summary

OT — 1. God Almighty. The Hebrew word that the English versions translate "God Almighty" is *šadday*. It is found forty-eight times in the OT as a divine title, thirty-one of them in Job. Seven times it is connected with God ('*ēl*), and forty-one times it appears alone. The word comes from a root meaning "mountain." It expresses the idea "God of mountains"; that is, one seated above all human authority. God appeared to each of the patriarchs and identified himself to them by this name (Ge 17:1; 28:3–4; 35:11; Ex 6:3). Thus the promises made in each context are guaranteed by God's power and overarching authority.

Occurrences of *šadday* in the Hebrew Bible can be identified in modern versions by "Almighty" standing alone or by "Almighty" (rather than "Lord") associated with "God."

2. LORD Almighty. The Hebrew word *ṣābā'* is also translated "Almighty" in the NIV, though the traditional translation "of Hosts" is retained in the RSV and NASB. The word means "armies."

This word occurs 486 times in the OT, over half of these associated with Yahweh as a title of God. Clearly the concept is a significant one!

First, the connection of this term with Yahweh is important. Yahweh identifies God as the living, active, ever-present Lord, who intervenes in history on behalf of his people. This name was revealed at the time of the Exodus, when God acted to "free [the people of Israel] from being slaves" and redeemed them with "an outstretched arm and with mighty acts of judgment" (Ex 6:6). ▶ **Lord** It is significant that the word "armies" is linked with this particular name of God; this affirms his active presence in history.

Second, the concept of armies extends beyond massed human military forces. The forces of heaven as well as of earth are at God's command, and nature itself may be called into battle on behalf of God's people (Jos 5:13–14; 10:10–19). The conviction that "it was the LORD . . . God who fought for" Israel (Jos 23:3) and was the unseen but real leader of Israel's forces (1 Sa 17:47) was basic to the OT believer's understanding of Israel's relationship with God.

Third, the concept LORD of Armies (LORD Almighty) affirms God's rule over every earthly power. God is the universal King. Even those armies that later overcame Israel and Judah did so as God's instruments, used by him to discipline a sinning people (Isa 10:5–6). The universal power of God over all humanity is masked now and unacknowledged by those who refuse to believe. But history will end, and God will appear as LORD of Armies. Through a final exercise of his power, the Lord will establish his power and set up his endless visible kingdom (Isa 29:5–8; 34:1–12; Zec 9:14–16; 14:2–21).

"LORD Almighty," or "LORD of Hosts," then, presents God as living and active, the present, though hidden, ruler of the universe who one day will be fully known when he establishes his visible kingdom.

NT — 3. The Almighty. The Greek word translated "Almighty" is *pantokratōr*. The compound links *pan* ("all") with *kratos*, a word for power, strength, and might. *Pantokratōr* signifies the unmatched greatness of God, who has power over all humankind and every competing authority (Eph 1:19–21). Occurrences of this word predominate (9 of the 10 uses) in Revelation. There they pick up the OT theme of God's final, decisive intervention in history, when he acts to destroy this world's kingdoms and to establish his own.

4. Summary. As the Almighty, God makes promises to people and commits his own power to see these promises carried out. This God is ever-present, hovering over history and free to act within it, even though his authority may be unacknowledged by those who do his will.

Ultimately, he will undertake a great, final intervention. Then every competing power will be visibly crushed, and God's hidden authority will be overwhelmingly visible. When this happens, the irresistible power that makes God almighty will be known and acknowledged by all (cf. Php 2:9–11; Rev 19:6).

ALTAR

The altar played a central role in Israel's worship of God, as it also did in other ancient peoples' idolatrous worship. The regulations surrounding the altar of Israel help us to better understand our own relationship with God through Jesus Christ.

OT 1. The nature of the altar
    2. The significance of altars
    3. Two types of altars
    4. Symbolic altars
NT 5. NT references to altars
    6. Summary

OT — 1. The nature of the altar. The essence of the altar is revealed in its Hebrew name: *mizbēaḥ*. The word comes from *zābaḥ*, "to sacrifice." The altar is "the place of sacrifice."

God himself instituted sacrifice in Eden when he used a covering of animal skins to clothe the fallen Adam and Eve (Ge 3:21). The first recorded instance of an altar built to worship the Lord was the one Noah built after the Flood (Ge 8:20), and each of the three patriarchs followed this practice after meeting with the Lord (Ge 12:7–8; 26:25; 35:3,7).

The law of Moses (c. 1450 B.C.) contains detailed instructions about the construction of the altar to be used by Israel and about the sacrifices to be offered on it. Instructions about sacrifice were given immediately after the moral and civil regulations of the law were announced. Once God's standards were inscripturated in the law, every violation was sin and brought guilt. The altar was a place where guilty people could come to bring the sacrifices that would reestablish a harmonious relationship with the Lord. ▶ *Offering and Sacrifice*

2. The significance of altars. In early Genesis the altar seems to have been both a place of sacrifice and a memorial, reminding the worshiper of some special experience with the Lord. The altar of sacrifice that the law instituted had a deeper significance. God says of the sacrificial animal: "The life of the creature is in the blood, and I have given it to you to make atonement for yourselves upon the altar; it is the blood that makes atonement for one's life" (Lev 17:11). It was through this—the altar and the covering of one's sins provided by the atoning sacrifice—that a sinner might approach a holy God. The altar thus was the point of contact with God: the place at which a sinning humanity might meet God in safety, with full assurance of forgiveness. ▶ *Atonement*

This significance is underlined in the design of the tabernacle and the temple. In each worship center the plan called for an enclosed court. There was only one door to permit entry. It was immediately inside this door that the altar of sacrifice was located. The lesson to Israel was clear: no one could approach God apart from sacrifice; that is, apart from the confession of sin and the atoning blood that the sacrifice involved.

The law also made it clear that there was to be only one worship center and one altar of sacrifice for God's OT people. The tabernacle served this purpose during the wilderness years; the temple did so after it was completed in the rule of

King Solomon. The other peoples of the ancient Middle East had many altars and worshiped their gods and goddesses in local groves and on the tops of hills. Israel was to destroy all such local worship centers. The pagan altars were to be broken down and the sacred stones and symbols smashed. Israel was not to worship God in pagan ways.

In the place of the many altars, there was to be only one, located in "the place the LORD your God will choose" to put his dwelling. Only to that place and only on that altar were burnt offerings and sacrifices to be brought (Dt 12:1–7). There were subsequent occasions, before the Jerusalem temple was established about 959 B.C., when offerings were made on temporary altars (1 Sa 7:7–17; 1 Ch 21:26). There were even exceptions afterward (1 Ki 18:16–40). But God's insistence that there be only one altar in Israel's worship is significant. The one altar, like the one door opening into the temple court, showed Israel (and it shows us) that God is the only one who can establish the way humans are able to approach him and that their approach can be made only through a sacrifice God himself ordains.

3. Two types of altars. Israel's worship involved two altars. One was the great bronze altar of sacrifice, visible to all the people at the place of entry into the temple. The second was the gold-overlaid altar within the holy building, hidden from public view, where incense was burned. The inner altar (Ex 30:6; 40:5) is sometimes called the "altar before the LORD" (Lev 16:12). The incense that was burned on the inner, hidden altar symbolizes prayer (Rev 8:3).

4. Symbolic altars. Not all altars in Israel were intended to be used for sacrifice. By long tradition, altars were used as memorials, reminders of some act of God or spiritually significant event. The tribes who lived east of the Jordan river built an altar by the riverside, "not for burnt offerings or sacrifices" but as evidence of their common religious heritage with the tribes living in Canaan (Jos 22). Gideon erected an altar in Ophrah as a memorial of the time God appeared to him (Jdg 6:24). Such memorial altars were carefully constructed on the pattern called for by OT law (Ex 20:24–26).

NT — 5. NT references to altars. The Greek word translated "altar" is *thysiastērion,* meaning "place of sacrifice." Usually the altar referred to in the Gospels is the sacrificial altar in the Jerusalem temple of Jesus' day.

In 1 Co 9:13, Paul argues by analogy for financial support of Christian ministers. The OT priests who served the altar were given a share of the animals they sacrificed; this was for feeding their families. Paul points out in 1 Co 10:18 that the worshipers also shared by eating the meat of some sacrifices. This was considered participation in the sacrifice. The young believers at Corinth were warned that attendance at the feasts linked with pagan worship constituted participation—and idolatry.

The whole argument of the Book of Hebrews is built by comparisons between the OT system instituted by law and the better "system" inaugurated by Jesus. Jesus' priesthood is superior to that of the Levites who served the old altar (7:11–28). The earthly worship center was itself merely a copy of realities that exist in heaven—and Jesus serves as priest in that realm of ultimate reality (9:1–24). The OT tabernacle was never more than a shadow cast by reality, an illustration for the present time. The sacrifices there could never really take away sins; so Jesus himself became the sacrifice on the real altar (9:9–14). Jesus went outside the walls within which the temple and its altar lay, to offer up his life on the altar of Calvary. Those who believe in Jesus must follow him outside the confines of the old system, abandoning its now-empty practices, and bear any disgrace that that may involve (13:10–13).

The Book of Revelation focuses on another aspect of the altar. Blood sacrifices were offered at the altar to make atonement for sin. The sacrifice thus speaks not only of forgiveness but also of judgment. Sacrifice shows that God can-

not dismiss sin lightly. Death is the necessary consequence of sin. In the OT and NT, the altar portrays God's willingness to accept the death of a substitute in place of the sinner. We discover that God himself became the sacrifice, as Christ at Calvary offered himself in payment of the penalty justice decreed.

But what of those who reject the forgiveness offered on the basis of the sacrificial altar at Calvary? For them the altar carries only a message of doom. In Revelation we see burning coals, which had consumed the sacrifice, hurled upon the earth (Rev 8:5) as the final judgment of humanity begins.

6. Summary. Both Testaments present the altar as a place of sacrifice. The OT describes in detail the altar and its placement in the tabernacle and the temple. The NT makes it clear that the pattern given in the OT is intended to communicate spiritual truths; it is a shadow, but one cast by spiritual reality. Both the placement of the altar and the fact that Israel was to offer sacrifices on only one altar picture for us this great truth: there is only one way to approach Israel's God. It is the way of a sacrifice that he himself ordained.

ALWAYS

Is "always" really forever? Or do the OT and NT uses of the word indicate something other than eternality?

OT 1. **For all time**
    2. **Continually**
NT 3. **At every time**
    4. **Summary**

OT — The focus of the OT is on history, both past and future. Life on this earth, including God's plan for his people here, captures the attention of the prophets. How to live each day while expecting God to bring his promised future to pass is the burden of the OT's teaching.

There are glimpses of eternity in the OT, but God's eternal purposes are unveiled with the death and resurrection of Jesus and in the writings of the apostles. It is not surprising, then, to learn that "always" in the OT is a word dealing with time more often than with eternity.

1. For all time. Two different Hebrew constructions translated "always" suggest the passage of time. Day follows day, and season follows season. "Always" is often "for all *days*" (*yôm*) or "through every *season*" (*'ēt*).

Israel was told by God to do two things always: "Keep all my commandments" (Dt 5:29) and "Revere the LORD your God" (Dt 14:23). NIV and NASB translate the Hebrew phrase "(through) all day(s)" as "always" in the following references: Dt 11:1; 14:23; 18:5; 19:9; Jos 4:24; 1 Sa 2:35; 1 Ki 5:1; 9:3; 11:36; 12:7; 2 Ki 17:37; 2 Ch 7:16; 10:7; Ps 37:26; 56:5; Pr 23:17; Jer 32:39.

2. Continually. Three different Hebrew expressions communicate the idea of continuity, or continuation. One is *'ôlām*, which in this sense denotes unlimited continuance into the future. A second is *tāmîd*, best translated "continually." This word is translated "always" in 2 Sa 9:7,10,13; 1 Ch 16:11; Ps 16:8; 34:1; 35:27; 40:11,16; 51:3; 70:4; 71:3,14; 73:23; 105:4; 119:117; Pr 5:19; Isa 58:11; 60:11. A third and similar term, *neṣaḥ*, has a wide range of meanings, but in Ps 9:18; 103:9; Isa 57:16; Jer 3:5; and La 5:20 it means "perpetually," "constantly." In these passages, "always" is not "forever" but "continually."

NT — 3. At every time. Five different words or expressions are translated "always" in the NIV NT. They too focus attention on this present age rather than on eternity. The two most common words are *pas*, meaning "all" (and thus in some contexts "always"), and *pantote*, literally "every when." The term "always" adequately expresses the idea of these and the other Greek expressions.

4. Summary. "Always" in the Bible does not link time with eternity. It is a word that focuses attention on experience within the world of time and space. "Always" may direct our attention to that which is stable over a period of time or to that which is to be experienced continually. When the issue is God's

relationship with us, "always" reminds us powerfully that God is present at every moment in time and thus is with us constantly. When the issue is our relationship with God, "always" calls us to continual commitment and to consistent holiness.

AMAZED/AMAZING

Four different Greek words tell us of the reaction of amazement described in the Gospels and in Acts. These words are synonyms, and so it is unwise to make sharp distinctions between them. It would be just as difficult for us to try to distinguish clearly between the English words "amazed," "astounded," "astonished," and "stunned." Yet there are fascinating insights suggested in the ways NT writers use the Greek terms.

Thaumazō. In the first three Gospels and in Acts *thaumazō* is usually linked with miracle stories. The word depicts the utter astonishment that Jesus' powers aroused. There is evidence that *thaumazō* suggests a hint of fear mixed with wonder (Mt 15:31; Lk 8:25; 9:43). Jesus is recorded as being amazed on two occasions: at the unbelief found in his hometown (Mk 6:6) and at the total faith demonstrated by the Capernaum centurion (Mt 8:10; Lk 7:9).

John's Gospel uses this word in a way that is distinctive from the other three Gospels and Acts. In John, *thaumazō* is not related to specific miracles but is used to describe the general impact of Jesus' words and his works. In John's report of observers' amazement we find no hint that *thaumazō* indicates budding belief. Instead the word suggests hesitation and doubt. Confronted by the unexplainable, Jesus' observers held back. Thus when Jesus explained that one must be born again, he urged Nicodemus not to be amazed (Jn 3:7); and he urged his hearers not to hold back in amazement at his announcement that he himself is the source of eternal life (Jn 5:20).

Although it is not always translated "amazed," *thaumazō* appears in the Gospels and Acts in the following places: Mt 8:10,27; 9:8,33; 15:31; 21:20; 22:22; 27:14;

Mk 5:20; 6:6,51; 12:17; 15:5,44; Lk 1:21,63; 2:18,33; 4:22; 7:9; 8:25; 9:43; 11:14,38; 20:26; 24:12,41; Jn 3:7; 4:27; 5:20,28; 7:15,21; Ac 2:7; 3:12; 4:13; 7:31; 13:41. John also uses the word in 1 Jn 3:13 and Rev 13:3; 17:6,7,8. Other occurrences are Gal 1:6; Jude 16. Finally, Paul uses it in 2 Th 1:10 to refer to the time of Jesus' return as "the day he comes to be glorified in his holy people and to be *marveled at* among all those who have believed."

Ekplēssō. This word expresses a stunned amazement that leaves the subject unable to grasp what is happening. It is used twelve times in the Gospels and once in Acts. It is usually used to describe the reaction of the uncommitted listener to Jesus' teaching. Only once is *ekplēssō* used to describe a reaction to a miraculous act (Lk 9:43). It is found in Mt 7:28; 13:54; 19:25; 22:33; Mk 1:22; 6:2; 7:37; 10:26; 11:18; Lk 2:48; 4:32; 9:43; Ac 13:12.

Existēmi. This verb suggests astonishment mixed with anxiety, stimulated by extraordinary events that cannot be explained. In one form it means to be "out of one's senses" (Mk 3:21; 2 Co 5:13). This word is found in Mt 12:23; Mk 2:12; 3:21; 5:42; 6:51; Lk 2:47; 8:56; 24:22; Ac 2:7,12; 8:9,11,13; 9:21; 10:45; 12:16; 2 Co 5:13.

Thambeō. This term focuses on the fright caused by an amazing event. It occurs four times in the NT (Mk 1:27; 10:24,32; Ac 9:6), its noun form is used three times (Lk 4:36; 5:9; Ac 3:10).

This family of words helps to remind us that Jesus' acts and words were "amazing" primarily to those who did not believe in him. As the disciples grew in their understanding of who Jesus is, they began to see them as acts performed by a God who has always been able to work in this world of space and time. And as we look back at Jesus' wonders from the perspective of the resurrection, we can also see them as such. Jesus' works were indeed wonderful. But they do not surprise those who know Jesus to be the Son of God. ◆ *Miracle/Sign/Wonder*

AM (I AM) ◆ *Lord*

AMBITION

There are two different Greek words translated "ambition" in the NIV and the NASB. One word is strongly negative, the other just as strongly positive.

Selfish ambition. The word *eritheia*, is translated "selfish ambition" in Gal 5:20; Php 1:17 (1:16, KJV); 2:3; Jas 3:14,16. The word appears elsewhere in the NT only in Ro 2:8 ("self-seeking") and 2 Co 12:20 ("factions"). It portrays a contentious struggle for personal profit or power, with no redeeming hint of service to others. Ro 2:8 suggests that such ambition demonstrates not only a wrong attitude but also wrong goals. Selfish ambition battles others for immediate gains and empty honors, which have no eternal value.

Godly ambition. The word here is *philotimeomai* and is used only three times in the NT. The NIV translates it "ambition" twice (Ro 15:20; 1 Th 4:11) and "goal" once (2 Co 5:9). The word suggests eager, continuing efforts for something that is good.

Paul aspired to preach the gospel where Christ was not known (Ro 15:20) and always tried eagerly to please the Lord (2 Co 5:9). The apostle urges believers to strive to live a quiet life filled with the honest work that wins the respect of outsiders and maintains independence (1 Th 4:11). Each of these ambitions is closely linked with the idea of service to others. Each calls us to focus our life on things that have eternal value.

AMEN

This word sounds nearly the same in Hebrew, Greek, and English. Its meaning is rooted in the Hebrew term, which indicates firmness, dependability, certainty, and truth.

The OT uses "amen" some twenty-five times. Typically, God's people respond to some warning or promise from God with "Amen." This identifies them with the warning or promise and also confirms that what has been said is true and binding (cf. Dt 27:15–26).

In the Gospels, only Jesus used this word, often in the formula "Amen, I say to you. . . ." The phrase was clearly understood by his Jewish hearers. It was a strong affirmation that what Jesus was about to say was certain and reliable and that what he taught must be considered binding on himself and his hearers.

The Epistles also use "Amen." It occurs at the close of prayers and as punctuation in praise (Gal 1:5). Used this way, it is almost the same as an exclamation point, bold print, or underlining. It strengthens and emphasizes.

"Amen" is also the response of a congregation to prayers or teaching. It is an expression of endorsement. When we say "Amen," we express our own participation in, and our commitment to, the shared faith and life of the people of God.

AMENDS

The making of "amends" is something done to compensate for a loss or injury a person causes others. This notion is suggested in passages where "amends" is found in some modern versions. But there is no Hebrew term that quite expresses the concept. The closest parallels are found in "atonement" and in "restitution." ♦ *Atonement* ♦ *Restitution*

"Make (making) amends" is found three times in Scripture. The word *atone* (*kāpar*) is translated "make amends" in 2 Sa 21:3. The idea in Job 20:10 is "to seek to please" (RSV). The Hebrew text of Pr 14:9 is obscure and may even be rendered, "God scorns the wicked."

Perhaps the reason why "amends" did not seem to fit in more OT or NT passages is that the Bible takes such a serious view of sin. There is really nothing anyone can do to make amends for sin. All we can do is to acknowledge our guilt and turn to God for forgiveness. There is really nothing we can do to make up for the hurt we cause others, though the OT stresses the importance of restitution and the NT presents the con-

stant need for mutually extending and accepting forgiveness. When making amends is not really possible, it is most important to live with others in sensitive, loving ways that enrich their lives rather than in ways that bring hurt.

ANCESTORS

Roots and lineage are extremely important to Bible history. Their importance is illustrated in the many genealogies found in the OT and in constant references to the forefathers. Their importance is particularly found in the distinctive covenant relationship that God established between himself and the descendants of Abraham.

OT 1. **The Hebrew words**
     2. **The significance of ancestry**
     3. **Biblical genealogies**
NT 4. **NT references to ancestry**
     5. **Summary**

OT — 1. The Hebrew words. The OT tells the story of God's dealings with one family called out of all humankind to be the avenue through whom God would redeem humanity. God established a special relationship with this family and formalized the relationship in great OT covenants. Membership in the covenant community, therefore, was a matter of physical descent from the family founders—Abraham, Isaac, and Jacob. The identity of the individual, and his claim to special relationship with God, rested on ancestry.

The word most commonly translated "ancestor" or "forefather" is *'āb*. This word occurs over twelve hundred times in the Hebrew OT and means "father." Usually used of one's parent or more remote ancestor, the term is also applied out of respect to someone in authority. It may be used of a founder, such as of a guild of musicians or metal workers (Ge 4:21).

The phrases "tribes of their fathers" and "inheritance of the fathers" are thus appropriately rendered "ancestral tribes" in Numbers and "ancestral inheritance" or "ancestral property" elsewhere.

A few times the word *yālad* ("to bear, beget") is used of ancestry. The idea is that by giving birth to a child, one becomes the ancestor of all who descend from the child (Nu 1:18).

A final word, translated "ancestry" in Eze 16:3, is a noun from the *yālad* root: *môledeṯ*. It can be understood as "relatives," or sometimes as "birthplace."

Each of these terms fits solidly within the pattern of Hebrew thought about the vital importance of one's ancestry.

2. The significance of ancestry. God makes a promise that illustrates the importance of ancestry to the Hebrew people. In Lev 26, Moses reviews God's promise of reward for obedience to the Mosaic Law and God's warnings about punishment for disobedience. After describing the troubles sin would bring, God said that if the Israelites would confess their sins, this is what he would do: "I will remember my covenant with Jacob and my covenant with Isaac and my covenant with Abraham, and I will remember the land. . . . I will remember the covenant with their ancestors whom I brought out of Egypt in the sight of the nations to be their God" (26:42,45).

The basic promise was given to the ancestors. Each generation might appeal to God, but it must be on the basis of the ancient promises. Ancestry became the foundation on which the community and the individual might have confidence that God would hear their confession and appeal.

Membership in the family of Abraham did not guarantee an individual a personal relationship with God. That was won by faith and was demonstrated in obedience to the Mosaic code. But those outside the Jewish family had no claim on God and no basis for guaranteed access to him. Paul describes their situation as "excluded from citizenship in Israel and foreigners to the covenants of the promise, without hope and without God in the world" (Eph 2:12). ◆ *Gentile*

It is clear, then, that ancestry is a basic and absolutely essential aspect of OT faith and life. God is the "God of Abraham, of Isaac, and of Jacob." Relationship of the OT believer to God was

mediated by physical descent from these ancestors.

3. Biblical genealogies. Since physical lineage is so important in the OT, it is not surprising to find a number of genealogies recorded in Scripture. These provided evidence that an individual or group had the right to membership in the community of Israel, a right that could be established only by proof of descent from the patriarchal ancestors.

The compelling urgency of racial purity is illustrated in a report recorded by Ezra. There some who claimed to be of priestly descent "searched for their family records, but they could not find them and so were excluded from the priesthood as unclean" (2:62). This demand for racial purity explains why those returning from captivity rejected the offer of the people who were then settled in Palestine to help in building a temple to the Lord. The settlers argued that they should help, "because," they said, "like you, we seek your God and have been sacrificing to him since the time of Esarhaddon king of Assyria, who brought us here" (4:2). But these were a mongrel people who followed the common custom of paying tribute to whatever gods were associated with the land in which they lived. Their ancestry did not go back to Abraham, Isaac, and Jacob. Thus they had to be excluded; and the animosity caused by this exclusion is reflected in the hostility that still existed in Jesus' day between the Jews and the Samaritans (descendants of these resettled peoples).

Genealogies, therefore, were essential. They alone could guarantee the right of Jewish individuals and families to membership in the community and in relationship with God.

Key OT genealogies are found in Genesis (chaps. 5 and 11). They trace history from Adam to Noah and from Noah to Abraham. Also, the first ten chapters of 1 Chronicles provides a detailed ancestry list, with genealogies collected from various records. There are two genealogies of Jesus in the NT (Mt 1 and Lk 3). Matthew records Jesus' lineage from Abraham through David and his descendants, while Luke goes back to Adam to demonstrate Jesus' full humanity. It is generally accepted that the Matthean genealogy is of the line of Joseph and the Lukan genealogy of the line of Mary.

Biblical genealogies are frequently schematic and incomplete. Often only chief persons, not every individual in a line, are recorded in biblical records. Generally these names have been arranged in easily memorized groups of ten or fourteen. The fact that genealogies are incomplete is illustrated by comparing Ex 6:16–20, which reports only four links between Levi and Moses, with Nu 3:39, which states that some twenty-two thousand male descendants of Levi were living in Moses' day.

NT — 4. NT references to ancestry. Four passages in the Epistles speak of ancestry. In two the Greek word is *patēr*, usually rendered "father." Ro 9:5 and Heb 7:16 use "ancestry" to express the meaning of the phrase "fleshly descent."

Heb 7:10 portrays Levi as "still in the body of his ancestor" (Abraham) at the time of Melchizedek. This reflects the Jewish concept noted above: in giving birth to a child, one becomes the ancestor of all who descend from him. Levi was the child of Abraham's grandson Jacob. The writer's argument from this fact is fascinating. The theme of Hebrews is that Jesus is superior in every way to the old Mosaic system. It follows that his must be a superior priesthood. To prove this, the writer remembers an incident reported in Ge 14. Abraham met and paid tithes to a person named Melchizedek, who then blessed Abraham. The writer argues from Ge 14 and Ps 110:4 (which speaks of a Melchizedekian priesthood) that the Bible shows Jesus' priesthood to be superior to the Levitical priesthood of the OT. Abraham, whose descendant Levi received tithes from Israel, paid tithes to Melchizedek. Levi, "in" the loins of his ancestor, participated in paying tithes and receiving the blessing given his ancestor. If the one who is paid tithes under the Mosaic system himself paid tithes to another, it follows that that other priesthood is superior. As the priesthood of Melchizedek was a universal priesthood, so

Christ's priesthood, following the interlude of the limited priesthood of Aaron, is also universal—that is, it includes the Gentiles in full participation in the covenant.

This reasoning may be hard for modern people to grasp. But in the context of the way God's OT people thought of ancestry, it is a valid and compelling argument.

5. Summary. In our day, relationship with God is viewed as an individual issue. What our parents did or did not believe does not change the fact that each of us must make a personal faith-commitment to Jesus and establish our own personal relationship with him. Faith was the basis for a personal relationship with God in OT times too. ◗ *Belief/Faith* But faith existed then in the context of covenant. The individual knew that God had made promises to the ancestors, and it was because the individual was a member of the covenant family that he or she had the right to call God his or her own.

The great historic promises of God were made to Abraham, to Isaac, and to Jacob. It was the individual's descent from these patriarchs that made it possible to share in the blessings God committed himself to make available to the chosen people.

ANCHOR

Heb 6:19 says of God's sworn promise, "We have this hope as an anchor for the soul, firm and secure." "Anchor" was often used in the NT world as the symbol of hope. The words "firm and secure" are important. The first describes the anchor as firmly settled on the ocean bottom. The second describes the quality of the anchor's construction. This anchor will not tear from insubstantial moorings, nor will it break because of internal flaws. ◗ *Hope*

ANCIENT

Were ancient times the "good old days" to Bible writers? Or isn't nostalgia appropriate to the biblical world view?

OT 1. Idyllic times
    2. Long ago
NT 3. The ancient and the new
    4. Summary

OT — The Hebrew people looked back into history and found their identity in the covenant promises God made to the patriarchs. ◗ *Ancestors* The past was thus the foundation for the present and the future and was deeply respected. Respect is shown in 1 Ch 4:22 for "ancient" records. Daniel, in a phrase suggesting enduring eminence, used a word three times (the only occurrences in Scripture) for "ancient" (*'attîq*) to speak of God as "Ancient of days." But two different OT words most commonly translated "ancient" suggest other aspects of the Hebrew view of the past.

1. Idyllic times. The word *qedem* is a noun found sixty-one times in the OT. It means either "east" or "ancient times." The verb from which it comes means "to precede," either in time or geographically. When used in its temporal sense, *qedem* suggests an idyllic state—a time when God acts, as in Creation or in the days of the Exodus. Old times were good times when God involved himself in history on behalf of his people. This Hebrew word is translated "ancient" in Dt 33:15; Ps 68:33; Isa 19:11; 46:10; Mic 5:2.

2. Long ago. A second Hebrew word translated "ancient" is *'ôlām*. It is used 418 times in the OT, in almost all cases indicating something that stretches continuously into the future. It refers to the past about twenty times. The basic idea is that of great distance—temporal distance that puts the event or thing described beyond the knowledge of the living. There is no indication that these events of the distant past are especially desirable or undesirable. This must be determined from the context. Passages in which *'ôlām* is translated "ancient" are Ge 49:26; 1 Sa 27:8; Ps 24:7,9; Pr 22:28; 23:10; Isa 44:7; 58:12; 61:4; 64:4; Jer 5:15; 6:16; 18:15; Eze 25:15; 26:20; 35:5; 36:2; Hab 3:6.

NT — 3. The ancient and the new. OT faith interpreted the past as a guide for the present. What was new and contemporary was often viewed with suspicion. The reaction of the Pharisees when investigating the healing of a man born blind is revealing: "We know that God spoke to Moses, but as for this fellow, we don't even know where he comes from" (Jn 9:29). The miracles of Jesus were rejected. The old ways and the old interpretations were grasped tenaciously.

Archaios, rendered "(of) long ago" in the Gospels (Mt 5:21,33; Lk 9:8,19) is translated "old" (2 Co 5:17) and "ancient" (2 Pe 2:5) in its two occurrences in the Epistles, always with a negative connotation. In Rev 12:9 and 20:2 the word is used to describe Satan, "that ancient serpent," who leads the world astray but who will one day be destroyed by God.

It is used in 2 Co 5:17 in Paul's announcement that "the old is gone, the new has come." Everything within and without that locked the believer in sin's grip has been shattered by the dynamic new life brought to us by Jesus. Here we see a striking transformation of attitude. The resurrection of Jesus does not make the old irrelevant, for history's report of God's acts helps us know and respond to him. But the resurrection of Jesus means that God's power has broken into our world in a new and fresh way. We must approach faith from the perspective provided by the new, not by the old. In the NT, the ancient no longer is as significant as the present, for we are to experience God's resurrection power in our present life!

4. Summary. How we look at the past will color our view of the present. It is possible to look back with deep appreciation and see all that God has done in history. But it is also possible to idealize the past and see yesterday as the locus of all that is good and meaningful. The Bible helps us to avoid this trap. Yesterday is beyond our capacity to experience. Yet the fact that God was active in history's yesterday does confer on the past an idyllic quality that appeals to the believer. How good, then, to hear the wonderful message given us in Jesus.

His power is available to us now! The ancient is past. And because of Jesus, our now is ever new.

ANCIENTS

Unlike the passages that use the Greek word *archaios* (♦ *Ancient*), Heb 11:2, in speaking of the faith "the ancients were commended for," uses the word *presbyteros*. It is used the same way in the Gospels. It indicates a generation to which the speaker looks back as ancestral and identifies a tradition in which the speaker is found.

In Mt 15:2 and Mk 7:3,5 it is the Pharisees who appealed to the past and focused on the "tradition of the elders." Specifically in view is the practice of eating only after a ceremonial washing of hands. Heb 11:2 sets the Christian firmly in another tradition. Those to whom we look for our example are not those who glory in legalistic practices but those who have lived by faith, for it is living by faith that wins God's commendation. ♦ *Pharisees* ♦ *Belief/Faith*

ANGELS

Both the OT and the NT speak of created beings with individuality and personal identity who exist in a spiritual dimension that touches, but is not the same as, our material universe. Our attention is not focused on these beings, but the veil between us and the unseen world is pulled back slightly, and we can see glimpses of a reality that is closed to us now. What we glimpse is a spiritual universe within which an invisible war is continually being waged. This universe touches our own, for God is the Creator of both, and a single act is being played out on each stage. According to the Scriptures, although hidden from us, angels play a significant role both in our lives and in the whole course of history.

OT 1. The angels
2. The role of angels in the OT
3. The angel of the Lord
4. Daniel 10
NT 5. The angels, good and evil
6. The role of angels in the NT
7. Jesus and the angels
8. Humanity and the angels

OT — 1. The angels. The Hebrew word *mal'āk* means "messenger," "representative," or "angel." It is used of both human and supernatural messengers, and the context will usually determine which is intended. The mission of a *mal'āk* is to (1) carry a message, (2) fulfill a special, specific commission, and/or (3) represent the one sending him.

The supernatural beings called angels are also referred to by other names. They are called "sons of God" (KJV), a phrase meaning direct creations of God (Job 1:6; 2:1; and possibly Ge 6:2–4). They are also called "mighty ones" in Ps 29:1 and "heavenly beings" in Ps 89:6, as well as "holy ones" in Ps 89:5,7; Da 4:13,17,23; 8:13 (twice).

The angels were created by God and were witnesses to the creation of the material universe (Job 38:7). They serve as members of God's eternal court (Job 1:6; Isa 6:2–4), and they are exhorted to praise him (Ps 103:20–21; 148:2).

There are different orders and different types of these powerful beings. The cherubim, for example, have traits of both humans and animals (Ge 3:24; Ps 18:10; Isa 6:2; Eze 1:5–14; 10:19–22). One powerful archangel, Gabriel, is identified by name four times in Scripture (Da 8:16; 9:21; Lk 1:19,26).

Satan was created an angel and named Lucifer. The NT tells us what the OT hints at. Satan led a great rebellion in the unseen universe and was followed by many of the angels who fell with him. ♦ *Satan* ♦ *Demons/Evil Spirits*

2. The role of angels in the OT. While angels are not a major theme of the OT, there are many indications of their importance to sacred history. Angels were associated with God's deliverance of his people from slavery in Egypt. God promised Israel, "I am sending an angel ahead of you to guard you along the way and to bring you to the place I have prepared" (Ex 23:20). On a similar mission of protection an angel aided Shadrach, Meshach, and Abednego in the fiery furnace (Da 3:28) and Daniel in the lions' den (6:22). One of the most graphic OT stories of angelic protection is found in 2 Ki 6. The king of Aram had sent an army to capture the prophet Elisha. Elisha's servant stepped outside one morning to find the town of Dothan surrounded by an enemy force. He ran in terror to the prophet. Elisha quieted his fears and then asked God to open the servant's eyes. Suddenly the servant saw "the hills full of horses and chariots of fire all around Elisha" (6:17). An angelic army was present to protect the Lord's prophet.

In addition, angels were involved in God's dramatic judgments on sinful people (Sodom, Ge 19:1; a plague decimating Israel, 2 Sa 24:17; 1 Ch 21:15; destruction of an Assyrian army, 2 Ch 32:21; Isa 37:36). Abraham reassured his servant by saying that God would send an angel to help the servant get a wife for Isaac (Ge 24:7,40). Angels clearly are given assignments to guard and guide believers and to carry out God's judgments on sin. Also, the "angel of the Lord" is intimately linked with revelation.

3. The angel of the Lord. A number of references in the OT single out a being identified as "the angel of the Lord." This distinctive personage is especially active at critical times in OT history and is identified when contact with angels involves revelation of some special message from God to man.

The angel of the Lord is linked with key events in the lives of each of the patriarchs (Abraham and Isaac, Ge 22:11,15–18; Jacob, Ge 31:11). The angel of the Lord called Moses to his mission (Ex 3), appeared to Gideon (Jdg 6), empowered Samson (Jdg 13), strengthened Elijah (1 Ki 19), and was the agent of revelation in a prophecy about Israel's future (Zec 1). He can be called on to protect (Ps 34:7) and to do battle against implacable enemies (Ps 35:5–6).

There has been much speculation about the identity of the angel of the Lord. Many suggest that he is actually the Second Person of the Trinity, appearing before the Incarnation. This interpretation is supported by the fact that the angel of the Lord not only serves as the

agent of revelation in most contexts where he appears; he also speaks as the God of the covenant (Jdg 2:1–4). He is often viewed as God by those to whom he appears (Ge 16:9–13; Ex 3:2,6; Jdg 13:20–22). Two conclusions seem evident: no clear distinction can be made between this angel and Yahweh, and where human beings encounter God in the OT, they meet him not in unmasked glory but in the person of the angel of the Lord.

4. Daniel 10. This chapter makes an important contribution to OT angelology. Daniel records that after three weeks of prayer and partial fasting, he was visited by an angel who brought an extended message concerning the far future. This angel, like others, was humanoid in form but burned with flame. The impact of the angel's presence was so traumatic that Daniel trembled, helpless and unable to move. The angel touched and strengthened Daniel and then explained that he was sent in answer to Daniel's prayers. But for twenty-one days this powerful being had been blocked from accomplishing his mission by a prince of the unseen universe, one who had been assigned [by Satan] to influence the course of the Persian Empire. The angel who spoke to Daniel had been able to break through only with the aid of Michael, one of God's faithful angels of even higher rank than this "prince of Persia." After delivering the message, Daniel's visitor returned to the battle he had just left, to struggle against added forces coming to the aid of the angel of Persia.

What this chapter adds to the OT's teaching on angelology is significant. It shows that angels were created by God with varying powers—or ranks—in angelic armies. Da 10 reveals that an invisible war is taking place between the angel armies of God and those of Satan, fought with forces whose numbers and power we cannot begin to imagine. It shows that nations as well as individuals are participants in the invisible war and that one facet of the hidden battle is waged to influence political events in our world of space and time.

What we are shown here and in the rest of the OT is at best a glimpse—a hint of wonders hidden from us, trapped as we are in the material universe. But what we are shown is compelling evidence that there is a spiritual universe that exists alongside the universe we know through our senses. The angels and other spiritual beings are real. And our God is the ultimate ruler of the invisible as well as of the visible.

NT — The NT assumes all that the OT teaches about angels and goes on to add fresh information. The NT word *angelos* also means "messenger." It is used some 175 times. The activity of angels in the NT concentrated around the birth of Christ (Mt 1–2; Lk 1–2) and will again be prominent at Jesus' return and the judgment to take place then (cf. Mt 13, 24–25, 1 Th 1, Rev).

Jesus' statement that those raised from the dead are "like the angels" (Mt 22:30; Mk 12:25; Lk 20:36) simply affirms that, like angels, the resurrected are not subject to the limitations of mortal life on earth.

5. The angels, good and evil. The NT makes explicit what is hinted at in the OT. Satan leads a host of angels (Mt 25:41). Like him, they fell from their original state; they choose not to "keep their positions of authority but abandoned their own home" (Jude 6) and as a result are condemned to eternal judgment (also 2 Pe 2:4). Many believe that fallen angels are the demons that are spoken of in the NT. ♦ *Demons/Evil Spirits* The angels who remained committed in their allegiance to God continue to serve him and carry out the missions they are assigned.

6. The role of angels in the NT. As noted above, the NT associates angels closely with the first and second comings of Jesus. In the meanwhile, they are "all ministering spirits sent to serve those who will inherit salvation" (Heb 1:14). Angels seem to have a special ministry in relation to children (Mt 18:10). An angel was instrumental in releasing Peter from prison (Act 12) and in preparing the way for the conversion of Cornelius (Ac 10–

11). Most references to the present ministry of angels, however, are oblique, and little attention is paid in the NT to angels. When believers at Colosse turned aside to follow a heresy that stressed special honor given angels as divine intermediaries, Paul sent a stern warning (Col 2). Jesus came in person into man's world and in the full majesty of his deity he brought us life. Jesus freed us from sin's deadly grip so that we might share through him the fullness of all that God has for us. Angels in the unseen world are all under Jesus, "who is the head over every power and authority" (Col 2:10). Jesus, not angels, is the focus of our faith. He is the one in whom we find fulfillment (Col 3:1–4).

7. Jesus and the angels. Jesus Christ, the Son of God, ranks far above the angels by virtue of his nature (Php 2:6; Heb 1:4–14). In the Incarnation, Jesus took on human nature. In the Resurrection, Jesus the God-Man took his place as Lord, being set in authority over angelic beings of every rank and title (Eph 1:20–22; Php 2:9–11; Col 2:10–11). The superiority of Jesus to angels is developed in the first chapter of Hebrews. This book was written to converted Jewish believers who were steeped in OT lore and needed to be reminded that Jesus and the new covenant he inaugurated were superior to the system that existed under the old (Mosaic) covenant. ♦ *Covenant* The writer of Hebrews begins by comparing Jesus with angels, because the angels were viewed by the first-century Jew as mediators of revelation and as higher beings who deserve great respect. The writer launches his argument by affirming Jesus as "the radiance of God's glory and the exact representation of his being" (Heb 1:3), that is, as God himself. The new revelation is given, not by angels, but by the God of the angels!

The superiority of Jesus is demonstrated by the following facts: (1) God calls Jesus "Son"—a title not shared with angels (1:5); (2) the angels offer the Son worship (1:6); (3) whereas angels are referred to as servants, Jesus is given a throne and a kingdom (1:7–8); (4) the angels were witnesses to the Creation, but Jesus both shaped and will outlast all of creation (1:10–12; cf. Job 38:7; Pr 8); and (5) Jesus is now seated at the Father's right hand, while angels are serving saved human beings (1:13–14). Since Jesus as the Son of God is so vastly superior to the angels, who were communicators of the old revelation (Heb 2:2), it is clear that the new revelation must be vastly superior to the old. The Jewish convert thus can rest secure in his Christian faith.

8. Humanity and the angels. It is clear from the Bible that angels are superior to human beings in many ways. As direct creations of God, these beings have unlimited lifetimes and unusual powers. Yet the writer to the Hebrews points out, in awed tones, that "it is not to angels that he [God] has subjected the world to come" (Heb 2:5). Jesus chose to share our humanity so that he might free us from sin's grip. "Surely it is not angels he helps," the writer says in wonder, "but Abraham's descendants" (2:16). Alive now in Jesus, we will be brought to glory and lifted far above the angels.

Angels, then, are not only God's ministers, assigned to serve the heirs of salvation; they are also eager witnesses to all that God is doing in this world (Lk 15:10; 1 Co 11:10; 1 Ti 3:16). Ultimately human beings will be called on to judge the angels (1 Co 6:3).

What we glimpse about angels is intriguing and stimulates speculation. But the thrust of the OT and NT is clear. Human beings, not angels, are the focus of God's concern. In return, God invites us to fix our thoughts and our faith on Jesus—not on angels. We can trust Jesus as Lord to supervise the unseen universe for his good purposes and for our benefit. We can concentrate our efforts on coming to better know and love the one who truly is Lord of all.

ANGER

Anger is viewed today as a "negative emotion." Christians often identify anger as sin and feel a sense of guilt when they become angry. Yet the Bible presents God as sometimes angry. It speaks of his wrath. How are we to understand the anger of God and to deal with our own angry feelings? How can we distinguish anger from sin?

OT 1. Hebrew words for anger
     2. The OT view of human anger
     3. The OT view of God's anger
NT 4. Greek words for anger
     5. The NT view of human anger
     6. The NT view of God's anger
     7. Summary

OT — 1. Hebrew words for anger. The OT has a rich variety of words to express the idea of anger. Often a word for anger is linked with strong descriptive words: God "burns with anger"; his "anger is fierce." OT words for anger are often used interchangeably; any of them may be translated "anger," "wrath," or "fury" in various English versions. Yet there are distinctions that should be noted.

The words *kā'as* (verb) and *'ap* (noun) are the most common OT words for anger. The verb is often used to describe God's anger when his covenant people sin. ◆ *Covenant* The noun portrays flaring nostrils and emphasizes the emotional impact of anger.

Qāṣap (verb) and *qeṣep* (noun) are perhaps the strongest terms and are often translated by the use of the word "wrath." The verb occurs thirty-two times in the OT. This word focuses attention on the relational damage done when one party has said or done something that causes hot anger or deep displeasure.

Hēmâh and *ḥarôn* (from *ḥārâh*) both mean "burning" and thus describe anger as heated emotional passion. *Ḥarôn* is always used in reference to anger and occurs forty-one times. It is often linked with other words, as in "burning anger," though "burning" may stand alone and may be translated "anger."

The word *'ebrâh* means "an overflow," or "fury." This word lays stress on the fierceness of the anger. Used of human anger, it suggests an arrogant pride expressed as implacable fury.

Taken together, these synonyms present a picture we know all too well.

Anger is a physical and emotional reaction, felt as a hot rush of fury. Anger is relational: we become angry when something is said or done that seems to violate a relationship. Anger is expressed: it overflows not only in emotional marks seen on one's face or in one's stance but also in actions.

The OT words for anger do not tell us whether anger is right or wrong, nor do they explain the anger of God. They simply tell us that anger exists. Anger is a potential emotion in any relationship, whether it is a relationship between human beings or between God and some person.

2. The OT view of human anger. The OT describes a number of incidents of human anger. These descriptions, along with the divine commentary on anger found in several OT passages, help us develop a distinctively biblical view of human anger.

Anger may be justified. Both justified and unjustified anger are described in the OT. Moses was angry with the people of Israel after they (while he was with God on Sinai) had shaped a golden calf to worship (Ex 32:19); and Jonathan was angry with his father Saul for treating David shamefully (1 Sa 20:34). Each of these is an illustration of justifiable anger.

Although certain other instances of anger in the OT can be understood, many cannot be justified. Fear and jealousy stimulated Saul's anger with David (1 Sa 18:8). It was probably a sense of shame that moved Eliab, David's older brother, to utter his angry words of accusation against the young shepherd (1 Sa 17:28). If we summarize the impression given in the OT, we see that some persons become angry about the same things that anger God: injustice, idolatry, and betrayal. This is justifiable anger. But anger that is an expression of personal pride or is generated by some baser emotion is not justifiable. Instead, such anger is an empty attempt at self-justification when the situation calls for acknowledging sin and seeking forgiveness.

Anger can be expressed righteously or sinfully. In Ps 4:4, believers are told, "In your anger do not sin." The OT, like the NT, makes a distinction between righteous anger and sinful anger, as well as between right and wrong reactions to righteous anger.

For instance, Potiphar—not realizing that his wife was lying—felt justifiable anger when she claimed that Joseph had attempted to rape her. Rather than taking personal revenge, the angry Egyptian reacted correctly by imprisoning Joseph (Ge 39:19–20).

The anger of Simeon and Levi when their sister was raped (Ge 34) was justifiable. But their action—tricking and murdering all the men in the rapist's city—is sternly condemned: "They have killed men in their anger and hamstrung oxen as they pleased. Cursed be their anger, so fierce, and their fury, so cruel! I will scatter them in Jacob and disperse them in Israel" (Ge 49:6–7). Even justifiable anger does not justify any sinful actions that the anger may stimulate.

This principle is illustrated beautifully in the story of David and Abigail. David and his men had guarded the flocks of a wealthy rancher, Nabal. When harvest time came, David asked for a fair share for his men. Nabal churlishly refused, and he insulted David. The furious David set out with his fighting men to kill Nabal and his household. While he was on the way, Nabal's wife, Abigail, was warned by her husband's anxious employees. She quickly packed supplies and set out to find David. Intercepting David, Abigail admitted Nabal's fault and asked David to forgive. "Let no wrongdoing be found in you as long as you live," she said, urging David to let the Lord avenge him so that David would "not have on his conscience the staggering burden of needless bloodshed or of having avenged himself" (1 Sa 25:28,31). David blessed her for her good judgment, took the gift of food, and returned to the hills. The next day Nabal heard what had happened and suffered a fatal stroke.

The story illustrates two vital OT principles. First, the person who feels anger must not let that anger result in sin.

Second, rather than taking revenge for the hurt, the individual is to trust God. David summed up these principles in Ps 37, especially in verses 8–9: "Refrain from anger and turn from wrath; do not fret—it only leads to evil. For evil men will be cut off, but those who hope in the LORD will inherit the land." A person may not be able to prevent a sudden rush of angry feelings. But each of us can choose to turn from the course that anger suggests. We can choose not to harbor anger and not to do the evil that anger urges us to do. We can rest our hope instead in the Lord.

Anger is dangerous. There are many warnings against anger and what anger may lead to. Anger stirs up strife (Pr 30:33) and dissension (Pr 29:22). Anger is by nature cruel (Pr 27:4), and a hot-tempered man will commit many sins (Pr 29:22). While we are to control our anger and turn away from it (Pr 29:8), we are also to avoid stimulating anger in others. This is done by keeping our answers soft and avoiding harsh words (Pr 15:1).

We must deal with our own anger. Several suggestions are found in the OT that can help us deal with legitimate anger. The first focuses on individual responsibility for choices. We are to "refrain from" and "turn away from" anger (Ps 37:8). Rather than concentrate on an affront that stimulated our anger and thus "fret" over it (Ps 37:8), we are to deal with our feelings in a completely different way. The second suggestion in the OT shows us that positive way. When we are angry, we are to accept the fact that we are angry and to express our feelings to God. This approach is often seen in those psalms that call on God to judge enemies. In expressing our feelings to God we consciously relate our situation to him and thus change our perception of it. The change of perception is the third OT prescription. When we remember that God rules the world of people, peace will come as we turn our situation over to him. Psalm 37 is rich in such expressions and encourages us by saying: "Be still before the LORD and wait patiently for him; do not fret when men succeed in their ways, when they carry out their wicked schemes" (Ps 37:7). This psalm summarizes powerfully the OT's prescription for relating anger and frustration to the Lord. It shows us how to let the realization of who God is reshape our perspective and reshape our emotions as well.

3. The OT view of God's anger. All the words for anger that are used to describe human emotions and actions are also used of God. But the picture the Bible paints is far from the stereotype of the "angry God of the Old Testament" we sometimes hear spoken of so blithely.

The causes of God's anger. One of the first facts to establish is that God's anger is no capricious thing, nor is it expressed in temper tantrums. God's anger is provoked: it is his righteous response to specific human failures and sin. OT law clearly specifies actions that arouse God's anger. Thus the law says: "Do not take advantage of a widow or an orphan. If you do and they cry out to me, I will certainly hear their cry. My anger will be aroused" (Ex 22:22–24). In addition to being related to injustice, God's anger is intimately linked with the violation by Israel of the covenant relationship the Lord established among them (Dt 4:23–26). These and many other warnings (e.g., Dt 29:23–28; Jos 23:16) laid out for God's OT people those sinful actions that provoked God's anger. Knowing God's moral character, his people could avoid his anger by being obedient to the covenant in which he carefully defines right and wrong.

A survey of OT incidents that stimulate God's anger shows that the Lord is angry when he is not trusted (Ex 4:14), when his people complain against him (Nu 11:1,33; 12:9), when he is disobeyed (Nu 32:10), and particularly when he is rejected in favor of idols (Ex 32:7–12; Nu 25:3; Dt 11:16–17).

God's anger is a measured response to sin—a response about which his OT people were thoroughly warned.

The interpretation of God's anger. The OT sees God's anger in a positive rather than a negative light. God's anger expresses itself in rebuke and discipline (Ps 6:1; 38:1; 78:31–38). It is God's righteous reaction to those who persecute his people unjustly (Ex 15:7; Ps 7:6). His anger is provoked by wicked deeds (Ps 106:29). The psalmist says, "Surely your wrath against men brings you praise, and the survivors of your wrath are restrained" (Ps 76:10). God's anger is thus viewed as completely justified and also as of ultimate benefit to people.

But the Bible does not present anger as an essential characteristic of God. In fact, God's wrath is set aside when God forgives (Ps 85:2–3), and even his acts of anger show restraint (Ps 78:38). Compared to his favor, which lasts a lifetime, God's anger is momentary (Ps 30:5). God intends only good to humanity, and when it is necessary to act in anger, the intention to do good is never lost.

The concept of righteous anger. The Bible's positive view of God's anger brings us to the concept of righteous anger. God's anger is righteous in several senses. It is provoked only by sin. It is expressed with only good in mind. And, strikingly, the Bible insists that God's anger is never a controlling element in his choices.

It is impossible for human beings to exhibit truly righteous anger, because in us anger tends to dominate and to control. Exodus 34:6–7 describes God in this way: "The LORD, the LORD, the compassionate and gracious God, slow to anger, abounding in love and faithfulness, maintaining love to thousands, and forgiving wickedness, rebellion and sin. Yet he does not leave the guilty unpunished." This significant statement places anger in a distinctive relationship with other qualities of the Lord. He is compassionate, gracious, loving, faithful, forgiving, just. God's anger never dominates to the extent that these other character traits no longer function. God's anger is always in harmony with his compassion, grace, love, faithfulness, eagerness to forgive, and commitment to do justice. Nine times the OT reminds us that God is "slow to anger" (Ex 34:6; Nu 14:18; Ne 9:17; Ps 86:15; 103:8; 145:8; Joel 2:13; Jnh 4:2; Na 1:3). Human beings are unable to

maintain the balance that God does—a balance that makes it possible for him to be lovingly angry and to show compassionate wrath.

God's anger is expressed in judgment. Just as real events elicit God's anger, so God's anger is expressed in real events in history. God's anger at the Egyptian persecution of Israel was expressed in the ten plagues (Ex 15:7; cf. 10:14; 11:1). Armies served as the rod of God's anger (Isa 10:5). History has shown again and again the impact of his fury at persistent rebelliousness (Dt 4:25; 9:1–8; 2 Ki 21:1–26). At the end of time, God's anger will be fully expressed in final judgment (Isa 63; Zep 2).

NT — The NT also speaks of divine and human anger. Although the two Testaments are consistent in viewpoint, there are differences in emphasis. In the OT, God's anger is linked with violations of the covenant relationship. Thus the Jewish people are often the objects of his wrath. But in the NT, God's wrath is focused on those who will not believe. This and other differences make it important for us to study the Testaments separately as well as together.

4. Greek words for anger. In the NT, the two common words for "anger" are synonyms. The Septuagint (the Greek translation of the OT used in Jesus' time) uses each of the Greek words to translate any of the Hebrew words for wrath or anger.

All the occurrences of *orgē* in the writings of Luke and Paul and in the Book of Hebrews describe human anger (except Ro 2:8). In Revelation the word is used of divine anger expressed in the judgments at history's end. Typically the writers of the NT prefer this word when *outbursts* of anger are in view.

This Greek noun (used 36 times) and its related verb (*orgizomai*, used 8 times) and adjective (*orgilos*, used only once) are variously indicative (1) of human anger (Mt 5:22; 18:34; 22:7; Lk 14:21; 15:28; 21:23; Ro 13:4–5; Eph 4:26; 4:31; 5:6; Col 3:6,8; 1 Ti 2:8; Tit 1:7; Jas 1:19–20), (2) of divine anger (Mt 3:7; Mk 5:3; Lk 3:7; Jn 3:36; Ro 1:18; 2:5,8; 3:5; 4:15; 5:9; 9:22;

12:19; Eph 2:3; 5:6; Col 3:6; 1 Th 1:10; 2:16; 5:9; Heb 3:11; 4:3; Rev 6:16–17; 11:18; 12:17; 14:10; 16:19; 19:15), and (3) of satanic anger (Rev 12:17).

The word *thymos* is preferred when the anger in view is more deliberate—a conscious response. It is condemned in human beings (Eph 4:31; Col 3:8). This Greek word is used (1) of human beings (Lk 4:28; Ac 19:28; 2 Co 12:20; Gal 5:20; Eph 4:31; Col 3:8; Heb 11:27; Rev 14:8; 18:3), (2) of God (Rev 14:10,19; 15:1,7; 16:1,19; 19:15), and (3) of Satan (Rev 12:12).

5. The NT view of human anger. The NT views unjustifiable anger and fits of rage as originating in sinful human nature. Such anger and rage, characteristic of the old nature, are to be decisively rejected by the new persons we have become in Christ. "Get rid of all bitterness, rage and anger, brawling and slander, along with every form of malice," Paul writes. "Be kind and compassionate to one another, forgiving each other, just as in Christ God forgave you" (Eph 4:31–32). It is important to adopt this attitude, for unchecked anger is a root of interpersonal bitterness, the very source of murder (Mt 5:21–22). James writes, "Everyone should be quick to listen, slow to speak and slow to become angry, for man's anger does not bring about the righteous life that God desires" (Jas 1:19–20). Revenge is ruled out for the believer, not only by the principle of forgiveness (Eph 4:32) but also to "leave room for God's wrath" (Ro 12:19). God alone is judge; he alone has the right to repay.

Although we may become angry, there is no question that anger is a signal to us to examine and to deal with ourselves, not justification for striking out at others. As Paul says, "In your anger, do not sin. Do not let the sun go down while you are still angry" (Eph 4:26).

6. The NT view of God's anger. The OT teaching on anger stresses the covenant people's rejection of God and views wrath as something their actions provoked. The NT does not continue this theme. Instead, it is the unsaved, those who refuse to respond to the gospel, who are pictured as the objects of God's wrath (Jn 3:36; Ro 1:18; 3:5; Eph 2:3). Believers are assured that "since we have now been justified by his blood, how much more shall we be saved from God's wrath through him!" (Ro 5:9). According to Paul, "God did not appoint us to suffer wrath but to receive salvation through our Lord Jesus Christ" (1 Th 5:9).

There are two reasons for this shift in emphasis. First, Christ's self-sacrifice dealt so completely with sin that, as forgiven men and women, we are outside the sphere in which God's wrath operates. God does discipline believing men and women. But that discipline is totally an expression of love, not of anger (Heb 12:6). ◆ *Discipline*

Second, in the NT, wrath is linked exclusively with final judgment. The wrath of God is viewed as something that will come at the end of the age, not as something that operates in the present (except through such human agencies as government [Ro 13:4–5]). While Heb 3:11 and 4:3 quote an OT passage that mentions God's anger against Israel, the reason is to underline the seriousness of unbelief. It is not to import the OT concept of wrath against Israel into NT relationships between the believer and God. Instead, we are shown again and again in the NT that God's wrath is coming, not present. The time when God will again unleash his wrath is at history's end (Mt 3:7; Lk 3:7; 21:23; Ro 2:5,8; 9:22; 1 Th 1:10; 2:16).

The second chapter of Romans is particularly revealing. Paul demonstrates there that a lost and sinful humanity lies under God's wrath. Continued rejection of God is "contempt for the riches of his kindness, tolerance and patience" (2:4). God's purpose, however, is to withold judgment in order to extend the opportunity for repentance. Those who remain stubbornly unrepentant actually store up "wrath . . . for the day of God's wrath, when his righteous judgment will be revealed" (2:5). Before that day is the day of grace. In regard to believers, the forgiveness that is theirs in Christ has removed them forever from the sphere of God's wrath. In regard to unbelievers, God graciously is holding back expression of deserved wrath, to give everyone opportunity for repentance. Those who will not respond to grace store up wrath, a wrath to be experienced in the day of final judgment.

It is clear, then, why the Book of Revelation speaks so often of God's anger and wrath. It is at history's end that the anger God now withholds will be fully displayed (cf. 2 Th 1:6–10).

7. Summary. The Bible deals with both human and divine anger. Anger, as a feeling that may be provoked by others' actions, is something all human beings experience. Anger may be justified or unjustified. But the feeling of anger is never justification for sinful actions. The OT gives us guidance for dealing with our anger, and the NT underlines the importance of choosing to respond as Jesus' own renewed persons, treating others with compassion and forgiveness rather than angrily seeking revenge.

God too knows the feeling of anger. The OT clearly specifies what human actions provoke God to anger. The NT treats wrath as a basic relational state, showing that the unsaved are under God's wrath. But God never acts capriciously in his anger. He always acts in full harmony with his character as a loving, forgiving, compassionate, and just person.

Each of these divine traits is clearly seen in the NT's age of grace. Believers are no longer under God's wrath, having been fully forgiven on the basis of Jesus' death. The unsaved are currently given the opportunity to repent as God holds back expression of his anger. Only at the end of history, when final judgment comes, will God's wrath be poured out—and then only on those who simply will not believe.

ANGUISH

The OT is rich in words that express suffering. Over a dozen of them underlie the modern versions' use of "anguish." The Hebrew language offers such contributing ideas as dismay, panic, terror, agony, pain, grief, sorrow, vexation, distress, ruin, and complaint. These words communicate a sense of deep pain and inner turmoil, with mental distress caused by external circumstances that create great pressure on the individual. While there are differences in shades of meaning of the Hebrew terms, the English word "anguish" appropriately captures the depth of feeling the OT words express.

ANIMALS

What is our relationship with other forms of life that share our planet? How does Scripture view animal life? Insights come from both the OT and the NT.

1. **Hebrew and Greek words for animals**
2. **The place of animals in the created order**
3. **Distinctions between humans and animals**
4. **Summary**

1. Hebrew and Greek words for animals. It has been estimated that there are over three thousand biblical references to animals. Many are to specific kinds: dogs, ponies, donkeys, sheep, lions, camels, etc. But there are also generic terms, usually translated "animal" or "beast" in both OT and NT.

The Hebrew word *bᵉhēmâh* means four-footed animals as distinct from birds. These animals may be wild or domesticated: the term refers collectively to the animal kingdom. The Hebrew word *ḥayyâh* means "living thing" and is normally used of wild animals in contrast to domestic ones. The Greek word *thērion* is used to translate this Hebrew term. Revelation uses *thērion* some thirty-eight times (of forty-six NT occurrences) to identify the fierce, ruthless, beastly powers that will be ranged against God at history's end.

The Hebrew words *miqneh* (larger cattle) and *ṣōneh* (smaller cattle, like sheep and goats) identify domestic animals. The NT uses the Greek word *ktēnos* for domestic animals. The Hebrew word *be'îr* is typically translated "beast" but is a generic term for cattle, and does not imply brutishness. It is a synonym for *behēmâh* and *miqneh*.

A survey of the Hebrew and Greek words tells us that the people of Bible times made a number of distinctions among creatures of the animal kingdom. But the words themselves tell us nothing of the theological questions often raised today. For answers, we must see how these words are used in Scripture and what is taught there about the creatures who share our world.

2. The place of animals in the created order. The creation story told in early Genesis presents God as the originator of both human and animal life. The story, however, makes several important distinctions. Animals and man were created on different "days." Human beings were created in a unique way and in God's own image and likeness. Humanity was given dominion, to "rule over the fish of the sea and the birds of the air, over the livestock [*behēmâh*], and over all the creatures that move along the ground" (1:26). The right to rule is not the right to exploit. ◆ *Rule/Dominion* But the superiority of humanity is clearly taught. It is also important to note that nowhere in the Bible is the human race classed among the animals.

Within the creation framework that is provided by Scripture, animals are viewed as valuable property (Ex 21,22; Lev 27). They are used for food and for sacrifice and are classified as "clean" or "unclean," depending on their suitability for these uses. ◆ *Clean and Unclean* Israel was warned not to make an idol in any shape—including that of an animal (Dt 4:16–17). One who has sexual intercourse with animals is considered worthy of death (Ex 22:19; Lev 18:23).

The biblical picture of creation and the concept of animal life as created within fixed boundaries of role and purpose are completely foreign to the evolutionary notion that higher orders of animal life developed from lower orders. Genesis says that God commanded the land to produce animals "according to their kinds . . . each according to its kind" (Ge

1:24). The Hebrew word *mîn* ("kind") occurs thirty-one times in the OT. It suggests that the form (whether of animal or vegetation) has its own generic group in which it was placed by the Creator. However, the biblical data does not enable us to match "kind" with any of the modern biological classifications (such as genus, species, family, or order). It seems that *mîn* is used at one time or another in each of these senses, but it is very clear that *mîn* is never used in the sense of kingdom, phylum, or class.

God has structured his universe with order and regularity. In this ordered universe animal life has its own place—and will stay in that place.

3. Distinctions between humans and animals. When Solomon in his search for life's meaning limited himself to what he could observe in the material universe, he was puzzled at the relationship between humanity and the animals. Ecc 3:18–21 reports his thoughts: "I also thought, 'As for men, God tests them so that they may see that they are like the animals. . . . The same fate awaits them both. As one dies, so dies the other. All have the same breath; man has no advantage over the animal. . . . All go to the same place; all come from dust, and to dust all return. Who knows if the spirit of man rises upward and if the spirit of the animal goes down into the earth?' " The fact that these thoughts are located in Ecclesiastes—a Bible book that records the struggle of the human mind to understand the meaning of life—tells us that Solomon's conclusions are not necessarily correct. In fact, the rest of Scripture assures us that Solomon was not correct and that there are vital differences between humanity and the animal creation.

Difference in image. This is the first and most basic difference. In creating the world, God made living creatures after a model that existed in his own imagination (Ge 1:24–25). The passage goes on to point out that the animal kingdom is now destined to reproduce "according to its kind." But the same passage says that man was created in God's image. The model after which humanity was shaped was God himself. Those capacities that mark God as a person with emotion, intellect, will, self-consciousness, etc., were given uniquely to mankind. This basic difference sets human beings completely off from the animals, over whom they are to rule (Ge 1:26–27).

Difference in destiny. The Bible teaches that each human being will retain his personal, self-conscious existence after death. ♦ *Resurrection* It is significant that in the key passage on resurrection, Paul points to the fact that human and animal creations are different (1 Co 15:39). It is the human body and human flesh that will be raised to imperishability (15:42–49) in a resurrection intended to restore the original image of God in all its fullness, unmarred by the sin inherited from Adam after the Fall (15:45–59). No such hope is ever suggested for animals.

Difference in mind. When God brought his judgment of temporary madness on Nebuchadnezzar, the curse stated: "Let his mind be changed from that of a man and let him be given the mind of an animal, till seven times [years] pass by for him" (Da 4:16). Given the mind of an animal, Nebuchadnezzar apparently lost all self-awareness; he lived with the wild donkeys and ate grass until the day God restored his sanity (4:34; 5:21).

There are several other passages in the Bible that help us better define the differences in mind that Daniel identified. The psalmist Asaph describes his depression when he was torn with envy at the prosperity of the wicked. In his despairing state, Asaph looked only at external circumstances, and felt self-pity at the apparent uselessness of his own commitment to holiness. Asaph recovered perspective when he gained God's perspective: "I entered the sanctuary of God; then I understood their final destiny" (Ps 73:17). Later, looking back at his time of depression, Asaph said, "I was senseless and ignorant; I was a brute beast before you" (v. 22). Asaph's expression here is important. He had looked at the present with no perspective either on God or on the future. His evaluations had been

based only on immediate experience. But he recovered his perspective when he considered God.

The animal mind (brute beast) is locked into present experience and must react to the present without awareness of the spiritual universe and without ability to project from the present to the future. An animal may learn from past experience; but it cannot draw on information beyond experience, nor can it reason from information to the end of a chain of probable cause-and-effect events.

A similar point is made by both Peter and Jude. They describe false teachers as being "like brute beasts, creatures of instinct" (2 Pe 2:12) who "understand by instinct, like unreasoning animals" (Jude 10). The animal mind is capable of understanding. But its understanding is of a different order from that of human understanding. Animal experiences are interpreted by instinct, and animals lack the capacity to reason from experience to a deeper understanding of the past or of the future.

While man and beast depend on God and are under his care (Ps 36:6), the animal creation is of a distinctly different order from that of humanity.

4. Summary. Animals share with human beings the world that God has created, and they have been placed under humanity's rule. Animals have a different place and role in the creation order from those of human beings, for they are distinctly different in original image, in destiny, and in nature, as shown by differences in mind.

There is no evidence in Scripture to indicate that animals (even the most loved of pets) will share in our resurrection or have an eternal destiny. There is no evidence in Scripture that animals, which are recognized as sensient beings, have "rights" that correspond to human rights. Yet there is evidence that God does have concern for the living beings in the animal creation (Jnh 4:11; Mt 6:25–26). We are called, by the responsibility of rule, to share God's concern for the animals. ♦ *Rule/Dominion*

ANOINTING/ANOINTED

The ancient practice of anointing is deeply rooted in the culture of the OT. We are likely to associate it primarily with the word *Messiah* ("the anointed one"), a title by which we know Jesus. But we make a mistake if we read our NT perspective back into the OT. Anointing had its own distinctive place in the ancient world of the Bible.

OT   1. The OT practice of anointing
      2. The OT purpose of anointing
      3. The "anointed one"
NT   4. Anointing in the NT
      5. Jesus as the Anointed One
      6. Summary

1. The OT practice of anointing. The Hebrew word translated "anoint" in the NIV and the NASB is *māšah*. The word is used sixty-nine times in the OT and means "to apply oil" by pouring or spreading.

The practice was common in many cultures of the ancient Middle East. We see it first in Scripture when Jacob anointed a pillar he had set up as a memorial of his meeting with God at Bethel (Ge 28:18). The practice is linked ritually with the worship of Israel at the tabernacle, where priests (Ex 28:41; 30:30; Lev 8:12) and the altar (Ex 29:36; 40:10; Lev 8:10) were anointed with a specially prepared sacred oil (Ex 35:8,28). Later, anointing with oil was extended to kings (e.g., Jdg 9:8,15; 1 Sa 9:16; 15:1; 16:3,12; 1 Ki 1:34) and at times to prophets (1 Ki 19:16).

Anointing was also associated with hospitality and the treatment accorded an honored guest (Ps 23:5; Lk 7:46; Jn 11:2).

2. The OT purpose of anointing. Anointing was used in religious ritual and for induction into leadership offices. The act has several functions. First, it consecrated religious items and served to ordain religious leaders. In each case the idea is that of setting aside, or authorizing for God's service. Thus a functioning priest is an "anointed priest," one who has been consecrated to his ministry (Lev 4:3,5). Second, while anointing was done

by a human agent (such as Samuel, who anointed both Saul and David), it was considered to be done by Yahweh himself (1 Sa 10:1; 2 Sa 12:7). Because God himself set the anointed person apart to be his servant, that person was worthy of special respect. Thus, David refused to kill his enemy Saul when he had the opportunity to do so (1 Sa 26:9–23). Third, anointing, at least in the case of David, was accompanied by a special divine enablement to carry out the mission for which one was commissioned. This is not stated directly but may be inferred from 1 Sa 16:13, which tells of David's anointing and then says, "From that day the Spirit of the LORD came upon David in power" (cf. 1 Sa 10:6–8).

Thus, anointing in OT times was an act of great significance. It set objects and persons—prophets, priests, and kings—apart for God's use. The one anointed was considered chosen by God to carry out his appointed service.

3. The "anointed one". The Hebrew term *māšîah*, transliterated "messiah," means "anointed one." It appears only thirty-nine times in the OT, and then it identifies a range of individuals. Included is even the pagan King Cyrus (Isa 41:1), who was appointed by Yahweh for a specific task relating to Israel.

Māšîah is used primarily in the books of 1 and 2 Samuel and Psalms to designate Israel's king. In Psalms it is often a poetic synonym for the royal office. Particularly, it is used to identify the royal line of David (Ps 2:2; 18:50; 84:9; 89:38,51; 132:10,17). There is no totally clear reference to an "anointed one" who will be Israel's coming deliverer, although it is evident in the OT that a ruler from David's line will come and will establish an eternal kingdom (e.g., Isa 9:7; 11:1–5). While there is evidence for pre-Christian use of "the anointed one" to identify the coming king, it is the NT that makes this connection obvious.

4. Anointing in the NT. Three different Greek words are translated "anoint" in the NT. Each expresses the same basic idea of rubbing or spreading oil, perfume, or ointment. *Chriō* is used five times in the NT, always figuratively and always in the sense of some special appointment or commission by God that sets the person(s) apart (Lk 4:18; Ac 4:27; 10:38; 2 Co 1:21; Heb 1:9).

The eight occurrences of *aleiphō* are all quite literal, referring to the rubbing of oils or ointment on the body (Mt 6:13; Mk 6:17; 16:1; Lk 7:38,46; Jn 11:2; 12:3; Jas 5:14). The use of this word in Jas 5:14 is significant: "Is any of you sick? He should call for the elders of the church to pray over him and anoint him with oil in the name of the Lord." The particular oil here is olive oil (*elaion*), which was used in a medicinal way in NT times. The passage seems to suggest that both prayer and medical treatment should be provided for the sick. The promise "the prayer offered in faith will make the sick person well" (5:15) indicates that the power to make well belongs to God, whatever means he may choose to use.

Chrisma is used only three times in the NT (1 Jn 2:20,27). A study of the word helps us to understand the puzzling verse 27: "As for you, the anointing you received from him remains in you, and you do not need anyone to teach you. But as his anointing teaches you about all things and as that anointing is real, not counterfeit—just as it has taught you, remain in him" (2:27). *Chrisma* focuses, not on the act of rubbing or spreading (anointing as a process), but rather on that with which one has been anointed. Traditionally, the anointing in 1 John has been understood to be the Holy Spirit, who is given to believers and who is identified in John's Gospel as the Teacher (Jn 16:12–15). Because the Spirit links each believer intimately with Jesus, the Head of the church, we can count on the one with whom we have been anointed to "guide [us] into all truth" (16:13).

The NT does not view anointing in the same way as does the OT. Physical anointing is not used in worship nor to consecrate persons for leadership. But there is a spiritual anointing. By it God himself consecrates each believer to himself and equips us with his Holy Spirit.

5. Jesus as the Anointed One. The Gospels quickly identify Jesus of Naza-reth with the OT concept of one anointed for a distinctive mission. In fact, Jesus is identified as the ultimate Anointed One, the one who will rule as king over a restored Davidic kingdom. This convic-tion is expressed in Jesus' title "Christ." This is not a name but a title that means "the anointed"; it is literally the same as *māšîaḥ*.

The identification of Jesus with the Anointed One is made explicit by John, who reports that Andrew, after meeting Jesus, hurried to find Simon (Peter) and told him, " 'We have found the Messiah' (that is, the Christ)" (Jn 1:41). John reports that the woman at the well said the following to Jesus: "I know that Messiah" (called Christ) "is coming" (Jn 4:25). It is clear from these references that in NT times, Palestinians had linked the title "Anointed One" with the OT prom-ises of a king from David's line who would restore Israel's kingdom. The real-ization that Christ is also the Son of God (Mk 14:61; Lk 20:41; Jn 20:31) placed OT prophecy in a bright new perspective. Later repeated use of the title "Christ" as Jesus' name affirms the belief that he sums up in himself both the promises and the eschatological hope of the OT.

▶ *Christ*

6. Summary. Anointing in the OT involved pouring or sprinkling with oil in order to consecrate a person or thing to God's service. Priests and prophets were anointed. In the time of the kingdom the practice focused on the consecration of kings. In that period "anointed one" came to serve as a title for a ruling monarch, especially for rulers in the Davidic line.

The NT uses anointing in different ways. In some cases literal anointing with ointments or oil is in view. In others the term is used figuratively. Yet the ritual uses of anointing do not reappear, nor does anointing as induction into leadership.

In the Gospels and the rest of the NT, Jesus is affirmed as God's Anointed One. As the Christ, Jesus fulfills the OT prom-ises of a ruler from David's line.

ANTICHRIST

The word "antichrist" appears only five times in the NT, all in John's writings. Yet the concept is woven deeply in apocalyptic literature and looms large in books and sermons on prophecy.

1. Antichrist in John's letters
2. False Christs in the Gospels
3. The apocalyptic background
4. Antichrist in the Epistles

1. Antichrist in John's letters. The word "antichrist" is a transliteration of the Greek *antichristos*. The prefix *anti* first meant "in place of," then "against." This word occurs only five times in the NT, all in the writings of John (1 Jn 2:18,22; 4:3; 2 Jn 7). He speaks both of the "antichrist," who is coming, and of "many antichrists," who have already come (1 Jn 1:18). The spirit and motivation that will animate the Antichrist are presently at work!

John identifies the present activity of antichrists. They eat away at the fellowship of believers from within by substituting lie for truth. Antichrists can be particularly detected by their denial of both Father and Son (2:22). These teachers of false doctrine reject the claim of Jesus to be the Christ, the Son of God, and reject the doctrine of the Incarnation—"that Jesus Christ has come in the flesh" (2 Jn 7). This denial constitutes rejection not only of the Son but also of the Father, for the Father is the one who showed his love by sending the Son to become the atoning sacrifice for our sins (1 Jn 4:7–15).

2. False Christs in the Gospels. The term *pseudochristos* appears only two times in the Gospels, but each time it is clearly linked with the Antichrist (Mt 24:24; Mk 13:22). The prefix *pseudo* means "false, deceptive, spurious, pretended."

Jesus is the speaker in each instance of the use of this word in the Gospels. In each case Jesus is talking about the end of the age, when God's OT promises given through the prophets are to be fulfilled. Jesus refers specifically to Daniel's prophecy about the end of the age (Mt 24:15; Mk 13:14). During this end time of great distress, "false Christs and false prophets will appear and perform great signs and miracles to deceive even the elect—if that were possible" (Mt 24:24). The culmination of this trend, according to Daniel and Revelation, is in the appearance of two specific individuals, one of whom is the Antichrist.

3. The apocalyptic background. The apocalyptic writings in the Bible focus on history's end. They provide powerful but often obscure descriptions of God's judgments on an unbelieving world. Jesus made reference to Daniel's apocalyptic vision (Da 11–12) in his description of the end of the age (Mt 24; Mk 13). Jesus clearly regarded the OT pictures of the future as trustworthy descriptions of what will indeed happen, thus assuring us that the Bible's apocalyptic literature is not mere symbolism: like other prophecy, it portrays actual events before they happen.

In apocalyptic literature, particularly in Da 11 and Rev 13, it is made clear that a certain individual will appear at the climax of history. This individual will be energized by Satan and lead humanity in rebellion against God and his people. Students of prophecy identify this individual as the Antichrist. He is most probably the one whom Jesus and John referred to.

4. Antichrist in the Epistles. The word "antichrist" is not used in the Epistles (other than those by John). But Paul clearly describes this individual in 2 Th 2. He writes there to correct the Thessalonians' misunderstandings of his early teaching on the future. Paul, like Jesus, refers to Daniel's apocalyptic vision and calls the Antichrist "the man of lawlessness" and "the man doomed to destruction" (2:3). Paul describes this man and his motivations: "He will oppose and will exalt himself over everything that is called God or is worshiped, so that he sets himself up in God's temple, proclaiming himself to be God" (2:4). The description 2 Th 2:1–12 provides of this person and his acts is in full accord with the descriptions in the apocalyptic material.

We may leave it to God to deal at history's end with the Antichrist of the future. We resist the antichrists now among us by remaining faithful to Jesus, the Son of God, our Savior.

ANXIETY/WORRY

"Anxiety" and "worry" in the NIV and the NASB almost always translate a single NT Greek term. But these same English words in the OT capture the meaning of a number of different Hebrew expressions. The Hebrew ranges from "the multitude of my thoughts" (tumbling, anxious thoughts) to "care," "thoughts," and "trouble, heaviness, or vexation of heart." In each of the OT settings, the sense of anxiety can be felt. But it is in the NT that a specific term focuses Scripture's teaching and helps us grasp the nature, cause, and solution of our own feelings of anxiety.

1. The Greek term
2. The nature of anxiety
3. Jesus' teaching on anxiety
4. The subject of anxiety in the Epistles
5. Summary

1. The Greek term. The Greek words translated "anxiety" or "worry" in modern versions (and often translated "cares" in the KJV) are *merimnaō* (verb) and *merimna* (noun). The verb originally meant "to care," or "to be concerned about." When used by the Greeks concerning the future, both words came to connote anxious expectation. When used of the present, the words expressed an aching sense of grief. The meaning of any term, however, is defined by the way it is used. It is the way that Jesus and the writers of the Gospels and Epistles, guided by the Holy Spirit, used words that filled them with their biblical meaning.

Either *merimnaō* or *merimna* is used in each NT passage where "anxiety" or "worry" appears, aside from Php 2:28 (*alypos*, "without grief") and Lk 12:29 (*meteōrizomai*, "to hang suspended in mid-air," thus, "to be worried"). Specifically, *merimna* is used in Mt 13:22; Mk

4:19; Lk 8:14; 21:34; 2 Co 11:28; 1 Pe 5:7. Lk 10:41; 12:11,22,25,26; 1 Co 7:32,33,34; 12:25; Php 2:20; 4:6. These words are not always translated "anxiety" or "worry," but the thought of anxious concern is expressed in each context. Mk 13:11 uses *promerimnaō*, meaning "to be anxious ahead of time."

2. The nature of anxiety. According to the Bible, anxiety is often legitimate. The word indicates first of all a sense of concern for self and/or for others. In 1 Co 7, for instance, it is used to express the commendable concern of a person for his or her spouse (7:33–34) and the concern of each "about the Lord's affairs," that is, how to "please the Lord" (7:32). Paul speaks of the daily "pressure of [his] concern [*merimna*] for all the churches" (2 Co 11:28) and states that God's purpose in the body is that each part have "equal concern [*merimnaō*] for each other" and that "if one part suffers, every part suffers with it" (1 Co 12:25–26). Even in speaking of the "worries of this life" (Mt 13:22; Mk 4:19), Jesus is simply stating a fact of life. We are living in this present world, and there are necessary concerns that each individual must attend to.

But while it is legitimate to have concerns that we will at times experience as demanding pressures, there is a limit to their legitimacy. The "worries of this life" may so dominate our attention that they make God's Word unfruitful in our lives (Mt 13:22; Mk 4:19). The pressures of legitimate concerns can cause us to so focus on worldly matters that we forget to relate our needs and our worries to the Lord.

3. Jesus' teaching on anxiety. In his ministry, Jesus dealt directly with the subject of legitimate concern. His teaching is reported in two places especially (Mt 6:25–34; Lk 12:22–34).

Each passage begins with an admonition: "Do not worry about your life, what you will eat." Jesus is talking here about necessities, not luxuries. They are thus objects of legitimate concern for one living in the material universe. But Jesus releases believers from the bondage of anxiety over necessities. God is a heavenly Father whose care extends even to vegetation and to animal life; we human beings are much more valuable to God than those other parts of his creation. Worry over what we will eat or drink or wear—all those things the pagans pursue—is unnecessary because we have a heavenly Father who knows our needs and loves us dearly.

By linking legitimate concerns to God, believers are freed from anxiety and worry. This freedom allows us to concentrate on seeking God's kingdom and his righteousness, knowing that "all these things will be given to [us] as well." So Jesus concludes, "Do not worry about tomorrow, for tomorrow will worry about itself."

What the pagan Greeks experienced as anxious concern over a tomorrow they could not control, the believer who knows God as a loving Father can experience in calm confidence. Released from fears about tomorrow, we can concentrate on doing God's will today, as obedient subjects of a kingdom over which the Almighty rules.

4. The subject of anxiety in the Epistles. The Gospels recognize the tendency of legitimate human concerns to lead to a loss of perspective; we can forget God and adopt a pagan materialism that looks ahead anxiously and concentrates on running after the material things that seem to offer security. In order to avoid this tendency, believers must orient life to God and realize that life's meaning is to be found in living as subjects who are responsive to their loving, wise, and powerful King.

The Epistles recognize that human beings must live with and under some degree of pressure (1 Co 12:25; 2 Co 11:28; Php 2:20). But we must learn how to handle pressure so that anxiety does not become a dominating or distracting concern. In Php 4:6 Paul uses the present imperative: "Do not be [keep on being] anxious about anything." Instead of letting our concerns nag at us, we are "in everything, by prayer and petition, with thanksgiving, [to] present [our] requests to God" (Php 4:6).

The alternative to being anxious is to bring to God those things that trouble us and then to leave them in his hands. We do this "with thanksgiving" for the release from worry that prayer provides, and we do it with confidence because we know that God hears and will act for us. Paul goes on to promise, "The peace of God, which transcends all understanding, will guard your hearts and your minds in Christ Jesus" (Php 4:9).

The same prescription is repeated in 1 Pe 5:7: "Cast all your anxiety on him because he cares for you."

5. Summary. Both anxiety and worry spring from natural and legitimate concerns that are part of life in this world. But legitimate concerns are handled wrongly when they do one or more of the following: (1) become dominating concerns in our life and lead to fear, (2) destroy our perspective on life and cause us to forget that God exists and cares, or (3) move us to drift into an attitude of constant worry and concern over a future that we cannot control.

Jesus deals with anxiety by calling us to an awareness of God. God does exist, and he cares. He is aware of our needs and is committed to meet our needs. Remaining aware of God frees us from the tyranny of things. It enables us to focus our lives on our relationship with God and go on living a righteous and productive life.

The Epistles add to our understanding by pointing out that areas of legitimate anxiety exist even for the strongest of believers. But the pressures of even legitimate concerns are not to dominate us or to make us habitually anxious, worried people. We escape by using anxiety creatively. This means that we must recognize the feelings of pressure and concern as a call to prayer. We should immediately turn to God to lay our needs and the needs of others before him. We then turn back to live our lives encompassed by his peace. Anxiety, rather than drawing us away from God, draws us to him and thus fulfills his purpose for it in our lives.

APOSTLE

Many people are uncertain about the role of apostles. The meaning of the word is clear. But just who should be called an apostle and whether there are apostles today are questions that continue to be debated. We cannot answer all the technical questions that scholars ask. But the basic biblical meaning of apostleship is relatively clear.

1. The Greek word and its background
2. The apostles in the Gospels and Acts
3. The apostle Paul
4. Other uses of "apostle" in the NT
5. Summary

1. The Greek word and its background. The Greek word that is most commonly translated "apostle" is *apostolos*. The verb *apostellō* and a compound of it, *exapostellō*, as well as a synonym, *pempō*, are sometimes used with the same meaning: to send one on a mission as an envoy.

At first these Greek words described the sending of a delegation of several representatives. Later the focus shifted, to emphasize the idea that an *apostolos* was the personal representative of the one sending him. Eventually *apostolos* came to be used in some Greek philosophical schools with a religious significance: the one sent spoke with divine authorization.

The translators of the Hebrew OT into Greek used *apostellō* as the equivalent of a particular Hebrew verb that also expresses divine authorization to accomplish some well-defined and specific task. *Apostolos* is used in the Septuagint some seven hundred times in this sense to fix our attention on God as the one who gives his envoy authority.

Apostellō was very seldom used in ordinary conversation in NT times. Those familiar with the Greek translation of the OT immediately identified the word with the OT concept of divinely authorized messengers sent by God and acting on his authority.

The verb *apostellō* is used 131 times in the NT, while *pempō* (usually synonymous) is used 81 times. The noun *apostolos* is also found frequently (81 times); it is translated "apostle" and helps us understand the nature of the special individuals who played such an important, foundational role in the establishment of the Christian church.

2. The apostles in the Gospels and Acts. The Gospels report that Jesus chose twelve men and designated them his apostles (Mt 10:2; Mk 3:14; Lk 6:13). These twelve were with Jesus through his years of earthly ministry and were witnesses to his resurrection. When Judas betrayed Jesus and then committed suicide, another was chosen to bring the number back to twelve. "It is necessary," Peter explained, "to choose one of the men who have been with us the whole time the Lord Jesus went in and out among us, beginning from John's baptism to the time when Jesus was taken up from us. For one of these must become a witness with us of his resurrection" (Ac 1:21–22).

Both the qualifications and the mission of the Twelve are identified here. They had to be followers of Jesus from the beginning of his public ministry through his ascension, and they had to witness the fact of Jesus' resurrection.

In Acts we see the twelve apostles evangelizing (Ac 2), performing miracles (Ac 2:43; 5:12), teaching converts (Ac 2:42), and proposing a way for the church to create a structure needed to handle distribution to the needy so the apostles themselves could concentrate on prayer and the ministry of the Word (Ac 6:1-4). The apostles served not as rulers but as wise guides. They were not directors but were participants with the whole church in seeking God's guidance in the significant decisions affecting the believing community (Ac 11:1–18; 15:1–35).

The role and identity of the Twelve was never transformed into institutional roles or offices. The Twelve remain a group of a dozen unique individuals, and Revelation tells us the foundation of the heavenly Jerusalem will have engraved on them "the names of the twelve apostles of the Lamb" (Rev 21:14).

3. The apostle Paul. While the Gospels and Acts focus on the Twelve, the Epistles introduce Paul as a thirteenth apostle. Paul too had seen the risen Jesus and thus could be a witness to his resurrection (Ac 9:1–6; 1 Co 15:3–7). Although not one of Jesus' original followers, Paul, like them received his commission directly from Jesus (Ac 26:15–18).

Paul's commission was as a "herald and an apostle . . . and a teacher of the true faith to the Gentiles" (1 Ti 2:7). These functions parallel the ministry of the Twelve as described in Acts, but with the Greek world rather than the Jewish people as Paul's particular constituency (Gal 2:8). In a number of NT passages, Paul explains and defends his unique position as an apostle—one who by virtue of his calling spoke with God's own authority (1 Co 9; 2 Co 11–13; Gal 2). Peter clearly recognized the validity of Paul's claim: he classified Paul's letters with the "other Scriptures" (2 Pe 3:14–16). In some significant sense, Paul ranks with the Twelve, and his apostleship is as unique as their own.

4. Other uses of "apostle" in the NT. The term "apostle" is applied to the Twelve and to Paul in a distinctive way. The calling of these individuals to witness to the Resurrection and their commissioning by Christ himself make it plain that no institutional office is in view. The authority of Paul and of the Twelve was a unique authority and is without parallel in the church today.

Yet it is clear that the underlying concept of apostleship is extended in the NT beyond these thirteen. Luke speaks of "the apostles Barnabas and Paul" (Ac 14:14). Writing personal greetings at the end of his letter to the Romans, Paul identifies Andronicus and Junias as "outstanding among the apostles" (Ro 16:7). Paul also writes heatedly about persons who are "masquerading as apostles of Christ" (2 Co 11:13). This involved the apostles' claim to a significant role, for Paul says in 1 Co 12:28: "In the church God has appointed first of all apostles."

In general, the title "apostles" seems to identify the original Twelve, who maintain a unique calling and position and share it only with Paul. The NT indicates that others besides *the* apostles typically had an itinerant ministry related to both founding and strengthening new churches. It is quite likely that our modern term "missionary" is very close in meaning to the general use of "apostle" in NT times. Perhaps one of the most significant uses of the word "apostle" in the NT is the reference to Jesus as "the apostle and high priest whom we confess" (Heb 3:1).

5. Summary. "The apostles" are the twelve followers of Jesus whom he selected when he began his public ministry. Each of these twelve men observed all that Jesus said and did during his years of ministry on earth, and each was a witness to the Resurrection. The ministry of the Twelve in the early church focused on prayer and the teaching of the Word, not on organization or administration. Paul was an apostle in this same unique sense, having also seen the resurrected Jesus and having been personally called by Jesus to a ministry of evangelizing and teaching.

But "apostle" has general as well as specific meaning. An apostle is an envoy, sent on a mission to speak for the one sending him and having the sender's own authority. Although not numbered with *the* apostles, other believers in the early church were considered apostles—God's envoys, set apart for special ministry. These early apostles were itinerants, who founded and taught new churches much like modern missionaries.

There is no indication in the NT that the office of apostle was an institutional one or a role to be filled in the local congregation. There is no indication that other envoys, sent by churches to their mission fields, had an authority similar to that of the Twelve or of Paul.

APPALLED

The English word "appalled" appears about twenty times in the NIV and the NASB. Each time it translates the Hebrew word *šāmēm*, which is used ninety-five times in the Hebrew OT. The Hebrew word usually applies to places or things; it describes total devastation resulting from some great disaster that is often associated with divine judgment. When the word is used of persons, it describes their emotional reaction to the shattered wáste around them. They are appalled, stunned by the horror of it all.

APPEAL

In the OT, appeal is generally used in the sense of making a request. It translates a variety of Hebrew phrases, such as "to cry to" or "to seek."

In the NT, "appeal" is used in several senses. Acts tells us that Paul appealed to Caesar (Ac 25:11,12,21,25; 26:32; 28:19). This involved Paul's invoking his right as a Roman citizen to be tried before Caesar's court in Rome rather than by an inferior court—a right called *provacatio*. The Greek word that Luke chose is *epikaleomai*. It means to "call out to" or "appeal to." It was not normally used in the NT world in the technical sense of a legal appeal, and only in the above-mentioned verses is it translated "appeal" in the NT.

In most of the passages where "appeal" is found in the NIV and the NASB, it is used to translate the verb *parakaleō* (1 Co 1:10; 2 Co 5:20; 10:1; 13:11; Phm 9,10; 1 Pe 5:1) or the noun *paraklēsis* (2 Co 8:17; 1 Th 2:3). This word group is used extensively in the NT. Besides signifying appeal, it is used to express comfort and exhortation. Typically Paul's appeals are made to believers and are based on his readers' experience of his own and of Christ's love. Typically too the appeals focus on a call to a distinctively Christian life.

The NIV renders two other Greek words by forms of "appeal." In Ro 11:2, Paul speaks of Elijah's historic "appeal to God against Israel." The word here is *entynchanō*. It means to approach, to meet with a person, or to intercede for or against someone. When Peter speaks of false teachers "appealing to the lustful desires of sinful human nature" (2 Pe

2:18), he uses the word *deleazō*, which means "to allure."

How striking, then, that God's appeals through the apostle are significantly different. Paul's words reflect the difference. "By the meekness and gentleness of Christ, I appeal to you . . ." (2 Co 10:1). "Although in Christ I could be bold and order you to do what you ought to do, yet I appeal to you on the basis of love" (Phm 8–9). God appeals to people in a variety of ways, especially by addressing the highest capacities enjoyed by redeemed human beings. God's appeals never coerce but always invite people to experience what is best for them, for other people, and for God's kingdom.

APPEAR/APPEARANCE

We human beings are limited in our view of the universe in which we live. We meet the world through our senses. Sight, smell, hearing, taste, and touch are the avenues that provide us with information, but they do not always enable us to grasp the reality of what we experience. Words about appearance relate to such sensory perceptions. The passages in which they are found help us to examine a number of things about God's relationship to this world in which we live. ♦ *Appearance of Jesus: the Second Coming*

OT 1. The Hebrew words
    2. God's appearances to people
    3. People's appearances before God
    4. Description of prophetic visions
    5. Appearances versus reality
    6. Appearing, as fulfillment of prophecy
NT 7. The Greek words
    8. Appearances versus reality
    9. Jesus' incarnation as an appearance
    10. Appearing, as fulfillment of prophecy
    11. Jesus' second coming as an appearance

OT — 1. The Hebrew words. The Hebrew words usually translated by a word in the "appear" group are *rā'âh* ("to see, look at, inspect") and its derivatives *r°'î* ("looking, appearance") and *mar'eh* ("sight, appearance"). The verb literally means "seeing with the eyes," but it has multiple extended and metaphorical uses. These include special religious uses, such as "seeing" God's Word (a metaphor for believing acceptance) and "seeing" as the act of a prophet who receives revelations from God (a seer).

In relation to general perception, the word also has many meanings. In various Hebrew stems the verb can mean to perceive; to feel; to understand; to learn; to be seen; to reveal oneself; to cause someone else to see, feel, know, or enjoy; to be shown; and even to look at (one another). Which of these extended senses is intended in a particular passage is usually made clear by the stem used and by the context, but the fact that "appear" is linked to the broadest possible range of human perceptions is important background as we look at different contexts in the Bible in which "appear" occurs. Another word, *'ayin*, is less frequently translated by the appear group. It means to "see with the eyes" and thus is synonymous with *rā'âh* in its relationship to perception.

2. God's appearances to people. A number of times the OT speaks of the fact that God has appeared to human beings. He appeared to the patriarchs (Ge 12:7; 17:1; 18:1; 26:2,24; 35:1,9; 48:3; Ex 6:3), to Moses in Eygpt (Ex 4:1), a number of times during the Exodus (Ex 3:2,16; 4:5; Lev 9:4,6,23; Nu 14:10; 16:19), and less frequently afterward (Jdg 6:12; 13:3,10; 1 Sa 3:21; 2 Ch 1:7; 3:1; 7:12). These passages do not always tell us how God appeared, and they do not suggest that God was seen in his essential being. Moses heard a voice speaking from a burning bush. All the people of Israel saw the glory of God as blazing brightness over the tabernacle (Nu 14:10). God appeared as the angel of the Lord both to Gideon and to the wife of Manoah (Jdg 6:12; 13:3). ♦ *Angels* The significant thing about such passages is that in some way God acted so that he could be perceived and experienced by human beings, who are limited to sensory capacities that function only in the physical universe. God acted to make himself known, and in the encounter God also communicated information about himself.

3. People's appearances before God. The OT often refers to such. For instance, during the three annual festivals all the men of Israel were required to appear before the Lord (Ex 23:17; 34:23–24). When Korah and his followers violated God's commands, Moses told them to "appear before the LORD" on the following day (Nu 16:16). Moses referred to all the people appearing before the Lord during the Feast of Tabernacles (Dt 31:11). In each case the phrase is related to the worship center at which God promised to be uniquely present (cf. Dt 12:7). When God's OT people wished to worship or to appeal to God, it was to the tabernacle and, later, to the temple that they came. Coming to these structures for some specific religious purpose is always implied in the OT when people "appear[ed] before God." ♦ *Tabernacle and Temple*

4. Description in prophetic visions. We often feel that OT prophets, as well as John in Revelation, struggled as they attempted to communicate what they saw in their prophetic visions. Ezekiel saw an immense cloud surrounded by brilliant light, and "what looked like four living creatures" (Eze 1:5). He attempted to describe them, saying, "The appearance of the living creatures was like burning coals of fire or like torches" (1:13). Joel describes what may be a locust army or a demonic horde and says, "They have the appearance of horses; they gallop along like cavalry" (2:4). The point in these and similar prophetic visions is that what the prophets actually saw was often difficult for them to describe. In seeking to communicate some image of the vision, the prophets had to find words that could form a link between what they saw and what their readers may have experienced and thus could relate to. We need to be careful in interpreting such prophetic descriptions. They are approximations; they are as accurate as the prophet could be in framing his report in images that would enable readers to catch some glimpse of the reality of what he experienced.

5. Appearances versus reality. In gathering data, we humans are limited to our senses. And what we sense in this limited way is further open to misinterpretation. Jacob expresses this concern to his mother as the two plot to deceive the now-blind Isaac. Jacob feared that his masquerade might be discovered and he "would appear to be tricking him" (Ge 27:12). In this case the conclusion would be justified: the two actually were tricking Isaac. When Samuel was sent by God to anoint the next king of Israel (1 Sa 16), he was impressed by the physique of Eliab, and he thought, "Surely the Lord's appointed stands here" (v. 6). But God corrected Samuel. He told him, "Do not consider his appearance or his height." God explained that "the Lord does not look at the things man looks at. Man looks at the outward appearance, but the Lord looks at the heart" (v. 7). Appearances may be deceiving. Only God, who sees beyond them, is able to consistently know reality.

This is a vital reason why revelation is essential to faith. What we experience in this world is open to misinterpretation. Even God's mighty acts in history would be open to misunderstanding if their true meaning were left to those who saw and experienced them. But God does not leave us confused or uncertain. In his Word, God through the prophets and apostles explains and interprets what his people experienced. God has spoken in the Scriptures to communicate in words the shape of a reality our senses can never grasp. ♦ *Revelation*

6. Appearing, as fulfillment of prophecy. The OT looks back to God's appearances in history to find the anchor for faith. But the OT also looks forward. The prophets spoke of what was to happen in the future, and "appear" words often occur in prophetic contexts. The point is that what has been foretold actually will be visible to human beings (at least some of them) when it happens in our world of time and space. Thus Daniel describes world empires that would arise (Da 7:23; 11:2–4).

But the prophets also speak of God's once again becoming plainly visible through his own unmistakable acts. God will appear as his glory is seen in a restored and righteous Israel (Isa 60). Likewise, he will appear in the judgments preceding and during the restoration (Hos 6; Zec 9; Mal 3:1–4). Just how complete the appearance of God to people has been and will be is unveiled in the NT.

NT — 7. The Greek words. Although the range of Greek words translated "appear" in modern versions seems wide, the words retain the traditional emphasis of the OT. All are linked with sight and the notion of becoming visible in an optical or spiritual sense. What is in view in the NT as in the OT is human perception of events in the real world. Thus angels appear to people (Mt 1:20; Ac 11:13) and individuals appear before a tribunal for an audience (Ac 5:27; 19:30).

Among the words commonly translated by forms of "appear" is *phainō*. The word means "to shine or gleam," "to manifest," and thus "to show." It is commonly used in the general sense of being visible. Typical uses of *phainō* are found in Mt 1:20; 13:26; Mk 16:9; Jas 4:14.

Phaneroō is extremely common in the NT and in early Christian writings. It, too, basically means "to make visible," as of Jesus in 1 Ti 3:16 ("He appeared [was made visible] in a body"). John explains that in Jesus' incarnation, "the life appeared," and he goes on to say that "we have seen it and testify to it" (1 Jn 1:2). *Phaneroō* is often used of God's revelation of himself in Jesus.

Epiphainō and *epiphaneia* reflect the root *phainō* and also mean "to show oneself" or "to appear." *Epiphaneia*, however, has a distinct and special theological use in the NT. It is used only to refer to the future appearance of Jesus in his second coming. ◆ *Appearance of Jesus: the Second Coming*

Emphanizō, yet another variation on the *phainō* root, is used a few times in the sense of "to show oneself" or "to appear."

The Greek word *optomai* is also translated a number of times by "appear" words (Mt 17:3; Mk 9:4; Lk 1:11; 9:31; 22:43; 24:34; Ac 7:2,30,35; 9:17; 26:16; 1 Co 15:5,6–8; Heb 9:28; Rev 12:1). Although it is from a different root, the word has a similar meaning: to appear to someone. Several times *optomai* is used to describe Jesus' showing of himself to believers after the Resurrection.

In a few cases *egeirō*, which means "to raise up, rouse," is used in the sense of appear (Mt 24:11,24; Mk 13:22; Lk 7:16). In each case the phrase is used of the coming of a prophet.

8. Appearances versus reality. In several places, the NT deals with the problem of appearances versus reality. Jesus called the rigidly religious Pharisees and teachers of the Mosaic Law who criticized him hypocrites: "You are like whitewashed tombs, which look beautiful on the outside but on the inside are full of dead men's bones and everything unclean. In the same way, on the outside you appear to people as righteous but on the inside you are full of hypocrisy and wickedness" (Mt 23:27–28). The contrast between what things seem outwardly to be and what they are within is picked up in the Epistles. "God does not judge by external appearance," Paul writes in Gal 2:6. The Greek phrase is literally "by the face [*prosōpon*] of man." This word is used in similar phrases in 2 Co 10:1,7 and also in Lk 12:56, which speaks of the religious leaders being able to interpret "the appearance [face] of the earth and the sky" but not being able to interpret the meaning of Jesus' appearance in Israel (cf. Mt 16:3). In each case, what is visible to the eye is emphasized, along with the fact that some observers are unable to interpret correctly what they see.

Scripture warns us that Christians too are susceptible to mistaking appearances for reality. In Colosse the young church was attracted to a teaching that called for an ascetic approach to life. To be spiritual, the Colossians were told by the false teachers, one must be rigorous in choosing what he eats and drinks, must cut himself off from all pleasures, and must keep a strict religious calendar. Paul attacks this ascetic perversion of spirituality based on human commands and teachings and not on God's Word: "Such regulations indeed have an appearance of wisdom" (lit., "passes for wisdom"), but they "lack any value in restraining sensual indulgence" (Col 2:23). These merely human notions of how one grows in his or her relationship with God actually feed the sinful aspects of our personality and have no value for true spiritual growth. ◆ *Soul and Spirit*

How do we avoid the traps set by appearances? Paul's comment to the Colossians is the key. We are to avoid notions "based on human commands and teaching" (Col 2:22). We are to turn instead to the reliable Word of God and let God's inspired writings open our eyes to a reality that lies beyond what we can see or even imagine.

9. Jesus' incarnation as an appearance. There are two senses in which the NT speaks of Jesus' incarnation as an appearance. The first is reflected in Tit 2:11 ("The grace of God that brings salvation has appeared to all men") and 3:4 ("The kindness and love of God our Savior appeared").

These passages look at the Incarnation as an event with timeless impact. When the Son of God became a man, he made visible in a fresh, totally compelling way the grace, kindness, and love of God of which all the Scriptures testify. As Paul writes in 2 Ti 1:9–10, "Grace was given us in Christ Jesus before the beginning of time, but it has now been revealed through the appearing of our Savior, Christ Jesus, who has destroyed death and has brought life and immortality to light through the gospel."

The second sense in which Jesus' incarnation is spoken of as an appearance is found in Php 2:8 (Jesus being "found in appearance as a man") and 1 Ti 3:16 ("He appeared in a body"). Some have wrongly argued that these passages deny the true humanity of Jesus, saying that they imply that Jesus only "seemed" to be a man. The familiar *epiphaneō* is used in 1 Ti 3:16; a different word, however, in Php 2:8 (*schēma*, rendered "appearance") lays stress on outward appearance. Both passages emphasize the fact that the eternal Son of God became visible to humanity in human form, appearing to us as one of us. The rest of Scripture makes it clear that his appearance was in full harmony with reality. In the Incarnation, Jesus truly is both totally God and fully human.

9. Appearing, as fulfillment of prophecy. At times the NT uses the word "appearing" as does the OT to predict future events (Mt 24:11; Mk 13:22; Col 3:4; Rev 12:1–2).

10. Jesus' second coming as an appearance. The NT looks forward to the visible reappearance of Jesus on planet Earth. As noted above, the word *epiphaneia* is used in the NT exclusively in a theological sense—to stress one aspect of Jesus' coming. ◆ *Appearance of Jesus: the Second Coming*

APPEARANCE OF JESUS: THE SECOND COMING

The news that Jesus had to go away stunned the disciples. But Jesus immediately reassured them, "Do not let your hearts be troubled. Trust in God; trust also in me. In my Father's house are many rooms; if it were not so, I would have told you. I am going there to prepare a place for you. And if I go and prepare a place for you, I will come back and take you to be with me that you also may be where I am" (Jn 14:1–3).

These words of promise have brought comfort to generations of believers since the first century. Jesus lives. He is preparing a place for us. And when the time is right, he will return for those who trust him.

The promise of Jesus' return is found in the early church's proclamation of the gospel (e.g., Ac 3:19-21), and the Epistles

are aglow with excitement at the prospect of his appearing.

1. **Coming to be present with us**
2. **Coming to intervene in history**
3. **Coming to unveil reality**
4. **Summary**

1. Coming to be present with us. One of the Greek words associated with Jesus' second coming is *parousia*. The word means "presence" or "coming" and emphasizes both the idea of "being there" and the idea of "having come."

Paul uses the word in its everyday sense when he observes that some of the Corinthians say of him, "His letters are weighty and forceful, but in person [*parousia tou somatos*–"his bodily presence"] he is unimpressive" (2 Co 10:10). *Parousia* is sometimes used in a technical sense as the term for an official visit or the arrival of a person of high rank. But even then the word does not normally emphasize the person's arrival but the fact of that person's physical presence with those to whom he or she has come (1 Co 16:17; 2 Co 7:6,7; Php 2:12).

When *parousia* is used to describe the return of Jesus, our thoughts are directed to the fact that he will return in person and that his being with us will have a transforming impact on our lives.

Parousia is found four times in the Olivet Discourse (Mt 24:3,27,37,39). The context makes it clear that Jesus' initial appearing is intended, for the disciples asked how they would recognize the sign of his coming. Jesus explains that he will appear suddenly (v. 27), unexpectedly (v. 37), and with devastating impact on those who do not believe (v. 39). Yet the emphasis in the total passage (Mt 24–25) is not on the meaning of the second coming but on the fact that, until Jesus does come, we are to watch, committing ourselves to serve our absent Lord (cf. the four illustrations in Mt 24:42–25:46).

The NT's basic passage on resurrection is 1 Co 15. "When he comes" (15:23), his appearance in person will initiate our own resurrection and mark the beginning of history's end. Jesus, our resurrected Lord, being here, he "must reign" and must destroy every competing authority. No enemy can stand in the overpowering presence of the glorified Son of God.

First Thessalonians three times refers to Jesus' coming as a *parousia*. Paul speaks of the joy he will know when he sees his dear converts standing in Jesus' presence when Jesus is again present with us (1:19). He asks God to strengthen the converts so they will be blameless and holy at that time (3:13). But it is in 4:13–18 that Paul unveils more of the exciting meaning for us of Jesus' return. Paul describes the resurrection of the believing dead and the transformation of those who are still alive when the trumpet of God announces the return of Jesus. Caught up and transformed to meet the Lord in the air, "we will be with the Lord forever" to experience the joy of his presence.

Second Thessalonians corrects misunderstandings of the Thessalonian church, which was confused by the teaching of some that Jesus had already come (2:1–2). Paul explains that Jesus will not appear in person until the Antichrist (called the "lawless one" here) has been clearly identified by his actions (2:3–12).
‣ *Antichrist* Then Jesus will return and "by the splendor of his coming" (the splendor of Jesus personally being here) will destroy this satanically energized enemy.

James views Jesus' return in a different perspective. He observes the injustice and oppression experienced by God's people and calls for patience. When Jesus is personally present (5:7–8), the oppressed will experience a rich harvest of reward.

Peter speaks of the *parousia* three times in his epistles. He recalls his experience on the Mount of Transfiguration (Mt 17; Mk 9; Lk 9), where he witnessed Jesus shining in the unveiled glory that will be seen at his coming (1 Pe 1:6). Peter exposes the foolishness of those who hold that the physical universe and its laws are all there is to reality and of those who deride the promise of a personal appearance by Jesus (2 Pe 3:4). For unbelievers, Jesus' promised presence holds out no hope, for they can expect only the certainty of cataclysmic judgment (2 Pe 3:5–7). For us who believe, however, the prospect of Jesus' return glows with hope. We are moved to live close to him, "so that when he appears we may be confident and unashamed before him at his coming" (1 Jn 2:28; cf. 2 Pe 3:11–13).

Parousia, then, (1) emphasizes the fact that when Jesus appears again, he will come in person to be with us, and (2) it focuses our attention on the impact that Jesus' return will have on believers. We will be transformed at his coming, to share the glory of his resurrection and to participate in the joy that comes when the world is at last set right.

2. Coming to intervene in history. The word *epiphaneia* means quite simply "appearing," or "appearance." As a religious term, it indicates a visible manifestation of a hidden deity, either in person or by some great act through which his presence is revealed. Jesus will come in a starburst of power, burning his image on the retinas of faithless, blinded humanity. The kindness and love of God have already appeared (Tit 2:11; 3:4), but our "blessed hope" is focused on the day when Jesus himself will appear in glory to all (Tit 2:13).

Titus makes the point that our experience of saving grace has taught us to reject ungodliness and worldly passions, for we have been redeemed from wickedness that we might be purified as God's own people (2:11–14). Having recognized the glory of God in Jesus' first coming, we have also seen the warped and twisted shape of a sin-filled world. But to those without faith, only the personal intervention of Jesus at his return will expose the corruption.

In 2 Th 2:8, Paul combines *epiphaneia* and *parousia* in a most instructive way. He writes of the Antichrist, whom Jesus will overthrow and destroy "by the splendor [*epiphaneia*—flaming, visible manifestation of power] of his coming [*parousia*—personal presence]." The presence of Jesus, which means comfort and joy to us, means the overthrow of the evil personage who typifies the sinful world system. ‣ *World*

In 2 Timothy, Paul again contrasts the glory visible to the eyes of faith and the glory that will be unmistakable at Christ's coming. The eyes of faith recognize the birth of life and immortality in Jesus' first coming (1:10). When Jesus and his kingdom appear at last, in unmistakable power, all will be subject to judgment (4:1). There will be a crown for those who have seen beyond this world's illusions and who long for Jesus' appearing as something that will shatter the empty hopes of humanity and evaporate the empty values by which this world operates.

Epiphaneia, then, emphasizes the fact that Jesus' return will constitute a disrupting intervention in a world that remains blind to God's grace. Shattered by his appearance, the world system of today will be replaced by the long-awaited kingdom of righteousness, and evil will be judged. For the believer, *epiphaneia* contains a challenge. We are to look at the ways of the world in which we live and to utter a decisive no! to human society's values. We are to commit ourselves simply to doing good while we long for Jesus to return to intervene and at last restore the tangled world to its intended beauty.

3. Coming to unveil reality. The last word linked closely with Jesus' appearance at his second coming is *apokalypsis*. It means "to disclose, or bring to light." In the Bible, *apokalypsis* is used particularly to mean the disclosure of supernatural secrets—the unveiling of truths that people (unaided) could not have discovered but that the Holy Spirit shared with us through Scripture (1 Co 2:10). ◗
Revelation Associated with Jesus' second coming, *apokalypsis* highlights the fact that while information about Jesus has been shared with humanity and recorded in the Bible, it is Jesus himself who will be disclosed when he comes again. Then all preceding revelation about him will be unmistakably confirmed. The coming of Jesus as God's final, culminating disclosure will vindicate every promise and affirmation of the Word of God.

Lk 17:22–35 describes the shock of that day when Jesus is suddenly revealed, visible to all mankind in his second coming. As at the devastation of Sodom, humanity will again be caught unaware, engrossed in daily affairs. Again in 2 Thessalonians, the disclosure of Jesus to all mankind is associated with judgment (1:7). Jesus will be seen then in blazing fire, accompanied by his powerful angels, punishing with "everlasting destruction" those who have refused to respond to the gospel. Ro 8:19 makes it clear that we too will one day be disclosed as children of God. Thus we will share in Jesus' glory (1 Pe 5:1), while he will be "glorified in his holy people" and "marveled at among all those who have believed" (2 Th 1:10).

Written against the background of the sufferings we experience in the present world, 1 Peter also stresses the fact that Jesus' return will display to all people the glory of a personal relationship with the Lord. The trial of our faith will result "in praise, glory and honor when Jesus Christ is revealed" (1:7). Today we may know "an inexpressible and glorious joy" (1:8). Then all that we experience subjectively will have its objective manifestation. Knowing this, we rest the full weight of our hope on the return of Jesus and long for "the grace to be given [us] when Jesus Christ is revealed" (1:13). If we participate today in Jesus' sufferings, we will "be overjoyed when his glory is revealed" (4:13).

Apokalypsis, then, emphasizes the following facts: (1) Jesus' return will be witnessed by all, his glory at last unmistakable. (2) For the unsaved, this unveiling of Jesus initiates the day of vengeance; for believers, Jesus' unveiling means that the moment of fulfilled hope has come. (3) For God, Jesus' final disclosure as Lord means full vindication of his gospel and his warnings to humanity. Jesus will come. Every eye will see him. Every knee will bow before him. And every tongue will confess that Jesus Christ is Lord, to the glory of God the Father (Php 2:10–11).

4. Summary. The second coming of Jesus is a rich and complex NT theme.

Like Jesus' first coming, it does not take place as a single act but stretches over a span of time as God's many purposes are worked out at time's end. But NT words associated with Jesus' reappearance help us to see what that return means for us and for others.

The most wonderful truth for believers is that Jesus will come in person for them. In the resurrection, we will be transformed, enabled at last to share fully in joyful fellowship with God forever.

For unbelievers, Jesus' appearing will constitute a jarring intervention. All mankind's values and hopes, settled as they are on the narrow confines of this life, will be exposed as empty and meaningless. The glory of our personally present Lord will dispel the illusions that captivate humanity, and mankind will come face to face with reality at last. By yearning for this intervention, believers can escape the passions that move the lost, and they can learn to say no to evil and yes to good.

Finally, the return of Jesus is God's final and ultimate self-disclosure. All that God has shown us in the words of Scripture will be experienced then by all mankind. Both the delayed judgments and the delayed rewards will be given out, and God will become all in all.

As we meditate on Jesus' appearance, we find our own lives enriched. Our present sufferings seem increasingly unimportant in view of the glory to come. We toss aside the playthings of the world, with childhood's toys, and we build our lives on those solid realities that, when Jesus comes, will remain.

APPETITE

No single word in either Hebrew or Greek is the basis for the word "appetite" in modern English versions. A number of picturesque expressions underlie the OT use of this word: e.g., a dried-up soul (Nu 11:6), a mouth that craves (Pr 16:26), a mouth open too wide to measure (Isa 5:14). The OT speaks of an appetite that "is never satisfied" (Ecc 6:7) and also one that "will be satisfied" (Jer 50:19). In the NT, Paul speaks contemptuously of people who do not serve Jesus but rather their own belly (Ro 16:18; cf. Php 3:19). Physical hunger can move us, but feeding our bodies can never truly satisfy the deeper needs every human being feels.

APPOINT/APPOINTED

Appointing implies an official act of recognizing a person or thing for a particular purpose. This meaning is reflected in both OT and NT usage. About two dozen different Hebrew or Greek words are used to express the concept. It is difficult to determine if the words are used synonymously or if there may be shades of difference in meaning implied in various passages.

In the OT, appointments were made by God or by human beings. God appointed the annual feasts his people were to keep (Lev 23:4,37; 2 Ch 2:4) at the times he appointed (Lev 23:4; Nu 9:2,7). God also appointed prophets (Jer 1:5) and other leaders, while kings appointed their own military staff (2 Ch 32:6). Authority carried with it the right of appointment. The OT also makes it clear that God has appointed a time when his purpose for the universe will be realized: history will end as he has planned (Da 8:19; 11:27,29,35; Zep 2:2).

In the NT, we continue to see God active in appointing. God appointed Jesus as the Messiah (Ac 3:20), as humanity's judge (Ac 17:31), as head over everything for the church (Eph 1:22), and as heir to all things (Heb 1:2). Jesus appointed the Twelve (Mk 3:14), and believers are "appointed for eternal life" (Ac 13:48; cf. 1 Th 5:9). ◆ *Predestine* God appointed Paul as a herald of the gospel (2 Ti 1:11–12).

In the NT, believers also appoint. It may be significant that church members suggested the individuals (Ac 6:3) who then were officially appointed by the apostles as the first deacons (v. 6). Also worthy of note is the fact that the Greek word used of Paul's appointing elders on his second missionary journey (Ac 14:23) is *cheirotoneō*; this verb originally meant to elect by a show of hands. Another verb, *kathistēmi* ("authorize, put in charge"), is used in a parallel passage (Tit 1:5). ◆ **Elders**

APPROACH

The word "approach" usually describes a commonplace event. A man looked up and saw camels approaching (Ge 24:63). Jesus approached a boat pulled up on the shore (Jn 6:19). But in some specialized uses, this word is anything but commonplace—particularly in what we are taught about approaching God.

OT 1. The Hebrew words and their uses
2. The OT on approaching God
NT 3. The NT on approaching God

OT — 1. The Hebrew words and their uses. The two Hebrew words most often translated "approach" are *qārab* and *nāgaš*. *Qārab* is found some 289 times in the OT and is translated "come near," "approach," "enter," etc. Its basic idea is a coming into intimate contact with. *Qārab* can be used in reference to time, two armies joining battle, or sexual relationships (Lev 18:6,14,19). *Nāgaš* also means to come into close proximity—close enough to touch, or eat, or kill. This word too is used euphemistically of sexual intercourse. Among the most significant technical uses of these two words are their use in the worship system that God established for his OT people. It is here that we learn much of the wonderful privilege we enjoy in Christ.

2. The OT on approaching God. The OT makes it plain that approach to God (seeking intimate contact with him) is a distinct privilege, a privilege not lightly granted. God called to Moses from the burning bush, but when Moses came over to see the phenomenon, God stopped him and said, "Do not come any closer [*qārab*, "approach"]" (Ex 3:5). Moses was told instead to remove his shoes, for he stood on holy ground. ◆ **Holy/Holiness** When God thundered from Sinai, the people were warned not to approach the mountain in an attempt to see God, lest they be struck down (Ex 19:16–25). When the tabernacle was constructed to serve as the place for Israel to corporately worship God, only the priests were allowed to enter the tabernacle or serve at its altar (Nu 18:1–7), and even they had to approach with extreme care and follow exactly the ritual established by God. Two sons of Aaron who "offered unauthorized fire before the Lord, contrary to his command," were destroyed in flames that "came out from the presence of the Lord and consumed them" (Lev 10:1–3). Even the high priest was warned that he must rigorously follow the established pattern when entering the Most Holy Place, and then just once a year, or he too would be struck down by the Lord (Lev 16).

All of these experiences and warnings to early Israel were intended to underline the fact that approaching a holy God is never to be lightly undertaken. Looking back, the NT explains that the rigid walls of ritual, like the inner curtain of the tabernacle and temple, were erected because the way into the holiest—into God's very presence—had not yet been manifested (Heb 9:8). Human beings could approach the Lord only with fear, bearing offerings that reminded them of their sin and that God was willing to forgive.

It is clear from the OT that the ritual observances were never enough to ensure a welcome from God. So the prophets spoke, condemning an unwelcome generation that drew near to God with words but whose hearts were far from him (Isa 29:13; Jer 12:2). But even with a pure heart, ritual was required.

NT — 3. The NT on approaching God. It is striking to move into the NT and read: "In him [Jesus] and through faith in him we may approach God with freedom and confidence" (Eph 3:12); "Let us then approach the throne of grace with confidence" (Heb 4:16); and "This is the confidence we have in approaching God: that if we ask anything according to his will, he hears us" (1 Jn 5:14).

The OT's wall of ritual is gone, even as the curtain that separated the Holy Place from the Most Holy Place in the Jerusalem temple was supernaturally torn from top to bottom when Jesus died (Mt 27:51). That tearing signified that, on the basis of Christ's death, the way of approach to God is open to all. Jesus' death dealt finally and decisively with the sins that separated us from God. Now, as forgiven persons, we can approach God freely and without hesitation.

This freedom that we have in Christ is emphasized in each of the three theologically significant "approach" passages in the NT (Eph 3; Heb 4; 1 Jn 5). In each, our approach to God is described by the Greek word *parrēsia*. The word signifies outspokenness or plainness in speech, openness to others, and confidence and boldness when in the presence of those of higher rank.

We now come into the very presence of God with joyous confidence (Heb 10:19), sure that Jesus has opened a new and living way for us to draw near to God (Heb 10:19–22).

APPROVE/APPROVAL

How do we win the approval of God? This is the focal issue in the NT's use of the word group that the translators render "approve" in modern versions. While OT uses involve the paraphrase of a number of expressions, NT use is particularly significant and draws on a distinctive Greek word group.

1. The Greek words
2. The approval of people
3. The approval of God

1. The Greek words. The occurrences of "approve/approval" in modern versions almost always signal the appearance in the original of a distinctive Greek word group. *Dokimos*, the noun, is used in the NT in the sense of recognition, of being officially approved and accepted. It is found in Ro 14:18; 16:10; 1 Co 11:19; 2 Co 10:18; 13:7; 2 Ti 2:15; Jas 1:12. *Dokimazō*, the verb, implies putting to the test with a view to approving the genuine. That which has been tested is demon-

strated to be genuine and trustworthy. This verb is used twenty-three times in the NT. Three times (Lk 11:48; Ac 8:1; 22:20) Luke uses a compound word that expresses complete approval: *syneudokeō*. This word is used in only three other places in the NT (Ro 1:32; 1 Co 7:12–13). In 1 Co 7:12–13, Paul says that if an unsaved spouse is "willing" to live with the partner who has become a believer, no divorce should be initiated. Only in Jn 6:27 is the idea of approval not a rendering of some word in the *dokimos* word group. There the Greek word is *sphragizō*, "seal," correctly interpreted by the NIV as "has placed his seal of approval."

What seems important in the notion of approval is its linkage with testing. Approval is not lightly given; it is won. Our character and our commitments emerge over time. It is only on evidence provided by experience and the passage of time that approval can be extended. ◗ *Temptation/Test/Trial*

2. The approval of people. Time and experience provide the evidence on which one can be approved. But the criterion by which a person is evaluated is also important. The NT warns against trying to "win the approval of men," even when these persons are fellow believers (Gal 1:10). There are a number of reasons for this warning. Christ alone is our Master; it is he whom we are to serve (Gal 1:10). It is dangerous for us to even try to evaluate ourselves. Only God's evaluation and commendation counts (2 Co 10:18; cf. 1 Co 4:3–5). As for the standards of unbelievers, Paul's preconversion approval of the stoning of Stephen shows how questionable their standards were (Ac 8:1; 22:20)! Clearly the warped consciences of the unsaved will often lead them to overlook serious sin or even to approve of those who today may be called "beautiful people," whose lifestyles deny righteousness (Ro 1:32).

3. The approval of God. Since the approval of God is so vital for us, what does the Bible say about winning it? Several NT passages link God's approval to a subjective attitude and an objective standard.

The subjective attitude is one of commitment to serve Christ (Ro 12:2; 14:18). The objective standard is the Word of God. In Romans, Paul writes of Jewish reliance on the law and of the fact that through the Scriptures the Hebrew people knew God's will. They even approved of it as superior. But, in fact, the Jewish people failed to do what they knew to be the will of God (Ro 2:17–29).

Paul warns Timothy against chattering on in theological dispute while drifting into ungodly behavior. An approved workman "correctly handles the word of truth" and demonstrates God's approval by turning away from wickedness (2 Ti 2:14–19). Romans 12:1–2 sums it up: we are to commit ourselves to be living sacrifices, dedicated to pleasing God. We must no longer conform to this world's patterns; our whole perspective on life is to be reshaped by God. Then we "will be able to test and approve what God's will is." Paul's point is a vital one. The Word of God—through which we come to know God's will—must itself be put to the test by us. We put Scripture to the test by acting on what it says. When we do this, we experience God's good, pleasing, and perfect will. When we do God's will, he will be able to approve of us as good workers who have no need to be ashamed.

Ro 14:22 is discussed in another article.
▶ Conscience.

ARGUE/ARGUMENTS

Both testaments express the idea of argument in a variety of ways. Perhaps the single most significant teaching is found in the NT: argument does not provide an effective way to uncover truth—or to build a believing community.

OT 1. Descriptive uses
NT 2. Argument and truth
   3. Argument and fellowship
   4. Summary

OT — 1. Descriptive uses. The Hebrew root yākâh, which means "to plead,

reason, dispute, or rebuke," and thus "to argue," is found in some places where modern versions read "argue." But often in the NIV and NASB, "argue" is an interpretation of a longer phrase, such as "Let not your voice be heard among us" (Jdg 18:25). While the context will suggest either a positive or a negative connotation, the OT basically used "argument" in a descriptive way. The conflict arose and is reported. But the OT says little about the nature of argument itself.

NT — 2. Argument and truth. The NT uses a fascinating array of Greek words to explore dimensions of the interaction that we call arguing. It is important that we examine the Greek word translated "argue" to discern just what is meant.

Dialogizomai (verb) means "to hold a discussion" or "to reason." This word (or its related noun, *dialogismos*) is rendered "argue" or "argument" only three times in the NIV (Mk 9:33; Lk 9:46; Php 2:14). In the NT this process of arguing is always looked on with distrust and with some distaste. *Dialogizomai* is found sixteen times in the NT (Mt 16:7,8; 21:25; Mk 2:6,8; 8:16–17; 9:33; Lk 1:29; 3:15; 5:21,22; 12:17; 20:14; Jn 11:50). *Dialogismos* is found fourteen times (Mt 15:19; Mk 7:21; Lk 2:35; 5:22; 6:8; 9:46–47; 24:38; Ro 1:21; 14:1; 1 Co 3:20; Php 2:14; 1 Ti 2:8; Jas 2:4).

Another pair of words—*syzēteō* (verb) and *zētēsis* (noun)—reflects an even more negative view. This is particularly fascinating in view of the fact that the Greeks thought of argument quite positively and saw questioning and disputation as a way to discover truth. The NT looks at the process as an empty war of words, without power to enrich faith or to build a loving community.

Among its ten occurrences in the NT, *syzēteō* is found twice in Mk 9:14,16, where a heated discussion of the disciples' failure to heal a boy became an argument in which the child's needs were forgotten. In Ac 6:9, *syzēteō* expresses the antagonism and anger of those who stoned the first Christian martyr, Stephen. Besides its use in three other places (Ac 25:20; 1 Ti 1:4; 6:4), zētēsis ("argument") is found in Jn 3:25; 2 Ti 2:33; Tit 3:9, where angry verbal battles are linked with quarreling, envy, slander, and godlessness.

In Col 2:4, *pithanologia* (used only here in the NT) picks up the same theme. The arguments of people, while seeming plausible, may be false. Ultimately, only a decisive word from God clarifies all debatable issues, answers all arguments, and silences all contradiction (Heb 6:16).

3. Argument and fellowship. The contexts in which the words noted above are found suggest that it is impossible to arrive at truth by a process of inner or interpersonal questioning and argument. The contexts also suggest that argumentation brings great interpersonal danger! The danger is made completely clear in 1 Ti 6:4 and 2 Ti 2:14, the only places in the NT where *logomachia* and *logomacheō*, respectively—meaning "(to do) battle with words"—are found. Such arguments are unhealthy, Paul says, and "result in envy, strife, malicious talk, evil suspicions and constant friction between men of corrupt mind" (1 Ti 6:4).

Paul's instructions to the Corinthians, who were arguing about eating food sacrificed to idols, contains a positive alternative to argument. Paul says that we all possess knowledge, but human knowledge is limited. When we approach a difference of opinion on the basis of knowledge, we forget that (1) our knowledge is inadequate and (2) the claim we know better promotes pride.

Paul's solution does not neglect truth but calls us to approach our differences with mutual love. Paul shows us that love draws us into a relationship of openness with God and with one another. In such a relationship, each person can grow in knowledge and be built up in the faith (1 Co 8:1–3).

Arguing, even about truth, does not help us know truth better, nor does it build the close, loving community that we Christians are called to become.

4. Summary. It is not wrong to explore and to seek to understand the teachings and the meanings of our faith. But human reasoning has limits. Our most cherished interpretations may well be inadequate or fail to take every relevant factor into account. Argumentation, as a way of approaching our differences in understanding, fails to help one distinguish truth and has the unfortunate effect of driving brothers and sisters apart rather than drawing them together.

How good, then, that God has spoken and that he has spoken plainly. We may differ on details, but there is a great body of truth about Jesus that all believers hold in common. By affirming those truths and continuing to love one another, we open up our lives to God and to growth.

We can talk about our differences and learn from each other. But we dare not fall into arguments that rob others of our love.

ARK

Two arks have significant roles in Bible history. Each is from the OT era, but each is also mentioned in the NT.

1. Noah's ark
2. The ark of the covenant

1. Noah's ark. Ge 6–8 relates God's call to Noah to build the large floating craft known to us as the ark. It was some 300 cubits in length, 50 in width, and 30 in height. Depending on which of several possible lengths is ascribed to the cubit, this massive boat displaced between 19,000 and 43,000 tons! The NT reports Jesus' references to Noah and his ark. Each report assumes that the story is historical (Mt 24:38; Lk 17:27). Hebrews speaks of the holy fear that led the believing Noah to commit some 120 years to preparing the ark, while God waited patiently for him to complete it before bringing on the cataclysmic judgment of the Flood (Heb 11:7 cf. Ge 6:3; 1 Pe 3:20).

2. The ark of the covenant. This ark is spoken of 195 times in the OT. It was a wooden chest overlaid with gold, probably measuring 3¾' x 2½' x 2¼'. The ark (*'ārôn*) was very significant in the worship conducted by God's OT people, and it had several special names: the ark of God (34 times in the OT), the ark of the Lord (30 times), the ark of God the Lord (once), the ark of the (Lord's) covenant (41 times), and the ark of the testimony (14 times).

The ark was constructed according to God's instructions (Ex 25:10–20) and was intended to rest in the Holy of Holies, the innermost room of tabernacle and temple. ♦ *Tabernacle and Temple* The chest contained (1) the stone tablets on which God had written the Ten Commandments and (2) a measure of the manna with which God fed his people in the wilderness (Ex 16:33–34). With the ark also was Aaron's staff, which had budded to show God's selection of his family for the priesthood (Nu 17:10).

The cover of the ark was particularly significant. It was overlaid with gold and decorated with two golden angels whose wings overshadowed the cover. It was on this cover that once a year on the Day of Atonement the high priest sprinkled sacrificial blood. ♦ *Atonement*

It was here, at the place that in some versions is called the mercy seat (in Heb 9:5), that the holy God of Israel met his sinful people. Thus the ark was understood in Israel's religion as the very focus of God's presence. Except when being moved from place to place, the ark, like God, was hidden from Israel's view. Even its location (the tabernacle tent or the temple building) could be approached only with blood sacrifice.

Several OT incidents feature the ark and tell us much about its meaning. In Joshua 3 and 4, we read that when the feet of the priests who carried the ark touched the waters of the Jordan, the river stopped flowing. Israel was thus shown in a graphic way that although Moses was now dead, God was still with his people.

Joshua 6 gives a prominent place to the ark when the Israelites marched around the walls of Jericho. The tumbling walls demonstrated that God would fight for his people as they invaded the Promised Land.

But Israel misinterpreted history. When they were being defeated by the Philistines some hundreds of years later, they took the ark from the tabernacle and brought it to the battlefield. The ark was mistakenly thought to guarantee God's active involvement in battle; the symbol was taken for the reality. Israel lost the battle, and the ark was taken. But after this, God brought a series of plagues on the victorious Philistines. In desperation, the Philistines finally returned the ark to Israel (1 Sa 4–6). God could not be manipulated by Israel. But neither could he be disregarded by Israel's enemies.

When David was made king, he attempted to transport the ark to Jerusalem. But the laws governing transportation were violated when Uzzah, one of David's men, attempted to steady the ark with his hand. When he touched the ark, he was struck dead (2 Sa 6; 1 Ch 13). David was angry about Uzzah's death, but it showed Israel that the Lord is a holy God, who must be respected. Later, when the laws governing the transportation of the ark were followed, it was brought without incident to Jerusalem (1 Ch 15–16).

When the Jerusalem temple was constructed, the ark was placed in the Holy of Holies. It remained there until the city and the temple were destroyed by Nebuchadnezzar (586 B.C.). There is no record of the ark after this time. What happened to it remains a mystery, though it may be inferred from Rev 11:19 that it was transported to heaven.

Hebrews 9 teaches us that the ark, like other features of OT religion, was significant because it reflected spiritual realities that have become clear only through Jesus. The blood sprinkled on the earthly mercy seat pictured the blood Jesus would one day spill to win entry for us to heaven itself (Heb 9:1–14).

ARM

The Hebrew word $z^e r \hat{o} a^{\cdot}$ generally means "arm" or "shoulder." In seventy-six of its ninety-one occurrences in the OT it is used metaphorically, usually as a figure of God's power. God "made the heavens and the earth by [his] great power and outstretched arm" (Jer 32:17). Deliverance from Egypt was accomplished "with an outstretched arm and with mighty acts of judgment" (Ex 6:6).

The Armor of God (Eph 6:14–17)

belt of truth	Openness and honesty are qualities that bind believers together. We are to be truthful with each other (4:25).
breastplate of righteousness	Righteous living is essential; we must have no trace of immorality or impurity (5:3).
feet fitted with the gospel	The gospel brings peace, which is the bond of peace that maintains our unity (4:3).
shield of faith	We place confident hope in God (3:20).
helmet of salvation	Salvation brings new life and identity; we are members of Jesus' body (3:6).
the Spirit's Sword	Only this piece of armor has not already been discussed in Ephesians, so it is defined ("which is the word of God").

Compared to God's power, humanity's "arm of flesh" is impotent indeed.

The symbolism of the phrase "break the arms of" is used of enemies and suggests destroying the enemy's capacity to make war.

ARMAGEDDON

This word, so prominent in books and sermons on prophecy, is found in only one place in the Bible: Rev 16:16. It is identified there as the place where the Antichrist mobilizes his armies for humanity's final battle against God. No one knows just where this site is located, though a number of locations have been suggested in modern times.

ARMOR

Twice in the NT the weapons and protective shielding of soldiers are referred to metaphorically as equipment for spiritual warfare. In Ro 13:12, Paul urges believers to "put aside the deeds of darkness and put on the armor of light." The word here, *hoplon*, is used five other times in the NT—Jn 18:3; twice in Ro

6:13 (where it is translated "instruments"); 2 Co 6:7; 10:4. In context, it is clear that the Christian's "weapons of light" are the qualities of love and decent behavior; they expose the origin of deeds of darkness, which are rooted in the desires of the sinful nature (Ro 13:8–14).

In Eph 6:11–13, the word twice translated "armor" is *panoplia*. Its only other NT use is in Lk 11:22. This word describes the full battle and display armor of the most heavily armed infantry in the Roman army. In Ephesians, Paul links various pieces of armor to God's equipment of the believer for a firm stand against the Devil's schemes.

There has been much discussion on how we are to understand each piece of equipment. Since this passage seems to be a summary of Ephesians, placed at the end of the book, it seems best to take each word in the sense in which Paul uses it in this letter. This principle of interpretation is the basis for the above chart on the Christian's armor.

In the context of Ephesians, an epistle that focuses on the church as a living body, we can see that Satan's goal is to distort relationships within the congregation and to weaken the new community within which believers can grow.

AROMA

The repeated OT phrase "an aroma pleasing to the LORD" is an expression affirming God's acceptance of a sacrifice brought to him. The idea of a pleasing aroma is used always connected with God: he is the one who smells the aroma and determines the acceptability of the sacrifice.

This OT symbolism is carried over into the NT in the three places where the Greek word *euōdia* ("aroma," "fragrance") is found. In two of the passages, *euōdia* is linked with *osmē* ("smell," "fragrance").

Eph 5:2 speaks of Jesus' death on Calvary as a "fragrant offering and sacrifice to God."

In Php 4:18, Paul views a money contribution from the Philippians as "a fragrant offering, an acceptable sacrifice, pleasing to God."

In 2 Co 2:15, Paul views himself and his ministry as "the aroma of Christ among those who are being saved and those who are perishing." The context extends the image. Just as the OT sacrifices for sin made on OT altars sent out an aroma that could be smelled by the worshipers, so Paul's ministry and life, though offered as a living sacrifice to God (cf. Ro 12:1), wafts the unique fragrance of the knowledge of God among mankind. The odor attracts some and repels others. One's response makes the difference between life and death.

God has accepted Jesus' death at Calvary as a sufficient sacrifice for sin. Those who reject what God has accepted will linger on in the realm of death. Those who accept the gospel by faith will live.

ARROGANCE/PRIDE

Arrogance and pride describe an attitude that Scripture carefully analyzes— and condemns. Both the OT and NT add to our understanding of the nature of these self-exalting traits, which draw us away from godliness.

OT 1. The Hebrew words
    2. The nature of arrogance and pride
    3. The ultimate example: Satan's fall
NT 4. The Greek words
    5. Summary

OT — 1. The Hebrew words. Where modern versions use "arrogance" or "pride," one most often finds a word from one of three Hebrew word groups. Words from the root *zîd* (*zēd, zûd, zādôn*) are usually translated in NIV by "arrogance." These words are used thirty-four times in the OT and convey the broad idea of a self-important pride, which leads to acts of rebellion and willful disobedience.

Words from the root *gā'âh* (those being *gē, gē'eh, gē'âh, ga'awâh, gā'ôn*) are usually translated "pride" or "proud." Used of Israel or of God, such words express excellence or majesty. But these words are usually applied to persons and are used in a negative sense. This word group is used most often by Isaiah, Jeremiah, and Ezekiel and in Psalms, Proverbs, and Job. The words imply an arrogant insensitivity to others, matched with overwhelming self-confidence. This attitude leads to conduct that in turn brings destruction, for only God can rightly be the source and object of our pride.

A third word group, from *gābah*, which means "to lift up," often expresses the lofty sense of self-importance identified with pride.

While there are shades of difference in the emphases of these words, they are usually used as synonyms. Often two are linked together to underline the extent of the arrogance and pride of the individuals described.

2. The nature of arrogance and pride. We sense the basic nature of these traits in Dt 1:42. There God warned a disobedient Israel not to attack the people of Palestine, "because," he said, "I will not be with you." Moses recalls Israel's sin: "You would not listen. You rebelled against the LORD's command and in your arrogance you marched up into the hill country" (Dt 1:43). The same theme is often found in the OT: "In his arrogance the wicked man hunts down the weak. . . . In his pride the wicked does not seek him; in all his thoughts there is no room for God" (Ps 10:2,4). The root of arrogance and pride is refusal to consider God or respond to him. Instead, the arrogant supposes that human beings can live successfully apart from an obedient relationship with the Lord.

The dangers of arrogance and pride are well documented. Even the godly can be drawn away from God when success stimulates pride (e.g., 2 Ch 26:16–17). According to Proverbs, pride is an evil to be hated (8:13), leads to disgrace (11:2; 29:23), breeds quarrels (13:10), and goes before destruction (16:18).

But pride is not only dangerous; it is sin. Pride and arrogance involve a denial of our place as creatures, living in a world shaped and governed by the Creator, who has given a Word that is to govern our lives. Thus the OT makes it clear: God is committed to punish pride and arrogance. In almost identical phraseology, Isaiah twice declared: "The eyes of the arrogant man will be humbled and the pride of men brought low; the LORD alone will be exalted in that day" (Isa 2:11; cf. v. 17). The theme of judgment is often associated with this sin, which involves not only a basic denial of the significance of God but also the foolish exaltation of the individual or the human race (e.g., Da 5:20; Lev 26:19).

3. The ultimate example: Satan's fall.
Many Bible scholars believe that two OT passages describe the fall of Satan. Each passage refers to a "king," who may be the unseen spiritual power behind the pagan ruler (cf. Da 10:12–15). ♦ *Angels* In Eze 28:11–19, this king is described as a guardian cherub who was created blameless but sinned and was expelled from the presence of God. The cause? "Your heart became proud on account of your beauty, and you corrupted your wisdom because of your splendor" (28:17).

Isaiah describes a morning star fallen from heaven and points out the swelling pride that led to its downfall: "You said

in your heart, 'I will ascend to heaven; I will raise my throne above the stars of God; I will sit enthroned on the mount of assembly, on the utmost heights of the sacred mountain. I will ascend above the tops of the clouds; I will make myself like the Most High' " (Isa 14:13–14).

The pride of the creature who seeks to displace God as the center of the universe and deny the Lord the glory due him may well be the root cause of all the evil that mars the universe and, specifically, of man's original sin (Ge 3:4–5).

4. The Greek words.
A number of Greek words are translated "arrogance" or "pride" in the NIV and the NASB. *Hyperēphania* is translated "arrogance" in Mk 7:22 (its only NT occurrence), and *hyperēphanos* (appearing five times in the NT) is translated four times "pride" or "proud" (Lk 1:51; 2 Ti 3:2; Jas 4:6; 1 Pe 5:5) and once "arrogant" (Ro 1:30). This word, with *hybris*, which is not found in the NT in the classical sense of pride, was used by those who translated the OT into Greek to express the meaning of each of the Hebrew words discussed above.

Hypsēlophroneō also means "proud" or "haughty." It is used in Ro 11:20 and in 1 Ti 6:17 of those who presumptuously rest their confidence in something other than God himself.

Physioō (found only in 1 Co 4:6,18,19; 5:2; 8:1; 13:4; and Col 2:18, and *physiōsis*, only in 2 Co 12:20) directs our attention to the inner impact of pride. Pride puffs us up, making us arrogant and conceited. Believers are warned against becoming puffed up about following one leader over another or for belonging to one particular group rather than another. The Corinthian church was warned against being puffed up while sin was permitted in the fellowship. Paul goes on to teach that love never puffs up (13:4). The seriousness of being puffed up is seen by its association in Scripture with quarreling, jealousy, anger, factions, slander, and gossip (2 Co 12:20).

Authadēs, found only in Tit 1:7 and 2 Pe 2:10, means "self-willed," "stubborn," and, in that sense, "arrogant."

Not all pride is wrong. *Kauchēsis* and *kauchēma* stress, not the individual's attitude, but the object or thing in which a person takes pride. Such pride can be good or bad, depending on its object. Paul wants the believer to take pride, not in externals, but in what God is doing in men's hearts (2 Co 5:12). Paul himself takes pride in the progress of the Corinthians in the faith (2 Co 7:4; 8:24). We believers can all take pride in ourselves, without comparing ourselves with others, when we lovingly support one another (Gal 6:4). Both poor and rich believers—for very different reasons—can take pride in their new position in the faith (Jas 1:9–10).

5. Summary. Pride as a self-exalting attitude is wrong. But God wants us to take a healthy pride, and to find joy, in what he is doing in our lives. As arrogance, pride is a source of sin, for only the humility that keeps us responsive to the Lord and his Word is appropriate in our relationship with the one who is truly the living God.

ASCEND

Although seldom found in our translations, the word "ascend" is always used with great theological significance.

OT 1. Approaching God
NT 2. Jesus' ascension
   3. Understanding key passages
   4. Summary

OT — 1. Approaching God. The Hebrew word translated "ascend" is *'ālâh*. The verb form alone appears almost 900 times in the OT and is translated in English versions in some 90 different ways! The most common translations are "go up" (about 300 times) and "come up" (about 150 times). Only in a few places is *'ālâh* translated "ascend." There is, however, a common element in these few passages. In each, the "going up" is linked with an approach to God's heavenly realm (Ge 28:12; Dt 30:12; Jdg 13:20; Ps 47:5; 68:18); an approach to the temple, God's earthly residence (Ps 24:3; cf. Eze 41:7 in connection with the temple being built in ascending stages); or a

rebellious attempt by some mere creature to approach and to usurp God's authority (2 Ki 19:23; Isa 37:24; 14:13–14).

NT — 2. Jesus' ascension. The Greek word in each instance where the NT uses "ascend" is *anabainō*. The word means simply "to go up" and is often used in a nontechnical, descriptive sense (e.g., "we got ready and went up to Jerusalem," Ac 21:15). Yet *anabainō* often carries a special spiritual significance, as in Jesus' coming out of the water of the Jordan or climbing some mountain. At such times, it precedes a special expression of God's power.

The most significant uses of *anabainō* are those directly linked with the ascension of Jesus. These include Jn 3:13; 6:62; 20:17; Ac 2:34; and Eph 4:8,9,10. Each of these affirms the ascent of Jesus to heaven, which the NT teaches was his return to the realm that was his by right of his deity (Php 2:5–11; 1 Ti 3:16). The ascension was witnessed by many of Jesus' disciples (Ac 1:1–11). Jesus' ascension is universally viewed in the NT as a victorious return to glory to minister to believers as their High Priest (Heb 7:23– 8:2) and to serve as the all-powerful head over all things for the church (Eph 1:15– 22). The ascension of Jesus thus stands with his incarnation, sacrificial death, and resurrection as a foundation of biblical Christian faith.

3. Understanding key passages. Ro 10:6 argues that Dt 30:12 demonstrates that righteousness comes by faith. In Dt 30, Moses reviews for a new generation the covenant under which Israel was called to live. This new generation, survivors of the wilderness wanderings, was made up only of those "who held fast to the LORD [their] God" (Dt 4:4). To this believing and faithful community, Moses gave the assurance that they were not called to an impossible task, as though someone had to ascend into heaven to bring down God's life-giving word. Instead, Moses says, it is "very near you; it is in your mouth and in your heart so you may obey it" (30:14).

In quoting this passage in Romans, Paul's point hinges on the fact that this was a unique generation. Only this generation in all Israel's history is specifically described in Scripture as serving the Lord (Jos 24:31; Jdg 2:7). It is to this group of people that God spoke of the law as being planted in their hearts so they might obey it.

As a believing generation, this group stands in contrast with modern Israel, which sees law not as something God will plant in believers' hearts, but as a means by which the individual may go about establishing his own righteousness through rigorous self-effort. This is a tragic failure. It has always been faith that brings God's Word near and plants righteousness in our hearts.

Eph 4 quotes Ps 68:18—with a significant modification. The original psalm is a victory hymn, expressing exultation in the final triumph God will surely win for his people. Paul picks up the image of the victor ascending to his throne to receive tribute from the defeated. But he changes the psalm to suggest that "when he ascended on high, he led captives in his train and gave gifts to men" (Eph 4:7). This reverses the original, which says that the conqueror *received* gifts from men, "even from the rebellious."

Rather than take this as a lapse of memory or a NT revision of a scribal error, it is best to view Paul's quotation in another light. God's OT people shared the spoil when a victory was won—even with those who merely guarded the baggage (1 Sa 30:21–25). Just so, Jesus' triumph means that we who believe on him have a share in those victory spoils! Moreover, the great gifts God bestows on believers, who are members of Jesus' body, are grace gifts that enable the individual and the community to grow in love and maturity (Eph 4:7–16).

4. Summary. God has always been recognized by believers as significantly "above" humanity. This spiritual relationship has often been expressed in special terms. Yet, from our standpoint, the gap between heaven and earthly spheres is uncrossable.

Only God's action in Jesus, coming to us in the Incarnation and returning in the Ascension, bridges the gap for us.

It is in this light that Hebrews presents Jesus, "now crowned with glory and honor" (2:9), as the one who, through his own death and resurrection, raised "many sons to glory" (2:10).

ASCRIBE

Of the ten biblical occurrences of this word, the Hebrew in each case (except in Job 36:3, where *nātan* is used) is *yāhab*. Both words mean "to give," but *yāhab* is translated "ascribe" only when "to the LORD" is part of the expression, or in similar constructions in which the object is an attribute of God (Job 36:3).

As used in the NIV and NASB, "ascribe" is a call to the purest kind of worship: giving praise to God for who he by nature is.

ASHAMED ♦ Shame

ASLEEP ♦ Sleep

ASSEMBLY/COMMUNITY

The people of Israel were both a community and a nation—a people linked together by a common law that governed their lives, and by a covenant relationship with the Lord, a relationship that provided their shared identity. Two Hebrew words are used for the calling together of this people.

1. The assembly
2. The community
3. NT uses of "assembly" and "community"

1. The assembly. The Hebrew word *qāhâl* (*qᵉhillâh, maqhēl*) is the word most often translated "assemble" and "assembly" in the NIV and NASB. An assembly might be called for any purpose, from preparation for war (1 Sa 7:7) to settling civil affairs (2 Sa 3:21). Normally, however, the assembly was called for religious purposes. A critical distinction between this word and the word usually translated "community" is that the assembly could involve representative groups, whereas the whole people were involved in gatherings of the community.

2. The community. The Hebrew word *'ēḏâh* is usually rendered "community" in modern versions and "congregation" in the KJV. It is essentially a synonym of the *qāhâl* group. In each, the summoning to an assembly could be for any purpose. But there are differences. For instance, *'ēḏâh* is sometimes used of a herd of animals, whereas *qāhâl* is not. The primary distinction between the two synonyms is the fact that *'ēḏâh* stresses a gathering of the whole people of Israel and implies the unity of the community of Israel as the people of God.

The covenant community was called together by the blowing of silver trumpets (Nu 10:2), to crown a king (1 Ki 12:20), or to send men to war (Jdg 21:10).

3. NT uses of "assembly" and "community". In most NT passages, no special theological conclusions should be drawn from the use of one or the other of these words. Five different Greek words are used in such passages, including *plēthos,* which simply means "a crowd," and *ekklēsia,* which is usually translated "church" and is used in a technical religious sense in the NT. ♦ **Church** But as "assembly," *ekklēsia* is found only in Ac 7:38, where it refers to the whole people of Israel gathered to hear God's Word, and in Ac 19:32,41, where it is used in its pagan political sense as the assembly of the citizens of a Greek city.

While the OT words translated "assembly" and "community" do carry a special significance and introduce us to a people bound together by their shared relationship with God, we find the NT parallel, not in either of these English words, but in the word "church," into which Jesus' resurrection has poured new meaning.

ASSIGN/ASSIGNED

Various Hebrew words expressing the idea of "give" are sometimes translated "assign" in the OT. When God is the actor, "assign" carries the binding force of law or, in prophecy, conveys the certainty that what has been announced will happen (e.g., Isa 53:9).

But Ps 16:5 shifts our attention to the fact that God assigns individuals their place in life. David realized what is also taught in the NT: God, he said, has "assigned me my portion and my cup."

The NT expresses this thought with the Greek word *merizō,* which means "to divide" and, at times, "to assign." The most significant passage where the word is used is 1 Co 7:17–23, which suggests that all the circumstances of our lives are assigned by God. We are not to be troubled by our lot, for whatever our circumstances, they provide us with opportunities to serve God and others.

In the same way, even the most noted leaders of the church (2 Co 10:13) are simply servants who have been assigned their place rather than winning it. We are hardly to view them with awe.

Two other NT passages that speak of assigning are significant: Mt 24:51 and Lk 12:46. Both use the word *tithēmi,* which means "to place or put." These passages speak of individuals who are "assigned a place" with the hypocrites and unbelievers respectively. But the context makes it clear that this is not predestination to eternal judgment. In the stories Jesus told, each individual made the choices and took the actions that led to his assignment.

ASSOCIATE

How important are our associations? The OT demanded that distance be maintained between Israel and the surrounding pagan peoples. This demand was introduced to maintain religious and moral purity: "Do not associate with these nations that remain among you; do not invoke the names of their gods or swear by them. You must not serve them or bow down to them" (Jos 23:7; cf. v. 12).

The separationist attitude that developed from this proscription is reflected in both Jn 4:9 and Ac 10:28. John relates that the Samaritan woman was surprised that Jesus would ask her for a drink, "for Jews do not associate with [from *syn-*

chraomai, "to have dealings with"] Samaritans." Luke reports in the Acts passage that it required a special revelation from God to prepare Peter to go to the house of the Roman military officer Cornelius: Peter explained, "It is against [the Jewish interpretation of] our law to associate with a Gentile or visit him." Here the word is *proserchomai*, "to assemble or come together."

This tradition of separation posed obvious questions for the new church. With whom are Christians to associate? Or are believers to form themselves into an enclave and cut themselves off from unbelievers? Paul uses the Greek word *synanamignymi* when he deals with this issue. The word means "to mix together" or "to be mixed up with." It is used only in 1 Co 5:9,11 and 2 Th 3:14, and at first Paul's teaching in these passages seems surprising.

Christians are warned not to associate with fellow believers who live immoral lives (1 Co 5:1–9; cf. 2 Th 3:14). But Paul does not tell us we should not associate with "the people of this world who are immoral, or the greedy and swindlers, or idolaters" (1 Co 5:10). Why does he make this distinction?

The community of faith also existed as a nation in OT times. That nation was to maintain its purity by isolation from the surrounding pagan lands. But the NT church exists as multitudes of tiny communities scattered throughout, and surrounded by, pagan society. Isolation in this situation is virtually impossible; and of course it would be wrong, for it is only by contact with people of the world that we can share the gospel of God and demonstrate goodness by our lives. Today, separation is a matter of heart commitment to God rather than isolation, and God is able to keep us pure despite the evil influences among which we live.

ASSURANCE

As commonly used by some Christians, this word suggests an "assurance of salvation" that comes when a person knows he or she is saved. There should be no lingering doubts about one's personal relationship with God.

But while three Greek words are translated "assurance" in the NIV (four in the NASB), in none of the passages where these words are found is attention focused on assurance about an individual's relationship with God.

Parrēsia, which means "confidence" or "boldness," is translated "assurance" in 1 Ti 3:13 and 1 Jn 5:14. The word is used in this same sense in Heb 10:35 (there rendered "confidence"). This particular assurance is a buoyant confidence that comes with faithful service or by acting on God's promises.

Plērophoria (found four times in the NT) means "full assurance" or "certainty." In the NT the satisfying conviction of *plērophoria* comes to us through the gospel (1 Th 1:5), and in a close-knit Christian community it grows with our growing understanding of God (Col 2:2–3). *Plērophoria* is also found in a trust in God that grows with committed Christian living (Heb 6:11; 10:22–24).

Plērophoreō is a parallel verb that means "to achieve certainty." It is used in this sense in Ro 4:21 and 14:5. Ro 4:21 uses this word to teach the nature of faith: Abraham was completely certain that God was able to do what he promised— and would surely do it.

Hypostasis is translated in the NASB as "assurance," in the NIV as "being sure." Faith provides an inner certainty about things that simply are not open to empirical verification but are communicated by God's Word (Heb 11:1).

The usage of these Greek words in their various contexts points us to an exciting Christian life. A growing and joyful sense of conviction is available to us. This comes to us with the gospel, is nurtured through the life we share with others in a close-knit believing community, and is confirmed as we continue to live by God's will despite difficulties and severe challenges. There may be no visible reason for our joy. But the confident satisfaction we have is very real and is shared by others who have also come to know and experience Jesus Christ.

What about the assurance of salvation? The scriptural passages on assurance deal with a confidence that comes *with* our salvation, but the Bible also speaks plainly about the fact that we can be sure *of* salvation. "This is the testimony: God has given us eternal life, and this life is in his Son. He who has the Son has life; he who does not have the Son of God does not have life" (1 Jn 5:11–12).

ASTONISH/ASTONISHMENT

The same Greek words translated "astonish" are also translated by our English synonym "amaze." The terms are discussed thoroughly under that entry. Of interest, but without special significance, is the fact that the words the NIV tends to translate "astonished" are usually translated "amazed" in the NASB. ◗ *Amazed/Amazing*

ASTRAY

This word is found in both Testaments, always with "go" or "lead." Four principal Hebrew words are reflected in our modern English translations of the OT. *Tā'âh* is the most common and is found mainly in the Psalms and in the Prophets. It means "to err" or "to stray" in a physical, mental, moral, or spiritual sense. The most famous occurrence is in Isa 53:6, which says, "We all, like sheep, have gone astray, each of us has turned to his own way; and the LORD has laid on him the iniquity of us all."

Synonyms used less frequently are *śāṭâh*, *šāgâh*, and *šāgag*. *Sāṭāh*, "to turn or go aside," is used in Nu 5:19,20 and Pr 7:25 of sexual impurity. Both *šāgâh* and *šāgag* mean "to err." They emphasize sins committed inadvertently, in ignorance. The causes suggested in the OT are alcohol (Pr 20:1; Isa 28:7) and seductive women (Pr 5:20,23).

Each of these OT words pictures an individual or a group that turns from the way of goodness. It is clear from the OT that both the individual who goes astray and those who lead others astray are held responsible by God.

The writers of the NT Epistles pick up the thought and language of the OT. All but Paul use a verb (*planaō*) that means "to lead astray" or "cause to wander" (Heb 3:10; 5:2; Jas 1:16; 5:19; 1 Pe 2:25; 1 Jn 2:26; 3:7; Rev 12:9; 18:23). Paul chooses another word, *apagō*, which means "to lead away" or, in passive forms, "to be misled" (1 Co 12:2; Gal 2:13, with prefix *syn*). The one thing that the NT identifies as leading a believer into intentional sin is a hard and unresponsive heart, which will not trust God or act on his Word (Heb 3:10–19).

ASTROLOGY

The NIV speaks of "astrologers" in the Book of Daniel and so translates the Hebrew '*āššap* (twice) and the Aramaic '*aššāp* (6 times). The NASB translates these same words as "conjurers." The difference stems from the fact that these words appear only here in the Bible and their meaning is uncertain. All we really know is that the astrologer/conjurer is linked in the context with magicians and sorcerers. The specific practices they followed are uncertain. Both the NIV and the NASB, however, translate the Hebrew for "diviners of the heavens" (Isa 47:13) as "astrologers."

Does the Bible make any definite statement about the modern practice of astrology? Today many believe that the position of the stars at a person's birth influences his or her life. By daily consulting the current position of the stars, believers in astrology expect to find guidance for the decisions they must make and to gain insight into their future.

While there may be no specific biblical prohibition of astrology as such, Scripture does prohibit God's people from looking to any source but the Lord himself for personal guidance. Dt 18 calls all such practices "detestable" and says, "Let no one be found among you . . . who practices divination or sorcery, interprets omens, engages in witchcraft, or casts spells, or who is a medium or spiritist or who consults the dead" (18:10–11). The people of Israel were reminded that God himself had spoken to them and had pledged to continue to speak through prophets he would send (18:14–20). ◆ *Prophecy/Prophet*

There are a number of ways through which God is able to lead believers today. These include the completed Word of God, the indwelling Holy Spirit, the insights of other Christians, circumstances, and the proper use of our renewed minds (Ro 12:2). These sources provide all the guidance we need. To turn to astrology is to insult the living Lord and to reject the guidance he has provided.

ATONEMENT

How can a sinful human being approach God? How do we deal with the sins and the failures that alienate us from him? God's solution to this basic problem is pictured in the atoning sacrifices of the OT. All those sacrifices picture what became a reality in the death of Jesus on Calvary.

OT 1. Atonement in the OT
    2. Atonement and sacrifice
    3. The Day of Atonement
NT 4. Atonement in the NT
    5. Jesus' death as atonement
    6. Summary

OT — 1. Atonement in the OT. The Hebrew words universally translated "atonement" in modern English versions are *kippur* (noun) and *kāpar* (verb). The root (*kāpar*) and its related words are used about 150 times in the OT and are intimately linked in the Bible with forgiveness of sin and with reconciliation to God. It is often said that the idea expressed is one found in a possibly related Arabic root that means "to cover or conceal." Atonement would then denote a covering that conceals a person's sin and makes it possible for him to approach God. Although this relationship is possible, the language link is not at all certain. What is certain is the role that atonement played in the religion of Israel—a role given to atonement by God to carry a vital message about our faith.

In the OT, atonement was made to purify objects ritually and set them aside for God's service (e.g., the tabernacle altar [Ex 29:36–37]). Atonement was also associated with ordaining persons for God's service (e.g., the priests [Ex 29:35–36]). But the primary connection of atonement was with sin, guilt, and forgiveness.

Lev 4 deals with unintentional sins that were committed by priests (Lev 4:3–12), the whole community (Lev 4:13–21), the leaders (Lev 4:22–26), and the humblest members of the faith community (Lev 4:27–35). In each case the formula is repeated: the one who sins unintentionally, "he is guilty." The guilty sinner then brings an animal to the priests, who offer it in sacrifice. "In this way he [the priest] will make atonement for the man's sin, and he will be forgiven" (4:26).

Lev 14 makes it clear that this sacrificial prescription was to be followed for both ritual and moral uncleanness and that the atoning sacrifice restored the guilty party or unclean object to harmonious relationship with God and the believing community.

Whatever the root meaning of *kāpar*, it is clear that atonement involves a sacrifice that in some significant and just way deals with guilt so that God extends forgiveness, reconciling the person or group to himself. ◆ *Forgive* ◆ *Guilt* ◆ *Reconcile*

2. Atonement and sacrifice. In the OT, atonement for sin is consistently linked with the sacrifice of some living animal. Even references to "atonement money" make a link with sacrifice, for Israel was told to "use it for the service of the Tent of Meeting" (Ex 30:16).

Leviticus 17:11 teaches that the death of a sacrificial animal was required for atonement. The Israelites were told not to eat blood, "for," God told them, "the life of a creature is in the blood, and I have given it to you to make atonement for yourselves on the altar; it is the blood that makes atonement for one's life."

The images in the OT worship system, then, are quite plain. As soon as God introduced law (Ex 19–24), the reality of sin as law-breaking was established. Persons who broke the law became guilty before God (Ro 7:7–13). It thus became necessary for God to deal with guilt, for implicit in the OT notion of sin is not only guilt as personal responsibility for one's actions but also the conviction that God must act to punish sin. ♦ *Sin* At Sinai, God acted immediately to deal with this problem. He gave Moses plans for the tabernacle (Ex 25–26). Worship there involved sacrifices that would be offered in atonement (Ex 27, 30). The priesthood was established to make the sacrifices (Ex 28–29) ♦ *Priesthood*

With the establishment of the tabernacle, the sacrificial system, and the priesthood, atonement could be made after a person sinned, and the guilty individual could thus be restored to right relationship with God.

OT atonement called for the life of an animal. The guilty party laid his hand on the head of the animal, identifying himself with it (Lev 4:4,15,24,29). Then the animal was slain, symbolically taking the sinner's place. The imagery tells us that sin merits death but that God will accept another life in place of that of the sinner.

3. The Day of Atonement. Members of Israel's community could come to the tabernacle to seek forgiveness when they discovered they were guilty of some unintentional sin. But what could be done about intentional sins?

Lev 16 gives instructions for a special sacrifice to be offered just once a year, on the tenth day of the seventh month, Tishri. On that day, the whole community was to gather at the tabernacle to fast and to do no work. The high priest, following carefully the prescribed steps, brought the blood of the sacrifice into the inner room of the tabernacle and there sprinkled the blood on the cover of the ark. ♦ *Ark* The sacrificed animal was a "sin offering for the people" (Lev 16:15) and is specifically said to have been "because of the uncleanness and rebellion of the Israelites, whatever their sins have been" (16:16; cf. 16:21). That annual sacrifice, made before the Lord, was an "atonement . . . to be made once a year for all the sins of the Israelites" (16:34). Following it, Israel was told,

"You will be clean from all your sins" (16:30).

The OT sacrificial system made provision, then, for atonement of both unintentional and willful sins. It assured Israel that God could and would forgive sins when his people came to him in the way he prescribed.

NT — 4. Atonement in the NT. In the NIV, "atonement" translates the Greek words *hilastērion* (Ro 3:25; Heb 9:5), *hilaskomai* (Heb 2:17), and *hilasmos* (1 Jn 2:2; 4:10), whereas the NASB has "mercy seat" in Heb 9:5 and "propitiation" in the other passages.

In Greek culture, the word group denoting "propitiation" carried with it the idea of acting in some way to avert the terrible, destructive powers of the gods and, if possible, to win the gods over to act favorably. The Greek translation of the OT (the Septuagint) chose this word group when translating *kippur*. Thus, the NIV's "atonement" reflects the OT, and the NASB's "propitiation" reflects the Greek emphasis. When we look into the NT passages themselves, we learn much about how the coming of Jesus filled the OT sacrifices with special meaning.

In Ro 3:25, Paul raises a question: How can God justly have left past sins unpunished? The implication of this question is that sacrificial animals surely could not have fairly satisfied the justice of God. People and animals are of different orders and value. ♦ *Animals* Yet from the beginning, God was willing to accept a person's faith in the place of righteousness, and, admittedly, this seems unfair. Paul's answer is that we can understand the fairness of it now that Jesus has been presented as "a sacrifice of atonement." It is on the basis of the atonement Jesus accomplished that God is shown to have been just and fair in forgiving those who have faith.

Heb 2:17 argues that Jesus must have become a true human being to serve both as the High Priest who offered the atoning sacrifice to God and as the sacrifice itself. Heb 9 develops this theme. The ark, with its golden cover on which atoning blood was spilled (9:5), was "an illustration for the present time" (9:9). All the sacrifices offered there were "not able to clear the conscience of the worshiper" (9:9).

In fact, those repeated sacrifices only reminded Israel that they were sinners who constantly needed forgiveness. But these sacrifices have now been superseded by the single sacrifice of Jesus Christ himself. This sacrifice does make the believer holy and takes away all sins (Heb 9:23–10:14).

John explores the meaning of Jesus' atonement for you and me as we live in this world and, at times, continue to fall into sin (1 Jn 1:8–9). When we come to God and confess our sins, he forgives and cleanses us, for Jesus, "the atoning sacrifice for our sins" (1 Jn 2:2), speaks up in our defense (1 Jn 2:1). The love that God has for us is fully and decisively seen in the fact that God "sent his Son as an atoning sacrifice for our sins" (1 Jn 4:10).

Each of the elements found in the OT doctrine of atonement is present in the NT. Here too are guilty human beings who have sinned and deserve punishment. Here too is a sacrifice, provided by God. Here too is forgiveness for sins, won by identifying by faith with the atoning sacrifice. The wonder of the NT revelation is that at last we see the glory of God's eternal plan. He has himself in Christ chosen to become the sacrifice through which humanity can be released from the grip of sin and death.

5. Jesus' death as atonement. The history of theology has seen several theories advanced to explain how the death of Jesus wins forgiveness. One early theory noted that Jesus' death frees the believer from the dominion of Satan (Col 2:15). Therefore some assumed that Jesus died to pay a ransom to Satan. But this completely overlooks the need for forgiveness.

In the twelfth century, a "moral influence" theory was promulgated. According to this theory, the life and death of Jesus demonstrated God's love so dramatically that human beings, who mistrusted God, were relieved. They learned in Jesus that God was never angry with them, and it is this discovery that moves human beings to love God and to turn from their sins. But this theory completely overlooks the fact of guilt and the need for forgiveness.

Anselm of Canterbury clearly stated the orthodox theory in the eleventh century: he taught that Jesus' death was substitutionary. God's justice demands that sin's debt be paid. God's love sent Jesus to pay this debt for us.

The whole Bible speaks to these theories. The teaching of the NT corresponds, as reality does to shadow, with the practices of the OT. By faith the sinner, guilty and deserving punishment, identifies with the one who died as a sacrifice in place of the sinner. That sacrifice, which is ordained by God, is accepted by God, and the sinner is pronounced forgiven.

The symbolism as well as the direct teaching of the NT shows that Jesus did take our place on the cross and died there as our substitute. United now with Jesus by faith, we are considered both to have died with him and now to be raised to new life with him (Ro 6:1–10).

6. Summary. The OT shows us that atonement calls for a sacrifice: a life given for our life. The guilty must come in God's prescribed way, trusting God to accept the substitute that he himself has ordained and trusting him to extend the promised forgiveness. The NT shows us that the sacrificial practices ordained in the OT were instructive: they foreshadowed the death of Jesus on Calvary and prepared us to understand the meaning of that death.

Jesus died as the Lamb of God, as our substitute, and it is on the basis of his shed blood that God offers full and free forgiveness to all who accept him by faith.

ATTAIN

The NIV and the NASB seldom use "attain" and "attained" in the same passages. Why?

In the OT, the English translators selected "attain" as one of several possible equivalents for the way a number of different Hebrew words function in various expressions. Some nine different Hebrew constructions—ranging from those generally signifying "to know, to take hold, to be found, to reach or overtake, to rest, to grasp," to those signifying "to do or to accomplish"—are in the original when we read "attain" in English. It is clear we should not attempt to build any theological theories on the "attain" group found in any OT version.

The situation is similar in the NT. Only three passages use "attain" in both the NIV and the NASB (Eph 4:13; Php 3:11,16), though in other contexts each version uses a word from the "attain" group. Actually, six different Greek words are found where the two versions choose to use some form of "attain." But there is a theological consistency in NT passages where the idea of attaining is found. In looking at these passages, we discover how we cannot attain spiritually—and how we can!

Ro 9:30–32 is Paul's explanation of why OT Israel failed to attain righteousness. It was because they approached righteousness as if it were to be won by works rather than received by faith.

In Gal 3, Paul warns the young church that they are making this same mistake (Gal 3:1–14, esp. v. 3). These believers have accepted salvation by faith, but now they want to try to go on in the Christian life as if growth were a matter of keeping the law. Paul shows that the law cannot help: faith is the key after salvation as well as for salvation.

In Eph 4:13–16, Paul examines Christian growth. We attain maturity by growing up into Christ. Our growth comes in the context of warm, loving relationships with other believers in the body of Christ—those who support us by caring and ministering.

In Php 3:11–16, Paul looks again at the idea of spiritual attainment. He himself has turned his back on his own considerable accomplishments under law. He has tossed them aside and considers them worthless. His goal now is simply to be found in Christ and so to "attain to the resurrection from the dead." This expression does not refer to the coming physical resurrection but to Paul's present experience of a power for righteous living that can be found only by faith and only as Jesus shares his own resurrection life with the believer (cf. 3:9; Ro 6:8,13). This experience of power comes as we seek to follow Jesus and put into daily practice whatever level of understanding and maturity we may arrive at (*phthanō*).

The picture that emerges as we connect these passages is an exciting one. God does have a high calling for Christians. But we attain it, not by self-reliant attempts to live by the law, but rather by humble commitment of ourselves to Jesus, asking and believing by faith that he will give us the power to follow him.

ATTENTION/ATTENTIVE

Several Hebrew words are translated "give (or pay) attention." In each case, the thought expressed is the same. The key to understanding passages in which such phrases occur is not found in the original words but in the relationship between the persons involved.

When a superior is the speaker, and particularly when God is speaking to people, "pay attention" or "give attention" calls not merely for listening but for obedience. When Proverbs exhorts, "My son, pay attention to what I say; listen closely to my words" (4:20), it is clear that the desire of the writer is to affect the readers' behavior rather than simply to communicate information.

It is also clear that when God speaks to his people and calls them to pay close attention, he speaks as a sovereign. Isa 42 explains: "You have seen many things, but have paid no attention; your ears are open, but you hear nothing." By refusing to listen to God Israel turned to sin, and so God acted: "They would not follow his ways; they did not obey his law. So he poured out on them his burning anger, the violence of war" (42:20–25).

When human beings call on God to pay or to give attention, this also is a call to action. The difference is that human beings come as supplicants, not as sovereigns. God hears us but remains free to respond or not as he chooses (though he has willingly bound himself by his loving promises). In contrast, God's call to mankind to hear carries the imperative of a divine command.

Some NT uses of "pay attention" or "give attention" are simply descriptive: they tell us that some person was listening but do not imply that any action might follow (e.g., Ac 3:5; 8:6,10). At other times the context makes it clear that paying attention is directly linked with response: "They paid no attention and went off" (Mt 22:5).

Heb 2:1, which says "we must pay more careful attention," picks up the OT sense, conveying the binding nature of the message brought by Jesus, which calls hearers to obedience (Heb 2:2–4). In all of these cases (except Mt 22:5 and Ac 3:5), the Greek word is *prosechō*, which can mean both "pay attention" and "be warned." It is often used in the sense of warning by the Gospel writers (Mt 6:1; 7:15; 10:17; 16:6,11,12; Lk 12:1; 17:3; 20:46; 21:34; Ac 5:35; 20:28).

Two NT passages render other Greek words by "pay attention." One is 3 Jn 10, which uses *hypomimnēskō*, found only seven times in the NT and meaning "remember." Jas 2:3 warns us that we sin if we give special attention to the rich and discriminate against the poor in our fellowships. The word here is *epiblepō*, which means "to look favorably on" or "to pay special attention to." It is found only three times in the NT: here, Lk 1:48 (Mary's song), and in Lk 9:38.

It is wise for us to pay attention—to our own lives, to each other, and especially to God. Learning to listen and to obey his Word is the key to fellowship and to growth.

ATTITUDE

No single term is found in the OT to express the idea of attitude. The translators of both the NIV and the NASB, however, did recognize this idea in the Greek word *phroneō* (NIV, Php 2:5; NASB, Php 2:5; 3:15). The Greek word means "to think," "to form an opinion or judgment." *Phroneō* thus leads us through the process of evaluating a situation and, on the basis of our evaluation, adopting an attitude or disposition to act.

Paul urges the Philippians to adopt an attitude of consideration for others that will be like Jesus' own willingness to give himself for others. Maintaining such an attitude will bring unity and joy to the local fellowship (Php 2:1–11). Later Paul urges this same group to maintain Paul's attitude toward life: we are to press on toward the goal of living out our calling in Christ (3:12–17).

The NIV also translates another Greek word as "attitude": *ennoia* is found in only two places in the NT and is translated "intentions" and "purpose" by the NASB (1 Pe 4:1; Heb 4:12). Like *phroneō*, *ennoia* relates to thought, especially to the development of a perspective that will provide insight and so shape our attitude and guide our actions. We are to adopt the attitude of Jesus, Peter writes, and live by the will of God rather than by the desires that struggle in our sinful nature to express themselves (1 Pe 4:1–2). Every thought and attitude of our heart is evaluated—and thus corrected—by the living Word that God has given us (Heb 4:12–13).

Each of these original terms clearly indicates that, from a biblical perspective, an attitude is no mere mental feeling. It is an outlook that carries with it a disposition toward action.

It is also significant that in each passage exhorting Christians to have a certain attitude, that attitude is to be shaped by observing the living example of a model—one who demonstrates that attitude by his daily choices. In two passages the model is Jesus (Php 2 and 1 Pe 4), and in one it is Paul (Php 3).

Another key passage where the NIV has "attitude" is Eph 4:23. The original phrase reads the "spirit of your mind." Here too we see that the mind as the organ of perception is involved in shaping our attitudes and that God himself is referred to as the one providing our example. It is good to know that new and godly attitudes are possible for us, for we have been given new life so that we "might be like God in true righteousness and holiness" (v. 24).

AUTHOR

Twice Hebrews refers to Jesus as "author." He is the author of salvation, made perfect through suffering, who brings many sons to glory (2:10). And he is the "author and perfecter of our faith" (12:2), who endured the cross and in due time knew its triumph.

The word translated "author" here is *archēgos*. In the Greek world it often referred to a city's traditional founder, who located and named it and became its guardian. *Archēgos* was often used of founders of philosophic schools. It is clear from the way the word is used in Hebrews that *archēgos* is intended to identify Jesus as a leader who by his death has opened up a new way—a way that has bridged the gap between earth and heaven itself. Jesus is the pioneer who has created the path that we now follow by faith into the very presence of God.

The same meaning is seen in Ac 3:15, where Jesus is said to be the *archēgos* of life. This does not refer to his resurrection but to the fact that as the eternal Son of God, Jesus is also the originator of life in the universe and himself the founder of humanity (cf. Jn 1:3–4).

AUTHORITIES

The NT identifies two different authorities. One is secular human government, which expresses its power to control in legal, political, social, and moral areas. The other authorities are supernatural beings who influence the course of human events, including exerting influence on governments. The Greek word used to identify each is *exousia*, which identifies a power based on position, in contrast to inherent physical or spiritual strength.

There are only a few NT passages that refer directly to either human governments or supernatural authorities. But they introduce us to a topic that is important for daily life and is touched on throughout Scripture. We are particularly concerned about the relationship of believers to secular governments. Is government good or bad? Should we be politically involved or seek to withdraw? How can believers resist unjust laws? Or should we simply submit? Such questions must often be answered by the individuals involved in a conflict situation. These questions call for seeking God's personal guidance. But even to think about them we need to know what the Bible says about the authorities under which human beings must live.

1. **Human government initiated**
2. **Human responsibility under theocracy**
3. **Delegation of power to secular government**
4. **Supernatural authorities and their link with human governments**
5. **Relationship of believers to secular authorities.**

1. Human government initiated. Genesis outlines an idyllic state in Eden. The first pair was given the responsibility of rule over the creation. In the beginning there was only harmony between Adam and Eve.

When sin entered, discord and strife were introduced (cf. Ge 3:11–13). God revealed one impact of sin when he introduced for the first time the notion that one human being may have rule over another (3:16). ◆ *Head* Genesis 4 describes the chaos in society when each individual acted without any restraint (cf. 4:19–24). Anarchy led to a civilization in which man's sin nature was given free expression and "every inclination of the thoughts of [man's] heart was only evil all the time" (6:5).

God himself acted then. He judged and cleansed the world by means of the Flood. After the Flood, as Noah and his family stood in the fresh new world, God announced, "From each man, too, I will demand an accounting for the life of his fellow man. 'Whoever sheds the blood of man, by man shall his blood be shed; for in the image of God has God made man'" (Ge 9:5–6). This statement is widely viewed as the formal institution of human government. With the responsibility that God gave human beings for punishment of the actions of one another, structures had to be developed through which violators could be punished and standards of behavior enforced.

The institution of human government provided no guarantee of righteousness. The rulers are sinners, just as are the citizens. But the mission of government is to restrain the expressions of man's sinful impulses by structuring a society in which what is harmful to order (and thus a threat to the self-interest of government) will not be permitted.

There have been many forms of human government, including Israel's theocracy, Greece's democracy, and the absolute personal dictatorship represented in Nebuchadnezzar's Babylon. But each system has had to deal with ways to control the behavior of its members and to punish those whose wrongdoing threatens the body politic.

2. Human responsibility under theocracy. The law, which we find in three of the books of the Pentateuch (Exodus, Leviticus, and Deuteronomy), did more than just state the Ten Commandments. It structured all of society. It provided wide-ranging laws that dealt with situations involving servants (Ex 21:2–11), personal injury cases (Ex 21:12–36), property rights (Ex 22:1–15), destructive social relationships (Ex 22:16–31), conducting law suits (Ex 23:1–9), and religious duties (Ex 23:10–19). Other extended passages touch on other aspects of national and community life. By following the social order laid down in the law, Israel was to create a just, moral community, in which even poverty would be eliminated. ▶ *Poor and Oppressed*

Under the theocracy, the burden of making laws and establishing the social order was accepted by God himself. The people of Israel were not given legislative powers. But the other function of government, that of enforcing the laws on the community, was delegated in accordance with the principle laid down in Ge 9. The individual is to be held responsible for his actions by others. Society is accountable for punishing wrongdoers.

The unique feature of Israel's theocracy in regard to administration of law is that no central control structures were originally established to administer justice. The responsibility to hold members of the community accountable to God's laws was distributed to the whole community.

This meant that individuals who had some personal knowledge of a situation were to be called as witnesses and were to tell the truth if an individual was brought to suit or trial. Suits were conducted within the community, with the elders of the local community serving as judges and jury. The community leaders were responsible for settling the cases, based on principles expressed in the law's codes.

In the case of sins like idolatry, which threatened the well-being of Israel itself because it provoked God's anger (cf. Jos 7), it was the responsibility of individuals to bring charges and thus to discharge the community of responsibility.

When a case was too difficult for local elders to settle, it was possible for the elders to take it to the priests, who served God at Israel's single place of worship. There were also provisions by which a case that could not be settled in any other way might be brought directly to God, who would serve as final judge.

The most significant element in the system was the principle of distribution of responsibility to every member of the community. In ancient Israel no one could stand by while a crime was being committed and then give the excuse that he did not want to become involved or that it was police business. In Israel each person was to hold himself responsible for the holiness of society. Each was to accept personal responsibility for seeing that all the people carried out God's just and holy laws.

This theocratic system, despite its wise structure and beauty, was never implemented in Israel. With the exception of a single generation (cf. Dt 4:4 with Jos 24:31), Israel failed to follow the Lord. The social order that depended on the presence of a majority of righteous persons was warped and twisted by sin, and God's good laws could not be administered as he intended (cf. Hab 1:4).

The fault was not in the system. The fault was in the weakness of sinful flesh (Ro 8:3). No system of government that attempts to rely on innate human goodness for its operation can ever succeed in maintaining the social order.

3. Delegation of power to secular governments. Several NT and OT passages give us insight into the delegation of power to secular rulers.

Romans 13. The NT church found itself existing as scattered communities, seeded in a pagan world ruled by hostile authorities. The overarching authority was that of Rome. But within the empire, national, ethnic, and even city units were permitted to maintain their own traditional systems of laws and customs.

Neither the content of these laws nor the modes of their administration would be in harmony with the standards of righteousness revealed by God. Conflict seemed certain, so there must be principles given by God to guide his people to live his way, often in hostile states.

The first problem was to define the relationship of secular governments to God and from that base to explore how believers would relate to the authorities in the land in which they lived.

Paul deals with the first problem directly. He tells the church at Rome to submit to governing authorities and adds, "For there is no authority except that which God established" (Ro 13:1). The Greek wording suggests that God has been active in arranging the state of affairs in which the believer lives, including the system of government that he or she is subject to. This does not imply divine approval of any particular form of government, but it does remind us that God is sovereign. God permits his people to live and to serve him in every type of society and under every possible form of government.

The passage emphasizes the function of government rather than its form. Human beings have been permitted to organize themselves in a variety of ways, but the common mission of all government is to serve as an agent of God, "an agent of wrath to bring punishment on the wrongdoer" (13:4). In this way governments carry out the intention expressed in Ge 9:5–6, and, as entities carrying out God's will, they can be called his servants.

Daniel 2,4,5,7. Daniel lived under a series of autocratic empires that combined the dictatorial and the bureaucratic elements so likely to disturb us today. Daniel's experience near the center of power is most instructive.

Daniel teaches that God is involved in setting up specific governments. He said to Nebuchadnezzar, "The God of heaven has given you dominion and power and might and glory: in your hands he has placed mankind . . . " (2:37–38). The same concept is emphasized in Da 4:17: "The Most High is sovereign over the kingdoms of men and gives them to anyone he wishes."

These rulers remain responsible to God. When Nebuchadnezzar's pride required judgment, God struck him with madness for seven years. Later restored, Nebuchadnezzar at last recognized God as ultimate ruler and confessed, "He does as he pleases with the powers of heaven and the people of the earth" (4:35).

The theme is found again in the next chapter (5:26–28); there it is recorded that the aging prophet announced that Belshazzar, a later king, had been weighed and found wanting. His kingdom would be taken away from him by God.

Two chapters later we find recorded a dream in which the prophet was shown future history and the governments that would rule until the Messiah should come. But he was also promised that in the end all secular powers will be overthrown, and "the Most High will receive the kingdom and will possess it forever—yes, for ever and ever" (7:18).

Daniel, like Paul, affirms God's sovereignty and views the Lord as actively permitting the growth of various world powers. This does not make God responsible for a particular governmental system nor for what a government does. Because all humanity is captive to sin, we can expect evils as well as benefits from governments. Daniel shows that even those secular powers that do not acknowledge God are responsible to him. God judges governments whose evil requires judgment.

Revelation 18. This passage, using the image of Babylon the Great, describes the final destruction of human government. We gain significant insight here into the values we can expect to be expressed by governments. The consistent emphasis in this passage is on the material wealth and the prosperity experienced by the citizens of the society under the government of "Babylon."

Human governments are valued by their citizens when they maintain a social context in which citizens can prosper materially. We cannot expect human governments to have spiritual goals or to seek to implement God's standards of righteousness. Laws are enacted and enforced to protect life and property and to encourage the prosperity of all classes of citizens. This is not done because of any sense of responsibility to God or commitment to what is right. It is done because people will rebel against a society in which citizens are not protected or are not given the opportunity to prosper. "Good government," which provides security and promotes prosperity, will willingly be granted more and more power by its citizens. Thus it is in every government's self-interest to provide "good government."

These biblical glimpses into government suggest the following: God is sovereignly involved and permits the existence of whatever government a believer may happen to live under. Whatever its form, government is charged by God with the responsibility of maintaining order and punishing evildoers. God holds governments responsible for performing this function and will act when a government institutionalizes evil. At the same time secular government cannot be expected to formally adopt God's standards or biblical values. Secular government must deal with secular humanity, whose basic values are materialistic. In self-interest, governing authorities must seek to provide a good government that protects its citizens and permits them to prosper.

4. Supernatural authorities and their link with human governments. The NT uses the word "authorities" along with other terms (e.g., "rulers," "powers") to identify supernatural beings who inhabit the unseen world of angels. ◆ *Angels* These powers may at present be good or evil (cf. Eph 3:10), but they were all originally created by and for the Son of God (Col 1:16). Today, even though the evil angelic authorities have been disarmed" and have been overcome in the Cross (Col 2:15), believers must "struggle against the rulers, against the authorities, against the powers of this dark world and against spiritual forces of evil in the heavenly realms" (Eph 6:12).

While little is said of the role of these authorities in the life of the individual, the Bible does speak of their relationship to human governments. Paul has said they exercise their authority over the dark world, and John adds that "the whole world is under the control of the evil one" (1 Jn 5:19). The world system with its values and its institutions is the focus of Satan's efforts to influence humanity.

Thus the world of the unsaved is said to be a kingdom, a "dominion of darkness" from which believers have been rescued to be brought into "the kingdom of the Son he loves" (Col 1:13).

The fact that Satan at least claims the right of control over governments is seen in the Gospel reports of Jesus' temptation. "I will give you all their authority and splendor," Satan said to Jesus, as he showed him the kingdoms of the world, "for it has been given to me, and I can give it to anyone I want to" (Lk 4:5).

Satan's claim is hardly decisive. He is "a liar and the father of lies" (Jn 8:44). But Daniel 10 unveils for a moment the fierce warfare in the hidden universe between the armies of God and the armies of Satan. In each force there are beings specifically assigned to influence governments. ◆ *Angels*

The picture that emerges from Scripture is perhaps best summed up in the Daniel passage. There are spiritual beings who struggle to influence governments and societies. Humanity responds naturally to those influences that appeal to human nature; societies as well as individuals are soon trapped in illusions shaped by Satan and his minions (cf. Eph 2:1–6).

Despite the apparent victories of evil, God remains in control. He is the ultimate authority. Jesus, now raised again to his place at the Father's right hand, is "far above all rule and authority, power and dominion, and every title that can be given." It is Jesus who is "head over everything for the church, which is his body" (Eph 1:21–22).

5. Relationship of believers to secular authorities. Christians today live in tension between secular society and government (which reflect the values of an unsaved world) and God's call to live out his holiness. In some nations this tension is far greater than in others. What does the Bible say about how a Christian is to relate to the government under which he or she lives? Among the important principles provided in Scripture are the following:

Obedience. Paul argues in Ro 13 that since God has ordained human government, both conscience and a healthy fear of consequences of disobedience should motivate the individual to keep human laws. The same theme is found in 1 Pe 2:13–15. Here Peter suggests that living good lives as responsible citizens will "silence the ignorant talk of foolish men."

Responsibility. The believer is responsible for supporting his government by the payment of taxes and by acting with respect (Ro 13:6–7). We are also to support our government by prayer (1 Ti 2:1–2). The role that Daniel played in the administration of three successive world powers provides an example suggesting that believers today too can participate politically within their system without compromising their commitment to God.

Dual citizenship. While believers are citizens of God's heavenly kingdom, they are also citizens of earthly nations. Paul sets an example for us by the full use of his own Roman citizenship and his insistence on his citizenship rights (cf. Ac 16:35–39; 22:22–29; 25:1–12). Paul's actions make it clear that in whatever way a government permits its citizens rights, it is appropriate for a Christian to claim and to exercise those rights. In a democracy this implies more than the demand for legal rights; it implies also political activity and serious efforts to influence law making.

Unjust governments. How are Christians to respond when their convictions come into direct conflict with unjust laws or unjust governments? Peter deals with this problem. According to him, legally established authorities should be obeyed when possible. But ultimately each of us must choose to do the right thing, even when the right thing leads to suffering. After all, Jesus too suffered unjustly. Like Jesus, we must then simply entrust ourselves to God, knowing that God is the final judge (1 Pe 2:13–23).

Normally when we do what is good, no troubles will follow. But there will be times when doing what is good will lead to suffering (1 Pe 3:13–14). In the context it is clear that "good" is ultimately determined by God and that his revealed will must be our final guide (1 Pe 3:16–18).

In summary, Scripture is ambivalent about human government. Governments are necessary and have a God-ordained function. Although they are ordained by God, governments are strongly influenced by Satan and tend to express materialistic values. The Christian living in a secular state will experience tensions between Christ and Caesar. But by commitment to living good and quiet lives, most of us will be able to keep the tensions to a minimum.

AUTHORITY

How to exercise and respond to authority has, almost from the beginning of time, troubled governments and citizens, employers and employees, parents and children. To some people the notion of authority is frightening. It conjures up the image of some distant, impersonal, uncaring power. To others the image is comfortable, suggesting security. Again, others may be excited, desiring to have authority over others. What, then, does the Bible say? What is the nature of authority? And how is authority used— and misused?

OT 1. OT concepts
NT 2. The Greek words
   3. The authority of Jesus
   4. The authority of people over people
   5. Difficult passages on authority
   6. Summary

OT — 1. OT concepts. A number of words and expressions communicate the idea of authority in the OT. One of the most commonly used words is *yād*, "hand." The word literally refers to the physical hand but is usually used in a figurative way. One usage suggests that coming under someone's hand indicates coming under that person's authority (e.g., Ge 41:35; Jer 5:31; and NASB: Ge 16:9; Jdg 9:29; 2 Ch 23:18; 31:13,15; Jer 38:10–11). Other words translated "authority" in English versions denote strength, power, majesty, dominion, or rule.

It would be difficult to develop a theology of authority from the meaning of the Hebrew words. This is partly because every culture's authority-linked words will be influenced by the institutions that exist in that society and the specific functions taken on by government.

The importance of context is illustrated by the range of meanings of just one word translated "authority" and "rule" in English versions. This word, *māšal*, can communicate the idea, depending on context, of oppression (Jdg 14:4; Isa 19:4), of self-control (Pr 16:32), of management of a business operation (Ge 15:2), and of God's providential care in governing events (Ps 89:10).

Perhaps it is best to summarize by saying that the way authority-linked words are used in the OT suggests (again, depending on context) any or all of the following ideas: responsibility, care, superiority, dominion, power.

Authority can be divine or human, exercised wisely or foolishly, for the benefit of others or to exploit them. Authority can be given or it can be imposed by force. It can be accepted or rejected. It can shape a healthy society or an oppressive one. But nowhere does the OT indicate that authority in itself is wrong. In a world corrupted by sin, human beings need limits, and God has ordained authorities to restrain sin. ◆ *Authorities*

NT — 2. The Greek words. With few exceptions, the word "authority" in the NIV and NASB is a translation of Greek word *exousia*. Unlike the OT terms with their wide range of meaning, this Greek word conveys a basic concept that has important connotations for our understanding of the nature of authority.

The basic idea in the word *exousia* is freedom of choice. The greater the *exousia*, the greater the possibility of unrestricted freedom of action. A person without *exousia* has little freedom of action, for others maintain a right to control him and determine what he does. A person with maximum *exousia* will have total freedom of action and thus the right to control the actions of others. It is easy to see why, when used of secular authorities, this word commonly means the "power to give orders" (Mt 8:9; Lk 7:8; 19:17; 20:20; Ac 9:14; 26:10,12; 1 Pe 2:13).

When used of God's overarching authority, *exousia* makes no claims about his inherent strength or nature as God. But it does claim for God ultimate freedom of action. God is totally free to make decisions that cannot be frustrated by any natural or personal power in the universe.

Passages in which other words for authority are used are discussed under 5, below.

3. The authority of Jesus. A Roman soldier came to Jesus to ask for help. His statement then penetrated to the heart of the authority issue. He expressed the belief that if Jesus would simply speak the word, his servant would be healed, because "I myself am a man under authority, with soldiers under me. I tell this one 'Go' and he goes; and that one 'Come,' and he comes. I say to my servant, 'Do this,' and he does it" (Mt 8:9).

The point is this: As a military officer this man derived his authority from Rome, i.e., from the empire itself, which had chosen to extend to him the freedom of action he enjoyed in controlling the behavior of his troops. The officer's request for Jesus to simply speak a healing word was a confession of faith. The officer recognized that the authority Jesus derived from God was so complete that he was able to exercise control even over diseases. Jesus spoke and acted with full divine authority and authorization.

The Gospels tell us that Jesus' very freedom of action in teaching and healing stunned and disturbed the Jewish people (cf. Mk 1:22,27; Lk 4:32–36). Instead of constantly referring to tradition as the authority for his actions, Jesus relied on his own unmistakable aura of power. When Jesus scandalized his listeners by pronouncing the sins of a paralyzed man forgiven, he proved his authority to do so by healing him: "so that you may know that the Son of Man has authority [*exousia*, freedom of action] to forgive sins . . ." (Mt 9:6–8; Mk 2:10; Lk 5:24).

Despite Jesus' miracles, at the end of his ministry on earth he was still being challenged by the religious leaders who were unwilling to accept him as God's Son and messenger (Mt 21:23–29; Mk 11:28–33; Lk 20:2–8).

The Gospels, however, report many statements made by Jesus that define his authority, and the Epistles extend the authority of the now-risen Lord. While Jesus was on earth, his miracles showed his authority over nature, sickness, sin, demons, and even death itself. ▶ *Miracle/Sign/Wonder* Jesus has authority to judge all humankind (Jn 5:27). The Father has "granted him authority over all people that he might give eternal life to all those you [the Father] have given him" (Jn 17:2). Human beings might appear to have the power to snatch Jesus away from his friends and to take his life.

But Jesus claimed, "I lay down my life— only to take it up again. No one takes it away from me, but I lay it down of my own accord. I have authority to lay it down and authority to take it up again" (10:17–18).

After his resurrection Jesus told his followers, "All authority in heaven and on earth has been given to me" (Mt 28:17). Jesus now has total freedom to act (cf. Col 2:10), and he does act on behalf of his body, the church (Eph 1:21–23).

Ultimately Jesus will exercise his freedom to act and will destroy every competing power, making everything subject to the direct, active will of God the Father (1 Co 15:24–28).

4. The authority of people over people. The Scriptures teach and assume that in a world warped by sin, governing authorities are a necessity. ▶ *Authorities* But a vital question for Christians has to do with the nature of authority within the body of Christ. In its philosophical and theological sense as freedom of action to control or limit the freedom of action of others, do Christian leaders really have authority within the church?

The issue is an important one and deserves much study and debate. But a number of observations should be made to help us think about this issue.

For instance, Jesus delegated authority to his disciples (cf. Mk 3:15; 6:7; Lk 9:1; 10:19), but this was authority over demons and diseases. No passage suggests freedom to exercise control over other human beings. In fact, the freedom of choice of those to whom these disciples came is clearly protected (cf. Mk 6:11; Lk 10:8–12).

One incident reported in the Synoptics is especially significant. Mt 20, Mk 10, and Lk 22 all tell of a heated debate among the disciples over which of them would be greatest. Jesus took that opportunity to instruct them on leadership and its character within the church. Each passage reports that Jesus said, "You know that the rulers of the Gentiles lord it over them, and their high officials exercise authority over them." In each passage Jesus bluntly rules out this kind of leadership authority for them: "Not so with you!"

The alternative that Jesus spells out is a servant leadership. ♦ *Leadership* And a servant is a far cry from a ruler!

It is fascinating to compare these three passages and to note that one of them uses *exousia* to indicate the authority exercised by secular officials. The other two (Mt 20:25; Mk 10:42) use *katexousiazō*, found only here in the NT. The latter word means "authority over" but it also implies a tendency toward whatever compulsion is required to gain compliance. These passages suggest strongly that whatever authority Christian leaders may have, their freedom of action does not include the right to control the actions and choices of their brothers and sisters.

The apostle Paul is deeply aware of the fact that as an apostle he does have authority. He speaks of it in 2 Co 10,13. He told the Corinthians that the Lord gave him authority with a specific purpose: "for building you up, not tearing you down" (10:8; 13:10). In 2 Co 13 Paul speaks of his concern not to be "harsh in the use of [his] authority" (13:10). The context shows that the Christians in Corinth refused to admit that Christ was speaking through this servant leader. Paul did not respond by threatening. He did not try to manipulate or to coerce. He simply reminded them, "[Christ] is not weak in dealing with you, but is powerful among you" (13:3).

Paul had no need to resort to manipulation or to coercion, because Jesus was alive and acting as Head of his church. Jesus remained powerful among his people and was free to exercise his authority in disciplining ways. Paul relied on Jesus to bring about a response to the words that he, Jesus, had given to Paul to speak to the Corinthians.

These passages, and studies of Paul's style of leadership, suggest strongly that in the church God limits the authority given to leaders. The leader's authority is not an authority to control, but an authority to help the believer use his or her freedom to respond willingly to Jesus. ♦ *Free/Freedom* ♦ *Leadership* ♦ *Lord*

5. Difficult passages on authority. A few passages in which "authority" appears do not read *exousia* in the Greek manuscripts. Among them are Mt 20:25; Mk 10:42; Ro 7:1; 1 Th 2:6; 1 Ti 2:2,12; Heb 13:17; 1 Pe 2:13; 2 Pe 2:10; Jude 8. The original text in these passages uses words whose emphasis ranges from a stress on the eminence of the one in authority to a stress on the awesome power that is exercised in ruling (2 Pe 2:10; Jude 8).

Several passages in which *exousia* is used have at times been misunderstood or have raised questions.

Authority to become God's children: Jn 1:12. The *exousia* to become the children of God is given to all those (and only to those) who receive Jesus. Sin has limited the freedom of action of those who do not believe, and they remain dead in their trespasses and sins (Eph 2:1–2).

Pilate's authority: Jn 19:8–13. Only Pilate, as Roman governor, had the legal right to pronounce the death sentence. But as Pilate interviewed Jesus, he became more and more disturbed. The shouts of the people outside the judgment hall could not overcome the awe he sensed as he faced Jesus. Finally, in frustration, Pilate blurted out to Jesus: "Don't you realize I have power [*exousia*] to either free you or crucify you?"

Jesus made a puzzling reply: "You would have no power [*exousia*] over me if it were not given you from above. Therefore the one who handed me over to you is guilty of a greater sin" (19:10–11).

After this strange exchange Pilate struggled to have Jesus released. Finally, threatened with being accused before Caesar for releasing someone who claimed to be a king (19:12), Pilate surrendered and permitted the crucifixion. The questions focus on the exchange between Pilate and Jesus and particularly on Jesus' words that limit to some extent Pilate's responsibility.

The passage is clarified when we note the following: The one handing Christ over to Pilate was Caiaphas, the high priest, with all the leaders of the Jewish nation. Pilate's claim to have freedom of action (*exousia*) was true, yet false. Technically he had the authority under law. In fact, however, as Pilate's actions demonstrate, Pilate was not free. His legal freedom was itself limited by his personal vulnerability to being accused in Rome. Ultimately Pilate acted against his own convictions: an empty *exousia* indeed! The source of Pilate's *exousia* was "from above," derived from Rome, and Pilate found himself limited in his freedom to act by his belief about how Rome would react if he freed Jesus.

This is striking indeed! The person claiming to have the power of life or death faces a prisoner threatened with execution. Yet all Pilate's prating about his *exousia* is shown to be empty when under pressure from the people he is supposed to rule, he is forced to act against his will. How empty is this kind of power of which people boast! How meaningless it is when all the power in the world fails to give an individual the freedom to act according to his own conscience!

Paul and his rights: 1 Co 9:4–18. Paul stands in bold contrast to Pilate. In Corinthians Paul discusses his *exousia* as an apostle. With the word translated here as "right," Paul points out that he had the freedom to eat or drink what he chose, to marry and travel with a wife, and to be supported financially by those to whom he ministered. But Paul voluntarily chose not to exercise any of these freedoms. He ate sparingly, remained unmarried, and even worked to support himself so others would realize that the gospel truly is free.

Pilate, who claimed to have freedom of action, found himself bound by the demands of others. Paul, who surrendered some of his freedoms in order to reach his goals, was a truly free human being. We too will often find our greatest freedom in not using our *exousia*, even the *exousia* that we have been given by God. Note Paul's exhortations along these lines (e.g., 1 Co 6:1–7; 8:8–13; 10:23–25).

Women and authority in the church: 1 Co 11:10. The Greek noun for "authority" in this verse is again *exousia*. The verse has been understood to imply that women are inferior to men. But what it says is that "a woman ought to have a sign of authority on her head." Women in Corinth were excited about the new equality offered in Christ. Some women went to the extent of marching into church meetings with heads uncovered—something customary for men but not for women. Paul responds by pointing out that men and women are different from each other (11:3–9). But difference does not imply inferiority. In fact, Paul states that men and women are also interdependent (11:11–12).

However, it is not appropriate for a woman to declare her equality by acting as if she were a male. This would involve denial of the worth and value of womanhood. A woman could be a woman and still participate in the life of the believing community.

In 1 Ti 2:12, in which Paul makes a strong statement that he does not "permit a woman to teach or have authority over a man," he uses the word *authenteō*, its only occurrence in the NT. ◆ **Women in the Church**

6. Summary. Our primary insight into the nature of authority comes from the NT. There we see it portrayed as unrestricted freedom of action. God has unlimited *exousia*, which he exercises as he chooses to direct or to permit. Jesus demonstrated his deity by proving that his own freedom of action was likewise unlimited. Although Jesus delegated *exousia* to his disciples, their freedom of action did not involve a right to manipulate or to coerce other persons. In fact, Jesus never acted in this way himself. He did not compel, but he invited his hearers to believe him and to obey.

When Jesus taught his disciples about how authority would be experienced in the church, he specifically ruled out the kind of power-based authority that is exercised in the secular world for personal gain or glory. Jesus gives Christian leaders authority to build up believers, not to enslave or smother them. Built up in the faith, Christians will freely choose to be obedient to Jesus as living Lord.

Not all of our questions about how authority functions in the world or in the Christian community are answered in passages where *exousia* is found. But it does seem clear that granting true freedom of choice and action to every believer is of great significance to the Lord (e.g., Jn 8:32,36; Gal 5:1,13).

AVENGE ♦ Vengeance/Revenge

AVENGER OF BLOOD

OT law established no central or local police forces. Responsibility for keeping and enforcing the law was distributed through the whole community. In the case of murder, defined as intentionally or with hostility causing another person's death, the responsibility of dealing with the wrong was usually given to a member of the family of the one slain. The goal of the avenger of blood was not to take revenge. It was rather to impose the penalty that God's law decreed, so that the community as a whole would not become guilty of complicity in murder (Nu 35; Dt 19; Jos 20). ♦ Murder/Kill

AVOID

OT occurrences of "avoid" reflect terms meaning "to let alone" or "turn aside." NT occurrences are appropriate to the thrust of the original words in each context. To avoid something means one must prevent contacting or being contacted by it.

AWAKE

Typically, one of two Hebrew words is found where English versions have "awake." *Qûṣ* appears only in a stem indicating "cause to awake." Three of the OT's few references to resurrection use this word (Job 14:12; Ps 17:15; Da 12:2).

The other word is *'ûr* ("to arouse," to "waken," or "to incite"). It occurs seventy-six times in the OT, often in Psalms as a cry of appeal to God, urging him to act at times when he appears unresponsive to the plight of his people (e.g., Ps 7:6; 35:23; 44:23). The call or warning to a people to awaken is often an idiomatic expression calling for spiritual renewal and responsiveness to God.

AWARD ♦ Reward

AWE/AWESOME

There is no instance in the OT or NT where "stand in awe" could not accurately be translated "be afraid" or where "awesome" could not be translated "fearsome."

Several Hebrew words are translated by the NIV and NASB as "awe." Malachi calls on the priests to stand in awe (*gûr*, "be in terror") and to demonstrate reverence by teaching and by living God's truth (Mal 2:5–6). Isaiah tells of a coming day when the ruthless and those with an eye for evil will be cut off. This will be recognized as the work of God. Then God's people will acknowledge his holiness and "will stand in awe [*'āraṣ*, "terror"] of the God of Israel" (Isa 29:23). The psalmist remains unmoved by the rulers who persecute him without cause, for his heart remains in awe (*pāḥad*, "fear") of God's Word (Ps 119:161).

In most cases, the word translated "awesome" in the NIV and NASB is *yārē'*. It too means "to be afraid," "to fear," or "to revere." In most contexts this widely used word is translated "fear." ♦ Fear Often fear of God, as awed awareness of who he is, is intimately linked with godly living (Lev 19:14; 25:17; Dt 17:19; 2 Ki 17:34).

In the NT the word translated "awe" in the NIV is usually *phobos*, "fear." *Deos*, which also means "fear or awe," is found only in Heb 12:28.

The awe felt by God's people is an appropriate response to who God is. But awe does not drive us from God. We know that this majestic one whose being and glory are immense and awe-inspiring has chosen to love us and to invite us into the most intimate of relationships with him. Somehow we need to keep in balance our sense of the tender love of God unveiled in Jesus, and the blinding, overpowering holiness and power that are God's by his very nature.

B

BAAL

This Hebrew word denotes owner, master, lord, or husband. In the English versions, "Baal" designates a Canaanite deity. Israel displaced the Canaanites when they conquered the Promised Land (c. 1450 B.C.).

Baal is sometimes found linked with a place name, such as Baal-Peor ("the Baal of Peor"). Usually the OT title refers to the most powerful god of the Canaanites, who was thought to control rains and fertility.

There is a strong sexual and sensual note found in the worship of such nature gods, often including prostitution as a part of the religious ritual (Jdg 2:17; Jer 7:9; Am 2:7). The immorality associated with the worship of the Baals permeated Canaanite society and is one of the reasons for God's commands to Israel to destroy the Canaanite people completely (Ge 15:16; Jos 23:6–13; Jdg 1:27–2:3). Israel failed to comply, and the pagan practices with their appeal to sensual appetites corrupted the faith and the life of God's OT people. Only after two major reforms (2 Ki 18:4–6; 23:4–15) and the purging experience of national exile from Palestine did most of Israel reject most aspects of Baal worship.

BABYLON

The Bible knows Babylon both as an ancient city and as a symbol. Ancient Babylon's ruins lie some fifty miles south of modern Baghdad. In Nebuchadnezzar's day it was the capital of a great world empire; it shattered Judah and carried the Jewish people captive. Babylon was thus a place of exile for God's people, but it also pictures monolithic human government that stands in opposition to God's kingdom.

The historic role of Babylon as a place of exile was probably in Peter's mind in 1 Pe 5:13, for he wrote to a people who were also dispersed throughout the Roman Empire (cf. 1 Pe 1:1).

But Babylon is spoken of in Revelation in a clearly symbolic way (cf. 17:5,7). Descriptions of Babylon found in Rev 14, 17–19 introduce us to a center of world power that will be existing at history's end. Then, as in Nebuchadnezzar's day, centralized power (cf. 14:8; 17:1,15–18) will have produced great material prosperity (18:3,11–19). But the final Babylon will be morally corrupt and an enemy of God's people. It will suffer sudden, complete destruction.

Historical and symbolic Babylon are linked by several common themes. Both represent consolidated human governmental power. Both are hostile to the kingdom of God. Both produce material prosperity but moral decline. And both suffer God's judgment of destruction.

BACKSLIDING

In popular theology the term "backsliding" is often given a prominent place. Depending on one's theological tradition, it may be used to describe a person's return to questionable habits, to a loss of the sense of God's presence, or even to the "down" times that seem to be part of so many believers' emotional experiences. But popular theology does not always reflect biblical meanings. In the Bible's use of "backsliding" there is an important, but different, message.

1. The Hebrew words
2. The nature of backsliding
3. Summary

1. The Hebrew words. "Backsliding" seldom occurs in modern English translations (6 times, NIV; 2 times, NASB), and only in the OT. Yet the root terms express an important biblical idea.

Three forms from the same root communicate the idea of backsliding. Two of them, *šôbāb* (4 times in the OT—Isa 57:17; Jer 3:14,22; 50:6) and *šôbēb* (2 times in the OT—Jer 31:22; 49:4), mean "backsliding" or "apostasy." The most commonly used word, *mᵉšûbâh*, occurs twelve times in the OT (Pr 1:32; Jer 2:19; 3:6,8,11,12,22; 5:6; 8:5; 14:7; Hos 11:7; 14:4). It means "backsliding," "disloyalty," or "faithlessness."

2. The nature of backsliding. A study of the use of these words makes it clear that this is one of the many OT words intimately linked with the belief that God has established a covenantal relationship between himself and Israel. Backsliding is disloyalty by the OT community to the covenant relationship and involves a refusal to live by the terms of the covenant.

The focus in references to backsliding is on the central element of the covenant: the commitment of God's people to him personally. Texts that refer to backsliding repeatedly describe a faithless community that has rebelled against the Lord and has "scattered [its] favors to foreign gods" (Jer 3:13).

Backsliding also involved rejection of the social and moral requirements of the covenant. Jeremiah shows this as he condemned the leaders who had consciously rejected "the way of the LORD, the requirements of their God" (Jer 5:5).

It is important to note that each OT cry against backsliding portrays the state of the OT community, not of individuals (except Pr 1:32). Each description of the backslidden people implies their willful choice to turn away from the God of the covenant to other gods and therefore to other moralities.

3. Summary. In the Bible "backsliding" is a word used to describe the corporate condition of God's OT people during periods of apostasy. The backslidden community had sinned by choosing to worship other gods, and a moral decay marked the backslidden society. This particular concept is never carried into the NT: "backsliding" is not found there as a description of the experience either of an individual Christian or of a particular congregation.

However, any who feel a sense of alienation from the Lord can find release in the prescription Jeremiah shares with God's OT people: " 'Return, faithless Israel,' declares the LORD, 'I will frown on you no longer, for I am merciful,' declares the LORD, 'I will not be angry forever. Only acknowledge your guilt' " (Jer 3:12–13). In confession and trust in the mercy of God we, like Israel, can find restoration and peace.

BALAAM

Balaam is a historical character whose story is told in Nu 22–25. A noted seer with reputed religious powers, Balaam was summoned by the king of Moab to curse the people of Israel at the time of the conquest of Palestine. God would not permit Balaam to curse Israel but instead used him to announce intended blessings.

Balaam is referred to three times in the NT. Each time what he did is strongly condemned—his "way" (2 Pe 2:15), his "error" (Jude 11), and his "teaching" (Rev 2:14).

A comparison of the NT texts and the OT story helps us to determine the nature of each of these strongly condemned practices.

The "way of Balaam" is the way taken by the false teachers against whom Peter warns, those who see religion as a way to seek and gain wealth.

The "error of Balaam" is also characteristic of false teachers. Jude sees them as individuals who, like Balaam, are so dominated by greed that obedience to God is viewed as irrelevant.

The "error of Balaam" is suggested in Nu 25. Unable to curse God's people, the pagan seer apparently counseled the king of Moab to entice Israel into immorality, hoping God would be forced to punish his sinning people. The error of Balaam involves the sanctioning of immorality by religion, for whatever reason (see Rev 2:14).

BALM

A number of plants have been suggested as possible source of balm (ṣºrî), valued in biblical days for its medicinal value when compounded as an ointment.

BANISH

This is another word found only in the OT. It is intimately linked with God's special covenant relationship with his OT people. "Banish" is used more extensively in the NIV than in the NASB. But in each version it is normally a translation of the Hebrew nādaḥ or a synonym. Nādaḥ is a powerful term. It means to forcefully drive or push something away.

Most often it is God's people who are banished, and banishment is a terrible and clear punishment for sin (e.g., Jer 8:3; 27:10,15). But what is most striking is that nādaḥ usually occurs in the context of a promise rather than a threat. After the punishment God will restore banished Israel from the lands where he has driven and scattered them (Dt 30:4; Jer 16:15; 23:8; 29:14; 32:37).

God was never indecisive in dealing with Israel when they sinned. But in his judgment he always remembered—and emphasized—his mercy.

BANNER/STANDARD

Two Hebrew words are translated "banner" and "standard" in the English versions of the OT. Neither the NIV nor the NASB is consistent in translating these words even though they have different meanings.

Degel occurs primarily in Numbers (13 of the 14 times it appears in the OT) and is translated "standard" there by both the NASB and the NIV. The degel was an upraised symbol that seems to have functioned like a flag identifying a military batallion. It was used to identify each of the tribes of Israel.

The well-known phrase in Song of Songs proclaiming "his banner over me is love" (SS 2:4) uses this Hebrew word. The banner proudly upraised by the shepherd in Solomon's poem announces to all that love binds the happy couple.

Nēs is the more significant of the words translated "banner" or "standard." It is especially significant in the later prophets, where the NIV retains "banner" and the NASB turns to "standard." The nēs was an upraised standard used as a rallying point. It called the whole people together to hear some vital message or to assemble for some important action.

The earliest occurrence, in Ex 17:15, announces that the Lord himself is the rallying point for his people.

The nēs is also important prophetically. The later prophets are dreadfully aware that God will discipline his people through exile from the Promised Land. Yet they also know that one day God will raise the standard and call for war against the oppressors (Jer 51:27). But the standard raised is also a symbol of God's recall of Israel to the Promised Land and to renewed fellowship with the Lord. "I will lift up my banner to the peoples," God promises as Sovereign Lord; "they will bring your sons in their arms and carry your daughters on their shoulders" (Isa 49:22; cf. 62:10–12).

Perhaps the most beautiful use of this symbolism is in Isaiah. The prophet takes the Exodus statement that the Lord is himself Israel's nēs and extends the symbol through the Messiah to all people. Isaiah promises, "In that day the Root of Jesse [Jesus, the descendant of Jesse, King David's father] will stand as a banner for the peoples; the nations will rally to him, and his place of rest will be glorious" (Isa 11:10; cf. vv. 11–16).

As we rally to Jesus in faith to hear and respond to the divine message of grace, we find God's own promised place of rest.

BANQUET

The OT banquet is usually a *mišteh*, which means "drink," "banquet," or "feast." In the early OT we meet the *mišteh* as a special meal prepared for honored guests or joyful celebrations (e.g., Ge 19:3; Jdg 14:10–17). As the word implies, drinking had a place in the joyous feasting known in OT times, though the wine of that era was only some eleven percent alcohol. In SS 2:4 the word translated "banquet" is actually the word for wine. ◆ **Wine**

In the NT, one Greek word is translated "banquet" by the NASB, and two by the NIV. *Deipnon* is usually translated "supper" and is a theologically important term. Both the NIV and NASB translate *deipnon* as "banquet" in Mt 23:6; Mk 6:21; 12:39; Lk 20:46.

The NIV also translates *gamos* as "banquet." The word means "wedding" and is often extended to include the celebration associated with the Jewish wedding. The NASB has "wedding feast" where the NIV has "wedding banquet."

The word is found primarily in a story told by Jesus and reported in Mt 22 and Lk 14. It is the story of a king whose invitation to a wedding banquet was refused by his chosen guests. But the celebration would still be held. When those chosen refused to come, servants were sent out with the command, "Invite to the banquet anyone you find" (Mt 22:9). How good it is to be among the "any" who have responded to God's invitation and will share the endless celebration held for his Son!

BAPTISM

Church history reports many disputes about baptism. There have been arguments about the way a person should be baptized. There have been debates over whether baptism is also for infants or only for adults who are able to make a conscious choice to follow Jesus. Baptism has been viewed by some as a sacrament and by others as an ordinance. Some have even argued that water baptism is essential to salvation.

Typically the positions taken in different traditions have been derived by inference from the Bible. But it is difficult to say that one position or another is definitely *taught by* Scripture. Each involves reasoning from the biblical texts, and in the process of deduction and induction fallible human beings do make errors. For that reason it is important for us to observe just what the Bible says about baptism and how the word is used in the NT. An understanding of the biblical usage of this significant term will help us to evaluate the arguments of theologians and the emphases found in various Christian traditions.

1. **Baptism in Greek and Jewish religions**
2. **The NT word and its meaning**
3. **The biblical uses of "baptize"**
4. **John's baptism**
5. **The baptism of Jesus**
6. **Water baptism in the church**
7. **Baptism by the Spirit**
8. **Baptism as union with Jesus**
9. **Difficult passages on baptism**
10. **Summary**

1. Baptism in Greek and Jewish religions. Both Greek and Jewish religions at the time of Jesus knew the use of ritual washings for purification. However, different Greek words were used in each tradition to describe these washings.

Some have linked Christian baptism to a Jewish practice that was followed when a man converted to Judaism. The individual was circumcised and then took a ritual bath. However, this practice is directly linked with OT commands about washing for purification. In neither the Greek religions nor Jewish practice was there a parallel to Christian baptism, nor was the term "baptism" used to describe ritual washings.

Baptism more or less as we know it today was first instituted by John the Baptist. It was a religious innovation, intended to communicate a content and concept present neither in the faiths of the Hellenistic world nor in Judaism.

2. The NT word and its meaning. Two Greek verbs that are closely related are linked with baptism. *Baptō* is the basic verb. It means "to dip in" or "to dip under." It is often used of dipping fabric in a dye. *Baptizō* is an intensive form of *baptō*. From early times it was used in the sense of immersing.

As noted above, other Greek words were commonly used of the religious washings in pagan and Jewish religions. ▶ **Wash/Bathe** In the NT, *baptō* is used only in its literal sense of dipping (Lk 16:24; Jn 13:26; Rev 19:13). *Baptizō* is the Greek word translated "baptize" and is always used in a special religious sense. It is used infrequently of the ritual washings of the Pharisees (Mk 7:4; Lk 11:38) but is primarily a word coined to be used in a technical and theological sense. As such, *baptizō* communicates aspects of God's working through the Christian gospel. "Baptism" is a special term infused with new meaning in the language of faith. It carries much more depth of meaning than with any meanings it may have had in the religions of the NT world.

3. The biblical use of "baptize". It is likely that the average person who reads the word "baptize" in the Bible is likely to suppose it refers to water baptism. But not every occurrence of this term is linked with water baptism. The Bible speaks of a baptism by the Holy Spirit and a baptism into Christ. When reading the Bible, we must be careful that we understand the way the passage we read uses this special theological term.

The different uses of "baptism" in Scripture are considered in the next five items in this article: the special baptism of repentance offered by John, the baptism of Jesus, water baptism, baptism by the Spirit, and baptism as union with Jesus.

4. John's baptism. All of the Gospels contain a report of the ministry of that stern prophet known as John the Baptist (Mt 3; Mk 1; Lk 3; Jn 1). His name was derived not from his message but from a striking new practice he instituted: John baptized in the waters of the river Jordan those who responded to his preaching by believing his message.

The message John preached helps to establish the meaning given to his baptism. John called for the people of Israel to repent and to turn to God wholeheartedly as a preparation for the coming of the Messiah, whose day was rapidly approaching. Those who accepted John's message were called on to acknowledge their commitment publicly. As John preached repentance, those who went into the waters to be baptized acknowledged their sins and made a commitment to live righteously. Ever blunt, the stern John warned them to "produce fruit in keeping with repentance" (Lk 3:8). The ritual itself had no merit. It must be the changed lives of the baptized that testified to the inner sincerity of their hearts.

John's baptism, then, seems to have involved three significant factors: (1) public identification with his message, (2) a public commitment to live by God's well-known standards of righteousness, and (3) a public expression of eagerness to welcome the Messiah (who, according to John's preaching, was near).

John's call to repentance and readiness was carried to the Jewish communities scattered throughout the Roman Empire. Years later the early missionaries would meet Jewish believers who had heard and responded to John's warning and had identified themselves with his message by accepting "John's baptism" (cf. Ac 10:37; 18:25; 19:3-4). Invariably, when they heard about Jesus as the one of whom John had spoken, these disciples of John responded to the gospel by believing in Jesus as the Messiah.

John's baptism is not the same in nature or intent as Christian baptism. But the new practice John introduced was picked up by the early church and given new significance—to reflect a reality that goes far beyond the meaning that John gave to baptism.

5. The baptism of Jesus. The meaning of John's baptism of Jesus at the beginning of Christ's public ministry has troubled some. Why should a sinless person accept a baptism of repentance?

The answer is suggested in Matthew's report of the dialogue between Jesus and the Baptizer. John, knowing the blameless character of his cousin (Lk 1:36) but not yet realizing that he was the Messiah, objected to baptizing him. But Jesus answered, "It is proper for us to do this to fulfill all righteousness" (Mt 3:15).

John's baptism was not itself equivalent to repentance. But the person who was baptized identified himself publicly with the total message of the prophet. Jesus found it fitting to be baptized, for he would thus identify himself with the call to righteousness issued by John and thus also would take a public stand with that austere preacher and his warnings.

6. Water baptism in the church. John's baptism has been spoken of a number of times in the Gospels and in Acts. Acts and the Epistles make it clear that the early church also practiced water baptism. This practice is spoken of in a number of NT passages (Ac 2:38,41; 8:12,13,16,36,38; 9:18; 10:47,48; 16:15,33; 18:8; 19:5; 1 Co 1:14–17; 15:29; Heb 6:2).

Yet each of these passages is simply a report of what the early church practiced. None of the passages attempts to define what water baptism meant to the early Christian community. We do know from these passages and from the writings of the church fathers that when a person received Christ as Savior and joined the community of faith, he or she was baptized. We can conclude that water baptism, like the Lord's Supper, was practiced and is to be practiced in the church. But we cannot conclude from these passages just what water baptism was intended to convey.

Certainly the early church did not see water baptism as necessary for salvation, for Paul himself expressed relief that in his mission to Corinth he himself "did not baptize any . . . except Crispus and Gaius" (1 Cor 1:14).

While Scripture is silent on the exact meaning of water baptism as practiced in the church, it speaks very clearly about supernatural works of God in the life of the believer, works that are also called baptism. It seems best to understand the meaning of the practice of water baptism by studying the meaning of the theological baptisms revealed in Scripture.

7. Baptism by the Spirit. When John came preaching and baptizing with water, critics asked him if he claimed to be the Messiah. John answered that he was not. Each time John announced that there was a person living even then in the land of Palestine who, he said, "is more powerful than I." That person would appear and baptize, not with water "but with the Holy Spirit" (Mt 3:11; Mk 1:8; Lk 3:16).

The Book of Acts describes the fulfillment of that promise. The baptism took place at the coming of the Spirit on Jesus' followers as reported in Ac 2 (cf. Ac 2:1–4 with 10:45–47 and 11:15–17). Acts describes a number of phenomena that took place at that time. The Spirit came. The Spirit filled the believers. There was an outward sign of fiery tongues and a rushing wind. The Spirit empowered the believers to speak in languages other than their own. But again, this is description, not definition. This was the time when Jesus' baptism with the Spirit took place. But the description does not tell us what that baptism is nor whether it is relevant to Christian experience today.

In the Epistles, however, we do find a definition of baptism by the Spirit. The definition is given in 1 Co 12:13, and the context makes it clear that the Spirit's baptism was neither the historic incident itself nor any of the associated phenomena. Writing of the body of Christ, a living organism into which Christians are formed, Paul says that "we were all baptized by one Spirit into one body — whether Jews or Greeks, slave or free — and we were all given the one Spirit to drink." The baptism of the Spirit began at Pentecost but is a continuing work of the Holy Spirit. Each individual who believes in Jesus experiences the baptism, for it is that work of the Holy Spirit by which he joins us to Jesus and to one another as members of a spiritual body.

This theological definition helps us see how appropriate the term "baptism" is: we are immersed in the Holy Spirit, and in Jesus himself by the Spirit.

8. Baptism as union with Jesus. The baptizing work of the Spirit that unites us as one body also unites us to Jesus, the head of the body. This aspect of baptism, union with Jesus himself, is picked up in several NT passages. The most notable is Ro 6:3–8, where Paul writes: "Don't you know that all of us who were baptized into Christ Jesus were baptized into his death? We were therefore buried with him through baptism into death in order that, just as Christ was raised from the dead through the glory of the Father, we too may live a new life. If we have been united with him in his death, we will certainly also be united with him in his resurrection. . . . Now if we died with Christ, we believe that we will also live with him."

Paul is not writing here of the rite of baptism; rather, he is dealing with what happens within the person who trusts Jesus. God acts and so unites the believer to Jesus that Christ's death and resurrection become his. Freed from bondage to the old life, believers are given power by Jesus to live a new kind of life.

Other NT passages also refer to baptism in this theological sense as real union with Jesus. Eph 4:5 speaks of the "one baptism" that, with the Spirit's other work, enables us to live in unity with other Christians. Col 2:12 picks up the language of Ro 6 and describes the believer as "having been buried with him in baptism and raised with him through . . . faith in the power of God, who raised him from the dead." Gal 3:27 announces, "All of you who were baptized into Christ have been clothed with Christ."

Each of these passages is best understood as speaking not of the rite of water baptism but of a work performed by God, uniting us with Jesus so completely that his death and resurrection become our own.

It may well be that the great theological reality of union with Jesus in death and resurrection are intended to be affirmed by the water baptism practiced by the church. But as in the case of John's baptism, it is clear that the efficacy of Christian baptism does not lie in the ceremony but in an inner work of God within the heart of the person.

9. Difficult passages on baptism. A number of NT passages have been misinterpreted or have raised questions about baptism.

Mk 10:38–39. Jesus asked a pair of eager disciples if they were able to drink the cup intended for him or to be baptized with the baptism he was baptized with. Jesus was speaking of his coming death and of his immersion in that experience of total suffering.

Mt 3:11. This and parallel passages that speak of Jesus' baptizing with the Holy Spirit add "and with fire," an expression generally taken to refer to the final judgment reserved for those who will not believe.

Mk 16:16. This verse is sometimes taken to teach that baptism is required for salvation. The two clauses of the verse make it clear that belief alone is the issue on which salvation hinges.

Ac 22:16. Instead of teaching that baptism washes away sins, as some have taken the verse to say, the truth here is simply that it is calling on the Lord that effects the cleansing.

1 Co 15:29. Paul is here referring to the practice of the living being baptized for those who have died. He does not mention the practice to give apostolic approval of it. Instead, he mentions it in the context of an argument for the truth and importance of the doctrine of the resurrection. In a church in which some doubt the reality of resurrection, it is foolish for others to have initiated a practice of being baptized for the dead. If there is no resurrection, why would they introduce this strange practice?

1 Co 10:2. This verse refers to the Exodus generation, who traveled under God's cloudy pillar and—when God opened a way—passed through the sea, as having been "baptized into Moses." The expression indicates that they were immersed with Moses in a relationship marked by sharing common experiences of God's supernatural activity.

1 Pe 3:21. Many have understood this verse to teach that the ceremony of water baptism saves. The passage speaks of the Genesis flood and the ark that Noah built, in which "a few people, eight in all, were saved through water, and this water symbolizes baptism that now saves you also—not the removal of dirt from the body but the pledge of a good conscience toward God. It saves you by the resurrection of Jesus."

To understand this statement we need to note that in the OT story, the waters of the Flood were the agency of judgment, not the agency of deliverance. The eight people in the ark were carried through the waters safely, to be deposited in a new world, purified by the judgment. In context Peter says that our salvation is wrought by Jesus' resurrection, a resurrection that we who are united with him share. The waters of the Genesis flood symbolize what happens when we are baptized by the Spirit into Jesus. We are carried by Jesus through God's devastating judgment on sin and are deposited in virtue of his resurrection in a fresh, new spiritual universe in which we are expected to live according to the will of God (1 Pe 4:2).

10. Summary. Water baptism has been practiced by the church since its beginning. But water baptism has not always been understood by believers. Many notions about baptism are not supported by the teaching of the Bible. If we are to reach adequate conclusions about baptism, we need to recognize the following basic facts: Christian baptism has no parallel in the OT. The "baptism of John" described in the Gospels and Acts is distinct from Christian baptism. The NT uses the term "baptism" to speak of great spiritual realities as well as the rite of water baptism. The spiritual realities communicated by the word "baptism" concern our true union with Jesus in his death and resurrection and our present union in vital organic relationship with all believers in the living body of Christ.

The basic truth of our union with all believers and with Jesus is so vital that it places our differences with others about the practice of baptism in distinct perspective. We are one in and through our relationship with Jesus. We may disagree about details. But our disagreements do not destroy the reality of a spiritual unity that makes us truly one.

BAR/CROSSBAR

The Hebrew word usually is *bᵉrîah*, meaning "something that is thrust through." In most OT cases it is used literally, as of the crossbars holding the tabernacle framework together or of the crossbars used to lock and strengthen city gates. By implication, a barred city is a strong, well-defended community, but a city whose bars are broken is defenseless.

BARE ◆ *Nakedness*

BARREN

OT people considered childlessness a terrible curse. Thus it was very significant to Israel that God promised generations that were obedient to his law: "None will miscarry or be barren in your land" (Ex 23:33) and "none of your men or women will be childless, nor any of your livestock without young" (Dt 7:14).

Later God's disobedient people found life itself to be barren. But even at times of greatest despair the prophets promised the barren a song and a shout of joy, for God would surely restore those who had been rejected (Isa 54:1–8).

BARRIER

Eph 2:14 speaks of a barrier, a "dividing wall of hostility" between Jew and Gentile. The word is *phragmos*, which means "a fence" or "a wall." In Eph 2 the hostility is caused by the law, not law as a moral code but law as the total OT system that made a sharp distinction between the Jewish people and the rest of mankind. As the context states, the rest of humanity were "excluded from citizenship in Israel and foreigners to the covenants of promise, without hope and without God in the world" (2:12). Israel's privileged position created hostility—on both sides.

But the death of Jesus destroyed the barrier. Now, through the blood of Christ, Jew and Gentile both have access to God. And even more, the old barrier of privilege was completely removed, as both are brought by the Spirit into unique relationship with Jesus as members of his one body.

Through Jesus, every possible barrier that separates groups and classes are made meaningless. Through Jesus every person has access to God and becomes part of that single living organism that is the body of Christ.

BASED ON

Both the NIV and NASB use "based on" in theologically significant passages. But each version uses this phrase in completely different passages (NIV, Ro 2:2; 10:2; Gal 3:12; Col 2: 22; NASB, Ro 10:5–6; Gal 3:18,21). Why the difference between the versions?

The Greek NT does not use a particular word corresponding to our "based on." Instead it expresses shades of the idea by the use of prepositions. The NIV translators chose to translate one preposition "based on," whereas the NASB translators chose the other preposition to be so translated.

In three passages the preposition is *kata* (Ro 2:2; 10:2; Col 2:22). As used in these passages *kata* identifies a norm or standard "according to" which something conforms. Ro 2:2 thus says that God's judgment on those who judge others will be according to (based on) truth. ♦ *Truth* Ro 10:2 commends the zeal of Paul's fellow Israelites but warns that their eager pursuit of God is not in accord with (based on) knowledge. Col 2:22 dismisses an ascetic approach to spirituality practiced by some in Colosse, pointing out that the norm used to measure spiritual achievement was never established by God but was established by mere "human commands and teaching."

The other preposition is *ek*, "from." In these contexts *ek* indicates the origin or source from which something flows.

In Ro 10:5–6, Paul notes that a righteousness that claims law as its source will always fall short. Galatians picks up the theme. Law fails because it does not have its own origin in faith (Gal 3:12). The inheritance of God's blessing can come from no other origin than his promise, and the promise can be appropriated only by faith (Gal 3:18,21).

The message of these verses is clear. Our relationship with God or our approach to him can never be in accordance with human norms and standards. We must come to God in the way he established. And his way does not involve finding righteousness by a struggle to conform to the divine law. His way is to simply appropriate the promise of our Lord by faith.

BASIS

Where "basis" is found in English translations of the NT it is either supplied as an equivalent of the Greek expression (as in the NIV Gospel usages) or it is the rendering of one of a number of Greek prepositions. ♦ *Based On*

Epi is translated "basis" four times (Ac 3:16; Php 3:9; 1 Ti 5:19; Heb 7:11). In these cases the preposition means "on the basis of" or "in accord with."

Ek is translated "basis" twice (Ro 11:6; Tit 3:5). This usage indicates the origin or source from which something flows.

Kata is translated "basis" once (Heb 7:16). This word directs our attention to a norm or standard that something accords with.

BATCH

The Greek word is *phyrama*, which means "batch" or "lump" (NASB). It is used in Ro 9:21 of a lump of clay and in other passages of a batch of bread dough. In each of the "batch" passages an OT practice is used to illustrate some NT principle.

Ro 11:16 returns to the OT for an image to support Paul's argument. In Ro 11,

Paul insists that one day Israel as a people will turn again to God, and the ancient promises of all the prophets will be kept. The fact that even now many Jewish people are turning to Jesus (11:1–5) shows that there will one day be a national recovery (11:11–24). In the context of this argument, Paul refers to Nu 15:18, which directed that a portion of ground meal from the firstfruits of every harvest be offered to God. The offering sanctified not only what was presented but the whole harvest. So Paul says those now being saved are like a firstfruits offering: they testify to the fact that the whole harvest to follow will be holy.

In two other passages (1 Co 5:6,7; Gal 5:9), Paul discusses another OT practice. Each year as Passover approached, every Israelite family carefully searched the house to find and remove every bit of leaven. The Passover must be celebrated with unleavened bread, and no leaven could be left in the home to slip into and spoil the bread being prepared for the feast.

Paul sees the Passover, the ancient feast celebrating God's deliverance of his people from death in Egypt (Ex 12), as a picture of the redemption we experience. We believers are also delivered from death. And, like that ancient generation, we too set out on a journey to God's Promised Land.

Paul calls on us in Corinthians and Galatians to be just as careful as the Israelites were about leaven to see that no sin slip into our fellowships. Evil, like leaven, is an active agent that quickly permeates a community. As God's redeemed people, we are to live holy lives, in which there is no place at all for sin.

BATHE ♦ *Wash/Bathe*

BATTLE ♦ *War*

BEAR/BEARING

Every language has words that carry multiple meanings. In English "bear" is one of those words. It is not surprising, then, that a number of Hebrew and Greek words are reflected in the passages where we find "bear" and "bearing."

OT 1. **"Bear" and "bearing" in the OT**
NT 2. **Bearing fruit**
    3. **Bearing with one another**

OT — 1. "Bear" and "bearing" in the OT. Glancing through the NIV or the NASB shows how wide a range of meanings there are for "bear" and "bearing." We read of bearing fruit (Ge 1:11) and of the crushing emotional pain that makes a person feel he is unable to bear his problems (Dt 1:12) or punishment (Ge 4:13). We read of bearing a child (Ge 17:17). The OT speaks often of bearing guilt (Ge 43:9; Isa 53:11) and of the related bearing of consequences (Nu 5:31), disgrace (Eze 16:52), and shame (Eze 32:24). We read of bearing a grudge (Lev 19:18), bearing in mind (Ex 16:29), and bearing arms (1 Ki 3:21), as well as bearing up (Ps 30:21) and bearing with (Ne 9:30).

All of these are common English expressions. All accurately pick up and reflect the meanings of the dozen or so different Hebrew words found in the original text.

NT — 2. Bearing fruit. Also in the NT, "bear" and "bearing" translate several Greek terms, most of which have the same flexibility of meaning we find in the English words.

Although the Greek words may not in themselves be especially significant, they become significant when they present a common image that is repeated in a number of NT passages. One of the repeated images of the NT is that of bearing fruit.

Mt 7:15–20 and Lk 6:43–45 report Jesus' words about goodness. The good person will be recognized by his words and actions, just as the good tree is recognized by the good fruit it produces. But producing fruit is a supernatural enterprise.

John 15:1–8 pictures believers as branches, in intimate union with Christ. It is he, the vine, who is the source of the life that enables us to bear fruit. Our fruitfulness depends on remaining in close, intimate relationship with the Lord. The passage makes it clear that the intimate relationship we need is maintained as we respond obediently to Jesus' words.

Ro 7:4 also presents union with Jesus as essential to fruitfulness. The Spirit of God energizes the new life Christ provides, enabling us to bear fruit for God (cf. 7:6 and Gal 5:22). Col 1:10 also links fruitfulness to relationship with God—a relationship that grows as we relate his words to life and put them into daily practice (cf. Col 1:9–10).

The NT, then, views goodness as a visible fruit growing out of a person's inner character. But for a person to be able to produce good fruit calls for a personal relationship with Jesus. Jesus Christ is the source of true goodness, and the source of good fruit in our lives. The specific relationship that issues in good fruit is clearly defined: it is a trusting relationship expressed as responsive daily obedience to God's guiding Word.

3. Bearing with one another. The NT speaks several times of believers bearing with one another. Three times the Greek word is *bastazō*, which means "to take up and carry." In the fellowship of the church we are willing to work for the good of others, even when this means we are burdened with the failings of our weaker brothers and sisters (Ro 15:1). We will also be willing to help carry the unusually heavy burdens (*baros*) that others may have at times, while accepting responsibility to bear our own normal burdens (*phortion*, the pack a soldier is expected to carry) (Gal 6:2,5).

The other word translated "bear with" or "bearing with" is *anechomai*, which means "to tolerate or put up with." Not every believer is as yet made beautiful by Jesus' touch: the process of transformation may be slow. Thus we are called on to "be patient, bearing with one another in love" (Eph 4:2) and are exhorted, "Bear with each other and forgive whatever grievances you may have against one another. Forgive as the Lord forgave you" (Col 3:13).

It is helpful to remember that while our brothers and sisters may be flawed, you and I are flawed as well. The gracious, loving way with which God puts up with our faults is the model for the way we are to treat others.

BEASTS ♦ Animals

BEAT/BEATING

A number of Hebrew words are translated "beat" or "beating" in the NIV and the NASB of the OT. The range of meanings of these synonyms is broad: to pound on (or beat), to attack, to crush, to batter, to pulverize. The NT uses fewer different Greek words but shows a similar flexibility.

It is interesting to note the context in Isaiah of the often-quoted saying about beating swords into plowshares (Isa 2:4; cf. Mic 4:3). International peace will come "in the last days" (2:2), when the nations stream to the mountain of the Lord, eager for God to "teach us his ways, so that we may walk in his paths" (2:3). But that great day will not come until after a final battle in which the nations, prepared for war, have beaten their plowshares into swords (Joel 3:10). The appearance of these sayings in unmistakably prophetic contexts means they give little guidance for international affairs today. ♦ War

One use of "beat" in the NT merits comment. In 1 Co 9:27, Paul speaks of beating his body and making it his slave. Is he encouraging some kind of ascetic self-denial? Paul here alludes to athletic training, in which the athlete, eager to excel, rigorously disciplines himself, punishing his body in training so it will be toned for the race. Christians are not to reject the material or deny their physical needs but are to use every asset to reach their goal of serving and pleasing Jesus.

BEAUTY/BEAUTIFUL

The OT has a rich and extensive vocabulary of beauty. God, who planned Eden with beauty in mind (Ge 2:9), has given human beings his own capacity to appreciate what is aesthetically pleasing. But beauty has its problems as well as its blessings. Externals can distract us from a deeper, inner beauty that is the most desirable of all.

OT 1. The OT concept of beauty
      2. The beautiful woman
      3. The beauty of the Lord
NT 4. The NT concept of beauty
      5. The beautiful person

OT — 1. The OT concept of beauty. The concept of beauty is likely to be complex and wide-ranging in any culture. It certainly is so in the Hebrew. In one of its aspects, beauty is *ṭôḇ*, "good, pleasant." The word itself implies that which is useful and pleasant. In many uses, *ṭôḇ* has a moral component as well. In aesthetic or sensual contexts, the word connotes something desirable. Thus in one sense, a beautiful thing creates desire in the beholder.

Yāpeh denotes the quality of beauty that has to do with outward appearance. It is probably best understood as "good looking." Persons, cattle, trees, and a piece of land can all be described by OT writers as good looking—as are the redeemed of the Lord (Zec 9:17).

But beauty involves more than appearance. The quality of one's beauty may extend to character and to relationships and can be expressed as kindness or pleasantness. The word that captures this aspect of beauty is *nō'am*. It is used of good words (Pr 15:26; 16:24) and to describe the Lord (Ps 27:4; 90:17).

But also whatever is splendid and glorious can be described as beautiful. *Sᵉḇî* is the word that expresses this beauty; it is often translated "glory" in the NASB and RSV. This is a particularly mystical beauty. The kind of beauty that human beings try to generate must fail (Isa 23:9), for human efforts produce only a fading flower (Isa 28:1–4). It is the Lord himself who glows with true beauty, and his people find their beauty in the reflection of his splendor (Isa 4:2; 28:5).

In all of the OT's portrait of beauty there is another common theme: that which is beautiful is pleasing (*šeper*, Ge 49:21 being its one OT occurrence). God has implanted in you and in me the capacity to recognize and respond to the beautiful and to derive pleasure from it. The beautiful and our enjoyment of it are among his good gifts to humankind.

2. The beautiful woman. Two Hebrew words are typically used to describe the beautiful woman and the handsome man, but they are most often used of women.

Yāpeh is the word most often chosen. This rather mild term describes a person's appearance and indicates that he or she is good looking. Sarah and Rachel in Genesis are called good looking, as is Joseph (Ge 12:11,14; 29:17; 39:6). Abigail is described both as good looking and intelligent (1 Sa 25:3).

OT usages suggest a warm approval of good looks. But the OT also reminds us that looks are far from all-important. Some of the reminders are graphic: A beautiful woman without discretion is like a gold ring in a pig's snout (Pr 11:22). Beauty can be appreciated but is not to be lusted after (Pr 6:25). The wise man looks beyond physical appearance, for "charm is deceptive, and beauty is fleeting; but a woman who fears the LORD is to be praised" (Pr 31:30). It is a great tragedy if the person who has been given beauty is deceived and trusts in her beauty or uses it as a means for gain (Eze 16:15).

The other word applied to women's looks carries the thought of sensual appeal. A person described as *ṭôḇ* is one whose beauty awakens desire. The OT describes Rebekah with this term, although in the same context Sarah and Rachel are simply called good looking. The Book of Esther also uses this word when it describes the consort who was to be sought for King Xerxes: the king's servants were to search out sexually desirable young virgins so that the king might choose one who would be specially pleasing to him.

It is not only women who are characterized as desirable. When Moses' mother saw her infant son, she felt that "he was a fine [desirable] child," and she hid him from the Egyptians (Ex 2:2). Achan sinned at Jericho when he was enticed by a "beautiful [desirable] robe" that he saw in the plunder and took it despite the Lord's command (Jos 7:21).

It is interesting that this word for beauty (*tôb*), which emphasizes desirability, is used very seldom to describe an attractive person (Ge 6:2; 24:16; 26:7; Jos 7:21; Jdg 15:2; 2 Sa 11:2; 1 Ki 20:3; Est 1:11; 2:2,3).

It seems that according to the OT a beautiful appearance is to be appreciated. But it is not considered all-important. It is interesting that whereas such beauty is not in the eye of the beholder, desire or lust very likely is. The reaction of the individual to beauty may be good or bad.

3. The beauty of the Lord. God's beauty is usually described by only a few of the possible Hebrew words. *Nō'am* emphasizes the pleasantness of the thing described. It communicates the idea of grace and of overflowing favor when describing God or his name as beautiful (Ps 27:4; 90:17).

The word *ṣᵉbî* emphasizes the beauty of whatever is splendid and glorious. God himself is the crown of beauty that shines with splendor as the focal point in the life of his people (Isa 4:2; 28:5).

God's beauty, then, is found in his splendor but also in his character as a warm and gracious person who is favorable toward his people.

NT — 4. The NT concept of beauty. The words "beauty" and "beautiful" seldom appear in our translations. This is somewhat misleading. In fact, the OT concepts of beauty are drawn into and expressed by a Greek word normally translated "good."

There are two basic words for "good" found in the NT: *agathos* and *kalos*. *Agathos* indicates the good as useful and came to have a strong ethical and religious emphasis. On the other hand, the other word meaning "good," *kalos*, stresses the aesthetic. The person or thing that is *kalos* is beautiful, fine, noble, and praiseworthy. As a thing of beauty, such a person or object is pleasing to God and to his people and is a source of joy. This happy tone in *kalos* is captured in Jesus' words about the woman called Mary who washed his feet and anointed

him just before he was betrayed: "She has done a beautiful thing to me," he said (Mt 26:10; Mk 14:6).

Because of their link with the good, *kalos* and *agathos* are often used synonymously and usually both are translated "good." Thus the aspect of beauty found in goodness and revealed in the Greek language is often lost in our English translations. ♦ *Good*

Beauty is always present in the Bible narrative. It is frequently seen in those acts described in Scripture as good and loving.

Another word that appears in English as "beauty" is *hōraios*. It is found only in Mt 23:27; Ac 3:2,10; Ro 10:15. The word originally meant "seasonable," or "appropriate to its time." It came to take on the meaning of "agreeable" and, finally, "lovely." According to Jesus, the Pharisees of his day were like decorated tombs, which appeared fittingly beautiful on the outside but were corrupt within and full of deadness (Mt 23:27). But the feet of those who trudge over the mountains to spread the gospel's good news are truly beautiful; the arrival of these emissaries is timely, for they have been sent by God to bring the harvest season's joy.

5. The beautiful person. The NT does not speak often of good looks. Unlike the the writers of the OT, NT writers do not speak of individuals as being beautiful or handsome. But one NT passage does capture the NT's emphasis on an inner beauty that outshines any external appearance. Peter writes: "Your beauty should not come from outward adornment, such as braided hair and the wearing of gold jewelry and fine clothes. Instead, it should be that of your inner self, the unfading beauty of a gentle and quiet spirit, which is of great worth in God's sight. For this is the way the holy women of the past who put their hope in God used to make themselves beautiful" (1 Pe 3:3–5). No specific Greek word for beauty is used in this passage; beauty is implied, and the word was supplied by the translators. The passage undoubtedly captures the thrust of the NT's joyful promise of a transformation toward the very likeness of Christ.

You and I are called to experience God's work in our lives. We can be sure that as God works in us, he will bring forth beauty.

BEER/STRONG DRINK

The word translated "beer" in the NIV and "strong drink" in the NASB is *šēkār*. It comes from a verb that means "to be or make drunk." The word *šēkār* is found only twenty-two times in the OT, and in all but two it is in a phrase that links it with wine. ♦ *Wine*

There is no evidence that the strong drink of the Bible was a distilled liquor. Distillation is a process developed at a much later date. But the ten or eleven percent alcohol content of drink made from grains or fruit was sufficient to cause drunkenness.

Of the sixty or so references to the use of strong drink in the OT, a very few have anything definite to suggest on this subject (note the positive or neutral attitude in Ge 43:34; Nu 28:7; Dt 14:26; Pr 31:6). Most warn against strong drink and its capacity to lead the user astray (e.g., Pr 20:1). ♦ *Drunkenness*

BEG

The Hebrew and Greek words translated "beg" in modern English versions are general terms for asking or requesting. The person asking is a supplicant, who requests what he or she needs from someone able to provide it.

In most instances in the OT the person who begs for help is asking a favor from the Lord.

BEGGAR/BEGGING

There are very few biblical references to begging. Ps 109:10 calls for reduction of the families of the wicked to begging as a just punishment. And God's disciplinary wars, which shattered Israel periodically, did bring some generations to this state. But Ps 37:25 reveals David's observation and his conviction regarding the people of God: "I was young and now I am old, yet I have never seen the righteous forsaken or their children begging bread."

Although individuals may be reduced at times to begging, the Mosaic Law makes no provision for the professional beggar. Instead, the social and economic system incorporated by law was designed to keep the specter of poverty from the land. ♦ *Poor and Oppressed*

But God's people failed to live by the law, and by NT times the little land of Judah was marked by great gaps between the rich and the poor and by an oppressive taxation system that further crushed the people. In the NT, we meet several people who were forced by illness or disability to beg regularly as a way to maintain life (Lk 16:20; Jn 9:8; Ac 3:2–11). In Jesus' day the giving of alms to the perpetually poor—often in a highly public way so that others would admire the giver's piety—was considered a deed that gained great merit with God (Mt 6:1–4). How much more God would have been pleased had Israel followed the economic principles established in the law and thus had provided for all the needy of the land. ♦ *Poor and Oppressed*

BEGINNING

We often find the phrase "from the beginning" in the OT and the NT. What does the phrase mean? And what ideas are communicated in our Bible about beginnings?

OT 1. Beginnings in OT thought
   2. The beginning of the world
   3. The beginning of wisdom
NT 4. Beginnings in NT thought
   5. Jesus as existing from the beginning
   6. The beginning of salvation
   7. Summary

OT — 1. Beginnings in OT thought. The translators of the NIV and NASB usually translate two Hebrew words as "beginning." *Rē'šît* occurs fifty-one times in the Hebrew Bible. It indicates the first, as the beginning of a series.

When used of a principle or concept, it affirms that this "beginning" principle is foundational, a necessary condition for what is being discussed. *Tᵉhillâh*, likewise, indicates the beginning in a series or a first principle. It is also used of a beginning of a specific time, such as harvest time or the beginning of a year.

The way these words are used as well as their meaning tells us something important about the OT view of history. Events are never seen as random happenings. History is no boiling cauldron of random ingredients. Instead history moves in a measured way through a sequence of events that had a definite beginning and move toward a determined end. History is under God's control, and it is his active involvement as much as the operation of cause and effect that links events into a unified whole. Because history is purposive and God exercises his moral control in man's world, the Lord is able to make known the end from the beginning (Isa 46:10). The past marches into the future with a measured tread from the beginnings God has initiated.

2. The beginning of the world. "In the beginning you laid the foundations of the earth," the psalmist affirms, "and the heavens are the work of your hands" (Ps 102:25). This is, of course, the affirmation of the opening words of the Bible: "In the beginning [*rē'šît*] God created the heavens and the earth" (Ge 1:1).

But the purposive aspects of creation preceded the beginning. God's purposes have unfolded as history has progressed. Wisdom gave birth to God's grand design "from eternity, from the beginning, before the world began" (Pr 8:23).

The portrait of God as creating a universe within which history unfolds according to his purpose and plan is seen also in Isa 40 and 41. There the prophet calls on Israel to consider and honor the Lord, "who has done this and carried it through, calling forth the generations from the beginning" (Isa 41:4). The earth was founded by God (40:21), but God's hand did more than create the stage on which history plays. The hand of God has also created history (41:20), and the

end is so surely woven into the beginning that God is able with unerring accuracy to tell us the future (41:26).

The beginning of the world was not simply God's creating and forming the elements that our universe consists of. Rather, the beginning of the world was his setting in motion a sequence of events that move inexorably toward his intended end.

3. The beginning of wisdom. The OT speaks several times of the fear of the Lord as a beginning. It is the beginning of wisdom (Ps 111:10; Pr 9:10) and the beginning of knowledge (Pr 1:7). This use of "beginning," noted in 1 above, identifies the fear of the Lord as an absolutely necessary ingredient if a person is to gain wisdom or knowledge. We cannot guide our own life or have a penetrating insight into the real nature of things unless we know God and take him seriously. Reverential awe, which takes the existence of God and his active involvement in human affairs into constant account, is necessary for a person to be truly wise or knowledgeable.

NT — 4. Beginnings in NT thought. Where English versions read "beginning," the Greek word is *archē*. This is an important word in Greek thought, with roots in every philosophical tradition. The NT usage of the word is in harmony both with Greek thought and the OT view of beginnings as the initiation of a sequence of events.

Archē is often rendered "rule" or "authority" in the NT. The relationship between this translation and that of "beginnings" is found in the idea of priority. *Archē* implies that something is first, or has priority. In time, that which is first either is the beginning of a sequence or the starting point of a phenomenon. At times the word is used to move beyond time to affirm the first cause, or basic principle, that underlies and infuses the laws of the universe in which we live. In terms of relationship with others, to have priority is to have authority or power.

Where *archē* is translated "beginning" or "first," it has a temporal force. The common use, identifying the commencement of a series of events or a period of time, is seen in phrases like "the beginning of birth pains" (Mk 13:8; cf. Lk 1:3; Jn 15:27; Ac 26:4). In each case, just what series a particular event commences is clear from the context.

Archē also can indicate the absolute beginning. In such uses it carries us to the beginning, before time was, to introduce God as originator and first cause. Many passages that speak of Jesus use *archē* in this sense.

Three passages help us see what the recognition of God as originator of the universe implies. In Mt 19 and Mk 10, Jesus refers to the beginning in his discussion of marriage and divorce. When God created Adam and Eve and initiated the marriage relationship, his intention was for marriage to be a lifelong union between one man and one woman. This principle, implicit and explicit in the beginning framed by God, continues on through all time as the governing principle that establishes the ideal. The meaning and intended course of the marriage relationship was established for all time by and in its beginning.

This argument seems to be turned against the believer by the scoffers of 2 Pe 3:4. They reject the idea of coming judgment, because "ever since our fathers died, everything goes on as it has since the beginning of creation." Peter responds by declaring that these scoffers are deliberately forgetting that God has already intervened in the course of natural events. They must go back beyond remembered history (their fathers) and remember the cataclysmic judgment of the Flood. God who himself was the beginning of creation continues to exercise active control over the universe. We can understand beginnings only by looking beyond a supposedly eternal natural world to the person who gave nature its origin and continues to subject it to his purposes.

5. Jesus as existing from the beginning. John quotes Genesis 1 in the opening phrase of his Gospel: "In the beginning." These words return us to the era before creation, when Jesus existed as God and with God. John goes on to show

that the eternal Word, through whom God has ever expressed himself, took on human flesh and entered the world that he had made (1:9–10). ♦ *Word*

The writer of Hebrews also identifies Jesus as the one who "in the beginning" as Lord "laid the foundations of the earth." He will continue long after the universe is gone (Heb 1:10).

Other statements that present Jesus as the preexisting first cause in creation include 1 Jn 1:1; 2:13–14; Rev 21:6; 22:13; and possibly Col 1:18.

6. The beginning of salvation. We have seen that most NT passages with the word "beginning" call attention to the commencement of events and that others present a preexistent Jesus. Some show us that God establishes principles in the beginnings he initiates and that he remains in full control of history. Three passages make statements that relate to our salvation and raise theological questions.

Paul speaks of God's calling of his people to a holy life and says that "this grace was given to us in Christ Jesus before the beginning of time" (2 Ti 1:9). Eternal life was "promised before the beginning of time" (Tit 1:2) and brought to light at God's appointed time (1:3). Although these verses have been used to argue for predestination, it seems that they need only be taken to locate the origin of God's grace and his promise in eternity, making it a feature of his eternal plan established before the era of time.

A third passage, 2 Th 2:13 may be taken in one of two ways. The passage speaks of the brothers at Thessalonica as "brothers loved by the Lord, because from the beginning God chose [them] to be saved through the sanctifying work of the Spirit and through belief in the truth." The interpretation of this verse depends on whether the beginning referred to is the point at which these brothers believed or whether it is some "point" in "eternity past." If the former, *archē* is used in the sense of commencement of faith; if the latter, it is used in the sense of the ultimate beginning. ♦ *Predestine*

7. Summary. The Bible locates the beginning of all things in God. He is the originator and the controller of events. Because of God's involvement, events are not random, and history is no cauldron of random ingredients. The end is known to God from the beginning, and all history moves along its intended path to the end he determined long before the world began.

BEHAVIOR

The Greek word for "behavior" or "conduct" is *anastrophē*. It is found in Gal 1:13; Eph 4:22; 1 Ti 4:12; Heb 13:7; Jas 3:13; 1 Pe 1:15,18; 2:12; 3:1,2,16; 2 Pe 2:7; 3:11. The phrase in Col 1:21 is literally "wicked works" (*ergon*).

The NIV tends to render *anastrophē* as "way of life." Before one comes to know Christ, his or her way of life is both empty (1 Pe 1:18) and corrupted by the desires of the old self (Eph 4:22). But because of Christ, believers are called to be holy in all they do (1 Pe 1:15) and to live lives of dynamic goodness (Jas 3:13; 1 Pe 2:12). The beauty of the good *anastrophē* is a winning quality (1 Pe 3:2) and will silence the slurs of the pagan (1 Pe 2:12).

Several passages suggest that Christian *anastrophē* is not simply learned from the content of the gospel but is learned by the modeling of leaders whose examples are to be followed (1 Ti 4:12; Heb 13:7).

BELIEF/FAITH

Few words are more central to the Christian message or more often used to describe Christian experience than "belief" and "faith." Yet these words are often corrupted by a misunderstanding of their biblical meaning. People today may use "faith" to indicate what is possible but uncertain. The Bible uses "faith" in ways that link it with what is assuredly and certainly true. Christians may sometimes speak of "believing," as if it were merely a subjective effort, as if our act of faith or strength of faith were the issue. But the Bible shifts our attention from subjective experience and centers it on the object of our faith—God himself.

It is exciting to look into the Scriptures and there rediscover the full meaning of faith and belief. There we grasp the great promise that faith holds out to all mankind: transformation through a personal relationship with God in Jesus Christ.

OT 1. The OT concept of faith
    2. Abraham's faith
    3. Israel's unbelief
    4. Faith under the law
    5. Summary
NT 6. The NT concept of faith
    7. Faith, in the synoptic Gospels
    8. John's use of "believe"
    9. Faith, in Romans and Galatians
    10. Faith, in James
    11. Faith, in the other Epistles
    12. Summary

OT — 1. The OT concept of faith. Where we read "belief" and "faith" in the OT in the NIV and NASB, the original usually has the Hiphil stem of the Hebrew word *'āman*. The root indicates firmness and certainty; in this stem the verb means "to be certain," "to believe in," or "to be assured." Other forms of the root denote faithfulness, fidelity, steadiness, faith, certainty, firmness, and truth. This powerful OT term, which captures the biblical meaning of faith, affirms certainty, never doubt. It expresses firm conviction—conviction based on the reliability of what is believed.

The Hiphil stem of *'āman*, which carries the meaning "believe in," is found in the following verses: Ge 15:6; 45:26; Ex 4:1,5,8–9,31; 14:31; 19:9; Nu 14:11; 20:12; Dt 1:32; 9:23; 28:66; Jdg 11:20; 1 Sa 27:12; 1 Ki 17:14; 2 Ch 9:6; 20:20; 32:15; Job 4:18; 9:16; 15:15,22,31; 24:22; 29:24; 39:12,24; Ps 27:13; 78:22,32; 106:12,24; 116:10; 119:66; Pr 14:15; 26:25; Isa 7:9; 28:16; 43:12; 53:1; Jer 12:6; 40:14; La 4:12; Jnh 3:5; Mic 7:5; Hab 1:5.

The closest Hebrew parallel to the NT word for "faith" and "belief" is *'āman*. Yet other aspects of our faith relationship with God are expressed in other Hebrew terms. Two words, *bāṭaḥ* and *maḥseh*, express the idea of trust in or reliance on another.

Bāṭaḥ turns our attention to the believer and expresses the inner result of having someone or something in which to place confidence. That outcome is a feeling of well-being and security. The word *'āman* captures the fullest meaning of religious faith: it portrays an informed decision to commit oneself to God. *Bāṭaḥ* captures the release that comes with our surrender.

But just as *'āman* can be false if the object of faith is something other than the true God, so *bāṭaḥ* is false if what we have trusted ourselves to is unable to guarantee our safety. The OT speaks of several false sources of security. It holds each of them up and examines them in contrast to the security that is ours in the Lord. We are foolish if we turn from reliance on God to seek security in man (Ps 118:8; 146:3; Jer 17:5), in violence (Ps 55:23; 62:10), in riches (Ps 49:6; 52:7), in military power (Dt 28:52; Ps 44:6; Jer 5:17), or in our own goodness (Eze 33:13; Hos 10:13).

The other word related to trust, *maḥseh*, means "to seek refuge." It suggests that a person is helpless and in danger and is rushing to find a secure hiding place. The psalmists speak words of hope to the insecure and fearful, reminding them that God, our rock and strength, is himself the refuge of his people (e.g., Ps 14:6; 46:1; 62:8; 71:7; 91:9). ♦ *Hope*

The OT concept of faith as certainty and safety is deeply rooted in the OT view of God. Faith fastens on God as one who by his nature is the sole certain and sure reality. God is faithful and unchanging, established in eternity; and because he is who he is, we can commit ourselves to him.

Because this God also commits himself to us in covenant relationship, placing our confidence in him brings us true well-being and safety.

The OT views human response to God as vital in the matter of true faith. But the OT emphasis (as expressed in the words chosen to express faith) is on this fact: our response to God has validity because

God himself is utterly faithful and trustworthy.

2. Abraham's faith. When we look into the OT to see how "faith" words are used, we are drawn at once to the experience of Abraham. Not that "faith" is used often to describe Abraham's relationship with God. In fact, it is so used only in Ge 15:6. But we turn to Abraham because of the pivotal nature of that verse and because the NT again and again points us to Abraham as faith's primary example.

Ge 15 describes Abraham, then a very old man, in dialogue with God. Abraham complained that God had given him no children of his own, despite an earlier promise (Ge 12:2). God responded by amplifying the promise. Abraham looked to the sky, filled with its numberless stars, and heard God say, "So shall your offspring be" (15:5). The next verse tells us, "Abram believed the LORD, and he credited it to him as righteousness" (15:6). The apostle Paul says of this incident: "Against all hope, Abraham in hope believed. . . . he faced the fact that his body was as good as dead—since he was about a hundred years old—and that Sarah's womb was also dead. Yet he did not waver through unbelief regarding the promise of God, but was strengthened in his faith and gave glory to God, being fully persuaded that God had power to do what he promised" (Ro 4:18–21). Abraham examined the circumstances and, despite everything, decided that God was to be trusted. Abraham consciously chose to put his trust in God, and this act of saving faith was accepted by the Lord in place of a righteousness that Abraham did not possess. ♦ *Righteous/Righteousness*

Abraham was not perfect, by any standard. But his life, as reported in the OT, shows again and again that he trusted God and acted on God's promises, certain the Lord could be counted on (Heb 11:8–12).

The example of Abraham stands as *the* biblical illustration of faith as believing response to God. God spoke in promise and command. Abraham trusted himself to God. And Abraham's faith was demonstrated as he subsequently acted on what God had said (Ge 12–22).

3. Israel's unbelief. A study of Abraham's life helps us to understand the nature of belief. By contrast, the history of the generation that was redeemed from Egypt helps us understand the nature of unbelief.

Ex 4:1–8 is foundational, and Nu 14 is the culmination of a theme. Exodus 4 reports a dialogue between the Lord and a hesitant Moses. Moses had been told to return to Egypt. He would become the instrument of Israel's deliverance. But Moses objected: "What if they do not believe me or listen to me?" (4:1). God gave Moses the power to perform three minor miracles and explained, "If they do not believe you or pay attention to the first miraculous sign, they may believe the second" (4:8).

Moses returned to Egypt and, through many striking wonders, delivered the people of Israel. That generation experienced many miraculous events, all providing unmistakable evidence of God's reality and his power. Yet these miracles failed to produce anything beyond moments of belief (e.g., Ex 14:31). Instead, when led to the edge of the Promised Land, these people, who had experienced many miracles, refused to respond to God's command to go up and take the land. Angrily, God exclaimed, "How long will these people treat me with contempt? How long will they refuse to believe in me, in spite of all the miraculous signs I have performed among them?" (Nu 14:11).

The OT and NT return to this incident often, just as they return again and again to Moses. In a review of history for the next generation, Moses reminded them, "You did not trust him or obey him" (Dt 9:23; cf. 1:32). Ps 78 speaks of God's being angry because the Exodus generation would "not believe in God or trust in his deliverance" (78:22) "in spite of his wonders" (78:32). The writer to the Hebrews warns NT believers not to permit a hardened heart to drag them into error so that they would become like the evil generation that heard God's word, but whose "unbelieving heart" (Heb 3:12) was shown by their refusal to obey.

The stories of Abraham and of the Exodus generation show the meaning of faith in positive and negative frames. Through them we see several basic aspects of faith.

First, faith is not some response to evidence, even when that evidence is clearly miraculous. Abraham believed *God*. His faith was a response to God himself, who met Abraham directly in a word of promise. That word from God is far more compelling for faith than any miracles performed in the material universe.

Second, faith in God engages the total person. It is expressed in perception and action. Abraham was well aware of his and Sarah's advanced age. But Abraham also considered God's power and faithfulness. The fact of God so transformed Abraham's perspective that he easily accepted God's promise, although fathering a son was humanly impossible for him. But Israel, poised on the borders of Canaan, could see only the military strength of that land's inhabitants. They treated God "with contempt" (Nu 14:11; 16:30) by refusing to consider his power and reality.

Faith is also expressed in actions. When Abraham was told to go to Canaan, he packed up and went (Ge 12). When the Exodus generation was told to conquer the land, they refused even to try. They were betrayed by their "unbelieving heart."

Third, the outcome of faith is demonstrated. When a person responds to God's self-disclosure, faith-generated obedience leads to blessing. Abraham believed God and knew God's protection during his lifetime. The unbelieving generation wandered back into the wilderness, to die in its desolate wastes.

4. Faith under the law. We read little of faith under the OT law. There are several reasons why *'āman* is not as prominent in the OT as *pistis* (representing the Greek word group for "faith") is in the NT.

For one thing, the OT focuses on the covenant that God established with the whole community of Israel. Law is to Israel the "word of promise" spoken by the living God to that community. The aspect of faith that is expressed as obedience was expressed in keeping the commandments and decrees that governed the life of the community. In the same way, lack of faith found expression in one's disobedience to the law. Looking at Israel's defeat and exile and remembering the refusal of the people to listen to warnings delivered by the prophets, Scripture says, "They would not listen and were as stiff-necked as their fathers, who did not trust in the LORD their God. They rejected his decrees and the covenant he had made with their fathers and the warnings he had given them" (2 Ki 17:14–15).

The fact that Israel was called to relate to God through the Word uttered in law should never be taken to suggest that the OT pictures anything less than trust in the Lord himself. In times of crisis the godly relied on the person of the Lord, as when Jehoshaphat led Judah's forces against a vast army. "Listen to me, Judah and people of Jerusalem," the king cried. "Have faith in the LORD your God and you will be upheld; have faith in his prophets and you will be successful" (2 Ch 20:20). The underlying reality in which true OT faith always rests is God himself, who meets each generation in words of promise. Encountering the Word, each generation must respond in obedient faith.

5. Summary. The OT term for faith introduces us to certainty—certainty as subjective conviction, a conviction that is possible because of the objective reality of God.

Two OT examples show us the nature and impact of responding to God as trustworthy. First, Abraham believed God. He took the Lord at his word, and his whole perspective was transformed. Because he took God into account, Abraham's life was changed as he translated faith into obedience.

Second, the Exodus generation was given many miraculous evidences of God's presence and power. Yet that generation fell short of faith. They re-

fused to take God into account when they faced a superior military force in Canaan, and their unbelief was translated into disobedience. As the people of that generation acted out their unbelief, they died in the wilderness.

Thus each OT individual and generation faced a choice between belief and unbelief. God spoke to every generation anew, in the law and by the prophets. Those who believed and put their trust in God demonstrated their faith just as Abraham had done, by obedience to the word of promise, and they were blessed. Those who disbelieved disregarded the written and prophetic Word and experienced God's judgments.

In the OT, then, faith is essentially a response to God. He comes to the individual and to the community in his Word. Belief means taking God seriously—to count on him as real and commit ourselves to him—and to act in accordance with the particular message he has given to us. Faith's inner conviction about God is always translated into action and results in a lifestyle through which the reality of faith is expressed.

NT — 1. The NT concept of faith.
One word group was used in classical Greek and in the common Greek of the NT era to express the idea of faith. That word group encompassed a wide range of secular and religious ideas, but the underlying thrust is clear. *Pistis* ("faith," "belief") and related words deal with relationships established by trust and maintained by trustworthiness.

Originally this word group seems linked with a more formal contract between partners. It stressed faithfulness to the agreement made or trustworthiness in keeping promises. In time the use expanded. In the classical period, writers spoke of trust in the gods as well as trust in people. In the Hellenic era, "faith in God" came to mean theoretical conviction about a particular doctrine, a conviction expressed in one's way of life. As different schools of philosophy and religion developed, the particular emphasis given *pistis* was shaped by the tradition within which it was used.

The NT retains the range of meanings. But those meanings are refined and re-shaped by the dynamic message of the gospel.

In the *pistis* word group as used in the NT are verbs, nouns, and adjectives that have the following general meanings. Looking over these meanings, we catch sight of the breadth of ideas linked with belief and faith.

These words are used in the NT in a variety of constructions. For instance, to "believe" is used with the accusative to mean "be convinced of" or "entrust." It is used with "that" to indicate something of which the individual is convinced. With the dative, to "believe" can mean "give credence to" or "entrust oneself to."

The verb and noun are also used with a number of prepositions. "To believe through" (*dia*) indicates the way by which a person comes to faith (Jn 1:7; 1 Pe 1:21a). "Faith *en*" indicates the realm in which faith operates (Eph 1:15; Col 1:4; 2 Ti 3:15). The most important construction is unique to the NT, an invention of the early church that expresses the inmost secret of our faith. That construction links faith with the preposition *eis*, "to" or "into." This is never done in secular Greek. In the NT it portrays a person committing himself or herself totally to the person of Jesus Christ, for our faith is *into* Jesus.

One other aspect of the NT's use of faith words is fascinating. Usually the object of faith is Jesus. Only twelve verses have God as the object of faith (Jn 12:44; 14:1; Ac 16:34; Ro 4:3,5,17,24; Gal 3:6; 1 Th 1:8; Tit 3:8; Heb 6:1; 1 Pe 1:21). Why? The reason is clearly expressed by Jesus himself: "I am the way and the truth and the life. No one comes to the father except through me" (Jn 14:6). God the Father has revealed himself in the Son. The Father has set Jesus before us as the one to whom we must entrust ourselves for salvation. It is Jesus who is the focus of Christian faith.

In the context of our faith and in our relationship with Jesus, "believing" has come to mean (1) the happy trust that a person places in the person of Jesus

Christ and (2) the allegiance to him that grows out of that very personal commitment.

7. Faith, in the synoptic Gospels. The Gospels report many signs (miracles) that Jesus performed as he traveled and taught. Often, but not always, Jesus' healings were intimately associated with the faith of the sick person (Mt 9:2,22,29; Mk 2:5; 5:34; Lk 17:19; 18:42). ◗ *Healing*

However, a survey of the Gospels shows that for most of the people, Jesus' miracles failed to produce true faith (see 8, below). Even as Jesus hung on the cross, the mocking promise of his watching enemies was a lie. "Come down from the cross," they pledged, "and we will believe" (Mt 27:42; cf. Mk 15:32). And when Jesus was raised from the dead what happened? These men were the first to attempt to hide the evidence (Mt 28:11–15).

In this we see the phenomenon we noted in the OT report of ancient Israel's unbelief. The Exodus miracles provided incontrovertible proof of God's power and his presence. Yet the Exodus generation would not commit themselves to him. The nation in Jesus' day saw his healings, watched him cast out demons, and even saw him raise Lazarus from the dead; yet they refused to believe.

But belief in the full flow of God's power was difficult, even for the disciples. They had trusted themselves to Jesus as Son of God. But when the Lord was crucified, their hope and confidence drained away. They could not, on the day of the Resurrection, bring themselves to believe that the one they trusted had come to life again (Mt 28; Mk 16; Lk 24).

But in the Gospels, one vital fact is made clear in Jesus' words about faith: a lack of trust in the God in whom we have faith closes off life's possibilities. When we fail to believe, we do not experience the full range of God's activity (Mt 21:22). But when we trust, we open up our future to a full experience of God's power in and through us (Mt 17:20; 21:21; Lk 7:9–10). All things are possible to the one who believes.

For you and me, faith in Jesus does not come through an observation of miracles. Faith is born as we learn about Jesus, find out what he said, and put our trust in him. We then go on to deeper faith, an active reliance on the power and presence of God. And as we trust, our life opens up to all sorts of possibilities. Miracles follow faith. Believing, we experience God at work in our lives. ▶ *Miracle/Sign/Wonder*

8. John's use of "believe". While other sections of the NT focus attention on faith, John explores the verb *pisteuō*. John is primarily concerned with believing.

Several aspects of John's emphasis are especially important. John looks at the relationship between believing and evidence. He examines superficial belief. And he connects true faith with life and death. In addition, several passages of John's Gospel call for careful study (particularly Jn 3,5,8,11).

Believing and evidence. In Christian faith knowing and believing are linked. We respond to testimony about Jesus with our intellect as well as with our heart. John's gospel looks at two kinds of testimony. There are the testimony of Jesus' miracles and the testimony of Jesus' words.

At times these two lines of testimony enhance each other. Thus the Twelve, who were already committed to Jesus, saw the miracle at Cana (Jn 2:11) and found their belief in Jesus strengthened. It is not unusual to find that many of the observers of Jesus' works were moved to some kind of belief. The testimony of his miracles was compelling (Jn 7:31; 11:45; 12:11). Yet others who saw the same signs chose not to believe, rejecting Jesus *against* the evidence of the Lord's works (Jn 10:38; 14:11).

In John we see that the testimony provided by miracle and sign forced observers to take Jesus seriously. But signs and miracles alone did not bring about saving faith.

Superficial belief. John distinguishes between two types of "believing." His gospel was written, he told his readers,

"that you may believe that Jesus is the Christ, the Son of God, and that by believing you may have life in his name" (20:31). Yet when John describes the response of the crowds to the testimony of Jesus' miracles, it is clear that those who "believed" did so in a way that fell short of life-giving belief in Jesus as the Son of God.

John 2:22–23 tells of many who saw his signs and "believed in him." But later, after that same crowd of shallow disciples heard Jesus speak about himself as the Bread of Life (Jn 6), they complained: "This is a hard teaching. Who can accept it?" (Jn 6:60). John observes that "from this time many of his disciples turned back and no longer followed him" (6:66).

Superficial faith came in response to the miraculous, and it died when Jesus communicated the divine content of his message.

Just so Nicodemus, a religious leader, confessed, "We know you are a teacher who has come from God. For no one could perform the miraculous signs you are doing if God were not with him" (Jn 3:2). Yet when these leaders heard the message that Jesus spoke (Jn 7:16–17), they refused to go on to the belief that involves commitment to Jesus as Lord (Jn 7:45–47).

Wonder at Jesus' powers and even agreement that God must have sent him falls far short of saving faith.

Only when he recognizes Jesus as the Son of God and commits himself completely to him does a person believe in the fullest, saving sense. This commitment involves accepting his words and making them the framework of one's life.

Belief and life. Over and over in his writings, John links faith with life, and unbelief with death. The one who believes in Jesus has eternal life. The one who does not believe is already condemned to eternal death.

The intimate connection between life and believing is as marked in John's gospel and epistles as is the connection between faith and righteousness in the writings of Paul. ▶ *Life and Death*

John 3. In this passage, Jesus explained to Nicodemus that all people must be "born again." This concept should not have surprised the religious leader: the OT speaks of a "new covenant" under which the forgiven are given a new heart (Jer 31). ♦ *Covenant*

Jesus explained to Nicodemus that the new life God had promised from ancient times comes from the "one and only Son" whom God gave so "that whoever believes in him shall not perish but have eternal life" (Jn 3:16). Jesus spoke very plainly. The Son came to save. No one who believes in the Son is condemned. Whoever does not believe continues in his present state of condemnation. Believing in Jesus is the one and only doorway to eternal life.

John 5. Jesus again announced that life is available only through the Son: "Whoever hears my word and believes him who sent me has eternal life and will not be condemned; he has crossed over from death to life" (5:24).

John 8. This passage explores the link between the testimony of the miraculous and the testimony of the message. Jesus teaches clearly that he and the Father are inseparably one. Thus, belief in Jesus is the critical issue for every hearer: "If you do not believe that I am the one I claim to be, you will indeed die in your sins" (8:24).

The miracles of Jesus cannot be argued away. But when Jesus spoke the truth, the religious leaders attacked him. Unlike Abraham, who heard God speak and responded with belief in the Lord, this generation did not respond to the word of truth.

When the physical descendants of Abraham rejected the fresh word of God that came through Jesus, they proved themselves to be of a different spiritual family, for Abraham believed God, and these men refused to believe God's Son.

John 11. This chapter tells the story of the raising of Lazarus. While many accepted the testimony of this miracle and accepted Jesus' word about himself, the story itself looks at believing from a slightly different perspective. Mary and

Martha, the sisters of Lazarus, did believe in Jesus. They believed that Jesus as the source of life would raise Lazarus "at the last day" (11:24), for Jesus was the Christ and the Son of God (11:27). But although saving faith was present, the women still failed to understand the life-giving power of Jesus, power that enabled him to raise their brother then and there, recalling him to life even though he had been dead for four days.

We may have saving faith in Jesus and yet limit his power. When we put our trust in Jesus, the Son of God, we enter a relationship with one who is Lord and whose ability to act in our world is without limitations.

Summary of John's view of believing. John sees believing as an active, continuing trust in Jesus. The act of believing draws an individual across the dividing line between death and eternal life. That act of faith is described by John as receiving Jesus (Jn 1:12) and as coming to him (Jn 6:35), as well as loving him (1 Jn 4:19).

There is counterfeit belief, which exists as a limited trust in Jesus. Counterfeit belief acknowledges that there is something special about Jesus but refuses to accept Scripture's full testimony about him. Saving faith goes beyond limited belief. It recognizes Jesus as Son of God and trusts completely in him as he is unveiled in God's Word. Saving faith demonstrates belief by acting on the words Jesus has spoken (Jn 8:31–32).

In making a faith commitment, a person considers the evidence and accepts God's testimony about who Jesus is. The one who does not believe may be impressed with the evidence but will hold back from entrusting himself or herself to Jesus.

Yet it is only by believing, as a total commitment of oneself to the Lord, that life can be found. How vital, then, that we consider the testimony of Scripture, accept it, and believe on the one who speaks words of promise there.

9. Faith, in Romans and Galatians. Paul's task as missionary strategist and theologian of the young churches was not simply to present the gospel. To Paul fell the task of giving testimony—and explanation. In Paul's two great theological expositions, there is a clear explanation of the nature and role of faith in the Christian life. There the relationship between faith and salvation, faith and righteousness, and faith and fellowship with God is made clear.

In his introduction to the Book of Romans, Paul announces his concern with faith: "I am not ashamed of the gospel, because it is the power of God for the salvation of everyone who believes: first for the Jew, then for the Gentile. For in the gospel a righteousness from God is revealed, a righteousness that is by faith from first to last" (Ro 1:16–17).

We find "faith" words clustered in Romans and in Galatians. So in order to understand the faith that brings us salvation and righteousness, it is best to look at the chapters in which these clusters appear.

Romans 3: the role of faith. In the first three chapters of Romans, Paul demonstrates the fact that all humanity is lost, without a shred of righteousness that would permit God to accept any individual. "Therefore no one will be declared righteous in [God's] sight by observing the law" (3:20). Yet God has determined to bring mankind a salvation that necessarily involves that sinners become righteous in his sight. This, Paul explains, is accomplished in the death of Christ, which was a sacrifice of atonement. ◗
Atonement Through "faith in his blood" the individual who believes is declared righteous. Thus salvation and righteousness come through faith in Jesus; and through faith, salvation and righteousness are available to all.

Romans 4: the nature of faith. But what is that "faith" that provides the believer with salvation and cloaks him with righteousness? In this chapter in which "faith" and "believe" are found no fewer than fifteen times, Paul argues that faith is the same thing today that it was when it was exercised by OT saints such as Abraham and David. And faith has the same result. Abraham and David won

forgiveness by faith (4:1–8); and for us today, forgiveness is also found by faith. In Romans 4 we see that to believe means simply to count on God's promise. We accept the word of the God who spoke, and we accept that God himself.

Paul shows that the God who spoke with promise to Abraham is the same God who, in Jesus, speaks with promise to us: the God "in whom [Abraham] believed—the God who gives life to the dead and calls things that are not as though they were" (v. 17).

Verses 18–25 are critical to Paul's definition of faith. Here he analyzes Abraham's faith. Abraham faced the fact of his and Sarah's advanced age. He knew this meant that conceiving a child was impossible. But Abraham "did not waver through unbelief regarding the promise of God." Instead he was "fully persuaded that God had power to do what he had promised." And so Paul concludes, "This is why 'it was credited to him as righteousness.' "

Abraham heard the promise. He looked beyond the impossibility of its fulfillment and considered God. Abraham, confident that God would keep his promise, expected that what God announced would come to pass.

The promise Abraham believed was the promise that he would father a child. The promise held out today in the gospel in which we are to believe is the promise that God, who has delivered Jesus up for our sins and raised him to life again for our justification (v. 25), will save us because of Jesus. We look beyond the impossibility that the natural person sees. We consider God. And we too are confident that what God has announced will come to pass.

Believing, we receive the gifts of salvation and righteousness.

Romans 10: the word of faith. Paul saw the enthusiasm of his fellow Israelites for God. He admitted their zeal but pointed out that their attempt to establish their own righteousness by works was a refusal to submit to God's righteousness. God's righteousness comes to man through faith (5–8), specifically a faith that confesses Jesus as Lord and believes that God has raised him from the dead. It is only through accepting this promise by faith that a person will be saved (9–13).

Throughout history, God has given promises to humanity. Throughout history, faith has been a trusting response, a confidence in the God who has promised. "Consequently," Paul says, "faith comes from hearing the message, and the message is heard through the word of Christ" (v. 17).

Galatians 3: faith and fellowship. Paul teaches that faith is a believing response to God's word of promise. The believer trusts God to act as he has said he would, and so he commits himself to the Lord. Paul reminds the Galatians that Abraham received righteousness as a gift through this kind of faith. Righteousness is ours as well through faith.

But then Paul goes on to argue that our relationship with the Lord is also maintained by faith. We are not to attempt to live in fellowship with God by trying to keep the law. Paul reminds us, "The righteous will live by faith" (v. 11; Hab 2:4). Law is based on a contrary principle: reliance on human activity. It is not based on promise. Since we must relate to God through his promise rather than through his works, we must continue on in our relationship with the Lord by faith. We must hear the words of Scripture as promise, and we must rely on them as promise. ▶ *Law*

In personal testimony Paul says, "I have been crucified with Christ and I no longer live, but Christ lives in me. The life I live in the body, I live by faith in the Son of God, who loved me and gave himself for me" (Gal 2:20). The life of faith is ours as we continue to count on God's words to us. We hear them as promise and believe that God will do in us all that he has spoken.

As we live by faith, the righteousness of which the Bible speaks as being ours in God's sight gradually infuses our life and character, and we become righteous persons in fact and in deed. ▶ *Right-eous/Righteousness*

10. Faith, in James. Paul's task in Romans and Galatians was to explain the nature and role of faith. James had a simpler mission. James wrote to believers who were members of that first church at Jerusalem. He did not try to explain faith or its role in Christianity. He simply wrote as a pastor, concerned that believers conduct themselves in ways that harmonized with their confession of Christ.

To James, a person with a living faith will find guidance in prayer (1:2–7), will act on the divine promise rather than simply hear it (1:19–25), will have compassion for the powerless (1:26–27), will control his or her tongue (3:1–12), will adopt God's peaceable wisdom rather than the contentious wisdom of the world (3:13–18), will turn from any worldly motives, which conflict with godliness (4:1–6), will find patience in suffering (5:7–11), and will find relief in prayer (5:13–18).

Nestled among the practical pastoral matters is a discussion of faith (2:14–26) that some have felt conflicts with Paul. But when we look at James's concerns and see how he develops his argument, we see that there is no conflict.

James makes his concern clear from the start. He asks what good it is "if a man claims to have faith but has no deeds" (v. 14). James, then, is examining a "faith" that fails to produce good and loving conduct.

In his argument, James establishes the fact that faith as mere "belief about" God is empty: "Even the demons believe [that there is one God]—and shudder" (v. 19).

Looking into history, James shows that the believers the OT recognizes as examples of faith are those whose faith found some expression in action. Abraham's "faith and his actions were working together, and his faith was made complete by what he did" (v. 22). In the same way, Rahab can be considered righteous, not because of some mere claim to belief, but because she acted on her conviction that the Lord is God—she hid the Israelite spies.

By each illustration, James shows that one's claim to "have faith" is justified (demonstrated valid) "by what he does."

◗ *Justify/Justification* Biblical faith is a dynamic, transforming force. It brings the believer into living relationship with God. Infused by the Holy Spirit, the believer's attitudes, values, and conduct change, to come more and more into harmony with the Lord.

11. Faith, in the other Epistles. The range of meanings of the *pistis* word group, noted in 6 above, is expressed throughout the Epistles. Yet there are emphases that we can distinguish.

At times, faith statements focus our attention on the gospel message itself: "the faith" is the totality of what Scripture affirms about God and his relationship to humanity (1 Co 16:13; Col 2:7; 1 Ti 2:7; 3:9; 4:1,6; 5:8; 6:10,12; 2 Ti 3:8; 4:7; Tit 1:4,13; 3:15; Heb 4:14; 1 Pe 5:9; Jude 3).

At times, faith statements focus our attention on our relationship with God. Faith is seen as that initial and continuing act of trusting ourselves to him (e.g., 2 Co 1:24; 10:15; Eph 1:15; 2:8; Php 1:25; Col 1:4,23; 2:5; 1 Th 1:8; 3:2,5–7,10; 2 Th 1:3,4; 1 Ti 2:15; 6:11; 2 Ti 1:5,13; 2:18; 3:15; 4:7; Phm 5–6; Heb 4:2; 10:38; 13:7).

At times faith statements focus our attention on the impact of believing: what it is that faith produces in the heart and life of the believer (e.g., 2 Co 5:7; Eph 3:12,17; 4:13; Php 2:17; 3:9; Col 2:12; 1 Th 1:3; 2 Th 1:11; 2 Ti 3:15; Heb 6:12; 10:22; 1 Pe 1:5,21; 1 Jn 5:4).

Of course, these categories overlap. You and I have committed ourselves to a God who is known through the gospel message. Trust and its content cannot be isolated from each other. Nor are the wonderful products of faith in the heart and life of the Christian ever found in isolation from trusting reliance on Jesus as living Lord.

Along with statements about faith that dot the NT, the Scriptures have one other grand exposition—Heb 11. Faith, the writer says, is "being sure of what we hope for and certain of what we do not see" (11:1). It is faith that lets us look beyond the visible and realize that "the universe was formed at God's command" (11:3). Faith moves us to a realm inaccessible to the senses and not open to ordinary means of verification. In faith

there must be that inner assurance that God does exist and that he rewards those who seek him, and this assurance makes possible the believer's response to promise. Faith never rests in a doctrine but always in a person and in the trustworthiness of that person (11:6).

Then the writer of Hebrews goes on to show what faith produces in the lives of those who do believe. Over and over we are shown that the obedient, who hear the promise and act on it, experience the reality of the unseen God (11:4–40). In each case, there is both that trusting of oneself to God's message, as Romans emphasizes, and—what is so important to James—the evidence of trust in obedient action.

12. Summary. The OT picture of faith as a personal, trusting response to God who speaks words of promise, is reflected in the NT. The NT explains in depth the role God has given to faith.

Although the basis on which God is free to forgive human beings in every era is the sacrifice of Jesus on Calvary, the object of faith has differed from age to age. For in different ages, God has spoken different words of promise. To Abraham, there was the promise of a son and multiplied descendants. To those under law, there was the promise of blessing to accompany obedience. To us, there is the promise of cleansing and acceptance through Jesus. In each age, faith is man's response to the promise. In each age, faith is trusting oneself to the God who has spoken. In each age, faith is accepted by God in place of a righteousness that no human being could have.

In the NT, we see with unmistakable clarity that it is through faith that God gives salvation and righteousness. It is in the NT that we see with unmistakable clarity that faith is a personal response to God and a complete commitment of ourselves to him. There also we see that faith calls for a continuing relationship of response to Jesus' word. It is in the NT that we see with unmistakable clarity that faith transforms human beings, bringing us a life that is eternal *and* can be experienced now. Through faith we come into a relationship with God in which he commits himself not simply to declare us righteous but also to make us truly good persons.

Trusting God is the heart and soul of the faith that centers in our Lord Jesus Christ.

BELIEVER

In Scripture a "believer" is not a person who holds a certain set of beliefs about God as if it were merely some theoretical conviction. A believer is a person who has responded to the gospel message by trusting Jesus and joining the company of others whose lives have found new focus in relationship with the Lord. A believer is a person who "has faith in Jesus" in the fullest, most biblical sense. ▶ *Belief/Faith*

BELONG/BELONGS

In both Testaments the idea of belonging is most often communicated by a grammatical construction rather than a specific word. What is most fascinating to us, however, is not those constructions, but what the Bible teaches about belonging.

1. What belongs to God
2. Who belongs to God
3. Where we belong

1. What belongs to God. Both OT and NT make statements about things that belong, or pertain, to God. To God belongs the interpretation of dreams (Ge 40:8) and the secret things he has planned but not revealed (Dt 29:29). To God belonged the sacred articles of the temple (1 Ch 22:19) and the firstborn of Israel (Lev 27:26). To God belongs judgment (Dt 1:17; Jer 46:10) and restitution (Nu 5:8). This God, the psalmists affirm, is more exalted than all, for to him belong the kings of the earth (Ps 47:9), the mountain peaks (95:4; 104:18), the highest heavens (115:16). God is the possessor of every living soul (Eze 18:4), as well as "everything under heaven" (Job 41:11), and to him belongs salvation (Rev 7:10). All things belong to God, and he is the unquestioned Lord of all.

Most often the Bible writers, aware of God's greatness, focus on his attributes rather than on his possessions. To God belong wisdom and power (Job 12:13), strength and victory (12:16), dominion and awe (25:2; cf. Ps 22:28). To God belong glory and power (Rev 19:1) and eternal praise (Ps 111:10).

2. Who belongs to God. One of the great prophecies of the OT is found in Isa 44:5: "One will say, 'I belong to the LORD.' " The verse looks ahead, during a time of apostasy, to a day when God will pour out his Spirit on humanity. Then human beings will know God in a deeply intimate way (44:3–4). For you and for me, that day has come. The NT is rich in affirmation that, in a unique way, we do belong to God—not as his possessions, but as his dearly loved children.

We have been "called to belong to Jesus Christ" (Ro 1:6). As Jesus' own people, we bear fruit to God (Ro 7:4), for Jesus breaks the power of our sinful nature (Ro 8:9). As a people belonging to God, we who know Jesus are chosen to bring him praise (1 Pe 2:9).

The new relationship with Jesus replaces all the old relationships that once entangled us. Once we were in the grip of our sinful nature (Ro 7:5), the Devil (Jn 8:44), and the world (Jn 15:19). As those who belong to Jesus, we enter a new world of light.

3. Where we belong. Belonging to Jesus, according to the NT, has to do with relationship, not possession. Although Jesus is Lord, we are no longer slaves. We are children and friends (Jn 15:15). The NT makes it plain that in this relationship, those who belong to Jesus also belong to each other. When we ask where we belong, the Bible's answer is in "the family" (Ga 6:10). Having come to know Jesus, we have been drawn into relationship with God the Father. And as children of a common Father, we are thus one another's brothers and sisters. We belong in close fellowship with other members of God's family. ▶ *Church*

We grow in our relationship with the Lord when we keep close company with others who also hear and respond to what God says (Jn 8:47). Participation in the believing community is vital for our growth and our sense of belonging.

BETRAY

Two Hebrew words are usually found where the NASB and NIV OT read "betray." *Bāgad* means "to deal treacherously" and indicates unfaithfulness in a variety of relationships (Ps 73:15; Isa 24:16; 33:1; Jer 12:6; La 1:2). *Rāmâh*, in the Piel stem, means "to beguile or deceive" or "to deal treacherously." It is translated "betray" in 2 Sa 19:26; 1 Ch 12:17.

In the NT the Greek word translated "to betray" is *paradidōmi*. It means "to hand over, or deliver up." Unlike the OT terms, which suggest betrayal of a relationship, the NT term simply describes an action. *Paradidōmi* is used in the Passion story to report the betrayal of Jesus by Judas (Mt 26–27; Mk 14; Lk 22; Jn 18). It is also used of Pilate's handing Jesus over to the crowds and to the soldiers for execution (Lk 23:25; 24:7; Jn 19:16).

BETTER

Comparisons are important in Christian experience. Christian life is not simply a matter of turning away from what is bad. We must also choose between what is good and what is better.

OT 1. "Better" in the OT
NT 2. "Better" in the Gospels
3. "Better" in the Epistles

OT — 1. "Better" in the OT. The Hebrew people had an interesting way of expressing the notion of something being better than something else. They used the word "good" (*tôb*) with a preposition or other indicator of comparison. The verb "to be good" (*yātab*) is used in the same way.

The OT notes some foolish comparisons. The people of the Exodus generation thought it was better to return to Egypt than to venture on with the Lord (cf. Ex 14:12; Nu 14:3).

Often "better than" statements speak of the commonplace. But at times the comparatives carry a powerful spiritual message. For instance, Samuel told Saul, "To obey is better than sacrifice" (1 Sa 15:22). And the psalmist points out that "better [is] the little the righteous have than the wealth of many wicked" (Ps 37:16). Other psalms add, "Your love is better than life" (Ps 63:3); "It is better to take refuge in the LORD than to trust in man" (118:8; cf. v. 9); and "The law from your mouth is more precious to me than thousands of pieces of silver and gold" (119:72).

The Proverbs also are filled with statements of comparison (e.g., Pr 3:14; 8:11,19; 12:9; 15:16–17; 16:8,16,19,32; 17:1; 19:1,22; 21:9,19; 22:1; 25:7,24; 27:5,10; 28:6).

NT — 2. "Better" in the Gospels. The Gospels tend to use a construction like that of the OT to express the idea of better. They use *kalos* ("good," "beautiful") with a comparative. Four times Matthew uses *sympherō*, which means "it is advantageous," and therefore "better" (Mt 5:29–30; 18:6; 19:10).

Most of the Gospels' use of "better" is concentrated in three parallel passages (Mt 5, 18, and Mk 9). In these passages is the warning of Jesus in regard to the seriousness of sin and of causing others to sin. He teaches that it is better to be blinded than to suffer judgment for sins stimulated by the wandering eye (Mt 5:29; 18:8–9; Mk 9:43–47) and it is better for one's life to end early than for that person to live to lead others astray (Mt 18:6–7; Mk 9:42). ♦ *Heaven and Hell*

The disciples had an interesting reaction to Jesus' prohibition of divorce. "In that case," they exclaimed, "it is better not to marry!" (Mt 19:10). ♦ *Divorce and Remarriage*

3. "Better" in the Epistles. In most cases, the Epistles use the word *kreissōn* where the NASB reads "better." This Greek word means "more prominent," "more useful or advantageous," and thus "superior" or "better." Exceptions are in Ro 3:9 (*proechomai*, "to excel" — only here in the NT); 1 Co 8:8 (*perisseuō*, "to have an advantage"); and Heb 11:4 (*pleiōn para*, "better than").

Usually *kreissōn* is used in its ordinary sense. Paul believed it is better for engaged couples inflamed with sexual desire to marry than to burn (1 Co 7:9), even though he is also convinced that if it is possible, it is better not to marry at all (*kreissōn*, v. 38—only here in the NT). Peter encourages us by saying that it is better to suffer for doing good, if that be God's will, than for doing evil (1 Pe 3:17).

But in Hebrews, *kreissōn* is used with definite theological significance. The writer of Hebrews penned his letter to encourage and to strengthen wavering Hebrew Christians. His argument to those converts who were deeply rooted in OT traditions is that the gospel of Christ is superior and that Jesus in fact fulfilled what the OT merely promises. In this argument, the writer often uses *kreissōn* to show ways in which faith in Jesus is superior to the faith of the OT that it supplants.

Jesus' gospel is superior, for Jesus is superior to the angels, who are considered mediators of the OT message to man (1:4). Jesus brings a superior hope, which enables us to approach God himself and does not leave us standing outside a drawn veil (7:19). Jesus provides a superior covenant relationship (7:22; 8:6), anchored in better promises (8:6). All this is guaranteed by a better sacrifice than that of the animals offered on OT altars (9:23). All the OT saints were commended for their faith, but we have more: we are recipients of what they hoped for, as God in Jesus has planned something better for us (11:40).

It is good to exercise our faculties to choose the better or best of various options. But how wonderful it is to realize that in Jesus, God has provided the very best for you and me!

BEWARE

The OT and NT words for this concept have the same meanings: "Keep watch" (*šāmar*) lest you forget the Lord (Dt 8:11), lest your hearts be deceived (Dt 11:16), lest there be a base thought (Dt 15:9). The NT warns, "Give attention" (*prosechō*); that is, watch out for false prophets (Mt 7:15) and the leaven of the Pharisees (Mt 16:11). "Look out" (*blepō*) for evil workers who would distort the gospel (Php 3:2).

BIND/BOUND

1. Binding in the OT. Several Hebrew words are translated "bind" and "bound" in the NIV and NASB. They appear with the full range of our English terms. But there are some differences, which are reflected in the emphases of the Hebrew words.

The word *qāšar* means "to bind or league together." It is used in Dt 6:8 of tying Scripture verses on one's arm as a symbol, and it is used figuratively in Pr 6:21 of taking a parent's instructions to heart.

Ḥābaš means "to bind," or "to wrap with a bandage." One of the great prophetic passages in the OT portrays the Messiah's announcement of his mission—a passage quoted by Jesus in the synagogue at Nazareth (Isa 61:1; cf. Lk 4:16–21): "He has sent me to bind up the brokenhearted, to proclaim freedom for the captives and release from darkness for the prisoners."

The Hebrew word most often found where the NIV and the NASB read "bind" is *'āsar*. It means "to tie, or bind," "to harness," or "to imprison" and is found seventy-one times in the OT. It is used of binding with an oath (Nu 30:3–11), of hitching an animal to a cart (1 Sa 6:7), and of binding on a sword (Ne 4:18). Most often *'āsar* suggests imprisonment and is used of such things as binding a sacrifice (Ps 118:27) or putting a person in prison (Jdg 15–16). The ministry of the Messiah is not only to bind up the brokenhearted (*Ḥābaš*) but also to announce release for the prisoners (for "them that are bound," *'āsar*).

This Hebrew word is closest in meaning to the word used in the NT to express binding and bondage.

2. Binding in the NT. The Greek word is *deō*. This is an everyday word, used often in the NT and in the common speech of the NT era. Like the OT *'āsar*, which is translated by *deō* in the Septu-

125

agint, *deō* suggests the broadest range of meanings of "to imprison" and thus the notion of limiting one's freedom of action, as one might do in making an oath. (A different word, however, *anathematizō*, is used of the oath mentioned in Ac 23:12,14,21—its only other NT occurrence being in the account of Peter's denial, Mk 14:71.)

Two uses of *deō* in the NT have raised questions. In one instance it is linked with the marriage bond, and the question is whether, or in what situation, that bond is broken so that one may be free to remarry. The passages in question are Ro 7:1–8 and 1 Co 7. In Ro 7, Paul notes that the marriage bond is broken when one party of the union dies. He argues that the believer's relationship with Jesus is also a union and that in Jesus' death and resurrection the bond that obligates the individual to live by the Mosaic Law was also broken. ◗ *Law* In 1 Co 7:39, Paul restates the principle that death dissolves the marriage bond so that one is "free to marry anyone she wishes, but he must belong to the Lord." ◗ *Divorce and Remarriage*

The most controversial use of "bind" is found in the Gospel of Matthew. Both Mt 16:19 and 18:18 announce, "Whatever you bind on earth will be bound in heaven, and whatever you loose on earth will be loosed in heaven." In Mt 16 this is said to Peter and is associated with the "keys to the kingdom of heaven" (16:19). In Mt 18 the binding and loosing power is given to the Twelve. What is this power?

The early church fathers believed that binding and loosing referred to a rarely mentioned but recognized rabbinic authority—to expel persons from, and to receive them back into, a congregation. This understanding is supported by the flow of Mt 18:15–18. There Jesus establishes a process for correcting faults within the believing community. If we follow that process, and a person still "refuses to listen even to the church," he or she is to be expelled from fellowship. It is at this point, as a culminating statement, that Jesus says such exclusion from fellowship [not exclusion from salvation!] is

binding in heaven and on earth. God himself has been at work in the process, and the one rejecting correction steps out of fellowship with the Lord as well as with the brethren on earth.

BIRTH ◗ *Born*

BIRTHRIGHT

The word *bᵉkôrâh* designates the legal right of the firstborn son of an OT family to a double portion of what each other child would inherit and to other rights that might belong to the firstborn. This word is found only fifteen times in the OT. And at times it is used to designate the firstborn of flocks or herds (Ge 4:4; Dt 12:6,17; 14:23; Ne 10:36). In other passages it indicates the birthright, or right of the firstborn (Ge 25:31–34; 27:36; 43:33; Dt 21:17; 1 Ch 5:1–2).

The most significant use of *bᵉkôrâh* is in Ge 25. There we read the story of Esau's selling his birthright to Jacob for a bowl of stew. That birthright was far more than the material possessions of their father Isaac: it was first and foremost the promise of God, the covenant oath given to Abraham and passed down from generation to generation. In despising his birthright, Esau showed that he was a complete materialist and had no concern at all for the special relationship with God granted under the covenant.

Later, Jacob was far from blameless in plotting to have the birthright confirmed to him by his father. But his actions showed that he considered relationship with God an important thing.

BITTER/BITTERNESS

We have all known bitter persons. And we have all had bitter feelings. We know that bitterness is unpleasant and wrong. But how do we deal with bitterness? Although the NT has an answer, the OT explores an aspect of bitterness that we may not have considered.

OT **1. Bitterness in the OT**
NT **2. Bitterness in the NT**
   3. Dealing with our bitterness

OT — 1. Bitterness in the OT. The Hebrew words that are translated "bitter" and "bitterness" come from the roots *mārâh* and *mārar.* They mean "to be bitter" and, occasionally, "to be strengthened." Some suggest that Ex 1:14 should be understood to say that the Hebrews were "toughened" by their slavery in Egypt rather than "made bitter."

Sometimes "bitter" is used in the literal sense to indicate the sharp taste of an herb. But usually the word is used figuratively, to describe an emotion. In the OT, that emotion is not the one we usually think of when we use the word "bitterness." In its OT meaning, bitterness is close to despair, an anguish felt as one is crushed by overwhelmingly painful circumstances.

We can sense the feelings that bitterness conveys in the OT when we look into some of the situations it is associated with. Naomi moved from her homeland and saw her husband and her two sons die in a foreign land. "The Almighty has made my life very bitter," was her complaint (Ru 1:20). The death of an only child left the Shunammite woman in "bitter distress" (2 Ki 4:27). Job, suffering his crushing tragedies, longed for release from misery, for he was "bitter of soul" (Job 3:20). The troubles of the psalmist were "many and bitter" (Ps 71:20), and Jeremiah declared of the coming destruction of Jerusalem: "How bitter it is! How it pierces to the heart! Oh, my anguish, my anguish! I writhe in pain. Oh, the agony of my heart!" (Jer 4:18–19)

When we read of bitterness in the OT, then, we are invited to look deeply within the heart of a person crushed by circumstances. There we sense, not anger or resentment, but helpless pain.

NT — 2. Bitterness in the NT. The Greek word translated "bitter" is *pikros.* Its verb form, *pikrainō,* is found only in Col 3:19 (translated "be harsh with" in the NIV) and in Rev 8:11; 10:9–10. *Pikros* (masc. noun) is found only in Jas 3:11,14, and *pikria* (fem. noun) occurs in Ac 8:23; Ro 3:14; Eph 4:31; Heb 12:15. Although this word group is used to translate the OT Hebrew words for bitterness, the NT meaning is different from that of the OT.

Like *mārâh,* the literal meaning of *pikros* and its related words has to do with sharp and bitter taste. This literal use is found in Jas 3:11 and Rev 8:11. Other passages have a figurative use. But while bitterness in the OT focuses on inner emotional responses to crushing circumstances, bitterness in the NT focuses on that angry and resentful state of mind that can develop when we undergo troubles.

We see this emphasis in the words that the NT associates with bitterness. In Col 3:19 it is contrasted with love and suggests harsh treatment. In Ro 3:14 bitterness is linked with cursing, and in Eph 4:31 with rage, anger, and malice. Jas 3:14 ties bitterness to jealousy. The developed portrait in the NT reveals bitterness to be an angry, hostile outlook on life, an outlook expressed in resentment and in attacks on others.

The OT use of "bitterness" focused on the hurt caused by painful experiences. The NT use of the word directs our attention to the way such experiences can warp our personality, turning us into hardened and hostile human beings.

3. Dealing with our bitterness. One passage that gives us God's prescription for dealing with bitterness is Heb 12. The writer there describes the hardships that come into our lives and speaks of them as God's discipline. They are a form of training that God in love has determined we need for our own good (12:7–10). Crushing experiences never seem pleasant at the time. They are painful. It is only later that we see their fruit in inner peace and righteousness (v. 11).

But an experience intended for our good can be twisted into bitterness. The writer points out that to profit as God intends, we must not surrender to hopelessness. We must keep on going so that we can experience God's healing (vv. 12–13). We must struggle, in God's holy way, to live at peace with all around us and not give way to bitterness. The writer gives us a warning and an implied promise: "See to it that no one misses the grace of God and that no bitter root grows up to cause trouble and defile many" (v. 15). The remedy for bitterness, then, is the appropriation of God's grace.

God's grace operates here in three ways. First, we are to see his grace as the reality beyond our circumstances. Even our trials are his gifts. Second, we are to be sure to call on God for the grace we need in our time of need (Heb 4:16). And, third, we are to look beyond the present and be aware of the grace of God in the good outcome he intends.

When we recognize and rely on the grace of God, we will avoid the bitter resentment that not only spoils our own life but also darkens the lives of others (Dt 29:16–18). Released from bitterness, we will continue to live by God's Word, and we will win through to that healing of our inner hurt and to the blessing that God has planned for us.

BLAME/BLAMELESS

The word "blame" in the OT of the NIV and the NASB is a translation of the Hebrew word for sin. The thought in each passage is that the individual accepts responsibility for a shortcoming or for guilt.

We gain significant insights as we attempt to grasp what the Bible—OT and NT—means by "blameless."

OT 1. "Blameless" in the OT
NT 2. "Blameless" in the NT
    3. Blameless in God's sight
    4. Blameless in fact and deed

OT — 1. "Blameless" in the OT. The Hebrew words translated "blameless," usually *tām* or *tāmîm,* share a common root, *tāmam.* The underlying concept of blamelessness is that of completeness, or soundness. The complete truth involves telling all, honestly and correctly. Moral completeness involves a life that is upright and ethically sound.

Sometimes we read of OT saints, such as David and Nehemiah, who mention their own blamelessness to God in prayer (e.g., Ps 18:23; 26:1). Such expressions are no claim of sinlessness. Rather, they affirm pure motives and the choice of a way of life that rejects wickedness. The blameless OT believer accepted God's

way and sought to live by it. When he or she fell short, God's way prescribed confession and provided sacrifices for restoration. ◗ *Confession of Sins*

2. "Blameless" in the NT. Several Greek words are used in the NT to express the idea of blamelessness. *Amōmos* (Eph 1:4; 5:27; Col 1:22; Heb 9:14; 1 Pe 1:19; Jude 24; Rev 14:5) means "faultless," "without "blemish." *Amōmētos* is found only twice (Php 2:15; 2 Pe 3:14). *Anenklētos,* a significant word, is used five times (1 Co 1:8; Col 1:22; 1 Ti 3:10; Tit 1:6–7). In the Pastoral Epistles, it describes an elder and in context simply indicates a reputation for respectability. A synonym, *anepilēmptos,* is found three times in the NT (1 Ti 3:2; 5:7; 6:14). The usages in Colossians stress the legal sense of the word and signify one's being beyond accusation and thus not able to be called to account. A fourth term, *aproskopos,* means "without offense" and occurs in three passages (Ac 24:16; 1 Co 10:32; Php 1:10).

Although these words express a common concept and can be treated as synonyms, G. R. Berry, *A Dictionary of New Testament Greek Synonyms* (Grand Rapids: Zondervan, 1979), p. 17, suggests the following emphases: (1) *Amōmos* means *"faultless, without blemish, free from imperfections.* It refers especially to character." (2) *Amemptos* "is strictly *unblamed,* one with whom no fault is found. This of course refers particularly to the verdict of others upon one." (3) *Anenklētos* "designates one against whom there is no accusation, implying not acquittal of a charge, but that no charge has been made." (4) *Anepilēmptos* has the idea of *"irreprehensible,* designating one who affords nothing upon which an adversary might seize, in order to make a charge against him."

3. Blameless in God's sight. In the Pastoral Epistles, Paul is concerned with the reputation Christian leaders maintain in the wider community. But other passages speak of one's being blameless in God's sight (1 Co 1:8; Eph 1:4; 5:27; Col 1:22). Usually such references draw us to the day of final judgment, when human beings will appear before the Lord.

But how can we be blameless in God's sight? Like the OT saints, we are hardly sinless. In answer to this question the Book of Colossians calls attention, not to our own goodness, but to the person of Jesus. God has "reconciled you," Paul declares, "by Christ's physical body through death to present you holy in his sight, without blemish and free from accusation" (Col 1:22). It is God's action in Christ that blankets us with his own holiness and lets us stand blameless before God.

In a number of NT passages, then, blamelessness is positional. It is only because of our relationship to Jesus that we are able to appear before God, for Christ's blood has purified us and provided us with a blameless standing.

4. Blameless in fact and deed. But God gives us more than positional holiness. Looking ahead to history's end, Peter asks, "Since everything will be destroyed . . . , what kind of people ought you to be?" (2 Pe 3:11). He answers that we "ought to live holy and godly lives" (v. 11) and urges, "Since you are looking forward to this, make every effort to be found spotless, blameless and at peace with him" (v. 14). Here blamelessness is not positional but practical. It involves living the life of ethical and moral completeness that the OT stresses, so that we can keep a clear conscience (Ac 24:16). It is exciting to know that we can develop a blameless character that reflects our spotless standing with God in Jesus Christ.

BLASPHEME/BLASPHEMY

Today we are likely to think of blasphemy as swearing. But there is more to blasphemy than the casual curse.

OT 1. The OT concept of blasphemy
NT 2. The NT concept of blasphemy
    3. The charge that Jesus committed blasphemy
    4. Blasphemy as the "unforgivable sin"

OT — 1. The OT concept of blasphemy. Several Hebrew words are translated "blasphemy" in both the NIV and the NASB. In Lev 24:11,16 the word is *nāqab*, "to utter a curse against." In a number of passages the Hebrew word is *gādap*, "to revile" (Nu 15:30; 2 Ki 19:6, 22; Ps 44:16; Isa 37:6,23; Eze 20:27). But the word that is closest to the meaning of the NT term and captures the fullest meaning of the concept of blasphemy is *nā'aṣ* (also *nᵉ'āṣâh*), "to spurn or treat with contempt."

In the OT, God is viewed with awe, not only because of his power but also because that power is exercised in the world of people. God has committed himself to keep covenant with Israel and has thus become the focus of his people's lives. He is to be counted on, respected, and obeyed. All this is reflected in the commandment "You shall not take the name of the LORD your God in vain" (Ex 20:7; Dt 5:11, NASB). In essence, in the OT to blaspheme is to speak of God with contempt or to act in ways that show one views him as irrelevant to the issues of life.

OT — 2. The NT concept of blasphemy. The Greek words are *blasphēmeō* (verb), "to slander" or "to speak lightly of the sacred"; *blasphēmia* (noun), "slanderous, abusive, and damaging speech"; and *blasphēmos*, "slanderous."

In the NT, blasphemy indicates a hostile attitude toward God that is expressed directly or indirectly in contemptuous or slanderous ways. The verb is found some thirty-five times of the fifty-nine occurrences of the word group. What we call swearing may be categorized as blasphemy in that it treats God's name contemptuously or lightly. But the hostility implied in the NT use of the word shows us that, biblically, blasphemy is far more than a casual curse.

It is striking that one cause of the contempt in which unbelievers may hold the Lord is the actions of those who claim to believe. The Gentiles blasphemed God's name because of the hypocrisy they saw in the Jews (Ro 2:24). How important it is, then, that our lives honor the Lord so that we elicit praise, rather than contempt, for him.

3. The charge that Jesus committed blasphemy. In reading the Gospels, we make the startling discovery that the religious leaders of Jesus' day accused him of blasphemy (Mt 26:65; Mk 2:7; 14:64; Lk 5:21; Jn 10:33). This is because Jesus claimed rights and powers that belong to God alone and, as the leaders would not acknowledge Jesus to be the Son of God, he was charged with this religious crime.

4. Blasphemy as the "unforgivable sin". Jesus once warned those who observed his miracles and heard his teaching—and who then dared charge him with being in league with Satan— that they were treading on the edge of an unforgivable sin. "All the sins and blasphemies of men will be forgiven them," Jesus said, "but whoever blasphemes against the Holy Spirit will never be forgiven; he is guilty of an eternal sin" (Mk 3:28,29; cf. Mt 12:31; Lk 10:12).

Jesus had appeared as a human being, his essential deity disguised. But he had performed miraculous signs by the Spirit's power, and these signs gave unmistakable evidence that God was present and active in him. The unforgivable sin needs to be understood in this historical context. Those who charged that Jesus was in league with Satan rejected, consciously and willfully, the God who met them in Christ and in his words and the acts empowered by the Spirit.

Many people believe that the unforgivable sin is limited to the time of Jesus and to the unique events of that era. But an attitude that disregards the reality of God and leans toward contempt for his power and his presence is a dangerous one. It is a real danger for all who have not come to know him as a living reality through Jesus Christ.

BLEMISH

The symbolism in the word "blemish" comes from the OT. The animals offered to God on the sacrificial altar were to be perfect, without defect or cosmetic blem-ish (Ex 29:1; Lev 14:10; Dt 17:1; Eze 43:22). The symbolism finds expression in the NT's stress on the blameless and unblemished character God expects of believers. ◗ *Blame/Blameless*

BLESS/BLESSING

"Bless" and "blessing" are common in the OT and are found frequently in the NT. But these words are not part of ordinary speech today. When we read these words in the Bible, they seem a little strange, almost archaic. When we meet them in passages such as the Beatitudes, we may be puzzled by them. We wonder what all the "blessed are" statements mean.

However, when we search the Scriptures, we find in the roots of our faith a rich meaning for the word "bless" and a deeper understanding of all that God has given us in Christ.

OT 1. The OT concept of blessing
     2. God, the source of all blessing
     3. Who are the blessed?
NT 4. The NT concept of blessing
     5. The blessed in the Beatitudes
     6. "Blessed with all spiritual blessings"

OT — 1. The OT concept of blessing. The word in Hebrew is *bārak*, "to kneel" or "to bless." The root and its derivatives (*brākāh* and *brekāh*) occur 415 times in the OT, with the meaning of kneeling found only 3 times! It is clear that "bless" and "blessing" had an important place in the thought of the people of the OT.

According to *Theological Wordbook of the Old Testament* (ed. R. Laird Harris [Chicago: Moody Press, 1980]), 1:132, to bless means "to endue with power for success, prosperity, fecundity, longevity, etc." In essence, the one who is blessed is given a rich and abundant life.

In OT practice, blessings were pronounced on the children or subordinates by heads of households or others in authority (e.g., Ge 49). Yet God is recognized as the only source of blessing, and in the OT blessings were offered in his name.

2. God, the source of all blessing.
"LORD, you bless the righteous," says the psalmist (Ps 5:12). God not only gives life but also enriches life. Even the power to get wealth (Dt 8:18) comes from the Lord. We are totally dependent on him.

However, the OT believer saw God as the source of blessing within a unique relationship. The Creator, who gave and sustains life, entered into a covenant relationship with Abraham and his descendants. ♦ *Covenant* He committed himself to bless them (Ge 12, 17). But the covenant had to be accepted by faith by each succeeding generation, and blessing was found in obedience to a way of life that God later laid down. "I am setting before you today a blessing and a curse," Moses said in restating God's law to one generation, "the blessing if you obey the commands of the LORD your God that I am giving you today; the curse if you disobey . . . and turn from the way . . . by following other gods" (Dt 11:26–28). This truth, restated often in Deuteronomy (Dt 12, 15, 28) is basic to the OT concept of blessing. The abundant life, enriched by God, is to be found in the Lord and experienced as we live his way.

There are occasions when believers are called on to bless the Lord (e.g., Ps 103:1–2,20–22). In such settings, *bārak* is translated "bless" in the NASB and "praise" in the NIV. The thought in this usage is that the believer recognizes the Lord as gracious and faithful and acknowledges his goodness with praise.

3. Who are the blessed?. The Psalms contains a number of descriptions of the blessed. The blessed person is the one who "does not walk in the counsel of the wicked" (Ps 1:1), whose "sins are covered" (32:1), who "takes refuge in [the LORD]" (34:8). The blessed one makes the Lord his trust (40:4; 84:12), has regard for the weak (41:1), and possesses the strength of the Lord (84:5). The blessed have learned to acclaim the Lord (89:15), are disciplined by the Lord (94:12), maintain justice (106:3), and fear the Lord (112:1; 128:1). The ways of the blessed are blameless (119:1), for they keep God's statutes (119:2). The blessed are those

whose help and whose hope is in the Lord (146:5).

These are descriptions of the qualities that bring blessing. They are qualities of a faith relationship with God and of obedience to him. To such persons, God is free to give his richest, most abundant life.

NT — 4. The NT concept of blessing.
Two word groups are translated "bless" and "blessed" in the NT. One is from *eulogia,* which means "to speak well of," "to bless," or "to praise." Over forty of the sixty-eight occurrences of this word group in the NT are used in the sense of praise.

According to other passages, we believers are called on to bless others rather than to curse them (e.g., Lk 6:28; Ro 12:14; 1 Co 4:12). No matter how we may be treated, we are to respond in a positive way and to seek to introduce others to that life in Christ that brings blessing. *Eulogia* and its derivatives are used in the Septuagint to translate *bārak.*

The other word translated "blessed" in the NT is *makarios.* It means "blessed," "happy," or "fortunate." It is used in the Greek translation of the OT to render a Hebrew word group that means "happiness" or "well-being," but it is not used to translate *bārak.*

4. The blessed in the Beatitudes. It would be logical to suppose' that the "blessed are" statements of Jesus in the Beatitudes (Mt 5:3–11; Lk 6:20–22) parallel the "blessed" statements of the Psalms. However, this conclusion is not valid, for the Beatitudes use *makarios* ("happy"), which is not used by the LXX to translate the OT *bārak.* There are some similarities but also some significant differences. First, the similarities. The "blessed are" statements in the Psalms describe human attitudes or actions that lead to blessing. The Beatitudes also look at human attitudes. The *makarios* are poor in spirit, they mourn, are meek, hunger and thirst for righteousness, are merciful, are pure in heart, are peacemakers, and are persecuted because of righteousness (Mt 5:3–10).

But the OT rightly assumes from God's covenant promises that the enriched life includes material blessings. These will come later as the individual lives by faith and in obedience to God. Jesus moves beyond the OT covenant. He makes the startling statement that God's kingdom is a present kingdom and that his blessed ones already know ("are happy" with) a unique joy, which comes from living in that kingdom. Some of Jesus' "blessed are" statements do point to the future (esp. Mt 5:5). But the others are intended to describe the present inner experience of the believer, who, in comforting others, knows the supernatural comfort provided by God (2 Co 1:3–6) and senses the healing touch of God that rests on those who mourn.

The OT describes the path that leads to God's blessing. Jesus describes that blessing itself. God's blessing comes to us in all our circumstances and makes us fortunate no matter how others may view our lives.

The *bārak* of the OT was a straightforward blessing. The *makarios* of the NT is a divine paradox: an experience of the kingdom's inner riches amid external poverty and trial.

6. "Blessed with all spiritual blessings". Eph 1:3 announces it. God has "blessed us in the heavenly realms with every spiritual blessing in Christ." Because our blessing is found in personal relationship with Jesus and because that relationship is so intimate and real, we have in Jesus himself the abundant life for which we yearn and which God has ever yearned to give straying mankind.

BLINDNESS

The Hebrew word for blindness is *'iwwēr*. It is used both literally and metaphorically in the OT. Blindness has been common in the Near East since before biblical times, and OT law protected the blind (Lev 19:14; Dt 27:18). Metaphorically blindness indicates spiritual insensitivity. The prophets especially use the word in this way. Spiritual blindness can be a cause for judgment and a judgment itself (Isa 29:9–10), but

God is able to heal spiritual blindness (Isa 29:18–19).

The NT Greek word for blindness is *typhlos*. It too is used both literally and metaphorically. Jesus gave sight to the blind, but he often struck out verbally against the hostile religious leaders, calling them blind guides (Mt 15:14) and blind fools (Mt 23:16–17,19,24,26).

John's report of Jesus' healing the man born blind (Jn 9) contrasts physical blindness with the spiritual blindness of the onlookers. They saw the miracle but could not recognize Jesus as God's Son.

BLOOD

Blood—*dām* in Hebrew and *haima* in Greek—is theologically significant in both Testaments. In both, this word is linked with life and death. In both, blood introduces us to the depths of God's love for us and to his unique forgiveness.

OT 1. Blood in the OT
NT 2. Blood in the NT
    3. The blood of Christ

OT — 1. Blood in the OT. The word *dām* occurs about 360 times in the OT. It is found most often in the Pentateuch and in Ezekiel. "Blood" is used generally in one of two ways. Often it indicates violence (the shedding of blood in war or murder), the usual outcome being death. In other instances it is associated with the shedding of blood done in making a sacrifice to the Lord. Three OT passages show the respect for life that God demanded from human beings, and they show the significance of blood.

Ge 9:6. "Whoever sheds the blood of man, by man shall his blood be shed." In context, the blood of every living creature must be accounted for, because that fluid is "lifeblood." To shed the blood is to take the life; and although all life is precious, the life of human beings, made in God's image, is uniquely precious (9:4–6). ♦ *Murder/Kill*

Lev 17:11. "The life of a creature is in the blood, and I have given it to you to make atonement for yourselves on the altar." In OT sacrifices the blood of the sacrificial animal was drained, then sprinkled on the altar or ground, and the lifeless body was burned. The blood represented life; blood sustains mortal life and may be offered to God in place of the sinner's life. ♦ *Atonement*

Dt 12:23. "Be sure you do not eat the blood, because the blood is the life, and you must not eat the life with the meat." Blood is neither to be drunk nor eaten with meat (cf. also Ge 9:4). Blood is sacred fluid: once taken from an animal, its sole use was the sacrifice through which the OT saint was assured of the forgiveness of his sins.

2. Blood in the NT. The word *haima* occurs ninety-nine times in the NT. Often it refers to human bloodshed, representing violence and death. Five times the NT speaks of "flesh and blood" to indicate human limitations and weakness. Blood is used in Revelation to express the terrors of those days of judgment and is found fourteen times in references to OT sacrifices. Thirty-eight times the word is used in reference to the blood of Christ.

3. The blood of Christ. When the blood of Christ is mentioned, it is always in reference either to the institution of the new covenant or to Jesus' death as a sacrifice of atonement.

Christ's blood and the new covenant. The covenant plays a central role in the theology of the OT. A covenant is an agreement or contract. The OT covenants entered into by God took on the character of an oath or promise, for in them God bound himself to do certain things for his people. He also told individuals how they can experience the benefits promised. ♦ *Covenant*

There were a number of ways to make a covenant in OT times, but the most binding was a covenant instituted and sealed by blood (e.g., Ge 15:8–21).

In the OT, God promised that one day he would make a new covenant with his people. Under the new covenant, God promised to provide forgiveness and a new heart (inner transformation, Jer 31:33–34). The death of Jesus (more specifically, the blood that he shed on Calvary) instituted this new covenant. Christ's blood sets the seal of God's promise on his offer of forgiveness through faith in the Son (Heb 9:15–28).

We meet the new covenant again in the cup of communion (Mt 26:28; Mk 14:24; Lk 22:20; 1 Co 11:25,27). We are told to drink, recognizing the blood of Jesus, as a sign of our "participation in the blood of Christ" (1 Co 10:16). This language reflects Jesus' discourse on the Bread of Life, where he urged his hearers to "drink" his blood (Jn 6:53–56). The metaphor calls for appropriating by faith the sacrifice by which Jesus instituted the new covenant, while communion affirms our faith in that sacrifice.

Christ's blood and sacrifice. Most references to the blood of Christ are linked directly with Calvary and recall the OT link between blood and sacrifice. Thus, Ro 3:25 calls Christ's blood the "blood of atonement." Jesus offered himself up as a sacrifice for our sins. ♦ *Offering and Sacrifice*

The emphasis in many NT references is laid on the benefits won for us by Jesus' blood. It is by the blood of Christ that we are justified (Ro 5:9). ♦ *Justify/Justification* Through the blood of Christ we have redemption (Eph 1:7; Heb 9:12) and have been delivered from our old, empty way of life (1 Pe 1:19). Jesus' blood has brought us near to God in the most intimate of relationships (Eph 2:3) and has made peace for us by bringing us into harmony with our Lord (Col 1:20).

The blood of Christ has been effective in doing away with sin (Heb 9:24–26). This involves forgiveness (Eph 1:7), continual cleansing (1 Jn 1:7), and freedom from sin's binding power so that we can actively serve God with a cleansed conscience (Heb 9:14; Rev 1:5).

Against the background of the OT, we understand the meaning of the sacrifice of Jesus on Calvary. It is through the teaching of the NT that we grasp the wonderful benefits won for us by the blood of our Lord.

BOASTING

We cringe when we meet a boastful person. Arrogance and self-importance are hardly attractive. But there is more to the notion of boasting that we meet in the Scriptures. Boasting is a concept directly linked with a person's understanding of himself and of God.

1. Boasting, in the OT. The word most often translated "boast" in the OT is *hālal*. It means "to praise" and portrays the act of praising superior qualities or great acts.

Most often God is the one praised in the OT, though it is legitimate to praise also the admirable qualities of human beings (1 Ki 20:11; Pr 31:28,31). The kind of glorying or praise that is not appropriate is boasting about oneself.

The context makes it clear when glorying is not appropriate. It is foolish, suggests 1 Ki 20:11, for a person strapping on a sword for doing battle to glory (boast) as though he were taking it off after winning a victory. The boasting of the wicked in their evil (Ps 52:1), like the boasting of those who worship idols (Ps 97:7), is likewise wrong. God's words to Israel, recorded in Jer 9:23–24, give a proper perspective on the subject: "Let not the wise man boast of his wisdom or the strong man boast of his strength or the rich man boast of his riches, but let him who boasts boast about this: that he understands and knows me, that I am the LORD, who exercises kindness, justice and righteousness on earth, for in these I delight."

2. Boasting, in the NT. The key word group here includes *kauchaomai* (verb), "to boast, exult, glory, take pride in," and the nouns *kauchēma* and *kauchēsis*, which mean "boasting, pride, exultation." This verb, with the related verb *enkauchaomai* (found only in 2 Th 1:4), appears forty-one times in the NT, and the nouns eleven and twelve times respectively.

Finally, *alazoneia* (meaning "boastfulness" or "arrogance") is found in Ro 1:30 and 2 Ti 3:2, and *alazōn* ("boaster") is found in Jas 4:16 and 1 Jn 2:16.

It is clear from the NT that some things are suitable for Christians to take pride in. Paul exults over the growth of the young Christians he has led to the Lord (1 Co 15:31; 2 Co 7:4,14; 8:24). He is proud when they remain strong despite persecutions and trials (2 Th 1:4), and he hopes these brothers and sisters will take similar pride in him.

But it is Paul's theological use of the term "boasting" that is most significant. In Paul's letters, boasting typically represents the empty confidence of those who seek to win salvation by their own good works or by adherence to the details of the Mosaic Law. We may boast of our good actions, Paul admits, "but not before God" (Ro 4:2). Salvation comes only as a gift, totally divorced from any human righteousness or accomplishments. "For it is by grace you have been saved, through faith—and this not from yourselves, it is the gift of God—not by works, so that no one can boast" (Eph 2:8–9). Expecting that salvation might be accomplished by any action of ours reflects the same arrogant attitude and foolish self-importance that the OT condemns. Since Jesus "has become for us wisdom from God—that is, our righteousness, holiness and redemption," Paul, like Jeremiah, says, "Let him who boasts boast in the Lord" (1 Co 1:30–31).

Boastfulness is an unattractive trait. It alienates others. Spiritual boastfulness is especially onerous. Only by recognizing our own helplessness and relying completely on Jesus can we find the salvation that God is so eager to give us.

BODY

From the straightforward use of the term "body" in the OT, the NT launches us into a whirlwind of ideas and concepts about our life in this world.

OT **1. Body in the OT**
NT **2. Body in the NT**
     3. Jesus' body
     4. The body of sin
     5. The mortal body
     6. The importance of life in the body
     7. The resurrection body

OT — 1. Body in the OT. The two Hebrew words most often translated "body" are *bāśār* and *beṭen*. The basic meaning of *bāśār*, usually translated "flesh," is "animal musculature." The word is used often in this sense in discussions regarding the OT sacrifices. *Bāśār* occurs about 270 times in the OT, with it meaning extended to indicate the human body, living things, and life itself. ♦ *Flesh*

The word *beṭen* is translated "belly" in the KJV and indicates human inward parts. Often it means "womb." ♦ *Born*

OT passages use the word "body" in the full range of meanings the word expresses in English, from physical self to corpse.

NT — 2. Body in the NT. The Greek word is *sōma*. It occurs almost 150 times in the NT, 92 of them in the thirteen epistles known to be Paul's. The word *ptōma*, meaning "body" or "corpse," is found in Mt 24:28; Mk 6:29; Rev 11:8–9.

In the Gospels and non-Pauline letters, *sōma* is used much like *bāśār* in the OT. This includes the sense of "corpse" (Mk 15:43; Lk 17:37; Heb 13:11) and the concept of physical life (Mt 10:28; Lk 12:4). *Sōma* is also used to indicate the sphere in which we live out our life on earth.

The Pauline letters introduce a number of special theological uses of *sōma*. Some of these pick up and amplify concepts implicit in the OT. Some uses are distinctly related to fresh revelations of the gospel. These special uses are discussed below.

3. Jesus' body. Several times Paul emphasizes the fact that Jesus lived and died in the body. Paul reminded the Colossians, "[God] has reconciled you by Christ's physical body through death to present you holy in his sight" (Col 1:22). This teaching is vital because some people in NT times argued that Jesus "came" only in appearance. He seemed to be human but was not. However, it is vital to the gospel that Jesus became human in fact, died in fact, and was raised in fact. Thus Paul and the writer of Hebrews insist that "we have been made holy though the sacrifice of the body of Jesus

Christ once for all" (Heb 10:10; cf. 1 Co 10:16–17; 11:27,29; Eph 2:16; 1 Pe 2:24; 3:18; 4:1).

4. The body of sin. Paul was deeply aware of the ruin the fall had caused. Humanity is trapped, forced to live with a moral warp, pulled always toward sin and rebellion. This warp is not located in our physical nature alone. "Body" is not used here in that sense, nor does Scripture separate the human being into isolated elements that we can label body, soul, and spirit. ♦ *Soul and Spirit* Rather, the "body of sin" is the person himself in his bodily existence; that is, his life on earth, warped and twisted by a sinful nature inherited from our first parents.

The "body of sin" calls our attention to man's nature as sinner and acknowledges the weakness that we must struggle with (Ro 6:6; 7:24; 8:10).

5. The mortal body. This phrase also emphasizes the weakness inherent in human nature. But despite our weakness, believers are told, "Do not let sin reign in your mortal body so that you obey its evil desires" (Ro 6:12). Victory is possible because now the Holy Spirit has come to empower us. "If the Spirit of him who raised Jesus from the dead is living in you, he who raised Christ from the dead will also give life to your mortal bodies through his Spirit" (Ro 8:11; cf. Gal 2:20).

6. The importance of life in the body. Against the backdrop of man's lost and hopeless condition, the news that God can render sin inoperative and bring life where there was only death is stunning indeed. Our bodily life is the arena in which spiritual death has been experienced. Now our bodily life is to be the arena in which the new life that comes from Jesus must also be demonstrated. Because we have been raised with Jesus, we are told, "Do not let sin reign in your mortal body so that you obey its evil desires" (Ro 6:12). Each of us is to offer our "bodies as living sacrifices" (Ro 12:1), so that "Christ will be exalted" in our bodies (Php 1:20; cf. 1 Co 6:16–20).

Those who view spirituality as something related only to a person's inner life are in tragic error. It is in our bodily life on earth that sin found expression; and it is in our bodily life on earth with all of its relationships that Christ's gift of newness is also to find expression and in which Jesus is to be revealed (2 Co 4:11).

Spirituality can never be isolated from the daily life you and I live in the world. A certain wise Christian used to say that the Christian should be "natural in spiritual things, and spiritual in natural things." ♦ Soul and Spirit

7. The resurrection body. Paul also speaks of a resurrection body (1 Co 15:33–44; Php 3:21). We will not be disembodied in the eternal state but will experience eternal life in a resurrection body that will be like Jesus' own (1 Jn 3:1–2).

BODY OF CHRIST

The NT introduces a concept basic to our understanding of the Christian community. That concept is not hinted at in the OT. The body of Christ as the fellowship of believers is a distinctively NT revelation.

The body of Christ is a mystical but real union. It is a living organism, composed not of cells but of human beings. Christ is the head of this living organism, and each believer is linked to him and to one another within it. The NT does not treat the body of Christ as a mere metaphor. The church is not *like* a body; it *is* a body. The implications of this mystical reality are seen in two different emphases in "body" passages.

1. **Relationship of body members to one another**
2. **Relationship of body members to Jesus Christ**
3. **Analogies and implications**

1. Relationship of body members to one another. "Body" passages stress the fact that the Holy Spirit unites every believer to Christ's living body (1 Co 12:13; Eph 4:4). The members of that body are intimately linked with one another. "Each member belongs to all the others" (Ro 12:5). This true union is to find expression in interpersonal relationships among Christians. We believers have been joined together in the body according to God's grand design, "so that there should be no division in the body, but that its parts should have equal concern for each other. If one part suffers, every part suffers with it; if one part is honored, every part rejoices with it" (1 Co 12:25–26).

The passages that explain membership in the body tend to stress three things. First, each of us has a role (function) within the body. Second, God has a purpose in giving us those roles. Finally, close interpersonal relationships are called for if the body is to work properly.

The believer's function in the body is linked with the concept of spiritual gifts. ♦ Gift/Gifts Each Christian has a divine enablement, a God-given ability to minister in a supportive way to others. Enablements differ, but each person is sovereignly placed in the body so that his or her ministry will contribute to the growth of others.

"Growth" is the key to understanding the purpose of the gifts. Believers are to be equipped to exercise each God-given function (Eph 4:11) "so that the body of Christ may be built up" (v. 12).

Living in close, loving fellowship is also stressed in each passage in which the body is discussed. Love is called for so that members "will in all things grow up into him who is the Head, 'that is Christ," from whom "the whole body . . . grows and builds itself up in love, as each part does its work" (Eph 4:15–16).

To function as God has intended, the Christian community must understand itself as a body and develop intimate, loving relationships within which each person can minister to and serve the others.

2. Relationship of body members to Jesus Christ. A number of NT passages stress the fact that Jesus himself is the living head of his body on earth. "God has placed all things under his feet and appointed him to be head over everything for the church, which is his body, the fullness of him who fills everything in every way" (Eph 1:22–23). This theme is repeated in Eph 4:15; 5:22–32; Col 1:15–20; 2:19. The implications of this great truth are seen in every passage in which Jesus is presented as Lord.

The NT emphasizes the fact that Jesus is the living head of the church. Not only is he the source of her spiritual life and growth. Significantly, Jesus is to be recognized as "head over everything" regarding the church, with "all things under his feet."

The reality of the living presence of Christ with his people has great implications for understanding spiritual leadership within the body. Nowhere in the NT are Christian leaders designated "heads" of local organizations. Somehow human leadership must be exercised under, and with full acknowledgment of, the headship of Jesus, who through the Word and through the Holy Spirit can lead both local leaders and individual members of his body.

3. Analogies and implications. The NT affirms that the church *is* a living organism, and, like a physical body, the church has members with different functions. Each function is necessary to the health and growth of the whole. Like a physical body, the body of Christ is intended to mature. Spiritual gifts given to body members are intended to enable them to function in ways that promote the growth of the whole. This suggests that maturity is essential if believers and the Christian community are to be effective as instruments of mercy and testimony in the world.

The picture of the body also stresses the importance of unity. Only as parts of one's physical body are joined together can nourishment pass from one part to the other, and only so can the spiritual body work in concert.

Jesus' headship suggests his active role in directing the individual and the church in mission. Because Jesus lives, the church is far more a supernatural organism than an institution, and the lifestyle of the Christian community must be such that it supports and affirms the supernatural nature of its own, and

every individual believer's, relationship to Jesus Christ.

BOLD

The translators of the NIV and the NASB disagree on where to use this English word and its cognates (such as "boldness" and "embolden"). Yet each group of translators draws from one of three Greek words when selecting "bold" as a rendering (*tharreō, parrēsia, tolmaō*). Each Greek word shares a common cluster of meanings and is translated in the NIV and the NASB in a number of ways: confidence, courage, openness, boldness, and outspoken frankness. The rendering used depends on the sense of the passage and the translators' judgment of what best expresses the meaning of the original.

Only in 2 Pe 2:10, which describes false teachers as "bold and arrogant" (NIV), is one of these three confidence/courage-linked words not found. There the original reads *tolmētēs*. The boastful false teacher is not bold in the sense of being courageous or confident; he is reckless and headstrong.

But when "we say with confidence [*tharreō*], 'The Lord is my helper; I will not be afraid. What can man do to me?' " (Heb 13:6) we are not being reckless. We are simply taking God at his word and acting confidently in full assurance of his love.

BOND

At times, the bonds spoken of in Scripture are chains that hold captive (Jude 6, *desmos*). In Ro 8:21 the bondage is figurative, a graphic way the NIV chooses to represent the fact that our universe is subject to (*hypotassō*) decay. *Syndesmos*, "that which binds together," occurs in only four NT passages (Ac 8:23; Eph 4:3; Col 2:19; 3:14). In one, Simon the sorcerer, who wanted to buy from Peter power to convey the Holy Spirit, was rejected. He was a bundle of bitterness, wrapped tight and held together by sin.

The church of Jesus is far different. We are a united fellowship, tied together by peace (Eph 4:3). We are a living body, united to our head and held together by spiritual ligaments and sinews (Col 2:19). We have compassion, kindness, humility, gentleness, and patience—all virtues that are bundled together and kept intact by love.

Some bonds chafe and burden us. But the bonds that unite the body of Christ are a joy.

BONES

In the OT, "bones" is used literally and in a number of extended senses. It may be found in expressions indicating close relationship (Ge 2:23) or indicating the person as a self (Ps 6:2). Likewise, it is often used where intense emotion is expressed ("constant distress in his bones," Job 33:19; cf. Ps 42:10; 51:8; Jer 20:9).

BOOK

The word for "book" is *sēper* in Hebrew (*sᵉpar* in Aramaic) and *biblos* in Greek. Meanings range from "a writing," "report," or "legal document," to "archives" or "book." The *sēper* was usually recorded on a scroll, and its particular nature is clear from the text, as in "the Book of the Covenant" (Ex 24:7), "this book" (Dt 29:27), etc.

BORE ◆ *Bear/Bearing*

BORN

The OT inaugurates the use of the image of spiritual birth. The NT amplifies it, explaining what it means to be "born again" and "born of God."

OT 1. "Born" in the OT
    2. When does human life begin?
NT 3. Being born again
    4. Being born of God

OT — 1. "Born" in the OT. The word "born" is used to translate one of several forms of the Hebrew word *yālad,* which describes the act of giving birth.

But this word is used in a variety of other senses as well. For instance, *yālad* can indicate the male role in conception (Ge 4:18; 10:8; Pr 23:22). It is often used figuratively. At times, Scripture speaks of Israel as having been given birth by God, in the sense of having been given life and provided with care during infancy (Dt 32:18). Thus the idea of being "born again" is implicit in the OT and should not have surprised Nicodemus as it did when Jesus used the phrase (Jn 3).

The grammatical form that *yālad* takes makes it clear whether the writer means actual parentage or another, but equally close, relationship. The Hiphil stem of *yālad* is used to indicate paternity, and the Qal stem is used when some other relationship is intended. Thus when Ps 2:7 announces, "You are my Son; today I have become your Father," the text does not suggest a point in time when the Son "began." The Qal stem here affirms the uniqueness of the relationship between the incarnate Jesus and the Father—a relationship not definable by parentage alone, for the Father and the Son are both God; they are one from eternity (cf. Heb 1:3–5).

2. When does human life begin? One modern question is raised by the meaning of the root *yālad,* indicating the birth process. Does this imply that life begins at birth? Or does life begin at conception?

The best answer is suggested by turning to another Hebrew word, *beten,* which indicates one's visceral parts and often means "womb." A significant statement from the *Theological Wordbook of the Old Testament* (ed. R. Laird Harris [Chicago: Moody Press, 1980]), 1:103, brings the issue into focus: "The references to God in connection with *beten* indicate that he is the one who shapes and forms the fetus (Job 3:3–11; 31:18; Ps 139:13; Jer 1:5; cf. Ps 51:15), who brings the child forth from the womb (Ps 22:9; Isa 46:3) and superintends its life from the earliest moments (Ps 71:6; Isa 49:1)." The fetus has been a person from conception, and God's hand rests lovingly on a child before, as well as during and after, its birth.

NT — 3. Being born again. The Greek word for giving birth is *gennaō*, which can mean to literally "beget" or "bring forth" but is often used figuratively in the NT.

The phrase "born again" is found in John 3, in Jesus' discussion with the religious leader Nicodemus. Jesus makes it clear that being "born again" describes the action God's Spirit takes when he transforms human beings (3:6). Peter uses the same language, reminding believers, "You have been born again, not of perishable seed, but of imperishable, through the living and enduring word of God" (1 Pe 1:23). ♦ *Life and Death*

4. Being born of God. This phrase is also found primarily in John's writings (Jn 1:13; 1 Jn 2:29; 3:9; 4:7; 5:1,4,18). The spiritual rebirth believers experience does not come through any natural process. God is the actor who effects the new birth in those who believe and receive the Son (Jn 1:12–13). New birth makes us children of God (v. 13) and leads to moral transformation. One who is born of God does what is right (1 Jn 2:29). While we may fail at times, no one born of God "keeps on sinning." God's life is planted within our reborn personality. "No one who is born of God will continue to sin, because God's seed remains in him; he cannot go on sinning, because he has been born of God" (1 Jn 3:6,9; cf. 1 Jn 5:18).

Another expression of the new life we receive from God is found in our love for one another (1 Jn 4:7; 5:1–2). Love and purity of life are sure to follow new birth, for God's own life swells within the twice born. We who have become God's children through faith are destined to grow into Jesus' likeness.

BORROW ♦ *Lending and Borrowing*

BOUGHT ♦ *Redeem/Ransom*

BOW DOWN

The words most commonly translated "bow down" are *šāḥâh* (Heb) and *proskyneō* (Gr). They are usually translated "worship." Scripture calls on all people to revere and bow down to God. ♦ *Worship*

BRANCH

The Hebrew words that are translated "branch" suggest the idea of growth (budding and sprouting). Metaphorically, the verbs picture one who will spring up from the line of David to fulfill the promise that there will be a descendant who will become God's ideal, endless ruler. In both Testaments the figure of branches is used metaphorically of persons.

OT 1. Messiah the Branch
NT 2. Believers as branches
    3. Israel as natural branches

OT — 1. Messiah the Branch. Six passages in the OT identify the coming Messiah as the Branch (Isa 4:2; 11:1; Jer 23:5; 33:15; Zec 3:8; 6:12). The NIV and the NASB capitalize "branch" in these verses to indicate the messianic identity. In Isa 11:1 the Hebrew reads *nēṣer*, ("shoot" or "descendant"). In the others it is *ṣemaḥ*, ("sprout," "growth," or "branch"). Isa 4 associates the day of the Branch with the washing away of sins and with subsequent kingdom glory (4:2–6). Isa 11 describes the appearance of the Branch in the line of David (Jesse was David's father)—the Messiah's relationship with the Spirit of God (v. 2) and his ministry of setting all things right by bringing justice and righteousness to the earth (vv. 3–9). Jer 23 also emphasizes the ultimate role of the Messiah (vv. 5–6), and Jer 33 is crucial in identifying the Branch as the one who was to fulfill the Davidic covenant (vv. 15–22). ♦ *Covenant* Zec 3:9 emphasizes the removal of sins "in a single day" (v. 9), while 6:12 pictures reestablishment of the Lord's temple by one who is both priest and king. Jesus alone fits every description. Jesus alone fulfills every role. ♦ *Christ*

NT — 2. Believers as branches. John 15 contains Jesus' picture of himself as a grapevine, God the Father as the farmer, and believers as the fruit-bearing branches (*klēma*). In this passage, Jesus is discussing fruitfulness, not salvation, and the images used must be interpreted with this in mind.

What Jesus describes is the conditions under which believers will produce spiritual fruit. ▶ *Fruit/Fruitfulness* He points out that the vine is the lifesource; a branch that is not "in" the vine cannot bear fruit, for "no branch can bear fruit by itself" (v. 4). Believers remain "in" (fruitful relationship to) Christ by loving and obeying him. One who does not maintain this relationship loses contact with the vine and will be unfruitful. Such a branch withers and, as far as bearing fruit is concerned, is useless. It is the kind of branch most farmers clip off and toss out to be burned.

It is wonderful that God the Father prunes our useless branches back (v. 2) to restore us to fruitfulness! We are not just servants to God. We are his dearly loved friends (v. 13).

3. Israel as natural branches. Paul uses the image of tree branches (Gr, *klados*) in Ro 11 to explain God's plan for the people of Israel. Israel's special relationship to God is affirmed in the OT. But Paul explains that throughout sacred history, never has all of physical Israel experienced spiritual conversion. Yet within the natural line there have always been those who have responded to God in faith (Ro 11:1–10), even as many have responded to the gospel.

But what about the promises given to Israel as a people? Paul goes on, using the analogy of an olive tree. He shows that Gentiles have been grafted as branches into a tree whose root and stock are Jewish. Surely one day God will act to graft the natural branches back into the tree. This will happen, Paul affirms, "and so all Israel will be saved" (Ro 11:26). Jesus will return as Israel's Messiah, and the promises given God's OT people will be kept, for "God's gifts and his call are irrevocable" (Ro 11:29).

In both Jn 15 and Ro 11, the image of branches is used to make points that are sharply defined in the context. Only with much caution should one consider extending the images of passages such as these to suggest they apply to issues that the passages do not deal with.

BREAD

Bread was the primary food of people in Bible times. Bread was baked from a variety of grains, and often the flour was mixed with beans or lentils. The bread was baked flat, perhaps a half-inch thick, in wide loaves. Bread has special significance in the Bible: it represents the sustenance of life in the world. The significance of bread as a sustainer of life underlies the metaphorical uses of "bread" in the Scriptures.

OT 1. Unleavened bread
     2. Bread of the Presence
NT 3. Expressions using "bread" in the NT

OT — 1. Unleavened bread. The normal word for bread in Hebrew is *leḥem*. A special term, *maṣṣâh*, is used for unleavened bread—bread made without yeast or without waiting for the dough to rise. *Maṣṣâh* was often served to unexpected guests. On the night of Israel's deliverance from Egypt, *maṣṣâh* was eaten because of the hurried departure.

Throughout its generations, Israel was to commemorate that deliverance, and on the day of Passover the people were to eat unleavened bread (Ex 12:8,39). The "days of unleavened bread" included the Passover itself and the seven days that followed. ▶ *Passover*

2. Bread of the Presence. In Israel's worship, fresh bread was baked each Sabbath and placed on a table within the tabernacle or temple. Twelve loaves were set before the Lord in two rows to represent the tribes of Israel, their worship being represented by incense along each row. This bread could be eaten later, only, however, by members of the priesthood.

Yet, 1 Sa 21 tells of David, in sudden flight from Saul, demanding five of the consecrated loaves from the priest at the tabernacle.

Jesus later commented on the incident, when his disciples were condemned by the Pharisees for plucking and eating ears of grain on the Sabbath. Jesus reminded them of David's actions, claimed personal lordship over the Sabbath, and announced that God has always valued mercy over sacrifice (Mt 12:3–8). Law was intended to serve human need. But the rigid Pharisees had twisted that intention and raised their questionable interpretations of Sabbath law above the needs of the human beings whom they, and law, were supposed to serve.

NT — 3. Expressions using "bread" in the NT. A number of expressions in the NT use the word "bread." Jesus reaffirmed an OT confession, "Man does not live on bread alone," when he was tempted by Satan (Mt 4:4; Lk 4:4; quoting Dt 8:3). Human beings are more than animals trapped within the material universe and dominated by physical needs. They have a spiritual dimension. To live as true human beings, we must respond to the Word of God and not be driven by our physical urges.

In the prayer Jesus taught his disciples, one familiar request is "Give us today our daily bread" (Mt 6:11; cf. Lk 11:3). The plea emphasizes constant dependence on God for everything we need to sustain us.

One of Jesus' great discourses followed his miracle of feeding the five thousand with only five small barley loaves and two small fish. The next day eager crowds searched for Jesus. But when they found him, he told them not to be so excited about food that spoils. There is a food that will sustain eternal life, he told them: "I am the living bread that came down from heaven. If anyone eats of this bread, he will live forever. This bread is my flesh, which I will give for the life of the world" (6:51). The symbolism finds constant repetition in our practice of communion (cf. 1 Co 11:23–28).

The phrase "break bread" is found several times in Acts. It often refers to communion rather than to sharing a meal (Ac 2:42,46; 20:7,11; 27:35).

BREAK

Over ten different Hebrew and ten different Greek words are rendered "break" and "broke" in our Bible. Their meanings range from violent shattering to tearing open to frustrating. All these, and other shades of meaning as well, are expressed in the English words also. The particular emphasis is normally made clear by the biblical context.

It is helpful, however, to note that wherever the OT speaks of "breaking" the covenant that God made with Israel, man is the actor, and the Hebrew word is *pārar*. *Pārar* means "to break," "to frustrate," or "to invalidate." No human being can break the covenant promises of God in the sense of annulling them (Gal 3:15–17), but by refusing to honor the Lord and by turning from his ways, individuals, or particularly generations of Israelites, could frustrate God's purpose to bless them. For they would have been blessed if only they had kept the covenant. The same word and thought is applied to the idea of "breaking" God's law (Ps 119:126).

How much better it is to hold tightly to God and keep his Word and so experience the blessings that flow as we maintain fellowship with the Lord.

BREATH

A number of different Hebrew and Greek words are translated "breath" and "breathe" in the NIV and the NASB. Some of these words mean "to expire": "Abraham breathed his last and died" (Ge 25:8). Other words convey graphic images, such as "puff out" (e.g., "breathing out violence," Ps 27:12). Perhaps the most significant of the slightly used words is *hebel*. This word means "vapor," "breath," "nothing." Human beings, looked at solely from the perspective of their days on earth, are little more than a morning mist. We are a vapor that disappears with the rising of the sun. David says it in Ps 39:5–6: "You have made my days a mere handbreadth; the span of my years is as nothing before you. Each man's life is but a breath. Man is a mere phantom as he goes to and fro: He bustles about, but only in vain; he heaps up wealth, not knowing who will get it." It is wonderful that we, like

David, can look beyond the brief flicker of our life span and express eternal confidence in God: "But now, LORD, what do I look for? My hope is in you" (Ps 39:7) ♦ **Soul and Spirit**

BRIDE AND GROOM

Both Testaments view marriage as a source of delight. Bride and groom are pictured as finding great joy in each other (SS; Ps 45:9; Jer 7:34; 16:9). This happy image is picked up by Isaiah and applied to the restored relationship between God and Israel that will come in the future (Isa 49:18; 61:10; 62:5; cf. Jer 2:2). The NT uses the image of bride and groom to explore the relationship between Christ and his church (2 Co 11:2; Eph 5:21–33; esp. Rev 19:7,9). The imagery suggests that betrothal has taken place. But the consummation of the marriage and the fullness of joy are yet to come. ♦ **Marriage**

BROTHER

The word "brother" dots both Testaments. It is prominent in the Bible, alerting us to the fact that the relationship of "brother" is very significant for any who venture out to live the life of faith.

OT 1. The OT concept of brother
     2. Brotherly responsibilities in Israel
NT 3. The NT concept of brother
     4. Brotherly responsibilities in the Christian community
     5. Special NT uses of "brother"

OT — 1. The OT concept of brother. The Hebrew word is 'āḥ. It appears 630 times in the OT, where it can be translated "brother," "relative," "fellow countryman," or "friend."

Usually 'āḥ designates either full brothers or half-brothers. The OT family relationship was particularly strong, despite normal stress within families, as is portrayed in the Genesis stories of Jacob and Joseph.

The word 'āḥ is also used to designate all the people of Israel. The Israelites were brothers in the extended sense because they shared a common descent from the patriarchs. They were also brothers in the sense of being fellow citizens, members of a distinct national community that was in fact a family. In this sense, 'āḥ is often used in contrast to "foreigner."

A third major use of the term is illustrated in the relationship of deep friendship between David and Jonathan (2 Sa 1:26).

The word 'āḥ is sometimes used in a polite or a political way. Thus a stranger might be greeted as brother (Ge 29:4). Archaeological finds suggest that in surrounding cultures "brother" was used to address persons of rank or occupation similar to the speaker or writer.

Finally, nations linked by treaty or common heritage were thought of as brother nations. The term was sometimes used by one ruler in addressing another (Nu 20:14; 1 Ki 9:13).

The concept of brother in the OT does more than acknowledge relationship. It also suggests a set of mutual responsibilities that were appropriate because of the special relationship. This is particularly seen in responsibilities of the people of Israel to one another.

2. Brotherly responsibilities in Israel. Every Israelite was bound to live by the Ten Commandments and thus to act lovingly to all mankind (cf. Ro 13:8–10). Yet within the community of Israel the brother relationship led God's people to treat fellow-countrymen with special concern, going beyond the duty owed to all persons.

That special concern did not make it right for the people to do injustice to others. Aliens who had settled in Israel were to be treated with scrupulous fairness. Disputes were to be judged fairly, the people were told, "whether the case is between brother Israelites or between one of them and an alien. Do not show partiality in judging; hear both small and great alike" (Dt 1:16–17).

But there was in the fact of brotherhood a call to go beyond fairness. For instance, every seven years the people of Israel were to cancel debts owed to one another: "You may require payment from a foreigner, but you must cancel any debt your brother owes you" (Dt 15:3). Even when the time of canceling debts was near, God's people were told, "Do not be hardhearted or tightfisted toward your poor brother. Rather be openhanded and freely lend him whatever he needs" (Dt 15:7–8). Grace, not fairness, is brotherhood's demand.

Similarly, if a brother Hebrew was sold into servitude, he or she was to be released in the seventh year and supplied liberally from the resources of the master (Dt 15:12–15).

Again, an Israelite might lend a foreigner money or food and expect repayment with interest. But the people were warned: "Do not charge your brother interest, whether on money or food or anything else that may earn interest" (Dt 23:19–20). Even that which a poor person might give in pledge of repayment was not to be kept if it would deprive the borrower of something he or she needed (Dt 24:10–13).

There are other details of life that show that a special concern was to be exhibited in the national family. Tragically, history records no generation that lived the life of love that law describes. There were individuals who exemplified the ideal (see Ne 5), but as a community, Israel never caught the vision of the brotherhood that is possible for the people of God.

NT — 3. The NT concept of brother. In the Gospels and in Acts we find echoes of the OT. The word *adelphos* may mean "brother," "neighbor," or "kinsman" and is used in these familiar ways. (A different word, *hetairos*, used only by Matthew [11:16; 20:13; 22:12; 26:50], expresses the idea of "friend" or "companion.") Near the end of his life Paul spoke to hostile crowds in Jerusalem and addressed them as "brothers and fathers" (Ac 22:1). They were brothers, "those of [his] own race, the people of Israel" (Ro 9:3).

Yet Jesus introduced the pivotal shift of meaning that shapes the concept as it developed within the church. "Who are my mother and brothers?" Jesus asked.

"My mother and brothers are those who hear God's word and put it into practice" (Lk 8:21; cf. Mt 12:46–50; Mk 3:32–34). Within the nation a sharp distinction was being drawn. It was not one's race but one's response to God that was the criterion of relationship.

Jesus made the stunning announcement to the Pharisees that failure to believe in him (and thus in the God who sent him) indicates that these religious men belonged to their "father, the devil" (Jn 8:44; cf. 31–47). By contrast, those who believe in Jesus are able to call God their Father. The image of family and the name "brother" were already becoming in Jesus' ministry what the Epistles reveal them to be, i.e., indicative of intimate relationship, applied within the fellowship to those who belong to God.

In most cases where we read "brother" or "brothers" in the Epistles, the meaning is simply "fellow Christian(s)."

The choice of the word "brother," carrying with it the image of the family, is important theologically and practically. Within the family of brothers and sisters an exciting pattern of shared life emerges to define the way we Christians are to live with one another.

4. Brotherly responsibilities in the Christian community. The writer of Hebrews admonishes: "Keep on loving each other as brothers" (Heb 13:1). Peter states it in a fuller way: "Now that you have . . . sincere love for your brothers, love one another deeply, from the heart" (1 Pe 1:22).

The dynamic for this relationship is best explained by John. God's own love infuses the true believer, expressing itself in deep caring for others in the Christian family. Thus, one who does not love his brothers is still stumbling in the dark (1 Jn 2:9–11).

How do we love our brothers? This is shown throughout the NT in nearly every Epistle and Gospel. Brotherly love is expressed in confrontation and forgiveness (Mt 18:15–35; Lk 17:3), as well as by exclusion for disorderly conduct (2 Th 3:6,15). Brotherly love is expressed by acceptance, by refraining from judging (Ro 14:10–13), and by considering others while exercising one's own freedom (1 Co 8:9–13). No brother should be spoken against (Jas 4:11), wronged (1 Th 4:6), or sued in a secular court of law (1 Co 6:5). Rather, the needs of others in God's family should be generously supplied when we are able to help (1 Jn 3:17; Jas 2:15–16). Many passages describe the way Christians are to live together in this new community that is also God's family. All the grace and love urged in the OT can now be known by Christians, in fellowships that are recognizable by their love (Jn 13:34–35).

5. Special NT uses of "brother". A few NT passages that use the word "brother" have raised questions. Let us consider some of them.

The Gospel of Matthew (13:55–56) makes reference to Jesus' brothers "James, Joseph, Simon and Judas" and "all his sisters." Since these individuals are seen in company with Jesus' mother, Mary, it seems natural to take them as the children of Mary and Joseph. Some traditions argue that these "brothers" are half-brothers, children of Joseph before he married Mary, or that they are cousins. Although the language makes this meaning possible, there is no clear use of *adelphos* in the NT in this sense of "kinsman." And there is no theological reason to suppose that Mary and Joseph should not have had children together after Jesus' birth.

Another use of "brother" is found in prophetic passages that announce a time when brother will battle brother, in one situation resulting from the divisive impact of the message of Jesus (e.g., Isa 9:19; Jer 9:4; Eze 38:21; Mt 10:21). A historical example is the OT incident in which the Levites, after one particularly evil lapse into rebellion by some of the Israelites, acted to destroy the sinners at God's command (Ex 32:19–29). Their loyalty to God surpassed even loyalty to family members, as all human relationships pale beside our responsibility to God.

How wonderful it is that an act of commitment to God gives you and me many brothers and sisters—an uncount-able number—to love and to be loved by them (Mt 19:29).

BRUTE ♦ Animals

BUILDING

Most often, "to build" and "building" are used in the Bible in an ordinary, literal sense. And then comes the excitement when we discover that, in some sense, *we* are God's building—and God's fellow builders.

OT 1. Building in the OT
NT 2. Building in the NT
3. The church as God's building
4. The believer as a builder

OT — 1. Building in the OT. The major Hebrew word is *bānâh*. In its verb form (to "build" or "rebuild") it is used in the OT 376 times for all kinds of constructions, from altars to cities. The word is also used metaphorically. Sarah spoke of "building" a family (Ge 16:2), and God promised Jeroboam, "I will build you a dynasty" (1 Ki 11:38), based on the condition that that king would observe the Lord's commands and statutes.

The most fascinating uses of the OT concept of building are found in those passages where God is pictured as the builder, the people of Israel being his building project. This imagery is found in the later prophets when they seek to explain God's devastating judgments and to offer hope to those exiled after the destruction of Jerusalem and the temple. Disaster came because of the evil ways of the people (Jer 18:9–10). But God promised, "I will bring Judah and Israel back from captivity and will rebuild them as they were before. I will cleanse them from all the sin they have committed. . . . Then this city will bring me renown, joy, praise and honor" (Jer 33:7–9). Reestablished, Israel would bring glory to God, her builder.

NT — 2. Building in the NT. One of two Greek roots are found wherever the NIV and the NASB speak of the act of building.

Kataskeuazō means "to make [something] ready." In six of its eleven NT uses it suggests building (Heb 3:3,4; 9:2; 11:7; 1 Pe 3:20). Hebrews 3:1–6 compares the role of Moses and Christ in God's grand design. Moses is honored as a faithful servant. But Jesus is worthy of far greater honor, for he is the builder of the house in which Moses served! And, the writer says, "We are his house" (v. 6). God's people are his building.

Two references are to the building of the ark. Noah followed God's plans. Building according to the Lord's specifications won him praise and provided safety for his family.

The more common Greek words for building are a pair of related words. The verb is *oikodomeō*, meaning "to build up." The related noun is *oikodomē*, which means "a building" in 1 Co 3:9 and 2 Co 5:1 but more commonly means the process of building. Often these terms are translated by some form of the word "edify," which means "to build up," and building takes on a distinctive theological significance in Paul's writings.

Two repeated uses of building imagery in the Gospels underline other concepts. The NT five times speaks of Jesus as "the stone the [or "you"] builders rejected." This phrase is found in Ps 118:22 and is quoted in Mt 21:42; Mk 12:10; Lk 20:17; Ac 4:11; 1 Pe 2:7. The psalmist exults in a gate that the Lord opened so that righteousness could enter. "I will give you thanks," he said, "for . . . you have become my salvation" (v. 21). Then follows this statement: "The stone the builders rejected has become the capstone."

This stone, the capstone, is the keystone that holds the whole structure together. God's keystone, Jesus, was carefully examined by the "builders" of Israel, the religious leaders, and they rejected (*apodokimazō*) it as worthless. But "the LORD has done this, and it is marvelous in our eyes" (v. 23). In awe, the NT points again and again to Jesus, the keystone that holds the whole structure of God's plan together, the one who is recognized by faith.

Another theme repeated in the Gospels is that of the wise and foolish builders (Mt 7:24–26; Lk 6:48–49). Here the life of each individual is pictured as a structure, and the foundation of life is a believing response to Jesus.

3. The church as God's building. This powerful metaphor is often used in the NT. It grows out of Jesus' statement in Mt 16:18 that on the foundation of Jesus' deity and messiahship (the truth expressed in Peter's confession) our Lord was to build his church.

The picture of believers linked together and built into a divinely designed structure is expressed both by *oikodomeō* (Ac 9:31; 1 Pe 2:5) and by *oikodomē* (1 Co 3:9; Eph 2:21). It is more commonly expressed by the image of "God's house" and of "temple," for God's house is that living structure within which and through which he is worshiped. ◗ *Family* ◗ *Tabernacle and Temple*

4. The believer as a builder. While God is the architect who designs his house, you and I are given the wonderful privilege of serving as his fellow builders. This ministry does not call for piling up bricks and mortar. It calls for strengthening God's people. Both verb and noun are often used in this sense in the NT (*oikodomeō*: 1 Co 8:1; 10:23; 14:4,17; 1 Th 5:11; *oikodomē*: Ro 14:19; 15:2; 1 Co 14:3,5,12,26; 2 Co 10:8; 12:19; 13:10; Eph 4:12,16,29).

The most extended passage on the subject is 1 Co 3. It links the images of a field and a building. Paul and other Christian leaders and evangelists were planting and watering God's fields, but God was making the new life grow (3:5–8). Paul was just a worker with God, but Christ is the foundation of God's building. Each of us builds on that foundation. The quality of life and ministry to others will be considered when God distributes eternal rewards (3:9–15).

Two very important concerns emerge from the use of the building metaphor in the NT. First, how do we build—that is, how do we contribute to the inner growth of the believing community? Second, what enables us to edify (build up)

145

our own and others' inner lives? A survey of "building" passages suggests a number of elements that are necessary if God's people are to build up one another in Christ.

Building up God's spiritual building, the church, takes place when we work at maintaining peace and harmony in our fellowship (Ro 14:19) and seek each other's welfare (Ro 15:2). Loving others is essential if building up is to take place (1 Co 8:1). It is also essential to choose those things that are constructive rather than simply permissible (1 Co 10:23–24). Verbal ministry to others is also important. We are to share insights and understanding in plain speech (1 Co 14:3–18). Leaders are to exercise the right kind of spiritual authority (2 Co 10:8; 12:19; 13:10). ▶ *Authority*

Living together in love and unity and sharing themselves fully with their brothers and sisters, believers contribute to the growth of individuals and the believing community toward Christlikeness (Eph 4:12–16,29). The wise builder seeks to grow close to others, for in the intimacy of shared lives God's building grows.

BURDEN

There are several Hebrew and Greek words that are translated "burden." Each suggests a load to be lifted and carried, as by a pack animal. The imagery is extended to one's assigned tasks (e.g., Nu 4:15,19) and to the burdensomeness or oppressive emotional weight of certain situations. But, as the psalmist reminds us, there is help in God: "Praise be to the LORD, to God our Savior, who daily bears our burdens" (Ps 68:19). The NT words generally convey the idea of a heavy weight. Paul uses the symbol of burden to express financial dependence and tells the Corinthians that he chose to support himself when ministering in Corinth rather than allowing himself to be a numbing burden (*katanarkaō*, used only in 2 Co 11:9 and 12:13–14). Paul uses the word *epibareō* in the Thessalonian letters, where he stresses his own struggle to support himself; he did not want to heap extra burdens on the young church, and

he hoped to provide an example of personal responsibility and love. Paul was also concerned about sharing others' burdens (Gal 6:2). ▶ *Bear/Bearing*

BURN

Fire isn't always in the writer's mind when the Bible speaks of burning. But nearly all the meanings of the original are adequately expressed by the English term.

Burning in the OT. More than fifteen different Hebrew words convey shades of meaning within the general idea of burning. The most common OT word, *śārap*, is always used of literal burning. *Qāṭar* means "to burn a sacrifice," and *bā'ar*, used often, means "to consume." *Bā'ar* is often used figuratively and may be accompanied by words that convey the idea of complete destruction.

While the Hebrew words suggest different emphases, the particular meaning of burning is usually clear from the context.

Burning in the NT. The NT also has a number of words to express the idea of burning. *Katakaiō*, used twelve times in the NT, means "to burn up." It is used to refer to chaff that is burned at harvest time (Mt 3:12; 13:30,40; Lk 3:17), the useless works of believers (1 Co 3:15), the earth and lost humanity at Christ's coming (Rev 8:7,9–10; 17:16; 18:8–9,18; 2 Pe 3:10), and the OT sin offering (Heb 13:11).

Burning is also used to express intense emotion, as one may be said to be set on fire (*pyroomai*) by legitimate sexual desire (1 Co 7:9) and as one may be said to be inflamed (*ekkaiomai*) by illegitimate passions (Ro 1:27).

Other phrases using the concept of "burning" in the NT call for interpretation. Ro 12:20 refers to heaping burning coals on the head of enemies by doing good. Most scholars believe this suggests injecting some stinging sense of remorse into the others' lives, thus recognizing kindness as greater and more appropriate than revenge.

At times, burning does describe the eternal state of the lost (Rev 19:20; 20:10). But passages that speak of burning useless branches (e.g., Jn 15:6) should not be taken as referring to hell. ♦ *Branch* ♦ *Chaff* ♦ *Heaven and Hell*

BURY

In the Jewish community of Jesus' day, burial was to take place on the day of death. How do we explain Jesus' reaction to the reluctant disciple who begged, "Lord, first let me go and bury my father" (Mt 8:21–22; Lk 9:59–60)?

The answer is simple: the man's father had not yet died. The reluctant disciple wished to put his obligation to his father before his obligation to God, and he was rebuked. "Follow me" takes priority over every human need.

BUSINESS

In our modern world, business is a major economic force. What is the biblical view of doing business?

Several Greek words are related to business. *Emporia* (Mt 22:5 only) means "commerce, or business," and the verb *emporeuomai* (Jas 4:13; 2 Pe 2:3) means "to engage in business." Two other verbs have the same meaning: *diapragmateuomai* (Lk 19:15 only) and *pragmateuomai* (Lk 19:13 only) also mean "to engage in business or trade." A final term, *ergasia*, means "work" or "effort," and it often means the outcome of work—"profit." This word is found in the business sense in Lk 12:58; Ac 16:16,19; 19:24–25.

Looking over the relevant passages, we note two instances in which doing business is viewed negatively. Ac 16 tells of the owners of a demon-possessed slave girl; these men wrongfully made a profit from her sayings. Ac 19 describes the guild of silversmiths in Ephesus, who were greatly concerned about the religion of Diana—concerned because they made their money fashioning idols and souvenirs of idolatry.

Only Lk 19 deals directly with doing business itself. Here Jesus tells of a man who left his community but provided investment capital for his servants. They were told to put the money to work until their master came back. Clearly, activity and earning a profit are expected and are commended in the parable.

Yet, although doing business is honorable and profits are commendable, an attitude of presumption is wrong. We cannot look into the future and guarantee the outcome of any venture. Jesus warns that engaging in business requires humility (Jas 4:13–17). The businessman's attitude about his plans must always take "if it is the Lord's will" into account.

BUSYBODY

The first-century reader of the NT recognized the busybody immediately. He or she was a *periergos*—a meddler (1 Ti 5:13; *periergazomai* in 2 Th 3:11). A busybody is no more a contributing member of the body of Christ today than such a person was then!

BYWORD

Two different thoughts are expressed in the Hebrew words translated "byword."

Sᵉnînâh is a sharp word, a taunt. It portrays the cutting remarks of enemies who were glad when Israel experienced troubles (Dt 28:37; 1 Ki 9:7; 2 Ch 7:30; Jer 24:9).

Māšāl, or *mᵉšōl*, is often translated either "proverb" or "parable." But when Israel's doom under the judging hand of God is in view, the best translation is "byword." In each case, God's people suffered a judgment that held them up as a public example, a judgment to be pondered and learned from by all who observed their calamity. The context suggests that "byword" is the best translation in several passages (Dt 28:37; 1 Ki 9:7; 2 Ch 7:20; Job 17:6; Ps 44:14; 69:11; Jer 24:9; Eze 14:8).

C

CALL/CALLED

"Call" is a common word, used in both Testaments in common ways. But as with many other common terms, Scripture often lifts "call" beyond the ordinary. Both Testaments invest this simple word and the ideas it conveys with special significance when it is used to describe our relationship with the Lord.

OT 1. The Hebrew words
    2. Calling by name
    3. Calling to a task
    4. Calling on God
NT 5. The Greek words
    6. God's call in the Gospels
    7. God's call in the Epistles
    8. "Calling" as a condition
    9. Summary

OT — 1. The Hebrew words. In most cases, the common Hebrew word *qārā'*, "to call," is found. In the few instances in which the OT speaks of calling on someone or something to bear witness, the Hebrew reads *'ûd*, "to bear witness."

The root *Qārā'* occurs 689 times in the OT. It suggests utterance of a specific sound or message. When *qārā'* involves a message, the one who receives it is expected to respond.

Within the context of the OT, many uses of *qārā'* are commonplace (e.g., "Let's call the girl and ask her about it" [Ge 24:57]). But at other times the word is used in ways that give us special insights into the OT world and life view.

2. Calling by name. "You are no longer to call her Sarai," God told Abraham (Ge 17:15). Abraham's wife's name was changed to Sarah, which means "princess."

The naming and renaming of things, places, and persons is seen often in the OT (e.g., Ge 1:5,8,10; 31:48–49; Ex 15:23). Such activity is always significant, for to the Hebrews a name was more than a label. A name was an identifier, expressing significant information about a quality or characteristic of the thing named. This thought is carried over into the NT. Jesus angrily drove the merchants out of the temple court, saying, "My house will be called a house of prayer" (Mk 11:17). The very nature of the temple, expressed in the name "house of prayer," was violated by those who bought and sold there in flagrant disregard of the sanctity of the temple.

Similarly, Luke (1:32) reports that Jesus is to be "called the Son of the Most High." This is a strong statement of Jesus' essential deity. The name affirms his identity.

It is also likely that in OT usage the right to name implies at least a limited authority over that which is named. God, by right of creation, assigned names to his works (Ge 1). Adam, given dominion over God's creation, was permitted to name the animals (Ge 2:19) and his wife (Ge 3:20). God reassured Israel, "I have called you by name; you are mine" (Isa 43:1). The Lord created, formed, and redeemed Israel and has sealed the relationship by calling Israel by name. He claims Israel as his own and asserts his sovereign care over them, even as he has called us to belong to him (Ro 1:6).

3. Calling to a task. The common Christian notion of a "calling" is expressed in the OT. The leaders of the tribes of Israel were "appointed [lit., "called"] from the community" for their roles (Nu 1:16). The story of Isaiah's commissioning (Isa 6:1–8) is just one example that, in the Bible, God set individuals aside for specific tasks. And Paul clearly expresses this conviction: he sees himself as one "called to be an apostle and set apart" (Ro 1:1; cf. 1 Co 1:1).

4. Calling on God. The OT often uses this phrase (e.g., Ge 4:26; 1 Ki 18:24; Ps 4:3; 18:3; 53:4). As in other instances where *qārā'* conveys a message, a response is expected. To call on God is to ask God to act.

Ge 4:26 reports the time when "men began to call on the name of the LORD." This was just after the Fall, at a time when the tragic events reported in Ge 4 (Cain's murder of Abel and Lamech's bigamy and self-justified killing) demonstrated the awful impact of sin. Truly lost, and aware of that condition, some men turned to God.

It is significant that most often when OT believers called on the name of the Lord, they were in a desperate situation in which only God could help. How good it is to know that God invites us to turn to him in the day of trouble and gives us his promise: "Call upon me in the day of trouble; I will deliver you, and you will honor me" (Ps 50:15).

NT — 5. The Greek words. One of two Greek verbs is usually found where the NIV and the NASB read "call." The most common is *kaleō*, "to call." The other is *proskaleō*, "to call to," or "to summon." From the same root are *klēsis*, "a calling" or "condition," and *klētos*, "called."

There is a significant shift in root meaning between the Hebrew and Greek terms. The OT word emphasizes the utterance or the message. The NT emphasizes the intent: to call is to speak to a person with the purpose of bringing him or her nearer. The nearness may be physical (Jesus "called the crowd to him," Mk 8:34) or relational ("those who are called to belong to Jesus Christ," Ro 1:6).

Despite the shift in emphasis in the root, "call" is used in the NT with all the commonplace meanings of our language and with the special meanings—naming, calling to a task, and calling on God—noted in the OT. What is especially significant for us is that the NT lifts the concept of calling out of both commonplace and OT contexts. In the Epistles, God's call is transformed into a technical theological term.

6. God's call in the Gospels. The idea of call, when involving communication of a message, has always carried significant implications. A call is issued by a person of higher rank to those of lesser rank (cf. Ge 24:58; Ex 1:18; 12:21). Thus a call is something more than an invitation: it is a command and requires a decision by the ones called. The called are to hear and respond. Yet, to call does not assure a response. Human beings can ignore or reject even the call of God.

The freedom to reject is illustrated in OT history and is seen clearly in some of the Gospel parables. Jesus told of a wedding banquet prepared by a king for his son (Mt 22:2–10). The king's servants invited (called) the intended guests. But when those invited refused to come, the king turned to the streets to find the crowds that were needed to fill the wedding hall. The same story is repeated in Lk 14:16–24, with the same lesson taught. Those who are called but refuse the invitation will be excluded from the final celebration of redemption.

In the Gospels, then, "call" is often used in the sense of invitation, with the response of the invited being uncertain. Indeed, Mt 22:14 says that "many are invited, but few are chosen." The invitation is broad and inclusive. But few respond. Not all accept the invitation that God extends to us in Jesus.

7. God's call in the Epistles. When we reach the Epistles, and especially Paul's letters, we find "call" and "called" used in a distinctive theological sense. There is nothing here of the gospel's invitation with its uncertainty about individual response. "The called" have heard and have responded. They are the saved, and to be called is to be already involved in salvation's great adventure.

We can note several important aspects of the use of this concept in the Epistles. First, God is always construed as the active person. He is the one who calls, who has uttered his powerful Word, drawing us to him. As the one calling, God has the right to define the relationship his call has established.

Second, at first glance the human beings who are the called seem almost passive in the process. This has led some to suppose that God's call is an irresistible invitation and that human beings cannot help responding to the Lord's efficacious call. This interpretation, however, misses the nature of "call" in the Epistles as a technical theological term. Here "call" is equivalent to "salvation." It is a term that encompasses the entire process that God has planned from eternity. In the Epistles, God is the actor, because salvation is entirely his work, from the original plan on into the culminating glory. Man appears almost passive, because "call" has nothing to do with how we respond to God's invitation. The called are those who have responded and are immersed in the salvation process that has been initiated and defined and is guided in every phase by God himself.

Third, the whole process of salvation is encompassed in the call. God acted to call believers to himself through the gospel (2 Th 2:14). Believers now, we belong to Christ (Ro 1:6); we are loved by him and named "saints" (Ro 1:7). As his very own, we are to live holy lives (1 Co 1:2; 1 Pe 1:15) so as to be worthy of our calling (Eph 4:1; 2 Th 1:11). God planned the unique salvation process from eternity (Ro 8:28–30). We are to live out the life he has planned for us (1 Ti 6:12; 1 Pe 2:21; 3:9) with other believers, united with them in the bond of peace (Col 3:15) and full of hope (Eph 1:18; 4:4), knowing that the end of the process means a share in God's own eternal glory (1 Pe 5:10).

8. Calling as a condition. A special use of "calling" is found in 1 Co 7:17–24. Here Paul wrote to individuals who were troubled by their situation in life. They were married or unmarried, circumcised or uncircumcised, slaves or freedmen. And many felt they could serve God better if one or more of these conditions were changed and if their life situation were changed. But Paul advised them, "Each one should retain the place in life that the Lord assigned to him and to which God has called him" (7:17; cf. vv. 20,24). Here, then, God's "call" is the Lord's sovereign action in placing individuals in specific circumstances or situations. While Paul left the door open for a change of circumstances (v. 21), he wanted the Corinthians to realize that a person can serve God and be spiritually significant whatever his or her circumstances. And he wanted them to know that God's sovereignty extends to ordering the details of each believer's life.

9. Summary. In both Testaments, "call" can have special significance. A call uttered by a superior demands a response from the one to whom it is addressed. In the Gospels, God's call is an invitation to personal relationship, and in response to this call individuals must make life's most significant choice.

In the Epistles, "call" becomes a technical theological term encompassing the whole process of salvation. The called are the ones who have heard and have responded and thus been plunged into the experience of the salvation that God has planned from eternity.

As God's called ones, you and I now recognize that salvation is from the Lord alone. As God's called ones, we joyfully submit to the one who alone defines and guides our experience of that salvation, until he ultimately brings us to share the glory.

CANAANITES/CANAAN

These familiar OT terms designate both a people and the land they possessed. The name Canaan comes from an ancestor of the peoples, identified in Ge 10:15–18. The Canaanites, with the Amorites, inhabited Palestine when the Israelites invaded the land c. 1400 B.C. under Joshua.

The Canaanites had a highly developed city-state culture at that time. They also practiced a nature- and sex-oriented religion, which continued to attract straying Israel for hundreds of years—in fact, until the time of the Babylonian captivity (c. 586 B.C.).

The conquest of Canaan was not only a fulfillment of God's promise to give Abraham's children the land of Palestine; it was also a divine judgment on the evils associated with the Canaanites' religion (Ge 15:16).

CANCEL

Col 2:14 is a theologically significant verse. Paul links the new life we enjoy in Christ and the forgiveness of our sins with God's act in Christ of "having canceled the written code, with its regulations, that was against us." "Regulations" connotes a posted edict, binding on all, while "written code" suggests an IOU, acknowledging personal debt. The binding word of Mosaic Law and the guilt that the law brings are both canceled in Christ.

The Greek word here is *exaleiphō*, "to wash out." It was used (1) of canceling a vote or a legal charge and (2) of annulling a law. Here it probably pictures washing away the writing inked on a piece of papyrus. Under the flowing water the words are simply washed out. This is a powerful picture of the fact that, for the Christian, law's decrees, which bring only guilt, no longer exist. ▶ *Law*

Exaleiphō is used four other times in the NT. Acts 3:19 speaks of washing out our sins. Rev 3:5 promises that Jesus will not wash from the Book of Life the names of those who walk with him. Rev 7:17 and 21:4 promise that one day God will wash away the tears from our eyes.

CAPSTONE

The NASB calls it the "chief cornerstone." In both the NASB and the NIV, the various NT references all suggest that the image is an important one for faith—and for unbelief.

Ps 118:22 and five NT quotes. Looking ahead to the coming Messiah, the psalmist cries, "The stone the builders rejected has become the capstone; the LORD has done this, and it is marvelous in our eyes." The NT quotes this verse five times, always relating it to Jesus. He was rejected by the Jewish leaders, though ordained by God as the foundation on which the Lord's new construction, the church, must rest.

Architecturally the "capstone" (Heb, *pinnâh*; Gr, *kephalēn gōnias*, "head of the corner") was most likely the large stone that lay at the top of the wall at the corner, binding the walls of a structure together. Some think it may have been the keystone that completes an arch or structure. Used figuratively as in these contexts, the capstone is clearly the one essential stone on which the integrity of the building depends.

The thrust of Ps 18 and the NT passages that quote it (Mt 21:42; Mk 12:10; Lk 20:17; Ac 4:11; 1 Pe 2:7) emphasize Israel's historic rejection of Jesus, despite his appointment by God. Peter points out that we who believe see the preciousness of Jesus, for we acknowledge him as essential to the structure of our faith. Unbelievers still stumble over the central role Jesus must have. Rejecting him, they disobey the gospel message and are lost.

Isa 28:16 and two NT allusions. In the Isaiah passage, God announces that he will himself "lay a stone in Zion, a tested stone, a precious cornerstone for a sure foundation." The promise is that "the one who trusts [in him] will never be dismayed."

The NT speaks twice of that cornerstone (*akrogōniaios*), once to stress the importance of faith in Jesus (1 Pe 2:6) and the other time (Eph 2:20) to uphold Jesus' role as the one in whom "the whole building is joined together and rises to become a holy temple in the Lord" (2:21).

Jesus is central to Christian faith. No one else and nothing else can serve to hold its structure, or our lives, together.

CAPTIVITY

Captivity is an uncomfortable theme, for captivity was a constant danger in ancient warfare, and it is a spiritual pitfall for the unwary today.

Captivity in Israel's history. God's people were wrested from slavery by God's own powerful action. God intended to release Israel from Egyptian bondage so they might serve him alone. But Israel's history is a story of constant unfaithfulness. And when the people of Israel turned from God to worship idols, what awaited them was captivity in the form of subjection to foreign powers (Dt 28:41).

Ultimately Israel's apostasy required their removal from the Promised Land. The people of the Northern Kingdom were removed from the land by Sargon (722 B.C.), and the people of Judah were deported by Nebuchadnezzar (586 B.C.). When they became a captive people, it was not God but a pagan world power that exercised immediate control over the destiny of the people of the Lord.

The historic lesson of captivity is clear in the sacred record. God intends his people to be directly subject and responsive to him. But failure to be obedient to God ripped Israel from the land of intended blessing. Disobedience led Israel into subjection to far less gracious powers than God.

Captivity as a NT theme. NT references to captivity reflect the message of sacred history. One who submits to a power other than God is taken captive, and his or her freedom is curtailed. ♦ *Serve/Servant/Slave* Thus captivity to sin (Ac 8:23) is tragedy indeed, for rather than obeying God, the believer finds himself obeying the evil desires of the mortal body (Ro 6:12–14).

Several NT passages use the theme of "captivity" in distinctive ways. One verse, 2 Co 10:5, speaks of taking "captive every thought to make it obedient to Christ." The Greek word *aichmalōtizō* denotes the taking of a captive in war, and the verse thus pictures our Christian life as a constant struggle to bring our

every purpose into subjection to Christ's will.

Col 2:8 warns against letting ourselves be taken captive (*sylagōgeō*, "to be carried away as booty") "through hollow and deceptive philosophy, which depends on human tradition and the basic principles of this world rather than on Christ." In context, the Colossians are warned against adopting limiting do's and don'ts as measures of spirituality (cf. 2:20–23). Spiritual achievement calls for personal allegiance to Jesus, not to standards invented even by a believing community.

A third verse, 2 Ti 2:26, warns that Satan seeks to trap (*zōgreō*) human beings in misunderstandings of the gospel and of its righteous way of life in order that such individuals may do his will (cf. Eph 4:8 with Ps 68:18). ♦ *Ascend*

In these and other NT passages, we see that we are to allow nothing to take us captive and thus win control over our actions. We remain free by being personally obedient to Jesus Christ as he speaks to us in his Word and by his Spirit.

CAUSE

There are two senses in which the word "cause" is used in the Bible. One (a noun) is reflected in the psalmist's cry, "Defend the cause of the weak" (Ps 82:3). The other is reflected in this dramatic question: "When disaster comes to a city, has not the LORD caused it?" (Am 3:6).

1. **The just cause**
2. **Causation: proximate cause**
3. **Causation: human responsibility**
4. **Causation: God beyond all circumstances**

1. The just cause. The Bible speaks of God as one who "defends the cause of the fatherless and the widow" (Dt 10:18; cf. Isa 1:17; Jer 22:16). The psalmists often call on God to act to uphold the cause of the weak (82:3), the needy (140:12), and the oppressed (146:7).

A number of different Hebrew words are translated "cause" in such passages. But each implies a dispute, controversy, or lawsuit that must be brought to someone to settle.

Typically, appeals to God to defend or uphold a cause are made by those who are powerless, or who are being unjustly persecuted. Such appeals are based on the OT believers' firm conviction that God is faithful to those who keep his covenant and that he is fully able to act in the world of men.

2. Causation: proximate cause.

All of us can look at a given situation and isolate factors that are causes of events. This is also common in Scripture. For example, according to Jn 12:18, "Many people, because they had heard that he [Jesus] had given this miraculous sign, went out to meet him." A miracle performed by Jesus was the proximate cause of the curious crowd going out to see him for themselves.

The OT is full of similar expressions. Ex 23:33 gives God's warning against letting the Canaanites remain after Palestine was conquered. Contact with their religion would cause them to sin against God. Elisha purified the tainted waters of a poisonous spring and gave the people God's promise: "Never again will it cause death or make the land unproductive" (2 Ki 2:21). Judah's king Amaziah was warned against the pride that prompted him to attack Israel, for it would cause his own downfall (2 Ki 14:10).

In each of these cases, Scripture looks at a given situation and points to choices or to events that cause other events. Cause and effect clearly do operate in our world of space and time. Anyone looking at a given situation will often be able to identify those things that serve as causes of subsequent events.

In both Testaments, cause and effect are spoken of within the framework provided by specific situations. But Scripture does not take the logical leap of faith made by many philosophers. Scripture never suggests that the idea of proximate cause (immediate cause within the given situation) can be extended to forge some endless chain in which every event can and must be explained only in terms of preceding causes. When the notion of cause and effect is so extended, we are left with a mechanical universe. In such a universe, human beings would be trapped, having neither freedom nor responsibility.

There is a great difference between, on the one hand, seeing cause and effect operate within the framework of specific situations and, on the other hand, imagining that history is nothing more or less than an unfolding chain of effects, each predetermined by preceding causes. ◗ *Predestine*

3. Causation: human responsibility.

The Bible makes it clear that individuals are responsible for their own actions and thus that no mechanistic "cause/effect" theory can explain away human choice. ◗ *Account/Accountable* Each of us has the freedom to choose, and the exercise of that freedom is not determined by circumstance.

At the same time, the Gospels repeat a warning of Jesus to his disciples: "Things that cause people to sin are bound to come, but woe to that person through whom they come" (Lk 17:1; cf. Mt 18:7). It is a serious thing to "cause one of these little ones to sin" (v. 2).

Ro 14:21 helps us sense the way in which "cause" is used in this and similar passages. Ro 14 deals with a dispute between those who felt that eating meat was wrong and those who believed it was right. Such personal convictions are not part of the gospel (14:14). But, even so, it would be wrong for a person holding a conviction to act against it.

In this context, Paul raises the question of our responsibility toward those with whom we differ. Paul gives no clear-cut answer. But he does say that if eating meat in front of a brother "causes" him "to stumble," "it is better not to eat meat" (14:21). Here "cause" is not used in either the sense of force or the sense of releasing the individual from responsibility for his own action. Paul's thought is that eating meat before such a brother might prove a proximate cause of leading him to start "passing judgment" or else to violate his conscience and follow the meat-eater's example.

There is a delicate balance here. Each individual is responsible to God for his choices and for his actions. However, others within the context of the situation in which the choices are made may influence the individual—for good or ill. Jesus' warning and Paul's reminder in Romans are intended to make us sensitive to the fact that our actions do have an influence on others.

While each individual is accountable to God for his own choices, all of us are called by God to influence others toward that which is truly good.

4. Causation: God beyond all circumstances.

The universe is never portrayed in Scripture as mechanical, with events determined by some endless cause-and-effect chain. Cause and effect do operate within specific situations. But, even here, human beings exercise personal freedom of choice, and it is the moral choice of individuals that most significantly affects the sequence of events.

But Scripture does provide a nonsituational view of the universe. Far from being dead and mechanical, the universe that the Bible describes is infused by the power of a living, moral Creator and Sustainer.

To the writers of the OT and NT, cause and effect can be found only beyond our material universe. The principles that govern events on earth are moral in nature and flow from the character and the purpose of God. Only when we see history in a perspective provided by our knowledge of God can we understand what has happened and why.

Essentially, a biblical view of cause and effect affirms that the universe operates on moral principles and that God ultimately (though indirectly) guides the course of history.

The moral nature of the universe and of history is often seen in the OT. It is seen when Moses warns Israel, "If you turn away from following him, he will again leave all this people in the desert, and you will be the cause of their destruction" (Nu 32:15). The moral choice of the adults of a generation will lead to preservation or to destruction, for God will shape history according to the righteousness of their acts. In the same way,

Moses explained that obedience to law would bring blessing, but if Israel should disobey, "the LORD," he told them, "will cause you to be defeated before your enemies" (Dt 28:25; cf. Eze 32:12).

The moral, rather than the mechanical, theory of causation is the one found in Scripture, and it demands that God be actively involved in the shaping of events. Again, the conviction that God is just this kind of being is expressed in both OT and NT. At times his intervention is miraculous and clear. But generally his intervention is quiet, and his causative actions are unnoticed by people. Only when we have the perspective of Daniel, who recognized God's presence in every situation, are we able to perceive in our own lives a principle that was true in Daniel's: "Now God had caused the official to show favor and sympathy to Daniel" (Da 1:9).

The message of the Bible is that there is a hidden supernatural aspect to cause and effect. God is beyond, and yet within, every circumstance. He acts to shape and to mold. The greatest impact that we can have on the shape of our future is to make truly moral personal choices, choices that express obedience to God's leading and his Word. It is our responsibility to obey. It is God's part to shape the results of our actions to fit his good purposes and his plan.

CELEBRATION

In Scripture, celebration is linked specifically with one of the three main religious festivals of Israel, during which all the people of Israel were to come to the temple for worship. The Hebrew terms are either ḥāgag ("to make a pilgrimage," "to keep a pilgrim feast") or the common word ʿāśâh ("to do or make"), associated with a feast.

The three feasts with which celebration is associated are: Passover and Unleavened Bread (Ex 13:3–10; Lev 23:4–8; Dt 16:1–8); Harvest, Weeks, or Firstfruits (Ex 23:16; Lev 23:9–21; Dt 16:9–11); and Ingathering, Booths, or Tabernacles (Ex 23:16; Lev 23:33–43; Dt 16:13).

CEREMONIAL ▶ *Clean and Unclean*

CHAFF

The image of "chaff" comes from agriculture in biblical times. After the harvest, the Palestinian farmer seeks out a flat area on a windswept hillside. There harvested grain is flailed and then tossed high into the air. The chaff (Heb, *mōṣ;* Gr, *achyron*) is swept away by the wind, and the precious kernels of grain fall to the ground, to be gathered and stored in granaries.

"Chaff" is often used figuratively in the Scripture. In every case, it has a negative connotation. The wicked, Ps 1:4 asserts, "are like chaff that the wind blows away." David looked around at his enemies and prayed, "May they be like chaff before the wind, with the angel of the LORD driving them away" (Ps 35:5). Daniel foresaw the end of pagan world empires and reported that all their elements "became like chaff on a threshing floor in the summer. The wind swept them away without leaving a trace" (Da 2:35).

In the NT, John the Baptizer's powerful words of warning make it clear that the chaff are the lost, who refuse to respond to God's message. The wheat, then, represents the believer, whom God will surely preserve and treasure.

CHANGE

Change threatens many of us, and we struggle to keep things the same. But change is built into the very structure of the universe. "That which is seen," Paul writes in 2 Co 4:18, "is temporary, but what is unseen is eternal." Anything that you and I can touch or see or feel can and will change. Only the God beyond the universe is stable and unchanging.

The theme of change and temporality is seen often in Scripture. The psalmist looks at the earth and heavens God has created, and says, "They will perish, but you remain; they will all wear out like a garment. Like clothing you will change them and they will be discarded. But you

remain the same, and your years will never end" (Ps 102:26–27). The fact of change is not viewed in Scripture as threatening. It contains a warning for us, and it offers hope.

The warning is implied in passages such as Jas 1:9–11. We cannot rest our confidence in anything in this brief life, lived as it is on the shifting sands of history (cf. Heb 12:25–29). Yet at the same time the fact of change provides a ground for hope. We are not trapped by our past, unable to change. In fact we "are being transformed into his [Jesus'] likeness with ever-increasing glory, which comes from the Lord, who is the Spirit" (2 Co 3:18). And, ultimately, "we will all be changed—in a flash, in the twinkling of an eye, at the last trumpet. For the trumpet will sound, the dead will be raised imperishable, and we will be changed" (1 Co 15:51–52).

Change, then, is viewed by Scripture as imbedded in the very nature of the created universe. It will always be part of the human experience. Yet the believer can still hope in an uncertain world. By God's will we even now experience an inner change, a growth toward godliness. And we will experience the ultimate change in the resurrection.

We are confident of this, for we have God's promise "I the LORD do not change" (Mal 3:6). ▶ *Repent*

CHARACTER

There is no specific word or concept translated "character" in the OT. But a very clear idea is found in the NT, expressed in the word *dokimē*.

The word group from which *dokimē* comes draws our attention to testing as a means of determining genuineness and thus as a grounds for giving approval. *Dokimē* is the quality of being approved and thus of having a demonstrated character. We see it used in this sense in Ro 5:4; 2 Co 2:9; 9:13; Php 2:22. Note also the use of *tropos* ("manner" or "way") in Heb 13:5 (NASB): "Let your way of life be free from the love of money."

What is the NT's message for us concerning character? It is that our character can develop only over time, through many testings. It is as we persevere in the life of faith that we develop a Christian character, of which God can approve. ♦ *Temptation/Test/Trial*

CHASTEN ♦ *Discipline*

CHEERFUL

The NT reserves this bright, happy word for use only in 2 Co 9:7. And the occasion is that of giving! Paul says our giving is not to be the reluctant act of one compelled by some grim demand. Giving is to be *hilaros*, a spontaneous response to need, a response that brings giver as well as receiver a glad sense of inner joy. ♦ *Giving*

CHERUBIM ♦ *Angels*

CHILDREN

Theologians have written books filled with questions about children in the church. Should children receive baptism? How old should children be to take communion? Is there an age of accountability? If so, what is that age? Can boys and girls really accept Christ as their Savior? How old must they be when they are allowed to do so publicly? And how much of the gospel do they have to grasp to be born again?

Despite all the books and learned arguments, there is little in Scripture to suggest answers, or even to suggest the questions. Children are viewed in the Bible as members of the community of faith. They grow up in believing families, and they grow up in faith. There is no theology of childhood suggested in either Testament. There is no special educational system outlined or taught.

Yet the Scriptures speak naturally and often of children—thousands of times. If we limit ourselves to what the Bible says about children, we find many fresh insights, though we find few answers for the theologians' questions.

OT 1. The Bible's attitude toward children

2. Hebrew words for "children"
3. Principles for the nurture of children
NT 4. Greek words for "children"
5. The weakness of children: *nēpios*
6. Children to age seven: *paidion*
7. Little children and Jesus' kingdom
8. Children between ages seven and fourteen: *pais*
9. Children in family relationship: *teknon*
10. Beloved children: *teknion*
11. Summary

OT — 1. The Bible's attitude toward children. The men and women of biblical times wanted large families. Children were viewed as a gift of God, a special blessing (Ge 22:2; Ps 127:3–4; 128:3; Isa 8:18). The emotional importance of children is underlined by the grief expressed by the childless and those who lost a child (Ge 30:1; 1 Sa 1:3–17; 2 Sa 12:14–25; Ps 113:9; Lk 1:24–25). Some of the blessings promised a person who fears the Lord and who walks in his ways are found in Ps 128:3–4,6: "Your wife will be like a fruitful vine within your house; your sons will be like olive shoots around your table. Thus is the man blessed who fears the LORD." And the culminating benediction is "May you live to see your children's children." Both Testaments make reference to the love and guidance to be provided by parents (Dt 4:9–10; Ps 78:4–6; Pr 4:3–4; 2 Co 12:14; Eph 6:4; 1 Ti 3:4; Tit 2:4) as well as to the responsibility of children (Pr 6:20; 13:1; Eph 6:4).

Jesus' own sayings about children clearly indicate that God views them as significant members of his kingdom, now and beyond time (Mt 18:2–5; Mk 9:33–37; 10:13–16; Lk 9:47–48).

2. Hebrew words for "children". A number of OT words are translated "child" or "children." Some are quite specific; for example, two that indicate very young children are '*ûl* and *yānaq*. Others indicate a wider span of ages, as *ṭap*, which can be a person from birth to age twenty but usually indicates someone younger. *Yeled* generally indicates young children, but may refer to teens or even young adults. *Na'ar* is sometimes translated "servant." But in its over two hundred OT occurrences it generally indicates a person between the age of weaning (about two) and marriageable age. Realizing this helps us understand that it was not little children who ridiculed Elisha and were attacked by bears (2 Ki 2:23–24); it was a gang of young hoodlums. The word *bēn* is found almost 5,000 times, and means "son" or "child." It is used some 630 times in the phrase "children of Israel," usually translated "Israelites" in the NIV and the NASB.

Despite the extensive vocabulary available in speaking about childhood, of which the above are examples, there seems to be little technical use that would permit us to develop an OT theory of childhood. The Bible uses terms about childhood with the same imprecision with which we use such words as the following: youngster, child, boy, girl, or toddler.

3. Principles for the nurture of children. Both the OT and the NT view children as members of the faith community. Each assumes that children will grow up in the context of relationships provided by that community. Within the community context, the OT defines a nurture process that intimately involves the family. The process is described in Dt 6:4–9. This process is especially important, since it gives guidelines for communicating faith in God through a written word, introduced here by Moses for the first time in salvation history.

The critical elements in the nurture process are the following: (1) parents who love God and have taken his Word to heart (Dt 6:4–6). The values, attitudes, and behavior of parents, shaped by the Word of God, providing the example needed by children to help them sense that God is real. (2) Conversation in the family about God's words so that these words are impressed on the children (Dt 6:7). (3) The relating of God's words to the daily experiences shared by parents and children. Scripture thus interprets life, and life experiences are guided by the words (Dt 6:7–9).

This significant interpersonal process for communication of Scripture in a nurturing way has never been superseded by any other system. It lies at the very heart of the effective communication of faith, today as well as in biblical times. The rest of the OT and the NT assume this process, for it is basic to bringing up children in the faith.

NT — 4. Greek words for "children". The NT words for "boys" and "girls" fall short of providing a technical vocabulary for a theory of childhood. Yet the words are more precise than those of the OT and offer many insights. *Nēpios,* the classical Greek word for an infant, stresses the weakness or helplessness of a child in contrast to the powers of an adult. *Paidion* designates a child up to age seven. *Pais* is a child between seven and fourteen, as distinct from a little child and an adolescent. *Teknon* is a child as viewed in relation to his parents or family. This word takes on special theological significance when the Bible calls believers the children of God. *Teknion* designates a little child. This word is used by John to address the followers of Jesus, who must have seemed like very little ones to the aged apostle.

Because these words are relatively precise, we gain many insights when we explore their use in the Gospels and the Epistles.

5. The weakness of children: *nēpios*. This word describes a very young child, characterized by weakness or helplessness when compared with an adult. *Nēpios* is found in Mt 11:25; 21:16; Lk 10:21; Ro 2:20; 1 Co 3:1; 13:11; Gal 4:1,3; Eph 4:14; Heb 5:13.

Divisions in the church at Corinth showed those believers to be spiritual infants (1 Co 3:1) whose reasoning and thought processes were immature (1 Co 13:11). A *nēpios* differs little from a slave, in that he or she must be under the authority of an adult (Gal 4:1–2)—a destiny not intended for us in Christ, in whom we receive "full rights as sons" (4:3). To grow beyond infancy and gain our inheritance calls for us to build close relationships with other believers and with Christ himself, for we grow to maturity together (Eph 4:14–16). Maturity comes only in community and only by a personal commitment to use our God-given capacity and choose between good and evil (Heb 5:13).

6. Children to age seven: *paidion*. The *paidion* is the "young child" and "little child" of the Gospels. In Jewish culture, the young child was not responsible to keep the Mosaic Law. The child accepted this responsibility when he reached the age of twelve, when he became *bar mitzvah* (a "son of the covenant"). *Paidion* occurs in the Epistles in 1 Co 14:20; Heb 2:13–14; 11:23; 1 Jn 2:13,18.

The Corinthians were again urged to "stop thinking like children." But the emphasis in other passages shifts from the fact of childhood to emphasize relationship. Believers are God's children: as we are flesh and blood, Christ came to share our humanity and free us from the deadly grip of Satan (Heb 2:13–14). As God's children, we know the forgiveness of sins, and we know God as Father (1 Jn 2:13–14). We may be too young to relate to God through the law, but we are still his children, and he knows us in warm and immediate relationship.

7. Little children and Jesus' kingdom. Several passages report Jesus' affirming statements about little children (*paidion*, the child from birth to seven). In a special way, "the kingdom of heaven [God] belongs to such as these" (Mt 19:13–15; Mk 10:13–16; Lk 18:15–17). To enter the kingdom of God, Jesus says, one must receive it "like a little child" (Lk 18:17).

The specific points of comparison on which these sayings rest is most clearly seen in Mt 18:1–5, which initiates an extended discussion of greatness (Mt 18:1–20:28). Jesus had preached to an unresponsive Israel. Yet when Jesus called a little child to stand among his disciples, the child responded immediately (18:2). An adult must "become like little children" and "humble himself like this child" (18:3–4) to catch a glimpse of Jesus' kingdom, and doubly so to find

greatness. It is the child's unhesitating response to Jesus' call, so different from the proud reluctance of the adults of Israel, that makes childlikeness such an attractive and necessary quality.

This understanding is reinforced by Mt 19:13–15. The Pharisees, whose boast was in their zealous keeping of God's law, came to test Jesus (Mt 19:1–12). Their very question brought a rebuke, for it showed how far they were from God's heart (19:3–4). Still the Pharisees argued, and they rested their argument on the Mosaic Law in which they trusted.

Jesus refuted their argument. And at this point, Jesus announced that the "kingdom of heaven belongs" to little children and those like them. Even the most zealous Pharisee never imagined that a seven-year-old's relationship with God was mediated through law. Yet for Jesus it is a childlike response to and trust in God, not an adult self-effort, that brings a person into relationship with God and into Jesus' kingdom. ▶ *Kingdom*

8. Children between seven and fourteen: *pais*. *Pais* in Greek identifies a boy or girl between seven and fourteen. At times the word also is translated "servant." It is used some five hundred times in the Septuagint to translate ten different Hebrew words. In the NT, *pais* is found only in the Gospels and in Acts and has no special theological significance. It occurs in Mt 2:16; 8:6,8,13; 12:18; 14:2; 17:18; 21:15; Lk 1:54,69; 2:43; 7:7; 8:51,54; 9:42; 12:45; 15:26; Jn 4:51; Ac 3:13,26; 4:25,27,30; 20:12.

9. Children in family relationship: *teknon*. This word underlies most English occurrences of "child" and "children." When *teknon* is used, it views the child in relation to his parents or family. The child is thus placed in a relational context, and in the Epistles this is theologically significant. Redeemed, we become the children of God (Ro 8:16). This does not affirm our childlikeness, but it affirms the fact that we are members of God's family and thus heirs (8:17). Soon we will experience full redemption and the liberty that is inherent in our relationship to the Lord (8:21).

Fleshly descent can never bring us into the spiritual family initiated with Abraham (Ro 9:7). Only faith can.

The thrust of *teknon*—whether the relationship of the child is to God, to Satan (Jn 8:39–41), to one's physical parents, or to one's spiritual parents (1 Th 2:7,11; 1 Ti 1:2)—is to assert the fact that we cannot understand an individual apart from understanding the family in which he holds membership.

Teknon occurs in the Epistles in Ro 8:16,17,21; 9:7,8; 1 Co 4:14,17; 7:14; 2 Co 6:13; 12:14; Gal 4:25,27,28,31; Eph 2:3; 5:1,8; 6:1,4; Php 2:15,22; Col 3:20,21; 1 Th 2:7,11; 1 Ti 1:2,18; 3:4,12; 5:4; 2 Ti 1:2; 2:1; Tit 1:4,6; Phm 10; 1 Pe 1:14; 3:6; 2 Pe 2:14; 1 Jn 3:1,2,10; 5:2; 2 Jn 1,4,13; 3 Jn 4; Rev 2:23; 12:4,5.

10. Beloved children: *teknion*. The word *teknion* is a diminutive, expressing affection, and is translated "little children." Paul used it in Gal 4:19. But the other uses are found in John's writings. Jesus used this word when he spoke to his disciples at the Last Supper (Jn 13:33). John used it to address that generation of disciples to which he ministered when he was approximately ninety years old (1 Jn 2:1,12,28; 3:7,18; 4:4; 5:21).

11. Summary. Children were highly valued in biblical times. They were seen as members of the believing community, and faith was shared naturally with them within the family and in the worship of the community.

The NT words indicating children make distinctions between age groups. These and other distinctions are important for understanding NT references to believers as children. The term *teknon* is particularly important, for it draws our attention to individuals not simply as children but as members of particular families, as those who must be understood within the context of their family and its character.

While differences between adult and childhood abilities are recognized, sometimes even highlighted to show the weakness of the faith of some, childlike-

ness is more often valued. In the kingdom of God it is a childlike faith, which responds unhesitatingly to Jesus and relies on his words, that brings us into full experience of life in God's kingdom.

CHOICE/CHOSEN

The Bible often uses the adjective "choice" to indicate quality. At a party, one serves only choice foods. But the use that most fascinates Bible students indicates an act of selection. Both Testaments emphasize God's choices more frequently than human choices. When we add to this the realization that the Greek word group rendered "choice" is also expressed as "elect," we understand that fascination. What does the Bible teach when it speaks of God's choice of places and, especially, of persons?

OT 1. The Hebrew word
2. Human choices in the OT
3. Divine choices in the OT
NT 4. The Greek word group
5. Freedom of the divine choice
6. Content of the divine choice
7. The question of election

OT — 1. The Hebrew word. The Hebrew word nearly always found where the NIV and the NASB speak of making a choice is *bāhar*.

The word and its derivatives have this meaning 198 times in the OT. The root may suggest taking a careful look at something. One form, *bāhîr*, always stresses the fact that by God's choice a relationship has been established between the chosen and the Lord (2 Sa 21:6; 1 Ch 16:13; Ps 89:3; 105:6,43; 106:5,23; Isa 42:1; 43:20; 45:4; 65:9,15,22).

2. Human choices in the OT. In the OT the stress is laid on God's choices; nevertheless, human beings are also portrayed as making choices. At times, choices are made within established limits: the sacrificial animals the Israelites chose had to meet specific criteria (Ex 12:5; cf. Dt 1:13; Jos 3:12). Sometimes the choice that is urged on one is clear and vital. Israel was urged to follow God and so choose life rather than death (Dt 30:19). The OT often returns to this theme. God's people are encouraged to choose what pleases the Lord (Isa 56:4; 65:12; 66:4) and fear of the Lord (Pr 1:29), not false gods (Jdg 10:14). Often the choices to be made are moral. Israel was to (in the words of the prophecy regarding the virgin's son) "reject the wrong and choose the right" (Isa 7:15,16). And the psalmist chose the way of truth (Ps 119:30), committing himself to keep God's precepts (Ps 119:173).

It is clear from this brief survey that the OT treats the community of Israel and individuals within it as able to make spiritually significant choices. God established criteria to guide choices. And he laid out the pathway his people were to select. But the choice of what God had provided and the responsibility for the choice made remained with the nation and its members.

3. Divine choices in the OT. The OT portrays God as one who makes a wide range of choices. A number of themes are repeated, and thus the often-mentioned choices are clearly significant.

God chose Israel (Dt 7:6; 14:2; 18:5; 21:5; Ps 33:12; Isa 14:1; 41:8,9; 44:1; 45:4; Eze 20:5).

God chose the city of Jerusalem, where his temple would be erected, as the nation's capital (cf. Dt 12:5,11,14,18,21; 14:23–25; 15:20; 16:2,6–7,11,15–16; 17:8,10; 18:6; 26:2; 31:11; Jos 9:27; 2 Ch 6:6,34,38).

God chose individuals: Abraham (Ge 18:19; Neh 9:7), Moses (Ps 106:23), David (1 Sa 16:9–10; 1 Ki 8:16; 1 Ch 28:4; 2 Ch 6:6; Ps 78:70), and even Saul (2 Sa 21:6).

In every instance, God's choices were completely free. They were not imposed by any necessity. They were not called for by the acts or merits of the ones chosen. Dt 7 protects Israel from misreading their having been selected by God. It stresses the fact that God's choice was internally motivated. His choices are a spontaneous act of love; the explanation for God's choices must be sought in the character of God and not in any quality of the chosen.

"The Lord did not set his affection on you and choose you because you were more numerous than other peoples, for you were the fewest of all peoples. But it was because the Lord loved you and kept the oath he swore to your forefathers that he brought you out with a mighty hand and redeemed you from the land of slavery. . . . Know therefore that the Lord your God is God: he is the faithful God, keeping his covenant of love to a thousand generations of those who love him and keep his commands" (Dt 7:7–9).

NT — 4. The Greek word group. In nearly all passages in the NT that speak of choice or election, it is a single word group that is so translated: *eklegomai*, "to select or choose"; *eklektos*, "chosen"; and *eklogē*, "a selection." Another term, *haireomai*, is found only three times in the NT. In 2 Th 2:13 it means "choice," but in Php 1:22 and Heb 11:25 the meaning is "prefer."

The words in the *eklegomai* word group are common in the Greek language. They imply options from which one can choose. And they suggest that the person making a choice selects freely, rather than being compelled by some circumstance.

Human beings are shown in the NT as making choices. The church chose Stephen to be a church officer (Ac 6:5; cf. 15:22). Companions were chosen for a missionary journey (Ac 15:40). Yet even more than the OT, the NT focuses our attention on the choices of God. It is God's choices that the writers of the NT are concerned with, and their use of these words consistently affirms God's freedom to act and affirms as well the grace that motivates his actions.

5. Freedom of the divine choice. Dt 7 affirmed the principle. In Ro 9, Paul argues strongly for it and against those who would try to find a reason for God's choice in some supposed human merit or inherited right. Paul looks back into sacred history and points out that physical descent from Abraham never guaranteed spiritual rights. God chose Isaac to be in the covenant line but rejected Abraham's other son, Ishmael (Ro 9:6–9). Isaac's sons (Jacob and Esau) were twins. Yet before their birth, before they "had done anything good or bad—in order that God's purpose in election might stand: not by works but by him who calls," their mother was told that Jacob was God's choice to carry on the covenant line. Esau was decisively rejected for this role (Ro 9:10–13).

In arguing this way, Paul proves that "it does not . . . depend on man's desire or effort, but on God's mercy" (Ro 9:16). Thus Paul makes the same point as that made in Dt 7. God's action in providing salvation and the existence of a people of God can be understood only by reference to God's own will. Salvation is completely his work, resting on grace alone. All comes from God's character, which is the sole explanation for his choice.

Thus Paul in Romans seeks simply to establish God's total freedom of action. No human being can claim as a right what God has spontaneously provided in his love and grace.

6. Content of the divine choice. God chooses freely. But what does God choose?

In the Gospels we read that Jesus is God's chosen one (Mt 12:18; Lk 23:35). Jesus himself then chose his disciples. The context stresses the sovereign nature of that choice. "You did not choose me," Jesus said to the Twelve, "but I chose you . . . to go and bear fruit—fruit that will last" (Jn 15:16; cf. Lk 6:13; Jn 13:18; 15:19). Jesus also spoke of the Son's freedom to choose those to whom he would reveal the Father (Mt 11:27; Lk 10:22).

At times the Gospels speak of the elect—the "chosen ones." The context is often eschatological. God will shorten the days of tribulation at history's end "for the sake of the elect, whom he has chosen" (Mk 13:20; cf. Mt 24:22,31).

The Epistles also speak frequently of the divine choice. God has chosen the weak, foolish, and lowly things of this world to confound the so-called wise (1 Co 1:27–28). God has chosen to bear patiently with rebels who are objects of his righteous wrath (Ro 9:22). He has chosen to provide a new birth for believers (Jas 1:18).

God's choice to give salvation to his church is expressed in many passages. In fact, the company of believers is often addressed as "the elect" or identified as "God's elect" (2 Ti 2:10; Tit 1:1; 1 Pe 1:1). Believers are reminded that they are recipients of God's grace. The Ephesians were "chosen, having been predestined according to the plan of him who works out everything in conformity with the purpose of his will" (Eph 1:11). The faith of the Thessalonians in response to the gospel message was evidence to Paul that God had chosen them (1 Th 1:4). Yet God's choice is never based on human merit. The divine choice was exercised "according to the foreknowledge of God the Father" (1 Pe 1:2), who determined before Creation that Jesus would redeem the church with his blood (1 Pe 1:20). In eternity, God acted freely and lovingly, and "he chose us in [Jesus] . . . to be holy and blameless in his sight" (Eph 1:4).

The consistent emphasis on God's choices, made in eternity, to provide the salvation his church now enjoys removes every ground for human pride. As God's chosen people, we realize that he alone is the source of salvation and that to him alone all glory belongs.

7. The question of election. Average folks and theologians alike have been troubled by the doctrine of divine election that is evident in the NT's strong statements about God's choice of believers for salvation. The fear is that this biblical theme rules out human responsibility and makes the universal gospel invitation a mockery. How can a valid invitation be extended to all if some have been preselected to respond? ♦ *Predestine*

Before coming to such a conclusion, however, it is important to make a few observations about how the *eklegomai* word group is used in the NT.

First, while statements about God's choices found in the NT may suggest a *logical* problem, they do not suggest a *biblical* problem. That is, we may feel that the fact of God's sovereign choice must predetermine how an individual will respond to the gospel and even that it must overrule a human being's exercise of free choice. This may appear logical to us. But that logic is not supported by any statements of Scripture limiting human freedom or responsibility. Biblically, the choice of faith or unbelief is called for in the gospel message, and each person is held responsible for his or her decision.

♦ **Belief/Faith** There is no suggestion that one is prevented from believing, or that one is forced to believe against his will. We must be careful never to exalt human reasoning· above Scripture, or to suppose that our logic can stand in judgment on the logic of God.

Second, some have noted that in most contexts, God's choices seem related to the believing community rather than the individuals that make it up. Election, in this view, deals with God's relationship to the saved in aggregate, and it is not intended to make a statement about a divine choice of individuals.

But most importantly, the passages affirming God's sovereign choices related to salvation should be read in the light of the writers' purposes. Each seems to emphasize the fact that God has chosen and acted to provide salvation. This emphasis precludes the notion that salvation is a joint enterprise, part from God and part from man. Long before the first man and woman looked around at God's fresh creation, God conceived, planned, and provided for a wondrous salvation for his church. This salvation is a work of God alone. It is rooted in his character of love and in his purposes. We human beings are simply the recipients of a free gift, prepared for us before we existed. The stress in the NT on God's choices, linked as they are with salvation, teaches us that we must seek to understand salvation in terms of God alone. We can never explain salvation by looking at human actions or choices.

We can explain salvation only by discovery of the loving heart and costly grace of our matchless God.

CHRIST

We tend to think of "Christ" as a name, just as "Jesus" is a name. In fact "Christ" is not a name, but a title.

1. The Greek word and OT roots

2. Messianic expectations in Jesus' day

3. The emerging NT meaning

1. The Greek word and OT roots. The Greek word is *christos* ("anointed"). In the NT, *christos* is intimately linked with OT anointing and with the thread of OT teaching that hints that a special Anointed One would come and set the world right. ♦ *Anointing/Anointed*

Where the Gospels read "Christ," or speak of the Christ, they give Jesus the title of God's Anointed One. The word "Christ" affirms that Jesus has been specially commissioned by the Father to an important office.

In the OT the word "anointed" is closely linked with two offices—that of king and that of high priest. It was prophesied that Jesus, from David's kingly line, would one day hold ultimate authority in our world. ♦ *King* As high priest, Jesus offered himself up for us and lives today to make intercession for us. ♦ *Priesthood*

2. Messianic expectations in Jesus' day. Just how clearly the OT presents a coming Messiah has been debated. Yet a look in the Gospels at references made to Christ, not by his followers but by others, suggests that the Jewish people saw a well-developed and popular doctrine in the OT.

One year at the Feast of Tabernacles even the common people loudly debated whether or not Jesus might be the Christ. The dissenters argued, "How can the Christ come from Galilee? Does not the Scripture say that the Christ will come from David's family and from Bethlehem, the town where David lived?" (Jn 7:41). Clearly the people expected a descendant of David to appear. God's plan for Israel's future was understood to include such a person as deliverer and ruler.

This expectation was so deeply imbedded in the faith of Israel that even a Samaritan woman said to Jesus, "I know that Messiah" (called Christ) "is coming. When he comes, he will explain everything to us" (Jn 4:25). When this expected deliverer would appear, God's hidden plans and purposes were to be unveiled.

Lk 24:21 further underlines the role of Christ as deliverer. After Jesus' resurrection, he walked unrecognized with two of his followers. Expressing their despair, one of the two said, "We had hoped that he was the one who was going to redeem Israel." The prophetic vision of spiritual and national renewal was associated in everyone's mind with the appearance of the promised Messiah—the Christ, God's Anointed One.

Perhaps the most revealing fact that the Gospels record is found in the utterance of an angry and frustrated enemy, the high priest. After futilely trying to convict Jesus on the testimony of false witnesses, the apoplectic ruler asked Jesus directly: "Are you the Christ, the Son of the Blessed One?" When Jesus answered, "I am," the triumphant priest charged Jesus with blasphemy (Mk 14:61–64). Although the rulers of Israel rejected Jesus' claim to be the Son of God, it is clear that their own interpretation of the OT led them to believe that the Messiah would be the "Son of the Blessed One."

In Jesus' day, then, the Christ was thought of as Israel's deliverer. God's Anointed would redeem Israel, rule as king over the restored kingdom, and answer all mankind's questions about God's plans and purposes. And this Redeemer would be the very Son of the Blessed One.

When Jesus, and later the early church, insisted that the man from Nazareth was in fact God's Christ, the people of Israel understood. The early preaching to the Jewish community emphasized their messianic hope. The Christ had suffered as the Scriptures had foretold (Ac 3:18), Peter announced in an early sermon. The people of Israel must now repent and turn to Jesus for the forgiveness of sins, so that the promised "times of refreshing may come from the Lord," Peter told them, "and that he may send the Christ who has been appointed for you—even Jesus" (3:19–20). The OT hope summed up in the title "Christ" was not abandoned by the church. The

promise of divine rule will be fulfilled, but in Jesus' second coming rather than the first. ▶ *Appearance of Jesus: the Second Coming*

3. The emerging NT meaning. As Christianity exploded beyond the narrow confines of Palestine, the OT roots of the title "Christ" were less clearly understood. The Epistles continue to emphasize this title but use it almost as a name. Sometimes it stands alone. More often it is linked, as in "Christ Jesus," or "Jesus Christ." Often Paul links it further in the phrase "Lord Jesus Christ." ▶ *Lord*

The Jewish people yearned for their deliverer. They focused on the political impact of setting up his kingdom. But the Samaritan woman suggests another aspect: "He will explain [*anangelō*] everything to us." The Greek word here implies announcement—a fresh revelation of divine truth.

In a sense, the Epistles are devoted to that revelation. They show us how Christ Jesus, the God-Man, unveils truth that was previously hidden and explains what had been revealed. In Christ, God's eternal plans, purposes, and love are shown with unmistakable clarity. Every aspect of God's eternal plan is brought into focus in Christ. He is the central figure, the focus of history, the climax of the sacred drama, the one through whom all things are at last explained (Col 1:15–20).

CHRISTIAN

The Greek word *christianos* occurs only three times in the NT. Becoming Christians (Ac 26:28), living as Christians (11:26), and suffering as Christians (1 Pet 4:16) were perhaps the three aspects of Christianity that stood out in the minds of the unbelievers. The NT emphasizes the family character of the church. So within the community fellow believers are primarily identified as brothers and sisters. But we find that the word "Christian" was used, as it is today, to identify Jesus' followers.

CHURCH

Anyone may be excused for being a bit confused about the meaning of the word "church"; we use the word in so many ways. It means a particular building (e.g., "the church on fourth street"), a denomination or organized faith (e.g., the Reformed Church in America), and even a Sunday meeting (e.g., "Did you go to church today?"). None of these uses is particularly biblical. The church is a basic NT theme, and we need to understand this meaning-filled word in its biblical sense.

1. The Greek word and its NT usages
2. The relationship between Jesus and the church
3. The church as a body
4. The church as a family
5. The church as a temple
6. The relationship between the church and Israel
7. The form of the local church
8. Summary

1. The Greek word and its NT usages. In Greek culture an *ekklēsia* was a political assembly. By the fifth century B.C. *ekklēsia* had come to mean an official gathering of the full citizens of a Greek city-state (*polis*) who were called together to make political and judicial decisions. The Greeks never used *ekklēsia* to refer to religious fellowships.

In the Septuagint, the word *ekklēsia* translates a Hebrew word most often used in the OT to indicate a ceremonial assembly of God's covenant people. ▶ **Assembly/Community** But by Jesus' time, another term (also used in the Septuagint to translate the same word and other Hebrew terms) was in common use. This word was *synagōgē*, "synagogue." "Synagogue" not only stood for the place of Sabbath meeting but in the Hellenistic world it was also identified with the Jewish faith.

The new community of Christians broke with Greek usage when it identified itself as an *ekklēsia*. It also broke with its Jewish roots by rejecting the term *synagōgē*. *Ekklēsia* was used in the NT in a way that infuses the word with new, distinctively Christian meaning.

The choice of *ekklēsia* was appropriate. The word links two Greek words to mean "a called-out assembly." The gospel proclamation called lost people out of the world to gather together in a unique fellowship. Joined-together believers formed a new community: a community committed to Jesus and to the radical lifestyle expressed in God's Word. It is the allegiance of the new community to Jesus that makes its members different from those "outside" (1 Co 5:12; cf. 6:4).

Ekklēsia appears only three times in the Gospels (Mt 16:18; 17:18 [twice]). It is the usage of *ekklēsia* in Acts and the Epistles that suggests how the early Christians understood the word "church."

Basically *ekklēsia* is an affirmation of a corporate identity. The *ekklēsia* is God's people viewed together as a new and whole community. *Ekklēsia* in the NT can encompass any number of believers. It is used of small groups that met in homes (Ro 16:5). It encompassed all believers living in a large city (Ac 11:22; 13:1; 1 Co 1:2); a large geographical district, such as Asia or Galatia, would include more than one church (1 Co 16:1,19).

The theologian's distinction between the church as local congregation and the church as universal body of all believers in all places and all time is not necessarily helpful for an understanding of the uses of *ekklēsia* in the NT. It is more fruitful to see *ekklēsia* as a technical theological term either for a specific Christian community or for Christians in community.

Geographical limitations (e.g., "the church at Jerusalem") may serve to identify a group functioning as a community. These groups too may be of varying size and not simply the house church of the NT era. Ac 20 is suggestive: Paul passed near the great city of Ephesus on his way to Jerusalem. Many elders and believers came from the city to meet with him. Paul charged the elders to shepherd God's *ekklēsia*. As overseers, they were to guard the flock committed to them by the Holy Spirit. It seems that the "church in Ephesus" is a single functioning community with a number of elders, though that community undoubtedly gathered as a number of small congregations in private homes.

Geographical extension (e.g., "the churches in the province of Asia") seems, in contrast, to make a broad statement about believers in a major district. The "Macedonian churches" (those gatherings of believers that functioned as communities within the "state" of Macedonia) responded with generous giving to the needs of fellow believers, despite their own poverty (2 Co 8:1–2).

When used without explicit or implied geographical reference, the word *ekklēsia* is also a corporate designation. Christianity can be understood only by exploring what Scripture says about the corporate identity of Christ's people as a mystical unity and as functioning communities. It is not enough to explore the identity of the individual as one of God's newborn. ♦ *Born*

In summary, then, *ekklēsia* is the company of believers. This word was chosen by the early Christians and the Scriptures to make a statement about community and the corporate identity of the people of God.

2. The relationship between Jesus and the church. The church and the churches belong to God (singular in 1 Co 1:2; 10:32; 11:16,22; 15:9; 2 Co 1:1; Gal 1:13; 1 Th 2:14; 2 Th 1:4; 1 Ti 3:5,15). Yet the *ekklēsia* stands in a unique relationship to Jesus. The church is Christ's body, a vital living extension of Jesus himself. Christ is "appointed head over everything for the church, which is his body" (Eph 1:22). Jesus thus relates not only to individual believers but also to believers in community. The community as well as the individual must recognize Jesus as Lord and corporately submit to him who is "head of the church" (Eph 5:23–24). ♦ *Head*

This theme in the NT is a corrective to Western culture's individualism. Christians must learn to live as a people called out of the world to be together, called to function in and as community. We must learn to discern Christ's will in and as communities. For whenever the word "church" is used in the NT, we are to discern our corporate identity and see how we are to function as community, not how an individual functions apart from community.

Three images found in Ephesians help us greatly to understand the corporate entity that is the *ekklēsia*. They also help us examine how believers function as constituent elements of God's special faith community.

3. The church as a body. Three major NT passages portray the *ekklēsia* as a body (Ro 12, 1 Co 12, Eph 4). Common elements found in these passages help us understand the implications of this image.

Each passage stresses interdependence, spiritual gifts, allegiance to one another, and love.

Members of the body of Christ, like parts of a human body, have different functions (Ro 12:4,5; 1 Co 12:4,5; Eph 4:11). God the Holy Spirit gives spiritual gifts—divine enablements for ministry—so that each person in the body can function in a ministering way toward other body members (Ro 12:6–8; 1 Co 12:7–11; Eph 4:11). ♦ *Gift/Gifts* Each member's contribution is essential (Ro 12:5; 1 Co 12:14–26): only as each believer's ministry is performed will the body grow and "build itself up in love" (Eph 4:14–16).

In each context the NT places great stress on the quality of interpersonal relationships in the body. Love, intimacy, and involvement in one another's lives are essential if we are to function as a body (Ro 12:9–21; Eph 4:25–32; 1 Co 13).

The image of the body in the NT teaches us that the *ekklēsia* is to function as an interdependent, ministering community, gathered so that the members can serve one another, and in this way the individual and community will grow to maturity. This is possible only in a relational context of closeness and love. We can meet Sunday mornings for worship and other activities and call this going to church, but unless we also come together to function as the body of the NT, we are not truly being Christ's *ekklēsia*.

4. The church as a family. The family is the second major image in Scripture that helps us understand the *ekklēsia*. Ephesians tells us that our corporate identity as family is derived from God's nature as Father (Eph 3:14). Paul says further in his letter to the Ephesians that his prayer is that believers might function as family: that "rooted and established in love," the family members might "have power, together with all the saints, to grasp how wide and long and high and deep is the love of Christ" (Eph 3:17–18).

Family terms are seen throughout the NT as primary identifiers of believers. Again and again believers are identified as brothers and sisters and at times even as mothers and fathers (1 Ti 5:1–2). In becoming children of one Father, each believer has been drawn into God's universal family of faith and thus into family relationship with one another.

This NT image portrays the *ekklēsia* as a network of intimate, loving relationships. We are family. Although there may be differences among members of a family, in practice and in convictions and even in doctrine, our basic identity comes from the fact that each person who trusts in Jesus becomes a child of God (Gal 3:26). As children of the same Father, each believer is to love other believers as brothers and sisters (1 Th 4:9; 1 Pe 1:22; 1 Jn 3:11–15; 4:7–21).

5. The church as a temple. Christ is the cornerstone in this image of a building being erected by God, rising to "become a holy temple in the Lord," a "dwelling in which God lives by his Spirit" (Eph 2:21–22). Peter uses the same image, calling believers "living stones, . . . being built into a spiritual house to be a holy priesthood, offering spiritual sacrifices acceptable to God through Jesus Christ" (1 Pe 2:5). The image of the temple portrays the relationship of the *ekklēsia* to God. The believing community is to be holy, in this way reflecting the very character of the Lord. Only as a holy people can we serve God as believer-priests. ♦ *Holy/Holiness* ♦ *Priesthood*

6. The relationship between the church and Israel. The NT portrait of the *ekklēsia* as a real spiritual entity, a living body of which the risen Jesus is head, has led many to emphasize differences between the church and Israel. The church, they say, began at Pentecost with the Spirit's coming (cf. Ac 2:1–4; 1 Co 12:13). The church thus functions as a supernatural entity, while Israel functioned as a nation. The church has a unique destiny as Christ's bride, while Israel has a unique destiny as Yahweh's wife. ♦ *Bride and Groom* ♦ *Marriage*

Others have stressed the similarities between the church and Israel. They insist that there are not two communities of faith, but one. Israel and the church were both intended to function as faith-communities. Each looks to Abraham as father (Gal 3:6–9; Ro 4:9–17). Each enjoys covenant relationship with God, and the new covenant governing Christian experience is the same new covenant promised to Israel (Jer 31:31–34). ♦ *Covenant*

Actually, both differences and similarities do exist. The church is not the same as Israel, and OT passages relating to Israel should not be spiritualized or forced out of context in an attempt to apply them to the church. But at the same time, emphasizing the differences at the expense of many vital similarities is wrong. However, to some extent the debate is not relevant to the thrust of the NT's teaching about the *ekklēsia*.

The NT emphasizes that believers ought to understand and experience life together (in community). We must learn to live as God's *ekklēsia* if we are to experience the full benefits of our relationship with God. Christianity cannot be understood simply by examining an individual's relationship with God. We must also examine the relationship of the community to Christ. We must understand how the community functions and how the believer lives in community.

7. The form of the local church. Believers are called to live in relationship with one another in a community that is the visible expression of a supernatural body. The local church of today is the geographically limited church of the NT: a congregation of believers who come together to function as God's called-out community.

We know a little of the form of the local NT *ekklēsia*. Early believers did not meet in public buildings ("churches") for at least the first 120 years of the Christian era. The typical meeting of the church was in a home. When such a congregation met, "everyone [had] a hymn, or a word of instruction, a revelation, a tongue or an interpretation" (1 Co 14:26). Individuals shared, and others would "weigh carefully what [was] said" (1 Co 14:29). In part because of the relatively small size of the group, the people could "all prophesy in turn so that everyone [might] be instructed and encouraged" (1 Co 14:31). Such sharing remains essential to the very existence of the church as the community of faith. Christians are not to "give up meeting together, as some are in the habit of doing." Instead, as individuals in community we are to "consider how we may spur one another on toward love and good deeds" (Heb 10:24–25).

The relatively small size of the congregation in the early church had advantages, but it also had disadvantages. On the positive side, individuals were not isolated members of a silent mass, seated on wooden pews, observing. Each person was expected to contribute and to serve others with his or her spiritual gift(s). Each would also be served by the concern of the community and spurred on to personal growth and commitment. On the negative side, the smaller groups could become factions—splinter groups, seeking separate identity by following some leader or by emphasizing a particular doctrine (cf. 1 Co 1:10–17; Col 2:16–19). The corrective to this is seen in the NT's stress on love and on the unity of the body of Christ (e.g., Eph 4:1–6). It also appears that maintaining unity was a task of the leaders and part of guarding the flock of God.

It is most likely that elders in the NT church served as a team to oversee the life of a wider community and were not "pastors" of a home-sized congregation. Thus the "elders of the church at Ephesus" were probably not leaders of household groups but overseers of a number of such congregations within the city. ♦ ***Elders***

While there are many unanswered and unanswerable questions about the way the NT church functioned as community, it is clear that the *ekklēsia* truly was a functioning community. It was marked by close-knit relationships and by the active ministry of each member to others.

8. Summary. Books have been written about the church, and many more will follow. Yet when we read the word *ekklēsia*, we need to clear our minds both of our own culture's idea of "church" and of most of the issues that theologians rightly debate. As used in the NT, "church" is a technical theological term. It does not reflect either Greek or OT meanings but is given fresh meaning by its use within the Christian community. This technical meaning can be summed up quite simply: *ekklēsia* calls us to see believers-in-community. The community is formed by God and exists as a spiritual reality. The spiritual reality of the *ekklēsia* finds expression in the gathering of believers to function as community.

To live together as Christ's church calls for the development of close personal relationships, for the ministry of members to one another, for the experience of family love, and for maturing in holiness. The believing community is to learn how to relate to Jesus corporately and is to build a lifestyle that reflects corporate as well as individual commitment to our Lord.

CIRCUMCISION

On the eighth day of life, a Hebrew boy was to have the fold of skin covering the end of his penis cut off. This rite was called circumcision. After God reconfirmed his covenant promise to Abraham for the third and last time, the Lord said of his descendants: "Any uncircumcised male, who has not been circumcised in the flesh, will be cut off from his people: he has broken my covenant" (Ge 17:14). The uncircumcised Israelite was not covered by the covenant promise given to Abraham. ♦ *Covenant*

The rite symbolized submission to God and belief in his covenant promise. But God also required a "circumcision of the heart" (Dt 10:16; 30:6; Jer 4:4), explained as a faith-rooted, heart-and-soul love for God that issues in obedience.

The NT argues that Abraham was justified by faith even while he was uncircumcised, years before the rite was given. Circumcision was a sign: "a seal of the righteousness that he had by faith while he was still uncircumcised" (Ro 4:11; cf. Ge 15:6; 17:10–27).

The sign of circumcision was not carried over into the church. Many Hebrew Christians struggled to impose circumcision, and the Mosaic Law as well, on Gentile Christians (Ac 15:1). This was rejected at the Jerusalem Council (Ac 15:1–29). Paul later wrote to the Corinthians, "Was a man already circumcised when he was called? He should not become uncircumcised. Was a man uncircumcised when he was called? He should not be circumcised. Circumcision is nothing and uncircumcision is nothing. Keeping God's commands is what counts" (1 Co 7:18–19).

Paul's point is that God has never been concerned for the symbol as a thing in itself. God cares about the reality. It is our heart response to him that counts. Thus, looking into hearts and examining those who have responded to Christ's gospel, the Bible says, "It is we who are the [true] circumcision, we who worship by the Spirit of God, who glory in Jesus Christ, and who put no confidence in the flesh" (Php 3:3).

CITIZEN

The concept of citizenship has special meaning in NT times: particularly when Paul uses it to affirm our position as citizens of heaven (Php 3:20; cf. Eph 2:19). Paul was a Roman citizen and was deeply aware of the privileges of that citizenship. The importance of being a citizen of the Roman Empire is illustrated by incidents reported in Acts (16:16–40; 22:22–29).

The citizen of Rome had a completely different legal standing in the empire than did a resident alien or citizen of one of the provinces. ♦ *Alien/Aliens* Only a citizen of Rome could hold office. Citizenship carried the right to free travel and the guarantee of protection wherever a person went within the empire. Citizens were not subject to local laws without their consent: they were governed only by the laws of the nation of which they were citizens. Roman citizens alone had access to Roman courts anywhere in the empire. They came under Rome's protection.

Against the background of NT times, Paul's statement that we believers hold citizenship in heaven has exciting significance. As citizens of heaven we are spiritually significant: we hold office as believer-priests, with spiritual gifts enabling us to minister to others. Wherever we may live or travel in this world, our heavenly citizenship guarantees us the protection of God himself. While we live as resident-aliens in human society, we are bound to obey the laws of the country in which we stay (Ro 13:1–7). Yet we can bring every need and every issue to the divine court, appealing to God in prayer as the one power higher than any earthly authority.

Understanding our heavenly citizenship brings us a sense of confidence and security. We can live boldly, committed to carry out our citizens' duty of obedience to heaven's laws.

CLAN

The NIV uses the word "clan" often in the OT (e.g., Nu 26). The Hebrew word is *'elep*. Originally it was used in censuses and in the listing of military units of a thousand men. It also is applied to family units of varying numbers of individuals.

CLEAN AND UNCLEAN

A common saying holds that cleanliness is next to godliness. Sometimes the statement is thought to have come from the Bible. It doesn't. Nor does the idea of some that sex is "dirty" have scriptural foundation. Yet the root of each of these notions may be traced to a misunderstanding of Scripture. In the OT, "cleanness" is associated with holiness. And persons who had sexual relationships were considered "unclean" until the evening initiated a fresh new day.

But neither a well-washed body nor the notion that sex is somehow wrong is implied in the biblical concept of the clean and the unclean.

OT 1. The Hebrew words
    2. Ritual or ceremonial
       uncleanness
    3. Moral uncleanness
    4. Cleansing
NT 5. The Greek words
    6. "Clean" and "unclean" in the
       Gospels
    7. "Clean" and "unclean" in Acts
    8. "Clean" and "unclean" in
       Hebrews
    9. "Clean" and "unclean" in the
       other Epistles
   10. Summary

OT — 1. The Hebrew words. A number of Hebrew words may be rendered "clean," including *nāqî* ("innocent" [e.g., Ps 24:4]) and *zākak* (e.g., Job 15:15). However, the word found in nearly all places where the NIV and the NASB read "clean" is *ṭāhēr*, which means "to be or to become clean, pure." The verb occurs 94 times in the OT; with its derivatives, *ṭāhēr* appears 204 times. The verb is linked almost exclusively with ritual or with moral cleanness. The adjective suggests unalloyed, as in its use to indicate "pure" gold (Ex 25:11,17).

The word *ṭāmē'* means "to be or become unclean, defiled." *Tāmē'* with its derivatives is found some 279 times in the OT, with about 80 percent of the occurrences in Leviticus, Numbers, and Ezekiel. This word designates ceremonial (ritual) uncleanness in the early books. Later the prophets use the term primarily of moral impurity.

The later prophets also use the word *gā'al*, "to defile or pollute," when speaking of Israel's moral condition (Ne 7:64;

Isa 59:3; 63:3; La 4:14; Eze 2:62; Da 1:8; Zep 3:1; Mal 1:7,12).

In the language of the OT, "clean" and "unclean" describe a state or condition, either ceremonial or moral, that has significant impact on one's relationship with God.

2. Ritual or ceremonial uncleanness. In the early books of the OT, cleanness and uncleanness are ritual issues. That is, calling a person or thing "unclean" was not a moral judgment. "Unclean" meant simply that a person or thing was unable to participate in Israel's worship of Yahweh. During the time of ceremonial uncleanness, one could not attend any worship ceremony or eat meat that had been offered in sacrifice (Nu 5:1–4; 9:6–12). Under certain circumstances an unclean person must be isolated from others in the community (Lev 13:45–46).

Ritual uncleanness could result from a number of different things—including giving birth (Lev 12), having various skin diseases (Lev 13–14), bodily emission or menstruation (Lev 15), and touching the dead (Nu 19).

Animals and foods were also divided into clean and unclean classes. The clean might be eaten; the unclean were forbidden (see Lev 11 for a list; cf. Ge 7:2; 8:20; Dt 14:3–21). Only clean animals might be offered to God as sacrifices.

A number of theories have been advanced to explain why the concept of the ceremonially unclean and clean was introduced into Mosaic Law. Did these rules serve to guard Israel against worship of animals? Were they designed to protect them from communicable diseases? The rules concerning the clean and the unclean seem to draw attention to central issues in human experience—to birth, death, sex, health, and food. In so doing, these ritual issues graphically demonstrated God's concern for everything in his people's earthly life.

There is no suggestion that the flesh of some animals is healthier to consume than that of others. When the clean and unclean animals are identified, Israel is simply told, "Do not defile yourselves by any of these creatures. Do not make yourselves unclean by means of them or be made unclean by them. I am the LORD your God; consecrate yourselves and be holy, because I am holy" (Lev 11:43–44). ♦ *Holy/Holiness* No additional explanation is offered. What we conclude is that Israel's God sets apart what he chooses for his people, and he sets them apart from whatever he rejects. Israel is God's people. Everything in their daily life is to testify to their exclusive commitment to the Lord.

3. Moral uncleanness. The Mosaic Law was intended to pattern the whole lifestyle of Israel. In the process, various aspects of the law taught deep spiritual lessons. Ceremonial and ritual uncleanness cut off an individual from participation in worship of the Lord. The lesson is clear: one must be clean to approach a holy God.

The same law extends the concept of clean and unclean to sin. The sacrifice of the Day of Atonement was made "to cleanse" the people so that, as Moses told them, "before the LORD , you will be clean from all your sins" (Lev 17:30–31).

The spiritually sensitive realized that cleanness was a matter of the heart and not simply a ritual issue. When King Hezekiah reinstituted the Passover after decades of neglect, many traveling to the festival failed to purify themselves, "contrary to what was written." Hezekiah prayed for the pardon of "everyone who sets his heart on seeking God . . . even if he is not clean according to the rules of the sanctuary" (2 Ch 30:18–19).

To the later prophets the concept of ritual uncleanness provided an illustration of sin's inner defilement. Reviewing history, the psalmist says, "They defiled themselves" (*ṭāmē'*, "made themselves unclean") by what they did (Ps 106:39). Idolatry and unresponsiveness to God polluted the land and its people (Ge 35:2; Jer 2:23; Eze 20:7,18,30–31). Israel's immorality made the land itself unclean (Mic 2:1–10), for whatever was touched by an unclean person became unclean (Hag 2:13–14).

One way to view Israel's exile in Babylon is through the perspective of the clean and the unclean. The unclean had to be sent outside the camp. An unclean Israel had to be sent outside the land on which the Lord had set his name.

Historically, when the law governing Israel's life was established, ceremonial and ritual cleanness was stressed. The prophets grasped the symbolic lesson taught and emphasized moral and spiritual cleanness. By Jesus' day, the Pharisees were preoccupied with the ritual and were insensitive to the spiritual lessons. Jesus' own pronouncements (e.g., Mt 15:10–20; 23:25–28; Mk 7:14–23) reaffirmed the prophets' emphasis. Cleanness and uncleanness are matters of the heart. The OT's message, imbedded in symbol in the worship and daily life of God's people, called for an inner cleanness that would permit the believer to approach and worship the Lord.

4. Cleansing. Ritual uncleanness did not bar an individual permanently from participation in Israel's worship. One who touched the dead body of an animal was to wash his clothes and would be unclean till evening. After giving birth, a woman was considered unclean for one to two weeks, and thirty-three or sixty-six days later was to bring an animal sacrifice as a cleansing offering. A man's emission of semen made him unclean: he must bathe and would be unclean till evening.

Cleansing from ceremonial uncleanness typically involved (1) a specific period of time during which one was unclean and (2) either washing with water or purification by a blood sacrifice. The most significant cleansings—of priests, of vessels for use in the sanctuary, from sin—demanded sacrificial blood. ♦ *Atonement*

There is an important spiritual message in ritual cleansing of the unclean: a person may be defiled and cut off from access to God, but such a person can be cleansed. The condition need not be permanent. There is hope that he or she will again be able to participate in worship of the Lord.

This message was not missed by the prophets. But understanding the depth of Israel's defilement by sin, the prophets held no hope for cleansing by ritual means. So the prophets looked to the future and conveyed God's promise of a supernatural work he would perform within the people of Israel—a work of changing hearts. "I will cleanse them from all the sin they have committed against me," God says through Jeremiah, "and will forgive all their sins of rebellion against me" (Jer 33:8). Using the symbolism of ritual cleansing, Ezekiel conveys the same message: "I will sprinkle clean water on you, and you will be clean; I will cleanse you from all your impurities and from all your idols. I will give you a new heart and put a new spirit in you" (Eze 36:25–26).

Thus ceremonial cleanness and uncleanness taught Israel that human beings must be right with God to approach him and that God himself is the only judge of what is clean or unclean. Yet the unclean can be cleansed. Lapses do not cut a person off forever from fellowship with God.

The lesson taught in ritual had moral implications. Sin made a person unclean in God's sight, and sacrifices must be offered for cleansing. ♦ *Offering and Sacrifice* ♦ *Sin*

The prophets saw clearly that the disasters that struck Israel resulted from Israel's moral and spiritual uncleanness. But the prophets looked ahead. The uncleanness was only for a time. One day God himself would act to cleanse his people within, where ritual cannot reach. God would then give his people a new heart. Then human beings would be clean indeed. ♦ *Heart*

5. The Greek words. A single word group expresses the notion of clean and unclean in Greek. Cleanness is expressed by *katharizo* (verb) and *katharos* (adjective). The negative prefix, *a-*, is added to make *akathartos*, "unclean."

In Greek culture this word group indicated physical, ritual, and moral cleanness. But the specific meaning of clean and unclean in the NT is rooted in OT thought and not in Hellenic culture.

6. "Clean" and "unclean" in the Gospels. The Pharisees complained that Jesus' followers ate with "unclean" hands. They meant that the disciples failed to follow the practice of ceremonial handwashing that tradition (not the Mosaic Law) prescribed before eating a meal. Jesus responded by confronting the Pharisees and the scribes. These men had substituted mere human interpretations for God's commands and missed the fact that all worship is empty if one's heart is far from God. Jesus also affirmed the message that God taught symbolically in the OT's regulations concerning the clean and the unclean (Mk 7:1–23).

Mark points out that Jesus "declared all foods 'clean' " (v. 19). But more importantly, Jesus reaffirmed the emphasis of the prophets. Ritual uncleanness was a symbol, designed to make Israel sensitive to God's holiness and to teach important lessons about a person's relationship with him. The reality with which God is truly concerned is the responsiveness of the human heart to him (cf. Mt 23:25–28; Lk 11:39–41).

Two other uses of "clean" and "unclean" in the Gospels deserve attention. First, the demonic beings whom Jesus cast out of so many ill and oppressed persons are consistently called "unclean spirits." The NIV takes the adjective to mean moral uncleanness and typically translates the phrase as "evil spirits." Second, the Gospels report incidents in which some with leprosy begged Jesus to make them "clean" (e.g., Mk 1:40; Lk 5:12). The appeal is rooted in the OT law, which made ritually unclean anyone suffering from an infectious skin disease. ♦ *Leprosy* To be made clean thus meant to be healed of the disease. Following their healing, Jesus told some who had had leprosy to go to a priest and, in accordance with the law, be certified as clean (cf. Mt 8:2,3; Mk 1:40; Lk 5:12; 17:11–14).

7. "Clean" and "unclean" in Acts. Incidents in Acts focus on a problem faced by the young Christian community as Gentile members were added. What is the relationship between the new faith and Israel's OT law?

Peter was given a vision of a sheet filled with unclean animals let down from heaven and a voice telling him to kill and eat. Horrified, Peter refused. "I have never eaten anything impure or unclean," he protested. The voice then told Peter, "Do not call anything impure that God has made clean." Immediately after the vision Peter was invited to the home of Cornelius, the Gentile centurion. Normally a pious Jew would refuse. Gentiles and their homes were considered defiling. But Peter understood the message of the vision: "God has shown me that I should not call any man impure or unclean" (Ac 10:9–28). The principle was clearly established. The "unclean" of the OT was unclean only because God chose to call it unclean for his OT people. God was free to remove that designation after Jesus came.

The counsel of the early church held in Jerusalem established the principle that customs associated with Israel's life under law were not binding on Gentile Christians (Ac 15). Now that God was dealing with the heart through the gospel of Christ, regulations about externals were no longer relevant.

8. "Clean" and "unclean" in Hebrews. The Book of Hebrews was written to help Jewish Christians see how life under Jesus' new covenant provides the reality that was only foreshadowed by the old, Mosaic covenant. ◢ *Covenant* The regulations associated with the OT system made persons only "outwardly clean." Christ's blood however, cleanses the conscience and makes one inwardly clean (Heb 9:10,14). ◢ *Conscience* OT cleansing was imperfect and temporary. But by one sacrifice Jesus "has made perfect forevermore those who are being made holy" (10:14). Rather than the body being sprinkled, as in OT ritual, we now have "our hearts sprinkled to cleanse us from a guilty conscience" (10:22).

OT symbol has been replaced by NT inner reality. Because of the work of God in our hearts, we no longer need the symbol. Thus, ritual cleansings—and ritual uncleanness—have no role in the Christian era.

9. "Clean" and "unclean" in the other Epistles. In the NT, the language of cleansing is found at times linked with Jesus' work for believers (Eph 5:26; 2 Pe 1:9; on 1 Co 7:14 ◢ *Sanctify/Sanc-*

tification). In Ro 14, Paul takes up the question of OT kinds of uncleanness and gives an explanation. "No food is unclean in itself." However, one who believes something to be unclean must not violate his conscience by eating it. We are to consider, not the thing itself, but our own heart and the impact of our actions on others who might have a tender conscience. So "whatever you believe about these things keep between yourself and God." A decision to eat or not to eat ought to be an expression of one's personal faith (14:14–23).

In this, Paul follows the principle expressed by Jesus (Mk 7:18–23) and enunciates his growing understanding of the startling relationship between the Christian and the law. ◢ *Law*

10. Summary. The concept of cleanness and uncleanness has roots in the ritual worship of Israel. God chose to identify some things and actions as "unclean." Individuals in an unclean condition were not permitted to participate in Israel's worship. But such individuals could be cleansed and again take part in worship.

The ceremonial concepts of cleanness and uncleanness were also used to clarify the concepts of sin and atonement. It is this moral aspect of the terms that the prophets emphasized. Israel was spiritually and morally unclean and had to look to the future, hoping for God to act and bring supernatural inner cleansing.

The religious leaders of Jesus' day were blind to the emphasis of the prophets. They focused on the ritual minutia. Jesus announced that cleanness and uncleanness are matters of the heart. He did away with the old classification of clean and unclean foods. This lesson was reiterated to the young Hebrew-Christian church through Peter's vision. God now deals with the heart: the OT symbols have been supplanted by the realities they symbolized but could never accomplish.

CLOUDS

God told Moses at Sinai, "I am going to come to you in a dense cloud, so that the people will hear me speaking with you and will always put their trust in you" (Ex 19:9). Paul looks back at the experience of Israel at Sinai and beyond, when Israel was led by God's cloudy-fiery pillar (e.g., Ex 13:21–22; 14:19–20), and views Israel as being "baptized" into Moses. The people participated with Moses in receiving God's law (1 Co 10:2–3).

Both Testaments associate clouds with appearances of God: he is both shielded by clouds and revealed by them (Ex 24:16; Lev 16:2; Ps 97:2; Mt 17:5; Mk 9:7). Clouds are associated in Jesus' life with the Transfiguration (Lk 9:34–35), the Ascension (Ac 1:9), and the Second Coming (Mt 26:64; Mk 13:26; Lk 21:27; 1 Th 4:17).

Not all references to clouds imply the special presence of God or of Jesus. False teachers are likened to "clouds without rain," which evoke hope but provide no life-giving moisture (Jude 12).

Heb 12:1 mentions a "great cloud of witnesses." This does not imply heavenly observers of the saints on earth. The image is drawn from the sports arena, and "cloud" is a common classical figure for a great number of persons. Envisioned here are OT persons who lived by faith; the record of their faith is given not only to testify to us but also to encourage us to "throw off everything that hinders and the sin that so easily entangles, and . . . run with perseverance the race marked out for us."

COLLECTIONS ▶ *Giving*

COMFORT

The Hebrew word for "to give comfort" is *nāḥam*. It portrays a person's deep feelings as he or she is moved to pity and compassion. Often *nāḥam* is used with a meaning of consoling (Ps 71:21; 119:82; Isa 49:13; 66:13). God is the one to whom the believer looks for comfort (Ps 23:4; Isa 40:1), for comfort can be found in God's unfailing love (Ps 119:76).

The Greek words translated "comfort" are *parakaleō* (verb) and *paraklēsis* (noun). The verb is found over a hundred times

in the NT. But this word group has several meanings besides that of comfort and encouragement. It can mean "to invite," "to call," and "to exhort."

Nine of the NIV's seventeen translations of this word group of "comfort" are found in 2 Co 1:3–7. Here Paul points out that in times of personal distress God comforts us. Our experience of troubles and suffering and of God's comfort equips us to comfort others "with the comfort we ourselves have received from God" (1:4). Paul goes on to show that to bring comfort to others, we must share our experiences and our feelings openly, as he does (1:8–10). In sharing our weaknesses, we also share the ability of God to meet every need. Only thus can we bring his comfort to other people. ▶ *Share*

COMMAND/COMMANDMENTS

In some people the word "command" evokes quick resentment. To them, even God's commandments seem restrictive, as if they are barriers that limit freedom. But such persons are unaware—or have forgotten—that God's commands were given to Israel for her own good (Dt 10:13).

OT 1. The Hebrew words
  2. God's commandments
  3. The Ten Commandments
NT 4. The Greek words
  5. Jesus and the commandments
  6. The commandments in Paul's epistles and in Hebrews
  7. The commandments in John's epistles
  8. Summary

OT — 1. The Hebrew words. Many different Hebrew words are translated "command" or "order." Some are ordinary words meaning "to speak or utter" (such as *dābar* and *'āmar*). With such words, context determines whether the utterance is a command, a revelation, a statement, a message, or some other entity.

Three Hebrew words are found most often when English versions speak of God's commands and commandments.

Peh means "mouth." Found some five hundred times in the OT, this word in fifty or so occurrences refers to God's mouth. In nearly every context in which God is speaking with his mouth, he is portrayed as Lord. Twenty-four times the phrase "according to the mouth of the Lord" is used as a formula to indicate the divine origin of a statement.

Where *peh* is found, the emphasis is on the fact that God speaks clearly and with authority. Whether an utterance is a prophecy (as Isa 40:5; 62:2) or a command (cf. Ex 17:1; 38:21; Nu 3:39; 14:41; Dt 1:26,43), the message comes from the Creator and Lord of the universe.

The use of the word "mouth" does not imply an anthropomorphic view of God. The mouth is the organ of speech. Used in relationship to God, *peh* affirms that God can and does communicate with his people.

Sāwâh means "to command" or "to charge." What God "commands" is always significant. God commanded the world into existence (Ps 33:9; Isa 45:12). He commanded the covenant (Ps 105:8; 111:9). He commands blessing to those who are faithful to him (Dt 28:8; Ps 133:3).

God's commands give structure to our universe. In commanding Creation, God established regularity and stability in the material realm. In commanding the covenant, he gave regularity and stability to his relationship with his people. In commanding human beings, God gives regularity and stability in the moral realm. Thus the OT warns Israel, "Be careful to do what the Lord your God has commanded you; do not turn aside to the right or to the left. Walk in all the way that the Lord your God has commanded you, so that you may live and prosper and prolong your days in the land that you will possess" (Dt 5:32–33).

The Hebrew word *miṣwâh* is found in nearly all instances where the English texts read "commandment." It is used almost exclusively in a religious way. Specifically, *miṣwâh* spells out the responsibilities of human beings who live in covenant relationship with the Lord. ▶

Covenant Thus the commandments,

though they unveil those moral principles on which the social universe is established, are ultimately rooted in relationship with God. Keeping the *miṣwâh* is a personal response to God, for the commandments show how his people must live to remain in harmony with the one who is holy.

2. God's commandments. God's commandments reveal the moral structure of our universe. More significantly, the *miṣwâh* defined how Israel was to live in covenant relationship with God.

The OT provides a number of important insights that shape our view of the commands and commandments of God.

a. The commandments express the moral character of God. As such they are pure (Ps 19:8), true (119:151), reliable (119:86), and righteous (119:172). The person in right relationship with God delights in the commandments (119:47,143), loves them (119:48), and finds comfort in them (119:52). Our conviction concerning God, that declares to him, "You are good, and what you do is good" (Ps 119:68) helps the believer realize that God's commands are intended to define for us what is morally good and to reveal the character of our Lord.

b. God's motive in giving the commandments is explained in the OT. The commands given to Israel "set before [them] life and death, blessings and curses" (Dt 30:19). God's own moral character demands that he punish evil and bless good. Thus, making the good clear to humanity is a distinct blessing: the commandments that express the good are clearly a rich gift.

So God's love for Israel was not only expressed in his sovereign choice of this family and in their redemption from Egypt (Dt 4:37). It was seen in the Mosaic Law. Moses told Israel to keep God's "decrees and commands . . . I am giving you today, so that it may go well with you and your children after you" (Dt 4:40).

c. Human beings can choose to respond obediently to or to reject God's commandments. The context in which the commandments are found promises blessing for obedience and warns against disasters to follow disobedience. But no individual is forced against his or her will to choose to live by the commandments.

d. Moral choices have consequences. The warnings and the promises provided with the *miṣwâh* make it plain that a moral law operates in the universe. In addition, God is personally involved in supervision of the consequences of moral choices. No wonder, then, that Moses warns, "Know therefore that the LORD your God is God; he is the faithful God, keeping his covenant of love to a thousand generations of those who love him and keep his commandments. But "those who hate him he will repay to their face by destruction; he will not be slow to repay to their face those who hate him" (Dt 7:9–10). More seriously, violation of the commandments is sin and requires atonement. ♦ *Atonement* ♦ *Sin*

e. Love alone is able to motivate a keeping of God's commandments. God's call to Israel through Moses is: "Hear O Israel: The LORD our God, the LORD is one. Love the LORD your God with all your heart and with all your soul and with all your strength. These commandments that I give you today are to be upon your hearts" (Dt 6:4–6). Love for God must be in our hearts before his commandments will be taken to heart (cf. Dt 10:12–13; 11:1).

Because God is a moral person and the universe he structured is intended to express his character, humanity needed a revelation of the good. OT commandments served as that revelation, setting before God's people the way of goodness and making possible intelligent personal moral choices. The giving of the commandments was motivated by divine love: keeping them is motivated by the believer's love for God.

3. The Ten Commandments. After Israel left Egypt and came to Mount Sinai, God gave the people his law. First, the LORD said to Moses, "Come up to me on the mountain and stay here, and I will give you the tablets of stone, with the law and commands I have written for [Israel's] instruction" (Ex 24:12). Those stone-etched commandments are recorded in Ex 20 and Dt 5. Although the OT contains many commandments in similar form ("You shall not . . ."), these ten words from Sinai are set apart as special. They were written by the finger of God and later enshrined in the ark of the covenant (2 Ch 5:10; Heb 9:4).

The Ten Commandments deal with relationships—with God and with other members of God's covenant community. Commandments one to five have to do with our relationship with God. The first: Yahweh alone is to be recognized as God (Ex 20:3). The second: No idol is to be made, to represent either Yahweh or any other supernatural power (Ex 20:4). The third: The name of Yahweh is not to be considered an empty symbol, as though God were not real and powerful (Ex 20:7). God is to be honored as Creator. The fourth: The seventh day is to be set apart for rest. Israel's life is patterned by the rhythm of a seven-day week (Ex 20:8–11). The fifth: Parents are to be honored by their children. This is often considered a command for the second tablet, which deals with relationships within the community. But the command adds the formula "so that you may live long in the land the LORD your God is giving you," a blessing that is associated with obedience to the Lord (Dt 4:40; 6:2; 11:9; 22:7; 25:15; 30:18; 32:47; cf. 4:1; 8:1; 12:10; 16:20; 18:16). It seems better to consider this fifth command as part of the first tablet, linked to our relationship with God. Briefly, children must be obedient to the authority of parents so they will learn to submit and later obey God's ultimate authority (Ex 20:12).

The next five commands governed interpersonal relationships in Israel. The sixth: God's people are to guard one another's lives ("You shall not murder," Ex 20:13). The seventh: God's people are to be faithful to covenant commitments ("You shall not commit adultery" [Ex 20:14]). The eighth: God's people are to respect others' property ("You shall not steal" [Ex 20:15]). The ninth: God's people are to guard one another's reputations ("You shall not give false testimony" [Ex 20:16]). The tenth: God's people are not to envy other people for their possessions (Ex 20:17). This final command defines the heart attitude that releases us to keep the other four in the second tablet.

There are several things to notice about the relationship of these Ten Commandments with other OT commandments.

a. Most commandments are given as negatives: "You shall not" (cf. Lev 18–19). The negatives describe a specific action rather than a general principle. In a list like that given in Lev 19 we are likely to find "Do not steal" (v. 11) and also "Do not defraud your neighbor or rob him" (v. 13) and "Do not hold back the wages of a hired man overnight" (v. 13). The list also contains "Do not lie" (v. 11) and "Do not show partiality . . . but judge your neighbor fairly" (v. 15). Why these multiplied examples rather than a simple general statement of principle? Probably because there are different ways of communicating meaning. A dictionary defines words by the use of other words, relying on concepts to communicate meaning. An operational or behavioral definition takes a different approach. It defines by providing a number of examples or illustrations, thus giving a feeling for, or a sensitivity to, meaning. The OT chooses to use this second approach to help God's people grasp the path of righteousness.

b. Some view the Ten Commandments as the essence of the commandments and believe that all the others can be derived logically from them. In a sense, then, the other commandments are illustrations of how God's people are to go about building moral sensibilities. It has been noted in support of this that the chapters immediately following the giving of the Ten Commandments (Ex 21–24) present case laws: they give illustrations of how principles expressed in the stone code can be applied to the daily life of God's OT people.

c. Within the Lev 19 list of "do nots" are two strong positive general statements: "Fear your God" (v. 14) and "Love your neighbor as yourself" (v. 18). These two statements express the core principles of love for God and for neighbor that find expression in the tablets of the Ten Commandments and in the other commandments of the OT.

NT — 4. The Greek words. A number of Greek words are found where the NIV and the NASB read "command" and "commandment." Some, like the Hebrew words, simply mean "to speak" or "to transmit a message." The nature of the message is determined by the context. Several other terms mean "to charge," "to command," or "to give orders" (*entellomai, epitassō, prostassō, keleuō*). But the word group that is particularly important to us is that of *entellomai* (verb) and *entolē* (noun). These Greek words were used in the Septuagint to translate most Hebrew words rendered "command," and especially for the critical *miṣwâh*. As is so often the case, the biblical meaning of God's *entolē* is defined within the Scriptures and is not derived from the cultural meaning of the term.

5. Jesus and the commandments. In Jesus' time there was debate about the commandments. Some rabbis attempted to distinguish between the vital and the less significant commandments of the law. Other rabbis sought to formulate foundational principles that would express the heart and soul of the law. Jesus' teachings take on special meaning against the background of these controversies.

On the one hand, Jesus warned that "anyone who breaks one of the least of these commandments and teaches others to do the same will be called least in the kingdom of heaven" (Mt 5:19). No commandment of God is irrelevant or to be ignored. But immediately Jesus went on to point out that an individual's righteousness must surpass that of the Pharisees and the teachers of the law, who took pride in keeping all the commandments. Jesus then gave illustrations (Mt 5:21–24) that show that while the commandments deal with behavior, God looks within at the motives of one's heart. The commandments must not be ignored, but neither should they be understood as God's last word on righteousness.

When Jesus was asked, "Teacher, which is the greatest commandment in the Law," he responded: " 'Love the Lord your God with all your heart and with all your soul and with all your mind.' This is the first and greatest commandment. And the second is like it: 'Love your neighbor as yourself.' All the Law and the Prophets hang on these two commandments" (Mt 22:36–40). All the commandments are important, for each commandment is an expression of God's basic concern: love for God and love for others.

The Pharisees misunderstood the unitary nature of the commandments. They invented one interpretation that permitted them to will property or income to the temple after their death. They then used the excuse "It is dedicated to God" to withhold help from their needy parents. By this traditional interpretation the Pharisees placed the commandments in a hierarchy and in effect argued that keeping a greater commandment (to honor God) made breaking of a lesser one (to honor parents) acceptable (Mt 15:1–9).

This hypocritical tradition denied the unity of God's commandments—a unity that rests on the fact that the commandments show man how to love God and how to love others. No Israelite who followed God's OT commands would ever be required to break one to obey another. The commandments were woven together into a unified whole, revealing to Israel love's lifestyle.

In view of this, Jesus' words at the Last Supper are uniquely significant. At this meal the evening before the Crucifixion, Jesus introduced God's new covenant, about to be instituted in his death (Mt 26:17–30; Mk 14:22–25; Lk 22:17–20). John takes us into the Upper Room with the Lord and records the conversation that took place. What is important to us is to remember that the commandments showed Israel how to live in covenant relationship with God. Now that a new covenant was to be instituted to replace the old Mosaic covenant, there had also to be new commandments to guide the believer. Jesus stated the believer's ultimate guideline with utter simplicity. "A

new command I give you: Love one another. As I have loved you, so you must love one another" (Jn 13:34).

What is significant here is not that the old commandments are set aside with the old covenant but that now believers are guided more by general principles and less by detailed instructions. Paul comments on this new commandment and on Jesus' remark that the Law and the Prophets hang on the command to love God and others: "Let no debt remain outstanding, except the continuing debt to love one another, for he who loves his fellow man has fulfilled the law. The commandments, 'Do not commit adultery,' 'Do not murder,' 'Do not steal,' 'Do not covet,' and whatever other commandment there may be, are summed up in this one rule: 'Love your neighbor as yourself.' Love does no harm to its neighbor. Therefore love is the fulfillment of the law" (Ro 13:8–10).

6. The commandments in Paul's epistles and in Hebrews. Paul's attitude toward the commandments in OT law is expressed in Ro 7. Viewed in themselves, the commandments are "holy, righteous and good" (v. 12). But when the system as a whole is examined, linking commandment, humanity, and sin, law itself is seen to be ineffectual. "We know that the law is spiritual," Paul says, "but I am unspiritual" (v. 14). Law with its commandments is powerless to release the individual from the principle of sin and death "in that it [law] was weakened by the sinful nature" (Ro 8:2–3).

The rabbis held that the law with its commands was a tool to subdue evil inclinations. Paul argues the reverse. Evil is in human nature. The commandment energizes that sinful nature rather than subdues it (Ro 7:5, 8–11). Just as a mother's warning to a small boy not to touch the cookies makes his mouth water, so God's "You shall not covet" provokes human desire.

The solution is not to deny the goodness of the commandments. The solution for Paul is to realize that *the external expression* of God's moral nature found in the written commandments is no longer relevant to faith. Jesus has abolished, Paul says, "in his flesh the law with its commandments and regulations" (Eph 2:15). Rather than relating to written commandments, the believer now lives in relationship to the Spirit of God, who personally guides him along the path the commandments also mark out (Ro 8:4–9a). Given a new nature and being supernaturally enabled by the Spirit, we today are to live a life of love, for "love does no harm to its neighbor" and thus "love is the fulfillment of the law" (Ro 13:10). ♦ *Law*

The writer of Hebrews makes the same points. The old covenant has been replaced, the "former regulation [*entolē*, "commandment"] set aside because it was weak and useless" (Heb 7:18). It is replaced with a better hope, linked to the priesthood of Jesus, who offered himself up as a sacrifice that God might keep his promise: "I will put my laws in their minds and write them on their hearts" (Heb 8:10; see Jer 31:31–34). What no external commandments could accomplish God has now made possible by planting love for him and for others deep within our renewed hearts.

7. The commandments in John's epistles. In the Gospel of John, unlike the Synoptics, "commandments" usually refers to an utterance of Jesus rather than to an OT commandment. Jesus is the revealer of the will of God and speaks with divine authority. Not only does Jesus' new commandment lay the basis for our understanding of all commandments, but Jesus himself demonstrated what he meant. He loved us unselfishly, to the death (Jn 13:33–34).

John's first letter focuses on fellowship with God. In a sense it is the NT's answer to Leviticus. That OT book explained how a person maintained fellowship with God under the Mosaic covenant. John explains how we live in fellowship with God under the new covenant. John emphasizes (1) Jesus' continual purification of our sins (1 Jn 1:5–2:2), (2) response to God that is demonstrated in keeping his commandments/word (1 Jn 2:3–8), and (3) response to God that is demonstrated in

love for our brothers (2:9–11). These last two themes are repeated again and again in John's epistles.

Unlike Moses in Leviticus, John does not detail numerous commandments that believers are to keep. John deals with principles, holding that believers know the truth, for they have been anointed by the Holy Spirit and thus given spiritual insight into all things (1 Jn 2:20–27). The specific commandments are of value, in that one who is unresponsive to God's inner voice can look to the OT code and, in the commandments imbedded in law, have an objective criterion against which to measure his or her actions (1 Jn 3:4). The Christian, however, develops a righteous life not by studying the commandments but by loving Jesus. We are children of God and have been given new birth by him. ♦ *Born* God's seed is within us, so we will not "go on sinning" but will do what is right (1 Jn 3:1–10). Like Paul, John places no trust in the OT system, which had to rely on a righteousness expressed in external commandments. John relies instead on the work of God within the heart of the believer.

8. Summary. God's commandments express his moral character and thus reveal righteousness to humanity. The OT commandments expressed the moral responsibilities of those living in covenant relationship with God. Although the commandments were in themselves holy, just, and good, they were unable to produce righteousness in members of the OT community because of human weakness.

Jesus affirmed the commandments. He taught that not one of them could be ignored. But he also taught that God is concerned with more than the behavior that the commandments regulated. God is concerned with our inner desires and motives. Moreover, Jesus showed that the specific regulations imbedded as commandments in OT law actually express two principles. God wants us to love him and to love one another. The OT commandments were pointers along the pathway of life and were designed to show Israel how to love.

When Jesus instituted his new covenant, he stated a new commandment. Believers are to love one another as Jesus has loved them. Paul points out that the one who loves in this way will fulfill the commandments. More importantly, Paul argues that the OT system, which relied on commandments to control human inclination to evil, was bound to fail. As long as the human heart is in bondage to sin, the commandments can only stimulate it to evil. God's solution has been to give human beings a new heart. He now writes his own morality, once expressed in stone, in the living person. As a believer lives in fellowship with Jesus, his actions flow from his new birth and he will spontaneously fulfill the requirements expressed in the commandments.

We should still study God's OT commands. They teach us about God and help us develop sensitivity to his will. And when our hearts wander from the Lord, the commandments give us objective evidence that we are not walking in fellowship with Jesus. Yet it is not the commandments but the new birth and a living relationship with Jesus that will transform us from within. Jesus alone will enable us to live the life that is truly good.

COMMIT

"Commit" appears many times in the NIV and the NASB. But it is not the translation of a specific Hebrew or Greek term. In each of these biblical languages the idea of "commit" is implicit in the verb form, or the word "commit" is the translation of some common term such as "do" or "make" (*'āśâh*, Heb; *poieō*, Gr). However, a few occurrences of "commit" are different, and a study of them offers enriching insights for us.

Three times the NASB translates *gālal* ("to roll, roll away") as "commit" (Ps 22:8; 37:5; Pr 16:3). One of these passages especially has brought inspiration and comfort to God's people. Ps 37:5–6 reads: "Commit your way to the LORD; trust in him and he will do this: He will make your righteousness shine like the dawn, the justice of your cause like the

noonday sun" (NIV). We can roll every burden, every concern for the future, on the Lord. We can be confident that he will accept that responsibility and will bless us.

In several places the NIV renders *paradidomai* ("to deliver") as "commit" (Mt 11:27; Lk 10:22; Ac 14:26). The NIV translation of 2 Co 5:19 reads, "He has committed to us the message of reconciliation." Here the Greek *tithēmi* is used; it means "to put or place" and at times "to appoint or ordain." We believers have been ordained as God's ambassadors, with the good news of the gospel placed in our hands.

On the cross, Jesus cried, "Father, into your hands I commit my spirit" (Luke 23:46). In this verse the Greek is *paratithēmi*, which means "to place beside," or "to present." A beautiful rendering is "to entrust." Not only can we roll our burdens onto the Lord but we can also entrust ourselves to him, just as Jesus entrusted himself to the Father.

COMMUNITY ♦ *Assembly/Community*

COMPASSION

The Bible makes many statements about God. One of the most comforting teaches us that "our God is full of compassion" (Ps 116:5).

OT 1. Compassion as response to need: *ḥāmal*
2. Compassion as expression of love: *rāḥam*
NT 3. Compassion, life's turning point: *eleos, oiktirmos, splanchnizomai*

OT — 1. Compassion as response to need: *hāmal*. *Hāmal* is translated "to have pity," "to spare," or "to have compassion." According to the *Theological Wordbook of the Old Testament* (ed. R. Laird Harris [Chicago: Moody Press, 1980]), 1:296, the word indicates "that emotional response which results (or may result) in action to remove its object ... from impending difficulty." The word describes human as well as divine emotion. Pharaoh's daughter, for example, was moved by *hāmal* when she saw the baby Moses in the rush basket and took him into her home to raise as her son (Ex 2:6).

Almost half of the occurrences of this word are in the negative: they speak of *not* having compassion. The Babylonian captivity had a good and purifying purpose, but to the exiles it felt as though God simply did not care (La 2:2; 3:43). But God does care, deeply, even for those undergoing discipline. So Malachi looks ahead and records God's promise of restoration: " 'They will be mine,' says the LORD Almighty, 'in the day when I make up my treasured possession. I will spare them, just as in compassion a man spares his son who serves him' " (3:17).

2. Compassion as expression of love: *rāham.*

The word means "to love deeply" and thus "to be compassionate," or "to have mercy." This word with its derivatives is found 133 times in the OT. Of the 47 uses of the verb, 35 speak of God's love for human beings (Ex 33:19; Dt 13:17; 30:3; 2 Ki 13:23; Ps 102:13; 103:13; 116:5; Isa 9:17; 13:18; 27:11; 30:18; 49:10,13; 54:8,10; 60:10; Jer 12:15; 13:14 31:20; 33:26; La 3:32; Eze 39:25; Hos 1:6–7; 2:23; 14:3; Mic 7:19; Zec 1:12; 10:6).

At times *rāham* portrays a lack of response to the helpless (Jer 21:7; 50:42). It clearly indicates the depth of the relationship God has with his children (Ps 103:13; Mic 7:19). But in the case of the Lord, it also reflects his sovereign choice. As God said to Moses, "I will have mercy on whom I will have mercy, and I will have compassion on whom I will have compassion" (Ex 33:19).

One fascinating OT theme links compassion with prophecy. The future that God has announced will not only bring him glory but will also show his deep love and compassion for his people (Isa 14:1; 49:13; 54:7; Jer 12:15; 33:26; Eze 34:25; Mic 7:19; Zec 1:16).

The concept of mercy is often found linked with both *rāham* and *hāmal*. ♦ **Mercy**

NT — 3. Compassion, life's turning point: *eleos, oiktirmos, splanchnizomai.*

These three Greek words communicate a sense of pity or compassion. *Eleos* is "mercy." ♦ **Mercy** *Oiktirmos* is a pitying exclamation torn from the heart at the sight of another's suffering. In the NIV and the NASB, *oiktirmos* is translated either "mercy" (Ro 12:1) or "compassion" (2 Co 1:3). God compassionately and truly cares about what happens to us (Ro 12:1; 2 Co 1:3). We are to imitate our heavenly Father (Lk 6:36) and let his kind of caring bind believers to each other in unity (Php 2:1; Col 3:12).

Oiktirmos and its cognates are seldom used in the NT. Besides the above verses, they are found in only three other verses (Ro 9:15; Heb 10:28; Ja 5:11).

The *splanchnizomai* word group is not used frequently in the NT. But its occurrences seem especially important. The noun is found in Lk 1:78; Ac 1:18 (in a physical sense); 2 Co 6:12; 7:15; Php 1:8; 2:1; Col 3:12; Phm 7, 12, 20; 1 Jn 3:17. The verb is used in Mt 9:36; 14:14; 15:32; 18:27; 20:34; Mk 1:41; 6:34; 8:2; 9:22; Lk 7:13; 10:33; 15:20.

The word originally indicated the inner parts of the body and came to suggest the seat of the emotions—particularly emotions of pity, compassion, and love. This is the word used in the Gospels to speak of Jesus' having compassion on someone in need.

When Jesus' response if such that he is described as being moved by compassion, the occasion is often the turning point in someone's life. A leper came to Jesus and begged for healing. Jesus, "filled with compassion," reached out to touch and heal (Mk 1:40–42). Traveling in the towns and villages of Judea, Jesus saw the confused crowds and "had compassion on them" because they were like sheep without a shepherd (Mt 9:33–38). Thereupon Jesus immediately gave his disciples authority to heal and drive out evil spirits. He sent his disciples to travel through the land (Mt 10:1–42). Compassion moved Jesus to take action that affected the lives of those whose needs moved him.

We see this same active aspect of compassion in two parables Jesus told. In Mt 18 there is the story of a servant who owed an unpayable debt. He begged the king to whom he owed the money to give him time to pay it. But the king was so moved by *splanchnizomai* that he canceled the debt. Lk 15 tells the story of the prodigal son. The wayward youth returned home to confess his sins and beg for a job as a hired man. But the father was "filled with compassion for him" and welcomed him back as a son.

The loving compassion of one person literally changed the life of another, for the person who cared was moved to act and so set the needy person on a new course in life.

God calls you and me to have compassion on others. That call is more than an appeal for us to feel with and for the needy. It is a call to care enough to become involved and to help by taking some action that will set others' lives on a fresh, new course.

COMPEL

Often the Greek word translated "compel" is *anankazō*. It means "to compel," or "to force," and occurs some nine times in the NT (Mt 14:22; Mk 6:45; Lk 14:23; Ac 26:11; 28:19; 2 Co 12:11; Gal 2:3,14; 6:12). In each context the word describes compulsion. But the compulsion is not one that involves the use of external, physical force. Instead, the compulsion comes from inner pressure—a positive response to moral force (Mt 14:22; Mk 6:45) or a reaction to the actions of others (2 Co 12:11). The *anank-* root words in the NT indicate all sorts of inner and outer pressures. ▶ *Necessary/Must*

Two NIV uses of "compel" are not translations of this word group. *Synechō*, which indicates a confining pressure as well as control, is used in 2 Co 5:14. Ac 20:22 uses a figure of speech: "I am bound in the Spirit."

God will not force us to any action. The compelling motivation for our choices comes from within.

COMPETENT

Different Greek words expressing the idea of strength or ability are translated in modern English versions as "competent" and "competence." ▶ *Ability/Able*

COMPLETE

A number of Hebrew terms are translated "complete" in OT versions. The NASB translators chose to use this word more often than did the NIV. However, one of two basic concepts is reflected where "complete" occurs in either version. The two concepts are seen in two Hebrew words, *kālâh* and *mālē'*.

Kālâh indicates bringing a process to completion. The process may be constructive, as in finishing the building of the temple (1 Ki 6:9). Or it may be destructive, as in the total devastation brought by war (Isa 10:23).

Mālē' means "to fill" or "to be full." Extended, it means completing a certain act in a fixed time or coming to the end of a designated time period (Est 2:12; Jer 29:10). This use is important theologically: in the fullness of God's time he brings his prophecies to pass.

Two NT roots are found where English versions read "complete." *Teleō* views completion as the reaching of a goal; when one's goal is reached, one has achieved a state of completeness. ▶ *Maturity* The other root is *plēroō*, often translated "to fulfill" or "to accomplish." This is an important word group, often used in a technical way to indicate the fulfillment of a prophecy of Scripture. ▶ *Fulfill* In passages where this word is understood as "complete," it is used in regard to persons being filled with an emotion (such as joy [Php 2:2; 1 Jn 1:4]) or with knowledge and understanding (Ro 15:14; Col 2:2). In both Testaments the context will suggest which emphasis is in view. ▶ *Finish*

CONCERN

When the NT speaks of a person being concerned, any of a range of feelings may be implied. *Melei* is the word used to express a general concern, whereas *merimna* carries a note of worry. ▶ *Anxiety/Worry* Usually "concern" in the

NIV and the NASB does not imply a lack of faith. Instead, such concern is natural and understandable, something appropriate to love and to a sense of responsibility (see 1 Co 7:32–34).

CONCUBINE

The concubine of the OT was not a mistress. In the polygamous world of OT times, a concubine was a woman who was married but who had fewer rights than a primary wife.

CONDEMN

Condemnation is an important concept. It is important both theologically and psychologically, for there are many persons whose sense of guilt leads them to fear condemnation. It is important even for those who need not fear condemnation, for too often Christians are tempted to take God's place and judge (condemn) others!

OT 1. The OT concept
NT 2. The Greek words
    3. Divine condemnation in the NT
    4. Condemning ourselves and others

OT — 1. The OT concept. The word usually translated "condemn" in the NIV and the NASB is *rāša'*. It means "to be wicked" or "to act wickedly." Another word, *'āšam,* which means "to offend" or "to be guilty," is also infrequently translated "to condemn" or "to be condemned." The thought is that the person who chooses a wicked rather than godly lifestyle has brought himself or herself under condemnation.

It is important to remember that the wicked can turn from their ways (Eze 18) and that confession can restore a right relationship with God. ♦ *Confession of Sins*

NT — 2. The Greek words. The NIV and the NASB read "condemn" for a large family of Greek words. The basic word is *krinō,* "to judge" or "to decide." There are a number of related words. The noun *krima,* "judgment," is usually rendered "condemnation" in the NASB. *Katakrinō* means "to give judgment against," and thus "to condemn." *Kataginōskō* means "to make a negative moral assessment," and thus "to blame," and *katadikazō* means "to pass judgment on."

Originally *krinō* and its cognates indicated simply an assessment. A person examined a matter and then came to a conclusion about it. By NT times these words had become part of the legal terminology used to speak of bringing charges, of judging, and of passing judgment. When used of God, *krima* ("judgment") is understood as "condemnation," for one judged by God is already condemned. ♦ *Judge/Judging*

3. Divine condemnation in the NT. The NT reminds us that Jesus did not enter our world to condemn us. He came because humanity was already condemned (Jn 3:17–18; Ro 5:15–16). Those who fail to respond to God's Word are in a state of condemnation (Jn 3:36; 12:48).

Jesus came to save the world. ♦ *Salvation/Save* His success is reflected in assertions such as this: "There is now no condemnation for those who are in Christ Jesus" (Ro 8:1). Because of Jesus, God's attitude toward believers is not one of condemnation. What God still condemns is the sin in sinners (Ro 8:3). We who respond to the gospel message in faith have the assurance that no one can successfully charge us. Jesus, "at the right hand of God," is "also interceding for us" (Ro 8:34).

4. Condemning ourselves and others. Those who remain outside the circle of God's grace by their refusal to respond to the gospel (Jn 3:18; 5:24) stand condemned; they are under judgment for their sinful actions (Mt 12:41–42; Jn 5:29; 12:48). But we who have trusted Christ have passed beyond condemnation (Ro 8:1). God views us as being in his Son, and no charge can be lodged against us. Yet two important truths are taught in the Scriptures about believers and condemnation. First, we are to be careful to do what is right so that our consciences will not condemn us for actions we believe are wrong (Ro 14:22; 1 Jn 3:20–

21). ◆ *Conscience* And second, we are not to condemn our fellow believers (Ro 14:3) ◆ *Judge/Judging*

Theologically, condemnation can be avoided only by trusting in Jesus, who bears our sin and thus removes us from the position of prisoners before the bar of divine justice. Psychologically, we are to recognize the freedom from condemnation that Jesus brings us and learn to live as forgiven men and women. Released from this burden ourselves, we are to bring the gospel to others so that they may be freed as well.

CONFESSION OF SINS

"Confess" is used in several ways in the NT. ◆ *Acknowledge* But for most of us, the confessing of sins is the first thing this word brings to mind.

The Greek word. The word translated "confess" in the NT is *homologeō*. It has a range of meanings, but the root idea is "to acknowledge." Used of confession of sins, *homologeō* drew on a meaning given to it in the contemporary legal system. To confess meant that one agreed with a charge brought against him; it was to acknowledge guilt before the court.

To "confess our sins" is to admit to God that our actions were indeed sin. We agree with him in his evaluation of our wrong actions. *Homologeō* does not mean to feel sorry or to promise never to do something again.

The context of 1 Jn 1:9. The primary NT passage that deals with the confession of sins is 1 Jn 1:5–2:2. The key verse promises us that "if we confess our sins, he is faithful and just and will forgive us our sins and purify us from all unrighteousness" (1:9).

In this Epistle, John explains the dynamic of fellowship with God. In the first chapter, John teaches that fellowship does not require sinlessness but does demand total honesty (vv. 5–7). When we claim sinlessness, we live in self-deceit (v. 8). On the contrary, we must confess (acknowledge) our sins to God. This kind of honesty with and about

ourselves means that God is free to help us. We experience his forgiveness and also his work within. That inner work is the continual process that God undertakes to keep on purifying us from all unrighteousness (v. 9).

If we deny our sins, we deny God's Word and block his inner working in our lives (1:10).

John explains that he writes this to his readers so that we will know the astounding truth. In Jesus, God has dealt decisively with our sins—past, present, and even future sins (1 Jn 2:1–2). We never pretend with God. Jesus not only has paid for our sins but also stands by our side, serving as our advocate when any accuse us. ◆ *Atonement*

The impact of this teaching is exciting. When you and I sin, we need not draw back from God, fearing his anger. We are invited to come to him, to acknowledge our sins, and to experience not only his forgiveness but also his ongoing work of purification within us.

An OT illustration. David's experience with Bathsheba illustrates this confession and forgiveness process. The story is told in 2 Sa 11, and David's inner feelings are shared in Ps 51. This psalm was written after David was confronted with his adultery by the prophet Nathan.

In Ps 51 David appealed to God for forgiveness and cleansing (vv. 1–2). He acknowledged that although he maintained a public façade, within he was plagued by guilt (v. 3). David at last admitted that his actions had been evil in God's eyes. He had sinned (vv. 4–6). David again appealed for cleansing (vv. 7–9) and looked to God to bring both purity and a restoration of salvation's joy (vv. 10–12).

This psalm was written for use in public worship. Nathan's confrontation of David had made David's failure public knowledge. Therefore, although David had sinned against God and confessed to God, it was necessary that he confess his sin publicly also.

We too are called on to confess our sins to God and thus to know the joyful restoration that David experienced. For private sins, private confession is appropriate. When our sins are public knowledge, then a public confession is called for (see also Ps 32).

CONFIDENCE

It almost sounds unspiritual to speak of having confidence. To many people, the word connotes self-confidence and smacks of self-efforts, of a denial of our human condition as sinners. But "confidence" is a word that occurs in Scripture—sometimes in very surprising contexts.

The Greek words. The primary word is *parrēsia*, which means "openness," "confidence," or "boldness." ♦ *Bold* Used thirty-one times in the NT, *parrēsia* indicates a sense of freedom in a situation or in a relationship. Jesus felt free to speak openly, despite opposition. So did the apostles.

In the places where the NIV and the NASB translate *parrēsia* as "confidence," the word indicates a boldness that comes from a relationship with God.

Parrēsia also indicates a bold view of the future. We look ahead with confidence because we know that Jesus is in control.

The other word commonly found where English versions read "confidence" is *peithō*, which means "to persuade." A person who is fully persuaded has confidence.

Confidence based on God's work in us. In Php 3:3–6, Paul makes it clear that we can have no confidence in mere human effort. ♦ *Flesh* Paul reviews his own experience and his faultless qualifications as far as legalistic righteousness is concerned. He concludes that his moral accomplishments are "rubbish." Only a righteousness that comes from God through faith in Christ will do. ♦ *Righteous/Righteousness*

Yet at other times, Paul speaks of his confidence in his fellow believers—even such poor specimens as the Corinthians (cf. 2 Co 2:3; 7:4,16). Paul's expressions of confidence, however, are not based on qualities he observed in these members of the Corinthian church. They are

founded on the fact that "if anyone is in Christ, he is a new creation; the old has gone, the new has come" (2 Co 5:17). The argument of the passage is that we should not evaluate our fellow believers by what we see of their lives. What we see is temporary (2 Co 4:18) and will change. Paul looks instead at the heart. There he finds Christ and is convinced that Christ's love is a compelling, motivating force that will surely bring about moral transformation (2 Co 5:12–15). It is because God was at work in the Corinthians that Paul could speak so confidently of their future.

Paul put it this way in Php 1:6: "being confident . . . that he who began a good work in you will carry it on to completion until the day of Christ Jesus."

John, in his first letter, looks at the question of Christian confidence from another perspective. Paul wrote of the theological certainty that God, who takes up residence in the believer, will do a transforming work. John explores the subjective basis for confidence that God is even now at work in us. John's stress is on following Jesus' commandments, especially the commandment that we love one another. If we live obediently, so that "our hearts do not condemn us," then we "have confidence before God" (1 Jn 3:21; cf. 4:16–17).

We may at times feel discouraged because we cannot see much progress in our transformation. God's message to us at such times is this: "Do not throw away your confidence; it will be richly rewarded. You need to persevere so that when you have done the will of God, you will receive what he has promised" (Heb 10:35–36).

Confidence based on God's work for us. Heb 4:16 invites us to "approach the throne of grace with confidence." We come boldly because we are assured of a welcome on the basis of the sacrifice offered for us by our High Priest, Jesus Christ (Heb 5:1–10). ♦ *Offering and Sacrifice* ♦ *Priesthood* Picking up the same theme, Heb 10:19 affirms, "We have confidence to enter the Most Holy Place by the blood of Jesus." Only through faith in Christ, and because of him, may people "approach God with freedom and confidence" (Eph 3:12).

It is their relationship with Jesus, then, that brings his people *parrēsia*. Because Jesus is resident within us, we have confidence that we and our brothers and sisters will grow in Christlikeness. Because Jesus has died for us, we are sure that we are always welcome when we turn to God.

CONFIRM

The Greek word for "confirmed" is *bebaios*, which means "sure, reliable, and certain." This word became part of the legal language of the NT world. It not only meant that a transaction or promise was valid but also implied a guarantee— some legally binding confirmation of intentions.

On the one hand, the gospel is confirmed by the testimony of those who experience its power (Php 1:7; Heb 2:3). On the other hand, God's promise in the gospel is guaranteed. He graciously chose not only to give us his Word but also to confirm that word by an oath (Heb 6:13–20).

CONFORM

The significant theological words are *symmorphos* and *syschēmatizō*.

Symmorphos is found in Ro 8:29 and Php 3:21, while the verb *symmorphoomai* appears only in Php 3:10. The first two uses speak of our ultimate transformation at the resurrection. This word implies more than a resurrection to similarity to Jesus and less than a resurrection to an identity with him. We retain our own individuality. But the qualities that make Jesus who he is will permeate us so that we truly will be "like him." Php 3:10 is exciting. Paul knows that in sharing Christ's sufferings and commitment now, we will be pervaded by our Lord's own qualities now. We do not need to await resurrection to become Christlike.

Syschēmatizō is found in Ro 12:2 and 1 Pe 1:14. Rather than being squeezed into this world's mold, the Christian is to undergo an inward transformation,

through which outward appearance and character also become Christlike.

God fully intends to do his work of grace within us. Without robbing us of our individuality, he will not leave us as we are. He will change us and enable us to share his glory.

CONGREGATION ♦
Assembly/Community ♦ *Church*

CONSCIENCE

We all know the inner nagging that drags our thoughts back to our past. But conscience is not quite what we usually think it to be. And most important of all, Jimminy Cricket's advice "Always let your conscience be your guide" is wrong!

1. The Greek word
2. The pagan conscience: moral faculty
3. The informed conscience: moral content
4. The inadequacy of conscience
5. The cleansed conscience
6. The clear conscience
7. Responsibility to the consciences of others
8. Summary

1. The Greek word. "Conscience" is a Greek concept, with a few of its aspects expressed by that complex OT term "heart." ♦ *Heart* For the average inhabitant of the NT world, the idea of conscience was familiar—and distasteful. The Greek word for "conscience" is *syneidēsis*. Originally the word signified a look back into one's past, an evaluation of remembered events in relationship to good and evil. To the Greeks, as reflected in their literature, conscience was usually a "bad conscience," one that relentlessly plagued its owner by accusations about past failures.

The noun *syneidēsis* occurs thirty-two times in the NT. The Bible shows how God deals with our bad consciences, and this revelation adds much to our understanding of human moral nature.

2. The pagan conscience: moral faculty. Paul argues that those with OT law and those without it are equally without righteousness; he writes that pagans "show that the requirements of the law are written on their hearts, their consciences also bearing witness, and their thoughts now accusing, now even defending them" (Ro 2:15). What Paul describes is the moral faculty that God has designed into human nature. Even those without specific knowledge of God's standards realize intuitively that moral issues exist, and they go on to establish standards in moral areas. But being sinners, pagans fall short of the goodness that is expressed in their standards. They do not do even the good they know of (2:1). Aware of guilt, they attempt to quiet an accusing conscience by blaming others and/or by excusing their own actions.

The pagan person has a conscience. Its existence stands as a witness to man's moral nature.

3. The informed conscience: moral content.

Paul also points out that the Jew took comfort in knowing God's will, being "instructed by the law" (Ro 2:18). The Hebrew people not only shared humanity's moral sense, but they also had unique access to true moral content. In the law, the Jews had a revelation from God of his own standards of right and wrong. Thus moral faculty was wedded with accurate knowledge of moral content.

But Paul goes on to argue that just as the pagans act against their uninformed conscience, the Jews have acted against their informed conscience. All humans break the moral code in which they themselves believe. Gentiles and Jews are sinners all.

Conscience serves as a witness to the rightness of moral standards. But conscience also serves as a witness against those who violate their standards. Yet, conscience has never succeeded in producing a truly moral person.

4. The inadequacy of conscience.

Scripture suggests a number of reasons why conscience is inadequate as a moral guide. First, conscience exists as a faculty of moral evaluation. There is no guaran-

tee that one's evaluation is correct. What a person's conscience says is right may not agree with what God says is right.

Second, even a believer's conscience may be weak. This concept is linked with the second point above, for a weak conscience is one that has not yet attained a mature understanding of Christian faith. In Paul's day, those with weak consciences were troubled about matters such as eating meat and determining which days should be considered special (Ro 14:1–6). By focusing on inconsequentials, such believers begin to judge or to look down on those who disagree with them (Ro 14:9–10). Thus a weak conscience may trap a person into serious sins.

Third, a person's conscience can be "defiled." Someone with a weak conscience is particularly susceptible to acting against what he or she believes is right, and thus this person is made to feel guilty (1 Co 8:7). Continual violation of conscience can corrupt a conscience and bring a constant state of defilement (Tit 1:15).

It should be clear from these observations that Scripture does not regard conscience as an infallible guide any more than as a motivator of good behavior.

5. The cleansed conscience.

The Book of Hebrews shows us another aspect of conscience. The writer looks back at the OT sacrificial system, with its repeated sacrifices for sins, noting that they were "not able to clear the conscience of the worshiper" (9:9). The endless sacrifices were in fact an "annual reminder of sins" (10:3), constant testimony to the worshiper that his past was with him and that he stood guilty before God. All of an individual's acts of sin were stored up in his conscience, shouting out his guilt and draining away any confidence in the possibility of a different future.

Guilt does this to us. It saps our strength and makes us unwilling to take a risk. It robs us of the hope that our future will be different from our past.

Hebrews presents this argument to show a contrast. What the OT sacrifices could not do, the blood of Jesus accomplishes. That blood, offered to God, does "cleanse our conscience from acts that lead to death, so that we may serve the living God" (9:14). Through Christ we are cleansed "once for all" (10:2,10,14). With our sins forgiven and ourselves cleansed, we have the assurance that God himself no longer remembers our lawless acts (10:17).

Cleansing is both objective, accomplished by Jesus' sacrifice, and subjective, experienced increasingly as we appropriate what Jesus has done for us. There will be times when our conscience will still drag our glance back to the past and shout out accusations. Then we must remember that our sins are forgiven (and the past gone). We must forget them (and it) and look ahead to how we can serve the living God.

As we continue to have confidence in God's Word and to act on the promise of a fresh future, our confidence will be rewarded. As we do the will of God, we will receive the fulfillment of that promise (10:35–36). Our consciences will be cleansed, never to nag us again. And we will be freed to look only ahead, enthusiastic about our opportunities to serve the Lord.

6. The clear conscience. God's forgiveness cleanses the conscience. A clear conscience is something else. It is the testimony of our conscience that we have chosen and have done what is right. Paul writes, "I strive always to keep my conscience clear before God and man" (Ac 24:16). The Christian maintains a clear conscience by living in harmony with the truths unveiled in God's Word (2 Co 1:12; 1 Ti 1:5,19; 3:9; 2 Ti 1:3; 1 Pe 3:16,21).

We of course want to keep our conscience clear. But we also need to remember that God, not the conscience, is our Judge. "My conscience is clear," Paul writes, "but that does not make me innocent. It is the Lord who judges me" (1 Co 4:4–5). Thus we see again the inadequacy of conscience. With all its other deficiencies, it is not even capable of penetrating to inner truth about our own guilt or innocence.

7. Responsibility to the consciences of others. Scripture is the objective criterion by which we evaluate not only our actions but also the content of our conscience. As we have seen, some believers have weak consciences. They have not matured to distinguish clearly between what is truly good and what is evil, nor to discern what is morally indifferent.

This is particularly a problem in matters of personal conviction. In matters about which God has spoken, believers should have no trouble seeing what is right. But there are many things about which God has no definitive word, and believers have different beliefs and convictions on these things. Such issues are considered in Ro 14. In each case discussed, believers are told to remember that Jesus alone is Lord. No one has the right to take Christ's place by judging or by imposing his or her own standards on others (14:1–10).

Thus, each person must act in accordance with his or her own conscience and be careful not to influence others to act against their convictions (14:13–16). We are to make every effort to "do what leads to peace and to mutual edification" (v.19). How are we to do this? Paul says, "whatever you believe about these things keep between yourself and God" (v. 22), warning us not to fall into foolish debates about secondary issues.

8. Summary. Conscience provides evidence of humanity's moral nature. But conscience is not an adequate guide to moral behavior. The conscience cannot move us to do right, and all too often its judgments are faulty.

Moreover, conscience reminds us constantly of past failures and of guilt. It robs us of confidence and hope for a better future. But God has acted in Christ to provide a forgiveness that cleanses our conscience, releasing us from bondage to our past. With God's forgiveness, that past is wiped away, and you and I can go on to live in obedience to God.

Believers want to maintain a clear conscience. This is accomplished by doing what we believe to be God's will. Our understanding of God's will grows, and our consciences become stronger as we mature in our faith.

Within the Christian community, conscience can become a problem. This happens when some insist that their personal convictions are the standard that should govern the believing community. God's Word on this issue is clear. We are to recognize the inadequacy of conscience and acknowledge the lordship of Jesus. ♦ *Lord* Where there is no clear word from God, each individual must be free to respond as he or she believes Jesus desires. Rather than make such matters issues in the Christian community, "whatever you believe about these things keep between yourself and God" and build unity through love for one another and by mutual commitment to Jesus.

CONSECRATE ♦ *Holy/Holiness*

CONSIDER

A number of different Greek and Hebrew words are translated "consider" in English versions. An overview of several of these words gives us a good picture of this biblical concept of "consider." The OT at times translates the following by the word "consider": *rā'âh,* "to see"; *yāda',* "to know"; *ḥāšaḇ,* "to think," "to calculate"; *bîn,* "to discern"; and *śîm,* "to put, or place." At times the NT translates the following words "consider": *katanoeō,* "to take note of," "to look closely at"; *hēgeomai,* "to suppose"; *logizomai,* "to reckon, consider"; *noeō,* "to perceive"; and twice *enthymeomai,* "to reflect on, ponder."

The word "consider," then, suggests careful examination with a view to discerning and coming to some conclusion. As used in the Bible, "consider" can focus on the process (as in Jesus' exhortation, "Consider the ravens" [Lk 12:24]) or on the conclusion reached (as in Php 2:6, which asserts that Jesus "did not consider equality with God something to be grasped at").

A quick survey of the NT shows a few of the realities that we believers are to consider: (1) Our present sufferings are inconsequential in view of the glory God has in store for us (Ro 8:18). (2) The needs and the qualities of others are to be considered before our own (Php 2:3). (3) There is always more for us to experience in Christ. Let us press on to find God's highest (Php 3:13). (4) We are not only to be considerate of others (Jas 3:17; 1 Pe 3:7) but also to find ways to spur them on to love and to good works (Heb 10:24).

CONSTRUCTIVE

The NIV translation of 1 Co 10:23 considers the freedom God has won for us and observes, "Everything is permissible," quickly adding, "Not everything is constructive." The key word is *oikodomeō* ("to build up, to edify"). Although everything may be permitted to us who are Christians, not everything will help us advance spiritually. Mature use of freedom calls for us to choose those things that will help us grow.

CONSUME

Where the NIV and the NASB read "consume," one of two words is found in the Hebrew Bible. One of these words is *kālâh,*which means "to bring [a process] to an end." So "consume" may portray the utter destruction brought by way of plague or other divine judgment.

The other word, *'ākal,* also means "to consume," in the sense of "to eat, or devour." Figuratively *'ākal* is often used of the devastation brought by famine, war, drought, fire, and other disasters.

CONTEMPT ♦ *Despise*

CONTEND

In most OT instances, "contend" is a translation of the Hebrew word *rîḇ.* This word sometimes indicates fighting between two persons but is often used in the sense of a verbal argument or a legal dispute. When the psalmist begs God to contend with his enemies, he asks the Lord to enter the case and act as an advocate, settling the affair in the petitioner's favor (Ps 35:1,23).

Perhaps the most interesting use of "contend" (NIV) or "strive" (NASB) is found in Ge 6:3. The verse reads, "Then the LORD said, 'My Spirit will not contend with man forever, for he is mortal; his days will be a hundred and twenty years.' " The Hebrew here is *dîn*, or *dûn*. This word is used only twenty-three times in the OT, usually in close connection with a synonym that, like it, represents some governmental function, either executive, legislative, or judicial. Genesis portrays humanity before the Flood as struggling against God's moral rule (Ge 6:5–6). Finally God announced that he had brought his case to court and had decided. No more evidence was required: there was nothing more to dispute. In one hundred twenty years, the judge announces, that age of man would come to an end, and the world would be destroyed by a devastating flood (cf. 6:11–14).

CONTENTMENT

The root word *arkeō* means "to be enough," "to be sufficient." At times the NT shifts the emphasis. It is not simply that something is in sufficient supply. It is that we have an attitude that lets us be satisfied with whatever is available. Paul sums it up in 1 Ti 6:6–8: "Godliness with contentment is great gain. For we brought nothing into the world, and we can take nothing out of it. But if we have food and clothing, we will be content with that."

CONTINUAL ♦ Always

CONTRIBUTION ♦ Giving

CONTROL

There is no specific word for "control" in most places where that word appears in the NIV. Instead, a number of different Greek constructions are accurately interpreted as indicating the concept of "control." Most of these constructions indicate the controlling influence of some factor, whether of the flesh (Ro 7:5; 8:6) or of an individuals' own will (1 Co 7:37; 14:32).

The issue of control in human experience is discussed elsewhere. ♦ *Free/Freedom* ♦ *Serve/Servant/Slave*

CONVICT/CONVICTION

The Greek word is *elenchō*, which is used in the NT to express both the convicting work of God's Spirit and the ministry of rebuke within the Christian community.

Generally *elenchō* means "to convince" or "to refute." It gradually took on additional meanings: "to correct," often by accusing, and "to convict." *Elenchō* is used in the Septuagint to translate the OT term the NIV and the NASB translate "to correct." ♦ *Correct*

God's correcting is a powerful ministry; it confronts human beings in their sin (Jn 16:8; Jude 15). The Holy Spirit is the active agent in this ministry. John 16:8 gives us Jesus' promise that when the Spirit comes, "he will convict the world of guilt in regard to sin and righteousness and judgment."

This active ministry of the Spirit carried out since his "coming" at Pentecost does not guarantee conversion. A person may hear the gospel, recognize his or her personal sin and need, and yet may choose not to believe. Even the brilliant light of God's revelation, directed by his Spirit to reveal an individual's heart, does not release that individual from the responsibility of personal choice.

Within the Christian community, believers are to exercise some responsibility for one another (cf. Jas 5:19–20). This responsibility is expressed by the other meaning of *elenchō*: "to correct" or "to reprove." The theme of reproof is often seen in the Pastoral Epistles (e.g., 1 Ti 5:20; 2 Ti 4:2; Tit 1:9,13; 2:15). The process outlined in Mt 18:15–17 is to be followed. ♦ *Discipline*

Scripture makes it clear that the ministry of reproof cannot be undertaken by a person with the wrong attitude. Paul provides this guideline: "Those who oppose [the Lord's servant] he must gently instruct, in the hope that God will grant them repentance leading them to a knowledge of the truth" (2 Ti 2:25). In our ministry of rebuke, performed when we see a brother or sister turn from the pathway that God's Word marks out, as in the Spirit's ministry of conviction, it is the knowledge of God's Word alone that will bring understanding and lead to life-transforming change.

CONVINCE ♦ Persuade/Convince

CORNERSTONE ♦ Capstone

CORRECT

In the OT, the idea of correction is expressed by Hebrew words normally translated "discipline." ♦ Discipline

Three different words are found where the NIV and the NASB use "correct" in the NT. One reflects the OT emphasis. ♦ Discipline

The other two words are found in 2 Ti 3:16 and 4:2 and give us an insight into our ministry of correcting others. Each context views correction as something that can be accomplished by a study or use of Scripture.

In 2 Ti 3:16, Paul affirms that all Scripture is God-breathed and useful for "teaching, rebuking, correcting and teaching in righteousness." "Rebuke" here is elegmos, which means to refute error or rebuke sin. "Correction" is epanorthōsis, "setting straight." "Training" is paideuō, "to instruct, or train" or "to discipline." The verse shows a progression. Scripture brings awareness of sin (with the purpose of leading to conversion); sets a person upright on his feet by correcting his wrong attitudes, ideas, and values; and then, like a servant who is given the task of guiding a child, leads us as we seek to live righteously.

In 2 Ti 4:2, which speaks of preaching this God-breathed word, there is a change. Elenchō means "to convict," that is, "to correct." ♦ Convict This verb means to make an issue so clear that, even though an individual may not re-spond with confession and faith, he or she will be convicted. This ministry takes "great patience." Paul warns that "the time will come when men will not put up with sound doctrine" (4:3).

In practice, then, the Scripture's own word of truth is the correcting agency. The believer who responds to God's word of correction will find himself lifted up and set on his feet, ready to travel along faith's pathway toward righteousness. The unbeliever who will not respond to God's Word will still be convicted by the Word and is responsible for his rejection of it.

As ministers of correction, we can share the wonderful teachings of the Word with "great patience" and so "discharge all the duties" of our ministry (2 Ti 4:5).

CORRUPT

The root concept in both the Hebrew šāḥat and the Greek phtheirō is that of destruction. These words are often used of moral corruption (Ge 6:11–12; Dt 31:29; Ps 14:1; Eph 4:22). The image is powerful. It reeks of decay, as inner death and ruin gain a grip on individual and society, promising not progress but a continual rotting away.

The NT portrays sin's corruption as something that affects every aspect of the personality—those desires that are at its root (Eph 4:22; 2 Pe 1:4), the mind and conscience (1 Ti 6:5; Tit 1:15), and the character (1 Co 15:33). What is the Bible's solution to corruption? It is "to be made new in the attitude of your minds; and to put on the new self, created to be like God in true righteousness and holiness" (Eph 4:23–24).

COUNCIL

In Ac 25:12 the council (symboulion) is the panel of advisors employed by all Roman governors. In other occurrences in the Gospels and Acts, "the Council" refers to the Sanhedrin (synedrion). This Jewish body was made up of seventy-one men, with the high priest as the chairman. In Jesus' day the Jerusalem Sanhedrin served as a court that had authority to maintain the purity of Jewish custom and practice. As OT law deals with every aspect of personal and social life, as well as with religious ritual, the Sanhedrin had wide powers. It could punish and even impose the death sentence, which, however, had to be confirmed by the Roman authorities. We read in Acts that the Sanhedrin gave Paul (then Saul) letters authorizing him to travel to Damascus (in Syria) and to bring any followers of Jesus back to Jerusalem as prisoners (Ac 9:1–2). It was possible for Saul to compel such people to return to Jerusalem because in the Roman Empire one was considered a citizen of the land of his origin, and wherever a person traveled he was considered to be subject to the law of his homeland.

COUNSEL/ADVICE

The NT church was a close-knit fellowship. Believers were deeply involved in one another's lives. Yet the NT says almost nothing about giving advice—or acting on another's advice.

OT 1. **The Hebrew words**
     2. **Taking counsel: planning**
     3. **God's counsel: purposing**
NT 4. **The Greek words**
     5. **Giving counsel: mature opinion**
     6. **The Counselor: divine guidance**
     7. **Summary**

OT — 1. The Hebrew words. At times, context suggests that a general word such as "speech" (*dābār*) or "mouth" (*peh*) should be translated "advice" or "counsel" (Nu 31:16 [*dābār*]; Jos 9:14 [*peh*]). But the Hebrew word that best communicates the concept is *yā'aṣ*, with its derivative *'eṣâh*. The root means "advice, counsel, purpose, or plan." It is used both of God's counsel and of human counsel, and the ways in which it is used reflects the OT's view both of God and of human beings.

2. Taking counsel: planning. Two incidents from OT history illustrate this use of *yā'aṣ*. The rebellion of Absalom against his father David is told is 2 Sam 17. Ahithophel, Absalom's adviser, presented Absalom with a plan to take the fleeing David. Hushai, David's undercover agent in Absalom's camp, presented another plan, which was actually designed to give David time to escape. The young usurper wavered—and then chose Hushai's plan.

In this situation, "counsel" is used of each adviser's plan. The word clearly means to give one's opinion on how to best deal with the specific situation. *Yā'aṣ*, then, is a plan for dealing with a problem. But a plan presented is only an option. The one given the counsel must decide which option to act on.

We see the same interplay in 1 Ki 12. Solomon's son and successor, Rehoboam, was confronted by his overtaxed people. His older advisers counseled him to reduce taxes and win the people's hearts. The fiery younger men of Rehoboam's own age saw complaint as rebellion and urged stern repression. Rehoboam followed the advice of the younger men and tried to implement their plan. He succeeded only in splitting the kingdom into two separate nations.

In each of these cases, there is also a relationship of the purpose of God to the counsel given and accepted. The rebellious Absalom and the hasty Rehoboam each freely chose the course of action that fit the plan of God.

Usually the OT portrays counsel as being given to kings (e.g., 1 Ch 13:1; 2 Ch 25:17). Proverbs suggests that one should seek counsel from many. The thought is that human beings are limited and need many contributors to be sure all alternatives are thought of and explored (Pr 11:14; 15:22; 20:18; 24:6). When we face important decisions, we need counsel (*yā'aṣ*) to help us explore all the options. However, no advice frees the person responsible from the necessity of making his or her own choice.

3. God's counsel: purposing. Although *yā'as* is used of both the counsel of humans and the counsel of God, when God is the subject there is a definite shift of meaning. God's counsels are not options. They are sure purposes that he has determined. So Ps 33:10–11 says: "The LORD foils the plans [*ēṣâh*] of the nations; he thwarts the purposes of the peoples. But the plans of the LORD stand firm forever, the purposes of his heart through all generations." This is the critical difference between the counsel of humans and the counsel of the Lord. Human beings may sort through options suggested by advisers, but there is no certainty to be found in the best of human plans. Nor can any human plan alter what God has purposed (Isa 14:24,27). God's counsel is sure: what he purposes will come to pass.

The implication is exciting. God knows the future, and he knows the best course for his child to follow in every situation. Thus the psalmist expresses joy when he says, "I will praise the LORD, who counsels me" (16:7). And the psalmist also gives us this promise, a promise for all who trust the Lord: "I will instruct you and teach you in the way you should go; I will counsel you and watch over you" (32:8). Our one infallible counselor is God, who shows us how to make our choices in harmony with his purpose and will.

NT — 4. The Greek words. Usually the word that conveys the idea of giving advice is from *bouleuō*, "to take counsel, or deliberate," or from a compound, *symbouleuō*, "to take counsel together." When used of God, *bouleuō* is a theologically significant term and has the impact of "to will" or "to purpose." ▶ *Will*

5. Giving counsel: mature opinion. There are only a few NT examples of giving advice. When Paul says, "Here is my advice about what is best," he is giving his considered opinion, based on his maturity and knowledge (2 Co 8:10). The same tone of mature consideration is found in Ac 5:38–39: When Gamaliel was advising the Sanhedrin regarding Jesus' followers, he said, "In the present case I advise you: Leave these men alone! Let them go! For if their purpose or activity is of human origin, it will fail. But if it is from God, you will not be able to stop these men."

6. The Counselor: divine guidance. The OT views God's counsel as his fixed purpose. It was important that Israel, when facing national crises, received guidance from God. His word provided instruction concerning the pattern of normal living. But when God's people were facing crisis situations, the prophets often provided special direction (cf. Dt 18:14–21; Jer 49:30). ▶ *Prophecy/Prophet*

The NT picks up the theme of guidance. God wants to guide his people with his counsel. John is the one who develops this thought. His gospel reports Jesus' promise that after he would return to the Father, he would send the Holy Spirit as Counselor (NIV, RSV; "Helper," NASB). "Counselor" is an appropriate translation of the Greek word *paraklētos*, which has many shades of meaning. In context, the Spirit is seen as the one who interprets God's truth by helping the disciples recall needed teaching (Jn 14:26; 15:26; 16:14) and also by introducing new truth (Jn 16:12–15). The emphasis in this ministry of the Spirit is on his helping believers relate God's truth to present situations, thus guiding them in action they are to take.

Although the Spirit may use any of a number of avenues to help us sense his direction, it is clear that the Spirit himself takes on the role given the OT prophet. The Spirit guides us to decisions that are in harmony with what God purposes for us.

7. Summary. When referring to human activity, to counsel or advise means to suggest some plan of action to deal with a specific situation. The OT suggests procuring a number of advisers so that all options can be explored. But the one responsible for making the decision must ultimately choose among the options and decide what to do.

In reference to God's activity, however, "counsel" suggests that there is no choice among options. Because God is sovereign, his counsel is in fact his sure and certain purpose. No human plan can succeed if it goes against God's plan. No purpose of God will be thwarted by any choices made by human beings.

Both the OT and NT recognize the need of God's people for divine counsel. We need to know God's plan so that we can act in harmony with it. A number of OT mechanisms made this guidance possible. ♦ **Will** Often the prophets were sent to give Israel's kings clear instructions (counsel) from the Lord. In the NT this ministry of guidance is performed by the Holy Spirit, who dwells in every believer. Because of the Spirit, each of us can receive personal counsel from the Lord.

COUNTERFEIT

The NIV uses this word in only two verses. When 2 Th 2:10 speaks of Satan's energizing "counterfeit miracles" to be performed by the Antichrist, the Greek word is *apatē*, which means "deceitful." The miracles will be real; their purpose will be to deceive the observer.

On the other hand, the believer's anointing by the Holy Spirit is "not counterfeit" (1 Jn 2:27). ♦ **Anointing/Anointed** Here the word is *pseudos*, "a lie." The Holy Spirit is a real presence in God's people. He truly does teach and guide us. This is a mystical concept, and there are times when we may doubt the reality of his leading. But the Spirit's presence and his leading are real and no lie. God will guide and teach us as we look to him.

COURAGE

Courage is a commendable quality. But what exactly is it? The Hebrew words translated "courage" in the NIV and the NASB are linked with the idea of strength. A person who lacks or loses courage (Jos 2:11; 2 Sa 4:1) feels himself to be weak, unequal to the task. The courageous person acts with confidence to attack vigorously the challenges before him.

The NIV and NASB translate four different Greek words as "courage." Two of them focus on the inner attitude. *Tharseō* (Mt 9:2,22; 14:27; Mk 6:50; 10:49; Lk 8:48; Jn 16:33; Ac 23:11) and its derivatives (Ac 28:15; 2 Co 5:6,8) and also *euthy-*

meō (Ac 27:22,25; Jas 5:13) mean "to be encouraged," "to be of good cheer." When persons are discouraged or frightened by what they face, then the phrase "be courageous" reminds them that in Christ they can abandon their negative attitudes and face life's issues with a confident, optimistic attitude that disposes them to act in faith.

Tolmaō, translated "courage" only by the NASB (Mk 15:43; Lk 20:40; Php 1:14), focuses on action. It denotes moral and physical courage, expressed by taking risks. The same thought is expressed in the NIV translation of *parēssia* as "courage" in Ac 4:13; Php 1:20; Heb 3:6. ♦ **Bold**

Courage, then, weds a positive outlook with bold action. With courage we can be willing to take risks when our objective is worthwhile.

COURT

In the OT a court was usually the large rectangular enclosure created within the walls surrounding the tabernacle or temple, Israel's house of worship. Sacrifices were made in the court, and there worshipers gathered. When the reference is to a court of law (Job 9:32) or the court of rulers (Jer 29:2), the context makes the meaning clear.

In the NT, the NIV and the NASB do not make clear the specific nature of the various courts referred to. In three passages (Mt 26:3; Jn 18:15; Rev 11:2), "court" denotes a courtyard. The court mentioned in Mt 5:22 is the Jewish Sanhedrin. ♦ **Sanhedrin** In two passages in Acts (18:12; 25:6), the court is the "judgment seat" where justice was dispensed in the cities of the Roman Empire. In several other verses (Mt 5:21–22,25; 1 Co 6:2,4; Jas 2:6), the court is the local court where civil suits were heard.

COVENANT

The notion of a covenant is unfamiliar today. But the concept of covenant is utterly basic to our understanding of Scripture. In OT times this complex concept was the foundation of social order and social relations, and it was particularly the foundation for an understanding of humanity's relationship with God.

1. The biblical concept
   a. OT roots
   b. NT references
2. The Abrahamic covenant
3. The Mosaic (law) covenant
4. The Davidic covenant
5. The new covenant foretold
6. The new covenant instituted
7. Human response to covenant
8. Summary

1. The biblical concept. The concept of covenant (*bᵉrît*) is not found exclusively in the Bible. Other cultures in early biblical times used the covenant concept as a basis for a wide range of interpersonal and social relationships. Between one nation and another, a covenant was a treaty (Ge 14:13; 31:44–55). Among individuals, a covenant expressed a pledge of friendship (1 Sa 18:3; 20:8; 23:18) or served as a business contract. When a ruler and his subjects were the parties to a covenant, such a covenant served as a national constitution and spelled out the responsibilities of the ruler and the ruled (cf. 2 Sa 3:21; 5:3; 1 Ch 11:3). It should not be surprising that in a world in which covenant was such a fundamental idea God would select the concept of covenant to clarify the relationship that he sought to establish with his people.

There would of course be distinctive aspects to any covenant that defined divine/human relationships. We noted above that the meaning of *bᵉrît* varies to some extent, depending on whether it is describing treaties, friendships, business agreements, or national constitutions. Surely there must be unique aspects when the parties to a *bᵉrît* are God and human beings. The distinctives are captured in the following definition of a biblical (divine/human) covenant: a biblical covenant is a clear statement of God's purposes and intentions expressed in terms that bind God by solemn oath to perform what he has promised.

a. OT roots. The nature of the biblical *bᵉrît* as a statement of God's intentions is seen in each of the four major covenants (Abrahamic, Davidic, Mosaic, new). In each of these covenants, God states what he will do. In three of the four, the purposes announced will be accomplished at history's end. These are eschatological covenants. In the other covenant (the Mosaic, or law covenant), God's purpose is essentially existential. He states the blessings he will give when the people of Israel obey and the disasters that will come when they disobey.

The nature of the biblical *bᵉrît* as something in which God binds himself by solemn oath is seen in the rituals followed in making the covenants. In OT times a covenant was "cut," perhaps referring to the fact that the most binding covenants were enacted in a ceremony that involved the offering of a sacrifice. Ge 15 describes how God followed this cultural form, passing between the halves of sacrificial animals as Abraham lay in a deep sleep. In this way God bound himself to keep the promises made to Abraham.

The Mosaic covenant followed another binding pattern, that of a suzerainty treaty made between a ruler and his subjects. The written law served as the constitution of the nation thus formed.

The use of these culturally binding forms to express relationship into which God entered with human beings provided a foundation to believer in God's full commitment to his Word. He bound himself to Israel by solemn oaths.

The nature of the biblical covenant as promise is stressed in the NT by the apostle Paul (Ro 4:13–17; Gal 3:15–18). The promises that God makes are not dependent on human reaction to them: he will do what he has promised.

We see something of this sense of binding commitment in Israel's response to the Gibeonites, who had tricked them into a political covenant ("treaty"). Despite the deceit of the Gibeonites, the covenant once made was not set aside, and the people of Israel kept their promise to help when the Gibeonites were attacked (Jos 10).

Throughout history, Israel's own repeated sins often brought God's discipline on the nation. But even the sternest warnings were tempered with restatements of the promises that one day God would act to fulfill the covenant promises given to Abraham and the patriarchs. This pattern in sacred history cannot be explained if the biblical covenants are conditioned on human behavior.

God gave his promises, and the OT celebrates his *ḥeseḏ* ("grace"—i.e., his faithfulness to his covenant obligations).

▶ **Grace** As Paul writes in Romans after reviewing Israel's history of unfaithfulness: "As far as election is concerned, they [Israel] are loved on account of the patriarchs, for God's gifts and his call are irrevocable" (Ro 11:28–29).

b. NT references. The Greek word for covenant is *diathēkē*. It is used over 270 times in the Septuagint (the Greek translation of the OT) to render the Hebrew *bᵉrîṯ*. Although *diathēkē* occurs only 33 times in the NT, many other passages base arguments on different aspects of the covenant that God established with Abraham and his descendants (e.g., Ro 5, Gal 3). One cluster of NT uses of *diathēkē* is connected with the Lord's Supper. Other uses are found in Paul's epistles and especially in the Book of Hebrews.

From early times the Greeks used *diathēkē* in the sense of a will. In contrast to a *synthēkē*, which spelled out terms of a partnership, a *diathēkē* permitted an individual to dispose of possessions any way that person chose. The decision, once expressed in a will, could not be annulled by another party. But the will became effective only after the person making it died. The writer of Hebrews (9:13–22) builds on this aspect of the OT covenants. He points out that the old covenants were confirmed with blood. Jesus' death instituted a new covenant—a covenant that serves as Jesus' own unbreakable will, "the promised eternal inheritance" (v. 15).

The writer of Hebrews also speaks of the Abrahamic covenant as an oath (*orkos*). This is understood to be a legally binding guarantee. As the writer says, "Because God wanted to make the unchanging nature of his purpose very clear to the heirs of what was promised, he confirmed it with an oath" (6:17).

This, combined with Paul's insistence that "promise" sums up the essential aspect of the Abrahamic covenant, gives us strong evidence that the Bible regards a covenant as a statement of God's purposes and intentions, expressed in terms that bind God, by solemn oath, to perform what he has promised.

2. The Abrahamic covenant. Presumably, Abraham was a pagan, a worshiper of Nannar, the moon-god, in the city of Ur. God told him: "Leave your country, your people and your father's household and go to the land I will show you" (Ge 12:1). God gave Abraham promises (vv. 2–3) that were later formally confirmed, God working in line with the human custom of making a binding covenant (Ge 15:1–21). Still later, Abraham was given a sign of that covenant (circumcision) and was told that that all his male offspring must be circumcised (Ge 17:1–22).

The call of Abraham is one of Scripture's theological turning points. Prior to that time, God dealt with the human race as a whole. From that point on, God's plan was carried out through the family of Abraham. Through that family, God gave his biblical revelation to humanity, and from that family the Savior of all has come.

The covenant passages in Genesis show a typical interplay between human beings and God as sovereign Lord. God announces his purposes, which no action of man can thwart. Abraham responds to God's revelation with faith and obedience. Thus Abraham personally experienced the blessings that God promised.

The interplay is implicit in circumcision: "Any uncircumcised male, who has not been circumcised in the flesh, will be cut off from his people," God announces. "He has broken my covenant" (17:14). The failure of an individual to respond with faith and with obedience to the stipulations in God's covenant remove that covenant-breaking individual from an experience of covenant blessings. But the failure of an individual or an entire generation of Israelites did nothing to alter God's commitment to do what he had announced. Human disobedience affects human participation in a covenant but does not release God from his covenant oath.

What are the provisions of that initial, Abrahamic covenant? These are the promises given to Abraham, most of which will be fulfilled only at history's end: "I will make you into a great nation and I will bless you; I will make your name great, and you will be a blessing. I will bless those who bless you, and whoever curses you I will curse; and all peoples on earth will be blessed through you" (Ge 12:2–3). When Abraham arrived in Palestine, God reappeared and added one other clause of promise, "To your offspring I will give this land" (Ge 12:7), later confirmed by covenant oath (Ge 15:7–21).

The conviction that God spoke to the forefather Abraham and that Israel inherited the covenant promises through Isaac and Jacob is basic to the Old Testament account. It was also basic to the sense of special identity that has preserved Israel as a separate and distinct race to this day.

3. The Mosaic (law) covenant. Moses led Israel out of Egypt and through the wilderness on their way to the land that God had promised to Abraham so many centuries before. But from the beginning, the Israelites proved almost impossible for Moses to manage (Ex 15–17). It was while they were at Sinai that God, the divine Ruler, established a constitution for the nation-to-be.

That constitution, the Mosaic Law, follows the pattern of the suzerainty treaties of the ancient Middle East. The features of such documents are:

(1) Preamble: author identified and his titles given. *Ex 20:1*

(2) Historical prologue: the recounting of the deeds of the ruler on behalf of his people. *Ex 19:4–5*

(3) Stipulations: principles that govern relationships between the parties. *Ex 20:2–7; 21:1–23:19*

(4) Blessings and cursings: announcement of results of keeping and of breaking covenant conditions. *Ex 23:20–33*

(5) Oath: promise given by the people as they accept the covenant. *Ex 24:1–8*

The Book of Deuteronomy also seems to follow the structure provided by a suzerainty treaty.

The law covenant is detailed. It regulates the personal, social, and civil life of Israel and spells out religious obligations.

There are a number of things about the law covenant that are important for us to understand:

a. Like the other biblical covenants, the Mosaic includes an announcement by God of what he intends to do. As such, law is an unconditional covenant.

b. Unlike the other biblical covenants, the Mosaic Law had an existential focus. The other covenants announce what God will do at history's end. This covenant announces how God will respond during history to each generation of Israelites, his response being based on their keeping of the law.

What God intends to do is to bless those generations that keep his covenant and to discipline severely those generations that fail to do so.

c. Unlike the other biblical covenants, the Mosaic covenant was to be confirmed (renewed) by the people. Each generation had to commit itself to live by the law given on Sinai (e.g., Ex 24, Dt 29, Jos 24). Each new generation had to choose whom it would serve. And even today in the Jewish tradition a twelve-year-old makes his personal choice. When he becomes *bar mitzvah,* a "son of the commandment," he accepts responsibility to live in accord with the stipulations laid down in the ancient Mosaic code.

d. Unlike the other biblical covenants, that of the law was never intended to be permanent. Paul argues that law is not even implied in the Abrahamic covenant, which is different in nature from the covenant of law. It was introduced some 430 years after Abraham's time. It is a performance code and not a gift offered and confirmed by promise. It neither replaces nor modifies the initial promise (Gal 3:15–25). ▶ *Law* And the OT itself contains God's announcement that there was to come a day when a new covenant would replace the covenant of the Mosaic Law. " 'The time is coming,' declares the LORD, 'when I will make a new covenant with the house of Israel and with the house of Judah. It will not be like the covenant I made with their forefathers when I took them by the hand to lead them out of Egypt' " (Jer 31:31–32). The Mosaic covenant has been replaced today by the new covenant and is the only biblical covenant that is not currently in force.

4. The Davidic covenant. David was Israel's model king. Under David the tiny land expanded some ten times and became a powerful state and came to occupy most, but not all, of the land that God had promised to Israel under the Abrahamic covenant. As 2 Sa 7 reports, the prophet Nathan came to David with a promise from Yahweh: "Your house and your kingdom will endure forever before me; your throne will be established forever" (7:16). This was a commitment made by Israel's sovereign Lord, whose words are trustworthy (7:28). David and the prophets who followed Nathan viewed this promise as a covenant. The psalmists celebrate both Abrahamic and Davidic covenants: "He remembers his covenant forever, the word he commanded, for a thousand generations, the covenant he made with Abraham, the oath he swore to Isaac. He confirmed it to Jacob as a decree, to Israel as an everlasting covenant: 'To you I will give the land of Canaan as the portion you will inherit' " (Ps 105:8–11); and "I will declare that your love stand firm forever, that you established your faithfulness in heaven itself. You said, 'I have made a covenant with my chosen one, I have sworn to David my servant, I will establish your line forever and make your throne firm through all generations' " (Ps 89:2–4). Because of this covenant promise, the Jewish people of Jesus' day believed firmly that the Messiah was to be a Davidic ruler who would establish the long-promised kingdom. ▶ *Christ* The

genealogies of Jesus in Matthew and Luke are important to authenticate not only his claim to be truly human but also his descent from David and thus his right to the promised throne of the eternal kingdom. ▶ *Kingdom*

5. The new covenant foretold. The promise of a new covenant to replace the Mosaic covenant was made at a critical point in Israel's history. The prophet Jeremiah transmitted God's promise during a time of national disaster.

It was about 1450 B.C. that God's people received the Mosaic Law. But Israel consistently disobeyed and therefore experienced the promised disciplines. Finally the Northern Kingdom, Israel, established at the breakup of David and Solomon's unified land around 931 B.C. , was defeated by the Assyrians; the people were deported in 722 B.C. The Southern Kingdom, Judah, survived. But despite sputtering revivals under a few godly kings, these people too drifted into idolatry, immorality, and injustice. Jeremiah followed up generations of prophetic warning by announcing that the foretold judgment was to fall on his own generation. Jeremiah's words came true. Judah was devastated, the temple in Jerusalem was destroyed, and a final group of people were carried captive to Babylon (c. 586 B.C.).

For the first time since the conquest (c. 1400 B.C.), God's people were torn from the Promised Land, the place associated with God's covenant promises. One question must have dominated the thoughts of the frightened captives: Had Israel's sin at last caused God to withdraw the promises made to Abraham and David?

Jeremiah gives two answers: (1) The Exile had initiated a "time of trouble for Jacob," but (2) "he will be saved out of it" (30:7). The people who had broken God's covenant would be punished, but afterward they would be restored. This is God's promise: "I have loved you with an everlasting love; I have drawn you with loving-kindness. I will build you up again" (Jer 31:3–4). Jerusalem would be rebuilt by another generation, and the land would be Israel's, as God had promised (chs. 30–33). " 'Only if the heavens above can be measured and the foundations of the earth below be searched out will I reject all the descendants of Israel because of all they have done,' declares the LORD" (31:37).

Nestled among these words of comfort is this unique and unexpected announcement: "The time is coming when I will make a new covenant with the house of Israel" (31:31). The law, relying not on promise but on human performance, has been shown to be unable to produce righteousness. Now God would replace it with a more effective approach. Like the other promise covenants, this covenant states boldly and clearly what God would do: "I will put my law in their minds and write it on their hearts. I will be their God, and they will be my people. No longer will a man teach his neighbor, or a man his brother, saying 'Know the LORD,' because they will all know me, from the least of them to the greatest," declares the LORD. "For I will forgive their wickedness and I will remember their sins no more" (31:33–34).

6. The new covenant instituted. The new covenant, though prophesied by Jeremiah about six hundred years before Christ, was not actually made at that time. The covenant was made, and confirmed, at the Cross.

At the Last Supper, the night before the Crucifixion, Jesus explained the symbolism of the communion cup. He said, "This is the blood of the [new] covenant, which is poured out for many for the forgiveness of sins" (Mt 26:28; cf. Mk 14:24; Lk 22:20; 1 Co 11:25). Just as the other covenants were oath-confirmed, so the new covenant would be made by a covenant-initiating sacrifice. But this time the offerer and the sacrifice were one, and the blood that sealed God's commitment was that of his own Son. The new covenant has now been made and confirmed. The promise of forgiveness is assured. Although only at history's end will we realize the full meaning of what Jesus has done, we can today experience the promised forgiveness and transformation made available in the new covenant.

The difference between the old and new is striking. The old covenant knew a law that was carved in cold stone. The new covenant takes the righteousness that was expressed in law and supernaturally infuses that righteousness into the very character of the believer. Thus Hebrews quotes the OT foreview as something that is now, through Christ, our own: "I will put my laws in their hearts and I will write them on their minds. . . . Their sins and lawless acts I will remember no more" (Heb 10:16–17).

There is none of the law's cold "Do this and live" in the new covenant. Instead we meet again the great "I will" of God, who promises that he himself will transform us from within.

Paul carefully explains that all of God's promises are appropriated by faith. Today, to us who, like Abraham, are "fully persuaded that God [has] power to do what he promises" (Ro 4:21) comes the promised salvation, and with it come forgiveness and inner transformation. Such are the benefits of covenant relationship with the Lord.

7. Human response to covenant. In Ro 4 and Gal 3, Paul argues that the essence of covenant is promise. What can we do to respond to the promise of God? Only one thing. We are to believe the promise and consider God's Word trustworthy. We are to consider God's Word so trustworthy that we step out to act on what he says.

It was this faith that saved Abraham, long before either circumcision or law was introduced. It is faith alone—faith in Jesus, the seal of God's new covenant—that saves us today.

But what is the relationship of faith to obligations under the old covenant, such as circumcision and Israel's obligation to keep the Mosaic Law? What is the relationship of faith today to keeping Jesus' commandments?

Scripture argues that it is the nature of true faith to express itself in action. ◆
Belief/Faith Those Israelites who heard and believed God's covenant promises to Abraham were circumcised. Those who loved God in the age of law followed the law's commands willingly; and when

they sinned, they offered the required sacrifices. ◆ *Atonement* Today we who trust Jesus also find our faith expressing itself in similar loving obedience to Jesus, through obedience to Scripture and the Spirit.

Faith enables human beings to appropriate God's promises and experience their benefits personally. But whether or not we believe in God's promises, his covenant promises stand. God will accomplish his purposes in history and in all who believe.

8. Summary. The biblical covenants are clear statements of God's purposes and intentions, expressed in terms that bind God by solemn oath to perform what he has promised.

The basic biblical covenants are the Abrahamic, the Mosaic (old, law), the Davidic, and the new. All but the Mosaic covenant look forward to history's end for their ultimate fulfillment.

The Mosaic covenant was a temporary covenant, the constitution of the nation Israel. It was based on human effort, not on promise, for its performance. It was intended to define for Israel the lifestyle that would enable God to bless them until the new covenant was made. Then the requirements of the law would at last be fulfilled in persons whom God was transforming, that they might be righteous indeed.

From the beginning, faith has been the only correct response people can make when God speaks in promise. Faith alone is able to bring human beings to personal relationship with God. It is through faith that we today can experience the blessings of God's new covenant: the forgiveness of our sins and the Spirit's work of engraving righteousness on our hearts.

COVER

In both Testaments the verb "to cover" is used with a full range of meanings, from "spread over" to "conceal." A few times in the OT it is used in the sense of "forgive" (cf. Ps 32:1; 85:2). There are three NT uses that deserve comment.

Covering women's heads (1 Co 11). In this passage on worship, Paul argues that women should follow custom and participate in worship with their heads covered. The passage is best understood against the background of an early "women's lib" movement. Affirmed in the church as gifted members of the body (1 Co 12:7), some women reacted by insisting that their new significance must be demonstrated by rejecting traditional "feminine" roles and acting like men. Paul responds by making several statements: A woman would feel disgraced if her hair were cut off (11:6). God created men and women different (11:7). Men and women are interdependent, not superior or inferior to each other (11:11–12). The point of these arguments is that a woman does not have to reject her femininity and become a man to be important. The Corinthian women were overreacting; they should continue to wear their veils proudly, as society and theology suggested was appropriate for women.

Covering of our sins (Ro 4:7). Here Paul, in order to demonstrate that righteousness has always been a gift, quotes a psalm of David: "To the man who does not work but trusts God who justifies the wicked, his faith is credited as righteousness." (Ro 4:5).

Some have taught that the sins of OT saints were "covered" but were not forgiven. ◆ *Atonement* But Romans teaches that forgiveness has always been extended to OT and NT saints who simply trust God's promises. The basis of that forgiveness has always been the sacrifice of Jesus on Calvary. Forgiveness was extended to Abraham and David and to the host of other OT believers on the basis of a sacrifice that *would be* made, just as forgiveness is extended to you and me on the basis of a sacrifice that *has been* made. ◆ *Forgive*

Covering "a multitude of sins" (1 Pe 4:8; Jas 5:20). The two NT references seem to paraphrase Pr 10:12: "Hatred stirs up dissension, but love covers over all wrongs." James suggests that love brings a closeness that enables one person to help another turn from his or her errors, and in this sense the first person covers many sins. The proverb may indicate that, as hatred stimulates sin, so love blankets those emotions that might lead us to sin against others.

COVET

The Hebrew *hāmad* and the Greek *epithymeō* both mean "to desire" or "to take pleasure in." The usage of derivatives that mean "pleasant" or "desirable" assures us that desire is not wrong in itself. Nor is it wrong for us to appreciate the good things of life.

But covetousness is desire running riot. The commandment makes it clear that it is wrong to desire the wrong things: "You shall not covet your neighbor's house. You shall not covet your neighbor's wife, or his manservant or maidservant, his ox or donkey, or anything that belongs to your neighbor" (Ex 20:17). But it is eminently right to desire and take pleasure in your own house, wife, and possessions.

Scripture identifies other inappropriate objects of desire, such as the prostitute (Pr 6:25) and the gold that coats the pagan idol (Dt 7:25). But Ro 7 argues that there is a fault within which is the real origin of covetousness. It is a fault that transforms pleasure in good things into a passionate longing for what we do not have.

The tenth commandment, rather than making us less covetous, actually stimulates "every kind of covetous desire" (7:8). To say "don't" makes us aware of desire; it does not quench it. It takes a work of God's Spirit to redirect our passions and to give us contentment in those things that God intends us to have.

How good it is that God's Spirit is with us! Like Paul, you and I can learn "the secret of being content in any and every situation" (Php 4:12).

The NASB translates each occurrence of *pleonektēs* as "covetous" (1 Co 5:10–11; 6:10; Eph 5:5). The word describes a person desirous of having more. It is better translated "greedy," as in the NIV.

CREATE

To many of us, the word "create" generally implies an action by which something that has not existed before is brought into being. The biblical words do not necessarily mean "to create out of nothing." But the key Hebrew and Greek words unquestionably teach the traditional Christian doctrine of creation.

OT 1. The Hebrew words
    2. The OT view of creation
    3. Genesis 1 and creation
NT 4. The Greek words
    5. Original creation
    6. God's new creation
    7. Summary

OT — 1. The Hebrew words. A number of Hebrew words are used of fashioning, shaping, or making an object; the word *bārā'*, however, is distinctive. In the Qal stem it is used only of God's activity, thus making it a technical theological term. The emphasis in *bārā'* is not on making something from nothing but on initiating an object or project. There are certain things that only God is capable of initiating and thus of giving being.

God's great acts of initiating indicated by *bārā'* include: (1) initiating the heaven and the earth and all natural phenomena; (2) initiating humanity, with male and female sharing the image of God; (3) initiating through forgiveness a cleansed heart; (4) initiating Israel as a distinct people; (5) initiating (in the future) new heavens, a new earth, and a new Jerusalem; and (6) initiating (within the flow of history) peace, the possibility of evil, the destroyer, and praise on the lips of mourners.

Bārā' occurs in the Qal stem, indicating actions that fall outside the realm of human competence, in the following Scripture passages: Ge 1:1,21,27; 2:3; 5:1–2; 6:7; Nu 16:30; Dt 4:32; Ps 51:10; 89:12,47; Ecc 12:1; Isa 4:5; 40:26,28; 41:20; 42:5; 43:1,7,15; 45:7–8,12,18; 54:16; 57:19; 65:17–18; Jer 31:22; Am 4:13; Mal 2:10.

2. The OT view of creation. The OT views God as the all-powerful creator of the universe. This image of God as sovereign over the material universe permeates the entire OT and shapes the OT believer's view of the Lord. We catch something of the sense of awe in the expressions of praise in Ps 89:5–13: "The heavens praise your wonders, O LORD, your faithfulness too, in the assembly of the holy ones. For who in the skies above can compare with the LORD? Who is like the LORD among the heavenly beings? In the council of the holy ones God is greatly feared: he is more awesome than all who surround him. O LORD God Almighty, who is like you? You are mighty, O LORD, and your faithfulness surrounds you. You rule over the surging sea; when its waves mount up, you still them. You crushed Rahab like one of the slain; with your strong arm you scattered your enemies. The heavens are yours, and yours also the earth; you founded the world and all that is in it. You created the north and the south; Tabor and Hermon sing for joy at your name. Your arm is endued with power; your hand is strong, your right hand exalted."

Isa 40:28–31 shows how this image of God as omnipotent Creator is applied to bring comfort and encouragement: "Do you not know? Have you not heard? The LORD is the everlasting God, the Creator of the ends of the earth. He will not grow tired or weary, and his understanding no one can fathom. He gives strength to the weary and increases the power of the weak. Even youths grow tired and weary, and young men stumble and fall; but those who hope in the LORD will renew their strength. They will soar on wings like eagles; they will run and not grow weary, they will walk and not be faint."

Knowing God as Creator is a source of confidence and encouragement. Surely the one who shaped the universe and offers human beings his covenant love can be trusted completely to do all that he has promised.

3. Genesis 1 and creation. There has been much debate about the first chapters of Genesis. Does chapter 1 describe the actual creation process, or is it intended—without making a scientifically or historically valid statement about

events—as a myth to affirm truths about the relationship between God and the universe? Another article discusses the seven days of creation. ◆ *Day*

Even for those who are convinced that in Ge 1 there is a literal history of the divine work, the teachings of the chapter about the relationship between God and his universe are most important. First, God himself is independent of the material universe. He is the active agent who not only calls all things into being but also organizes and orders them. Ge 1 shows God as one who plans and establishes a complex but stable universe, makes moral and aesthetic value judgments, and actively involves himself in the shaping of all things. The God who is distinct from the universe shows himself completely involved in its order and functions.

NT — 4. The Greek words. A number of Greek words are included in the vocabulary of creation. The basic idea is expressed by *ktizō*, "to create," "to produce," and by *katabolē*, "foundation." ◆ *Foundation*

Ktizō and its derivatives occur thirty-eight times in the NT. The contexts provide insight into the distinctive creation emphasis of the NT, which totally accepts the OT view of God as originator of all things.

5. Original creation. The Gospels contain several references to creation. Jesus referred to "the creation of the world" (Mt 13:35; 25:34; Jn 17:24) and to "the beginning" (Mt 19:4,8; 24:21; Mk 10:6; 13:19; Lk 11:50; Jn 8:44). Here as always the OT revelation is validated as accurate by Jesus.

Of particular note are Mt 19:4 and Mk 10:6. In these passages Jesus refers to God's creation of human beings as male and female and to his institution of marriage. The point in each argument is that in the original creation God initiated a particular order and that such patterns are not to be changed by human beings (cf. 1 Co 11:9; 1 Ti 4:3–4). ◆ *Divorce and Remarriage*

In Romans, Paul makes two fascinating assertions about creation. The created universe is unmistakable evidence of the power and divine nature of God (Ro 1:20). One can reason from the material universe and its features to the existence of God as first cause. But Paul is careful not to suggest that we can reason from creation to the *goodness* of God. The reason is that the entire universe was twisted when Adam's act introduced sin. The present world does not give clear witness to God's goodness: it itself needs to be redeemed and "liberated from its bondage to decay" (8:21; cf. 8:18–23).

The Epistles also invite us to look back "before the creation of the world" (Eph 1:4; cf. Heb 4:3; 1 Pe 1:20). God existed before the material universe. His plans were completely laid before the first creative act brought matter into being.

Col 1:16 tells us that Jesus was the active agent as well as the reason for creation. "For by him all things were created: things in heaven and on earth, visible and invisible, whether thrones or powers or rulers or authorities; all things were created by him and for him" (cf. Jn 1:1–5). But Jesus' role in the created universe was not completed with the acts of creation. "He is before all things, and in him all things hold together" (1:17). The power that binds atom and galaxy alike is provided by Jesus, "the ruler of God's creation" (Rev 3:14).

Peter argues that God's power enables him to intervene in the material universe. Peter rejects the scoffers' position that "everything goes on as it has since the beginning of creation" (2 Pe 3:4). Such people forget that God destroyed creation's original pattern by a great flood and that God has declared that he will destroy the present heavens and earth by fire (3:6–7).

The emergent picture of creation is significant. God existed before the material universe came into being. He not only caused it but also designed and ordered it according to his own plan and purposes. A change in the order that God initiated—whether the disastrous change Adam and Eve introduced in the Garden or contemporary changes in the created order of relationships—is wrong and courts disaster.

Jesus, the active agent in the Creation, remains active. He holds the universe together. So our universe is not some massive clockwork machine, wound and left to run by an absentee God. God's own power is required to maintain material existence. It should not be surprising, then, that God can and does intervene in his creation, bringing judgment and initiating events within history, as he initiated history itself. Although the creation is now flawed by sin, God will one day act to liberate it from its bondage to decay and will purge it by fire. In everything, God remains God. And his creation remains subservient to him.

6. God's new creation. The OT foretells a new heaven and a new earth, to be created after this present universe is folded up and put away like a worn and ragged cloak (Isa 65:17–25). But the NT focuses our attention on a new creation that is taking place now. This is creation in the sense of divine initiation of a new order, as well as in the sense of originating a new thing. ♦ *New and Old*

God's new creation takes place within human beings. Anyone in Christ "is a new creation; the old is gone, the new has come" (2 Co 5:17). Eph 2:10 says believers are "created in Christ Jesus to do good works." God has shaped us to glorify him and has even laid out the works he has designed for us to do. The theme of inner renewal by a new creation is found often in the NT (cf. Gal 6:15; Eph 2:15; 4:24; Col 3:10).

No mere human reformation will do. God must initiate something within us so new that only the image of a new birth or new creation can adequately describe it.

7. Summary. In Scripture, "creation" (Heb, *bārā'*; Gk, *ktizō*) is a work of initiation, whether of the material universe or patterns to be established within it and in social relationships. God is understood in both Testaments to be the cause of physical material, calling into being by his power the things that now exist. God is completely sovereign over his universe. He can and does intervene, as he chooses, in the natural course of events. ♦ *Miracle/Sign/Wonder*

The created universe continues to give testimony to God. His glory glows in the stars, which are set so securely in the heavens (Ps 19:1–4; 104:2). The delicate balance of nature witnesses to God's loving provision for the needs of living creatures (Ps 104:10–30). Evidences of caring in the animal world are additional reflections of God's sensitivity and continuing concern for his creation. Even the imperfections of our world cannot mask God.

But the universe that God formed has been warped by the introduction of sin. The world as we know it, as well as the human personality, is twisted and misshapen. The material universe witnesses clearly to the existence and the power of God, but his goodness is not as easily seen in a broken world.

Yet God is good. He promises redemption of the material creation as well as our own spiritual transformation. And he has begun his renewing work within us. He causes those who believe to be reborn, and their rebirth is in fact a new creation. Our very faith and our new life in Christ are expressions of the creative power of the living God.

CREATURE

The Hebrew and Greek words translated "creature" in the NIV and the NASB do not mean simply a "created being." Rather, "creature" is a translation of words with such meanings as "living being" (*nepeš*, Heb; *zōon*, Gk), "animal" (*ḥay*), "desert creature" (*ṣî*), and "wild beast" (*thērion*). All living things are understood to have come from other living things that were the work of the Creator.

CREDIT/CREDITED

By a glance at the NIV concordance we can see that the word "credit" has theological significance. Again and again Ro 4 speaks of faith being "credited" to someone as righteousness. The Greek here is *logizomai*, "to reckon." The word was an accountant's term in NT times, a word in common usage. It means "to make an entry in the account book."

As sinners, you and I have no righteousness that would be acceptable to God. But God has given his Word of promise. When we respond to him in faith, against our name in his account book he makes an entry that says in effect, "This person is righteous in my sight!" Our faith has been credited to us as righteousness.

CRIME

Today "law and order" issues are very important in our society. How does the Bible view crime? Are there guidelines that might help our society with its criminal justice system?

OT 1. OT view of crime and punishment
NT 2. Crime in the NT
3. Summary

OT — 1. OT view of crime and punishment. The Hebrew words translated "crime" in the OT are usually words that mean "sin" or "wickedness." This is because the social life and the religious life of Israel were interwoven. A wrong committed against one's fellow-man was first and foremost a sin against God, for God was the giver of the law that governed all of life in Israel.

A criminal act, as a sin, had to be brought to God so that the fabric of society would not be destroyed. Aside from law suits to settle disputes, there were three mechanisms in the law to restore social harmony.

The first was restitution. A person who stole or destroyed another's property was required to pay back double (e.g., Ex 22:4,7,9).

The second mechanism was compensation. In personal injuries and some other noncapital crimes, the "eye for an eye" principle was established. In most situations, however, money compensation could be offered. A financial settlement for an injury could cover loss of income and medical care and be substituted for the prescribed retribution.

In general, capital offenses were seldom what we call criminal acts, which harm persons or property. Rather, capital crimes were those that threatened the moral and social order that God had established. Included in this category are such evils as incest, adultery, and idolatry (Lev 20). However, in the case of murder (as distinguished from manslaughter) the law did prescribe execution. ◆ *Murder/Kill*

2. Crime in the NT. NT terminology is quite sophisticated and reflects the Greek/Roman legal system. The word *adikēma* occurs in Ac 18:14 and 24:20, where the NIV reads "crime." (It is rendered "iniquities" in its other occurrence, Rev. 18:5.) The root indicates a failure to conform to the social order and thus denotes a violation of the recognized rights of others. Actions so labled in the Hellenistic world were considered legally and ethically wrong. In each passage, Paul stands before a pagan court, charged by his Jewish enemies with what might be considered a religious crime (i.e., against Jewish tradition). In each case he argues that nothing he has done is a crime within the definition of crime as *adikēma* against the fabric of the Empire, and that therefore he should be acquitted.

Kakos is found in the Synoptics where a frustrated Pilate, shouting to the crowds who shriek for Jesus' death, bursts out: "Why? What crime has he committed?" (Mt 27:23; Mk 15:14; cf. Lk 23:22). The word "crime" here indicates something evil, destructive. According to Ro 13:3–7, human government is assigned the mission of punishing evil (*kakos*). In Jesus' trial, particularly as described by John, Pilate had insisted that the Jews state some legal ground (*aitia*) for their accusations against Jesus (Jn 18:38; 19:4,6). The Jewish leaders responded with only threat and bluster, and Pilate announced that he found no legal basis for the death penalty. But still the crowd shouted. It was then that Pilate burst out, begging these men who had frightened him with their threat of political reprisal (Jn 19:12–15) to at least provide him with some excuse. Couldn't they at least demonstrate the evil Jesus had done? They could not. In spite of this, the weak Pilate finally surrendered to their pressure.

In places where the NIV reads "criminals," the Greek has a compound of *kakos*, meaning "evildoers, or evilworkers."

3. Summary. The criminal justice system of the Roman world was much closer to that of the modern Western world in the ways it dealt with crime than either of these systems is to the OT approach. But we can learn much that is of value to our society from the OT. Particularly, we could apply the principle of restitution instead of imprisonment for nonviolent crimes.

CROSS

The two Greek words used for the cross are *xylon* ("wood") and *stauros* ("stake," or "cross"). In the Roman world the cross was used to execute only slaves and foreigners. Those with Roman citizenship were protected from the shame and the pain associated with crucifixion.

As practiced by the Romans, crucifixion involved either tying or nailing the convicted person to a crossbeam, which was attached to the *stauros* ("pole"). The cross might be in the form of a **T** or, as it is more traditionally represented, as a **†**.

Death came slowly to a crucified person, through exhaustion or by suffocation. And it came with great pain. Death by crucifixion was also considered a great disgrace. It is the theological implications of Jesus' crucifixion, however, that are of most concern to the Christian. ◆ *Crucifixion of Jesus*

CROWN

The significant Hebrew words for "crown" are *nēzer* and *'ăṭārâh*. Both words signify some type of headgear, but they also carry a significant message.

Nēzer is from a root meaning "consecration." It can refer to the long hair that marked the person who took a Nazirite vow or to priests' headgear. It can also refer to the royal crown of Israel's king (2 Sa 1:10; 2 Ki 11:12; 2 Ch 23:11; Ps 89:39; 132:18; Pr 27:24; Zec 9:16). This use of the word is significant. It underlines the fact that Israel's kings were consecrated by God to the sacred task of leading God's people.

The word *'aṭārâh* is also translated "crown." But it is never used to designate the crown of a king of Israel or of Judah. An *'aṭārâh* might have been made of gold, and it might have been worn by a queen or a noble, but it did not signify divine consecration.

The word *'aṭārâh* is also used figuratively, to indicate honor and blessing. Gray hair (Pr 16:31) and wisdom (Pr 4:9; 14:24) are considered such a crown. The figure is extended further as Isaiah looks toward history's end and says, "In that day the LORD Almighty will be a glorious crown, a beautiful wreath for the remnant of his people" (28:5).

Only three NT passages use the word "crown" to suggest authority. They are the three NT occurrences of *diadēma* (Rev 12:3; 13:1; 19:12). Usually where the English NT speaks of a crown the Gk word is *stephanos*, which denotes either a wreath or a crown. Probably *stephanos* is used both literally and figuratively when referring to the circlet of thorns that was pressed on Jesus' brow (Mt 27:29; Mk 15:17; Jn 19:2,5).

When Paul speaks of believers' rewards as crowns, he picks up the symbol from both pagan and Jewish cultures. For the Jew, the word *stephanos* recalled the OT *'aṭārâh*. For the pagan, it brought to mind the garland of leaves awarded the victor in Greek athletic games. In both cultures it expressed honor and blessing.

God intends to honor his faithful saints and to bless them with crowns of life (1 Co 9:25; 2 Ti 2:5; Jas 1:12; Rev 2:10), of righteousness (2 Ti 4:8), and of glory (1 Pe 5:4).

Paul, looking ahead to his appearance before Christ at his coming, says that the believers he has won to Jesus in his missionary efforts will themselves be his crown of rejoicing (1 Th 2:19). There can be no greater honor for Paul than to meet Jesus in the company of those his efforts had won to the Lord.

CRUCIFIXION OF JESUS

The execution of Jesus on the cross is a historical event. We may debate the exact configuration of the cross and dispute the precise location of Jerusalem's public execution grounds. ◆ *Cross* But we cannot debate the clear teaching of the Bible about the meaning of the cross in God's plan and in our lives today.

The meaning of Jesus' crucifixion. The story of the Crucifixion is told in all of the Gospels (Mt 27, Mk 15, Lk 23, Jn 19). What at first seemed to the disciples to be a tragedy was recognized after the Resurrection as the source of salvation and hope.

In his first recorded evangelistic sermon after the Ascension, Peter presented Jesus' crucifixion as something determined "by God's set purpose and foreknowledge" (Ac 2:23). Forgiveness can be found only in the crucified and risen Lord (2:38–39; 4:10–12).

That first message called on the people of Jerusalem to put their trust in the person of the crucified and risen Savior. Later Paul explained that the Cross is God's means for reconciling "all things, whether things on earth or things in heaven, by making peace through his blood, shed on the cross" (Col 1:20). ◆ *Blood* ◆ *Reconcile* Through the Crucifixion, we have been offered life, and those who put their trust in Christ have been forgiven for all their sins. All that could condemn us was washed away at Calvary (Col 2:13–17). In addition, the barriers that divide humanity and create hostilities were abolished, for people of every culture are brought to God through the Cross (Eph 2:16). Because of the Crucifixion we have peace with God and access to the Father and have become members of God's own household (Eph 2:17–19). Jesus' crucifixion and resurrection were God's only way to bring all these benefits to humanity.

In view of all that Jesus has accomplished, it is no wonder that the writer of Hebrews confronts Jews who did not grasp it all and were tempted to turn back to an OT faith to find in OT law the means for completing their salvation. Will they crucify Jesus again? Are they shamelessly implying that the Cross did not accomplish all that God says it has (Heb 6:6)?

The Cross, the Christian message. When the apostle Paul evangelized Corinth, he refused to rely on his training and rhetorical skills. He preached the gospel simply and plainly and relied on the divine power inherent in the message of the Cross (1 Co 1:17; cf. Ro 1:16). Those who perish will think the Cross is foolishness, but those who are being saved will recognize it as the message that bears the stamp of God's own authority (1 Co 1:18).

Because the Cross is central to the Christian gospel, Paul often uses "the cross" as a term for the gospel itself (1 Co 1:18; Gal 5:11; 6:12,14; Php 3:18).

The Christian's crucifixion with Jesus. The NT speaks of our crucifixion with Jesus (Ro 6:6; Gal 2:20; 5:24; 6:14). The key to understanding the reference is the concept of identification. The union that each believer has with Jesus is so close that everything that happened to Jesus is considered to have happened to us. Through our union with Jesus and by the divine power that raised Jesus from the dead, we experience not only crucifixion but also renewal (Ro 6:1–14; 8:1–4).

Marriage provides an illustration of identification. A poverty-stricken woman who marries a millionaire becomes a millionaire when the wedding takes place. Even if the couple divorce later, the law treats his millions as though she had participated in earning them, and that participation will be reflected in the divorce settlement. But God will never divorce us. All that Christ has done and all that he now is, are ours through our relationship with him.

The Christian's daily cross. This enigmatic concept must be important, for all three Synoptics report Jesus' encouragement to his disciples to take up their cross and follow him (Mt 10:38; 16:24; Mk 8:34; Lk 9:23; 14:27).

In all of these reports "cross" is used symbolically. When Jesus was faced with imminent crucifixion, he prayed in Gethsemane, "Father . . . , take this cup from me. Yet not what I will, but what you will" (Mk 14:36). Here the cross is the ultimate symbol of Jesus' commitment to do the will of God, whatever suffering that might bring for him. Taking up our cross to follow Jesus simply means that we are to imitate daily Jesus' total willingness to do the will of the Father, whatever that will may hold for us. ◆ *Cup*

CRY ◆ *Prayer*

CUBIT

The cubit is the standard linear measure of the OT. It was probably about 17 1/2 inches.

CUP

Usually in the Bible this word indicates a vessel that holds liquids. When used figuratively, the cup is imagined to be filled with an experience that someone is to undergo.

The "cup of his wrath" is an image of the judgment of God that earth's faithless are about to experience (Rev 14:10). The communion cup is called the cup of thanksgiving (1 Co 10:16), for with it our thoughts are drawn to the Cross and we experience a fresh appreciation for Jesus.

What was Jesus' cup, about which he asked his too-eager disciples if they were ready to share it (Mt 20:22,23; 26:39; Mk 10:38,39; 14:36; Lk 22:42; Jn 18:11)? At first glance it seems to be a cup filled only with suffering and sorrow, for when Jesus spoke of his cup, his thoughts were clearly turned toward his coming crucifixion. But the cup of Jesus' agony on the cross was the cup that God the Father personally poured out for him (Jn 18:11). His was to be an unspeakably terrible experience, though afterward it led to resurrection glory and joy (Heb 12:2).

When you and I share Jesus' cup, we willingly accept what God has prepared for us. If that experience should involve suffering, let us consider Jesus and remember that beyond every cross lies resurrection joy.

CURE ♦ Healing

CURSE

What does it mean that God cursed the ground? And why was there an immediate reaction, as reported in Deuteronomy, when a young man of mixed parentage cursed his parents? And what about the curses that stand in contrast to the blessings listed in Mosaic Law?

Our English concept of "curse" is complicated. The OT concept is even more complex. But we can understand the various meanings of "curse" by considering Hebrew and Greek words and the context of the biblical world.

OT 1. The solemn warning: 'ālâh
    2. The binding act: 'ārar
    3. The blessing withdrawn: qālal
NT 4. NT uses of "curse"
    5. Summary

OT — 1. The solemn warning: 'ālâh. The Hebrew word means "to swear a solemn oath." It is used of promises that people make and of testimony they give in court. It is also found in passages that speak of the covenant that exists between God and his people (Dt 29:12). Although an oath statement may make a promise as well as define a penalty, 'ālâh is most often used in warnings. A curse made God's people aware ahead of time of the judgments that would follow should they break their covenant obligations (cf. Dt 29:14–21; Isa 24:6; Jer 23:10; Da 9:11).

2. The binding act: 'ārar. This verb is found sixty-three times in the OT, and a derivative noun, me'ērâh, is found five times (Dt 28:20; Pr 3:33; 28:27; Mal 2:2; 3:9). Twelve times 'ārar stands in opposition to bārak, "to bless." In such passages it functions much like 'ālâh as a statement of consequences imbedded within the framework of God's law (Dt 27:15–

16; 28:16–18). Such warnings are bold and clear: "The LORD will send on you curses, confusion and rebuke in everything you put your hand to, until you are destroyed and come to sudden ruin because of the evil you have done in forsaking him" (Dt 28:20).

But this word goes beyond the definition of the consequences of disobedience. It also serves to announce punishments that God has imposed.

The root idea expressed in 'ārar is to bind so as to reduce ability or to render powerless. When God announced that because of sin his curse was on the earth, he declared that earth's original spontaneous fertility had been stunted. The land was no longer able to produce to its earlier capacity. Human beings were no longer able to enjoy earth's produce without labor.

Two other examples deserve mention. One is the curse on Cain the farmer (Ge 4:2–3,11–12), which included driving him from the ground (i.e., banning him from enjoying the land's productivity). The second is that of Balaam; he was hired by Balak to curse Israel, because Balak wanted the seer to neutralize Israel's military power (Nu 22:4–6).

A person or thing that is cursed, then, is in some significant way bound: that person or thing is unable to do what he, she, or it was once able to do.

Peoples of the ancient world considered that curses were magic tools to be used to gain power over enemies. In Scripture the curse is notably a consequence of violating one's relationship with God. Thus "curse" is a moral rather than a magical term.

The association of the curse with magic is sometimes reflected in the term qābab. All of its eight OT uses are associated with the story of Balaam. Certainly Balak wanted the seer to utter magical words that would immobilize his enemy.

3. The blessing withdrawn: qālal. The basic meaning of this word is "to be slight." The one cursed experiences reduced circumstances. Often this curse of reduced position, power, wealth, or honor is occasioned by the breaking of God's covenant. The noun qelālâh emphasizes the loss or absence of the state of blessing, a state that God yearns for his people to enjoy.

The verb may be used in the sense of pronouncing a curse or to indicate that someone is in the state of being cursed. Again, the pagans felt that by uttering magical words they could attack and diminish an enemy. This may be reflected in the phrase in the Abrahamic covenant "he who curses [qālal] you." It is also likely that the case reported in Lev 24:11, in which "the son of an Israelite woman blasphemed the name of the LORD with a curse," reveals an attempt to use God's name in a magical incantation against someone the young man viewed as an enemy. But God says, "He who curses you, I will curse" ('ārar). The use of "magic" against believers is done before Almighty God, who himself puts persons and competing powers in a state of powerlessness or reduced ability.

When we understand the background of the ancient Near East, the command "If anyone curses his father or mother, he must be put to death" (Lev 20:9) takes on a different meaning. The individual is not uttering careless oaths in anger. He is turning to magic in a conscious effort to harm his parents, whom God has commanded him to honor in context (cf. vv. 6–8).

NT — 4. The NT use of "curse". Two different Greek roots are reflected in the use of this word by the NIV and the NASB.

One concept is expressed in words linked with *anathema*, "accursed." The root indicates dedication to destruction: an anathematized object or person is delivered up to the judgment of God.

Paul, touchingly eager for the salvation of his Jewish brethren, wished that, if such a thing were possible, he might be accursed that they might be saved (Ro 9:1–3). But the wish could not be granted–for him or for anyone else who has been saved through the blood of Jesus.

Words compounded with "anathema" are generally translated "accursed." Usually the words found where the NIV and the NASB read "curse" are *katara* or

kataraomai. These Greek words correspond closely to *qālal* and suggest the opposite of blessing.

In Paul's argument in Gal 3:10–14 he looks back into history at the blessings and curses of law. Paul says that law requires us to "continue to do everything" written in it if we are to be blessed. We all fall short of doing everything. Thus all who rely on the law must in fact fall under the curse rather than the blessing! Thus law itself, when taken as a means to life, becomes a curse, from which we can be released only by faith in Jesus.

According to the NT's instructions about those who curse us, we are to do nothing that might diminish their situation nor wish them ill ("bless and do not curse" [Ro 12:14]). What about the believers, mentioned in Heb 6:8, who were in danger of being cursed? They were in danger of slipping out of the realm of blessing into the opposite experience, for they were considering turning back to the OT ways of worship, away from Jesus. Jesus himself provides all the blessings the OT holds out—and more!

5. Summary. When we read "curse" in the Bible, the reference is not to swearing. Usually it does not even refer to that magical kind of curse that is pronounced by witches and warlocks.

The peoples of the biblical world thought of curses as magical incantations that harnessed supernatural power to harm enemies. At times the OT uses the word "curse" in this pagan sense, as in the prohibition against cursing one's parents. But the biblical meaning of "curse" is quite distinct.

A curse is essentially a divine judgment. A curse may be uttered as a solemn oath, warning of what God will do if his covenant is violated. A curse may also be the judgment itself, spoken of after it has been imposed. Such a curse binds and limits its object. It brings about diminished circumstances that stand in contrast to the blessing God yearns to provide.

In the OT, blessing and cursing are intimately associated with the Mosaic Law. That law defines the way of life that those in relationship with a holy God must follow. Those who obey are to be blessed; those who will not obey are to experience the curse. But, as the NT points out, with these conditions the law itself proved to be a curse, for no one could keep it perfectly.

It is wonderful that in his death, Jesus won release for us from the curse of the law. Through faith in Christ, we have been given blessings that we could never have earned. And it is significant that though the OT speaks often of curses that God's sinning people must endure, there is no hint in the NT of a curse for those who continue to follow Jesus.

D

DARKNESS ◆ *Light and Darkness*

DAY

The word "day" is commonplace. But it is also a surprising key to the uniqueness of the Bible's view of time. And it is a key to help us see how freely and purposefully God intervenes in history.

OT 1. The Hebrew term
   2. The seven days of creation
   3. "The day of the Lord," "that day"
NT 4. The Greek term
   5. "The last days"
   6. Summary

OT — 1. The Hebrew term. The word *yôm* is the Hebrew term that best communicates the OT concept of time. *Yôm* is translated "day," "time," or "year" and can express either a point in time or a period of time (e.g., "during those days"). Specifically, *yôm* can stand for (1) the daylight hours, (2) a twenty-four-hour period, (3) an undetermined period of time encompassing months or years or even centuries, and (4) a particular point in time. In the plural, *yôm* may mean years rather than days.

The word is theologically important in at least three ways. First, *yôm* is linked with the Bible's unique concept of time, which has become that of the Western world through our Judeo/Christian heritage. In the ancient Near East, however, the myths that provided a framework for life envisioned time as a cycle. There was a repeated yearly cycle, and life's meaning was sought in the repeated rounds of the seasons, marked by winter's death and spring's rebirth.

The Hebrew concept, expressed in the OT, is a dramatic contrast to that of the surrounding nations. In Scripture, time is not viewed as a cycle but as a line, springing from a definite beginning (Creation) and moving toward a divinely revealed and purposed end. Scripture sees the meaning of the universe and of our lives as outside the repetitive patterns that mark human experience. The meaning of it all is in the sweep of a history that had a definite beginning and will have a promised end.

Second, we find a distinct relationship between time (history) and God. God, the Ancient of Days, stands outside time. He existed before it; he is both creator and shaper of time's flow.

Third, the phrase "the day of the Lord" or "that day" is often used by the prophets to indicate a period of time during which God personally intervenes in history to carry out some specific aspect of his plan.

2. The seven days of creation. Because of the range of meanings given *yôm*, one cannot argue from the word alone to the nature of the seven days of creation mentioned in Genesis. However, many do build an argument for seven literal days on the use of "evening" and "morning" to define *yôm*.

Theories about the seven days include: (1) a gap theory, which proposes an original creation, ruined by Satan, and a literal seven-day process setting it to rights; (2) the hypothesis of an indefinite age, depending on the figurative use of "day" to represent geologic eras; (3) a day-age theory, which supposes each day represents a period of twenty-four hours in which new additions to creation were initiated, followed by millennia before the next creative day arrives; (4) the idea of a creation *in situ*, with the Creation having taken place only several thousand years ago in seven literal days but with a "false history" built into the earth at that time; (5) a revelatory-day theory, according to which Moses was told about each stage of creation on seven successive literal days; and (6) a revelatory-device idea, which says that the human author chose to organize his material by the use of "days."

No one knows for sure how long the creation days were, but there is no doubt that the Bible does teach a special creation by God and that he is the author of all things in the universe. ♦ *Create*

3. "The day of the Lord," "that day".

The theologically significant phrases "the day of the LORD" and "that day" occur often in the Prophets. They usually identify events that take place at history's end (Isa 7:18–25). The key to understanding the phrases is to note that they always identify a span of time during which God personally intervenes in history, directly or indirectly, to accomplish some specific aspect of his plan.

What events do OT prophets most often link to these phrases?

Briefly, the day of the Lord is seen as a day of terror, during which Israel would be invaded and purged with an awful destruction. Amos warned those of his day who hoped God would intervene soon: "Woe to you who long for the day of the LORD! Why do you long for the day of the LORD? That day will be darkness and not light" (Am 5:18). Zephaniah adds, "The great day of the LORD is near—near and coming quickly. Listen! The cry on the day of the LORD will be bitter, the shouting of the warrior will be there. That day will be a day of wrath, a day of distress and anguish, a day of trouble and ruin, a day of darkness and gloom, a day of clouds and blackness" (1:14–15). The dark terror of divine judgment was to be poured out on unbelieving Israel (Isa 22; Jer 30:1–17; Joel 1–2; Am 5; Zep 1) and on the unbelieving peoples of the world (Eze 38–39; Zec 14).

But judgment is not the only aspect of that day. When God intervenes in history, he will also deliver the remnant of Israel, bring about a national conversion, forgive sins, and restore his people to the land promised Abraham (Isa 10:27; Jer 30:19–31:40; Mi 4; Zec 13). ♦ *Remnant/Survivors*

And what will be the outcome of the day of the LORD? "The arrogance of man will be brought low and the pride of men humbled; the LORD alone will be exalted in that day" (Isa 2:17).

NT — 4. The Greek term.

The Greek word *hēmera* is used to indicate literal days and may also be extended to indicate indeterminate periods of time. Naturally, the Gospels use the word "day" in the OT sense of "that day" to indicate eschatological judgment and the return of Jesus (cf. Mt 7:22; Mk 13:32; Lk 17:31).

When using the word "day" in an eschatological sense, the Epistles tend to identify particular aspects of the end time. Thus, the writers speak of the day of wrath (Ro 2:5; Rev 6:17), the day of judgment (2 Pe 2:9; 3:7), the day of redemption (Eph 4:30), the day of the Lord (1 Th 5:2; 2 Pe 3:10), the day of Christ (Php 1:6,10; 2:16), the great day of God (Rev 16:14), and the day God visits his people (1 Pe 2:12). ♦ *Appearance of Jesus: the Second Coming*

5. "The last days".

A number of passages in the NT seem to suggest that the writer and readers were then living in the "last days" (e.g., Ac 2:17–18; 3:24; 2 Ti 3:1; Heb 1:2; 2 Pe 3:3; 1 Jn 2:18). What do the writers mean?

The concept that we live in history's final day is not to say that the eschatological period that marks history's end has come. Instead, the writers view history as a process that will culminate in "that day," and they view this present age as the final moment before the intended climax. John sees principles of evil at work now that will be given full reign in the end period (1 Jn 2:18). A hostility to truth will prevail at history's end and is incipient in this age as well (2 Ti 3:1–13). The distinctive difference between these days and the day of the Lord, in which

God's purposes are drawn together and brought to their conclusion, is this: our age, which began with the resurrection of Jesus, is the last great historical epoch before God's final intervention.

6. Summary. The term "day" in both Testaments is used in the literal twenty-four-hour sense and in other senses as well. The way in which the word is used in the OT introduces us to a distinctive concept of time and history—a concept that has been adopted by Western culture and thus seems less striking than it is. According to the Bible, history had a beginning and moves toward an end.

The Bible uses the phrase "that day" to identify a time when God personally intervenes in history. History's end is the ultimate "day of the Lord," when with wondrous power God will punish evil and fulfill all his promises. But "that day" can also identify other periods in which God personally intervenes to accomplish some aspect of his plan.

Our present age is also a day. It is the last day (age) before the time of the end. As Peter reminds us, we live in a temporary universe, one that is about to be destroyed. How shall we then live? We need to "live holy and godly lives, as [we] look forward to the day of God and speed its coming. That day will bring about the destruction of the heavens by fire, and the elements will melt in the heat. But in keeping with his promises we are looking forward to a new heaven and new earth, the home of righteousness" (2 Pe 3:11–13).

DEACONS ♦ Minister/Ministry

DEAD/DEATH ♦ Life and Death

DEAR

The NIV uses this word of endearment in contexts where someone addresses Christian friends. The NT writers used *agapē*, the prevailing NT word for love. In the body of Christ, relationships of intimacy and caring and deep affection can be adequately expressed only by "beloved." However, in two instances when Jesus addressed his mother, the NIV uses the phrase "dear woman," whereas the original simply has "woman" (Jn 2:4; 19:26).

DEBAUCHERY

"Aselgeia" (Mk 7:22; Ro 13:13; 2 Co 12:21; Gal 5:19; Eph 4:19; 1 Pe 4:3; 2 Pe 2:7,18; Jude 4) is usually translated "licentiousness" or "sensuality" in the NASB. *Aselgeia* means the unrestrained indulgence of greed or of animal lust in whatever one's passions desire.

The word in Eph 5:18 is *asōtia*, which suggests a loss of self-control, leading one to squander both finances and life.

DECEIT/FALSEHOOD

There is more than a "lie" involved in the complex web of ideas expressed by "deceit" or "falsehood" in the Bible. The deceitful and the false are always wrong. But they are not always the same thing.

OT 1. Deception and falsehood: the Hebrew words
NT 2. Deceit: the Greek words
    3. Falsehood: the Greek words

OT — 1. Deception and falsehood: the Hebrew words. The best way to build our understanding of the OT concept is to note that the same Hebrew words are translated by the English words "false," "falsehood," "deceit," and "deception" and to realize that the Hebrew words often more clearly define shades of meaning only implied in our language.

Rāmâh and its several derivatives are common. The root means "to mislead" or "to deceive," and its participle (Ge 34:13; Ps 10:7) and a noun (Zep 3:13) are used of misleading speech and the participle (Am 8:5) of shady business practices.

Sāqar means "to deceive" or "to tell a falsehood." This verb implies breaking a promise or a commitment. It is found six times in the OT (Ge 21:23; Lev 19:11; 1 Sa 15:29; Ps 44:17; 89:33; Isa 63:8). A derivative, *šeqer*, is used of groundless words or actions. Such things are deceiving because they have no basis in fact. This common word occurs often in Psalms,

Proverbs, and Jeremiah and is frequently used to identify a false accusation or a false prophecy. NASB often renders it "deceit" or by some form of the word "false" (Ex 5:9; 20:16; 23:7; Lev 6:3,5; 19:12; Dt 19:18; Job 36:4; Ps 7:14; 27:12; 33:17; 52:3; 101:7; 119:29,104,128,163; 144:8,11; Pr 6:19; 12:17; 13:5; 14:5; 19:5,9; 20:17; 25:14,18; 29:12; 31:30; Isa 9:15; 57:4; 59:3; Jer 13:25; 14:14; 20:6; 23:14,25–26,32; 27:15; 29:9,21,23; Eze 13:22; Mic 2:11; Hab 2:18; Zec 5:4; 13:3; Mal 3:5).

Sāw' appears fifty-three times in the OT. It is usually translated "vain, or empty." It means "emptiness" and "deceit" in the sense of presenting as real something that is unsubstantial and unreal. *Sāw'* appears as "deceit" or a form of the word "false" in the NASB in Ex 23:1; Dt 5:20; Job 11:11; 31:5; Ps 12:2; 24:4; 26:4; 41:6; 144:8,11; Isa 5:18; La 2:14; Eze 12:24; 13:6–9,23; 21:23,29; Zec 10:2. The NIV renders *šāw'* "deceit" or a form of the word "false" in Ex 23:1; Dt 5:20; Job 11:11; 15:31; 31:5; Ps 24:4; 26:4; 41:6; Pr 30:8; La 2:14; Eze 12:24; 13:6–9; 21:23,29; 22:28; Hos 10:4.

Nāšā' indicates deceptions that lead a person astray. This is the word used in Eve's excuse: "The serpent deceived me" (Ge 3:13). This Hebrew word occurs in the sense of "deceive" in fourteen of its sixteen occurrences in the OT (Ge 3:13; 2 Ki 18:29; 19:10; 2 Ch 32:15; Isa 19:13; 36:14; 37:10; Jer 4:10; 29:8; 37:9; 49:16; Ob 3,7).

Kāhaš occurs twenty-eight times and its derivative *kehaš* once in the OT with a wide variety of meanings. In those passages indicating deceit or falsehood, the word suggests undependable behavior in a given relationship. The person who thus deals falsely causes harm to others. The verb is used in this sense in Ge 18:15; Lev 6:2–3; 19:11; Dt 33:29; Jos 7:11; 1 Ki 13:18; Hos 4:2.

In addition, there are the words *pātâh*, which suggests enticing to do wrong, and *tā'âh*, "to err" or "to wander."

The portrait of falsehood and deceit suggested by the Hebrew words is far from pretty. Actions and words designed to deceive are not supported by reality. Worse, they violate the basic relationship of trust and honesty that are to exist between human beings, and they are often intended to mislead and so to harm another person.

NT — 2. Deceit: the Greek words. There are several different Greek terms are associated with the idea of deceit. The most common is *planaō*, which means "to lead astray or deceive [by words or behavior]." The NT almost always uses this word when speaking of the influence of false teachers. It is also the word chosen to speak of Satan's final effort to deceive at history's end. When the NT warns, "Don't be deceived," this statement expresses the writer's concern that we might be led away from the Christian message or lifestyle.

Planaō (verb) is found in Mt 18:12–13; 22:29; 24:4–5,11,24; Mk 12:24,27; 13:5–6; Lk 21:8; Jn 7:12,47; 1 Co 6:9; 15:33; Gal 6:7; 2 Ti 3:13; Tit 3:3; Heb 3:10; 5:2; 11:38; Jas 1:16; 5:19; 1 Pe 2:25; 2 Pe 2:15; 1 Jn 1:8; 2:26; 3:7; Rev 2:20; 12:9; 13:14; 18:23; 19:20; 20:3,8,10. *Planē*, "error," is found in Mt 27:64; Ro 1:27; Eph 4:14; 1 Th 2:3; 2 Th 2:11; Jas 5:20; 2 Pe 2:18; 3:17; 1 Jn 4:6; Jude 11. *Planos*, "deceivers," is found in Mt 27:63; 2 Co 6:8; 1 Ti 4:1; 2 Jn 7.

Apataō and its derivatives indicate ethical enticement. These words are found less frequently in the NT: *Apataō* (Eph 5:6; 1 Ti 2:14; Jas 1:26), *apatē* (Mt 13:22; Mk 4:19; Eph 4:22; Col 2:8; 2 Th 2:10; Heb 3:13; 2 Pe 2:13), and *exapataō* (Ro 7:11; 16:18; 1 Co 3:18; 2 Co 11:3; 2 Th 2:3).

Another word, *dolos*, picks up the metaphor from hunting and fishing. Deceit is an attempt to trap or to trick and thus involves treachery. *Dolos* occurs in the NT in Mt 26:4; Mk 7:22; 14:1; Jn 1:47; Ac 13:10; Ro 1:29; 2 Co 12:16; 1 Th 2:3; 1 Pe 2:1,22; 3:10; Rev 14:5. The verb *doloō* occurs only in 2 Co 4:2, and another verb, *dolioō*, is found only in Ro 3:13.

Deception sometimes comes from within, as our desires impel us to deceive. But more often in the NT, deceit is error urged by external evil powers or by those locked into the world's way of thinking.

3. Falsehood: the Greek words. There are some fifteen different words in the

NT built on the root *pseudō*, "to be false." The verb *pseudomai* means "to deceive by lying."

The concept underlying the truth-falsehood dichotomy in Scripture is important, particularly to those who live in a relativistic world that can speak of something as being "true for you" (subjective) while denying absolute (objective) truth. The Bible clearly affirms objective truth, and it grounds that belief in the biblical concept of God. God is Truth. All that he says is in strict accord with reality. His words are therefore firm and trustworthy. ♦ *Truth* By contrast, we human beings are trapped in illusion. We struggle to understand the meaning of the world around us and of our experiences. But, unaided, we cannot distinguish between the real and the counterfeit, the truth and the lie. Only reliance on God's Word, which is true, enables us to build our lives on a firm foundation. The *pseud*-root places whatever it is associated with—teaching, prophecy, etc.—in the realm of illusion, far from the foundation of reality unveiled in God's Word.

Strikingly, the NT appeals to us to throw off falsehood and speak the truth to each other (Eph 4:25; Col 3:9–10). This exhortation calls for far more than a refusal to lie. It is a call to live openly with each other, honestly sharing the reality of our lives rather than attempting to project illusions that make us appear better than we are.

DECIDE ♦ *Judge/Judging*

DECLARE

A number of Greek and Hebrew words are translated "declare" in English versions. The most common OT word is *nāgad*, "to tell" or "to make known." When used of that which God reveals, the declaration carries God's own authority. Often the OT uses the formula "declares the Lord." Here the word is *ne'um*, an utterance or an oracle. This pronouncement by the prophet stressed the origin and the authority of the message delivered.

NT words generally mean "to announce," "to disclose," or "to speak."

DECREE

We find this word most often in the OT. ♦ *Predestine* The root concept is that of a command or judgment. Many of the Hebrew words translated "decree" carry the image of cutting or engraving on rock. Thus, God's decrees (see especially the use of this word in the Psalms) are presented as divine judgments, irrevocably inscribed in the bedrock of God's moral character or his eternal purpose. ♦ *Purpose*

DEDICATE

"Dedicate" and "dedication" are generally used in translating one of two Hebrew words. One is *hānak* (and its related word *hanukâh*), "to dedicate or consecrate." But the underlying idea seems to be one of initiation. The OT lays special stress on those ceremonies of dedication that inaugurated the use of something for God's service. *Hānak* occurs in Dt 20:5; 1 Ki 8:63; 2 Ch 7:5; Pr 22:6. We might paraphrase Pr 22:6 in this way: "Get a child started [*train*] in the way he should go, and when he is old he will not depart from it."

Hanukâh is found in Nu 7:10–11,84,88; 2 Ch 7:9; Ezr 6:16–17; Ne 12:27; Ps 30 title; and Da 3:2–3.

The other Hebrew term is *qādaš*, "to set apart," "to be holy." *Qādaš* indicates something set apart for God's special use. ♦ *Acts/Actions* ♦ *Holy/Holiness*

DEEP

Usually the word "deep" is found in the NIV and the NASB as an adjective. Often it is added to a word to intensify its meaning. The word "deep" can also stand alone as a noun: "the deep," as in Ge 1:2; 7:11, or "the deep [things] of darkness" (Job 12:22).

In Genesis, "the deep" (*tehôm*) is prominent in the accounts of Creation and the Flood. It means "ocean," "sea depths," and, at times, "abyss." The story that the

Flood presents is one of subterranean waters shaken by cataclysm. The deep surges and breaks forth in great fountains as the very crust of the earth is shaken.

The NT's "deep things of God" (1 Co 2:10) refers to those things concerning God that cannot be discovered by human beings apart from special revelation, such as his attributes and his intentions. It is wonderful that these hidden things, including God's very thoughts, have been revealed to us in the Spirit-taught words of the Bible (1 Co 2:10–13).

DEFECT

The word "defect" seems to be reserved in the NIV and NASB to describe the animals to be offered in OT sacrifices. *Tāmîm*, from the root *tāmam*, means "complete, or perfect." In the context of sacrificial animals, this is often translated "without blemish." When this same Hebrew word is used to describe human beings, it is usually translated "upright" or "perfect," meaning that the person so described has met God's standards as far as the subject under consideration is concerned. ♦ *Perfect*

DEFILE

For a discussion of the meaning of the Hebrew concept of defilement, see ♦ *Clean and Unclean.* However, there are several verses in the NT that may deserve separate comment.

Defiling a believer's conscience is mentioned in 1 Co 8:7. The Greek *molynō* means "to contaminate, or defile." As water from a polluted well is unsafe, so the convictions of a polluted conscience are unsafe guidelines for godly action. The cause of the pollution in this passage is one's acting against the dictates of conscience. Disregarding our sense of right and wrong corrupts us.

Tit 1:15 also speaks of corrupted minds and consciences. Here the word translated "defile" is *miainō*, which also means "stained" or "polluted." Here unbelievers' minds and consciences are the subject. Paul warns that only those who are pure can view life purely: "To those who are corrupted and do not believe, nothing is pure." Without an experience of God's purifying, saving work, mind and conscience will both be polluted. The product of the mind and conscience warped by inner sin must be impure.

Heb 12:15 also uses the word *miainō*. The verse warns against bitterness, which "grows up to cause trouble and defile many." A bitter attitude has an impact on our relationship with other persons. Bitterness can pollute their lives as well as our own.

Keeping alert to recognize the grace that God gives us to live holy lives can free us from bitterness and keep our consciences clear (Heb 12:14–15). ♦ *Conscience*

DELIGHT

Several Hebrew words are translated "delight" in some English versions. *Ḥāpēṣ* suggests strong emotional involvement. It emphasizes one's feeling about the object of delight. The *hapēṣ* root is translated "delight" by the NIV in Ge 34:19; 1 Sa 15:22; 2 Sa 22:20; 1 Ki 10:9; 2 Ch 9:8; Est 6:6,7,9,11; Ps 1:2; 16:3; 18:19; 35:27; 51:16,19; 112:1; 119:35; 147:10; Isa 13:17; 58:13; 62:4; 66:3; Jer 9:24; Mic 7:18; Mal 3:12. God is not emotionally moved by sacrifice, but he delights in our obedience (Ps 51:16,19). We are to find our delight in his words (Ps 1:2; 112:1) and in his people (16:3). Another article has further discussion of the root. ♦ *Desire*

Rāṣâh is also translated "delight," this being one of three basic meanings of the root. ♦ *Favor* ♦ *Will* The underlying idea is to be favorably disposed toward, either to meet a need or after examination and approval. When various versions of the OT speak of God's taking "delight" in a sacrificial offering, the word actually means that God finds the sacrifice acceptable.

This root is translated "delight" in the NIV in Ps 51:16; 62:4; 147:10–11; 149:4; Pr 3:12; 11:1,20; 12:22; 14:35; Isa 42:1.

Sā'a' and its derivative *ša'ᵃšu'îm* suggest great pleasure. Fifteen verses use them in the sense of delight (Ps 94:19;

119:16,24,47,70,77,92,143,174; Pr 8:30; Isa 5:7; 11:8; 29:9; 66:12; Jer 31:20).

Other words translated "delight" are likewise associated with desire, pleasure, and joy.

NT words generally mean "to take pleasure in" (see 2 Co 12:10) or "to rejoice." Paul picks up the emphasis of Ps 119 when he says in Ro 7:22, "In my inner being I delight in [*synēdomai*, "joyfully agree with"] God's law." But Paul goes on to point out that no matter how much his inner self may resonate in harmony with the law's unveiled righteousness, there is a principle of evil at work within him. He is imprisoned by sin and cannot do that which delights him as an ideal. It takes God's work within us through Jesus to free us to live out the righteousness that we sense in God's law and that we desire.

DELIVER

Both Hebrew and English have a number of synonyms for this concept. We understand the overlap of words like "rescue," "save," and "deliver." Each indicates help from another that releases from danger.

OT 1. Delivered from
     2. Delivered to
NT 3. Betrayal and rescue

OT — 1. Delivered from. When the writers of the OT wanted to express a cry for help or to describe rescue and escape from danger, they were most likely to choose one of three words, though others were available. ♦ *Redeem/Ransom*

Nāṣal means "to deliver, or rescue." This is the word found in Ex 3:8, which describes God's response to the misery of his people in Egypt: "I have come down to rescue them . . . and bring them up out of that land into a good and spacious land." In most references a literal deliverance is in view. But, like God's rescue of Israel at the Exodus, physical deliverance has spiritual application. In the several uses of this root in Psalms, spiritual salvation from sin is clearly in view (Ps 39:8; 51:14; 69:14; 79:9).

Pālat means "to escape," "to save," or "to deliver." The use of this verb is limited to OT poetry, and the word appears often in Psalms. Nouns built on the root are sometimes translated "deliverance," but typically they are translated "escape," and the persons who have escaped are known as survivors.

Yāša' means "to deliver, or save." It and its derivatives are used 353 times in the OT. While the NASB often translates *yāša'* "deliver"—and its nouns as "deliverance"—the NIV translators preferred, somewhat more consistently, to translate it "saved." ♦ *Salvation/Save*

Any of the above Hebrew words may be used of a rescue effected by human beings. But usually God is the subject, and human beings the object, for God alone is capable of delivering us in any situation. Many OT references contain requests for God's deliverance, while others celebrate what God has done in the past (e.g., Jdg 6:9). Typically, human agents of deliverance are thought of as acting in the name and with the power of the Lord.

2. Delivered to. A number of uses of "deliver," especially in the NASB, indicate defeat rather than deliverance. The Hebrew usually has the common word *nātan*, "to give." The expression is "give [deliver] them into your hand." This word for deliver is found in those narratives in which God gives Israel victory over their enemies (Dt 23:14; 31:5) and in which Israel is being disciplined by foreign invaders (2 Ki 21:14; Eze 11:9).

The context makes it clear in which sense "deliver" is being used in the English texts.

NT — 3. Betrayal and rescue. Both senses of "deliver" are also found in the NT. The word *paradidōmi* indicates a deliberate giving over to another's power. This is the word used in passages that describe Jesus' being handed over for crucifixion. Its basic use in the NT is to suggest delivering up to judgment and death, as in Ro 4:25: "He was delivered over to death for our sins and was raised to life for our justification."

Two Greek words are used to convey the idea of rescue, or deliverance from danger. One is *sōzō*, which is used 111 times in the NT and is usually translated "save" or "salvation." ◆ *Salvation/Save*

The other word is *rhyomai*, which occurs only 18 times in the NT. In seven of these *rhyomai* is found in OT quotes or allusions. The Greek translation of the OT in use in Jesus' day (the Septuagint) used *rhyomai* to render the Hebrew *nāṣal*, "to deliver or rescue." *Rhyomai* is found in Mt 6:13; 27:43; Lk 1:74; 11:4; Ro 7:24; 11:26; 15:31; 2 Co 1:10; Col 1:13; 1 Th 1:10; 2 Th 3:2; 2 Ti 3:11; 4:17–18; 2 Pe 2:7,9.

Perhaps the most fascinating use of *rhyomai* is found in the interplay between Mt 6:13 and Col 1:13. Jesus taught his disciples to pray, "deliver [*rhyomai*] us from evil." Paul, after the death and resurrection of Jesus, announced the deliverance joyfully: God "has rescued [*rhyomai*] us from the dominion of darkness and brought us into the kingdom of the Son he loves!"

DEMONS/EVIL SPIRITS

Demons seem to hold a strong fascination for some of us—as well as for the makers of horror movies. Although the Gospels contain many references to demonic activity, both the OT and the NT epistles are almost silent on the subject.

1. **Common beliefs about demons**
2. **Demons in the OT**
3. **Demons in the Gospels**
4. **Demons in the Epistles**
5. **Demon possession and exorcism**
6. **Origin and fate of demons**

1. **Common beliefs about demons.** The Hebrew word for demon (*šēḏ*) is borrowed from the Babylonian (*šēḏu*). In Babylon, demons were thought to be supernatural powers, neither particularly evil nor particularly good. Demons were distinguished from the gods only by being somewhat less powerful than they.

In Greek thought, demons (*daimonion*) were supernatural powers that inhabited the air close to earth—an order of beings between men and gods. But the Greeks believed that demons had an evil influence on human affairs. They caused misery and disasters; they were agents of madness and the cause of many sicknesses. The Greeks viewed demons as hostile beings that must be appeased or controlled by magic.

Later Judaism showed considerable interest in demons. Demons were thought of as malignant beings distinct from angels, and a number of theories were suggested to explain their existence. One theory held that demons were the offspring of a primeval mating of fallen angels with human women (Ge 6:1–4). The rabbis thought of demons as beings eager to lead humanity into sin. They were also believed to be the cause of much but not of every sickness.

2. **Demons in the OT.** In view of the common beliefs about demons in most ancient cultures, it is striking to find only two specific references to demons in the OT. Dt 32:17 says of the rebellious generation that died in the wilderness: "They sacrificed to demons, which are not God—gods they had not known, gods that recently appeared, gods your fathers did not fear." And Ps 106:36–37 says, "They worshiped their idols, which became a snare to them. They sacrificed their sons and their daughters to demons." Both of these passages suggest that real demonic beings existed behind the gods and goddesses of the pagans. This is in fact something that Paul affirms in 1 Co 10:20, saying that "the sacrifices of pagans are offered to demons."

There are other OT passages that may allude to the demonic. The OT contains prohibitions against all spiritism and magic, which were linked with the demonic in every ancient culture (cf. Dt 18:9–12). There are other hints in such passages as 1 Sa 28:13 and Isa 8:19.

But still, very little attention is paid to demons by the OT. The OT concentrates instead on God, the Creator and Redeemer, who is sovereign over every power—natural and supernatural.

3. **Demons in the Gospels.** Although the OT is relatively silent about demons, the Gospels are full of references to

demonic activity. This is possibly because Jesus, in his ministry of healing and restoring, exposed many demons as he expelled them from those they oppressed. Or it may be that Satan's kingdom concentrated unusual forces on Palestine when Jesus walked that land. The level of demonic activity *was* unusual. The religious leaders' charge that Jesus must be in league with the prince of demons was probably based on the unusual level of demonic activity associated with his earthly ministry (Jn 7:20; 8:48–52; 10:20).

Gospel references to demons show them possessing or oppressing human beings (e.g., Mt 8:16,28,33; 9:32; 12:22–28; Mk 1:32; 5:16–18; Lk 4:33–35; 8:27–29, 36; 9:42). Such demonic influence was expressed in various sicknesses and in madness. When some observers argued that Jesus was mad or in league with Satan, others said, "Can a demon open the eyes of the blind?" (Jn 10:21). The Gospels also show Jesus driving out demons whenever he met them (Mt 9:33; 17:18; Mk 7:26,29–30; Lk 11:14). Jesus' own defense against the charge is based on this fact. How could Satan's kingdom stand if Jesus drove out demons by demonic powers? Any divided kingdom must soon fall (Lk 11:14–22).

So the Gospels do picture demons as living beings with malignant powers. Demons are personal beings, not impersonal influences (Mt 8:31). Jesus demonstrated his total mastery of demons, expelling them with a word. He is the "stronger" being of his own illustration, able to "attack and overpower" the demons in their own realm (Lk 11:21–22). However fearsome demons may be, the person who walks with Jesus has nothing to fear.

4. Demons in the Epistles. After Jesus returned to heaven, little demonic activity is reported by the Bible. Acts 5, 8, and 19 mention evil spirits. The Epistles do not. Yes, there is some teaching. Ro 8:38 establishes a dichotomy between angels and demons. In 1 Co 10:20–21 Paul warns that demonic beings are the spiritual realities behind the facades of idolatry. In 1 Ti 4:1 he suggests that

demons distort truth and encourage the spread of twisted doctrines of their own. Aside from brief views of increased demonic activity at history's end, given in the Book of Revelation, this is all that the NT has to say about demons!

Of particular note in the Epistles' comparative silence on the demonic is the fact that in the many passages that deal with Christian life and ministry, none speaks of demons. There are no guidelines for exorcism. There are no warnings against demon possession. There is no hint of terror or awe, no suggestion that we should fear or pay special attention to these unseen evil powers.

Why this silence? Perhaps it is because Jesus truly is the Head over all things for the church, which is his body. He is "far above all rule and authority, power and dominion" (Eph 1:21). Perhaps he personally restrains the activity of demonic powers that would seek to touch his church.

4. Demon possession and exorcism. There is no doubt for those with a high view of the Bible that demons do exist. There are evil spiritual beings who can and do influence events on the earth. We learn from the Gospels that they can possess—or perhaps more accurately, oppress—human beings. They can bring misery and cause sickness. The Gospels show that some madness, though surely not all, may be related to demon oppression.

There is also no doubt that Jesus has total power over demons. He exercised that power in NT times and cast out demons. Jesus relied on no rite or magical words. He simply commanded, and the demons obeyed. Even later, when the disciples cast out demons, they apparently commanded the demons in Jesus' name. But the name was not enough: a personal relationship with Jesus was also essential (Ac 16:16–18; cf. 19:13–16).

An important question remains: Can a believer be demon possessed or oppressed today? And is exorcism something normal, to be commonly experienced in the modern church? Opinions differ considerably—and heatedly! But the relative silence of the Epistles regarding demons and healing, both emphasized in the Gospels and in early Acts, suggests that we should not expect open warfare with demonic powers today.

It may well be that John's comment in his first letter is also something of a promise: "The one who is in you is greater than the one who is in the world" (1 Jn 4:4). It is hard to imagine a demon, or Satan himself, settling comfortably into any association with a person indwelt by the very Spirit of God!

6. Origin and fate of demons. It seems most likely that the demons and evil spirits of the NT are the angels who fell with Satan. ♦ *Angels* ♦ *Satan* The NT speaks of real spiritual powers and real forces of evil operating in our dark world (Eph 1:21; 6:12). The Devil and his fallen angels are the only evil spiritual beings about which we have any information in Scripture. Surely if the demons of the Gospels were different from the fallen angels, there would be some mention of them when Jesus describes hell as "the eternal fire prepared for the devil and his angels" (Mt 25:41). Even as Satan is free to trouble humanity, so too are the fallen angels.

If demons and fallen angels are the same, then their origin, their place in the ordered realm of created beings, and their fate are all defined in the Scriptures.

DEMONSTRATE

The word "demonstrate" is seldom used in English versions of the Bible. But each use is theologically significant, with three different Greek words reflected in our translations.

Endeiknymi means "to demonstrate" in the sense of placing evidence on display. God placed evidence of his power on display in the events of the Exodus (Ro 9:17,22). The evidence of his unlimited patience is viewed in the salvation of Paul, the "worst of sinners" (1 Ti 1:16). And the evidence that God is righteous in forgiving sins is displayed in Jesus' death as a sacrifice of atonement. (*endeixis*, Ro 3:25). ♦ *Atonement*

Synistēmi suggests drawing the evidence together, to sum it up in a single exhibit. Human unrighteousness is a backdrop against which God's righteousness is so displayed (Ro 3:5). The evidence for God's love is focused, for its grandest display, in Jesus' death for us (Ro 5:8).

Apodeixis is a strong word. It appears only once in the NT. It indicates compelling proof: evidence that demands agreement. God's acts demonstrate his power, his patience, and his love. But it is the Holy Spirit, working through the gospel, who awakens faith with compelling proof (1 Co 2:4).

DENY/DISOWN

Many passages that use the word "deny" may puzzle or concern us. What about those warnings against denying Jesus? What do they mean? And how about denying ourselves? What is it that Jesus demands from those who want to follow him? And what of Jesus' statement that he will deny in heaven those who deny him on earth?

1. **The Greek words**
2. **Denial as rejection of Jesus and the gospel**
3. **Denial as a fall from fellowship**
4. **Self-denial as the path of discipleship**

1. The Greek words. The basic word is *arneomai*, which means "to deny" or "to disown." *Aparneomai* is a stronger form of the same word, ordinarily used in the sense of "to renounce or disown." In the NT the two are often used interchangeably as synonyms (Lk 12:9 and Mt 10:33). When used in a context in which a person must make a decision, these Greek words indicate rejection. But when the subject of the verbs is a person who has an established faith in Jesus, denial means unfaithfulness in the relationship, an abandoning of fellowship.

2. Denial as rejection of Jesus and the gospel. John writes of those who deny "that Jesus is the Christ." He calls them antichrists, and says that no one who denies the Son has the Father (1 Jn 2:22–23). Here "denial" stands in contrast with "confess" ("acknowledge," *homologeō*). These persons refused to acknowledge that Jesus is the Christ, the Son of God. ♦ *Acknowledge*

The same sense of rejection is found in Jude 4. Certain individuals who were not believers had slipped into the believing community. They had distorted the message of grace, twisting it into a license for immorality, and they denied Christ as sovereign Lord. They were not believers: they had rejected Jesus as he is presented in the gospel.

It is likely that a similar rejection of Jesus in the saving sense is meant when Christ warned the crowds, "Whoever disowns me before men, I will disown him before my Father in heaven" (Mt 10:33; cf. Lk 12:9).

3. Denial as a fall from fellowship. Peter's denial of Jesus in the high priest's courtyard (Mt 26, Mk 14, Lk 22, Jn 18) was not a rejection of his Lord. But it was a definite step back from the commitment Peter had made to die for Jesus if necessary, and that he would never, never disown him (Mt 26:33–35). Later Jesus gently restored Peter, leading his repentant disciple to reaffirm the love that Peter always had for Christ, even though fear had gained momentary control. Each of us, no matter how firm our personal commitment to Jesus is, is just as vulnerable to the momentary lapse.

In the context of the church's early creedal statement in 2 Ti 2:11–13, Paul is speaking of believers, eager that each might experience the full meaning of the salvation we have in Christ. Here he repeats this trustworthy saying of the early church: "If we died with him, we will also live with him; if we endure, we will also reign with him. If we disown him, he will also disown us; if we are faithless, he will remain faithful, for he cannot disown himself." If we remain in fellowship ("endure"), we will experience his ruling authority. But if we abandon fellowship with Jesus (deny him or disown him), then he will withdraw from fellowship with us. Yet even should we prove unfaithful, he remains faithful in his commitment to us, for relationship with God does not depend on our own fallible character but on his flawless and faithful nature.

Peter experienced all this when he disowned Jesus in a moment of fear. Jesus continued committed to Peter. Christ not only restored Peter to fellowship but also restored him to his place of leadership in the early church.

4. Self-denial as the path of discipleship. Mt 16 reports Jesus' first announcement to his disciples that he must die and be raised again. It also contains an instruction that is repeated in each of the Synoptics: "If anyone would come after me, he must deny himself and take up his cross and follow me" (Mt 16:24 and Mk 8:34; Lk 9:23 inserts "daily" after "cross"). The thought reflects the NT teaching on transformation. Jesus brings each of us new life. He makes possible an inner transformation that enables us to grow in Christlikeness (2 Co 3:18). As Jesus works within us, we learn to reject the desires and motives that swell up from our old nature. We turn from them and commit ourselves to live by the will of God, as Jesus did. In taking daily steps of obedience, we deny ourselves and choose instead the will of God. And in doing so we find ourselves being transformed. ♦ *Soul and Spirit*

DEPOSIT

"Deposit" is a theologically significant word in the NT. Each of the three times the word *arrabōn* is found in the NT it refers us to the Holy Spirit. The word is a legal/business term. It means a deposit that guarantees that the full amount due will be paid. The Holy Spirit has been given to us as God's personal guarantee of our ultimate redemption (2 Co 1:22; 5:5; Eph 1:14).

The other NT word translated "deposit" occurs in 1 Ti 6:20 and 2 Ti 1:14. *Parakatathēkē* means "something given into another's charge," deposited with that person. Here the contexts suggest that what has been deposited with Timothy is a position of leadership and the responsibility that that position carries.

DEPRAVITY

Each of the five passages where "depravity" occurs in the NIV has a different Greek word from which it was translated. These words mean "judged and disapproved," "evil," "perversion," and "corruption." In each case, the sense of the passage is well expressed by the English term "depravity."

DESCENDANTS ◆ Offspring

DESERT

Only one of the three Hebrew words translated "desert" (y'šîmôn) identifies the hot, arid sands brought to mind by the English word. Another word, 'ªrābāh, identifies a desert plateau, or steep. The most common word, midbār, is used of three types of terrain: of pasture land, of barren, empty lands, and of large areas that are only sparsely populated. A number of such lightly populated areas are identified in the OT: the Sinai, the Negeb (the area south of Palestine toward Egypt), the Jordan Valley, and a few others. Although not every biblical desert should be thought of as desolate, none is pleasant. Desert living is hard on people and on beasts. Often the desert lands or wilderness (as midbār is translated some 257 times in the NASB) are contrasted to the lands flowing with milk and honey that God promises his obedient people.

Another article discusses the verb "desert," meaning "to leave." ◆ Abandon/Abandoned

DESIRE

Looking over the biblical passages that contain the word "desire" raises a number of questions. Is it the object of desire that makes desire good or bad? Is there something suspicious about the very act of desiring? Are our desires intrinsically evil? The original languages, especially the Greek, help us find important answers.

OT 1. Hebrew words for "desire"
NT 2. Desire as a choice

3. Desire as an expression of human beings' sinful nature
4. Summary

OT — 1. Hebrew words for "desire". The two basic words for "desire" are 'āwâh and hāmad. 'Awâh means "to desire," "to long for," "to want," "to wish." It is used with both good and bad objects of desire.

Hāmad emphasizes the desirability of the object as a source of delight (◆ Delight) but is used often in a strongly negative sense. It is this word that is translated "covetousness": desire running riot, trapping the subject in an evil passion. ◆ Covet

The use of these words makes it clear that human desires are often twisted out of the pattern God established. But the words themselves make no statement about fallen human nature.

There are other, special words that are also translated "desire" in the OT. T'šûqâh means "desire or longing." It appears only in Ge 3:16; 4:7; SS 7:10. In Ge 3:16 it describes the changed relationship that sin introduced in husband-and-wife relationships. A hierarchy is imposed where none existed; it is expressed in the phrase "your desire will be for your husband, and he will rule over you." In Ge 4:7 sin is portrayed as a wild beast gazing hungrily at Cain, desiring to devour him if he fails to respond to God's instructions.

Miš'ālâh is a petition. It is found only in Ps 20:5 and 37:4, in which God grants the desires and petitions of those who love him.

Another major term is rāṣôn. It has three basic meanings: (1) it represents God's favor, (2) it expresses his acceptance of a sacrifice or a person in a ritual sense, and (3) it means "desire," in the sense of that which motivates a choice of one's will. It is used in one or more of these senses in Ge 49:6; Lev 1:3; 19:5; 22:19,29; 2 Ch 15:15; Ezr 10:11; Ne 9:24,37; Est 9:5; Ps 40:8; 51:18; 143:10; 145:16,19; Da 8:4; 11:3,16,36.

NT — Desire as choice. Several times the NIV and the NASB translate thelō as "desire" (in the NIV, at Mt 9:13; 12:7; Jn

8:44; Ro 7:18; 9:16; 2 Co 8:10; Gal 5:17; 1 Ti 5:11; Heb 13:18). This word means "to want" or "to will." There is a strong dimension of choice in *thelō*. When Jesus quoted the OT in saying, "I desire mercy, not sacrifice (Mt 9:13; 12:7), he was not speaking of God's feelings but of the Father's conscious choice of what is truly important in a relationship with him (cf. Heb 10:5,8).

At times in the NT, "desire" is supplied by the translators (Ro 8:5; Jas 1:20) to communicate the sense of the passage but not to represent any specific word.

Ro 10:1 has *eudokia* ("good pleasure") and 1 Co 12:31 has *zēloō* ("to be jealous for," "to seek eagerly"). ♦ *Jealousy/Zeal*

3. Desire as an expression of human beings' sinful nature. The word most often translated "desire" in the NT has definite theological implications. *Epithymeō*, "to desire," was originally used in an ethically neutral sense. Long before the time of Jesus, however, *epithymia* came to be used in an ethically bad sense. It suggested dangerous passions growing out of one's false evaluation of the world and its contents.

In the NT, *epithymia* and *epithymeō*, are used in a positive or neutral sense only in Lk 15:16; Php 1:23; 1 Th 2:17; 1 Ti 3:1; Heb 6:11. In other passages, the words are used in its ethically bad sense. Furthermore, the passages where they are used develop a picture of human nature that reveals a truth the Greeks sensed when they used this word to mark their suspicion of their own passions.

The NT reveals that the desires that drive human beings lie deep within sinful human nature (Gal 5:16; Eph 2:3; 4:22). Driven by passions, human beings fall under sin's power (Ro 6:12; Eph 2:3). What is more, human beings create a world (society) that institutionalizes as values the tragic misinterpretations of what is truly important, for these values are derived from the passions of our twisted nature (1 Jn 2:16; Mk 4:19). Temptation thus does not come from the things that attract us: it is found in our response to them (Jas 1:14–15). ♦ *Temp-*

tation/Test/Trial Only by turning to God and learning to rely on the Holy Spirit can we resist our warped passions and develop a new system of values (Ro 8:9; Gal 5:16; Eph 4:23).

The biblical teaching that the Fall warped and twisted human nature is underlined by the treatment given *epithymia* in the NT. Human personality is wholly infected by sin. Mind, heart, and will are all corrupt: even the desires that motivate us are twisted by our inability to evaluate what is truly good for us.

4. Summary. It is not wrong for us to have desires. The capacity to feel pleasure and delight has been given to us by God, a reflection of his own rich emotional capacity. But both Testaments indicate that we may desire the wrong things. The NT helps us realize that we cannot explain away our actions by an appeal to the desirability of the thing that motivated them. Our desire for what is desirable is often tainted, for we are flawed by sin. The flaw includes those desires that lead us to many wrong evaluations. Thus the desires of sinful human beings are shaped by the sin nature and all too often impel us toward what is both evil and bad for us.

But there is release for those who are in Christ. We can let the Holy Spirit shape our desires. We can reject the old and choose those things that God holds to be of value, and so we ourselves may in this way be purified and cleansed.

DESOLATE/DESOLATION

The word *šāmēm* with its derivatives occurs 195 times in the OT. It defines the concept that is reflected in the few NT uses of "desolate."

The image *šāmēm* casts is one of a barren, empty land, wasted and made bleak by some disaster. The disaster may be natural or a result of war. But usually this word group is associated with divine judgment.

Normally "desolate" applies to places and things. A few times a person is pictured as desolated by events (e.g., Isa 54:1).

One derivative, *šammâh*, is a noun that emphasizes the horror experienced by a person viewing desolation. The view may be of future or past events brought on by judgment. *Sammâh* is found in a number of passages (Dt 28:37; 2 Ki 22:19; 2 Ch 29:8; 30:7; Ps 46:8; 73:19; Isa 5:9; 13:9; 24:12; Jer 2:15; 4:7; 5:30; 8:21; 18:16; 19:8; 25:9,11,18,38; 29:18; 42:18; 44:12,22; 46:19; 48:9; 49:13,17; 50:3,23; 51:29,37, 41,43; Eze 23:33; Hos 5:9; Joel 1:7; Mic 6:16; Zep 2:15; Zec 7:14).

DESPISE

The words translated "despise" in both the OT and the NT present a common image.

Bāzâh is found forty-three times in the OT. It means to place little value on something and implies contempt. According to custom, Esau, Abraham's oldest son, should have had first son's rights to his father's possessions. But Esau had only contempt for the most important thing his father had: God's covenant promise. Esau despised this birthright and was willing to trade it to his brother for a bowl of stew (Ge 25:34).

Disobedience and other sins are portrayed in the OT as nothing less than evidences that we despise God. When we disobey, we show that we place little value on the Lord. Thus David's adultery with Bathsheba was a display of contempt for God (2 Sa 12:10). It is good to read of David's confession of his sin and of his confidence in the forgiving grace of God in Psalm 51: "A broken and contrite heart, O God, you will not despise" (Ps 51:17). ▶ *Confession of Sins*

Qālal is a common root that is translated "despise" only three times in the NASB. It means "to be slight," or "to curse." ▶ *Curse* After Hagar gave birth to Ishmael, she despised Sarah, for Sarah could not conceive (Ge 16:4–5). Sarah had a wife's position but was unable to perform the wife's function of giving her husband children. So Hagar's attitude toward her mistress subtly changed.

Nā'aṣ is the most unusual of the words translated "despise." It describes a change in actions or in attitude. A person or thing that once was viewed and treated favorably is now treated with contempt. *Nā'aṣ* occurs twenty-nine times in the OT. The NIV translates it "despise" in Ps 107:11; Isa 60:14; Jer 14:21; 23:17.

Continuing the OT emphasis, the NT translates both *kataphroneō* and *exoutheneō* as "despise."

Kataphroneō means "to think little of," "to despise." When Jesus warned against trying to serve two masters, he used this word (Mt 6:24; Lk 16:13). In time, one master will win our allegiance, and we will think less and less of the other.

Exoutheneō means "to set no value on," and thus "to regard with contempt." *Exoutheneō* describes the attitude of the Pharisee who considered himself righteous and despised others (Lk 18:9). We are warned not to have a similar attitude toward fellow Christians even though we may disagree with their thoughts or ways (Ro 14:3,10). *Exoutheneō* appears only in Lk 18:9; 23:11; Ac 4:11; Ro 14:3,10; 1 Co 1:28; 6:4; 16:11; 2 Co 10:10; Gal 4:14; 1 Th 5:20.

DESTINE ▶ *Predestine*

DESTROY/DESTRUCTION

The word "destroy" appears often in English versions. It should. Many different words in the original languages convey our English idea. The KJV translates some thirty-eight different Hebrew words "destroy" or "destruction," though many have this meaning in only certain stems or certain contexts.

OT 1. Death and destruction
NT. 2. Theologically significant passages

OT — 1. Death and destruction. A number of Hebrew words have "destruction" as their primary meaning or are frequently so translated. Although each of these words may have a distinctive shade of meaning and may be used at times in distinctive settings, they are treated as synonyms in that all of them convey the idea of violent death and destruction.

NT — 2. Theologically significant passages. A number of Greek words are found in the NT where the NIV and the NASB use "destroy" and "destruction." At times the difference in meaning is theologically significant and NT verses are clarified and enriched when the Greek word translated "destroy" is known.

Mt 6:19–20. The word here is *aphanizō* (elsewhere in the NT only in Mt 6:16; Ac 13:41; Jas 4:14). Its basic meaning is "to render invisible or unrecognizable." The thought is that moth and rust attack material objects, changing them so that their value is lost. How much better to lay up heavenly treasures, which can never suffer such corruption.

Ro 14:15. This passage discusses our reaction to differences in Christian convictions. It teaches that we are not to judge others and that nothing is evil in itself. But it also calls on us to be sensitive to the impact our actions may have on others: "Do not by your eating destroy your brother for whom Christ died." The word translated "destroy" is *apollymi,* usually meaning "to cause to become lost or destroyed." The thought is, Do not bring about the ruin or downfall of your fellow Christian.

In what sense do we bring ruin to others? The thought is further developed in 14:20, "Do not destroy the work of God for the sake of food." Here the word is *katalyō,* "to tear down," and it is used in contrast to *oikodomē,* "to build up" (14:19). Together these verses show us that we must be careful in our relationships within the Christian community. God wants our relationships to enrich others and build them up, not do anything that would be destructive of spiritual growth.

1 Co 3:17. This verse warns, "If anyone destroys God's temple, God will destroy him." The word in each phrase is *phtheirō.* This means destruction in the sense of ruin, or corruption. We might translate this statement in this way: "If anyone brings ruin to God's temple, God will bring ruin on him."

1 Co 5:5. This verse relates that an unrepentant brother was, by a judicial act of the local Christian community, released to destruction (*olethros*) to experience physical death. ⟩ *Judge/Judging*

1 Cor 15:26. This great passage on resurrection proclaims Christ's ultimate victory. It declares that "the last enemy to be destroyed is death." Here the word translated "destroyed" is *katargeō,* used almost always in theologically significant contexts. The word means "to abolish," "to nullify," and so to render something inoperative or ineffectual. The power that death has to quiet human beings will be forever nullified. ⟩ *Life and Death*

The same word is found in 2 Ti 1:10. Jesus has already rendered spiritual death inoperative in those who turn to him. We truly can experience now the life and immortality we have in him (cf. Heb 2:14).

2 Ti 2:18. Paul warns Timothy against those who spread false doctrine that would "destroy the faith of some." The word here is *anatrepō,* which means "to upset" or "to ruin" (used elsewhere only in Tit 1:11). False teaching results in, not the loss of saving faith, but a failure to build experience on faith's sure foundation of truth; this, in turn, limits the individual's Christian experience and usefulness (cf. 2:19–21).

1 Jn 3:8. Christians need to, recognize that all sinful actions reflect the character of Satan, for sin was introduced in the universe by his original act. ⟩ *Satan*

John argues that "the reason the Son of God appeared was to destroy the devil's work." The word for "destroy" here is *lyō,* "to undo." The thought is that the harm Satan has done is now being undone by Jesus. The Devil's structure of sin and corruption is crumbling as you and I, given new life in Jesus, break the pattern that Satan's work imposes on humanity. How wonderfully the pattern is being unraveled, for "no one who is born of God will continue to sin, because God's seed remains in him; he cannot go on sinning, because he has been born of God" (3:9).

The OT occurrences of "destruction" use the word in its straightforward sense. But we must be careful when interpreting NT passages that contain the word "destroy" or "destruction." Our English word can carry many shades of meaning. We need to determine by careful study which shade of meaning is intended in the context of each passage we explore.

DETESTABLE ▶
Abominable/Abomination

DEVIL ▶ *Satan*

DEVOTE/DEVOTION

The OT concept of "devote" is expressed by *hāram*. The word means "to set aside solely [for God]." *Hāram* is used both of those things set aside for God to use and of things placed under a ban, to be completely destroyed.

Jos 6–7 provides an example. Everything in Jericho was to be destroyed. But Achan took some silver and an expensive garment. As a result of his breaking the ban, Israel suffered defeat until Achan's sin was exposed and punished. *Hāram* is typically found where any object, person, or thing is devoted to destruction.

When the English OT versions use the concept of devotion in a positive sense, the Hebrew often has a phrase such as "prepared his heart" (Ezr 7:10), "continued in" (Ne 5:16), or "set apart" (Ps 86:2).

A number of Greek words are found where English versions read "devoted" and "devotion." None of these Greek words picks up the OT meaning of setting aside for destruction. But Mt 15:5 and Mk 7:11 use "devote" in the OT sense of setting apart for God's service.

Other NT words translated "devoted" suggest such ideas as attending constantly, finding time for, following after, and—when personal relationships are in view—being tender or loving toward.

DEVOUR

The Hebrew word is *'ākal*, "to eat, or consume." One major use of the word is symbolic, to indicate hardships that ensue when an individual or a people's resources are consumed. Usually the consuming force is some disaster, such as a foreign invader, a plague, a fire, or drought. At times the consuming force is a person who oppresses others.

Some Greek words mean "to consume" or "to devour" and are used figuratively in the same way as *'ākal*. Satan is graphically portrayed (1 Pe 5:8) as looking about for someone to devour (*katapinō*), and the religious hypocrites of Jesus' time "devour [*katesthiō*] widows' houses and for a show make lengthy prayers. Such men will be punished most severely" (Mk 12:40).

DIE ▶ *Life and Death*

DIRECT ▶ *Lead/Guide*

DISAPPEAR

When Jesus says that not the smallest letter in the Hebrew alphabet in which the Scriptures are written will disappear from the law (Mt 5:18), he uses the word *parerchomai*. The term means "to pass away" or "to come to an end." God's Word will outlast the heavens and the earth.

The same word is used in 2 Pe 3:10 to relate the passing of the universe, describing as a roar the final, tumultuous, unimaginable fury of the elements as billions of billions of suns burn themselves out of existence. Heb 8:13 uses the word *aphanismos* (only here in NT) to affirm that the earth is ready to "vanish." The context suggests utter destruction.

Another word—*katargeō*—is used in 1 Co 13:10 when Paul declares that the old will be abolished, set aside to make room for something infinitely better. It is good to know that the disappearance of the world we know will be no loss, for "when perfection comes, the imperfect disappears."

DISASTER

The NIV consistently translates the noun *ra'* as "disaster." The word means "evil," "misery," or "distress." The root is a powerful ethical and moral term that usually identifies something that is evil in God's eyes. But evil can also be experiential: something that seems evil to us because it brings us misery and distress. It is in this subjective sense that *ra'* is translated "disaster" in some English versions. And it is in this sense that God accepts responsibility for some of the evils that befell Israel. Many national disasters were a result of Israel's unfaithfulness and were decreed by God as a punishment and as discipline (e.g., Ex 32:12; 2 Ki 6:33; Isa 45:7).

DISCERN

The key Hebrew word is *bîn*. It and its derivatives are used some 247 times in the OT and are usually translated "understanding." The basic idea is that of understanding gained by evaluating. Thus, words like "discern," "distinguish," and "judgment" capture the basic meaning of *bîn*. ◆ **Understand/Understanding**

DISCIPLE

The word "disciple" seems to fill the Gospels and appears often in Acts. But then the word disappears. "Disciple" is not used in the Epistles—even by John, who uses it frequently in his Gospel. Today, however, many speak and write about discipleship. What does "disciple" mean in the NT? And is there a message of discipleship for the church today?

1. **The Greek word**
2. **The Twelve and others**
3. **Discipleship today**

1. **The Greek word.** The Greek word *mathētēs* ("disciple") is from the verb *manthanō* ("to learn"). Thus, a disciple is a pupil or learner. In Greek culture prior to Socrates, *manthanō* described the process by which a person sought theoretical knowledge. A *mathētēs* was one who attached himself to another to gain some practical or theoretical knowledge, whether by instruction or by experience. The word came to be used both of apprentices who were learning a trade and of adherents of various philosophical schools. After the time of Socrates, the word lost favor with the philosophers, who were not at all happy with its association with labor.

But the concept of discipleship was most popular in the Judaism of Jesus' day. Rabbis had disciples who studied with them in a well-defined and special relationship. The need for training was intensely felt in the Jewish community, which believed that no one could understand Scripture without a teacher's guidance. A disciple in Judaism had to master—in addition to the Scriptures of the OT—the oral and written traditions that had grown up around the Scriptures. Only after being so taught might a person become a rabbi himself or teach with any authority. This notion is expressed in the Jews' amazed reaction to Jesus' public teaching: "How did this man get such learning without having studied?" (Jn 7:15). Jesus taught with authority without having gone through the only process that the Jews felt could qualify anyone to teach.

Several aspects of the rabbi-disciple relationship in first-century Judaism are significant. The disciple left his home and moved in with his teacher. He served the teacher in the most servile ways, treating him as an absolute authority. The disciple was expected not only to learn all that his rabbi knew but also to become like him in character and piety (Mt 10:24; Lk 6:40). The rabbi in return provided food and lodging and saw his own distinctive interpretations transmitted through his disciples to future generations. So when Mark says that Jesus chose twelve men "that they might be with him" (Mk 3:14), he accurately reflects contemporary understanding of how future leaders should be trained.

2. **The Twelve and others.** The word *mathētēs* is used in several different ways in the Gospels. First, it designates the Twelve whom Jesus chose to be with him. The Twelve are unique in that Jesus

chose them and trained them to both teach and serve (Mk 3:14). In responding to Jesus' call, the Twelve made a disciple's total commitment. They surrendered everything to live in obedience to Jesus (Lk 14:26).

Second, *mathētēs* identifies followers of various schools or traditions. There were the disciples of the Pharisees (Mt 22:16; Mk 2:18; Lk 5:33) and the disciples of John the Baptist (Mt 11:2ff.; Mk 2:18; Lk 5:33; Jn 1:35–37; 3:35). Used in this sense, "disciple" does not identify a student in a traditional teacher-learner relationship; rather, it identifies persons who are adherents of a movement.

Third, our NT describes a much wider circle beyond the Twelve who are also called disciples. These are adherents of the movement associated with Jesus. At times the word "disciple" may seem to carry the sense of "believer" (cf. Jn 8:31; 13:35; 15:8). But it would be a mistake to think that all those who were called disciples in the Gospels were persons who had made a firm commitment to Jesus. In fact many were only initially attracted to Jesus. When they found his teachings difficult, as after his discourse on the Bread of Life, "many of his disciples turned back and no longer followed him" (Jn 6:66).

After the Resurrection, Jesus charged his followers to "go and make disciples of all nations" (Mt 28:19). The mission was not to win loose adherents for a movement. Instead, Jesus said to his disciples that they were to teach those who believe "to obey everything" he had commanded them (v. 20).

3. Discipleship today. Acts continues to use the word "disciple," but there *mathētēs* is synonymous with "believer." Luke even records the point at which the believing community began its break with the language of both Jewish and Greek culture. He tells of the time at Antioch when "the disciples were first called Christians" (Ac 11:26). Although it is dangerous to build on silence, it does seem significant that the term "disciple" is simply not used in the Epistles. This may be because it carried too many associations at a time when a new proc-

ess was demanded within the church to equip God's people for growth and ministry.

Jesus defined the goal of discipling when he said, "A student [*mathētēs*] is not above his teacher, but everyone who is fully trained will be like his teacher" (Lk 6:40). Likeness, not simply knowledge, was the goal of Jewish discipleship. And likeness to Jesus himself is the goal God has for you and me (Ro 8:29; 1 Jn 3:2). Although complete likeness to Jesus awaits our resurrection, even now God is actively at work within believers. We "are being transformed into his [Jesus'] likeness with ever-increasing glory" (2 Co 3:18). A number of NT passages give insight into the processes that are involved in individual and community growth toward Christlikeness (e.g., Eph 4:11–16).

The NT has several images that replace the image of disciples gathered around a rabbi. The Epistles speak of the Christian community as family, teaching us that we must build intimate relationships with our brothers and sisters. There is the image of Christ's body, a living organism, and this teaches us to look to each other for ministries that will facilitate our transformation. There is the image of a holy temple, indicating that we are to serve God and others. ♦ *Church* The Epistles, especially in contexts that emphasize the family and the body, present new interpersonal processes that in effect supplant those by which the disciples of Judaism were trained.

We can learn much from a study of Jesus' relationship with the Twelve. But just as the word "disciple" was discarded when new terminology was needed to express new truths, so we should study the Epistles for nurture principles by which modern men and women of faith and commitment can be developed. ♦ *Teaching/Learning*

DISCIPLINE

Often when we speak of discipline we mean punishment. But biblically, discipline is much more than painful correction.

OT 1. The Hebrew words
    2. The character of OT discipline
NT 3. The Greek words
    4. The character of NT discipline
    5. Guidelines for family
       discipline
    6. Church discipline

OT — 1. The Hebrew words. The key Hebrew word for discipline is *yāsar*, which means "to discipline," "to chastise," or "to instruct." A derivative, *mûsār*, means "discipline." These Hebrew words are translated in the NIV and the NASB by both "discipline" and "chastisement." The root denotes correction that contributes to education. Biblical discipline (chastisement) is goal oriented: it seeks to develop a godly person who is responsive to the Lord and who walks in his ways.

2. The character of OT discipline. Discipline (chastisement) involves correction that contributes to one's education and training in righteousness. The goal of OT discipline is well expressed in this stated purpose of Proverbs: "for attaining wisdom and discipline, for understanding words of insight; for acquiring a disciplined and prudent life, doing what is right and just and fair" (Pr 1:2–3). OT discipline is exercised in the context of close family relationships. God urged Israel to view his own discipline of them in a family framework: "Know then in your heart that as a man disciplines his son, so the LORD your God disciplines you" (Dt 8:5).

The Deuteronomy context makes it very clear that discipline is not primarily punishment. Dt 8:1–5 reminds Israel of how God cared for his people in the Exodus years. God caused them to hunger—but then he gave them manna, "to teach [them] that man does not live on bread alone but on every word that comes from the mouth of the LORD" (8:3; cf. Dt 11:1–7). This illustrates a major aspect of OT discipline. God provided instructive experiences for his people. Throughout Scripture, Israel is called to look back into their history and to learn not only from God's punishments but also from his provisions.

Both biblical history and the Proverbs make the point that there is an element of punishment in God's discipline of his people—when this is required. God corrected with punishment (Lev 26:18,28; cf. Isa 8:11; Hos 5:2; 7:12). And Proverbs recommends the rod of correction to parents with unresponsive youngsters (Pr 22:15; 29:15,17). But the rod is reserved for those who will not respond to verbal lessons. And verbal instruction remains the primary resource for discipline and correction.

Proverbs also identifies another vital element in discipline. It must be administered in love. In his relationship with Israel, God has set an example for us to follow: "My son, do not despise the LORD's discipline and do not resent his rebuke, because the LORD disciplines those he loves, as a father the son he delights in" (Pr 3:11–12).

NT — 3. The Greek words. The Greek word that most closely corresponds with *yāsar* is *paideuō*. This verb is used forty-one times in the Septuagint to translate *yāsar*. The noun *paideia* is used thirty-seven times to translate *mûsār*. The Greek word means "to bring up, or train," and in this sense "to discipline."

▶ **Teaching/Learning**

This Greek word group is used some twenty-one times in the NT. Twice the meaning is "to instruct" (Ac 7:22; 22:3), and twice "to whip, or beat" (Lk 23:16, 23). The rest of the time the OT sense of corrective guidance as a means of training or educating is intended.

4. The character of NT discipline. The key NT passage on discipline is Heb 12:4–13. In the context of the Christian's struggle against sin, the writer quotes Pr 3:11–12. God's rebuke, and even his punishments, flow from love. God accepts the parent's responsibility: he will discipline (train) his sons.

The suggestion in verse 7 that God's discipline is often experienced as hardship harks back to the OT. God continues to use circumstances that cause us pain in a positive way, even as he used a variety of hardships to correct Israel. The writer tells us that we should submit to the Father. He "disciplines us for our good, that we may share in his holiness" (v. 10). The painful experiences of today are intended to produce "a harvest of righteousness and peace for those who have been trained by it" (v. 11). Because of this, we are not to become discouraged in our difficulties, but are to "strengthen . . . feeble arms and weak knees" (v. 12).

The Heb 12 picture of discipline emphasizes the same elements that are so prominent in the OT. There is a special family relationship from which discipline flows. There is a distinctive goal: discipline is guidance toward holiness. Discipline uses circumstances and experiences as well as verbal instruction to correct. Evidence of God's love helps us respond appropriately when hard times come.

Both the verbal and historic elements that we see so prominently in the OT are also presented in the NT. Scripture is given by God for "teaching, rebuking, correcting and training [discipline] in righteousness" (2 Ti 3:16). We need the guiding words of the Bible to correct us and to point us toward holiness.

Tit 2:11–13 points back to Jesus, as Dt 8 points back to the God of the Exodus. Paul writes that "the grace of God that brings salvation has appeared to all men. It teaches [disciplines, guides] us to say 'No' to ungodliness . . . to live self-controlled, upright and godly lives in this present age." Knowledge of God's love in Christ creates the climate of love in which we can accept discipline experiences. We are brought to the path of righteousness by consideration of God's grace as well as by the pain of his punishments.

5. Guidelines for family discipline. Little is said in either Testament of specific child-rearing practices or of parental discipline. But much is implied. God's relationship with his children provides a model for our relationship with our own children. In general, the guiding principles are: (1) Be sure children have many experiences that prove parental love and commitment. (2) Be sure children have clear verbal guidance. (3) Be sure to pro-

vide corrective experiences when children need help to apply verbal instructions or when they resist them. (4) Be sure discipline used is in harmony with the long-range goal of developing godly character, rather than with short-range goals or for our own convenience.

It is important to remember that no discipline can be effective out of the context of loving relationships and that caring enough to let each child know that he or she is truly important is essential.

5. Church discipline. Church discipline is in the same corrective tradition as that characterized in the OT and in Heb 12. But church discipline is the responsibility of the Christian community. It too involves words and actions designed to correct a straying brother or sister. The purpose of church discipline is to restore rather than to condemn. Church discipline is exercised only in matters that the Scriptures clearly identify as sin, and only when the sin is continuously practiced and the individual rebelliously refuses to respond when verbally confronted. Another article discusses church discipline more fully. ◆ *Judge/Judging*

DISEASE ◆ *Sickness and Health*

DISGRACE

Just as English has a number of synonyms to express the idea of disgrace, so does Hebrew. These Hebrew words are likely to be translated into English by any of several terms: "disgrace," "shame," "reproach." The overlap is shown by the fact that thirteen of the NIV uses of "disgrace" are rendered "shame" in the NASB.

But there are differences in emphasis implicit in the Hebrew, just as the English word "disgrace" tends to emphasize public evaluation whereas "shame" emphasizes one's feelings. What are the Hebrew words and their emphases?

Kelimmâh is translated both "dishonor" and "shame." It emphasizes public humiliation and the embarrassment that that causes. It is found in fifteen passages where the NIV reads "disgrace" or "disgraced" (Ps 35:26; 44:15; 69:19; 71:13; Pr

18:3; Isa 30:3; 45:16; 61:7; Jer 3:25; 20:11; 51:51; Eze 16:52,54; 32:30; Mic 2:6).

Ḥerpâh means to blame or to scorn someone; to harm his reputation and character. It appears some seventy-three times in the OT and is often translated "reproach." It is found in twenty passages where the NIV reads "disgrace" or "disgraced" (Ge 30:23; 34:14; 1 Sa 11:2; 17:26; 2 Sa 13:13; Ne 1:3; 2:17; Ps 69:19; 119:39; Pr 6:33; 18:3; Isa 4:1; 25:8; 30:5; 54:4; Jer 23:40; 31:19; La 3:30; 5:1; Eze 36:30).

Qālôn views disgrace in relation to social position. A person who is disgraced is made to appear to be in a lower social position than he actually is. This Hebrew word is found where the NIV uses the word "disgrace" or "disgraceful" only in Pr 6:33; 11:2; 18:3; Isa 22:18; Hos 4:7; Hab 2:16.

Neḇālâh focuses on an act and identifies it as both disgraceful and sinful. This word is linked with immorality and comes from a root that means "foolish" or "senseless." Homosexuality, rape, and Achan's theft at Jericho are all called disgraceful in this sense of foolish sin. The term occurs only thirteen times in the Hebrew Bible (Ge 34:7; Dt 22:21; Isa 7:15; Jdg 19:23,24; 20:6,10; 1 Sa 25:25; 2 Sa 13:12; Job 42:8; Isa 9:17; 32:6; Jer 29:23). The NT has a smaller vocabulary to convey this concept. It relies on one or two words that are most often translated "shame." ▶ **Shame**

DISHONEST ▶ *Honest/Dishonest*

DISHONOR ▶ *Honor/Dishonor*

DISOBEY ▶ *Obey/Disobey*

DISOWN ▶ *Deny/Disown*

DISPUTE

Two Hebrew words are found where English versions read "dispute." *Rîḇ* means "controversy." It may be a fight or a quarrel, but the word is easily extended to include a dispute in court. This is the emphasis in the NIV and the NASB: a

dispute between two or more people that requires some kind of adjudication.

The other Hebrew word translated "dispute" is *dāḇār*. It simply means "word." In verb and noun form it occurs over 2,500 times in the OT. The particular nature of the word is determined from its context.

DISQUALIFY

This word has a disconcerting sound. What do the two NIV uses of it suggest?

In 1 Co 9:27 the Greek word is *adokimos*. It means "to be rejected as unusable." Paul's whole life had been spent telling others of the prize that could be theirs in the gospel. Like an athlete in training, Paul concentrated his efforts on his own experience of the blessings promised in the gospel. Like the athlete in his analogy, disqualification would take the prize out of his reach.

In Col 2:18 the word is *katabrabeuō*, "to give judgment against." In Colosse some members of the church had adopted a futile approach to spirituality and were pressuring others to adopt their system. They disqualified all others either (1) by passing judgment on those who refused them or (2) by actually influencing those who responded so as to cause them to miss the path to spiritual reality. ▶ *Soul and Spirit*

DISTINCTION/DISTINGUISH

Two concepts are found where English versions read "distinguish" and "distinction." One is expressed in the Hebrew words *pālâh* and *bāḏal*. Each means "to separate" and thus to divide or make a distinction between. Often God is the subject of one of these active verbs. They indicate his action in making a distinction between Israel and all other peoples (Ex 8:23; 11:7). God's people are also to make distinctions—between the clean and unclean, the sacred and the unholy.

The other concept has to do with perception. This sense is illustrated in Mal 3:18: "You will again see the distinction between the righteous and the wicked, between those who serve God and those who do not." Here the meaning is "to discern." ♦ **Discern**

Those of us who belong to the Lord have been set apart for him. We must be sensitive and alert, ready to discern the way of life that will truly distinguish us from the lost.

DISTRESS/TROUBLE

Like many other biblical terms, "distress" and "trouble" have a range of meanings. Some passages have a Hebrew word that may be translated by either English word. In other passages the original words have different shades of meanings that the translators have chosen to render by only one of the English pair.

OT 1. Hebrew words translated by either "distress" or "trouble"
    2. Hebrew words translated "trouble" but not "distress"
NT 3. "Trouble" and "distress" in the NT

OT — 1. Hebrew words translated either "distress" or "trouble". The noun *ṣārâh* and the verb *ṣārar* suggest confining, narrow circumstances. Both words draw attention to the emotional response of the person who is under pressure. The pressure may come from enemies, adverse circumstances, wrong decisions, or passion run awry.

These Hebrew words appear frequently in the OT and are translated in the NIV and the NASB by both "distress" and "trouble." In the NIV *ṣārâh* is translated "distress" (or "distresses") in Ge 35:3; 42:21; 1 Sa 10:19; 2 Ki 19:3; 2 Ch 15:6; 20:9; Ne 9:37; Ps 20:1; 77:2; 81:7; Pr 1:27; Isa 8:22; 30:6; 33:2; 63:9; Jer 14:8; 15:11; 16:19; Da 12:1. It is translated "trouble" in 1 Sa 26:24; 2 Sa 4:9; 1 Ki 1:29; Ps 9:9; 10:1; 22:11; 37:39; 46:1; 50:15; 86:7; 91:15; 116:3; 138:7; 142:2; 143:11; Pr 11:8; 12:13; 24:10; 25:19; Jer 30:7; Ob 12,14; Na 1:7,9; Zep 1:15; Zec 10:11. In addition, of its approximately sixty occurrences in the OT, the verb *ṣārar* is rendered "distress" five times (1 Sa 28:15; 2 Sa 24:14; 1 Ch 21:13; Ps 31:9; Jer 10:18) and "trouble" four times (Nu 33:55; Jdg 11:7; 2 Ch 28:22; Ps 69:17).

2. Hebrew words translated "trouble" but not "distress". The concept of bad, or evil, has a subjective as well as an objective aspect. In a nonmoral, subjective sense, something is experienced as an evil if it causes physical or mental pain, or if it affects one's condition adversely. Often the word "trouble" in the NIV and the NASB is a translation of a Hebrew word for evil (*ra'*, *rā'a'*), as in Pr 19:23: "The fear of the LORD leads to life: Then one rests content, untouched by trouble." This Hebrew root is found where the NIV reads "trouble" in Ge 43:6; Ex 5:19,22,23; Nu 11:11; 1 Ki 11:25; 20:7; 2 Ki 14:10; 2 Ch 25:19; Ne 1:3; 2:17; Job 2:10; 31:29; Ps 10:6; 27:5; 41:1; 88:3; 90:15; 94:13; Pr 28:14; Ecc 12:1; Jer 2:27,28. It is rendered "distress" only in Ps 35:26 and La 1:21.

Another concept expressed by "trouble" in English versions is seen in *'āmāl*. This word concentrates attention on the frustration of difficult work (toil) that, despite struggle, offers no fulfillment. This word is translated "trouble" some sixteen times in the NIV, as in Ps 10:14: "But you, O God, do see trouble and grief; you consider it to take it in hand. The victim commits himself to you; you are the helper of the fatherless." *'Amāl* is translated "distress" in Ps 25:18, and "trouble" in Ge 41:51; Job 3:10; 4:8; 5:6,7; 11:16; 15:35; Ps 7:14,16; 10:7,14; 90:10; 140:9; Pr 24:2; Isa 59:4; Jer 20:18.

A third major concept translated "trouble" is expressed by *'ākar*. This word draws attention to the social impact of a person's action. It is found where the text speaks of troubling someone. The thought is that of influencing a person or group to act in such a way as to bring judgment on them. The NIV tends to express this as "bring trouble on." *'Ākar* is found in Ge 34:30; Jos 6:18; 7:25; Jdg 11:35; 1 Sa 14:29; 1 Ki 18:18; 1 Ch 2:7; Ps 39:2; Pr 11:17,29; 15:6,27.

3. "Trouble" and "distress" in the NT. Both the NIV and the NASB translate several Greek words "distress" and "trouble."

The primary word is *thlipsis*, which is often translated "tribulation." The NIV uses "distress" in Mt 24:21,29 and Mk

13:19,24, where *thlipsis* is used as a technical theological term for the Great Tribulation of the end times. *Thlipsis* is also used in a nontheological, figurative way to convey the idea of the great emotional and spiritual stress that can be caused by external or internal pressures. Of the fifty-five uses of this root in the NT, fifty-three are figurative and correspond closely to the Hebrew words *ṣārar* and *ṣar*.

The NASB also frequently translates *tarassō* as "troubled." The word means "to be disturbed, to be stirred up" (by spiritual and emotional confusion). In passages such as the familiar Jn 14:1 ("Let not your heart be troubled"), the meaning is that of being "anxious." ◗ *Anxiety/Worry*

A number of other concepts are expressed by the English word "distress" or "trouble." Ac 17:16 suggests Paul was greatly distressed at the sight of the idols that filled Athens. The Greek word is *paroxynomai*, which suggests a distress akin to anger (used elsewhere only in 1 Co 13:5). Later, when Paul concluded his letter to the believers in Galatia with the phrase "let no one cause me trouble" (Gal 6:17), he used the word *kopos*, "laborious toil."

When Jesus said that "each day has enough trouble of its own" (Mt 6:34), the text has *kakia*, "evil." In this context the subjective experience is emphasized, and the meaning is "misfortune."

In Heb 12:15, which warns that bitterness can cause trouble, the word used is *enochleō* (its only use in the NT). It means "to crowd in" or "to press" and has the sense of harassing or annoying.

Life on earth is filled with all sorts of troubles and distress. Each of us will experience our full quota. It is good, then, to share Paul's conviction that "our present sufferings are not worth comparing with the glory that will be revealed in us" (Ro 8:18).

DIVINATION

One of two Hebrew words is usually found where the OT speaks of divination or diviners.

Nāḥaš seems to suggest fortunetelling or consultation of omens for information to direct one's choices. Like other occult practices, this is forbidden to God's people (Dt 18:10; cf. Ge 30:27; Lev 19:26; 1 Ki 20:33; 2 Ki 17:17; 21:6; 2 Ch 33:6). God's people are to rely on the Lord for guidance and to reject every other supposed source of supernatural aid.

Qāsam is translated "divination" and sometimes "witchcraft." It too is forbidden in Dt 18:10,14, though the noun *qesem* is used in a positive sense in Pr 16:10. The exact character of the occult practices indicated by *qāsam* are not known. But in the story of Balaam, *qesem* was to be used in an offensive way against Israel, as well as for a source of information (Nu 23:23).

Modern occult practices that promise guidance or supernatural power over others should be repugnant to God's people. Our trust is in the Lord, and we rely only on his unseen control over all the days of our lives.

DIVORCE AND REMARRIAGE

The Bible says surprisingly little about divorce. Yet divorce and remarriage are important issues today. The tragedy of shattered homes and crushed hearts is seen more and more often within the church. As Christ's people, we wish to be compassionate, but we are also committed to remain true to our Lord and to his revealed Word.

Part of the problem arises from differences in interpretation of key Bible passages. Some Christians are convinced that the Bible permits no divorce for believers under any circumstances. Others believe that divorce, while not God's ideal, may be necessary and that remarriage may be justified. And there are many variations within these two camps.

The very fact that there are different interpretations among those who do honor the Scriptures suggests that the Bible's teaching may not be unequivocably clear on this subject. Yet we must thoroughly explore what God says, within the framework provided by Jesus' revelation of his constant grace.

1. The covenant character of marriage
2. Biblical provision for divorce
3. The Bible and remarriage
4. The NT passages
5. Conclusions

1. The covenant character of marriage. The OT introduces marriage as a lifelong link between two persons. The two so share their lives that they become one in their experience here on earth. Many OT allusions make it clear that in marriage the commitment of husband and wife to each other reflects God's covenant commitment to his people. Thus when Mal 2:16 reports God's statement "I hate divorce," it is in the context of an emphasis on covenant faithfulness—to the Lord and to "the wife of [one's] marriage covenant" (2:14). God has made two one: each partner is to preserve the commitment that makes marriage the enriching relationship that God intends (2:15). ◆ *Marriage*

There is no question that God's ideal is that of an unbroken covenant: a lifelong relationship that mirrors on earth God's faithfulness to those whom he has chosen to love. When Jesus was questioned about divorce, he pointed back to the ideal established at the creation: "Haven't you read that at the beginning the Creator 'made them male and female' and said, 'For this reason a man will leave his father and mother and be united to his wife, and the two will become one flesh'? So they are no longer two, but one. Therefore what God has joined together, let man not separate" (Mt 19:4–6).

2. Biblical provision for divorce. Despite strong OT and NT affirmation of the covenant character of marriage and of God's creation ideal, the OT did permit divorce. Dt 24:1–4 lays down a procedure by which a husband may write a certificate of divorce and send a wife from his home. The basic Hebrew words for divorce, *gāraš* and *šalaḥ*, are used in many different contexts in the OT. But their basic meaning is "to drive out or away," or "to send away."

In Jesus' time there was a debate over the exact conditions under which a divorce might be lawfully granted. Was divorce allowed only in the event of adultery, or could a divorce be obtained also for incompatibility (e.g., for "any and every reason" [Mt 19:3]). Although the conditions were debated, there was no doubt that OT law permitted divorce.

When the Pharisees tried to involve him in this debate over the legalities, Jesus reaffirmed the sanctity of the marriage covenant. Still his questioners probed. "Why then did Moses command that a man give his wife a certificate of divorce and send her away?" (Mt 19:7).

Jesus' answer is important. "Moses permitted you to divorce your wives because your hearts were hard" (Mt 19:8). Jesus' point is that sin warps the most sacred of relationships. Humanity, in the grip of sin's hardening power, can twist the wonderful gift of marriage. Its healing and enriching design can be distorted into a warped parody that crushes and destroys.

Divorce is by no means the best solution to marital problems today, nor was it so in biblical times. Divorce is not God's will for a couple, even if adultery is involved! God's solution is forgiveness and continuing love, which mirrors the Lord's own faithfulness despite untold hurts.

But there will sometimes be relationships in which one partner or the other *will not* respond to love and will reject commitment to the other. In such cases, in which heart commitment to covenant love is consistently rejected, a legal divorce may follow. In such cases it is not the divorce that is the sin, but the sin that necessitates the divorce. God, then, has provided divorce for those whose marriages have already been destroyed by the hardness of a human heart.

We should note here that hardness of heart has many aspects. It need not suggest active hostility. Like other sins, hardness of heart may involve falling short. ◆ *Sin* The inability to give and receive love—something that may be imposed by a loveless childhood home— is probably the greatest destroyer of marriages today.

233

3. The Bible and remarriage. Most Christian leaders recognize that certain conditions may call for the divorce or separation of married persons. But what about remarriage? It is clear from the OT that those who divorced were permitted to remarry (Lev 21:14; Dt 24:2–4). Jesus also spoke of remarriage in his statements on divorce (Mt 5:31–32; 19:3–12). And 1 Co 7 calls on believers to remain unmarried in the hope of reconciliation, at least until that hope is gone. Yet these NT passages raise a specter unmentioned in the OT. Both Testaments seem to expect that remarriage will follow divorce. But the Gospels link remarriage with adultery! ▶ **Adultery**

Several aspects of passages that suggest this link should be explored before one concludes that remarriage is sin.

a. The OT provided for divorce and limited remarriage only in special cases (Lev 21:14; Dt 22:29; 24:2–4). Adultery was condemned in the OT, and the adulterer was to be put to death. Why weren't the remarried to be put to death under the law—a law that provided for divorce?

b. Two of Jesus' statements about divorce and remarriage contain an "exception clause." Jesus taught that those who remarry after a divorce, "except for marital unfaithfulness," commit adultery (Mt 5:32; 19:9). Does this mean that not every remarriage is adulterous, but that some are?

c. Mt 19 reports the shocked reaction of Jesus' disciples to his statements about divorce and remarriage: "If this is the situation between a husband and wife, it is better not to marry!" (Mt 19:10). Jesus responded by saying that "not everyone can accept this word" (v. 11). Verses 11–12 seem to suggest that to remain unmarried is a special gift (as Paul says in 1 Co 7:7).

d. Mt 12 reports an attack by Pharisees on Jesus' disciples. The disciples were eating grain as they walked through the fields on a Sabbath Day. Jesus defended his followers from the petty charge that they were working on the Sabbath—a charge that was based on a questionable interpretation of the OT rather than on a clear OT prohibition. In his defense,

Jesus pointed to two clear violations of law: "Haven't you read what David did when he and his companions were hungry? He entered the house of God, and he and his companions ate the consecrated bread—which was not lawful for them to do, but only for the priests. Or haven't you read in the law that on the Sabbath the priests in the temple desecrate the day and yet are innocent? . . . If you had known what these words mean, 'I desire mercy, not sacrifice,' you would not have condemned the innocent" (Mt 12:3–7).

David's need was seen by God as more important than the law's regulation. And the priests' service to Israel was, of course, more important than the Sabbath prohibition against work. In each case a principle of mercy—of deep concern for human need—took precedence over what was technically a violation of law. David and the priests broke the law but were adjudged innocent.

Isn't it possible that those who suffer the tragedy of divorce and who remarry do commit adultery, as David committed sacrilege, and yet are adjudged innocent? Doesn't the law's provision of divorce and its expectation of remarriage indicate that God can and does deal with divorce and remarriage with a mercy quite unlike the attitude of ancient and modern Pharisees who are preoccupied with legalities?

Certainly divorce and remarriage are tragic violations of God's ideal. They do involve sin. But often the ideal escapes us. When it does, we must find healing in God's forgiveness, and faith in his mercy. We acknowledge our failure, but we affirm God's willingness to give us another chance.

4. The NT passages. Several NT passages deal with divorce and remarriage. The context of each is significant. A more complete discussion of this issue is found in the author's book *Remarriage* (Waco: Word, 1981).

Mt 5. Jesus identifies remarriage after divorce as adultery. The context contains a series of sayings in which Jesus shows that OT law only imperfectly expressed God's ideal of righteousness. It is clear from the context that none of the statements in this series is intended to be codified as law for Israel or the church.

Mt 19. Jesus points out that the Pharisees' concern with legalities misses the true issue: failure to achieve God's ideal. Mt 18 presents principles for healing hurts in intimate relationships. But the Pharisees were not concerned with hurts or with ideals. They cared only about legal technicalities. It is here that Jesus points out that divorce was permitted because human hearts are hard, not because God desires divorce. Divorce was an expression of God's mercy, not an affirmation of his ideal will.

Mk 10; Lk 16. These passages report the sayings of Jesus without a clear context like that provided by Matthew.

1 Co 7. Paul deals with questions raised by believers in Corinth. He begins by commending marriage as a way to meet valid needs of both husband and wife. However, he especially commends singleness, talking of it in terms of a special gift from God (v. 7).

Paul then moves on to deal with divorce. Some in Corinth mistakenly thought that Paul called on them to divorce unbelieving spouses. Paul explains: Christians are not to initiate divorce. Those who do separate (the word here means divorce and does not suggest our modern concept of legal separation) are to remain unmarried or to be reconciled to their spouse (7:10–14). Paul then moves on to explore a situation in which an unbelieving spouse is unwilling to live with the believer. Paul says, "If the unbeliever leaves, let him do so. A believing man or woman is not bound in such circumstances."

The critical question here is, How much difference does it make that the one who leaves is not a believer? Or is it the leaving—that is, abandonment of the marriage—that is the controlling circumstance? Since believers are to remain with unbelievers who are willing to live with them (7:13), it seems that the controlling circumstance is abandonment of the covenant relationship by one of the partners in the marriage.

It seems that a refusal to live as a married person, like the death of one partner (Ro 7:2–3), breaks the covenant bond and releases the willing partner to remarry.

5. Conclusions. It is clear that divorce is not God's best for his people. Those who are able to live in God's way within the marriage relationship will not divorce. But sin corrupts society and individuals—even believers. Some may be unable to keep the marriage covenant; others may be unwilling to. Recognizing the hardness of human hearts, Scripture provides for divorce as a last resort. It is clear from both Testaments that remarriage often follows divorce.

Jesus reaffirmed the ideal. He made it clear that remarriage involves at least technical adultery, and thus it is sin. But Jesus also suggested to his disciples that he was not establishing a higher rule of law (Mt 19:10–12).

There is no direct answer to the often-asked question concerning grounds for divorce. One passage, 1 Co 7, may suggest that only an abandonment of the marriage relationship releases a person to remarry. If that is true, the legal divorce and remarriage can follow only when one or both partners are unwilling to live together as spouses.

Divorce and remarriage are particularly sensitive issues today. Nothing should be done to encourage or justify divorce. Yet those who have suffered the agony of marital breakup should not be treated with a Pharisee-like condemnation. God has forgiveness for our sins and a mercy that can meet the needs of the divorced and make up for the sorrow involved in termination of a marriage.

The church must not legislate divorce or remarriage. We can only affirm the standards of Scripture, help those in difficulty learn to express Christ's forgiveness within marriage, and—should sin shatter a home—offer love and support to the sufferers.

DOCTRINE

The Greek word translated "doctrine" is *didaskaleia.* It means "teaching." It is found twenty-one times in the NT—

fifteen of them in the Pastoral Epistles. It seems most probable that this word indicates Christian doctrine, which is binding on the Christian community as faith's divinely communicated content.

DOMINION ▶ Rule/Dominion

DOUBLE

There are specialized biblical uses of the word "double." Under the OT's criminal justice system, a thief was to repay double what he stole, rather than to be placed in a prison at public expense (Ex 22:4–9).

The firstborn son must be acknowledged as a man's heir and be given a double share when the estate is divided (Dt 21:17). When Elisha begged the prophet Elijah, "Let me inherit a double portion of your spirit" (2 Ki 2:9), he was asking to be acknowledged as Elijah's successor and God's prophet in Israel. This request was honored. Not only did Elisha become Elijah's successor, but the OT records fourteen miracles of Elisha and only seven of Elijah.

The NT passage that declares that "the elders who direct the affairs of the church are well worthy of double honor, especially those whose work is preaching and teaching" (1 Ti 5:17) refers to respect and to payment. Some elders are supported by the church so they can be free to devote their working hours to the believing community.

When the NT speaks of being double-minded (Jas 1:8; 4:8), it uses the word *dipsychos* ("of two minds"). This word describes one who wavers uncertainly rather than making a commitment. The uncommitted person, holding back uncertainly, "should not think he will receive anything from the Lord" (1:7).

DOUBT

The NT does not commend doubt. "Doubt" in the NT is a technical religious term that looks specifically at relationship with God and his Word.

Several Greek words were commonly used in NT times to express our idea of doubt. One, *distazō*, is used twice and means "to waver uncertainly" (Mt 14:31; 28:17).

The distinctive biblical term is *diakrinō*. In ordinary speech it meant "to judge," "to evaluate," "to make a distinction." Although these meanings are also found in the NT (Ac 15:9; 1 Co 4:7; 11:29; 14:29; Jas 2:4), the word takes on a unique Christian meaning where it indicates doubt (Mt 21:21; Mk 11:23; Ac 10:20; 11:12; Ro 4:20; 14:23; Jas 1:6; Jude 22). Uniquely in the NT, *diakrinō* suggests uncertainty about something set forward as an object of faith. Rather than the quiet confidence that rests completely in God's Word and thus responds with an obedience capable of giving focus and direction to life, *diakrinō* suggests a defective faith—a faith that believes and yet cannot bring itself to trust.

This religious doubt is not expressed in some intellectual quest for logical certainty. It invades experience, hindering prayer (Mt 21:21; Jas 1:6) and trapping us in actions about which our consciences are unsure (Ro 14:22–23).

What is the antidote to the wavering faith the NT calls doubt? In Ro 4 Paul points to Abraham and describes the patriarch as being fully aware of his own advanced age and of Sarah's having gone far beyond menopause. The fact is clear: no child can possibly be conceived by these two. Yet God appears to them and promises that Abraham will father a multitude. Paul says of him, "Without weakening in his faith, he faced the fact that his body was as good as dead— since he was about a hundred years old— and that Sarah's womb was also dead. Yet he did not waver through unbelief regarding the promise of God . . . , being fully persuaded that God had power to do what he had promised" (Ro 4:19–21).

We need only to realize that whatever our circumstances, the overriding fact is the reality of God. He has power to do what he has promised. When we commit ourselves to the Lord and acknowledge him as the ultimate reality, we find an assurance that quiets every doubt and frees us to live obedient lives.

DRAGON

The Greek *drakōn* means "serpent" or "sea monster." The word occurs only in Revelation, where it is the dominant image representing Satan.

This image has biblical roots in the events of the Garden of Eden. But it also has roots in the mythology of the Greeks, the Babylonians, and the Egyptians, whose beliefs linked the *drakōn* with the demonic or the gods and with the struggle between chaos and order.

In Revelation the image suggests that Satan's evil character is finally unveiled as he openly uses his vast powers to energize the final struggle against God.

DREAM

The OT contains reports of different kinds of dreams (*ḥªlôm*). There are ordinary dreams (Job 7:14; Ecc 5:3), and there are dreams through which God revealed information. Nu 12 suggests that dreams may have been a primary mode by which the Lord spoke to his prophets: "When a prophet of the LORD is among you, I reveal myself to him in visions, I speak to him in dreams" (12:6). But receiving a revelatory dream did not make a person a prophet. The pagan Pharaoh of Egypt and Babylon's Nebuchadnezzar had dreams that were given to them by God. These dreams had to be interpreted, Pharaoh's by Joseph and Nebuchadnezzar's by Daniel.

The OT reports different kinds of revelatory dreams. At times God seemed to speak directly to an individual by means of a dream (Ge 20:3–7; Mt 1:20; 2:12–23). At other times, dreams feature symbolic representations of the divine message (Ge 40–41; Da 2). Such dreams required interpretation, and in each case God revealed the symbolic meaning to one of his people. The dream in Da 7 was a symbolic dream, but it was interpreted by an angel who appeared within the dream itself.

Yet, after the events associated with Jesus' birth, we read no more of revelatory dreams in the NT. Why?

Heb 1 suggests an answer. "In the past," the writer begins, "God spoke to our forefathers through the prophets at many times and in various ways, but in these last days he has spoken to us by his Son" (1:1–2). In Christ, ultimate revelation has been given. In the now-completed canon of the OT and NT, all the special revelation that God intends for humanity has been provided and preserved. The revelatory dream, conveying truths not before revealed, is no longer required.

Can dreams be a divine vehicle not of special revelation but of individual guidance? It is unwise to limit God and to say that he cannot or will not use dreams to guide us. At the same time, the silence of the NT about dreams suggests that we would not be wise to interpret our dreams as personal messages from the Lord. ♦ *Lead/Guide*

DRINKING

Several words for drinking appear in Hebrew and in Greek. Aside from references to "strong drink," the words normally are used in their ordinary, literal sense. ♦ *Drunkenness*

There are symbolic uses of the image of drinking in the OT. *Šāqâh*, indicating the giving of a drink, is used to picture the joy of fellowship with God (Ps 36:8) and the bitterness of his punishments (Ps. 80:5; Jer 8:14). Typically, the context makes any symbolism clear, as in Isa 22:13 where the other common Hebrew word for "drink," *šātâh*, is found in the sentence (quoted in 1 Co 15:32) " 'Let us eat and drink,' you say, 'for tomorrow we die!' "

In the NT the word "drink" is used in several ways. It is of course used in the literal sense, but, in addition, there are social implications in eating and drinking. To eat and drink with others suggests a close association, and this was something that upset the Pharisees when they saw that Jesus ate and drank with sinners (Mk 2:16; Lk 5:30–33). But Jesus' association with sinners did not imply his participation in the ways of sinners, nor did it imply the commitment of the sinners to Jesus (Lk 13:26–27). Close association was a part of Jesus' identity with the fallen human race, and it provided the opportunity for them to be exposed to Jesus and his teaching.

The NT also uses the image of drinking in a stronger symbolic sense. That use does indicate a participation in Christ and moves us into the realm of faith (Jn 6:53–55; 7:37; 1 Co 10:16–17; 11:23–26). To drink of Christ is to take him into our lives and by faith to take part in all that he is and all he has done for us.

DRIVE OUT ◗ Demons/Evil Spirits

DRUNKENNESS

Both the OT and the NT speak of drunkenness and of strong drink. The OT root is šāk̲ar, "to be intoxicated." The noun šēk̲ār indicates strong or intoxicating beverages. The strong drink of biblical times was not distilled liquor, as distilling was unknown. Instead, strong drink was any fermented drink made from grain (beer) or fruit.

The root is used almost sixty times in the OT. Only four or five of these references are favorable. Joseph's reunion with his brothers was marked by a party (Ge 43:34), and strong drink is recommended for those who are dying or in anguish (Pr 31:6). But "it is not for kings, O Lemuel—not for kings to drink wine, not for rulers to crave beer, lest they drink and forget what the law decrees, and deprive all the oppressed of their rights" (Pr 31:4–5). The images associated with drunkenness in the OT—such as reeling and staggering (Ps 107:27; Isa 19:14), wild spending and poverty (Dt 21:20; Pr 23:21)—suggest a loss of physical control and a loss of judgment. The words to Lemuel also suggest a loss of moral control. Thus, although drinking is not forbidden in the OT, drunkenness is unquestionably condemned.

The NT does not condemn drinking in moderation. ◗ Wine But drunkenness is viewed in the same negative way as in the OT. Drunkenness is associated with evil practices (1 Th 5:7) and mention of it is found in lists of sinful practices that believers are not to engage in (1 Co 5:11; 6:10; Ro 13:13; Gal 5:21; 1 Pe 4:3). Paul's best-known statement on drunkenness is "Do not get drunk on wine, which leads to debauchery. Instead, be filled with the Spirit" (Eph 5:18). Christians are to surrender control and judgment, not to alcohol, but to the Holy Spirit, who will teach us how to glorify God.

For many people the association of alcoholic beverages with drunkenness seems a decisive argument against all drinking. Whatever one's personal convictions about drinking in moderation, there is no doubt that drinking until one becomes drunk is not God's will for believers.

DUST

The Hebrew word 'āp̲ār means "dust" or "loose, dry earth." It is often used in its literal sense. But many of the 109 occurrences of this word in the OT have theological significance.

According to Genesis, man's physical body was made from dust (Ge 2:7), and at the time of death the body will return to dust (Ge 3:19). Thus dust is at times an image that stands for death (Ps 22:15; 30:9). Dust also represents human frailty and weakness, and we are told that God has compassion on those who fear him, "for he knows how we are formed, he remembers that we are dust" (Ps 103:14).

But human beings are more than dust. In the creative act, God not only formed the human body but also "breathed into his [man's] nostrils the breath of life, and man became a living being" (Ge 2:7). Human beings are unique among living creatures, for the life that God created and with which he endowed them is a reflection of his own image and likeness (Ge 1:26). The body may die, but our individual essence will never be dissolved. This is in part the significance of God's words to Satan at the fall: "You will eat dust all the days of your life" (Ge 3:14). Satan's hatred for human beings, who are living on the earth he claims as his own kingdom, is doomed to frustration. When death occurs, the body will return to dust (Ge 3:19), but the living personality will continue into eternity, forever beyond the limited powers of the Evil One. ◗ Life and Death

Other OT passages use the word "dust" figuratively to represent poverty and helplessness (1 Sa 2:8; Ps 113:7; 119:25).

The disciples were told to shake the dust off their feet if a community rejected the message they were charged by Jesus to communicate Mt 10:14; Mk 6:11; Lk 9:5; cf. Ac 13:51). This Jewish custom suggests complete abandonment. Those who choose not to receive Jesus' messengers must be abandoned to the fate they have chosen.

DUTY

OT references to duty (usually *mišmeret*) imply assignment: e.g., "The duty of the Levites was . . ." (1 Ch 23:28). The root (*šāmar*) means "to keep" or "to watch."

The OT also speaks of the "duty of a brother-in-law." Here a specific word, a verb form of "husband's brother," is found. In OT times, lineage and family were very important. If a man died without children, his brother had the duty of taking the dead man's wife in what was called a levirate marriage. The child of that union was considered the child of the dead brother and would carry on his line.

The idea of duty in the NT is more philosophical. It is expressed in a number of different words. ◗ *Should*

DWELL

The words in Hebrew and Greek all suggest being in a residence. They are most often used in the ordinary sense of dwelling (living) in a particular city or place. But the OT raises a theological question, which the NT answers in an exciting way.

The OT word *yāšab* means "to sit," "to remain," or "to dwell." It is found some 1090 times in the OT; when used of God, it usually indicates his residence in the heavens. As Solomon asks: "Will God really dwell on earth? The heavens, even the highest heaven, cannot contain you. How much less this temple I have built!" (1 Ki 8:27). The other Hebrew word translated "dwell" is *šākan*. This word occurs 129 times and suggests a permanent stay. It is used 43 times with God as the subject and emphasizes his faithfulness to his commitments. The tabernacle and the temple were constructed as divine dwelling places so that God's people might always approach him (Ex 25:8; 29:45–46; 2 Ch 6:1). Still, God announces, "I live [*šākan*] in a high and holy place, but also with him who is contrite and lowly in spirit" (Isa 57:15). It is in the NT that this last theme is developed. And in the NT the emphasis shifts from God dwelling *with* his people to his dwelling *in* them. Two Greek words are used in this special sense. *Enoikeō*, meaning "to take up residence," is used in this connection in four of its five occurrences in the NT (Ro 8:11; 2 Co 6:16; Col 3:16; 2 Ti 1:14). The NT tells us that God now settles down in the hearts of his people. It is no longer the OT temple, nor is it the modern church building, but it is the personality of the believer that is the residence filled with God's living presence.

But there is another word translated "dwell" in the NT: *katoikeō*. The word means "to establish permanent residence," implying a permanence that stands in contrast to the making of occasional visits. In the Gospels this word is used in its ordinary sense, as when it is said that one dwells in Nazareth (Mt 2:23) or Jerusalem (Lk 13:4). But in the Epistles the word has special theological significance. Through faith, Christ takes up permanent residence in our hearts (Eph 3:17). "In Christ all the fullness of the Deity lives [*katoikeō*] in bodily form, and you have been given fullness in Christ" (Col 2:9–10). The permanent, living presence of Jesus and his Spirit (Jas 4:5) is now established in the hearts of his people.

E

EAR

When we read "ear" in the OT, and in many NT passages, we should read from the perspective of the Hebrew people. To "hear" in a biblical sense meant not only to take in information but also to respond appropriately to it. Appeals to God to hear the cry of his people were prayers for help, not attempts to tell God something he did not know. When we say that a believer "hears" the Word of the Lord, it is tantamount to saying that he responds with faith and with obedience.

♦ Hear/Listen

In the world of the Bible, where hearing was of supreme importance, it was the ear (not the mind) that was viewed as the organ of response. So the Lord laments: "To whom can I speak and give warning? Who will listen to me? Their ears are closed so they cannot hear. The word of the LORD is offensive to them; they find no pleasure in it" (Jer 6:10). Likewise, Revelation's repeated "He who has an ear, let him hear" (Rev 2:7,11, 17,29; 3:6,13,22; 13:9) suggests that only one who is equipped with the spiritual organ needed to perceive God's voice will hear his message. And this warning teaches us that he who has that capacity must respond to the divine message.

In the Bible, then, the ear is represented as a person's capacity to respond. This view establishes the figurative and at times the symbolic meaning of "ear." God, who made the ear, has a living being's capacity to respond to the appeals of his people (Ps 94:9). But dumb idols have no ears for hearing (Ps 115:6; 135:17).

The symbolic significance of ears is seen in a special feature of OT law dealing with voluntary servitude. If a Jew were sold into service to a countryman, the law prescribed a limit on his service. He was to be released the seventh year and given funds to establish himself in society as a self-supporting individual (Dt 15:12–18). But the servant had an option. He might choose to stay in service because he loved his master and his family and considered himself well off with them. If he made this choice, the master was to take an awl and push it through the servant's ear lobe, into a door, and he would become that man's servant for life. Why this symbolic act? Because the ear is the organ by which orders are heard and with which choice of obedience is made. The pierced ear symbolizes the servant's choice to open his ear in lifelong obedience to that master (Ex 21:6).

In a real sense, we Christians are to be a people of pierced ears. Our commitment to Jesus is not made simply that we might enjoy the benefits of salvation. Our commitment acknowledges Christ as Lord. It is because Jesus is Lord that our spiritual ears are to be always open to him. Our obedience is to be the lifelong mark of our choice of Jesus as Savior and Lord.

EARTH/EARTHLY

The Hebrew word 'eres means "earth" or "land." It appears about 2,400 times in the OT. The Greek word, gē, has the same range of meanings as the OT word and is used 251 times. Often "earth" simply means the ground in which we plant crops. But it does have specialized meanings as well. Let us consider these meanings.

1. **Earth as an aspect of the created universe**
2. **Earth as a political unit**
3. **"Earthly"**

1. Earth as an aspect of the created universe. The Bible often uses the phrase "the heavens and the earth" to express our concept of "universe." The heavens and the earth are the handiwork of God. He called them into being and shaped each realm (Ge 1 ♦ *Create*). To affirm that God is "the God of heaven and the God of earth'.' (Ge 24:3) asserts the Lord's continuing control over the universe he has shaped. Scripture tells us that one day God will create "new heavens and a new earth" (Isa 65:17; cf. 66:22; Rev 21:1). In origin, in continuing dependence, and in ultimate disposition, the universe is the Lord's (Ps 24:1; 47:7; Isa 54:5).

Within the framework provided by this OT conviction, it is clear that earth is the portion of the universe that has been given to human beings. Our experience during our lifetimes is limited to the surface of our planet. Human beings were shaped from the dust of the earth, and our physical form returns to dust. But our destiny lies beyond. Our inheritance is not laid up on earth but is deposited in heaven (Mt 6:19).

In speaking of the earth the NT introduces words with a strong theological orientation, words that refine the concept of "earth." Earth is more than that part of creation committed to man; it now also involves warped social systems shaped by sinners. It is identified in the NT by the word *kosmos*. ♦ *World* There may be OT passages that hint at this aspect of life on our planet (e.g., Ge 6:11; Ps 58:11), but the Jewish scholars who translated the OT into Greek (the Septuagint) did not choose *kosmos* as a translation of 'eres.

What the OT emphasizes is that God's unfailing love is demonstrated on the earth (Ps 33:5) and that righteousness will be established there (Isa 42:4). Ulti-

mately all the earth will bow down to the Lord (Isa 66:23).

2. Earth as a political unit. The OT often uses the phrase "the land of" and then adds the name of a nation, such as Israel, Egypt, Assyria, often with theological implications. ♦ *Land*

3. "Earthly". The usual Greek word for "earthly" is *epigeios*. Literally it means "on the earth" but is to be understood as "of the earth." It is found seven times in the NT (Jn 3:12; 1 Co 15:40; 2 Co 5:1; Php 2:10; 3:19; Jas 3:15). In these and other occurrences the contrast is usually between that which has its origin in, or is characterized by, limitations imposed on this earthly sphere and that which flows from the heavenly realm infused by God and thus is pure in origin and character.

EAT

Eating and drinking were significant acts in the biblical world. Besides satisfying physical needs, they were symbolic of both friendship and of participation.

OT   1. **The Hebrew word and its meanings**
NT   2. **The Greek word**
      3. **Eating as friendship and participation**
      4. **Summary**

OT — 1. The Hebrew word and its meanings. The Hebrew word 'ākal means "to eat, consume, or devour." One of its major OT uses is to indicate times of hardship, during which resources and hope are consumed. ♦ *Consume* ♦ *Devour* It also has the common meaning of eating food.

In addition, eating is associated with theologically significant concepts. Ritually, the worshiper of OT times ate portions of some of the animals offered in sacrifice. Participation in such a ritual meal was limited to true believers. It was the mark of acceptance of, and acceptance by, the Lord. As God said of the Passover meal: "No foreigner is to eat of it. Any slave you have bought may eat of it after you have circumcised him, but a temporary resident and a hired worker may not eat of it" (Ex 12:43–44).

The significance of the ritual meal in the OT is seen in the psalmist's commentary on a generation that rejected the Lord: "They yoked themselves to the Baal of Peor and ate sacrifices offered to lifeless gods" (Ps 106:28). To participate in a worship or ritual meal was to yoke oneself either to idols or to the true God; i.e., to whomever the meal was dedicated.

In addition, Israel was given instructions concerning which mammals, birds, and fish might be eaten. Israel was limited to the flesh of "clean" animals. ◗ Clean and Unclean This did not have a dietary or health purpose but was a constant reminder to Israel that they were linked with Yahweh, and everything they did was to express their position as his special people.

The sense of association or fellowship that was expressed by eating affected interpersonal relationships in the biblical world. Those who shared a meal entered into a closer relationship with each other, and such a meal implied real mutual obligations. Against this background, Jesus warned those he taught during his earthly ministry: "You will say, 'We ate and drank with you, and you taught in our streets.' But he will reply, 'I don't know you or where you came from. Away from me, all you evildoers!' " (Lk 13:26–27).

It is not the social obligation imposed by a shared meal, but the commitment symbolized by the ritual meal that stands for saving faith and for participation in all that Jesus brings to humanity.

The meaning of full participation is emphasized in other contexts. One who takes part in wickedness will be judged: he will "eat the bread of wickedness" (Pr 4:17; cf. 1:31; Jer 9:15; 23:15). On the other hand, one can participate in the rewarding aspects of work: "You will eat of the fruit of your labor" (Ps 128:2).

NT 2. The Greek word — The NT word for eating is esthiō. Although OT ritual requirements for eating clean animals are done away with in the NT, the link between food and participation is not. Partaking in the Lord's Supper continues as a symbolic affirmation of commitment to Jesus. And there is no room for believers to take part in a feast offered in honor of an idol (1 Co 10:14–22).

3. Eating as friendship and participation. The frequent meals shared by members of the early church (Ac 2:46; 11:3; 1 Co 5:11; 11:33) were indications of the deep fellowship that developed in the believing community. They were also symbolic of the commitment of believers to one another and to the Lord.

4. Summary. Eating meets a basic need of all living creatures. But eating also meets other needs. In human society, eating is an occasion for fellowship, and shared meals carry connotations of social obligation. Eating is also linked with worship in the OT. The one who eats of a sacrificial animal affirms his being yoked to God. In the OT, only God's people were permitted to take part in ritual meals. And no true believer would take part in a ritual meal provided in honor of an idol.

In the NT the Lord's Supper is a worship occasion. Only those who belong to Jesus share in it, for eating is an affirmation by the true believer of his or her faith commitment to Jesus as Savior and Lord.

EFFORT

Salvation, the Scriptures insist, "does not, therefore, depend on man's desire or effort, but on God's mercy" (Ro 9:16). Good works give no access to relationship with God. ◗ Works

Yet in a number of places the NIV repeats the phrase "make every effort" (Lk 13:24; Ro 14:19; Eph 4:3; Heb 4:11; 12:14; 2 Pe 1:5; 3:14). This appeal is made despite the fact that even spiritual development cannot be attained simply by human effort (Gal 3:3).

Part of the solution to the apparent dilemma is found in the Greek words translated "make every effort." In Lk 13:24 the writer takes an image from the sports stadium: agōnizomai means to expend all one's energy to reach a significant goal. In the Epistles there are three different words translated "effort." *Diōkō* is a call to actively pursue some course. It is variously translated "hurry," "run," and "press on." We are to be actively engaged in activities of the Christian faith; for example, doing those things that lead to unity (Ro 14:19) and to interpersonal peace (Heb 12:14).

Spoudē (noun) and *spoudazō* (verb) suggest zealous concentration and diligent effort. We Christians are to be zealous to mature in our character (2 Pe 1:5) and in those qualities that mark godliness (cf. 1 Th 2:17; Heb 4:11; 2 Pe 1:15; 3:14).

The concept of effort, whatever the term used, is important. Christian living is no passive abandonment of personal responsibility. The believer realizes that he must depend on God for all. But true dependence energizes. Faith is expressed as we accept responsibility and channel our energies in ways directed by God's Word. To simply do nothing is not an expression of faith. If we have faith, we believe so fully that we are released to expend every effort in joyful obedience.

ELDERS

The nature of leadership in the church is a critical issue in any age. ◆ *Leadership* The organizational structures used by the churches today and in history reflect different understandings of leadership and different understandings of the words Scripture uses to identify leaders. "Elder" is one of the critical terms. It has implications for our understanding of the local church and how the church should function today.

OT 1. The elders of the OT
NT 2. The Greek word in its context
3. The elders of the Gospels
4. Elders in the Christian community
5. The elders of Revelation
6. Conclusions

OT — 1. The elders of the OT. The adjective *zāqēn* is from a verb that means "to be or to become old." *Zāqēn* is the OT word for elder, someone of advanced age and who, in that culture, thus deserved

respect and would be valued as a counselor. ◆ *Age (Old Age)*

But *zāqēn* is also a technical term that designated persons who were members of local or national ruling bodies in Israel. Although there is no biblical statement of age requirements or of other qualifications, it is clear that elders had a significant judicial and governing role throughout Israel's history. Israel had elders when Moses returned to Egypt to lead the enslaved people to freedom (Ex 3:16). The law speaks of local elders (Dt 19:12); they functioned during the Exodus period (Ex 24:14; Lev 4:15), at the conquest of Canaan (Jos 8:33), in the dark days of the judges (Ru 4:2), and during the monarchy (1 Sa 8:4; 2 Sa 19:11; 1 Ki 21:8). There were elders during the Babylonian captivity (Jer 29:1) and after Israel's return to Palestine (Ezr 10:8), and they continued to play a role in local and national government during Jesus' days on earth (see 3, below).

No complete picture of the role of the elder can be drawn from Scripture. And that role undoubtedly changed with historical conditions. Yet it is clear that local elders, who assembled at the city gates to do their business in public (Dt 21:19; 22:15), handled both civil matters (Dt 22:15; Ru 4:9,11) and criminal cases (Dt 19:12; 21:1–9; Jos 20:4).

Two things about the early elder system are worth nothing. First, supervision of the life of the community was placed in the hands of a group of elders, not in the hands of a single elder. The wisdom of several rather than of one was considered necessary for those matters that an elder team had to deal with. Second, the elder system settled matters within the community. The elders were members of the community; their judgments would flow not only from knowledge of law and custom but also from intimate knowledge of the persons who might stand before them. This community aspect of the elder system stands in contrast to modern bureaucracy, which tends to create increasing distance between individuals and those who decide civil or criminal issues that might affect them.

NT — 2. The Greek word in its context. The word "elder" translates a word group that originally also described older persons. Then "elder" came to indicate the rank and importance typically gained by older persons. Older men with seniority served as ambassadors to other states and as advisors within the Greek political community. In the Greek world as among God's OT people, the particular duties or privileges associated with eldership shifted with changes in culture. But there was apparently a less significant role for elders in the pagan world.

3. The elders of the Gospels. The elders spoken of in the Gospels and in the early and late chapters of Acts were apparently lay members of the council responsible for administering Jewish law. This council of seventy was located in Jerusalem but had authority over all Jews wherever they might live, in or out of Judea. ♦ *Counsel/Advice*

4. Elders in the Christian community. Acts quickly picks up the term "elder" (*presbyteros*) and applies it to leaders in the Christian church. Missionaries appointed elders in relatively new Christian communities (Ac 14:23; Tit 1:5). The elders in Jerusalem functioned with the apostles as a council to consider how to respond to various crises that faced the young church (Ac 15:2–23). Clearly, the elders performed an important function, leading the local body as well as the wider Christian community.

The role of the biblical elder is indistinct to us, but a number of features are clear. These men were spiritual leaders of a congregation and of the wider community. They functioned in teams rather than individually in directing the affairs of a local community. They were carefully selected to meet specific moral and personal criteria.

Personal and moral requirements. Paul's letters to Timothy and Titus outline personal requirements for leadership in the church (1 Ti 3, "overseer"; Tit 1, "elders"). In each passage, demonstrated Christian character is emphasized. Spiritual leaders are to provide living examples of the truths they teach. Leaders are to be models of that Christlikeness to which all believers are called.

Appointment of elders. The appointment of elders is mentioned in both Acts and Titus. The term "appoint" need not imply apostolic selection of elders; but it does indicate official apostolic recognition and installation. ♦ *Appoint/Appointed* Apparently elders were appointed only on subsequent visits of the missionaries to congregations they had established (Ac 14:21–23; Tit 1:5). It was necessary for a congregation to exist for some time before those whose growth toward maturity and whose gifts could be recognized by the local community could properly be appointed as elders. The religious con man might temporarily deceive with smooth words. But within a community that shared life intimately, time would reveal true character and motivations.

Tasks of elders. Scripture gives no well-defined job description for elders. We do know that elders functioned within local congregations and assembled with other elders to consider matters that affected Christians everywhere. The word "elder" probably suggests age, and certainly indicates spiritual maturity.

The role of elder requires distinctive spiritual gifts, as well as developed Christian character. After all, every one of God's people is called to spiritual maturity. But not every mature believer is called to serve as an elder.

One critical ministry of elders is mentioned in 1 Ti 5:17: "The elders who direct the affairs of the church are well worthy of double honor, especially those whose work is preaching and teaching." Some elders preached and taught. But all "directed the affairs of the church." A hint about this directing role is found in the concept of overseer (*episkopos*). By the way it was used in the secular society, this word, often translated "bishop," suggests both administrative and judicial functions. The same meaning seems applicable to the church, particularly when the concept is linked by Peter with the image of shepherding (1 Pe 2:25).

Although we have no detailed description of the tasks of an elder, the hints found in the NT are suggestive. The church is a body, with its own unique organic kind of life. ♦ **Church** Gifts of overseeing are needed to understand and to guard those processes and relationships that permit the local community to function in an organic way. Thus, being an elder calls for insight into the nature of the church and an understanding of how the body functions and the way the gift of administration operates. ♦ **Leadership** ♦ **Minister/Ministry**

5. The elders of Revelation. The Book of Revelation draws back the veil between the natural and the supernatural universe. It mentions twenty-four elders gathered around the throne of God (Rev 4:4,10; 5:8; 11:16; 19:4). The origin of these elders is never defined. It is most likely, however, that they represent the founding fathers of both major dispensations: the heads of the twelve tribes of Israel and the twelve apostles of Jesus.

6. Conclusions. It is apparent that several aspects of governing or leadership by elders has been maintained throughout the ages and carried into the NT era. The significant characteristics of elder leadership that remain constant seem to be the following:

Mature members of the local community, whose age and character have won respect, were recognized as elders.

Elder-style leadership was not exercised by individuals but entrusted to groups of men who served as a team in overseeing community life.

Elders of the church were drawn from the local community and were required to have a character that merited respect. Elders in the church also functioned in teams: one-man oversight is not biblical, though gifted individuals may make significant contributions to the life of a local congregation.

While the specific tasks entrusted to elders remain undefined, the Bible's teaching on the function of leadership within the body of Christ provides clues not only to the elder role but also to the gifts required for effective team leadership.

No passage in either the OT or the NT suggests that women have historically functioned as elders. ♦ **Women in the Church**

Whatever we may call our local church leaders and whatever form of government our tradition may involve, harmony with Scripture suggests that (1) there should be a team (2) drawn from the local congregation (3) that functions to guard the processes that make for a healthy, spiritually growing local expression of the body of Christ.

ELECTION ♦ *Choice/Chosen*

EMPTY

A number of Hebrew words are translated "empty." In most cases, the meaning is both literal and clear. There are a few references that have theological significance.

Ge 1:2 reads, "Now the earth was formless and empty." The word "empty" is *bōhû*, which appears only three times in the OT and is always paired with *tōhû*. Together these words portray the chaos that marked the universe before God created the present world order. Both Isaiah and Jeremiah look back on this early state and draw on that image to communicate the devastation that accompanies divine judgment. Jeremiah writes: "I looked at the earth, and it was formless and empty; and at the heavens, and their light was gone. . . . I looked, and there were no people; every bird in the sky had flown away. I looked, and the fruitful land was a desert; all its towns lay in ruins before the LORD, before his fierce anger" (Jer 4:23–26; cf. Isa 34:11).

Another word is found in Isa 55:11. The Lord says that his word "will not return to [him] empty." The word here is the adverb *rêqām*, from *rûq*, "to make empty." *Rêqām* (sixteen times in the OT) means "vainly" or "emptily" and has the sense of "unsuccessfully." As waters nourish the earth "so that it yields seed for the sower and bread for the eater"

(v. 10), so God's Word will accomplish what he desires. And God has announced that desire. It is his intention for his people to "go out in joy and be led forth in peace" (v. 12).

Occurrences of the word "empty" in the NT are translations of the *kenos* word group. That which is empty is without significant content. Even more, it is often something that is ethically and morally futile. Empty words may lead some astray (Eph 5:6; 2 Pe 2:18), but God's Word fills and enriches our lives.

ENABLE ◆ *Ability/Able*

ENCOURAGE

The Hebrew words translated "encourage" mean "to strengthen." The Greek words are somewhat more complex. *Euthymos,* found only in Ac 27:36, means "to be of good cheer" or "to cheer up." *Symparakaleomai* is found only in Ro 1:12 and means "to encourage together." *Paramytheomai* occurs four times (Jn 11:19,31; 1 Th 2:11; 5:14) and conveys a strong sense of comfort or consolation.

The basic NT words are *parakaleō* (verb) and *paraklēsis* (noun). This word group appears over a hundred times in the NT and carries three different meanings: *parakaleō* can mean (1) "to summon, invite, or ask," (2) "to exhort or encourage," and (3) "to comfort."

Traditionally "encourage" is linked with comfort rather than with exhortation. But the NIV particularly tends to use the word "encourage" where older versions read "exhort" (except in Lk 3:18; 1 Ti 5:1; Heb 13:22). In those passages where the context suggests that *parakaleō* denotes comfort or consolation, the word that is usually used is "comfort." ◆ *Comfort*

But what does "encourage" mean? Encouragement strengthens and calls forth renewed commitment. Typically believers are encouraged to some godly course of action. Many were encouraged by Paul's chains to "speak the word of God more courageously and fearlessly" (Php 1:14). The apostle encouraged believers in Thessalonica to "walk worthy of God" (1 Th 2:12). God's grace and love are intended, he told them, to "encourage your hearts and strengthen you in every good deed and word" (2 Th 2:17).

There is a subjective aspect to encouragement. The purpose of encouragement is that we may be strengthened for fresh faith and obedience.

How beautiful, then, is the gift of encouraging (Ro 12:8). Those with this spiritual gift are able to strengthen others, enabling them to win fresh victories in their Christian lives.

END

Like many other common words, "end" reveals much about the view of the universe shared by users of a language.

OT 1. The OT concept of ending
NT 2. The NT concept of ending
   3. Significant NT verses

OT — 1. The OT concept of ending. A number of different Hebrew words are translated "end" or "ends." The most frequent specific words are derivatives of *qāṣâh,* "to cut off." The underlying concept is that of extremity: the point at which a thing is cut off. *Kālâh* stresses the completion of a process. Here too the idea of extremity is implicit: a process has gone on as long as it could.

What is particularly significant is that this view of ending is applied not only to distance ("the ends of the earth," Dt 33:17) and to the human life span ("show me, O LORD, my life's end," Ps 39:4) but also to time itself. The universe in which we find ourselves has experienced a beginning and will come to an end. The processes of life and the processes imbedded as natural law within inanimate matter stretch from the past into the future. But these processes are not eternal. Each extremity—beginning and end—is an essential aspect of the creation.

We cannot understand ourselves, or reality, without the perspective that focuses our attention on one who stands beyond the material universe and controls not only present processes but also the beginning and the end.

2. The NT concept of ending. The Greek word group (*teleō* [verb], *telos* [noun]) has two basic emphases. The primary concept of "end" is that of achievement of an intended goal. Particularly in eschatological passages the NT picks up the thought of process implicit in the OT. But the NT draws our attention to the conclusion of the process. That end is an extremity, but it is an extremity infused by purpose. Nothing is random; nothing is purposeless. When the end comes, it will bring the achievement of all of God's purposes. The end will be marked by the consummation of God's plans. ▶ *Age/Ages*

The other concept implicit in the Greek words indicating "end" draws our attention to persons or to things that have reached an intended goal. In a limited but real sense, achieving a goal means that a thing or person is completed, or perfect. Thus "perfect" in the NT does not suggest sinlessness or flawlessness; rather, it is a mature stage of development in which one's potentials are achieved. ▶ *Perfect*

3. Significant NT verses. There are several "ends" in the NT. The NT often speaks of the "end of the age." ▶ *Age/Ages*

In another connection, Ro 10:4 says that "Christ is the end of the law so that there may be righteousness for everyone who believes." The passage may be understood in one of two complementary ways. The law has come to an end in Christ because he has superceded it. Law no longer has a function in relationship to righteousness. ▶ *Law* Or it may be that Christ is the logical end of the law. Law unveiled sin in such a way that human beings were forced to turn to Jesus to obtain righteousness.

A beautiful promise is found in 1 Co 1:8. This universe is moving toward God's intended end. Even now we may be near history's final extremity. Yet we still struggle on within the process. But as we struggle, we are comforted. We "eagerly wait for our Lord Jesus Christ to be revealed" (1 Co 1:7), sure that "he will keep [us] strong to the end, so that [we] will be blameless on the day of our Lord Jesus Christ" (v. 8).

ENDURE/ENDURANCE

A number of Hebrew and Greek words are translated "endure" or "endurance." The NT terms especially suggest patient waiting, but they do not imply passivity. Inspired by hope (1 Th 1:3), the believer finds an inner strength that enables one to hold up under persecutions and hardship (2 Ti 2:3; 3:10). Although it is God who gives endurance (Ro 15:5), patient endurance remains one of the virtues by which Christian character can be measured (2 Co 1:6; 1 Ti 6:11; 2 Ti 3:10; Tit 2:2). ▶ *Patience*

ENEMY

The OT promises the defeat of the enemies of God's people. The NT instructs us to leave vengeance to God and shows us instead how to win a unique victory over those who are our enemies and the Lord's.

OT 1. The Hebrew words and their context
NT 2. The Greek word for "enemy"
    3. The origins of antagonism
    4. Treatment accorded to enemies

OT — 1. The Hebrew words and their context. There are a number of words in Hebrew that suggest the idea of enemy or adversary.

The word '*āyab* means "to be an enemy," and the derived word '*êbâh* means "enmity, hatred." These words imply active hostility that issues in angry, harmful acts.

Sārar means "to show hostility toward," and *şār* indicates an adversary or enemy. This word group tends to emphasize hostile actions.

Sānē' emphasizes an emotional attitude and indicates strong antagonism and opposition. ▶ *Hate/Hatred*

All these words are used in the OT to speak of relationships between individuals and the hostility of the unbelieving to God. But they are primarily used in the OT to describe relations between Israel and other peoples. Biblical Israel was surrounded by hostile nations, much as is modern Israel. But biblical Israel had a covenant relationship with God. ▶ *Covenant* God chose Israel, gave them the land, and made promises to them through the patriarchs. In the law, God committed himself to provide victory over Israel's enemies—when Israel was obedient (e.g., Lev 26:7–17; Dt 1:42). Thus when the OT speaks of enemies, it typically views them in a theological rather than a political context. The enemies of Israel are God's enemies, and he is known through his rescue of his people (Nu 10:9; 1 Ch 17:10). But if Israel is disobedient and unresponsive, God may use those enemies to discipline his people. ▶ *Discipline*

It is at history's end that the OT shows God dealing finally and decisively with all his enemies. The OT portrays hostile nations gathered to battle against Israel and her God. In the judgments the enemies among Israel would be destroyed, but pagan enemies would be totally crushed.

The prophets describe the final judgments of the end time very graphically; we can almost hear and see the terrors as Isaiah cries, "Hear that uproar from the city, hear that noise from the temple! It is the sound of the LORD repaying his enemies all they deserve" (66:6).

NT — 2. The Greek word for "enemy". The word translated "enemy" in the NT is *echthros*. *Echthra* is translated "hostility" and "hatred." These words describe that extreme negative attitude that is the opposite of love and friendship. The NT views this attitude as the source from which hostile acts flow. It is the inner source rather than the acts themselves that are focused on.

Indeed, the NT takes us beyond national rivalries. It probes for the source of hostilities in the individual and in the race. In the process, the NT unveils God's unique way of dealing with *echthros* during this age of grace.

3. The origins of antagonism. The Bible locates the origin of hostility in sin. Human beings have been twisted and our original form distorted. We were created to love God and others. But sin's warping power has distorted this natural order of interpersonal relationships. Sin has also created hostility to God. We have become rebels in thought and action. "We were God's enemies," Paul affirms (Ro 5:10), and he develops this thought in other passages. "The sinful mind is hostile to God. It does not submit to God. It does not submit to God's law, nor can it do so" (Ro 8:7). Hostility spilled over into every human relationship (Eph 2:14–16), for this was the fate of sinful humanity, as Paul wrote to the Colossians, "You were alienated from God and were enemies in your minds because of your evil behavior" (Col 1:21). Selfishness displaced love, leading to quarrels, to tensions, and to wars (Jas 4:1–3).

So the Bible teaches that hostility toward others, and the resultant interpersonal and international tragedies, have their origin in sin. Sin has distorted humanity and created hostility toward God and toward others.

4. Treatment accorded to enemies. The NT joins the OT in warning of final judgment. "God is just," suffering saints are reminded, "he will pay back trouble to those who trouble you and give relief to you who are troubled." But "this will happen when the Lord Jesus is revealed from heaven." God's judgment is reserved until that time (2 Th 1:6–7).

Until then God has chosen to go with a radical solution to hostility. He will deal directly with sin, and by changing us within he transforms hostile people into friends. "While we were still sinners, Christ died for us. . . . When we were God's enemies, we were reconciled to him through the death of his son" (Ro 5:8–10). God has acted in Christ to transform his enemies into his friends. ▶ *Reconcile*

During this age in which grace rules, anyone can respond to the offer of salvation in Jesus. Anyone can experience an inner transformation that frees his or her heart from hostility and replaces hostility with love. *Echthra* is an expression of man's sinful nature (Gal 5:19–21). But God's Spirit produces an overcoming love, patience, and kindness (Gal 5:22–23).

God's approach to the transformation of enemies into friends is to be copied by Jesus' followers. In Christ's days on earth the popular understanding of "love your neighbor" included the corollary "hate your enemy" (Mt 5:43). Jesus corrected this notion, which was never taught in the OT (OT believers were, in fact, advised not to be glad when their enemies suffered misfortunes [Pr 24:17]). Jesus taught, "Love your enemies and pray for those who persecute you, that you may be sons of your Father in heaven. He causes his sun to rise on the evil and the good, and sends rain on the righteous and the unrighteous" (vv. 44–45).

God does not allow the antagonism of a hostile humanity to turn him from his chosen course of love. If you and I are to bear the family resemblance as children of God, we must model our interpersonal relationship on the example his actions provide. We must not respond to hostility with hostility, but instead we must respond with love.

When we respond to our enemies with love, we become partners in God's radical solution to hostility and hatred. Our love communicates his, and we become agents of reconciliation, introducing our enemies to the transforming power of God.

ENVY

The green-eyed monster is familiar to us all. *Phthonos* is that bitter feeling roused by another's possession of what we want but do not have, whether material possession, popularity, or success. The verb, *phthoneō*, occurs only once in the NT (Gal. 5:26). The noun occurs nine times (Mt 27:18; Mk 15:10; Ro 1:29; Gal 5:21; Php 1:15; 1 Ti 6:4; Tit 3:3; Jas 4:5; 1 Pe 2:1), most often on lists of those vices that emerge from sinful human nature. We all have reason to know

the truth of the Scripture's judgment, "The [human] spirit he caused to live in us tends toward envy." It is wonderful—and necessary—that God "gives us more grace" (Jas 4:5–6).

EPHOD

The ephod was a complex vest worn by the OT high priest. It featured twelve gems that represented Israel's twelve tribes. It also contained the Urim and Thummim, used at times to determine God's will by a process that we do not understand but that may have involved casting lots. Because of its role in seeking God's guidance the ephod was particularly valued.

EQUAL

The Greek words *isos*, "equal" and *isotēs*, "equality," appear seldom in the NT. Yet they represent extremely important concepts that were woven into Greek thought.

At first, equality was simply a numerical concept. But it developed into a philosophical and political concept. The Greeks came to believe that all citizens should enjoy equal standing in society and be treated impartially under the law. The NT teaching that believers are fellow citizens of heaven and are members of a body in which there is an essential unity despite differences in function (1 Co 12:4–26) must have appealed to the Greek churches.

Two passages that use the concept of equality bear on the issue of who Jesus is. John 5 reports Jesus' defense of his miracles. He identified them as the work of his Father. The Jews understood his meaning. Jesus was claiming equality of will and nature with God. "For this reason the Jews tried all the harder to kill him; not only was he breaking the Sabbath, but he was even calling God his own Father, making himself equal with God" (5:18; cf. Jn 8:48–59).

Php 2:6 views the Incarnation in relation to prehistory. It reveals Christ Jesus as "being in very nature God" and becoming a human being. It explains that he "did not consider equality with God something to be grasped." In becoming a human being, Jesus did not surrender his nature as God, but he did abandon the glory, the rights, and the worship that are the prerogatives of the Lord alone.

ERROR

The Hebrew words translated "error" suggest inadvertent sins and wandering. The NT concept is expressed in the Greek word *planē*, derived from a root that also means "to wander." The biblical image is of a person who has lost his way and is deluded or deceived about reality.

James puts Scripture's view of truth and error in perspective in the last verses of his letter: "My brothers, if one of you should wander from the truth and someone should bring him back, remember this: Whoever turns a sinner from the error of his way will save him from death and cover over a multitude of sins" (Jas 5:19–20).

ESCAPE ♦ Remnant/Survivors

ESTABLISH

The concept "establish" is significant because of its associations. In the OT the covenants are described as established by God (e.g., Ge 6:18; 9:9,11; 17:7; Eze 16:60–63). David's throne is established "forever" (1 Ch 17:12; Ps 89:29). God's throne (Ps 9:7; 93:2; 103:19), his faithfulness (Ps 89:2), and even the earth are spoken of as having been established by God (Ps 78:69; 93:1; 96:10; 119:90).

Yet the OT has no single word to communicate the idea of establishing. Instead, a number of ordinary terms are translated "establish" or "established" because this meaning is suggested by the context. What is the root meaning of these Hebrew words? Two of them mean "to stand, or take one's stand." Another means "to be firm"; yet another means "to give." Included also are words that mean "to abide," "to plant," and "to confirm, or support."

What is established has been given by God, and because of him it stands firm and certain.

A number of different Greek words are found where the NT reads "establish." Their special meanings give us insight into several NT verses.

Ro 13:1 teaches that human authorities have been "established" (*tassō,* "ordered, arranged") by God (Ro 13:1).

Where the NASB says that we through faith establish the law (Ro 3:31), the Greek has *histēmi,* "to make valid." Christ's death puts law into correct perspective. Law is not, as the Jewish people thought, a way of salvation. The law is valid only as a warning, engraved in stone, reminding humanity of the need for faith.

The Christian community is rooted in and founded on (*themelioō*) love (Eph 3:17; Col 1:23). Believers are to remain firmly fastened (*stērizō*) to the truth that God has given (e.g., 2 Pe 1:12).

ETERNAL

The Greek word for "eternal" is *aiōnios.* Its roots and the OT concept form the background for the NT teaching involving this word. ♦ *Age/Ages* ♦ *Always*

In the NT, "eternal" and "eternity" come into focus. Essentially, the eternal is that which is not limited by time. The eternal has no beginning and no end but stands outside of and beyond time.

God is like this. His nature (Ro 1:20) and his purposes (Eph 3:11) are timeless, for he created the material universe and set in motion the processes by which time is measured.

Paul points out that everything that can be seen is temporary. It is subject to change within the flow of time's passing stream. But there are realities that exist outside of and uncorrupted by time— realities not perceived through the senses. "For what is seen is temporary, but what is unseen is eternal" (2 Co 4:18).

The Christian makes a commitment to act on the basis of the conviction that what cannot be seen has far greater reality than the things that can be seen.

Thus, we live as citizens of an eternal kingdom (2 Pe 1:11). We accept by faith an eternal life (Mt 25:46), won in an eternal redemption (Heb 9:12). We are sure that because of Jesus we are no longer in danger of going to hell.

Faith, hearing God's Word announce unseen but eternal realities, believes.

EVANGELIST

The Greek word is *euangelistēs.* It means "one who brings good news," i.e., the gospel. ♦ *Gospel* The word appears only in Ac 21:8 (which identifies Philip as an evangelist), Eph 4:11 (which views evangelists as gifted individuals given to the church), and 2 Ti 4:5 (where Timothy is told to "do the work of an evangelist").

It is likely that the person called to be an evangelist carried the gospel to new regions as a missionary. ♦ *Apostle*

EVER/EVERLASTING ♦ *Always*

EVIL

Philosophers debate the origin and nature of evil. How can evil exist with good in the universe? The Bible takes a different approach. Scripture turns us from the speculative to observe the character of evil and its tragic impact on humanity. Both the OT and the NT make important contributions to our understanding. And the NT in particular offers a unique hope.

OT 1. The Hebrew words
    2. The nature of evil
    3. The tragic consequences of evil
    4. God and evil
NT 5. The Greek words
    6. *Kakos:* evil and a damaged humanity
    7. *Ponēros:* evil and a hostile humanity
    8. The evil one
    9. The divine solution to evil
    10. Summary

OT — 1. The Hebrew words. A single family of Hebrew words focuses the OT concept of evil. *Rā'a'* is the verb, which means "to be evil, or bad," or more often, "to act wickedly," "to do harm." The masculine noun *ra'* means "evil," or "bad." The feminine noun *rā'âh* means "evil," "misery," or "distress" and includes every kind of calamity and wickedness. Other words in the family are *rŏa'*, "badness, evil"; *rešaʻ*, "wickedness, evil"; and *rāšāʻ*, "wicked, criminal."

These words are used throughout the OT. They focus on two aspects of evil. Morally, they identify actions that violate God's intentions for human beings. The words are also used to describe the consequences of doing evil; the tragedy, distress, and physical and emotional harm that come as a result of wrong moral choices are, like the choices themselves, labeled evil.

The OT does not explore the great philosophical or theological questions raised by those who are intrigued with the problem of evil. Instead it is bluntly practical. Evil is something that is expressed in a person's relationship with God and with other human beings. Evil is what one does when he or she chooses a course of action that is wrong because it violates God's intentions for us. And evil also encompasses all the tragic effects of such choices.

If we wish to explore the origins of evil, we must look at the OT's doctrine of sin. ♦ *Sin* When we examine evil, we are forced to focus on the implications of the choices we human beings must make daily.

2. The nature of evil. If we look into the OT to determine the nature of evil, we find an answer unexpected by the philosophers. There is no talk here of evil either as a lack or as inherent in the gap between creature and Creator. There is no hint of the modern notion that good and evil are simply matters of personal preference; that is, that something can be good for me but evil for you. Instead of relativism, the OT observes that "there is a way that seems right to a man, but in the end it leads to death" (Pr 14:12). Only God is capable of making truly moral judgments. Thus the OT defines wrong actions as that which is evil "in the eyes of the LORD" (e.g., Nu 32:13; Jdg 2:11; 1 Ki 15:26; cf. Dt 4:25; 2 Sa 3:39). It is God's evaluation of good and evil that the OT calls you and me to deal with.

Because God is the moral measure of all things, an objective revelation of morality is essential. Thus Moses completes his review of OT law with these words: "See, I set before you today life and prosperity [*tôb*, "good"], death and destruction [*ra'*, "evil"]" (Dt 30:15). God's written Word communicates all we need in order to develop a moral sensitivity that will enable us to know what is good and what is evil.

Because Scripture does reveal God's perspective, Isaiah can validly warn, "Woe to those who call evil good and good evil, who put darkness for light and light for darkness, who put bitter for sweet and sweet for bitter" (Isa 5:20). What is moral evil? Moral evil is that which God regards as wrong. God, the Creator and the Judge, has the right and obligation to make this determination. We creatures have the obligation to understand his standards—and to choose them.

We are not to legislate right and wrong. We are simply to choose what God says is right, and do it (cf. Dt 4:5–9; 39–40; 7:12–15).

The simplicity of the OT portrait of moral evil is reflected in the OT's view of evildoers. The OT does describe "evil men" (e.g., Job 16:11; "man" in Ps 10:15). But this should be understood not so much as a theological statement but rather as a descriptive one. Evil men are evil because they are evildoers: it is their choice of evil that leads God to identify them as evil.

Moses might have wondered in amazement: "How prone these people are to evil!" (Ex 32:22). But Moses did not ask why.

Thus evil in the OT remains an objective issue. Evil is located in human choices to "do evil," an expression that occurs over and over in the OT. It may be that a person chooses evil because he or she is evil. Or it may be that the choice is caused by one's upbringing, or by a failure of the society. But on such questions the OT is relatively silent. Whatever the root, the issue remains one of choice. An individual chooses to do either good or evil. ♦ *Account/Accountable*

3. The tragic consequences of evil. A look through an English concordance might lead one to believe that the OT uses "evil" only in the sense of moral choice. This is because the translators of the NIV and the NASB chose other words to express the second major meaning of the *ra'* word group. That meaning expresses the consequences of evil choices and is intended to drive home the fact that evil choices ultimately bring evil results.

This second major meaning of *ra'*, "evil," in the OT is expressed in the NIV and the NASB in words such as "harm," "distress," "disaster," "troubles," and a number of similar terms. The extent to which the OT explores this aspect of evil is illustrated by the following list of passages in which the adjective *ra'* carries the meaning of trouble or harm: Ge 19:19; 26:29; 31:29,52; 47:9; 50:15,17,20; Ex 5:19; Nu 11:15; 35:23; Dt 7:15; 29:21; 31:17,21,29; 32:23; Jos 23:15; Jdg 2:15; 20:34,41; 1 Sa 10:19; 20:7,9,13; 24:9,17; 25:17,21; 2 Sa 12:11,18; 17:14; 18:32; 19:7; 24:16; 1 Ki 5:4; 9:9; 11:25; 14:10; 20:7; 21:21,29; 22:8,18; 2 Ki 8:12; 14:10; 21:12; 22:16; 2 Ch 7:22; 18:7,17,22; 20:9; 21:19; 25:19; Ne 1:3; Job 2:11; 6:2; 13:18,27; Ps 10:6; 15:3; 21:11; 27:5; 28:3; 34:19,21; 35:26; 37:19; 38:12; 40:12; 41:1,7; 49:5; 54:5; 70:2; 71:13,20,24; 88:3; 90:15; 91:10; 94:13; 107:26,39; 121:7; 140:11; 144:10; Pr 3:30; 12:21; 13:21; 15:15; 16:4,30; 19:23; 22:3; 27:12; 28:14; 31:12; Ecc 1:13; 5:13,16; 6:1; 7:14; 8:6,9; 9:3; 10:5; 11:2; 12:1; Isa 3:9,11; 45:7; 47:11; Jer 1:14; 2:3,19,27,28; 4:6; 5:12; 6:19; 11:11,12,14, 15,17,23; 16:10; 17:17,18; 18:8,11; 19:3,15; 21:10; 23:17; 24:9; 25:7,32; 26:3,13,19; 28:8; 29:11; 32:23,42; 35:17; 36:3,31; 38:4; 39:12,16; 40:2; 42:10,17; 44:2,11,23,27,29; 45:5; 48:2,16; 49:37; 51:2,60,64; La 1:21; 3:38; Eze 5:16; 6:10; 7:5; 14:22; Da 9:12, 13,14; Am 3:6; 5:13; 6:3; 9:4,10; Ob 13; Jnh 3:10; 4:2,6; Mic 1:12; 2:3; Zep 3:15; Zec 1:15; 7:10.

We cannot really understand the Bible's view of evil until we sense the extent of the personal tragedy—the physical and psychological disaster—that results from abandoning God's way.

4. God and evil. Although the OT does not explore theoretical questions, it does make clear statements about God's involvement with evil.

In regard to choices that are morally evil, the OT agrees with Elihu's evaluation: "Far be it from God to do evil" (Job 34:10). Habakkuk goes so far as to say, "Your eyes are too pure to look on evil" (Hab 1:13). God does not condone or participate in evil and certainly is "not a God who takes pleasure in evil" (Ps 5:4). Instead, the OT reports God's commitment: "I will punish the world for its evil" (Isa 13:11).

While the OT rejects the notion that God is responsible for moral evil, it strongly affirms that the Lord is involved in supervising the consequences that result after evil is chosen. A number of passages indicate that God will accept responsibility for many of the consequent evils that trouble us. For example, "I form the light and create darkness, I bring prosperity and create disaster [evil]; I, the LORD, do all these things" (Isa 45:7). Again, "I am preparing a disaster [evil] for you and devising a plan against you" (Jer 18:11). Note also Am 3:6: "When disaster [evil] comes to a city, has not the LORD caused it?"

Such statements reveal a basic aspect of the OT concept of God. God is the measure of what is morally right, and he is responsible for the consequences of doing evil.

The divine responsibility for consequences may be direct, as when God intervened in Egypt in the time of the Exodus. But normally God's responsibility is indirect, worked out through natural consequences. In our morally ordered universe there are moral laws, even as there are natural laws. And violation of the moral laws as well as of the natural laws brings inevitable consequences.

But whether consequences that come from doing evil are direct or indirect, the OT is confident that God, who defines the good and the evil, acts righteously. He is right to bring on us those evils that come as a result of our violation of his moral order.

NT — 5. The Greek words. Two word groups are used in the NT to express the idea of evil. Although the two (*kakos*, with its derivatives, and *ponēros*, with its derivatives) are synonyms, they have different shades of meaning. *Kakos* represents evil in a negative way. It is a lack of those qualities that make a person or thing what it should be. Thus *kakos* looks at evil from the perspective of the nature of a thing. *Ponēros* is a stronger concept. It represents evil as an active force. *Ponēros* takes pleasure in injuring others and is both dangerous and destructive. This word looks at evil from the perspective of its effects.

Each of these Greek words is used with equal frequency to render the OT *ra'* in the Septuagint.

6. *Kakos:* evil and a damaged humanity. The words in this group are variously translated to represent the full range of biblical concepts associated with evil. However, one passage in Romans is theologically definitive in explaining the *kakos* done by human beings who know what is good and who want to do it.

Ro 7:7–25 contains Paul's report of his personal struggle with sin. In this passage he links the law of God, expressed in commandments, with "another law [principle] at work in the members of [his] body" (v. 23). ▶ *Law* Paul sees in Scripture the divine revelation of righteousness and agrees that God's will is both right and beautiful. But when Paul tries to do what this revelation unveils, he discovers that he cannot. "I know that nothing good lives in me, that is, in my sinful nature" is the apostle's agonized confession (v. 18). Thus he says, "What I do is not the good I want to do; no, the evil [*kakos*] I do not want to do—this I keep on doing. . . . When I want to do good, evil [*kakos*] is right there with me" (vv. 19,21).

This is Paul's explanation of the moral gap that exists between what human beings recognize as good and what they actually do. The problem is that sin has warped human nature: *"kakos* is right there with me."* There is a flaw within us that keeps the best of us from being what we should be and what we want to be.

There is a solution to this miserable, soul-vexing situation, however. Paul goes on in Ro 8:1–11 to describe deliverance. For believers there is the presence of the Spirit of God. He alone releases us and enables us to live truly good and righteous lives.

The words in the *kakos* family, and the ways they are rendered in the NIV and the NASB, follow:

Kakia is translated "evil, or wickedness" and in the NIV often "malice." It occurs eleven times in the NT (Mt 6:34; Ac 8:22; Ro 1:29; 1 Co 5:8; 14:20; Eph 4:31; Col 3:8; Tit 3:3; Jas 1:21; 1 Pe 2:1,16).

Kakopoieō means "to do harm or evil" and occurs in Mk 3:4; Lk 6:9; 1 Pe 3:17; 3 Jn 11. *Kakopoios* means "doer of evil" and is found in Jn 18:30; 1 Pe 2:12,14; 3:16; 4:15.

Kakoō means "to do harm or evil" and is found in Ac 7:6,19; 12:1; 14:2; 18:10; 1 Pe 3:13.

Finally, *kakos* itself is variously translated: "evil," "wicked," "crime," "bad things," "harm," and "ill effects." A key passage is Ro 13:3–10. Human government has been structured by God to restrain the harm and ill effects that would result were persons free to express the evil that warps human character. *Kakos* is found in Mt 21:41; 24:48; 27:23; Mk 7:21; 15:14; Lk 16:25; 23:22; Jn 18:23; Ac 9:13; 16:28; 23:9; 28:5; Ro 1:30; 2:9; 3:8; 7:19,21; 9:11; 12:17,21; 13:3,4,10; 14:20; 16:19; 1 Co 10:6; 13:5; 15:33; 2 Co 5:10; 13:7; Php 3:2; Col 3:5; 1 Th 5:15; 1 Ti 6:10; 2 Ti 4:14; Heb 5:14; Jas 1:13; 3:8; 1 Pe 3:9,10,11,12; 3 Jn 11; Rev 2:2; 16:2.

7. *Ponēros*: evil and a hostile humanity. Words in this group are variously translated: "evil," "bad," "wicked," and "wickedness." But this Greek term is stronger and more active than *kakos*. The difference is illustrated in the fact that *ponēros* is chosen to describe the character of Satan (see 8, below). *Ponēros* portrays active rebellion against God and thus

raises a number of theological questions. Particularly it poses the question of the origin of evil as active malevolence.

Although the NT teaches that there is a link between lost humanity and Satan (Mt 6:13; 1 Jn 3:12), it locates human rebellion in the heart, the biblical center of the personality. Matthew and Mark both report this statement from Jesus: "The things that come out of the mouth come from the heart, and these make a man 'unclean.' For out of the heart come evil thoughts, murder, adultery, sexual immorality, theft, false testimony, slander" (Mt 15:18–19; cf. 12:34–45; Mk 7:22–23). The human heart not only lacks an essential capacity for good but is also so distorted that the energy generated within the human personality is channeled toward evil.

But this thrust of Scripture must be balanced by another. Jesus also makes it clear that the depravity worked by original sin did not completely quench the good that God planted within humanity. We can see, even in evil people, reflections of the beauty that God intended to flourish in us all. Notice what Jesus taught: "Which of you, if his son asks for bread, will give him a stone? Or if he asks for a fish, will give him a snake? If you, then, though you are evil, know how to give good gifts to your children, how much more will your Father in heaven give good gifts to those who ask him" (Mt 7:9–11; cf. Lk 11:12–13). The rebelliousness of *ponēros* calls the natural man to turn against God and against good. But the beauty of God's own goodness is still glimpsed in his fallen creations.

The two primary words used in this family are *ponēria*, translated "evil" and "wickedness," and *ponēros*. *Ponēria* appears only seven times in the NT (Mt 22:18; Mk 7:22; Lk 11:39; Ac 3:26; Ro 1:29; 1 Co 5:8; Eph 6:12), whereas *ponēros* is found frequently (Mt 5:11,37,39,45; 6:13,23; 7:11,17,18; 9:4; 12:34,35,39,45; 13:19,38,49; 15:19; 16:4; 18:32; 20:15; 22:10; 25:26; Mk 7:22,23; Lk 3:19; 6:22,35,45; 7:21; 8:2; 11:4,13,26,29,34; 19:22; Jn 3:19; 7:7; 17:15; Ac 17:5; 18:14; 19:12,13,15,16; 28:21; Ro 12:9; 1 Co 5:13;

Gal 1:4; Eph 5:16; 6:13,16; Col 1:21; 1 Th 5:22; 2 Th 3:2,3; 1 Ti 6:4; 2 Ti 3:13; 4:18; Heb 3:12; 10:22; Jas 2:4; 4:16; 1 Jn 2:13,14; 3:12; 5:18,19; 2 Jn 11; 3 Jn 10; Rev 16:2).

8. The evil one. This phrase identifies Satan. The NT always uses *ponēros* to represent the active malevolence of Satan's personality. As the leader of the "spiritual forces of evil" that are ranged against God and his saints (Eph 6:12), Satan is the chief "evil spirit." ♦ *Demons/Evil Spirits* ♦ *Satan*

9. The divine solution to evil. The Bible gives different answers, each showing us an aspect of God's plan for dealing with evil.

a. Evil in the universe, represented by Satan and unredeemed humanity, will be dealt with in judgment. The evil personalities will be punished and will be isolated in what the Bible calls the "lake of fire." ♦ *Heaven and Hell*

b. Evil in the human personality, both as *kakos* and as *ponēros*, is dealt with through Christ's great act of redemption. Those who believe are brought into harmony with God and are given new life. Rebelliousness is replaced by love for God, and human inadequacy is overcome through the power of the indwelling spirit (Ro 8:1–11). Made new and reshaped through personal relationship with God, believers are to "avoid every kind of evil" (1 Th 5:22) and indeed to "hate what is evil [and] cling to what is good" (Ro 12:9).

c. Human government has been established to restrain the full expression of evil (Ro 13). In order to exist, government must act to provide a context within which its citizens will be safe from each other and surrounding nations.

d. Believers are to follow God's example in dealing with evil people during this age of grace. In our personal relationships with hostile persons we are to show love, seeking to introduce them to the redemption that can change them from within (Mt 5:43–44; Lk 6:35). ♦ *Enemy* Ultimately those who do not respond to love will suffer divine judgment. But the Christian's calling is not to

condemn but to communicate the gospel in vital, loving ways.

10. Summary. Neither the OT nor the NT deals with the classic issues posed by the existence of evil in the universe. As far as the OT is concerned, evil includes (1) actions that violate God's intentions for mankind and (2) the consequences that follow moral violations and bring physical and psychological harm to evildoers.

NT references to evil operate within the context established by the OT, but they add to our understanding of the evil found within human beings. *Kakos* views evil as a tragic lack. Something missing within us keeps us from achieving our potential as beings created in the image of God. *Ponēros* views evil as an active, rebellious drive, also found within human nature. Sin has brought a bent toward what is wrong and harmful. Only God's transforming work within can change the direction in which our energies are channeled.

One day every question raised by the existence of evil will be answered. But God does not concentrate his attention in Scripture on the philosophical. Instead, he seeks through his Word to concentrate our attention on the reality of evil and its impact on our experience. When we see what evil is and does to us, we may turn to Christ and find in a personal relationship with him God's ultimate solution to release us from the power of evil within us and in this present evil world.

EXALT/EXALTED

One of two complementary notions is expressed in OT and NT occurrences of this word. One set of original terms means "to become or to declare great." God shows himself great through his acts; faith recognizes and affirms his greatness and exalts him by praising him for what he has done and for who he is.

Another set of biblical words means "to lift up, or raise," or "to be high." It is appropriate that God be exalted, for he is great and lifted up. It is not appropriate for mere human beings to exalt themselves. "The arrogance of man will be brought low and the pride of men humbled; the LORD alone will be exalted in that day, and idols will totally disappear" (Isa 2:17).

EXAMPLE

A number of different Greek words are found where the NIV and the NASB read "example." The basic meaning of the most significant words (*hypodeigma* and *typos*) is that of a figure or pattern, which can serve as a model. In the NT the pattern is nearly always established by a person whose words and actions provide a living expression of that which Scripture calls for from all believers.

At times the example found in the Bible is negative (Heb 4). But the concept of example is essentially positive.

Jesus set his followers an example of humility and love (Jn 13:1–17). Christians are urged to follow the example of their leaders. In fact, providing an example is a primary task of leaders (1 Ti 4:12; 1 Pe 5:3). The truths leaders teach must be given living expression so that the truths taught may be fully understood.

◆ *Leadership* But Jesus remains the believer's prime example (Jn 13:15; 2 Pe 2:8). Leaders can call on others to imitate them only as they themselves imitate the Lord (1 Co 11:1).

Paul links the importance of words and example in Php 4:9: "Whatever you have learned or received or heard from me, or seen in me—put it into practice. And the God of peace will be with you."

EXCUSE

"Excuse" is theologically significant in three passages. In Jn 15:22 Jesus describes the hatred with which the world responded to him. Antagonized by the Lord's teaching, the men of the world persecuted him. Thus Jesus' coming stripped his listeners of every defense: "They have no excuse for their sin." The Greek word is *prophasis*. It is a word related to appearances. Humanity's sin and its hatred of God might have remained masked had not Jesus appeared.

But Jesus did come, and he spoke the truth. The hatred his words evoke strip away every pretense and reveal a mankind that is far from God.

The other two important passages are Ro 1:20 and 2:1. In each, the word is *anapologētos* (its only two occurrences in the NT). In Romans, Paul examines the concept of righteousness. In chapter 1 he traces humanity's hostility toward God and demonstrates it in the choices made by individuals and by cultures. Paul begins with the affirmation that God has revealed himself to all: "Since the creation of the world God's invisible qualities—his eternal power and divine nature—have been clearly seen, being understood from what has been made" (1:20). This revelation of God leaves humanity without excuse; that is, without a legal defense, for "although they knew God" (1:21), they turned from him.

In Ro 2 Paul turns to the Jew. The Jew has special revelation to accompany general revelation. Yet the Jew too is without a legal defense (excuse) because, while condemning the sins of others, the Jews have committed the same sins.

God wants each of us to realize that we stand guilty before him. Why? So that rather than offering excuses, we will accept the forgiveness that he is so eager for us to find in Jesus Christ.

EXILE

The Hebrew verb *gālâh* means "to uncover" or "to remove" and thus "to be led into captivity [exile]," a significant concept in OT history. ◆ *Captivity*

EXHORT ◆ *Encourage*

EYE

The eye is a physical organ. But the word expresses far more than that in both the OT and the NT.

OT 1. "Eye" in the OT
NT 2. "Eye" in the NT

OT — 1. "Eye" in the OT. The Hebrew word is *'ayin*. It indicates both the physical organ and sight. But it expresses more than this. Figuratively the eye represents the character and attitudes of individuals, as in phrases like "My eyes are fixed on you" (Ps 141:8) and "I will hide my eyes from you" (Isa 1:15).

The eyes also represent one's capacity to perceive. When the OT speaks of God's eyes, it is not being crudely anthropomorphic, but rather it affirms that he is fully aware of all that happens on earth. And God is personally involved, as an actor, in events.

The eyes also represent people's spiritual faculties. When Adam and Eve fell, the reference to the opening of their eyes indicated their loss of innocence (Ge 3:5,7). Closed eyes represent an unresponsive attitude toward God (Jer 5:21), whereas open eyes represent sensitivity to the Lord (Ps 119:8).

Also, the phrase "in your eyes" is a way the OT expresses a personal or divine opinion.

NT — 2. Eye in the NT. *Ophthalmos* is found 101 times in the NT. Here too the eyes are spiritually significant organs. Eyes reveal much about a person and that person's orientation to life.

As an organ of perception, the eye can lead an individual astray (Mt 5:29; Mk 9:47). Jesus called the eye the "lamp of the body." Then he added, "If your eyes are good, your whole body will be full of light. But if they are bad, your body will be full of darkness" (Mt 6:22–23; cf. Lk 11:34). There is no hope for someone whose spiritual perceptions are distorted. It is no wonder that Paul prays for the Ephesian believers "That the eyes of your heart may be enlightened in order that you may know the hope to which he has called you, the riches of his glorious inheritance in the saints" (Eph 1:18).

Spiritual perception will open our whole life to the light of God's presence. But Jesus warned that we should not think that spiritual awareness conveys the right to judge others. True spiritual perception enables us to examine our own relationship with God. "Why," Jesus asks, "do you look at the speck of sawdust in your brother's eye and pay no attention to the plank in your own eye? How can you say to your brother, 'Let me take the speck out of your eye,' when all the time there is a plank in your own eye? You hypocrite, first take the plank out of your own eye" (Mt 7:3–5; cf. Lk 6:41–42).

Having eyes to see is a great gift from God. We are to use this gift by directing our eyes to those things that God wishes us to observe and examine.

F

FACE

A number of OT expressions use the word "face" (*pānîm*) to express a person's attitudes or feelings. These expressions describe God's face in various ways, such as shining on (showing favor), turned away from (in rejection), hidden from (in disgust), or set against (in judgment). The intimacy of a right relationship with God is expressed by God's turning his face toward people, or being seen. "In righteousness I will see your face," the psalmist says (17:15), confident in God's promise that "upright men will see his face" (11:7).

Such OT expressions also express human feelings and attitudes. Warned by the Lord, Cain's face was "downcast" (angry). Fear causes the face to turn pale. A face lifted up represents confidence or acceptance. An evil face reveals deep anxiety or worry, and a hard face shows defiance.

One thing the OT makes clear: human beings cannot meet God face to face. This expression indicates direct and full experience of one person by another. Thus God says to Moses, "You cannot see my face, for no one may see me and live" (Ex 33:20). Yet God did permit Moses some direct experience of himself, even though it is represented as merely seeing God's back as the Lord's glory passed by (Ex 33:12–23). Ge 32:22–31 reports an experience of Jacob with the Lord, who appeared in the form of a man and wrestled with the patriarch. Jacob's awed expression, "I saw God face to face, and yet my life was spared" (32:30) expresses his feelings but not the facts. Jacob's experience was with God masked, not unveiled in his essential glory.

In the rest of the OT, expressions of seeking or seeing God's face usually refer to the people's coming to the tabernacle or the temple to worship, or they are euphemisms for prayer (2 Sa 21:1; Ps 24:6; 27:8).

It is in the NT that the awe felt by Jacob is realized. John expresses that awe in the first chapter of his Gospel: "The Word became flesh and made his dwelling among us. We have seen his glory, the glory of the One and Only, who came from the Father, full of grace and truth" (1:14). In one sense the glory of God was masked in the Incarnation. In another, it was unveiled. The fullest revelation of who Jesus is was glimpsed only by the disciples (cf. Mt 17:2; Lk 9:29; Rev 1:16), and Jesus could say to them and to us, "Anyone who has seen me has seen the Father. . . . I am in the Father, and . . . the Father is in me" (Jn 14:9). In Jesus we come face to face with God!

There is one last NT teaching that arouses our awe and awakens praise. In 2 Co 3 Paul looks back to the OT and reminds us that after Moses spent forty days with the Lord on Sinai, he returned with a glorious (shining, radiant) face. But the splendor began to fade, and Moses put a veil over his face, to hide the fact that the glory was fading.

Paul then pointed up the contrast between the believer's experience of God and Moses' experience of God. In our intimate relationship through Jesus and God's Spirit, "we are being transformed into his [Jesus'] likeness with ever-increasing glory." Thus, Paul can say that we "with unveiled faces all reflect the Lord's glory" (3:18). Jesus is at work, shaping us to be more and more like him, so that others will see God's face in our transformed personalities.

FACTIONS

In 2 Co 12:20 and Gal 5:20, "factions" is included in listings of the works of the flesh. The Greek word *eritheia* also occurs in Ro 2:8; Php 1:16; 2:3; Jas 3:14,16 and is usually translated "selfish ambition." The word portrays partisanship or intrigue that is not motivated by love for God or others but by a fierce passion for self-advancement.

FAIL/FAILURE

The word "fail" is used in the OT in a number of ways: Individuals may fail to carry out God's commands (Lev 26:15; Nu 15:22). David's family will never fail to have a man for the throne of Israel (1 Ki 2:4). One's flesh and heart may fail (Ps 73:26).

The Hebrew language does not have any single or specific words for such failures or for failure in general. Instead, "fail" is an interpretation of words that signify one or more of the following concepts: to be at an end, to be cut off, to pass over, to sink or relax, to be at a distance, or to stumble.

There is no specific Greek word for "fail" either. In the statement "Love never fails" (1 Co 13:8) the Greek word translated "fails" (*ekpiptō*) means "to become ineffective." The same word is used in Ro 9:6, where Paul points out that Israel's refusal to respond should not be interpreted "as though God's word had failed." Human rejection of God's message is a sign of failure in mankind, not in the efficacy of God's Word.

In 2 Co 13:5–7 Paul says, "Examine yourselves to see whether you are in the faith; test yourselves. Do you not realize that Christ Jesus is in you—unless, of course, you fail the test? And I trust that you will discover that we have not failed the test . . . that people will see that we

have stood the test but that you will do what is right even though we may seem to have failed." Here Paul uses *dokimazō* (to put something to the test in order to approve it) and *adokimos* (to be disqualified as not standing the test, and thus to fail).

Paul's authority had been challenged by many in Corinth. The dissidents had demanded proof that Christ did indeed speak through the apostle. Paul's answer focuses attention on the indwelling Christ, who is powerful within and among his people and will deal with those who reject one whom he sends.

So Paul calls the Corinthians to put themselves to the test of exploring this inner reality: "Do you not realize that Christ Jesus is in you?" (v. 5). If Jesus was not within them, these rebels were pretenders and were not "in the faith." If Jesus was within them, he would bear inner witness to the validity of the message Paul communicates.

FAITH ♦ *Belief/Faith*

FAITHFULNESS

Faithfulness is a quality that the OT praises highly. It is a divine quality that the NT urges us to remember—and to develop.

OT 1. Hebrew words for "faithfulness"
NT 2. Greek words for "faithfulness"

OT — 1. Hebrew words for "faithfulness". The Hebrew words for "faithfulness" are derivatives of one of the OT's great theological terms. The root is *'āman,* which in the Qal stem means "to confirm or support"; in the Niphal stem, "to be established, faithful"; and in the Hiphil stem, "to be certain," "to believe in." ♦ *Belief/Faith* One of the derivatives is the OT word that we translate "truth." ♦ *Truth*

In addition to the Niphal verb stem, "faithful" and "faithfulness" are translations of *'emûnâh. Emûn* also means "faithful" but is found only in Dt 32:20; Pr 13:17; 14:5; 20:6; Isa 26:2.

The word *ʿemûnâh* means "firmness, steadiness, fidelity." The OT often uses this word as an attribute of God, to express the total dependability of his character or promises. Its first use in describing the Lord is found in Dt 32:4: "He is the Rock, his works are perfect, and all his ways are just. A faithful God who does no wrong. Upright and just is he." Many other passages apply this great OT term to God or to his words and works (1 Sa 26:23; Ps 33:4; 36:5; 40:10; 88:11; 89:1,2,5,8,24,33,49; 92:2; 98:3; 100:5; 110:75,86,90,138; 143:1; Isa 11:5; 25:1; La 3:23; Hos 2:20).

NT — 2. The Greek word for "faithful".

The Greek word translated "faithful" is from the NT's belief/faith word group. ♦ *Belief/Faith*

Pistos has both an active and a passive use. In its active sense it means "trusting, believing." More often, though, it is passive, meaning "trustworthy, reliable, faithful." *Pistos* portrays an unshakable loyalty, which is displayed in a number of ways.

We see *pistos* in the faithful servants of Mt 24:45 and 25:21–23, who prove trustworthy in carrying out their assignments. Most often, however, the NT calls our attention to God and describes him as faithful. Because God is faithful, he can be trusted completely to carry out his commitments to us in Christ (1 Co 1:9; 10:13; 2 Co 1:18; 1 Th 5:24; 2 Th 3:3; 2 Ti 2:13; Heb 2:17; 10:23; 11:11; 1 Pe 4:19; 1 Jn 1:9; Rev 1:5; 3:14; 19:11).

"Faithful" is also a word used to commend believers for their quality of steadfast endurance (e.g., 1 Co 4:17; Eph 6:21; Col 1:7; 4:7). Indeed, "the faithful" is used in some passages as a way of saying "believers" (e.g., Eph 1:1).

Paul is particularly aware that God has committed to him, as to every believer, the responsibility of using his gifts to serve others. "It is required that those who have been given a trust must prove faithful," he writes in 1 Co 4:2.

We know that we can trust God to remain faithful to his commitments. It is wonderful that God entrusts so much to us. Let us use our opportunities to show loyalty to him.

FALL

The use of the word "fall" as we often give it theological weight, describing Adam and Eve's sin and its impact on the human race, is not the biblical use of it. But many theological questions are linked with "fall," especially in such NT phrases as "fall beyond recovery" (Ro 11:11) and "fall from grace" (Gal 5:4).

OT 1. The OT words and usages
NT 2. The NT words and usages
   3. Analysis of sensitive NT passages
   4. Summary

OT — 1. The OT words and usages. "Fall" is used in the OT in a literal sense and in a number of idiomatic phrases. The most common Hebrew word is *nāpal*, found 428 times. It means "to fall," "to lie down," or "to be cast out." Besides describing the physical act of falling, the word is used idiomatically in such phrases as "fall in battle" and "fall into the hands of [an enemy]." A number of other Hebrew words have also been translated "fall" when the context suggested this meaning to the translators.

NT — 2. The NT words and usage. "Fall" has the same range of uses in the NT as it does in the OT. It is used literally to describe the fall of a person or building. It is used idiomatically in such phrases as "fall into the hands of" (Heb 10:31) and "fall under . . . judgment" (1 Ti 3:6). In the former phrase it means to be given up to. In the latter phrase it means to act in ways that provide grounds not only for trial but also for a guilty verdict.

In addition, there are figurative uses of "fall," uses that cause believers some degree of consternation. We wonder about the implications of falling from grace or falling away in our relationship with the Lord.

The Greek words translated "fall" provide only limited help in understanding the figurative uses that are sometimes made of the concept. *Skandalizō*, found where the NIV and the NASB read "fall" in Mt 26:31,33; Mk 4:17; 14:27,29; Lk 7:23; 1 Cor 8:13, means "to anger or offend," or "to cause a person to stumble [into sin]." Most verses that read "fall" have *piptō* or one of its compounds (*empiptō, ekpiptō, katapiptō, parapiptō, peripiptō*). The basic meaning of all of these words is modified by added prepositions to indicate falling into, falling away or down from, falling down, or falling aside. As these words are given a full range of literal, idiomatic, and figurative uses, we must turn to the context of any significant passages to define their theological implications.

3. Analysis of sensitive passages. A number of NT passages raise theological questions in their use of "fall." As these questions focus on the nature of our relationship with God, it is important to study these verses carefully.

Ro 14:21. This passage explores the responsibility of Christians to one another. Paul announces freedom but urges the believers of Rome, "[Do nothing] that will cause your brother to fall." The word here is *proskoptō*. It pictures a traveler who bumps against an obstacle and is caused to stumble. The context makes Paul's meaning clear. Believers will have different convictions about matters on which Scripture is silent. Each of us is free to follow his or her conscience in such matters. But we are never free to influence others to act against their personal convictions and thus cause them to stumble into sin.

1 Co 10:12. Paul uses the common word *piptō* to represent committing sin. Paul has reviewed the failure of Israel on its Exodus journey, telling how they succumbed to temptation (10:1–10). We too will face temptations. But Israel's failure and the resulting punishments they suffered should move us to look for God's "way out so that [we] can stand up under" our temptations (10:13).

Heb 4:11. This passage also uses *piptō*. As with 1 Co 10:12, the context warns against slipping into sin and experiencing the discipline that must follow. Here too the writer looks into history, this time to an Israel poised on the border of the Promised Land. There God called on

Israel to enter, but the people hesitated and then turned away. If only they had listened and obeyed God's word, that generation would have found rest in the Promised Land.

Today too God speaks to us. We find rest in our Christian life by listening to and obeying the Lord. So the writer concludes, "Let us, therefore, make every effort to enter that rest, so that no one will fall by following their example of disobedience."

Heb 6:6. Here the Greek word for "fall," *parapiptō* (used only here in the NT), means "to fall aside."

Heb 6:4–6 is best understood as posing a hypothetical case for Jewish believers who are tempted to turn back to the OT faith. If they should turn aside and later seek repentance, what would they do then? Would they crucify Jesus again, as though his sacrificial death recorded in the Gospels were not enough to satisfy the justice of God? How impossible that would be!

The writer makes it clear that he does not view these believers as lost (6:9). But he does confront them. They must realize that once faith is founded on Christ, there is no need to return to basic teachings. Now believers can and must move on toward maturity (6:1–3).

Gal 5:4. This passage uses *ekpiptō*, "to fall out of," "to fall down from." The verse says, "You who are trying to be justified by law have been alienated from Christ; you have fallen away from grace."

What does falling away from grace mean? This passage and most of Galatians deals with the struggle in the early church to understand the believer's relationship to OT law. Many zealous Jewish Christians felt that the Christian life was a matter of keeping the law, and they brought this doctrine to Gentile congregations. Paul argues throughout his letters that the key to vital Christian experience is to be found not in the law but in Christ's living within the believer (Gal 2:20). We experience that relationship and know its vital power for righteous living through faith (2:21). Paul points out several key issues. Did salvation come through the law or through faith (3:1–2)? Why then expect God to abandon the faith principle when it comes to living as saved men and women (3:3)?

Then, in Gal 3–4, Paul explores the great contrasts between law and faith. His conclusion is expressed in the troublesome verse 5:4. To turn to law as a pathway to spiritual growth is to reject the pathway of grace. To struggle to keep the law is to cut oneself off from Jesus, for it involves abandoning that daily faith in him by which grace operates in our lives.

It is thus that Paul speaks of "falling away from grace." The Christian life is a matter of grace from first to last, and grace is appropriated only by faith. For the Christian to "fall from grace" in this context is not to lose salvation; rather, it indicates a turning from daily reliance on Jesus, which in turn results in being cut off from that daily fellowship that is the source of spiritual power.

2 Pe 3:17. This passage also uses *ekpiptō*. Peter warns, "Be on your guard so that you may not be carried away by the error of lawless men and fall from your secure position." He continues, "But grow in the grace and knowledge of our Lord and Savior Jesus Christ" (3:18).

This passage raises the same issue as that raised in Gal 5:4. There a return to law threatened to cut believers off from that sphere of relationship in which grace operates. Here Peter warns of the danger of false teachers who also seek to turn believers from Jesus. Peter urges his readers not to be enticed from that relationship in which we are always secure. Instead we are to hold to our position in Christ by faith. Holding to him, we will grow in grace and in knowledge of the Lord.

4. Summary. Like many common words found in Scripture, "fall" cannot be understood out of context. To fall does not mean, in itself, to lose salvation, to sin, or even to turn from grace. It is the argument of each passage that determines how we interpret the meaning of

"fall," especially when it is used in a figurative sense.

Peter helps to make it clear that, although warnings against falling into sin or away from grace are valid, God wants us to concentrate our energies on the positive aspects of our Christian lives. In 2 Pe 1 we are encouraged to "make every effort to add to [our] faith goodness" and such other Christian virtues as knowledge, self-control, kindness, godliness, and love. Growth in these qualities, Peter wrote, "will keep you from being ineffective and unproductive in your knowledge of our Lord Jesus Christ" (1:5–8).

Vital, personal growth through a relationship with Jesus brings us a sense of the reality of our calling. And, Scripture promises, "if you do these things, you will never fall" (2 Pe 1:10).

FALSE ◆ *Deceit/Falsehood*

FAMILY

The family is viewed in both Testaments as a basic unit of the believing community. In the NT the image of the family is one of the primary ways in which Scripture explains the nature of Christians' relationships with God and one another.

OT 1. The Hebrew concept of family
NT 2. The Greek words translated "family"
    3. The church and the family
    4. The church as family
    5. Household salvation
    6. Summary

OT — 1. The Hebrew concept of family. The foundation for the biblical view of family is laid in Ge 2. There God instituted marriage as a permanent union between one man and one woman. ◆ *Marriage* This stable relationship is the foundation of a stable society. The larger groupings of OT society—the tribe and the clan—are expressions of extended family relationships. It is particularly significant that the OT focuses on the family as central in communicating faith to children. ◆ *Teaching/Learning*

Two Hebrew words are typically used to indicate the family: *mišpāḥâh* is translated "family" in the NIV and NASB and *bayit* means "house" but is often used in the sense of "family" (as in "the house of" someone; e.g., Ex 2:1; 2 Sa 21:1; 2 Ch 10:19; Hos 1:4) or is translated "household."

In American culture, the family is increasingly perceived as the nuclear unit of husband and wife and their children. Both *mišpāḥâh* and *bayit* are terms with much more flexible meaning. Depending on context, a family or household in the OT might be the nuclear family, an extended family of three or more generations plus any servants living with them, or an even wider circle of relatives who trace their family bond back to a common male ancestor. Thus when we read "family" or "household" in the OT, we need to let the context determine how many persons this very flexible term is intended to include.

NT — 2. The Greek words translated "family". The most common words to express the concept of family in the NT are *oikos*, "house," and its derivatives. This parallels the use of *bayit* in the OT. *Oikos* may indicate the couple, their children, and any servants or relatives living in the home (1 Ti 3:5,12). It may also represent an entire people, such as Israel (Lk 1:33; Ac 7:42), or the Christian community (1 Ti 3:15; 1 Pe 4:17; cf. Eph 2:19, "household" [*oikeios*]).

The significant term *patria* is found only three times in the NT. This term for family means "father's house" and focuses attention on the particular forefather who is the origin of the family group and who also provides it with its identity (Lk 2:4; Ac 3:25; Eph 3:15).

3. The church and the family. The house, or family, is the smallest natural group in the NT congregation. In the church the family remains basic in the nurture of children in the faith. ♦ *Teaching/Learning* In NT times the house was the primary place of meeting and fellowship for believers (e.g., Ac 2:46; 16:15; Phm 2). For the first centuries of the Christian era, believers did not meet in church buildings but in smaller, more intimate groups in homes. Thus, the greeting in Ro 16:5 to the "church that meets at" the house of Priscilla and Aquila is a reflection of the normal pattern of early church life. It was very natural for early Christians, meeting in household groups, to sense deeply the family quality of their mutual relationship as children of God.

It is also significant that the NT pays attention not only to relationships within families (Eph 5:22–6:9; Col 3:18–24; 1 Pe 3:1–7 ♦ *Marriage*) but also to relationships between believers who are called on to live together and to "love as brothers" (e.g., Ro 12:9–16; Eph 5:1–21; Col 3:12–15; 1 Ti 5).

4. The church as family. Eph 3:15 uses the theologically significant term *patria* to affirm that God's "whole family in heaven and on earth derives its name" from him whom we know as Father. ♦ *Father* As children of the same Father, we believers have a common origin and common identity that is shared with all other believers everywhere. Paul goes on to pray that, "rooted and established in love," we who are God's family may grow "together" to experience Jesus' love and so be "filled to the measure of all the fullness of God" (3:16–19). We *are* family. Experience of the intimacy and love appropriate to family members is basic to personal and corporate spiritual growth (4:12–16).

Images of the family relationship abound in the NT. Believers are addressed as brothers and sisters; the church is considered to be the household of God (Eph 2:19–20).

The intimate link between the family and the church is also seen in Paul's instructions concerning recognition of spiritual leaders. A leader is to "manage his own family well and see that his children obey him with proper respect. (If anyone does not know how to manage his own family, how can he take care of God's church?)" (1 Ti 3:4–5). The same emphasis is found in Titus, which suggests that a leader be "a man whose children believe and are not open to the charge of being wild and disobedient"

(1:6). Because the church is a family, leadership in the church has strong parallels to the leadership to be provided by a parent for his or her children.

5. Household salvation. One of the theological questions posed by some Christians focuses on the link between natural family relationships and God's plan of salvation. The OT covenant provided a special relationship between God and the descendants (family) of Abraham, Isaac, and Jacob. ♦ *Covenant* Is there also established between the Lord and the believer a special relationship that extends beyond the believing individual to encompass his or her family too? Two NT passages are used to support such a relationship.

Ac 16:31 records Paul's promise to the Philippian jailer: "Believe in the Lord Jesus, and you will be saved—you and your household." The passage continues: "Then they spoke the word of the Lord to him and to all the others in his house. At that hour of the night the jailer took them and washed their wounds; then immediately he and all his family were baptized. The jailer brought them into his house and set a meal before them; he was filled with joy because he had come to believe in God—he and his whole family" (16:32–34).

There seems no need to understand this passage to teach household salvation. The promise was given to the jailer and his whole household. All were there to hear the gospel presented, and all believed.

What is possibly suggested here is the influence of the head of a household. In many cultures, individual decisions are strongly influenced by what the head of a family or clan decides to do. In this sense certainly the faith of the head of a household has significant impact on family members.

The other passage used is 1 Co 7:14. This says that the unbelieving partner in a mixed marriage is in some sense sanctified by the believer, as are any children. This is a difficult passage. But there is no compelling reason why its meaning should be pressed beyond the fact that each family with a believing member is in

a unique position to hear the gospel. ♦ *Sanctify/Sanctification*

The basic reason for questioning the concept of household salvation, however, comes from the nature of the very OT covenant on which the doctrine is based. The Abrahamic covenant did establish a special relationship between God and the people of Israel, but each individual Israelite was still called on to make a personal choice. Each had to either trust the God of the covenant and obey him or else remain in unbelief and disobedience. The covenant promises to Israel never, in themselves, guaranteed the salvation of any given individual. In fact, Israel's history is marked by the massive unbelief of whole generations, despite the covenant. Thus the OT covenants can hardly be used to support the notion that the salvation of the head of a modern household, or the salvation of one of its members, is a divine guarantee that other family members will be saved.

6. Summary. Both OT and NT view the family as the basic unit of society and of the believing community. The family is the first and most significant influence in the spiritual training of children.

The concept of family is flexible in the OT and may indicate a number of widening blood relationships. The NT concept reflects both OT thought and the culture of the NT world.

In the NT we see that the family is particularly important in the Christian congregation. The early church met in homes, an ideal context for building household and family-type personal relationships. The church saw itself as family—a relationship based on common spiritual birth into the household of God. NT descriptions of relationships among believers constantly stress the intimate and sharing love that is appropriate among brothers and sisters.

The modern church cannot and should not try to reproduce every structure of the early Christian community. But there are certain things that are basic to the very nature and identity of the church. Whatever structures a local congregation evolves, it is clear that these structures must help members live together and love one another as family. This is utterly basic to what it means to belong to Jesus and his church. ♦ *Church*

FAMINE

The Hebrew word for "famine" is *rā'āb*. It occurs over one hundred times in the OT, always indicating human hunger. Because of poor distribution systems and a lack of methods for preserving foods, the ancient world was particularly vulnerable to famine.

The OT makes it clear that God would provide abundant food when Israel obeyed his commandments (Dt 30:9–10). The disobedient were disciplined by "wasting famine," pestilence, plagues, and wild beasts (Dt 32:24). The best-known biblical famine was precipitated by the sins of King Ahab. It lasted for three years and came and ended at the word of the prophet Elijah (1 Ki 17–18).

FASTING

The Hebrew word *ṣûm*, or *ṣôm*, means "to abstain from food." OT fasts usually lasted from sunrise to sunset. They might be partial fasts, abstaining from meat or other specific foods rather than from all foods.

Fasts described in the OT are religious in character and never for the purpose of losing weight. There were four common reasons for fasting: (1) Fasts expressed depth of feeling. Many were linked with times of great grief or mourning (1 Sa 31:13). (2) Fasts were undertaken in times of deep trouble and underlined the seriousness of personal (2 Sa 12:16–22; Da 9:3–19; Ne 1:4) and national (2 Ch 20:1–29; Jer 36:1–10) appeals to God. (3) Fasts were a sign of honest repentance (1 Ki 21:27; Jnh 3:5–10; Joel 2:12–15). (4) Fasts also expressed the solemn character of the Day of Atonement ("deny yourselves"—Lev 16:29,31; 23:26–32). Later other fasts, associated with commemorative days, were added (Zec 8:19).

In Jesus' day, the religious Jews expressed their zeal by fasting each Monday and Thursday (Lk 18:12). But Jesus warned against the common practice of marking one's face to show others that one is fasting (Mt 6:16–18). There is no merit in fasting as such. It is one's heart attitude and the focus of attention on God that make fasting acceptable and helpful.

Jesus' own forty-day fast is the longest reported fast in Scripture, though Moses (Ex 34:28) and Elijah (1 Ki 19:8) also went without food for forty days. It took place just before Christ began his public ministry (Mt 4:1-2; Lk 4:1–3). The hunger Jesus felt after his forty-day experience is a physiological sign of exhaustion of the body's stored resources. This typically occurs between the thirtieth and the fortieth day of a total fast. Christ thus had become weakened prior to his temptation by Satan. Overcoming Satan's temptations demonstrated Jesus' personal qualifications to rule God's kingdom. Jesus showed control over his human needs and passions, and he promises others victory. ♦ *Temptation/Test/Trial*

The practice of fasting as a distinctive adjunct to worship is suggested in Lk 2:37; Ac 13:2; and 14:23. But fasting is not taught in any of the Epistles.

FATE

In many ancient cultures the universe was perceived as hostile to human beings, and people were perceived as helpless before malevolent spiritual forces or impersonal fates. There is no such concept in the OT or the NT. Both picture the universe as a divine creation and reveal a God who is in full control. Those who live in harmony with God's will will be blessed. Those who sin will be punished.

A quick survey of the thirteen OT verses that use the word "fate" show that the term is used in the sense of "what happens" or is used to indicate a ruler's determination. It does not indicate a fatalistic attitude, such as is often found among pagans.

FATHER

The word "father" is precious to believers, who realize that they have an intimate family relationship with God, who has revealed himself as their Father. But "father" is a complex term in the OT and a theologically significant term in the NT. When we read the Bible, we need to understand the ways this word is used as well as the ways it is not used.

OT 1. **The Hebrew words and their uses**
    2. **The role of fathers in OT times**
    3. **"Father" as a term of respect**
    4. **God as Father in the OT**
NT 5. **The Greek words and their uses**
    6. **God as the Father**
    7. **God as the Father of Jesus**
    8. **God as our Father**
    9. **Unusual NT uses of the word "father"**
      a. **Father as founder**
      b. **The prohibition against calling anyone on earth "father"**
      c. **Fathers honored and rejected at the same time**
      d. **Melchizedek: man "without father"**
    10. **Summary**

OT — 1. The Hebrew words and their uses. The OT provides a number of genealogical lists in which we read that *x* was the father of *y*. An often-repeated Hebrew word in these lists is *yālaḏ*, which means "to beget or bring forth a child." ◆ *Born* In such uses the emphasis is on physical descent, but the "father" may be a grandfather or an even more distant ancestor.

The key word for "father" in the Bible is *'āḇ*. It occurs 1,191 times in Hebrew and 9 times in an Aramaic form. It is a complex word. Although it usually indicates a literal father or grandfather, it may also be used as a title of respect for a governor or prophet or priest. It may also indicate the respect of a servant for his master. *'Aḇ* is also used to indicate the founder of a tribe or family group. Similarly, it can mean the originator or founder of a guild. Thus Ge 4:21 identifies Jubal as "father of all who play the

harp and flute"; i.e., he was the first musician.

God is identified as Father only a few times in the OT. In those instances the relationship is between God and Israel as a people or between God and Christ as the seed of David's line. In the OT, God is not viewed as being in a father-son relationship with individuals or as the father of mankind in general.

It is probable that the title "Everlasting Father" ascribed to Messiah by Isaiah (Isa 9:6) is better understood as "father of eternity," i.e., founder of the ages. ◆ *Age/Ages*

2. The role of fathers in OT times. OT culture was patriarchal. The father was the dominant family member. He was the head of the house (Jos 24:15 ◆ *Head*) and, with his wife, was to be respected and honored by their children and other members of the household (Ex 20:12; 21:15,17; Dt 5:16; 27:16). The father was responsible for the well-being of the family unit (Dt 1:31) and for its discipline (Dt 8:5).

The primary goal of the godly in OT times was to bring up children who would choose that holy life to which Israelites were called. Thus the father's prime responsibility was religious, as family priest and as teacher of the faith (Ex 12:3–28; 13:14–16; Dt 6:4–9,20–25; 32:7,45–47; Isa 38:19). The Book of Proverbs reveals much of the pattern of parental guidance, as well as the fulfillment a godly Israelite felt in seeing his children grow up to follow the Lord (cf. Pr 10:1; 15:20; 17:21; 23:24).

Although the father was responsible to teach, children were also responsible for certain familial attitudes and actions: "Listen, my son, and be wise, and keep your heart on the right path. . . . Listen to your father, who gave you life" (Pr 23:19,22). Eze 18 makes it very clear that each individual is responsible for his own response to God and for his own moral choices. A father can instruct and model the faith, but each child will make his or her own choices (Eze 18:14–20). ◆ *Account/Accountable*

In biblical times the father guarded and provided for his family. But his primary responsibility was to communicate a living faith in Yahweh to the next generation.

3. "Father" as a title of respect. In a number of cases, persons with governmental or spiritual authority in the OT are addressed, "My father." Priests (Jdg 17:10; 18:19) and prophets (2 Ki 2:12; 6:21; 13:14) as well as kings were sometimes called father as a sign of respect.

This usage also generated idiomatic phrases. The "father to those who live in Jerusalem" was the governor of that city (Isa 22:21). "Father to the needy" (Job 29:16) indicates one who is generous in providing for the poor. The statement that Joseph became a "father to Pharaoh" (Ge 45:8) indicates his position as advisor and chief executive in Egypt.

4. God as Father in the OT. Jeremiah reports God's words to a rebellious Israel in 3:19–20: "How gladly would I treat you like sons and give you a desirable land, the most beautiful inheritance of any nation. I thought you would call me 'Father' and not turn away from following me. But like a woman unfaithful to her husband, so you have been unfaithful to me, O house of Israel." In this and other passages where the OT ascribes the title "Father" to God, that relationship is corporate rather than individual. God is the Father of Israel, the covenant people, for "is he not your Father, your Creator, who made you and formed you?" (Dt 32:6). It is in this distinctive sense of originator, the one who called Israel into being as a people, that God is Father to his OT people (cf. also Isa 63:16; 64:8; Jer 31:9; Mal 1:6; 2:10). In the same sense, God is father to David, for God called his royal line into being by the Davidic covenant (2 Sa 7:14; 1 Ch 17:13; 22:10; 28:6; Ps 89:26).

Thus when Malachi cries out, "Have we not all one Father? Did not one God create us?" (2:10), he does not suggest a universal fatherhood for God. Malachi instead reminded Israel that they were called into being as a people by God's divine act and that thus their very identity was owed to the Lord their Creator.

Yet, although the OT does not teach what we think of as a father-child relationship, there are many indications that within the covenant God fulfills a father's responsibilities. It was "as a father carries his son" that God brought Israel through the years of wilderness wandering (Dt 1:31). History reveals that "as a man disciplines his son," so God disciplined them (Dt 8:5).

David said with confidence, "As a father has compassion on his children, so the Lord has compassion on those who fear him" (Ps 103:13). And Pr 3:12 again insists that we understand trials in a perspective that releases us from resentment, because we know that "the Lord disciplines those he loves, as a father the son he delights in." In each of these passages, family relationship is used to shed light on God's motives and actions. God has acted "as a father." Yet each passage carefully refrains from teaching that an actual father-child relationship exists between God and his OT worshipers (Ps 68:5; Pr 22:22–23; Jer 31:9–10).

Prophetic psalms indicate a real father-son relationship—between God and the Messiah (2:7; 89:26). But it is not until the NT era that we discover the wonder of the relationship that God has planned for those who come to him in faith.

NT — 5. The Greek words and their uses. The primary Greek word, which corresponds to the OT *'āḇ*, is *patēr*. Another term, striking in its intimacy, is *abba*. ◆ **Abba** A quick survey of NT uses of *patēr* shows a significant shift from the OT use of *'āḇ*, which is seldom applied to God. In the NT, God is spoken of as Father about 250 times, with the remainder of the over 400 occurrences of *patēr* having a secular or natural meaning.

The secular uses parallel the uses of *'āḇ* in the OT. The NT reaffirms the ties of each person to father and mother (Mk 7:10–12; 10:29–30; Mt 10:37; 15:3–9; Lk 14:26) and the responsibilities of parents to children (Eph 6:1–4; Col 3:21). God's OT people are "our fathers" in a spiritual sense (1 Co 10:1; Heb 1:1; cf. Ro 9–11), even as Abraham, the founder of that family that exists through faith in God, is the father of believers (Ro 4:1,11–12). In

267

this same sense the NT speaks of a spiritual family bond between new believers and those who introduced them to Christ and nurture them (1 Co 4:14–17; 1 Ti 1:2,18; 2 Ti 1:2; 2:1; Tit 1:4; Phm 10; 1 Pe 5:13). Some of the passages that explore this spiritual relationship are discussed under 8, below.

The most significant feature of the NT use of *patēr* is its profuse use in reference to God. OT references to God as Father focus on his creative acts that constituted him as originator (and thus "father" in this sense) of the people of Israel. NT references to God as Father are completely different (except Heb 12:9 and Jas 1:17; and perhaps Eph 3:14). In the NT, references to God as Father unveil aspects of God's very nature and reveal the depth of that relationship to which he invites us.

6. God as the Father. The OT characteristically identifies the Lord as "God of our fathers" or as "God of Abraham." It is a shock to one steeped in the OT to discover that in the NT God is known as "the Father." God is revealed as the Father in his intrinsic relationship within the Trinity, in which Jesus is the Son. And God is revealed as Father in the stunning relationship he establishes with believers.

The passages in which God is spoken of as the Father are typically Trinitarian in character. They focus on the First Person of the Trinity either in his relationship with Jesus, or in distinction from the other members of the Trinity. Despite the fact that Jesus and the Father are, together with the Spirit, one God (Jn 10:30; 14:10–11), the Father is said by Jesus to be greater than he (Jn 14:28). When Jesus was on the earth, only the Father knew the day and hour of Jesus' return, or the schedule of history's end (Mt 24:36; Mk 13:32; Ac 1:7). The exact character of the differences between the persons of the Trinity are and will remain mystery. But the first person of the Trinity has from eternity been "the Father," and the Second has been "the Son." This stunning revelation of the hidden nature of God is a major contribu-

tion of the NT and is central in identifying God as the Father.

Although the Bible does not go into detail on distinctives within the Trinity, some things are specified as uniquely the Father's. John says that all those who come to Jesus come because the Father has enabled them to do so (Jn 6:37,44,65). Col 1:12–13 says that it is the Father who qualifies us to share in the inheritance of the saints, and it is he who rescues us from the dominion of darkness by bringing us into the kingdom of the Son he loves. Eph 1:4–5 portrays the Father as the architect of the plan of salvation. He "chose us in him before the creation of the world" and "predestined us to be adopted as his sons through Jesus Christ."

Despite the theological significance of the use of *patēr* to distinguish the first person of the Trinity from the others, the overwhelming personal impact of the name in the first century cannot be overestimated. The distant God of the fathers was suddenly shown in a new light. The awesome one whose name Yahweh the pious Jew would never pronounce (and even the writing of whose name by a scribe called immediately for a ritual bath) was now presented to humankind in the most intimate and loving way. Even today, if we pause to consider, we must hear Jesus' words in awe and wonder: "When you pray, say: 'Father' " (Lk 11:2).

7. God as Father of Jesus. The revelation of God as Father is introduced by Jesus. He often spoke of God as "my Father in heaven" (only recorded in Matthew—7:21; 10:32,33; 12:50; 16:17; 18:10,19; cf. 15:13; 18:35). In addition, in his public and private prayers Jesus addressed God as Father (cf. Mt 11:25–26; 26:39,42; Mk 14:36; Lk 10:21; 22:42; 23:34; Jn 11:41; 12:27–28). This claim that he had a Father-Son relationship with God was shocking to the religious leaders of the first century. When Jesus spoke of God as his Father, the Jews (John's term for the religious leaders) "tried all the harder to kill him." Jesus not only violated their traditions "but he was even calling God his own Father, making himself equal with God" (Jn 5:18).

Many of the things Jesus taught explore the relationship between the Father and the Son. When Jesus claimed, "I and the Father are one" (Jn 10:38), he aroused hostility. Rather than accept his claim, the Jews made attempts to stone Jesus because, they told him, "You, a mere man, claim to be God" (10:33). Yet the claims of Jesus were authenticated over and over again. The oneness existing between Jesus and the Father were expressed in Christ's words and in his miraculous works (Jn 14:10–11; cf. 8:28). God the Father was at work in all Jesus did so that Christ perfectly expressed the will and character of the Father (Jn 5:17–23). The Father and Jesus were one in authority and power. Jesus has the divine right to judge and the divine power to give life (Jn 5:21–22). Preexistent as God with the Father (Jn 1:1–5; 8:56–58), the Son is one with the Father as object of our love and worship (Jn 14:21–23).

The statements made by Jesus and recorded in the Gospels affirm the Son's identity with the Father. Jesus could say, "Anyone who has seen me has seen the Father" (Jn 14:9), for he is in the Father and the Father is in him (14:10). Jesus fully and perfectly expresses the very character of God the Father. And yet Jesus remains, as the Second Person of the Trinity, distinct from the Father. Jesus said the Father is greater than he (Jn 14:28), portrayed himself as sent by the Father (Jn 5:36–37; 6:57; 8:16,18,42; 12:49) and lived his life on earth according to the Father's will (Mt 26:39–42; Jn 5:36; 12:49).

While the existence of one God as a Trinity of Father, Son, and Holy Spirit involves concepts beyond our understanding, what is most important is that in the coming of the Son we have a stunning revelation of the fact that God is Father. This could come only through Jesus. As Christ said, "No one knows the Son except the Father, and no one knows the Father except the Son and those to whom the Son chooses to reveal him" (Mt 11:27; cf. Lk 10:21–22; Jn 14:1–13). In presenting himself as Son, Jesus pre-sented an aspect of God completely unknown before the Incarnation. He spoke of God as his Father—the one they claimed as their God—saying to the Jewish leaders, "Though you do not know him, I know him" (Jn 8:54–55). Only in Jesus do we learn that God is Father. Only in seeing God as Father do we begin to realize the intimacy of the relationship that can exist between the believer and the Lord.

8. God as our Father. Jesus used the term "Father" carefully. He spoke of "my Father," and to the disciples he referred to God as "your Father." He never used the phrase "our Father" in a way that would link himself with them: the relationship of Jesus with God is unique, for he is the eternal Son of God. Yet, through Jesus, human beings have been welcomed into a family relationship with God the Father. ♦ *Born*

The NT authors who wrote the Epistles, typically in their introductions and in other formulas, remind believers constantly of their position as children of God. The family language of the Bible shows us that our relationship with God and with one another is rooted in the fact that God is Father of a family that encompasses all whom faith makes his children. ♦ *Family*

But what are the implications of a relationship with a God who is now revealed to be the Father by his very nature, as well as our Father by redemption? The Gospels in particular suggest a number of ways in which God acts as our Father. He rewards us (Mt 6:1) and disciplines us (Jn 15:2; Heb 12:7–11). God the Father listens to our prayers (Mt 6:6; 18:19). He knows and he meets our needs (Mt 6:8; Lk 12:30), thus fulfilling the father's obligation to provide for his family. God has lavished love on us (1 Jn 3:1; Jude 1) and has given us good gifts (Mt 7:11; Lk 11:13). He numbers the very hairs of our head and remains in such total command of the universe that not even a sparrow can fall without his permission (Mt 10:29–30). As our Father, God is merciful (Lk 6:36) and is pleased to give the kingdom to Jesus' disciples (Lk 12:32). Yet though our Father loves us (Jn 16:27), he also judges each person's work (1 Pe 1:17).

Jesus, revealer of God as our Father, spells out other implications of this exciting relationship. A father sets the pattern for his children. Thus we are to be like our father in showing love, even to our enemies (Mt 5:43–48). The Father accepts responsibility to meet the needs of his family. Thus we are released from anxiety and from the necessity of focusing our energies on obtaining material things. We can seek God and his kingdom first (Mt 6:25–34; Lk 12:22–31) and be free to share our possessions with the poor (Lk 12:32–34). We have confidence in our new relationship with God, for we have access to his presence at any time (Heb 4:16). And when we come into the presence of the Lord of the universe, we are free to address him as "our Father" (Mt 6:9).

9. Unusual NT uses of the word "father". Among the many appearances of *patēr* in the NT are some that raise questions.

a. Father as founder. One OT concept expressed by "father" is that of the founder of a family or line. When the Jewish leaders angrily shouted at Jesus, "Abraham is our Father" (Jn 8:39; cf. Mt 3:9; Lk 3:8), they were claiming to be in the religious tradition of the founding father of Israel.

Jesus pointed out that Abraham did not respond to God's truth with hatred and rejection (Jn 8:39–41). The Jewish leaders' protest that the only Father they had was God himself echoes another OT use of this title: God was creator of the covenant people in whose ranks they claimed membership (8:41). Jesus challenged their claim when he said, "If God were your Father, you would love me" (8:42). The attitudes and values of anyone who has a real relationship with God are shaped by that relationship. The leaders' reaction of angry hatred and their plans to kill Jesus for telling them the truth show that their true spiritual kinship was with Satan (8:43–47).

Ro 4 expressly calls Abraham the "father" of those who have faith in Jesus.

Abraham is the first person identified in Scripture as having been made righteous by faith. All who have faith can look to Abraham as the founder of their spiritual line. Faith, not spiritual descent, makes one a member of Abraham's spiritual family and makes Abraham one's spiritual father.

b. The prohibition against calling anyone on earth "father". This practice reflects another OT usage. "Father" became a term of respect to honor one who had authority.

In Mt 23, Jesus discussed the Pharisees and their claim to spiritual authority in Israel. He then turned to the disciples and instructed them about relationships within the new family of faith. Believers are not to recognize others as rabbi (Mt 23:8) or father (23:9) or teacher (23:10). These terms of respect served to create hierarchies in Israel. But in the church, he told his followers, "You are all brothers" (23:8), and Christ is the only Teacher. And the great within the fellowship of faith are simply servants (23:11). Hierarchies and words that foster them are wrong for NT believers.

c. Fathers honored and rejected at the same time. The NT repeats the OT injunction to honor father and mother (Mk 10:19). But Jesus also made several blunt statements that seem to contradict these commands: "Anyone who loves his father or mother more than me is not worthy of me" (Mt 10:37); "If anyone comes to me and does not hate his father and mother, . . . he cannot be my disciple" (Lk 14:26; cf. Mk 10:29–30).

Each of these statements is found in a context in which the possible cost of discipleship is explored. If a choice must be made between family ties and loyalty to Christ, the disciple must choose to "hate" (decisively reject) the family ties in favor of Jesus.

While such a conflict may exist in unusual situations (Mk 13:9–13; Lk 12:49–53), there is normally little tension between loyalty to parents and loyalty to Jesus. The reason is that both loyalties are God's will for us, and usually they will not be in conflict. An illustration of the harmony is found in Mt 15:3–6. This passage reports Jesus' reaction to a misuse of the tradition of Corban, which provided that resources dedicated to God need not be used to support one's old parents. Some in Israel claimed that all their possessions were devoted to God (but to be enjoyed by them during their lifetimes) and so refused on this basis to help their parents. Jesus angrily told the Pharisees that this practice broke "the command of God," whose express will it is that children honor their parents.

d. Melchizedek: man "without father". Heb 7:3 bases an argument about Jesus' high-priesthood on the Ge 14:18 reference to the ruler of Jerusalem in Abraham's day. The phrase "without father" is derived from the NT writer's use of a rabbinic principle of OT interpretation: What is not mentioned in the Torah does not exist. The writer of Hebrews argues that the fact that Melchizedek's birth and death are not mentioned in the Torah implies he had an endless priesthood. ♦ *Priesthood*

10. Summary. The term "father" is significant in both Testaments. It is most significant in the ways in which it is applied to God.

In the OT, God is conceived of as the Father of Israel, in the special sense of being creator or founder of the nation. In the NT, the Incarnation reveals the fact that God exists in three persons and that the First Person of the Trinity is to be known as the Father. God is not only Father in nature; he is also the Father of Jesus, the Second Person of the Trinity. While the nature of this relationship is shrouded in mystery, it is clear that the Father and the Son are one and yet that the Father has primacy.

Another stunning and wonderful revelation given in Jesus is that God is the Father of those who come to him by faith in the relational sense. Relationship with God as our Father brings us both awesome blessings and family responsibilities. But through Jesus' revelation of the Father and through his self-sacrifice on Calvary, you and I never again need doubt God's love or the intimacy of the relationship that we now have with him.

FATHERLESS

The Hebrew word for "fatherless" is *yāṯôm*, "orphan." It occurs forty-two times in the OT and, often in conjunction with the word "widow," portrays the helpless ones of society. The OT shows great concern for the fatherless and insists that they be given justice (Dt 24:17; 27:19; Ps 82:3). Lack of concern for the poor and helpless who lack a father to provide for them is a sign of corruption in any society (Job 31:17; Ps 94:6; Isa 1:17,23; Zec 7:10; Mal 3:5). Because of their helplessness, God has special concern for the fatherless (Dt 10:18; Ps 68:5).

FAVOR

Several Hebrew words are translated "favor" in the NIV and the NASB. At times the word is found in an idiomatic phrase like "entreat the face [seek the favor] of the Lord" (cf. 2 Ki 13:4). Most often the Hebrew reads either *ḥēn* ("grace") or *ḥānan* ("be gracious"). ♦ *Grace*

Another common word is *rāṣôn* ("good will," "favor," or "acceptance"). ♦ *Acceptable/Acceptance*

Phrases that indicate having, finding, or showing favor are reasonable ways of expressing these terms in the context where "favor" appears in the OT.

FEAR

Fear is a complex quality, swirling with emotions and pointing to real or imagined terrors. The concept is complicated in Scripture by its use in a religious sense, "fear" expressing an attitude toward God. Perhaps surprisingly, the antidote to most of our fears is in fact fear—fear of the Lord!

OT   **1. The Hebrew words**
      2. Fear as an emotion
      3. Fear of anticipated evil
      4. Fear of the Lord
NT   **5. The Greek words**
      6. The behavioral impact of fear

7. Fear of God's working
8. Fear in the believer's relationship with God
9. Summary

OT — 1. The Hebrew words. Several Hebrew word groups express the ideas of fear and being afraid. The most common is the *yārē'* group, which conveys all the meanings of fear. *Gûr* and *mᵉgôrâh* mean "terror." Both words suggest a cringing fear, a falling back before superior force in man, animal, or God. *Paḥad* and its derivatives are poetic synonyms for *yārē'*. This group suggests both the presence of a feared object and the trembling that that presence causes. These words may focus on one's feelings or on the object of fear. Unlike *yārē'*, this word group is not used to suggest anticipated evils.

2. Fear as an emotion. OT uses of "fear" often indicate the all-too-familiar feeling of terror. Adam and Eve fled from God in the Garden of Eden, Adam later explaining, "I heard you in the garden, and I was afraid because I was naked" (Ge 3:10). A basic cause of this emotion is awareness of vulnerability because of sin or because of the perceived power of another to do harm. The Hebrew people experienced such terror at Sinai (Dt 5:5), and Saul was gripped by fear when he saw the size of the massive Philistine army (1 Sa 28:5).

The antidote for the emotion of fear is the conviction that God is for us and with us. God told Israel he would be with his covenant people. So Moses exhorted Israel, "Do not be faint-hearted or afraid; do not be terrified or give way to panic before them. For the LORD your God is the one who goes with you to fight for you against your enemies to give you victory" (Dt 20:3–4).

There are many situations in which fear is most appropriate. We should never berate ourselves because of our fears. David reported a time of personal fear in Ps 56. In that psalm, he presents fear as an opportunity rather than a weakness. It is only when we are afraid that we can experience the meaning of trust in God. David traces his own emo-

tions and shows a pattern that we can duplicate: "When I am afraid, I will trust in you. In God, whose word I praise, in God I trust; I will not be afraid. What can mortal man do to me?" (56:3–4). The pattern is this: (1) David experiences fear. (2) He turns to God with a statement of trust. (3) He recalls God's self-revelation in the Word. (4) He determines not to anticipate evil, for he knows that God is in control, and no mere mortal can overcome the Lord.

3. Fear of anticipated evil. Many passages portray the emotion of fear as aroused by an intellectual anticipation of what might happen. At times, such anticipation does not create terror but finds expression in worry or anxiety.

Abraham was "afraid to say, 'She is my wife,' " for he anticipated that the local ruler of the Philistines might want Sarah for himself and might murder him to get her (Ge 26:7). Moses, when he was told by God to return to Egypt to lead Israel to freedom (Ex 3–4), raised many objections. He anticipated all sorts of problems that might arise, and his actions made it clear that he was afraid.

The antidote to such fear of anticipated evil is also found in looking to the Lord with trust. Ps 112 celebrates the blessings given to the person who honors and remembers God. It says of such a person: "He will have no fear of bad news; his heart is steadfast, trusting in the LORD. His heart is secure, he will have no fear; in the end he will look in triumph on his foes" (112:7–8).

God, who commands events in his universe, is in control of each believer's future. Whatever trials the future may hold, the person whose trust is in the Lord will have hope and a sense of personal security.

4. Fear of the Lord. This religious fear, or awe, is God's answer to the ordinary fears that master human beings.

Such fear is reverence for God. We who fear God recognize him as the ultimate reality, and we respond to him. Fear of God is called the "beginning of knowledge" (Pr 1:7), meaning that taking God into account is the foundation of a disciplined and holy life (Pr 1:3; cf. Ge 20:11; Ps 36:1–4). To fear God means to reject every competing deity and to serve him only (Dt 6:13). Fear of the Lord is expressed by walking in all his ways, by loving him, and by serving him with all our heart and soul (Dt 10:12; Job 1:1; Ps 128:1).

While fear of God is closely linked with morality and with obedience to God's commands, it is also freeing. To fear God means to recognize him as Creator and to know that his plans stand firm forever (Ps 33:8–11). God has a special concern for all who fear him (vv. 18–19; cf. Ps 31:19; 34:9). Thus those who fear God can say with the psalmist, "We wait in hope for the LORD ; he is our help and our shield. In him our hearts rejoice, for we trust in his holy name. May your unfailing love rest upon us, O LORD , even as we put our hope in you" (Ps 33:20–22).

NT — 5. The Greek words.
The Greek *phobos* (noun) and *phobeomai* (verb) indicate fear, terror, fright, or reverence; and *deilos* has the idea of dread. As in the OT, fear in the NT carries a full range of meanings. The disciples were terrified at the storm on the sea of Galilee (Mt 8:26). Paul was afraid (concerned) that when he came to Corinth he might not find the Corinthians as he wanted them to be (2 Co 12:20). And, of course, there is in the NT as well as the OT a fear of God that is in essence the reverence and the awe felt by those who know and who love him.

Although uses of "fear" in the NT parallel the uses of this word in the OT, the NT makes distinctive contributions to the understanding of our fears.

6. The behavioral impact of fear.
The OT points out that those who fear God show their awareness of who he is by their moral choices as well as by their worship. The NT helps us to further explore ways that fear shapes human behavior.

The enemies of Jesus are portrayed several times holding back their hatred and resisting the impulse to attack him for fear of the crowds who thought him to be at least a prophet (e.g., Mt 21:46;

Mk 12:12). Some who believed in Jesus were afraid and so would not acknowledge him openly (e.g., Jn 7:13; 12:42). King Herod wanted to execute John the Baptist, but he held back for a time out of fear of the people (Mt 14:5). Even Peter so feared the members of the circumcision party in Jerusalem who came to visit the new Gentile church in Antioch that he stopped eating with the non-Jewish believers (Gal 2:12).

Each of these instances involves a fear of what others will think or how they will react to us. Such fear is a primary source of conformity in society. But Jesus told his disciples to put this kind of fear behind them, even if some would hate them because of him (Mt 10:26). We are to be in awe of God, not of others, for he alone holds the ultimate power (Mt 10:28; Lk 12:4). Such fear of the Lord releases us from bondage to the opinions of others and frees us to act spontaneously and to choose what is right.

So, Jesus taught, "Don't be afraid," even of those who seem to have the power to kill. God is in control of even the sparrow's fall, and, he told them, "You are worth more than many sparrows" (Mt 10:31; Lk 12:7). When we are aware of God's power and of his love, we are released from those lesser terrors that might move us to compromise or to disobey the Lord.

7. Fear of God's working.
We can understand the amazement and the initial fright that overtook those who first observed Jesus' miracles. In some cases, fear was transformed to adoration, as bystanders praised God for what Jesus had done (e.g., Lk 5:26). But all too often we see a different reaction.

In Gadara, Jesus released a demon-possessed man and sent the horde of evil spirits that had dominated him into a herd of pigs. The people saw their neighbor "sitting there, dressed and in his right mind," and "they were afraid" (Mk 5:15). Because of this they began to plead with Jesus to leave their region! They were uncomfortable with God's work, even though his power had been used for good.

When Felix, the Roman governor at Caesarea, listened to Paul speak about faith in Christ and the coming judgment, he "was afraid" (Ac 24:25). Felix sent Paul away from him.

John helps us to understand such reactions, which are so much like the reaction of Adam and Eve in Eden. "Light has come into the world," John wrote, "but men loved darkness instead of light because their deeds were evil. Everyone who does evil hates the light, and will not come into the light for fear that his deeds will be exposed" (Jn 3:19–20).

Man's reaction to God's action and to God's Word is often to reject them or to try to flee from God. Sin has so warped our perception that God's love is difficult to see. Instead, an often-unacknowledged sense of guilt creates in us a fear of exposure and leads us to flee headlong from the only source of healing.

8. Fear in the believer's relationship with God. Two themes concerning fear are found in the NT. The first is a reflection of the OT's presentation of the fear of the Lord as reverent awe. This attitude is still wholly appropriate for believers. When Ananias and Sapphira lied to the Holy Spirit and immediately died, this kind of fear gripped the Jerusalem church and "all who heard about these events" (Ac 5:11). Acts reports that immediately there was renewed spiritual vitality that generated healings and stimulated evangelism (5:12–16).

Peter calls us to remember the holiness of God and the fact that God "judges each man's work impartially"; being aware of who God is and being in awe of him, we are to "live [our] lives as strangers here in reverent fear" (1 Pe 1:17; cf. 2:17).

While this theme of a reverent awe as being an appropriate fear of the Lord is found in the NT, there is a second theme, one that stresses release from fear. Paul reminds us that the Spirit, whom we received at conversion, does not "make [us] a slave again to fear." Instead, the Spirit testifies to our sonship. As children we can approach God

confidently and call on him as Father (Ro 8:15).

John adds this thought: "There is no fear in love. But perfect love drives out fear, because fear has to do with punishment. The one who fears is not made perfect in love" (1 Jn 4:18).

The impact of the statements of both Paul and John is to purify our concept of religious fear. The OT concept of the fear of God must be understood in the context of covenant relationship with God. ♦ *Covenant* God promised both to remain the loyal protector of his people and to shower them with lovingkindness. Those who truly feared God would keep his commandments and, because they did not violate the covenant, did not need to fear punishment.

But when Jesus came, the unlimited depth of God's love was unveiled. Love originated in God, for God is love (1 Jn 4:7–8,16). God then showed himself to be love by sending his son to be the atoning sacrifice for sin (vv. 9–10) ♦ *Atonement* By accepting Jesus as that atoning sacrifice and acknowledging him as God's Son, we can "rely on the love God has for us" (4:15–16).

The impact of John's argument is this: When our fear of God—that is, our wonder and awe and deep respect for the Lord—grows out of fear of punishment, we have not fully grasped the nature of God or the meaning of Jesus' sacrifice. Our fear of God is purified when what motivates us is not fright but love.

9. Summary. We experience fear as fright and also as anxiety about what might happen in the future. God is the antidote for each of these aspects of fear. Both the OT and the NT show us a God who is in complete control of every event. When we are in a right relationship with God, we can be sure that he supervises everything that happens to us.

Trust in God's power and in his commitment to our best interests releases us from all competing and lesser fears.

Fear of God is a religious concept, with an intimate link to right relationship with God. To fear God means to acknowledge his power and his authority. To fear God also means to adopt a godly lifestyle out of respect for him. One who fears God makes those moral choices that reflect the character of the Lord.

In the NT, fear is seen as a source of human motivation. Fear of others' opinion will pressure many to make choices they would not otherwise make. Believers are to remember that only one opinion is important. Ultimately we are answerable only to the Lord. Thus we are released by a healthy fear of God from those inferior terrors that hold so many of us in their grip.

The NT also purifies and further explains the meaning of the fear of the Lord. True fear of God does not include a fear of punishment. Jesus has shown us that God is love. It is love, not dread, that moves us to respond obediently to the Lord. ♦ *Love*

At the same time, our love for God must always be blended with awe. We must not take God lightly. He is one whose voice shakes the very earth and will soon shatter the heavens (Heb 12:26–28). Thus the exhortation comes: "Let us be thankful, and so worship God acceptably with reverence and awe, for our God is a consuming fire" (v. 29).

And let us never forget that the consuming fire we worship is also our Father.

FEAST/FESTIVAL

Several Hebrew terms are translated "feast" or "festival." *Mišteh* is a secular feast or banquet, such as a wedding feast (*gamos*) of the NT. ♦ *Banquet*

Other terms are specifically religious. *hāgag* and *hag* refer to the three pilgrim festivals that all Israel was to celebrate (Ex 23:14). *Mô'ēd* can refer to one of the three, but it means "appointed time" or "meeting," and can also indicate other worship occasions.

The three annual festivals were times of religious joy, when whole families made pilgrimages to Jerusalem to celebrate their faith. These festivals are the Passover, with its days of unleavened bread (Ex 13:3–10; Lev 23:4–8; Dt 16:1–8); Firstfruits, also called the Feast of

Weeks and Pentecost (Lev 23:9–21; Dt 16:9–11); and Tabernacles, also called Booths or the Feast of Ingathering (Ex 23:16; Lev 23:33–43; Dt 16:13). Although linked with agricultural seasons, these festivals were holidays during which Israel relived salvation history and reaffirmed their commitment to God with gifts and shared worship.

The Greek word for the religious feast or holiday is *heortē*. The verb *heortazō* "to celebrate," occurs only in 1 Co 5:8. Nearly every use is found in the Gospels or Acts and refers to one of Israel's three pilgrim festivals. Col 2:16 refers to religious special days in general, and 1 Co 5:8 is a call to celebrate relationship with God by a commitment to holiness.

FEEL/FEELINGS ♦ *Heart*

FELLOWSHIP

Fellowship is a particularly significant concept in the NT. There it expresses shared participation in Christ and the bond that Christ creates between believers.

OT 1. Fellowship in the OT
NT 2. Fellowship in the NT

OT — 1. Fellowship in the OT. The NIV uses the word "fellowship" frequently in its translation of the OT. Most often this word is a translation of *šelem* as "fellowship offering." The NASB translates this word as "peace offering."

This particular sacrifice was a fellowship offering in two senses. (1) The offering was made by those at peace with God, in contrast with the sin offering, which was designed to restore peace. ♦ *Peace* Thus, the fellowship offering represented the blessing of wholeness, which comes through a right relationship with God. (2) The offering was a communion sacrifice. That is, the priests and the worshipers ate of this offering. By this shared meal the worshipers expressed their fellowship with each other in the bond of their common faith.

NT — 2. Fellowship in the NT. The Greek word translated "fellowship" is *koinōnia*. It is variously translated "fellowship," "sharing," "partnership," and "contribution." Although not often used, *koinōnia* is a theologically significant term. It appears in Ac 2:42; Ro 15:26; 1 Co 1:9; 10:16; 2 Co 6:14; 8:4; 9:13; 13:14; Gal 2:9; Eph 3:9; Php 1:5; 2:1; 3:10; Phm 6; Heb 13:16; 1 Jn 1:3,6–7.

Ac 2:42–47 gives us a beautiful picture of participation in the life of the believing community at Jerusalem. It portrays a mutual commitment to God that helps us sense the deeper meaning of fellowship: "They devoted themselves to the apostles' teaching and to the fellowship, to the breaking of bread and to prayer. Everyone was filled with awe, and many wonders and miraculous signs were done by the apostles. All the believers were together and had everything in common. Selling their possessions and goods, they gave to anyone as he had need. Every day they continued to meet together in the temple courts. They broke bread in their homes and ate together with glad and sincere hearts, praising God and enjoying the favor of all the people. And the Lord added to their number daily those who were being saved."

The Greek philosophers chose the word *koinōnia*—which means "association," "fellowship," or "participation"— to depict the ideal of a harmonious secular society. But such a utopia has never been realized. Sin always twists the reality of interpersonal relationships, leaving mankind hungry for the realization of its dreams. There is hope only in the NT and the church.

Paul uses *koinōnia* fourteen times in his epistles (fifteen times if he wrote Hebrews). Paul's usage does not echo the philosopher's dream. Instead, the NT affirms a new reality. God has called us "into fellowship with his Son Jesus Christ" (1 Co 1:9). We are drawn into relationship with God and participate in a unique fellowship won for us by the blood of Christ (1 Co 10:16). Everything in life is an expression of our mystical but real participation in all that Jesus is. This mystical union is what overflows into our relationship with other believers. Recog-

nizing that others are also in Christ, we extend to them the right hand of fellowship (Gal 2:9), sensing a partnership in the gospel (Php 1:5). Even Christian giving must be understood in the context of fellowship. In this context, financial gifts become sharing, not "giving" (Ro 15:26; 2 Co 8:4; 9:13; Heb 13:16). ◆ *Giving*

Paul's use of *koinōnia* emphasizes the reality of our mystical union with Christ. But John in his first epistle focuses on our experience of fellowship. John begins with the fact that fellowship "is with the Father and with his Son, Jesus Christ" (1 Jn 1:3). But we do not have (experience) fellowship with God if we walk in darkness. Here darkness represents not sin but self-deceit, as light represents not sinlessness but honesty in our relationship with the Lord. ◆ *Light and Darkness* When we do live honestly in our relationship with God, we have fellowship with God and with God's people as well (1:7).

The bonds that link us to Jesus bond us to one another. The fellowship we experience in the community of faith goes far beyond friendship.

In the NT, then, fellowship begins with our relationship with the Lord in mystical union with Jesus. We experience that union as we live close to the Lord and with honesty in our dealings with him. Our union with Jesus is the basis for a bond with our fellow Christians. Because that bond is so vital and real, we can live with each other in an intimacy impossible in every other setting.

FEMALE ◆ *Male and Female*

FESTIVAL ◆ *Feast/Festival*

FIERCE

The word translated "fierce" most often is *hārôn*, which means "burning anger." Other Hebrew words indicate the strength or intensity of that emotion. Another article discusses the fierce anger of God. ◆ *Anger*

FIGHT/FIGHTING ▶ War

FILL/FULLNESS

The common meanings for these quite ordinary words is found throughout Scripture. But their common use is often enriched by their figurative application to God and to the believer's spiritual experience. In the NT they are lifted beyond their common meanings and in some cases become technical theological words with most significant meaning.

OT 1. Hebrew words for "fill" and "fullness"
NT 2. Greek words for "fill" and "fullness"
   3. Filling with the Spirit
   4. The fullness of Christ

OT — 1. Hebrew words for "fill" and "fullness". A number of Hebrew words or phrases are translated "fill" or "full." Most are so translated rather infrequently; thus when we read one of these words in the OT in the NIV or the NASB, it is most likely that "fill" and "fullness" are translations of one of two Hebrew word groups.

a. *Mālē'* means "to fill" or "to be full." The verb occurs 249 times in the Qal and Niphal stems. Its basic meaning is spacial: locusts fill up the space in a house; liquid fills up the space in a cup. But the word is also extended and used of time, indicating a set number of elapsed days or weeks—prophetic and theological significance. ▶ *Fulfill*

Mālē' and its derivatives are usually translated "fullness." The word is used of abstract qualities as well as material things. God's omnipresence is expressed in passages that announce that the Lord fills heaven and earth (Jer 23:24). The spiritual condition of the preflood generation is explained by the statement that the whole earth "was full of violence" (Ge 6:11). Israel's spiritual condition is described by the assertion that the land is full of idols (Jer 16:18). But the earth has a beautiful future. One day the whole earth will be full of the knowledge of the glory of the Lord (Hab 2:14).

b. *Sāḇēa'* focuses on our subjective experience of fullness. The verb means "to be satisfied," usually by nourishing food. Its derivative, *śoḇa'*, is translated "fullness." The concept of being satisfied, or full, shifts easily from the literal to the metaphorical. A person can be full of troubles or horror (cf. Ps 88:3; Eze 20:26). But the OT emphasis is on the positive. There is a deep satisfaction that is ours through a relationship with the Lord. Thus God is praised for his endless love, and the material images are transcended, becoming symbols for who God himself is in our lives. We are filled, for God "satisfies the thirsty and fills the hungry with good things" (Ps 107:9; cf. Mt 5:6). Ultimately, only God can satisfy us, for in his presence there is "fullness of joy" (Ps 16:11, NASB).

NT — 2. Greek words for "fill" and "fullness". A number of words are used in the NT to indicate filling or fullness. The most significant are:

plēroō	to fill, complete, fulfill
plērophoreō	to accomplish, satisfy fully, give full measure
pimplēmi	to fill, complete, fulfill
empiplēmi	to fill full, satisfy
plērēs (adj)	full, complete
plērōma (n)	that which has been completed, fullness
plērophoria (n)	fullness, full assurance

The literal meaning of the verb was early extended to include a wide variety of meanings. It might mean any of the following: to fulfill a wish or a promise, to finish a task, to satisfy a desire, to meet an obligation, or to describe the quality of a person's life as filled with love, joy, virtue, or even with God.

In the NT the verb *plēroō* becomes a technical theological term when used to indicate the fulfillment of prophecy. ▶ *Fulfill*

The NT often uses this word group to characterize human experience or to describe an individual's character. We can be filled with a knowledge of God's will. We can also be filled with joy, awe, grief, greed, compassion, wonder, and the fruits of righteousness.

All the meanings of "fill" and "fullness" expressed in the Greek NT are found in English as well and thus are easily understood when translated. But two uses have special theological significance. The NT speaks of believers being filled with the Spirit and of their possessing the fullness of Christ.

3. Filling with the Spirit. The OT speaks of the Spirit of God coming upon various OT leaders (Jdg 6:34; 11:29; 14:19); these leaders subsequently performed special tasks. Then the NT unveils one of the great wonders of our present age: every believer is given the gift of the Holy Spirit. Each of us can be filled with the Spirit, and by the Spirit we are qualified and equipped both for any service to which we are called and for living a victorious Christian life.

When used in connection with the Spirit's filling, the verbs *plēthō* (Lk 1:15,41,67; Ac 2:4; 4:8,31; 9:17; 13:9; used in other connections in Mt 22:10; 27:48; Lk 1:23,57; 2:6,21,22; 4:28; 5:7,26; 6:11; Jn 19:29; Ac 3:10; 5:17; 13:45; 19:29) and *plēroō* (Eph 5:18) always appear in the passive voice. We are filled, and this filling is a work of God. It is God who is the active giver of this wonderful gift. The adjective *plērēs* is used in relation to the Spirit's filling in Lk 4:1; Ac 6:3,5; 7:55; 11:24 (other uses occur in Mt 14:20; 15:37; Mk 4:28; 6:43; 8:19; Lk 5:12; Jn 1:14; Ac 6:8; 98:36; 13:10; 19:28; 2 Jn 8).

"Filling" is one of several distinctive terms used in the NT to describe the work of the Holy Spirit in and for believers. ♦ *Spirit (Holy Spirit)* This word has implications for both ministry and character. John the Baptist's filling is directly linked with his mission "to make ready a people prepared for the Lord" (Lk 1:17). Being filled with the Spirit was a necessary qualification for the service to be performed by the first deacons (Ac 6:1–6).

Ac 6 also gives us a hint of how filling affects character. The men chosen as Spirit-filled men were known for their wisdom (6:3) and their faith (6:5). Paul in Galatians focuses our attention on how the Spirit shapes character. Sinful nature shows itself in immorality, interpersonal discord, jealousy, anger, selfish ambition, and lack of self-control. But someone filled with the Spirit—led and enabled by him—demonstrates love, joy, peace, patience, kindness, goodness, faithfulness, gentleness, and self-control (5:19–23).

God has given his Spirit to us. The Spirit fills us, not only that we may serve him but also that our own character may reflect Jesus Christ.

4. The fullness of Christ. The word used to express the fullness of Christ is *plērōma*. This word is capable of a wide range of meanings (e.g., that which fills, full measure [the whole], completeness, and maturity). So the particular meaning of the *plērōma* of Christ must be determined from the argument and context of each passage in which the phrase is found.

The key passages are in Paul's two christological letters (Colossians and Ephesians). Col 1:15–20 affirms the nature and supremacy of Christ as God. In this context the statement "for God was pleased to have all his fullness dwell in him" (1:19) emphasizes the complete expression of God himself through Jesus. Col 2:9–10 is another affirmation of who Jesus is. But this time Paul speaks of Jesus' nature as it affects us. In context, Paul is denouncing the empty approach to spiritual fulfillment, the approach touted by some who relied on human philosophy and tradition to construct their own spiritual pathway. Paul offers a totally different way: Jesus. All that God is can be and is summed up in Jesus Christ, "for in Christ all the fullness of the Deity lives in bodily form" (2:9). All that we need in order to be filled with God is ours already, in Jesus: "You have been given fullness [*plēroō*] in Christ" (2:10). How futile, then, to look for spiritual fulfillment or maturity in religious practices (2:16–23) instead of in our personal relationship with the Lord.

Ephesians focuses on the relationship of Jesus to his church. What does it mean for Christ, who is fully God, to exist in an organic relationship with human beings who, through faith, have been joined to him as a body is joined to its head?

Paul's prayer that we may come to understand this relationship is recorded in Eph 1. Through this relationship with Jesus we have become God's treasure, and also through it God's power is released within us and for us (1:15–23). Paul's prayer concludes with his statement that the church as Jesus' body is "the fullness of him who fills everything in every way." Jesus, who fills all things, is in a unique and mystical sense himself fulfilled (completed) by us who are his body.

The next occurrence of *plērōma* in Ephesians is also found in a prayer. Paul prayed 'that members of the Christian community might experience the love of Christ "that surpasses knowledge." In experiencing the reality of this love, which we can never really comprehend, we will "be filled to the measure of all the fullness of God" (3:19). Paul desires that as Jesus is completed by the body, so we might find our completion in being wholly filled with God.

The final use of *plērōma* in Ephesians is in 4:13. Here the apostle discusses how the body functions in such a way as to "in all things grow up into him who is the Head" (4:15). Christ gives the body leaders, who are to "prepare God's people for works of service" so that as God's people exercise their spiritual gifts in ministry to one another, the body of Christ is built up (4:12). In the process of serving and being served, both the individual and the Christian community achieve unity, gain knowledge of God's Son, and "become mature, attaining to the whole measure of the fullness of Christ" (4:13). This shows that although the bonds that link members of the church to Jesus and to one another always exist, coming to maturity and experiencing the fullness of Christ come by a process. Growth does not come automatically. It comes as we function as Christ's body.

Yes, fullness of life is to be found in Jesus. That fullness is possible because Jesus himself is the fullness, the full and complete expression of Deity. How won-derful that Scripture shows us how to live in relationship with Jesus and with each other, so that we may be fulfilled.

FIND/FOUND

The common Hebrew word for "find" is *māṣā'*. It occurs 455 times in the OT, usually with the meaning of finding or being found. The OT assures God's covenant people that even after they had sinned and had been punished for it, they could "seek the LORD [their] God," and they were promised, "You will find him if you look for him with all your heart and with all your soul" (Dt 4:29; cf. 2 Ch 15:2; Jer 29:13). Such seeking of the Lord involved repentance: "Seek the LORD while he may be found; call on him while he is near. Let the wicked forsake his way and the evil man his thoughts. Let him turn to the LORD, and he will have mercy on him, and to our God, for he will freely pardon" (Isa 55:6–7). This promise is echoed by Jesus in Lk 11:10.

What do we find when we seek the Lord? There is much that we discover in him and in him alone. According to Scripture, we find favor (Ge 33:10; 2 Sa 15:25; Lk 1:30), rest (Ps 62:1,5), refuge (Ps 36:7; 91:4), delight (Ps 112:1; 119:35), comfort (Ps 119:52), salvation (Ac 4:12), and a great store of grace to help in time of need (Heb 4:16).

The Greek word translated "find" is *heuriskō*. Although it is an ordinary word, it is used in an exciting way in many NT passages. For example, often it indicates a spiritual discovery. When it is so used, it means that one becomes suddenly aware of one of God's great mysteries—a fresh and enriching link between the kingdom of God and our own human experience.

FINISH

One of two common Hebrew words is usually found where the NIV and the NASB have "finish." *Kālâh* means "to bring [a process] to completion." *Tāmam* means "to be complete or finished," often in the sense of consumed or destroyed.

The Greek *teleō* signifies bringing to an end or reaching a goal. It is usually the word found where the NIV and the NASB read "finish."

One notable exception is Heb 4:3. The word in this verse is *ginomai*, which is a common word usually meaning "to come into being, or happen," and at times meaning "to accomplish, or carry out." The Hebrews passage records God's promise of rest to those who listen to his voice and obey it, for his works have been "finished since the creation of the world." The thought is that the whole of history is implicit in God's original creative act: the end exists in the beginning. For us this means that we face no problem for which God does not already have the solution. We need not struggle against circumstances, but within our situation we can rest. We can rely on Jesus to guide us to the solution God has provided from the very creation of the world.

FIRE/FLAME

Fire is a basic necessity in every culture. Yet fire, the servant of humanity, is also used in most cultures to express religious ideas. In the OT and the NT, fire is linked with worship and is associated with judgment.

OT 1. Fire in the OT
NT 2. Fire in the NT
    3. Unusual NT expressions using "fire"

OT — 1. Fire in the OT. In addition to the commonplace uses of fire (*ēš*), it is associated in the OT with four theologically significant ideas.

a. Fire is associated with God's revelation of himself to fallen humanity. God spoke to Moses from the burning bush (Ex 3:2). Flames encompassed Sinai's peak (Ex 19:18–19; 24:15–18). The prophets' visions often portray God as a burning glory (Eze 1). This fiery image communicates the holiness of a God whom human beings did not dare to approach (Dt 5:23–27) but could only gaze on in awe and wonder (Dt 4:24; Isa 33:14).

b. Fire is associated with the sacrifices offered when people approached God. **▶ Offering and Sacrifice** The word *'išeh*, the offering made by fire, is found sixty-four times in the OT.

c. Fire is associated with divine judgment. Fire from the Lord destroyed Sodom (Ge 19:24). Fire flamed out to destroy those who approached the tabernacle for unauthorized worship (Nu 11:1–3). These and other incidents describe the destroying fire of the Lord (2 Ki 1:10–14; Job 1:16). It is not surprising that the prophets picked up the image of flames to symbolize divine judgment (e.g., Isa 9:19; 26:11; 66:15; Jer 4:4; 15:14; Eze 15:7; 19:14; Joel 1:19,20; Am 1:4,7,10,12,14; Zep 3:8).

d. Fire is associated with the purification of God's own people. It is a burning coal from the altar that cleanses Isaiah (Isa 6:6,7). Whereas God's breath is a fire that consumes the wicked (Isa 33:11), the divine fire heals and refines God's own people (Mal 3:2–4).

The consuming fire that terrifies others is transformed by personal relationship with God to be experienced as a love that warms and transforms the Christian.

NT — 2. Fire in the NT. Associations developed in the OT are repeated in the NT, with several delicate modifications.

a. Fire is a sign of God's essential glory, linked not only with his appearance (e.g., Ac 7:30; Rev 1:14) but also with his works (e.g., Ac 2:3). The symbol of fire is selected when the writer of Hebrews wishes to impress his readers with the essential awesomeness of the Lord (Heb 12:18,29).

b. Fire is a portrait of divine judgment, an image that features prominently in the preaching of John the Baptist (Mt 3:10,12; 7:19; Lk 3:9,17). When the judgment involves believers, it is applied as a test of the quality of their works (Jn 15:6; 1 Co 3:13–15). When the NT speaks of judgment involving unbelievers, it is final judgment that is in view. This is different from the meaning in the OT. There the judgment threatened is typically to be worked out within the flow of history. The NT looks beyond to final judgment at history's end (e.g., 2 Th 1:7–8). Here fire refers to the eternal judgment of individuals who persist in unbelief (cf. Mk 9:43; Lk 16:24; Jude 7; Rev 20:14). ♦ *Heaven and Hell*

c. Fire in the NT as in the OT is associated with the purification of believers (1 Pe 1:7; Rev 3:18). The experiences through which God cleanses and shapes us are often painful. But the product of God's purifying fires is a character of gold (Job 23:10).

3. Unusual NT expressions using "fire". Most NT verses fall into one of the above categories. But several passages deserve comment.

a. The Gospels tell of baptism with the "Holy Spirit and with fire" (Mt 3:11; Lk 3:16). Later, on the Day of Pentecost (Ac 2:3), tonguelike flames appeared over those who experienced what the NT defines as the Spirit's baptizing work (1 Co 12:13 ♦ *Baptism*). On this unique occasion, the visible flames were outward signs of the Holy Spirit's activity.

The activity of the Spirit in modern believers can also be thought of in the same symbolic way, for Paul warns us not to "put out the Spirit's fire" (1 Th 5:19).

b. Heb 1:7 calls angels God's servants and "flames of fire." This verse, quoting Ps 104:4, is sometimes taken to indicate the forms that God's angelic servants may take. But it is probably best to understand the phrase (in this passage, designed to exalt Christ) as a reference to the glory of those powerful beings who still are far below Jesus in nature, power, and glory.

FIRST

In both Testaments, "first" indicates priority. This may indicate either priority in time or sequence or priority of rank in a class. Believers are to "seek first" God's kingdom (Mt 6:33), giving the Lord a priority that makes every other concern of secondary importance.

Any Christian who wants to be first in rank in the church of Jesus must seek to serve others rather than to rule them (Mk 10:44).

The Christian life is "by faith from first to last" (Ro 1:17). What Paul means by this is that the Christian life is a process that is begun by faith and calls for faith at every step.

The Greek work translated "first" (*prōtos*) occurs some 160 times in the NT. No use is more significant than those that affirm Jesus as the first and last (Rev 1:17; 2:8; 22:13). Our faith is in one who has first place in the universe and is to be given first place in our lives.

FIRSTBORN

The Hebrew word for "firstborn" is *bākar*, "to be born first." *Bākar* and its derivatives occur 158 times in the OT. In the ancient world the firstborn son held a special position in the family. He received a double portion as his inheritance (Dt 21:17) and had a right to the special blessing of his father (Ge 27).

When Israel was constituted a nation, God established the principle that every firstborn male belonged to the Lord (Ex 13:2–15). The firstborn males of clean animals were sacrificed to the Lord; the firstborn son of the family was redeemed. The picture is a beautiful one. God exercises his right of ownership, but he does not do it by killing. Instead, he gives life!

The beauty of this rite is further enhanced when we discover that the members of the tribe of Levi, who were dedicated to serving God, were accepted by the Lord as a substitute for the firstborn of all the other tribes (Nu 3:1–45). God drew this tribe into a special place of closeness to him and of service to their fellows. It was from the tribe of Levi that the priests and all others who served in God's temple would be drawn. ♦ *Priesthood*

In the OT, then, the concept of the firstborn communicates the idea of special position within the family. It also portrays God's redeeming grace, for God transforms the right to take a life into the gift of a new life, rich with meaning through fellowship with him and service to others.

In the NT the word "firstborn" (*prōtotokos*) appears only nine times. Twice it refers to Jesus in a literal way—that is, as the first child in the family of Joseph and Mary (Mt 1:25; Lk 2:7). This word occurs one time in the plural, to identify believers as "the church of the firstborn" (Heb 12:23). This phrase suggests a position of special intimacy with God. One other use of *prōtotokos* is historical, a reference to the events of the redemption of Israel from Egypt (Heb 11:28).

In most cases, however, *prōtotokos* serves as a technical theological term, applied only to Jesus (Ro 8:29; Col 1:15,18; Heb 1:6; Rev 1:5). This use is not literal but is intended to suggest Jesus' supreme rank and the uniqueness of his special relationship with the Father. In connecting the title of firstborn with the Resurrection (Col 1:18; Rev 1:5), Scripture also offers us hope. Jesus has entered the realm of glory. We too, though junior members of the family, will also share in the glory Jesus now enjoys.

FIRSTFRUITS

People in the ancient Near East considered local or national deities to be owners of the land. In Israel, a portion of the initial harvest was given as an offering to God. These firstfruits (*bikkûr*) were partly used to provide the Lord's priests with food (Lev 2:14; Nu 18:12–14).

FLEE

Three words are used in the OT to express the idea of fleeing. *Bārah* almost always indicates hurried flight from an enemy. *Nûs* and *nādad* indicate rapid movement or motion away from someone or something. People flee to escape some real or imagined danger.

The NT word for flight or escape is *pheugō*. When used literally, the word means "to seek safety in flight." *Pheugō* is also used in a moral sense in such verses as 1 Co 6:18 ("Flee from sexual immorality") and 2 Ti 2:22 ("Flee the evil desires of youth"). In such passages the word

means "to avoid," "to shun," "to have nothing to do with."

Perhaps one of the most encouraging of NT verses is Ja 4:7. God's promise there is as follows: "Resist the devil, and he will flee from you." Those who live in terror of Satan can be encouraged.

FLESH

The word "flesh" is suggestive. For some people, it implies sexuality. For others, the word seems to indicate the seat of sin in human nature, in contrast to the seat of good in the spiritual aspect of our makeup.

"Flesh" is theologically significant in both the OT and the NT. It expresses important aspects of the biblical view of human nature. Surprisingly, the biblical view differs in very significant ways from the ideas associated with the word's use in our society.

OT 1. The Hebrew *bāśār* and its meanings
2. The view of humanity suggested by *bāśār*
NT 3. The Greek *sarx* and its meanings
4. The view of humanity suggested by *sarx*
5. Summary

OT — 1. The Hebrew *bāśār* and its meanings. The two Hebrew words translated "flesh" are *bāśār* and *šᵉʾēr*. The latter occurs only sixteen times in the OT (Ex 21:10; Lev 18:6,12,13; 20:19; 21:2; 25:49; Nu 27:11; Ps 73:26; 78:20,27; Pr 5:11; 11:17; Jer 51:35; Mic 3:2–3). It is without special theological significance and often means "kin."

Bāśār is found 273 times in the OT. When used to indicate something essential about human beings, the word does have theological significance.

Among the many meanings of *bāśār* are the following: the physical body (as in Ge 40:19; Nu 19:7; 1 Ki 21:27; 2 Ki 9:36), the self (as in Ps 16:9–10), all living creatures (as in Ge 6:12,19; Ps 145:21), and intimate interpersonal and family relationships (as in Ge 2:23–24; 29:14).

2. The view of humanity suggested by bāśār.

"Flesh," "heart" (lēḇ), and "soul" (nepeš) are key biblical words affirming something about the nature of human kind. We should not take them to indicate that we human beings are made up of three or more separate parts, such as soul, spirit, and flesh. In fact, the OT generally understands human beings as undivided wholes. So what the OT does with terms like bāśār is to look at persons from particular perspectives. To view a human being from the perspective of flesh means that we try to understand ourselves in view of our mortality. This perspective calls us to look at human beings as those who, with us, live out their present life in the material universe.

Given this perspective, the statement that a man and a woman in marriage become "one flesh" (Ge 2:24) affirms far more than sexual union. That act of joining is a symbol of the fact that the married couple are called by God to live in this world now as those who share every blessing and tragedy that life in the world may have for them. ♦ Marriage

While "flesh," as I said, focuses our attention on human beings as persons who must live in the physical universe and who are a part of it, it also draws our attention to human frailty. Because we are flesh, we are mortal, weak, and frail. In his mercy, God "remembers that they were but flesh, a passing breeze that does not return" (Ps 78:39). The notion that the flesh is the root and source of sin is not found in the OT. In fact, Ezekiel's report of God's promise to give Israel a "heart of flesh" (Eze 36:26) is a promise that God will make his people responsive to him. Here flesh is a positive thing, standing in contrast to an unheeding "heart of stone."

The OT's emphasis in its use of the word "flesh" is on our frailty as creatures. This line of teaching does more than underline our differences from the eternal, all-powerful God. This line of teaching shows us that we must not rest our hope on that which is essentially so frail. Jeremiah records the Lord's words: "Cursed is the one who trusts in man, who depends on flesh for his strength

and whose heart turns away from the LORD" (17:5). The prophet adds, "But blessed is the man who trusts in the LORD, whose confidence is in him" (v.7). This realization of the essential frailty of man can bring us comfort when we are threatened by danger. As the psalmist reminds us, "In God, whose word I praise, in God I trust; I will not be afraid. What can mortal man [bāśār] do to me?" (Ps 56:4).

NT — 3. The Greek sarx and its meanings.

Sarx, with sarkinos and sarkikos (both translated "fleshly"), can be found many more times in the original than is reflected in a modern version like the NIV. The reason for this is that the translators of such a version are willing to accept responsibility for communicating the meaning of the word in its context in the English rendering. This is complex for a word like sarx, which has so many possible translations. For instance, the eleven occurrences of sarkikos ("fleshly") are translated "carnal" nine times and "fleshly" two times in the KJV, but in the NIV they are variously translated "unspiritual" (Ro 7:14), material (Ro 15:27; 1 Co 9:11), worldly (1 Co 3:1,3; 2 Co 1:12; 10:4), "mere men" (1 Co 3:4), "ancestry" (Heb 7:16), and "sinful [desires]" (1 Pe 2:11).

Sarx thus is a complex concept. It carries all the OT meanings of bāśār into the NT. In the NT, too, sarx can indicate literal flesh (1 Co 15:39), the physical body (Gal 4:13), a human being (Ro 3:20; 1 Co 1:29), life in this present world (1 Co 7:28), and family relationships (cf. Ro 4:1; 9:3; 1 Co 10:18).

The most significant uses of sarx in the NT are found in Paul's epistles. Here a number of passages expand implications of the OT view of human nature expressed in bāśār. According to Paul, human nature is not just frail and weak; human nature is also twisted and tangled. Human perspectives, human understanding, and human efforts are actually hostile to the perspective, understanding, and plan of God. We are morally inadequate, and we are driven toward rebellion.

4. The view of humanity expressed by sarx . Ancient philosophers and popular psychology contrast the flesh with the spiritual part in human nature. The NT, however, makes no such comparison. Instead, the NT uses *sarx* to denote human nature apart from God. The contrasts drawn are between human powers, perspectives, and abilities and the powers, perspectives, and abilities of God, most importantly his ability to enable people to do his will. The whole of human nature, not merely a "part" of human beings, is in view when Scripture uses "flesh" in a moral or theological sense to make statements about human nature.

Sarx sees human beings in isolation from God. Essentially, when human beings are cut off from the Lord, they are morally inadequate (Ro 6:19; 7:7–11,15–20; 8:3). To live according to the flesh (*kata sarx*) is completely different from living according to God's Spirit (Gal 5:16–26; Ro 8:4–13).

Apart from God, humanity is characterized by a complex web of thoughts, desires, values, and actions that are in opposition to God's intended pattern for us.

Several extended passages in Paul's letters explore the nature and meaning of the flesh.

Ro 7:4–25. Exploring his own struggle with sin, Paul faced his moral inadequacy. The law of God is spiritual, but Paul was *sarkikos* (characterized by the flesh) and thus was trapped in sin. Paul realized that "nothing good" lived in him, that is, in his "flesh" (NIV, "in my sinful nature"). Trapped by his moral frailty, Paul cannot live the righteous life that is revealed in God's law, even though he acknowledges its beauty.

Gal 5:16–26. Sarx is translated "sinful nature" five times in the NIV reading of this passage. Paul here describes the flesh as energized and motivated by desires that find expression in a number of actions, ranging from sexual immorality to jealousy and fits of rage. In contrast, believers are called on to "live by the Spirit." God himself is the source of transformed desires that can motivate a new life. What's more, he is also the source of power for such a life. When we keep in step with the Spirit rather than the flesh, God will fill us and our actions with love, joy, peace, and the other aspects of the fruit of the Spirit.

1 Co 3:1–4. Sarkikos, "fleshly," occurs four times in these verses. It is descriptive of the behavior of the Christians at Corinth. Their bickering and factions show that despite their relationship with Jesus, the Corinthians were acting like "mere men." Their outlook was human, rather than being shaped by God's perspective on the issues they found so important.

We Christians do have the potential to live beyond the possibilities of our human nature. But such an enabled life is not guaranteed. We make daily choices, beyond our initial choice of trusting and loving Jesus, that affect our experience of the Christian life.

To break out of the fleshly pattern these Corinthians had to return to God's Word and search out his perspective.

Release from the limits of our human nature is possible. Ro 8:3–14 explains God's remedy for the limitations and sins of the flesh. That remedy is not found in the law. Law was unable to lift us to righteousness, because it was "weakened by our sinful nature (*sarx*)" (v. 3). So God through Christ provided the Holy Spirit to believers. Now we have the possibility of being controlled by the Spirit, not by the flesh. It is the Spirit whose life-giving power raised Jesus from the dead. It is the Spirit who can bring us life and power despite our mortality.

If we choose to rely on the Spirit and if we commit ourselves to his control, we will experience a resurrection kind of life—now. The limits imposed by our fleshly human nature will no longer contain us, and we will be freed from the mastery of the flesh.

5. Summary. In both Testaments, "flesh" is a complex word with many meanings. Most significant is the way that *bāśār* in the OT and *sarx* in the NT are used to make statements about human nature.

The OT emphasizes the frailty of human beings. Because of our weakness, we must look to God for everything good. He alone is the source of our help. To recognize his power brings us release from fear of other persons, who are ultimately as powerless as we are.

The NT emphasizes humanity's moral inadequacy. When they are isolated from God, human beings are energized by evil desires and guided by perceptions that distort God's will and his nature. The word "flesh" reminds us that we are caught in the grip of sin. Even a desire for righteousness cannot enable us to actually become righteous.

God deals with our flesh in a surprising way. He does not free us now from the fleshly nature. Instead, he provides a source of power that will release us from the domination of the flesh. Jesus has paid for sins generated by our flesh, whether sins of our past or those yet in our future. But Jesus has also provided us with his Holy Spirit. The Spirit lives within us, and he is the source of new desires and a new perspective. Even more, the spiritual power unleashed in the resurrection is made available to us in the Spirit.

The bonds of our mortality and all that mortality implies can be shattered if we live according to the Spirit, with our desires and motives shaped by him, with his power enabling us to do what is truly good. ◆ *Spirit (Holy Spirit)*

FLOCK ◆ *Sheep/Shepherd*

FLOOD

Sometimes the word "flood" simply refers to waters that overflow natural boundaries (Jos 3:15; 4:18; Isa 8:7). At other times it is used metaphorically: tears flood the psalmist's bed (Ps 6:6); events at the end of time will come like an irresistible flood (Da 11:10,40). But the Bible also knows of a unique flood, and technical terms in both the OT and the NT refer to that single event.

In the OT, the Genesis flood is the *mabbûl*, an overwhelming cataclysm that totally destroyed prediluvian culture and

wiped out all of humankind except for the single family of Noah. The word *mabbûl* occurs very seldom in the OT (Ge 6:17; 7:6–7,10,17; 9:11,15,28; 10:1,32; 11:10; Ps 29:10). Its use in Ps 29:10 portrays the God of judgment "enthroned over the flood."

In the NT the technical term for the Genesis flood is *kataklysmos*. It occurs in Mt 24:38–39; Lk 17:27; 2 Pe 2:5; and in verb form in 2 Pe 3:6.

Thus, the very vocabulary of Scripture makes a distinction between the destructive flood of Genesis and all other floods.

Whatever we may believe about the universal extent of the Genesis flood, we cannot doubt that this flood stands unparalleled in the history of the world as well as in salvation history.

FOES ◆ *Enemy*

FOLLOW

In the OT the verb "to follow" is normally taken in part from ' *ahar*, which means "behind" or "after." It is often found in a phrase with *hālak*, "to walk." Believers demonstrate faith by following (walking after) God's ways, laws, statues, and decrees. But the apostate makes the tragic mistake of following false gods.

In the NT, "to follow" is from the Greek *akoloutheō*. It is often used in narrative passages with a common, descriptive meaning. But it also has a special spiritual impact, linked with discipleship. The Christian disciple is one who has chosen to follow Jesus. The disciple expresses that basic commitment by daily choices of obedience to the Lord. *Akoloutheō* expresses a disciple's commitment in quite a number of NT passages (Mt 4:20,22; 8:19,22; 9:9; 10:38; 16:24; 19:21,27,28; Mk 1:18; 2:14; 8:34; 10:21,28; Lk 5:11,27,28; 9:23,57,59,61; 18:22,28; Jn 1:43; 8:12; 10:4,5,27; 12:26; 21:19,22; Rev 14:4). ◆ *Disciple*

In some cases, English versions supply "follow" where *akoloutheō* is not found. In 1 Co 1 and 3, verses that indicate that the Corinthian believers were following different leaders use this thought to render the Greek phrase "I am of." The church was forming cliques, each claiming to be disciples of a different leader of that era. But the NT knows only one discipleship: we are disciples of Jesus Christ.

Other words translated "follow" (such as *exakouloutheō* in 2 Pe 1:16; 2:2,15 and *mimeomai* in 2 Th 3:7,9; Heb 13:7; 3 Jn 11) mean "to imitate an example." But *akoloutheō* is found outside the Gospels and Acts only in 1 Co 10:4; Rev 6:8; 14:4,8–9,13; 18:5; 19:14.

FOOD

The basic words in Scripture for "food" indicate that which is used for nourishment.

It appears that preflood civilization was vegetarian, but God allowed humanity to expand its diet after the Flood to include the flesh of animals (Ge 9:3).

There are a number of religious regulations associated with food in the OT era (♦ *Bread* ♦ *Clean and Unclean*), but the Epistles of the NT make it clear that Christian faith has nothing to do with what a person does or does not eat (Ro 14:14; 1 Co 8:8). Instead, the believer, recognizing God as the source of all that he or she needs to maintain life, is released from anxiety and is free to put God's kingdom first (Mt 6:15–33).

Discussions of other important matters regarding food are found in other articles (e.g., the social implications of sharing food). ♦ *Eat*

FOOL/FOLLY

We think of a fool as someone who lacks intelligence or common sense. But mental deficiency is not suggested when the OT uses this morally significant term.

OT 1. The Hebrew words and their meanings
NT 2. The Greek words and their meanings

OT — 1. The Hebrew words and their meanings. Three Hebrew words with their derivatives are translated "fool," "foolish," and "folly."

'*Iwwelet,* like the other Hebrew terms, views foolishness as a moral rather than a mental issue. The fool is morally deficient. The particular moral fault suggested by '*Iwwelet* is insolence or rebelliousness. The trait is revealed by a quick temper, which stands in contrast to the wisdom of one who is slow to anger (Pr 14:29). Impetuosity and insistence on one's own way are also suggested by this word. Pr 22:15 says that such impetuosity is "bound up in the heart of a child, but the rod of discipline will drive it far from him."

Kesîl is also a moral term. It portrays the obstinate person, who persists in making choices that lead to destruction. This kind of fool refuses to learn proper ways or to concentrate on what is right. This fool rejects fear of the Lord. The Book of Proverbs often points to sexual immorality to illustrate this kind of folly.

Nābāl is the third kind of fool. This moral term draws attention to a person's inner disposition. This fool denies God (Ps 14:1; 53:1) and is closed to God, to morality, and to reason. This person's folly (*nebālâh*) is shown in sins of gross immorality, such as homosexuality (Jdg 19:23–24) and rape (2 Sa 13:12), and by Achan's violation of God's direct command (Jos 7:15).

It is clear that whenever we read "fool," "foolish," or "folly" in the OT, we are confronted by a moral concept rather than an intellectual one. The fear of the Lord is the beginning of knowledge (Pr 1:7), for relationship with God provides a necessary orientation to life. Human beings differ in moral capacity and proclivity, as well as in intellectual capacity and potential. The basic choices we make display our wisdom or our folly. ♦ *Wisdom*

NT — 2. The Greek words and their meanings. There is a delicate shift in emphasis in the NT's use of "fool" and "folly" from the way the OT used these words. Three Greek words normally are used to express the concept. Each suggests that a person has misperceived reality because he or she has failed to take God into account or to see things from God's perspective.

Aphrōn is found eleven times in the NT (Lk 11:40; 12:20; Ro 2:20; 1 Co 15:56; 2 Co 11:16,19; 12:6,11; Eph 5:17; 1 Pe 2:15). Jesus called the Pharisees fools for their preoccupation with externals and for their unconcern with character warped by greed and wickedness (Lk 11:40). Jesus called the rich farmer a fool for laying up material possessions and ignoring God, the appellation of fool being especially poignant because he was to meet God that very night (Lk 12:20). In each case, willful ignorance is involved. The Pharisees and this farmer refused to take into account what God had revealed to his OT people.

No wonder Paul objected to the attitude of some of the Corinthians and told them, "Let no one take me for a fool" (2 Co 11:16). Despite the hostility of some in Corinth, even they could hardly believe that Paul would fail to take God seriously.

Anoētos occurs only six times in the NT (Lk 24:25; Ro 1:14; Gal 3:1,3; 1 Ti 6:9; Tit 3:3). Despite the use of this word in Tit 3:3 to describe the intellectual and spiritual condition of humans before salvation, *anoētos* is usually used of believers. The two disciples who walked the Emmaus road with Jesus were "fools and slow of heart to believe" the Scriptures (Lk 24:25, KJV). The Galatians were foolish to be distracted from faith to law as if law were a pathway to spiritual achievement (Gal 3:1,3). In these passages the word "fool" makes no moral judgment as it does in the OT. Instead, it warns that the foolish individual is seeing things in a distorted way and has lost the divine viewpoint.

Mōros, "fool," and *mōria*, "foolishness," are the most commonly used NT words and are the strongest. *Mōros* is used thirteen times in the NT (Mt 5:22; 7:26; 23:17,19; 25:2,3,8; 1 Co 1:25,27; 3:18; 4:10; 2 Ti 2:23; Tit 3:9) and *mōria* five times (1 Co 1:18,21,23; 2:14; 3:19). This word group again calls our attention to those whose perspective is distorted because they fail to take God into account. The foolish virgins of Jesus' parables miscalculated their supply of oil (Mt 25:2,3,8). The Pharisees are called blind fools by Jesus for their complete insensitivity to

God's values (Mt 23:17,19). These spiritual leaders concentrated on legalistic arguments while they neglected "the more important matters of the law—justice, mercy and faithfulness" (23:23).

The key passage that helps us understand the meaning of *mōros* and *mōria* is 1 Co 1–4. Here Paul contrasts divine wisdom and human wisdom. He shows how essential it is that we adopt God's perspective rather than looking at life's issues from some mere human viewpoint. To humanity, the Cross itself seems foolish. But this particular foolishness of God is the ultimate wisdom. The Cross alone puts the great moral issues of the universe—sin, justice, and salvation—in complete perspective.

You and I must search the Scriptures for God's revelation of his own unique wisdom. Only by looking at our life from God's revealed point of view can we avoid those foolish notions about life's meaning that distort the lifestyle of the lost.

FOOTSTOOL

The footstool of Bible times was a low support for one's feet. It was used by a person on a high seat such as a throne. Except for 2 Ch 9:18, "footstool" (found thirteen times in the NIV) is used metaphorically in Scripture to express the subordinate relationship of persons and of the earth itself to the Godhead or the exalted Jesus.

FORCE

Both Testaments use "force" with a normal range of meanings. To force is to compel. Forces of natural and spiritual enemies are arranged in battle order (Eph 6:12). A will is in force (i.e., valid) only on the death of its maker (Heb 9:17).

It is difficult to understand what the Bible says should be the Christian attitude toward the use of force in war. But Paul does give us an admirable example of refraining from any use of force in dealing with another believer. In his brief letter to Philemon, in the midst of his discussion of returning the runaway slave Onesimus to his master, Paul expresses this thought: "I did not want to do anything without your consent, so that any favor you do will be spontaneous and not forced" (Phm 14).

FOREFATHER ♦ Father

FOREIGN

Most instances of "foreign" are translations of *nēkār* or *nokrî*. "Aliens," "foreigners," and, in older versions, "strangers" are translations of the same Hebrew root.
♦ *Alien/Aliens*
Generally the implication is that the foreign god, thing, or practice is outside the lifestyle that God had prescribed for his OT people. This is clearly seen in the use of *nokrâh* (literally "foreign woman") in Proverbs to identify a prostitute (Pr 2:16; 5:10,20; 6:24; 7:5; 20:16; 23:27; 27:2,13). The prostitutes referred to were almost surely Jewish. But the practice was completely foreign to the life God intended for his own.

The Greek word *allotrios* makes the same point. Foreign practices are not for God's people, for the citizens of heaven live by heaven's laws.

FOREVER ♦ Always

FORGET

The Hebrew verb *šākah* is used 102 times in the OT. At times a literal lapse of memory is intended, as in the story of the released butler who forgot his former fellow prisoner Joseph (Ge 40:23).

At times God is the subject of this verb. It may seem to believers that God has forgotten them, and they may express their apparent abandonment in cries to him (Ps 10:11; 42:9). But God neither neglects nor ignores his own. ♦ *Abandon/Abandoned*
What is more likely is that human beings will forget the Lord. Thus *šākah* is often used in warnings. God's people must not forget the Lord nor his covenant. They must not forget his laws and statutes. Nor may they forget the helpless.

These illustrations help us realize that the OT idea of forgetting indicates not a psychological state but a moral one. The focus is on a person's choices, not memories. To forget God's laws and statutes is to choose to ignore them; it is to act without considering God's revealed will. In this context, "forget" indicates a complacent neglect of the Lord, perhaps linked with a material prosperity that dulls awareness of our need of his blessing (Dt 8:11–19).

In the NT, the words translated "forget" (*epilanthanomai* in Mt 16:5; Mk 8:14; Lk 12:6; Php 3:13; Heb 6:10; 13:2,16; Jas 1:24, and *eklanthanomai* in Heb 12:5) may indicate a literal forgetting, but often they suggest neglect or overlooking. We may neglect or overlook important issues. But God is incapable of overlooking even the death of a sparrow (Lk 12:6). How good to know that we, who are so precious to the Lord, can never be forgotten by him (though he does "forget" our sins ♦ *Forgive*).

FORGIVE

Forgiveness is often misunderstood. Yet forgiveness is one of the most basic of Christian qualities. Forgiveness can transform our relationship with God, with others, and even with ourselves.

OT 1. Hebrew words for forgiveness
    2. God's forgiveness in the OT
NT 3. Greek words for forgiveness
    4. God's forgiveness in the NT
    5. Forgiving one another
    6. The inner dynamics of
       forgiveness
    7. Summary

OT — 1. Hebrew words for forgiveness. Several Hebrew words are associated with the OT teaching about forgiveness and at times are translated "forgive" in the NIV and the NASB.

Kāpar has the basic meaning of "atonement." The verb, derived from a root that is found about 150 times in the OT, suggests the removal of sin or of ritual defilement. ♦ *Atonement*

Nāśā' is found almost six hundred times in the Qal stem alone. This common word means "to lift up," "to carry or support," or "to take up or away." In three distinct ways the OT links *Nāśā'* with sin. (1) Human beings "take up" sin or inequity by their evil actions. (2) The guilt or punishment for sin is "taken up" and "carried" by the sinner or by a substitute (Lev 10:17; Isa 53:4). (3) God can act to "take up" or "take away" sins. This is the root of forgiveness and pardon. Forgiveness is possible because God acts to take away the sin that makes us guilty. Thus God releases us from guilt and from punishment.

David, deeply aware of his own sins, meditated on forgiveness in Ps 32:1–5: "Blessed is he whose transgressions are forgiven, whose sins are covered. Blessed is the man whose sin the LORD does not count against him and in whose spirit is no deceit. . . . I said, 'I will confess my transgressions to the LORD ' and you forgave the guilt of my sin."

Sālaḥ and its derivatives mean "to forgive, or pardon." This word group is used only of the divine offer of pardon to sinners. The offer is extended to all: "Seek the LORD while he may be found; call on him while he is near. Let the wicked forsake his way and the evil man his thoughts. Let him turn to the LORD, and he will have mercy on him, and to our God, for he will freely pardon" (Isa 55:6–7).

It is important to notice that in the OT the offer of pardon is closely linked with atonement. When atoning sacrifices had been made, forgiveness was assured to God's OT people (cf. Lev 4:20,26,31,35; 5:10,12,16,18,26; 6:7). ▶ *Atonement*

2. God's forgiveness in the OT.
Moses, in praying for a sinning Israel, based his appeal to God on the Lord's love and on his record of gracious actions: "In accordance with your great love, forgive the sin of these people, just as you have pardoned them from the time they left Egypt until now" (Nu 14:19). God's motive in forgiving is clear in the OT, and there is celebration of God's character as a forgiving Person (Ex 34:7; Nu 14:18; Ne 9:17; Ps 86:5; 99:8; 130:3–4; Da 9:9).

Solomon, in his prayer at the dedication of the temple, asked God to forgive when his straying people would turn to him (1 Ki 8:30–50). Both the nation and individuals were invited to seek and to experience forgiveness.

But although the doctrine of atonement links forgiveness with sacrifice, there is no clear explanation in the OT of how a holy God can forgive sinning human beings.

NT — 3. Greek words for forgiveness. Three different Greek words are translated "forgive" in the English versions of the NT.

Charizomai means "to be gracious," or "to give freely." It is used in the sense of "forgive" (2 Co 2:7,10; 12:13; Eph 4:32; Col 2:13; 3:13). The word is also used in regard to canceling a debt, a concept analogous to forgiving a sin (Lk 7:42–43).

Paul not only urged the church at Corinth to be gracious to a repentant brother who had sinned seriously (2 Co 2:7–10); he also insisted that the believers in every church show the same compassion to each other that God had showed in forgiving them: "Bear with each other and forgive whatever grievances you may have against one another. Forgive as the Lord forgave you" (Col 3:13; cf. 2:13; Eph 4:32).

Aphiēmi is a verb that occurs 146 times in the NT. It has the sense of "forgive" 49 of these times, 44 of which occur in the Gospels; but it has this meaning only once in Paul's writings (Ro 4:7). It is used in the sense of forgiveness of sins, of debts, and of crimes. The majority of the occurrences of *aphiēmi* convey a meaning other than forgiveness: i.e., dismiss, release, leave, or abandon.

Divine forgiveness does not overlook sin or dismiss it lightly. Rather, forgiveness is an act of God by which he deals, not with our guilt but with sins themselves. In forgiveness God removes the sins and makes the guilt moot. No wonder the teachers of the law objected when Jesus said to a paralytic, "Your sins are forgiven" (Mk 2:5). The offended onlookers thought angrily, "Who can forgive sin but God alone?" (v. 7). You and I may be compassionate to another who falls, but we cannot remit his sins. To demonstrate his authority to act as only God can, Jesus healed the paralytic. His miracle demonstrated not only his power but also his claim to "authority on earth to forgive sins" (v. 10).

Aphesis is found seventeen times in the NT. In fifteen of these occurrences it expresses forgiveness (often "remission" in KJV) of sins (Mt 26:28; Mk 1:4; 3:29; Lk 1:77; 3:3; 24:47; Ac 2:38; 5:31; 10:43; 13:38; 26:18; Eph 1:7; Col 1:14; Heb 9:22; 10:18), it being rendered "freedom" and "release" in its other two occurrences (both in Lk 4:18). The preaching of the early church always linked forgiveness with Jesus. He alone is able to "give repentance and forgiveness of sins to Israel" (Ac 5:31; cf. 2:38). The death and resurrection of Jesus put the promises of the OT prophets in perspective, for "all the prophets testify about him that everyone who believes in him receives forgiveness of sins through his name" (10:43). Paul specifically links forgiveness with the death of Christ. He announces it twice in rather similar terms: "we have redemption through his blood, the forgiveness of sins, in accordance with the riches of God's grace" (Eph 1:7; cf. Col 1:14).

4. God's forgiveness in the NT. Both Testaments extend the promise of forgiveness to the human race. In the OT as well as the NT, human beings are recognized as sinners in need of pardon. The OT links God's forgiveness with sacrifices of atonement. The NT relates forgiveness to Jesus, specifically to his sacrificial death. The basis on which God can forgive sin and remain righteous has been provided by Jesus' sacrifice of himself as an atonement, in that ultimate sacrifice to which OT offerings merely pointed. As Hebrews puts it, "By one sacrifice he has made perfect forever those who are being made holy" (10:14).

The context of the Hebrews quote is an extended passage that runs from Heb 9:1 to 10:18. The writer carefully discussed the meaning of Jesus' death on Calvary. Jesus' sacrifice did bring us forgiveness (10:18). But Jesus also provided us with the possibility of a dynamic inner transformation. Jesus has done a perfecting work for us, to make us new and holy; it was not simply a remedial work, wiping out past sins. It is important when thinking of forgiveness to realize that it is simply the doorway through which we pass into a new life. Jesus' sacrifice did take away our sins (9:28). They are so completely gone that God no longer recalls them against those whom he has decided to save, for he says, "Their sins and lawless acts I will remember no more" (10:17).

The blood of Christ is the basis on which God can righteously provide the promised forgiveness (Ro 3:25–26) ♦ *Justify/Justification* . Christ's atoning death is also the basis for our continuing relationship with God (1 Jn 2:1–2). We will stumble and fall as we journey in our new life toward holiness. But even though we do, we have the promise of forgiveness for every sin. All anyone needs to do is to confess sin; then God will forgive and the Holy Spirit will keep on working to cleanse from all unrighteousness (1 Jn 1:7–9). ♦ *Confession of Sins*

This is exciting indeed! God's forgiveness opens up our lives to his inner transformation, and God himself begins to release us to live truly good lives.

5. Forgiving one another. The NT places considerable stress on the importance of forgiving others. In Mt 18, Jesus tells three stories to illustrate forgiveness. He portrays human beings as sheep, prone to go astray. When this happens, we are to seek the straying. We are to bring the straying home, bearing them in our arms, rejoicing. The image is of a forgiveness that frees us from bitterness or recrimination and provides a joy that is able to heal every hurt (18:10–14).

Jesus then spoke of the hurts and sins that mar family relationships. "If your brother sins against you" (v. 15), he began, and then he went on to explain that we are to take the initiative when we are hurt, and we should seek reconciliation. Peter recognized the difficulty of this teaching, and objected. He asked how often such hurts should be forgiven.

Jesus answered, "seventy times seven" (v. 22, KJV)—a phrase indicating unlimited forgiveness.

Following this, Jesus told a parable about a servant with a debt equivalent to several million dollars (in modern terms and rates). When the servant could not pay and begged for time, the ruler to whom he owed the sum simply forgave the entire obligation. But the same servant later demanded the minor amount a fellow servant owed him (equivalent to a few hundred dollars). He actually went so far as to throw the fellow servant into prison for nonpayment. Jesus' intention is clear: we who are forgiven an unimaginable debt by God surely must be so moved by gratitude that we treat our fellows as we have been treated.

This theme—forgive as you are forgiven—is often stressed in the NT, and the theme has two applications. First, God's treatment of us provides an example that we are to follow in our relationships with other persons. We are to be "kind and compassionate to one another, forgiving one another, just as in Christ God forgave [us]" (Eph 4:32).

The second application seems to introduce a conditional aspect to the promise of forgiveness. In Mt 6:14–15 we read, "For if you forgive men when they sin against you, your heavenly Father will also forgive you. But if you do not forgive men their sins, your Father will not forgive your sins." In Mk 11:25 the thought is expressed this way: "And when you stand praying, if you hold anything against anyone, forgive him, so that your Father in heaven may forgive you your sin." Such passages trouble many. Elsewhere in the Scriptures, forgiveness is spoken of as something provided freely through Jesus. It is promised to all who come to him. How can the gospel offer and these warnings of Jesus both be true?

The best answer seems to lie in the way in which forgiveness affects our personality. Just as every coin has two sides, never only one, so forgiveness has two aspects that can never be separated. Those two sides of forgiveness are accepting and extending.

The person who accepts forgiveness becomes deeply aware of his own weakness and need. Pride is ruled out as we take our place as supplicants before the Lord. This basic attitude releases us from our tendency to become angry with, or judgmental of, others. We begin to see others as creatures who are, like us, flawed by weakness. Rather than react with inflamed pride ("He can't do this to *me!*"), we are freed to respond as God does, with loving concern and forgiveness.

It isn't that God will not forgive the unforgiving. It is simply that the unforgiving lack the humble attitude that both permits them to accept forgiveness and frees them to extend forgiveness.

6. The inner dynamics of forgiveness. The foregoing discussion should demonstrate something of the transforming impact of forgiveness. One who accepts forgiveness adopts an attitude toward himself that transforms his or her attitude toward others. The person who accepts forgiveness becomes forgiving.

But there are other effects of forgiveness as well. Jesus once confronted a critical Pharisee who observed with contempt the tearful devotion a prostitute had for Jesus. The Pharisee thought, "If this man were a prophet, he would know who is touching him and what kind of woman she is" (Lk 7:39). Jesus responded to the Pharisee's unexpressed thought. He told a story of two men in debt to a money lender. The one owed fifty denarii and the other five hundred (a denarius was equal to a day's wage). If the money lender should cancel the debts, Jesus asked, which man would love him more? The Pharisee answered, "I suppose the one who had the bigger debt canceled" (7:43). Jesus then nodded toward the weeping prostitute and confirmed the principle. Her sins were many, but when she was forgiven, she knew the wonder of God's gift of love, and she responded with love. As we meditate on God's forgiveness and realize how much we have been forgiven, love for the Lord is nurtured in our hearts.

Hebrews develops yet another aspect of forgiveness. The writer compares the sacrifice of Jesus with the OT sacrifices that prefigured him. Had the earlier sacrifices had the power to make the worshipers perfect, they "would have been cleansed once for all, and would no longer have felt guilty for their sins" (10:2). But Jesus' sacrifice does make us perfect! Through Jesus our sins are actually taken away! Thus the believer who realizes that he is truly forgiven is released from a sense of guilt and from bondage to past mistakes. Because God has forgiven our sins (10:17), we can forget our past. Forgiven, we can concentrate all our energies on living a godly life.

7. Summary. Both Testaments portray God as a forgiving person. In the OT, forgiveness is associated with atoning sacrifices. In the NT, we are shown that Jesus' death enables God to take away our sins. In both Hebrew and Greek, key words for forgiveness express this idea of taking away.

The NT develops the doctrine of individual forgiveness more completely than does the OT. Forgiveness is part of the process of salvation. Forgiveness opens our hearts to God and opens our lives to his working within us. Forgiveness is a wellspring nurturing our love for God. And forgiveness provides us with release from bondage both to guilt feelings and to guilt itself.

The outlook that forgiveness engenders changes our relationship with others. We who keep it in mind that we are forgiven have a humility that enables us to see others as weak and needy too. We feel compassion, and we offer others the forgiveness that is so essential in our own lives—and so near to the heart of God.

FORM ♦ *Acts/Actions*

FORSAKE ♦ *Abandon/Abandoned*

FORETELL/FORETOLD ♦ *Prophecy/Prophet*

FORTIFIED ♦ *Fortress/Stronghold*

FORTRESS/STRONGHOLD

A number of Hebrew words indicate fortified cities. In the ancient Near East, principal cities were enclosed with walls that might be from 15 to 25 feet thick and over 25 feet high. Trenches were often dug in front of the walls, and towers were built at their corners. These fortified cities were virtually impregnable. The psalmists and prophets called on God's people not to rely on their fortified cities but to remember that "God is our refuge and strength, an ever-present help in trouble. . . . The LORD Almighty is with us. The God of Jacob is our fortress" (Ps 46:1,7; cf. Jer 5:17).

FORTY

The number forty is symbolic at times. It is primarily linked with divine testing or punishment (Ge 7:4,12,17; 8:6; Nu 14:33; 32:13; Jnh 3:4; Mt 4:2). It is also associated with the giving of law (Ex 24:18) and is the span of time within which Jesus showed himself on earth after the Resurrection.

FOUNDATION

The Hebrew verb *yāsad* means "to lay a foundation," "to establish," or "to found." But its underlying meaning is "to fix firmly." *Yāsad* indicates an immovable base on which a solid structure can be erected.

In the OT, most uses of this family of words are metaphorical. A literal foundation is, among other things, spoken of in reference to Solomon's palace (1 Ki 7:10), the temple in Jerusalem (1 Ki 5:17; 2 Ch 3:3; Ezr 3:10,11,12; Isa 44:28; Hag 2:18; Zec 4:9; 8:9), the city of Jericho (Jos 6:26; 1 Ki 16:34), the nation of Egypt (Ex 9:18), and the earth (Job 38:4; Ps 104:5; Pr 3:19; 8:29; Isa 24:18; 48:13; 51:13,16; Zec 12:1). To affirm that in the beginning God "laid the foundations of the earth" (Ps 102:25) is to say that God established the universe and the unchangeable laws by which it operates.

Two Greek words are translated "foundation": *katabolē* and *themelios*. The emphasis of the Greek words is less on the immovability of what has been established than it is on the act of founding. What is important in the NT is the point of beginning. Paul's role as an expert builder, laying the foundation of the church at Corinth, is as the evangelist who first brought the gospel (1 Co 3:10–12). The Ephesian reference to the church as "built on the foundation of the apostles" (Eph 2:20) in no way suggests that the apostles have replaced Jesus as the unshakable base of our faith (1 Co 3:11). Rather, Paul reminds us believers that the church had its origin in the ministry that the apostles had after Jesus' resurrection.

FREE/FREEDOM

"Freedom" is an attractive word. It implies a release from restriction, an opportunity to act without restraint. But all too often the freedom that human beings seek so urgently is nothing but another form of slavery. It is only in Scripture, and particularly in the NT, that we begin to grasp the meaning of the "glorious freedom of the children of God" (Ro 8:21).

OT 1. The Hebrew words and their uses
NT 2. The Greek words and concept
    3. Of human bondage
    4. Common uses of freedom
    5. Freedman and slave
    6. The glorious freedom of the children of God
    7. False promises of freedom
    8. Summary

OT — 1. The Hebrew words and their uses. Several different Hebrew words are translated "freedom" in the NIV and the NASB. Those used most often include the following:

Šālaḥ. The basic meaning of this word is "to send." It is used in the sense of letting go, or setting free (as in Ex 4:21; Ps 81:12; Isa 45:13; Zec 9:11).

'Azaḇ. This word means "to leave, forsake, abandon" or "to set loose." It is

translated "free" where the context indicates the act of setting loose or releasing, as in Dt 32:36; 1 Ki 14:10; 21:21; 2 Ki 9:8; 14:26.

Nāqî. This word means "to free [one from], or to exempt." It is a derivative of *nāqâh,* which means "to be clean, clear, or acquitted," and thus free. In contexts of morality, *nāqâh* indicates release from guilt or punishment (as in Nu 5:31). In a political or social sense, *nāqî* indicates release from a legally binding obligation (e.g., Dt 24:5). In an interpersonal sense, these Hebrew words can mean release from an oath or promise (as in Ge 24:8; Jos 2:17,19,20). ♦ *Innocent*

Ḥāpšî. This adjective occurs seventeen times in the OT and in all but four instances (1 Sa 17:25; Job 39:5; Ps 88:5; Isa 58:6) indicates freedom from slavery (as in Ex 21:2,5 ♦ *Serve/Servant/Slave*).

Considered together, these OT words provide a portrait of freedom as release from external or internal restrictions imposed by others, by social convention, or by the principle of responsibility for one's wrong actions. However, the OT use of the words focuses on specific situations, and we cannot say that there is an abstract concept or doctrine of freedom in the OT.

NT — 2. The Greek words and concept. The family of Greek words translated "free" and "freedom" were originally political terms. The root idea was that of membership within a community, a membership that conferred rights not possessed by slaves or outsiders. In the world of the Greek city-state (*polis*), freedom meant the right to debate public policy and the right to carry on one's own affairs within the structure of the community. City law and custom were not opposed to freedom but provided the order and structure required for a citizen to exercise freedom.

But history showed the Greeks that the ideal of freedom was flawed. Gradually the words that indicated freedom were taken over by the philosophers and used in new senses. No human being can really control the external factors that place pressure on his life. For example, everyone is subject to breakdowns in society, to war, to injustice, and to crop failure. Since there is no way to gain control over such things, some philosophers concluded that freedom must be found within a person. The Stoics taught that freedom could be experienced only if one detached himself or herself from the external world and even from one's individual passions. The detached attitude of withdrawal from the affairs of this world offered people their only possible hope of freedom.

In the world of the NT, the Greek words for freedom were used in their old political sense and in the skeptical mode of the philosopher. In common speech, "liberty" and "freedom" seemed to denote simply the opportunity to do whatever one wants. These words took on special political meaning to the Zealots, who were committed to the goal of national independence and were sure that only with release from domination by any pagan power could religious freedom be won.

The Greek words used in these ways, and found in our NT, are *eleutheria* ("freedom," "independence from others"), *eleutheros* ("free, not bound," indicating one who is his own master), and *eleutheroō* ("to set free, to release"). The first of these words occurs eleven times in the NT; the second, twenty-three times; and the third, seven times.

In no NT passage is any of these words used in a political sense. Nor are they used in the Stoic's sense; that is, freedom from emotion and desire. Nor is freedom conceived of in the Bible as license to do whatever one wants, without hindrance or consequences. In the NT, freedom is a spiritual and relational concept. NT freedom takes its meaning from the fact that the NT sees human beings as locked in terrible bondage—a bondage beyond our ability to overcome.

3. Of human bondage. The NT's teaching on freedom can be understood only against the background of human bondage. According to the Bible, human beings are definitely not free. There are some powerful forces to which people (especially unbelievers) are in bondage. First, Satan and his "powers of this dark world" and "spiritual forces of evil" are ranged against us (Eph 6:12; cf. Lk 13:16; 2 Ti 2:26). Second, the law, though righteous and holy and good, can do no more than hold us in its grip: while it shows us the moral ideal and urges us on, it can never help us to achieve what it requires (Ro 7:3–6; 8:3; Gal 2:4; 4:21–31; 5:1–13).

◆ *Law* Moreover, the Bible also speaks of a spiritual death that maintains an icy hold on humanity (Ro 6:2–23; 8:21). ◆

Life and Death And then there is the "old man" (KJV; "old self" in NIV; Ro 6:6; Eph 4:22; Col 3:9), the complex swirl of passions that masters the unredeemed. Perhaps most important, the Bible speaks of sin as a principle that is active within our personalities. Sin's active force propels an eager humanity into acts that express fallen human nature and bring people into even deeper bondage (Ro 6:18–22; 8:2–3; Gal 5:1; 2 Pe 2:19). ◆

Serve/Servant/Slave

It is tragic that these masters of the lost not only corrupt but also bring terrible consequences. They cause hurt and misery in this life and cause people to be brought into future judgment (Ecc 11:9).

Images of this bondage that pervade the NT focus our attention on the real issue raised by the concept of freedom. What men and women need is not the removal of external restraints, but release from the chains of the inner bondage that keeps them from being the persons that God intends them to be and that they yearn to be.

4. Common uses of "freedom". At times the Greek word group is used in quite ordinary ways. Paul talks about being free to marry (1 Co 7:39) and about presenting the gospel free of charge (9:19). He explores our freedom to exercise various rights that are ours (1 Co 9:1). There are also many references to freedom in contrast to slavery (see 5, below). But the truly significant uses, by which we will be able to build a biblical concept of freedom, are those that are intimately linked with the bondage of human beings to the inner and outer spiritual forces that hold us captive.

5. Freeman and slave. There are many references in the NT to free people in contrast to slaves (1 Co 7:22; 12:13; Gal 3:28; 4:22–23,26,30–31; Eph 6:8; Col 3:11; 1 Pe 2:16; Rev 6:15; 13:16; 19:18). Slavery was entrenched in NT times, and its governing principles were established in law. The NT references to free people and slaves are made against this background. In Roman law, all people were either free or slaves. Slaves were in the power of their masters. Slaves lacked rights as human beings and might legally be punished or even killed by their masters. But when a slave was freed, he or she possessed the freedoms of the free-born citizen (with certain additional obligations).

It is striking that from the perspective of the NT, true freedom is not viewed as independence from a master. Freedom is found only in taking a new master, Christ. The Christian is never to serve his old masters (especially sin and the law).

The death of Jesus is the price by which we were purchased from slavery to become servants of the Lord. "You are not your own," Paul says; "you were bought at a price" (1 Co 6:19–20). As a slave of Jesus Christ (Ro 1:1; Php 1:1), the apostle realized that only in submitting to his new "Master in heaven" (Col 4:1; cf. Eph 6:9) could the freedom that people yearn for and need be achieved.

6. The glorious freedom of the children of God. The NT proclaims a message of freedom for God's people. "For freedom . . . Christ has set us free," Paul says in Gal 5:1, and in 5:13 he sees us as a people "called to be free." The nature of our freedom is defined in several significant passages.

Jn 8:31–36. Jesus promises that those who believe in him will experience a freedom that comes from holding to (i.e., doing) his teaching: "You will know the truth, and the truth will set you free." Jesus' point is that humankind blunders on in a world of illusion, with no way to discover or recognize reality. But Jesus' words are truth, in full harmony with reality. ♦ *Truth* We experience truth by accepting Jesus' version of reality and then living according to his words. This,

and this alone, is the pathway to freedom for the believer.

Some who overheard this teaching objected. "We . . . have never been slaves," these descendants of Abraham insisted. How, then, they argued, could they be set free?

Jesus pointed to their murderous hatred of him. "Everyone who sins is a slave to sin." The freedom that Jesus promises, which can be found in obedience, is release from the sin that surges within us and release from wicked acts and the tragedy and punishment that sin brings.

Ro 6:15–23. Paul develops Jesus' point: "You are slaves to the one whom you obey—whether . . . to sin, which leads to death, or to obedience, which leads to righteousness." No matter how great our past bondage to sin, now that we belong to Jesus we are set free to become slaves to righteousness.

In this passage the great contrast is found in the rewards of the two forms of slavery. Serving sin results in shame and the living death that sin pays as wages. On the other hand, slavery to righteousness leads to holiness. It is wise to evaluate the master we choose to serve and to examine the wages he pays.

Ro 8:2–11. In Ro 7 Paul has explored his own bondage to indwelling sin. No matter how he tries, he cannot find a way to serve righteousness.

Then he discovers the freedom to become Jesus' slave, and he explains this transformation in Ro 8. The Spirit of God enters the believer's life. The Spirit becomes the source of a dynamic that can wrestle with inner sin and death and overcome them (8:2). One must give control to the Spirit of God to be released from the control of sinful human nature. The Holy Spirit, who raised Christ from the dead, can make us alive in our mortality. The Spirit can enable us to do what we could never do unaided. As 2 Co 3:17 says, "Now the Lord is the Spirit, and where the Spirit of the Lord is, there is freedom."

Gal 5:1–26. Paul has shown that the OT law offers neither salvation nor a way to spiritual achievement. ♦ *Law* He has also shown that while law served as a guardian slave during faith's childhood, now that Jesus has given believers full rights as sons, the guardian is no longer needed to direct us. Paul concludes first by emphasizing that "it is for freedom that Christ has set us free" (5:1) and then by calling on us to stand firm in our freedom.

But what is the nature of our freedom? It is not release from all restraint. It is not license to indulge our sinful nature. Our freedom is the freedom to "serve one another in love" (5:13). It is possible to do so, because the Holy Spirit enables us to act in ways that are contrary to the natural impulses of our sinful nature. Walking by the Spirit, we are released from the old master that produces hatred, jealousy, fits of rage, envy, and such. We are released to be loving, patient, kind, faithful, and good.

The emphasis in this passage is on our choice between two masters. We must serve one or the other. It is either God or our sinful nature. Also, the Holy Spirit is again presented to us as the key to this new freedom to do good. It is our responsibility to choose the master we will obey, underlined by Paul's injunction to "keep in step with the Spirit" (5:25).

7. False promises of freedom. The idea of freedom is attractive to sinful human nature, especially when misunderstood. Mankind's view of freedom is distorted, for true freedom is found in responsible discipline rather than in reckless dissipation. Peter warns, "Live as free men, but do not use your freedom as a cover-up for evil; live as servants of God" (1 Pe 2:16).

False teachers lure followers with promises of the freedom that humanity thinks it wants. The Bible describes these teachers in this way: "By appealing to the lustful desires of sinful human nature, they entice people who are just escaping from those who live in error. They promise them freedom, while they themselves are slaves of depravity—for a man is slave to whatever has mastered him" (2 Pe 2:18–19). The false promise of free-

dom that is license to indulge ourselves is actually an invitation to disaster.

8. Summary. The Christian concept of freedom is developed against the background of the Bible's revelation of human bondage. Lost humanity is in slavery to the demands of unkeepable law, to sin within, to death, to inner passions, and to distorted perceptions.

The freedom that Scripture offers does not include independence, and there is no hint of release from restriction. Instead, the NT insists that freedom is to be found only in willingly choosing to submit to a new master, to Christ. We are his by right of blood purchase. We must choose to obey him daily and keep his words, permitting God's will to provide structure and meaning for our lives.

How can slavery to Christ be, in actuality, true freedom? In several significant ways. First, only by submitting to Jesus and living by his words are we free to experience truth. Only thus can we be guided away from what hurts to what is truly beneficial for us. ▶ *Truth*

Second, only by submitting to Jesus can we experience the immense power for true goodness that is provided for us in the Holy Spirit. What we could never do in our own strength, the Spirit can enable us to do. In a real sense, freedom is freedom to achieve beyond our human potential.

Third, the kind of freedom that would release us from all restraint could never free us from the consequences of our actions. The Christian knows that the consequences of his actions carry over even into eternity. Any freedom that is meaningful must release us from actions that lead to tragedy or judgment.

A commitment to serve Jesus promises us holiness, and the consequences of holy actions are blessings—now and forever. The blessing that slavery to Jesus produces helps us realize that servitude provides the most real and wonderful freedom there can be.

Finally, we human beings are creatures. We have been shaped by God to love him and to enjoy him forever. Only by choosing to serve God can we become the people we were created to be. This freedom to experience our destiny is a wonderful freedom indeed.

Only when you and I willingly submit to the lordship of Jesus Christ can we learn what freedom truly is.

FREEWILL OFFERING

The Hebrew word for "freewill offering" is *nᵉdābâh*. It is used twenty-six times in the OT. It is used of voluntary contributions—as materials for building the tabernacle (Ex 36) and as the offering of prayer (Ps 119:108). One beautiful use of this word is in describing God's blessings. God does not bless us out of obligation, but his blessings are voluntary gifts to his dearly loved people (Ps 68:9; Hos 14:4).

FRIEND/FRIENDSHIP

The idea of friendship is relatively well defined in our culture. A friend is a person whom we know well and with whom we spend time. We are obligated to each other in various ways by our friendship. The various words translated "friend" or "friends" in the OT and NT are more flexible and have a wider range of meanings.

OT 1. *'Ahēb:* friendship as love
    2. *Rêa':* friendship as acquaintance
NT 3. *Philos:* friendship as a sharing of experiences
    4. *Agapē:* friendship as loving fellowship
    5. Summary

OT — 1. *'Ahēb:* friendship as love. The participial form of this word means "lover," but it is translated "friend(s)" or "friendly" in 1 Ki 5:1; 2 Ch 20:7; Est 5:10,14; 6:13; Pr 18:24; Isa 41:8; Jer 20:4,6; and Zec 13:6. The participle is used also in a negative sense, with "lover" suggesting "prostitute." But no sexual relationship is implied in positive uses. Thus Abraham was not merely an acquaintance of God but a "friend" who loved God deeply (2 Ch 20:7). The same bonding or commitment of affection joined David and Jonathan, their friendship

being the OT's prime example of human friendship (1 Sa 18–20).

2. *Rêa':* friendship as acquaintance. This most common Hebrew word for friendship occurs 187 times in the OT. It indicates the relationship of those who are friends, companions, associates, or neighbors. *Rêa'* and its derivatives are very flexible. Although not used to describe the deep friendship of a David and Jonathan, the words are used to describe most other relationships. Such a friend might be a chance acquaintance or a long-term friend. In its breadth, this word can be taken to indicate anyone with whom one comes in contact in daily life.

The flexibility of the term is significant, for it helps us to grasp the full import of God's commandment in Lev 19:18: "Do not seek revenge or bear a grudge against one of your people, but love your neighbor as yourself." Obligation to others extends both to "one of [our] people" and to our "neighbor" (friend!), who is anyone we may contact.

Jesus' story of the Good Samaritan (Lk 10:25–37) is the divine commentary on this OT verse. Jesus showed that the obligation to love a neighbor, and thus the principle of friendship, extends to any fellow human being one meets who is in need, whether that person has been known socially or not.

NT — 3. *Philos:* friendship as a sharing of experiences. In the Greek world the ideal of friendship was well developed. Aristotle, in his *Ethics*, described the noble individual as one who is willing "to do all things for the sake of his friends . . . and, if need be, he gives his life for them." But the word *philos*, "friend," was used in the broad sense of "acquaintance," as well as in the more intimate sense of a personal and deep bonding of real affection.

Philos is found twenty-nine times in the NT, usually in Lk and Jn. The twenty-nine occurrences are: Mt 11:19; Lk 7:6,34; 11:5,6,8; 12:4; 14:10,12; 15:6,9,29; 16:9; 21:16; 23:12; Jn 3:29; 11:11; 15:13,14,15; 19:12; Ac 10:24; 10:31; 27:3; Jas 2:23; 4:4; 3 Jn 14. It is not always translated "friend." The emphasis in the NT seems to be sharing experiences that make a person more than a mere acquaintance. Thus Jesus eats with social outcasts and is accused of being a "friend of publicans and sinners" (Mt 11:19, KJV). And Jesus told at least two parables that suggest that neighbors have a friend's claim on one another (Lk 11:5–8; 15:6–9).

Most significantly, Jesus spoke of laying down his life for his friends, and he called his disciples friends rather than servants (Jn 13–15; cf. Jas 4:4).

While friendship among humans may be expressed in table fellowship and neighborliness (Lk 10:38–42; 11:5–8; 15:6–9; Jn 12:1–8), friendship with God is expressed in commitment to Jesus and in a life lived by his words.

4. Agapē: friendship as loving fellowship. The NIV translates agapētos (derived from agapē) as "dear friend." Literally, agapētos means "beloved," and it occurs over sixty times in the NT. This is an appropriate way to address fellow believers, for the ties that bind Christians together go beyond the ties of normal friendship. Christians are brothers and sisters, members of a single family, bound together by an allegiance that is deeper than that called for by friendship. ♦ *Church*

5. Summary. Friendship in the OT and NT is a significant and yet flexible concept. It includes the closest of personal relationships and yet is extended to chance acquaintances.

What is perhaps most significant is the underlying conviction expressed in the concept that we human beings have an obligation to all our fellows. The neighbor whom the OT calls on us to love may be a stranger lying hurt along the roadside, fully as readily as it may be a close companion.

We may recognize the chance acquaintance as a friend and accept the fact of obligation to him or her. But it is also true that friendship deepens as we share experience with others. In one sense, the expectation that we will respond to another's needs increases as we share experiences together. But the obligation to

care and to act is not based on the depth of one's friendship. It is based on the fact that God has placed the highest value on every human being. Everyone is neighbor and friend, and we are to respond to every human being in need.

FRUIT/FRUITFULNESS

The metaphorical use of "fruit" is significant in both Testaments. For Christians who are convinced that "being fruitful" means winning others to Christ, the description of fruit in Scripture may come as a surprise.

OT   **1. Fruit in the OT**
NT   **2. Fruit in the NT**
      3. Spiritual fruit and fruitfulness
      4. Summary

OT — 1. Fruit in the OT. The two main Hebrew words having to do with fruit are pārâh (verb) and p⁽e⁾rî (noun), the latter indicating (1) the product of plants, trees, and vines, (2) the offspring of animals and human beings, and (3) the consequences or outcome of human acts. The figurative use (the third meaning) predominates in the Psalms (11 times) and in Proverbs (10 times). It is also found often in the prophets.

The primary example of the image is found in Isaiah. In chapter 5 the prophet describes the Lord's complaint against Israel. Israel was the Lord's vineyard, lovingly planted and tended. God looked for good fruit (justice and righteousness) from his vines. But Israel produced bitter fruit (bloodshed, cries of distress).

2. Fruit in the NT. The Greek word karpos is used in the same three senses as the Hebrew p⁽e⁾rî. In the NT, as in the OT, metaphorical uses predominate. This is particularly true in the Gospels, where human actions and words are viewed as fruit growing out of a person's essential being or character.

One example of this is found in the preaching of John the Baptist (summarized in Mt 3 and Lk 3). John called for repentance and insisted that any inner change produce fruit as evidence of its reality.

Mt 7 and Lk 6 report Jesus' explanation to his followers that true character is recognized in a person's acts. "The good man brings good things out of the good stored up in his heart, and the evil man brings evil things out of the evil stored up in his heart" (Lk 6:45; repeated almost identically in Mt 12:35). A parallel passage, Mt 12:33–37, expands on this theme. One's character is betrayed by one's words (vv. 33–34), and "every careless word" (v. 36) will be judged.

3. Spiritual fruit and fruitfulness. It is in the Gospel of John and the Epistles of Paul that the concept of fruitfulness shifts from that of the product of character to the product of God's work within us.

Jn 15:1–16. Jesus takes the image of the vine, with God as gardener, from Isaiah. We believers are carefully tended by the Father, pruned and cared for that we may "bear much fruit." Fruitfulness is possible, he said, if we remain in him and his words remain in us. The point Jesus makes is that fruitfulness is rooted in our personal relationship with him, and our personal relationship with him is maintained by living his words: "If you obey my commands you will remain in my love" (v. 10).

God has chosen us. It is his intention that we be fruitful. It is for this reason that he has given us the most intimate of relationships and Jesus' own words to guide us, and it is our responsibility to walk in close fellowship with our Lord.

Ro 7:4–6. This passage explains that human actions are energized from one of two sources. We can, on the one hand, be energized by our sinful nature; but when we are, we produce "fruit for death." Or we can be energized by the Holy Spirit. When we are controlled by the Spirit, we bear "fruit to God."

Gal 5:16–26. This vital passage defines the fruit of sinful human nature and the fruit that the Spirit-energized nature produces. It is striking that the fruit God seeks, as defined here, is exactly the fruit sought in his OT people! Bad fruit, the acts of the sinful nature, are "sexual immorality, impurity and debauchery; idolatry and witchcraft; hatred, discord,

jealousy, fits of rage, selfish ambition, dissensions, factions and envy; drunkenness, orgies, and the like" (vv. 19–21). The fruit of the Spirit is both inner (in the quality of our personal experience) and external (in the quality of our relationships); because "the fruit of the Spirit is love, joy, peace, patience, kindness, goodness, faithfulness, gentleness and self-control" (vv. 22–23).

4. Summary. Fruitfulness is a consistent concept in the OT and the NT. The fruit God seeks in human beings is expressed in righteous and loving acts that bring peace and harmony to the individual and to society. But that fruit is foreign to sinful human nature. Energized by sinful passions, fallen humanity acts in ways that harm and bring dissension.

God's solution is found in a personal relationship with Jesus and in the supernatural working of God's Spirit within the believer. As we live in intimate, obedient relationship with Jesus, God's Spirit energizes us as we produce the peaceable fruits of a righteousness that can come only from the Lord.

FULFILL

In both Testaments the word meaning "to fill" or "to be full" is typically used where the NIV and the NASB read "fulfill." Infrequently the Hebrew or Greek words so translated denote bringing a process to completion or reaching a goal.

Some specific denotations of "fulfill" in our versions are (1) to accomplish an act or keep a vow, (2) to indicate a period of time that must pass between a prediction and its accomplishment, and, most important, (3) to indicate God's fulfillment of his expressed purposes. The third use is a technical one found in both Testaments. It affirms that God is fully able to keep every promise he has made. God is able to finish every work he begins.

The two Testaments are woven together as a whole by the OT's expression of divine intention and by the NT's record of the historic fulfillment in Christ of many OT predictions. And, where

FULL

there are still expressed purposes to be completed, the authors of both Testaments agree on what they expect the future to hold. The Bible invites us to be filled with its own confidence that God is able to do all that he has announced and that he will do it.

FULL ◆ *Fill/Fullness*

FURY ◆ *Anger*

FUTURE

The Hebrew word most closely linked with the idea of "future" is *'aḥªrît*. It comes from a root meaning, variously, "after," "ending," "past," and "future." Used in a phrase such as "end of days," it suggests the future in general. Used alone, it can represent a life beyond this one (Pr 23:18; 24:14,20).

The NT renderings of "future" in the NIV and the NASB reflect a number of different Greek expressions but no specific or single word for the future. Even so, the Bible does have a distinct and powerful view of the future. Past and future are both expressions of God's master plan. His promises give shape to the future, just as his mighty acts have given form to the past. God can speak decisively about the future, for he is in firm control of all history. "No man knows the future" (Ecc 8:7), but God does.

God's control extends to the individual as well. Thus the psalmist is sure that "there is a future for the man of peace" (Ps 37:37). Just as God spoke positively of the future awaiting the Babylonian exiles, so we take comfort in the certainty that God desires only good for us. "For I know the plans I have for you," Jeremiah quotes the Lord, "plans to prosper you and not to harm you, plans to give you hope and a future" (Jer 29:11).

G

GAIN ◆ *Wealth/Riches/Possessions*

GATE

The significant cities of biblical times were walled for protection. Entrance was possible only through fortified gates. But city gates had additional significance in Bible days.

OT 1. Gates in OT times
NT 2. References to gates in the NT

OT — 1. Gates in OT times. There are three images suggested by the role of city gates in OT times.

The first image is that of controlled access. OT cities had one main gate, though larger cities often had others as well. The city gate was strongly fortified; it was closed at night and in times of danger. Thus, the people of the city could control access and egress. The image of access is picked up in such OT phrases as the "gate(s) of [i.e., entrance to]" heaven (Ge 28:17), death (Job 17:16; 38:17; Ps 9:13; 107:18; Isa 38:10), and the Lord (Ps 118:20).

The second image is legal or governmental in character. The leaders of a city sat at its gates. There the elders or the king handed down judicial decisions (Dt 21:19; 22:15; 25:7; Est 2:19,21; 3:2,3; 4:2,6; 5:9,13; 6:10,12). Thus the psalmist's reference to "those who sit at the gate" (Ps 69:12) indicates the recognized leaders of the community.

The third image is that of business and social functions. It was at the city gates that business contracts were made and witnessed (Ge 34:24; Ruth 4:1,11). Also, markets were set up just outside the city gates. OT prophets sometimes took their stand at this key social location to sternly announce God's messages (e.g., Jer 17:19). The city gates were important in the life of OT peoples.

NT — 2. References to gates in the NT. Most NT references to gates reflect OT images.

In John 10, Jesus speaks of the gate to the sheep pen, referring to a yard attached to a dwelling. There is a single gate for the sheep, and the high stone walls surrounding the yard are topped with thorn bushes. Jesus portrays himself as both guarding the gate (opening it for his own sheep) and being the gate itself, the only way one can enter to be saved (Jn 10:9).

In Mt 16:18, Jesus assures us that "the gates of Hades" will not "overcome" (*katischyō*, "be stronger than"—used only here and Mt 23:23 in the NT) the church, founded as it is on "the Christ, the Son of the living God." This promise should give confidence to believers as they seek both to live in and also to evangelize the world. The forces from hell that battle against the congregation of God will ultimately fall before the advancing church.

Jesus also speaks of wide gates and broad highways that lead to destruction, in contrast to the gate to life, which is small, and the path to life, which is narrow (Mt 7:13–14). Jesus' point is that the way to life is through a portal providing controlled access, along a narrow way defined by God. The wide and wandering highways that humanity substitutes for the way to life end, every one, in death.

GATHER

GATHER ♦ Assembly/Community

GAVE ♦ Gift/Gifts ♦ Giving

GENEALOGY ♦ Ancestors

GENERATION

There are several meanings to this simple word. But the context in Scripture usually makes its meaning in a particular verse clear.

OT 1. The Hebrew words
   2. Metaphorical use
NT 3. "This generation"

OT — 1. The Hebrew words. Two Hebrew words are translated "generation" in the NASB; one is so translated in the NIV.

The NASB translates *tôlḏôt* (found 39 times in the OT) as "generations" in several places. The word means "genealogical records," and its use can usually be recognized by some such phrase as "the account of _____'s line" (e.g., Ge 5:1; cf. 6:9; 1 Ch 7:9).

The key Hebrew word is *dôr*. Literally, *dôr* indicates the span of a single life. Life span can be measured from birth to death, or from the birth of a person to the birth of his offspring. This basic meaning of a lifetime shapes most extended uses of the word "generation" in the OT.

In extended senses, "generation" is used to indicate (1) a period of time, past or future or unending (e.g., Ex 3:15; Lev 23:14; Ps 45:17; La 5:19), (2) a family line traced through history ("the generations to come," Ex 12:14), and (3) a particular group that was alive during a distinctive period of sacred history (Ps 95:10).

2. Metaphorical use. The metaphorical use of *dôr* is the most significant. Here "generation" is used with a characterizing adjective, such as righteous (Ps 14:5 KJV) or stubborn (Ps 79:13). In this use the phrase is intended to identify a specific group of persons, marked by a dominant moral or spiritual trait. This identification not only identifies this group but also defines its relationship as a class with God and with others, and it indicates

their destiny. This use is particularly important because it finds such frequent use in the NT.

NT — 3. "This generation". The Greek word *genea* (used 42 times in the NT) is translated "generation" and means "generation," "family," "race," or "age." These meanings reflect the OT use of *dôr*, with its basic, extended, and metaphorical uses. Thus in the NT, "generations" may indicate the distant past (Col 1:26) or endless future (Lk 1:50), or it may identify a specific historic time (Ac 13:36; Heb 3:10).

The most common NT use of *genea* is in the phrase "this generation." Jesus described his generation as adulterous, wicked, unbelieving, perverse, and sinful. Paul speaks of his own life among "a crooked and depraved generation" (Php 2:15).

This is clearly a metaphorical use, intended to characterize and classify those who heard Jesus' message and rejected him. "This generation" is that group of people whose hearts remained hardened to God. It is a type of people, not the totality of those alive in Jesus' day or at any other particular time.

Recognizing this metaphorical use helps us to understand Jesus' ambiguous remark, repeated in three of the Gospels, that "this generation will certainly not pass away until all these things have happened" (Mt 24:34; Mk 13:30; Lk 21:32). What does this remark, focused in each context on the time of history's end, mean?

Two interpretations seem possible, given the way the phrase is used in the Gospels and in Acts: (1) "This generation" in the Gospels is unbelieving Israel, Jesus' own people, who did not receive him (Jn 1:11). So Jesus may be promising the preservation of the Jews as a distinct people until the time of the end foretold by the OT prophets. (2) "This generation" as a class is unbelieving and perverse. Jesus may have been speaking of the persistence of unbelief throughout human history, until unbelief is shattered and the rebellious are judged at Jesus' appearing. Either view seems justified linguistically, theologically, and by the witness of history.

GENTILE

The Greek word *ethnos* signifies Gentile, pagan, or, in the plural, a nation or nations as distinct from Israel.

The root of the concept is found in the OT, in the words *gôy* and *gôyim*. These Hebrew words, usually translated "nation" or "nations," originally indicated any people who could be distinguished as a group by their political, territorial, or ethnic identity. In the early books of the OT these terms are applied to Israel as well as to other nations. But increasingly as sacred history moves on, God's OT people develop a sense of their unique identity as a covenant people. ♦ *Covenant* Israel was bonded to the Lord and was significantly different from the pagan peoples surrounding the Jewish homeland. Increasingly history shows that the pagan peoples around Israel seduced them from faith in the Lord and were the antagonists and persecutors of Israel. After the Captivity, Gentile world powers were dominant over the Holy Land, a fact that galled the Jews of Jesus' time. The prophets portrayed the Gentiles as enemies, the objects of divine judgment. And yet the prophets testified of a day when even the Gentiles would know God's salvation. ♦ *Nation*

Ethnos occurs 164 times in the NT. Some occurrences designate all peoples (e.g., Lk 7:5; Ac 10:22). Several times the word specifies believers won from paganism (e.g., Ac 15:3,23; Gal 2:12,14; 3:8; Eph 2:11; 3:1; 1 Ti 2:7; 2 Ti 1:11). Typically, however, it is used to designate pagan peoples who stand in contrast to the Jews or to Christians.

The NT portrays the Gentiles as people who are without God's written revelation (cf. Ro 2:14), who are led astray by futile thoughts (Ac 14:16; Eph 4:17), and who are captive to idolatry (1 Co 12:2). The Bible's moral description of the Gentiles is found in Ro 1:18–32, and their spiritual condition is portrayed in Eph 2:11–22. Gentiles were "separate from Christ, excluded from citizenship in Israel and

foreigners to the covenants of the promise, without hope and without God in the world" (v. 12). Yet the message of Christ is announced to the Gentiles, so that those "who were once far away" may be "brought near" (v. 13), to be united with believing Jews in the one body of Christ. ♦ *Body of Christ* The message of the gospel breaks down the wall of hostility and antagonism that has divided humanity, and it unites people from every culture and society in the single spiritual organism created by the death and resurrection of Jesus.

GENTLE/GENTLENESS

"Be completely humble and gentle," Eph 4:2 commands. But what is the quality of gentleness?

1. **The Greek words**
2. **The usage of these words in the NT**

1. The Greek words. The English words "gentle" and "gentleness" often represent the Greek *praus* (3 times in the NT) or *prautēs* (also 3 times in the NT). The word in 2 Co 10:1 is *epieikia,* and the NASB translates *epieikēs* (translated "temperate" and "considerate" by the NIV) as "gentle" in 1 Ti 3:3; Tit 3:2; Jas 3:17; 1 Pe 2:18.

What do these families of Greek words mean, and how are they used in the NIV and the NASB of the NT?

Praos, praus, prautēs, praotēs. These words indicate a mild, soothing quality, a quality that is to be expected in friends, benevolent rulers, tame animals, and mild medications. These Greek words occur in Mt 5:5; 11:29; 21:5; 1 Co 4:21; 2 Co 10:1; Gal 5:23; Eph 4:2; Col 3:12; 1 Ti 6:11; 2 Ti 2:25; Tit 3:2. Jas 1:21; 3:13; 1 Pe 3:4,15.

Epieikēs, epieikia. These words originally indicated a thoughtful, considerate, and decent outlook. Rather than hotly demanding his or her rights, whatever the cost to others, a person with this trait seeks peace in a calm way. These Greek words are found in Ac 24:4; 2 Co 10:1 Php 4:5; 1 Ti 3:3; Tit 3:2; Jas 3:17; 1 Pe 2:18.

The words from both groups are seen as opposites of an angry harshness that grows out of personal pride and a dominating selfishness.

2. The usage of these words in the NT. Gentleness and consideration are qualities ascribed to Jesus himself (2 Co 10:1), even though he is the all-powerful King (Mt 21:5). In describing those who are blessed, Jesus spoke of the meek (*praus*) and announced that they will inherit the earth (Mt 5:5).

Strikingly, this is one of the traits required in spiritual leaders (1 Ti 3:3; Tit 3:2) and is a mark of spiritual maturity and of responsiveness to God's Spirit (Gal 5:23). It is also the way set out in the NT for believers to respond to opposition (2 Ti 2:25). It is "of great worth in God's sight" (1 Pe 3:4).

GIFT/GIFTS

These are simple words. They imply the willingness and ability of one person to give something to another. Yet these words have rather deep theological significance, particularly when used to describe the special endowments that Jesus gives to his people.

OT 1. "Gift" in the OT
NT 2. "Gift" in the NT
    3. Corban
    4. Spiritual gifts
      a. Basic passages on spiritual gifts
      b. Function of spiritual gifts
      c. Questions about spiritual gifts
      d. Discerning an individual's spiritual gift(s)
    5. Summary

OT — 1. Gift in the OT. A number of Hebrew words are translated "gift." But two word groups best express the underlying concept.

Minḥâh is a gift in the sense of an offering or tribute. In common use it is a present (sometimes a bribe) that one person might give another. Such gifts are typically expressions of submission to, or attempts to gain the favor of, a powerful personage. The word is also used of gifts given to God, in recognition of his greatness, or in the daily grain offerings prescribed by law (e.g., Lev 2:1–16; 5:13; 6:14–23).

Nātan is a common verb with a variety of meanings, "to give" being primary among them. A number of words derived from *nātan* mean "gift." Depending on the context, they may also denote a present, a bribe, or a reward.

What is most significant about the use of these Hebrew words is the pattern visible within the culture. Gift giving was regarded as an act with definite social significance, for gifts were viewed as an appropriate way for an inferior to express submission to, or to seek to win the favor of, a superior. A superior may deal generously with an inferior, but that behavior is not described in terms of giving gifts.

NT — 2. Gift in the NT. The common word for giving, *didōmi* (found over 400 times in the NT), is used with all shades of meaning. ♦ *Giving* There are also several words translated "gift." Although these terms for gifts are within the same family of words, each has a special emphasis.

Dōron (found 19 times in the NT) is used very much in the OT sense and most frequently of an offering or gift given by man to God. Only one time (Eph 2:8) is God portrayed as the giver, and in that reference we are shown that salvation comes through faith ("not from yourselves, it is the gift of God"). *Dōron* occurs nineteen times in the NT (Mt 2:11; 5:23–24; 8:4; 15:5; 23:18–19; Mk 7:11; Lk 21:1,4; Eph 2:8; Heb 5:1; 8:3–4; 9:9; 11:4; Rev 11:10).

Dōrea (11 times in the NT) is used less in Scripture; but wherever it is found, God is the giver. God's gifts in and through Jesus include salvation, righteousness, enablement, and the Holy Spirit. *Dōrea* occurs in Jn 4:10; Ac 2:38; 8:20; 10:45; 11:17; Ro 5:15,17; 2 Co 9:15; Eph 3:7; 4:7; Heb 6:4.

Dōrean occurs only eight times. However, it is a significant word. It emphasizes the free character of the gift, given spontaneously and without reference to human merit. Thus, "we are justified freely by his grace" (Ro 3:24) on the basis of what Jesus has done. *Dōrean* is found with this meaning in six of its occurrences (Mt 10:8; Jn 15:25; Ro 3:24; 2 Co 11:7; Rev 21:6; 22:17). In Gal 2:21 it means "not without impact," and in 2 Th 3:8 it means "without payment."

What is significant about the idea of gift giving in the NT is the sudden and jolting reversal of the flow. Gifts are no longer presents offered by an inferior to a superior. God, the ultimate superior in the universe, is seen giving gifts to humanity. His gifts are freely and spontaneously offered, without reference to the merit of the one who receives and without the intention of later profiting from the transaction. The impact of the NT revelation is its demand that we see God in a new light: God is one who is suddenly presented to us as *given*.

The teaching of the NT makes it clear that the ultimate gift of God is Jesus himself. All other gifts come to us through the Son. Accepting Jesus, we step into the relationship with God that Paul describes in Ro 8:32: "He who did not spare his own Son, but gave him up for us all—how will he not also, along with him, graciously give us all things?"

3. Corban. Mark's Gospel (7:11) uses this technical term, where it is described as a gift vowed to God (cf. Mt 15:5, *dōran*). The thing vowed was not actually transferred to the temple treasury. All that was called for was the pronouncement of the vow, and others were thereupon barred from benefiting from the property or person so committed to God.

The rabbis of Jesus' day held that such a vow was always binding, even if it denied one's parents the resources required for their support. Jesus condemned this interpretation. His strong words about Corban need not imply that the practice was widespread. Instead they condemn the willingness of the religious leaders to set aside for a technicality God's command to honor parents. Jesus' complaint was that these interpreters of Israel's faith did "many things like that" (Mk 7:13).

4. Spiritual gifts. The Greek word involved in this subject is *charisma*. It indicates a grace gift, one bestowed only by God to people in the NT. ◆ *Grace* In Romans, Paul speaks of "the gift that came by the grace of" Jesus, eternal life (Ro 5:15; cf. 6:23). But in most occurrences in the NT, *charisma* is God's special endowment of believers for service to the community of faith. This Greek word occurs seventeen times in the NT (Ro 1:11; 5:15–16; 6:23; 11:29; 12:6; 1 Co 1:7; 7:7; 12:4,9,28,30–31; 2 Co 1:11; 1 Ti 4:14; 2 Ti 1:6; 1 Pe 4:10).

Because of the unusual character of some of the spiritual gifts identified in Scripture, the real significance of this biblical teaching has often been clouded.

a. Basic passages on spiritual gifts. The two major passages are Ro 12 and 1 Co 12.

Ro 12 calls on believers to look at life from God's perspective (vv. 1–2). Immediately Paul moves to explain God's view of the individual believer within the community (vv. 3–8). Individuals are to see themselves as members of a body— parts of a living organism, within which each person has a distinct function. God has endowed each believer with a gift, an enablement that makes him or her able to contribute to others in the body. Thus the church is an interdependent community, a living body, within which each of us "belongs to all the others" (v. 5) and is to serve others. In 12:9–18 Paul describes the interpersonal relationships that members of the body are to develop. Only loving and intimate personal relationships create a context for that loving service in which spiritual gifts operate.

The same themes are picked up in 1 Cor 12. There are different gifts (v. 4), sovereignly distributed by God (v. 7). Each believer is given a gift to be used for the common good (v. 7). The passage emphasizes the importance of each person to the body, a corrective in a church that tended to exalt some gifts over others (vv. 14–26). As in the discussion in Romans, Paul moves on to speak of the climate of love that is to mark the believing community (13:1–13). It is in the context of interpersonal relationships shaped by love that spiritual gifts function freely.

Peter sums up the personal impact of the Bible's teaching on gifts: "Each one should use whatever gift he has received to serve others, faithfully administering God's grace in its various forms" (1 Pe 4:10).

b. Function of spiritual gifts. The grace gifts of the NT are always seen within the context of the Christian community. Although believers are called on to witness to, and to do good to, all people, the passages that explore spiritual gifts are focused on the shared life of members of the body of Christ. It is within the body that spiritual gifts function "for the common good" (1 Co 12:7).

According to Eph 4, the "works of service" of Christians are called for "that the body of Christ may be built up, until we all reach unity in the faith and in the knowledge of the Son of God and become mature, attaining to the whole measure of the fullness of Christ" (vv. 12–13). Vitalized by the spiritual life that flows from Jesus, the whole body "grows and builds itself up in love, as each part does its work" (v. 16).

It is important that we see spiritual gifts as spiritual endowments that function within the body, focused on the maturing of our fellow Christians and the believing community. God surely works through his people to serve and witness to him in the world. But spiritual gifts are in Scripture a family concern.

c. Questions about spiritual gifts. Many questions are asked about spiritual gifts, questions that cannot be fully answered here. But some observations are called for in response to major questions raised.

(1) Do the more obviously supernatural gifts of the Spirit operate today? No decisive answer can be given to this much-debated issue. But surely there is not enough biblical evidence to say with certainty that the more spectacular gifts mentioned in the NT *cannot* operate today. ♦ *Tongues*

(2) Are all the spiritual gifts listed in the Bible? It is best to take the various gifts listed in Ro 12 and 1 Co 12 as representative rather than as an exhaustive listing of God's endowments. Any way in which we serve others and contribute to their lives must depend on the Holy Spirit's working through us and should be considered a *charisma*.

(3) Where do spiritual gifts operate? The context defined in the Bible is relational. Spiritual gifts operate as we lovingly respond to others and seek to serve them. At times we mistakenly identify spiritual gifts with church offices or institutional roles. We should not assume that the spiritual gift of teaching is summed up by functioning in a Sunday school classroom. ♦ *Teaching/Learning*

(4) Can a person have more than one spiritual gift? It is clear that Paul had more than one gift (1 Co 14:18; 2 Co 12:11–12). We know that each believer has at least one spiritual gift. There is no reason to believe that any individual is necessarily limited to one gift.

(5) What is the difference between the spiritual gifts and persons who are called God's gifts to his church? Both 1 Co 12 and Eph 4 speak of such gifted persons: apostles, evangelists, etc. These persons were set aside in the early church to a full-time and probably itinerant ministry. They had to be gifted spiritually to fulfill their ministries. But the offices are not gifts in the sense of *charisma*. For a discussion of each role, see the appropriate entry; e.g., ♦ *Apostle.*

d. Discerning an individual's spiritual gift(s). Many believers wonder what their spiritual gifts are. How can they find out?

It is important to remember that spiritual gifts operate in a relational context. It is in a climate marked by intimate sharing and love that we respond to others' needs and that God the Spirit ministers through us to serve them. Given this, we can outline the way that spiritual gifts can be identified.

First, Christians must develop close relationships with other believers. Within this context a person will respond appropriately to shared needs.

Second, Christians must be willing to reach out and serve others, seeking to help and to minister to personal, emotional, material, and spiritual needs. In responding to others and in seeking to serve them, God the Holy Spirit has opportunity to work through the individual.

Third, the ministry of God the Spirit through the individual will eventually be recognized by others in the community of faith. It is the testimony of others concerning how God has worked through an individual that is decisive in identifying that person's spiritual gifts.

Fourth, as gifts are identified, each believer must seek opportunities to minister in appropriate ways that use his or her gifts for the benefit of others.

5. Summary. The Bible's teaching on gifts gives us a unique appreciation for God. In the OT, giving gifts is seen as an appropriate way for an inferior to approach a superior person, especially God. In the NT, we are shown the stunning fact that God has reversed this flow. God has taken the initiative and in Christ has bestowed wondrous gifts on humanity. The NT, then, introduces us to God as the great giver of every good and perfect gift (Jas 1:17).

God's gifts are focused in and through Jesus. Jesus himself is God's greatest gift, for through Jesus we are redeemed and given eternal life. But God also blesses us with gifts that come to us through Jesus. *Charisma* is a special term for grace gifts. It focuses attention on how we are called to function within the body of Christ. God has given each believer a special endowment of the Spirit, so that he or she can make a distinctive contribution to individuals and to the community of faith. Living together, united by the bonds of brotherly love, each of us is used by God to enrich our brothers and sisters and to stimulate their growth to Christian maturity.

GIVING

Do Christians owe a tenth of all income to the local church? How are believers to gauge their giving? Both the OT and the NT help us resolve the confusion many feel about giving.

OT 1. Tithes
2. Freewill offerings
3. Care of the needy
NT 4. The social context
5. Sharing
6. Cheerful giving
7. Conclusions

OT — 1. Tithes. At first glance, the concept of tithing seems simple. Lev 27:30–33 says: "A tithe of everything from the land, whether grain from the soil or fruit from the trees, belongs to the LORD; it is holy to the LORD. If a man redeems any of his tithe, he must add a fifth of the value to it. The entire tithe of the herd and flock—every tenth animal that passes under the shepherd's rod—will be holy to the LORD. He must not pick out the good from the bad or make any substitution." Ten percent of everything the land produced was to be set aside, to be used as God commanded.

Other passages expand our knowledge of OT tithing. Nu 18:21–32 instructs that tithes were to be used to maintain the Levites. That tribe was set apart to serve God, and its members were not given a district when Israel possessed the Promised Land. Dt 12:5–14 and 14:22–26 indicate that the tithes are to be brought to the central sanctuary, later established at Jerusalem. Dt 14:27–29 and 26:12–15 introduce another tithe, to be collected every third year for local distribution to the needy. Some argue for as many as three separate tithes designated in these passages. It is likely that there were at least two: the annual ten percent taken for the support of those who served the Lord, and the third-year tithe taken to sustain the widow and orphan.

These tithes were not to be viewed as a burden. They were to express both love and trust for God, as the Lord promised to bless the works of his people's hands (Dt 14:29). Giving was thus no threat to security. In fact, it showed confidence that God would make the land produce. As Malachi announced to a struggling generation that withheld the payment of the tithe, "'Test me in this,' says the LORD Almighty, 'And see if I will not throw open the floodgates of heaven and pour out so much blessing that you will not have room enough for it' " (3:10).

2. Freewill offerings. The OT reports giving that goes beyond the tithe. This is most clearly expressed in the *nᵉdābâh,* or voluntary contribution. The emphasis here is on a giving that flows spontaneously, expressing devotion to the Lord. It is not a gift given out of a sense of duty, nor to win promised blessings. The voluntary contributions are most often associated with the construction of the tabernacle (Ex 36) or the temple (2 Ch 35; Ezr 1:4). Ps 119:108 speaks of prayer as a voluntary offering, and God is praised for his own generous voluntary offerings to man (Ps 68:9), even when his people have not been faithful to their covenant commitments (Hos 14:4). ◆ *Covenant*
◆ *Freewill Offering*
The Lord has always been concerned with the heart attitude of worshipers. The grateful believer who did not find the required tithes enough to express his or her devotion was invited to bring freewill offerings as well.

3. Care of the needy. The annual tithes were dedicated to support the people set aside to serve the Lord. ◆ *Priests and Levites* The third-year tithe, stored and distributed locally, was for the care of the needy (Dt 14:27–29; 26:12–15).

OT law established a social system with several mechanisms designed for care of the needy. Interest-free loans were encouraged, and those unable to repay were forgiven their debts every seventh year. ◆ *Lending and Borrowing* Fallen grain was to be left in the fields at harvest for the poor to gather. A person in extreme need could bind himself to a fellow Israelite to work as a servant. After a set number of years, such a person was to be freed and provided with money to reestablish himself. It was hoped that with training received, such a person could make his own way.

To understand giving as practiced in OT times, we need to be aware of the distinctives that the law established in that society. Giving had a unique purpose within that system. It supported those set aside to lead in worship. And it was one of several different social mechanisms designed to meet society's obligation to the poor and oppressed.

NT — 4. The social context. There are many obvious differences between OT and NT faith communities.

The OT faith community was a sovereign nation. It was a society whose civil structures were ordered by the Mosaic Law. In Israel those who served God were set aside to minister and were not given lands of their own. Worship took place in a single, national worship center, supported by a tithe from all the people. Tithing also served as a triennial tax, to be collected and distributed locally for the care of the poor. But this tax was only one of several social mechanisms established to do justice to the oppressed in society.

The NT faith community has no national identity. It is composed of little companies of believers scattered through all the world's nations and cultures. Christians are subject to the laws of the nation in which they live, participating in the obligations and privileges of citizenship. Secular governments cannot be expected to conform to the principles for a just moral society that are outlined in the OT. Nor does the scattered church know a central temple. For the first two hundred years or so of the Christian era, believers met in small groups in private homes. Instead of a special priestly class, the NT announces a priesthood of all believers. ◆ *Priesthood* Although some men and women may be supported so they can provide full-time service (2 Co 9:7–12), even Paul did not elect this option.

These are dramatic differences between OT and NT faith communities. In view of these differences, it is not surprising that the NT does not transfer the tithe into the new era. Although the principle of the tithe predates the law (Ge 14:20; 28:22), no instruction in Acts or in the Epistles suggests that tithing is to be practiced by Christians. Instead, a new set of principles that reflect new theological and social realities is introduced.

5. Sharing. One of the theologically significant terms of the NT is intimately linked with giving. The term is *koinōnia* (which occurs 20 times in the NT; its corresponding verb is *koinōneō*, which occurs 8 times). In Greek culture, this term expressed the ideal of mutuality, of a brotherly bond forged by sharing in the common life. Thus the word expressed the idea of sharing and of fellowship.

In the NT this is a distinctively theological term. It affirms the reality of a bond created with faith in Christ—a bonding to God and to those who belong to God. Thus the NT speaks of a fellowship with God's Son (1 Co 1:9), a fellowship of the Holy Spirit (1 Co 13:14), a fellowship in the gospel (Php 1:5), and a fellowship of faith (Phm 6). "Our fellowship," John says, "is with the Father and with his Son, Jesus Christ" (1 Jn 1:3). Our fellowship with others is based on the fact that all who come into relationship with God as Father also come into relationship with those who are God's children, becoming brothers and sisters linked with the most significant of all bonds.

We see this reality of a shared family identity applied first in Ac 4:32–37. Members of the early church in Jerusalem responded spontaneously to the needs of others and "shared everything they had" (v. 32). The passage goes on to say that "there were no needy persons among them," as those with various properties sold them and brought the money to be "distributed to anyone as he had need" (vv. 34–35).

This passage suggests neither an organized social program nor a shared ownership of property. Instead, it reveals a sensitive concern for others and a spontaneous willingness to share material things with those in need.

It is striking that the NT writers continue to select this concept of "fellowship" to speak of Christian giving. We see it in *koinōneō* (Ro 12:13; Gal 6:6; Php 4:15) and in *koinōnia* (Ro 15:26; 2 Co 8:4; 9:13; Heb 13:16). These and other passages show that as believers in distant places experienced desperate need, Christians everywhere responded and shared generously with them.

In the NT's major passage on giving (2 Co 8–9), Paul expresses the principle that governs our giving-as-sharing: "Our desire is not that others might be relieved while you are hard pressed, but that there might be equality. At the present time your plenty will supply what they need, so that in turn their plenty will supply what you need. Then there will be equality, as it is written, 'He who gathered much did not have too much, and he who gathered little did not have too little' " (2 Co 8:13–15).

So then giving is portrayed in the NT as a way to provide support for those who give their full time to ministry (Gal 6:6; 1 Ti 5:17–18). It is also a way to meet the needs of local people who have no family to help them when they cannot care for themselves (1 Ti 5:16). But the major emphasis in the NT is given to world-wide concern: Christians are to share with others who, because of natural disasters, are not able to survive without help.

6. Cheerful giving. The NT presents the idea of systematic giving. Paul exhorts one church to give by setting aside weekly "a sum of money in keeping with . . . income" (1 Co 16:2). But how is that sum of money to be determined? Instead of suggesting the tithe as a measure, Paul (2 Cor 8 and 9) provides several principles for our guidance:

a. Giving is an expression of love. It is to be prompted by an inner concern for others that cannot be commanded but must be a free and spontaneous act (8:8).

b. Giving is to be a balanced response, measuring what a person has against the current needs of others (8:12–15).

c. Giving is an act of faith. It shows trust in God, who is "able to make all grace abound to you" (9:8). As we give generously, God will supply our needs and enable us to "be generous on every occasion" (9:11).

d. Giving has many benefits. It meets the needs of our brothers and sisters and stimulates praise to the Lord. It also stimulates prayer both for the giver and the receiver (9:11–14).

e. Giving follows the example of Jesus. "Though he was rich, yet for your sakes he became poor, so that you through his poverty might become rich" (8:9). Giving is an appropriate way to express our appreciation to God for his own indescribable gift (9:15).

These NT principles for cheerful giving call for serious consideration. We must measure our attitude toward material things, measure our own needs, and measure the needs of our brothers and sisters. In the process, we must be sensitive to the Holy Spirit. Through this process that calls for the most responsible of behavior, we must each come to our own conclusion about how—and how much—God is leading us to give.

7. Conclusions. The OT pattern of giving was an integral part of the social system that was established in the Mosaic Law. It provided for the specific needs of persons within the nation Israel—needs for a central worship center, for a large company of persons set aside for religious service, and for the poor who were not fully cared for by other social mechanisms.

The early NT church existed in a different social context, and thus the principles regarding giving were suited to the new setting and new theological realities. Churches were responsible for the support of those set aside for full-time ministry and for those whose families could not meet basic needs. There were no buildings to maintain, as Christians simply met in house-churches. But collections were taken to aid fellow believers made destitute by natural disasters or economic conditions in other parts of the world. No set amount was required for giving, but individuals were taught to be aware of principles that should guide their giving and to be sensitive to others with needs.

Conditions are different today, as the church exists in institutionalized form and as all citizens are called on to contribute to the needs of the poor through government taxes. Yet the basic NT principles of giving must still be applied, for each person is responsible to use material possessions in ways that honor God. Today too we must remain sensitive to others and commit ourselves to giving

generously for those needs we believe are closest to God's heart.

GLORY

"Glory" is not a word that is heard often in our conversation. Yet in the Bible it is a vital and rich term. It provides perspective on our values. And it calls us to deepening worship of our God.

OT   1. The Hebrew words
      2. The glory of the Lord
NT   3. The Greek word
      4. The roots of God's glory
      5. Giving God glory
      6. Our journey toward glory
      7. Summary

OT — 1. The Hebrew words. The primary Hebrew word translated "glory" in the English OT versions is *kābôd*. It comes from a root that means "heavy" or "weighty." The word is normally used in a figurative sense to suggest an impressive or worthy person. Typically, someone honored in ancient cultures had high position and consequent wealth. Kings of Bible times are perhaps our prime example, for they were treated with deferential awe and surrounded with regal splendor (e.g., Ps 4:2; cf. Da 4:30,36, where the Chaldean word used is *yᵉqār*).

Both the NIV and the NASB also use "glory" to translate *tip'ārāh*, from a root verb that means "to glorify or beautify." The root suggests also glorying in someone or something (Pr 17:6; 28:12). The OT tells us that the Lord views Israel as his glory (Isa 46:13; 62:3; Jer 33:9), in the sense that Israel will ultimately adorn the Lord and bring him praise. ◆ *Beauty/ Beautiful*

In the OT, the glory of human achievement is an ascribed glory. It exists in the eye of the beholder. But the glory of God is objective. It is rooted not in the evaluation of others, but in his very nature. When God's glory is unveiled and recognized, all those things in which human beings take pride fade to nothingness.

2. The glory of the Lord. In the OT, the glory of God is intimately linked with the Lord's self-revelation. There is much imagery: a blazing splendor and flaming holiness mark his presence (e.g., Ex 16:10; 40:34,35; 2 Ch 7:1,2). But neither raw power nor burning holiness adequately express God. Thus Exodus links God's glory with an unveiling of his loving character. When Moses begged God to show him his glory, the Bible reports: "The LORD said, 'I will cause all my goodness to pass in front of you, and I will proclaim my name, the LORD, in your presence. I will have mercy on whom I will have mercy, and I will have compassion on whom I will have compassion. But,' he said, 'You cannot see my face, for no one may see me and live'" (33:19–20). In the same sense of unveiling, God says, "I will gain glory for myself" in the case of Pharaoh's refusal to let Israel go (Ex 14:4). God's great redemptive power was displayed in the Exodus (Nu 14:22), even as his creative power is displayed when "the heavens declare the glory of God" (Ps 19:1).

But "glory" implies more than a disclosure by God of who he is. It implies an invasion of the material universe, an expression of God's active presence among his people. Thus, the OT consistently links the term "glory" with the presence of God among Israel in tabernacle and temple (e.g., Ex 29:43; Eze 43:4–5; Hag 2:3). God's objective glory is revealed by his coming to be present with us, his people, and to show us himself by his actions in our world.

And what is our response to be? We are to "ascribe to the LORD glory" (1 Ch 16:28; Ps 29:1) and to "glory in his holy name" (1 Ch 16:10). We are to worship him by recognizing his presence and praising him for those qualities that his actions for us unveil.

NT — 3. The Greek word. The Greek word is *doxa*. In Hellenic cultures *doxa* expressed primary values of vital importance to the Greek people. *Doxa* focused attention on the opinion held by others: it expressed the valuation placed by others on one's actions or achievements. A high valuation—i.e., fame—exalted an individual over others. It was a goal of the Greeks to be honored and praised by others.

This meaning is completely transformed in the Bible. When the translators of the Hebrew OT into Greek chose *doxa* to translate *kābôd*, glory as mere human opinion was transformed into glory as the majesty associated with God's self-revelation. In the NT it is this OT concept that is generally reflected. Perhaps the Greek notion is suggested in a few passages, however, such as that describing the temptation in which Satan showed Jesus "all the kingdoms of the world and their splendor" (*doxa*) (Mt 4:8). What men consider splendor and fame fades into insignificance when compared to the true glory of God.

4. The root of God's glory. The OT has shown us the root of God's glory in his essential nature and in the display of that nature as he acts in the material universe. His qualities are glorious in themselves (e.g., Eph 1:6; 3:16; Col 1:11), as is Jesus himself (Jas 2:1). But it is in God's actions and his works that we discover and are awed by the splendor of the Lord.

The NT speaks of two differing expressions of the divine glory. One expression is visible, yet is perceived only by the eyes of faith. Thus the Incarnation can be described in these words: "The Word became flesh and made his dwelling among us. We have seen his glory, the glory of the One and Only, who came from the Father, full of grace and truth" (Jn 1:14). Yet the unbelieving saw only the carpenter from Nazareth. It was the believing who saw in his person and in his actions the ultimate unveiling of God (cf. Jn 2:11; 8:50–54; Heb 1:3).

The Bible also tells of an expression of God's glory in Jesus that will be experienced by all. This is an eschatological unveiling; an unmasked demonstration of the bright and flaming splendor that was dimmed even as Sinai burned. In that day, God's presence will be known, as his unsheltered holiness sears every conscience not washed by Jesus' blood (Mt 16:27; 24:30; 25:31; Mk 8:38; 10:37; 13:26; Lk 9:26; 21:27; Col 3:4; 1 Th 2:12; 2 Th 1:9; Tit 2:13; 1 Pe 4:13; 5:1; 2 Pe 1:17; Rev 15:8; 21:11,23). To the saved in that day the Lord's *doxa* will be beauty; to the lost, terror. But all will recognize his essential glory then, and "at the name of Jesus every knee [shall] bow, in heaven and on earth and under the earth, and every tongue confess that Jesus Christ is Lord, to the glory of God the Father" (Php 2:10–11).

5. Giving God glory. Throughout the Bible we find commands to glorify God (e.g., 1 Ch 16:28; Ps 34:3; Jer 13:16; Jn 9:24; Rev 14:7). In one sense we give God glory when we recognize his presence and praise him for the qualities his acts unveil (e.g., Rev 4:9–11; 5:12–13). But there is another NT sense in which we give God glory. Jesus spoke of his own actions as bringing glory to God (Jn 14:13) and called on his disciples to bear fruit to the "Father's glory" (Jn 15:8). Expressions like these occur frequently in the NT (see "glorify," "glorified," and "glory" in a concordance, noting especially Jn 9:24; 14:13; 15:8; 17:4,10; Ro 3:7; 1 Co 10:31; 2 Co 1:20; Eph 1:12,14; 3:21; Php 1:11; Col 1:27). These expressions force us back to our basic concept to discover a beautiful and wonderful fact: God's glory is displayed in his acts in our world. Because God is present in believers today, he is able to display his qualities in our lives and so to glorify himself in us. How wonderful that you and I can be agents of God's grace, displaying in our character and in loving works of service those Spirit-wrought qualities that God uses to make himself known to those around us.

6. Our journey toward glory. In 2 Corinthians, Paul explores the great wonder that you and I are on a journey toward glory. Speaking of the work of the Holy Spirit in us, Paul says we "reflect the Lord's glory." This is because we "are being transformed into his likeness with ever-increasing glory, which comes from the Lord, who is the Spirit" (2 Co 3:18). This process is hinted at in many passages (e.g., Ro 2:7,10; 5:2; 8:17,30; 2 Co 4:17; Php 3:21; Col 1:27; 3:4; 1 Th 2:12; 2 Th 2:14; 2 Ti 2:10; Heb 2:10; 1 Pe 1:7). The reality underlying it all is that, through our personal relationship with Jesus, the very splendor of God's presence enters our lives. Because of his presence, we are new creations, on a journey toward the very likeness of Christ (Ro 8:29; 1 Jn 3:1–2), to enter and to share the ultimate presence—the glory—of God, there to display in our transformed selves the beauty of our God.

7. Summary. The world is impressed by appearances. Wealth and position are equated with glory, and fame—the admiration of others—is eagerly sought.

The Christian has a different set of values. To the believer, true glory is found only in the splendor of God. It is recognized as his character is displayed in his actions, and it is reflected back to him as praise. ♦ *Praise* We say with the psalmist David: "You are a shield around me, O LORD; you bestow glory on me and lift up my head" (Ps 3:3). We glorify God by recognizing his presence in his actions and by offering him our praise. And we glorify God by being channels through which the Holy Spirit, who lives within us, can communicate God to those whose lives we touch.

GOD

Multiplied volumes have been written to explore this short word. Who is God? What is he like? What reasons are there to believe that God exists? What concepts does the word "God" convey?

While the answers given are often complex and vary with culture and faith, the uses of "God" in the Bible introduce the believer to a unique person, who is alike the center of the universe and the center of our lives.

OT 1. OT words for God
    2. The word 'ēl
    3. The word 'elôah
    4. The word 'elōhîm
NT 5. The NT word for God
    6. Summary

OT — 1. OT words for God. A cluster of three words, possibly from the same ancient root, are translated "God" or "god" in the NIV and the NASB. These are 'ēl, 'elôah, and 'elōhîm. Each is a generic term, meaning "god" or "mighty one." Normally when one of these words occurs in the OT, it designates either the true God or something the pagan nations viewed as a god. In only a few instances are these words used of angels or of mighty human beings.

In the OT, God has a proper name as well as a generic designation. God's name is Yahweh, typically represented as Lord in the NIV and NASB (some 6,400 times!). About 315 times, in phrases where it is linked with 'ādôn, which is also translated "lord," Yahweh is rendered "God." ♦ **Lord** These occurrences can be recognized by a phrase like "O Lord God" or "the Lord God."

Because the generic words for God were used by other nations in the OT world to indicate their gods, the OT is usually careful to distinguish Israel's God. This is done by linking each word for God with a number of descriptive terms. Thus God is defined—and the OT concept of God is developed—by attached words or phrases that set the Lord apart from every competing deity. It is in these descriptive adjuncts that the true God is gradually unveiled for us and honored. By looking at each of the three generic God words and the ideas linked with them, we can build our awareness of who our God is and who he has shown himself to be for us.

2. The word 'ēl. Words associated with this basic Semitic word for God teach us much about the Lord. He is spoken of in the OT as almighty (Ge 17:1), jealous (Ex 20:5; Dt 4:24), faithful (Dt 7:9), living (Jos 3:10; Ps 42:2; Isa 37:4), holy (Isa 5:16), and righteous (Isa 45:21). God is also seen in his relationship to other persons and things. The true God is God Most High (Ge 14:18–19) and the God who sees me (Ge 16:13). He is God of eternity (Ge 21:33), of knowledge (1 Sa 2:3), of truth (Ps 31:5), of glory (Ps 29:3), of miracles (Ps 77:14), of heaven on high (Ps 136:26). He is God of gods (Da 11:36). Moreover, God is known through his relationship with us. He is our source (Dt 32:18), our fortress (2 Sa 22:2), our Rock (2 Sa 22:3; Ps 42:9; 89:26), our Savior (Ps 89:26; Isa 12:2).

No human mind can comprehend God fully. Yet in these and other descriptions we begin to sense something of the wondrous person who has shown himself to us as Creator and Redeemer as well.

3. The word 'ĕlôah. This is the least-often used of the three terms. It is found primarily in Job—in dialogue between Job and Eliphaz, and by Elihu. It also occurs in other very early poetic sections.

The word seems to convey the idea of strength. Outside of Job it is linked with descriptions of God as Rock and Savior (Dt 32:15) and shield (Pr 30:5) for his people, but as terror to sinners (Ps 50:22).

4. The word 'ĕlōhîm. This word for God is used more frequently (some 2,570 times) than either of the others in the OT. It is a plural form—a form used in other religions to suggest fuller manifestation of a deity. It is often called the "plural of majesty" and in the OT, although normally used with singular vowels, probably implies that more than one person is involved. For instance, Ge 1:1–2 introduces God and the Spirit of God. Ge 1:26 reports that God said, "Let us make man in our image, in our likeness. . . ." While this might be considered a royal "we," it is more likely an early indication of the triune nature of God who, though one Person, exists forever as Father, Son, and Holy Spirit.

The doctrine of the Trinity is never clearly taught in the OT, however many hints there may be. What the OT does is continue to use this name, with others, as a means of developing the concept of God by linking with it descriptive terms and phrases. Many such descriptions are linked to 'ĕlōhîm.

The OT presents 'ĕlōhîm as the Lord God of heaven and earth (Ge 24:3). He is God of all the kingdoms of earth (Isa 37:16; cf. 54:5). As sovereign, God is Judge (Ps 50:6; 58:11). He is also the Savior (Isa 45:15). He is holy (1 Sa 6:20), living (Jer 10:10), strong (Ps 81:1), the God of justice (Isa 30:18), the God of eternity (Isa 40:28), and the God of truth (Isa 65:16; Jer 10:10).

God is so involved in human affairs that he can be known by those with whom he has established a covenant relationship. ♦ **Covenant** God is the God of Abraham (Ge 26:24) and of all the patriarchs (Ex 3:6,15; 4:5). He is God of salvation (1 Ch 16:35; Ps 18:46) and God of the armies of Israel (1 Sa 17:45). In his saving relationship with the human beings who trust in him, he is God nearby and far away (Jer 23:23), the God who disciplines (Dt 8:5), the God who is gracious and righteous and full of compassion (Ps 116:5). The psalmist cries out, "O my Strength; . . . you, O God, are my fortress, my loving God" (Ps 59:17).

As the OT develops the concept of God in this distinctive way, it also calls on us to respond to God. Because God is faithful, we are to trust him. Because God is a God of salvation, we are to turn to him for help. Because God is holy, we are to do good. Something of the impact the revelation of God is to have on his people can be seen in this announcement that Moses made to Israel: "The LORD your God is a God of gods and Lord of lords, the great God, mighty and awesome, who shows no partiality and accepts no bribes. He defends the cause of the fatherless and the widow, and loves the alien, giving him food and clothing" (Dt 10:17–18). Immediately Moses applies this affirmation of God's identity: "And you are to love those who are aliens . . ." (10:19).

This is one great impact of knowing God as he is revealed in Scripture. God becomes the standard by which all things are to be measured. God becomes the one after whom our character is to be patterned. We respond to this God with trust. But we also respond by seeking to be like him (e.g., Lev 20:26).

NT — 5. The NT word for God. The NT refers to God by using the common Greek term *theos*. The Greeks had believed in many gods and goddesses. These deities were shaped in the image of human beings, with both base and honorable passions. They were limited in their powers. Typically, Greek gods were not concerned with mortals, though they might be influenced to help them at times.

In later Greek philosophy, the gods and goddesses of mythology were discounted, and the deity was thought of more as an abstract principle or force. The biblical concept of God, as defined in the OT, was foreign to Greek thought.

Thus when *theos* was used in the Septuagint and in the NT, it was purified and transformed. The vague notions of the Greeks were cleansed, and the clear images of the OT were imported. The God of the NT is the God of the OT.

But additional development of our concept of God takes place in the NT. God is still the same eternal, sovereign, loving, and righteous person. But God's attributes are further explored, and the implications of each is developed. We have known God as righteous and have seen his righteousness in the way he dealt with sinning generations in Israel. Now we see his righteousness in a new light, as the Son offers up himself in payment for the sins of a lost humanity (Ro 3:21–26). We have seen God's love operate in his free choice of Israel as his own special people. But now we see God's love in its full burst of glory as Jesus comes with the gospel's call to all mankind.

Some concepts undergo a transformation. In the OT, the idea of God as Father is limited to the conviction that he is the source of everything. ♦ **Father** In the NT, "Father" is a relational term and emphasizes the intimacy of the relationship we have with God through Jesus.

The OT hints at God's triune nature. The NT presents the Son and Holy Spirit as persons in their own right, yet linked in undivided unity with the Father.

The God who began to communicate himself to us in OT acts and descriptive words shares himself fully with us in Jesus and in the NT. As we explore both Testaments, we come to know him as he is; and are moved to worship him in spirit and in truth (Jn 4:23–24).

6. Summary. How is God known? The concept of God is developed gradually in Scripture. God is unveiled as we trace his actions and see the descriptions of him linked with the ancient world's common words for God. How clear it is! This God, who meets us in the Bible and who stepped into history in the person of Jesus, is the true God, unique among all that humanity has ever dreamed of acknowledging as deity.

To strengthen our concept of God and to strengthen our faith, there is no better way than to read through the Bible. There we can note God's acts and mark each descriptive term that gives insight into his nature and character. In the NT, we can trace the full unveiling in Jesus of every attribute of God. Only in him can we recognize the full extent of the endless love, righteousness, and goodness of God.

GODLESS

The word "godless" occurs seldom in the NIV and the NASB. The Hebrew word used in the OT is *ḥānēp*. It means "irreligious" but suggests an active course in opposition to all that God says is right. The Book of Job makes it clear that a terrible fate awaits the godless (8:13; 13:16; 15:34; 20:5; cf. 17:8; 27:8; 34:30; 36:13; Ps 35:16; Pr 11:9; Isa 9:17; 10:6; 33:14).

Two Greek words are translated "godless" in the NT. *Bebēlos* (found 5 times in the NT) means "irreligious" in the sense of the unhallowed in contrast to the sacred, as the worldly in contrast to that which is rooted in spiritual realities (1 Ti 1:9; 4:7; 6:20; 2 Ti 2:16; Heb 12:16). Another term translated "godless" is *asebēs* (found 9 times in the NT but rendered "godless" only in Jude 4); and *asebeia* (found 6 times in the NT) is rendered "godlessness" twice (Ro 1:11; 11:26). These two terms suggest the condition of the pagan, whose thoughts and actions take no account of God.

GODLY/GODLINESS

In the OT the word translated "godly" is *ḥāsîd*. ♦ *Grace* It is often rendered "saints" as well. It indicates those who were recipients of God's grace and who as a result showed the impact of grace in their lives. This word, found most often in the Psalms, occurs thirty-two times in the OT (Dt 33:8; 1 Sa 2:9; 2 Sa 22:26; 2 Ch 6:41; Ps 4:3; 12:1; 16:10; 18:25; 30:4; 31:23; 32:6; 37:28; 43:1; 50:5; 52:9; 79:2; 85:8; 86:2; 89:19; 97:10; 116:15; 132:9,16; 145:10,17; 148:14; 149:1,5,9; Pr 2:8; Jer 3:12; Mic 7:2).

In the NT, "godly" and "godliness" are found only in Paul's final letters (the Pastorals) and in 2 Peter. This common pagan moral and religious concept had finally been cleansed and adopted to make a statement about Christian experience.

The Greek words are from a single family (*eusebeia*, "godliness"; *eusebēs* and *eusebōs*, "godly"). To the Greek they indicated fulfillment of obligations and resultant acceptability to God. When used by translators of the Septuagint, these words usually were used to convey the idea of the fear of God. This OT concept is rooted in deep faith: a reverential awe, expressing itself in obedience to God. ♦ *Fear* In the NT use, we find the thought that the godly person has restructured his life around Jesus and is living that life as a disciple, worshiping the Lord and doing good works (1 Ti 5:4; cf. 2:10). ♦ *Works*

GOOD

"Good" is a deceptively simple term. We all have a feel for what a person means when he says that something is good, feels good, or looks good. Yet philosophers have puzzled for centuries over the nature of the good and how that which is truly good can be determined. The Bible is no book of philosophy, but it affirms basic ideas we need to understand when looking for the good in our own lives.

OT 1. The Hebrew words and their meanings
NT 2. The Greek words and their meanings

OT — 1. The Hebrew words and their meanings. The words translated "good" in the OT are forms of *tôb*. This simple word means "good" in the broadest possible sense. It includes the beautiful, the attractive, the useful, the profitable, the desirable, the morally right.

The concept that links all these uses of "good" is evaluation. To determine the good, one must compare things, qualities, and actions with other things, qualities, and actions. One must contrast beneficial and the right with other things, qualities, and actions that are not beneficial and are wrong.

The account of the Creation introduces *tôb* biblically, as God views each day's work and pronounces it good (Ge 1). God too evaluates. It is in fact because God shared his image and likeness with mankind that human beings have the capacity to make value judgments. But sin has distorted humanity's perceptions. Because of this, only God is able to evaluate perfectly. The writers of the OT were convinced that not only was God the giver and the measure of good but also that he alone knows what is truly beneficial for us and what is morally right. Only because God has shared his evaluation of the good in his Word are we who rely on him able to affirm with confidence that a certain thing, quality, or course of action is beneficial.

NT — 2. The Greek words and their meanings. NT occurrences of "good" in the English versions are translations of one of two Greek words, standing alone or in compounds. There are shades of difference between the two. Yet they are normally used as synonyms in the NT, and both were used to translate the Hebrew *tôb* in the Septuagint. Each of the two words—*agathos* and *kalos*—occurs 102 times in the NT.

Agathos views the good as useful or profitable and is the word chosen when moral goodness is being considered. *Kalos* tends to stress the aesthetic aspect of good. Good is not only beneficial but also beautiful. Evil is a warping of the divine pattern; whatever is good is free from flaw, in full balance and harmony with the ideal.

In the ultimate sense, only God is good (Mt 19:17; Mk 10:17–18). Although human beings may be "good" in comparison with one another (Lk 6:45; 19:17),

nothing in any human action can be beneficial to God, in the sense that it will merit salvation. But all believers are called by God to do good works enthusiastically and so to glorify the Lord. ◗ *Works*

GOSPEL

The Greek words that are relevant for a study of "gospel" are *euangelion* (good news) and *euangelizō* (to share the good news, to evangelize).

In most NT uses, "the gospel" is the sum total of saving truth about Jesus as it is communicated to lost humanity. The gospel is called the good news about Jesus (Mk 1:1) and the gospel of God (Ro 1:1; 15:16; 2 Co 11:7; 1 Th 2:8–9; 1 Ti 1:11), of Christ (1 Co 9:12; 2 Co 2:12; 10:14; Gal 1:7; 1 Th 3:2; 2 Th 1:8), and of our salvation (Eph 1:13). Through Jesus, the good news comes. His shed blood on Calvary's cross allows God to forgive sinners of all their sins. In Jesus the invitation is given to accept that forgiveness as a free gift and so to come into personal relationship with God.

When distorted by a denial of who Jesus is or by rejection of the truth that everything that God works in us is of grace, appropriated by faith, the gospel is "a different gospel—which is no gospel at all" (Gal 1:7).

While in the Epistles the word "gospel" is clearly focused on the saving work of God in Jesus, it is important to note that at times in the Gospels a different message of good news is in view. This is the good news that God's kingdom is at hand and that God may act at any moment to establish his rule on earth. It is important when reading the Gospels to note that when the phrase "of the kingdom" is added to "gospel," a different message is in view than that intended by the Epistles. ◗ *Kingdom*

GOSSIP

The OT words denote a talebearer, one who rushes around telling stories. The NT word is "whisperer," or "babbler." The gossip whispers poisonous reports in someone's ear in private that he or she would not dare to say in front of the person talked about. In 2 Ti 3:3 and Tit 2:3, the word translated "malicious gossip" in the NASB ("slanderers" and "slanderous" respectively in the NIV) is from the Greek word for slanderer, or false accuser.

GOVERN/GOVERNMENT ♦
Authorities ♦ *Judge/Judging*

GRACE

"Grace" is a dominant NT theme. Salvation is by grace, not works (Ro 11:6; Eph 2:5). Grace releases us from the dominion of sin, for believers are "not under law, but under grace (Ro 6:14). NT letters begin and conclude with the wish that grace will be with the readers, and the NT closes with these words: "The grace of the Lord Jesus be with God's people. Amen" (Rev 22:21).

It is clear that if we are to appreciate the message of the NT, we need to have some understanding of the concept of grace.

OT 1. OT roots of grace
NT 2. The developed concept
    3. Transformed perspective
    4. Transformed experience
    5. Conclusions

OT — 1. OT roots of grace. The word "grace" seldom appears in the English OT versions. There is no full parallel to this NT concept in the OT. The closest parallel seems to be drawn by the Hebrew *hānan*, "to be gracious," "to be merciful" (*hēn*, "grace," "favor").

The verb portrays the compassionate response of one who is able to help another person in need. In human society it is often used in statements concerning helping the poor.

The Book of Psalms best illustrates the theological use of this Hebrew term. Ps 51:1 expresses David's appeal to God for forgiveness: "Have mercy on me [*hānan*], O God, according to your unfailing love; according to your great compassion blot out my transgressions." This appeal is uttered out of a sense of helplessness. It turns away from self and looks to God as a loving and compassionate person. God's own nature is the basis on which help is expected. As David says, "Turn to me and have mercy [*hānan*] on me, as you always do to those who love your name" (Ps 119:132).

Our appreciation for God's name leads us to turn to him, but it is his love itself that moves him to respond to us.

When we look through the psalms we gain insight into the weakness that causes those who love God to cry out to him. The psalmists speak of their distress (Ps 4:1; 31:9), of agony (6:2), persecution by enemies (9:13; 56:1), loneliness and affliction (25:16), disaster (57:1), the contempt of others (123:3), weakness and trouble (41:1; 86:16), and sin (51:1) as aspects of the human condition that hold us in bondage. Only God can act to release us and enable us to overcome the foes within us and around us.

But God is who he is. He is compassionate and loving. We are confident that when we call on God, he will respond. He will act, not because we merit help, but because he recognizes our desperate need and love moves him to exercise his power to meet our need. This indeed is grace!

NT — 2. The developed concept. In the Greek language, "grace" is *charis*. It means a gracious favor or benefit bestowed, and at the same time it means the gratitude appropriate to the grace received. The verb *charizomai* means "to show kindness or favor." The concept came to include both the gracious action and agreeable human qualities.

In the NT, Paul fastens on this word and develops it as a technical theological term. It is clear that Jesus' teachings provide a solid basis for Paul's affirmation of the grace of God. Jesus shows that God stoops to help the undeserving and pardons the helpless sinner (e.g., Mt 11:28–12:13; 18:21–34; 20:1–16; Lk 7:36–50; 15). But in the Gospels, these actions are not termed grace. Even in Acts, "grace" is used in a different way, namely, to indicate the visible expression of God's power in action, an expression that marked his presence in the early church.

Yet as the church expanded beyond Palestine and penetrated the Roman world, Paul fastened on *charis* to communicate the truth that lies at the heart of God's saving work in Jesus. To Paul, "grace" is a transforming reality. It transforms the way we think about a person's relationship with God. It transforms our present and eternal destiny.

3. Transformed perspective. By Jesus' time, OT faith had been seriously distorted by centuries of misinterpretation. The religious Jew relied on his physical descent from Abraham and on his knowledge of the law. Relationship with God was considered an issue of ritual piety and obedience to the letter of the law. The religious man had a claim on God, established by membership in the covenant community and based on his own merits. The sense of helplessness that moved the psalmist to call out to God, pleading only that the Lord show mercy and stoop to meet his needs, was replaced in the religious life of the Pharisees by a smug sense of self-righteousness.

The apostle Paul was thoroughly trained in this way of thinking and in rabbinical interpretation. But he was dramatically converted to Christ on the Damascus road and was driven to re-examine the beliefs of a lifetime. His perspective on a person's relationship with God was transformed, and as Paul was committed to missionary work, he was driven to the word "grace" for a way to express the vital difference between human attempts to win God's favor and the way in which personal relationship with God is actually established and developed.

Paul's letters to Romans and Ephesians most clearly show the dramatic perspective that grace provides on God's past and present actions. Let us look at some of the teachings of these books, referring also to Paul's epistle to the Galatians.

In Ro 3, Paul quotes the OT to show that all people are sinners. Law offered no way of salvation, for law stands as humanity's silent accuser, making us conscious of our sin (3:19-20). So in Jesus, God acted to reveal a righteousness that has no relationship to law. This is a righteousness that comes from God and through faith in Jesus is given to all who believe (3:21-22). Because all have sinned, only God's spontaneous and decisive act in Christ—an act of grace—could win our redemption (3:23-26). ▸
Redeem/Ransom

Then Paul, in Ro 4, reviews sacred history. He shows that Abraham's relationship with God was not based on his works but on his faith. Law and all human achievements are ruled out as avenues to a felicitous relationship with God. That can come only through faith in God, who has promised to do for us what we could not do for ourselves. This whole process—the promise and the faith—are rooted in grace (4:16).

Ro 5:15-21 again portrays salvation as a gift that comes to us through Jesus and is an expression of God's grace.

Ro 11:1-6 argues that the concept of grace in no way contradicts OT revelation, which was so badly misunderstood by Israel. God has always acted freely, and those who have found a personal relationship with God have not found it by works but in grace.

Eph 2:1-11 sums up the human condition and holds up the essential elements expressed by "grace." Mankind lies "dead in . . . transgressions and sins" and follows "the ways of this world and of the ruler of the kingdom of the air" (2:1-2). But "because of his great love for us, God, who is rich in mercy, made us alive with Christ even when we were dead in transgressions—it is by grace you have been saved" (2:4-5). This comes to us "through faith—and this not from [ourselves], it is the gift of God—not by works, so that no one can boast" (2:8-9).

The affirmations grace makes about God and human beings stand in bold contrast to the normal human approach to relationship with the Lord. Grace holds that human beings are helpless, so locked in sin that their state can only be represented as death. Grace declares that God is merciful and loving and that he is

The Two Perspectives

	Grace	*Religion*
View of mankind	basically sinful, unable to please God	basically good, able to please God
Associated concepts	promise gift faith	law works obligation
Focus	Jesus	self
Result	forgiveness life righteousness	condemnation death sin
Definition	God's free action—based on Jesus' death and motivated by love—to redeem all who believe and to make them righteous.	Man's effort to do good and by his own works to merit salvation as a deserved reward for his behavior.

able to act to meet our deepest need. Grace teaches that God has acted in Jesus to bring us forgiveness and new life through his atoning sacrifice on Calvary.

♦ **Atonement** Because of motives rooted deeply within his own character, God has reached out in Jesus to save sinners.

For the religious people of Paul's day and for all people of every time, the message of grace is a powerful warning of our absolute need, and it is an affirmation of the overwhelming love of God that acts in Jesus to meet our need and provide forgiveness and life.

4. Transformed experience. The grace affirmed in the NT is always mediated by Jesus. This grace is a dynamic force that does more than affect our standing with God by crediting us with righteousness.

♦ **Righteous/Righteousness** Grace affects our experience as well.

In Ro 6, Paul traces something of the transforming impact of grace. He shows that when we are united with Jesus, we are removed from the realm of law, with its emphasis on works, and are established in the realm of grace. Grace is marked always by God's enabling work within us to overcome our helplessness. We yield ourselves to God and trust him to do what we are unable to do. This walk of faith releases us from the domination of sin, and we become slaves to God, doing his will and reaping the benefit of holiness (6:22).

Ro 6 shows us that grace is not simply a basic orientation to relationship with

God. It is also a practical approach to living the Christian life. This aspect of grace helps us to understand the warning found in Gal 5:4, that those "who are trying to be justified by law have been alienated from Christ; [they] have fallen away from grace." Any attempt by believers to struggle toward a life of goodness by works of the law means a return to the futile way of religion. It involves reliance on ourselves and an abandonment of reliance on Christ, who alone can enable us to live righteous lives. We cannot approach Christian experience from the old perspective, for grace and religion are contradictory. We can only live by full commitment to the way of grace and all that grace involves.

5. Conclusions. The biblical concept of grace is much greater than is suggested in the common definition of "unmerited favor." "Grace" is a word that expresses a radical view of life and of relationship with God.

Grace teaches that God's attitude toward us is one of acceptance and love; knowing God's heart, we can "approach the throne of grace with confidence" (Heb 4:16) with every sin and need.

Grace is a dramatic statement about the human condition. Each person is helpless, trapped in sin and incapable of pleasing God or winning his favor.

Grace is a proclamation. It is the triumphant announcement that God in Christ has acted and has come to the aid of all who will trust him for their eternal salvation. ♦ *Belief/Faith*

Grace is a way of life. Relying totally on Jesus to work within us, we experience God's own unlimited power, vitalizing us and enabling us to live truly good lives.

The message of grace found in the NT calls us to a completely different outlook on relationship with God and on spiritual achievement than is found in any religion of human invention. Understanding the nature of grace, we decisively reject any confidence in ourselves, and we trust ourselves totally to Jesus, who alone is able not only to declare us truly righteous men and women of God but also to make us so.

GREAT/GREATNESS

The Hebrew and Greek words translated "great" in the NIV and the NASB are general terms. In the OT, *gādal* and its derivatives suggest growth: an increase in size, importance, and power. *Rābab* and *rābâh* have uses parallel to *gādal* but approach the concept from the point of view of numerical increase. Any of these terms can indicate greatness of intangible qualities, such as great goodness or great evil.

In the NT, *polys* means "many," "much," "a large quantity"; and *megas* suggests greatness in size. Each can be applied to abstract qualities, though normally *polys* is used when speaking of a high degree of strength, severity, depth, etc., and *megas*, of length of age, or greatness in rank or importance.

Actually, the English words "great" and "greatness" accurately express the shades of meaning found in OT and NT original terms, so knowing the particular Hebrew or Greek word used in a text is not generally important to our understanding of the biblical text.

It is instructive, however, to look at these words in the Bible and so to sense various emphases in Scripture. The NT underlines certain qualities of God—for example, his great patience (Ro 9:22), great power (Eph 1:19), and great love for us (Eph 2:4; 1 Jn 3:1). God has given us a great salvation (Heb 2:3). In Jesus we have a great High Priest (Heb 4:14) and a great Shepherd (Heb 13:20), and believers are looking forward to seeing their great God (Tit 2:13).

It may be even more instructive to explore the teaching of Jesus on greatness itself. Various portions of Mt 18–20 present Jesus' response to a question posed by the disciples: "Who is the greatest in the kingdom of heaven?" Jesus answered that it is the one who humbles himself as a little child. In context, this involves responding immediately to the Savior's voice (18:2–5). Jesus then gives three pictures of how those who are his "little ones" will live together to achieve greatness. He reminds us that human beings are like sheep, prone to wander, and we ought to both seek and bring back with rejoicing the one who strays (18:12–14). He reminds us that when a brother sins against us, we are to take the initiative to restore the shattered relationship, and we are to let forgiveness heal the hurt (18:15–18). Jesus reminds us that if we find forgiveness difficult, we are to recall how much we ourselves have been forgiven by God and then forgive others as freely (18:21–35).

When the mother of James and John asked Jesus that her sons be given the highest positions in his coming kingdom, Jesus used the occasion to contrast human and divine concepts of greatness: "You know that the rulers of the Gentiles lord it over them, and their high officials exercise authority over them. Not so with you. Instead, whoever wants to become great among you must be your servant, and whoever wants to be first must be your slave—just as the Son of Man did not come to be served, but to serve, and to give his life as a ransom for many" (Mt 20:25–28).

Finally this passage shows a burdened Jesus (20:29–34). He had turned toward Jerusalem, knowing that crucifixion lay ahead. But he stopped at the cries of two blind men to ask, "What do you want me to do for you?" (v. 32). In this action we see the heart of God—and true greatness. Greatness is found in a willingness to set aside our needs in order to minister to others' needs.

GRIEF ♦ Sorrow

GROW/INCREASE

Three key terms are associated in the NT with the ideas of growth or increase: *pleonazō, plēthynō,* and *auxanō.*

Pleonazō suggests an abundance, an increase in number; the NT uses it nine times (Ro 5:20; 6:1; 2 Co 4:15; 8:15; Php 4:17; 1 Th 3:12; 2 Th 1:3; 2 Pe 1:8).

Plēthynō means "to multiply," "to abound," and it is occurs twelve times in the NT (Mt 24:12; Ac 6:1,7; 7:17; 9:31; 12:24; 2 Co 9:10; Heb 6:14; 1 Pe 1:2; 2 Pe 1:2; Jude 2).

The most fascinating of the terms is *auxanō,* which, together with its related term *auxō,* means "to grow." These words (occurring 22 times in the NT) suggests the natural process that God has structured into his universe. In the Gospels, they are used of the growth of lilies, trees, and the child Jesus (Mt 6:28; 13:32; Mk 4:8; Lk 1:80; 2:40; 12:27; 13:19). In recording John the Baptist's response to his disciples, the apostle John includes the fact that Jesus must increase, but John the Baptist must decrease (Jn 3:30). These words are also used of the growth of the church, spoken of as the increase of the Word of God (Ac 6:7; 12:24; 19:20) and as the increase of the number of people (Ac 7:17). In the Epistles we see another dimension of this concept. Believers, and the church as an entity, are also involved in a growth process, superintended by God himself (1 Co 3:6–7; Eph 2:21; 4:15). Individually, we grow in faith (2 Co 10:15), in knowledge of God (Col 1:10), and in grace (2 Pe 3:18). Corporately, we grow up into a holy temple (Eph 2:21), and we mature as the body of Christ (Eph 4:15–16).

The suggestion of growth as a natural and a supernatural process is exciting. In the natural world the shape of the mature plant or animal is stamped in its genetic code. Each seed and each infant grows in an ordered way toward a maturity appropriate to its nature. The use of *auxanō,* which emphasizes the growth process, to speak of spiritual development is exciting. God has designed the individual and the church according to his perfect specifications. As we grow, we move toward a perfection that he has planned for us. ♦ *Mature/Maturity*

But Christian growth is not automatic. The NT makes it clear that we need to feed on the Word of God (1 Pe 2:2; Heb 5:11–14). We need to root ourselves deeply in the shared life of the believing community (Eph 3:17–19; 4:13–16). We are also called on to make personal choices that will facilitate our growth (Heb 5:14; cf. 2 Co 9:6–11). God is deeply involved in the process of our growth, and he has ordained its direction. Moreover, he has given us the privilege of cooperating with him as he works within us. ♦ Sanctify/Sanctification

GUARANTEE

The word "guarantee" (or a related form) occurs only five times in the NIV NT. Heb 7:22 calls Jesus the "guarantee of a better covenant." The Greek word (*engyos*) appears only here in the NT. It was used in legal documents to indicate a bond or collateral. It meant that the signer of the guarantee pledged his resources as security for the commitment made. Jesus is the living promise that the forgiveness offered us under the new covenant will be ours. ♦ Covenant

Three other occurrences (2 Co 1:22; 5:5; Eph 1:14) are the three NT uses of the Greek word *arrabōn*. This word indicates a deposit given as a guarantee that full payment will be made. In each of these passages the Holy Spirit, who has been given to believers, is presented as "a deposit guaranteeing our inheritance until the redemption of those who are God's possession" (Eph 1:14).

Ro 4:16 translates the word *bebaios*, "firm or established," as "guaranteed." The words in this word group (including *bebaioō* and *bebaiōsis*) occur nineteen times in the NT and stress certainty or the established character of the subject. Words in this group speak of the confirmed nature of the Word and of God's promises (Mk 16:20; Ro 15:8; 1 Co 1:6,8; Heb 2:2–3; 6:19; 2 Pe 1:19) and of believers being firmly established in the faith (Ge 2:7; Heb 3:6,14; 13:9; cf. 2 Pe 1:10).

There is a passage in Hebrews that perhaps best sums up this theme as it is found in Scripture. It reads: "Because God wanted to make the unchanging nature of his purpose very clear to the heirs of what was promised, he confirmed it with an oath. God did this so that, by two unchangeable things in which it is impossible for God to lie, we who have fled to take hold of the hope offered to us may be greatly encouraged" (6:17–18). We can be confident in our faith in the Word of God, for all that it promises is guaranteed by God himself.

GUARD

In most cases in the English versions the phrase "to guard" means either "to keep confined" or "to protect [as something precious]." The warnings to "be on guard" are from several different Greek words that mean "to be watchful" or "to pay close attention to."

GUIDE ♦ Lead/Guide

GUILT

In ordinary speech today, "guilt" most often indicates a feeling. Typically, counsel (therapy) tries to get rid of that uncomfortable feeling. But in Scripture, "guilt" is a fact, not a feeling. For believers, God forgives the sin that makes people guilty.

OT 1. Guilt in the OT
NT 2. Guilt in the NT
3. The divine remedy for guilt

OT — 1. Guilt in the OT. While Hebrew words that mean "iniquity" and "wickedness" are sometimes translated "guilt" in the NIV and NASB, the Hebrew term that means "to be guilty" is *'āšam*. This word and its many derivatives focus our attention on the full impact of guilt, which always involves three distinct aspects: (1) there is an act that brings guilt, (2) there is the condition of guilt that results from the act, and (3) there is the punishment that is appropriate to the act. The stress in a particular verse may lie on the act itself, on the human condition, or on the punishment. But the biblical concept of guilt always includes these elements.

Because all sin is an offense against him, guilt can be understood only by relating it to God. ♦ Sin The issue in guilt is not how a person may feel about his or her actions; rather, the focus is on the fact that each human being is responsible and will bear the consequences of his or her actions. In order to avoid those consequences, each person must let God deal with the sin and guilt. ♦ Atonement
♦ Offering and Sacrifice

NT — 2. Guilt in the NT. In the NT, "guilt" is a judicial concept, affirming criminal responsibility. This is true whether the court is human or divine. Two Greek word groups express this idea. *Aitia, aitima,* and *aition* speak of charges made before the court. When used in nonjudicial settings, they mean the cause or reason of a particular action. Words in this group are most often found in the judicial context in the Gospels, speaking of the accusations brought against Jesus (Mt 27:37; Mk 15:26; Lk 23:4,14,22; Jn 18:38; 19:4,6), and in Acts, in reference to the accusations brought against Paul (Ac 22:24; 23:28; 25:7,18,27; 28:18).

Another legal term, *hypodikos,* is found only in Ro 3:19. It means "to be guilty," or "to be held accountable," in the sense of being forced to answer to the divine jurisdiction.

Enochos (used 10 times in the NT) assumes the person's conviction and liability for punishment. It occurs in some verses in which NIV and NASB read "guilt" (Mt 5:22 [NASB only]; Mk 3:29; 1 Co 11:27; Jas 2:10).

In the two occurrences of "guilt" in Heb 10 (vv. 2,22), the NIV unfortunately adopts the modern notion of *feeling* guilty when it translates original constructions that speak of consciousness or awareness of sin.

3. The divine remedy for guilt. The Bible's message that human beings are accountable and must bear the consequences of wrong moral choices is taught in many ways. ▶ *Account/Accountable* ▶ *Sin* But the divine emphasis is not on our failure. Instead, God comes to us with his unique message of hope. Even though you and I are guilty before God, we can be acquitted in the divine court! ▶ *Acquit* God shares with us in Scripture, especially in the teaching and actions of Jesus, his willingness to forgive. ▶ *Forgive*

Guilt is a reality. But so is forgiveness. In Jesus we find the perfect remedy for those tragic choices that have made us liable to judgment. In Jesus we have the promise that no one can bring any charge against those whom God has chosen (Ro 8:33).

H

HAND

The hand is viewed in the OT as the part of the body that carries out a person's will. Thus "hand" is found in many idiomatic OT expressions. To give something into someone's hand is to place it under his authority (e.g., Ge 9:2) or to surrender it into his power. Uplifted hands suggest prayer but are also linked with taking an oath or giving a blessing. Symbolically, "hand" expresses strength and power, especially God's great power (e.g., Ex 3:19–20) when that power is used to perform his will.

Two significant expressions regarding "hand" are found in both Testaments: (1) the laying on of hands and (2) being seated at the right hand of another.

In the OT, laying hands on someone has several connotations. Sometimes it suggests an aggressive act that does violence to another person or his property (Ex 22:11; Isa 5:25). It is also used in ritual blessing (Ge 48:18; Isa 44:3) and in commissioning for an office (Nu 27:12–23; Dt 34:9). Most significant in the OT is the act of the worshiper in laying hands on an animal about to be sacrificed. The act symbolizes the substitution of the animal for the sinner, who by that act confesses his sin and his trust in God's promise of forgiveness. ♦ *Atonement*

In the NT the idea of touching with the hand(s) is found over forty times. It is seen in connection with healings performed by Jesus and the apostles (Mt 9:18; Mk 6:5; 8:23; Lk 13:13; Ac 28:8). It is seen in Jesus' act of blessing the children (Mt 19:13,15). It is seen in the context of baptism (Ac 8:17; 9:17; 19:6). ♦ *Baptism*

Of special interest is its association with the ordination of individuals for special tasks or for offices. This use is found in Ac 6:6; 13:3; 1 Ti 4:14; 2 Ti 1:6. We should note that these acts of ordination were performed by different groups: the apostles (Ac 6), the prophets and teachers in Antioch (Ac 13:3), local church elders (1 Ti 4:14), and Paul (2 Ti 1:6). In no case was the transfer of one's office in view, so no case for "apostolic succession" can be made from these NT references

Perhaps the most exciting common use of "hand" is in the expression "at the right hand of." In Ps 110 the Messiah is invited by God to be seated at his right hand. In OT idiom this symbolizes coregency. God, the king of the universe, calls on Israel's Messiah to possess and to exercise divine power. This vivid image is repeated often in the NT, in those passages where Jesus is shown to be "at the right hand of God" (Ac 2:33; 7:55,56; Ro 8:34; Col 3:1; Heb 10:12; cf. Ac 2:34; 5:31; Eph 1:20; Heb 1:3,13; 8:1; 12:2; 1 Pe 3:22). Seated, Jesus exercises the full power of God and uses it on behalf of his church. We can fully trust him! For Jesus even now is "far above all rule and authority, power and dominion, and every title that can be given, not only in the present age but also in the one to come" (Eph 1:21).

HARM

In both Testaments, most nouns and verbs of the root "harm" in the original suggest either (1) evil done to a person or persons or (2) the doing of evil to a person or persons. ♦ *Evil*

324

HARDEN ◆ *Heart*

HARVEST

Harvest time in Palestine occurs in the period from April to June. One of Israel's three worship festivals held at Jerusalem was associated with the harvest. ◆ *Feast/Festival*

In the OT, the word "harvest" is sometimes used as a picture of judgment (Jer 51:33; Hos 6:11; Joel 3:13). Jesus also used the image in speaking of the time of final judgment (Mt 13:30,36–42; cf. Rev 14:15).

But in most NT uses the image of the harvest is positive. Humanity is pictured as a field of ripening grain, and those who share the good news of Jesus are the workers who harvest men and women for God's kingdom (Mt 9:37–38; Lk 10:2).

In the Epistles the harvest is viewed as the end result of growth within the believer. The harvest is the promise of righteousness made to those who live God's way (2 Co 9:10; Gal 6:9; Heb 12:11; Jas 3:18).

HATE

In both Testaments the word for hatred (*śānē'*, OT; *miseō*, NT) describes an emotional response or attitude toward persons or things. The hated thing is decisively rejected; it is detested, and the individual wants no contact or relationship with it.

The fact that both God and human beings hate brings up a series of theological questions.

OT 1. The objects of God's hatred
    2. Hatred's affect on human beings
NT 3. The dynamics of hatred
    4. The meaning of "Esau have I hated"

OT — 1. The objects of God's hatred

It is not surprising to read that God hates wickedness and will have no relationship with the evildoer. God, who loves justice, rightly hates robbery and iniquity (Isa 61:8). The Bible tells us that God also hates hypocritical worship of-

fered by those whose lifestyles show that his moral standards have been ignored (Isa 1:13–15; Am 5:21). God's hatred of idolatry is also well established.

Usually we human beings are fearful of hatred. Both in ourselves and in others it becomes a dominating emotion that robs one of judgment and of compassion. But God's hatred is different. His hatred is always appropriate, focused on evil and the evildoer. And God's hatred is always balanced by his attributes of love and compassion. Because God is the moral judge of the universe, he must make distinctions between good and evil. Because God is wholly committed to good, he must react to wickedness and act passionately but wisely to punish. As the psalmist says: "You are not a God who takes pleasure in evil; with you the wicked cannot dwell. The arrogant cannot stand in your presence; you hate all who do wrong. You destroy those who tell lies; bloodthirsty and deceitful men the LORD abhors" (Ps 5:4–6).

2. Hatred's affect on human beings. OT occurrences of the word "hatred" usually depict this emotion in human beings as directed against other people. While the psalmist can say he hates those who hate the Lord (Ps 139:21), hatred generally is recognized as a destructive emotion. Hatred is associated with violence (Pr 29:10), with interpersonal strife (Pr 10:12), and with lies (Pr 10:18). The OT specifically commands that God's people are not to hate their brothers, as we read in Lev 19:17. The passage goes on: "Do not seek revenge or bear a grudge against one of your people, but love your neighbor as yourself" (v. 18).

Believers are, however, called on to join God in his hatred of evil ways. This is to be expressed by a decisive rejection of that which is wrong. When a moral issue is involved, as in the statement "I hate every wrong path" (Ps 119:128), we can best understand hatred not so much as an emotion but as a value judgment expressed in a choice to have nothing to do with what is "hated" (cf., Ps 119:163; Pr 8:13; 13:5).

In a few instances the OT speaks of man's hatred for God (Dt 7:9–11; 2 Ch

19:2). This aversion for the Lord is expressed in Israel's history by idolatry and by rejection of the holy way of life regulated by the Mosaic Law. Speaking of the final judgment against Judah in the Babylonian captivity, Jeremiah reports God's description of his people's antagonism and the tragic results of their rejection of God: "Again and again I sent my servants the prophets, who said, 'Do not do this detestable thing that I hate!' But they did not listen or pay attention; they did not turn from their wickedness or stop burning incense to other gods. Therefore, my fierce anger was poured out; it raged against the towns of Judah and the streets of Jerusalem and made them the desolate ruins they are today" (Jer 44:4–6).

NT — 3. The dynamics of hatred. In human beings, hatred is a dangerous emotion. It is listed in Gal 5:20 among the works flowing from the old fleshly nature. It describes the antagonisms that are so deeply rooted in human society (Tit 3:3).

The NT is clear that when Christ enters our life, we are to control hatred. As John points out twice in his first epistle, our lives are to be marked by love for our brothers (1 Jn 2:9–11; 3:14–15). These passages show that the experience of hatred transformed to love is one of the evidences that Christ has entered our life! In fact, divine renewal of our capacity to love even frees us to love our enemies, something that went against the common wisdom of the religious leaders of Jesus' day, who said, "Love your neighbor and hate your enemy" (Mt 5:43–48).

The transformed attitude toward people does not, however, mean that believers are freed from making value judgments. We are still called on to "hate what is evil" (Ro 12:9). At times, even more difficult choices are called for. We best understand Jesus' call to "hate . . . father and mother, wife and children, brothers and sisters—yes, even [our] own life" (Lk 14:26) in this context of choice. Where there is conflict between the disciple's commitment to Jesus and

other commitments, Jesus has prior and total claim on our lives.

Finally, John shifts our attention back to the raw emotional reaction of despising, which is part of the concept of hatred. He reports Jesus' warning that the unregenerate world is deeply antagonistic to him (Jn 15:25). John has earlier explained that "everyone who does evil hates the light" (Jn 3:20). It should be no surprise that if we follow Jesus closely and live his kind of holy life, the world will hate us as well (Jn 15:18–25).

Hatred, as an emotional reaction to persons, and particularly as a reaction that spills over into antagonistic acts, is wrong for believers. Hatred, as a value judgment that guides us to have no contact with that which is wrong, is another matter entirely.

4. The meaning of "Esau have I hated". Many have been troubled by the quote in Ro 9:13 of Mal 1:3: "I have loved Jacob, but Esau I have hated." It is important here to note both the historical and logical context of each quote. In the original incident, God chose Jacob, rather than his older twin, Esau, to inherit the covenant promises given Abraham. This choice was made before the birth of the children (Ge 25:19–23).

Malachi the prophet answers the skeptical query of a spiritually wandering Israel, which says in response to God's affirmation of love, "How have you loved us?" (Mal 1:2). The prophet's answer is to point to the evidence of history. Jacob (Israel) and Esau were brothers. But God chose to give Jacob's children the land they were then enjoying, while Esau's ancient land became a desert.

In Romans, Paul is arguing that God exercises sovereign choice. He points to history for several illustrations. God chose Jacob (Israel) over Esau before the twins were born. Thus his choice could not rest on any action or moral superiority of one of the twins. The choice was free, not based on any human works.

We have seen in earlier discussion that the biblical idea of "hate" has both emotional and volitional components. Hatred is an emotional attitude toward a person or thing. And it also involves a decision to have no contact or relationship with the hated person or thing. However, we best understand the reference to Israel and Esau as a statement about God's choice rather than as a statement of his emotional attitude toward Esau.

HEAD

This is a sensitive word for women today. Too often they have heard "head of the house" used in a rigid, hierarchical way. Too often a claim of headship has been used to justify domineering or selfish behavior by men or to deny women their full partnership in church or home. So it is important that we look at the concept of head in both the OT and the NT. How can we affirm what Scripture teaches and avoid the tragedies that are associated with selfish misinterpretation?

OT 1. "Head" in the OT
NT 2. "Head" in the NT
　　 3. Christ, the head of the church
　　 4. "Head" in 1 Co 11
　　 5. "Head" in Eph 5

OT — 1. "Head" in the OT. The word that means "head" in Hebrew is *rō'š*. Other words are at times translated "head" in the NIV and the NASB. But these are specific terms, meaning "skull" or "scalp." Although *rō'š* denotes the head of a person or animal (e.g., Ge 3:15), the idea is extended in many ways, making "headship" a complex idea indeed.

For instance, *rō'š* can mean the first in a series. Or it can mean the beginning, the source. It is often used to indicate the top of a mountain or building (e.g., Ex 17:9). It is commonly used to indicate the chief of a family or clan (e.g., Nu 1:4). This may be the current living head or it may refer to the ancestor of the group. *Rō'š* can suggest priority, as in God's promise to make Israel the head and not the tail among the nations (Dt 28:13; Isa 9:14). In the OT, the word is also used to indicate bureaucratic rank or position. This is found in the organization of

ancient Israel for judicial, military, and religious matters (Ex 18:25; 2 Ki 25:18). Thus our image of a hierarchical order is certainly justified, as far as the OT is concerned.

NT — 2. Head in the NT. The Greek term is *kephalē*. It is used much like *rō'š*, to indicate the head of a person, the beginning of a month, the source or mouth of a river, etc. The Greeks viewed the head as the superior member of the body, the seat of reason and authority.

Kephalē appears over seventy-five times in the NT, usually to designate the literal head of a person or animal. In certain passages, we need to know the background of certain NT sayings before we can understand them. For example, "Do not swear by your head" (Mt 5:36) is a reference to a rabbinical judgment that one who makes an oath "by his head" (i.e., by his very life) cannot be released from the oath under any circumstances. Other sayings, such as Jesus' assurance of God's care as expressed in the statement "the very hairs of your head are all numbered" (Lk 12:7), are easily understood.

There are, however, three theologically significant uses of "head" to which we need to pay careful attention. They help us gain insight into issues of great concern for Christians today.

3. Christ, the head of the church. The NT pictures the church as a living organism, a body of which Jesus is the head (Eph 1:22; 4:15; 5:23; Col 1:18; 2:10,19). A review of these passages suggests that Christ's headship emphasizes his role as sustainer, protector, organizing principle, and source of the church's life. The passages emphasize Jesus' exalted position so that we may have complete confidence in him. We respond to him because he is Lord and the only one with wisdom and motive to direct us into God's perfect will.

In the OT, rank within bureaucratic structures and organizations was indicated by the word "head." On the other hand, the NT pictures the church not as an institution but as an organism. In the place of institutional principles of organization, the NT advances organic principles of organization for the church (Rom 12; 1 Co 12). ◆ **Body** In fact, Jesus stressed the importance of rejecting all thought of rank in relating to fellow believers (Mt 20:25–28; 23:8–12; cf. Ro 12:3–8).

In thinking about leadership in the church it is important to recognize the fact that Jesus is the sole head of the church, the only Lord. Whatever leaders are within the body of Christ, they are not superior persons of higher rank whose office gives them a right to direct and control other believers. ◆ **Leadership**

4. "Head" in 1 Co 11. The passage (11:2–16) explores what is proper in worship. Paul argues that the women in Corinth should wear a veil, as the women in the other churches did (v. 16). There is a mix of the cultural and theological reasons for this. Within the culture, and especially by those with a Jewish background, appropriate feminine dress on such a public occasion called for a veil. The women of Corinth were apparently so excited about the Christian message of freedom and equality that they reacted by rejecting feminine dress and asserting their equality by traditionally masculine behavior.

In the above passage, Paul protects this freedom of women. But he clearly does not approve of their symbolizing their liberation by praying and prophesying with their heads uncovered (v. 5). It is in effect a denial of their femininity. He refers to creation and shows that there is a creation order that includes both men and women (vv. 3,7–10). Men and women are interdependent in God's design for the universe (vv. 11–12). It is the glory of each being within creation to proudly take the place God has assigned.

Paul writes that "the head of every man is Christ, and the head of the woman is man, and the head of Christ is God" (v. 3). This defines the flow of the creation order: Christ flowed from God the Father, man came into being by Christ's activity as Creator, and woman was taken from the side of man. In this verse, then, the order of creation is established. There is no suggestion here of inferiority, for Jesus is and always was the complete equal of the Father.

Thus Paul's appeal is not that women take a subordinate place in the church. His appeal is that they recognize the fact of an order in creation that is unchanged by the wonderful message that in Christ all are equal (Gal 3:26–28).

What is a woman to do? Simply this: she must live within the culture *as a woman* rather than deny her womanhood by dressing as would a man. A woman in the Corinthian church was to pray and prophesy with head veiled, and a man in Corinth was to function with head unveiled. Neither need deny his or her identity within the creation order to affirm significance in the body of Christ. A man can be proud of his place as a man. And a woman can be equally proud of her place as a woman.

5. "Head" in Eph 5. In Eph 5 Paul continues his instruction on how to be "imitators of God" and live a life of love (5:1). There is to be harmony and mutual submission in the church (5:15–21). Then Paul shows how to maintain harmony within marriage (vv. 22–33).

Each partner in a marriage is to seek to imitate Jesus. The wife takes the lead in imitating the virtue of submission (1 Pe 2:21–3:6), responding to the husband as the church does to Jesus (Eph 5:22–23). ◆ **Subject/Submission** The husband has the challenging task of imitating Christ in his headship.

It is very critical here not to read into this passage hierarchical notions. Instead, it would appear that "head" is used in its well-established sense of source and nourisher of life. Rather than demand from the church, Christ "gave himself up for her" (v. 25). His purpose is not to rob the church of her identity but to help her achieve her full potential: "to make her holy, cleansing her by the washing with water through the word, and to present her to himself as a radiant church, without stain or wrinkle or any other blemish, but holy and blameless" (vv. 26–27). The husband imitates Christ by loving his wife—"feeds and cares for" her (again in the sense of head as source and nourisher)—"just as Christ does the church" (v. 29).

HEALING

The biblical accounts of healing can answer many of our questions about this subject. How much of what we see the Bible saying on this subject is colored by our doctrinal heritage? Can we be healed from our diseases if only we have faith enough to believe? Devoted Christians differ on their answers to such questions. But we can hardly be dogmatic without a careful examination of biblical material.

OT 1. Healing in the OT
     2. The role of medication
     3. The healing in the atonement
NT 4. Healing in the NT
     5. The gift of healing
     6. Sickness among believers
     7. Conclusions

OT — 1. Healing in the OT. The OT word *rāpā'* appears sixty-seven times in the OT, and its cognates occur another nineteen times (*repu'âh*, 2 times, *rip'ût*, once, and *marpē'*, 16 times). The basic meaning, maintained throughout history, is "to heal" or "to make healthy."

In many OT uses of this word, physical healing of a sickness or disease is in view (e.g., Ge 20:17). But the image of sickness is used in other passages to portray the ravages of sin. In these contexts, healing speaks of forgiveness and of the restoration of a harmonious relationship with God, as well as of the blessings that follow such a relationship. Thus Isaiah cries out to his countrymen, to a people "loaded with guilt" (1:4). He describes their condition in their rebellion against God: "Your whole head is injured, your whole heart afflicted. From the sole of your foot to the top of your head there is no soundness— only wounds and welts and open sores, not cleansed or bandaged or soothed with oil" (1:5–6). To be healed, God's people must turn to him and be cleansed (1:18). Then, in fellowship again, "if you are willing and obedient, you will eat the best of the land" (1:19). Thus, spiritual sickness is equated with sin, and healing is equated with

forgiveness and relationship with God (cf., 2 Ch 7:14–16; Hos 6:1).

The prophets announced God's firm intention to heal his sinning people spiritually (Isa 57:18–19; Jer 33:6). But it is also clear that God is viewed as the source of physical healing as well. Both are in view in God's announcement of this distinctive name to his people, recorded in Ex 15:26: "I am the LORD who heals you."

2. The role of medication. In view of the radical conviction that both spiritual and physical health come from God, what role was there for medicine and healers in OT times? In later Judaism, medicines were viewed with considerable suspicion. What do we find in the OT?

There is very little evidence to appeal to. Ge 50 mentions the physicians of Egypt, and 2 Ch 16:12 criticizes King Asa because, "though his disease was severe, even in his illness he did not seek help from the LORD, but only from the physicians." The thought here is not that seeking medical help was wrong. What was wrong was failing to seek help from the Lord.

The OT mentions medical practices such as the cleansing and binding of wounds and the use of soothing oil (Isa 1:6). There are references to healing balm (2 Ch 28:15; cf. Jer 51:8). Isaiah was told by God that a poultice was to be applied to King Hezekiah and he would recover (Isa 38:21). But although common remedies were in use in Israel, no medical science or practice as such developed.

3. The healing in the atonement. The OT always recognizes God as healer, and in their distress the godly looked to the Lord for restoration. A critical question, however, is raised by Isaiah's prophetic portrait of Jesus' crucifixion and its impact (Isa 53). He wrote, "Surely he took up our infirmities and carried our sorrows" (v. 4). Mt 8:17 says that this was fulfilled (at least partially) in Jesus' acts of healing while he was on earth. But Isa 53 goes on and says, "By his wounds we are healed" (v. 5). The issue is this: does the Isaiah passage indicate that the healing in the atonement is physical healing and that this is the right of every believer today, along with other benefits of the atonement? ♦ *Atonement*

The complete text of Isa 53:5 reads: "But he was pierced for our transgressions, he was crushed for our iniquities; the punishment that brought us peace was upon him, and by his wounds we are healed." It seems clear that the primary focus of the healing referred to here is spiritual healing from the sickness of sin. Yet OT thought linked spiritual and physical sickness and healing, so this is not decisive. We can only go on to the NT and see if there is any evidence in the Epistles that suggests that healing is the believer's blood-won right.

4. Healing in the NT. Besides *sōzō* and *diasōzō* (which are usually used in the sense of "save"), five Greek words are used in the NT to express the idea of healing. *Therapeuō* and *therapeia* are used in the NT only in the sense of "healing" or "curing." *Iaomai* ("to cure or restore"), *iama* ("healing"), and *iasis* ("healing," "cure") are used in the Gospels and Acts with the same meaning as *therapeuō* and *therapeia*. What is significant is that of the eighty-two times these five words occur in the NT, no fewer than seventy-three are found in the synoptic Gospels and in Acts!

The reason these Greek words are so clustered is simple: healing was a significant part of Jesus' ministry before the Ascension and in the ministry of the apostles in the early church. The magical elements associated with healing stories in the literature of the ancient world are not found in the NT. Instead, we find that the Gospels, in straightforward narrative, simply tell what happened, describing healings that were obvious to Jesus' followers and enemies alike.

In the Gospels and Acts, healings are often associated with the faith of the person who was healed (Mt 9:21–22; 15:28; Ac 14:9; cf. Mt 8:1–3). But the NT reports other miracles of healing without reference to faith or even to the conversion of the persons healed (Mt 9:23–26; Mk 6:5; Ac 3:1–10; 5:16; 8:7; 28:8). It is clear that Jesus' works of healing were an integral part of his primary ministry: to present himself to Israel as the Messiah and to demonstrate God's power and love. ♦ *Miracle/Sign/Wonder*

It is also clear from the NT that Jesus did endow his disciples with his own healing power (Mt 10:1,8; Mk 6:13; Lk 9:1,6). The early church saw this healing power exercised after the resurrection of Jesus, as the apostles preached Jesus in Palestine (Ac 3:16; 4:9–30; 5:16; 8:7; 9:34) and beyond (Ac 14:9; 28:8). These demonstrations of healing power were one element in authenticating the apostles and their message about Jesus.

In view of the prominent place given healing in the Synoptics and Acts, it is startling to find almost nothing about healing in the rest of the NT. Heb 12:13 speaks of healing in its inner, spiritual sense. James calls on the sick to have the elders of the church pray over them and anoint them with oil in the name of the Lord, and he promises healing in response to the prayer offered in faith (Jas 5:14–16). In 1 Co 12, Paul mentions the gift of healing, but he does not explain it. The idea that healing is ours by right certainly is not taught explicitly in the NT.

5. The gift of healing. In 1 Cor 12:9,28,30, Paul includes the gift of healing (*iama*) in his list of spiritual gifts given to believers. ♦ *Gift/Gifts* It is clear that healing can be carried out by those gifted for this purpose. But the NT says nothing more about this gift or how it is exercised.

6. Sickness among believers. With so little prescription in the NT regarding how to deal with illnesses, we must turn to examples for insight. What do the Epistles tell us of how believers reacted to sickness after the early apostolic period? Three cases are instructive.

Paul suffered from a serious disease that affected his appearance and probably his eyesight. He "pleaded with the Lord to take it away" (2 Co 12:8). But God did not. Instead, Paul was given grace to live with his disability.

Timothy suffered from chronic stomach trouble. Paul advised him, "Stop drinking only water, and use a little wine because of your stomach and your frequent illnesses" (1 Ti 5:23).

Epaphroditus came to Paul with a gift from the church at Philippi. He became sick and nearly died. Paul wrote after his recovery: "Indeed he was ill, and almost died. But God had mercy on him, and not on him only but also on me, to spare me sorrow upon sorrow" (Php 2:27).

In none of these cases reported in the NT do we see a believer claim healing as a right won for him by Christ on Calvary. In each case we see a dependence on God and a recognition of him as healer. Paul prescribed to Timothy a course of treatment rather than exhorting him to "claim" healing. In only one case is there evidence of recovery, while in the other two there is some suggestion that God was using the illness for his own gracious purpose.

7. Conclusions. Healing will probably always be a debated issue. We can be sure of only a few basic realities. Spiritual and physical health are linked. Spiritual and physical healing are linked. God is the supervisor and source of it all. The believer is expected to bring every need to God in prayer and can be confident that God will hear. There may be no guarantee of healing to those of us who have faith, but there is a guarantee that God loves us and will act for our good.

HEALTH ♦ *Sickness and Health*

HEAR/LISTEN

At times these words are used in the Bible in their simplest descriptive sense: Adam and Eve "heard the sound of the LORD God as he was walking in the garden" (Ge 3:8). But the text goes on to report that they immediately tried to hide. Because we human beings have been shaped as we are by God and have been given minds that process the data of our senses, we go beyond the simple act of hearing to interpret what we hear and to act on it. In both Testaments the words "hear" and "listen" recognize this fact and thus have special significance.

OT 1. The Hebrew concept
    2. Hearing God
    3. Asking God to hear
NT 4. The Greek concept
    5. Hearing as perception
    6. Hearing and faith
    7. Summary

OT — 1. The Hebrew concept. The root word of both "hear" and "listen" is *šāma'*. The verb occurs some 1,050 times in the OT, in addition to many occurrences of its derivatives. The basic thought is that of effective hearing. In most contexts the act of hearing is extended beyond (1) the physical act of hearing to suggest (2) processing and (3) responding to what is heard. The emphasis of "hear" or "listen" may be on any of these three aspects. The statement that Adam and Eve "heard the sound of the LORD" focuses on the act of hearing. In Ge 3:17 God introduced an announcement of judgment on the fallen pair by saying to Adam, "Because you listened to your wife." Here there is an emphasis on the response: Adam listened, considered, and paid attention to what Eve said. He let her view shape his action, rather than paying attention to the command of God. In Ge 11:7 the emphasis is on processing. God acted on the minds of the people at Babel "so they [would] not understand [*šāma'*] each other." Usually the context will make the focus of the word (on the act, the processing, or the response) clear. Often the translators of the NIV and the NASB chose a word that gives one of those specific meanings.

2. Hearing God. The Christian religion is a revealed religion. The Creator of the universe, who has acted to redeem mankind, has spoken in a clear and decisive Word. ♦ *Word* Man is called to perceive, process, and respond appropriately to God's Word. Because God is Lord, the appropriate response to his Word is obedience.

This stress in the OT is so deeply established that in most cases where the NIV and NASB read "obey" the Hebrew has *šāma'*. ♦ *Obey/Disobey* Wherever the words "hear" and "listen" are used of human relationship with God, obedient response is implied. Response is not only appropriate but essential to truly "hearing" the Lord.

Pharaoh, who did not recognize God, reacted understandably to Moses' demand that he let Israel go. "Who is the LORD, that I should obey [šāma', "hear"] him and let Israel go?" (Ex 5:2). But even after a series of divine judgments demonstrated to all Egypt who Israel's God was, Pharaoh would neither listen nor respond.

As God's chosen people, Israel knew God. It was on their behalf that the Lord did all his wonderful works. Thus Israel would be responsible to hear, grasp, and respond to God's Word. This call was basic to the relationship between God's people and the Lord. "Now if you obey me fully [šāma', "hear"] and keep my covenant, then out of all nations you will be my treasured possession" (Ex 19:5). Much later in history the disasters that struck the nation were explained by Jeremiah as happening because of Israel's failure to hear, in the sense of responding appropriately, to the Lord: "They did not obey [šāma'] you or follow your law; they did not do what you commanded them to do. So you brought all this disaster upon them" (Jer 32:23).

So we remember as we read. The call to hear God, which runs as a bright thread through the OT, is a call to know what he said, to grasp the meaning of what he said, and to respond by putting God's Word into practice.

3. Asking God to hear. The OT presents a living God, who can and does act in the world of people. Thus God's people can pray to God and expect his intervention. Often in the prayers recorded in the Bible this expectation is expressed in cries to God to hear the worshipers.

The link between hearing and action is clearly seen in Solomon's prayer at the dedication of the temple. Hearing is extended in this prayer and is defined in context as forgiving (2 Ch 6:21,25,27,30), as repaying the guilty and establishing innocence (6:23), as bringing Israel back to the land (6:25), as teaching the right way to live and sending rain on the land

(6:27), as dealing with each person according to all he does (6:30), as doing whatever the petitioner asks (6:33), and as upholding the worshipers' cause (6:35,39).

The psalmist finds it impossible to believe that "he who implanted the ear" cannot hear or that "he who formed the eye" cannot see (Ps 94:9). As judge, God is aware of all that happens on earth, and he is well able to intervene. Thus we can pray to him with confidence, expecting him to hear, to understand our need, and to respond by giving us the help we require.

NT — 4. The Greek concept. The Greek akouō is not as inclusive as the Hebrew šāma'. In Greek culture, akouō involved the act of hearing and was extended to include processing what was heard. But the further extension to response is expressed in Greek by the compound word hypakouō, which means "to listen," "to obey."

The NT uses "hear" in this Greek sense rather than carrying over the Hebrew sense in which response is implied and included in hearing.

This variance is helpful in enabling us to analyze more carefully the various relationships between hearing the Word of God and responding to that Word.

5. Hearing as perception. Several incidents in the Gospels help us to explore the relationship between hearing and perception. Exploring the unresponsiveness of Israel, Jesus told the Parable of the Sower (Mt 13:1–23; Mk 4:1–20; Lk 8:4–15). Jesus linked his use of parables to Isaiah's prophetic picture of an unresponsive Israel: "This people's heart has become calloused; they hardly hear with their ears, and they have closed their eyes" (Mt 13:15). In Jesus' parable, he likens the Word to seed spread by a sower. It falls on different soils, representing the way different hearers process the message. Some (the rocky ground) are unable to perceive or grasp anything of the meaning of the message (v. 19). Some readily receive the Word; but then, when persecution comes to the believers on account of the Word, they cease living

by the Word (vv. 20–21). Others receive the Word but soon become unfruitful because of the "worries of this life and the deceitfulness of wealth" (v. 22). The good soil represents the "man who hears the word and understands it" (v. 23). Understanding involves reshaping one's whole perception of the meaning of life. Only when the Word is allowed to reshape perception will it produce a crop over an extended period of time in the hearer's life.

John's Gospel reports another confrontation of Jesus with those who refused to hear. "Why is my language not clear to you?" Jesus asked. "Because you are unable to hear what I say" (Jn 8:43). He explained that these men who rejected and resisted him were in the family line of Satan, who also is committed to lies and cannot comprehend truth. Jesus concluded, "He who belongs to God hears what God says. The reason you do not hear is that you do not belong to God" (8:47).

A person's perceptual field—how one views life and attends to the multiple messages that each of us hears—is ultimately shaped by one's attitude toward God. If God has the central place that is rightly his, all other things fall into place. But if God is not given his rightful place in our life and recognized for who he is, the message of the Word of God cannot be heard, in the sense of truly being understood.

6. Hearing and faith. The NT makes it clear that hearing God's Word also necessarily involves responding to it, just as the Hebrew šāma' implies.

Jesus emphasizes response in his story of the two builders (Mt 7:24–27). The wise builder builds on rock and pictures "everyone who hears these words of mine and puts them into practice" (7:24). The foolish builder builds on sand; he represents "everyone who hears these words of mine and does not put them into practice" (7:26). James puts it in terms of self-deceit: only the one who looks into the Word "and continues to do this [i.e., maintains the perception that the Word shapes], not forgetting what he has heard, but doing it [acting in harmony with the new perception]—he will be blessed in what he does" (Jas 1:25).

But with this emphasis, the NT adds in Hebrews 3 and 4 an analysis of what it is that moves the individual beyond understanding to response. Looking back in history, the writer describes the Exodus generation. They heard God's voice but hardened their hearts and did not obey. The writer explains, "We see that they were not able to enter [the Promised Land], because of their unbelief" (3:19).

Continuing, the writer points out that "we also have had the gospel preached to us, just as they did; but the message they heard was of no value to them because those who heard it did not combine it with faith" (4:2). It is faith, a settled confidence that God's spoken Word is reliable and can be trusted, that is a necessary attitude as we approach God. We hear, we understand the implications as the Word reshapes our perceptions, and then we express trust in God by acting on the Word and putting it into practice.

7. Summary. Both the OT and the NT place great theological significance on hearing. In the OT the physical act, the mental process of grasping meaning, and the appropriate response of obedience are all included when hearing or listening to God is mentioned.

The NT uses a Greek word that focuses on the first two of these aspects. The mental process is pictured as a shaping of perspective, so that the Word determines the way the hearer views all the issues of life. The goal of hearing is to have our outlook completely reshaped, so that God's Word will determine our values and attitudes.

But the NT also focuses on the third aspect of hearing: putting into practice what was heard. The first two are considered to be futile unless they issue in appropriate action—in doing God's Word. The key to response is a believing heart. When we hear what God says, see its meaning, and trust his outlook as being in fullest harmony with reality, we will put his Word into practice. Then, in the doing of the Word we have heard, we will be blessed.

HEART

The Bible seems to say little about human emotions, attitudes, or values. The complex vocabulary of technical terms we use today is not found in the OT and NT. But the Bible is hardly silent about man's inner life. The Bible says much, and the key to our understanding is the word "heart."

OT 1. "Heart" in the OT
    2. Pharaoh's hardened heart
NT 3. "Heart" in the NT
    4. Sayings about the human heart

OT — 1. "Heart" in the OT. The Hebrew word *lēb* is usually found where the NIV and the NASB read "heart." Infrequently, other words for internal organs or the inner person are also translated "heart."

The Hebrew *lēb* is a broad, inclusive term. In our culture we tend to divide a human being into isolated functions, such as the spiritual, the intellectual, the emotional, the rational, and the volitional. But Hebrew thought maintains the unity of the person. It looks at a human being as a whole and expresses all of these and other inner human functions by use of the word *lēb*. In the OT the heart is thus the conscious self — the inner person with every function that make a person human.

2. Pharaoh's hardened heart. One often-debated passage in Exodus describes the response of Pharaoh to God's demand that Israel be released. The reaction to this message delivered by Moses is described in the following ways:

> 4:21 I [the LORD] will harden his heart
> 7:3 I will harden Pharaoh's heart
> 7:13 Pharaoh's heart became hard
> 7:14 Pharaoh's heart is unyielding
> 7:22 Pharaoh's heart became hard
> 8:15 He hardened his heart
> 8:19 Pharaoh's heart was hard
> 8:32 Pharaoh hardened his heart
> 9:7 Yet his heart was unyielding

The same interplay continues for a few chapters (9:12; 9:35; 10:1,20,27; 11:10; 14:4,8).

In context, Pharaoh's will is clearly in view. The question is whether Pharaoh (1) operated as a free and responsible person in refusing Moses' requests or (2) was caused to act against his will.

The OT views God as a causal force in all that happens, but it also views human beings as fully responsible for their attitudes and actions. ♦ *Account/Accountable* ♦ *Predestine* In a sense, God caused the response of Pharaoh, even if in no other way than by confronting him with the choice. Whenever God speaks, we are driven to make a choice, to open our hearts to God's Word or to harden them.

Whatever the implications of the Lord's announcement that he would harden Pharaoh's heart, it is clear from the fact that Pharaoh "hardened his heart" that any influence exerted by God did not force Pharaoh to act against the inclination of his own character and the free choice of his own will.

What is perhaps more significant is Jeremiah's frustrated description of humanity: "The heart is deceitful above all things and beyond cure. Who can understand it?" (17:9). In looking at the inner man, the OT remains aware that every aspect of personality — mind, emotion, will, etc. — has been affected by the Fall and is so warped that we cannot trust ourselves.

NT — 3. "Heart" in the NT. The Greek *kardia* is used in the OT sense, with all the meanings found there. The heart of man is his very person: his psychological core. The conscious awareness each of us has that makes us persons and the spiritual dimension of responsiveness or unresponsiveness to God are both expressed by the word "heart." This significant term occurs in 158 NT passages.

4. Sayings about the human heart. The NT's many expressions about the human heart are especially rich when read with understanding. These verses make statements about our essential identity and God's relationship to the very core of our being.

Mt 6:21; Lk 12:34. The thing that we treasure will become the focus of our life and our personality.

Mt 12:34; 15:18–19; Mk 7:19; Lk 6:45. The inner personality of human beings, warped toward sin, is the source of sin and of sinful actions. We are not to look for causes of sin in externals. We are to look within.

Ro 1:21–32. It is failure to respond to God that causes the full development and expression of the inner, sinful bent to human nature.

Ro 10:8–13. A heart response to God begins with belief that Jesus is Lord and that God has raised him from the dead. This new beginning redirects our total life and experience.

Ro 5:5; 2 Co 1:22; Gal 4:6. God's Spirit comes into our renewed personality, bringing God's own strength and vitality, his own pure motives and desires.

In these and other NT passages speaking of the heart, we sense how deep a need exists in lost humanity. And we discover with awe how wonderful is the provision of God. He moves with his Spirit into the very core of our being and makes all things bright and new.

HEAVEN AND HELL

Most Christians have definite, though hazy, notions about heaven and hell. We are confident of our resurrection. We are sure that just and unjust alike are everliving persons. Saved and unsaved will exist forever as self-conscious, aware individuals.

Usually we speak of "heaven" as the place where believers go at death, and "hell" as the place where unbelievers go. But when we explore the use of these words in the OT and NT, we discover how little is said about heaven and hell as we usually understand them!

OT 1. The heavens
    2. S'ôl: the realm of death
NT 3. Heaven
    4. Hell
    5. Conclusions

OT — 1. The heavens. The Hebrew word translated "heaven" or "the heav-

ens" is *šāmayim*. It is used in two primary senses.

First, the heavens are part of the created universe. Specifically, the heavens are everything above the earth, that is, (1) the sky and (2) the lights seen in the sky. In OT thought the earth is below, the heavens above. While a number of figures are used, such as heavenly sluice-gates ("windows") through which rains come, such expressions reflect Hebrew imagery and not a set of literal beliefs about cosmology.

Second, the heavens are viewed as the realm of God. Thus the physical and spiritual universe parallel to some extent the pattern set by earth and sky. The spiritual universe too is above, beyond the ability of humanity to experience directly. Thus Isaiah says: " 'For my thoughts are not your thoughts, neither are my ways your ways,' declares the LORD. 'As the heavens are higher than the earth, so are my ways higher than your ways and my thoughts than your thoughts' " (55:8–9).

Continuing the parallelism, the phrase "hosts of heaven" indicates, depending on context, either the stars (the multitude of lights in the sky of the material universe) or angels (the multitude of bright beings inhabiting the spiritual universe).

▶ *Angels*

Although God inhabits the heavens, he does exercise complete control over events in the physical universe (e.g., Isa 40:10–31). It is God who is the unifying factor between material and spiritual realms, for he is Creator and sovereign Lord of both.

The OT does not speak of "heaven" as a place to which the believing dead go, but it does look forward to eternity. In the end, God will restructure the universe, earth and heavens alike, for righteousness: "The heavens will vanish like smoke, the earth will wear out like a garment and its inhabitants die like flies" (Isa 51:6). But, as God goes on to say in the same verse, the spiritual universe is stable: "My salvation will last forever, my righteousness will never fail."

The OT message of hope is found in God's hints about resurrection and in his

plans for the future. ♦ *Resurrection*
" 'Behold, I will create new heavens and
a new earth. The former things will not
be remembered, nor will they come to
mind' " (Isa 65:17). " 'As the new heavens
and the new earth that I will make
endure before me,' says the Lord, 'so will
your name and descendants endure' "
(Isa 66:22). God's plan for humanity
extends beyond the end of time as we
know it. But the OT is almost silent
concerning the destiny of the individual
who dies before history's end.

2. Šᵉôl: the realm of death. A look at
the concordance shows that the OT says
little about hell. Some feel that the OT
term Šᵉôl (found 65 times in the OT),
transliterated *sheol* in the NASB but
translated "the grave" or "the realm of
death" in the NIV, represents the OT
conception of hell.

However, such arguments are unsatis-
factory, and it is best to understand šᵉôl
as a poetic synonym for *qeber*, "grave."
Thus there are no references to eternal
destiny but simply to the grave as the
resting place of the bodies of all people
(e.g., Job 17:13–16; 24:19–20). Deliverance from šᵉôl is rescue from impending
death or future punishment (e.g., Ps
89:48).

So while the OT does indicate a resurrection for the blessed dead, it has little
to say of the destiny of the lost or of what
happens to the human personality when
the body dies and goes to the grave.

NT — 3. Heaven. The average Christian expects to go to heaven at death.
This popular view expresses much truth,
but it is not intended or taught in the
Bible's use of "heaven" (*ouranos*).

The basic concept of heaven is rooted
in the heavens-and-earth duality of OT
thought. In the NT too the heavens and
the earth are aspects of material creation.
Heaven is the spiritual realm. It is the
abode of God, where he and his throne
are (e.g., Mt 3:17; 5:16,34,45; 6:1,9;
7:11,21; 10:32,33; 12:50; 16:17; 18:10,14,19;
23:9; Lk 11:13; Heb 1:3; 8:1,5; 9:24).

The vision of the NT writers corresponds with the OT when the destiny of
the heavens and the earth are in view.

One day this creation will be swept
away, and there will be new heavens and
a new earth (2 Pe 3:10,12; Rev 21:1; cf. Mt
24:35; Lk 21:33). But when the NT writers
speak of "heaven" in the spiritual sense,
there is a definite sharpening of focus.

In the NT, heaven is that supernatural
realm in which God dwells and over
which he exercises direct control. Both
Testaments view God as sovereign and
as "Lord of heaven and earth" (Mt
11:25). But it is in heaven where his will
in done perfectly, that is, without sin (Mt
6:10). On earth his control is indirect, and
the wills of lost men and demons vigorously oppose him. In heaven, every will
is joyfully subject to God's own will.

In Jesus, heaven established a bridge-
head on earth. Throughout history the
supernatural has at times directly altered
affairs on earth, as evidenced in the
manna that "came down from heaven"
(Jn 6:42). We see this same breakthrough
in Jesus' miracles, each of which was "a
sign from heaven" (Mt 16:1). In the
Gospels, Jesus speaks often of the "kingdom of heaven," which he represented
and established on earth. ♦ *Kingdom* It
is best to understand this kingdom as
having present existence through the
church, the body of Christ. Although
Jesus himself is physically resident in
heaven (Ac 1:11; Col 4:1), he is vitally
and truly present in the members of his
body here on earth. When we are responsive to his will, we represent the
continuing direct breakthrough of the
spiritual realm into the material: we
represent the kingdom of heaven on
earth.

While "heaven" in the NT is a timeless, locationless concept representing
the breakthrough in Christ of the spiritual realm into the material, "heaven" is
more than this. The spiritual realm is the
location of our true life and our hope. We
maintain our citizenship in heaven (Php
3:20). ♦ *Citizen* It is not in the material
realm of earth but in the spiritual realm
of heaven that our treasures lie (Mt 6:20).
It is there we will receive our rewards
(Mt 5:12; Lk 6:23); it is there that our
names are inscribed (Lk 10:20; Heb
12:23). Our true home is not on earth but

in heaven (Gal 4:26; Heb 12:22; Rev 21:2). So we look forward eagerly to that time when Jesus will come again from heaven (Acts 1:11; 1 Th 1:10; 4:16; 2 Th 1:7). Then and only then will the material realm be remolded to be in perfect harmony with the spiritual, when after final judgment God will create new heavens and a new earth.

Very little in these uses of "heaven" suggest the common notion of the place we go while we await the resurrection or after the resurrection. But it is clear from the NT that the blessed dead *do* enter the presence of God, existing with him until the time of the resurrection (2 Co 5:1; 1 Th 4:14). It is also clear that, whatever "heaven" is like, after the final apocalyptic battle between God and the forces of evil, there will be a new creation and the enjoyment of eternal life in God's presence (Rev 21–22). However, by our use of "heaven" in the limited sense in which we use it, we lose much of the rich meaning the NT invests in this term.

4. Hell. The popular notion of heaven and hell as the abodes of the souls of the dead is more or less correct. But as we have seen, "heaven" is used in a much broader, more significant sense. How then is "hell" used?

Three Greek words in the NT are most often used to express concepts associated with hell. The two most significant are *gehenna* and *hādēs*. ▶ **Abyss** *Gehenna* occurs twelve times in the NT (Mt 5:22,29–30; 10:28; 18:9; 23:15,33; Mk 9:43,45,47; Lk 12:5; Jas 3:6). It is always translated "hell" in the NIV. The Greek word translated "sent . . . to hell" in 2 Pe 2:4 appears only there in the NT; it is *tartaroō*, which means "to confine in Tartaros." Tartaros was the Greek name for the mythological abyss where rebellious gods were confined.

Hādēs occurs eleven times in the NT (Mt 11:23; 16:18; Lk 10:15; 16:23; Ac 2:27,31; 1 Co 15:55; Rev 1:18; 6:8; 20:13–14). It is translated "Hades" in the NASB and variously by "death," "the grave," and "Hades" in the NIV.

The reason for the wider scope of translations in the NIV is that this version adopts the OT sense of the grave when quoting OT passages that contain *š'ôl* (Mt 11:23; Lk 10:15; Ac 2:27,31). These passages and 1 Co 15:55 refer to the place where the body goes after death.

But in other uses, *hādēs* means the temporary residence of the persons awaiting final judgment. Luke 16 contains Jesus' story of the rich man and Lazarus. Both of these men died. The rich man found himself in *hādēs*, "where he was in torment" (v. 23; cf. v. 28). He was in "agony" and in "fire" (v. 24). But Lazarus was comforted and was in Abraham's very arms. Between those in *hādēs* and the blessed dead there is a great and uncrossable gulf (v. 26).

Many believe that Jesus, at the time of his resurrection, released the saved of OT times from their place of waiting, causing them to go directly into God's presence (cf. 1 Th 4:14). Also, in Revelation's prophetic portrayal of the end it is only those awaiting final condemnation who are in *hādēs* when the "dead [will be] judged according to what they [have] done as recorded in the books" (Rev 20:12).

In NT times, the rabbis used the word *gehenna* to indicate the place of final punishment. Jesus maintained this meaning in the Gospels. In his warnings to his listeners Jesus often spoke of *gehenna* in association with fire (Mt 5:22; 18:9; Mk 9:43,48). The phrase "eternal fire" is also used of hell, and human beings will be punished there in a fire prepared for "the devil and his angels" (Mt 25:41).

The most striking picture of eternal punishment is found in the Book of Revelation. There the state of the condemned is described. They are in a "fiery lake of burning sulfur" (19:20; cf. 20:10), a "lake of fire" (20:14–15), where "they will be tormented day and night for ever and ever" (20:10).

5. Conclusions. Scripture views each human being as a person with an eternal destiny. Each life is too significant to be simply snuffed out. There will be a resurrection of the saved and of the lost. ▶ *Resurrection*

Resurrected individuals will be self-conscious, aware persons, destined for eternal existence. That endless life will be lived in the presence of God or in alienation from him. To the extent that we represent these realities by our use of "heaven" and "hell," we correctly state the Bible's position. But as we read the NT we need to be careful not to read this limited, though accurate, concept into the word "heaven." Heaven is a significant theological term in the NT and does not simply designate the destiny of the blessed.

Against the background of the certainty of endless life comes the gospel's good news. If we were left alone, we would all go to hell. ▶ *Belief/Faith* By his death, however, Christ has made perfect atonement for sin and provided the basis to forgive all who believe. ▶ *Atonement* Anyone and everyone who turns to him is assured of eternity in the presence of the Lord and avoids having to face condemnation.

HEBREW

Abraham (Ge 14:13) and Joseph (Ge 39:14) are the first persons in the Bible to be called Hebrews. The word appears in Babylonian and Egyptian texts, probably to mean immigrants or foreign contract workers. When Potiphar's wife used this term in speaking of Joseph, it seems to have been a term of racial contempt: "this foreigner!" Only later did "Hebrew" develop as an ethnic term for the Jewish people. Paul calls himself "a Hebrew of Hebrews" (Php 3:5; cf. 2 Co 11:22). "Hebrew" is also used of the language by that name (e.g., Rev. 9:11; 16:16).

HEIR

The Hebrew word for "heir" is *yāraš*, "to inherit" or "to take possession." ▶ *Possess* The NT word is *klēronomos*, "one who takes possession of or inherits." The emphasis is on the heir's right to possess.

God has given us wonderful rights. In Jesus we have a right to God's promises,

for we become his children in Jesus (Gal 4:7). ▶ *Inheritance*

HILLS/MOUNTAINS

The Hebrew words *gib'âh* ("hill") and *har* ("mountain") are taken at times as interchangeable by the translators of the NIV and the NASB. Both words have some theological significance.

Gib'âh indicates higher ground, a prominence in the landscape. Such locations were often sites for the rites of the pagans who inhabited Palestine before Israel and who lived in surrounding nations. The Bible's condemnation of worship "on every high hill" is not directed against high hills but against the pagan rites associated with them.

Har indicates a mountain that is majestic and impressive in its rugged power. In other cultures in the ancient world, mountains were seen as the home of the gods and goddesses. In Isa 14:13 this pagan symbolism is mockingly placed in the mouths of the rulers God would soon destroy. Scripture presents God as greater than the most mighty; he is able both to create and to destroy them (e.g., Ps 65:6; Isa 41:15; Hab 3:6). "Mountain" is sometimes used symbolically in the Bible to represent strength and authority (e.g., Jer 51:25).

Mountains provided the impressive background for many of Israel's experiences with God (e.g., the blessings and curses recited on Ebal and Gerizim—Dt 11:29; Jos 8:33). Some were also significant in Jesus' life and ministry (Mt 4:8; 17:1; 24:3; 27:33; 28:16).

The two most significant mountains in Scripture are associated with God's acts of revelation. Mount Sinai was central in the past history of Israel, for there God met with Moses and gave his people the law. ▶ *Law* Mount Zion will be central in future history. It is not only the site of the Jerusalem temple, at which the OT people were called to worship; it is also the mountain of God to which Christ will return and from which his rule will extend throughout the world (Isa 2:2–3; Mic 4:1–2).

HOLY/HOLINESS

Believers in every age have been called by God to be holy. There is no contradiction between OT and NT concepts of holiness, but there is a change in emphasis on what holiness involves.

OT 1. The OT concept of holiness
2. Ritual holiness
3. Moral holiness
NT 4. The NT concept of holiness
5. The holy life
6. The Holy Spirit
7. Conclusions

OT — 1. The OT concept of holiness. The root of the words translated "holy" and "holiness" is *qādaš*. The verb means "to be consecrated," "to be dedicated," "to be holy." Anything that is "holy" is set apart. It is removed from the realm of the common and moved to the sphere of the sacred.

The focus of the sacred realm is God himself, Israel's Holy One (2 Ki 19:22; Job 6:10; Ps 16:10; 22:3; 71:22; 78:41; 89:18; Pr 9:10; 30:3; Isa 1:4; 5:19,24; 10:17,20; 12:6; 17:7; 29:23; 30:11,12,15; 31:1; 37:23; 40:25; 41:14,16,20; 43:3,14,15; 45:11; 47:4; 48:17; 49:7; 54:5; 55:5; 60:9,14; Jer 50:29; 51:5; Eze 39:7; Hos 11:9,12; Hab 1:12; 3:3; cf. Lev 20:26; Jos 24:19; Ps 22:3; 99:9). "Holy" becomes a technical religious term used of persons, places, times, and things that were considered sacred because they were associated with and consecrated to God. The seventh day was holy, to be reserved for worship and rest (Ge 2:3; Ex 20:8–11; Dt 5:12). Mount Sinai was holy, for God appeared there in fire to give the Ten Commandments (Ex 19:23). The priests of Israel were holy (Lev 21:7), and everything associated with worship and sacrifice was to be considered holy. In a very significant sense Israel itself was considered holy, for this people was chosen by God to be his own special possession (Dt 7:6; 14:2,21).

It is important to realize that great stress is placed in the OT on maintaining the distinction between what is sacred and what is secular. The holy must never be used in a common or profane way.

That which was consecrated to God must be for his use alone—forever.

2. Ritual holiness. The religion of Israel was both cultic and moral. The cultic element established religious ritual and many aspects of the lifestyle of God's people. A person was in a state of holiness when he observed cultic restrictions. It was a responsibility of the priests to "distinguish between the holy and the common, between the unclean and the clean, and [they were required to] teach the Israelites all the decrees the LORD [had] given them through Moses" (Lev 10:10–11). Both essentially nonmoral practices, such as not cooking a young goat in its mother's milk (Ex 34:26), and religious ceremonies were aspects of ritual holiness. ▸ *Clean and Unclean*

3. Moral holiness. Two aspects of God's nature are associated with holiness in the OT. One is his essential power and splendor. When two of Aaron's sons violated the ritual regulations governing worship, God, as quoted by Moses, announced: "Among those who approach me I will show myself holy; in the sight of all the people I will be honored" (Lev 10:3). Fire flared from the Lord on that occasion and consumed the men who had treated him with contempt by ignoring his commands. God's holiness was displayed in this exercise of awesome power.

Lev 19:2 displays a moral dimension to God's holiness. "Speak to the entire assembly of Israel," the Lord told Moses, "and say to them: 'Be holy because I, the LORD your God, am holy.' "

The commands that follow this statement are not ritual but are moral in character. They deal with idolatry, theft, lying, fraud, slander, revenge, etc., and include the command to love one's neighbor. These commands are punctuated regularly by the reminder, "I am the LORD."

In this OT passage and many others, God's holiness is directly linked with his own moral character. That holiness is displayed in his moral perfection and faithful commitment to good and in his judgment on those who desert the way of goodness for sin. As Isaiah says: "The LORD Almighty will be exalted by his justice, and the holy God will show himself holy by his righteousness" (Isa 5:16). When Israel was set apart to God by God's sovereign choice, both the ritual and moral aspects of obedience to God were essential in their life of holiness.

NT — 4. The NT concept of holiness. Three main words in Greek culture were associated with the idea of the holy. *Hieros* reflected the OT emphasis on the ritually holy. This word is rarely used in the NT (found only twice—1 Co 9:13; 2 Ti 3:15). *Hagios* reflected the law's expression of the divine will and human obligation to God. It had a strong moral overtone. It is this word that is the dominant one in the NT. *Hosios* reflected piety or devoutness. It is used only eight times in the NT—Ac 2:27; 13:34,35; 1 Ti 2:8; Tit 1:8; Heb 7:26; Rev 15:4; 16:5—four of them in quotations from the OT. In addition, *hosiotēs* is used twice in the NT (Lk 1:75; Eph 4:24), and *osmē* is used once (1 Th 2:10).

In the NT the most frequent use of "holy" is in the designation of God's Spirit as the Holy Spirit. It is also used often in reference to believers as God's "saints." In the Gospels and Acts "holy" may have either a ritual or a moral emphasis, just as *qādaš* words do in the OT. It is in the NT, however, that we see a dramatic shift in the concept of the nature of practical holiness.

5. The holy life. In the OT, holiness is expressed in strict separation. The clean were not permitted to come in contact with the unclean. Israel had to fiercely guard its differences from the surrounding nations. Cultic commitments were, in part, designed to underline the uniqueness of Israel as a people set apart from all others to God.

The NT also has an emphasis on separation. ♦ *Separation* But Christians do not live in a separate nation. The church is scattered as tiny communities planted in every kind of human society. Paul wrote to Corinth: "I have written you in my letter not to associate with sexually immoral people—not at all meaning the people of this world who are immoral, or the greedy and swindlers, or idolators. In that case you would have to leave this world" (1 Co 5:9–10).

Rather than viewing separation as isolation, as lack of contact between the clean and the unclean, the sacred and the common, the NT presents a dynamic concept of holiness as moral purity expressed in contact with the common and profane! Believers are to separate themselves from evil while living among people who remain uncommitted to the divine standards.

This is an extremely important reorientation. In Christian experience the holy is not kept rigorously distinct from ordinary life. Instead, the essence of holiness is a dynamic expression of the divine within the normal processes of daily life.

We see this emphasis in nearly all of the Epistles. Peter expresses God's call to holiness in these words: "Just as he who called you is holy, so be holy in all you do; for it is written, 'Be holy, because I am holy' " (1 Pe 1:15–16). Peter goes on to explain this holiness "in all you do" in the second chapter of the same letter: "You are a chosen people, a royal priesthood, a holy nation, a people belonging to God, that you may declare the praises of him who called you out of darkness into his wonderful light. . . . Dear friends, I urge you, as aliens and strangers in the world, to abstain from sinful desires, which war against your soul. Live such good lives among the pagans that, though they accuse you of doing wrong, they may see your good deeds and glorify God on the day he visits us" (2:9,11–12). It is as God's obedient children, living by his will as strangers within our cultures, that we fulfill the call to holiness. ♦ *Alien/Aliens*

This theme is developed in many of Paul's epistles. Colossians is a good example. After presenting Jesus as the center of our lives and our Christian experience, Paul looks at empty avenues to spiritual achievement. He dismisses ritualistic and ascetic religious practices as lacking any value (Col 2:20–23). Instead, he describes the holy life as one involving an inner separation from those passions that bubble up from our sinful natures (3:5–11). What marks believers as "God's chosen people, holy and dearly loved" (3:12) is their commitment to compassion, kindness, humility, gentleness, and patience. It is these things, with mutual forgiveness and deepening love, that express the reality of holiness (3:12–14).

In the NT, God's people are called "saints"—his holy ones. This reflects our standing as those who have been set aside by God's actions in Christ to be his own personal possessions. But the term is also to reflect our experience. We are daily to live out that moral holiness and active love that is revealed so beautifully in God's own character. The call to holiness in the NT is a call to let our Father be seen and glorified in our lives.

6. The Holy Spirit. Most NT uses of "holy" are in the title "Holy Spirit." ♦ *Spirit (Holy Spirit)* In the NT the Father and Son are sometimes also called holy (Jn 17:11; Lk 1:35), but almost every mention of the Spirit includes the word "Holy"—thus, "Holy Spirit." This title is more than a reference to the Spirit's deity; it is more specifically a reference to the nature of his work.

OT cultic holiness focused attention on holy persons (priests), places (the temple, Jerusalem), and things (the altar, the temple furniture, etc.). In the NT the sacred is no longer seen in places or things. The focus of the holy shifts dramatically to persons. "Don't you know," Paul writes emotionally, "that you yourselves are God's temple and that God's Spirit lives in you?" (1 Co 3:16). In the NT, holiness is linked with the Spirit's working and with the product of his work within human beings. ♦ *Sanctify/Sanctification* The Spirit is the Holy Spirit because he himself is the source of the holy. Thus NT holiness is always rooted in a relationship with Jesus and with the Spirit, whom Jesus sends to be within every believer.

7. Conclusions. The idea of holiness in both Testaments is one of consecration

to God. In the OT, holiness involves keeping both cultic (ritual) and moral commandments. Places and things and even persons were set aside as sacred, to have no contact with the common or ordinary. But the OT consistently reminds us that the key to understanding holiness is found in the character of God. Holiness is expressed in his power and his own moral character. So true holiness in his people will necessarily have a strong moral component.

In the NT the cult of the OT is set aside. ♦ *Law* ♦ *Clean and Unclean* The emphasis in NT teaching about holiness is squarely on the moral. There is another shift in emphasis as well. The OT maintained strict separation between the holy and the profane. In the NT, holiness is true goodness woven through the lifestyle of the believer and expressed in every daily activity and in every relationship.

In the OT, God's people consecrated persons, places, and things solely for God's use. In the NT, God's Spirit himself acts in salvation to set us apart to God. In addition, the Holy Spirit continues to act in our lives to infuse us with Christ's own likeness and to enable us by his power to express Christlikeness in our daily lives. It is here that we find the true holiness of the NT: joyous commitment to God and to the truly good, expressed in everything we say and do.

HONEST/DISHONEST

One of the main Hebrew words for "honest" is kēn (5 times in the OT—Ge 42:11,19,31,33,34), which means either "honest" or "right." "Dishonest" is bāṣa' (16 times in the OT), whose root meaning is probably "to cut off," as of cloth, adapted (like the slang expression "rip off") to indicate the making of illicit profit or gain through violence. Habakkuk speaks to those who have such a passion for money that it replaces one's commitment to God as the central focus of life: "Woe to him who builds his realm by unjust gain to set his nest on high, to escape the clutches of ruin! You have plotted the ruin of many peoples, shaming your own house and forfeiting your life" (Hab 2:9–10).

HONOR/DISHONOR

Honor and dishonor are important social concepts in any culture. They are important in the Bible too, where they are intimately linked with character and behavior.

OT 1. Honor and dishonor in the OT
NT 2. Honor and dishonor in the NT
   3. Honoring parents

OT — 1. Honor and dishonor in the OT. Most occurrences of "honor" in the OT are translations of some form of *kābôd*. The root means "to be heavy," a concept that Israel extended figuratively in a number of ways.

Heaviness sometimes indicated severity, as in the proverbial heavy hand. It sometimes suggested magnitude or greatness. It also came to connote honor and glory. ♦ *Glory*

The idea of honor is a social one, reflecting how people within a society evaluate someone. In every society, wealth and position are closely associated with honor, and in some references "honor" may suggest material splendor. But the OT consistently says that someone in an honorable position should have an appropriate personal character. As Proverbs says: "Like snow in summer or rain in harvest, honor is not fitting for a fool" (Pr 26:1). ♦ *Fool/Folly*

The concept of honor is also closely linked with the idea of responsibility. The psalmist exclaims in wonder about God's gift of dominion to humanity: "You made him a little lower than the heavenly beings and crowned him with glory and honor. You made him ruler over the works of your hands; you put everything under his feet" (Ps 8:5–6). To honor someone thus implies more than to be impressed with his wealth. It means to respect the person and to give him or her appropriate attention and obedience. Thus God complains about Israel: "These people come near to me with their mouth and honor me with their lips, but their hearts are far from

me. Their worship of me is made up only of rules taught by men" (Isa 29:13). To truly honor God, his people must show him respect by obeying his commandments from the heart.

Two different Hebrew words are translated "dishonor." *Kālam* and its derivatives suggest the feelings of disgrace associated with some public humiliation. The other, *qālâh* (with its derivative *qālôn*), is the opposite of *kābôd*. It is a perception of a person that is lower than appropriate for his social position.

"Honor" and "dishonor" are important concepts. It is important for God's people to honor that which is honorable in God's sight and to see as disgraceful that which he sees as disgraceful. The wealth and power associated in human cultures with honor are never in themselves indicators of whom we should respect. It is the character and the commitment of a person to God that makes that one worthy of respect and honor.

NT — 2. Honor and dishonor in the NT. The words translated "honor" are *timaō* and its derivatives. These are also social terms, referring to the proper respect gained through one's position or wealth, or to the position itself. The use of "honor" in the NT parallels the concept in the OT and in secular Greek. God is honored when we respect his Word and do those things that please him (e.g., Jn 8:49–51; 1 Co 6:20). We are to obey governing authorities and treat them with due respect (Ro 13:1–7). Believers are encouraged to "honor one another above" themselves (Ro 12:10) and indeed to "show proper respect [*timaō*, "honor"] to everyone: Love the brotherhood of believers, fear God, honor the king" (1 Pe 2:17). We are to treat everyone with whom we come in contact with appropriate respect.

Except in 1 Co 11:4–5 (where the word means "to put to shame" or "to disgrace"), the Greek word is *atimaō* where the NIV and the NASB read "dishonor." God is dishonored, robbed of his due respect, when people who claim to be his commit sin (Ro 2:23). While others may wrongly lose respect for someone (1 Co 4:10; 2 Co 6:8), we need to be sensitive to the impact of our actions on those around us.

3. Honoring parents.

When we understand the meaning of "honor," we see in a fresh way what the repeated command to honor parents implies (Ex 20:12; Dt 5:16; Mt 15:4–6; Mk 7:10; 10:19; Lk 18:20; Eph 6:2). Listening, respecting, and obeying are all implicit in the concept of honor. So is the dimension of support for needy parents that occasioned Jesus' rebuke of legalists who resorted to Corban to withhold such support. Pr 3:9 calls on us to "honor the LORD with [our] wealth." The same financial support seems to be a way in which one's parents are honored (1 Ti 5:8).

HOPE

When we use the word "hope" in casual conversation, it often has a wavering, uncertain sound. "I hope I can make it," we say doubtfully. At times we sense the same uncertainty in Scripture. Herod "hoped" he would see Jesus do some miracle (Lk 23:8). Felix "hoped" Paul might offer him a bribe (Ac 24:26). Both men were disappointed.

The Bible seldom uses "hope" in this doubt-filled way. Instead, hope focuses attention on God and fills us with eager expectation. No one who learns to hope in a biblical way will ever be overcome by disappointment but will be filled with patience, encouragement, and enthusiasm.

OT 1. "Hope" in the OT
     2. The content of the believer's hope
NT 3. "Hope" in the NT
     4. The objects of our hope
     5. Summary

OT — 1. "Hope" in the OT. Most often where we find "hope" in the English versions, the Hebrew word is *miqweh*, *tiqwâh* (from the common root *qāwâh*), or *yāhal*. Each Hebrew word invites us to look ahead eagerly with confident expectation. Each also calls for patience, reminding us that the fulfillment of hope lies in the future.

Qāwâh forms focus attention on what it is that awaits us. In the Book of Job, perhaps the oldest OT book, Job expresses the sufferer's fears as tragedy shatters his sense of comfortable relationship with God. "If the only home I hope for is the grave," Job cries, "where then is my hope? Who can see any hope for me?" (17:13,15). As Job faces his fears of the future, he rejects the suggestion of Eliphaz: "Should not your piety be your confidence and your blameless ways your hope?" (4:6). Ultimately he finds the solution of the psalmist: "LORD, what do I look for? My hope is in you" (Ps 39:7).

The psalmist, living after the time of Moses, was familiar with God's commitment to his people expressed in the covenants. ♦ *Covenant* God had always shown himself faithful to his commitment. God's specific plan for the future might not be fully understood; nevertheless, many psalms express an overflowing confidence in God personally. How God will deliver, in this life and for the life beyond, was not completely clear to these OT believers. But surely God was himself the kind of person who could be trusted.

Yāhal forms dominate the psalms and the later prophets. This word for hope focuses on our present experience as we look ahead. At times translated "wait," *yāhal* invites us to link our present relationship with God to hope. In this relationship the OT suggests that (1) God is a deliverer, who will act in the future to save the one whose hope is in him, and (2) it is appropriate for us to wait confidently until God acts.

Because the believer knows God and trusts him, the psalmist can say, "I will always have hope" (Ps 71:14). When we have hope, we have courage to face each new day, for "the LORD preserves the faithful. . . . [Therefore,] be strong and take heart, all you who hope in the LORD" (Ps 31:23–24).

In a most basic way, then, "hope" is a relational term. It is a great affirmation of trust in God, not because the believer knows what is ahead, but because God is known as wholly trustworthy. David

343

writes in Ps 119:49–50, "You have given me hope. My comfort in my suffering is this: your promise preserves my life." Again and again the OT exhorts us to hope. "O Israel," comes the invitation, "put your hope in the LORD, for with the LORD is unfailing love, and with him is full redemption" (Ps 130:7).

2. The content of the believer's hope.

As the centuries drifted by, the prophets revealed more and more of God's plan. The shape of the hoped-for future took on clearer and clearer form. When Jerusalem fell to the Babylonians, Jeremiah's words reassured the Jews: "[You] will return from the land of the enemy. So there is hope for your future" (31:16–17). God had not rejected his people.

Despite sharpening images of what was to take place in the near and distant future, the OT never shifts from the conviction that relationship with God is the ultimate ground of hope. It is God himself who is the hope of Israel (Jer 14:8; 17:13). It is only by focusing our gaze on him that we find a source of confidence and patience. "Find rest, O my soul, in God alone," encourages the psalmist. "My hope comes from him. He alone is my rock and my salvation; he is my fortress, I will not be shaken" (Ps 62:5–6). Locked tight in the grasp of history as it slowly unfolds, the individual can only wait expectantly. "I will wait [yāḥal] for the LORD who is hiding his face from the house of Jacob. I will put my trust in him" (Isa 8:17).

3. Hope in the NT.

The Greek words translated "hope" are elpizō (verb) and elpis (noun). Of the eighty-five times these Greek words are found in the NT, only five are in the Gospels, ten are in Acts, and seventy are in the Epistles. They are seldom used in the Gospels, for Jesus, the object of the believer's hope, was present with his disciples. It is Paul who most carefully examines hope and develops its meaning for the NT age.

In the NT, "hope" is always the expectation of something good. It is also something we must wait for. In the NT, unlike the OT, just what we hope for is carefully explained. The mystery that the OT does not solve is untangled in the NT, and we are told about the wonders God has in store for us.

4. The objects of our hope.

The NT is a revelational nova. It caps the slowly unfolding OT with a three-decade starburst of light, illuminating long-hidden aspects of God's master plan. Hope today is still rooted in a relationship with God. But we know clearly what it is we are waiting for.

Resurrection is a reality. Some in Israel denied this doctrine. But with Jesus' resurrection, all doubts were settled. Acts glows with the specific hope of bodily resurrection for all (Ac 2:26; 23:6; 24:15; 26:6–7). Because believers will be raised to be with the Lord, we do not "grieve like the rest of men who have no hope" when death invades our circle of relatives or friends (1 Th 4:13).

Many exciting NT doctrines are associated with this hope of resurrection: Jesus will appear in glory (Ro 5:2,4–5; Tit 2:13); our bodies, and the creation itself, will be liberated from bondage to decay (Ro 8:20,24); we will then have the full experience of our eternal life, entering into the inheritance he guards for us in glory (Tit 1:2; 3:7; 1 Pe 1:3; 1 Jn 3:2–3).

There is also progressive transformation. The NT emphasizes a present as well as a future hope, a growing experience of renewal that we can expect as we take each struggling step toward the future. In 2 Corinthians, Paul explores this aspect of the new covenant. ♦ **Covenant** The Holy Spirit is at work now, writing God's holy law on our hearts rather than on cold stone. God the Spirit even now is transcribing Jesus' own character within our personalities, so that we are progressively becoming more like Jesus. ♦ *Sanctify/Sanctification* This theme is found often in the NT. Because of the Spirit's present work in us there is a "righteousness for which we hope" (Gal 5:5). Christ in us becomes not only our hope for the distant future but our expectation for tomorrow as well: a "hope for all the glorious things to come" (Col 1:27, PHILLIPS; cf. Eph 1:18–23).

The NT also shows us that there is a vital need for us to have hope. NT hope has not only an objective content but also a subjective impact. When we fix our eyes on the future that God has in store for us, we taste the wonders of his transforming power. John promises that as we realize that God intends for us to be like Jesus, our lives will change: "Everyone who has this hope in him purifies himself, just as he [Jesus] is pure" (1 Jn 3:3). We are told that "faith and love . . . spring from the hope that is stored up for [us] in heaven" (Col 1:5) and that faith rests "on the hope of eternal life, which God, who does not lie, promised" (Tit 1:2).

The NT also associates hope with character. In the NT, character development is linked with patient endurance: doing the right thing despite delay in reaching goals or receiving rewards. So it is particularly significant when we are told that "endurance [is] inspired by hope in our Lord Jesus Christ" (1 Th 1:3; cf. Ro 5:4–5). We are exhorted to "hold on to our courage and the hope of which we boast" (Heb 3:6) and to make our hope sure by showing "diligence to the very end" (Heb 6:11).

What is more, hope brings us a deep sense of joy (Ro 12:12). With hope we can maintain an optimistic outlook even when things go wrong (1 Pe 3:15; cf. vv. 13–17). Our life will still have its stress and its personal tragedies. But the believer whose hope is in the Lord and who has a grasp of God's plan will not be overcome.

5. Summary. In what do we hope? The OT saints knew less of God's plans than do NT saints. But psalmists and prophets called on believers to anchor their hope in the Lord himself. Most NT references either explore the objective content of the Christian's hope or examine the subjective impact of hope on our spiritual growth. Yet it is clear that there has been no basic change in the basis for hope. It is God who is the focus and object—and the ultimate guarantee—of our hope.

Everything you and I hope for is wrapped up in Jesus. He is the power who works our present transformation. He is the one whose return marks history's furthest horizon. He is the one through whom each believer will experience both the resurrection of the body and the future's full expression of eternal life. Our share of glory awaits his appearing.

The only significant difference between the testimony of the OT and that of the NT is that the NT contains additional facts about the future, facts God chose to not reveal to his OT people. Knowing more of his magnificent gifts tells us even more than they knew about the giver, the God of the universe. When we know how good God is, we can only respond with grateful praise and worship, as we are moved to awed wonder by the extent of his love. But it is always our sovereign and loving God who is the ground and focus of our hope. As Hebrews reminds us, "Let us hold unswervingly to the hope we profess, for he who promised is faithful" (10:23).

Like the OT saints, you and I will know hurt and uncertain tomorrows. We may suffer and experience tragedy, yet we can face the future expectantly. We may have to wait a while for the full experience of the good that God intends for us, but God is fully committed to everyone who makes a faith commitment to him.

" 'For I know the plans I have for you,' declares the LORD, 'plans to prosper you and not to harm you, plans to give you hope and a future' " (Jer 29:11).

As long as our hope is in God, we have hope. And a future.

HORN

Except when indicating a horn for blowing (*šôpār*), the OT word for horn is *qeren*. It indicates the horn of an animal. In the OT the horn is a symbol of power or of a person with power. Teeth and claws represent violence, but the horn symbolizes the possession of power. This symbolism is often used in prophecy (e.g., Da 8:20–21, where "horn" represents rulers, and Zec 1:18–21, where it represents world powers).

In the NT, the word *keras* ("horn") occurs eleven times—once in Lk 1:69 and ten times in Revelation.

HORRIBLE/HORROR ♦ *Appalled*

HOST/HOSTS

Both *ṣābā'* and *ṣᵉbā'ôt* are translated "host" (army) and "hosts" (armies). Although associated with warfare, "host" can indicate any large, ordered array, including the "host of heaven" (i.e., the stars, Ge 2:1; or angelic hosts, 1 Ki 22:19).

The NASB typically translates these Hebrew words as "host" or "hosts." The NIV translators emphasize the sense of masses, organized and placed under command. Thus Israel's organization in Egypt or in its wilderness journey by tribes is "in its divisions" rather than "in its hosts." Their military units compose the army of Israel rather than the host of Israel (e.g., Ex 1:26; Jos 5:14).

The title given God as "Lord of hosts" is very significant. It emphasizes not only his supreme personal power but also his power over everything in the material and spiritual universe. All is organized and under his command. Thus the NIV translates "Lord of hosts" by "Lord Almighty," rightly recognizing that this title ascribes to God supreme power.

HOUR

Why isn't "hour" found in the OT? The reason is that the Jewish people didn't divide the day that way but spoke of morning and noon and evening. By NT times the Greek-speaking world had adopted the Babylonian system of dividing the day into twelve equal parts. It is this system—where the third hour corresponds to 9 A.M., the sixth to noon, and the ninth to 3 P.M.—that is reflected in the Gospels.

"Hour" (*hōra*) is also used in extended ways. It is an indefinite point of future time when a significant event will take place (e.g., the hour of Jesus' return [Mt 24:36,44]). It is a pivotal or significant time in the life of a person or of the race (Jesus' hour had come [Jn 12:23,27; cf. Ro 13:11]). Generally the meaning of "hour"

in any specific passage is made clear by the context.

HOUSE/HOUSEHOLD ♦ *Family*

HUMAN/HUMANITY ♦ *Mankind*

HUMBLE/HUMILITY

The Bible places a high value on humility. God saves (Ps 18:27), sustains (Ps 147:6), and gives grace to the humble (Pr 3:34). Still, we are a little uneasy with the concept of humility and not quite sure just what it involves. Both Testaments give us insight into this virtue.

OT 1. The Hebrew words for humility
2. The blessings of humility
NT 3. The Greek words for humility
4. The humble lifestyle

OT — 1. The Hebrew words for humility. A number of Hebrew word groups are translated by "humble," "humbled," "humility," and "humiliation." It is best to view these words as synonyms conveying the same general meaning, though there are variations of emphasis.

'Anâh and its derivatives suggest being bowed down, oppressed. We find the word group translated "poor" and "afflicted," as well as "humble" and "gentle." The root suggests a submission that is forced. The force may be exerted by someone who is hostile or by God, who uses affliction to encourage his people to turn to him. ♦ *Affliction*

But the force that brings the humbled into a state of submission may also come from within. God's people are called to humble themselves and so to face the pain of self-examination and confession of sins. ♦ *Sin* Humbled before God, human beings are able to experience the blessings he has for all who will submit completely to him.

At times this word group is also used to express the poverty that accompanies forced submission to enemies.

Kāna' and its derivatives suggest public humiliation. A person who is humbled in this way is wounded because of a crushing defeat or public humiliation. In the uses of this word there is a strong undertone of shame and dishonor. ♦ *Honor/Dishonor* Still this root has a positive sense when used of a person's humbling himself, as in 2 Ki 22:19: "Because your heart was responsive and you humbled yourself before the LORD when you heard what I have spoken against this place and its people . . . and because you tore your robes and wept in my presence, I have heard you, declares the LORD."

Ḥāpār, like this word group, also suggests shame and disgrace. Other Hebrew words translated "humble" pick up the image of being low or bowing low and extend it to a low economic or political estate, including *šāpēl* and *šāḥaḥ*.

2. The blessings of humility. The OT speaks of the humility of Moses with commendation: "Now Moses was a very humble man, more humble than anyone else on the face of the earth" (Nu 12:3). The key to our interpretation is not so much in knowing which root is used as it is in noticing whether the person so described has humbled himself (and thus is characterized by humility) or has been humbled by God or enemies.

NT — 3. The Greek words for humility. In Greek culture, *tapeinos* and its derivatives were words of contempt. The Greeks saw man as the measure of all things. Thus, to be low on the social scale, to know poverty, or to be socially powerless was seen as shameful. Only seldom in classical Greek do these words have a positive tone, commending an unassuming or obedient attitude.

Scripture, however, sees the universe as measurable only against God. Compared to him, human beings are rightly viewed as humble. Thus in Scripture *tapeinos* and its derivatives are nearly always used in a positive sense (exceptions are in 2 Co 10:1; Col 2:18,23). *Tapeinos* represents a person's proper estimate of himself in relation to God and to others. In this sense, Jesus himself lived a humble life, depending completely on God and relating appropriately to all around him (Mt 11:29). It is the humble, Jesus says, whom God will exalt in his

good time (Lk 14:11; 18:14). While the thought of the OT about humility infuses the NT, we learn more about humility in the Gospels and the Epistles.

4. The humble lifestyle. What does the NT add to our understanding of humility?

Mt 18:1–4 helps us see humility expressed in relationship with God. The disciples asked Jesus who was greatest in the kingdom of heaven. The text tells us that Jesus "called a little child and had him stand among them." Jesus then told them that unless they were to "change and become like little children" they would be unable to enter heaven's kingdom. He explained, "Whoever humbles himself like this child is the greatest in the kingdom of heaven." Just before this, Jesus had presented himself to Israel as God's Son and their promised Messiah. ♦ *Christ* Israel refused to respond. But what of the child? When he was called, he came immediately, responding to Jesus' word. Humility in our relationship with God is seen when we refuse to stand in judgment on his Word but instead respond immediately, recognizing God as the ultimate authority in our life. The dependence and responsiveness of the child is to mark our attitude in our personal relationship with the Lord.

The NT often exhorts humility in relationships with other believers (e.g., Eph 4:2). Paul gives the example of Jesus' humility (Php 2:5–8) to encourage compliance with his exhortation: "In humility consider others better than yourselves. Each of you should look not only to your own interests, but also to the interests of others" (vv. 3–4).

This attitude is explored further in Ro 12:3–16. The introductory instruction goes like this: "Do not think of yourself more highly than you ought, but rather think of yourself with sober judgment, in accordance with the measure of faith God has given you" (v. 3). That faith is to find expression within the body of Christ, as each member of the body uses his gifts to serve his fellows. Moved by a sincere love, each is told, "Honor one another above yourselves" (v. 10), and "Do not be proud, but be willing to associate with people of low position. Do not be conceited" (v. 16).

It is in seeing others as persons of great worth because they are loved by God and in seeing ourselves as their servants that we find the fulfilling lifestyle of humility.

HUNGER AND THIRST

Famine and drought were among the most feared calamities of biblical times. Hunger and thirst represent humanity's most basic needs for survival. In a culture that saw God as the central reality, it is not surprising to find hunger and thirst linked in a number of ways with God.

In the material realm, God is looked to as the source of food and drink. At times God withholds food and drink for the benefit of his people. "He humbled you," Moses reminds the new generation, "causing you to hunger and thirst and then feeding you with manna . . . to teach you that man does not live on bread alone but on every word that comes from the mouth of the LORD" (Dt 8:3). When Israel would not learn dependence, she was judged for her sin by being made to endure hunger and thirst (Dt 28:47–48). The satisfaction of these basic needs is associated with restoration to the place of blessing (Isa 49:10).

God's concern for the basic needs of his people is to be reflected in their sensitivity to the needs of one another. Instruc..ng Israel on the worship God desires, Isaiah communicates this message from the Lord: "Is this not the kind of fasting I have chosen: to loose the chains of injustice and untie the cords of the yoke, to set the oppressed free and break every yoke? Is it not to share your food with the hungry and to provide the poor wanderer with shelter—when you see the naked, to clothe him, and not to turn away from your own flesh and blood?" (Isa 58:6–7). Both the OT and the NT give us this rule: "If your enemy is hungry, feed him; if he is thirsty, give him something to drink" (Ro 12:20; cf. Pr 25:21).

Hunger and thirst are extended in Scripture to represent basic spiritual needs that also require satisfaction. Often references to hunger or thirst express both physical and spiritual needs. "You still the hunger of those you cherish," the psalmist says (Ps 17:14). Only God is able to meet every need.

In both Testaments there are places where the focus is purely spiritual. For example: "As the deer pants for streams of water, so my soul pants for you, O God. My soul thirsts for God, for the living God. When can I go and meet with God?" (Ps 42:1–2). Jesus called those blessed who have a great inner hunger and thirst for righteousness and promised they would be satisfied. Awareness of spiritual need turns us to God, and it is in dependence on him that our needs will be met.

How exciting it is to read our Bible and to realize that in Jesus we have an endless supply of the Bread of Life (Jn 6:25–58) and that in the Holy Spirit we have an inexhaustible source of the Water of Life, bubbling up from within (Jn 7:37–39).

HUSBAND ♦ Marriage

HYPOCRITE

The Greek words hypokrinomai (appears once in the NT), hypokrisis (6 times in the NT), and hypokritēs (20 times in the NT) denote someone acting out the part of a character in a play. In Greek drama the actors held over their faces oversized masks painted to represent the character they were portraying. In life, the hypocrite is a person who masks his real self while he plays a part for his audience.

What characterizes the religious hypocrite? In Matthew's Gospel (where 16 of the 27 occurrences of these Greek words occur) we note these things:

1. A hypocrite does not act spontaneously from the heart but with calculation, to impress observers (Mt 6:1–3).

2. A hypocrite thinks only of the external trappings of religion, ignoring the central, heart issues of love for God and others (Mt 15:1–21).

3. A hypocrite uses spiritual talk to hide base motives (Mt 22:18–22).

Jesus gives this warning that to the hypocrites of every age: "Woe to you" (Mt 23:13,15,16,23,25,27,29).

I

IDOL/IMAGE

It is stated in the commandments: "Do not make for yourself an idol in the form of anything in heaven above or on the earth beneath or in the waters below. You shall not bow down to them or worship them" (Ex 20:4; cf. Dt 4:15–19).

The idol, or image, is anything that one may shape for use as an object of worship. The basic reason for this prohibition is that idols necessarily distort one's concept of God, who is spirit (Jn 4:24) and who must be worshiped in harmony with his nature. Human beings who worship idols are led from dependence on God to reliance on something that expresses their own religious thoughts and motivations. In Isa 2:8–22 the prophet asserts that idolatry is an expression of human pride and arrogance. He insists: "Stop trusting in man, who has but a breath in his nostrils. Of what account is he?" (v. 22).

Although idolatry is essentially a spiritual sin, representing rejection of the true God, it is a sin that has moral implications. This is seen clearly in Ro 1:18–32. Here Paul clearly rejects the theory that sees idolatry as "primitive" religion, which in time must naturally develop to "higher" forms. Paul portrays mankind as having a knowledge of God but suppressing the truth by their wickedness (1:18). People reject creation's testimony to the Creator and, instead of worshiping and thanking him, creates images to worship. This rejection of God cuts human beings off from a knowledge of their own moral character and denies them a standard against which to measure choices. Consequently they turn to all forms of immorality (1:26–27) and sin (1:28–31). Deep within these God-rejecters is a sense of sin, but rejection of a knowledge of God renders them unable and unwilling to repent (1:32).

This process of alienation had its culminating expression in Canaan and in Canaanite religion. Yet it was in Canaan that God led Israel to settle. The stern warnings against idolatry and the original inhabitants' practices linked with idolatry, are found throughout the OT. These passages, which use some ten different Hebrew terms for "idol" and "image," are found in nearly every Bible book up to the time of the Babylonian captivity. That exile purged Israel: after the exile, idolatry was no temptation to the Jewish people.

For a powerful satire on the futility of idolatry, see Isa 44:6–23.

Idolatry was widespread in the world of the first century. Paul warns believers to stay away from events featuring idol worship (1 Co 10:14). Although the idol has no real existence (1 Co 10:19; 12:2; Gal 4:8; 1 Th 1:9) and idol worship accomplishes nothing (1 Co 10:19), demonic beings are involved in pagan worship (1 Co 10:20–22), and immorality was often interwoven with it (1 Co 10:6–13).

The gospel's impact on pagan culture was powerful. In Ephesus, riots were stimulated by silversmiths whose business—producing and selling miniatures of the goddess Artemis—was ruined by the conversion of many people to Christ. This is particularly significant because Ephesus was one of the religious centers of Asia, and the great temple there was on the itinerary of tourists and pilgrims alike.

The condemnation of idolatry in the OT and the NT warns us against trusting ourselves to anything but God himself. In his powerful words interpreting Israel's history, Hosea shows the psychological impact that worship has on a people: "When I found Israel, it was like finding grapes in the desert; when I saw your fathers, it was like seeing the early fruit on the fig tree. But when they came to Baal Peor, they consecrated themselves to that shameful idol and became as vile as the thing they loved" (Hos 9:10). The potential for fruitfulness was destroyed as God's OT people became like that which they worshiped. How wonderful that we who believe can consecrate ourselves to the living Lord! Worshiping the Lord, we can, like him, become lovely and pure! ▶ *Holy/Holiness*

IGNORANCE

The Greek word *agnoeō* and its derivatives are used to express the idea of ignorance. While some argue that in a few instances *agnoeō* implies an ignorance that comes from lack of knowledge, all agree that human ignorance in spiritual affairs cannot be corrected simply by learning unknown facts.

The problem in spiritual ignorance is a misunderstanding that comes from a wrong perception of available data. Jesus' listeners heard what he told them, but they could not understand its meaning for them (Mk 9:32; Lk 9:45). Ignorance lies at the core of pagan worship (Ac 13:27) and explains the failure of all the lost to realize that it is God's kindness only, designed to lead them to repentance, that delays God's judgment (Ro 2:1–4).

These significant Greek words that express the concept of ignorance as misperception are as follows: *agnoeō*, "to be ignorant" (Mk 9:32; Lk 9:45; Ac 13:27; 17:23; Ro 1:13; 2:4; 6:3; 7:1; 10:3; 11:25; 1 Co 10:1; 12:1; 14:38; 2 Co 1:8; 2:11; 6:9; Gal 1:22; 1 Th 4:13; 1 Ti 1:13; Heb 5:2; 2 Pe 2:12), *agnoēma*, "a sin of ignorance" (Heb 9:7), *agnoia*, "ignorance" (Ac 3:17; 17:30; Eph 4:18; 1 Pe 1:14), and *agnōsia*, "lack of knowledge" (1 Co 15:34; 1 Pe 2:15).

What is the Bible's antidote to an ignorance that comes from failure to perceive spiritual realities? Rom 12:2 says, "Be transformed by the renewing of your mind" (*nous*, the mind as the organ of perception). It is by listening to God's will expressed in his Word and putting that will into practice that we will have a totally new outlook on life's issues. But inner transformation requires both a grasp of what the Word says and an obedient response to the Word. Only by a commitment to obedience to God can our ignorance be replaced by firm knowledge. ▶ *Know/Knowledge*

ILLNESS ▶ *Sick/Sickness*

IMAGE AND LIKENESS

These are theological words in both the OT and the NT. In the OT they are used to make important statements about the nature of man. In the NT they are used to make important statements about Jesus and about the destiny of those whose lives have been renewed through faith in him.

OT 1. Mankind in God's image and likeness
NT 2. Christ in God's image
 3. Christ in mankind's likeness
 4. Renewal of the image and likeness

OT — 1. Mankind in God's image and likeness. Two Hebrew words are used in OT passages that assert that man was made in the "image and likeness" of God (Ge 1:26–27; 5:1–3; 9:6).

The word *ṣelem* means "image," "representation." It is used five times in the OT (the passages cited above) in reference to people. Most of its uses are to designate an idol shaped in the form of a person or an animal.

Demût, translated "likeness," is a word of comparison. It is used to attempt to explain something by referring to something else that it is like. Although God makes it very clear that there is no way we can understand him by comparing him to a person or thing (Isa 40:18), we can understand the nature of man by comparing human beings with the Lord (Ge 1:26).

Only some biblical statements about human nature use ṣelem and dᵉmût together (Ge 1:26; 5:1,3). It is best to understand these words as necessarily linked in this theological statement. Man is a likeness–image of God.

The creation story makes it clear that the likeness–image is not of physical form: material for creation was taken from the earth. It is the inner nature of human beings that reflects something vital in the nature of God. Thus theologians generally agree that the likeness is rooted in all that is required to make a human being a person: in our intellectual, emotional, and moral likeness to God, who has revealed himself to us as a personal being.

It is this likeness–image that sets human beings apart from (the rest of) the animal creation, and it is transmitted through the process of reproduction to succeeding generations (Ge 5:1–3). It is this likeness–image of God that makes each human life so precious that nothing of however great value can possibly be offered in compensation for the taking of another's life (Ge 9:5–6).

Both Ge 1 and Ps 8 make it clear that with the likeness–image, God gave humanity a place of unique responsibility in the universe. Moved by wonder at God's gift of personal capacity to humanity, the psalmist writes: "What is man that you are mindful of him, the son of man that you care for him? You made him a little lower than the heavenly beings and crowned him with glory and honor. You made him ruler over the works of your hands; you put all things under his feet" (8:4–6).

NT — 2. Christ in God's image. The NT teaches that Jesus perfectly expressed the image of God. The Greek word for image is eikōn, which means "representation." In classical Greek thought, the eikōn had a share in the reality it expressed. This word is used several times to speak of Jesus' relationship with God. Paul calls Jesus "the image of God" (2 Co 4:4) and "the image of the invisible God" (Col 1:15). The word expresses the rela-

tionship of a coin to its die; that is, there is no comparison here but rather an exact expression of the thing from which the coin is molded. In Heb 1:3 Jesus is described as the "exact representation of his [God's] being" (charaktēr being the Greek word here—its only use in the NT—for "exact representation").

God is so perfectly expressed in Jesus that when Philip asked to be shown the Father, Jesus could say, "Anyone who has seen me has seen the Father" (Jn 14:9).

3. Christ in mankind's likeness. The NT word group expressing likeness is homoioō. It is often used in statements making comparisons, such as Jesus' frequent statements beginning "The kingdom of heaven is like. . . ." This word of comparison suggests similarity of kind, resemblance. Several times the NT affirms that in the Incarnation, Jesus was made "like his brothers" (Heb 9:17) and "in the likeness of sinful man" (Ro 8:3) or "in human likeness" (Php 2:7).

Although the NT never speaks of Jesus as being in the image of man, we should not conclude that he simply seemed to be human; for he is never said to be in the likeness of God, but he is fully God. ♦ *Appear/Appearance* (In the Bible we find the full deity and true humanity of Jesus [e.g., Jn 1:1,14; Heb 1–2].) Instead, we should note the delicacy of the distinction. Jesus in his person perfectly represented God as he truly is. Jesus could not perfectly represent man as he is, however, for humanity is tainted by sin. Jesus' human nature was untainted by sin. Thus, Jesus is in the image of humanity as it will be renewed when the drama of redemption is complete.

4. Renewal of the image and likeness. Even as sinners, human beings bear something of the ṣelem and the homoiōsis of God. The fall has not robbed us of personhood, though sin makes each person a sad mockery of the beauty that might have been ours.

Yet the gospel brings the bright promise of full restoration. The believer has "put on the new self, which is being renewed in knowledge in the image [eikōn] of its Creator" (Col 3:10). God's Spirit even now is at work within us, and we "are being transformed into his likeness [eikōn] with ever-increasing glory" (2 Co 3:18). When resurrection comes, we will know our destiny and be "conformed to the likeness [eikōn] of his Son" (Ro 8:29; cf. 1 Co 15:49–54). And John adds, "When he appears, we shall be like [homoios] him, for we shall see him as he is" (1 Jn 3:2).

IMAGES ♦ Idol/Image

IMITATE

Originally the Greek words translated "imitate" suggested an awkward attempt to ape someone else's behavior. But mimeomai (4 times in the NT) and mimētēs (7 times in the NT) are used only in a powerful, positive sense in Scripture. There "imitate" is an ethical concept. It is a call to reproduce in our own way of life those godly qualities that result from salvation and that we see in others. The idea is intimately linked with the thought that teachers and leaders ought to be clear, living examples of the practical implications of commitment to Jesus. ♦ Leadership ♦ Teaching/Learning

These Greek words are found in 1 Co 4:16; 11:1; Eph 5:1; 1 Th 1:6; 2:14; 2 Th 3:7,9; Heb 6:12; 13:7; 1 Pe 3:13; 3 Jn 11.

IMMORAL ♦ Adultery ♦ Evil

IMMORTAL ♦ Imperishable

IMPERISHABLE

Two Greek words are translated either "immortal" or "imperishable." The Scripture teaches that persons, like the universe in which we live, are now subject to decay and are under the control of sin. Aphtharsia (occurs 8 times in the NT) and aphthartos (occurs 7 times in the NT) indicate immunity to the decay that infects all of creation.

The NT declares that God is imperishable (Ro 1:23; 1 Ti 1:17) and has brought the possibility of imperishability for hu-

man beings to light in the gospel (2 Ti 1:10). God has planted new life in believers through his own incorruptible seed (1 Pe 1:23). The core of our personality now is beyond the forces associated with death. Finally in the resurrection we will be completely clothed with immortality (1 Co 15:42,50,52–54).

These interesting Greek words are rendered by various English words. Aphthartos is rendered "unfading" in three passages (1 Pe 1:4; 1:23; 3:4), "that will last forever" in three passages (Ro 1:23; 1 Co 9:25; 15:52), and "integrity" once (1 Ti 1:17). Aphtharsia is rendered "undying" in five passages (1 Co 15:42,50,53,54; Eph 6:24), "integrity" in two passages (2 Ti 1:10; Tit 2:7), and "that will last forever" once (Ro 2:7).

IMPOSSIBLE

The Greek words rendered "impossible" are adynateō (verb, 2 occurrences in the NT) and adynatos (adjective, 10 occurrences in the NT). These words indicate that, because the nature of a person or thing lacks a certain ability, that person or thing cannot do some specified action. Thus the adjective means "powerless, or impotent." What is impossible for unaided human beings (Mt 19:26; Mk 10:27) is possible with God (Mt 17:20; Lk 1:37). It is of course impossible for God to lie, for his nature lacks that capacity (Heb 6:18).

What are the impossible things mentioned in the NT? See Mt 19:26; Mk 10:27; Lk 18:27; Ac 14:8; Ro 8:3; 15:1 (where the noun means "weaknesses"); Heb 6:4,18; 10:4; 15:3.

IMPURE ♦ Pure/Impure

INCENSE

A number of Hebrew words meaning "incense" or the "odor of burning sacrifice" are found in the OT. Incense was burned as something especially pleasing; in both Testaments it is used to symbolize prayer (e.g., Ps 141:2; Lk 1:10).

Incense was usually made by mixing various aromatic substances. Some incense was pure frankincense, the resin of certain trees. Incense was used by the wealthy and is associated with luxury. It was burned at parties (Eze 23:41) and at funerals (2 Ch 16:14; cf. Jer 34:5). It was also used in the worship of pagan deities (e.g., 1 Ki 11:8; 2 Ch 30:14).

Incense was used in several ways in worship of the Lord. The priests prepared a special mixture of incense to be used only in worship and offered it on incense burners (Ex 30:35–37). It was also added to some of the offerings burned in sacrifice (e.g., Lev 2:1–2; 6:15; 24:7).

The figure of incense is used in the NT to indicate that which is especially pleasing to God, a special gift added to basic commitment (Php 4:14–19). The knowledge of Jesus spread by the evangelists is viewed as the rich fragrance of incense permeating the known world (2 Co 2:14–17). And the prayers of the saints are symbolized as rising clouds of incense drifting up to heaven (Rev 5:8; 8:3–4).

INCREASE ♦ Grow/Increase

INHERITANCE

The concept of the believer's inheritance is significant in the Bible. Although the nature of the inheritance shifts, as does the context of the legal system under which the believer inherits, there is an exciting message communicated in the OT and NT alike that portrays our relationship with the Lord.

OT 1. The Hebrew terms
    2. The material and spiritual inheritance
NT 3. The Roman legal system
    4. Heirs of God
    5. Our joint inheritance

OT — 1. The Hebrew terms. Two Hebrew word groups are linked with the idea of inheritance. *Yāraš* means "to become an heir" or "to take possession." *Nāḥal* indicates giving or receiving property as a permanent possession. It is usually but not always used of property transmitted as a result of succession. Of special note is the stress on the idea of permanent possession. A central OT concept is that God gave Israel the land of Palestine as a *naḥᵃlâh*. That gift established Israel's claim to Palestine "forever." Modern Israeli expansion within Israel's biblical borders, even into land currently occupied by Arabs, is considered by many in Israel to be simply exercising an ancient right.

2. The material and spiritual inheritance. The covenant God gave to Abraham, and later expanded and confirmed, emphasizes possession of Palestine. ♦ *Covenant* Most references to inheritance or possession in the OT focus on transmission of material objects or property. The inheritance that God gave Israel is usually understood as the land of Palestine, which was divided among the tribes in the time of Joshua, with plots given to each family as a permanent possession. Although disobedient generations of Israelites might be driven from the land, God committed himself by covenant to give to the descendants of Abraham, Isaac, and Jacob "all this land" to be "their inheritance forever" (Ex 32:13). The psalms praise God for his commitment and remind Israel that it is those who are in right relationship with God — the meek and the righteous (e.g., Ps 37:11) — who will ultimately take full possession of the promised inheritance.

While the OT focuses on tangible possessions as inheritance, there is also a model for intangible inheritance. The priests and Levites were not given plots of land as their inheritance. They were to be supported by the offerings and sacrifices made by their brothers at the temple, for, the OT says, "The LORD is their inheritance" (Dt 18:2).

NT — 3. The Roman legal system. Passages in the Gospels that refer to heirs and inheriting most likely reflect the OT legal system, which sees inheritance as the passing of property at a person's death to those who at that time become his heirs. Paul's use of the metaphor seems to reflect principles drawn from Roman law. Under Roman law the inheritance is made up of the total tangible and intangible assets of a person. While these will pass to heirs on his death, it does not require the parent's death to make his children heirs. In fact, under Roman law, birth into the family establishes a person's right as an heir. What is more, while the parent retains the right to manage his property, the children are in a sense considered co-owners of all that is their father's. Relationship itself establishes one's right to a share of all that is possessed by the family.

4. Heirs of God. When Paul writes in Ro 8:17, "if we are children, then we are heirs," he reflects a principle of Roman inheritance law. In the OT system, as in ours, a person must die before others become his heirs. In Roman law, it was birth, not death, that established heirship. Because we have been born again through faith in Jesus and have become God's children, we have full rights as heirs to all that is our Father's (Ro 9:6–8; Gal 3:6–7,28–29).

As God's heirs we are in a real sense currently "owners" of all the good things, tangible and intangible, to be found in God. The blessings we receive now are from the rich store of his wealth, distributed at his will, but truly our own. One day we will possess fully what we currently own.

5. Our joint inheritance. Eph 3:6 says that believers of every age are "heirs together" and are "sharers together in the promise in Christ Jesus." As joint heirs in a family whose father lives now and forever, we have the certainty that the tangible and intangible property that belongs to God will be used to benefit all in the family.

It is exciting to see in the NT those things that are our inheritance. The main emphasis is on the kingdom of God (Mt 25:34; 1 Co 6:9–10; 15:50; Gal 5:21; Eph 5:5; Jas 2:5). ♦ *Kingdom* There is also an emphasis placed on salvation (Heb 1:14; cf. Eph 1:14). Because of the unique character of Roman law, the NT can affirm both that we already do own this wonderful inheritance and that we will come into a full experience of it in the future. Because inheritance law was based on birth and not on the determina-

tion of one's heirs at the time of his death, we can be sure *now* that in Christ, and through the new birth, we have already come "into an inheritance that can never perish, spoil, or fade—kept in heaven for [us]" (1 Pe 1:4).

INIQUITY ♦ *Sin*

INJUSTICE ♦ *Justice/Injustice*

INNOCENT

The Hebrew word for "innocent" used most frequently in the OT is *nāqî*. It is derived from a root that means "to be clean." The extended judicial meaning is "to be innocent"; that is, clear of a charge, or acquitted, or exempt from an obligation.

The NT occurrences of "innocent" in the NIV and the NASB are actually translations of a number of different Greek words with various meanings.

In Mt 10:6 and Ro 16:19 (and in Php 2:15, where the NIV reads "pure") the word is *akeraios*. It means "simple," "pure," "unadulterated by evil."

The two NT occurrences of the word *anaitios* are in Mt 12:5,7. It means "innocent" in the sense of "guiltless."

The word *athōos* (found only in Mt 27:4,24) also means "guiltless." Judas and Pilate both realized that Jesus was guiltless, but each played a role in Jesus' crucifixion.

In Lk 23:47 the centurion observing Jesus' execution said, "Surely this was a righteous [*dikaios*] man," as the NIV customarily and correctly translates the Greek word.

In Ac 20:26 the word is *katharos*, "clean." Paul could not be charged with the blood of any, for, he said, "I have not hesitated to proclaim to you the whole will of God" (v. 27).

In 1 Co 4:4 the word is *dikaioō*, "to justify or declare to be in the right." ♦ *Justify/Justification*

In 2 Co 7:11 the word is *hagnos*, "to be free of ceremonial defilement."

In Heb 7:26 it is *akakos,* here meaning "without any taint of what is bad or wrong."

Finally, in Ja 5:6 the word is *dikaios,* "righteous."

INQUIRE ◆ *Lead/Guide*

INSIGHT

Several OT terms are translated "insight" in the NIV and the NASB. Their emphasis is on a practical wisdom that leads to successful actions. Thus a counselor with insight is one who is able to advise a course of action that will be best in a specific situation.

In the NT, "insight" is *synesis* (except in Eph 1:8, where NASB so translates *phronēsis,* the other occurrence of this Greek word being in Lk 1:17). Insight has to do with understanding in the spiritual realm, with an emphasis on how spiritual truths can be applied to guide action in life situations. The people marveled at Jesus for his insight (Lk 2:47), and believers have been given insight into spiritual realities through Christ and his Spirit. This significant Greek word occurs seven times in the NT (Mk 12:33; Lk 2:47; 1 Co 1:19; Eph 3:4; Col 1:9; 2:2; 2 Ti 2:7).

INSTRUCT ◆ *Teaching/Learning*

INSULT

In the OT, "insult" most often is either *kālam* or *ḥārap. Kālam* is associated with disgrace, shame, and public dishonor and is an attempt to humiliate another publicly, with the intention of wounding his spirit. ◆ *Honor/Dishonor Ḥārap* is to insult by reproaching, by heaping public blame or scorn on another.

In the NT a number of different word groups give different shades of meaning to the passages in which the NASB and the NIV read "insult."

Loidoreō means "verbal abuse." It is found in Jn 9:28; Ac 23:4; 1 Co 4:12; 1 Pe 2:23. Two related words appear twice each in the NT—*loidoria* (1 Ti 5:14; 1 Pe 3:9) and *loidoros* (1 Co 5:11; 6:10).

Oneidizō and its derivative *oneidismos* are strong words; they indicate being publicly reviled and insulted. Jesus suffered this fate, and believers may also be reviled for the name of Christ. This root is found where the NIV and the NASB read "insult" in Mt 5:11; 27:44; Mk 15:32; Lk 6:22; Ro 15:3; 1 Pe 4:14; Heb 10:33. It is also found in Mt 11:20; Mk 16:14; Lk 1:25; 1 Ti 3:7; 4:10; Heb 11:26; 13:13; Jas 1:5.

Hybrizō (5 occurrences in the NT), *hybris* (3 occurrences in the NT), *hybristēs* (2 occurrences in the NT), and *enybrizō* (once in the NT) suggest harm done to another by mistreatment or by insults meant to shame. This root is found where the English versions read "insult" at Lk 11:45; 18:32; 2 Co 12:10; 1 Th 2:2; Heb 10:29. In this last passage a deliberate choice to "keep on sinning" amounts to "trampling the Son of God under foot" and "insulting" in a most arrogant and violent way "the Spirit of grace." This root is also found in Mt 22:6; Ac 14:5; 27:10,12; Ro 1:30; 1 Th 1:13.

Other words are translated "insult" only in the NIV. The Greek word in Mt 27:39 and Lk 23:39 is *blasphēmeō* ("to slander, revile"). In Jas 2:6 the word is *atimazō* ("dishonor"), which is found a total of six times in the NT.

In both the OT and the NT, "insult" means more than casual or critical comment. It means an active and vindictive attempt to slander and thus to harm the person insulted.

INTERCEDE

In the OT, the words translated "intercede" are usually either *pālal* or *pāga'.* Both are used for prayer, the first stressing intervening or interposing, the second denoting a meeting or encounter. Key examples of intercessory prayer are found in Abraham's prayer for the inhabitants of Sodom (Ge 18:16–33) and Moses' prayer for a sinning Israel (Nu 14:10–19).

In the NT, the main word for "intercession" is *entynchanō* (5 occurrences), which means "to plead on behalf of someone." Besides being used in Ro 8:27,34; Heb 7:25, it is found in Ac 25:24 (in regard to the Jewish community's petition to Festus against the apostle Paul) and in Ro 11:2 (to describe Elijah's appeal to God against a sinning Israel). The Holy Spirit exercises this ministry in its most intensive degree (*hyperentynchanō*, only here in the NT), according to Ro 8:26.

INTERPRET

Diermēneuō (6 occurrences in the NT) means "to translate." As used in the NT it means "to explain." Except for Lk 24:27, it involves the utterances of a person speaking in tongues. ♦ *Tongues*

ISRAEL

The name Israel is used in a number of closely linked ways in the OT. At times the meanings are so interwoven that it is difficult to say which is to be emphasized.

As a personal name. Jacob, the son of Isaac and grandson of Abraham, wrestled with the angel of the Lord when returning to Palestine. ♦ *Angels* After the night-long struggle, his name was changed to Israel (Ge 32:28; 35:10). This compound name is usually taken to mean "prince with God."

As a tribal name. The descendants of Israel's sons retained their family identity. This is theologically important, as God's covenant promises were given to the progeny of Abraham, Isaac, and Jacob (Israel). In the OT, "Israel" is often used in this sense, thus affirming the identity of the people of God as a distinct religious community (e.g., Ex 1:1; 3:16; 12:3; Dt 1:38).

As a national name. The people of Israel (as a family) were delivered from slavery in Egypt. They were led by God to Palestine, the land promised to their forefathers by the Lord. ♦ *Inheritance* There the family took on another dimension, becoming a nation as well as a people. The Mosaic Law was the national code as well as the religious code for Israel. At times in the OT, "Israel" stands for the nation (e.g., Jdg 19:1; 2 Sa 1:12; 1 Ki 9:5). In the same sense, it stands for

the land occupied or claimed by the nation.

As a splinter kingdom. After the death of King Solomon, the nation was divided geographically. The territory occupied by the ten northern tribes became the separate kingdom of Israel. The territory occupied by the two southern tribes became the separate kingdom of Judah. During this era, the history of which is given from 1 Ki 11 through 2 Ki 25, "Israel" is sometimes used to designate this northern kingdom, sometimes it is used in other senses.

As a restored people or district. The northern kingdom was destroyed in 722 B.C., and in 586 B.C. the people of the southern kingdom were deported to Babylon. After a time of exile, a group of the Jewish people returned to the Promised Land. They did not set up an independent nation but remained a province in a larger empire. In the books of Ezra and Nehemiah and in the Gospels, "Israel" is used in most of the OT senses to indicate the religious community, the land, and the ethnic entity that looked forward to a restored national identity.

As a prophetic entity. The OT portrays a bright destiny for the descendants of Jacob. This destiny involves a religious conversion, reestablishment of a national identity, reoccupation of the Promised Land, and many associated blessings. Often in the OT the prophets speak of "Israel" in ways that incorporate all these meanings (e.g., Isa 44:21–23; 45:17; Jer 31:21–37; Amos 9:7–15).

As believers within the national community. Many of the physical descendants of Israel had no vital personal relationship with the Lord. Paul argues in Ro 9 that "not all who are descended from Israel are Israel. . . . It is not the natural children who are God's children, but it is the children of the promise who are regarded as Abraham's offspring" (vv. 6,8). This concept is expressed in the OT doctrine of the remnant and is evidenced in history (e.g., 1 Ki 19:14–18; Zep 3:13). ♦ *Remnant/Survivors* Paul also presents the stunning fact that through the gospel, Gentiles are brought into the covenant and thus into the religious community (Eph 3:6; cf. Heb 8:1–13). In this limited religious sense, all believers are "Israel" and Abraham's spiritual descendants.

The many different ways in which "Israel" is used has naturally led to confusion about the promises given Israel in the OT. Are these metaphors? That is, do they present a spiritual meaning that is presently experienced by Christians? Are Israel of the OT and the church of the NT distinctive aspects of God's plan, or do they blend together into one? Is the future of the nation of Israel as it is presented in the OT still to be realized in history?

These questions are important, for the answers a person gives shape many aspects of his theology and of his understanding of Scripture. While the NT does not go into detail about the future, Jesus' own prophetic statements are in harmony with the OT picture. When the question "Are you at this time going to restore the kingdom to Israel?" was asked by his disciples (Ac 1:6), Jesus replied that only the Father knows the times and dates (Ac 1:7).

Dealing with the question in depth, Paul devotes chapters 9 through 11 of Romans to examine the situation of Israel. He portrays the opening of the door of faith to the Gentiles as the grafting of wild olive branches on a cultivated tree and promises that this purposeful setting aside of Israel is not permanent. Looking back to the OT, Paul praises God, for "God's gifts and his call are irrevocable" (11:29). Thus, the OT picture of Israel's future still awaits realization at the return of Christ.

J

JEALOUSY/ZEAL

One Hebrew word and one Greek word can both be translated either "jealousy" or "zeal." The distinction is not in the terms (*qānā'*, Hebrew; *zēloō*, Greek). Instead, it is found in the relationship of the person to the thing that is desired.

OT 1. Jealousy and envy
      2. The jealous zeal of God
NT 3. Jealousy
      4. Zeal
      5. Summary

OT — 1. Jealousy and envy. The Hebrew root meaning "jealousy" portrays a very strong emotion, a passionate desire. The word is used in both a positive and a negative sense. In the negative it is a desire for something that properly belongs to another (e.g., Ge 30:1; 37:11). When referring to the emotion itself, and not to the relationship between one person and another or between a person and an object, *qānā'* is often translated "envy" (e.g., Pr 3:31; 23:17).

The strong emotion represented by *qānā'* can be viewed positively as a high level of commitment when it describes the feeling of a person for something that is rightly his or her own. Here "jealousy" has the sense of intense love. When applied to God, "jealousy" communicates the fierce intensity of his commitment to his people, even when they turn from him.

2. The jealous zeal of God. In the Mosaic Law, special provision was made for testing the faithfulness of a wife if her spouse should begin to feel jealous (Nu 5). Jealousy in marriage is an image used in the OT to describe the relationship between God and his covenant people, paralleling the relationship between husband and wife.

In giving the Mosaic Law, the Lord announced to the people of Israel that they must remain committed to him and not turn to idolatry, and he gave this reason for it: "I, the LORD your God, am a jealous God" (Ex 20:5). The jealousy of God is expressed in OT history both in "punishing" and in "showing love" (vv. 5–6).

In the OT, God is said to be jealous for his people, for his land (Joel 2:18), and for Jerusalem and Zion (Zec 1:14). While the anger of God is an expression of God's jealous wrath, the acts of judgment recorded in the OT continue to be for the ultimate benefit of a people who must be brought back to a right relationship with God if they are to experience blessing. ♦ *Anger* ♦ *Punishment*

NT — 3. Jealousy. In NT passages where *zēloō* and its derivatives are translated "jealous," the tone is nearly always negative. The Jews were jealous of the Gentiles' response to the gospel (Ac 5:17; 13:45; 17:5). In each case this jealousy motivated hostile acts. It may be this link with sinful actions that is stressed in the NT. Jealousy is often found linked with "outbursts of anger" (2 Co 12:20; cf. Gal 5:20) and dissension (Ro 13:13; 1 Co 3:3) in the NT's lists of the behavior that springs from man's fallen nature.

Stephen refers to the patriarchs' jealousy of Joseph (Ac 7:9), and Paul makes mention of Israel's attempt to provoke God to jealousy (1 Co 10:22). Only in 2 Co 11:2, where Paul speaks of his own jealousy over the Corinthians as being like God's jealousy (a fierce desire for what is best for them because they are his own), is the word used in a positive way.

4. Zeal. In a few NT cases, *zēloō* appears to focus on the emotional drive itself. The translators tend to translate this as "zeal." Thus Paul uses this word to describe the zeal of his fellow Jews and his own passionate persecution of the church (Ro 10:2; Php 3:6). In Ro 12:11 he urges believers, "Never be lacking in zeal." But he adds a warning in Galatians: "It is fine to be zealous, provided the purpose is good" (4:18).

5. Summary. Neither God nor humans are cold, computerlike beings. Persons have emotions as well as intellect and will, and often these emotions are strong. Jealousy, or zeal, is one of the stronger emotions.

God's jealousy, although it issues in punishment as well as blessing, is viewed as something both righteous and good. In general, human jealousy is viewed with suspicion. Our emotions are too often tainted by the sin that twists human personalities. But we can experience strong emotional commitments to what is good, as well as strong emotional desires for what is not our own.

It is good to remember that God's desire, as he works in our lives, is not to rob us of our emotions. Instead, he wants to capture and channel our capacity for intense commitment. He wants us to have a godly jealousy for others, and to be zealous for everything that is good.

JERUSALEM

The name of this city recurs again and again in both the OT and the NT. A survey of the Testaments suggests the reasons for this.

1. Jerusalem's historical significance
2. Jerusalem's theological centrality
3. Jerusalem's prophetic destiny

1. Jerusalem's historical significance. In the time of David, the city of Jerusalem was occupied by Canaanite peoples. It lay secure on mountainous heights in a wedge of land between the southern and northern sections of the land then occupied by the twelve tribes of Israel. David took the city by force. His action was politically motivated: there was historic jealousy between the two sections of Israel. By establishing his capitol in the captured city of Jerusalem, David was able to avoid the jealousy that might have occurred if he had chosen a site in either the north or the south.

It was during the reign of David and Solomon that this city was developed not only as the capital of a united Israel but also as its worship center. Throughout subsequent sacred history, Jerusalem was viewed as the place where God had established his name, and succeeding temples were always built on the original site. ♦ *Tabernacle and Temple*

Most of the events of Bible history have their focus in Jerusalem, which became the central location that represents for all time Israel's occupation of the Promised Land.

2. Jerusalem's theological significance. Jerusalem became the political and religious center of the life of Israel. Israel's kings ruled here, and it was here that the temple, which symbolized the unity of the people and its faith, was constructed. Most of the events of OT history after the monarchy was established focus on Jerusalem, and it is in part from these events that Jerusalem derives her theological significance.

Historic revivals were initiated in Jerusalem by godly kings, and here too apostasy was spread by evil rulers. In a real sense, the spiritual condition of Jerusalem at any time in history was a barometer of the spiritual condition of the nation. The ministry of the great OT prophets, such as Isaiah and Jeremiah, took place in Jerusalem—as did the murder of so many of the messengers God sent to warn his people.

Much of Jesus' ministry took place in Jerusalem. Jerusalem was the home of the leaders who so fiercely resented him and who plotted to achieve his execution. It was outside the walls of the Holy City that Jesus died, was buried, and rose again. And it was in Jerusalem that the gospel was first preached and the first church formed.

Both the magnificent and the dreadful events of sacred history combine to give Jerusalem a unique place in Scripture, and they give it its distinctive theological associations. Paul saw the historic Jerusalem and the Jerusalem of his day as representative of slavery. Again and again the freeing power of God was rejected by Israel, and her experience demonstrates the destructive power of law when law is confused with faith as a way of salvation (Gal 4:21–31).

3. Jerusalem's prophetic destiny. The OT portrays a distinctive future for God's people. The children of Israel will be restored to nationhood, to be exalted over the other nations of the world. Jerusalem will be the worship center of the world when the promised time of renewal comes. The Messiah will take his waiting throne, and the nation will be secure. This future is affirmed by most of the prophets (especially Zec 12–14).

The NT introduces the concept of a heavenly Jerusalem. All that Jerusalem has been in sacred history as a political and religious center has foreshadowed what God intends to do on earth. That perfect future world center of political and religious life is spoken of as the new or heavenly Jerusalem (Heb 12:22; Rev 3:12; 21:2,10).

JESUS

The name Jesus is a transliteration of the Greek form of the Hebrew name Joshua. The meaning of the Hebrew name is "Yahweh is salvation." The name was chosen by God and communicated to Joseph and Mary by an angel. ◆ *Angels* The child was to be named Jesus because he was to "save his people from their sins" (Mt 1:21; cf. Lk 1:31).

In the context of the story of Jesus' birth it was also announced that Jesus would be "God with us" (Mt 1:23) and that he would fulfill all the messianic

prophecies associated with the Davidic throne (Lk 1:32–33). ◆ *Christ* ◆ *Covenant*

The deity, the humanity, and the work of Jesus are explored through many of the words in this volume. See "Jesus" in the index for a complete listing of words to study to develop an understanding of who Jesus is and what he has done for us.

JEW

Today the word "Jew" indicates an ethnic group or a religious group. But the name is used in several senses in the NT, leading to some confusion when we read the Gospels.

OT 1. Origin of the designation "Jew"
NT 2. Uses of "Jew" in the Gospels
    3. Uses of "Jew" in the Epistles

OT — 1. Origin of the designation "Jew". The name is derived from the name "Judah." Judah was one of the sons of Israel. But it is only at the time of David that this tribal name became important to denote the southern section of the land of Israel. ◆ *Israel* After Solomon's death, when the land was divided into two kingdoms, the southern section became known as Judah. This name in later OT history is the source of "Jew," which means "a citizen of Judah." Even after the Babylonian captivity the name was retained, and the Hebrew people were known as "men of Judah"—i.e., Jews.

NT — 2. Uses of "Jew" in the Gospels. After the return of a remnant from Babylon to rebuild Jerusalem, the province in which they lived was known as Judah, and they continued to be known as Jews.

However, additional meanings of the name developed. A survey of its uses in John's Gospel shows us the different ways in which it is used in the NT. In any given context we need to look carefully to distinguish the writer's intended meaning. In John's Gospel, "Jew" can indicate:

a. The Jewish people (2:6,13; 3:1,25; 4:9,22; 5:1; 6:4; 7:2; 8:52; 11:55; 18:12,35; 19:21,40,42)
b. Judeans, the people who lived in and around Jerusalem (11:8,19,31,33,36, 45,54; 12:9,11; 19:20)
c. People hostile to Jesus (6:41,52; 8:48,52,57; 10:19,24,31,33; 18:20,38; 19:7, 12,14)
d. The authorities in Jerusalem who exercised political and religious control (1:19; 2:18,20; 5:10,15,16,18; 7:1,11,13, 15,35; 8:22; 9:18,22; 13:33; 18:14,31,36; 19:31,38; 20:19)

3. Uses of "Jew" in the Epistles. In the Epistles, references to the Jews are made on the assumption that they are a well-defined group with a distinctive racial heritage and religious outlook. In nearly all the cities of the first-century Roman Empire, well-defined Jewish communities were established early. ♦ *Citizen* ♦ *Alien/Aliens*

JOY

A number of words in both Testaments express the joy that human beings experience. Joy is found in the good things of this life and in expectation of God's work in the future. Tracing the concept of joy through the Bible helps us realize that our happiness, like our hope, is founded on realities that are unaffected by conditions in this world.

OT 1. Hebrew words for joy
2. Relationship with God as the source of a believer's joy
NT 3. Greek words for joy
4. Insights into the believer's joy
5. Summary

OT — 1. Hebrew words for joy. A number of different Hebrew words are translated "joy." Some of the key terms are (1) *gîl*, which is joy at God's works or attributes, (2) *rānan*, jubilant shouts expressed at times of sacrifice and over God's saving works, (3) *śûś*, glad enthusiasm provoked by God and his Word; and (4) *śāmah*, a glad or joyful disposition.

Often in the OT, joy is not so much a private emotion as it is the enthusiastic response of a feasting company or wor-

shiping community to God's tangible and intangible blessings. This joy is an expressed joy: it is expressed in glad shouts, in praise, in laughter, and in enthusiastic commitment to God's ways.

2. Relationship with God as the source of a believer's joy. There is no doubt that the OT portrays joy, like every other aspect of life on earth, as dependent on God's goodness. Although there is a direct joy that comes from a personal relationship with the Lord (Ps 16:11), all other joy is from him as well.

Obedience to God led to rich harvests and to joy expressed in celebration of the Feast of Tabernacles. "The LORD your God will bless you in all your harvest and in all the work of your hands, and your joy will be complete" (Dt 16:15).

The memory of God's saving acts was a constant source of joy. We sense the joy of praise in David's psalm recorded in 1 Ch 16: "Sing to the LORD, all the earth; proclaim his salvation day after day. Declare his glory among the nations, his marvelous deeds among all peoples. For great is the LORD and most worthy of praise; he is to be feared above all gods. For all the gods of the nations are idols, but the LORD made the heavens. Splendor and majesty are before him; strength and joy in his dwelling place. Ascribe to the LORD, O families of nations, ascribe to the LORD glory and strength, ascribe to the LORD the glory due to his name. Bring an offering and come before him; worship the LORD in the splendor of his holiness. Tremble before him, all the earth! The world is firmly established; it cannot be moved. Let the heavens rejoice, let the earth be glad; let them say among the nations, 'The LORD reigns!' " (16:23–31).

The believer's relationship with God was a source of joy in another way. The obedient believer finds God's Word to be a source of joy (Ps 19:8; 119:14); likewise, the trusting believer rejoices in God's promises (Ps 119:162). It is in commitment to God that the believer finds an inner and hidden spring of joy bubbling up within the heart.

In the OT as well as the NT, a person's relationship with God is characterized by hope and by faith. Often one's situation is difficult or even dangerous. In times of trouble the believer finds joy in the expectation that God will act to deliver. Ps 33 expresses this theme beautifully: "No king is saved by the size of his army; no warrior escapes by his great strength. A horse is a vain hope for deliverance; despite all its great strength it cannot save. But the eyes of the LORD are on those who fear him, on those whose hope is in his unfailing love, to deliver them from death and keep them alive in famine. We wait in hope for the LORD; he is our help and our shield. In him our hearts rejoice, for we trust in his holy name. May your unfailing love rest upon us, O LORD, even as we put our hope in you" (33:16–22).

NT — 3. Greek words for joy. There are three different word groups in the NT that express the idea of joy. *Agalliaō* is a loud, public expression of joy in worship. It focuses attention on God and his past and future work for the believer. *Euphrainō* emphasizes a community joy, expressed by believers in times of religious festival or neighborly banquet. It does not describe the feelings of the individual as much as the atmosphere of shared enjoyment. *Chairō* is the word for joy that is used most often in the NT. It has reference to both the subjective state of joy and the things that bring joy. Each of these words is used in the Septuagint to translate several of the OT terms for joy. The NT retains the basic OT outlook on joy.

4. Insights into the believer's joy. Every human being is hungry for joy. The NT provides a number of insights into how those who know Jesus can experience joy through faith.

Intimate relationship with Jesus is a source of joy. Two teachings of Christ, reported by John, describe this relationship: "If you obey my commands, you will remain in my love, just as I have obeyed my Father's commands and remain in his love. I have told you this so that my joy may be in you and that your joy may be complete" (Jn 15:10–11). "Until now you have not asked for anything in my name. Ask and you will

receive, and your joy will be complete" (Jn 16:24).

The believer's joy is produced within, by the Holy Spirit (Lk 10:21; Ro 14:17; Gal 5:22; 1 Th 1:6). The joy of the pagan is found in God's material blessings (Ac 14:17), but the Christian's joy is unique in that it is an outcome of salvation (Ac 8:8; 16:34) found through trust in God (Ro 15:13).

The NT often links joy with persecution. Jesus spoke in prayer of the antagonism of the world to him and to his followers and asked that his followers might have "the full measure" of his joy within them (Jn 17:13). The reaction of the early missionaries to persecution was a glowing, inner joy that seemed to deny circumstances (Ac 13:52; cf. 2 Co 7:4; Jas 1:2). In his first epistle, Peter describes the believer's joy despite suffering: "In this [salvation] you greatly rejoice, though now for a little while you may have had to suffer grief in all kinds of trials. These have come so that your faith—of greater worth than gold, which perishes even though refined by fire— may be proved genuine and may result in praise, glory and honor when Jesus Christ is revealed. Though you have not seen him, you love him; and even though you do not see him now, you believe in him and are filled with an inexpressible and glorious joy, for you are receiving the goal of your faith, the salvation of your souls" (1 Pe 1:6–9). The saving work of God within us provides an inexpressible joy, whatever our circumstances.

Joy is most often linked in the NT with God's work in fellow believers whom we love and whom we serve. This thought is behind the joy spoken of in a number of passages (Ro 16:19; 2 Co 1:24; 7:7; Php 1:4,25–26; 2:2,29; 4:1; 1 Th 2:19–20; 3:9; 2 Ti 1:4; Phm 7; Heb 13:17; 1 Jn 1:4; 2 Jn 4,12; 3 Jn 3–4).

5. Summary. A sense of joy pervades the Bible. The OT looks most closely at the joy of the believing community gathered to worship and praise God. Joy is an emotion that is evoked by remembering God and his work and by the confident expectation that God will act to deliver when troubles come. One's relationship with God, maintained by obedient response to his Word, is a source of joy. Joy is surely associated with an abundance of the good things of this life. But joy is essentially a religious experience. The NT suggests that pagans find joy in God's material blessings. But, again, true joy is essentially a religious experience. It is found in a saving relationship with God and in maintaining fellowship with him. Love, expressed in prayer and obedience, is the key to the Christian's full experience of joy. The NT sees joy as something that is independent of circumstances. The believer's joy is found in the inner work of the Holy Spirit, who, despite trials or suffering, is bringing us to salvation. Thus joy, like peace, is rooted in trust in the Lord. As for externals, the greatest source of joy for the Christian is found in serving other believers and in seeing God work in their lives.

JUDAH ▶ Jew

JUDGE/JUDGING

Don't judge one another, the NT warns. Yet we are also told to maintain church discipline! Does the Bible solve such puzzles? Yes. And it adds an insight that will enrich our reading of the OT.

OT 1. The OT concept
NT 2. The NT concept
    3. God alone is judge
    4. What we are not to judge
    5. What we are commanded to judge
    6. Church discipline
    7. Summary

OT — 1. The OT concept. Two Hebrew synonyms are translated "judge" and "judgment." *Dîn* is a poetic form that occurs forty-three times, usually in the Psalms and the Prophets. More common are forms of *šāpaṭ* ("to judge," "to govern") and the derivative *mišpāṭ* ("judgment," "decision").

Each of these synonyms expresses the idea of governing and implies every function of government. Each includes

executive and legislative as well as judicial functions.

In our culture the various functions of government are divided, and the separation of powers is fiercely guarded. In the OT world such departmentalization did not exist. A ruler decided disputes and acquitted or punished the accused. But the ruler also had legislative and executive responsibility, and he led his people. So we are misled if we think of the biblical "judge" only in a modern judicial sense. Like the "judges" who ruled Israel after Joshua, such persons were governors in the fullest sense. So when *dîn* or forms of *šāpaṭ* occur, translators of the English versions often selected an English word that emphasizes the aspect of government suggested by the context. Even so, when we read the word "judge" in the OT, we need to keep the broad meaning of "rule" or "ruler" in view.

The OT makes it clear that the ultimate ruler of the universe is God. All human governing authority is derived from him. Often where the OT speaks of God as judge, it is his ultimate sovereignty as governor of the universe, and not simply his role as moral arbiter, that is in view. We see the interplay clearly in Ps 96:10–13, where God is pictured as "judge" in all the rich meaning of that word. "Say among the nations, 'The LORD reigns.' The world is firmly established, it cannot be moved; he will judge the peoples with equity. Let the heavens rejoice, let the earth be glad; let the sea resound, and all that is in it; let the fields be jubilant, and everything in them. Then all the trees of the forest will sing for joy; they will sing before the LORD, for he comes, he comes to judge the earth. He will judge the world in righteousness and the peoples in his truth."

God's judicial acts are but one aspect of his rule. To affirm God as judge is to assert that he is governor of all, not only with every right to command but also with responsibility to vindicate and to condemn.

NT — 2. The NT concept. A single family of Greek words is used to express the many shades of meaning in the NT references to judging. *Krinō,* the verb, means one or more of the following in a given usage: to judge, evaluate, decide, assess, distinguish between, pronounce judgment, select, or prefer. The whole process of evaluation is thus expressed by this one word, with the context helping to determine if the focus is on process or product. Various derivatives mean "to investigate or examine" (*anakrinō*), "to condemn" (*katakrinō*), "to be a judge" (*kritēs*), "decision" (*krisis*), or "verdict" (*krima*). By NT times these words were entrenched in the legal system and are often used in the NT in reference to some aspect of the judicial process—of bringing to trial, condemning, and punishing.

But "judge" is not used in the NT only in a legal or semilegal way. This family of words is used where the Bible speaks of evaluating, considering, making a decision, approving, and preferring. Often the translators use an appropriate English equivalent when *krinō* or one of its compounds has one of these meanings. But in other cases, "judge" is used as in the original, the context being depended on to make the meaning clear.

Still, when a word like "judge" or "judgment" has a number of possible meanings, it is easy to become confused, as many Christians are, about the Bible's teaching concerning judging others. The best way to develop our understanding of what the Bible teaches on this important subject is to examine key passages in the NT.

3. God alone is judge. The NT, like the OT, strongly affirms God as ultimately the only qualified judge. James emphasizes the OT concept of a judge as a ruler when he writes, "There is only one Lawgiver and Judge, the one who is able to save and destroy. But you—who are you to judge your neighbor?" (Jas 4:12). In this dominant legal or judicial sense, only God has the right or knowledge to judge (Jn 8:15–16). All will have to "give an account to him who is ready to judge the living and the dead" (1 Pe 4:5; cf. 2 Ti 4:1,8; Heb 10:30; 12:23; 13:4). The fact that God alone is competent to pronounce judgment on human beings is

basic to our grasp of what the Bible says about judging.

Yet God is not eager to judge. John writes that Jesus was sent into the world, not to condemn, but so that all who believe might be saved (Jn 3:17). The verdict of condemnation is passed on the lost by their own condition and actions. Jesus, the Light, has come into the world; those who love darkness will reject him and turn away (Jn 3:19–21). The Father "has entrusted all judgment to the Son" (Jn 5:22). A person's response to Jesus has become the dividing line between life and death (Jn 5:19–30). So Jesus announced to the crowds during the week of his death: "As for the person who hears my words but does not keep them, I do not judge him. For I did not come to judge the world, but to save it. There is a judge for the one who rejects me and does not accept my words; that very word which I spoke will condemn him at the last day. For I did not speak of my own accord, but the Father who sent me commanded me what to say and how to say it" (Jn 12:47–49).

Romans picks up the theme and portrays God, moved by kindness, waiting patiently in order that people will respond and repent (Ro 2:4). But "for those who are self-seeking and who reject the truth and follow evil, there will be wrath and anger" (Ro 2:8). Those who reject the divine pardon must in the end stand before God as judge. In that judgment, based on evaluation of each person's works (Rev 20:12), God will "give to each person according to what he has done" (Ro 2:6). Those who know the revealed law of God will be judged by its standard. But even those who do not know the will of God as unveiled in the written Word have "the requirements of the law . . . written on their hearts" (Ro 2:15). God has created human beings with a moral sense, which gives inner testimony to right and wrong. Tragically, human beings are so warped by sin that the inner witness accuses but does not lead to righteous living.

And so the day is coming when God will act as the moral governor of our universe. He will put aside his patience to carry out the verdict that people pronounce against themselves by their actions and by their refusal to accept God's pardon in Jesus.

4. What we are not to judge. In affirming God as judge, the Scripture also limits those ways in which human beings are to judge others. A number of passages help us understand the limitations.

Mt 7:1–2; Lk 6:37–38. The verses in Matthew record Jesus' warning as follows: "Do not judge, or you too will be judged. For in the same way you judge others, you will be judged, and with the measure you use, it will be measured to you." The thought is that we must not assume the right to condemn others. Luke adds, "Forgive, and you will be forgiven." The faults of others are to occasion forgiveness, not condemnation.

Ro 2:1–3. Paul speaks passionately of passing judgment on others. He warns, "At whatever point you judge the other, you are condemning yourself" (v. 1). To pass judgment implies the assumption of a moral superiority that we simply do not possess. We are all sinners; no human being is able to judge others without becoming vulnerable to the same judgment.

Ro 14:1–18. Paul looks at convictions in the Christian community. Then, as today, believers differed about what was right to eat or drink or do. While each person should develop his or her own convictions and live by them, no one has the right to look down on or condemn a brother or sister for his or her practices. Paul says we must see Jesus as sole Lord and each other as his servants. So each believer is responsible to the Lord, not to the conscience of other Christians. Paul does appeal for unity. But Christian unity is based on (1) the freedom of each individual to be responsible to Jesus, (2) a nonjudgmental approach to differences of conviction, and (3) a willingness to consider others when deciding whether or not to use one's freedom to follow one's own convictions.

1 Co 4:3–5. Paul himself was being judged by believers in Corinth. He wrote, "I care very little if I am judged by you or by any human court" (v. 3). The word here is *anakrinō*, which refers to undertaking an investigative process that is intended to lead to a verdict. Paul rejected the right of the Corinthians to convene such a court or call his faithfulness as Jesus' servant into question. Paul, though his conscience was clear, was not even competent to judge himself and his possibly hidden motives. What were Paul's conclusions? "It is the Lord who judges me," he said; "therefore judge nothing before the appointed time: wait till the Lord comes" (vv. 4–5).

1 Co 5:12. Paul taught the Corinthians not to relate to non-Christians in a judgmental way. Their sins might be many, but it is not the business of Christians to "judge those outside the church." The issue in the case of unbelievers is not their morality but their relationship with Jesus. When Jesus enters their lives, their practices will change (cf. 1 Co 6:9–11).

Col 2:16. Judging creates pressure that is designed to force conformity. Paul urged the believers in Colosse to resist this kind of thing. It denies not only Christian freedom but also Jesus' Lordship. "Therefore do not let anyone judge you by what you eat or drink, or with regard to a religious festival, a New Moon celebration or a Sabbath day."

Jas 4:11–12. James sees a critical approach to others as slander. Talking against our brothers is wrong because it implies becoming a judge of the law rather than a doer. James's argument is that God gave us the law, not to use against others, but that we might be responsive to it. Only God, who as governor of the universe gave the law, has the right to judge human beings by it.

In each of these passages, "judging" carries quasi-legal meanings. The choices or the motives of others are called into question, and a condemning verdict is passed in each. Each part of this process is ruled out by the above Scripture passages. Human beings are not competent to call another's motives or practices into question. Even when actions are clearly wrong, forgiveness, not condemnation, is the appropriate response. A judgmental attitude and punitive attempts are both wrong. We are to draw back, remembering that God alone is competent to judge, and to stop judging others.

5. What we are commanded to judge. Christians are not to judge others. But this does not mean that we are not to use the capacity God has given us to evaluate and make judgments. It does not even mean that "judging" is wrong in every circumstance!

a. *Ro 13:1-7*. God has established human government. He has given to governing authorities responsibility for all functions of rule, including the judicial functions. Thus the administration of criminal and civil law by judges is a right and a responsibility delegated to organized society. The ruler is "God's servant, an agent of wrath to bring punishment on the wrong doer" (v. 4).

b. *1 Co 2:15*. Paul says that "the spiritual man makes judgments about all things, but he himself is not subject to any man's judgment." The word here is *anakrinō*, "to examine or discern." Believers possess God's Holy Spirit, and they also have been given the very mind of Christ (v. 16). Believers can thus evaluate from the divine perspective and can also sense God's individual guidance.

c. *1 Co 5:12-13*. Is the church to stand in judgment on fellow believers? The apparent contradiction is resolved when we understand the nature of church discipline (see 6, below).

d. *1 Co 6:2-5*. The fellowship of believers in Corinth was being marred by some of the believers taking their disputes into secular law courts. Paul urges Christians to ask other believers to serve as a panel to resolve such "trivial matters" rather than to go to court before unbelievers.

e. *1 Co 10:15; 11:13*. Paul's exhortation "Judge for yourselves" suggests here that the right answer is obvious. But not every matter Christians are called on to examine has an obvious answer. However, God expects us to examine the issues of our lives and develop convictions based on principles found in God's Word.

f. *1 Co 11:31-32*. Paul calls on us to judge ourselves. He points out that at times God disciplines us because we have not evaluated our own actions, recognized them as sin, and confessed the sin. "If we judged ourselves," he writes, "we would not come under judgment."

6. Church discipline. In 1 Co 5, Paul expresses shock because the Corinthians were passively accepting sexual immorality. Looking at one specific case, Paul wrote, "I have already passed judgment on the one who did this, just as if I were present" (v. 3), and he goes on to command, "When you are assembled in the name of our Lord Jesus . . . hand this man over to Satan" (vv. 4-5). The believers are "not to associate with anyone who calls himself a brother" and consistently practices sin; Paul says, "With such a man do not even eat" (v. 11).

How does this teaching square with the many NT passages that tell Christians not to judge one another?

The answer is found in the affirmation of Scripture that God is the ruler of the universe and is the final moral arbiter. He, the Judge, had already announced his verdict on the practices of which Paul was writing. He had identified these practices as sin. What the church is called on to do is to agree with God in the divine assessment of the actions of this one who "calls himself a brother." As a community, the church is to "expel the wicked" from its fellowship (1 Co 5:13).

Condemning someone by calling into question that person's motives, actions, or personal convictions is vastly different from accepting God's verdict that certain actions are sins and that those who practice them must be ostracized.

A number of aspects of NT church discipline help us understand Paul's insistence that the immoral person be expelled.

a. What necessitates discipline is an individual's choice to practice what the Bible identifies as sin. We may fail often and come to God in confession. For this there is no call for discipline. Discipline is applied only when a person refuses to acknowledge that his practices are sin and refuses to change his ways.

b. The goal of church discipline is restoration. In the case mentioned by Paul, the "punishment inflicted on [the offender] by the majority" (2 Co 2:6) was sufficient, and the guilty man repented. Paul then called on the Corinthians to accept him back and "to reaffirm" their love for him (v. 8).

c. The rationale for church discipline is found in spiritual reality. Sin in fact alienates from God, cutting off the individual from fellowship (1 Jn 1:6). In church discipline, the body of Christ acts out this spiritual reality in its relationship with the sinner. A person expelled from the local community senses the fact of lost fellowship.

d. The occasion for church discipline is moral fault: the practice of sin. The church is not permitted to discipline for other deviations. Difference in convictions or even doctrinal differences do not call for church discipline. ◗ **Doctrine** It is only the consistent practice of sin without acknowledgment of the fault that occasions discipline.

e. The responsibility for church discipline rests on the local Christian community. Mt 18:15–17 is generally understood to outline a process that Christians should follow. An offended person should approach the sinner and explain the fault. One or two members of the congregation should go with the first member if the sinning saint refuses to listen. The whole church is to be informed if the individual still refuses to listen. Then the person is to be ostracized. This joint responsibility is reflected also in Corinthians, where Paul writes of expelling the sinning person when the church is "assembled in the name of our Lord Jesus" (1 Co 5:4).

Exercising church discipline is very different from adopting the judgmental and condemning attitude against which Scripture speaks. In church discipline we see the loving action of the Christian community, committed to obedience, intending through the discipline to help the brother or sister turn from sin and find renewed fellowship with the Lord.

7. Summary. The OT presents God as governor of the universe when it speaks of him as the judge. In the OT, all the functions of rule—the executive and legislative as well as the judicial—are summed up in this word.

The OT law sketches a society directly governed by God. But Israel's unwillingness to respond to the Lord first led to the introduction of human governors ("judges") and later to the monarchy. The judges and the kings were viewed as ruling Israel for God and were to be subject to the Lord and to his Word.

The NT maintains the perspective of the OT. God is indeed the ruler of all. And he is the ultimate judicial officer. But when the word "judge" is used in the NT, its meaning is shaped more by the meanings found in Greek culture than those found in the OT. NT uses of "judge" emphasize the judicial functions of God rather than his overall rule. Thus, it is often a legal or quasilegal term. But it is also an ordinary word having to do with evaluation: all persons are called on to make choices based on nonjudicial judgments.

The NT helps us make distinctions about judging that have an important impact on our interpersonal relationships. God has established human government and assigned it judicial functions relating to criminal acts in society (Ro 13). But God has not given believers any right, apart from Scripture, to examine or condemn other persons. No one but God is competent to measure motives or to establish convictions for others. Jesus is Lord and, as God, he is able to discern rightly. Thus we are freed from the responsibility of judging others in these areas. We can instead relate to them in love, with acceptance, and freely extend forgiveness. We are not burdened with the responsibility of punishing others or of forcing them to conform to our notions of what God desires. God will judge—at the appointed time (1 Co 4:5).

Yet there are certain practices that God has already spoken about. It is our responsibility on moral issues to take our stand with the Lord. Thus, when one who claims to be a believer habitually practices sin, the believing community is to expel that person. In church discipline, the church judges, not the person, but the actions of that person. When the actions are those that God has identified as sin, then the church must act in obedience and expel the unrepentant person.

Every Christian has a need for wisdom to make judgments about how to live from day to day. How wonderful to know that God through His Word has already equipped us to judge. By judging only those things that God calls on us to judge and by refusing to be trapped into judging others, we will be enabled to live productive and peaceful lives.

JUDGMENT SEAT

The Greek word for judgment seat is *bēma*. It indicates a raised platform on which an official is seated when rendering judgment on certain legal cases. The Greek word is found a dozen times in the NT: Mt 27:19; Jn 19:13; Ac 7:5; 12:21; 18:12,16–17; 25:6,10,17; Ro 14:10; 2 Co 5:10.

The last two occurrences are significant, for they speak of a judgment each believer will "give an account of himself" to the Lord. But Paul makes it clear that it is the quality of our works as believers that is under consideration (2 Co 5:10; cf. 1 Co 3:10–15). Jesus has borne in his own body on Calvary the eternal condemnation due us for our sins.

JUSTICE/INJUSTICE

In our culture, "just" and "justice" are often used as political code words. To some, justice means that there should be harsh punishment for criminals. For others, justice is a social issue: it demands a war on poverty and ridding the "system" of inequities. But in all of the talk about justice, we must be careful to read the Bible so that it speaks with its own meanings. It is all too easy to let contemporary issues so color our notion

of what justice is that we fail to develop a biblical perspective.

OT 1. Hebrew words for justice
    2. God and justice
    3. Doing justice: an OT perspective
    4. Injustice and the unjust
    5. Teachings on legal justice
    6. Teachings on social justice
NT 7. Greek words for "just" and "unjust"
    8. God is just
    9. Summary

OT — 1. Hebrew words for justice. Where the English versions read "just" or "justice," one of two Hebrew terms is usually found.

Mišpāṭ, which occurs over four hundred times in the OT, is usually found where the NIV speaks of "doing what is just" or of justice. The root, *šāpaṭ*, encompasses all functions of government. ▶ *Judge/Judging* Among these functions are the judicial. Thus *mišpāṭ* can be a case in litigation, a judicial decision, the execution of a judgment, and even a statement of the code against which actions are to be judged. In essence, then, justice has to do with one's rights and duties under law.

A number of words formed from the root *ṣādaq* are also translated "just" and "justice." This family of words has in common the idea that moral and ethical norms exist and that actions in harmony with the norms are "just," while actions not in harmony with the norm are unjust or constitute injustice. This important OT root and its derivatives is also translated "right" and "righteous." The concept is discussed at length in another article. ▶ *Righteous/Righteousness*

2. God and justice. It is important when we read of justice and of just behavior in the OT to remember that these are not abstract philosophical concepts. People today struggle to find an acceptable definition of what justice is. God's OT people knew what it meant. The writers of the Bible were convinced that the Lord himself revealed the norms and standards by which all human behavior can be judged. Justice, then, is doing what is in harmony with the divinely revealed norms of interpersonal behavior. God has given "regulations and laws that are just and right" (Ne 9:13), and it is these that define justice for mankind.

But the concept of justice has even deeper roots. Ultimately our understanding of justice has its source in the person of the one who gave mankind his law. "He is the Rock, his works are perfect, and all his ways are just. A faithful God who does no wrong, upright and just is he" (Dt 32:4). God's historic punishments of Israel for deviation from the revealed norms are also an aspect of justice. Again and again Israel was forced to admit, "In all that has happened to us, you have been just" (Ne 9:33; cf. 2 Ch 12:5-6)..

Justice, then, is rooted in the very nature of God, and his character is the true norm or standard. All his acts are just and right, even those we may not be able to understand. But in Scripture, God has given us norms that we can grasp. These standards, expressed in the OT in the Mosaic Law and in the Prophets, take justice from the realm of the abstract and make it a practical issue indeed.

3. Doing justice: an OT perspective. Often the prophets called Israel back to a just lifestyle. Their call is rich in illustration of the actions of a just individual and the just society. Listening to the prophets, we can sense the perspective of the OT: "They ask me for just decisions and seem eager for God to come near them. 'Why have we fasted,' they say, 'and you have not seen it? Why have we humbled ourselves, and you have not noticed?' Yet on the day of your fasting, you do as you please and exploit all your workers. Your fasting ends in quarreling and strife, and in striking each other with wicked fists. You cannot fast as you do today and expect your voice to be heard on high. Is this the kind of fast I have chosen, only a day for a man to humble himself? Is it only for bowing one's head like a reed and for lying on sackcloth and ashes? Is that what you call a fast, a day acceptable to the LORD? Is not this the kind of fasting I have chosen: to loose the chains of injustice and untie the cords of the yoke, to set the oppressed free and break every yoke? Is it not to share your food with the hungry and to provide the poor wanderer with shelter—when you see the naked, to clothe him, and not to turn away from your own flesh and blood? . . . If you do away with the yoke of oppression, with the pointing finger and malicious talk, and if you spend yourselves in behalf of the hungry and satisfy the needs of the oppressed, then your light will rise in the darkness, and your night will become like the noonday" (Isa 58:2-10).

Jeremiah picks up the same themes. "This is what the LORD says: Do what is just and right. Rescue from the hand of his oppressor the one who has been robbed. Do no wrong or violence to the alien, the fatherless or the widow, and do not shed innocent blood in this place" (Jer 22:3). Jeremiah goes on to commend the godly king, for "he did what was right and just, so all went well with him. He defended the cause of the poor and needy, and so all went well. Is that not what it means to know me? declares the LORD. But your eyes and your heart are set only on dishonest gain, on shedding innocent blood and on oppression and extortion" (Jer 22:15-17).

In passages like these (see also Am 5), we see expressed the underlying principles of both OT law and of justice. OT law was a divine revelation of good, teaching Israel how to love God and how to love their neighbors. ♦ *Law* This loving way of living by the law is doing justice. Justice is doing good to others and showing an active concern for the well-being of the weak. The just society and the just individual alike demonstrate this active concern to meet the needs of the powerless and to defend the oppressed.

It is important to note that justice and injustice have an impact on one's relationship with God. God is the one who calls humanity to do justice. He is also the governor of the universe, who must enter into judgment with evildoers. ♦ *Judge/Judging* For God to be just means that he will both act according to his own standards in his treatment of human beings and exercise his responsibility to punish those who are unjust.

In summary, then, justice is an interpersonal concept in the OT. Doing justice has to do with how human beings treat one another, individually and in society. The norm or standard that defines just behavior is a moral and ethical one. It is derived from God's character and is expressed in those commands of the law and exhortations of the prophets that reveal how God expects his people to relate lovingly to those around them.

4. Injustice and the unjust. As we might expect, justice and injustice are mirror images of each other. Honesty in business practices is just; dishonest practices are unjust. Impartial courts are just; courts that show partiality to any individual or social group are unjust (Lev 19:15; cf. Hab 1:4). Oppression of others is also injustice (1 Ch 17:9; cf. Hab 2:12).

In the Hebrew, "unjust gain" is *tarbît* (which occurs 6 times in the OT), a profit made by violent or criminal acts (e.g., Pr 28:8). But where the English versions speak of injustice or the unjust, the Hebrew nearly always has a word constructed on the stem ʿ *āwal*. The underlying concept is also the mirror image of the concept underlying the idea of "just." A moral or ethical norm exists. Unjust acts or acts of injustice are those that violate the norm or deviate from it.

5. Teachings on legal justice. One major emphasis on justice in the OT finds focus in the legal system. The Mosaic Law established a system in which responsibility to deal with criminal matters was distributed throughout the society. Each community was to have its own panel of elders who would serve as judges in civil and criminal matters. The OT emphatically enjoins the judges to show no partiality and to accept no bribes (Dt 16:18–20). Rules of evidence were established for serious cases (Dt 17:1–7; 19:15) and a "supreme court" of priests was established to inquire of the Lord in cases "too difficult" for the judges. Later, when the monarchy was established, the king became the chief judicial officer. In biblical times, all governing functions were considered to be located in the king as the head of the nation. But the king, like the lower courts, was to be subject to God. The law established the standards according to which the ruler must judge.

How were criminal matters dealt with? The OT justice system, unlike our own, did not rely heavily on imprisonment to punish criminals. The OT does report a number ˋof cases of imprisonment— many of them under foreign jurisdiction (Ge 39:20–22; 40:3,5,14; 42:16,19; Jdg 16:21,25; 2 Ki 17:4; 25:27,29; Jer 52:11,31,33; Eze 19:9) and some under rulers in Israel and Judah (1 Ki 22:27; 2 Ch 16:10; 18:26). Confinement could involve simply restriction to one's residence or city (1 Kg 2:36), but in other instances it seems to have been in a room or pit in some official's residence (Jer 20:2; 32:2; 37:4,15,18; 38:6).

The OT justice system relied more on restitution than on imprisonment. A person who was responsible for another's loss was to reimburse the value of the property destroyed (Ex 22:1–15). Property that was stolen or obtained illegally had to be returned, and a penalty of one to four times its value was added. Murder and accidental homicide were special cases with a distinct code to govern how they were to be judged. ◆ *Murder/Kill*

Other penalties were prescribed for various personal-injury and civil violations, including provisions for covering a person's loss of income if an injury prevented work.

With many such guiding principles provided in the Mosaic Law, local judging elders were to call on witnesses within the community to establish the facts of a case and to supervise payment of the appropriate restitution or penalty.

The OT justice system relied heavily on the existence of a community in which individuals were responsive to God and to his laws. History shows that, with few exceptions, God's kind of justice was not administered during the OT era.

6. Teachings on social justice. OT law is not concerned only with individual justice. It is concerned with social justice.

Thus a number of mechanisms were built into the law that were designed to create a just moral community. Individuals were urged to have a generous concern for those less fortunate than they were. And the community was to maintain structures to meet needs as well. The spirit of justice continues to be that of concern for one's neighbor, and God shows his deep concern by designing a social system within which justice can be done. ♦ *Poor and Oppressed*

NT — 7. Greek words for "just" and "unjust". The concept of justice is expressed by *dikaios*, which means "just," "upright," "righteous." ♦ *Righteous/Righteousness* Words in this family reflect the meanings of the OT root *ṣādaq*. At times the NT uses *dikaios* in a purely OT sense to describe persons whose lives conform to the divine norm expressed in law. At times too *adikos* ("unjust," "unrighteous") indicates one who deviates from the norm. Thus Joseph is spoken of as a *dikaios* man (Mt 1:19), and God is described as sending rain on the *dikaios* and *adikos* alike (Mt 5:45). However, the translators of the NIV and the NASB have chosen to use "righteous" and "unrighteous" in these as in almost all other cases where these Greek words are used of human beings. This may be because the NT concept of righteousness is so dynamic and significant. It moves beyond evaluation of behavior, even by the divine standard, and looks deeply into character, which is the wellspring of actions.

8. God is just. The translators of the NIV invariably chose "righteous" rather than "just" to express the meaning of *dikaios* when it is applied to human beings. In three instances they used "just" when describing God's dealings with humankind. Thus, the NT affirms God as just, on the one hand justifying those who believe in Jesus (Ro 3:26) and forgiving those who confess their sin (1 Jn 1:9), on the other hand punishing those who persist in unbelief (2 Th 1:6).

Ro 3 develops the first theme. Because all have sinned, human beings must be redeemed. ♦ *Redeem/Ransom* Salvation

is given freely, as a gift of grace, through "the redemption that is in Christ Jesus." Paul explains that "God presented him as a sacrifice of atonement, through faith in his blood. He did this to demonstrate his justice, because in his forbearance he had left the sins committed beforehand unpunished—he did it to demonstrate his justice at the present time, so as to be just and the one who justifies those who have faith in Jesus" (Ro 3:24–25). ♦ *Justify/Justification*

Paul's point is that God, as governor of the universe, is morally bound to condemn the guilty. Since all have sinned, God might be criticized for failure to condemn OT saints. The death of Christ has at last demonstrated that there is a basis on which God as judge could validly leave sins unpunished. And Jesus' self-sacrifice provides a basis on which God can be just and offer salvation to people today. Because of the Cross, God can remain true to his own moral commitment to what is right, and still freely acquit sinners (cf. 1 Jn 1:9).

The second theme is found in a number of NT passages. God is not unfair in punishing sinners. In 2 Thessalonians, Paul graphically portrays the destiny of those "who do not know God and do not obey the gospel of our Lord Jesus Christ" (1:8). When Christ returns, they will be punished everlastingly. Paul affirms, "God is just: he will pay back those who trouble you and give relief to you who are troubled" (1:6–7). The emphasis on just punishment is also seen elsewhere in the NT (e.g., Ro 3:5–6; 9:14; Heb 2:2; Rev 15–16).

Considering the positive side of the subject, the writer in Heb 6:10 uses fact of God's justice to encourage believers. God is not unjust. So he will "not forget your work and the love you have shown him as you have helped his people and continue to help them."

It is important to note that in these passages the Bible is neither defending God nor trying to explain his actions. After all, God is the standard of morality in the universe. Human beings may resist and challenge the "humanity" of God's decisions. But God is himself the measure of righteousness. Thus the Bible simply affirms that God is just. In both salvation and condemnation, God's actions are in full harmony with his righteous character.

9. Summary. God has communicated to human beings his standards of behavior. Within the context of his covenant relationship with Israel, God shared his norms for a people who would live in intimate relationship with him. A nation and a person that was identified with the Lord must do justice and live in accordance with the divine standards of what is loving and right. OT law, which expresses these standards, is an expression of God's own character as well as his explanation of how his OT people were to live a life of love.

Justice in the OT is both a personal and a societal issue. Law not only shows individuals how to act toward each other but also lays the foundation for a moral society. Thus the OT law contains developed legal justice and social justice mechanisms.

The NT says less about society. This is in part because the church, unlike Israel, is not a nation. It is also in part because in the NT the emphasis shifts from just behavior (behavior in conformity to a standard or norm) to righteousness. The NT emphasis on righteousness focuses attention on the character, the inner person, from which behavior springs. And God shows us that his solution to injustice is not to be found in life regulated by law; rather, it is found through God's action in Christ to change human character. ♦ *Righteous/Righteousness*

What is the importance of studying the OT for insights into justice? For one thing, we are immediately confronted with the importance to God of the way we treat other persons. Justice is a concept that calls us to loving concern for those who are weak and oppressed, not simply to moral action in our interpersonal dealings. What is more, the social mechanisms that God established for Israel suggest positive ways that our society might act to correct inequities in both our legal and social justice systems.

JUSTIFY/JUSTIFICATION

These are key theological terms. They lie close to the heart of the gospel. When we understand them, we have a clear insight into the nature of God's stunning plan of salvation.

OT 1. Justification in the OT
NT 2. Justification in Romans and
          Galatians
       3. Justification in James

OT — 1. Justification in the OT. The Hebrew root is *ṣāḏaq*. ♦ *Righteous/Righteousness* The word "justification" has important judicial meanings. A person whose actions are in question will be justified if those actions are examined and found to have been right. Thus "justify" can mean both "found innocent" and "vindicated" in a particular course of action.

The theological meaning of justification rests heavily on the judicial concept. God is the ultimate judge of all beings in the universe. He will evaluate their actions and will not clear the guilty. Yet David, in Ps 51, appealed to God for forgiveness. David relied on God's mercy (vv. 1–2), despite the fact that a sentence of condemnation would have been completely justified by the fact of David's sins (vv. 4–5). David faced this dilemma and expressed his conviction that it is God's saving action alone that could free him from guilt and restore his joy (vv. 7–14). Thus, David called on God to justify him—to declare him innocent—despite his sin and his guilt.

Passages like Ps 51 prefigure the doctrine of justification as it is developed in the NT. But already in Isa 53 the OT gives a clear picture of that developed doctrine. Isaiah looked ahead to the suffering of Jesus. He saw, at least in some measure, Christ's sacrificial death, in which "the Lord . . . laid on him the iniquity of us all" (v. 6) and described some of the events of Calvary in graphic detail. And then the prophet concludes: "After the suffering of his soul, he will see the light of life, and be satisfied; by his knowledge my righteous servant will justify many, and he will bear their iniquities. Therefore I will give him a portion among the great, and he will divide the spoils with the strong, because he poured out his life unto death, and was numbered with the transgressors. For he bore the sin of many, and made intercession for the transgressors" (vv. 11–12). On the basis of that poured-out life, God will declare many righteous, despite their sins and failures.

NT — 2. Justification in Romans and Galatians. The Greek word is *dikaioō*, which means "to acquit," "to vindicate," or "to pronounce righteous." The early church rejoiced that God pronounced righteous all those who believed in Jesus (Ac 13:39). But it is the apostle Paul who developed the doctrine of justification.

Paul begins his argument in Romans by showing that no human being is righteous in God's sight (Ro 1–3). Since all are sinners, salvation can come only if God acts to justify—to pronounce sinners righteous. Ro 3:21–31 announces a "righteousness from God" that is given freely, received by faith in Christ Jesus. Paul shows that the substitutionary death of Jesus provided a basis on which God can make this judicial pronouncement. As human beings always fall far short of the divine standard of righteousness, humanity's only hope is a righteousness that comes apart from human actions.

Paul then goes back in history and shows that his presentation of justification by faith is in harmony with the OT. "Abraham believed God," Paul quotes from Genesis, "and it was credited to him as righteousness" (4:3). Moving on through history, Paul shows later in Ro 4 that justification has always come through faith, not through human efforts to live by the law.

In ch 5 the apostle returns to the death of Christ and says, "Since we have been justified through faith, we have peace with God through our Lord Jesus Christ" (v. 1). Note the significant "we have been." God, the judge, has already announced his verdict. The person who has faith in Jesus stands acquitted *now*. The judge has spoken, and no one can annul the divine decision. Through faith we are declared righteous and stand acquitted of every charge that might be brought against us.

This same teaching is repeated in Galatians: "A man is not justified by observing the law, but by faith in Jesus Christ" (2:16). No one's behavior can win a verdict of "righteous" if it is God who is evaluating the behavior. "By observing the law no one will be justified" (v. 16). Here Paul introduces another dimension of divine justification. Christ now actually lives in the believer. Through personal relationship with Jesus, the believer not only is declared to be righteous but also becomes righteous by God's working within!

In Gal 3, Paul argues that the principle of faith, which operates in justification, must also be applied as the believer seeks to live a righteous life: "All who rely on observing the law are under a curse" (3:10) and "the righteous will live by faith" (3:11). Paul then shows how the principle of faith infuses the entire OT as well as the NT. Only by misunderstanding the message of the OT could God's people have imagined that righteousness can be won by their efforts to conform to the law. Only by misunderstanding the doctrine of justification can believers today imagine that they may become righteous by a modern struggle to live by law. Reliance on God both for salvation and for power to live a righteous life is the only option the believer has.

3. Justification in James. Church history has seen attacks on the Book of James, based on supposed conflict between its teaching on justification and that of Romans and Galatians. Luther called James a "right strawy epistle," for he was unable to accept the apparent implications of Jas 2:24: "You see that a person is justified by what he does and not by faith alone." To Luther, justification had to be faith alone, and he was totally convinced that salvation by faith alone as explained by Paul is the centerpiece of the Christian faith.

The apparent conflict is resolved when we note that James is contrasting "faith" with "faith." He describes a faith that is mental agreement with a set of facts about God but that produces no change in the life of such a believer. As for that kind of faith, James asks, "What good is it?" (2:14). He is concerned with a different kind of faith. He views faith as total commitment. The kind of faith the Bible speaks about is a faith that produces a dramatic change in human lifestyle (2:14–19). And so James returns to biblical characters who were persons of faith and points out that these men and women *acted* on their faith (2:20–26). James says of Abraham, "His faith and his actions were working together, and his faith was made complete by what he did" (v. 22), thus fulfilling the Scripture that pronounced him righteous (v. 23).

It is not beyond our efforts to resolve the apparent conflict between Romans and James. Consider the following: (1) James does not teach that Abraham was pronounced righteous on the basis of his actions. James teaches that Scripture's announcement that Abraham *was* righteous is vindicated on the basis of Abraham's subsequent obedience. He did right because God's action actually worked within to make him righteous! (2) James is speaking of two kinds of faith, only one of which is saving faith. He teaches that a person's claim to have saving faith will be vindicated by the actions that flow from it and in this sense complete it. ◆ *Belief/Faith*

What is particularly significant to us here is that James joins Paul in suggesting that justification is something more than a judicial declaration. True, in response to faith, God does declare sinners acquitted and righteous before him; but he does more than that. God acts within the believer to make righteousness a reality. Thus the gospel offer of salvation by faith includes more than a pardon: it includes also a transformation. God will declare the sinner righteous, and then God will act to *make* the sinner what God has declared him to be.

K

KEEP/KEPT

"Keep" expresses a range of meanings. It is the same with the Greek and Hebrew words translated "keep" in English. In all three languages the words mean one or more of the following: to preserve, to watch, to guard, to maintain or hold to. Thus, one keeps God's laws (Lev 18:5) and Jesus' words (Jn 12:47). God keeps his covenant promises (Dt 7:12), which includes his keeping (in another sense of the word) believers safe (Ps 12:7; 16:1). We are kept from terror (Jer 17:18), and the lost are kept for judgment day (2 Pe 3:7). Perhaps best of all is the Bible's good word that God "is able to keep [us] from falling and to present [us] before his glorious presence without fault and with great joy" (Jude 24).

KILL ♦ Murder/Kill

KIND

Genesis affirms, "God said, 'Let the land produce living creatures according to their kinds: livestock, creatures that move along the ground, wild animals, each according to its kind' " (Ge 1:24). Despite the often-stated truth that the Bible is "not a book of science," it is clear that Scripture is in conflict here with modern evolutionary thought. The conflict is even more clear when we explore other passages in which the word "kind" (mîn, 31 times in the OT) is used (particularly Ge 6–7, Lev 11, Dt 14). In Scripture, mîn designates what biologists would identify as species, genus, family, and even order. And in each case the Bible affirms that God created and maintains the identity of the form within the creation order. Whatever we may conclude from Scripture's affirmation, we find no support for the evolutionary hypothesis that calls at the least for development and change across kingdoms and phyla.

KINDNESS

What does the term "kindness" mean in the Bible? In the NIV and the NASB, "kindness" is usually a translation of hesed. This key OT term indicates faithfulness to a relationship. To show kindness is to act in a loyal, loving way to a person. This is true of kindness in human relationships and of the kindness God shows us. God's love moves him to be kind to those with whom he has established a covenant relationship. ♦ Covenant ♦ Love

The Greek words most often translated "kindness" are chrēstos and chrēstotēs. The Greek word for "good" (agathos) is rendered "kind" or "kindness" a few times; and ēpios is rendered "kind" once (2 Ti 2:24), it meaning "gentle" or "mild" and appearing only one other time in Scripture (1 Th 2:7, where it is rendered "gentle").

Chrēstotēs (appearing 10 times in the NT) conveys the idea of a moral goodness that enables a person to be friendly and kind toward others. God's own kindness is unlimited, enabling him to act as a friend even to those who are his enemies (Ro 2:4; 11:22; Eph 2:7; Tit 3:4). Christ's willingness to offer himself to help the spiritually destitute shows the extent of God's kindness. And, as God's chosen, we are to imitate his kindness in our relationships with others (Col 3:12). *Chrēstotēs* is used three other times in the NT—as "kindness" twice (2 Co 6:6; Gal 5:22) and as "good" once (Ro 3:12). The sense of kindness is also communicated by *chrēstos* (Ro 2:4; Eph 4:32; 1 Pe 2:3).

KING

"King" is, in a sense, an archaic word. In these modern days of constitutional monarchy, we can sense little of the awesome power and responsibility of the kings of the ancient world.

OT 1. King in the OT
    2. God as King
NT 3. Jesus the King

OT — 1. King in the OT. The Hebrew word is *melek*. It, along with other Hebrew words (words often translated "governor," "chief," or "prince"), indicates a person with civil authority. *Melek* does not suggest a specific office or form of government. Nebuchadnezzar, head of the great Babylonian Empire, was called *melek*, but so also were the governors of subprovinces and even the leaders (mayors?) of the tiny city-states that dotted Palestine during the time of the Conquest. This is due to the fact that *melek* designates a ruling magistrate. In biblical times this was a person who was responsible for all the functions of modern government—the legislative, the executive, and the judicial. In essence, the *melek* provided whatever leadership and control were required to govern the people. Of course, the ancient kings ruled in harmony with the customs of their culture, as Israel's kings were to rule by, and be personally subject to, the Mosaic Law. But in ancient times, royal power was the power of life and death, and the king's word was final in civil matters. In Israel's long history, evil kings showed their influence by leading God's people to abandon him, and good kings led revivals that called the people back to God. Thus, the chief ruler set the moral and religious tone for the nation.

In earliest Israel, civil authority was decentralized. It rested in local elders and tribal heads. During the age of the judges, charismatic leaders emerged in times of crisis and, after affecting deliverance, exercised civil authority during their lifetimes. ◗ *Judge/Judging* But the hereditary monarchy was not introduced in Israel until about 1,100 B.C., in the days of Samuel, Saul, and David.

The ancient Book of Deuteronomy (c. 1450 B.C.) does speak of a monarchy for God's people (Dt 17:14–20), but the motives of the people who insisted that the last judge, Samuel, anoint them a king, were wrong. The people wanted a king to lead them so they could be like other nations. God, the invisible but true *melek* of Israel, was implicitly rejected (1 Sa 8). The first king, Saul, was seriously flawed. David, who succeeded him, was devout and was highly successful. God established David's dynastic right to the throne of Israel forever (2 Sa 23:1–16; Ps 89:3; ◗ *Covenant)*. Jesus, born in the family line of David, was destined to become King, in the fullest biblical sense of *melek*, over the entire earth. ◗ *Kingdom*

2. God as King. On the day that Samuel presented Saul to Israel as their first king, he recalled sadly, "You said to me, 'No, we want a king to rule over us'—even though the LORD your God was your king" (1 Sa 12:12). Samuel affirmed that God had committed himself to personally provide the judicial, legislative, executive, and military leadership that his people needed. But God was invisible, and the enemies that surrounded Israel were all too visible. God was overtly rejected; Israel demanded a ruler they could see. They would rely on a human being rather than on the Lord.

Samuel warned against reliance on mere human leadership (1 Sa 8:10–20). And biblical history records recurrent tragedies, with evil and inept kings leading Israel into apostasy.

The prophets, many of whom lived in the days of the monarchy, called Israel back to its original vision of God. God was Israel's Creator, King, and Redeemer (Isa 43:15; 44:6). He had to be recognized as the great King (Mal 1:14; cf. Zep 3:15). But it is Zechariah who sums up most clearly Israel's future hope: "The LORD will be king over the whole earth. On that day there will be one LORD, and his name the only name" (Zec 14:9). After God personally intervenes to destroy Israel's wicked enemies, he will be personally present on earth. "Then the survivors from all the nations that have attacked Jerusalem will go up year after year to worship the King, the LORD Almighty, and to celebrate the Feast of Tabernacles" (Zec 14:16).

Thus, in speaking of God as King, the OT sees both his invisible but real rule over the course of human events and a coming day when he will appear on earth to bring everything under his personal authority.

NT — 3. Jesus the King. After carefully tracing Jesus' genealogy, the introduction to Matthew's Gospel quotes or alludes to many OT passages. His purpose is to demonstrate that Jesus of Nazareth truly was Israel's promised Davidic King, the Messiah (Mt 1:1–2:6). ♦ *Christ*

In the Gospels, "king" is most often used of Jesus in the context of his trial and crucifixion. The very words "King of the Jews" were inscribed on the plaque attached to his cross (Mt 27:37; Mk 15:26; Lk 23:38; Jn 19:19,21).

It was when Christ's enemies brought him to Pilate that they charged him with claiming to be "the Christ" and added, for clarity, "a king" (Lk 23:2; cf. Jn 19:12). Pilate's questioning focused on this issue; he asked Jesus, "Are you king of the Jews?" (Mt 27:1; Mk 15:2; Lk 23:2; Jn 18:33). The charge and the question are significant in historical context. The Jews charged that Jesus saw himself as a king, one with supreme civil authority. Even though Jesus' explanation that his kingdom "is not of this world" (Jn 18:36) was not understood by Pilate, the Roman governor tried to free him (Jn 18:38–19:16). Ultimately it was the political danger to himself that pressured Pilate to let Jesus be crucified. The danger to the Roman was real. The shout of the people was a threat: "If you let this man go, you are no friend of Caesar. Anyone who claims to be a king opposes Caesar" (Jn 19:12).

While the Gospels and the very title "Christ" establish Jesus as Israel's promised king, the full meaning of his rule is understood only by a study of the NT's teaching about the kingdom. ♦ *Kingdom*

KINGDOM

The NT tells us that Jesus came preaching a gospel of the kingdom. What was his good news? Was that early word of the kingdom only for Israel or does it have meaning for us today? Theologians differ on their answer. But the many references in the Gospels to the kingdom of heaven and to the kingdom of God make one thing clear: Jesus shares significant truth with us when he speaks of the kingdom.

OT 1. "Kingdom" in the OT
NT 2. "Kingdom" in the NT
    3. The gospel of the kingdom
    4. The present kingdom
    5. The coming kingdom
    6. Summary

OT — 1. "Kingdom" in the OT. Several Hebrew words are translated "kingdom" in the English versions. They come from the same root as *melek,* king: *mal°kû, mal°kût,* and *mamlākâh.* ♦ *King*

In modern thought, a kingdom is a specific geographical area, with national identity. In the OT, however, "kingdom" is best expressed by the idea of reign or sovereignty. One's kingdom is the people or things over which he or she has authority or control.

In the OT, "kingdom" is most often used in the secular sense, to indicate the sphere of authority of human rulers. But the Bible does speak of God's kingdom, in two significant ways.

First, the entire universe is God's kingdom, for he exercises sovereign rule over all things at this present time. Ps 103:19 affirms, "The LORD has established his throne in heaven, and his kingdom rules over all." Similarly: "They will tell of the glory of your kingdom and speak of your might, so that all men may know of your mighty acts and the glorious splendor of your kingdom. Your kingdom is an everlasting kingdom, and your dominion endures through all generations" (Ps 145:11–13).

The same theme is developed in Nebuchadnezzar's praise after he recovered from a madness given as divine judgment: "How great are his [God's] signs, how mighty his wonders! His kingdom is an eternal kingdom; his dominion endures from generation to generation" (Da 4:3). The overarching sovereignty of God may not always be expressed in mighty acts. It also operates in quiet providence, as history marches toward God's intended end. But all is God's kingdom. And he is the ultimate ruler of all (2 Ch 13:8; Da 4:17; 5:21; 6:26–27).

Second, the OT does look forward to a future expression of God's now-disguised sovereignty. Then the kingdom will have a visible, earthly form. Daniel speaks of a time when "the God of heaven will set up a kingdom that will never be destroyed, nor will it be left to another people. It will crush all those kingdoms and bring them to an end, but it will itself endure forever" (Da 2:44). Essentially the same vision is repeated in Da 7, and the establishment of God's visible kingdom is again foretold. In fact, OT prophecy uniformly and consistently pictures a time when earth will be ruled by the Messiah, when "the kingdom will be the LORD's" (Ob 21).

In the OT, therefore, God is seen as the present, though often unacknowledged, ruler of the universe. The universe and everything in it constitute his kingdom, for he exercises sovereign control over all beings. At the same time, the OT anticipates a day when God will establish a visible kingdom on earth. In that day his sovereignty will be recognized, and his authority will be acknowledged by all.

NT — 2. "Kingdom" in the NT.

The import of "kingdom" (basileia) in the NT is derived from OT thought rather than from Greek culture. A kingdom is a realm in which a king exerts control and authority. The "kingdom of God," rather than being a place, is the realm in which God is in control.

The OT draws attention to two aspects of God's kingdom. As king of the created universe, God is always at work, actively shaping history's flow according to his will. This expression of the kingdom of God is usually hidden. Only at times, as at the Exodus, has God visibly broken into time and space to set his unmistakable imprint on events. But the OT looks forward to a time when God's Messiah will step boldly into history. Then with raw power he will act to establish God's open rule over the whole earth. Then Israel's enemies will be shattered, the Davidic successor established on the throne in Jerusalem, and God will enforce peace on all peoples.

In Jesus' day, Palestine lay under Roman rule. Rome was only the latest in a centuries-long series of pagan overlords. Understandably, Israel longed for the kingdom the prophets foretold. No wonder Jesus was looked to at first as the one who would establish the prophesied kingdom. Jesus' own disciples, even late in his ministry and after his resurrection, expected him to establish the visible kingdom soon (Mt 20:21–23; Ac 1:6–7). So when Jesus came, at first preaching the "gospel of the kingdom," it was natural that he was not understood. His listeners' perceptions were shaped by their vision of the kingdom to come, and they could not grasp the fact that Jesus actually spoke, not of one of the two OT forms of the kingdom, but of yet another expression of God's rule, yet another way in which God would act in human affairs.

In reading the NT it is important to remember the basic meaning of "kingdom." It refers to the realm in which a ruler acts to carry out his will. If we operate from this basic definition, Scripture will break down our stereotypes as well and reveal an exciting aspect of the kingdom of heaven that Christians too often miss.

3. The gospel of the kingdom. When it was time for Jesus to begin his public ministry, John the Baptist began to preach, "Repent, for the kingdom of heaven is near" (Mt 3:2). God was about to break into history, to act in a bold, fresh way. This message, which was also the theme of Jesus' early ministry (Mt 4:17; Mk 1:15), is "the good news of the kingdom" (Mt 4:23).

Jesus' message was stronger than that of John. John said the kingdom was coming. Jesus announced that it had arrived! Confronting men who accused him of doing his miracles by Satan's power, Jesus said, "If I drive out demons by the Spirit of God, then the kingdom of God has come upon you" (Mt 12:28; cf. Lk 11:20). Most of Jesus' miracles belong to this time period, the time of his preaching the gospel of the kingdom. The king had come and had demonstrated his power to act, revealing his authority over every natural and supernatural power. In the NT, the kingdom and Jesus are inseparable, even as the concept of kingdom is meaningless apart from the person of the king.

In a significant sense, then, any announcement of the gospel of the kingdom must focus on the person of Jesus, promising that he is or soon will be present, able to act in all his sovereign power.

There seem to be two periods of time when this particular message is presented. The first is seen in Jesus' own historic announcement of his presence. Israel was called on to acknowledge the heavenly king and thus by faith step into that realm in which he would freely exercise his power for them (e.g., Mt 3:2; 4:17,23; 9:35; 10:7; Mk 1:15; Lk 4:43; 8:1; 9:2,11,60; 10:9,11). Jesus summed up this era by saying, "The Law and the Prophets were proclaimed until John. Since that time, the good news of the kingdom of God is being preached" (Lk 16:16).

The second time will be just before Jesus' return. Mt 24 records Jesus' answer to his disciples' questions about history's end. Jesus reviewed OT prophecy and said of that future time: "This gospel of the kingdom will be preached in the whole world as a testimony to all nations, and then the end will come" (Mt 24:14). It is clear from the context that this preaching is not of the Christian gospel of salvation but is the announcement to all that Jesus is again about to appear on earth.

There are, of course, other NT references to preaching and teaching about the kingdom (Ac 8:12; 19:8; 20:25; 28:23,31). Thus, the gospel of the kingdom—the good news that the king is at hand or is already present—is preached when Jesus personally is about to, or already has (at the First Advent), stepped into history.

The gospel of the kingdom may be a technical theological term with narrow focus. But the NT teaching about the kingdom itself has a broader significance and touches our lives today.

4. **The present kingdom.** While he was on earth, Jesus taught much about an expression of the divine kingdom that was unrecognized in the OT. When it was clear that Israel would not accept Christ as Messiah/King, Jesus began to speak of the kingdom in parables. And he began to speak of his death. When asked why he used parables, he told the disciples that "the knowledge of the secrets of the kingdom of heaven has been given to you, but not to them" (Mt 13:11). Matthew points out that Jesus' use of parables fulfilled the OT: "I will open my mouth in parables, I will utter things hidden since the creation of the world" (Mt 13:35; cf. Mk 4:10–13). It is best to take this "secret" as a previously unrevealed expression of the divine kingdom—a way in which God acts in man's world that is not known from the OT.

The NT has much to say about this form of the kingdom, for this is the kingdom in which you and I are called to live today.

The present kingdom in the Epistles. Most of what the Epistles have to say about the Christian life does not mention the kingdom. Yet it is clear that believers have been rescued by the Father from the domain of darkness and have been brought "into the kingdom of the Son he loves" (Col 1:13). In Heb 12:28 the writer uses the present active participle to affirm, "We are receiving a kingdom that cannot be shaken." A number of passages speak of inheriting the kingdom (1 Co 6:9–10; 15:50; Gal 5:21; Eph 5:5; Jas 2:5). With the possible exception of Ja 2:5, the matter of inheritance is viewed in the context of Roman law. At birth a child becomes an heir and has an established right to the possessions controlled by his father. ◆ *Inheritance* Clearly, the NT presents another kingdom in addition to (1) the universal rule of God through providence and (2) the yet-future kingdom of prophecy (cf. Ro 14:17; 1 Co 4:20; Col 1:12,13; 4:11; 1 Th 2:12; 2 Th 1:5; Rev 1:6; 5:10). Still, the Epistles say less than the synoptic Gospels do about this other kingdom, possibly because it was necessary for Jesus to speak in kingdom terms before the language of resurrection could be established by his death and coming to life again.

Kingdom lifestyle in the synoptic Gospels. A number of extended passages in the Gospels explore life in Jesus' present kingdom. Using Matthew's Gospel as a framework, we see these major teaching passages.

Mt 5–7. The Sermon on the Mount has been interpreted in a number of ways. Is it a salvation message? Was it given to show Christians how they ought to live? Is it a picture of life in Jesus' future and coming kingdom? Is it a combination of the above? In view of the nature of the kingdom, it seems best to understand this Sermon as Jesus' statement of how people of every age live when they abandon themselves to God's will. This last view seems to best integrate the Sermon's many teachings with the NT's view of the kingdom.

The Beatitudes describe the values of a person living a kingdom lifestyle (Mt 5:3–12). Jesus then gives a series of illustrations, showing how inner values find expression in lifestyle (5:17–42). As king, Jesus acts to transform the character of his subjects. Jesus in the present kingdom is working in our inner selves to change our outward behavior. Jesus goes on to show how we can experience this transforming power. We focus on our "in secret" relationship with the Lord, not on visible piety (6:1–18). We give priority to seeking God's kingdom

and righteousness, and we trust our Father to supply our material needs (6:19–33). We relate to other kingdom citizens as brothers and sisters and reject every claim of a right to judge or control them (Mt 7:1–14). Instead of relying on human leaders, we rely on the simple words of Jesus and commit ourselves to obey them (7:15–27).

Mt 13. Jesus explained in parables how the present form of the kingdom compares with and differs from the expected, prophetic vision of God's direct rule on earth. The kingdom teaching of the parables is summarized in the accompanying chart (p. 381).

Mt 18–20. Jesus explains how one becomes great in God's present kingdom. ◆ *Great/Greatness*

There are other significant verses and insights. For instance, we read in the Lord's prayer: "Your kingdom come, your will be done on earth as it is in heaven" (Mt 6:10). In context, this is no prayer for the end of time. It is the believer's request that for the ability to do God's will now, here on earth, as it is done in heaven, so that God's kingdom may find expression in divine acts here and now. The kingdom is the realm in which the king acts with sovereign power. In Christ, you and I can experience that kingdom here and now. We can know God's power at work in our own lives as we adopt the lifestyle of the kingdom over which Jesus rules.

The theological basis for the present kingdom. It is clear that God's sovereign touch rules the universe, now and always. So the present kingdom of Jesus does not supersede or replace providence. Yet in speaking of the still-future kingdom over which Jesus will rule visibly, Scripture introduces a unique expression of the divine kingdom. God's providential supervision of the universe usually leaves him hidden. In the future, however, his rule on earth will be unmistakable and visible. The NT's introduction of a kingdom currently ruled by Jesus presents another unique expression of the divine kingdom: a mode in which God has chosen to act and through which his control will be expressed.

Parables of the Kingdom

The Parable	Expected Form	Unexpected Characteristic
1. sower 13:3–9,18–23	Messiah turns Israel and all nations to himself.	Individuals respond differently to the gospel invitation.
2. wheat/tares 13:24–30, 36–43	The kingdom's righteous citizens rule over the world with the King.	The kingdom's citizens are among the men of the world, growing together till God's harvesttime.
3. mustard seed 13:31–32	The kingdom begins in majestic glory.	The kingdom begins in insignificance; its greatness comes as a surprise.
4. leaven 13:33	Only righteousness enters the kingdom; other "raw material" is excluded.	The kingdom is implanted in a different "raw material" and grows to fill the whole personality with righteousness.
5. hidden treasure 13:44	The kingdom is public and for all.	The hidden kingdom is for individual "purchase."
6. priceless pearl 13:45–46	The kingdom brings all valued things to men.	The kingdom demands abandonment of all other values.
7. dragnet 13:47–50	The kingdom begins with initial separation of righteous and unrighteous.	The kingdom ends with final separation of the unrighteous from the righteous.

The theological basis for Jesus' action in the present form of his kingdom is laid in the new birth. "No one can see the kingdom of God unless he is born again" and "no one can enter the kingdom of God unless he is born of water and the Spirit" (Jn 3:3,5). The new birth gives entrance into the kingdom—the realm in which Jesus' sovereign power is translated into action on behalf of his people.

But why this stress on being born again? Perhaps because of the fact that when a person is born again, Jesus enters his or her life. And there he takes up permanent residence. ▶ *Born* Now and for all time Jesus is present in his people—in each believer and in the corporate body of Christ. In a mystical but real way, Jesus is present on earth in us. He is the key to release of the power needed to transform us and to shape the events that affect our lives according to his will.

The kingdom is here because Jesus is here. Because Jesus is here, the possibility of a new kind of life is laid open before us.

5. The coming kingdom. The NT never rejects the OT's portrait of the future. There will be a kingdom on earth, and Jesus will rule over it in person. Although this is not a dominant theme in NT teaching, Jesus himself confirms the OT vision of history's end (Mt 8:11,12; 16:28; 25:1,34; 26:29; Mk 11:10; 14:25; 15:43; Lk 13:28–29; 14:15; 21:31; Ac 1:6–7; cf. Mt 20:21; Mk 11:10; 15:43; Lk 14:15; 17:20; 19:11; 23:43,51).

6. Summary. When we read the word "kingdom" in the Bible, we must not import modern notions of a geographical area. The word simply indicates a realm in which a king exercises his power to act and control. The OT knows two different forms of God's sovereign rule, or kingdom. (1) There is a universal kingdom. God controls all events in the universe but does so nearly always through providence, so that his rule is hidden. (2) There is to be a visible earthly kingdom. In the future, Jesus will return to earth to rule in person over the whole world.

The NT adds another, previously unknown, form of the divine kingdom. This form, like that of the prophetic kingdom, is intimately linked with Jesus, for he is its king. When Jesus was on earth, this kingdom existed here. Although Jesus did not take up earthly political power (Jn 18:36), the miracles he performed showed his authority over every competing power. But Jesus the king was rejected and crucified, as his enemies struggled to force his kingdom out of history.

But Jesus' death was not the end. During his days on earth, Jesus explained what life under his rule (i.e., in his kingdom) would be like. It is best to take most Gospel descriptions of the kingdom of heaven and the kingdom of God (which should be treated as synonyms) as explanations of life in Jesus' present kingdom. Here we are given powerful insights into how we can live today as Jesus' subjects and experience his power. Because the new birth brings us into union with Jesus and brings Jesus in a unique way into our experience here on earth, we live in a day in which the king is present, though still disguised. Because Jesus *is* present, the unmatched power of God can find supernatural expression in and through our lives.

KNOW/KNOWLEDGE

The word "know" has multiplied shades of meaning in English. We know the information that we need to pass a test. We know how to drive. We know our friends. We should not be surprised to find that in the Bible "knowing" carries the same wide range of meanings.

OT 1. The Hebrew concept of knowing
   2. Knowing God in the OT
NT 3. The Greek concept of knowing
   4. Knowing God in the NT

OT — 1. The Hebrew concept of knowing. The basic Hebrew word is *yāḏaʿ*, "to know." The root appears almost 950 times in the OT and is used in referring to all kinds of knowledge gained through the senses. *Yāḏaʿ* is used also to indicate a knowing of information and facts, the learning of skills, acquaintance with persons, and even the intimacy of sexual intercourse. Although Hebrew is not a philosophical or speculative language, it is clear that "to know" calls for more than direct experience. Knowing implies the process by which human beings structure experience—the process by which one recognizes, classifies, and systematizes the data gained from experience. Thus, the phrase "knowing good and evil" (Ge 3:5,22; cf. Dt 1:39) focuses attention on the process of making moral distinctions and coming to conclusions about what is good and what is evil. To know, then, means far more than raw experience. It means to organize experience and, from that organized experience, to develop a perception of the world that provides a basis for response to different life situations.

2. Knowing God in the OT. It is clear from reading the OT that "knowing" God incorporates every dimension of this human capacity. When Moses first confronted Pharaoh with God's demand to let Israel go, the Egyptian snorted in derision: "Who is the LORD, that I should obey him and let Israel go? I do not know the LORD and I will not let Israel go" (Ex 5:2). In a series of divine judgments, Pharaoh and the Egyptians experienced God's power. Reluctantly Pharaoh released Israel, only to change his mind. He sent his army to compel his slaves to return. But at the Red Sea, God announced that he would destroy the Egyptian army: "The Egyptians will know that I am the LORD when I gain glory through Pharaoh, his chariots and his horsemen" (Ex 14:18).

Here we see a significant interplay of the factors involved in knowing. Pharaoh had no acquaintance with the Lord. Thus Yahweh played no part in his thinking or planning. Yahweh's acts provided the king with a direct experience of his power. Now Pharaoh was forced to revise his view of the world and take God into account. But Pharaoh would not accept a universe in which Yahweh was the ultimate reality. He acted against what he knew of God, and in the destruction of his army the Egyptian people saw clearly the result of a failure to truly "know" God.

Later Moses reviewed history and recounted for a new generation the record of God's mighty acts. Moses also shared the revealed meaning of these acts, and then he went on to review knowledge about God's moral nature revealed in the now-written Word. There is presently enough information available for all generations to hear about and come to know the Lord. So Moses went on to warn, "Acknowledge [yāḏaʿ] and take to heart this day that the LORD is God in heaven above and on the earth below" (Dt 4:39). The available information about God transmitted to each new generation must lead them to take his reality to heart and to let the vision of God shape their lives.

In the OT, a person's conduct gives evidence of whether or not that individual really knows God. Where God is not known, sins abound (e.g., Hos 4:1–2). Where God is known in the full biblical sense (knowledge "taken to heart"), a person is moved to do justice and to help the poor and needy (Jer 22:15–16).

NT — 3. The Greek concept of knowing. A number of words are used to express the Greek concept. *Ginōskō* and *oida* are the basic terms. Each indicates knowing and understanding. Each emphasizes the organization of one's perceptions so as to grasp the true nature of an issue, concept, or thing. In Greek thought, knowledge comes through the senses, and that which is known can be verified by observation. Words in these two families contrast with words that mean raw perception (*aisthēsis*, "experience") or a mere opinion (*dokeō*). Thus, traditionally in Greek culture, "knowing" meant intelligent comprehension, with the assumption that knowledge is a true assessment of reality insofar as reality can be known in this world. Despite distinctions suggested by some scholars, it is not really possible to show any significant difference in the way *ginōskō* and *oida* were used in ordinary speech; so it is best to treat them as synonyms.

Epiginōskō is also translated "know" in the NT. This is an intensive form of *ginōskō* and implies a fuller or more nearly complete knowledge.

In ordinary speech, *ginōskō* and *oida* carried most of the meanings found in English usage. Often translators of modern versions select an English equivalent that captures a particular shade of meaning. Thus, for instance, the word "knew" in Paul's statement that none of the princes of this world "knew God's secret wisdom" is translated in the NIV as "understood" (1 Co 2:8). The statement that Jesus "knew no sin" reads "him who had no sin" (2 Co 5:21). But ordinarily "know" is used, and it has the same breadth of meanings—from knowing facts to recognizing persons to enjoying a deep friendship with them.

There are, however, philosophical and theological dimensions to "know" in Greek thought that are not implied in ordinary speech. Often these philosophical issues are reflected in the NT. The ancient Greeks placed great reliance on human ability to understand the universe. By rational analysis of what they observed, they believed that mankind would ultimately arrive at an understanding of the universe. This view is rejected by Paul in 1 Co 2.

But over the centuries, Greek culture itself had come to doubt the assumptions of the old philosophers. By NT times, Hellenistic culture questioned the possibility of arriving at truth about reality through rational processes. Now humanity was looking inward, convinced by its unease that the source of human existence must lie outside the material universe. Focusing on people rather than on the universe, moderns asked, Who are we? Where did we come from? and Where are we going? So by the time of the NT, a variety of answers were suggested, and a number of mystical and speculative beliefs about origins, salvation, and theology sprang up. The belief systems of these thinkers could not be verified by observation. They rested on claims of special knowledge (*gnōsis*) from beyond the material world. The movement took its name from the Greek term: it is called the Gnostic movement. Its belief system is called Gnosticism.

There were several varieties of Gnosticism. Its supposed sources of knowledge ranged from mysticism and sacramentalism to magic and pseudo-philosophical speculation. But, basically, Gnosticism made a sharp distinction between the material and immaterial universes, between the physical and the spiritual. All matter was considered evil, while "good" was ascribed only to the unseen and spiritual realm. Human beings were viewed as "good" spirits trapped in bodies that, because they were physical, were necessarily evil. Inevitably, this dualism destroyed the basis for ethics laid down by earlier philosophers. The result was a variety of approaches to life, ranging from the strictly ascetic to the libertine. According to one view, if the flesh is evil, it must be crushed. According to another view, if the flesh is evil but the "true" person good, why not permit the flesh its excesses? What else could be expected of it? It cannot corrupt the spirit.

Paul appears to deal directly with the Gnostic views that infected the early church in Colosse. In the Epistle to the Colossians, he insisted that reconciliation came "by Christ's physical body through death" (1:22). His affirmation that "in Christ all the fullness of the Deity lives in bodily form" (2:9) strikes directly against Gnostic dualism and the Gnostic view of the material. Paul also insists that true goodness is the practice of compassion, kindness, and love in daily life. Thus, morality is something that calls for holiness in the most ordinary aspects of our life on earth; it is emphatically not a matter of "self-imposed" religious practices (2:9–23; 3:1–4:1).

Despite the claims of some to see Gnostic tendencies in the NT, Scripture rejects the Greek philosophical concepts of knowledge. Instead, it adopts the view of the OT. Knowledge is gained through the senses, but knowledge of God is based on a personal encounter with God through his historic acts and his inscripturated revelation of himself. To know God or spiritual truth in a biblical sense, one must perceive truth about God, let that truth shape one's understanding of life, and respond appropriately with faith and obedience. ♦ *Truth* ♦ *Obey/Disobey* Knowledge of God that incorporates all of these aspects will shape our lives in time and in eternity.

Probably the best way to explore the nature of religious knowledge, particularly the nature of knowing God, is to look at key NT passages where the argument rests on a distinctly biblical view of knowing.

4. Knowing God in the NT. John and Paul are the two NT writers who deal most significantly with the question of knowing God. A survey of their thought gives insight into how basic OT concepts of knowing are developed in the NT.

John. The writings of John usually employ "to know" as a relational term. It is used when explaining the nature and the implications of a personal relationship with Jesus.

Jn 8:19,31–47. The Jewish leaders saw the evidence of Jesus' miracles and heard his teachings but were "unable to hear" (v. 43) what he said. Their failure to respond to Jesus and to acknowledge him demonstrates their lack of a personal relationship with God. Jesus declared to them, "You do not know me or my Father" (v. 19). Instead, their antagonistic response to Jesus showed that they were in the grip of sin, replicating the response of Satan to God rather than the response of Abraham, whom they claimed relationship with.

But here Jesus also spoke to those who did believe, calling on them to hold to (do) his teachings. Those who believe and obey will "know the truth, and the truth will set [them] free" (v. 32). The first "know" (v. 19) indicates a personal relationship: a recognition, acknowledgment, and believing response to God presented in Christ. The second (v. 32) indicates a personal experience. Only obedience will bring those who know Jesus personally into a full experience of all that that relationship promises.

Jn 10:4,14–15. Jesus' relationship with believers is compared to that of a shepherd and his sheep. The sheep recognize the shepherd's voice and they respond to follow him. This is because an intimate relationship exists between sheep and shepherd, just as an intimate relationship exists between Jesus and the Father. Relational knowing is demonstrated by response: "My sheep listen to my voice" (v. 27).

1 John. John's first letter is about fellowship. ▶ **Fellowship** Here "knowing" expresses an intimate relationship of continual sharing that exists within the believing community and between the believer and God. Rather than indicating saving faith, in 1 John the idea of "knowing him" usually represents continuing fellowship.

About this aspect of knowing God, John says, "We know that we have come to know him" if we respond to his commands with obedience (2:3; 2:4–6,29). Additional evidence is found in love for others in the Christian community, for "everyone who loves has been born of God and knows God" (4:7).

Relationship with God comes only through Jesus. God's act of sending his only Son into the world is history's decisive act of self-revelation by God: "If anyone acknowledges that Jesus is the Son of God, God lives in him and he in God. And so we know and rely on the love God has for us" (4:15–16).

John emphasizes the absolute importance of the Holy Spirit. It is through the work of the Spirit within that we who believe in Jesus have the ability to recognize, understand, and respond to God's words and actions (2:20–23; 3:24; 4:13).

At the end of 1 John there is a summary of truths that we know in and through our personal relationship with Jesus. These are truths that shape our perspective on reality and thus shape our lives. We know that anyone born of God does not continue in sin. We know that we are the children of God, while the world around us lies in the grip of Satan. ▶ **World** We know that the Son of God has come to make it possible for us to have a personal relationship with God. We know that we are in Jesus, the true God and source of eternal life (5:18–20).

For John, then, knowing God is a matter of (1) God's initiating acts of self-revelation, particularly his act of sending Jesus; (2) the individual's recognition of these acts and subsequent acknowledgment of Jesus as God's Son and his Savior; (3) the Spirit's inner testimony within the believer enabling him to recognize and grasp the meaning of truth; and (4) the individual's daily life of obedience and of love. ▶ **Truth**

Paul. Paul's exploration of the nature of knowledge includes the strong emphasis of John on personal relationship. But it ranges to include other issues as well.

Ro 1:18–32. Paul shows that God has revealed himself to humanity in creation. God's invisible qualities "have been clearly seen, being understood from what has been made" (v. 20). The thought here is significant. Paul says both that creation reveals the Creator and that man's nature is such that this message is understood! But Paul adds, "Although they knew God, they neither glorified him as God nor gave thanks to him" (v. 21). This refusal to respond to God is culpable ignorance (cf. 2 Th 1:8). Humanity chooses not to acknowledge

God. But failure to acknowledge and respond to God has consequences. Mankind's thinking has been distorted by refusal to fit God into its perception of the world, and this in turn has led to intellectual and moral folly. Although God has given mankind a nature that also recognizes moral issues, man continues to act against that innate knowledge (v. 32).

Ro 7:7–25. God has also revealed himself to mankind in words. Thus, some revelation is natural revelation and some is special revelation. ▶ *Reveal/Revelation* When God revealed his own moral standards in the words of the Mosaic Law, he intended to give man not only more knowledge about himself but also self-knowledge. Both in the Mosaic Law and in his own failure to keep it, Paul discovered the fact that he was a sinner. His perception of himself was reshaped when he observed his inner and outward reaction to the Mosaic Law and so came to the place of relying totally on Christ and not on his own moral potential.

1 Co 2. In this vital passage, Paul criticizes the philosopher's approach to knowledge. The Greek thinkers supposed that they could grasp the nature of reality by applying rational processes to evaluate the data they gained by observing the universe. Paul says that the shape of reality can be known only through revelation, for God's Spirit must communicate the things known only to God. Some information about reality is simply not available to humanity through the senses, for "No eye has seen, no ear has heard, no mind has conceived what God has prepared for those who love him" (v. 9).

Often this statement is taken to be a paraphrase of Isa 64:4. But it seems better in context to see it as Paul's commentary on philosophy (the world's wisdom), picked up from Empedocles, who in the fifth century B.C. wrote the following: "Weak and narrow are the powers implanted in the limbs of man; many the woes that fall on them and blunt the edges of thought; short is the measure of the life in death through which they toil. Then are they borne away; like smoke they vanish into air; and what they dream they know is but the little that each has stumbled upon in wandering about the world. Yet they boast all that they have learned the whole. Vain fools! For what that is, no eye hath seen, no ear hath heard, nor can it be conceived by the mind of man." One cannot move from data obtained from the material universe to deduce the whole, for only God knows the reality beyond the material. It is wonderful that, as 1 Co 2:10 makes clear, God has chosen to reveal reality, and himself, to us now!

1 Co 6. Again and again in this passage, Paul poses a question: "Do you not know . . . ?" He expresses shock over what he saw the Corinthians doing. His point is that knowing such revealed truths as that "the saints will judge the world" (v. 2) and "the wicked will not inherit the kingdom of God" (v. 9) has implications for one's lifestyle. If one truly "knows" such truths, one will see their relevance to daily life. Knowing changes perspective and thus changes one's response to ordinary situations.

1 Co 8. Paul examines a doctrinal dispute over whether or not it is right to eat meat previously offered to idols. Each side in the dispute based its case on revealed truths. Each made deductions from such truths and tried to apply them in a practical way.

Paul insisted that this approach to resolving doctrinal differences in the believing community is not adequate. Why? First, because the claim to superior knowledge puffs us up. Pride and arrogance then close us off from our fellow believers and dampen love. This is tragic, for love within the believing community is the key to future spiritual development. Second, "the man who thinks he knows something does not yet know as he ought to know" (v. 2). Our knowledge even of revealed truths is incomplete. Thus we cannot claim to have all the perspective needed to make dogmatic statements. Paul's solution is unique: deal with the dispute on the basis of love. Differ if you must, but remain committed to love one another. While caring for each other and listening to each other, those involved in a dispute will grow spiritually and enrich their perspectives on the issue.

Eph 1:17–23; 3:14–19. Paul's prayers for the Ephesians focus on a personal relationship with God and on a right perspective of him. Paul asks God to help the Ephesians "know [God] better." In each prayer, knowing God is linked with truth about God. With knowing God comes an opening of the eyes of the heart, "enlightened in order that you may know the hope to which he has called you" (1:18). Paul knows that it is through relationships within the family of God that believers will experience God's love as a reality. Thus, they can "know this love that surpasses knowledge" (3:19).

Here rational process is set aside. It is never possible for us to encompass the nature of divine love, for it is beyond comprehension. Still, just as a little child cannot grasp the meaning of forgiveness but can experience it as his parents forgive him, so the believer will experience God's love within the family as Christ, through others, reaches out to touch that person.

Col 1:9–12. Paul's prayer for the Colossians shows more of the link between knowing truths about God and knowing God personally. Paul asked the Lord to fill the Colossians with a knowledge of what God had willed. That objectively revealed truth was to be processed with "all spiritual wisdom and understanding" (v. 9). The result would be a daily life marked by bearing fruit in every good work. ◗ **Fruit** This kind of life itself issues in growth in knowing God in a personal, experiential way.

Paul's teaching about knowledge of God and of spiritual truths reinforces the basic view of knowledge presented in the OT. There is no dichotomy between information about God and knowing God: the two are linked in human experience. God has acted to communicate with mankind. He has shown himself in creation, in his written Word, and in Jesus. Human beings are called on to acknowledge and respond appropriately to what God has revealed. It is in the interaction between revelation and response that a human being comes to know God personally and to grow in that personal relationship.

Each truth revealed by God calls for an appropriate human response. For instance, the appropriate response to God's revelation of himself in nature is to glorify him and give thanks. An appropriate response to God's revelation in the Mosaic Law is self-examination, with acknowledgment of one's sin. An appropriate response to the truth that "the saints will judge the world" (1 Co 6:2) is for the church to take responsibility to settle worldly disputes between believers. And the appropriate response to the good news of Jesus is to trust him as Savior and Lord.

Making an appropriate response calls for spiritual wisdom and insight. ◗ **Wisdom** An appropriate response will also issue in a life of good works—that is, in bearing fruit to God. These responses to truths from God will have an exciting impact on our personal relationship with the Lord. While never able to grasp the whole, we will grow to know God better and better in a personal, relational way.

It is knowing God in personal relationship that is, in fact, the goal on which the biblical view of knowledge focuses. This is the ultimate goal of God's self-revelation. He lets us know about himself in revelation in order that we may respond appropriately and know him in a deeply personal way—in salvation and fellowship. No wonder, then, that Paul gladly threw away everything on which he had once based his hope of gain, looking instead only for the "surpassing greatness of knowing Christ Jesus [his] Lord" (Php 3:8).

L

LABOR ♦ Work/Labor

LAKE OF FIRE ♦ Heaven and Hell

LAMB

In the OT, the lamb is presented as an animal to be offered as a sacrifice to God, particularly at the Passover. In the NT, three different Greek words for "lamb" are found: *amnos, arēn,* and *arnion. Amnos* is the sacrificial lamb. This word is found in a quote from Isa 53 that presents Jesus as a sacrificial lamb (Ac 8:32). It is also used in 1 Pe 1:19, where it emphasizes Jesus' perfection, qualifying him to offer his blood as a sacrifice. In its other two NT occurrences (Jn 1:29,36), Jesus is called the Lamb of God. In all of these passages, Jesus' death as a sacrifice for our sins is clearly in view.

Arēn speaks of the harmless nature of the animal. It is a word that is not linked with sacrifice. It is used only once in the NT (Lk 10:3).

Arnion is the third word for lamb in the NT. One of its thirty occurrences is in Jn 21:15; the other twenty-nine are in Revelation, where it identifies the judge and lord of the universe as the Jesus who was crucified for the fallen human race.

Where the NIV reads "passover lamb," the Greek simply reads "passover." "Lamb" is supplied for clarity. ♦ *Passover*

LAMP/LAMPSTAND

The OT lamp (*nēr*) was a small clay bowl, holding oil and a bit of flax or linen as a wick. God's Word is said to be like a lamp to the psalmist's feet (Ps 119:105); this is a graphic image of guidance, as the flickering light revealed only enough of the path for one to safely take the next step. The OT lampstand is the *mᵉnôrâh,* a seven-branched holder of lamps that was placed in the tabernacle or temple. The lampstand often symbolically represents God's perfect leadership in showing his people their way. It also represents the Holy Spirit.

In the NT, "lamp" is *lychnos* or *lampas,* and "lampstand" is *lychnia.* In the Gospels the lamp is usually symbolic. It speaks of the impact of the believer's obedience on the world (Mt 5:15–16; Lk 8:16–18; 11:33–36). The eye is the "lamp of the body" in that it is the instrument enabling persons to see. Jesus warns that when the spiritual eye is blinded, man lies in terrible darkness (Mt 6:22–23; Lk 11:34).

LAND

The Hebrew word translated "land" is *'ereṣ.* It is the fourth most common noun in the OT, occurring some 2,526 times. It is translated "earth," "land," and "world." ♦ *Earth/Earthly*

The word is often used to indicate geographical areas, such as "the land of Egypt" and "the land of Babylon." It is in this usage, applied to the land of Israel, that we find "land" theologically significant.

The OT presents Israel as a chosen people, selected by God as his own special possession. ♦ *Israel* From before their beginning as his people, the Lord promised to commit himself to give them a particular land to possess. The promise is originally stated in Ge 12:1 and Ge 15:7, but it is repeated often throughout the OT. ♦ *Covenant*

Ex 13 sets the Exodus in the context of slavery versus freedom. Moses told them: "Commemorate this day, the day you came out of Egypt, out of the land of slavery. . . . He [God] brings you into the land he swore to your forefathers to give you, a land flowing with milk and honey" (vv. 3,5). Throughout the OT, the land of Canaan (modern Palestine) is viewed as Israel's by right of the divine gift.

Disobedience kept the generation of the Exodus from entering the Promised Land. But their children were reminded of God's commitment: "See, I have given you this land. Go in and take possession of the land that the LORD swore he would give to your fathers . . . and to their descendants after them" (Dt 1:8).

Disobedience led to a later generation's being dragged captive from the land. But even as God's people suffered exile, Jeremiah promised that there would be a restoration to the land (Jer 32–33). In addition, before the exile (Am 9:15) and after (Zec 14:10), Israel's destiny is linked with the Promised Land.

In the OT, Canaan (Palestine) is *the* land of God's people, an inheritance from the Lord that will be possessed forever. ♦ *Inheritance*

LAST DAYS ♦ *Day*

LAUGH/LAUGHTER

The Hebrew *ṣāḥaq* and its derivatives mean "laughter in joy" or "incredulity." In increasingly intensive steps these words can be understood as play or sport or revelry, or as mocking and derision. Thus there is nothing in the Hebrew words to help us explain God's rebuke of Sarah's laughter when she heard his promise of a son (Ge 18:12) and his failure to rebuke Abraham's involuntary laugh when he first heard the same promise (Ge 17:17). Each was at first incredulous. We can only conclude from context that Abraham's response did not spill over into mockery, whereas Sarah's

may have done so. How wonderful that God blessed each, and when we next read of Sarah's laughter, it is clear that it is a laughter stimulated by joy in the birth of Isaac, the child who was promised to them both.

LAW

We sing about law in our hymns. "Free from the law, O happy condition, Jesus has bled, and there is remission." And yet we hear the OT believer affirm, "O how I love thy law!" (Ps 119:97, KJV).

What is law? Is it a good thing or a bad thing? Are Christians today truly free from the law? And, if so, what does that freedom involve?

There are few questions as significant to us as those we must address in seeking to understand what the law of God is—and what it is not!

OT 1. Law in the OT
     2. Law and covenant in Israel
     3. The extent of the law
     4. The OT believer's attitude toward law
NT 5. Law in the NT
     6. Jesus and the law
     7. Law as a total system
     8. Three functions of law
     9. The weaknesses and inadequacy of law
    10. The Christian alternative to law
    11. Summary

OT — 1. Law in the OT. The Hebrew word is *tôrâh.* Its basic meaning is "teaching" or "instruction." It denotes instruction focused on how one should live rather than on abstract or academic subjects.

The basic meaning of the word is reflected in passages that speak of parents or the aged instructing youth. "My son, do not forget my teaching [*tôrâh*], but keep my commands in your heart, for they will prolong your life many years and bring you prosperity" (Pr 3:1). Again, "The teaching [*tôrâh*] of the wise is a fountain of life, turning a man from the snares of death" (Pr 13:14).

It is important to keep this basic meaning in view when we turn to the law (*tôrâh*) of God. This too is instruction. It is teaching focused on how one should live.

The OT looks in wonder at the fact that God stooped to instruct Israel. If we have thought of God's law as some cold, rigid set of rules brutally applied, we miss the heart and soul of law. Moses reveals the warm heart of law in Dt 4, when he said to an expectant new generation about to enter Palestine: "See, I have taught you decrees and laws as the LORD my God commanded me, so that you may follow them in the land you are entering to take possession of it. Observe them carefully, for this will show your wisdom and understanding to the nations, who will hear about all these decrees and say, 'Surely this great nation is a wise and understanding people.' What other nation is so great as to have their gods near them the way the LORD our God is near us whenever we pray to him? And what other nation is so great as to have such righteous decrees and laws as this body of laws I am setting before you today? (vv. 5–8).

Moses' words introduce the derived meaning of *tôrâh*. To most of us, "law" is not simply instruction. It is the specific instruction given to Israel through Moses, carrying with it the full force of all that "law" means to us. It is the Mosaic code, with its Ten Commandments and with its instructions covering every aspect of Israel's personal and national life. It is the moral, ceremonial, and civil way of life God ordained for his OT people.

In this sense the law consists of all the statutes, ordinances, precepts, commandments, and testimonies given by God to guide his people. But the Mosaic Law—those teachings included in the first five books of the OT—includes even more. It includes Moses' review of and interpretation of history, his record of God's mighty acts, his report of Creation. In time, "the Law" came to indicate everything that God revealed through Moses, and in one sense it indicates the Pentateuch.

When we read the word "law" in the OT, it is helpful to remember that it may have many referents. It may refer to God's revelation in a general way. It may point to a specific set of instructions— e.g., the law of Passover, or the Ten Commandments. It may indicate the moral or ceremonial codes, or the writings of Moses.

What is clear, however, is that whatever a particular use of "law" points to, the OT views *tôrâh* as divine instruction. *Tôrâh* is God's gift, intended to show Israel how to live a holy and happy life in this world.

2. Law and covenant in Israel. In OT history and theology, covenant precedes law. God made his historic commitment to Abraham some 430 years before the law was introduced at Sinai. And law made no basic change in the covenant.

▶ *Covenant* It is the covenant that stands as the basis of Israel's relationship with the Lord, and it is the covenant with Abraham to which God will remain faithful.

Law was introduced to meet a need that existed within the context of the covenant. God acted in covenant faithfulness to bring Israel out of Egypt. But Israel's unresponsiveness to God demonstrated that this people needed guidance and structure. At Sinai, God provided the needed structure. He established guidelines for Israel for living with him and with others, as individuals and in community. God also made clear the consequences of obedience and disobedience. The individual or generation that lived in harmony with the divine teaching would receive blessing. The individual or generation that wandered away from the path marked out by law would be disciplined.

The OT often has this emphasis on law as marking out the path by which one might experience blessing within the covenant relationship. For instance:

Moses to Israel	The Lord will delight in you and make you prosperous . . . if you obey the Lord your God and keep his commandments and decrees that are

written in this Book of the Law and turn to the Lord your God with all your heart and with all your soul (Dt 30:9–10).

God to Joshua

Be strong and very courageous. Be careful to obey all the law my servant Moses gave you; do not turn from it to the right or to the left, that you may be successful wherever you go (Jos 1:7–8).

David to Solomon

Observe what the Lord your God requires: Walk in his ways, and keep his decrees and commands, all his laws and requirements, as written in the Law of Moses, so that you may prosper in all you do and wherever you go (1 Ki 2:3).

Observing the revealed will of God shared in the law of Moses was the way to blessing. The law was a great gift to Israel, for it was their key to the experience of God's best.

To understand the OT, we need to grasp the relationship between law and covenant. Covenant is the basis for relationship between God and human beings. But the covenant was made with Abraham, and its fulfillment promised his descendants blessings at history's end. What about those generations that follow one another across the intervening millennia? It is to these generations that the law is addressed. Law was designed to teach each generation of God's people how to live so that they might experience in their day the blessings that God promised will be provided at history's end. A generation might disobey the law and violate God's commandments, but the covenant itself was unaffected. All that the disobedient generation would do is to bring down upon itself the punishments established when the law was given (Dt 28:15–68).

3. The extent of the law. At times we may think of the law as merely the moral code delivered by Moses. As we have

seen, law encompasses far more than that. In its prescriptive elements the Mosaic Law functioned as (1) the constitution of the nation, (2) the basis for determining civil and criminal cases, (3) a guide to worship, (4) a personal guide to good family and social relationships, and (5) a personal guide to relationship with the Lord. Law comprised not only those regulations that defined sin and established guilt but also the sacrificial system through which the believer might find atonement for sins. In essence, everything in the experience of the people of Israel was guided by the law.

Despite the all-encompassing nature of law and despite the fact that law is seen in the OT as one of God's good gifts, Israel fell far short of becoming a just and holy community. The prophets looked back and viewed history only as an unbroken series of disasters and tragedy, as generation after generation turned from the Lord and his ways. Looking ahead, Jeremiah saw a new day when the Mosaic Law would be supplanted. Then an effective and powerful guide to holiness, "not like" the Mosaic Law, would be introduced. The Lord declared through the prophet: "I will put my law in their minds and write it on their hearts. I will be their God, and they will be my people" (Jer 31:33). Law in the OT is good. But law is not permanent, for law has never been effective in making the people of God righteous.

4. The OT believer's attitude toward law. While law was unable to make a generation or individual good, law was deeply appreciated by the person who trusted the Lord. Two of David's psalms show us how highly esteemed the law was among believing Israelites. Ps 19 says this: "The law of the LORD is perfect, reviving the soul. The statutes of the LORD are trustworthy, making wise the simple. The precepts of the LORD are right, giving joy to the heart. The commands of the LORD are radiant, giving light to the eyes. The fear of the LORD is pure, enduring forever. The ordinances of the LORD are sure and altogether righteous. They are more precious than gold, than much pure gold; they are sweeter than honey, than honey from the comb. By them is your servant warned; in keeping them there is great reward" (vv. 7-11).

Many similar thoughts and words of praise for the law are found in Ps 119. David perceived God's law in the context of personal relationship. The law is not a stern external demand, but David experienced it as the caressing voice of a God whom he loved and whom he rejoiced to obey. In the context of this kind of relationship, all who trusted the Lord could say: "Praise be to you, O LORD; teach me your decrees. With my lips I recount all the laws that come from your mouth. I rejoice in following your statutes as one rejoices in great riches. I meditate on your precepts and consider your ways. I delight in your decrees; I will not neglect your word" (vv. 12-16).

NT — 5. Law in the NT. The Greek word for "law" is *nomos*. Its roots in Greek culture assume a social process by which members of a community develop patterns of expectations, which become traditions, and finally are incorporated as norms that define a person's duties to others and the state. By the fifth century B.C., laws were written laws, which if not obeyed brought punishment.

The philosophers were disturbed by the uncertainty and change they saw in laws generated by society. They looked for a source of law outside history—a source of law that would be in harmony with the nature of the universe itself. Their conviction was that life could be meaningful only if it were lived in harmony with universal principles.

At times this sense of "universal principle" best captures the meaning of *nomos* in the NT. Paul described his inner struggle with sin in these terms. He found within himself a "law [*nomos*, principle] of sin and death." He wanted to respond to the revealed law of God, but his own fallen nature betrayed him. So Paul turned to another universal principle operating in God's universe: "the law of the Spirit of life in Christ Jesus" (Ro 8:2, KJV). He had to rely on the principle of divine enablement to lift him beyond his own powerless state.

Usually, however, the meaning of *nomos* in the NT is shaped by OT thought and the various meanings of *tôrâh*. In the NT too, law is a word of instruction from God, coming from outside, that authoritatively marks out the path of righteousness and blessing.

6. Jesus and the law. In Jesus' time the rabbis (the teachers of the law we meet so often in the NT) focused their faith on law. God had given the *tôrâh*, the first five OT books, to Moses. All else (the Writings and the Prophets) were but commentary on this core. The religious leaders in Jesus' day were sure not only that these Mosaic books were the key to life and death but also that the individual could keep the law and please God. The young ruler's question, "What must I do to inherit eternal life?" (Lk 18:18) sums up the understanding of religion held by most of the religious people in his generation.

When Jesus appeared, he did not deny the Law (the books of Moses). But he did directly challenge the understanding of the OT on which contemporary Jewish faith was based. To understand the challenge and to sense Jesus' own view of "law" as the term is used in the Gospels, we need to examine several significant gospel passages.

Mt 5:18-48. Jesus began by stating his own allegiance to the OT. But then he made this dramatic declaration concerning his purpose for coming to earth: "Do not think that I have come to abolish the Law or the Prophets; I have not come to abolish them but to fulfill them. I tell you the truth, until heaven and earth disappear, not the smallest letter, not the least stroke of a pen, will by any means disappear from the law until everything is accomplished" (5:17-18). ◆ *Fulfill* Jesus continued with a warning: the commandments are to be practiced (5:19). But then he said, "I tell you that unless your righteousness surpasses that of the Pharisees and the teachers of the law, you will certainly not enter the kingdom of heaven" (5:20).

Jesus then illustrated what he meant. He picked commands from the law, saying, "You have heard. . . ." And then he went on, "But I say to you. . . ." In each case, Jesus shifted the focus from a behavior regulated by law (e.g., "Do not murder") to inner attitudes (e.g., anger) from which the actions flow. His point is clear: law looks on the outside, but God is concerned with the heart. It is the human heart that must be transformed and not merely expressions of sin that must be restrained.

Mt 7:12; 22:36–40. Jesus taught that the Law and the Prophets can be summed up simply: "In everything, do to others what you would have them do to you" (v. 12). An expansion on this statement came when Jesus was questioned by one "expert in the law" (v. 35). Asked which is the greatest commandment, Jesus answered: "Love the Lord your God with all your heart and with all your soul and with all your mind. This is the first and greatest commandment. And the second is like it: Love your neighbor as yourself. All the Law and the Prophets hang on these two commandments" (vv. 37–40). Again the issue shifts from strict compliance with the detailed instructions of the OT to one's heart attitude. Love for God and love for others is the key to godliness.

Jn 1:17; Mt 11:13; Lk 16:16–17. The NT indicates that with the appearance of Jesus, the foretold day in which the Mosaic Law would be superseded had arrived. John wrote that "the law was given through Moses; grace and truth came through Jesus Christ" (Jn 1:17). Luke quotes Jesus: "The Law and the Prophets were proclaimed until John. Since that time the good news of the kingdom of God is being preached" (Lk 16:16). The OT economy was not rejected. Not at all. Instead, all that the OT foretold had come with Jesus. He is the Prophet who was destined to bring the message that supersedes that of Moses (Dt 18:15). The way of life he introduced did not abolish the Mosaic code but supersedes it with the new covenant that the prophets promised (Jer 31). ♦ *Covenant*

Mt 19:3–9. When Pharisees came to Jesus to raise a point of law concerning divorce, Jesus answered them by stating God's intentions for marriage. From the time of creation God has intended marriage to be a permanent union. The Pharisees insist, "Why then did Moses command that a man give his wife a certificate of divorce and send her away?" (v. 7). Jesus' response is stunning, cutting the ground from underneath those who saw the Mosaic Law as a perfect expression of God's righteousness. "Moses permitted you to divorce your wives because your hearts were hard" (v. 8), Jesus replied.

The point of Jesus' response is this: God in the law established a requirement for his people that was *less than his ideal.* Rather than being the highest possible standard, the Mosaic Law is a divine compromise. What God truly desires is utterly beyond possibility for people whose hearts are hardened by sin. To make it possible for Israel to even approximate God's real standards, he gave them a law that made allowances for less-than-perfect righteousness!

No wonder, then, that Jesus taught that our righteousness must surpass that of scribes and Pharisees. God calls on the believer to find a righteousness that is greater than that expressed in law: a righteousness that flows from and finds expression in love for God and love for others.

In the Gospels, then, "Law" usually means the first five books of the OT, although at times it means the commandments contained in them. Jesus denied that his teaching threatened the OT revelation. Instead, Jesus fulfilled the OT, both in the sense of explaining it correctly and in the sense of being himself the goal toward which the OT points. As far as the specific commands contained in the Mosaic Law are concerned, Jesus introduced a righteousness surpassing them. This is possible because the moral regulations of the law are simply practical guidelines on how to love God and neighbor. When love fills the believer's heart, the reality to which law points will come.

7. Law as a total system. Both the Book of Hebrews and the apostle Paul approach law from a systems perspective.

For the writer of Hebrews, law is that perfectly balanced OT system that includes commands, sacrifices, priesthood, and tabernacle worship. Hebrews argues that this OT structure is like a modern mobile, which suspends a number of objects in balance with each other. The writer introduces Jesus as a priest "in the order of Melchizedek" (7:11) rather than of Levi and argues that "there must also be a change of the law" (v. 12). The system is so balanced that a change in any single element implies a change in all other elements within the system. Under the new covenant there must be a new sanctuary, new sacrifices, and even a new approach to righteousness. The laws that the older covenant engraved on stones will be "put in their minds" and written "on their hearts" (8:10).

The writer's constant contention is that what we now have is "better than" what was provided by the OT system—better at every point. The old was merely "an illustration for the present time" (9:9), replaced now by the reality to which it testified. In saying that "the law is only a shadow of the good things that are coming—not the realities themselves" (10:1), the writer includes the total OT system—ceremonial (10:2–14) and moral (10:15–18).

The apostle Paul also takes a systems approach in his use of "law." But the system implicit in Paul's use of *nomos* has different elements. Paul is concerned with the interaction between the revealed moral code and human nature. Viewed objectively and in isolation from human experience, the law is "holy, righteous and good" (Ro 7:12). But when looked at in its impact on human beings, the law is a word of destruction and death (7:9–19). The very establishment of a standard stimulates human beings to efforts to achieve righteousness, turning them from faith to works as an approach to a relationship with God. Thus the objectively "good" law, when viewed in its interaction with humans beings, is "powerless" because "it was weakened by the sinful nature" (Ro 8:3).

In Paul's letters this evaluation of *nomos* as a system of interaction between the word of divine command and human beings is explored again and again. We cannot understand Paul's use of "law," as we will see, unless we realize that he includes in his use of the term the commandments that express righteousness via statutes, the human beings who hear this word, and every interaction between the word and the natural man.

8. Three functions of law. Theologians distinguish three functions of law, using law in the sense of the OT's moral code. The first of these functions is to reveal the nature of God. The thought is that God's own character is revealed by the standards he establishes. The God who gives laws and announces "Be holy because I, the LORD your God, am holy" (Lev 19:1) clearly expresses his own character in the commandments he calls on Israel to keep.

The second function of the law is to reveal sin. In the OT, one who discovered he had violated a commandment in the Mosaic code was to come to the Lord with sacrifice. Paul picks up and emphasizes this function of the law: "Now we know that whatever the law says, it says to those who are under the law, so that every mouth may be silenced and the whole world held accountable to God. Therefore no one will be declared righteous in his sight by observing the law; rather, through the law we become conscious of sin (Ro 3:19–20).

Paul describes the psychological process in Ro 7: "I would not have known what sin was except through the law. For I would not have known what coveting really was if the law had not said, 'Do not covet' " (7:7). In revealing sin, law points us away from our own efforts and directs our gaze to Jesus so that we may be saved by faith.

This view of law contradicts the common view of the religious Jews of NT times. They held that law marks out God's way of salvation, and Paul's preaching of faith seemed to them a great heresy. But Paul asked, "Do we, then, nullify the law by this faith? Not at all! Rather we uphold the law" (Ro 3:31).

Paul's point is that the gospel restored faith to the place it had always had in one's relationship with God, and the gospel restored law to its rightful place as well! ♦ *Belief/Faith* Law does not make anyone righteous. Law brings to all who hear its demands and who honestly examine their own lives a consciousness of sin.

The third function of law is debated. This function is to guide the believer to a holy life. We have already seen that this third function did operate in OT times. But there is clear and convincing biblical evidence that the law does not function this way today. "Sin shall not be your master," declares the apostle, "because you are not under law, but under grace" (Ro 6:14).

The same thought is expressed elsewhere in other ways. Believers died to the law with Christ (Ro 7:1–4). We are released from the law so that we serve in the new way of the Spirit (Ro 7:6). Christ is the end of the law (Ro 10:4). Believers die to the law so that they may live for Christ (Gal 2:19). Redeemed from under the law, we now have full rights as sons and daughters (Gal 4:5). The law is not for good people (1 Ti 1:9).

These statements of release from obligation to law do not explain how or why Christians are not to relate to the law as a moral guide. But they do indicate that the law is not to have the same role in the life of the NT believer that it played in the life of the believer of the OT.

The early church recognized the issue in its first decades. A decision was necessitated by the fact that some people were insisting that the Gentile converts be required to accept circumcision and keep the Mosaic Law. ♦ *Circumcision* In council at Jerusalem the church agreed not to put "on the necks of the disciples a yoke that neither we nor our fathers have been able to bear" (Ac 15:10). With Christ, a new way is opened up, and the believer finds a principle of life that supersedes the way of law.

9. The weakness and inadequacy of law. One problem we have in understanding the NT view of law is rooted in the shifting meanings of *nomos* throughout the NT. "Law" sometimes indicates the books of Moses or Scripture itself (Ro 3:21b). Law can be a universal principle (Ro 3:27; 7:21). In Hebrews, law usually means the total way of life prescribed in the OT, including the moral, cultic, and other regulations.

Paul gives us our greatest difficulty. In his writing, the meaning of *nomos* shifts often and subtly. At times he clearly means the moral requirements of God that are established by the OT. Then in the same context he seems to shift, to mean a "works" approach to righteousness, which assumes that one's actions provide the basis for acceptance by God or a means to become righteous. This tendency to shift emphases makes it difficult to interpret a verse such as Ro 6:14: "Sin shall not be your master, because you are not under law, but under grace." Is Paul talking of freedom from the OT's moral code? Or is he referring to the cultic aspect of the OT? Or is he simply saying that sin will not master us because we no longer approach righteousness as if it were something we could attain by our own efforts?

But we should not try to make this kind of distinction. In fact, Paul realizes that we cannot separate an expression of morality in commands and a works approach to righteousness. The reason he shifts focus so often and so subtly when he writes of law is that each meaning is implicit in the other! To express righteousness in commands creates a necessity for effort to achieve. This is why the law is so effective in convicting of sin. We see the standards. We try to attain a degree of obedience, and we see how far short we fall. Thus it is in the very nature of law to stimulate effort. When righteousness is expressed in a form that by its nature stimulates human effort, looking to law will bring moral defeat, even to the believer.

With this in mind we can explore key passages in which Paul critiques the weaknesses and the inadequacy of law. *Ro 4:13–16.* Blessing comes through the divine promise, accepted by faith. Paul says, "If those who live by law are heirs, faith has no value and the promise

is worthless, because law brings wrath"
(v. 14). Law and faith are totally different
approaches to relationship with God,
and elements of the two systems cannot
be mixed.

Ro 7:4–6. Paul says that man's sinful
nature is stimulated (energized) by the
law. The result is "fruit for death" (v. 5).
Paul contrasts systems when he says,
"We have been released from the law so
that we serve in the new way of the
Spirit" (v. 6). The two operating systems
Paul describes are diagramed below,
showing his conviction that no elements
of the systems can be mixed.

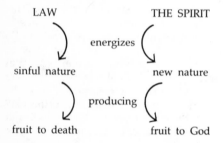

In the context of this teaching we see
the force of 1 Co 15:56: "The power of sin
is the law." Law relates to the old nature
and arouses it to sin.

Ro 7:21–25; 8:3. Paul recognized the
law's commandment as "holy, righteous,
and good" (7:12). Although as a believer
he yearned to keep the law, he found
that the principle of sin was so firmly
rooted in his personality that his efforts
fell desperately short: "I myself in my
mind am a slave to God's law, but in the
sinful nature a slave to the law [principle]
of sin" (v. 25). In Ro 8:3, as Paul is
sharing his solution to the dilemma, he
explains that the law was "powerless . . .
in that it was weakened by the sinful
nature."

There is nothing wrong with law. But
the law system falls short where it
touches humanity. A ship's anchor may
be carefully cast and its size matched to
the vessel. But if the ocean bottom is soft
mud covering a hard, impenetrable surface, there is no way the anchor can grip.
The anchor is useless to hold the vessel.
Just so, the law is good and righteous,

but there is no feature in human nature
where it can obtain a grip.

Gal 2:21; 3:21–22. Paul said that if
righteousness could come by law, then
Christ died for nothing. But law could
not impart spiritual life.

Gal 3:10–14. Paul criticized those believers who, having come to Jesus by
faith, were trying to attain spiritual goals
by human effort (i.e., by observing the
law [3:2–3]). Paul showed that "the
righteous will live by faith" (v. 11), while
"the law is not based on faith: on the
contrary, 'The man who does these
things will live by them' " (v. 12). Here
again Paul insisted that one cannot mix
faith and law in approaching Christian
experience.

Gal 5:1–6. Developing the thought
that law and faith are opposing principles, whose system elements cannot be
mixed, Paul insists that "it is for freedom
that Christ has set us free" (v. 1). One
who seeks to be justified (to become or
be declared righteous) by the way of law
has "been alienated from Christ" (v. 4).
Paul does not threaten loss of salvation.
He teaches that the source of righteousness is known through intimate relationship with and dependence on Jesus. To
turn to law as a path to righteousness is
to turn away from Jesus.

Each of these passages develops a
common view: law must be seen as a
total system and evaluated as a system. It
is inadequate because (1) it cannot give
life, (2) it is opposed to faith as an
approach to a relationship with God,
(3) it actually energizes man's sin nature
and produces sin, and (4) it cannot produce righteousness.

In view of these flaws the NT argues
against what theologians call law's third
function. Yes, looking into the law, we
do catch a glimpse of the beauty of God's
holiness. Yes, gazing at law, we sense
our own sinfulness and are convicted of
our guilt. But no! We are not to look to
the law to help us become the truly good
persons that God intends us to be.

10. The Christian alternative to law.
To argue against the third function of law
is not, as some fearfully believe, to reject
righteousness. Both Testaments witness

powerfully to God's desire that we who are his live holy and righteous lives. ♦

Righteous/Righteousness

The issue raised in the NT, particularly by Paul, is whether or not law can help the believer attain to righteousness. As we have seen, Paul's answer is a decisive no! So it is important to go on to see what the NT provides as an alternative to the way of law. To discover this, there are two different questions we must ask and answer: (1) Can we conceive of righteousness apart from law? (2) How do we achieve righteousness apart from law?

Can we conceive of righteousness apart from law? The Testaments agree that we can. There is the witness of the OT. Enoch "walked with God" before the Flood (Ge 5:22). Abraham was credited with righteousness long before the law was given (Ge 15:6). Also long before law existed to mark out God's way, the Lord said of Abraham, "I have chosen him, so that he will direct his children and his household after him to keep the way of the LORD by doing what is right and just" (Ge 18:19). Jeremiah looked to a day when the Mosaic Law would no longer be relevant, and he communicated God's promise: "I will put my law in their minds and write it on their hearts" (Jer 31:33). Someone who is righteous within does not need to look at an external standard for direction on how to live.

There is the witness of the Gospels. Jesus' teaching shifted the focus of righteousness from behavior to character and motivation. God is concerned with a righteousness that surpasses that of the rabbi and the Pharisee. That it is not necessary to express such righteousness by detailed commandments is shown in Jesus' response when he was asked the greatest commandment. Love God and love others, Jesus replied. And he added, "All the Law and the Prophets hang on these two commandments" (Mt 22:40).

There is the witness of the Epistles. Paul writes in Ro 13: "Let no debt remain outstanding, except the continuing debt to love one another, for he who loves his fellow man has fulfilled the law. The commandments, "Do not commit adul-tery," "Do not murder," "Do not steal," "Do not covet," and whatever other commandment there may be, are summed up in this one rule: "Love your neighbor as yourself." Love does no harm to its neighbor. Therefore love is the fulfillment of the law" (vv. 8–10). Parallel passages, such as Gal 5:13–26, make it plain that we can talk about righteousness without depending on the law to define it. In fact, the Epistles of the NT are filled with descriptions of how God's people live together in love—descriptions that have no need to adopt the language or structure of law.

But there is still the second question: How does the Christian achieve righteousness apart from law? Paul answers this question just as carefully as he analyzes and rejects the third function of law.

Ro 6:1–10. Christians are persons who have been given new life by Jesus. United to Jesus in his crucifixion, so that his death is considered ours, we are raised to a new life in him. Righteousness now becomes a matter of living that new life, for the deadly and powerful grip of sin on our personalities has been broken by Jesus. The possibility of a righteous life is established by what Jesus has done and by the newness of life we have in him.

Ro 7:1–6. In these verses, Paul establishes a basis on which Christians can claim to be free from a responsibility to live under the law: in marriage, the death of one partner frees the other from "the law of marriage" (v. 2). By analogy, the death of Jesus, to whom we are united, frees us from obligation to the law. After all, law has no jurisdiction over the dead. Paul then shows the need to be free from the law; the reason is that law energizes our old nature. In contrast, the Spirit of God energizes the new nature so that we produce "fruit to God" (v. 4). It is by relating to the Spirit and not to the law that righteousness is produced.

Ro 8:1–14. Paul explains that the law was powerless to make us good. But he goes on to show that the death of Jesus established a basis on which "the righteous requirements of the law might be fully met in us, who do not live according to the sinful nature but according to the Spirit" (v. 4). God does intend to produce righteousness in human beings! But he will not do it through law. He will do it in those who rely on and yield to the work of the Holy Spirit.

Gal 5:16–25. Paul teaches that if we live by the Spirit, the Spirit will control our sinful nature. "If you are led by the Spirit, you are not under law," Paul says (v.18). He lists, first, the sins that sinful human nature generates (vv. 19–21) and then the fruit that the Spirit generates: "love, joy, peace, patience, kindness, goodness, faithfulness, gentleness and self-control" (vv. 22–23). In adding "against such things there is no law" (v. 23), Paul describes the law's approach to righteousness; it points to righteousness by standing *against* sin ("Do not murder," "Do not steal," etc.). In contrast, the Spirit generates righteousness by creating within us the love, patience, faithfulness, and simple goodness that move us to want to do what is right. No wonder Paul reminded Timothy, "We know the law is good if one uses it properly. We also know that the law is not made for the righteous but for lawbreakers and rebels" (1 Ti 1:8–9). Would there be any need for laws if everyone were truly good and only did the good?

God's solution to the problem of righteousness is to give us a new life in Christ. God tells us to look to Christ and rely wholly on him. He then gives us the Holy Spirit to guide us and to energize the resources of that new life. As we commit ourselves to doing good, the righteousness of which the law testifies will become a reality in our lives.

11. Summary. Law is a difficult and yet critical biblical concept. *Tôrâh* in the OT is the divine revelation itself, given to Israel through Moses. The commands and statutes of *tôrâh* established the moral, social, and religious foundations for national and individual life. As the revelation of the God committed by covenant to Israel, *tôrâh* was a great and wonderful gift. Through a study of *tôrâh*, true believers found the Lord and understood his way, and they knew that rich blessings would follow if they walked the way its commands and ordinances marked out.

But the warm breath of the faith relationship that breathes through the OT was stifled by the way many approached the OT revelation. They missed the message of forgiveness and took the law's careful description of life for God's OT people as a way to salvation. Jesus affirmed the authority and trustworthiness of the OT. But he directly challenged the rabbis' grasp of its meaning. The righteousness that Christ's contemporaries sought to establish by careful keeping of the law's detailed instructions is rejected by Jesus. He calls for a different kind of righteousness—one that flows from an inner transformation.

The Gospels also show us that the OT way is to be superseded and transformed by Jesus. He is the focus of the OT, the one of whom it testifies. Now that he has come, that era is brought to a close. It is fulfilled, and a new era with new patterns of life will replace it.

The new era is explained and developed in the Epistles. Paul shows that *nomos,* as the law's statement of righteousness in commandments and as an aid to being good, cannot function in the believer's life. Faith, not law, was always the way to salvation. Reliance on the Spirit, not a struggle to keep the law, is the way to live a righteous life. It seems clear from Paul's analysis of the weakness of the law that the OT saint, like the Christian today, lived a godly life by trusting God and having a personal relationship with him rather than by looking to law and trying to keep it.

How, then, are Christians today to regard the moral commandments of the Bible? With respect. We look at them and sense the holiness of God. We find them standing against us if we wander into sin. But they will not help us become good.

For becoming good we rely on Jesus and his Spirit. When we read "Do not" or "Do" in Scripture, we praise God, for we see the kind of person he intends to help us become. And then, without even trying, we simply give ourselves, reaching out to love and to share.

How marvelous that in our loving—of God and others—we suddenly realize the truth. The requirements of the law are finding expression in our lives—not because we are trying to be good, but because the love of Jesus is working to transform us from within, and the Holy Spirit is prompting us to acts of love that fulfill every demand of law.

LAWFUL/UNLAWFUL

The lawful (*exesti*, 32 times in the NT) is that which is permissible or permitted by law. The word is used most often in the Gospels and Acts.

The Pharisees of Jesus' day had developed a vast network of interpretations of OT statutes and commandments. The result was that these "commandments of men" (Mt 15:9 KJV) condemned many perfectly neutral actions as unlawful. This is well illustrated in Mt 12:1–14. Jesus rejected Pharisaical legalism and met the issue head on. When those who wanted to accuse Jesus asked him if it was legal to heal on the Sabbath, Jesus said, "It is lawful to do good on the Sabbath" (v. 12), and he healed. The Pharisees hated Jesus for cutting through their convoluted thinking to reestablish the original concern of law: to show people how to love God and others.

Paul uses *exesti* in a distinctive way in 1 Co 6:12 and 10:23. He says, "All things are lawful for me, but. . . ." His point is that while believers are not under the OT law—and thus technically all actions are lawful—there are still criteria by which one must evaluate his or her decisions.
♦ *Law*

LAWLESS/LAWLESSNESS

In the NT, "lawlessness" (*anomia*, 15 times in the NT), "lawless" (*anomos*, 10 times in the NT), and "lawlessly" (*anomōs*, 2 times in the NT) are active concepts. They reflect actions that are not outside the governance of law but are in active violation of either divine or innate moral principles. The apostle John says, "Everyone who sins breaks the law; in fact, sin is lawlessness" (1 Jn 3:4). The

seriousness of lawlessness is seen in its association with the virulent outbreak of Satanic power destined for history's end (2 Th 2:3,7–8).

LEAD/GUIDE

The question of leading is important to most believers. Do we really have a basis for the conviction that God leads his people and that as individuals you and I can look for the Lord to direct us as we agonize over decisions or as we take daily steps? For those who doubt, the Bible has an exciting word.

OT 1. The concept of leading
2. Examples of leading and guidance
3. Inquiring of the Lord
NT 4. The role of the Holy Spirit
5. Conclusions

OT — 1. The concept of leading. A number of Hebrew words express the idea of leading or guidance. The following are some of the most exciting. Although they can be treated as synonyms, each does have a special shade of meaning.

Nāhâh means "to lead" in the sense of conducting along the right path. A beautiful picture of this is found in Ex 13:21: "By day the LORD went ahead of them in a pillar of cloud to guide them on their way." This image of guidance stresses the presence of the Lord: God goes with believers to show the way.

Nāhag conveys the idea of shepherding. God conducts us to his intended destination, going before us when we are responsive to his voice and "herding" us when we stray.

Nāhal means "to lead with care." We sense the implications in Isa 40:11: "He tends his flock like a shepherd: He gathers the lambs in his arms and carries them close to his heart; he gently leads those that have young."

Dārak in the Hiphil stem is used of God's leading his people in righteous paths. The psalmist prays: "Show me your ways, O LORD, teach me your paths; guide [*dārak*] me in your truth and teach me, for you are God my Savior, and my hope is in you all day long. . . . He guides [*dārak*] the humble in what is right and teaches them his way" (Ps 25:4–5,9).

There are other words in the OT that express God's leading or guidance, almost any of which may be translated "lead" or "guide" in the English versions. But it is clear from this brief survey that the concept of divine leading is firmly established in the OT.

2. Examples of leading and guidance. The OT is rich in examples of divine leading. Providential leading—that quiet, hidden supervision of events—is illustrated in Ge 24. Miraculous leading is seen in the cloudy and fiery pillars of Exodus. With the introduction of the written Word, Israel was given general moral and social guidance.

However, the nation and individuals faced many situations in which very specific guidance was called for. Decisions were forced on them, and in such cases general principles were not enough. At times, individuals looked for signs. When Jonathan thought about challenging a Philistine outpost alone, he said to his armorbearer, "Come then; we will cross over toward the men and let them see us. If they say to us, 'Wait there until we come to you,' we will stay where we are and not go up to them. But if they say 'Come up to us,' we will climb up, because that will be our sign that the LORD has given them into our hands" (1 Sa 14:9–10).

Signs were not always necessary. When David was urged to kill Saul, who was momentarily in his power, David answered, "The LORD forbid that I should do such a thing to my master, the LORD's anointed" (1 Sa 24:6). God's will was made clear in his Word, and so no special guidance was necessary.

For the times when help in making a specific decision was needed, God provided two sources of help: the Urim (specifically mentioned 7 times in the OT—Ex 28:30; Lev 8:8; Nu 27:21; Dt 33:8; 1 Sa 28:6; Ezr 2:63; Ne 7:65) and the prophet.

Urim and Thummim were most likely two stones that were placed in a pouch worn by the high priest (Ex 28:16,30).

When a series of questions was asked, God guided the people by showing a consistent pattern of "yes" or "no" responses. "Thus," the OT says, "Aaron will always bear the means of making decisions for the Israelites over his heart before the LORD" (v. 30; cf. Nu 27:21). David sought this kind of guidance from the Lord when he had a particularly difficult decision to make (1 Sa 30:6–8).

In Dt 18, God warned Israel that none of the practices used by the pagan peoples of Canaan to seek guidance were to be adopted by Israel (vv. 9–13). ♦ *Astrology* ♦ *Divination* Instead, God promised to provide his own answers for Israel through prophets. ♦ *Prophecy/Prophet* God announced regarding each such future prophet: "I will put my words in his mouth, and he will tell them everything I command him" (v. 18). Thus, two special avenues were provided by which God's people could seek his guidance in specific situations.

3. Inquiring of the Lord. Asking the Lord for his guidance is an important aspect of leading. Two OT words express this concept. *Dāraš* means "to seek with care." Often what is sought is knowledge or advice, in order to gain insight into a particular problem. *Sā'al* is also often used in statements about going to God for guidance.

It is important to God that his people show reliance on him by requesting his specific guidance when difficult decisions must be made. God pronounces woe on those who rush to solve their own problems without looking to him: " 'Woe to the obstinate children' declares the LORD, 'to those who carry out plans that are not mine, forming an alliance, but not by my Spirit, heaping sin upon sin; who go down to Egypt without consulting me' " (Isa 30:1–2; cf. Jos 9:14).

The act of inquiring reveals two things about the concept of leading in the OT. First, it reveals the believer's faith that God is, that God is aware, and that God is involved in the life of the individual and the nation. Looking to God and seeking his leading is an act of faith. Second, it shows us the willingness of God to show us his best way. Some, like

Saul, who rejected and turned from God, might not be given guidance (1 Sa 28:6). But believers need have no doubt that when they approach God for guidance, he hears and is pleased.

NT — 4. The role of the Holy Spirit. The NT too contains examples of guidance. In a few unusual cases, God provided guidance in dreams, as to Joseph and the Magi (Mt 1:20; 2:12,13,19,22; cf. Ac 16:9–10). There were also prophets in the early church. ♦ *Prophecy/Prophet* There are, moreover, a number of places where guidance is said to have come from the Holy Spirit (Lk 4:1; Ac 13:2–3; 20:22; Ro 8:14).

5. Conclusions. The Bible does not provide a formula for believers to follow in seeking God's guidance. Nor does it provide a list of ways in which God leads. It does, however, provide a clear perspective that helps us to approach this vital and practical issue. The Holy Spirit may use any number of means (including circumstances, Scripture, and the advice of friends) to guide our lives.

LEADERSHIP

Leaders play a critical role in any human endeavor. This is as true in the church as it is in business or government or the military. But the NT sets church leadership apart from the leadership exercised in the secular realm. A failure to grasp the unique character of the leadership appropriate to the body of Christ has plagued Christianity through its long centuries. That same misunderstanding often creates difficulties for the local church today.

OT 1. The role of leaders in the OT world
NT 2. The role of leaders in the NT world
    3. The role of leaders in the church
    4. Responsibilities of leaders in the church
    5. Responsibilities of believers to leaders

OT — 1. The role of leaders in the OT world. The OT concept of leadership is best expressed in "judge" (*šāpaṭ*) and "king" (*melek*). ♦ *Judge/Judging* ♦ *King* Each of these terms focuses attention on an individual, in whose person all governing functions resided. Our modern concept of government separates legislative, executive, judicial, and military functions. In the OT world these were unified, and the leader—whether he was the ruler of a great empire or a tiny city-state—was viewed as the final authority in every area.

OT law established a system of distributed authority. God was the living, ultimate king of Israel. He governed through his revealed law. God acted to punish and reward his people, as well as to lead them to victory over their enemies. Authority was distributed to elders of every local community, who were responsible to resolve disputes and judge criminal cases according to the divine law. But this system never functioned as intended because of the waywardness and faithlessness of Israel. During the time of the judges, and later with the establishment of the monarchy, the prevailing cultural view of authority vested in a human leader prevailed. The judges and kings of Israel were to be subject to the divine law, and history tells us that there were indeed a few godly rulers. But the cultural concept of leadership was never intended to replace the ideal of a nation under a God who acted through every community to carry out the divine will. ♦ *Authority*

NT — 2. The role of leaders in the NT world. The NT world was dominated by Rome. The empire enfolded Western civilization, its armies a barrier against the barbarians beyond. Roman administrators supervised conquered provinces, and Roman law was supreme over local legal codes. Greek language and culture provided a medium for communication, and the empire policed the roads and seas, thus making free trade and travel possible.

Also in this world leadership was personalized. The Emperor Augustus was viewed as *the* ruler, in whom all governmental functions resided. In oriental provinces, the distant emperor might also be worshiped as a god. But the very size of the empire meant that here too the power of Augustus must be distributed.

The Roman solution was not that of the OT. Rather than opting for a system of local multiple leadership by elders who administered but did not create laws, the Romans developed a bureaucracy. One who served within the Roman system acted as the agent of Caesar. The system is expressed in the words a Roman army officer spoke to Jesus: "Lord, I do not deserve to have you come under my roof. But just say the word, and my servant will be healed. For I myself am a man under authority, with soldiers under me. I tell this one, 'Go,' and he goes; and that one, 'Come,' and he comes. I say to my servant 'Do this,' and he does it" (Mt 8:8–9).

In portraying himself as a "man under authority," the centurion made an important claim. Because he was in the military chain of command, he spoke to those under him with the full authority of empire and emperor. He was obeyed because he represented Caesar himself. His statement to Jesus was a profession of faith, for it expressed his conviction that Jesus spoke and acted with the full authority of the Father. This Roman officer was convinced that Jesus represented God himself on earth and that whatever he commanded would be done.

Peter expresses this view in his word to believers: "Submit yourselves for the Lord's sake to every authority instituted among men: whether to the king, *as the supreme authority, or to governors, who are sent by him to punish those who do wrong*" (1 Pe 2:13–14, emphasis mine).

3. The role of leaders in the church. Those living in the first century had secular models of leadership on which to draw. These models viewed authority as vested in a person. The Roman system was a highly developed bureaucratic model. Although there were checks and balances, an official in the system spoke as a representative of the supreme authority himself. A leader thus had the power to tell a person, "Do this," and he or she had to do it.

There was another model implicit in the pattern originally provided in the OT. In this model, God was the living king, and local elders acted to guide the community to live by his laws. But this model had never proven practical and was replaced in Israel by charismatic judges and later by hereditary kings.

We need to have some insight into the view of leadership prevalent in the NT world to sense the impact of some of the statements of Jesus. In a world where leaders spoke as representatives of a person with supreme power—with total authority to command the behavior of ordinary folk—Jesus told his disciples: "You know that the rulers of the Gentiles lord it over them, and their high officials exercise authority over them. Not so with you. Instead, whoever wants to become great among you must be your servant, and whoever wants to be first must be your slave—just as the Son of Man did not come to be served, but to serve, and to give his life as a ransom for many" (Mt 20:25–28).

Jesus' view of leadership is also reflected in his judgment on the religious leaders of Israel—"the teachers of the law and the Pharisees" (Mt 23:1)—who claimed that they had authority to command the faithful. Jesus, in light of their leadership, told his disciples: "But you are not to be called 'Rabbi,' for you have only one Master and you are all brothers. And do not call anyone on earth 'father,' for you have one Father, and he is in heaven. Nor are you to be called 'teacher,' for you have one Teacher, the Christ. The greatest among you will be your servant. For whoever exalts himself will be humbled, and whoever humbles himself will be exalted" (Mt 23:8–12).

These and other statements of Jesus stand in stark contrast to the cultural concept of leadership and raise many questions for us. What is the role of leaders in the church? How are they to function if the pattern provided in secular leadership is denied them? And what is the responsibility of the believer to leaders?

Christ, the living head of his body. Leadership in the church is viewed against a new reality. The church is an organism, with Christ the sole and living head. ♦ **Church** ♦ **Head** There is no need for intermediaries to represent him, for "Christ died and returned to life so that he might be the Lord of both the dead and the living" (Ro 14:9). ♦ **Lord**

Words for leader. The Bible uses general terms for leaders. In the OT, *śar* is used of every kind of secular and religious leader. *Nāśî'*, which means "one who is elevated," is also used of any ruler. The NT word translated "leader" in Heb 13 is also a general term used in secular culture to designate a governor or ruler. The point is that such terms take on their distinctive meaning from the culture and era in which they are used. Thus, we speak today of the American president as the "leader of the free world" and of the Soviet premier as the "leader of the communist world." The word "leader" is the same in each use, but the type of leadership is determined by the vast difference between Western and communist societies. In the NT, our understanding of "leader" must be developed by studying the way leadership is to function in that unique culture and society of the church.

Images of leadership. A number of images are provided that suggest aspects of leadership within the church. As seen above, Jesus decisively rejected the image of the secular ruler (Mt 20). Instead, he pointed to the servant and to his own servanthood as alternative models. ♦ **Serve/Servant/Slave** Along with this, the NT offers the image of a shepherd, with terms such as elder, deacon, and overseer. ♦ **Elders** ♦ **Minister/Ministry** ♦ **Overseer** ♦ **Sheep/Shepherd**

A study of these images and the way they are used in the NT continues to develop awareness that NT leadership truly is different from the leadership observed in either the OT or various human cultures. In a unique way the NT recaptures the OT ideal of God as king and through the resurrection of Jesus

makes possible its realization. Human leaders in the church must not hastily adopt the patterns and methods of their society if they are to provide effective church leadership.

4. Responsibilities of leaders in the church. Leaders in the church should be God's persons, able to "prepare God's people for works of service" (Eph 4:12). The responsibility of leaders is to build up believers, enabling them to be mature and to minister as members of the body of Christ (1 Co 3:1–9; 2 Co 10:8).

These responsibilities are carried out by modeling and teaching. Modeling calls for the leader to be an example. ♦ **Example** This is reflected in the biblical lists of qualifications for church leaders (1 Ti 3:1–7; Tit 1:5–9; 1 Pe 5:1–4). The theme is expressed elsewhere as well (e.g., 1 Ti 4:11–16; 2 Ti 3:10,14).

Besides being a model, the church leader must also be able to teach, though the NT concept of teaching differs from current ideas. ♦ **Teaching/Learning** The ability to communicate truth so that it can be lived is basic to being a leader.

In neither of these major responsibilities is behavioral control (which is the focus of the efforts of secular leaders) in view. Rather, the spiritual leader in Christ's church is to be concerned with the inner growth and development of the believer, so that acts of service will be an expression of a vital work of God within the believer's personality. The coercive power of the secular ruler is abandoned in the church, and the supreme power of God to change from within is relied on in its stead. For a discussion of how this leadership is exercised, see Lawrence O. Richards and Clyde Hoeldtke, *A Theology of Church Leadership* (Grand Rapids: Zondervan, 1980).

5. The responsibility of believers to leaders. Paul makes it clear that those who commit themselves to the full-time service of the believing community have a right to receive financial support (1 Co 9:7–14). More significantly, they are worthy of respect: "Respect those who work hard among you, who are over you in the Lord and who admonish you. Hold them in the highest regard in love because of their work" (1 Th 5:12–13). ♦ *Respect*

The Book of Hebrews adds two additional admonitions regarding leaders. First we are told, "Remember your leaders, who spoke the word of God to you. Consider the outcome of their way of life and imitate their faith" (13:7). Then the passage goes on to say, "Obey your leaders and recognize their authority. They keep constant watch over your welfare, and they have great responsibility. Try to make their work a pleasure and not a painful burden—that would be of no advantage to you" (13:17 PHILLIPS). Thus, besides being paid and respected, Christian leaders are to be obeyed.

It is the privilege of the people of God to give a free, rather than a coerced, response to leaders who teach and model the Christian way of life. Because of this, it is even more important that leaders be "worthy of respect" (1 Ti 3:8,11; Tit 2:2) and that they abandon the world's concept of leadership in favor of a distinctively Christian leadership for the people of God.

LEARN ♦ *Teaching/Learning*

LEAVEN/YEAST

Leaven (Greek, *zymē*) in Bible times is sourdough, which with added juices served as a fermenting agent to leaven new dough. It is used in a number of figurative and symbolic senses in the NT.

In Mt 13:33 (Lk 13:21) leaven is used to explain one aspect of Jesus' hidden kingdom. Rather than appearing openly and affecting all mankind, Jesus' kingdom operates like leaven, hidden in the mass of the dough and yet affecting it all. ♦ *Kingdom*

In several passages, Jesus spoke metaphorically of the leaven of the Pharisees. Here *zymē* represents the teaching and the hypocritical lifestyles of the Pharisees (Mt 16:6,11–12; Mk 8:15; Lk 12:1).

In 1 Co 5:6 and Gal 5:9, Paul quoted this proverb: "A little yeast works through the whole batch of dough." In each context there is a warning against

negative influences in the community of faith—those of undisciplined brothers and false teachers. We are to get rid of such leaven (1 Co 5:7).

These uses of *zymē* do not suffice to show that leaven is a symbol of evil in Scripture. Rather, the use of *zymē* draws attention to the way in which an influence works, infiltrating the whole until everything is affected—for good or for evil.

LEFT ♦ *Right/Left*

LENDING AND BORROWING

Lending and borrowing are moral rather than economic concepts in the OT. They express one way in which God sought to care for the poor among his people. Thus the Mosaic Law says (Ex 22:25–27): "If you lend money to one of my people among you who is needy, do not be like a moneylender; charge him no interest. If you take your neighbor's cloak as a pledge, return it to him by sunset, because his cloak is the only covering he has for his body. What else will he sleep in?"

The cloak was probably given as a security for the loan and taken to the local elders so that the deal would be registered as an official transaction. It was, however, a symbolic act. The cloak was to be returned rather than held to force repayment (cf. Dt 24:10–13).

In the OT system itself, repayment was not the central issue. In fact, the law provided that every seventh year all debts were to be canceled. Concern for the poor was to override thoughts of self protection: "If there is a poor man among your brothers in any of the towns of the land that the LORD your God is giving you, do not be hardhearted or tightfisted toward your poor brother. Rather be openhanded and freely lend him whatever he needs. Be careful not to harbor this wicked thought: 'The seventh year, the year for canceling debts, is near,' so that you do not show ill will toward your needy brother and give him nothing. . . . Generously give to him and do so without a grudging heart; then because of this the LORD your God will bless you in all your work and in everything you put your hand to" (Dt 15:7–10).

It is a trait of the righteous in the OT that they lend freely (Ps 37:21; 37:26; 112:5). This view of borrowing and lending not only encouraged generosity and sharing by those God had blessed; it also guarded the integrity of the poor. If they were able to repay, they would do so, so that they might not be the recipients of charity. Even the sense of obligation that might come with a loan (Pr 22:7) is dealt with as the entire society experienced the year of release. It is important to realize that borrowing and lending did not play the same role in the OT that they play in our modern credit economy.

The OT limits interest-free lending to the people of God. In Mt 5:42, Jesus restated the principle in a context that may suggest lending to others as well (cf. Lk 6:34–35).

NT giving has much of the spirit of lending and borrowing of the OT. A believing donor is to give out of personal prosperity to meet others' needs—to supply those fellow believers who are in need—so that others' generosity may in turn show itself in the time of the donor's need. ◗ *Giving*

LEPROSY

The Hebrew word *ṣāra'at* and the Greek word *lepra* are both translated "leprosy" in older versions. They actually include a wide variety of diseases that cause sores or eruptions on the skin. Probably the best translation is that adopted by the NIV, where these diseases are called "infectious skin diseases," of which clinical leprosy is only one form. The same Hebrew term is used of mildew on clothing (Lev 13:42–53) and mold in houses (Lev 14:47–52).

The person with such a disease in Bible times was considered unclean and unable to take his place in the worshiping community. ◗ *Clean and Unclean* In addition, a person with such a disease was to be isolated from others. In the case of such diseases as smallpox, isola-

tion may have saved the community from epidemic.

A person with a visible outbreak was to visit a priest, who was responsible for diagnosis (Lev 13). When an outbreak was healed, the person was to reappear before the priest (Lev 14). This does not suggest that the priests functioned as doctors; rather, they were responsible to establish the ritual qualification of an Israelite to appear before the Lord and to function in the believing community.

Theologically, what is significant about leprosy is its relationship to sin. ◗ *Sickness and Health*

LETTER

What did Paul mean in 2 Co 3:6 when, after writing of himself as minister of a new covenant, he added, "not of the letter but of the Spirit; for the letter kills, but the Spirit gives life"? In the context, Paul used *gramma*, "that which is written"—i.e., a letter, to represent the Mosaic Law "which was engraved in letters on stone" (3:7). ◗ *Covenant* ◗ *Law*

LEVITES ◗ *Priests and Levites*

LIES ◗ *Deceit/Falsehood*

LIFE AND DEATH

Life and death are basic issues. In the Bible, God has shown us the meaning of each. To hear his message helps us understand how truly significant each human being is. And it helps us realize how vital it is that we maintain a close relationship with the Lord—for today as well as for eternity.

OT 1. The Hebrew words for life and death
2. The meaning of life on earth
3. Eternal life in the OT
4. Key theological passages
NT 5. The Greek words for death
6. The source of death
7. The nature of death
8. The death of Jesus
9. Key theological passages

10. The Greek words for life
11. The source of life
12. The nature of life
13. Eternal life
14. Key theological passages
15. Summary

OT — 1. The Hebrew words for life and death. A number of Hebrew words are translated "lives" or "living." Often these are words that indicate residence: a person living in a certain place. But two Hebrew words focus on the nature of life itself.

Ḥāyâh is a verb that in the Qal stem means "to live," or "to have life." It can also convey the idea of remaining alive, of living prosperously, or even of living forever. In other stems the verb means "to quicken" or "to revive," often from a depressed or sickened state. Many derivatives indicate living things, or living itself.

Nepeš is translated many ways, one of the most common being "soul." It originally meant "to breathe." In most cases *nepeš* indicates an individual's personal existence. It encompasses all those drives and desires that an individual experiences. On many occasions, *nepeš* means a unique person (the living "I"). When *nepeš* is the object of a verb—such as to save or to deliver—it is usually translated "life."

References to death in the OT are derivatives of *mût*, "to die" or "to kill." Death in the OT is the antagonist and opposite of life. It is intimately linked with the separation from God caused by sin.

2. The meaning of life on earth. A number of significant themes help us sense the OT's view of life and death. In the first place, physical life was produced by God's original creative act (Ge 2:7). God remains the source of life for the race and the individual.

Next, because each person's existence can be traced to the Lord and each is stamped with his image, persons have unique worth and value. ♦ **Image and Likeness** The precious nature of each life is seen in God's command that one who violently snatches away the life of an-

other must pay with his or her own life (Ge 9:5–6; Ex 21:23; Dt 19:21). In the OT, life is a good in itself. But "life" is not simply an abstract, vitalizing principle that energizes the body. "Life" gathers up all human capacities and views people in their ability to experience and exercise emotions, intellect, sense, and will. "Life" is also a qualitative term in the OT. It implies health and vitality and the exercise of God-given capacities in a fulfilling way. Death, by contrast, shades into sickness and those other troubles that can rob a living person of the opportunity to use his or her potentials.

Physical existence and the quality of a person's life are both linked with God. Under the Mosaic covenant, God faithfully laid out for his people a pathway to blessing. One who obediently followed the pathway would have the opportunity to experience a fulfilling life. God's Word also identified sin, so that the people of Israel would be warned away from paths that would destroy the quality of their lives. Thus the OT often repeats a theme expressed in Dt 30: "See, I set before you today life and prosperity, death and destruction. For I command you today to love the LORD your God, to walk in his ways, and to keep his commands, decrees and laws; then you will live and increase, and the LORD your God will bless you in the land you are entering to possess. But if your heart turns away and you are not obedient, and if you are drawn away to bow down to other gods and worship them, I declare to you this day that you will certainly be destroyed. You will not live long in the land you are crossing the Jordan to enter and possess. This day I call heaven and earth as witnesses against you that I have set before you life and death, blessings and curses. Now choose life, so that you and your children may live and that you may love the LORD your God, listen to his voice, and hold fast to him. For the LORD is your life, and he will give you many years in the land" (vv. 15–20).

3. Eternal life in the OT. Scholars agree that the verb *ḥay* can at times mean "endless life." Conservative scholars are convinced that some of these references are to eternal life, stretching on endlessly beyond our brief moments on earth—though the passages in which this meaning may be intended are few (Ps 30:5; Pr 12:28; 15:24; Da 12:2; cf. Ps 16:11; 21:4–6).

♦ **Resurrection**

The idea that the dead do not praise God (Ps 115:17; Isa 38:18) is best taken to represent the simple observation that death ends one's worship on earth.

4. Key theological passages. Life and death are critical theological concepts, explored in a number of OT passages.

Ge 2:7: "The LORD God formed the man from the dust of the ground and breathed into his nostrils the breath of life, and man became a living being."

The creation story portrays God as the source of life for every creature (Ge 1:21). Human beings are one such type of creature, but their creation is special; God gave the human race his own image and likeness (Ge 1:27). Every capacity of personhood is now expressed in the context of the material universe, as man sets out on life's great adventure.

Ge 2:17: "You must not eat from the tree of the knowledge of good and evil, for when you eat of it you will surely die."

After Adam and Eve sinned in Eden (Ge 3:6–7), death was introduced into the universe. Death involves, but is more than, physical corruption. "Death" includes the process of dying and also all the pain and suffering associated with decay. Mankind is cut off from intimate fellowship with God, and human interpersonal relationships are warped and twisted. Ge 3–4 demonstrates over and over again the nature of this death that is rooted in sin and that cripples not only human beings but affects the universe itself (Ro 8:19–22). We see Adam and Eve run in fear from God and blame and betray each other. We see the ground cursed, so human beings must struggle with an unresponsive creation that shudders under the impact of sin. We see hatred and murder in the first family as Cain kills Abel. We see Lamech distort God's ideal by taking two wives, and we see him justify murder by claiming he was injured. The bright potential of humanity is suddenly darkened, as every gift of personhood is misused. It is all this, not simply the ending of existence on earth, that the OT views as death.

Dt 19:21: "Show no pity: life for life." This and parallel passages (Ge 9:5–6; Ex 21:23) show the importance of each individual life (*nepeš*). Capital punishment for murder shows the ultimate horror of the taking of a person's life. Restitution, usually in the form of payment, can be offered for other injuries and crimes, but there is no acceptable restitution for murder. Nothing can compare in value to a single human life. Thus, the death penalty is called for in the OT as an affirmation by God's people of the worth of individuals and of the preciousness of life on earth.

Lev 17:11: "For the life of a creature is in the blood, and I have given it to you to make atonement for yourselves on the altar; it is the blood that makes atonement for one's life." In the sacrifice, God provides a promise. Although human beings have sinned and deserve divine punishment, God will accept life for life. The sacrificial animal foreshadowed the final sacrifice—Jesus, who offered his life in payment of sin's debt so that God could give fresh life to all who believe.

Dt 30:19: "Choose life, so that you may and your children may live." Although they are a redeemed people, Israel must still choose whether to experience life or death in their earthly sojourn. Here the OT stresses the quality of life. The person who loves and obeys God will experience blessing and prosperity, as human potentials are fulfilled. The person who turns from God and rejects his way will know the meaning of death, that destruction and distortion of human potentials. Only in relationship with God can a person experience true life during his or her days on earth.

NT — 5. The Greek words for death.
The Greeks saw death as the end. One might turn inevitable death into an achievement by dying gloriously, but they believed that existence ended at the close of every life span.

A segment of society sought comfort in philosophy. Of these, some said that since death is natural, each person rightly journeys toward it. Some consoled themselves with the idea that people live on in their children. Some argued that death was a welcome end to human struggles and pains in an uncaring universe. Plato advanced the notion that personality, being moral and immaterial, must continue after the death of the body. But those who lived in the world of the first century held no common belief about immortality, and the notion of resurrection was completely foreign to them.

The words for death in the Greek language express and reflect cultural beliefs. *Nekros* simply means "dead," or "a dead body." In the Greek culture, *nekros* conveyed the idea that the dead has become mere matter. Whatever it was that had made the corpse a person and animated the body was gone. The dead had reached that final state that destiny has decreed for all people.

It is striking to see how *nekros* is used in the NT. In over half of the 133 times it is found it is linked with affirmations of resurrection. The NT triumphantly announces concerning Jesus that "God raised him from the dead" (Ac 13:30); but it goes on to promise that there is resurrection ahead for us as well (1 Co 15:12–52). Human beings are more than mere matter!

The word *thanatos* means "death." In the Gospels it is usually used of the death of Jesus. In Paul's letters its use focuses on the apostle's exploration of the meaning of human death. A number of derivative words are also found in the NT; these include *thanatoō* ("to kill"), *apothnēskō* ("to die"), and *thnētos* ("mortal").

As expected, the NT view of death builds on and expands concepts found in the OT. It stands in bold contrast to the views of the Hellenic world. Death is not simply a biological phenomenon. Death is a theological phenomenon, with impact in the spiritual as well as the physical realm. As for the physically dead, God is well able to raise them (Ac 26:8). Mankind's problem, and God's great challenge, has to do with the grim darkness of a living death that to some extent shrouds human existence for time as well as for eternity.

6. The source of death. Ro 6:23 says, "The wages of sin is death."

Like the OT, the NT traces the entry of sin into the world back to Adam. Looking at the Fall, Paul explains that "just as sin entered the world through one man, and death through sin, and in this way death came to all men, because all sinned" (Ro 5:12). Adam's sin was not his alone. He sinned for the race. The death that struck him and was expressed not only physically but in every relationship has been passed on to every succeeding generation. Paul states that even those who, before Moses, did not sin by breaking a commandment (5:14) still found themselves in the grip of death.

Death, then, is not "natural." It is not rooted in the nature of the universe; it is not simply an expression of the way things are. Death is unnatural, brought on mankind by a shattering event that shook the material universe (Ro 8:19–22) and so warped human nature as to affect the experience of every person ever born.

Death is the direct result of sin. And the fact of death testifies to the overwhelming importance of a personal, obedient relationship with God.

7. The nature of death. "Death" is a very complex term in the NT. One aspect of death is the biological end of life. Human beings sense their own uniqueness. They feel intuitively that somehow they are too significant to be simply snuffed out. The sense of death's wrongness, as well as the mystery of the unknown, arouses fear of death, and Satan uses this fear to enslave human beings (Heb 2:15).

But death is descriptive of what exists here and now and not simply of biological destiny. Eph 2:1–6 is theologically significant. It portrays people as "dead in [their] transgressions and sins" (v. 1). Man's sinful nature is dead. It is not responsive to God but is filled with corrupt cravings, desires, and thoughts. Human society itself is so twisted that it reflects Satan rather than God. Other passages too view death as an active principle (Ro 8:2), affecting man's outlook and warping his natural passions (8:5–8). Just as human beings are helpless in the grip of biological death, they are likewise powerless in the grasp of their inner moral corruption.

Death is also descriptive of man's relationship with God. As Eph 2 affirms, we, being dead in trespasses and sins, "were by nature objects of wrath" (v. 3). The dead are helpless and lie under the righteous judgment of God. What is more, death is a state of actual antagonism toward God. Paul shows that God has revealed himself to all human beings (Ro 1:18–20). But what reaction does he get? "Although they knew God, they neither glorified him as God nor gave thanks to him" (1:21). Death is marked not only by rejection of God but by actual antagonism, turning human beings against the only possible source of deliverance. Without God, man is carried inevitably into a religious and moral cesspool (Ro 1:21–32). Death, as a state of enmity with God, isolates human beings from personal relationship with him and subjects them to the divine judgment. An individual who remains in this state of death throughout his or her biological lifetime stands in eternal peril. "Man is destined to die once," Heb 9:27 says, "and after that to face judgment." The Book of Revelation graphically portrays the result of that judgment. It is, according to Rev 20:14, endless existence in "the lake of fire," and this is "the second death." ▶ Heaven and Hell

Like the OT, the NT views man as a whole being. The biological and spiritual are linked. Thus, even though Jesus has dealt with death in fact and in principle at Calvary, death maintains its foothold in the believer's personality. Only biological transformation or resurrection will cleanse the body from every taint of sin and complete man's release from the realm of death.

This leads to a danger to the believer. Death has its claim on Christians as well as on the lost. In Ro 7, Paul links sin and death with law and shares his struggle to do what law commands. He discovered that the principles of sin and death were so deeply rooted in his personality that he was unable to experience the righteousness that law portrayed. ▶ Law

The believer is released from condemnation and need not fear the second death. But even the believer must be rescued daily "from this body of death" (Ro 7:24). Paul finds the answer in Jesus, who introduces within us a power that will even "give life to [our] mortal bodies through his Spirit, who lives in [us]" (Ro 8:11).

Death, then, is a biological concept that is applied theologically to graphically convey the true state of humankind. The death that grips mankind is moral and spiritual. Death warps and twists man out of the pattern of original creation. Every human potential is distorted, every capacity—for joy, for relationships, for harmony with God, for true goodness—is tragically misshapen. And because each ugly twist and turn gives expression to sin, man—intended to reflect God's image and likeness—falls instead under God's condemnation. The striking and terrible image of death is designed to communicate how desperately we need God and how hopeless we are without him. It is as foolish to expect one who is spiritually dead to win God's favor by his works as it would be to expect a corpse to rise from his coffin and walk.

8. The death of Jesus. The Bible views Jesus' death, not as a tragedy or injustice, but as a mighty act of God. His death has a significance parallel only to the Fall. Adam's sin gave death its chilling grip on the race: Jesus' death for sin conquered death and breathed life into humanity again. As Ro 4:25 puts it, "He was delivered over to death for our sins and was raised to life for our justification."

Christ's substitutionary death breaks the power of death in all its aspects. We are reconciled to God "through the death of his Son" (Ro 5:10). We are even released from death's crippling impact on our present experience. "By sending his own Son in the likeness of sinful man to be a sin offering" God "condemned sin in sinful man, in order that the righteous requirements of the law might be fully met in us" (Ro 8:3–4). Through Jesus, believers experience a transition from death to life. Paul told the Colossians, "[God] has reconciled you by Christ's physical body through death to present you holy in his sight" (Col 1:22). Ultimately the complete meaning of this release will be known; for redeemed humanity will never experience death after their resurrection.

In view of the varied and terrible meanings that Scripture ascribes to death, it would be wrong to think of Jesus' death as a mere biological event. When the Bible teaches that Jesus suffered death and tasted death (Heb 2:9), a full experience of all that death involves is implied. That this extends even to the awful separation from God that tears the heart of the godly is revealed in Jesus' cry from the cross: "My God, my God, why have you forsaken me?" (Mt 27:46).

9. Key theological passages. Among the many NT references to death there are some key passages that develop aspects of the theme.

Ro 5:12–21. Two events dominate human history. Each event is summed up in a man. In Adam, death was introduced into the race. In Christ, death is defeated and life restored.

Ro 6:1–10. The believer is so completely identified with Jesus, and in such a perfect union through faith, that the death of Jesus is in fact the believer's own death. And the resurrection of Jesus is the believer's restoration to life.

Ro 7:7–25. The principle of death is still active within the believer. Death, with its companions, sin and the law, can still make the Christian's life ineffective and unproductive.

Ro 8:1–11. The Holy Spirit, present in the believer, breaks the grip of sin and quickens even mortal bodies. We can live a righteous and fulfilling life through the Spirit. Life—that full experience of human potential in intimate relationship with God—becomes possible for the Christian.

1 Co 15:12–57. The grip of death on the human personality will be broken when believers experience resurrection. Then, when the mortal is clothed with immortality, it will at last be true that "death has been swallowed up in victory" (v. 54).

Eph 2:1–10. The impact that death has on the personality is shown in Paul's picture of the cravings, desires, and thoughts of those who are corrupted by sin.

Heb 2:9–16. Jesus took on human nature so that by his death he might release mankind from death's power and lift believers to that glory God has always intended for humanity.

10. The Greek words for life. The Bible uses "life" in many ways. It speaks, for example, of a holy life, of life on earth, of eternal life. As we might have expected, a number of Greek words are used to express different shades of meaning. Still, there are three words the Greeks used to explore the concept of life itself: *bios, psychē,* and *zōē.*

Bios is seldom found in the NT (only 11 occurrences). It is an ethical term, which originally looked at one's lifestyle. In later times, *bios* focused on life's externals: one's wealth or possessions. Thus, Lk 8:14 warns against the impact of "life's worries, riches and pleasures," and John decries "the pride of life" (1 Jn 2:16, KJV). In many cases the NT uses *bios* and its derivatives to speak of wealth or possessions (KJV, one's "living"). But words from this root (including *bioō, biōsis,* and *biōtikos*) are found only in Mt 12:44; Lk 8:14,43; 15:12,30; 21:4,34; Ac 26:4; 1 Co 6:3,4; 1 Ti 2:2; 2 Ti 2:4; 1 Pe 4:2,3; 1 Jn 2:16.

Psychē (found 103 times in the NT) is typically translated "soul." But it is also often translated "life." In its developed meaning, *psychē*—which originally indicated the unconscious—came to stand for the basis of life and consciousness. It is often equated to the inner person or personality and so may have the force of a personal pronoun. Some of the NT passages in which *psychē* is translated "life" help us see this meaning. Jesus gave "his life [*psychē*] as a ransom for many" (Mt 20:28). This was not life as distinct from personality; it was life as possessed and expressed in the unique person he was. Jesus gave "himself."

Lk 12:22–23 reports Jesus' words on discipleship. He told his followers: "Do not worry about your life [*psychē*], what you will eat; or about your body, what you will wear. Life [*psychē*] is more than food, and the body more than clothes." Here too life is the self, the personal existence of the living individual. Because you and I have a Father who cares about us as persons, we are free to shift our concentration from ourselves to the Lord. We can "seek his kingdom," knowing that "these things [food and clothing] will be given to [us] as well" (Lk 12:31).

Significantly, *psychē* is also found in Jesus' enigmatic words on discipleship: "If anyone would come after me, he must deny himself and take up his cross and follow me. For whoever wants to save his life [*psychē*] will lose it, but whoever loses his life [*psychē*] for me will find it. What good will it be for a man if he gains the whole world, and yet forfeits his soul [*psychē*]?" (Mt 16:24–26; cf. Mt 10:39; Mk 8:35–36; Lk 9:24–25; 17:33; Jn 12:25). Jesus warns that the individual who struggles to hold on to the person he is, rather than surrendering himself to Jesus, will lose himself. It is only through the transforming power of Jesus that any of us can become the self (the person) that God wants us to become—and that we yearn to be.

As a general rule of thumb, passages that in the English speak of "his" or "their" or "my" life typically have *psychē* in the Greek.

The third significant Greek word is *zōē*. *Zōē* in classical Greek refers to natural life—the principle that enables living things to move and to grow. In the NT, *zōē* focuses on the theological meaning rather than on the biological. From the perspective of the NT, in every respect life is the counterpart of death. Each book of the NT speaks of *zōē*. In each, the principle of life lifts our vision beyond our earthly existence to reveal a unique quality of life that spans time and eternity and that has its roots in God. It is the biblical use and meaning of *zōē* that most concerns us as we examine what the NT says about life.

11. The source of life. Human sin was the source of death. God alone is the source of life, for God "has life in himself" (Jn 5:26). All other life is derived. As Creator, God is the source of biological life. Jn 1 presents Jesus as the active agent in creation and the source of life in the universe. "Through him all things were made; without him nothing was made that has been made. In him was life, and that life was the light of men" (Jn 1:3–4).

God is also the source of eternal life, the spiritual dynamic that shatters the power of death in the human personality. John reports Jesus' words: "I tell you the truth, whoever hears my word and believes him who sent me has eternal life and will not be condemned; he has crossed over from death to life. I tell you the truth, a time is coming and has now come when the dead will hear the voice of the Son of God and those who hear will live. For as the Father has life in himself, so he has granted the Son to have life in himself (John 5:24–26).

Jesus is also the source of vitality for the believer's experience of eternal life here on earth. As Paul writes, "I have been crucified with Christ and I no longer live, but Christ lives in me. The life I live in the body, I live by faith in the Son of God, who loved me and gave himself for me" (Gal 2:20; cf. Php 1:21). At every turn, the Bible's teaching on life points us to Jesus. As the Mediator sent from God, Jesus is the source in which the eternal life from God can be found (1 Jn 1:1–2).

12. The nature of life. The Greeks were fascinated with life as a principle that could animate matter. Plants, animals, and mankind were made from the stuff of this universe. For a time each lived, and, with the passing of life, each seemed to become nothing but inanimate matter again, a brother to the insensible earth.

The Bible too is fascinated with life. But according to the Bible, life is more than a passing quality: it is a vital principle that can shatter human bondage to both the biological and the spiritual corruption that were introduced into the world by sin.

To the sin-warped but hopeful personality, life means a new and different future. "If anyone is in Christ," 2 Co 5:17 reads, "he is a new creation; the old has gone, the new has come!" Daily experience becomes a matter of putting on "the new self, which is being renewed in knowledge in the image of its Creator" (Col 3:10).

Life to the struggling Christian means that vitalizing power of God, flowing within, which lifts us beyond our limitations. We have this promise: "[Since] the Spirit of him who raised Jesus from the dead is living in you, he who raised Christ from the dead will also give life to your mortal bodies through his Spirit, who lives in you" (Ro 8:11). Because of the new life from God, energized by the Spirit, you and I can actually "bear fruit to God" (Ro 7:4).

The dying Christian has the calm assurance that biological ending is nothing but a new beginning. When our earthly tent is destroyed, we go to be with the Lord "so that what is mortal may be swallowed up by life" (2 Co 5:4).

To every believer, life is the expectation of resurrection. God has powerfully proclaimed Jesus to be his Son by resurrection from the dead (Ro 1:4). Now we wait for the ultimate transformation, that glorious burst of power at the last sound of the trumpet, at which "the dead will be raised imperishable, and we will be changed" (1 Co 15:52). As the NT triumphantly announces, "The perishable must clothe itself with the imperishable, and the mortal with immortality. . . . Then the saying that is written will come true: 'Death has been swallowed up in victory' " (vv. 54–55).

13. Eternal life. We tend to think of eternal life as life with endless duration. That is part of it. But when the NT speaks of eternal life, its emphasis is on the quality or character of that life.

Eternal life stands in contrast to biological life. Biological life is derived and fleeting; it has no shaping impact on the personality. Eternal life is God's own life, burning brightly not only with his vitality but with his own character. The wondrous message of the Scripture is that God has chosen to share this life—to share himself!—with human beings. "You have been born again," Peter writes, capturing the wonder of it, "not of perishable seed, but of imperishable, through the living and enduring word of God" (1 Pe 1:23). ◗ *Born* God's life alone is able to break the grip of death on humanity. God's life alone can provide a basis for a warm personal relationship with the Lord. God's life alone can lift humanity to the destiny for which we were originally intended.

As the Bible presents the stunning possibility of eternal life now, that possibility is always linked with Jesus. It is only through faith in the Son of God that a person receives eternal life. It is only through faith that a close fellowship develops, and it is through this that God's life is released to find expression through us.

14. Key theological passages. There are many significant passages in the NT that explore God's gift of life. A few of the more important in John's and then Paul's writings should be noted.

Jn 3:15–36. The person who believes in Jesus is given eternal life. The person who rejects the Son "will not see life."

Jn 5:21–26. Jesus possesses eternal life "in himself" (v. 26), as does the Father. Life is given to us by the Son.

Jn 6:27–68. Jesus came from heaven, bringing life to people.

Jn 10:10–28. By giving his life for the sheep, Jesus the Good Shepherd provides eternal life for his followers.

Jn 11:1–44. Jesus demonstrated his power by restoring biological life to Lazarus. He affirmed the promise of resurrection and endless life for all who believe in him.

1 Jn 2–3. These chapters show that life from God will necessarily be expressed. God's life will show itself as believers love others and respond obediently to the Lord.

1 Jn 5:10–12. All who believe in the Son have eternal life now.

Ro 5:9–10. Justified by Jesus' death, we are being delivered by the vitalizing power of his life.

Ro 5:12–21. Adam's death-bringing Fall is countered only by Jesus' life-bringing Cross.

Ro 6:1–10. We are united with Jesus in his death and in his life. It is our union with Jesus that makes his own vital, resurrection life flow within our personalities.

Ro 8:1–11. The power of the Holy Spirit, used to raise Jesus from death, vitalizes our new nature and enables us to express our new life from God in righteous living.

2 Co 4:1–12. Because we are in a process of transformation toward Jesus' likeness (2 Co 3:12–18), God expresses Jesus through us in the world. The whole NT adds its testimony. We who have been given eternal life are called by God to express that life day after day by the loving and holy way we live.

15. Summary. Life and death are basic biblical themes. Even more, they are the concepts that explain both the human condition and the vital need of every person for a living relationship with God. It is unlikely that we will ever truly grasp the devastating impact that sin and death have had on the race and on the universe. But each glimpse afforded us in the Bible makes us grateful to God, who gave his Son that in him you and I may have life.

LIGHT AND DARKNESS

Light and darkness are natural phenomena, associated with day and night. All peoples also use the terms "light" and "dark" metaphorically. This is true in Scripture, where the two images are given theological significance.

OT 1. **Darkness in the OT**
    2. **Light in the OT**
NT 3. **Darkness and light in Greek thought**
    4. **Darkness in the NT**
    5. **Light in the NT**
    6. **Key theological passages**

OT — 1. Darkness in the OT. God acted at Creation to separate (make a distinction between) darkness and light, night and day (Ge 1:4,5,18). In the OT, darkness is theologically associated with a number of different things.

a. Judgment and distress. Ex 10:21 portrays the plague of darkness falling on the terrified Egyptians. Images of darkness are associated with God's displeasure (e.g., 1 Sa 2:9; Ps 91:6). Darkness is especially associated with the Great Tribulation, the time of world judgment to come at history's end (Joel 2:2,31; Am 4:13; 5:18,20; Zep 1:15).

b. God's hiddenness. Human beings cannot penetrate the mystery of God. Even when he showed himself in lightning at Sinai, God himself was masked "with black clouds and deep darkness" (Dt 4:11; cf. Ex 20:21; Ps 18:11). In contrast, nothing is hidden from God; as David says in addressing God: "If I say, 'Surely the darkness will hide me and the light become night around me,' even the darkness will not be dark to you; the night will shine like the day, for darkness is as light to you" (Ps 139:11–12).

c. Divine intervention. Because God can penetrate the darkness, he is able to act for his people. When Messiah comes, Isaiah prophesied, "the people walking in darkness [will see] a great light" (Isa 9:2). Even now, God illumines us with his Word and presence. "My God turns my darkness into light" (Ps 18:28).

2. Light in the OT. God set the sun in the sky to "give light on the earth" (Ge 1:15). He accompanied Israel through the wilderness in a fiery pillar "to give them light" (13:21). These historic acts provide images that are picked up and expanded by the psalmists. God is called "my light and my salvation" (Ps 27:1). It is only in relationship with the Lord that one's life is illumined, for "in [his] light we see light" (Ps 36:9). Light is linked with divine revelation (Ps 43:3; 119:130), with life (Ps 49:19; 56:13), with salvation (Ps 27:1), and with God's presence (Ps 89:15; 90:8). God's people are called to "walk in the light of the LORD" (Isa 2:5), and the prophets promise that one day God himself will live among men, to replace

413

the sun as their "everlasting light" (Isa 60:19–20).

NT — 3. Darkness and light in Greek thought.

"Darkness" (*skotos* in Greek) had no specific philosophical importance in itself except in contrast with light (*phōs*). It was associated with ignorance, with sinful doings, and particularly with man's fear of death, for death was often characterized as a realm of darkness. On the other hand, light symbolized life itself, as well as happiness. Plato compared the good with sunlight, and light developed a distinct relationship to the ethically good, as well as to healing and the illumination of one's thoughts and life. Strikingly, the Greeks did not relate light and darkness to the activities or realm of the gods. Later Gnostic thought transformed light and darkness into opposing and hostile powers. While the NT, particularly John, contrasts the realms of darkness and light, Scripture links each image firmly to the one who is Lord of both light and darkness.

4. Darkness in the NT.

Darkness is a powerful NT image. As a moral metaphor, it describes sinful acts and a sinful lifestyle. Believers are to put aside "deeds of darkness" (Ro 13:12; Eph 5:11). We do not "belong to the night or to the darkness" (1 Th 5:5).

But spiritual darkness is more than a lifestyle. It is an evil power, holding people in its dominion (Col 1:13). We sense the restless activity of sin within our personality. All people were once impelled by inner evil (Eph 5:8) and so chose to turn their backs on God's light and to embrace the darkness (Jn 3:19). It may be this that Jesus warned of when he pointed out that if one's eye (the organ that directs and guides the body) is darkness, the whole body (life) will be full of darkness (Mt 6:23; Lk 11:34–35).

There is only one hope for those in the grip of darkness: the light provided by Jesus (Jn 1:5). In God there is no darkness at all (1 Jn 1:5). He can release us from sin's power and illumine us, so that the person who follows Jesus "will never walk in darkness" (Jn 8:12). And how vital it is that we be drawn "out of darkness into his wonderful light" (1 Pe 2:9). The Greek word *zophos* is used four times in the NT—two times each by Peter and Jude—twice to describe the darkness in which fallen angels are now held (2 Pe 2:4; Jude 6) and twice to describe the coming final judgment (2 Pe 2:17; Jude 13).

5. Light in the NT.

In the NT, light is an image of both holiness and illumination. But most significantly, light characterizes Jesus. He is *the* light of the world (Jn 8:12); he is the light that shines in the darkness, bringing life (Jn 1:4–5). People who are in the grip of darkness may scurry away from his light (Jn 3:19–20). But only the good news of Jesus can provide perspective on reality. Only through Jesus can people recognize their lost state, come to God (Jn 14:1; 2 Co 4:4), and find their way to a righteous life (Eph 5:8–9).

Believers, who respond to Jesus, are rescued from the realm of darkness to become children of the light (Eph 5:8). They share a place in God's kingdom of light (Col 1:12) and are even lights in this dark world (Mt 5:14–16). Believers are to reflect Jesus and declare his praises (1 Pe 2:9).

6. Key theological passages.

The theological significance of light and darkness is shown in a number of NT passages, especially in the writings of John.

Jn 1:4–9. Jesus is the "true light," whose coming into the world puts the whole creation in perspective. In Jesus we discover who God is, and we are given the vital divine life that can overcome our darkness.

Jn 3:19–21. Despite the demonstration of God's love in the coming of Jesus, humanity scurries deeper and deeper into darkness. Man's love of darkness rather that light demonstrates the reality of human sinfulness: "Everyone who does evil hates the light, and will not come into the light for fear that his deeds will be exposed" (v. 20). But one who is willing to face reality comes to the light. Only believers, whose trust in Jesus has carried them beyond condemnation (Jn 3:16–18), will come.

Jn 8:12. Only through Jesus, the light of the world, are people released from darkness and given "the light of life"— that is, eternal life.

2 Co 4:4–6. Satan blinds the lost so they cannot see the light of the gospel of the glory of Christ, and so they fail to recognize Jesus "who is the image of God" (v. 4). For a person to respond to Jesus and be enlightened by "the knowledge of the glory of God in the face of Christ" (v. 6) calls for a divine creative act parallel to the original creation when God said, "Let light shine out of darkness" (v. 6).

Eph 5:8–9. Those who have been translated from darkness to light are expected to live "as children of light" (v. 8). This means bringing forth in one's life the fruit of the light—"all goodness, righteousness and truth"—and having nothing to do with the "fruitless deeds of darkness" (v. 9).

1 Jn 1:5–7. Maintaining fellowship with God calls for us to walk in the light and not in darkness, for God is unshadowed light. Walking in the light is not sinlessness, however; for as we walk in the light, "the blood of Jesus, his Son, purifies us from all sin" (v. 7). Because this passage associates light with truth, it seems best to take "walking in the light" in the sense suggested in Jn 3:19–21. ♦ **Truth** To walk in the light is to accept God's verdict on our actions and to come to him for cleansing and forgiveness when we fall short (1 Jn 1:9).

1 Jn 2:8–10. John makes it clear that any believer who hates other believers is not living according to God's way and is actually showing behavior typical of the moral realm of darkness. Christians can test their fellowship with the Lord by observing their relationship with other believers. Any believer who loves other Christians "lives in the light, and there is nothing in him to make him stumble" (v. 10; cf. Ro 13:8–10).

LIKENESS ♦ *Image and Likeness*

LION

Seven Hebrew words are translated "lion" in the OT. Their use often stresses the pride and ferocity of Israel's enemies (cf. 1 Pe 5:8). But the royal lion from the tribe of Judah, Jesus, overcomes every enemy (Rev 5:5).

LISTEN ♦ *Hear/Listen*

LOOK

The word "look" captures the emphases of the Hebrew and Greek terms it translates. But many puzzle over Mt 5:28: "I tell you that *anyone who looks at a woman lustfully* has already committed adultery with her in his heart."

What is Jesus saying? The troublesome Greek phrase is *pas ho blepōn gynaika pros to epithymēsai*. While *pros* may express purpose, it also may mean "with reference to," here "with reference to desire." Thus, Jesus is forbidding lustfully looking a woman other than one's wife. This is consistent with the context, in which Jesus is exploring the roots of sins rather than the acts themselves. As contempt and anger toward a brother is a source of murder (5:21–22), so lustfully gazing at a woman is a source of adultery (5:27–28). In God's eyes, the root of sin as well as its fruit calls for judgment.

LOOSE ♦ *Bind*

LORD

This significant word occurs again and again in OT and NT. What does it mean when the OT identifies God as Lord? And what does it mean when this name is ascribed to Jesus Christ? The answer to these questions initiates us into some of the wonders of our faith.

OT 1. The Hebrew words
2. Implications of the name Yahweh
NT 3. The Greek word
4. Jesus is Lord
5. Implications of Jesus' lordship
6. Summary

OT — 1. The Hebrew words. Two Hebrew words are translated "lord" in the OT. *'Aḏôn* means "lord" in the sense of a superior, master, or owner. It is also used as a term of respect. *'Aḏôn* is generally found in the OT in reference to human beings (e.g., Ge 18:12; 19:2; 24; 1 Sa 16:16). But at times, especially in a series of names such as "the LORD, the God of Israel" it is used of God. A special intensified form, *'aḏōnāy,* is found over three hundred times in the OT, and this plural form refers only to God. Where *'āḏôn* or *'aḏōnāy* refers to God, the English versions show it by capitalizing the first letter: Lord.

The other Hebrew word translated "Lord" is *Yâhweh,* God's revealed personal name. This name occurs 5,321 times in the OT in this form, and 50 more times in the poetic form *Yâh.* *Yâhweh* is particularly significant, and when it occurs, most English versions indicate this by the form LORD.

The pronunciation of *yhwh*—the Tetragrammaton, the four letters without vowels that compose the divine name— is not certain. But the common pronunciation, Jehovah, was surely not used in ancient times. The transcribers of the Hebrew OT in the twelfth century believed the divine name too holy to pronounce. They added the "o" and "a" from ' *aḏōnāy* to the four Hebrew consonants, and when they read the Hebrew aloud said *'aḏōnāy* in its place. It seems most likely that the original pronunciation is approximated in Yahweh.

2. Implications of the name Yahweh. Most scholars believe that the name is derived from an old form of the Hebrew verb meaning "to be" or "to become." The word stresses existence, with the meaning being that expressed in Ex 3:14: "I am." This has been taken to emphasize the unchanging nature of God, particularly his changeless commitment to his people.

But the name suggests more, especially in the context of its introduction to Israel. This came as Moses, standing before the burning bush, hesitated to accept God's commission. "Moses said to God, 'Suppose I go to the Israelites and say to them, "The God of your fathers has sent me to you," and they ask me, "What is his name?" Then what shall I tell them?' God said to Moses, 'I AM WHO I AM. This is what you are to say to the Israelites: "I AM has sent me to you."'" God also said to Moses, 'Say to the Israelites, "The LORD, the God of your fathers—the God of Abraham, the God of Isaac and the God of Jacob—has sent me to you." This is my name forever, the name by which I am to be remembered from generation to generation'" (Ex 3:13–15).

Later God revealed more to Moses. He told of his appearances to Abraham and Isaac and Jacob as God Almighty, but said, "By my name the LORD I did not make myself known to them" (Ex 6:3). It was in the Exodus that God unveiled his character as Yahweh. It was in his action bringing Israel out of Egypt and accompanying them to Palestine (cf. Ex 3:12) that his nature was unveiled.

The Exodus generation, which had only heard of God through tales passed on by their ancestors, would suddenly experience God as the one who IS—one who was present with them.

It is in this way, by this name, that God is "to be remembered from generation to generation" (Ex 3:15). What is the meaning of the name Yahweh? It is God's affirmation that he is THE GOD WHO IS ALWAYS PRESENT. He is not simply a God afar off, or a God of past history, or a God who will appear in that future the prophets foretell. He is a God who is present and who acts at every point of the history and experience of his people.

He is such a God for us as well. And we are to remember him by this name. For whatever our situation, whatever our need, our God is *one who is always present.* He is with us now—now and evermore.

3. The Greek word. The word translated "Lord" in the English versions is *kyrios.* In ordinary speech it may simply have been a term of respect or a form of address that emphasized superior position, as that of the master of a slave. When *kyrios* is so used, it is translated by an appropriate English equivalent, such as "master," "owner," or even "Sir."

When *kyrios* designates God or Jesus, it is rendered "Lord." In the Gospels, however, this should not be taken to mean that the speaker acknowledges Jesus as God (e.g., Mt 8:2,21; Lk 9:59). However, since the Septuagint uses *kyrios* for *Yâhweh*, it is clear that in many of its uses in the Gospels, the title Lord is equivalent to the divine name. It seems certain that when Jesus spoke of himself—e.g., the time he called himself Lord of the Sabbath (Mt 12:8)—he was ascribing deity to himself (cf. Lk 20:42–44). Some uses of the title Lord by the disciples may also reflect the growing awareness that Jesus truly was divine, as Thomas finally confessed when he exclaimed, "My Lord and my God!" (Jn 20:28).

It is after the Resurrection, and in the Epistles, that we discover the significance of *kyrios* as applied to Jesus.

4. Jesus is Lord. The earliest chapters of Acts testify to the fact that after the Resurrection, the church immediately confessed "Jesus is Lord"; and the rest of the NT constantly affirms Jesus' lordship. In Philippians, Paul traces the process of Jesus' self-emptying, the Crucifixion, and his subsequent exaltation. Jesus, "being in very nature God, did not consider equality with God something to be grasped, but made himself nothing, taking the very nature of a servant, being made in human likeness. And being found in appearance as a man, he humbled himself and became obedient to death—even death on a cross! Therefore God exalted him to the highest place and gave him the name that is above every name, that at the name of Jesus every knee should bow, in heaven and on earth and under the earth, and every tongue confess that Jesus Christ is Lord, to the glory of God the Father" (2:6–11). To recognize Jesus as Lord is to acknowledge his deity. And this is evidence that God the Spirit has accomplished his saving work within (cf. 1 Co 12:3).

5. Implications of Jesus' lordship. Jesus is Lord. What does this mean and imply? It implies that he has authority of various kinds.

Universal authority. The NT teaches us that the risen Christ is seated at God's right hand, the place of authority. His authority is universal, "far above all rule and authority, power and dominion, and every title that can be given, not only in the present age but also in the one to come" (Eph 1:21). All "angels, authorities and powers" are "in submission to him" (1 Pe 3:22).

Sovereign authority. The Lordship of Jesus is worked out in this present world. Peter explores the situation in which a believer does what is right but still endures suffering. He reminds us that the "eyes of the Lord are on the righteous" (1 Pe 3:12). Even if we suffer for what is right, we can "set apart Christ as Lord" in our hearts (v. 15); that is, we can remain confident that Christ, as Lord, is superintending events.

Personal authority. In Ro 14, Paul looks into the freedom of the Christian person. In matters of conviction each believer is to "be fully convinced in his own mind" (v. 5) and then must act on his convictions. It is not the Christian community but Jesus who is Lord, for this is the "very reason" that "Christ died and returned to life," that is, "so that he might be the Lord of both the dead and the living" (v. 9). Jesus' authority as Lord extends to the personal relationship that he has to each believing individual.

Pervasive authority. Both the church and the individual believer live "in" and "under" and "through" the Lord. These recurring prepositions in reference to one's relationship to the Lord remind us that it is only by the presence and power of Jesus, who is Lord, that present and future victories are made possible. The very fact of our existence is determined by the reality of Jesus as Lord.

Ultimate authority. The NT speaks of a coming day of the Lord. Jesus will appear again, and then his ultimate lordship over all creation will be demonstrated. ♦ *Appearance of Jesus: the Second Coming* ♦ *Day*

6. Summary. In the OT, "LORD" is the English rendering of the personal name of God, Yahweh. That name reminds us that he is the *God who is always present.*

417

God is not limited to past or future. He is with each of us now, to act in and through us.

In the NT, "Lord" is the English rendering of the title *kyrios*. In its ultimate meaning, that title belongs to Jesus alone (Php 2:9–11). It affirms his deity and his authority over every power—natural and supernatural. As Lord, Jesus governs the sweep of history and guards each individual's step.

One practical implication of Jesus' lordship is seen in Scripture's call to us to abandon judging or attempting to control others. Jesus died and rose again that he might actually be Lord in the life of each person who trusts in him.

LOSE/LOST

Most passages that use these words are easy to understand. There are some, however, that should be noted.

The thought of "losing one's life" is found in each of the Gospels (Mt 10:39; 16:25; Mk 8:35; Lk 9:24–25; 17:33; Jn 12:25). ◗ *Life and Death*

The statement "he will suffer loss" (1 Co 3:15) has puzzled some. The context makes it clear that this phrase is related to the believer's rewards, which are to be based on his or her works as a Christian. The loss of salvation is not in view in this passage. ◗ *Reward* ◗ *Salvation/Save*

In the verse that says "He has lost connection with the Head" (Col 2:19), the literal reading of the phrase translated "lost connection" is rather "not remained closely united." In the context, Paul sketches the futility of turning to religious observances for spiritual fulfillment, rather than relying on Jesus—who, as Head of a living body, fully supplies each part with all the nourishment required for growth to maturity.

As for the common use of the word "lost" to indicate the unsaved, the image of "lost sheep" from which it may be derived is used in Scripture more often of straying believers than of those who have no relationship with the Lord.

LOVE

Love is the grandest theme of Scripture. It is a divine motivation. It moved God to reach out to the lost; and it enables the lost to look up in response, as well as to reach out to others. What the Bible says about love cannot help but enrich our lives.

OT 1. The Hebrew words
      2. God's love for man
      3. Man's love for God
NT 4. The Greek words
      5. God's love in Christ
      6. Man's love for God
      7. Love's lifestyle
      8. Summary

OT — 1. The Hebrew words. The most common Hebrew word translated "love" in the NIV and the NASB is *'āhēb̲*. This is a general word for "love" or "like," and it varies in intensity with its subject and its object. *'Ahēb̲* is used to indicate the relationship between a father and son (Ge 22:2; 44:20) and a slave and master (Ex 21:5). It is the word chosen to exhort love for neighbor (Lev 19:18) as well as love for the stranger visiting the land (Dt 10:19). *'Ahēb̲* can also be used of a love for food (Ge 27:4,9,14), for wealth (Ecc 5:9), and for God's commands (Ps 119:47,48,127). This is the word used when the OT speaks of human love for God, and it is often used to indicate God's love for mankind. When used of God's love, the character of God infuses *'āhēb̲* with intensity and stability: God says "I have loved you with an everlasting love" (Jer 31:3).

The NIV also translates *hesed* "love" or "kindness." The NASB renders this theologically significant term "lovingkindness." Among people, *hesed* describes a bond of loyalty, such as is established between relatives, friends, or allies. An act of *hesed* is carried out by free choice in harmony with the relationship; thus *hesed* is an expression of love appropriate to a relationship.

The term is theologically significant because it is often used to express divine attitudes and actions. It is closely linked with covenant in the OT, and many believe it should be translated "covenant faithfulness." ◗ *Covenant* But "covenant faithfulness" is not an adequate explanation for God's actions. It was God's deep love that moved him to establish covenants with man in the first place. His acts of *hesed* are generated from his own loving character. Thus, in revealing himself to Moses, the Lord associated *hesed* with a constancy and forgiveness that went beyond the obligations to which the Mosaic covenant might bind him. God is "the LORD, the LORD, the compassionate and gracious God, slow to anger, abounding in love [*hesed*] and faithfulness, maintaining love [*hesed*] to thousands, and forgiving wickedness, rebellion and sin" (Ex 34:6–7).

Other words that are translated "love" include *rāham* (◗ *Compassion*) and *dôd*. *Dôd* is used when an individual is spoken of as one's love or beloved (SS; Isa 5:1).

The Hebrew words themselves give us some sense of the active commitment that is intrinsic to the biblical concept of love. But it is in seeing how these words are used to speak of God's love for a human being and a human being's love for God that we discover the role of love in human experience.

2. God's love for man. *'Ahēb* is given as the motive for God's choice of, and continuing commitment to, Israel. Moses told Israel, "Because he loved your forefathers and chose their descendants after them, he brought you out of Egypt by his Presence and his great strength, to drive out before you nations greater and stronger than you and to bring you into their land to give it to you for your inheritance" (Dt 4:37–38).

Love alone moved God to choose Abraham, and love moved God to bring Israel out of Egypt. As Deuteronomy also points out, it will be love that moves God to bless his obedient people with health, prosperity, and children (Dt 7:13–15).

Looking back on Israel's history, the prophets sense the mark of God's love in every event (e.g., Hos 11:1; Mal 1:2–3). Even God's discipline of his people is an example of parental love (Pr 3:12).

God's love also extends to the individual, especially to the righteous poor and oppressed: "The Lord loves the righteous. The Lord watches over the alien and sustains the fatherless and the widow" (Ps 146:8–9).

The prophets associate God's promise of a bright future for Israel with love. When the time of salvation comes at last, God will be free to love Israel as fully as he desires (e.g., Isa 43:1–7; Hos 14:4).

God's love as *hesed* is uniquely for those he has redeemed. His love is linked with his leading. He guided Abraham's servant to a bride for Isaac (Ge 24). At the Red Sea, Israel sang in assurance: "In your unfailing love you will lead the people you have redeemed" (Ex 15:13). The Sinai covenant is called a "covenant of love" (Dt 7:9,12; 1 Ki 8:23; 2 Ch 6:14; Ne 9:32), as is God's covenant commitment to David (cf. 1 Ch 16:34,41; Ps 89:24,28). This same quality—commitment—underlies every expression of divine love: "From everlasting to everlasting the LORD's love is with those who fear him" (Ps 103:17).

In the Psalms, *hesed* is associated with the call to people to worship (Ps 5:7; 26:3), with deliverance from enemies (Ps 6:4; 17:7; 44:26; et al.), with protection (Ps 21:7; 32:10; 36:5; et al.), with forgiveness (Ps 25:7; 51:1; 86:5; 130:7; Mic 7:20). In *hesed*, God is sensitive to our sufferings (Ps 31:7), answers prayers (Ps 66:20; 69:16), and remains slow to anger (Ps 86:15; 103:8; 145:8; Joel 2:13; Jnh 4:2). In love God provides redemption (Ps 130:7), teaches us his decrees (Ps 119:64,124), and remains committed to fulfill his purpose for us (Ps 138:8).

In the prophets, God's love is linked with the ultimate establishment of David's throne and kingdom (Isa 16:5; 55:3). In faithful love God will restore Israel (Jer 31:3).

3. Man's love for God. Only in Jer 2:2 do we find *hesed* used of man's response to God. There the prophet shares God's lament over Israel: "I remember the devotion [*hesed*] of your youth, how as a bride you loved [*'ahēb*] me and followed me through the desert." In the rest of the OT, human love for God is spoken of as *'ahēb*.

We sense that love's expression primarily is an obedience that demonstrates one's clinging to the Lord. Deuteronomy's great call to "love the LORD your God with all your heart and with all your soul and with all your strength" (Dt 6:5) is fulfilled by obedience: "These commandments that I give you today are to be upon your hearts" (v. 6). Moses later adds: "And now, O Israel, what does the LORD your God ask of you but to fear the LORD your God, to walk in all his ways, to love him, to serve the LORD your God with all your heart and with all your soul, and to observe the LORD's commands and decrees that I am giving you today for your own good?" (Dt 10:12–13).

This link between love and obedience is seen again and again in the OT (Dt 30:16–20; Jos 22:5; cf. Ps 119:113,119, 127,159,163,165,167). In the context of the OT, God's commands were given only after he had acted to redeem Israel. In the Exodus, God demonstrated his faithfulness to his ancient promises given to Abraham, and he showed his power. Thus when the people of Israel were called to love and to obey God, they were able to respond on the basis of God's clear self-revelation.

This is a basic feature of the call to love God. Love is to be a response to God's initiating acts of saving love. God initiates. Man responds.

It is also important to note that the commandments associate love for God with love for others. Thus Jesus placed love for neighbor second only to one's love for God in the two "great commandments" of the law (Mt 22:37–39).

NT — 4. The Greek words. Only two of the three common Greek words for love are found in the NT. The Greeks differentiated aspects of what English includes in the word "love." For example, *eros* indicates the love of a man and a woman for each other, embracing all aspects of sexual desire. This word, much used in Greek culture, is not found in the NT.

Philia was the most common word for love. It indicates a fondness, which develops as persons are attracted to each other and build a relationship within or outside the context of family. Loving behavior, which is appropriate between relatives or friends, ideally included such things as hospitality and common concern for one another. In the Greek world this word had no religious overtones or root.

The NT has a number of compound words built on this root (such as *philadelphia*, "brotherly love," and *philagathos*, "love of good"). The verb *phileō*, the noun *philia*, and *philos* as a substantive all occur in the NT. Some have tried to make distinctions between these words and the noun *agapē*, the NT's dynamic word for love (along with its corresponding verb, *agapaō*). But even when *phileō* and *agapaō* are used together in a passage such as Jn 21:15–19, it is difficult to interpret supposed shades of meanings. The great fact is that God's action in Christ has forever changed our understanding of love and has opened up a life of love for us—a life that is different from every culture's highest ideals.

For those who wish to study the question of possible differences in meaning between these two word groups, the verb *phileō* occurs twenty-five times in the NT (Mt 6:5; 10:37; 23:6; 26:48; Mk 14:44; Lk 20:46; 22:47; Jn 5:20; 11:3,36; 12:25; 15:19; 16:27; 20:2; 21:15,16,17; 1 Co 16:22; Tit 3:15; Rev 3:19; 22:15). The substantive use of *philos* ("friend") appears twenty-nine times in the NT (Mt 11:19; Lk 7:6,34; 11:5,6,8; 12:4; 14:10,12; 15:6,9,29; 16:9; 21:16; 23:12; Jn 3:29; 11:11; 15:13,14,15; 19:12; Ac 10:24; 19:31; 27:3; Jas 2:23; 3 Jn 14). The noun *philia* ("friendship") is found only once in the NT (Jas 4:4).

The third Greek word, already mentioned above, is the noun *agapē*. In ordinary speech this was a rather weak word, conveying fondness or pleasure. It was a helpful word in that it could be used to alternate with either *eros* or *philia*. But it was an orphan word, without any fixed heritage to give it special meaning within Greek thought. It is this word that the NT adopts and infuses with unique meaning. This word was chosen by the NT writers to convey to future generations the unique dimensions and overwhelming depth of God's love and to explore the impact of that love on human beings.

5. God's love in Christ. The NT affirms that "God is love" (1 Jn 4:16). It calls us to understand all that God does, even his discipline of believers, as an expression of love (Heb 12:6). This same conviction is expressed in the OT. There we are invited to understand events as demonstrations of God's love. It was love that impelled God's choice of Abraham, love that led God to establish the covenants, and love that underlies his acts of covenant faithfulness. ♦ *Covenant* But only in Christ do we grasp the fact that God's love encompasses all of humanity. Only in Christ do we realize the depth of the love that impelled him to sacrifice himself on our behalf. John puts it this way: "This is how God showed his love among us: He sent his one and only Son into the world that we might live through him. This is love: not that we loved God, but that he loved us and sent his Son as an atoning sacrifice for our sins" (1 Jn 4:9–10).

Paul emphasizes the same reality but adds a note of special wonder. It was not for God's friends that the Son sacrificed himself. It was for God's enemies: "At just the right time, when we were still powerless, Christ died for the ungodly. Very rarely will anyone die for a righteous man, though for a good man someone might possibly dare to die. But God demonstrates his own love for us in this: While we were still sinners, Christ died for us. . . . If, when we were God's enemies, we were reconciled to him through the death of his Son, how much more, having been reconciled, shall we be saved through his life" (Ro 5:6–8, 10).

In the Incarnation and Crucifixion, Christ is the ultimate expression of God's love. Looking at the Cross, we too can be sure that this God of love will, "along with [Christ], graciously give us all things" (Ro 8:32). Convinced that nothing "will be able to separate us from the love of God that is in Christ Jesus our Lord" (Ro 8:39), we face life and death with confidence. In Christ every event in our personal history takes on fresh per-spective, for the Cross assures us of God's endless love.

6. Man's love for God. The NT makes it all too clear that human beings do not naturally love God. The natural condition of human beings is that they are "alien-ated from God and . . . enemies in [their] minds" (Col 1:21). A humanity that lies dead in sin can only follow the desires and thoughts of the sinful nature (Eph 2:1–3). ♦ *Life and Death* Human beings in themselves are without hope and without God in the world; only Christ's blood can bring life, and with it a per-sonal, love relationship with the Lord (Eph 2:12–13).

The NT shows us that the first re-sponse to God, which marks the passage from death to life, is faith. ♦ *Belief/Faith* Once a person establishes a personal relationship with the Lord through trust, love can exist, and love will grow. John emphasizes this aspect of faith's life in his writings. Jesus confronted the Phari-sees with evidence that they had left the path marked out by Abraham. Abraham believed God and responded to him. If the Pharisees had had a relationship with God, they would respond as Abraham did. "If God were your Father, you would love me," Jesus explained (Jn 8:42; cf. 1 Jn 5:1).

Love for God is a response, closely linked with faith. It is created by an awareness of what God has done for us in Christ. As John says, "We love be-cause he first loved us" (1 Jn 4:19).

7. Love's lifestyle. While the NT speaks compellingly of God's love for us and of our love response to Jesus, most mentions of "love" in the NT focus on the Christian's lifestyle. We are to "live a life of love, just as Christ loved us and gave himself up for us as a fragrant offering and sacrifice to God" (Eph 5:2). Although we do well to draw on the model of Christ to develop several as-pects of the Christian's lifestyle of love, the NT makes the transforming impact of love very clear through explicit teaching. Each of the following themes is found in the NT and calls for our personal explora-tion.

LOVE

Love creates community. Jesus gave to his disciples a new commandment: "Love one another. As I have loved you, so you must love one another" (Jn 13:34). The call to or the commendation of love within the fellowship of Christians is repeated in every Epistle (e.g., Ro 12:9–10; 1 Co 13; 2 Co 8:24; Gal 5:13–14; Eph 5:2). God has through Christ laid the basis for a relationship more intimate than that experienced in many families. It is in the context of the family of God that, rooted and grounded in love, believers are to grow in their experience of God's love and reach Christian maturity (Eph 3:17–19). ♦ *Church* ♦ *Community*

Love prompts obedience. The OT link between love and obedience is seen in the NT as well. Jesus explains to his disciples: "Whoever has my commands and obeys them, he is the one who loves me. He who loves me will be loved by my Father, and I too will love him and show myself to him" (Jn 14:21). This repeated theme (Jn 14:23; 1 Jn 5:3) does not suggest that obedience wins us God's love or that obedience *is* love. It simply states that the one who loves is the one who obeys. Real love for God prompts obedience, and this in turn deepens our relationship with God and enables him to show us even more of himself.

Love provides motivation. In 2 Co 5, Paul explains one of the foundational convictions on which his ministry was based. He did not coerce or manipulate others in an attempt to motivate them to follow Jesus. Paul was convinced that "Christ's love compels us" (2 Co 5:14). Christ wants to bring us to that place where we no longer live for ourselves but for him. But the only motivating force that brings such a commitment is Christ's love within. This verse may also be saying that it is our love for Christ that compels us (the Greek allows for this interpretation). It is not the love of money or the love of power but the love of Christ that fills our hearts and moves us to love others. So too Paul speaks in 1 Th 1:3 of the believers' "labor prompted by love."

Love transforms character. The Christian is a person who is in the process of a transformation toward Christlikeness. Many passages in the NT provide a description of the kind of person the believer is becoming (e.g., 1 Co 13:1–7; Col 3:12–17). It is the fact of our transformation toward Christlikeness that explains the relationship that the NT postulates between love and law. The law expressed righteousness in the form of external commandments. Love moves the believer to actually be righteous in his every relationship. As Paul writes in Ro 13:10, "Love does no harm to its neighbor. Therefore love is the fulfillment of the law" (cf. Gal 5:23). ♦ *Law*

Love provides purpose. In a striking use of *agape*, John warns against love of the world (1 Jn 2:15). Love of things provides an inadequate goal to give life meaning (1 Ti 6:10). God calls us to love only God and our fellow human beings. Only such love can begin to capture the wonderful purpose that God has for us (1 Th 4:9,10; 2 Th 3:5; Heb 10:24; 1 Pe 4:8).

Love stabilizes relationships. It is love that maintains unity in the body of Christ (Php 2:2; Col 2:2). Love makes it possible for us to give others freedom in matters of personal conviction and to be sensitive when our convictions might cause offense (Ro 14:15; 1 Co 8:1).

Love compels concern. Love moves believers to share freely to help meet the spiritual and material needs of others (1 Jn 3:16–18).

8. Summary. God is portrayed in Scripture as the one who, moved by love, initiates a relationship with human beings. God's love prompts his free decision to reach out to sinful humanity.

In the OT, God's love is focused on the covenant people of Israel, and his love is demonstrated by his acts for them. In return, God's OT people are called to show their love for God by commitment to him alone and by obedience to his commands.

In the NT, the full scope and meaning of God's love is unveiled. God's love reaches out to embrace all humanity. But to redeem the lost God must take the full weight of sin's punishment upon himself. Despite the cost, the Father sent his only and dearly loved Son, and the Son chose to enter the material universe as a human being. It is love that impelled this divine act of self-sacrifice, culminating in Christ's death on the cross. In view of the compelling evidence of God's love for us in Christ, human beings respond with faith in the resurrected Lord. Transformed within by the Holy Spirit, the believer is now able to respond to God's love with a love of his or her own for the Lord.

But love awakened must find expression in a transformed lifestyle. The divine principle of love infuses the believer, moving Christians as it moved God to love even enemies (Mt 5:43). The NT explores in depth the impact of the divine love on our relationships in this world. Love creates a new community, as brothers and sisters in Christ's church are bonded together. Love prompts obedience and provides the motivation that moves believers to respond to the Lord. Love transforms the character of the individual and provides a sense of purpose. Love stabilizes relationships, enabling us to overcome the tensions that shatter friendships. Love compels that practical concern for others that leads us to reach out and meet their needs. It is love that moves us toward the righteousness that law calls for but cannot produce.

This brief sketch of a few of the functions of God's love as it is shed abroad in Christ should awaken us to, or remind us of, the power of love. If we who are already transformed by faith want to continue being transformed, let us focus on loving God and one another. If we want to help someone change, let us love

them as Jesus loves us and them. And let us seek in the pattern provided by Jesus the secret heart of that love that can make all of life fresh and new.

LOVINGKINDNESS ♦ *Love*

LUST

In the NASB as in older versions, "lust" is a translation of *epithymia*. This Greek word denotes any strong desire directed toward an object. In passages like Jas 1:14 (which speaks of a person "carried away and enticed by his own lust") or 1 Jn 2:16 (which warns against the "lust of the flesh"), a sexual association that is not intended may be supposed by the English reader. The object of *epithymia* is not necessarily sexual.

The translators of the NIV have chosen to restrict the use of the English word "lust" to passages in the OT and NT where sexual passion is implied (except in 1 Jn 2:16). In other passages, *epithymia* is rendered by a more general word such as "desire" or "craving." In addition, the NIV translates as "lust" other Greek words that can express sexual passions: the three NT uses of *pathos* (Ro 1:26; Col 3:5; 1 Th 4:5), the one NT use of *orexis* (Ro 1:27), and one of the ten NT uses of *pleonexia* (Eph 4:19).

In each NIV setting "lust" is used in a strongly negative sense. These passages deal with a sexual desire stimulated by the sin nature—a desire that seeks to possess and use persons who are not rightly objects of desire. This does not at all suggest that sexual desire itself is wrong. In marriage, sexual desire for one's spouse is good indeed. ♦ *Sex*

M

MAKE ♦ Create

MADNESS

Two Hebrew words are translated "madness" in the NIV and NASB: *šāga'* and *hôlēlâh*. *Šāga'* refers to the behavior of the person. It is used to describe how David acted when he fled Israel and went to Philistia, there pretending to be mad (1 Sa 21:14–15). When the madness of God's prophets is spoken of, it is mockery aimed at their message and is not a description of their behavior (2 Ki 9:11; Jer 29:26; Hos 9:7). Madness is one of the judgments that God brings on sin (Dt 28:28; Zec 12:4; cf. 2 Ki 9:20); however, mental illness should not be automatically viewed as divine judgment. ♦ *Sickness and Health*

Hôlēlâh looks at the irrationality of the thought processes of the mad individual; all four of its OT occurrences are in Ecclesiastes (1:17; 2:12; 7:25; 9:3). In view of God's revelation, sin is viewed as a kind of madness (Ecc 10:13, where we find the one OT use of the related word *hôlēlût*). *Hālal* (the root of *hôlēlâh*) is translated "arrogant" in Ps 5:5; 73:3; 75:4. The wicked who exalt themselves and boast are, in view of God's existence, acting irrationally.

The NT does not mention madness per se, but severe mental illness was described in NT times as demon possession. The Bible shows Jesus' power over even this supernaturally intensified illness. He expelled demons, in one case it being specifically recorded that he left the person "in his right mind" (Mk 5:15; cf. vv. 1–14). ♦ *Demons/Evil Spirits*

MAGIC

The occult has fascinated people of every age and culture. Is it possible to control persons and events supernaturally? Can one manipulate supernatural beings and forces? In the ancient world the majority were sure the answer was yes! Only a knowledge of God's true nature and his relationship to the world can place the occult in perspective and shatter the pretensions of those who dream of mastery through manipulation of the world beyond.

OT 1. Magic in ancient Eastern
   cultures
   2. The OT view of the occult
NT 3. Magic in Hellenistic culture
   4. NT view of magic
   5. Summary

OT — 1. Magic in ancient Eastern cultures. In the myths of the Babylonians, the gods themselves resorted to magic. This is because the gods themselves were viewed as limited, having to reach beyond their own powers to exercise control over the universe. Canaanite religion also possessed gods and goddesses who used magic.

In Egypt, magic was under the protection of the major gods and was taught to priests in the temple schools. While much of magic involved the use of charms and incantations, there are indications that supernatural agencies as well as trickery may have been involved in some instances. The OT tells that Egypt's magicians duplicated several of Moses' miracles "by their secret arts" (Ex 7:11,22; 8:7). But their resources soon failed to duplicate even the semblance of God's acts, and the magicians were forced to confess, "This is the finger of God" (Ex 8:19).

Although magic woven into their myth and the use of spells may have been part of the daily life of the ancients, magic was not always viewed as a good. The Code of Hammurabi (1728–1686 B.C.) proscribed sorcery and called for the death sentence for those who practiced it. Yet the possibility of influencing events by the supernatural was attractive, and astrologers and magicians were members of the official staff of advisers of world rulers such as Nebuchadnezzar of Babylon (Dan 1:20; 2:2,20; 4:7,9).

2. The OT view of the occult. The OT strictly forbade God's people to practice any magical or occult art or to consult those who did so. The practice was viewed so seriously that the death penalty was prescribed for any violation (Ex 22:18; Lev 20:27; cf. Lev 19:26,31; 20:6).

The nation of Israel was bluntly warned about all occult practices: "When you enter the land the LORD your God is giving you, do not learn to imitate the detestable ways of the nations there. Let no one be found among you who sacrifices his son or daughter in the fire, who practices divination or sorcery, interprets omens, engages in witchcraft, or casts spells, or who is a medium or spiritist or who consults the dead. Anyone who does these things is detestable to the LORD" (Dt 18:9–12). The passage moves immediately to God's promise to send prophets, who would be his messengers to his people. God's people have no need to turn away from him. He is committed to give them all the guidance they need and to act on their behalf.

The reason that the practice of the occult is such a serious sin is that it denies the basic nature of God. The God of Scripture is ruler of the material and immaterial universe. All is under his sovereign authority. To appeal by magic to spiritual forces is to deny God as master of all and to turn from God to other powers for help. For the person who knows God as sovereign Lord and has established a personal relationship with him, turning to magic or the occult

is a deadly insult. To turn to magic is to turn away from God and necessarily implies either a lack of trust in his power or doubts about his love.

NT — 3. Magic in Hellenistic culture. The myths of the Greeks are—like those of the Babylonians and the Canaanites—filled with references to magic practiced by their gods and goddesses. The ordinary person both believed in and was in awe of magic. Strikingly, ancient magic bears a close resemblance to magic as practiced today by the few who still believe in it. Books about modern magic express quite accurately the beliefs about magic held in and after Jesus' day.

The average person in the NT world thought that magic enabled the practitioner to control the gods, provide a defense against evil spirits, influence events, and manipulate other people. It is interesting to note that in the first centuries of the church, those who opposed the Christian message did not deny Jesus' miracles. Instead, they ascribed them to magic. Apologists in the early church often argued that Jesus' miracles were not accomplished by magic but by the power of God and that the miracles authenticated Jesus' claim to be God's Son.

4. NT view of magic. The Greek word for magic is *mageia* (its only NT use occurring in Ac 8:11). The NT identifies a few people as magicians. Of its six uses in the NT, the Greek term *magos* is used four times of the wise men who visited the child Jesus (Mt 2:1,7,16) and twice of Bar-Jesus (Ac 13:6,8). The passage concerning Simon the sorcerer employs two other words, each used once in the NT— *mageia* (Ac 8:11) and *mageuō* (Ac 8:9). Simon practiced sorcery and amazed the population of Samaria. He "boasted that he was someone great" (Ac 8:9), and the whole population seems to have accepted his claims. But Simon was himself amazed when Philip came to Samaria with the gospel and performed miracles Simon could not begin to match.

Acts also tells us that Paul's mission to Ephesus was marked by healing miracles (19:11–12). Some itinerant exorcists visiting Ephesus tried to use the name of Jesus in a magical way to expel a demon, and the person with the evil spirit "gave them such a beating that they ran out of the house naked and bleeding" (19:16). The passage goes on (v. 19) to tell that believers who had practiced magic (*periergos* in the Greek, rendered "sorcery" here by the NIV), impressed with Jesus' power, burned their books of magic publicly. We should take note of two things. First, in a society where magic was regularly practiced, "extraordinary miracles" were performed by God to demonstrate his power and authenticate his messengers. Second, the word *periergos* ("busybody" in 1 Ti 5:13, its only other NT occurrence) suggests the focus of the "magic" practiced by the general populace: it includes interfering with others. Thus the purpose of the magic, at least that practiced in Ephesus, was on obtaining psychic control of others. This type of magic often included such things as trying to make another person return love or harming or even attempting to bring about the death of an enemy. It is likely that the burning of the books in Ephesus shows not only a repudiation of magic and the occult but also a transformed attitude toward others. Christians were certainly taught by Paul and by the Holy Spirit to view others as persons, not objects, and to love even one's enemies.

5. Summary. The Bible consistently rejects all forms of occult practice. Such practices deny the nature of God as sovereign Lord. And for persons in a personal relationship with the Lord, occult practices are a contradiction of the role God wants to play in their lives.

The Bible does not deny that supernatural influences may be associated with some occult practices. Demons are viewed as realities in the NT, and demonic activity may partially explain achievements ascribed to the occult.

But the Bible also affirms that there is no power or authority that can compete with God. The believer is ready to abandon every attempt to manipulate events or other persons and to rely on God to work out his good and perfect will. The

believer submits to God's will in all things and seeks only to follow the Lord closely. As we love and obey the Lord, we can be confident that his good purposes will be worked out in our lives.

MALE AND FEMALE

Today we are particularly concerned about the roles of men and women. But it is clear that men and women do not have all roles in life in common in any society. But the problem for the believer is this: Are male/female roles simply defined by one's culture, or are there limitations imposed by God in relation to gender?

In this article we will look at one aspect of this problem and explore biblical testimony focused on the fact of maleness or femaleness. In other articles I discuss the relationship of the sexes in marriage and the role of women in the church. ◆ *Marriage* ◆ *Women in the Church*

OT 1. The Hebrew words
   2. The testimony of Genesis
   3. Male roles in the OT
   4. Female roles in the OT
   5. Significant women of the OT
NT 6. The Greek words
   7. Male and female in NT
     perspective
   8. Significant NT women
   9. Summary

OT — 1. The Hebrew words. The Hebrew `ādām` generally means "man," in the sense of mankind. Another word, `îš`, designates any individual male, whereas `zākār` is often used when a sharp sexual distinction is made. For instance, the male (`zākār`, 83 times in the OT) is the one that is to be circumcised (Ge 34:15,22,24,25); and the first male offspring of every animal was to be sacrificed to the Lord, to commemorate the Passover (Ex 12:5). ◆ *Passover* Also the first son of each family was to be purchased back from the LORD by a special offering (Ex 13:12,15). The burnt offering for sin had to be a male animal (Lev 1:3), though a fellowship offering might be an animal of either sex (Lev 3:1; cf. Ge 15:9). A census was taken in Israel by counting every male of twenty years or more (Nu

1:20,22). And genealogies were traced through the male line (Ezr 8:3–14).

The Hebrew word 'iššâh is translated "woman" or "female" in the NIV and the NASB. It designates any individual woman. Neqēbâh (22 times in the OT) is often used in the same way that zākār is used, that is, when a clear sexual distinction is to be made. Thus, God is said to have created humanity "male and female" (Ge 1:27; 5:2). In the OT the word for female is also used where differing time periods for ritual purification after the birth of male and female children is specified (Lev 12:1–5 ♦ **Clean and Unclean**). Also, persons making a vow are assigned different monetary values, according to age and gender (Lev 27:1–8). This should perhaps be taken to reflect their value as an economic unit rather than as an estimate of intrinsic worth.

2. The testimony of Genesis. In our search for biblical perspective on male and female we begin with the account of Creation. We see that God stated his intention to create humanity in his own image (Ge 1:26). Immediately Scripture reports that "in the image of God he created him; male and female he created them" (v. 27). ♦ **Image and Likeness**

Adam searched animal creation for a suitable helper. Finally God took one of Adam's ribs to shape Eve. Awakening, Adam affirmed, "This is now bone of my bones and flesh of my flesh" (2:23). Thus, the passage reinforces the essential identity ascribed to men and women as persons.

After the Fall, Genesis makes it plain that the wife is to be in subordination to her husband ("he will rule over you," 3:16). Whatever this may imply for marriage, it does not suggest some wholesale inferiority of women to men.

3. Male roles in the OT. Hebrew society, like the other societies in the ancient world, was patriarchal. Genealogies were reckoned through the male. The man was recognized as the civil and responsible head of the house. Civic responsibility for the community was also placed on male elders. Although there is no OT statement restricting this

eldership to males, there are no biblical examples of women who had been given this responsibility. This structure of society is reflected in, and—to the extent that existing patterns are sanctioned—is permitted by, OT commands and statutes.

The OT priesthood is a different matter. Only males from the tribe of Levi and the family of Aaron were to officiate at public worship (Ex 28:1–3; Nu 3:12–15). This pattern was specifically established by God, even though the whole people of Israel were holy (Nu 16:3). But we should not conclude that this implies that women are inferior to men. Creation's design excludes men from bearing children, but this does not imply male inferiority. OT law does not permit women from any tribe, nor men from any other tribe than the tribe of Levi, to serve as priests. But we cannot conclude from this that women are inferior, just as we do not consider the men of the other eleven tribes inferior to the men of the tribe of Levi.

4. Female roles in the OT. OT society was patriarchal in structure, and men historically filled most roles of leadership and influence. It would be a mistake, however, to conclude that women were passive, or inferior, or necessarily discriminated against.

Pr 31 praises the noble wife and provides an insight into the opportunities for women to find personal fulfillment in ancient agrarian society. The passage shows that the "noble wife" actually performed many of the roles of men in that culture. She supervised a staff of workers (v. 27). She served as buyer for her enterprises (v. 13). She sold what her staff produced (vv. 18,24) and she invested her profits (v. 16). She had the freedom to give to help the needy (v. 20). She was respected for her wisdom and responsibility (vv. 14–15,26–31). This picture is striking, for it shows the woman of OT times engaged in the functions of what today we call "business." The OT woman's activities were linked closely with her home and family, but she was not at all cast in what some think of when they suggest that women should "keep house and take care of the children." Women were viewed with far greater respect in biblical times than that!

It is true that OT women did not share all the legal rights and civil responsibilities of men. But active wives, and women who were heads of households, were not restricted to "women's work."

In most cases the OT civil laws governing the rights of men and women reflect cultural patterns. They fall short of what many believe to be a deserved "equality." But it is important to remember that no culture provides equality. Injustices exist in every culture. And OT law was not a perfect expression of God's ideal for the whole human race (Mt 5:21–43). OT law was an accommodation, bringing righteousness as close as possible to men and women who lived in a world in which all things were tainted and twisted by sin.

There are, however, three valid conclusions we can draw from the OT: (1) Women and men were created in the image and likeness of God, both having worth as human beings. (2) Women and men are given, within the framework of their society, opportunities to use their full potential as human beings. And (3) God ordained, in the specific case of the priesthood, that only men (and men of a specific tribe and family) would fill at least one religious-social role.

5. Significant women of the OT. The OT tells of a number of significant women. Some of these had roles within and some had roles outside of the framework of cultural expectations. Abigail (1 Sa 25) and Ruth won commendation within cultural roles. (Ex 15; 2 Ki 22:11–13). Miriam (Ex 15:20) and Huldah (2 Ki 22:14; 2 Ch 34:22) and Deborah (Jdg 4:4) served in roles usually associated with men—all three were prophetesses. And Deborah was far more: she was a prophetess who led Israel and functioned as a judge, "and the Israelites came to her to have their disputes decided" (Jdg 4:5). In addition to that, Deborah communicated instructions to Barak in the name of the Lord and then accompanied him on a military expedition that resulted in Israel's victory over their enemies

(4:6–10). Deborah's role may have been inappropriate culturally. But it was not a role from which her womanhood excluded her per se. Just as clearly, the people of Israel recognized her divine appointment and did not reject her leadership.

These and other women, such as Ruth and Esther, had important places in sacred history. In public office or private life, each demonstrated that spiritual significance is not a matter of gender. Significance and usefulness are determined rather by our being open to God and letting him use us in the place and position he chooses.

NT — 6. The Greek words. The word used to distinguish mankind from the gods and the animals is *anthropos*. Generally all humanity is indicated when this word is used, but it can also refer to an individual man. *Anēr* is usually used to indicate an individual man. But at times it shifts in meaning to include mankind. In the NT, *anēr* is often used to distinguish man from woman (*gynē*). *Gynē* is the general word for woman, which also includes the meaning of "wife."

Arsēn is a seldom-used word (only 8 times in the NT) that emphasizes maleness. It is found in three significant NT passages where it is contrasted with femaleness (*thēlys*). In Mt 19:4 and Mk 10:6, *arsēn* and *thēlys* are used when Jesus, referring to the Genesis account of Creation, says "God made them male and female." Both *arsēn* and *thēlys* are found in Ro 1:26–27, where Paul identifies homosexuality and lesbianism as unnatural and indecent perversions. Finally, both words are found in Gal 3:27–28. There we find this statement: "All of you who were baptized into Christ have clothed yourselves with Christ. There is neither Jew nor Greek, slave nor free, male nor female, for you are all one in Christ Jesus."

7. Male and female in NT perspective. In the Hellenistic world, a variety of attitudes toward women existed. Athens had a tradition of contempt for women. The Doric tradition gave women greater respect. The Orient contributed a significant role for women in religious cults: they served as priestesses who might be called on to remain virgins or to become cult prostitutes. But it is clear that in the Hellenic world, male and female were not equal. It was not uncommon during the Greek era for girl babies to be exposed (put out on some garbage heap) at birth—a practice that differs from abortion only in that death was delayed until the fetus reached full term.

Women were shown even less respect in the Judaism of NT times. A rabbi would not condescend to speak to women unless other men were present. Women were not allowed full access to the outer courts of Herod's temple in Jerusalem. For some three centuries before Jesus, women were isolated from men in the synagogues. One rabbi announced, "The woman does not read out of the Torah, for the sake of the honor of the congregation." But any male member might be called on to read. Teaching the law to women and even holding conversations with them were discouraged. In A.D. 150, Rabbi Judah ben Elai announced: "One must utter three doxologies every day: Praise God that he did not create me a heathen! Praise God that he did not create me a woman! Praise God that he did not create me an illiterate person!"

In view of the culture's view of women, it is striking to read in the Gospels that Jesus spoke naturally with women and taught them (e.g., Lk 10:38–42; Jn 4:7–27). He also uses many illustrations drawn from the daily life of women. Mary Magdalene and Mary the mother of James and Joses were among his closest followers (Mk 15:40–41). It is even more striking, in view of Paul's training as a rabbi, to note that he writes familiarly about seven women in Ro 16. And twice he named Priscilla before her husband, Aquila, perhaps acknowledging her significance in the church that met in their home (Ro 16:3; 2 Ti 4:19; cf. 1 Co 16:19).

All these attitudes and events, which we view as natural and normal from the perspective of modern attitudes, take on a stunning significance against the background of biblical times. For those who read a bias against women into the NT, unfamiliarity with NT times has blinded them to the marks of acceptance and respect expressed on the Gospel pages and in Acts, as well as in the Epistles.

There are a number of passages in the NT Epistles that deal with the question of relationships between husband and wife and with the woman's role in the church. These are better explored in other articles. ◆ *Marriage* ◆ *Women in the Church* But there is one passage that deals with male/female standing in the church in itself. This passage is 1 Co 11:2–16.

The women of Corinth became excited by the gospel's affirmation of their spiritual equality with men in Christ. They determined to show their equality by abandoning a head covering in church meetings. This involved either (1) wearing their hair loose rather than coiffured, as the culture suggested was appropriate for women, or (2) adopting a male hair style. Paul reacted strongly to this practice. He saw it as striking at the very heart of the gospel message.

Paul begins his discussion of this issue by stating that there is a headship relationship between Christ and man, man and woman, and God and Christ. ◆ *Head* He is simply noting the fact that God made humanity male and female. With this as a basis, he proceeds to note that women, if they pray or prophesy, are to have their heads covered, whereas men are not to have their heads covered during such religious activities.

Paul concludes with an argument for interdependence. Whatever the creation order, today men and women are not independent of each other. God has designed a universe in which each sex requires the other. Thus, it is proper for a woman to pray to God with her hair and dress proudly testifying to all the world that she is a woman.

8. Significant NT women. The Gospels mention a number of women who were significant. One of them, Mary Magdalene, was especially honored by Jesus by being the one to whom he first appeared after the Resurrection (Mk 16:9–11; Jn 20:1–18). Luke notes that some women—including Joanna, the wife of "the manager of Herod's household" (8:3)—traveled with Jesus, ministering to him out of their means.

The closing of Romans refers to specific women who are identified by Paul as his "fellow workers in Christ Jesus" (Ro 16:3) and as those who "work hard in the Lord" (v. 12). Phoebe was commended to the Roman church as a deacon (v. 1, the same term used of male leaders in 1 Ti 3:8–13). I have already referred to Priscilla, who was mentioned before her husband Aquila in a few NT passages. These references, and more, bear witness to the importance of women in the life of the early church, where every member possessed a spiritual gift and was an essential member of the body.

9. Summary. God made human beings in his own image and gave the first couple the charge to exercise rule over his creation (Ge 1–2).

The introduction of sin into the world distorted male/female relationships. Sacred history, including the Mosaic Law itself, testifies to the fact that God has historically made some definite distinctions between men and women. Even the OT ideal, as expressed in the law, failed to fully restore woman's worth and dignity, although OT society provided women with greater opportunity for self-actualization than is generally realized.

With the gospel came the announcement that in Christ "there is neither Jew nor Greek, slave nor free, male nor female, for you are all one in Christ Jesus" (Gal 3:28). This proclamation insists that there is spiritual equality in God's sight, despite those cultural distinctions made in every society. Yet believers remain male and female, slave and free. And each must live out his or her life within roles imposed by society as well as within the believing community.

For the church, the teaching of the gospel is a challenge to become the kind of community that Scripture says we are—one that values persons apart from their social role. For the woman today, the teaching of the gospel is a challenge to be comfortable with herself as a female. A woman, because she *is* sig-

nificant in Christ, can find worth and dignity by living life as a woman—without a need to act like a man.

MALICE

A range of ideas is suggested in the OT words translated "malice," including the ideas of hatred and violence. The basic Greek word for "malice" in the NT is *kakia*; it occurs eleven times, six of which NIV renders by "malice" (1 Co 14:20; Eph 4:3; Col 3:8; Tit 3:3; Jas 1:21; 1 Pe 2:1,16). The word means "wickedness," but in these contexts it is a wickedness that manifests itself in a hard and vicious disposition toward others. In Ro 1:29 the word is *kakoētheia* (its only occurrence in the NT), which tends to put the worst possible construction on others' words and actions.

"Maliciousness" is expressed by *diabolos* and *blasphēmia,* each of which suggests slander.

MANKIND

People today are curious about human nature. They raise questions in the categories of contemporary psychology and philosophy—categories the Bible does not really use. But the Bible holds the answer to the ultimate questions about mankind. Man is here as a product of God's creative act. Individuals live out a brief span. Yet Scripture looks beyond time to eternity and posits an endless existence for each individual personality.

OT 1. Hebrew words for "mankind"
    2. Human identity established at Creation
    3. Themes that provide insight
NT 4. Greek words for "mankind"
    5. Human destiny established in redemption and resurrection
    6. The old man and the new man
    7. Themes that provide insight

OT — 1. Hebrew words for "mankind". Where English versions speak of "humanity" or "man" in referring to the human race, the Hebrew word is most likely to be '*ādām*. This, the name of the first man, is also the Bible's primary word for humanity.

There are other Hebrew words that mean "mankind." One of them, 'îš, which views each person as an individual, asserts the great worth of every human being by establishing the death penalty for murder (e.g., Lev 24:17). ▶ *Murder/Kill* The word '*enôš* tends to emphasize mankind's mortality and weakness in contrast with the eternality and might of the Lord (e.g., Job 33:12; Ps 9:19–20).

The word *bāśār* is sometimes translated "mankind" (e.g., Job 12:10; Isa 66:23–24; Joel 2:28). The word means "flesh," and its use provides many insights into human nature. ▶ *Flesh*

2. Human identity established at Creation. Our understanding of the human race in biblical perspective must begin with the Genesis account of Creation. Here we discover a number of ways in which humanity is carefully distinguished from the rest of creation.

a. Man alone was created in the image and likeness of God (Ge 1:26–27). Even after the Fall, this image persists, continuing to set humanity apart and to make each individual life precious (Ge 9:6). ▶ *Image and Likeness*

b. Man alone was created with distinct elements, the body having been shaped from the earth and given the breath of life (Ge 2:7).

c. Man alone is described as directly and personally shaped by the Creator, rather than being simply called into existence by the Creator's spoken word (Ge 2:7).

d. Man alone was given the right to subdue the material creation and to rule all living beings as God's representative (Ge 1:26,28–30; cf. Ps 8).

e. Man alone has a nature that requires relationships with his fellows on multiple levels of personality (Ge 2:18–25).

f. Man alone was made morally responsible to obey God's commands and to care for the Garden of Eden (Ge 2:15–17).

There was a continuing and unique interaction between God and humanity. Human wickedness was judged in the Flood (Ge 6–8). God established a covenant with Abraham (Ge 12). God acted in faithfulness to the covenant and through his power released Israel from Egypt in the Exodus. God continues to be involved as history moves on. He announces a plan for his people, and he declares purposes of his own that stretch beyond time into eternity. Thus, sacred history reinforces Creation's affirmation of man's uniqueness. In the words of the writer of the Hebrews: "It is not angels he helps, but Abraham's descendants" (Heb 2:16). The focus of God's concern has been and remains, humanity.

3. Themes that provide insight. The account of Creation and the history of God's work in the universe require us to take a high view of human nature. But many different themes in Scripture explore man's present state and aspects of human nature that give insight into mankind's present state and motivations. ▶ *Account/Accountable* ▶ *Flesh* ▶ *Heart* ▶ *Sin* ▶ *Soul and Spirit*

NT — 4. Greek words for "mankind". Where English versions speak of mankind or humanity, the Greek is sometimes *sarx* (which primarily means "flesh") but usually *anthrōpos*. *Anthrōpos* distinguishes man from the gods and animals and includes women and children as well as adult males.

It would be wrong to think that such words import into Scripture a particular view of human beings. In fact, the flow is from the other direction. It is Scripture's theological perception of man and the universe that brings distinctive meaning to the Bible's use of such Greek words.

5. Human destiny established in redemption and resurrection. Human nature can be understood only when it is seen in its relationship with God. Any philosophical or psychological school that attempts to treat human nature apart from God must reach inadequate or wrong conclusions. In the OT, the focus of revelation rests on Creation, with mankind viewed as created in the image of God. In the NT, the focus of revelation is on man's alienation from God and on

God's remedy in Christ—redemption and resurrection.

Rather than look at mankind in the abstract, the Bible always reminds us that man is a creature. What's more, man is a fallen creature. Human potential and personality has been warped by sin. Rather than live in fellowship with God, human beings rebel and look at the Lord with enmity (Ro 1:18–32). Humanity is not and cannot be subject to God's law (Ro 8:14–25). "The sinful mind is hostile to God. It does not submit to God's law, nor can it do so" (Ro 8:7). As persons who are fully responsible for their acts, human beings are under the wrath of God, for he, as righteous judge, must punish sin.

But the vision of man as sinner is itself inadequate. Even those explorations of the impact of sin on personality and relationships, while they give insight into the current state of the race, do not adequately explain mankind. The Bible tells us that human beings remain the objects of God's love. In virtue of the uniqueness of humanity, which flows from a creation endowment, each individual has an eternal destiny. No individual is simply snuffed out of existence at death.

God's concern for us as unique beings is shown in the decision of the Triune God to effect our salvation. The Father planned and predestined; the Son entered the human family to die; and the Spirit breathes life into all who believe, bonding each believer to the body of Christ. To effect this plan, the Son himself actually took on humanity (Heb 2:14–18) and then died as a human being to effect our redemption. In his resurrection we have not only a guarantee of forgiveness but also a vision of our own final destiny.

So the Scripture draws our attention to Christ and to the redemption he provides and the resurrection he promises. Through Jesus, there is the possibility of an inner transformation, through which sin's impact will be canceled and our lives will bring forth beauty. Through Jesus, there is the prospect of full restora-

tion to God's ideal for mankind—when the resurrection occurs.

It is clear, then, according to Scripture, that mankind can never be understood simply by looking at man's present experience in this world. To grasp who and what human beings are, we must look back to Creation, look to the continuing impact of redemption, and look ahead to the ultimate transformation that will be effected by resurrection.

When each human being is understood as an ever-living person—unique, and precious to God—then and only then will we begin to understand the nature of mankind.

6. The old man and the new man. The Bible is realistic about man's natural capability. Human nature is presently in the grip of sin, twisted beyond hope. The NT term "old man" indicates all that is misshapen within the personality of the believer.

But the term "new man" represents God's dynamic new creation. That "new self" is "being renewed in knowledge in the image of its Creator" (Col 3:10). It recaptures in time what was lost in the Fall, and it gives a taste of the feast that awaits believers. ♦ New and Old

7. Themes that provide insight. Many themes run throughout the NT and fill in our understanding of humanity. Each must be seen in the perspective provided by the Bible's revelation of the creation and destiny of man, just as our personal experience can be understood only as we experience today the redemption provided for us in Jesus. ♦ Body ♦ Born ♦ Conscience ♦ Mind ♦ Redeem/Ransom ♦ Resurrection ♦ Sin ♦ Soul and Spirit

MARRIAGE

Marriage is a persistent institution. It is found in every human culture. The Bible presents marriage as a divine institution, ordained and regulated by God's Word. But marriage, even as reflected in the OT, often falls short of the ideal. Today many people have questions about the shape of the ideal. Can women be fully persons in what tradition says is a male-dominated relationship? Or does the Bible really teach male domination? What is the pattern in husband/wife relationships that enables a couple to experience all the good that God intended?

OT 1. The Hebrew words
     2. The institution of marriage
     3. Marriage and the Fall
     4. Polygamy
     5. Marriage in OT law
     6. Marriage as an image of relationship with God
NT 7. The Greek words
     8. The marital ideal
     9. Male headship
   10. Christian marriage: love, respect, submission
   11. Mixed marriages
   12. Marriage as an image of Christ and the church
   13. Summary

OT — 1. The Hebrew words. The OT views marriage as a natural state for the adult human. Marriage is so expected that the Hebrew word that indicates "husband" is simply *'îš*, which means "a man." And the word translated both "wife" and "marriage" is *'iššāh*. One aspect of being an adult male is to be a husband, and one aspect of being an adult female is to be a wife.

Sometimes *ba'al* ("master, or owner") is translated "husband(s)" (9 times in the NIV: Ex 21:22; Dt 24:4; 2 Sa 11:26; Est 1:17,20; Pr 12:4; 31:11,23,28). ◗ *Master* While we see from the words linked with marriage that it was an expected and natural state for both men and women in OT times, we must turn to key OT passages to develop a portrait of marriage as an ideal and as practiced.

2. The institution of marriage. Marriage is the first institution established by God and the only one established before the Fall. Ge 1:26–27 makes it clear that God intended humanity to have male and female expression. Yet after the creation of Adam, a period of time passed before Eve joined Adam. During this time, Adam explored creation but found no suitable "helper" for himself (Ge 2:20). It was then that God caused

Adam to sleep, and God shaped Eve from one of Adam's ribs. Three different aspects of the creation story provide insight into the divine ideal for marriage.

Shared nature. When God brought Eve to Adam, Adam declared, "This is now bone of my bones and flesh of my flesh" (Ge 2:23), recognizing her likeness to him. ◗ *Image and Likeness*

One flesh. The Hebrew expression "one flesh" includes sexual union but suggests far more. Husband and wife are united in their life on earth, sharing all experiences that may come. ◗ *Flesh*

A suitable helper. After creating him, God gave Adam an extended period of time to explore creation, that he might fully sense his need for another like himself. Then, in Eve, God provided a "suitable helper" (Ge 2:20). Eve was suitable because she shared with Adam the image and likeness of God—the image that permits human beings to relate on every dimension of personality (emotional, intellectual, spiritual, physical, etc.). Only another being who, like Adam, was shaped in the image of God would be suitable.

The word for helper here is *'ēzer*. It means "a help," "a support," "an assistant." Before we understand this concept to imply inferiority or subordination, we should note that the root is used in the OT to speak of God as helper of his nation and of individuals. God is man's helper in all kinds of distress (Ex 18:4; Dt 33:7,26,29; Ps 20:2; 33:20; 70:5; 89:19; 115:9,10,11; 121:1,2; 124:8; 146:5; Hos 13:9). We would hardly argue from this that God is inferior to the person he helps.

Ideally, then, the Bible views marriage as an intimate union of two human beings—one male and the other female. Marriage not only serves to populate the earth through reproduction (Ge 1:28) but it is also designed by God to meet the need of human beings for sharing.

3. Marriage and the Fall. The OT and the NT explore the damage Adam's fall inflicted on creation. The universe itself (Ro 8:20–22), plant life (Ge 3:17–19), animal life (Isa 65:25), and every human experience were dramatically affected by the entry of sin. ♦ *Sin* It is hardly surprising that marriage did not escape. The distortion of the sinless harmony that existed prior to the Fall can be seen in the first recorded dialogue of the first couple, as the husband accused and blamed his wife (Ge 3:8–13). We see it likewise in God's announcement of the consequences of Adam and Eve's disobedience. ♦ *Curse* Several aspects of marital distortion are suggested in Ge 3.

Ge 3:16a. "I will greatly increase your pains in childbearing." The pains of childbirth are proverbial in their unique intensity (1 Sa 4:19; Job 39:3; Isa 66:7; Hos 13:13; Mt 24:8; Mk 13:8; Ro 8:22; Gal 4:19,47; 1 Th 5:3). This curse may also refer to a modification of the menstrual cycle, imposing a monthly pattern.

Ge 3:16b. "Your desire will be for your husband, and he will rule over you." The word translated "desire" is *t^ešûqâh*. It occurs only three times in the OT (the other instances being Ge 4:7 and SS 7:10). Here, in the context of judgment, it is in parallel with "rule." Together, "desire" and "rule" describe a change in the psychological and social order. In sin-warped human society, the woman will seek refuge in her relationship with her husband, while her husband will dominate the marriage.

Ge 3:17–19. The curse on the ground is addressed to Adam. In the new order, Adam, who will dominate his wife, must also take responsibility to wrest a living from a resistant earth. Man's brief life span will be marked by toil and struggle, as well as by pain-filled distortions of the husband/wife relationship.

This grim interpretation of Ge 3 is not intended to suggest that God sanctions any shift of marriage away from the ideal. In Ge 3 we simply see foreshadowed what history (including sacred history) documents. Sin distorts every relationship, and we must not draw conclusions about what should be in marriage, or in any other realm, from OT descriptions of what actually was. Just as we make the land productive by whatever

means possible, so we must with all our effort seek to counteract the effects of the curse on marriage.

4. Polygamy. Three events are recorded following the Genesis account of the Fall: Cain killed his brother Abel (Ge 4:1–18), Lamech married two women (Ge 4:19–22), and Lamech justified his murder of a youth who injured him (Ge 4:23–24). Each event illustrates the meaning of the death that struck humanity when Adam sinned. ♦ *Life and Death* The intimacy of the first family was shattered by murder. And marriage, intended to be a vital union between one man and one woman, was distorted by polygamy (more precisely, polygyny, i.e., having more than one wife).

We know that polygamy was practiced by the patriarchs (Ge 29:21–30) and by some of Israel's kings (1 Sa 25:43; 27:3; 30:5,18; 2 Sa 2:2; 5:13; 12:11; 19:5; 1 Ki 11:1–11). This happened despite the law's clear command that the king "must not take many wives" or "accumulate large amounts of silver and gold" (Dt 17:17).

Writings from the time of Christ indicate that polygamy, along with the practice of taking concubines, was practiced in Israel and was sanctioned by some rabbinical schools.

But the practice of polygamy is never sanctioned in Scripture. The ideal of monogamy shines through clearly in the Creation account and in the prophets' image of a relationship between God and Israel that is like that of a husband espoused to one wife (Isa 54:5–6; Jer 3:14).

5. Marriage in OT law. OT law concerning marriage presupposes the patriarchal structure of that society. Yet the laws of the OT are significantly different from the laws of Assyria and Babylon, which were also patriarchal societies.

In OT society the extended family or clan was the basic unit. ♦ *Family* The patriarch (male parent) ruled his wife and children—and the families of his children as well. The father was legally responsible for the actions of his wife and children and had an authority appropriate to that civil responsibility. Early in Genesis, patriarchs were also family priests. One aspect of the father's responsibility is shown in the father's arrangement of marriages for children of both sexes (Ge 24; Jdg 14:1–2). This social structure does not imply either the inferiority or the incompetence of the wife— nor, incidentally, of the adult sons! But the wife and children were under the authority of the husband/father. The fact that no intrinsic female inferiority is implied is seen in the fact that widows in Israel were considered capable of caring for the family estate and raising children. But such widows were vulnerable, and so Scripture commands a special concern for the widow and fatherless in order to prevent them from being victimized. ♦ *Widow*

Furthermore, the sexual attitude of the OT is shaped by the concept that marriage reflects the relationship between God and his people. Thus, faithfulness is called for from both husband and wife. Neighboring cultures in those times had a double standard. Sex was not viewed as sinful in itself, and men could indulge in sexual activity with relative freedom; but wives were subject to brutal punishment should they stray. In Israel, however, adultery was a sin for both male and female. ♦ *Adultery*

In the cultures of the nations surrounding Israel, men maintained almost total control over their wives: they were free to devise whatever punishments they wished for various violations. By contrast, OT laws contained penalties as well as regulations (e.g., Dt 22:13–30). In this way the rights and person of the wife were protected.

We know little from the OT about the age at which marriage took place. Moreover, the OT does not establish a marriage ceremony as such. The typical pattern included a feast given by the bride's father, at which she was given to the groom (Ge 29:22,27; Jdg 14:10; Mt 22:1–10; Jn 2:2).

Lev 18:6–20 lists those with whom marriage should not be contracted. And Dt 7:3–4 forbids marriage to pagans and foreigners (cf. 20:16–18).

One special provision of OT marriage law calls for levirate marriage. If a husband died childless, his brother was to marry his widow. Their children were considered the children of the dead brother, and thus his line would not be lost and his estate would not pass out of the clan. This provision seems to assume that the brother who entered the levirate marriage had his own wife and family.

6. Marriage as an image of relationship with God. The prophets made an allegory of marriage. Turning from God to idols, they said, is like the sin of adultery (Jer 3:9; Eze 23:37). With this insight came the divine revelation that God was a husband to faithless Israel (Isa 54:5). Despite Israel's sin, God did not reject them but through the prophets (especially Hosea) called them back to renew their intimate marriage relationship with him.

This image underlines the grace of God. The sin of rejecting God violates the most intimate of relationships. Yet God continues to love and to forgive. ♦ *Divorce and Remarriage*

NT — 7. The Greek words. As in the OT, the word "husband" in the NT is the translation of the common Greek word for an individual man (*anēr*), and "wife" is the common word for a woman (*gynē*). ♦ *Male and Female* "Marriage" is *gamos*, "to marry" is *gameō*, and "to give in marriage" is *gamizō* or *gamiskō*. The way these words are used in the NT is in harmony with the OT view and practice of marriage.

8. The marital ideal. Marriage and family were highly prized among the Jews of NT times. Marriage was considered the normal state. When some Pharisees queried Jesus about grounds for divorce, his response reaffirmed the Creation ideal. God formed humanity as male and female. It is his intent that a man leave his father and mother to establish a permanent union with one woman. That bond is to be maintained as each couple shares the experiences of their common life on earth (Mt 19:1-9). ♦ *Divorce and Remarriage*

435

Jesus made a striking additional comment to the disciples. "Some," he said, "are eunuchs because they were born that way; others were made that way by men; and others have renounced marriage because of the kingdom of heaven" (Mt 19:12). This emphasis goes counter to the common Jewish view of marriage as a responsibility and lays a foundation for giving value to the single life.

Paul develops this theme in 1 Co 7:25–38. He argues that the single state has many advantages; thus, the unmarried should certainly not consider themselves obligated to marry. The married rightly concern themselves with the needs of their spouses, whereas the unmarried are free to concentrate every energy on pleasing the Lord. Paul's earnest endorsement of singleness is striking in view of the attitude of historic Judaism.

One reason why singleness may now be an option is seen in the nature of the church. Human beings need intimate fellowship with others. Marriage provides one avenue for such sharing. But now in the body of Christ, God's larger family on earth, none of us needs to be alone. ‣ Family

9. Male headship. To grasp the Bible's view of what we call male headship of the home, we need to deal with three lines of NT teaching. One line has to do with the nature of NT headship. Another line has to do with the wife's submission. A third has to do with spousal relationships that provide the basis for a renewal and transformation of marriage.

Head in the NT. Some have suggested that the word "head" in the NT may mean "source," while others maintain that it indicates something more like "authority." In either case, the emphasis in Eph 5 is on the loving exercise of the husband's headship by his giving himself up for the bride, committing himself to help her achieve her full potential and what is best for her. The term "head" in this passage and the rest of the NT lends no comfort to those who call for a tyrannically male-dominated household, with the wife merely an adjunct who exists for the benefit and pleasure of the husband. ‣ Head

Submission. When we read the passages in the NT that call for women to submit to their husbands, it is important to note a number of things about Christians and culture. In every society, Christians are surrounded by legal restrictions and social expectations. The NT's word to each of us is "Submit yourselves for the Lord's sake to every authority instituted among men" (1 Pe 2:13). Peter affirms Christian freedom but insists that freedom not be misused. We are to live within the confines of culture, and "show proper respect to everyone" (v. 17), even dictatorial leaders.

Although the NT does not expressly sanction slavery and in fact lays the basis for the rejection of slavery in the brotherhood of believers, Peter calls on slaves to submit to their masters. He does not say they should submit because slavery is right. He says they should submit because they are in fact slaves. This call for submission in no way gives approval for slavery, nor does it suggest the inferiority of the slave as a person. It simply teaches that one who lives as a Christian within a culture must do what is "right" by that culture's standards as long as such norms do not conflict with higher, divine law.

Not all agree on just how this idea of submission applies to marriage. As Peter has exhorted submission to government and (if a slave) to a slave master, so he goes on to tell wives, "be submissive to your husbands" (3:1). "A gentle and quiet spirit" is "of great worth in God's sight" (v. 4). In the world of the NT, husbands were legally and socially responsible for their wives. It certainly was appropriate for believing wives to offer the same submission to the laws and norms of society concerning marriage that their husbands and they were expected to offer in other culturally defined situations.

However, there is a problem when we try to argue from the cultural context of the NT to the context of our own culture. Are women still to be "like Sarah, who obeyed Abraham and called him her master" (1 Pe 3:6)? Or is a partnership, rather than patriarchal structure, in harmony both with biblical principles and with contemporary economic and cultural realities?

Spousal relationships. One may debate the interpretation of 1 Pe 2–3 and other passages that prescribe a wife's submission. But when it comes to interpersonal relationships, the worth and value of each partner is to be affirmed, and each is to be so treated by the other. Peter exhorts husbands, "Be considerate as you live with your wives, and treat them with respect as the weaker partner and as heirs with you of the gracious gift of life" (3:7). Paul calls on husbands to love their wives as Christ loves the church (Eph 5:25–30) and as each husband loves himself (v. 33).

Perhaps the most stunning statement is Paul's instruction concerning sex. He writes in 1 Co 7:3–4: "The husband should fulfill his marital duty to his wife, and likewise the wife to her husband. The wife's body does not belong to her alone but also to her husband. In the same way, the husband's body does not belong to him alone but also to his wife." The Jewish rabbis likewise said that a husband owed his wife a sexual duty; but they did not state it in such strong terms.

10. Christian marriage: love, respect, submission. The whole NT contributes to our understanding of basic Christian interpersonal relationships. We learn that we are God's extended family. We learn to love, accept, forgive, encourage, rebuke, build up, and in many other ways participate in one another's lives. Our view of relationships in marriage is necessarily controlled by this foundation laid so thoroughly in every NT Epistle. In marriage—the most intimate of Christian relationships—every quality is to be given its fullest and most beautiful expression.

Any perspective on Christian marriage that steps out of the context provided by the common voice of the NT on quality Christian relationships must, to that extent, be in error. Thus, it is unnecessary for Scripture to teach Christians how to have a successful marriage, or to give a special definition to marriage, as though that relationship were to be different in kind from other Christian personal relationships.

However, the NT clearly notes the responsibilities of husbands and wives. First, the emphasis for husbands is that they *love* their wives (Eph 5:25,28,33), though wives are also told to *love* their husbands (Tit 2:4). A related concept is that they *respect* (lit., "honor") their wives (1 Pe 3:7). Second, in connection with the general exhortation to proper submission to authority among believers (Eph 5:21), Paul specifies that wives are to *submit* to their husbands (vv. 22,24; cf. "be submissive" in 1 Pe 3:1). Along with this, wives are also to *respect* (lit., "fear") their husbands (Eph 5:33).

11. Mixed marriages. The NT carries over the OT injunction: Christians are not to yoke themselves to unbelievers (2 Co 6:14). The unmarried are free to marry, but the partner must "belong to the Lord" (1 Co 7:39).

But what of the case in which a person is converted while married to an unbeliever? When this situation arose in Corinth, Paul told the believer not to initiate divorce. If the unbelieving partner was willing to live with the believer, the latter must not "divorce" the spouse. In Paul's view, the presence of the believing partner consecrates the spouse and children of the union, in the sense that they are given a unique opportunity to hear and to see the gospel (1 Co 7:12–14). Should the unbeliever be unwilling to stay with the Christian, however, that decision leaves the believer free of any obligation to forcefully prolong the marriage, especially at the price of peace (1 Co 7:15–16).
▶ *Divorce and Remarriage*

12. Marriage as an image of Christ and the church. The OT portrays Israel as the wife of Yahweh. She has been unfaithful, but he remains faithful and at history's end will cleanse her and recall her to her holy estate. The NT uses a similar imagery. Husbands are to love their wives as Christ loved the church, for that spiritual union is the reality that the bonding of lives on earth is to reflect (Eph 5:29–33). Today the church lives on earth as a fiancée of Christ. At Christ's return, the marriage will take place, and the bride and groom will be united forever (Rev 19:6–9; 20:2,9).

13. Summary. Marriage was instituted by God before the Fall, with the marital ideal being the union of a man and a woman who would be committed through their lifetimes to share every challenge and experience of life on earth. The possibility of achieving this ideal was shattered in the Fall. With the entry of sin into the universe, all relationships were distorted. The patterns that developed in society reflect the distortions of sin far more sharply than they reflect the memory of the ideal.

The culture of the OT was patriarchal. The law, including the laws and statutes regarding marriage, reflect that culture. Believers have always been called on to live out their relationship with God in the real, rather than the ideal, world. The subordination of wives that was prescribed by the Mosaic Law did not deny women a significant role as persons, and, in fact, they had greater rights and protection than did wives in neighboring cultures. ♦ *Male and Female*

Moreover, Christians are likewise called on to live in the real world. Christian women do not deny their worth or value as persons by submitting to their husbands. Instead, they demonstrate their worth and value by fulfilling that role with beauty and grace. Women are persons of value, beings in God's image, indwelt and given gifts by his Spirit. Thus, Christian husbands are to love and respect their wives as persons.

When challenged by the Pharisees concerning divorce, Jesus simply reaffirmed God's ideal, established in Creation. When you and I adopt those attitudes toward others that Christ teaches and the Spirit makes real, our marriages too can be redeemed from the impact of sin, and our lives approximate the divine ideal. ♦ *Women in the church*

MASTER

The basic Hebrew word for "master" is *'ādôn,* and the basic Greek word is *kyrios.* Each is a term of respect and is used of a superior. Sometimes these words are used in direct address simply out of politeness (e.g., Ge 19:2; Mt 19:21; Lk 19:8,16,18,20,25). Often the context must define which usage is intended, that is, whether slave is contrasted with master or citizen with ruler.

Luke uses the Greek word *epistatēs* (its only occurrences in the NT) in his accounts of six of the instances in which Jesus is directly addressed as "Master" (Lk 5:5; 8:24,45; 9:33,49; 17:13). This word denotes "commander," "director," or "chief." Like *kyrios,* it implies authority to give orders.

The NASB also translates *despotēs* as "master" in three of the ten times it appears in the NT (2 Ti 2:21; 2 Pe 2:1; Jude 1:4). This word is stronger than *kyrios* and *epistatēs;* it indicates absolute or unlimited power. The NIV translates it as "sovereign" in the last two references.

MATURITY

The Greek words translated "maturity" are *teleios* (used 19 times in the NT) or *teleiotēs* (used twice in the NT). The root expresses an important Greek concept: that of end or goal. The thought is that a mature individual has reached the goal of the process of growth as a person.

The NT gives us insight into the process by which a Christian becomes mature. Maturity should come as a natural process of our being among a group of believers who are functioning properly (Eph 4:12–13), as we face trials and persevere (Jas 1:4), and through the constant exercise of our faculties by applying God's Word to guide our daily choices (Heb 5:14).

Why is maturity important? Because those who are mature Christians are able to grasp and apply spiritual truths (1 Co 2:6), establish right priorities in life (Php 3:15), and stand confident and firm in the will of God (Col 4:12).

MEASURE

The NT uses this word in three of the Gospels: "With the measure you use, it will be measured to you" (Mt 7:2; Mk 4:24; Lk 6:38). This is both a warning and a promise. The judgmental person will be judged by others. But the person who forgives will be forgiven.

MEDICINE ♦ Healing

MEDIUM ♦ Magic

MEEK

The Greek word for "meek" is *praus*, and "meekness" is *prautēs*. These words picture a humble, gentle attitude that maintains patience despite offenses and is untainted by vengefulness or malice. Each Greek word is found three times in the NT: *praus* (Mt 5:5; 21:5; 1 Pe 3:4) and *prautēs* (found in Jas 1:21; 3:13; 1 Pe 3:15).

A beautiful picture of this attitude as shown in Christ is found in 1 Pe 2:21–23.

MEMBER

The Greek word is *melos*. It means "a limb, or part, of the body." The term is theologically significant in its NT uses. On the one hand, our body with all its parts is seen to be in the grip of sin and death (Ro 7). Yet through Christ we are enabled to surrender our members to God, to be used by him to do righteousness (Ro 6).

The term is also intimately linked with the NT's teaching on the body of Christ (Ro 12; 1 Co 12). Individual believers live in an organic relationship with Jesus and one another, and Christian growth and service depend on drawing on the resources the body relationship provides. ♦ *Body of Christ*

The NASB consistently translates *melos* as "member." The NIV, in Ro 6 and 1 Co 12, adopts "parts of the body" or simply "parts."

MEMORY ♦ Remember/Memory

MEMORIAL ♦ Remember/Memory

MERCY

No one has a right to mercy. When we understand this fact and its implications, we gain a deeper appreciation of God's goodness to us. And we find a new freedom to "approach the throne of grace with confidence, so that we may receive mercy and find grace to help us in our time of need" (Heb 4:16).

OT 1. The Hebrew words
NT 2. The Greek words
    3. The Gospels: mercy demonstrated and demanded
    4. The Epistles: mercy provided and experienced
    5. Summary

OT — 1. The Hebrew words. The word "mercy" appears infrequently in the OT. This is because each of the Hebrew words translated "mercy" is usually rendered by a different English word. None of the Hebrew words has the same concentrated meaning of the Greek term that expresses the concept in the NT.

In the NASB, most occurrences of "mercy" are in the phrase "mercy seat." This in the Hebrew is a technical theological term, *kappōret*, the place of propitiation. ♦ *Atonement*

In the NIV, "mercy" usually is a translation of a word from one of two Hebrew roots: *rāham* and *hānan*. It is also found in phrases such as "cry for mercy" as a translation of *tepillâh* (used 76 times in the OT), which literally means "prayer" (e.g., Ps 6:9; 86:6; 143:1). ♦ *Prayer*

Rāham and its cognates express the love of a superior for an inferior. This love is seen in the deep feelings that move the superior to help. *Rāham* is most often translated "love" or "compassion." ♦ *Compassion*

Hānan and its cognates draw attention to the response of a person who is able to help another person who stands in need. Again there is the implicit assumption that the one who helps is moved by his feelings and that the one who is helped has no right to expect aid. ♦ *Grace*

Even though different Hebrew words may be found where English versions read "mercy," the underlying concept shines through. Mercy is condescending love, reaching out to meet a need without considering the merit of the person who receives the aid.

NT — 2. The Greek words. The verb "to show mercy" is *eleeō*, and the noun is *eleos*. Originally these expressed only the emotion that was aroused by contact with a person who was suffering. By NT times, however, the concept incorporated compassionate response. A person who felt for and with a sufferer would be moved to help. This concept of mercy— as a concern for the afflicted that prompts giving help—is prominent in both the Gospels and the Epistles.

3. The Gospels: mercy demonstrated and demanded. The use of "mercy" in the Gospels has a twin focus: Jesus' own contact with human need and his instruction in true religion.

In reading the Gospels, we often find that people with afflictions came to Jesus. One cried out, "Lord, Son of David, have mercy on me" (Mt 15:22); another pleaded, "Lord, have mercy on my son" (Mt 17:15). Jesus responded; in each case, he healed and met the need. There were two lessons for those who observed Jesus, and they are there for us as well. First, those with needs must recognize Jesus' ability to help them: each recorded cry for mercy is also an expression of faith in Jesus as the Son of God. Second, those who come to Jesus invariably have their needs met. This latter fact vividly expresses the attitude of God toward us.

▶ Compassion

Also, the Gospels often have Jesus encouraging others to have mercy. He calls the merciful blessed (Mt 5:7) and tells his followers, "Be merciful, just as your Father is merciful" (Lk 6:36). Particularly significant are the reports of his confrontation with the religious leaders of his day. He challenged them because they were preoccupied with the minutia of OT law and "neglected the more important matters of the law—justice, mercy and faithfulness" (Mt 23:23). Inci-

dent after incident underlies the fact that those who share God's heart will identify with the needy and show solidarity with the oppressed (e.g., Mt 9:9–13; 12:1–7; 18:21–33). Mercy is not merely something that God shows to us. Mercy is a quality that God expects in us, for those who live close to the Lord are to reflect his character.

4. The Epistles: mercy provided and experienced. According to Ro 9 and 11, God's mercy is the basis for his action. This does not take away from love as the primary motivation in providing salvation. **▶ Love** But, in context, Paul emphasizes that God was responding to the need of the helpless and was not moved by any merit on the part of those he chose to love. The NT continues to affirm that mercy has been provided for the believer: God, "who is rich in mercy, made us alive with Christ even when we were dead in transgressions" (Eph 2:4–5). "In his great mercy he has given us new birth into a living hope" (1 Pe 1:3). And "he saved us, not because of righteous things we had done, but because of his mercy" (Tit 3:5). There can be no doubt that mercy has been provided for every believer and that the salvation we enjoy is a vivid expression of the mercy of God. Moreover, his mercy is designed to transform our experience. On a few occasions the NT links "mercy and peace" (1 Ti 1:2; 2 Ti 1:2; 2 Jn 2; cf. Jude 2). Each of these occurrences comes in a letter designed to encourage those living in difficult times. When stress fills our lives, knowledge of God's mercy fills us with peace.

Heb 4:16 is a significant statement about mercy. We come with confidence to God's very throne "to receive mercy." The context suggests that we have failed, trapped by our human weakness, and have fallen into sin (4:15). Yet we come with confidence, for God will have mercy on us in our need and then will give "grace to help" so that we need not fall again.

By God's mercy we (1) have been accepted in Christ (Ro 15:9), (2) are given ministries to perform (2 Co 4:1; 1 Ti 1:16–18), and (3) have become God's own special people (1 Pe 2:9–10). No wonder Paul appealed to the believers at Rome to be aware of all that God has done for them and "in view of God's mercy . . . offer your bodies as living sacrifices, holy and pleasing to God" (Ro 12:1).

5. Summary. In both Testaments, mercy is compassion expressed to meet human need. The focus in both is on God's mercy to human beings. In the final analysis, God is the only one truly able to meet our needs. He is the one on whom we must depend.

Those who know Jesus have received mercy and continue to experience God's mercy. We follow the example of those men and women of the Gospels who came to Jesus, acknowledged him as Lord, and cried out to him for mercy in their time of need.

And, because in mercy God has brought us to life in Jesus, we too can show mercy to those around us, providing in our own compassion a witness to the loving mercy of God.

MESSAGE

Both the OT and NT typically have "a word" where the NIV and the NASB read "message" (Heb, *dābār;* Gr, *logos* or *rhēma*). In some OT passages the word is *šᵉmû῾âh,* which means "a report," or "news" (1 Sa 2:24; 4:19; 2 Sa 4:4; 13:30; 1 Ki 2:28; 10:7; 2 Ki 19:7; 2 Ch 9:6; Ps 112:7; Pr 15:30; 25:25; Isa 37:7; Jer 10:22; 49:23; 51:46; Eze 7:26; 16:56; 21:7; Da 11:44). In the other five of its twenty-six occurrences in the OT this word is used with the technical meaning of a prophetic message, received directly from the Lord and then passed on to the people (Isa 28:9,19; 53:1; Jer 49:14; Ob 1).

MESSIAH ♦ *Christ*

MIGHT ♦ *Strength/Might/Power*

MIND

OT 1. Personality as a unity
NT 2. *Phronesis:* one's way of
     thinking

3. *Nous:* one's capacity to perceive
4. *Dianoia:* the faculty or organ of perception
5. Summary

OT — 1. Personality as a unity. The OT views a human being as an indivisible whole, rather than making the distinctions between human functions that were made by the Greeks and are reflected in the NT. Thus, there is no specific word for "mind" in the OT. Instead, where the English versions read "mind," a variety of Hebrew words are found: heart (*lēb, lēbāb*); spirit (*rûah*); kidney, or inner part (*kilyâh*); and person, soul (*nepeš*) are all translated "mind" at times. Verbal concepts such as to "be sorry" (*nāham*) can be translated "change one's mind." Yet, throughout the OT, Hebrew thought sees human personality as a unity. ♦ *Heart* It is in the NT that subtle distinctions are drawn.

NT — 2. *Phronesis:* one's way of thinking. A number of Greek words are constructed using the *phroneō* root. The NT uses *phroneō* ("to think," "judge," "be minded") thirty times (Mt 16:23; Mk 8:33; Ac 28:22; Ro 8:5; 12:3,16; 14:16; 15:5; 1 Co 4:6; 13:11; 2 Co 13:11; Gal 5:10; Php 1:7; 2:2,5; 3:15,16,19; 4:2,10; Col 3:2), *phronēma* ("way of thinking") four times (Ro 8:6,7,27), *phronēsis* ("way of thinking," "good sense") two times (Lk 1:17; Eph 1:8), *phronimos* ("intelligent," "thoughtful," "prudent") fourteen times (Mt 7:24; 10:16; 24:45; 25:2,4,8,9; Lk 12:42; 16:8; Ro 11:25; 12:16; 1 Co 4:10; 10:15; 2 Co 11:19), and *phronimōs* ("wisely") once (Lk 16:8).

The verb *phroneō* is also found in compounds (e.g., in Ro 12:3; Php 2:3). The verb in particular expresses the idea of thinking or judging in a neutral way. The context indicates the content of what is being thought.

Theologically significant usage is found in Ro 8. There the apostle writes: "The mind of sinful man is death, but the mind controlled by the Spirit is life and peace; the sinful mind is hostile to God. It does not submit to God's law, nor can it do so" (Ro 8:6–7). The direction or orientation of human thought is warped by sin. Human beings without the Spirit are both unable and unwilling to grasp spiritual realities, and so they rebel against God.

Clearly, faith in Christ has a decisive impact on the way a person thinks. Thus, the direction and attitude of believers should be affected by their commitment to Christ (e.g., Php 2:5; 3:15; Col 3:2).

3. *Nous*: one's capacity to perceive. In the Greek language, *nous* may, depending on the context, incorporate any aspect of sensual or cognitive perception. The NT use of this word and its derivatives focuses on ability to grasp and understand the revealed will of God. Thus, *nous* appears in passages where one's spiritual or religious judgment is under consideration. The various words in this significant word group appear frequently in the NT.

Nous ("mind," "thought," "understanding") occurs twenty-four times (Lk 24:45; Ro 1:28; 7:23,25; 11:34; 12:2; 14:5; 1 Co 1:10; 2:16; 14:14,15,19; Eph 4:17,23; Php 4:7; Col 2:18; 2 Th 2:2; 1 Ti 6:5; 2 Ti 3:8; Tit 1:15; Rev 13:18; 17:9).

Noeō ("to grasp," "to perceive," "to understand") is used fourteen times (Mt 15:17; 16:9,11; 24:15; Mk 7:18; 8:17; 13:14; Jn 12:40; Ro 1:20; Eph 3:4,20; 1 Ti 1:7; 2 Ti 2:7; Heb 11:3).

Noēma ("mind," "thought") occurs six times (2 Co 2:11; 3:14; 4:4; 10:5; 11:3; Php 4:7).

The compound word *katanoeō* ("to consider," "to contemplate") is found fourteen times (Mt 7:3; Lk 6:41; 12:24,27; 20:23; Ac 7:31,32; 11:6; 27:39; Ro 4:19; Heb 3:1; 10:24; Jas 1:23,24).

A look at the contexts in which these words appear shows their theological significance. The first chapter of Romans speaks of the witness of creation, through which God's nature as Creator is understood (*noeō*). But although "they knew God" (Ro 1:21), humanity refused to respond to him. As a result, "since they did not think it worthwhile to retain the knowledge of God, he gave them over to a depraved mind [*nous*]" (v. 28). The NT continues to bear witness to the fact that humanity's mind, as the organ

of perception of spiritual realities, is futile (Eph 4:17), corrupt (1 Ti 6:5; Tit 1:15), and depraved (2 Ti 3:8). By faith in Jesus we must "put on the new self" (Eph 4:24), which alone allows for a renewing of human ability to perceive and act on the will of God (cf. Ro 12:2).

It is striking to see Paul share his personal discovery that, even as a believer, the principle of sin that infects us in our mortality wars against the "law of [our] mind" (Ro 7:23). Without an individual's faith commitment to respond to the Holy Spirit's promptings, even the believer is "a prisoner of the law of sin" (v. 23), also called "the law of sin and death" (8:2).

4. *Dianoia*: the faculty or organ of perception. This is one of the *nous* group in its root and has a meaning very close to *nous* itself. It focuses on one's ability to think or perceive and thus designates the mind with which one organizes perceptions. *Dianoia* is found thirteen times in the NT (Mt 22:37; Mk 12:30; Lk 1:51; 10:27; Eph 1:18; 2:3; 4:18; Col 1:21; Heb 8:10; 10:16; 1 Pe 1:13; 2 Pe 3:1; 1 Jn 5:20).

This is the word chosen in the Gospels where Jesus states the first and great commandment of the law: "Love the Lord your God with all your heart and with all your soul and with all your mind" (Mt 22:37; Mk 12:30). But again the NT witnesses against the bent of mind of the unsaved: "They are darkened in their understanding and separated from the life of God because of the ignorance that is in them due to the hardening of their hearts" (Eph 4:18). "Once you were alienated from God and were enemies in your minds because of your evil behavior" (Col 1:21).

Two passages remind us again that only God can open the human understanding to spiritual truth. Hebrews twice quotes God's promise under the new covenant: "I will put my laws into their minds" (Heb 8:10; cf. 10:16). ▶ *Covenant* An inner transformation of the human personality, accomplished by a work of God, is necessary to open man's mind to the Lord. This is why Paul focuses his prayers on the minds of the

Ephesian believers, that they might be "enlightened in order" that they might "know the hope to which he [had] called [them]" (Eph 1:18).

5. Summary. The NT explores human cognitive capacity. It has little to say about native intelligence or about human ability to master the physical universe in which all must live. Instead, the NT looks closely at human capacity for perceiving spiritual realities.

Sinful mankind has lost the ability to perceive truth about God. The natural mind is hostile to God (Ro 8:6). The capacity to perceive has become corrupt and futile through man's choice not to respond to God's self-revelation. Even the organ of perception is twisted and darkened, alienated from God.

The solution is found only in a renewal of the mind, a renewal that comes as a result of a faith commitment to Jesus. Only when God completely changes our thinking are we able by faith to respond to the gospel and begin to grasp reality as God knows and has revealed it. ◗
Know/Knowledge ◗ *Wisdom*

MINISTER/MINISTRY

Just what is meant when the Bible speaks of ministers or of ministry? Is a specific office or function in mind?

OT 1. The Hebrew words
NT 2. *Leitourgia*: echoes of the past
3. *Diakonia*: privilege of the present

OT — 1. The Hebrew words. The Hebrew word translated "minister" in the NIV is *šārat*. This word is used of persons who give personal service to a ruler, particularly of those who are set aside to perform some special service in the worship of God. It is of special note that such ministers, in the secular and sacred realms, are persons of high rank. They merit special respect, for they are in a very close relationship with the ruler they serve.

The NASB also translates *kāhan*, "to serve as a priest," by the verb "to minister."

NT — 2. *Leitourgia*: **echoes of the past.** Words of this group echo ministry in the cultic sense of service at the tabernacle or temple. They are seldom used in the NT but may be found as follows: *leitourgeō*, "to minister": Ac 13:2; Ro 15:27; Heb 10:11; *leitourgia*, "minister": Lk 1:23; 2 Co 9:12; Php 2:17,30; Heb 8:6; 9:21; *leitourgikos*, "ministering": Heb 1:14; *leitourgos*, "minister": Ro 13:6; 15:16; Php 2:25; Heb 1:7; 8:2.

3. *Diakonia*: **privilege of the present.** In most instances where "minister" or "ministering" is found in English versions, the Greek has some form of *diakonia* ("service" or "ministry"), which occurs thirty-four times. A related noun, *diakonos* ("servant," "minister," or "deacon"), occurs thirty times. The verb *diakoneō* ("to serve" or "to serve as a deacon") is used thirty-seven times.

These words are distinctive in that their focus is squarely on loving action on behalf of a brother or sister or a neighbor. A similar word, *doulos* (127 times in the NT) can mean either "slave" or "servant," and it focuses attention on our subjection to Jesus. But these ministry words call us to look at our fellow human beings as objects of the loving services we extend to them for Jesus' sake.

It was Jesus himself who set both the tone and the example for such Christian ministry. He called his disciples to find greatness through servanthood, " . . . just as the Son of man did not come to be served (*diakoneō*) but to serve (*diakoneō*), and give his life as a ransom for many" (Mt 20:28).

A survey of NT passages using the *diakoneō* word group reveals how we can serve others and what "ministry" involves. It will include the following activities: caring for those in prison (Mt 25:44), serving tables (i.e., meeting physical needs) (Ac 6:2), teaching the Word of God (Ac 6:4), giving money to meet others' needs (2 Co 9:1), and all the service offered by Christians to others to build them up in faith (1 Co 12:5; Eph 4:12). Although Paul and other apostles are called ministers, and although there was the office of deacon in the early church, there is a sense in which every

443

believer is a minister and is to use his or her gifts to serve others.

It should be noted that in a few places the NIV has the word "ministry" where the Greek has no corresponding word of the *diakoneō* word group (Lk 3:23; Ac 8:21; Gal 2:8), Gal 2:8 being of special interest (in that the Greek actually mentions the "apostleship" of Peter).

MIRACLE/SIGN/WONDER

Scripture never relates miracles hesitantly. There have been miracles worked in the world by God. It is fascinating to discover the nature of the miracles and what they are intended to teach us.

OT   1. The Hebrew words
      2. The message of miracles
NT   3. The Greek words
      4. The message of miracles
      5. Summary

OT — 1. The Hebrew words. Three different Hebrew words are closely associated with miracles. *Pālā'* is used seventy times in the OT and means "to be marvelous or wonderful." The root usually refers to God's acts, either in shaping the universe or acting in history on behalf of his people. The word focuses on people's reaction when they are confronted by a miracle. The believer sees the power of God, the God who has invaded time and space to do something too wonderful for humans to duplicate.

Môpēt occurs only thirty-six times and also means "wonder," "miracle," or "sign." It is used to recall God's acts in Egypt (Ex 4:21; 7:3,9) and the punishments and provision that testified to his perpetual care of Israel throughout their history (e.g., Dt 6:22; 7:19–24).

The Hebrew word *'ôt* means "sign." Of all the related Hebrew words, it has the widest range of meaning, but in almost all of its approximately eighty occurrences it clearly means "miraculous sign." Each plague inflicted on Egypt is described as an *'ôt*, as are the continuing acts of God for Israel on their travels (Dt 4:34; cf. 2 Ki 20:9; Isa 38:7).

2. The message of miracles. As the word *pālā'* indicates, miracles are intend-
ed to have an impact on the observer. They create a sense of awe and wonder, a sense of the inescapability of God as an active force within the world of time and space.

We gain insight into the impact of miracles by noting four results of the ten plagues in Egypt. First, the plagues focused Israel's faith; for from that time on, God was identified with these acts performed on behalf of his people (Ex 6:7). God exercised his power to fulfill his ancient covenant promises to the children of Abraham.

Two other purposes are seen in the fact that it would be through the plagues that the Egyptians not only would be confronted with the knowledge of who Yahweh is but also would allow Israel to leave Egypt (Ex 7:5). ▶ *Lord*

Fourth, the plagues served as a judgment on the gods of Egypt (Ex 12:12). The powerlessness of human religious invention would be displayed as the living God exercised his power.

Each of these purposes is clearly linked with God's revelation of his nature. The false images of believer and unbeliever alike are shattered as God steps from the mysterious beyond to enter our here and now. The God of miracle must be responded to and not ignored, for the God of Scripture is no being of tenuous spirituality whose influence is limited to a mystic, immaterial setting.

For believers, this affirmation of God's reality and power is comforting, and the psalms constantly call on worshipers to remember and tell of his works. As David expressed it, "Tell of all his wonderful acts. . . . Remember the wonders he has done, his miracles" and "declare . . . his marvelous deeds among all peoples" (1 Ch 16:9,12,24). God can be counted on by his people.

NT — 3. The Greek words. A number of Greek words are associated with NT miracles. Each is linked with acts that clearly violated what the people of the NT understood of natural law. Each produced wonder and the compelling conviction that the supernatural had been confronted.

Dynamis is often translated "miracle." It is from a root meaning "power" and emphasizes the miracle as a spontaneous expression of God's elemental power. *Sēmeion* (77 times in the NT) indicates "sign." Its basic meaning is that of an authenticating mark or token. When it refers to a miraculous sign (e.g., Jn 2:11; Ac 4:16,22; 1 Co 1:22), it emphasizes the authenticating aspect of the miracle as an indication that supernatural power is involved. ◆ *Prophecy/Prophet Teras* (16 times in the NT) is used only in the phrase "signs and wonders." Where "miracle" is clearly meant, the NIV so translates *ergon*, the Greek word for "work" (e.g., Jn 7:3; 10:25,32).

Another family of words describes the reaction of observers to Jesus' miracles.

◆ **Amazed/Amazing**

The NT, particularly the Gospels, describes a number of miracles. These were performed by Jesus or by his followers. They are distinctive in several ways. First, in contrast with contemporary reports of "miracle," the NT miracles are not associated with spells or incantations. Jesus simply spoke or gestured, and the work was done. The power was in Jesus, not in a formula for magical control of the supernatural. ◆ *Magic*

Second, the miracles were not performed to punish. Rather, Jesus' miracles were performed to rescue human beings from physical and spiritual forces that bound them. The gospel associated with Jesus is truly good news for humanity.

Third, in every way the miracles provide testimony to Jesus' supernatural power and authority, and they witness to his ultimate victory. The kingdom over which he rules will come at last, for neither hunger, sickness, madness, death, nor demon can stand against Jesus. All fall back before him. Because Jesus will return, the ultimate fate of all of man's enemies is sealed.

4. The message of miracles. The essential message of miracles is sketched above. God has shown us his power and has proved that his power will be used to benefit us. We can trust Jesus fully. He is able, and he wills only our good.

But there was also a perhaps surprising contemporary message to be found in miracles. Jesus was authenticated to follower and enemy alike as God's perfect man. Yet the reaction of each group was different. His disciples saw in the miracles Jesus' glory, and they "put their faith in him" (Jn 2:11). But his enemies did not do so. Both Nicodemus (Jn 3:2) and the man born blind (Jn 9:33) recognize and state that God must be enabling Jesus to do miracles, but the Pharisees do not see (or admit) this to be the case (Mt 12:24; Jn 9:34). This is reminiscent of Pharaoh; he was evidently convinced but not converted by the plagues on Egypt (Ex 12:31).

The NT speaks of a future burst of apparent miracles. As history nears its end, God's final enemy will appear with "all kinds of counterfeit miracles, signs and wonders" (2 Th 2:9). These will deceive "those who are perishing" (v. 10), not those whose faith is anchored in the living and written Word of God.

5. Summary. It is hardly surprising that the Bible's stories of miracles do not produce faith today in those who are unwilling to accept Scripture's testimony about Jesus. It is faith that brings us to Scripture's vision of God, as one who towers above the "natural law" that to the unconverted seems the ultimate reality. When God is seen as he really is, miracle—while it produces praise and wonder—hardly seems strange at all.

We do not expect miracles in our daily lives. Nor do the OT and NT report that every generation was given miraculous signs. In fact, few were. There are actually only three biblical periods (of less than a hundred years each) when we find miracles occurring. But what we do expect is that a God who is totally unlimited retains his freedom to act in and through natural processes as well as by miracle. And we believe that this God continues to exercise his power for his people.

MONEY

Money is important in every culture, and so are various items associated with it. Believers ought to know the biblical view of wealth and possessions. ♦ *Giving* ♦ *Wealth/Riches/Possessions*

In the OT, "money" is *kesep* ("silver"). This metal is basic also in the vocabulary of the NT. *Argyrion* ("silver or silver coinage") is often translated "money" in the English versions. A lover of money is a *philargyros* (used twice in the NT—Lk 16:14; 2 Ti 3:2). *Philargyria* ("the love of money") is used once in the NT (1 Ti 6:10), and *aphilargyros* is used twice— "not a lover of money" (1 Ti 3:3) and "free from the love of money" (Heb 13:5).

There are several different specific designations for coins in the NT. A *dēnarion* (denarius) was a silver coin worth about eighteen cents, an amount that represented a typical day's wage for a workman. A "talent" (NIV one time adds the words "of money"—Mt 25:15) represents about six thousand days' wages.

We gain fascinating insight into Mk 12:41–42 by looking at the terms Mark uses for coinage: "Jesus sat down opposite the place where the offerings were put and watched the crowd putting their money into the temple treasury. Many rich people threw in large amounts. But a poor widow came and put in two very small copper coins, worth only a fraction of a penny."

The "money" that the crowd was putting into the temple treasury was *chalkos*, copper or bronze money rather than silver. "Many rich people" threw in many pieces of coin, not necessarily a large amount of money. The image may suggest the wealthy ostentatiously throwing in many coins that would clink loudly, though these were cheap copper coins rather than valuable silver ones. The coins the widow put in were very small (*lepton*, a copper coin worth about one-eighth of a cent). Mark gives the Roman equivalent for his readers (*kodrantēs*, a coin worth about one-fourth of a cent). With this background, Jesus' comment is even more pointed: the wealthy simply threw in great handfuls of small change, while the tiny amount the widow contributed was more significant. "They all gave out of their wealth; but

she, out of her poverty, put in everything—all she had to live on" (Mk 12:44).

MONTH

The biblical month was a lunar month of twenty-eight days. The Hebrew *hōdeš* literally means "new moon," because the new moon marked the end of one month and the beginning of another. To fit the solar year, an additional month was inserted every three years. A lunar calendar is approximately eleven days shorter than the solar calendar.

MORTAL ♦ *Imperishable*

MOUNTAIN ♦ *Hills/Mountains*

MOURN

The OT uses a dozen words in connection with mourning. The most common words translated "mourn" or "mourning" are 'ābal and its derivatives, sāpad and qādar. These words suggest deep grief and lamentation, qādar adding a sense of darkness and gloom.

In each case, these words are closely linked with mourning for the dead. In Hebrew culture such mourning began at death and lasted for at least seven days after interment. Those who shared the sense of loss joined with the family for this period of time, openly and emotionally expressing their feelings, often with wailing.

In the Prophets, the image of such grieving is linked with God's coming judgments, as the nation itself would die before the promised rebirth would occur (see references to "mourn" in Isaiah, Jeremiah, and Ezekiel).

A number of Greek words also are used to express the idea of mourning or grief. Most of them can be used as translations of the key Hebrew words. In the Gospels, *koptō* is often found linked with Jewish funeral mourning customs (Mt 11:17; 24:30; Lk 8:52; 23:27). It is used similarly in Revelation (1:7; 18:9). In fact, in only two of its eight uses in the NT is it not directly associated with deep grief, and both of them relate to Jesus' triumphal entry (Mt 21:8; Mk 11:8).

It is indeed good to reflect on the changes that Jesus' more perfect vision of our future brings. Because we know that when Jesus returns we will arise to join him, we do not "grieve like the rest of men, who have no hope" (1 Th 4:13; the word for "grief" here is *lupeō*, "to feel deep emotional or physical pain"). And we look forward to eternity when "there will be no more death or mourning or crying or pain, for the old order of things has passed away" (Rev 21:4).

Another Greek word, *pentheō* ("to experience grief, mourning, sadness"), also needs to be considered. It is used ten times in the NT (Mt 5:4; 9:15; Mk 16:10; Lk 6:25; 1 Co 5:2; 2 Co 12:21; Jas 4:9; Rev 18:11,15,19). Most notable is the use of this word in the Beatitudes: "Blessed are those who mourn, for they will be comforted" (Mt 5:4). It is best to understand this phrase in the context of Jesus' purpose in the Beatitudes, where he contrasted the values of his kingdom with those of the world. This world considers blessed, not those who mourn, but the hedonistic and pleasure-seeking, who find "happiness" in transitory experience. It is the one who is dissatisfied and pained by what this world has to offer who will find the comfort that is offered by a living relationship with God.

MOUTH

The Hebrew word for "mouth" is *peh*. It focuses on the mouth primarily as the organ of speech. Some fifty times in the OT reference is made to God's mouth, emphasizing the fact that God speaks and thus reveals his will to man. It also emphasizes the authoritative force of what God's mouth utters. The NIV typically translates such phrases as "according to the mouth of the Lord" by "as the LORD commanded" (e.g., Ex 17:1) and renders the word "mouth" as "will" (e.g., Lev 24:12).

As far as the mouth of human beings is concerned, it is viewed as the revealer of one's character. We see this clearly in Proverbs. "A wise man's heart guides his mouth" (Pr 16:23), but "a fool's mouth is his undoing, and his lips are a snare to his soul" (18:7).

In the NT, "mouth" (*stoma*) has the same significance. Jesus said, "Out of the overflow of the heart the mouth speaks. The good man brings good things out of the good stored up in him, and the evil man brings evil things out of the evil stored up in him" (Mt 12:34–35). Jesus goes on to warn of giving account on the judgment day of "every careless word" (v. 36). His point is that the heart is revealed, not by the words one carefully frames and utters in public speeches, but by the words spoken carelessly without thought. A classic illustration is former President Nixon's speeches and books in contrast with the "careless words" captured on tape in the oval office, for it was the latter that revealed the flaws in his character.

In Ro 10:8–13 there may be a hint of this thought that the mouth is a revealer of character, for these verses speak of confessing with one's mouth the faith in Jesus that exists in the heart. But there is more involved here: To confess with one's mouth is *homologeō*, here used in a technical sense to mean a public declaration that establishes a relationship in a legally binding way.

MURDER/KILL

In the English language there are many words that portray the killing of human beings; they include "destroy," "kill," "massacre," "murder," "slaughter," and "slay." There is a similar range of terms in Hebrew and Greek. In fact, the very variety of terms and settings that have to do with the taking of life complicates the debates over the morality of killing.

This debate has extended throughout the Christian era. Some people just a few generations removed from the apostolic period refused to give evidence in capital cases lest they be responsible for an execution. Many in the Roman army refused to fight and were thereupon executed by their officers.

The moral issues are many and complicated. What about killing in war? Capital punishment? Killing in defense of one's life or property? The convictions that individuals hold on these and similar issues differ. But the testimony of the words of Scripture—and the way these words are used—may at least help us clarify our reasoning and evaluate one another's arguments. ♦ *Authorities* ♦ *War*

OT 1. The biblical ideal
    2. *Hārag:* killing as a fact of life
    3. *Rāṣaḥ:* manslaughter and murder
NT 4. The Greek words
    5. The heart of the issue
    6. The role of government
    7. Conclusions

OT — 1. The biblical ideal. The OT tells of God's personal and unique creation of human beings (Ge 1–2). Only man shares the image and likeness of God. ♦ *Image and Likeness* Humanity is granted dominion over creation, but the first two chapters of Genesis record no provision for the rule of man over man. Ge 1–2 establishes the ideal. But Ge 3–4 shows why the ideal has never been approached in history. Adam and Eve sinned, and death struck the race. ♦ *Life and Death* One expression of death was demonstrated when a jealous and angry Cain killed his younger brother, Abel (Ge 4). Cain was unable to master the sinful passions that gripped him (4:7). He did the unthinkable: he took the life of a being who, like himself, was shaped in the divine image.

The OT is filled with words that portray killing and death, because history is filled with events duplicating the first killing. We read in the Bible of *nāḵâh,* "to smite," "attack," "kill," and of *šāḥaṭ,* "slaughter." We read of those who caused the death (*mût*) of others, who killed (*hārag*) and who murdered (*rāṣaḥ*). The multiplicity of such words testifies to the awful impact of sin, which shattered our every hope of realizing God's ideal, even as Cain's blow shattered the body of his brother, spilling his blood on God's new, but now stained earth.

There is no way to justify murder. Any act of murder falls short of God's ideal and crushes a being shaped in God's image.

But man does not live in an ideal world. Each of us lives in a world in which killing does take place. The problem we face thus is clear, even though it is complex. How do we affirm the ideal and honor the image of God that is stamped on every human being, while at the same time responding to the reality of the killing that does take place?

To explore this question, we need to look at two of the key Hebrew words for "killing" and "murder" and, in another article, address the entire question of war. ♦ *War*

2. *Hārag:* killing as a fact of life. The word *hārag,* though one of several used for "to kill," is significant in that it is usually used of the violent killing of people by other people. It is used of Cain's killing of Abel (Ge 4:25), of Moses' killing of an Egyptian slavemaster (Ex 2:14), of Saul's murder of a family of priests (1 Sa 22:21), of the killing of the false prophets of Baal at Elijah's behest (1 Ki 19:1), and of the Jews' killing of their enemies in Esther's day (Est 9:6,10,12). It is used of Jezebel's killing of Yahweh's prophets (1 Ki 18:13) and of God's killing of the firstborn of Egypt in the culminating judgment on that people who held Israel in slavery (Ex 13:15).

This brief survey shows that the word is used of unjustified murder and of what might be considered justified killings, and it is even used of divine judgments. In this present world, warped as it is by sin, killing is a fact of life that we must deal with. Are there any theologically crucial passages that may guide us?

Ge 4:8–16. Cain killed (*hārag*) Abel. Confronted by God and driven from his farm, Cain complained of his fate: "I will be a restless wanderer on the earth, and whoever finds me will kill (*hārag*) me" (v. 15). But God placed a mark on Cain "so that no one who found him would kill (*hārag*) him" (v. 15).

Ge 9:5–6. God announced after the Flood, "From each man, too, I will demand an accounting for the life of his fellow man. Whoever sheds the blood of man, by man shall his blood be shed; for in the image of God has God made man." Although it uses none of the words for killing, this passage introduces the principle of social responsibility. Human beings are now charged by God as participants in the divine call for an accounting.

Those who see this as foundational to capital punishment argue that (1) capital punishment affirms the image of God in man by placing the only possible equivalent value on it—that of another life; (2) God has himself set the penalty that society is to require; and (3) the failure of society to accept this responsibility implies social consent to murder and a lowering of the value placed on human life.

In this view, David's execution (*hārag*) of the murderers of Ishbosheth (2 Sa 4:11–12) is not only a case of justified killing but also a case in which execution was a moral necessity.

Dt 13:6–11. This passage in the Mosaic Law shows how Israel is to protect itself from pagan influences. If anyone, no matter how close the relationship, suggests the worship of other gods, that person is to be put to death. "Show him no pity," the passage reads. "Do not spare him or shield him. You must certainly put him to death (*hārag*). Your hand must be the first in putting him to death (*hārag*), and then the hands of all the people" (vv. 8–9).

Again the concept of social responsibility is implicit. In a world marred by sin, there are actions that call for the taking of a life. Individuals and the community of Israel itself are called by God to accept responsibility for its own purification, and God himself passes sentence for his people, defining acts that call for the death sentence.

3. *Rāṣaḥ*: manslaughter and murder. In the OT, *rāṣaḥ* is the only uniquely Hebrew term for killing; it alone has no cognate (similar word/concept) in contemporary societies. Thus, this is a particularly important concept to explore in developing our own attitudes and convictions.

Rāṣaḥ is the specific Hebrew word for a range of what we may call "personal" killings, from manslaughter to premeditated murder. This word may be used of assassination (2 Ki 6:32) and revenge killings (Nu 35:27,30), but it is not used of killing in war or of judicial executions.

Two contexts in which it is employed are critical on this point. First, the Ten Commandments. Here we read, "You shall not kill [*rāṣaḥ*]" (Ex 20:13; Dt 5:17). What it means is, "You shall not murder" (or "You shall not kill a person")—more than simply killing.

Second, Nu 35. This passage is a judicial one, laying out clearly how Israel was to deal with murder when the nation was established in Palestine. No fewer than eighteen of the forty-seven OT occurrences of *rāṣaḥ* are in this passage. The passage establishes cities of refuge to which a person who killed another might flee. This protected the killer from the vengeance of a member of the family of the person killed, until a trial could take place.

The passage carefully establishes and defines the personal killing that merits a death penalty. There is motivation (hostility, intent), method (shoving, throwing, hitting), means (iron, wooden, or stone object, or fist), and result (death). In such cases the murderer (*rāṣaḥ*) is to be put to death by society.

The passage, however, goes on: "But if without hostility someone suddenly shoves another or throws something at him unintentionally, or without seeing him, drops a stone on him that could kill him, and he dies, then since he was not his enemy and he did not intend to harm him, the assembly must judge between him and the avenger of blood according to these regulations. The assembly must protect the one accused of murder" (vv. 22–25). So accidental homicide, while still *rāṣaḥ*, is not murder, and the killer deserves the protection of society.

Later in the passage it is specified that the facts of a capital case must be established "only on the testimony of witnesses. But no one is to be put to death on the testimony of only one witness" (v. 30). One other regulation is also worth noting: "Do not accept a ransom for the life of a murderer, who deserves to die. He must surely be put to death" (v. 31).

Although many would want to put off the drawing of conclusions until after examining the NT, we can and should note the following facts established in the OT: (1) Human beings, shaped in God's image, are precious to him. (2) The unwarranted taking of another's life is prohibited. (3) The OT recognizes the reality of war and does not expressly forbid killing in war. ◆ *War* (4) The OT recognizes offenses for which the death penalty is prescribed. (5) The OT holds the society of Israel responsible for carrying out the death penalty where it is ordained by God. (6) Personal killing is forbidden in the Ten Commandments. (7) The death penalty is prescribed when personal killing is premeditated or an expression of hostility. (8) Witnesses must give uncontrovertible evidence before the death penalty can be carried out. (9) Accidental killing of persons does not merit the death penalty, and the person who kills accidentally is to be protected by society.

NT — 4. The Greek words. Three Greek words are translated "kill" or "murder" in English versions. In twenty-one of its twenty-three occurrences in the NT, *anaireō* is used in the sense of "to kill" (all in Matthew, Luke, and Acts)— the two exceptions being Ac 7:21 and Heb 10:9. It is used, for example, of Herod's killing of the children after Jesus' birth (Mt 2:16), of the killing of Jesus (Lk 22:2; Ac 2:23), and of the plot to assassinate Paul (Ac 9:23).

Apokteinō is the most common term for "kill" in the NT; it includes any way of depriving another of life. Earlier generations of Jews killed the prophets (Mt 23:37), just as Jesus' own generation killed him (e.g., Mt 26:4; Lk 18:33; Jn 5:18; Ac 3:15; 1 Th 2:15). This word is also used figuratively, to indicate depriving something of its vitality, force, or power (e.g., Ro 7:11; 2 Co 3:6; Eph 2:16).

The distinctive word translated "murder" in the English versions is *phoneuō*. This word is used twelve times in the NT, including each occurrence of the commandment "Do not murder" ([where *rāṣaḥ* is found in Hebrew] Mt 5:21; 19:18; Mk 10:19; Lk 18:20; Ro 13:9; Jas 2:11). The Greek noun for "murder," *phonos* (used 12 times in the NT), is found in every list where killing as murder is identified as a sin flowing from man's corrupt and evil nature (Mt 15:19; Mk 7:21; Ro 1:29; Gal 5:21). The related noun for "murderer" is *phoneus* (7 times in the NT), two of its uses being in connection with Jesus' death—once in Jesus' parabolic prediction of his own death (Mt 22:7) and once by Stephen in his accusation of the Jewish leaders responsible for Jesus' crucifixion (Ac 7:52).

5. The heart of the issue. The NT uses none of the above three words in a positive or approving way. In each case, killing is seen to involve the guilty person's violating the rights of the innocent. Whether the slaughter of the innocents, the persecution of the prophets, or the plot against Jesus, the killings the NT deals with are criminal as well as sinful acts, whatever pseudo-legal justification such acts may have claimed.

Yet it is significant that *phoneuō*, "to murder," is used distinctively and is set apart in two ways from the more general words for "kill." First, it alone is in each case where the NT restates the OT commandment against *rāṣaḥ*. Second, it alone is used when the root of murder in the evil heart of humanity is examined. Jesus states clearly that murder is not a matter of circumstances caused by social or economic deprivation: murder is like adultery and evil thoughts, immorality, theft, false testimony, and slander. It comes "out of the heart" (Mt 15:19). It is a work of the flesh (Gal 5:21).

The way to deal with such evil is to deal directly with the human heart. It is only by the new birth that one's heart can be renewed, and it is only by the fruit of the Spirit that love can replace the hostility and hatred that stimulate murder. ◆ *Born* ◆ *Covenant*

6. The role of government. One of the striking differences between the OT and the NT is that the NT gives no suggestions as to how a society is to deal with the reality of murder.

The believer individually is to recognize that his faith commitment to Jesus may put his life in jeopardy (Mt 10:28; Jn 16:2). But this simply is an invitation to a deeper trust in God's sovereign power and goodness.

The Book of Revelation, which portrays God's terrible judgments on an unrepentant humanity, speaks of his killing the rebellious (6:8; 9:5,15,18,20; 11:5,13; 13:10,15; 19:21). This word for "kill" is not *phoneuō* but *apokteinō*.

Paul tells the Roman believers that human governments, as agencies instituted by God for the control of sin in society, "do not bear the sword for nothing" (Ro 13:4). More significantly, the same verse adds that government is "God's servant, an agent of wrath to bring punishment on the wrongdoer." This passage has been taken by most to imply government's right and responsibility for carrying out God's established principles of justice, which would include carrying out the punishment the OT indicates is appropriate for murder.

But the word "imply" in the preceding paragraph raises an important question. Why does the NT not include the same kind of social legislation that forms such a large block of OT teaching? The answer is simply that Israel was a nation under God. The church is a community that has no existence as a nation or state. Instead, the church exists across the ages as communities of God's people within many different states and subject to the laws of their respective states.

The Christian church does not control society, nor are the church's standards necessarily the standards a state will adopt. So, most simply put, the issue of how the state is to deal with murder or, for that matter, with embezzling is simply not vital or relevant to the NT. ◗

Authorities

Does this mean that OT social principles provide sufficient guidance and are still in force? Or does the spirit of the NT, which emphasizes forgiveness now but judgment to come, demand new social attitudes and a new approach to the reality of murder? Those who answer yes to the latter question must do so only after careful consideration, for God's OT commands concerning putting a murderer to death are stated in the strongest possible way. Those who answer no must likewise do so only after careful consideration, for the law that guided society in OT times was careful to protect the innocent by setting up evidential safeguards. Are we as careful today to condemn only murderers whose convictions are based on incontrovertible evidence?

This article cannot resolve the debate and is not intended to do so. But one who seeks to develop his or her own position must note that the NT harmonizes with the OT in certain significant respects: (1) The NT term for the murder of persons is different from other words for killing. (2) Only the murder of persons (which may be done by a group as well as an individual) is said to flow from the sinful heart, or to be a work of the flesh. Other terms, used more often of killing, are not so identified. (3) The existence of governing bodies with responsibility for punishing wrongdoers is an established and assumed fact in the NT. Thus, no instructions as to how society should deal with murder are found in the NT, nor would they be appropriate there.

7. Conclusions. The Bible distinguishes between killing and murder. Murder is a conscious, hostile act against another person (or persons). The OT emphasizes the death penalty as society's only responsible way to punish the murderer. But safeguards are provided that are designed to protect the rights of the killer. Only on clear evidence, involving the testimony of more than one person, can a person be convicted of a premeditated act. One should not ignore the OT data in setting up a new standard that is thought to be in closer harmony with the "spirit" of the NT. Our judgments of morality may not be as wise as those of God.

MUST ◗ *Necessary/Must*

MYSTERY

In the OT, the word *rāz* ("mystery" or "secret") occurs only in Daniel (2:18,19, 27,28,29,30,47; 4:9). It relates specifically to God's revelation through Daniel of dreams and visions whose meanings were hidden to others.

The NT word is *mystērion*. It occurs only twenty-seven times in the NT, twenty of them in Paul's writings (Ro 11:25; 16:25; 1 Co 2:7; 4:1; 13:2; 14:2; 15:51; Eph 1:9; 3:3,4,9; 5:32; 6:19; Col 1:26,27; 2:2; 4:3; 2 Th 2:7; 1 Ti 3:9,16). Its other seven uses (Mt 13:11; Mk 4:11; Lk 8:10; Rev 1:20; 10:7; 17:5,7) are found in connection with parables about God's kingdom or truths disclosed in the Book of Revelation. The word is always associated with a verb of revelation or proclamation. A "mystery" is an insight into some present-day Christian experience or future expectation not unveiled (as clearly) in the OT.

N

NAKEDNESS

Two Hebrew words are translated "naked" and "nakedness" in the English versions. The word ' *ûr* and its cognates indicate spiritual and physical nakedness. Symbolically nakedness can represent poverty or oppression. At times a person may be said to be naked ('*ārôm*) when he has simply laid aside his outer clothing (e.g., 1 Sa 19:24; Isa 20:2–4).

The other Hebrew word is '*ārâh*. This word and its derivatives are stronger terms, suggesting total nakedness and complete exposure. The OT strictly prohibited nakedness outside of marital relationships (Lev 18,20).

The OT's view of nakedness is established in early Genesis. Unfallen, Adam and Eve were "both naked, and they felt no shame" (Ge 2:25). But after the Fall, they looked at each other with new eyes. They "realized they were naked" and sewed fig-leaf coverings (3:7). Confronted by God, Adam confessed, "I was afraid because I was naked; so I hid" (3:10).

This linkage of nakedness with shame, exposure, and guilt makes no statement about sex or the human body per se. Instead, the statement is about human beings and our perceptions. Sin distorts the perspective with which we look at each other. Within marriage, with its total exposure of persons to each other, figurative and literal nakedness are appropriate and right. But because of the way sin has affected humanity, nakedness in other contexts is rightly linked with fear and shame.

In the NT, the Greek word is *gymnos*. It means "naked" or "poorly clothed" and is used particularly to express the material needs that should move believers to action to help the needy (Mt 25:36–44; Jas 2:15). It also is used in Heb 4:13 of the complete exposure of our thoughts and motives to the Lord. The NT associates nakedness with divine judgment and with shame (Rev 16:15; 17:16).

NAME

"Name" is a significant concept in both Testaments. The Hebrew *šēm* occurs some 864 times in the OT, and the Greek *onoma* appears 228 times in the NT.

In biblical cultures a name did more than identify; it communicated something of the essence, the character, or the reputation of the person or thing named. This is seen in a variety of personal names. Nabal means "fool," and the man Nabal was a fool (1 Sa 25:25). Abram means "father," and, despite his age and childless state, the patriarch accepted the name change ordained by God: Abraham, "high father," or "father of a multitude" (Ge 17:5).

Names become particularly significant when linked with revelation about God.

◆ **God** The Messiah would be called Immanuel ("with us is God"). Mary and Joseph are told to name her infant "Jesus" (meaning "deliverer"), "because he will save his people from their sins" (Mt 1:21; cf. Lk 1:31).

It is the linkage of the name with the identity and essential character of the person named that helps us to understand several misunderstood phrases in Scripture.

The third of the Ten Commandments is as follows: "You shall not misuse the name of the LORD your God" (Ex 20:7; Dt 5:11). The reference is not to cursing but to any use of the name of God that treats him as anything but what he is—the sovereign source of all things and the redeemer of his people. In addition, Christians, who bear the name of Christ, should not misuse the name by behavior that is unbecoming to it.

When Jesus encouraged the apostles to pray in his name (Jn 14:13,14; 15:16; 16:23,24,26), he was not referring to an expression tacked on to the end of a prayer. To pray "in Jesus' name" means (1) to identify the content and the motivations of prayers with all that Jesus is and (2) to pray with full confidence in him as he has revealed himself. Jesus promised that prayer in his name would be answered.

Baptism "in the name" of Jesus or of the Father, Son, and Holy Spirit is also an expression that calls for an act of total commitment to who Jesus is and what he has done. It is an affirming of the truth of Jesus' death and resurrection and of believers' identification with him. ▶ *Baptism*

Thus, in biblical cultures, a person's name is very important, and often special insight can be gained by learning the meaning of the names of those involved in various biblical events. More significantly, the importance of the name of God reminds us that we are to hold God in awe, for he is the sovereign Lord, who reigns supreme over the universe.

NATION

The Hebrew word for "nation" is *gôy*. It indicates a geographically, politically, or ethnically defined group of people. While God's OT people existed as a nation and are at times designated as *gôy*, it is most often used in the OT of the pagan peoples surrounding Israel. The context indicates it.

The Greek word is *ethnos*. This too is a general word for any nation, including Israel. In the plural, however, "nations" usually has the same meaning as Gentiles: it designates all mankind apart from, and in contrast to, the Jews.

NATURE/NATURAL

The concepts expressed by these terms are reflected in the NT but not in the OT. In OT thought, all is related directly to God and to his ordering. It was the Greeks who developed the categories by which the nature and origin of things in themselves might be explored. The NT uses the vocabulary of the philosopher in some places where English versions read "nature" and "natural." But this is not always the case.

The term *psychikos*, "soulish," is found six times in the NT. Four times the NIV renders it "natural" (1 Co 15:44,46; Jude 19), three of those being in contexts where the resurrection bodies are contrasted with the present bodies of believers. In the other two instances it is rendered "without the Spirit" (1 Co 2:14) and "unspiritual" (Jas 3:15). The word describes a person who acts in or is controlled by his old human nature, or that which is of that old nature.

The NIV, which is a "dynamic equivalence" translation, tends to search out modern thought equivalents and expressions for phrases in the original languages. Thus it often uses the words "nature" or "natural" where there is no specific equivalent Greek word. In such contexts the use of "nature" is not wrong, but one should not build an exegetical structure assuming that the original introduces this concept.

The Greek word for "nature" is *physis* (Ro 1:26; 2:14,27; 11:21,24; 1 Co 11:14; Gal 2:15; 4:8; Eph 2:3; Jas 3:7; 2 Pe 1:4), and the word for "natural" or "according to nature" is *physikos* (Ro 1:26,27; 2 Pe 2:12). The adverb in this family of words is *physikōs*, rendered "by instinct" by NIV in its only occurrence in the NT (Jude 10). In addition, *theotēs* is a term drawing together the attributes of deity and is appropriately translated "divine nature" in its one NT occurrence (Ro 1:20).

What does the NT mean to express by the words "nature" and the "natural"? Ro 1:26–27 affirms heterosexual union as being according to nature, whereas homosexuality is "unnatural" (v. 26). The word *physis* is used in one classical sense—that of origin. Thus, the NIV renders "Jews by nature" as simply "Jews by birth" (Gal 2:15).

A significant statement is made in Ro 2:14, which teaches that human beings have a moral sense implanted within human nature. This capacity does not save, but rather it proves human moral responsibility.

Human beings are spoken of as "by nature the children of wrath" (Eph 2:3 KJV) but are promised through Jesus a share in the "divine nature" (2 Pe 1:4).

James uses *physis* in the Greek sense to indicate "all kinds" of animal life (Jas 3:7). Here the concept is linked to the conviction that there is an orderliness in nature that can be seen in everything around us (cf. Ro 11:21,24).

What is significant, of course, is that while the pagans divorced the order of nature and the essence of things and beings from the notion of creation, Scripture takes no such radical step. Human beings are what they are "by nature" because of their own and God's historic acts. The world exhibits order and structure because that order was imposed by a personal being, to whom all the creation testifies. And so even the categories of skeptical exploration are carried captive by faith and are given fresh meaning as they are related to God and to his will.

NECESSARY/MUST

The language of necessity is always troubling to the Christian. For example, what did Jesus mean when he said that "he must go to Jerusalem" (Mt 16:21)? A number of Greek words are linked with this concept, which appears often in the NT. It is helpful to look beneath the surface and to examine the language of "must," "ought," and necessity very carefully.

NT 1. *Dei*: divine necessity
    2. *Opheilō*: debt and responsibility
    3. *Anankē*: inner compulsion
    4. *Prepō*: appropriateness
    5. Summary

NT — 1. *Dei*: divine necessity. In classical thought, the Greek word *dei* represents compulsion by a force or forces, the force or forces being defined by the context. In the NT, *dei* seems to refer to a necessity that is imposed by God's will. There is none of the Greek sense of an awesome and impersonal fate that rests with crushing weight on a helpless humanity. Instead, there is the loving, creative, purposeful will of a God whose intentions for humanity promise only hope and a bright future.

Dei appears over a hundred times in the NT (Mt 16:21; 17:10; 18:33; 23:23; 24:6; 25:27; 26:35,54; Mk 8:31; 9:11; 13:7,10,14; 14:31; Lk 2:49; 4:43; 9:22; 11:42; 12:12; 13:14,16,33: 15:32; 17:25; 18:1; 19:5; 21:9; 22:7,37; 24:7,26,44,46; Jn 3:7,14,30; 4:4, 20,24; 9:4; 10:16; 12:34; 20:9; Ac 1:16,22; 3:21; 4:12; 5:29; 9:6,16; 10:6; 14:22; 15:5; 16:30; 17:3; 18:21; 19:21,36; 20:35; 21:22; 23:11; 24:19; 25:10,24; 26:9; 27:21,24,26; Ro 1:27; 8:26; 12:3; 1 Co 8:2; 11:19; 15:25,53; 2 Co 2:3; 5:10; 11:30; Eph 6:20; Col 4:4,6; 1 Th 4:1; 2 Th 3:7; 1 Ti 3:2, 7,15; 5:13; 2 Ti 2:6,24; Tit 1:7,11; Heb 2:1; 9:26; 11:6; 1 Pe 1:6; 2 Pe 3:11; Rev 1:1; 4:1; 10:11; 11:5; 13:10; 17:10; 20:3; 22:6).

2. *Opheilō*: debt and responsibility.
Words in this group originally expressed the idea of a legal or personal obligation. The Greeks had both financial and, later, moral obligations in mind when they used this term.

In the NT, this language is used in the Gospels to explore the reality of man's debt to God. Thus, it is often (e.g., Mt 18:23–35) associated with forgiveness. It is only by accepting God's priceless forgiveness that human spiritual debts can be discharged.

In the Epistles, the language is used to explore Christian responsibility. Because we belong to Jesus now, we are to love one another (Ro 13:8) and bear with the weak (Ro 15:1). We who claim to live in fellowship with Jesus have a responsibility to live on earth as Jesus lived when he was here (1 Jn 2:6).

Opheiletēs ("debtor") occurs seven times in the NT (Mt 6:12; 18:24; Lk 13:4; Ro 1:14; 8:12; 15:27; Gal 5:3), *opheilē* ("debt") twice (Mt 18:32; Ro 13:7), and *opheilēma* ("debt") twice (Mt 6:12; Ro 4:4).

The verb *opheilō* is found in Mt 18:28,30,34; 23:16,18; Lk 7:41; 11:4; 16:5,7; 17:10; Jn 13:14; 19:7; Ac 17:29; Ro 13:8; 15:1,27; 1 Co 5:10; 7:3,36; 9:10; 11:7,10; 2 Co 12:11,14; Eph 5:28; 2 Th 1:3; 2:13; Phm 18; Heb 2:17; 5:3,12; 1 Jn 2:6; 3:16; 4:11; 3 Jn 8.

3. *Ananke*: inner compulsion. Words in this group indicate inner or outward pressures. In some cases the words simply refer to troubles or afflictions—pressures that cause suffering. In most cases, however, they are linked with the channeling of choices or the constraints that cause one to choose. In the NT, outward force is not primarily intended. One is not forced to choose against his will, but the forces suggested act on and with the will.

The NT uses three words in this word group. *Anankazō*, "to compel," is always used in this sense of inner pressure (Mt 14:22; Mk 6:45; Lk 14:23; Ac 26:11; 28:19; 2 Co 12:11; Gal 2:3,14; 6:12). *Anankaios*, "necessary," is used seven times in this sense (Ac 13:46; 1 Co 12:22; 2 Co 9:5; Php 1:24; 2:25; Tit 3:14; Heb 8:3) and once in the sense of "near" ("close" in NIV, Ac 10:24). *Ananke*, compulsion, necessity, has this idea in thirteen of its eighteen NT occurrences (Mt 18:7; Lk 14:18; 23:17; Ro 13:5; 1 Co 7:37; 9:16; 2 Co 9:7; Phm 14; Heb 7:12,27; 9:16,23; Jude 3.

4. *Prepō*: appropriateness. This seldom-found word emphasizes the fittingness or suitability of a thing or action. Jesus had to be baptized by John because identification with his message of the coming kingdom and its standards was appropriate (Mt 3:15). In the same way it is appropriate that there should be no hint of immorality or impurity among those who follow Jesus (Eph 5:3). *Prepō* is used five other times in the NT (1 Co 11:13; 1 Ti 2:10; Tit 2:1; Heb 2:10; 7:26).

5. Summary. The various words and ideas in Scripture that deal with the issues of necessity and obligation do not express a fatalistic view of the universe or of redeemed humanity. God's guiding will is what gives shape to history. True, past and future are determined, but it is only in the sense that they necessarily include those things that God has decided must be. It is God's gracious gift that his inner compulsions gently attract us, wooing us to choose that which our own best judgment knows is right, and which our renewed nature deeply desires.

NEIGHBOR

Love my neighbor? But "Who is my neighbor?" (Lk 10:29). The question posed by an expert in the Scriptures led to an explanation from Jesus that is particularly important to us today.

Two Hebrew words are most often found where English versions read "neighbor" in the OT. *Sākēn* simply indicates inhabitants of neighboring areas, whether they are friendly or unfriendly. The key word is *rēa'*. The basic idea is that of having something to do with one another. That is, neighbors are persons who in some way contact me and affect my experience. The verb *rā'âh* is generally taken to mean "to associate with or be a friend to." The noun *rēa'*, appearing some 187 times in the OT, has a very broad application. It is used both of the close friend and the chance acquaintance. While at times it seems to indicate relationships between members of the covenant people (e.g., Lev 19:18–32), in early times it was used to indicate a fellow Israelite (Ex 2:13) and also the Egyptian oppressors (Ex 11:2).

The broad use of *rēa'* actually made the question Jesus was asked unnecessary. "Love your neighbor as yourself" (Lev 19:18) should have been given the broadest possible interpretation. But out of a desire for self-justification, the expert in the law asked the question "Who is my neighbor?" in an attempt to narrow the responsibility that the term implied.

The answer Jesus gave used the most common Greek word for neighbor—*plēsion*. This word is used in each of the nine NT passages in which the OT injunction to love one's neighbor is repeated (Mt 5:43; 19:19; 22:39; Mk 12:31,33; Lk 10:27; Ro 13:9; Gal 5:14; Jas 2:8).

Jesus told of the good Samaritan (Lk 10:25–37), who, upon passing a Jewish stranger who had been stripped and beaten by robbers, took pity on him. The Samaritan stopped, helped him to the nearest inn, and took responsibility to pay for his care. After establishing the fact that the neighbor was one who had mercy on the needy stranger, Jesus told his questioner, "Go and do likewise" (v. 37).

The story extends rather than narrows the concept of neighbor. In the story, the injured man was a Jew, someone traditionally hostile to Samaritans. There was no bond of personal relationship between the two. They were simply two human beings, one in need and the other able to meet the need. Jesus' message was clear for those who heard him then, and it is clear for us today.

Our neighbor is any person we may come in contact with who has a need. And to love one's neighbor means to be moved by compassion to reach out and seek to meet that need.

NEW AND OLD

How you and I view new and old depends on our personality and perhaps on the age in which we live. To some, the old is best. What is "tried and true" promises stability. For others, the new holds out the exciting prospect of progress. Who wants to be stuck in history's rut? Each of us gives a weight of personal value to the new and to the old.

Does the Bible give a similar weight to old and new? Sometimes not. But in the NT particularly, it is more than weighing old versus new. There are vital theological affirmations as well.

OT 1. New and old in perspective
NT 2. The old
    3. The new
    4. The new wine and old bottles

OT — 1. New and old in perspective.
There seems to be no special loading of words translated "new" or "old" in the OT. Nevertheless, the key Hebrew word for "old" (*qedem*) does betray a nostalgia for the past. ◆ *Ancient* Also the use of *zākēn*, as with other terms that suggest old age, shows a pronounced respect for those whose old age is assumed to have given them a wisdom and insight denied the young. Still, the OT, while it may tend to look back to God's historic acts and his self-revelation in covenant and law as faith's foundation, also looks forward. History lays a foundation for the future. God's past acts take on meaning as his intentions for Israel and mankind are unveiled by those prophets who foretold the future. So we should not read too much into either "new" or "old" in the OT.

NT — 2. The old. In the NT, old and new take on a different coloration. The NT describes the coming of Jesus, and many of his teachings are "new" in the sense of being radically different from what the people steeped in the OT expected. It is not surprising, then, to find that words for both old and new suddenly become more than merely descriptive. They become terms that make a strong theological statement.

Two Greek words translated "old" participate in this theological interpretation of the old and the new. *Archaios* (12 occurrences in the NT) at times seems to be used in its secular Greek sense of "venerable" (Lk 9:8,19; Ac 15:7,21; 21:16). In other cases, it appears to carry the neutral meaning of simply "old" (2 Pe 2:5; Rev 12:9; 20:2). Elsewhere, however, the old belongs to the age that is passing away, replaced by a newness introduced by Jesus (Mt 5:21,27,33; 2 Co 5:17).

Another word, *palaios* (19 NT occurrences), has an even stronger negative weight when used in the Epistles, where it is typically contrasted with the new. In the Gospels, *palaios* is found in Mt 13:52 and in reports of Jesus' parables of the old wineskins and old garments (Mt 9:16,17; Mk 2:21,22; Lk 5:36–39; see discussion below). In the Epistles, *palaios* designates the "old man," who is corrupt and must be put to death by being crucified with Christ (Ro 6:6; Eph 4:22; Col 3:9). *Palaios* is associated with old leaven to be purged from the church (1 Co 5:7–8). It is used also in reference to the old covenant (testament), which

Israel cannot understand (2 Co 3:14). Only John uses *palaios* in a positive sense, speaking of the venerable roots of the commandment to love (1 Jn 2:7).

In its three NT occurrences, the related verb *palaioō*, "to grow old," suggests that which is obsolete through decay (Lk 12:33; Heb 1:11; 8:13). The only time *palaiotēs*, "oldness," is found in the NT it is used disparagingly of the "old way of the written [law] code" in contrast to the "new way of the Spirit" by which believers serve God (Ro 7:6). ♦ *Law*

3. The new. The way in which the NT uses "new" underlines the message communicated by its uses of "old."

There are two basic word groups translated "new" or "newness." *Neos* traditionally focuses on time. The thing it describes is "new" in the sense of being newly arrived, or just appearing. Thus *neos* wine is this year's crop. *Neōteros* is youth, fresh on the world's scene. While the word group does stress time of appearance, its uses in the NT are universally positive in theologically significant passages. The church is to expel the sinning brother that it may truly be what it is, a new community (1 Co 5:7). Believers have put off the old man and put on the new (Col 3:10). And the superior covenant that Jeremiah promised and that is so carefully described by the writer of Hebrews is also *neos* (Heb 12:24).

The classical word that indicates new (and superior) in quality is *kainos*. In secular Greek usage the *kainos* was definitely better than the old. This emphasis is carried over into the NT, particularly the Epistles.

Christ's death initiates a new covenant between God and man—a covenant that is vastly superior to the old Mosaic Code (Mk 14:24; Lk 22:20; 1 Co 11:25; 2 Co 3:6; Heb 8:8). Through Christ, human beings themselves become new creations (2 Co 5:17) and discover a realm of life in which all things become new (2 Co 5:17). These new creations wrought by Christ himself live as new people, God's renewed humanity (Gal 6:15; Eph 4:24). The believers form a new community (Eph 2:15) in which Jesus' new commandment, to love

as he loved us, is enfleshed (Jn 13:34; 1 Jn 2:7,8; 2 Jn 5). One day God will complete his new work of creation and call into being new heavens and a new earth (2 Pe 3:13; Rev 21:1–2,5). ♦ *Covenant*

Thus, "new" in the qualitative sense makes the strongest possible statement about the impact of the Good News that comes to us in Jesus. The gospel message is not a message of reform but of transformation. It is a fresh, powerful word from God. In contrast to all that God does in Christ, the "old" is obsolete and inferior indeed.

4. The new wine and old bottles. Each of the synoptic Gospels reports on Jesus' reference to new wine and old bottles (wineskins). Luke's version reads: "[Jesus] told them this parable. 'No one tears a patch from a new [*kainos*] garment and sews it on an old [*palaios*] one. If he does, he will have torn the new [*kainos*], and the patch from the new [*kainos*] will not match the old [*palaios*]. And no one pours new [*neos*] wine into old [*palaios*] wineskins. If he does, the new [*neos*] wine will burst the skins, the wine will run out and the wineskins will be ruined. No, new [*neos*] wine must be poured into new [*kainos*] wineskins. And no one after drinking old [*palaios*] wine wants the new [*neos*], for he says, 'The old [*palaios*] is better' '" (Lk 5:36–39; cf. Mt 9:16–17; Mk 2:21–22).

The parable explores the relationship of old and new and gives insight into the psychology of Israel. The generally accepted meaning of the first parable is that the new and better garment represents Christ and his gospel. The old and worn garment represents the OT pattern of faith and life. Jesus did not come to patch the old but to provide a new and superior garment.

The second parable looks not so much at the reality represented by the two systems (old and new covenants) but at human reaction to them. A fresh squeezing of wine must be put into wineskins that are superior because they are new, able to stretch and respond as the wine matures. New wine poured into the old wineskins will result in burst wineskins, and the fresh crop will be lost.

But what about the final statement showing how people evaluate the two wines? First, it shows a hasty decision, for the new wine has not had time to mature when it is rejected. Second, it shows a foolish decision. Wine is exhausted, even as the pattern of faith and life expressed in the Mosaic Code is now exhausted. The old skins are empty! The only wise decision one can make is to place the new crop in superior wineskins in which it can mature and take on its own unique character.

Jesus must be accepted on his own terms. We cannot cut him to fit the gaping holes in our garments: we must cast off the old and let him clothe us completely. And in the same way those old categories that shaped thinking must be set aside, as we let the gospel message infuse our lives and give us a fresh, new shape, chosen by God's Spirit, in which the new wine of God's work within us can mature toward beauty and holiness.

NIGHT

The main Hebrew word for "night" is *lāyil*. It does not evoke the image of unnamed terrors that gripped the contemporary civilizations of Israel's neighbors. Israel's God established night and day and filled both with his presence. As the psalmist promises those who dwell "in the shelter of the Most High" (Ps 91:1): "He will cover you with his feathers, and under his wings you will find refuge; his faithfulness will be your shield and rampart. You will not fear the terror of night, nor the arrow that flies by day, nor the pestilence that stalks in the darkness, nor the plague that destroys at midday" (vv. 4–6).

The Greek word for "night" is *nyx*. Night is usually the time of darkness, and the word suggests nothing more than the normal passage of time. Paul uses the term symbolically to indicate spiritual darkness and uncertainty (Ro 13:12; cf. 1 Th 5:5,7). But most NT occurrences of "night" indicate the literal time of darkness (e.g., Jn 3:2; 13:30; 21:3; 1 Co 11:23; 2 Co 11:25; 2 Th 3:8).

NOBLE

"Noble" is one of those fine-sounding words that has no precise equivalent in either Testament. Behind the English word "noble" in the NIV OT may stand the concept of being virtuous (e.g., Ru 3:11; Pr 12:4) or liberal (e.g., Isa 32:5,8). In the NT, only 1 Co 1:26 has the idea of high social status (*eugenēs*) in mind. In 1 Ti 3:2, "good work" is translated "noble task." *Semnos*, "worthy of honor," or most often *timēn*, which means "honor," have often been translated "noble" or "nobility." ◗ *Honor/Dishonor*

NORTH

The OT takes Israel as the center from which the directions are set. Thus, "north" is north of Israel. Some scholars believe that Job 26:7 and Isa 43:6 contain symbolic allusions to evil powers, whose spiritual and physical forces God will defeat. Many think the Soviet Union and her allies are the military force predicted to threaten Israel.

NULLIFY

The NIV uses the word "nullify" in several theologically significant passages.

Jesus condemns those whose interpretations of the OT make void or legally cancel (*akyroō*, used also in Gal 3:17) God's intentions as expressed in the Mosaic Law (Mt 15:6; Mk 7:13).

Paul uses a different term, *katargeō* ("to put out of action" or "to make inactive, invalid"), to insist that the lack of faith of those who were entrusted with God's Word hardly makes that Word invalid (Ro 3:3). He also shows that the principle of justification by faith does not put law out of action; instead, it establishes its valid function and thus upholds law (3:31). Law was not meant to save but to reveal sin and thus lead us to faith.

Finally, Paul points out that God has chosen the despised things, which the world claims do not even exist, to put out of action the "things that are" (1 Co 1:28). We are to reject human notions and commit ourselves to what God has revealed to us in Christ.

O

OATH/SWEAR

Most of us make a distinction between casual words that express an intention and the more formal expressions of a commitment. When the Bible uses terms like "oath" and "swear," it refers to solemn commitment.

OT 1. The Hebrew words
NT 2. The Greek words
3. Significant NT passages

OT — 1. The Hebrew words. Two Hebrew terms are translated "oath" and "swear" in English versions: *'ālâh* and *šāba'*.

Of the two, *'ālâh* is used less often. As a verb, it means "to make a solemn oath" and is found in six passages (Jdg 17:2; 1 Sa 14:24; 1 Ki 8:31; 2 Ch 6:22; Hos 4:2; 10:4). The noun indicates a solemn promise, or sworn testimony given in court. It is often used to indicate the certainty of disaster should God's people not keep their covenant obligations. In this context, *'ālâh* is often translated "curse." This noun is found in a number of passages (Ge 24:41; 26:28; Lev 5:1; Nu 5:21,23,27; Dt 29:12,14,19,20,21; 30:7; 1 Ki 8:31; 2 Ch 6:22; 34:24; Ne 10:29; Job 31:30; Ps 10:7; 59:12; Pr 29:24; Isa 24:6; Jer 23:10; 29:18; 42:18; 44:12; La 3:65 [as *ta'ªlâh*]; Eze 16:59; 17:13,16,18,19; Da 9:11; Zec 5:3).

Sāba' (found 184 times in the OT) means "to swear" and is usually used in a reflexive stem with the meaning "to bind oneself with an oath." This strong word means to give one's sacred, unbreakable promise as testimony that one will faithfully keep one's word to do or not do a certain thing.

The oath may be sworn to another person (as Ge 21:22–34), or it may be sworn to God (Ps 119:106) or "by the LORD" (1 Ki 1:17). The OT recognizes the pattern of making a binding oath using God's name (Dt 6:13; Isa 19:18) and shows how compelling this form of commitment was supposed to be to God's people (Jos 9:19).

The most striking use of the verb, and the most common, is in relating God's sworn commitment to mankind. Many times God's covenant commitments to Abraham and his descendants are spoken of as God's sacred word, sworn to his people. To make the certainty of God's promises even clearer, God has at times sworn by himself or his attributes (e.g., Ge 22:16; Ps 89:35; Isa 45:23; 62:8; Jer 22:5; 44:26; 49:13; Am 4:2; 6:8; 8:7). Such an addition to the bare promise was unnecessary; God will surely keep his word. But God graciously added the strengthening phrases to encourage those who, despite the promise, might hesitate to trust.

The close link between covenant and oath is significant. The covenant is the substance of God's stated intention—the constant reminder that God swore (bound himself by an oath) in making the covenant promise and so underlines his firm commitment to do all that the covenant defines. ♦ *Covenant*

The noun *šᵉbû'âh* is translated "oath" and occurs some thirty times in the OT. It includes (1) the oath made before judges, declaring that one will tell the truth (Ex 22:11), (2) pledges of loyalty (Ne 6:18), and (3) vows to perform certain acts (Jos 2:17,20). The vow is most solemn and not to be broken. Nu 30 gives an outline of the law governing oaths (vows). In general, a person could be released from an oath only if circumstances beyond his or her control made it impossible to keep it (Ge 24:8). Thus, any conditions limiting responsibility should be specified when the oath was first taken (e.g., Jos 2:17,20).

NT — 2. The Greek words. The verb "to swear" is *omnyō*. It means to bind oneself by an oath and is used mainly in two types of contexts. In one context there are warnings against swearing any oaths. In the other there are references to the oaths that God has sworn historically. For a discussion, see 3 below.

"Oath" is *horkos* or *horkomōsia*. *Horkos* is found ten times in the NT (Mt 5:33; 14:7,9; 26:72; Mk 6:26; Lk 1:73; Ac 2:30; Heb 6:16,17; Jas 5:12). *Horkōmosia* is used only four times, all in one passage (Heb 7:20,21,28).

Anathematizō also is translated "oath" in Ac 23:12,14,21 (Mk 14:71 being its other NT use, where it is rendered "call down curses"). The literal meaning of these verses is that those men who plotted to assassinate Paul placed themselves under a curse. They swore not to eat or drink until Paul had been killed.

3. Significant NT passages. Swearing and oath taking are found in two contexts in the NT. On the one hand, the Bible, particularly in Mt 5:34–37 and Jas 5:12, warns against swearing "at all." This appears puzzling at first, both because the OT recognizes the validity of oath taking and because God himself adds his oath to confirm his promises.

The best explanation of passages such as these is found in Mt 23:16, which reports a series of rabbinical interpretations designed to distinguish between valid (binding) oaths and invalid (nonbinding) oaths. For instance, a person might promise and bind himself "by Jerusalem." But the rabbis held that unless that person was actually facing Jerusalem when making the oath, it had no force. In essence, the way oaths were misused in Jesus' day made them a cloak for lies; they had lost that most solemn commitment found in the OT oaths. So

Jesus said in concluding his teaching, "Simply let your 'Yes' be 'Yes,' and your 'No,' 'No'; anything beyond this comes from the evil one" (5:37). In other words, stop lying. Be the kind of person whose expression of a commitment is so trustworthy that no one will ask for a binding oath.

On the other hand, a number of NT passages remind us that God swore with an oath (Lk 1:73; Ac 2:30; Heb 3:11; 4:3; 6:17; 7:20,21,22,28) in OT times. But God did not use an oath to cloak his real intentions. Rather, he used an oath to underline his intentions and to give us a basis for confidence that everything he has promised will come true. God's bare word is enough for us. But, in his grace, "to make the unchanging nature of his promise very clear to the heirs of what was promised, he confirmed it with an oath" (Heb 6:17). Now we who believe can be "greatly encouraged" (v. 18), for in God's word of commitment we have hope as an anchor for our souls (v. 19).

OBEY/DISOBEY

Often our understanding of the Bible is subtly colored. When we read the Bible, we often import a tone of voice into our reading. The words we read may seem harsh or impersonal, or strident and demanding, not because they are so used in the Bible, but because we intuitively feel this way about the words themselves. This is particularly a danger when we read of obedience or disobedience. All too often the warmth and love that infuse the passages that speak of them are replaced by a cold impersonality that we bring with us and that robs Scripture of its meaning.

OT 1. To hear and obey
NT 2. The Greek words
    3. Obedience and disobedience in Jesus' teaching
    4. The obedience of Jesus
    5. Obedience and faith
    6. Summary

OT — 1. To hear and obey. The basic word translated "obey" in the OT is *šāma*, "to hear." The biblical concept stresses effective hearing: one who truly hears will comprehend and will respond with obedience. ▶ *Hear/Listen*

The OT portrays obedience as the appropriate response of God's covenant people to his revelation. In this sense, obedience is the outward expression of a heart that has turned to God.

Throughout the OT, obedience is intimately associated with blessing. The person and generation that lives in intimate relationship with the Lord will experience the blessing he yearns to extend to his people. So God promises, "Follow my decrees and be careful to obey my laws, and you will live safely in the land. Then the land will yield its fruit, and you will eat your fill and live there in safety" (Lev 25:18–19; cf. Dt 4:30). God's call to obedience is, at the same time, a call to holiness and an invitation to blessing: "Hear, O Israel, and be careful to obey so that it may go well with you and that you may increase greatly in a land flowing with milk and honey" (Dt 6:3).

Obedience enabled God to bless his people, but disobedience led necessarily to discipline. "See," God told them, "I am setting before you today a blessing and a curse—the blessing if you obey the commands of the LORD your God that I am giving you today; the curse if you disobey the commands of the LORD your God and turn from the way that I command you today by following other gods" (Dt 11:26–28). The consequences of obedience and disobedience were fully explained for Israel in Dt 28 and 30.

We need to hear both the promises and the warnings as they were uttered—i.e., in the warmest and most loving of tones. This is how the OT believer who truly loved and trusted the Lord heard God's instructions on obedience and his warnings about disobedience. Thus, the psalmist did not regard God's call to obedience as a cold command that aroused resentment. Instead, his deep love for God enabled him to hear God's call as the loving invitation it truly was, an invitation filled with promise: "Do good to your servant according to your word, O LORD. Teach me knowledge and good judgment, for I believe in your commands. Before I was afflicted I went astray, but now I obey your word. You are good, and what you do is good; teach me your decrees. . . . The law from your mouth is more precious to me than thousands of pieces of silver and gold" (Ps 119:65–68,72).

NT — 2. The Greek words. Two different families of Greek words are linked with "obedience" and "disobedience."

Peithō means "to convince" or "to persuade." It is logically linked with obedience; a person who is persuaded to obey a demand obeys it. This root is translated "obey" only three times in the NASB (Ro 2:8; Heb 13:17; Jas 3:3).

Another word from the same root is much stronger and is used of obeying a superior. That word is *peitharcheō* and occurs four times in the NT (Ac 5:29,32; 27:21; Tit 3:1).

Disobedience is expressed by negative forms of this root: *apeithei, apeithēs,* and *apeitheō.* In most usages in the NT, disobedience is viewed as disobedience to God (except in Ro 1:30; 2 Ti 3:2). Strikingly, disobedience does not stand in contrast in the NT with obedience but in contrast with faith. The reason for this critical linkage is explored by the writer of Hebrews (see 5 below).

The other family of Greek words for obedience and disobedience is, like the OT concept, linked with hearing. The emphatic form of *akouō,* "to hear," is *hypakouō,* which in all its forms means "to obey." The sense here as in the OT is that of understanding and responding. Obedience can be spoken of as an attitude (2 Co 2:9; Php 2:12) and most particularly as a faith-rooted disposition. In many contexts obedience to Christ or the gospel has the same meaning as faith in Christ and a faith response to the gospel (e.g., Ro 15:18; 16:26; 2 Th 1:8).

3. Obedience and disobedience in Jesus' teaching. In Jesus' teaching, as in the OT, obedience is a relational term. Obedience flows out of a personal relationship and is motivated only by love. The reality of a relationship with God is demonstrated by one's obedience to him. This theme is developed in several key passages, particularly in the Last Supper discourse (Jn 14–17). The following are key statements in that discourse: "Whoever has my commands and obeys them, he is the one who loves me. . . . If anyone loves me, he will obey my teaching. . . . He who does not love me will not obey my teaching. . . . If you obey my commands, you will remain in my love, just as I have obeyed my Father's commands and remain in his love" (14:21,23,24; 15:10).

The picture provided here is vital. Obedience flows from a love relationship with God and cannot be generated by any other motivating force. Jesus maintained his own unique fellowship with the Father through that responsive relationship with him portrayed as obedience. We too maintain our fellowship with Jesus and the Father by responding to his words and teaching with obedience.

Later the apostle John picks up this theme and develops it. Obedience is one of those qualities that give the believer evidence that he is living in close fellowship with the Lord (1 Jn 2:3; 3:22,24; 5:3).

4. The obedience of Jesus. In his discourse on obedience, Jesus held himself up as an example. Two passages from the Epistles examine Jesus' obedience. Php 2 is a call to the Christian to adopt a Christlike attitude. Jesus, devoid of pride, took on human nature. Then, "being found in appearance as a man, he humbled himself and became obedient to death—even death on a cross!" (Php 2:8). Subsequently Jesus was raised from death and was exalted to the highest place in our universe.

The passage has two lessons. First, if we maintain this attitude of Jesus, we will be able to work out the fullest possible expression of our salvation (2:12). Only when we live in full accord with God's will can our actions be in accord with his good purpose (2:13). In Jesus' full commitment to God's will for him, he demonstrated the level of commitment we are to achieve. And he showed us the result: exaltation. This is the second lesson about obedience. It produces blessing, but this blessing may

not be experienced until resurrection occurs.

Heb 5:7–10 also speaks of Jesus' obedience, especially his "learning" obedience and his "being made perfect" through it. The thought is that Jesus established his integrity by living a normal human life in which obedience was demanded. By actually living out obedience he was "perfected" in the sense of being demonstrably qualified to become "the source of eternal salvation for all who obey [i.e., believe in] him" (5:9).

5. Obedience and faith. Jesus spoke of our personal relationship with the Lord in terms of a love that generates obedience. The writer to the Hebrews examines the relationship of obedience to the responsive hearing of God's Word that expresses faith and trust in him.

First, disobedience stems from a hard heart (Heb 3:7–11). The heart is further characterized as "a sinful, unbelieving heart that turns away from the living God" (v. 12). The modern reader is warned not to hear God today with a similarly hard heart. Both the attitude and the resulting disobedience of the earlier generation was located in unbelief (v. 19).

God has spoken in Scripture. One response to the Word is an expression of the sinful heart, which simply will not trust God. This response is disobedience. The other response, obedience, comes from a heart that trusts God, being persuaded that he is able to guide his people into rest (Heb 4:1–11).

6. Summary. Greek and Hebrew words view obedience as a response. One hears, grasps what is communicated, and acts on it. Thus, obedience is essentially linked to God's revelation. God initiates by speaking; creatures respond by obeying.

In both Testaments, obedience is also closely linked with relationship. It was God's intention to guide his OT people to blessing by speaking to them in statute and commandment. If they obeyed, they would find the blessing he yearned to give. If they disobeyed, they would find only tragedy and necessary discipline.

Thus, the call to obedience in the OT is God's loving invitation to blessing, and not some cold, impersonal command.

In the NT, obedience is further demonstrated and analyzed. Jesus lived a life of obedience and in so doing demonstrated the exaltation that comes at last to the person who obeys God. Jesus' teaching linked obedience to love; only the person who loves God will obey him. The NT goes on to link obedience with faith; only the person who trusts God will obey him. Thus, biblically speaking, there is a definite and vital connection between faith in God, love for God, and obedience to God, and all are a result of God's work in a person's life.

The NT testifies that today as well as in sacred history, an obedience that is motivated by love and exists as an expression of faith is necessary in order to stay close to God. We live in fellowship with God only as we obey him.

So obedience, properly understood, is never a cold or impersonal thing. God's call to obedience is a loving invitation to experience his best. Our response flows from a growing love for God and expresses our confidence that God is living and able. Only in a deep and loving relationship can the biblical import of obedience be understood.

OBSERVE

A number of different Hebrew and Greek words are translated "observe" in the NIV and the NASB. In each instance, the English meaning is clear and reflects the various meanings of the original: "keep," "watch," "do," "preserve."

The striking difference between the many OT calls to observe the Mosaic laws, festivals, and commands and the NT insistence that mankind "is not justified by observing the law" (Gal 2:16) is explained in the discussion on law. ▶ *Law*

OFFENSE

In the OT, the words translated "offend" or "offense" generally indicate a sin or a crime. Except for 1 Co 6:9 (where the word "offend" is not in the original), where these terms occur in the NIV NT, they are always translations of *skandalizō* (verb) or *skandalon* (noun).

Skandalizō can mean "to cause to sin or to fall." But in each NIV verse where it is translated "offend" or "offense," it has the meaning of causing anger, shock, or repulsion, and thus of giving offense.

OFFERING AND SACRIFICE

Sacrifices and offerings are mentioned often in Scripture. Yet, at times, Scripture's attitude seems contradictory. The OT, in careful detail, gives complex instructions for worshiping God with sacrifices and offerings. Later, the prophets scathingly condemned their people for mere ritualism—a condemnation repeated by Jesus. But in the NT we discover the true meaning of sacrifice and realize how God through the centuries clearly communicated his message of salvation; he did it by the sacrifice of those living animals who prefigured the ultimate sacrifice—that of God's Son.

OT 1. The Hebrew words
     2. The significance of sacrifice
     3. Historical roots of sacrifice
     4. Prophetic condemnations of Israel's sacrifices and offerings
NT 5. Sacrifice in the Gospels
     6. Sacrifice in Paul's writings
     7. Sacrifice in Hebrews
     8. Summary

OT — 1. The Hebrew words. The OT contains an extensive and technical vocabulary dealing with its various sacrifices and offerings. The prescribed rituals were a major means of expressing the worshipers' faith. They were also one of God's means for illustrating the nature of their relationship with him.

Often our words "offering" and "sacrifice" are used interchangeably. OT ritual involved offerings, in that everything brought for use in worship was viewed as being offered to God and thus as set apart and holy (Ex 28:38). ▶ *Holy/Holiness* The ritual system also featured sacrifice. The most significant offerings called for the sacrifice of a living animal.

Other ancient cultures also had clearly defined and complex rituals, including sacrifice. But these cultures tended to view the sacrifice as food for the gods, and their priests used the entrails of the animals for occult divination. In Israel, the sacrifice, while pleasing to God, was not his food (Ex 29:38–41; Ps 50:8–15). And only in Israel was the blood of the sacrificial animal central in the worship. In fact, in the OT the blood was crucial: it defined the significance of sacrifice itself. "For the life of a creature is in the blood," God says in Lev 17:11, "and I have given it to you to make atonement for yourselves on the altar; it is the blood that makes atonement for one's life." Thus, the worshiper, who with hands placed on the head of the living animal saw it killed and its blood sprinkled on the altar, was being graphically shown that sin called for the surrender of a life and was also made poignantly aware that God would accept a substitute. ◗ *Atonement*

An extended discussion of the OT sacrifices and associated rituals can be found in Merrill C. Tenney, ed., *Zondervan Pictorial Encyclopedia of the Bible* (Grand Rapids: Zondervan, 1976), 5:194–210.

2. The significance of sacrifice. Throughout sacred history, sacrifice has been the avenue by which a sinning humanity has approached a holy God. ◗ *Atonement.*

3. Historic roots of sacrifice. The practice of sacrifice precedes the Mosaic Law. Many believe that the first sacrifice was God's killing of an animal to provide skin coverings for Adam and Eve after the Fall (Ge 3:21). The story of Cain and Abel (Ge 4) seems to show that the way to approach God with sacrifice may have been made clear to the first family. Genesis tells us that Cain "brought some of the fruits of the soil as an offering to the LORD. But Abel brought fat portions from some of the firstborn of his flock. The LORD looked with favor on Abel and his offering, but on Cain and his offering he did not look with favor." God's rebuke to an angry Cain, "If you do what is right, will you not be accepted?" may suggest that Cain's offering was made in conscious violation of God's known will.

Animal sacrifices continued to be the norm. They were made by Noah after the Flood (Ge 8:20–21). Job, who may have been a contemporary of Abraham, offered sacrifices for sins (Job 1:5; 42:7–9). The Genesis record shows that the patriarchs called on the name of the Lord at altars they constructed (Ge 12:8; 13:4; 26:25).

History's most symbolic sacrifice is reported in Ge 22. To test Abraham, God sent him to a distant mountain, where he was to sacrifice his son Isaac. There, as Abraham was about to kill Isaac, God called out to him and stopped him. Abraham substituted a ram, which had been caught by its horns in a thicket, and he named the place "the LORD will provide." Abraham was not, after all, called on to surrender the life of his only son. That kind of surrender would be reserved for God himself.

Following their deliverance from slavery in Egypt, the Israelites were provided a law that established moral, social, civil, and other standards for them. That law clearly defined the way in which Israel was to worship. It set up a complex but well-defined system of sacrifice.

During the age of the judges and the reigns of Saul and David, sacrifices were offered at a number of locations, particularly where the tabernacle was set up. ◗ *Tabernacle and Temple* Despite the fact that only priests were to make sacrifices, families and clans did offer local sacrifices during this era (e.g., 1 Sa 16:2–5; 20:6,29; 2 Sa 15:12,24).

The most controversial passage linked with sacrifice during this period is Jdg 11:29–40. It tells of Jephthah's vow to make an ʿōlâh, a whole burnt offering, of the first creature to meet him after a notable military victory (v. 31). The first one to run to him was his daughter. This passage is variously interpreted. Was the girl killed despite the OT's rejection of human sacrifice? Or did Jephthah simply dedicate her to perpetual virginity and the service of the Lord?

A most significant sacrifice was offered by Saul (1 Sa 13). Told to wait for Samuel to come and make a burnt offering, Saul's courage ebbed as his troops deserted him. Finally, left with only six hundred men to face a massive Philistine force, Saul offered the sacrifice himself. His fear-motivated disobedience of God led to his being rejected as king. He had not kept "the command [of] the LORD" (v. 13). It is ironic that despite his army's desertion, Saul still had twice the number of men that Gideon had used to defeat an even larger army of Midianites (Jdg 7:7).

The era of David introduced dramatic changes in all of Israel. Jerusalem was established as a political and worship center. There David reorganized the ritual responsibilities of the priests and Levites (1 Ch 22–23). After David's death, his son Solomon built the magnificent temple in Jerusalem. ▶ *Tabernacle and Temple* This was to be the site at which required festivals would be held and the only site at which it was legitimate to offer sacrifices. The command to worship and sacrifice only at the place where God had put his name is strongly stated: "To that place you must go; there bring your burnt offerings and sacrifices, your tithes and special gifts" (Dt 12:5–6). After this injunction is repeated, the passage goes on: "Be careful not to sacrifice your burnt offerings anywhere you please. Offer them only at the place the LORD will choose" (vv. 13–14).

This injunction was later ignored. Many in Israel established their own local "high places" to worship Yahweh or some god or goddess of the Canaanites. The faithlessness of God's people, who ignored his guidelines for worship, contributed to their being exiled from the land.

The temple in Jerusalem was destroyed when Judah was taken captive to Babylon. It was rebuilt after their return. The sacrifices were still offered in Jesus' day—at the magnificent temple reconstructed by Herod. But that temple later was destroyed by Rome in A.D. 70, and the place ordained for sacrifice was lost to the Jewish people.

One striking aspect of OT prophecy is seen in Eze 40–48, which tells of a yet future rebuilding of Jerusalem's temple. There the prophet pictures the offering of perpetual memorial sacrifices and burnt offerings. How this picture of the future relates to the NT's affirmation that Christ's self-sacrifice has forever ended the need for animal sacrifice is debated by those who expect a literal temple to be established. The best suggestion seems to be that these are memorials, recalling the work of Christ but having no efficacy in themselves.

4. Prophetic condemnation of Israel's sacrifices and offerings. Sacred history records the failure of generation after generation to keep the Mosaic Law. It is not surprising to find the prophets condemning Israel's approach to worship, as they condemned their other failures.

At the division of Solomon's kingdom, Jeroboam, who became ruler of Israel's ten tribes, set up his own worship system. He feared that if Israel looked to Jerusalem as the religious center, they might reunite politically with the two tribes that composed the southern kingdom, Judah. Jeroboam established worship centers at Bethel and Dan, set up a non-Aaronic priesthood, and established new festival dates, thus counterfeiting the system established in the Mosaic Law. Despite the system's violation of every point of the divine command, Israel continued this supposed worship of Yahweh until the Assyrians destroyed the kingdom and dispersed the people (722 B.C.). No wonder prophets thundered forth in words such as these: "Go to Bethel and sin; go to Gilgal and sin yet more" (Am 4.4). God hardly could be pleased with sacrifices and offerings that were supposed to honor him but ignored and violated his commands.

There were other breakdowns as well. Even in Judah, where the form was maintained, the people's worship was contaminated by foreign elements. "High places" (local worship centers) continued to be used for sacrifice despite God's command that worship must take place only at Jerusalem. Isaiah reports God's reaction: "These people come near to me with their mouth and honor me with their lips, but their hearts are far from me. Their worship of me is made up only of rules taught by men" (29:13).

For insight into how corrupt worship finally became, read Ezekiel's description of what happened in the temple itself in the days just before the Babylonian exile (Eze 8).

But perhaps most serious of all, worship of the Lord was to be offered by a holy people, and the people had no concern for holiness. The sacrifices of expiation were ordained for those who fell into inadvertent sin and later discovered their failure (e.g., Lev 4:2). Sacrifice was to be the expression of a repentant heart, and offerings were supposed to overflow out of an ever-deepening love for the Lord. The prophet's primary thunder was directed against those who supposed that God was concerned only with the form of worship, not with the heart of the worshiper.

So Isaiah and the other prophets sought to reestablish the link between sacrifice and social concern, between worship and morality. Through Isaiah, the Lord cried out: "Stop bringing meaningless offerings! Your incense is detestable to me. . . . Your New Moon festivals and your appointed feasts my soul hates. They have become a burden to me; I am weary of bearing them. When you spread out your hands in prayer, I will hide my eyes from you; even if you offer many prayers, I will not listen. Your hands are full of blood; wash and make yourselves clean. Take your evil deeds out of my sight! Stop doing wrong, learn to do right. Seek justice, encourage the oppressed. Defend the cause of the fatherless, plead the case of the widow" (Isa 1:13–17; cf. Jer 7:20–23; Am 5:21–27; Mic 6:6–8).

Thus the prophets taught Israel, and thus they are still teaching us today. The worship of God is not a matter of ritual or form. Worship must be an expression of commitment to the Lord. But true commitment also finds expression in a lifestyle marked by justice and mercy. Worship is never acceptable if the worshiper has wandered from God's way of morality.

NT — 5. Sacrifice in the Gospels. In Jesus' day, the prescribed sacrifices were being offered at the magnificent Jerusalem temple, which had just undergone a forty-year reconstruction and beautification process. Nowhere does Jesus condemn the practice of making sacrifices and offerings. In fact, he told those he had healed to make the offerings required by law (Mt 8:4; Mk 1:44; Lk 5:14). And he angrily cleansed the temple court of profiteers so that God's house might be treated as a place for prayer and worship (Mt 21:12–13; Mk 11:15–17; Lk 19:45; Jn 2:13–17).

But Jesus also reestablished priorities. Among a people whose leaders put ritual first, Jesus agreed with the prophets. Twice he alluded to Mic 6:6–8, which reads: "With what shall I come before the LORD and bow down before the exalted God? Shall I come before him with burnt offerings, with calves a year old? Will the LORD be pleased with thousands of rams, with ten thousand rivers of oil? Shall I offer my firstborn for my transgression, the fruit of my body for the sin of my soul? He has showed you, O man, what is good. And what does the LORD require of you? To act justly and to love mercy and to walk humbly with your God."

Thus, Jesus challenged his critics and told them to "go and learn what this means: 'I desire mercy, not sacrifice' " (Mt 9:13; cf. 12:7). And he said that if one who is approaching the altar harbors anger against a brother, he must leave his gift and be reconciled with his brother. Then he can return to the altar and offer his gift to God (Mt 5:23–24). Jesus agreed with the teacher of the law who said that to love God and neighbor is more important than all burnt offerings and sacrifices (Mk 12:33–34).

But humanity failed in its calling to love. And so the great sacrifice that the OT system prefigured lay ahead, as Jesus knew (Mt 20:28; 26:28; Mk 10:45; 14:24; Lk 22:20). Jesus himself would soon be shown to be the sacrificial Lamb of God (Jn 1:29,36).

6. Sacrifice in Paul's writings. The apostle Paul uses the language of sacrifice in two contexts. First, and most important, Jesus' death is understood as a sacrifice. Jesus is our Passover Lamb, who has been sacrificed for us (1 Co 5:7). ♦ *Passover* God has provided redemption and justification for us in Christ Jesus, for "God presented him as a sacrifice of atonement, through faith in his blood" (Ro 3:25). ♦ *Atonement* Jesus died "for us," and he justified us "by his blood" (Ro 5:8–9). ♦ *Blood* ♦ *Justify/Justification* Often the Epistles state and assume that salvation has been won for mankind through God's great act of self-giving on Calvary, where the sacrifice of Christ is to be understood as fully efficacious. Thus the death of Jesus is seen, as symbolized in the great sacrifice of the Day of Atonement, as the ultimate sacrifice of expiation.

Second, Paul adopts the language of sacrifice to speak of the Christian lifestyle. Believers are to present themselves to God as living sacrifices (Ro 12:1). This "spiritual worship" corresponds to the OT 'ōlā2, the whole burnt offering of consecration. Like that OT sacrifice, our spiritual commitment can come only after the sacrifice of expiation has been offered for us. Using the same symbolism, Paul sees his approaching death as a libation (*nesek*) added to enrich the full commitment to service demonstrated by the Philippians (Php 2:17). Paul also uses the analogy of the 'ōlâh in speaking of the Philippians' gifts to him: such are fragrant offerings, acceptable sacrifices that please God (Php 4:18).

Thus, Paul uses the sacrificial system of the OT in a literal way to interpret the meaning of the death of Jesus and in a symbolic way to emphasize the significance of Christian commitment and service (e.g., Eph 5:1–2).

7. Sacrifice in Hebrews. The Book of Hebrews offers the Bible's definitive statement concerning sacrifice and offerings. Written to those who looked back nostalgically to OT faith, Hebrews seeks to demonstrate just how the gospel of Jesus is superior.

The passage that explores sacrifice is Heb 8–10. The writer begins in chapter 8 by affirming that the OT sanctuary where gifts and sacrifices were offered is simply "a copy and shadow of what is in heaven" (8:5). In fact, the whole Mosaic covenant under which the OT sacrifices were ordained has been replaced by a superior covenant, under which God will be able to work a full transformation of believers and so perfectly forgive that he "will remember their sins no more" (8:12).

Chapter 9 affirms that the elements of the earthly tabernacle and its worship regulations served as illustrations for the present time. They applied only until Christ established the new order, for "the gifts and sacrifices being offered were not able to clear the conscience of the worshiper" (v. 9). They were only "external regulations" that could not touch the inner person (v. 10).

But Christ entered the Most Holy Place in heaven. "He did not enter by means of the blood of goats and calves; but he entered the Most Holy Place once for all by his own blood, having obtained eternal redemption" (v. 12). The OT sacrifices made a person "outwardly clean" (v. 13) ♦ *Clean and Unclean* The blood of Christ, who offered himself, works within to "cleanse our consciences from acts that lead to death, so that we may serve the living God" (v. 14). ♦ *Conscience*

The writer goes on to show that the new covenant that has replaced the Mosaic was instituted by Jesus' sacrifice of himself (vv. 15–22). That sacrifice was so efficacious that "once for all at the end of the ages" Jesus was able to "do away with sin by the sacrifice of himself" (v. 26). This one sacrifice was enough to "take away the sins of many people" (v. 28).

In chapter 10 the writer returns to his theme: the OT patterns are "only a shadow of the good things that are coming—not the realities themselves" (v. 1). Thus, the repeated sacrifices could not cleanse the worshipers from sins, or they would not have needed to be repeated. But now "we have been made holy through the sacrifice of the body of Jesus Christ once for all" (v. 10). His one sacrifice perfects believers and provides a perfect forgiveness (vv. 11–18). "And where these [sins] have been forgiven, there is no longer any sacrifice for sin" (v. 18).

8. Summary. The OT shows that sacrifice has always been an element in sinners' approach to God. Sacrifice was institutionalized in the Mosaic Law and was an essential aspect of OT worship. But the ritual itself was not important to God. The prophets reminded Israel that God was concerned with the attitude of people's hearts. This attitude had to be revealed in a concern for justice and mercy as well as in faithfulness to ritual requirements.

The NT points out that aspects of OT worship, like other aspects of the Mosaic system, mirrored heavenly realities. They were important as illustrations, foreshadowing the present age and helping us see the significance of Jesus' death.

The NT consistently presents Jesus' death as a sacrifice—the ultimate sacrifice. His blood won forgiveness for human beings and laid the foundation for transformation. There is no more sacrifice for sin: "By one sacrifice he has made perfect forever those who are being made holy" (Heb 10:14).

The Bible's teaching on sacrifice gives insight into the true nature of sin. Sin can never be viewed lightly by God. He must call for the death of the sinner as the necessary penalty. But God is rich in love. And that love impelled him to an act of deliverance. The Son of God became a man and offered up his own life as a substitute for sinners.

All the blood spilled on Jewish altars over the centuries testifies to the necessity and the meaning of Calvary.

OFFSPRING

The Hebrew word for "offspring" in most verses is *zera'*. It is also translated "seed" and "descendants" in the NIV and the NASB, especially the latter. The theologically significant use of the term is found in certain Genesis passages that deal with the Abrahamic covenant (e.g., Ge 12:7; 13:15,16; 15:3,5,13,18; 17:7,9, 10,12,19). A great many OT uses of *zera'* are in connection with God's covenant promises to the patriarchs.

This Hebrew word always appears in the singular, even when it refers to many descendants. This distinctive aspect of *zera'* makes it possible to designate a single person who represents the whole group or all the persons in that group. The apostle Paul picks up on this feature of *zera'* in two passages. Using the common Greek word for "offspring" (*sperma*, also translated "seed" and "descendants" in the NIV and NASB), Paul states that "the promises were spoken to Abraham and to his seed. The Scripture does not say 'and to seeds,' meaning many people, but 'and to your seed,' meaning one person, who is Christ' " (Gal 3:16).

Elsewhere, Paul argues that the promise made to Abraham and his offspring is received by faith (Ro 4:13). The question, then, is, Who are Abraham's offspring? Who is in that group that the Scripture represents as his descendants? Paul's answer is that "all those who are of the faith of Abraham" (v. 16) constitute that single line to which God's promises were given.

In Acts 17:28–29 there is a different word from the theologically significant *sperma*. When Paul spoke to the Greeks in Athens, he referred to God's original creation of the human race. In quoting the pagan poets' claim that we are God's offspring, Paul uses the word *genos*. Humanity is God's offspring in that it is to Adam, the one man God made, that all humanity traces its origin (17:26). Not all of mankind is God's offspring in the significant relational sense of *sperma*.

OIL

The Hebrew word for "oil" is *šemen* (used 192 times) or a synonym, *yiṣhār*, which means "fresh oil." When the word "oil" was used, it usually referred to olive oil, which was very important in biblical days. Olive oil was used in cooking, called for in certain sacrifices and offerings, mixed with perfume, used to anoint some kings and priests, and associated with a few medical treatments. ▶ **Anointing/Anointed** James advised that the sick be anointed with oil (Jas 5:14). ▶ **Healing** Oil was also burned in the tiny lamps used for indoor lighting. Because of the everyday importance of oil, the abundance of oil became a symbol of joy and of prosperity.

OLD ▶ New and Old

OPPOSE

Where the NASB OT uses the word "oppose," the Hebrew is usually ʿāma_d_, "to take one's stand against." The NIV translates a number of different Hebrew expressions by "oppose," such as those that signify to gather against, to be an enemy, to be an adversary, to withstand, and to be against.

The NT also translates a number of Greek words by "oppose." The NASB makes the following differentiations: *anthistēmi* (used 14 times in the NT) is four times rendered "to set oneself against" (Ac 13:8; Gal 2:11; 2 Ti 3:8; 4:15), *antilegō* (used 10 times in the NT) once appears as "to speak against" (Tit 1:9), and the stronger word, *antitassō* (used 5 times in the NT), is either "to be an enemy of" or "to resist with assembled forces." This latter word is found in the significant statement that "God opposes the proud" (Jas 4:6; 1 Pe 5:5), as well as in three other NT passages (Ac 18:6; Ro 13:2; Jas 5:6). The NIV uses "oppose" to express the meaning of these words, but it also uses "oppose" for additional words, including *kōlyō* ("to hinder"), *symballō* ("to fight"), and *enantios* (to be in opposition to).

The passages that use the word "oppose"—especially Gal 2:11—teach us a simple lesson: we must stand for those things that God approves and stand with him in opposing everything that is wrong.

OPPRESS ▶ Poor and Oppressed

ORACLE

Two Hebrew roots are found where the NIV and NASB read "oracle." *Neʾum* means "an utterance." It is used 375 times in the OT, and only of divine speech. In older versions "Thus saith the Lord" is usually used when this verb appears. Use of this root emphasizes the divine origin and authority of the message delivered.

The other word is *maśśāʾ*, used to indicate a message of judgment. Thus, an "oracle against" persons or nations is an announcement that God is about to bring judgment on them.

In each case the oracle was delivered with a strong sense of divine authority, and the message was claimed to be God's and not the speaker's.

ORDAIN

The word used in connection with the installation of the Aaronic priests is *mālēʾ*. The OT focus is on the original ordination of Aaron and his sons (Ex 28–29; Lev 7–8), but there is evidence that later generations were also to be officially installed (Lev 21:10; Nu 3:3). This terminology is not used in the NT of setting leaders apart, though there was clearly some kind of official recognition (Ac 13:1–3; 14:23). ▶ **Leadership** Expressions that refer to God's ordaining his covenant, his plans, the life of individuals, etc., reflect words like *ṣāwâh*, "to command" or "to order."

ORDER

Most uses of the English noun "order" and the verb "to order" are common and self-explanatory. However, there are two contexts in which special meanings reflect specific words.

In Isa 28:10–13, the NASB reads "order," whereas the NIV has "do." The passage picks up the ridicule of Isaiah's listeners and shows how the prophet turns it back on them: "Do and do, do and do, rule on rule, rule on rule; a little here, a little there" (v. 10). In Hebrew, "to do" ("to order") is *şaw* and "rule" is *qaw*. Uttering these nonsense sounds in a singsong pattern, Israel pretended the prophet's message was itself meaningless. In judgment, God's message would indeed become meaningless to them, "so that they will go and fall backward, be injured and snared and captured" (v. 13). Anyone who rejects the divine message will lose his capacity to understand it and will fall into disaster.

In the NT, the word "order" in six verses (Lk 1:8; Heb 5:6,10; 6:20; 7:11,17) is *taxis*. In each of these references to the priesthood the word means a particular group or class. Zechariah came on duty with his "division" (NIV). Jesus' priesthood is classified as Melchizedekian and not Aaronic. *Taxis* is also used of orderly worship in the church (1 Co 14:40), of a harmonious and strong Christian community (Col 2:5), and of Jesus' everlasting priesthood (Heb 7:21).

ORDINANCE ♦ *Law*

ORDINATION ♦ *Ordain*

ORPHAN ♦ *Fatherless*

OVERCOME

The NT makes exciting statements about overcoming. We have a legacy of peace, for Jesus has overcome the world (Jn 16:33). We are to overcome evil with good (Ro 12:21), and through faith we have overcome both the world and the evil one (1 Jn 5:4; 2:13,14). In each of these passages, the Greek word is *nikaō*, "to win a victory," "to conquer."

Peter warns of promises of freedom that actually only enslave to depravity (2 Pe 2:19–20). One who is entangled in the corruption of the world will be overcome. Here the word is *ēttaomai* (used elsewhere only in 2 Co 12:13), "to be defeated" and thus "to be inferior."

Believers have different options. We can struggle futilely with the world on our own or surrender to it and be enslaved—or we can trust in the endless victory that Christ has won for us, through him conquering every enemy that would hold us back from a full experience of God's good will.

OVERFLOW ♦ *Abound/Abounding*

OVERSEER

The Greek word for "overseer" is *episkopos*, translated "bishop" in older versions. Of its five occurrences in the NT, one uses the word as a title of Jesus, who lives to guard and guide his church (1 Pe 2:25).

The concept expressed by this term is that of one who is continuously observing, scrutinizing, and watching out for something. In the NT, what is overseen by individuals with this ministry is the Christian community. Two parallel terms are *presbyteros* ("elder") and *poimen* ("shepherd"). These are so close in concept and so linked in NT usage that they probably should be treated as functional synonyms.

The NT has three passages that indicate multiple leadership among believers (Ac 6:1–6; 20:28; Php 1:1).

Although we do not know the specific duties of the overseer, this very important position involved working with a functioning, local church. The NT gives the specific principles that should guide any church leader in ministering among believers. ♦ *Elders* ♦ *Leadership* ♦ *Sheep/Shepherd*

P

PAIN AND SUFFERING

Pain and suffering have been themes for many a philosopher. But when we enter a time of suffering, all the wisest speculations of the philosophers seem empty and meaningless. We simply hurt. We struggle to cope with our pain. And sometimes when we look to Scripture to find a word on pain and suffering, hoping for a message that will heal, it may seem that we find little help.

Unlike the ancient Greek Stoics, who viewed suffering as man's fate in an impersonal universe, the Bible affirms a world ordered by a personal God. The OT consistently sets pain and suffering in the context of morality and the divine purpose. There is no hint there of chance or fate. The NT speaks more directly about human pain and suffering and explores the stunning theme of the suffering of God. But Scripture has no magic remedy to offer when suffering surprises and overwhelms us. There is no verse to read that will instantly heal us or even dull our pain. However, there is a perspective on suffering that, if we adopt it by faith, will enable us to cope and even to overcome.

OT 1. **Hebrew words for pain and suffering**
    2. **Job: why the good suffer**
    3. **Pain and childbirth**
    4. **Isa 53: the suffering servant**
NT 5. **Greek words for pain and suffering**
    6. **The suffering of Jesus**
    7. **The suffering of the believer**
    8. **Peter's perspective on suffering**
    9. **Summary**

OT — 1. Hebrew words for pain and suffering. One English meaning of "to suffer" is "to experience [something unpleasant]." Thus, there are such phrases in some English versions as "suffer vengeance," "suffer thirst," and "suffer shame." These statements simply assert that one will experience thirst or shame; they can be disregarded in our exploration of the meaning of pain and suffering.

One difficulty we face is that the Hebrew language has many different words to express the idea of pain and suffering. Some express the intensity of what is suffered. ♦ *Agony* ♦ *Anguish* Others are almost synonyms, with slightly different emphases. These, translated by a number of different English words in the NIV and the NASB, have a common characteristic: they speak in a general way of suffering or pain and often can be used interchangeably. ♦ *Affliction* ♦ *Distress/Trouble* ♦ *Sorrow* Usually when the NIV uses "suffering" in a verse where that word is not used by the NASB, the NASB will have one of the above words.

It is best, then, to simply look at the more frequently used Hebrew terms that these versions translate as "pain" or "suffering."

Kā'ab and *kᵉ'ēb* emphasize pain, while a derivative, *mak'ōb*, focuses on sadness or sorrow. Yet even those dealing with bodily pain are most concerned with mental anguish; the physical experience is of less concern (exceptions: Ge 34:25; Job 14:22; 33:19; Eze 28:24).

Several derivatives of *'āṣab* ("to grieve, trouble, or displease") mean "sorrow": *'eṣeb* ("sorrow," "labor"); *'ōṣeb* ("sorrow"); *'aṣṣebeṯ* ("sorrow," "wound"); and *'iṣṣāḇôn* ("sorrow," "toil"). Here too both physical and mental stress are in view, and the words are used in many contexts.

Particularly significant is the occurrence of this root in Ge 3:16–17. As a result of sin entering the human race, women experience greater pain in childbirth (*'iṣṣāḇôn* and *'eṣeḇ*), and men experience pain in their toil (*'iṣṣāḇôn*). The word *'iṣṣāḇôn* appears only one other time in the OT (Ge 5:29).

Several of the words for pain and suffering in the OT are associated with childbirth. *Ḥîl* is graphic, picturing an individual writhing in agony. It is often used to express mental anguish (e.g., Isa 23:5; Mic 4:10). It is also used of the shaking terror that grips us as disaster looms (Jer 6:24; Mic 4:9).

Eight of the sixty OT occurrences of *ḥēḇel*, from a root that means "to bring forth," focus specifically on the pain of childbirth.

Pain and suffering are concepts in the OT that draw attention to how human beings are affected by the tragedies of life. It is not the loss of a home or a loved one, nor physical agony, that seems devastating. It is how such an experience affects us within, causing doubts and fears and trembling as the pattern of our lives is shaken and our expectations fail.

2. Job: why the good suffer. The prime OT example of one who endured pain and suffering is Job. Although he was a person whom God himself called blameless and upright (Job 1:8), his long prosperity was suddenly transformed into tragedy. Wealth, family, the respect of his peers, and even physical health were torn away in a single day.

Most of the book is a dialogue in which Job and three of his friends probe for the reason for Job's suffering. All the speakers link suffering with God. God is active in the universe, a moral judge who shapes events. His commitment to goodness leads him to bless the righteous and to bring tragedy on the sinful. Thus, pain and suffering cannot be shrugged away, nor should they be borne stoically as being no more than

human fate in a harsh and mindless universe.

But Job was led to anguish by the conviction that God is personally involved on some level of causation when pain and suffering come. Job's friends argued that some secret sin must have been the cause of Job's suffering. His pain was his punishment. Job should repent, they said, and get right with God, and God would lift his crushing hand. Job accepted this reasoning, but knew within his own heart that he had not sinned intentionally. Searching his memory, he could not even locate unintentional sins. Job's integrity would not allow him to lie, even to protect God's "honor." And so Job was thrown into deepest anguish. His image of God and his justice was challenged at the deepest level of Job's personality. Job felt stripped of hope, alone in a universe he suddenly could not understand. In his shattered trembling, thoughts of God were no comfort; they seemed only a part of the curse of suffering.

Job's experience and his feelings have been shared by thousands of believers across the centuries. But the Book of Job only hints at an answer to the problem of pain. The window to hope is opened by a younger man who had sat and listened as his elders wrestled with Job on the ash heap. Elihu, the youth, broke the linkage between suffering and punishment by pointing out that God may at times use suffering to instruct human beings. Elihu did not explain why Job suffered. He merely said that in human suffering God may have a purpose that is separate from punishment. But that statement alone allowed Job to return in heart to God. Once again Job began to believe that God was good and would not act against his own character.

Finally, God appeared. In two magnificent discourses, Job was shown the greatness of God and the insignificance of human beings. God is not to be questioned by mere man. God is to be trusted—even when suffering comes.

God's discourses do not answer the question of just why Job suffered; but in this revelation of himself, God restored

Job's faith. Job took his place as a mere creature before the Creator. With restored trust came the restoration of blessing as well.

It is significant that the Book of Job never draws back from the conviction that somehow God is at work when suffering comes. His hand is there, in our days of darkness as well as in the sunshine. We may not understand his reasons for the pain that grips us. But we need not doubt his presence or his love.

3. Pain and childbirth. The OT's view of pain and suffering links disaster to God's moral governance of his universe. This is well illustrated in Nu 14. Israel had refused to enter the Promised Land at God's command. True, the Lord "is slow to anger, abounding in love and forgiving sin and rebellion," but "he does not leave the guilty unpunished" (v. 18). Thus, God announced, "For forty years—one year for each of the forty days you explored the land—you will suffer for your sins and know what it is like to have me against you. I, the LORD, have spoken, and I will surely do these things to this whole wicked community, which has banded together against me" (vv. 34–35). Suffering comes as a result of sin and is a punishment.

But this view is more complex than it might at first appear. Sinful choices resonate through history. A person's sins affect the character of his children, so warping their lives that God "punishes the children for the sins of the fathers to the third and fourth generation" (v. 18). ♦ *Account/Accountable* The innocent suffer along with the wicked. The disobedient's children, who were not responsible for their parents' choices, trudged through the wilderness too, as one by one that first generation died. In later centuries, prophet and psalmist cry out against the wicked whose sins cause the innocent to suffer. Amos shouts, "You oppress the righteous and take bribes and you deprive the poor of justice in the courts" (5:12).

The suffering of the innocent at the hands of the wicked is a reason for the believer to call on God. There will come a day when the Lord will give them "relief from suffering and turmoil and cruel bondage" (Isa 14:3).

While suffering may be punishment directed by God at the wicked, suffering may also come to the innocent through the actions of the wicked. The sinful choices that bring the individual pain may not be his or her own! Society too is twisted and warped, and injustice has its grip on every culture.

And so we come to the significance of the images of pain in the OT. Again and again the Hebrew words turn our attention to childbirth. Pain's essence is summed up in the writhing body and straining muscles of the woman in the pain of childbirth. The image is theologically significant. It offers hope, in that the outcome of that pain is the emergence of fresh life into the world. But it is also a constant reminder of sin's origin. Pain and the image of childbirth take us back to Eden and to God's announcement to Adam and Eve of the impact of their sin. To Eve he said, "I will greatly increase your pains ['iṣṣābôn] in childbearing; with pain ['eṣeb] you will give birth to children" (Ge 3:16). And to Adam, "Through painful toil ['iṣṣābôn] you will eat . . . all the days of your life" (Ge 3:17).

The pain and suffering of the human condition are an outcome and a reminder of man's shattered relationship with God. Pain and suffering are linked not only with individual choices but also with the sinful condition of man. How beautiful, then, the image of pain as childbirth's travail. The seed of our suffering was planted long ago. Pain testifies to our need for deliverance. And despite our pain, we have hope that it will one day bring new life (cf. Paul's use of this image in Ro 8:18–25).

4. Isa 53: the suffering servant. The OT introduces a theme that will be explained in the NT. God was to send his servant, who would be "a man of sorrows, and familiar with suffering" (53:3). Although he was innocent, it was God's will "to crush him and cause him to suffer" (v. 10). His suffering too was like that of giving birth. The seed of his suffering had been planted long before in

Adam's act of disobedience. The pain was intense, with many different words and images required to even begin to convey it. But the purpose and the result of his suffering has been the bringing of life: "After the suffering of his soul, he will see the light of life and be satisfied; by his knowledge my righteous servant will justify many, and he will bear their iniquities" (v. 11).

The suffering servant is Jesus. And every word of Isaiah's majestic account of what was to happen some seven hundred years later on Calvary reminds us that God has not left us to suffer alone. God has stepped into history. We have sinned. But it is God who suffers with us—and for us. "Surely he took up our infirmities and carried our sorrows, yet we considered him stricken by God, smitten by him, and afflicted. But he was pierced for our transgressions, he was crushed for our iniquities; the punishment that brought us peace was upon him, and by his wounds we are healed. We all, like sheep, have gone astray, each of us has turned to his own way; and the LORD has laid on him the iniquity of us all" (Isa 53:4–6).

5. Greek words for pain and suffering. The NT contains a number of Greek words from which we derive various words for the "pain and suffering" family of words in English.

In the Septuagint, *lypē* is used to translate thirteen different Hebrew words for pain. It describes both physical and emotional pain and is translated in the NIV by "distress," "grief," and "sorrow," as well as by "pain(ful)," in all except one (2 Co 9:7) of its sixteen occurrences in the NT (Lk 22:45; Jn 16:6, 20,21,22; Ro 9:2; 2 Co 2:1,3,7; 7:10; Php 2:27; Heb 12:11; 1 Pe 2:19).

The word *ōdin* means "the pangs of childbirth," so often reflected in Hebrew words for pain. In each of the four places it is used in the NT, the NIV and NASB read "pain" (Mt 24:8; Mk 13:8; Ac 2:24; 1 Th 5:3). A related word, *ōdinō*, is found three times in the NT (Gal 4:19,27; Rev 12:2).

Basanos is a strong word that is found only three times in the NT, twice ren-dered "torment" (Lk 16:23,28) and once rendered "severe pain" (Mt 4:24).

The word *ponos* means "the pain of exhaustion." It is used only in Revelation, where, as in the OT, pain is seen as an aspect of divine judgment (Rev 16:10,11; 21:4).

In most NT references to suffering, the Greek word is *paschō*. Other words used to express suffering include *kakopatheō*, "to suffer evil"; *sympaschō*, "to suffer together with," "to suffer the same thing"; and *pathēma*, "suffering." These are part of the same word group, which in Greek culture expressed the view that humanity is afflicted with experiences that are beyond our control and yet cause us physical and mental anguish. In the NT, these words for suffering are found most often in the Synoptics, sporadically in Paul, and frequently in Peter's letters. The passages are usually referring to the death of Jesus and the events associated with it. Here the strongest language is used to remind us that Jesus suffered by God's express will (e.g., Mt 16:21; Mk 8:31; Lk 17:25; 24:26; Ac 17:3) and that his suffering was foretold in the OT (e.g., Mk 9:12; Lk 24:26; Ac 3:18; 1 Pe 1:11).

English versions often use "suffer" to mean "experience"—e.g., the phrases "suffer loss" (1 Co 3:15), "suffer wrath" (1 Th 5:9), and others. These can be disregarded as we examine suffering and its meaning.

6. The suffering of Jesus. The NT's view of suffering is seen most clearly in Jesus' experience. Suffering, the OT teaches, is a direct or indirect result of sin. Either one makes the wrong choices that bring suffering as punishment or one is affected unjustly by the wrong choices of others. Jesus' suffering, of course, falls in this latter category. He died, "the righteous one for [*hyper*, on account of] the unrighteous ones" (1 Pe 3:18). The sins for which Jesus was punished were not his own. In the immediate context of history, it was the sins of Jesus' enemies that led to his suffering. In the grand context of eternity, it was your sins and mine that led him to Calvary.

The OT also sees the hand of God behind every experience of the individual. In Jesus' experiences the hand of God is undisguised. Jesus' suffering was "foretold through all the prophets" (Ac 3:18). He was in fact "handed over" to the wicked men who caused his death "by God's set purpose and foreknowledge" (Ac 2:23). God's hand is shown to operate even in the suffering that comes on us unjustly.

Finally, the suffering of Jesus is purposeful. Although an injustice, Jesus' suffering had as its purpose our being brought to God (1 Pe 3:18). To accomplish this, Jesus' suffering and death were a sacrifice of atonement (Heb 13:12; 1 Pe 2:21). ◗ **Atonement** Despite the gross injustice evident in Jesus' execution, God has purified and in fact used his Son's suffering to accomplish history's greatest mission, the salvation of the race.

The suffering of Jesus underlines his full humanity. Only by truly becoming man could God not only subject himself to the suffering that has invaded history but also, through Christ's death, lift all who believe beyond the vale of tears. ◗ **Mankind**

7. The suffering of the believer. The Christian, redeemed by Jesus, has been delivered, but not from earthly suffering. Rightly approached, "suffering produces perseverance; perseverance, character; and character, hope" (Ro 5:3–4). Confident of our inheritance through Jesus' resurrection, we rejoice "though now for a little while [we] may have had to suffer grief in all kinds of trials" (1 Pe 1:6). To produce its greatest benefits, suffering is not to be a consequence of our own sinful choices (1 Pe 2:19; 4:15).

Moreover, suffering should be viewed as fellowship (*koinōnia*, "participation"). Jesus suffered for his commitment to doing the will of God. A similar commitment on our part leads to a uniquely "Christian" suffering, which is linked with the completion of Jesus' mission on earth and which is in fact an aspect of fellowship (a close relationship) with our Lord (e.g., 1 Pe 4:1,13; Php 3:10). Thus, truly Christian suffering is also purpos-

ive: it is for the sake of Jesus, his kingdom, and his righteousness (e.g., Ac 9:16; Php 1:29; 2 Th 1:5; 1 Pe 2:19; 3:14; 4:14,16,19).

But what about the suffering that comes in the normal course of life? Or the suffering that comes when we have tried to do good, and some tragedy occurs? Here too the NT adds a distinct perspective. Grasping what the Bible teaches about suffering and how to meet it will not relieve our pain nor release us from circumstances beyond our control. But grasping the Bible's teaching will enable us to cope and will rekindle our hope.

8. Peter's perspective on suffering. A Christian perspective on suffering is presented in 1 Peter. Peter begins (1:3–9) by pointing out that our hope is fixed on Christ and the future he has for us, even though we may "suffer grief in all kinds of trials" now (1:6). These trials demonstrate the genuineness of our faith and will result in praise and glory when Jesus comes (1:7).

The apostle moves on (1:13–25) to show that our hope is to be fixed fully on the grace to be given us when Jesus returns. This will free us to commit ourselves to obedience and to holiness now. As we live good lives (2:13–25), in submission to existing authorities, suffering may come. Peter commends bearing up under unjust suffering because one is "conscious of God" (2:19). In consciousness of God, not only do we seek to be obedient and holy for his sake, but we also remember that Jesus too suffered. We are to follow his example and walk in his steps. Our attitude is to be one of simple trust in the ultimate justice of God.

God so supervises events that normally good comes to the one who does good (3:8–13). But at times one who does good will suffer for it. In such a case the believer is (1) not to fear, (2) to remember that Jesus is Lord and is in charge of all events, (3) to, despite suffering, display so much hope that others will ask about it, and (4) to always keep a good conscience. To encourage his readers, Peter points to Jesus. Jesus did only good. Yet he, not the unrighteous men who were his opponents, suffered. But God used Jesus' suffering to bring us to himself (3:18). Peter's point is that when we suffer despite doing good, we too can be sure that God has some good purpose in view.

Peter then reminds us of Noah and his family (3:20). They were delivered from judgment by hearing and responding to God's voice and were deposited in a new world. Spiritually speaking, we too have been carried in Christ into a new realm. In this new creation, we no longer live "for evil human desires but rather for the will of God" (4:2).

Christians are not to be surprised at suffering. When we live by the will of God, we "suffer as a Christian" (4:16), and this is a cause for praise rather than shame. Suffering is only for "a little while"; our destiny is to share "his eternal glory" (5:10).

9. Summary. The OT portrays suffering and pain as experiences that are in the immediate control of God. They also are aspects of the human condition and must be traced back to sin. It was the disobedient act of Adam and Eve that introduced sin and suffering into history. Since that time human beings have suffered because of their own wrong choices and because of the wrong choices and acts of others. Sin is so much an integral part of human experience that both individual and society are warped and twisted, and each is a constant source of injustice and suffering.

In the NT we discover God's attitude to suffering expressed in Jesus. Not only did God sympathize, hurting with our hurts and suffering with our suffering, but God in Jesus even entered the human race and took on himself the full weight of sin, and with it the weight of suffering. Christ's suffering was vicarious (in the place of others). And it was an atoning sacrifice. ♦ *Atonement* But in the NT, Christ's suffering is also presented as a model. Christians are to adopt his attitude of trusting obedience and to accept patiently the suffering that may come. Like Jesus, we will be vindicated by our righteous persistence in

doing God's will, and God's wisdom will one day be known as we discover the purpose for which he has led us into pain.

The mystery of why a particular individual suffers as he or she does remains shrouded and hidden. Let us remember that from God's perspective, time is fleeting. It is eternity that counts. And in eternity all mysteries will be known, and the bright glow of glory will wash out the last remaining stain of any despair.

PARABLE

The Greek word for "parable" means something "set alongside." Sometimes Scripture records people illustrating what they are saying by setting a concrete situation alongside an abstract concept (e.g., Jdg 9:8–15; 2 Sa 12:1–7; Isa 5:1–7). The most well-known parables in the Bible are those of Jesus. Many of these have an illustrative thrust, such as those of the good Samaritan (Lk 10:27–37), the prodigal son (Lk 15:11–32), and the talents (Lk 19:11–27). But some parables, related to a yet hidden form of the kingdom, were told in such a way that they concealed rather than illustrated Jesus' meaning. ♦ *Kingdom*

PARDON ♦ *Forgive*

PASSION

The notion of passion as desire is discussed elsewhere. ♦ *Desire*

Where "passion" is used in one or more English versions of the Bible, two Greek concepts are reflected. *Pathēma* and *pathos* (Ro 1:26; 7:5; Gal 5:24; Col 3:5; 1 Th 4:5) focus on the evil condition of the sinner, which is the source of the desires that move him. Of the thirty-seven times that *epithymia* occurs in the NT, it is translated "passion" only twice in the NIV (Tit 2:12; 3:3). This word refers to any natural desire with its goodness or evil usually designated in the context. Where the NIV reads "burn with passion" in 1 Co 7:9, the Greek has simply *pyroō*, "to burn or be inflamed."

PASSOVER

The historic roots of the Passover are found in Ex 12. When the destroying angel swept through Egypt, he "passed over" (*pāsaḥ*) the homes of the Israelites, which were identified by the blood of a lamb sprinkled on the doorposts.

Israel was given explicit instructions on how to keep the Passover so it would be an annual reminder of God's deliverance (Lev 23:5–8; Nu 28:16–25; Dt 16:1–8). This ritual was a reenactment of Israel's preparations for leaving Egypt and focused on killing the paschal lamb. It was to take place in the month of Abib (March/April). God's people were not faithful to this instruction, though the OT tells of several specific times when the Passover was observed; these were often linked with revivals (Nu 9:1–14; Jos 5:10–12; 2 Ki 23:21–23; 2 Ch 30:1; 35:1–19; Ezr 6:19–22).

The Passover is theologically significant to Christians as well as to Jews. To God's OT people, the Passover recalled a redemption linked with death and the shedding of blood. To the Christian, the Passover speaks of Jesus. Christ is our Passover Lamb, who has been sacrificed for us (1 Co 5:7). Our redemption is linked to his shed blood, as it protects us from the ultimate destroyer.
♦ *Blood*

PATIENCE

"Love is patient" (1 Co 13:4). The NT contains many exhortations to be patient. But just what is patience? The Greek word group (*makrothymeō / makrothymia*) focuses our attention on restraint: that capacity for self-control despite circumstances that might arouse the passions or cause agitation. In personal relationships, patience is forbearance. This is not so much a trait as a way of life. We keep on loving or forgiving despite provocation, as illustrated in Jesus' pointed stories in Mt 18. Patience also has to do with our reaction to the troubles we experience in life.

PATTERN

The interaction between the OT and the NT in regard to the pattern of the tabernacle is theologically significant. The OT says that Moses was given a *tabnît* by God himself. The word means "a plan" or "a layout." Scripture goes on to show that that plan included detailed specifications for the construction of this place of OT worship (Ex 25–26). ♦
Tabernacle and Temple The writer to the Hebrews looks back and fixes on that original affirmation (Ex 25:9,40). The fact that Moses was given a *typos* ("likeness," "model") to guide him indicates that the pattern is at best a copy. It indicates that the OT worship system itself "is a copy and shadow of what is in heaven" (Heb 8:5). Jesus as high priest has entered the reality, offering his own blood as the atoning sacrifice for our sins.

In Ro 5:14, Adam is a *typos* ("pattern") of Christ; that is, in certain respects Jesus' work is understood by comparison and contrast with the impact of Adam on humanity.

Three times Paul refers to himself as a type or pattern for believers. In one he boldly calls on the Philippians to live "according to the pattern" (*typos*) he had given them in word and deed (Php 3:17).

In another significant passage he calls on young Timothy to keep what he has learned from Paul as "the pattern [*hypotypōsis*] of sound teaching" (2 Ti 1:13). In NT times, *hypotypōsis* was used of a floor plan to guide a builder or of a first draft of written material used to guide fuller development. Paul's point is that life is to be founded on Scripture's revelation of reality. But each person and culture must move on to construction, not violating the principles laid down, but constantly seeking to flesh out the divine vision.

Only one other NT passage uses this word. In it Paul states that Christ chose both to save and "to display his unlimited patience in him as an example for those who would believe on [Christ] and receive eternal life" (1 Ti 1:16).

PEACE

Peace seems impossible to achieve in our troubled world and, for those struggling with anxiety or disappointment, in individual lives.

Peace is a complex concept. In the OT particularly, peace is a powerful theological term, with the nature of peace deeply rooted in Scripture's view of relationships and of humanity's deepest needs. The NT provides clear guidance as to how we can experience peace—a peace that our world neither understands, nor gives, nor can take away.

OT 1. The Hebrew concept of peace
      2. The peace offering
NT 3. The Greek word
      4. The peace that Jesus brings
      5. Summary

OT — 1. The Hebrew concept of peace. The Hebrew word for "peace" is *šālôm*. It is derived from a root that conveys the image of wholeness, unity, and harmony—something that is complete and sound. Although "peace" is essentially a relational concept in the OT, it also conveys the idea of prosperity, health, and fulfillment.

The word *šālôm* occurs over two hundred times in the OT. In fifty or sixty of these occurrences, the emphasis lies on the absence of strife. Thus, e.g., the tension and antagonism that had developed between Isaac's servants and the people of Abimelech, a Philistine king, were resolved with a feast and a treaty, after which the people of Abimelech "left him in peace" (Ge 26:31). The same use of "peace" affirms a lack of international strife, as well as the beneficial effect of such peace on a nation's citizens. "During Solomon's lifetime Judah and Israel, from Dan to Beersheba, lived in safety, each man under his own vine and fig tree" (1 Ki 4:25). This is the blessing that came from having "peace on all sides" (v. 24).

While most of the uses of *šālôm* in the narrative books of the OT focus on interpersonal or international harmony, the concept does expand to refer to an individual's or a nation's welfare. For example, when the prophet Elisha saw a close friend hurrying to him, he sent his servant to greet her with a series of questions: "Are you all right [*šālôm*]? Is your husband all right [*šālôm*]? Is your child all right [*šālôm*]?" (2 Ki 4:26). Thus, health, personal fulfillment, and prosperity are all included in the concept of peace. And, in the twenty-five or so times when "*šālôm*" is used as greeting or farewell, it is the extension of a blessing—a wish for the recipient's welfare.

Peace takes on its deepest significance as we move into the Psalms and the Prophets. Through the OT, some two-thirds of the uses of this word express the fulfillment that comes to human beings when they experience God's presence.

The sovereign God of Israel will bless "his people with peace" (Ps 29:11). But more than national blessing is involved in the peace that God gives. David, fleeing from Absalom during that son's rebellion, felt intense pressure (Ps 4:1–2). But David fixed his thoughts on God and remembered the joy that came with trust in him. Comforted and at rest despite overwhelming danger, David concluded, "I will lie down and sleep in peace, for you alone, O LORD, make me dwell in safety" (4:8). For us as for David, peace in difficult circumstances is a result of our relationship with the Lord. "Great peace," David says, "have they who love your law" (Ps 119:165). The one whose life is in harmony with God's revealed will experiences inner harmony as well. It is not surprising, then, to find Ps 37 contrast the wicked and ruthless with "the man of peace" (37:35–37). The man of peace lives in a right relationship with God, for God alone is the source of human rest and fulfillment. For those who have missed the way of faith and are struggling to find fulfillment apart from God, there is no such blessing. As Isaiah warns, "The wicked are like the tossing sea, which cannot rest, whose waves cast up mire and mud. 'There is no peace,' says my God, 'for the wicked' " (Isa 57:20–21).

The prophets added yet another dimension to the theological shape of "peace." God not only brings an inner harmony and peace to those who live in a right relationship with him but he also intends to bring peace to the nations. This peace too will come only with God's presence. The prophets promised the coming of a "Prince of Peace" (Isa 9:6) and looked forward to the day when "of the increase of his government and peace there will be no end" (v. 7). God says that when the Messiah comes to establish his kingdom and pour out his Spirit, "The fruit of righteousness will be peace; the effect of righteousness will be quietness and confidence forever. My people will live in peaceful dwelling places, in secure homes, in undisturbed places of rest" (Isa 32:16–17).

One OT prophecy (Eze 34:20–31) declares that God will be personally present and "will be their God" (v. 24) and that David's descendant (Jesus) will rule, confirming God's "covenant of peace" with his people (v. 25).

Peace in the OT, then, speaks of the blessing of inner and outer harmony that comes to a person or people who live in a close relationship with God. Believers can, like David, experience peace despite dangerous circumstances by being conscious of God's presence, or at least of his sure promises. Ultimately the world will know international and interpersonal peace as well, as the very presence of God in the person of Jesus halts strife and war.

But peace is not purchased cheaply. Alienation from God and antagonism toward others flows from twisted human nature. ◗ *Sin* Isaiah gives us a hint of the price of peace in his description of the suffering servant: "He was pierced for our transgressions, he was crushed for our iniquities; the punishment that brought us peace was upon him, and by his wounds we are healed" (Isa 53:5).

2. The peace offering. One of the OT offerings was called the peace offering (*šelem*). It is mentioned over eighty times in the OT. This offering, which came after the sacrifices for sin, was partially burned and partially eaten by the worshipers. Thus it symbolized the *šālôm*, the overflowing joy and fulfillment, that forgiveness brings us, causing us to be at peace with the Lord. ◗ *Offering and Sacrifice*

NT — 3. The Greek word. The Greek word *eirēnē* originally referred to that orderly, prosperous life that is possible when there is no war. Only much later did philosophers begin to apply the concept to an inner, personal peace. But the NT use of *eirēnē* (90 occurrences) does not reflect the culture of the Greeks. Instead, "peace" in the NT is defined and enriched by the OT's *šālôm*. In every theologically significant use, "peace" is something rooted in one's relationship with God and testifies to the restoration of human beings to inner harmony and to harmonious relationships with others. Our once-shattered lives are again made whole, and we become in Christ what God originally intended us to be. The vital health and wholeness of a restored humanity is available in Jesus.

4. The peace that Jesus brings. Multiplied greetings and farewells in the Epistles are wishes that the believing readers will receive grace, mercy, and peace. This peace is "from God our Father and from the Lord Jesus Christ" (Ro 1:7; cf. 1 Co 1:3; 2 Co 1:2; Gal 1:3; Eph 1:2; Php 1:2; Col 1:2; 2 Th 1:2; 1 Ti 1:2; 2 Ti 1:2; Tit 1:4; Phm 3; 2 Jn 3). As in the OT, the NT affirms that the Lord is "the God of peace"—the source and bringer of peace (Ro 15:33; 16:20; 1 Co 14:33; Php 4:9; 1 Th 5:23; Heb 13:20).

First and foremost, the peace human beings need is peace with God. This is ours in Jesus; "since we have been justified through faith, we have peace with God through our Lord Jesus Christ" (Ro 5:1). Eph 2:14 adds that Jesus "himself is our peace."

God's peace may be an inner experience, but the wholeness that is suggested by *šālôm/eirēnē* is also visibly expressed in the believing community. Among God's people, peace means that hostility has been replaced by unity (Eph 2:14–17; 4:3). It means order and harmony (1 Co 14:33). It means a commitment to harmony that is as much the Christian's calling as is holiness (Heb 12:14; 2 Ti 2:22). Paul beautifully portrays peace as it is experienced by the believing community living in fellowship with the Lord: "As God's chosen people, holy and dearly loved, clothe yourselves with compassion, kindness, humility, gentleness and patience. Bear with each other and forgive whatever grievances you may have against one another. Forgive as the Lord forgave you. And over all these virtues put on love, which binds them all together in perfect unity. Let the peace of Christ rule in your hearts, since as members of one body you were called to peace. And be thankful" (Col 3:12–15).

In the Epistles, "peace" is most often that restored wholeness that Jesus brings to our relationship with God and others, although this cannot be separated from the inner sense of well-being that accompanies them. The Gospels seem to show a slightly different emphasis. Sometimes "peace" is the absence of strife. Jesus warns his disciples not to imagine that his coming means they will be freed from external pressures and strife "on earth" (Mt 10:34; Lk 12:51). Instead, Jesus focuses on peace despite suffering.

John most clearly develops this theme. He reports Jesus' words of peace: "Peace I leave with you; my peace I give you. I do not give to you as the world gives. Do not let your hearts be troubled and do not be afraid" (Jn 14:27). "I have told you these things, so that in me you may have peace. In this world you will have trouble. But take heart! I have overcome the world" (Jn 16:33). Jesus provides an inner peace that lets the believer face danger and suffering without fear or a trembling heart. Through Jesus, an inner peace is possible, no matter how turbulent the external situation may be.

5. Summary. In the narrative passages of the OT, "peace" speaks primarily of harmonious relationships between persons and nations. As we move into the Psalms and Prophets, "peace" takes on strong theological overtones. There peace is found by the individual and the nation through the presence of God. Awareness of God's presence quiets the inner turmoil that comes with danger. Fellowship with God, and thus a life lived in his presence, brings material

blessings and the cessation of war. Ultimately God will be present in this world in the person of the Messiah. Then an era of universal peace for all mankind will become a reality. ▶ *Christ*

Because God's goal for humanity has always been to experience fellowship with him and in that fellowship to develop every human potential, "peace" also speaks of health, completeness, and fulfillment.

The NT links peace directly to Jesus. God, the God of peace, who alone brings peace, has acted in Jesus to bring the blessings of šālôm to man. Peace with God should overflow in the experience of Jesus' people—both in the quality of relationships among believers as a community of faith and in the inner life of each believer.

PENALTY ▶ *Guilt*

PEOPLE

The Hebrew word for "people" is *'am.* It refers to a larger grouping of people linked by relationships that give them unity and identity. Israel in the OT was a people united by family ties and, in time, a common homeland. But it is essentially Israel's relationship with the Lord as his people ('*ammî,* "my people," he called them) that provided the Jews with an identity that has persisted over millennia.

The NT word found in most places where English versions read "people" is *laos.* This word is found 143 times in the NT. In the church, God has acted to take "from the Gentiles a people for himself" (Ac 15:14). Jew and Gentile are united by Jesus to form a new people—his people.

The Gospels and Acts use the word "people" in a general sense, however. The aggregation of persons intended in most passages, unless otherwise indicated, is not necessarily God's own special people. On the other hand, in the Epistles the word "people" usually has theological significance, and those indicated are in a unifying relationship with the Lord.

PERFECT

Is it possible that we can be "perfect"? Some people believe so and postulate a sinlessness that is expected of the believer. Others hold to the possibility of perfection but remember human frailty. To them, forgiveness is a continual necessity as individuals grow in their capacity to love and respond to the Lord.

Often our theologies grow from a deep sense of our own need and a yearning desire to live in full commitment to God. These theologies may, or may not, be rooted in the meaning given to words in Scripture. So it is especially important in regard to such a word as "perfect" to be very certain just what Scripture is saying—and what it is not saying.

OT 1. The Hebrew words
NT 2. The Greek words
3. Becoming perfect

OT — 1. The Hebrew words. Two Hebrew words are most often found in the few settings where "perfect" is found in the English versions of the OT: *kālîl* and *tāmîm* or *tām*. *Kālîl* speaks of completeness or wholeness. Where it is translated "perfect" it expresses a quality that completely or wholly fills its subject (beauty, 4 times; a color, 3 times). But this term is definitely not associated with sinlessness. It is Israel's perfection that led her to trust her own beauty and turn to spiritual idolatry (Eze 16:14). Satan's original perfection did not protect him from choosing sin and from suffering a spectacular fall (Eze 28:12).

The word *tāmîm* or *tām* comes from a root that means "complete." As a moral concept, it speaks of uprightness or blamelessness, which, in a limited sense, humans can possess. God himself is completely perfect (Dt 32:4). His way, unveiled in his Word, is perfect (2 Sa 22:31), and by arming the believer with strength, God completely equips him for a righteous walk ("God arms me with strength and makes my way perfect" [2 Sa 22:33]). But human beings are "perfect" only in the sense that David and Job were. Each loved and responded to God as he knew him, yet each was flawed. David's passions swept him from the

path of holiness. And despite Job's exemplary life (Job 1:1), Job was aware of his own sins and imperfection (Job 9:28; 14:16–17; 42:6). The blameless man or woman, according to the OT, turned from evil to follow the Lord honestly and wholeheartedly. But even the *tāmîm* might fall, and sometimes did.

NT — 2. The Greek words. The Greek word group translated "perfect" in some English versions includes *teleioō*, *teleios*, and *teleotēs*. These words emphasize wholeness and completeness. In the biological sense they mean "mature," or "full grown": the person, animal, or plant achieved the potential inherent in its nature. The perfect is the thing or person that is complete, in which nothing that belongs to its essence has been left out. It is perfect because every potential it possesses has been realized.

This basic sense of the word group as it is used in the NT helps us put many passages in exciting perspective. A "perfect love"—one that drives out fear—is a complete one (1 Jn 4:18). God's power "made perfect in weakness" (1 Co 12:9) reminds us that his power is fully released in us when we do not hinder him by relying on our own supposed strengths.

The use of this word group in Hebrews is slightly different from its use in other NT passages. The law "made nothing perfect" (Heb 7:19), but in his sacrifice Jesus has made believers "perfect forever" (Heb 7:28; 10:14; cf. 10:1). The point is that the law was never able to bring to completion the task set for its sacrifices: to make it possible for a person to stand in God's presence. But Jesus' one sacrifice has accomplished that task, and now we who are perfected are completely cleansed and thus are able to stand before the Lord.

As for Jesus himself, he was "made perfect" (Heb 5:9; cf. 2:10) in the sense of being fully equipped for his saving ministry. Suffering added nothing to his essential character or nature. The OT high priest had to be drawn from humanity and had to be able to sympathize with mankind because he shared the human condition. So also Jesus had to become a man and suffer the common lot of humanity if he was to serve as our high priest.

3. Becoming perfect.

The Greek philosophers had various definitions of the perfect (complete) human being. Scripture too speaks of the perfect or mature individual. However, we should remember that the Bible defines its own terms, and we should resist the temptation to read into its verses some meaning of "perfect" that the word does not have. The perfect human being is not a sinless paragon, for the NT makes it clear that "we all stumble in many ways" (Jas 3:2). Yet "if anyone is never at fault in what he says, he is a perfect man" (Jas 3:2). How do we reconcile the apparent contradiction in these statements?

First, we realize that saints remain sinners. John says bluntly, "If we claim to be without sin, we deceive ourselves and the truth is not in us" (1 Jn 1:8). God deals with our failures by extending forgiveness and cleansing as we come to him (1 Jn 1:9). So "perfection" is not sinlessness.

Second, we realize that God holds out an exciting prospect for us. We can be "perfect" in the biblical sense of achieving our potential as Christian persons!

Matthew records Jesus' words to all those who yearn to experience God's kingdom. We are to love our enemies and pray for our persecutors, as God the Father sends rain and sunshine on both the evil and the good. "Be perfect," Jesus concluded, "as your heavenly Father is perfect" (Mt 5:48). God fulfills his divine potential and the potential of his love in his treatment of the wicked. As his children now, we are to fulfill our potential as Christian persons by loving even our enemies.

James says the same thing. The person who controls his tongue has reached maturity: he achieves his potential as a Christian and so in that sense is a perfect person.

So there is an exciting life ahead for us who believe! We will never reach here the state we will achieve in the resurrection. But we can stretch out to achieve our full potential as Christian persons.

There is a future for us. And that future is one of fulfillment and joy.

PERISH

The Hebrew word translated "perish" in English versions is most often '*ābad*, which means "to perish" or "to be destroyed." In most cases, and perhaps all, physical death rather than eternal punishment is in view. ◗ *Heaven and Hell*

In the NT, "perish" is usually *apollymi*. Occurring ninety-two times in the NT, this word too speaks of destruction and loss. It is often used in contexts that make it clear that the final, ultimate ruin that can be produced by sin is intended.

In two NT passages, *apollymi* is not the Greek word for "perish." In Ac 13:41 the word is *aphanizō*, "to vanish"; i.e., to be so completely destroyed as not to be visible. It occurs only four other times in the NT (Mt 6:16,19,20; Jas 4:14). In Col 2:22 the word (used only here in the NT) is *apochrēsis*, "to use up," thus emphasizing perishability.

PERSECUTION

In most NT references to persecution the Greek word is *diōkō*. It means "to run after or pursue," particularly to pursue with the intention of doing harm—thus, to persecute. Of its forty-four occurrences in the NT, the word is found some thirty times in this sense. On two occasions "persecute" is *thlibō*, "to put pressure on," "to oppress" (1 Th 3:4; Heb 11:37), and in one passage (Mt 24:9) it is a related word, *thlipsis*. In one instance the NIV translates *kakoō* "to do evil or harm to"; i.e., to persecute (Ac 12:1).

What does the Bible teach us about persecution? Jesus warned, "If they persecuted me, they will persecute you also" (Jn 15:20). One who lives as a Christian and actively represents God's point of view to a lost world should not be surprised if he or she is persecuted. The same active antagonism that Jesus experienced may, as Jesus warned, come to the believer (Mt 5:11; Lk 11:49; 21:12; cf. Ac 7:52; 22:4).

How do we respond to persecution? We remember that suffering persecution is part of what it means—in certain situations at least—to live as a Christian (1 Th 3:4; 2 Ti 3:12). Like Paul, "when we are persecuted, we endure it" (1 Co 4:12). We respond by loving and blessing our persecutors and praying for them (Mt 5:44; Ro 12:14). And through it all, we remember that we are surrounded by the love of Jesus. For no "hardship or persecution or famine or nakedness or danger" will ever be able to separate us "from the love of God that is in Christ Jesus our Lord" (Ro 8:35,39).

PERSEVERANCE

The Greek word *hypomenō* means "to patiently endure." In the Bible it usually has an active sense. Perseverance is overcoming difficulties: it is facing pressures and trials that call for a steadfast commitment to doing right and maintaining a godly life.

The NT encourages us to value trials and difficulties, for, taken in the right way, they can enable us to develop perseverance (Ro 5:3–4; Jas 1:3–4).

When we are under intense pressure, it is all too easy to become discouraged. At such times we need to remember the words of Hebrews: "Do not throw away your confidence; it will be richly rewarded. You need to persevere so that when you have done the will of God, you will receive what he has promised" (Heb 10:35–36).

PERSUADE/CONVINCE

The Hebrew language has no single word for this concept. The Greek word *peithō*, "to persuade or convince," is built on a word root that has the basic meaning of trust. To be persuaded is to put faith (in something) or to obey. The "ministry of persuasion" is an attempt to influence others to faith.

The emphasis in contexts where we find "persuade" or "convince" in the English versions may be on the process of persuading. Paul is pictured in Ac 18:4 and 19:8 as teaching and dialoguing in an attempt to bring others to Jesus. But the act of persuasion may not always be positive: some seek to draw God's people away from commitment (Gal 5:8).

The emphasis in other passages where we find these words may be on the outcome of the process. It affirms the faith of the one persuaded in that which is believed (Lk 20:6; 2 Ti 1:5).

In Ac 1:3, the "convincing proofs" (*tekmērion*) refer to "sure signs" and found only here in the NT. Attention is drawn to the intrinsic nature of the attesting miracles as valid evidence of the Resurrection. Luke is emphasizing the objective certainty of the signs, not drawing attention to their subjective impact.

Plērophoreō is found five times in the NT (Lk 1:1; Ro 4:21; 14:5; 2 Ti 4:5,17). This word means "to fill completely" and emphasizes the total conviction that fills the heart of the believer. In two of these verses (Ro 4:21; 14:4), both important passages, the idea is that evidence is considered and conclusions are drawn, conclusions to which the person commits himself or herself.

PETITION ♦ *Prayer*

PHARISEES

In Jesus' day, the Pharisees were the most respected and influential group in Judaism. Having originated about 135 B.C., they were a committed fellowship of men, determined to follow in exact detail everything required in the Mosaic Law.

The Pharisees would be called the theological conservatives of their day. They (1) believed in the resurrection, in angels, and in Satan, (2) looked for the Messiah, and (3) rejected the idea that force should be used to win freedom. Freedom must come through God's action and in his time.

But the Pharisees made a tragic mistake. It began with their scribes (the experts in Bible interpretation) constantly interpreting and reinterpreting the Mosaic Law to show how it might apply to every aspect of contemporary life. To the Pharisee, these interpretations and additions were the oral Torah (law), which they placed beside the written Torah as having equal authority. As the oral tradition focused on behavior, prescribing in detail each acceptable and each forbidden action, the attention of the Pharisees was drawn away from the great themes of the OT. Jesus faced the opposition of these committed and orthodox men, and in many confrontations he pointed up their errors. They had fallen into hypocrisy, as Jesus accused them: "You give a tenth of your spices—mint, dill and cummin. But you have neglected the more important matters of the law—justice, mercy and faithfulness" (Mt 23:23). The image is powerful. It pictures the religious leaders of Israel sitting in their gardens, squinting with great concentration so as not to miss a single tiny leaf of these common herbs but ignoring the cries of the poor outside in the street.

Jesus also attacked the Pharisee's devotion to the oral law. He pointed out how their interpretations actually nullified God's clear intent. He applied the words of Isaiah to them: "These people honor me with their lips, but their hearts are far from me. They worship me in vain; their teachings are but rules taught by men" (Mt 15:8–9).

Tragically, in attempting to establish their own righteousness, the followers of this approach to religion missed Scripture's great revelation of human need and divine forgiveness. Mistakingly thinking the Mosaic Law was a way of salvation, they wandered further and further from faith and further and further from the heart of God. There is no doubt that there were many sincere individuals among the Pharisees. But they were sincerely on the wrong path! Their spirituality and holiness were based on a total misunderstanding of what God requires; truly, they were "blind guides" (Mt 15:14; 23:16,24; cf. 23:17,19,26; Lk 6:39; Jn 9:39,40). Their final state is powerfully portrayed by Jesus in his last confrontation with this group, as reported in Mt 23.

PIT ♦ *Heaven and Hell*

PITY ♦ *Compassion*

PLEASING/PLEASURE

At times Christians are suspicious of pleasure: if one enjoys something, it must be wrong. But the Bible has a different attitude. Surely, human beings sometimes take pleasure in things that are wrong. But God has created a rich and beautiful world and given us the capacity to enjoy it. The Bible's rich vocabulary for pleasure, joy, and delight testify to the fact that God created men and women to experience the pleasure and joys of his world and his presence.

OT 1. The Hebrew words
NT 2. The Greek words
3. Summary

OT — 1. The Hebrew words. A number of Hebrew words are associated with the idea of pleasure or being pleased. Four of the words translated "pleased," "pleasing," and "pleasure" are significant.

Tôb is a very broad word in Hebrew, encompassing a sweeping range of concepts for which English has specific terms. These terms include the following: good, pleasant, glad, right, happy, righteous, and delightful. It is very seldom translated "pleased" or "pleasant." ♦ *Good*

The word śimḥâh means "pleasure" or "gladness." The basic idea is that of being glad or joyful with all of one's being. ♦ *Joy*

In Ecclesiastes, Solomon describes his search for meaning in life apart from God. In one part he describes how he committed himself to pleasures of every kind (Ecc 2:1–11). His pleasures included drinking wine, enjoying sinful delights, accomplishing great projects, amassing wealth, gathering a harem—"the delights of the heart of man" (v. 8).

What was the result? Solomon concludes: "I denied myself nothing my eyes desired; I refused my heart no pleasure. My heart took delight in all my work, and this was the reward for all my labor. Yet when I surveyed all that my hands had done and what I toiled to achieve, everything was meaningless, a chasing after the wind; nothing was gained under the sun (vv. 10–11). Solomon's despairing conclusion testifies to the inability of pleasure alone to give life meaning. Apart from a relationship with God, even life's good things prove to be only "vanity."

Rāṣôn, from the root *rāṣâh*, also means "pleasure." It comes from a verb that means "to be pleased with or favorable to." ♦ Delight ♦ Desire

Ḥāp̄ēṣ and its related words occur over a hundred times in the OT, denoting the feeling of great delight or favor. This is a more emotional family of words than the others, suggesting strong emotional involvement. These words also may be translated "desire" and "delight."

These are also the words often found in more theologically significant passages. God is not one who "takes pleasure in evil" (Ps 5:4). But neither does he take delight or pleasure in sacrifices aside from a repentant heart (Ps 51:16,19).

Ezekiel makes it clear that God is forced by his nature rather than by his desires to punish the wicked. "Do I take any pleasure in the death of the wicked?" God asks. No, God's pleasure comes "when they turn from their ways and live" (Eze 18:23).

These words, among others, communicate the message that human beings, like God, are emotional beings. Our life in this world is enriched by joys and pleasures; and our character, like God's, is revealed by that which fills us with delight.

NT — 2. The Greek words.
A number of Greek words are translated "pleasing" or "pleasure" in the NT.

Hēdonē simply means "pleasure," "something desirable." It was used most often in an ethically questionable or bad sense. It is found only five times in the NT (Lk 8:14; Tit 3:3; Jas 4:1,3; 2 Pe 2:13). In each case, pleasure that appeals to man's sinful nature is in view.

The noun *eudokia* (found 9 times in the NT) indicates one's choice as one's "pleasure," whether the choice was made by God or by a human being (Mt 11:26; Lk 10:21; Eph 1:5,9). The same

meaning of pleasure regarding one's choice expressed in that person's will or purpose is in the verb (*eudokeō*), translated "to be pleased" fifteen times in the NIV (Mt 3:17; 17:5; Mk 1:11; Lk 3:22; 12:32; Ro 15:26,27; 1 Co 1:21; 10:5; Gal 1:15; Col 1:19; Heb 10:6,8,38; 2 Pe 1:17) out of the twenty-one times it occurs in the NT. Thus, a statement that the churches to which Paul ministered were "pleased" to make a contribution to the poor (Ro 15:26–27) indicates not only their state of mind but also their determined choice.

What does it mean when the NT reports that God spoke of Jesus as one with whom he was "well pleased" (Mt 3:17)? It means, among other things, that Jesus was fulfilling the messianic role to which God had called him. In contrast, God was not pleased with the sacrifices and offerings of the OT system (Heb 10:6,8). They could not be established in his purpose as a way to cleanse humanity from sin.

Areskō, found seventeen times in the NT, is the other major Greek word translated "to please," "to be pleasing." In Greek culture it speaks of the pleasure that a person derives from something. In Paul's writings the word is used to describe one's attitude toward life (e.g., Ro 8:8; 15:1–3; 1 Co 7:32–34). A person seeks to please either himself or herself or else, like a servant, chooses to live to please God and others. *Arestos*, "pleasing," is found four times in the NT (Jn 8:29; Ac 6:2; 12:3; 1 Jn 3:22).

Another group of words are used in statements regarding how we can please God and others. The verb *euaresteō* ("to please") is used three times in the NT (Heb 11:5,6; 13:16), the adjective *euarestos* ("pleasing") is used nine times (Ro 12:1,2; 14:18; 2 Co 5:9; Eph 5:10; Php 4:18; Col 3:20; Tit 2:9; Heb 13:21), and the adverb *euarestōs* ("pleasingly") is used once (Heb 12:28).

Some other words are used less frequently in connection with the idea of pleasure. *Philēdonos* ("lover of pleasure") is found only once (2 Ti 3:4). Of the over two hundred times that *thelō* ("to will," "to desire") occurs in the NT, only once is it translated "please" in the NIV (Jn 3:8). *Spatalaō*, used twice in the NT (1 Ti 5:6; Jas 5:5), means "to live luxuriously" and suggests living for pleasure and for self.

3. Summary. The basic outlook of the OT on what we call pleasure is best explored by tracing what it has to say about joy and rejoicing. ♦ *Joy*

When the Bible, especially the NT, discusses pleasure and what pleases, it makes a vital point. You and I may orient our lives to that which gives momentary pleasure to our old nature, but this will never satisfy. Human beings have been created with a nature that cries out for a relationship with God and subjection to his will. Only by commitment to what pleases the Lord can we find the enrichment of our lives that God intends us to have. Only by such a commitment will our joys outlast the fleeting days of life here and provide pleasures forevermore.

POLLUTE/POLLUTION

In the OT, *ḥānēp* and *ḥālāl* express the idea of defilement or pollution. The former Hebrew word is a moral term; it indicates what happens to the land and the people when people turn away from right as God has defined it. The latter is associated with physical uncleanness. ♦ *Clean and Unclean* The NIV translates the stronger term as "to pollute" only twice (Nu 35:33) out of its eleven occurrences in the OT.

There are several Greek words for this concept. Ac 15:20 is the only time that *alisgēma* is used in the NT; it suggests ritual pollution. Out of consideration for their Jewish brothers' sensitivities, Gentile believers are asked to abstain from "food polluted by idols" (cf. 1 Co 8,10). In contrast, Jas 1:27 and Jude 8 use forms of *miainō*, which speaks of moral defilement. The NASB adds Jude 23 to the list of NT verses where English versions read "pollute." The word there is *spiloō* ("to contaminate" or "to stain"), its only other NT occurrence being Jas 3:6.

POLYGAMY ♦ *Marriage*

POOR AND OPPRESSED

In the United States, "poor and oppressed" is a political code phrase. Every society has its poverty and oppression. What must the Christian's attitude toward poverty and the poor be? Are we to seek social or personal solutions? Or is poverty not an issue for believers at all? There certainly is no current consensus on issues like these. For some, the reality of poverty and oppression demands a commitment to change the "system." For others, the problems demand a radical change of heart through conversion, after which renewed men and women will seek the good of their fellows. And for others still, only the return of Jesus to establish God's righteous rule can help. Such people feel that the Christian can, in the meantime, only seek to do good as an individual and abandon a corrupt world system to its expected injustices.

The issue is of course more complex than this. For some, the "oppressor" is "big business" and "corporations." For others, the existence of these institutions is the reason why there is so little poverty in the United States!

It should be clear that we can find few one-for-one correspondences between Israel's theocracy and modern America's capitalistic system. We can hardly look to Scripture to buttress our personal bias with proof texts. But we can look into the Bible and discover principles that provide guidance. Often the principles of the Word of God stand in judgment on the favorite theories of liberal and conservative alike!

OT 1. Hebrew words for "poor" and "poverty"
    2. The relationship between poverty and oppression
    3. Social responsibility for the poor in the theocracy
    4. Personal responsibility for the poor in the theocracy
NT 5. Greek words for "poor" and "poverty"
    6. The poor within the church
    7. Summary

OT — 1. Hebrew words for "poor" and "poverty". There is an extensive vocabulary for the concept of poverty in the OT. Together the words give us insight into the state of the person who lives in any society without material resources.

Dal, appearing nearly fifty times in the OT, is often translated "poor," describing one who is low. As a social term, it refers to the lower class within a society, made up of those who lack the material wealth of the upper classes. An associated word, *dallâh*, means "poorest" and is usually so translated. Except in the often repeated phrase "I am poor and needy," this word seldom indicates a spiritual poverty. Material lack is nearly always indicated. Only two or three passages (2 Sa 3:1; 13:3; Zep 3:12) use *dal* in a sense other than material poverty (Ex 23:3; 30:15; Lev 14:21; 19:15; Jdg 6:15; Ru 3:10; 1 Sa 2:8; Job 5:16; 20:10,19; 31:16; 34:19,28; Ps 41:1; 82:3,4; 113:7; Pr 10:15; 14:31; 19:4,17; 21:13; 22:9,16,22; 28:3,8, 11,15; 29:7,14; Isa 10:2; 11:4; 14:30; 25:4; 26:6; Jer 5:4; 39:10; Am 2:7; 4:1; 5:11; 8:6). *Dallâh* is used five times in this sense (2 Ki 24:14; 25:12; Jer 40:7; 52:15,16) and occurs only three other times (Gen 41:19; SS 7:5; Isa 38:12).

The word *'ānî* emphasizes the pain of the oppressed poor. It portrays a person who is socially powerless and thus unable to resist the socially powerful. It emphasizes also the additional difficulties and suffering that are associated with poverty. The root verb from which it comes, *'ānâh*, is translated "to afflict" or "to oppress." It implies a forced submission that involves great pain.

At times *'ānî* is used in the sense of "humility." "Spiritual distress" is also the meaning in some passages. Some of the passages in which this word has the primary meaning of "financial distress" with accompanying social impotence are Ex 22:25; Lev 19:10; Dt 24:12,14,15; Job 24:9; 29:12; Ps 10:12; 12:5; 14:6; 22:24; 68:10; 72:2; 74:21; Pr 14:21; 22:22; Ecc 6:8; Isa 3:14–15; 58:7; Eze 18:12,17; Zec 7:10. In these passages, *'ānî* may be translated "poor," "needy," or "afflicted." Of special note is Ps 102, which is introduced as

"a prayer of an afflicted man" [*'ānî*] "when he is faint and pours out his complaint before the Lord."

The word *'ebyôn* connotes a person in dire want. This person is needy in a material way and may lack food and clothing (Ps 132:15) and the resources to obtain them. Socially, this person is dependent and must rely on others for fair treatment and for loans (e.g., Dt 15:1–11). Twenty-three of the sixty-one occurrences of this word are found in the Psalms, in which the destitute individual is typically a righteous person who has suffered loss because of wicked enemies. Such a person looks to God as his or her only source of help.

This word, which pictures both want and dependency, refers to the poor and needy. Some of the verses where it is found are the following: Ex 23:6,11; Dt 15:4,7,9; 1 Sa 2:8; Est 9:22; Job 29:16; 37:14; 40:17; 69:33; 107:41; 109:31; 113:7; 132:15; Pr 14:31; Isa 14:30; 25:4; 29:19; Jer 2:34; 5:28; 20:13; Eze 16:49; 18:12; Am 2:6; 4:1; 5:12.

Another root that indicates deep poverty is *rûš*. This word and its cognates describe the all-too-frequent condition of the lower classes. This family of words appears some thirty-two times in the OT (1 Sa 18:23; 2 Sa 12:1,3,4; Ps 82:3; Pr 10:4,15; 13:7,8,18,23; 14:20; 17:5; 18:23; 19:1,7,22; 22:2,7; 24:34; 28:3,6,19,27; 29:13; 31:7; Ecc 4:14; 5:8).

The combined image that these words give of poverty is all too familiar. The poor are in need, often lacking adequate basic necessities. They always need those resources that provide for an improved quality of life. But more than material need is implied by poverty. Poverty assumes a low social status and a terrible vulnerability to the abuses of those with power. Because the poor lack resources, they are defenseless against those in the society who are above them. They are likely to be treated unfairly in the courts (Dt 15:1–4). They are assumed to have little spiritual insight (Jer 5:4). When defrauded by the well-to-do, they have no recourse but to appeal to the Lord. Because of their powerlessness, the poor are the most easily robbed in any society

(Ps 35:10). Poverty strips the individual of rights, respect as a human being, and a place in society.

2. The relationship between poverty and oppression. One of the constant debates in the area of social welfare concerns the question of who is to blame for poverty. The combatants seem to take one of two sides. To some, poverty is the fault of the individual. To others, poverty is the fault of social injustice.

In the OT, especially in Proverbs, there is sometimes strong emphasis on individual responsibility. See, for example, the following sayings: "Lazy hands make a man poor, but diligent hands bring wealth" (Pr 10:4). "Do not love sleep, or you will grow poor; stay awake and you will have food to spare" (20:13). "He who loves pleasure will become poor; whoever loves wine and oil will never be rich" (21:17). "Drunkards and gluttons become poor, and drowsiness clothes them in rags" (23:21; cf. 24:34). These thoughts express common wisdom. A person who is lazy and spends his time and resources on passing pleasures is destined for poverty; and such poverty—as a natural consequence of an individual's choices—is, of course, his own responsibility.

But the Book of Proverbs also recognizes causes of poverty that an individual has no control over. "A poor man's field may produce abundant food," Pr 13:23 observes, "but injustice sweeps it away." And, clearly, it is the injustice of those who oppress the poor and the helpless that the OT portrays as the most common cause of poverty.

Although certain laws were intended to guard the poor (see 3 and 4, below), Israel's failure is, in this regard, reflected both in history and in the OT prophets' pronouncements. Calling for a return to God, Isaiah communicated God's message that his people are to stop their practice of empty ritual and begin to live a life acceptable to the Lord: "Is not this the kind of fasting I have chosen: to loose the chains of injustice and untie the cords of the yoke, to set the oppressed free and break every yoke? Is it not to share your food with the hungry and to provide the poor wanderer with shelter—when you see the naked, to clothe him, and not turn away from your own flesh and blood? (Isa 58:6–7).

But in his review of history Zechariah had to confront those who oppressed the poor. God said, "Administer true justice; show mercy and compassion to one another. Do not oppress the widow or the fatherless, the alien or the poor" (Zec 7:9–10). Zechariah reports that "they refused to pay attention; stubbornly they turned their backs and stopped up their ears. They made their hearts as hard as flint and would not listen to the law or to the words of the prophets that the LORD Almighty had sent" (vv. 11–12).

The OT has an extensive vocabulary regarding oppression and poverty. A few of the more prominent terms should be noted.

Nāgaś speaks of intense pressure, causing intense pain. This was the experience of Israel itself as slaves in Egypt (Ex 3:7).

The noun *'ōšeq* implies a violent abuse of authority to oppress.

Rāṣaṣ pictures as a crushing weight the mistreatment that is brought on by oppression.

Daḵ also refers to those who are crushed, oppressed. Calling on God, Asaph cries, "Do not let the oppressed [*daḵ*] retreat in disgrace; may the poor and needy praise your name" (Ps 74:21).

Lāḥaṣ graphically pictures a squeezing of those whose social status leaves them vulnerable.

The verb *'āšaq* also involves the misuse of power to crush those of lower status. Despite the special heinousness of such behavior and the condemnation of that behavior by many tenets of the law, the widow and the orphan—i.e., the poor and vulnerable—were constantly misused and defrauded in ancient Israel. The writer of Proverbs cries, "He who oppresses the poor shows contempt for their Maker, but whoever is kind to the needy honors God" (Pr 14:31).

Yet the pattern is all too evident in the OT books of history and in the repeated message of the prophets to the oppressors to cease from injustice and to return to justice. ◆ *Justice/Injustice*

In the OT there is a strong linkage between sin entrenched in society and practiced by individuals and the crushing poverty that many suffered. God himself sometimes brought the nation to a state of poverty. This came as a judgment to those generations that would not serve the Lord in times of prosperity. Such judgment brought hunger and thirst, nakedness and dire poverty (Dt 28:48).

3. Social responsibility for the poor in the theocracy. Israel in the OT was a people governed by God in a society structured by him. The social structure of ancient Israel as revealed in the law is of great interest for the number of its interwoven social mechanisms provided to care for the poor and the needy.

The justice system. ▶ *Justice/Injustice* The OT justice system was distributive in that local communities were to deal with disputes within the community. The OT warns against all kinds of favoritism when making decisions in disputes between rich and poor. "Do not pervert justice," the law said. "Do not show partiality to the poor or favoritism to the great, but judge your neighbor fairly" (Lev 19:15). The local setting for the handling of disputes is significant. But so are the frequent admonitions that one is to decide disputes not out of pity or favoritism, but honestly according to the facts and the law (e.g., Ex 23:3,6).

Preservation of capital. This is one of the most significant of OT social mechanisms. Israel was an agrarian society: originally wealth was based on land and what the land could produce. OT law decreed that land was to remain perpetually in the family of the first settlers. "The land must not be sold permanently. . . . Throughout the country that you hold as a possession, you must provide for the redemption of the land" (Lev 25:23–24).

What the OT law did permit was sale of the *use* of the land. The value of a property was to be computed by the projected value of crops between the time of sale and the Year of Jubilee. Every fiftieth year was a Year of Jubilee. In that year, people were not to work the land but to enjoy a year of rest; and in that year everyone was to take possession again of his family heritage—his own land.

In addition, if a person needed funds and sold the use of his land and later prospered or found a rich relative who was willing to help him, that person could reclaim his property by recomputing its projected value to the Year of Jubilee and paying that sum.

The potential significance of this mechanism cannot be overestimated. A person might make bad decisions or squander his wealth, but there was always provision for capital for the next generation, to be reclaimed in the Year of Jubilee. Thus, every fiftieth year, wealth was in a sense redistributed, and the poor were given the means for making a fresh start.

Voluntary servitude. Another option that the poor in Israel had was to sell their personal services to a fellow Israelite. This relationship was carefully governed by OT law (Dt 15:12–18; Lev 25:39–54). Such a sale of services was paid for in an initial purchase price, but it was not a permanent sale of the individual. Rather, at the end of his seventh year a Hebrew servant was to be released. "And when you release him," that law stated, "do not send him away empty-handed. Supply him liberally from your flock, your threshing floor and your winepress" (Dt 15:13–14).

In a sense we can perhaps look at this as an apprentice program. A poor person who could not meet his financial obligations was given a sum of money to pay off his creditors. He bound himself to serve the person who had purchased him. During the seven years of service the servant should have learned skills, both for working and for managing his own finances, so that when he was released, he would be able to make it on his own. At the time of his release his former master supplied him "liberally" with the resources he needed for a fresh start.

Access to necessities. Two social mechanisms were designed to give the poor immediate access to life's necessities.

First, during the seventh Sabbatical year no crops were to be planted. Instead, the poor of the land were to be given access to any crops that had grown up (Ex 23:10–11). In addition, during regular harvests in other years, the landowner was to go through the fields one time only. Everything that had been missed and all that fell to the ground or was left on the vine or tree was to be made available to the poor. They were to be allowed to glean such fields freely (Lev 19:10; 23:22).

Interest-free, forgivable loans. Loans to other Israelites were to be made without charging interest (Lev 25:35–37; Dt 23:19–20) and were to be canceled when the Sabbatical (seventh) year came (Dt 15:1–3). Of course a person was to try to repay a loan he made, but if this was impossible, that debt was not to be permitted to weigh him down forever.

The proper and loving attitude toward a brother is indicated in Dt 15:7–11: "If there is a poor man among your brothers in any of the towns of the land that the LORD your God is giving you, do not be hardhearted or tightfisted toward your poor brother. Rather be openhanded and freely lend him whatever he needs. Be careful not to harbor this wicked thought: 'The seventh year, the year for canceling debts, is near,' so that you do not show ill will toward your needy brother and give him nothing. . . . There will always be poor people in the land. Therefore I command you to be openhanded toward your brothers and toward the poor and needy in your land.

Organized collections. A number of tithes were to be collected from the people of Israel. ▶ **Giving** One such collection, described in Dt 14:28–29, was to be undertaken every three years, and what was collected was to be stored in each locality. This was to supply the Levites and also "the aliens, the fatherless and the widows."

Taken individually, or together, these social mechanisms are extremely striking. They make provision for the immediate needs of individuals, for training of the ineffective, for the preservation of capital, and for the preservation of the respect of the poor as well as of the wealthy. It is fascinating to consider how the principles imbedded in these social mechanisms might find expression in modern society. Certainly they should stimulate a more careful search for social remedies to the problems of the poor and oppressed than many believers are ready to consider.

4. Personal responsibility for the poor in the theocracy. One of the striking features of most of the social mechanisms listed above is that they depended on the goodwill of individuals. The person approached for a loan must be openhanded and not hardhearted or tightfisted. The person who purchased a fellow Israelite as a slave had to be willing to let him go at the appointed time and had to choose to supply him generously. The farmer must not greedily close his fields or go over them even a second time. The person who had taken possession of another's land, and perhaps held it for four decades, had to be willing to give it up when the heirs came to claim it in the Year of Jubilee. Thus, none of the social mechanisms actually worked apart from the good will and the willingness of the wealthy to obey God in these areas.

As a matter of fact, *none* of the mechanisms worked on a society-wide scale in Israel's entire history! God's people remained hardened; and although individuals may have approached the ideal, no generation of Israelites ever achieved it.

This may be one reason why commitment to God is closely associated with concern for the poor and oppressed in Scripture. Only by putting God and his way first would someone exhibit compassion, surrendering material possessions to meet the needs of others.

Job, portrayed by Scripture as a "blameless and upright man," is also shown as a man with a heart for the poor. He testified: "Whoever heard me spoke well of me, and those who saw me commended me, because I rescued the poor who cried for help, and the fatherless who had none to assist him. The man who was dying blessed me; I made the widow's heart sing. I put on righteousness as my clothing; justice was my robe and my turban. I was eyes to the blind and feet to the lame. I was a father to the needy; I took up the case of the stranger. I broke the fangs of the wicked and snatched victims from their teeth. . . . Have I not wept for those in trouble? Has not my soul grieved for the poor?" (Job 29:11–17; 30:25). Job had never denied the desires of the poor or kept bread to himself without sharing. He had clothed the needy and warmed them with wool from his sheep (31:16–21). Clearly, the way in which Job lived revealed both his commitment to God and his compassion for his fellow human beings.

The OT introduces another theme associated with personal responsibility: God himself takes the part of the dispossessed. He can be expected to rise up and judge on behalf of the poor and needy (Ps 82). So too the OT looks forward to a day when God will act directly and decisively: "With righteousness he will judge the needy, with justice he will give decisions for the poor of the earth" (Isa 11:4).

Till then, God must act for the poor through his people. How can we be effective in ministry to the oppressed? We can work toward social structures that will provide opportunity for the poor and meet their needs. And we can, in our personal decisions, reflect the compassionate heart of a God who cares deeply for the widow and fatherless and all those crushed by their position within society.

NT — 5. Greek words for "poor" and "poverty". Two Greek families of words expressed the idea of poorness in the NT world: (1) penēs/penichros and (2) ptōchos and its related words.

Penēs and penichros indicated those who were poor in relation to the well-to-do. These poor were unable to make a living from any property they owned, and so they had to work for a wage, or as apprentices. Most freemen of society fell into this class. The NT uses words from this group only in Lk 21:2 and 2 Co 9:9.

Ptōchos, occurring thirty-four times in the NT, is the word we normally find

used there for "poor." Along with ptōcheuō, "to be poor," and ptōcheia, "poverty," it speaks of those reduced almost to a beggarly situation. These poor were unable to meet their basic needs and so were forced to depend on others or on society. It is striking to realize that during Jesus' years of ministry he went from being a member of the poor (penēs) class, earning his way as a carpenter, to the state of the truly ptōchos, being dependent on the gifts of others for his support (2 Co 8:9; cf. Mt 8:20; Lk 9:58). Similarly, in order to follow him and to live a life of dependency, Christ's disciples left employment (Mt 4:18–22; Mk 1:16–20; Lk 5:1–11,27–29; cf. Mt 10:1–16; Lk 10:1–17). Jesus and his disciples accepted this role in their eagerness to do the work of God's kingdom. They had made the choice freely in an awareness of God the Father's care (Mt 6:25–33).

The focus of this word on a dependent state helps us understand Jesus' blessing for the "poor in spirit" in the Beatitudes. These who have learned to be completely dependent on God will possess the kingdom of heaven (Mt 5:3; cf. Lk 6:20). ▶ *Kingdom*

6. The poor within the church. Regarding their teaching on poverty, the Epistles differ in several striking ways from the OT.

First, the OT links poverty in society with oppression and establishes social mechanisms that people of good will can use to reduce poverty. The NT does not explore the relationship between social oppression and the state of the lower classes. Nor does it suggest social mechanisms by which a society can deal with poverty. This is primarily because Israel was a nation as well as a community of faith. OT law was civil as well as ethical in nature. ▶ *Law* The NT church exists as a community of faith within a variety of societies and cultures. The Christian may influence his or her society, but the church is never envisioned as a state. Thus, no NT writer felt that it was his mission to set up the constitution of an ideal society.

Second, social class differences are assumed in the NT. But these differences are not to be considered within the fellowship of those who follow Jesus. James warns against showing favoritism to the rich (Jas 2:1–7). He reminds us that early Christianity was a movement of the lower classes and that the rich were exploiting the believers. Paul makes a similar point in writing to the Corinthians (1 Co 1:20–30): "Not many of you were wise by human standards; not many were influential; not many were of noble birth" (v. 26). They were instead "the lowly things of this world" (v. 28). Paul insisted that those now clothed with Christ "are all one in Christ Jesus" and not to be categorized as slave or free, male or female (Gal 3:28). It follows, then, that class distinctions are to be rejected in the body of Christ. As Paul says to the Romans, "Do not be proud, but be willing to associate with people of low position. Do not be conceited" (Ro 12:12–13).

Third, the NT definitely focuses on the plight of the poor and on the way in which the church and the individual believer are to respond.

The church, viewed as the larger community of faith in a geographical area, is to respond to the need of Christian communities in other areas. This process was evidently functioning (Ro 15:25–28; 1 Cor 16:1–4; 2 Co 8:1–7; Gal 2:10). When one part of the ancient world suffered famine or persecution, believers in more prosperous areas responded by sending funds to meet the survival needs of their brothers and sisters.

Each believer is also to respond to the immediate needs of individuals whom he or she knows (Jas 2:14–16; 1 Jn 3:16–18). It is seen in the structures that existed in the local community to meet the needs of widows (1 Ti 5:1–16) and the poor (Ac 6:1–7). Moreover, it is seen in the description of those in the early church who were willing to sell their possessions and goods to give "to anyone as he had need" (Ac 2:45).

The philosophy of giving is explored in 2 Co 8–9. In this context, giving is clearly designed to meet human need rather than to support institutions. Even those who are themselves poor can give to the more destitute (8:1–4). Their giving is viewed as a sharing modeled after Christ, who sacrificed himself to meet our needs (8:8–9). The goal of such giving is to meet the basic needs of others, realizing that when our time of need comes, we will have to depend on our brothers as they depend on us now. "Our desire is not that others might be relieved while you are hard pressed, but that there might be equality. At the present time your plenty will supply what they need, so that in turn their plenty will supply what you need" (8:13–14). Because God ultimately is the one who supplies our needs, we can give generously, sure that he will care for us when we have need. Then, "having all that you need, you will abound in every good work" (9:8–11). ◆ *Giving*

Although believers are exhorted to "do good to all people," they are to do so "especially to those who belong to the family of believers" (Gal 6:10). ◆ *Wealth/Riches/Possessions*

7. Summary. Poverty is associated with the vulnerability of the lower classes to exploitation and oppression by those with wealth or social or political power. God's Word shows a deep sensitivity to the poor, who are of special concern to our compassionate Lord.

OT law established a social system for the nation of Israel. In this system there were a number of social mechanisms established to meet the needs of the poor and to help them break out of their condition. But the OT also presents the plight of the poor as an individual ethical issue as well as a societal issue. Wealthy individuals were required to be generous if the social mechanisms of the OT were to function. Tragically, the history of Israel shows that the provisions that God had made for compassion were never widely used by his people. Thus, the prophets cried out against the hardheartedness and greed of the wealthy, who oppressed the poor instead of acting to relieve them in their need.

The NT focuses its attention on a community of faith, the church, which is to exist within a number of different societies. The NT explores how Christians are to respond to human need, particularly the needs of those who are brothers and sisters. The NT does not suggest mechanisms for the reduction of poverty in society at large, but it suggests several structures for dealing with poverty in the local church. It calls for the church in more prosperous parts of the world to respond to the needs of the destitute in other parts of the world. And it calls for a generous sharing of the individual's resources with those in the local community who are in need. This giving is not "charity," but sharing, designed to meet needs temporarily. ♦ *Work/Labor* The NT does not command the distribution of wealth to bring about a leveled society, but the rich are to see their wealth as a gift God has given them to alleviate the needs of brothers and sisters. ♦ *Wealth/Riches/Possessions*

A study of OT and NT teaching on poverty and oppression may not provide clear-cut directives on how we are to respond to these evils in our day; however, the OT does give us several models of structures for justice that our society might adapt. Individual businessmen as well as governments can find bases for innovation in the ideals expressed in the Mosaic Law. We also sense in both Testaments a clear call by God to deep compassion. Churches may need to rethink priorities when they make up their budgets; and individual believers may need to rethink personal priorities. It may well be that our involvement in the needs of others is too often through institutions, too little in deep personal caring and contact with the needy.

POSSESS

In the OT, the word "possess" is usually linked with the land, which was a key part of Israel's promised inheritance in her covenant relationship with God. ♦ *Covenant* ♦ *Inheritance* ♦ *Land*

The most sensitive use of this word in the NT is in connection with demon possession. This is expressed in two synonymous ways: by the use of the verb *daimonizomai* ("to be demon-possessed") or by the verb *echō* ("to have") plus the noun for "demon." According to the NT, demonic activity is one cause of sickness. More terrible is a possession that distorts the individual's personality, driving one to self-destruction or destructive attacks on others (Mt 8:28; 17:14–18; Ac 19:13–16). ♦ *Demons/Evil Spirits*

POSSESSIONS ♦
Wealth/Riches/Possessions

POWER ♦ *Strength/Might/Power*

PRAISE

Praise takes first place in the vocabulary of worship, as God comes first in the life and thoughts of believers. We need to understand praise and to practice it. For God is worthy of our praise. Nothing so deepens our awareness of his power and presence in our lives as to praise him.

OT **1. Hebrew words for praise**
NT **2. Greek words for praise**
　　3. Expressing love to God

OT — 1. Hebrew words for praise. A number of different Hebrew words are used in the OT to express the concept of praise. The common elements in these words focus our attention on the true nature of praise: (1) Praise is addressed to God or his "name." ♦ *Name* God himself, his attributes, or his acts are the content of our thoughts, words, and songs. (2) Praise is linked with the believing community's joy in the person of God. Most praise in the OT is corporate, though an individual certainly could praise God in private. Most praise comes from those who are filled with a sense of joy in who God is and in how deeply he is committed to his people. (3) Praise exalts the Lord. It is in praise that the believer implicitly acknowledges creaturely dependence on God and explicitly acknowledges God's greatness and goodness. Several central Hebrew terms give us these insights.

Hālal—in Piel, Pual, and Hithpael—means "to acclaim," "to boast of," "to glory in." It expresses our deep satisfaction in exalting the wonderful acts and qualities of the one being praised. Derivatives of this word (*hillûl, mahªlāl, tᵉhillâh*) are also translated "praise."

The constant use of the verb in the plural shows that the joy found in recognizing God's greatness is to be shared by the people who know and love him. An example of such praise is seen in Ps 65, which begins: "Praise awaits you, O God, in Zion; to you our vows will be fulfilled. O you who hear prayer, to you all men will come" (vv. 1–2). The psalm continues: "You answer us with awesome deeds of righteousness, O God our Savior, the hope of all the ends of the earth and of the farthest seas, who formed the mountains by your power, having armed yourself with strength, who stilled the roaring of the seas, the roaring of their waves, and the turmoil of the nations. Those living far away fear your wonders; where morning dawns and evening fades you call forth songs of joy" (vv. 5–8). How good it is to publicly exalt the person of God and sense his greatness!

Yādâh is translated "to praise," "to give thanks," and "to confess." With its cognate *tôdâh*, it focuses on our acknowledgment of God's works and character, often in contrast with human failures.

Like all other praise, this too is addressed to God himself. It is significant that the Hebrews expressed thanks to God in praise that included recounting God's actions on their behalf. ♦

Thanks/Thanksgiving Understanding that *yādâh* is essentially praise in expression of acknowledgment of God's goodness, we sense its power in Ps 118: "Shouts of joy and victory resound in the tents of the righteous: 'The LORD's right hand has done mighty things! the LORD's right hand is lifted high; the LORD's right hand has done mighty things!' I will not die but live, and will proclaim what the LORD has done. The LORD has chastened me severely, but he has not given me over to death. Open for me the gates of righteousness; I will enter and give thanks [*yādâh*] to the LORD. This is the gate of the LORD through which the righteous may enter. I will give you thanks [*yādâh*], for you answered me; you have become my salvation" (vv. 15–21).

Zāmar means "to sing praise," "to make music." One of its derivatives, *mizmôr*, is translated "psalm." *Zāmar* focuses on the use of instruments of music in praising God. It is found only in Bible poetry, usually in the Psalms. Again, this praise focuses on who God is and what he has done. Thus David calls to Israel in Ps 9:11, "Sing praises to the LORD, enthroned in Zion; proclaim among the nations what he has done."

The word *šābaḥ*, in Piel and Hithpael, means "to praise or commend." Again, this is praise directed to the Lord, this time rich with notes of adoration. This word also indicates praise for God's mighty and wonderful works for us. "Great is the LORD and most worthy of praise [*hālal*]; his greatness no one can fathom. One generation will commend [*šābaḥ*] your works to another; they will tell of your mighty acts. They will speak of the glorious splendor of your majesty, and I will meditate on your wonderful works. They will tell of the power of your awesome works, and I will proclaim your great deeds. They will celebrate your abundant goodness and joyfully sing of your righteousness" (Ps 145:3–7).

This, indeed, sums up the OT's revelation of praise. It tells of God's people gathered to adore and give glory to God for all he is and all he has done. It tells of God's people gathered to remember his works and to focus on him, stimulating the individual to personal praise. It tells of God's people, their eyes filled with the glory of the Lord, overflowing with joy.

NT — 2. Greek words for praise. The essential nature of praise is established in the OT. No NT passages modify its character. But a variety of words are used to express human awareness of and response to God's greatness.

Aineō (with *ainesis* and *ainos*) is the word most often used in the Septuagint (the Greek translation of the OT) to translate Hebrew words for praise. Its object is God alone in the NT, where it is found nine times (Lk 2:13,20; 19:37; 24:53; Ac 2:47; 3:8–9; Ro 15:11; Rev 19:5). *Ainesis* is found only once (Heb 13:15) and *ainos* twice (Mt 21:16; Lk 18:43).

Epaineō means "to commend," and thus "to praise." In the spirit of the OT, this word for praise involves commending God for himself, his qualities, and his works. This word is also used in commending people. Excitingly, we learn that God will commend believers for faithful service. This word is found six times in the NT (Lk 16:8; Ro 15:11; 1 Co 11:2,17,22). Its related noun, *epainos*, occurs eleven times in the NT (Ro 2:29; 13:3; 1 Co 4:5; 2 Co 8:18; Eph 1:6,12,14; Php 1:11; 4:8; 1 Pe 1:7; 2:14).

Eulogeō means "to bless" or "to speak well of." This word and its cognates— *eulogētos*, "blessed," and *eulogia*, "blessing"—are found frequently in the NT (44, 8, and 16 times respectively). In the NIV and the NASB, *eulogeō* is translated "praise" at Lk 1:64,68; 24:53; 1 Co 14:16; Jas 3:9,10; and by the NIV only in Rev 5:12,13; 7:12. Thus, for example, only one of the places where *eulogētos* is found (Mk 14:61; Lk 1:68; Ro 1:25; 9:5; 2 Co 1:3; 11:31; Eph 1:3; 1 Pe 1:3) has "praise" in either NIV or NASB.

Exomologeomai means "to confess" and is found eleven times in the NT. When such a confession is linked with sin or with public profession, it is translated "praise" (Mt 11:25; Lk 10:21).

Doxazō (62 times in the OT), "to give glory to" or "to glorify," is often translated "to praise," particularly in the NIV (e.g., Gal 1:24). Sometimes the noun *doxa* (162 times in the OT) is used with the verb "to give"; that is, "to give glory." These words are found where either the NIV or the NASB or both read "praise" in Mt 5:16; 9:8; 15:31; Mk 2:12; Lk 4:15; 5:25,26; 7:16; 13:13; 17:15,18; 18:43; 23:47; Jn 5:41,44; 12:43; Ac 11:18; 12:23; Ro 15:7,9; 2 Co 9:13; 1 Pe 1:7; 4:11.

There are other phrases and words translated "to praise" in the NIV or the NASB or both. *Hymneō*, "to sing a hymn" or "to sing praises," is found four times in the NT (Mt 26:30; Mk 14:26; Ac 16:25; Heb 2:12) and *hymnos*, "hymn," twice

(Eph 5:19; Col 3:16). *Psallō*, "to sing psalms," is translated "praise" in Jas 5:13. This word is found three other times in the NT (Ro 15:9; 1 Co 14:15; Eph 5:19). *Megalynō*, "to magnify," is translated "praise" three (Lk 1:46; Ac 10:46) out of the eight times it appears in the NT. The NIV renders a phrase in 2 Pe 2:9 that means "to set forth the virtues of" simply by "praise."

3. Expressing love to God. Praise in both the NT and the OT is essentially the response of the believer to God's self-revelation. God shows us his attributes in his mighty works, in his Word, and especially in Jesus. The believer recognizes the hand of God and acknowledges the person whose reality he has come to know.

But praise is more than acknowledgment. It is also an expression of delight. It is reveling in the God who has shown himself to us. It is expressing the love that wells up within us by speaking to him. We can speak to God privately, with others in our homes, or assembled in congregations. When we speak to him, we join with believers through the ages who have expressed their love for the Lord by praising him for his great and wonderful acts and for his great and wonderful self.

PRAYER

Prayer remains one of the mysteries of our faith. Yet prayer is a simple act and a comfort to believers, who from the beginning have turned with confidence and faith to God.

The mysteries are theoretical: How can prayer "change" the mind of God or modify events? How does prayer relate to divine sovereignty? Scripture hardly notices such questions.

Instead, the Bible emphasizes the simplicity of prayer. Believers are to pray about everything, confident that God hears prayers, cares, and is able to act.

OT   1. **Hebrew words for prayer**
      2. **The foundations of OT prayer**
      3. **Model OT prayers**
NT   4. **Greek words for prayer**

5. The foundations of NT prayer
6. Prayer conditions
7. Summary

OT — 1. Hebrew words for prayer.
The OT is filled with references to prayer. God's people speak to him, call on him, and cry out to him. In addition, a number of words are translated by such expressions as "prayer," "request," "petition," and "intercession." Some of the more prominent words are worth considering.

Pālal is usually translated "to pray." Eighty of the eighty-four uses of this verb are in the Hithpael, the stem most commonly used in verbs indicating prayer. While the root meaning is uncertain, it may emphasize (1) a call to God to assess a need presented and act on it, (2) the dependence and humility of the one praying, or (3) an appeal for a divine decision. The derivative noun *tepillâh* is used over seventy-five times in the OT and is translated "prayer." The word *pālal* is concentrated in narrative books and passages and is seldom used in prophetic address. These words are used of personal and corporate prayer with the sense of requesting intervention (Nu 21:7), of entreaty (1 Sa 2:1), of confession (2 Ch 33:18–19), and of thanksgiving (Ne 11:17).

Nā' is a particle expressing entreaty. It is often translated "I [or we] pray" (e.g., Ge 12:13), though it may also be rendered by the interjection "O" or similar expressions (Ps 118:25). This word is found about four hundred times in the OT.

The word *'ātar* means "to pray or entreat." It stresses the earnestness of the one praying and the intensity with which the request is made. Sometimes this word is associated with sacrifice (cf. 2 Sa 24:25), but sometimes with simple entreaty: "Moses . . . prayed . . . the LORD did" (Ex 8:30–31), which is literally "Moses entreated . . . the LORD was entreated by."

The common verb *šā'al* occurs over 170 times in the OT and means "to ask or inquire"—to ask someone for something. The one asked may be a person or the Lord, and the thing asked for may be some material object, a favor, or information. This word is often used in the OT of "inquiring of the LORD" (that is, asking God for direction and guidance). Many of Israel's difficulties came because the people failed to inquire of the Lord (e.g., Jos 9:14; contra 1 Sa 10:22). The historical passages that deal with David's life portray the shepherd king consistently inquiring of the Lord. It is clear from Isa 30:1–2 that the attitude of dependence suggested by this word is very important to God.

The word *'ānâh* has two distinct sets of meanings. The first relates to prayer. Sometimes the meaning is "to answer, or respond." In the imperative it is translated "Hear me" and is often used in a call or cry to God (e.g., Ps 4:1; 69:16,17). At times the more common word for "to hear, *šāma'*, is also used in addressing God. ♦ *Hear/Listen*

The second set of meanings is to afflict, oppress, or humble. ♦ *Poor and Oppressed* When used to indicate humbling oneself, this word indicates humility before, and submission to, God (e.g., Ezr 8:21).

Pāga' means "to meet" or "to encounter." However, in the Hiphil it often means "to use one's influence for" or "to entreat [God for another person]." Thus, the meaning is one of intercession (e.g., Isa 47:3; 53:12; Jer 27:18).

The verb *hānan* means "to be gracious," "to act favorably." In the Hithpael it is often translated "supplication." It is essentially a cry to one who is able to act to meet the need of the supplicant. It is closely related to showing pity or kindness and thus meeting a need. It is also found in the Qal stem as the plea "Be gracious to me."

Thus, the OT's extensive prayer vocabulary shows us how significant prayer was in the life of believing Israel. The uses of the words as well as their intrinsic meaning reveal a beautiful dependence on God as a person who cares for his people and who acts to help them.

2. The foundations of OT prayer.
Prayer in the OT is an expression of personal relationship. This relationship is initiated by God, who is recognized as

Creator and Redeemer. The core of the relationship—mutual commitment—is expressed in the OT concept of covenant.

♦ Covenant

As Creator, God is recognized as the source of each life as well as of the universe. His limitless power is expressed in the material world and in history itself, which unfolds according to his purposes. As Redeemer, God acted in history to deliver his people in their need. While the Exodus is the prime example of redemption, God continued to act on Israel's behalf. He is a God who saves, and his people can depend on his intervention. God's basic commitment to the descendants of Abraham was given formal expression in the covenant. God had chosen this race and blessed them. When Israel turned to God, they turned to the one who had made himself their God.

The law covenant did not modify the earlier promises but it did spell out the way of life for each individual and generation. Those living in harmony with law were sure of God's favor; they could call on him with confidence. Those falling short could also turn to God with confession. By recommitment to living in God's way, they too could assure themselves of his blessing.

All this—knowing God as Creator, Redeemer, and Covenant-giver—was the basis of the relationship within which God's OT people approached him in prayer. Knowing God also taught the Israelites their own place. Compared to God, the most exalted individual is but a humble supplicant. Matched against God's power, the greatest human force is wholly insignificant. It is appropriate, then, for God's people to depend completely on him. In the final analysis, his favor is all that matters. Every issue of life hinges on his grace alone. The OT believer was dependent on God in everything, just as a little child is completely dependent on his or her parents.

Prayer, then, is the appeal of a child who recognizes his dependence. It is made to an all-powerful person who cares. It is not surprising that OT prayers are personal, often motivated by need,

and beautiful in their childlike simplicity. Moreover, prayer in the OT is a spontaneous expression. God can be approached at any time, in any place. It is significant that the OT presents no prayer liturgy. Prayer is not a matter of ritual religion. Prayer is a living, vital expression of relationship. Thus, true prayer is always a matter of the heart (Jer 29:12–14), while false or meaningless prayer is only a matter of the lips (Isa 29:13; cf. 1:15–17; Am 5:23–24).

3. Model OT prayers. The Psalms are our primary source for model personal prayers and for prayers of corporate worship. Yet some other OT prayers, imbedded in specific historical contexts, are especially helpful in enriching our understanding.

a. Abraham's intercession for Sodom and Gomorrah (Ge 18:16–33)

b. Moses' prayer of intercession when Israel sinned at Sinai by making a golden calf to worship (Ex 32:11–14)

c. Moses' prayer of complaint to God about a rebellious Israel (Nu 14:11–19)

d. Hannah's thanksgiving for an answer to prayer (1 Sa 2:1–10)

e. David's prayer in response to God's promise of a dynasty (2 Sa 7:18–29; 1 Ch 17:16–27)

f. David's prayer for the sick son born to Bathsheba (2 Sa 12:13–23)

g. Solomon's prayer at the dedication of the temple (1 Ki 8:22–53; 2 Ch 6:12–42)

h. Hezekiah's prayer when Jerusalem was threatened by Assyria (2 Ki 19:14–19; 2 Ch 32:20; Isa 37:14–20)

i. Jehoshaphat's prayer at a time of national crisis (2 Ch 20:5–12)

j. Ezra's prayer of national confession (Ezr 9:5–15)

NT — 4. Greek words for prayer. A number of different Greek words are in the NT's vocabulary of prayer. Rather than denoting different kinds of prayer, most of the words can be used in reference to the same prayer to view it from slightly different standpoints.

Proseuchomai, "to pray, or entreat," is used of prayer to God in general. In classical Greek it was the technical term for calling on a deity. The NT transforms the classical stiffness into the warmth of genuine conversation. Such entreaty in the NT is addressed to God or Jesus and typically is both personal and specific. The verb is found eighty-seven times, *proseuchē* ("prayer") thirty-seven times, *euchomai* ("prayer," "vow") seven times, and *euchē* ("prayer," "oath") three times.

Aiteō means "to ask for, or request." The derived noun *aitēma* is "request." The idea is that of expressing a desire or want to other persons or to God. Although these words are often used in the NT of requests to God, they are never used of Jesus' prayers. The NT often emphasizes the fact that God hears and responds to the requests of his people (Mt 6:8; 7:7–11; 18:19; 21:22; Jn 14:13–14; 15:7,16; 16:23; Jas 1:5; 1 Jn 3:22; 5:14). For a discussion of the passages in which this theme is found, see 6, below.

Deomai, "to ask, request, beseech," is used of specific spoken requests to God or man. This verb and its cognate noun, *deēsis*, emphasize the existence of a need. The individual speaking is deeply aware of a personal need, and out of the need comes a cry for specific help. The cry for help may be addressed to Jesus or to the Father and is often uttered in intercession for others (cf. Ac 8:24; Ro 1:10; 2 Co 1:11; Eph 6:18; Php 1:19).

Erōtaō means "to ask," "to ask a question," or "to request." It is found fifty-eight times in the NT. It is often used of questions asked Jesus, but it is also used of intercessory prayer (e.g., 1 Jn 5:16).

Entynchanō, "to intercede," occurs five times in the NT, and *enteuxis*, "intercession," occurs twice. The NT emphasizes both our freedom to approach God and the Spirit's cooperative enablement.

The use of these and other words suggesting approach to God in prayer makes it clear that the view of prayer established in the OT also permeates the NT. As in the OT, prayer is an expression of relationship and must always be understood as an expression of fellowship between God and human beings, made possible by Jesus.

5. The foundations of NT prayer. The elements basic to OT prayer are carried over into the NT, where they are given even richer expression. In the NT, prayer is related to the intimate relationship that the believer sustains with the Father, the Son, and the Holy Spirit.

Prayer and the Father. Jesus condemns a ritualistic, hypocritical approach to prayer and presents true prayer as an intimate expression of relationship with a God who is one's Father (Mt 6:5–8). Jesus' model prayer, known to us as the Lord's Prayer, sums up the beautiful relationship we have with God.

We approach him as we would a father. We acknowledge and praise him as the hallowed one in heaven. We express our joyful submission to his will. We acknowledge our dependence on the Lord for material and spiritual sustenance, and we ask for forgiveness. We acknowledge his right to direct our lives (Mt 6:9–13).

Shortly after Jesus taught his disciples this prayer, he assured them by explaining the freedom from worry that believers have: "Your heavenly Father knows [what you need]" (Mt 6:32). Coming in prayer to a God who is Father and resting in all that this means, we are free to "seek first his kingdom and his righteousness" (v. 33).

Prayer and the Son. Jesus is seen in the NT as the key to that personal relationship with God that is central to prayer. Looking back on Jesus' death and resurrection, we understand what Jesus was saying when he taught his disciples, "I am the way and the truth and the life. No one comes to the Father except through me" (Jn 14:6). Through Jesus, and because of his cross, we can "approach the throne of grace with confidence," sure that we will "receive mercy and find grace to help us in our time of need" (Heb 4:16).

However, a continuing intimate walk with Jesus is vital to prayer. Jesus, using the image of the vine and branches (Jn 15), told the apostles, "If you remain in me and my words remain in you, ask whatever you wish, and it will be given you" (15:7). That intimate relationship with Jesus, enhanced as his words reshape our personalities to fit with his values and character, brings us into so rich a harmony with the Lord that what we wish is what God desires us to ask. Later that same night the apostles were told essentially the same thing: "My Father will give you whatever you ask in my name. . . . Ask and you will receive, and your joy will be complete" (Jn 16:23–24).

Prayer and the Holy Spirit. The Holy Spirit lives within believers. ▶ *Spirit (Holy Spirit)* He has a unique role in this intimate exchange known as prayer. "The Spirit himself intercedes for us with groans that words cannot express" (Ro 8:26), and "the Spirit intercedes for the saints in accordance with God's will" (v. 27). While the Spirit may assist us in prayer without our conscious awareness, our understanding clearly must be involved (1 Co 14:13–15). Jesus told the apostles that the Spirit would take from what belonged to Jesus and make it known (Jn 16:15).

Prayer is a continuous expression of relationship. The NT speaks of prayer as a continuous, constant experience for Christians (Ac 1:14; 1 Th 5:17; 2 Th 1:11; 1 Ti 5:5; cf. 1 Co 7:5). Just as we talk with members of our family naturally and spontaneously, so we converse with God, who also shares our lives.

One of the most striking features of NT prayer as it is portrayed in the Epistles is its intercessory nature. We read again and again of prayer being offered by believers for one another. In this we learn that prayer is an expression of relationship within the body of Christ as well as an expression of relationship with God. Out of the intimacy of shared lives grows a deep concern for others and their needs, and this provides the primary content for the prayers in the Epistles.

6. Prayer conditions. In much popular literature on prayer, "conditions for answered prayer" are laid down. Often the treatment suggests that only if certain obstacles are overcome will prayer be answered. If we do not successfully negotiate the obstacle course, God will not hear us. Too often the reader is given the impression that God stands watching like a tennis judge, ready to disqualify us if we are even slightly out of bounds. The relational nature of prayer is missed, and prayer is recast as a spiritual exercise, with answers depending on our efforts rather than on God's grace and good will.

What are the supposed "conditions," and how are we to understand them? The OT tells us that disobedience (Dt 1:43–45), unconcern (Isa 58:7–9), and injustice (Isa 1:15–17; 59:1–2,4,9; Mic 3:1–4) prevent God from hearing and answering prayer. Those whose lives are marked by such traits clearly do not live in fellowship with God, for the people who are close to him are obedient and loving and seek to do justice. It is in the context of a growing relationship with the Lord that prayer finds its place. Outside of such a relationship, prayer is a meaningless exercise.

The NT offers us encouragement that our requests (*aitēma*) will surely be answered. This encouragement comes as a listing of indicators that reassure us that our relationship with God is vital and real. Those who seek, knock, and ask receive what they request (Mt 7:7–11). Jesus told the apostles that when two agreed regarding a matter, it would be done by God (Mt 18:19). To pray "in Jesus' name" means to identify with his character and purposes (Jn 14:13–14; 15:16; 16:23). The trust that we have in God, which calms our doubts and uncertainties, also testifies to us that God's answer will come. Only those who show contempt for God by questioning his ability or willingness to act in human affairs, and thus violate the relationship, will not be answered when they call (Jas 1:5). As we obey the Lord, we are assured that we live in a relationship with him in which our prayers are heard and answered (1 Jn 3:22). As Scripture and the Holy Spirit testify to us that what we ask is in the framework of God's will, we can have confidence that what we asked for will be granted (1 Jn 5:14–15).

7. Summary. Both OT and NT show that prayer grows out of one's personal relationship with God. It is the spontaneous, heartfelt sharing by needy human beings with God, who is able and willing to help. The Book of Psalms—the prayer book of the OT—best captures the warmth and intimacy of the prayer that grows out of the believer's relationship with his God.

In the NT we are shown that each person of the Trinity is deeply involved in prayer. We come to the Father, through the Son, accompanied by the guidance of the Spirit. Significantly, the NT pictures prayer as a continuous expression of the personal relationship that has been established with God through Jesus; and the content of prayer grows out of our intimate relationship with others in the body of Christ.

While there are no "conditions" that a person must meet before God will hear prayer, the Bible provides indicators that force our attention back to the quality of our personal relationship with God. Those whose lives demonstrate that they have no significant relationship with God (the unjust, the unconcerned, and the disobedient) have no basis on which to expect prayers to be heard. But those who experience a growing relationship with God marked by trust, obedience, love, harmony with other believers, and a growing commitment to the revealed will of God can rest assured. God does hear the prayers of those who live close to him. Our prayers are heard, and they will be answered in his time.

PREACH

Two Greek words are translated "preach." One is *euangelizō*, "to announce good news." It is usually translated "preach the gospel" or "preach the good news" in the NIV and NASB. The other word is *kēryssō*, which means "to proclaim, to announce publicly."

When we study passages that speak of preaching, it is important to notice indications of the content preached. Often in the Gospels the subject is the "good news of the kingdom." ♦ *Kingdom*

The best examples of preaching by the early church are found in sermons recorded in Acts, especially two by Peter (Ac 2:14–41; 3:11–26) and two by Paul (Ac 13:16–43; 17:22–31). The common elements in these sermons reveal basic truths that were preached as believers in the early church set about evangelizing the world: Jesus, the historical person, was crucified and raised in accordance with Scripture. He, the promised Messiah, must be received by faith with repentance. ♦ *Faith* ♦ *Repent*

PRECEPTS

In the NASB the Hebrew word for "precepts" is always *piqqûdîm*, representing responsibilities that are laid on God's people. The NIV at times also uses "precept" to translate *ḥōq* and *mišpāṭ*. ♦ *Justice/Injustice* Divine responsibilities are not burdensome. In fact, "the precepts of the LORD are right, giving joy to the heart" (Ps 19:8).

PREDESTINE

The word "predestination" remains a focus of theological debate, but the Greek term for "to predestine," *proorizō* (which means "to mark out ahead of time" or "to predetermine"), occurs only six times in the NT (Ac 4:28; Ro 8:29,30; 1 Co 2:7; Eph 1:5,11). However, there are other words in Scripture that suggest the same concept—that God has sovereignly determined beforehand that certain things shall come to pass. Such words as *keimai* and *tithēmi* are variously translated "appointed" or "determined" or "destined." In context, these often affirm God's ultimate control of all things.

In the NT, *proorizō* is used with specific focus. That is, just what is predetermined is carefully identified. For example, Ac 4:28 asserts that the events associated with and culminating in Jesus' crucifixion were exactly what God's "power and will had decided beforehand should happen."

Ro 8:29 identifies those who love God as "predestined to be conformed to the likeness of his Son." The next verse adopts the divine viewpoint of timelessness. The aorist sums up what to us is a process, but what to God is so certain that it can be spoken of as a completed whole. We who love God have been chosen, predestined, called, justified, and glorified, with the whole process encapsulated as a single timeless event.

According to 1 Co 2:7, God's plan to redeem human beings through Christ was something "destined for our glory before time began."

In Eph 1:5, Paul affirms that God, out of love for believers, "predestined us to be adopted as his sons through Jesus Christ, in accordance with his pleasure and will." In the same chapter he adds that "in him we were also chosen, having been predestined according to the plan of him who works out everything in conformity with the purpose of his will" (v. 11).

Thus, the NT use of "predestination" focuses on salvation. That whole wonderful process—including specifically Jesus' death, our adoption into God's family, and our transformation into Jesus' own likeness—is in view.

Strikingly, these passages do not relate God's plan and the human will. Other passages make it clear that the choice to reject or respond to Jesus is the responsibility of those who hear the gospel. ♦ *Account/Accountable* In some way, God sovereignly orders history so that the uncoerced choices of human beings harmonize with his plan. Another striking fact is that the verb *proorizō* is nowhere used in Scripture to state that some people are predestined by God to be lost. What is clear is that each individual's choice invariably coincides with God's foreknowledge and his sovereign will.

PRESENCE

In the OT, being in God's or another's presence is indicated by a preposition (*l*) prefixed to the Hebrew word *pānîm* ("face"). The thought is to be "before the face of" the person. At times, entering the Lord's presence has ritual meaning, indicating his appearance at the tabernacle or temple (e.g., Ex 28:30; 34:34). More often the thought is that captured by the psalmists: we live in full view of God and

place ourselves joyfully at his disposal. The presence of the Lord is the place of blessing in the OT, and those who sin must be "thrust from" God's presence (e.g., Jer 7:15; cf. 15:1).

PRIDE ♦ *Arrogance/Pride*

PRIESTHOOD

The priesthood was one of the critical institutions of the OT. Priesthood was vital to the practice of OT faith; it also provides rich insights into the ministry of NT believers. In addition, it is significant for understanding the work of Jesus, who is presented in the NT as our High Priest. Thus, an understanding of the significance of OT and NT priesthood is important if we are to grasp vital Bible teachings.

OT 1. The ministry of OT priests
    2. The ministry of the high priest
    3. Significance of the priesthood
NT 4. The priesthood of all believers
    5. The high priesthood of Jesus
    6. Summary

OT — 1. The ministry of OT priests. The Hebrew word for "priest," *kōhēn,* occurs over seven hundred times in the OT. In the kingdom of Israel the priestly functions were the responsibility of one tribe, that of Levi. Of that tribe only the family of Aaron, the brother of Moses, served the altar of sacrifice. Dt 33:8–10 sums up the ministry of the priests as (1) watching over and guarding the covenant, (2) teaching God's precepts and law, and (3) offering incense and offerings at God's altar.

In performing their ministry, the priests served a dual mediatorial role. On the one hand, they looked toward God on behalf of the people. On the other, they looked toward the people on behalf of God.

The OT priests served under a covenant that called on God's people to be holy (e.g., Lev 19–20; Dt 7:6). Yet the law, in setting out a holy lifestyle, set a standard none could maintain. The priests taught this law in Israel (Lev

10:11; 2 Ch 17:9). Most significantly, when the people or an individual fell short, the priests offered the prescribed sacrifices that testified to God's acceptance of the sinner on the basis of shed blood (Lev 1–4). In teaching the law, the priests represented God to the people. In coming before the Lord at the altar of sacrifice, the priests represented the people to God; and in the many other sacrifices they presented to God the worship of his people. ◆ *Offering and Sacrifice*

2. The ministry of the high priest. By the time of Jesus the high priesthood carried with it considerable religious and hierarchical authority. But in the OT itself the high priest had two religious functions, and these summed up the mediatorial role of the whole priesthood. The high priest had in his vestments the Urim and Thummim, "the means of making decisions for the Israelites" (Ex 28:30). God spoke through these twin objects to provide special guidance and thus to communicate his will. Also, the high priest alone, with the name of each tribe etched on precious stones on his breastpiece, entered the Most Holy Place in the tabernacle. He did this once a year to make the unique sacrifices of the Day of Atonement for the forgiveness of the willful and the unintentional sins of all of God's people (Lev 16). ◆ *Atonement* Thus, the significance of the high priesthood is found in the sacrificial service that the high priest alone could provide.

3. Significance of the priesthood. The faith of Israel focuses on the people's relationship with God. The priesthood, occupying a mediatorial position between God and Israel, testifies to the holiness that God demands for access to him. The ritual system with its sacrifices shows the seriousness of sin and testifies that a life must be given before forgiveness can be obtained. The priesthood as an institution demonstrates the need for a mediator. No common person can make the sacrifice that provides access to God. Only one whom God has chosen and ordained can serve at the altar where sinful man meets a holy God.

NT — 4. The priesthood of all believers. Only four NT passages mention a priesthood of all believers. In one, Christians are called a "chosen people, a royal priesthood, a holy nation" (1 Pe 2:9). These titles of Israel are picked up and applied to the church with the comment that our identity enables us to "declare the praises of him who called [us] out of darkness into his wonderful light." While some take this as mediating Christ to the world, it is more likely that the reference is to worship. We, as a holy priesthood, are to offer "spiritual sacrifices acceptable to God through Jesus Christ" (1 Pe 2:5).

The other three references—all in Revelation—have a similar emphasis. As a kingdom of priests, we "serve his [Jesus'] God and Father" (Rev 1:5; cf. 5:10; 20:6). With direct access to God through Jesus, we who are God's priestly kingdom are freed to worship him continually.

5. The high priesthood of Jesus. Although the language of the priesthood is not carried over into the NT in reference to believers, the high priesthood is very significant in understanding the ministry of Jesus. The Book of Hebrews explores the significance of Jesus' high priesthood.

As a human being able to sympathize with our weaknesses, Jesus the Son of God is the source of eternal salvation for us. Through him we can approach God freely (Heb 4:14–5:10).

As a priest in the Melchizedekian rather than the Levitical tradition (Heb 7), Jesus "is able to save completely" those who come to God, because he lives always to make intercession for us (v. 25).

As a high priest who offered himself as a spotless sacrifice, Jesus does not need to make repeated sacrifices. One sacrifice was sufficient to provide us with eternal access to God (Heb 7:26–8:2).

As a high priest who offered his own blood, Jesus was able to do what the OT priests could not do; namely, "cleanse our consciences from acts that lead to death, so that we may serve the living God" (Heb 9:14). His sacrifice takes away sin forever, releasing us from guilt and making us truly holy (Heb 9:15,26; 10:10,18).

Thus, Jesus' high-priestly ministry fulfills all the OT priestly/sacrificial system implied. He is the Mediator, the only one who can bring us into full and complete relationship with God, for only through his sacrifice of himself could we become holy. ♦ *Holy/Holiness* ♦ *Offering and Sacrifice*

As an outcome of Jesus' ministry, believers are fully taught the law that the priests of the OT were to explain (Heb 8:10). Thus, every mediatorial role given the OT priesthood finds its fulfillment in Jesus.

6. Summary. The OT age required that generations of priests serve as mediators between Israel's holy God and his sinning people. But Jesus, who came as both high priest and atoning sacrifice, accomplished everything of which the OT priesthood speaks. With the sacrifice of himself, Jesus purified all who believe. Forgiven now, we have direct access to God. Christ, as living High Priest, continues to intercede for us, to assure us that we will receive every benefit he died to provide.

When we understand the priesthood, we realize how assured our salvation is. We have been perfected by the one sacrifice of Jesus and forever have access to God through him.

PRIESTS AND LEVITES

In the Exodus, the organization of God's people by tribes was maintained. One tribe—Levi—was set aside for ritual religious service. Within this tribe, priesthood was limited to the family of Aaron, Moses' brother. Other families in the tribe of Levi were assigned various duties linked with the tabernacle worship center (Nu 3). ♦ *Tabernacle and Temple* When the people of Israel entered Palestine, the Levites, instead of being given land, were provided with designated cities in various places in the territory of other tribes. The priests and Levites were to be supported by tithes from their fellow Israelites and were to give themselves to serving God.

The priests' ministry involved making the sacrifices prescribed by the law. ♦ *Offering and Sacrifice* The priests were also to communicate God's law to the nation (Lev 10:11; 2 Ch 17:9). In addition, the priests were charged with serving as judges in difficult disputes (cf. Dt 17:9). They also were involved in maintaining the health of the nation (Lev 13–15).

With the building of temple, the ministry of the Levites shifted. The Levites aided the priests in their functions, cared for temple property, offerings, and animals, and were in charge of music in worship (Nu 1, 3, 8, 16, 18, 31; 1 Ch 23, 26; 2 Ch 8; Ezr 8; Ne 8).

PROCLAIM

A number of different OT and NT words are translated "proclaim" in the NIV and the NASB. Each stresses a public announcement or a call to pay attention. Basic meanings of underlying NT terms include "to announce [something]" (*katangellō*), "to report or announce" (*apangellō*), and "to herald, or preach" (*kēryssō*). ♦ *Preach*

PROMISE

"Promise" is a theologically significant word, especially in Paul's letters. The verb, *epangellomai* ("to promise"), is found fifteen times in the NT; the noun *epangelma* ("promise") is found only two times, and the noun *epangelia* ("promise") is found fifty-three times. In nearly all cases, "promise" refers to the specific content or to the form of God's utterances to human beings. In Greek culture, this term of announcing an intention is sometimes used of human commitments made to the gods, never of divine commitments to humans.

In two passages (Ro 4 and Gal 3), Paul stresses the unique nature of God's relationship with human beings.

Paul points out in Romans that human effort cannot commend a person to God. Instead, God came to Abraham with a statement of his intentions, and this amounted to a promise. Abraham simply responded in faith. "Abraham believed

God, and it was credited to him as righteousness" (Ro 4:3). This exemplifies the principle and nature of God's promises; human beings are to trust God, "who justifies the wicked" (Ro 4:5). This principle of faith-response to God's announced intentions remains the pattern for every relationship with God. Promise is ever received by faith, "so that it may be by grace and may be guaranteed" (4:16).

Paul makes the same point in Gal 3. God's commitment to Abraham and his seed (Christ) stands, unmodified by the law given 430 years later. Our relationship with God is one of grace, depending on promise and not on law. People can respond to God's word of promise in either faith or unbelief (3:15–22).

"Promise," then, confronts us with the nature of God's Word and calls us to respond with faith to what he says to us.

PROPERTY ♦
Wealth/Riches/Possessions

PROPHECY/PROPHET

We often associate the biblical prophet with sweeping visions of the distant future. But to fasten only on this feature of biblical prophecy is to miss much of the message that biblical prophecy has for us today.

OT 1. **The Hebrew terms**
     2. **The role of the prophet in Israel**
     3. **Predictive prophecy**
NT 4. **The Greek terms**
     5. **The role of the prophet in the NT church**
     6. **Predictive prophecy in the NT**
     7. **Conclusions**

OT — 1. The Hebrew terms. The basic word for "prophet" in the OT is *nābî'*, which means "spokesman" or "speaker." Essentially a prophet is a person authorized to speak for another, as Moses (Ex 7:1–2; Nu 12:1–8) and the OT prophets were authorized to speak for God. Two other words to designate OT prophets are *hōzeh* and *rō'eh* (both meaning "seer"). In fact, Gad is called

both *nābî'* and *hōzeh* (2 Sa 24:15). At times, prophets are called messengers (*mal'āk*, also translated "angel") and men of God. The message of the prophet may be called a prophecy (*nebû'âh*), but it may also be called a vision, oracle, burden, or simply "the word of the LORD."

Each of these OT terms invites us to look at an important aspect of OT faith and life and the unique gift of the prophetic office that God gave to his people.

2. The role of the prophet in Israel. Moses is the prime OT prophet. He was called by God to lead Israel from Egypt and as God's spokesman to communicate the law that was to govern Israel's lifestyle. God warned Israeι not to turn to the occult sources consulted by pagan nations (Dt 18:9–13). He promised to send his own spokesmen to Israel, spokesmen who would meet certain tests. Each prophet (1) would be an Israelite (Dt 18:15), (2) would speak in the name of the Lord (vv. 20–22), (3) would be authenticated by predictions that came true (v. 22), and (4) would deliver a message in harmony with written revelation (Dt 13:1–5). Anyone claiming to have a message from God but not meeting these tests was a false prophet and could be safely ignored (Dt 18:22).

There is a critical thought in this passage. God promised to provide through his prophets the supernatural guidance his people would need. The prophetic movement was significant in Israel's history until the end of OT revelation (about 400 B.C.).

Women (Ex 15:20; Jdg 4:4; 2 Ki 22:14; 2 Ch 34:22; Ne 6:14) as well as men might serve as God's spokespersons. But this role, unlike kingship and priesthood, was not hereditary. Instead, God called individuals from every walk of life to bring his message to his people. Nor was the message of the prophets primarily predictive. God's messengers spoke whatever word was needed by the Lord's people at their moment in history. Often the message of the prophets was moral— a call to Israel to return to the holy ways established in God's law. But a prophet might deliver a simple message, even one concerning the location of lost donkeys (1 Sa 9:6–10). Most often the prophets ministered to the spiritual and political leaders of God's people, but they also preached powerfully to the citizenry. Thus, the prophets were a voice offering guidance and calling Israel to live more in line with God's Word.

While Israel seldom heeded the prophetic word, references to "sons of the prophets" may suggest that some prophets attracted followers or trained others to carry on their work.

3. Predictive prophecy. The primary ministry of the OT prophet was to the people of his own time. The predictive gift was used to declare what would happen in the near future and thus to authenticate a prophet's claim to speak in the name of the Lord (e.g., Isa 38:4–8; Jer 28:1–17).

But the prophets whose written works are found in the OT also looked beyond their contemporary situation to deliver messages that unveiled God's yet-future purposes—often those of the distant future. Through Isaiah, God made these sweeping assertions: "I am God, and there is no other; I am God, and there is none like me. I make known the end from the beginning, from ancient times, what is still to come. I say: My purpose will stand, and I will do all that I please" (Isa 46:9–10).

God alone not only knows the future but is all-powerful, able to bring to pass what he announces beforehand. Thus, he says, "What I have said, that will I bring about; what I have planned, that will I do" (Isa 46:11).

These and other passages link predictive prophecy (making known "the end from the beginning") with the divine purpose. We need to note several features of those predictions that outline beforehand what God purposes to bring to pass.

Interpreting predictive prophecy. A number of features make interpretation of predictive prophecy difficult. First, prophecy is often rich in figurative language. The images used may make it difficult to provide a literal interpretation. Second, prophecy is often fragmentary. Some details are given, but the complete situation is not sketched. Thus, relating details to one another without a future-history context may lead to differences in interpretation. Third, prophecy may have multiple references. That is, instead of focusing on a single event, a prophetic passage may focus on a series of events or on several events culminating in an end-time repetition.

These, plus other features of prophecy, such as its sometimes conditional nature, make it difficult to order chronologically the future that the OT unveils. Major elements in God's plan are clear, but the details and timing often escape us.

Examining fulfilled prophecy. Despite the difficulties one may face in interpreting yet-unfulfilled prophecy, we have fulfilled prophecy as a model. The most striking feature of fulfilled prophecy is its concrete, literal nature. Fulfilled prophecy may cover sweeping historical events, as do the prophecies of Daniel. Or it may be detailed, as are many prophecies about Jesus. Hundreds of years in advance, the OT foretold Jesus' birth from David's line (Isa 9:6–7; 11:1), the virgin birth (Isa 7:14) in Bethlehem (Mic 5:2), and the early years in Galilee at Nazareth (Isa 9:1–2; 11:1). Many prophecies focus on Jesus' death. He died with criminals (Isa 53:9,12) but was buried with the rich (Isa 53:9). He was offered vinegar on the cross (Ps 69:21) while soldiers gambled for his clothing (Ps 22:18). His dying words are prerecorded (Ps 22:1; 31:5); and Scripture clearly stated that though his side would be pierced (Zec 12:10), none of his bones would be broken (Ps 34:20).

As we look back on the events of Christ's life and death, we are stunned by the accuracy of these scattered prophecies. But no one looking ahead could have known with certainty how what was foretold would fit together.

The great array of fulfilled Bible prophecies fills us with confidence that God surely will bring all that he has announced to pass. All will be fulfilled—literally. But to understand yet-unfulfilled prophecy we must await history's unfolding.

The future portrayed in unfulfilled prophecy. While details remain uncertain, there are multiple passages that attest the future the OT prophets announced. Briefly, that future includes (1) world-wide tribulation, including a great conflict, and (2) the establishment of a glorious kingdom by God's intervention—a kingdom established on the new earth and marked by righteousness and peace. According to the premillennial view, it also includes a final gathering of Israel to her land at history's end.

We may be uncertain as to how God will order history to accomplish his announced purposes. But these themes are so often repeated in the OT that, on the basis of the model of fulfilled prophecy, we must believe that these things will happen.

NT — 4. The Greek terms. The Greek word *prophētēs* ("prophet") is the only word the NT uses to translate the Hebrew *nābî'*. Related NT words are *prophēteuō* ("to prophesy"), *prophētis* ("prophetess"), and *prophēteia* ("prophetic saying, gift, or activity").

In the NT, the appellation "prophet" is applied to OT prophets, to John the Baptist, to Jesus, and also to Christian prophets in the early church. Our primary difficulty in interpretation focuses on the meaning of "prophet" when applied to persons in the early church. John is clearly in the tradition of the OT's great spokesmen for God, as he warns Israel and calls for moral and spiritual reformation. Jesus served this same function when he announced previously hidden truth about God's purposes. But we are uncertain about the prophets of Acts and the Epistles.

5. The role of the prophet in the NT church. Many hold that prophecy in the early church is parallel to that in the OT. Individuals moved by the Spirit delivered special messages to God's people. Agabus warned Paul what would happen to him when he reached Jerusalem (Ac 21:10–11). The same man, with other prophets, foretold a famine, leading foreign churches to raise funds for believers in Jerusalem (Ac 11:27–30). Prophets

who were church leaders set Paul and Barnabas apart for missionary service (Ac 13:1–3). Clearly these individuals were channels through whom the Holy Spirit spoke, and the validity of their message was recognized by the young Christian community.

Prophets are gifted individuals within the church (1 Co 12), and 1 Co 14:29–39 sets down principles for the exercise of the prophetic gift in church meetings. The nature of the prophetic utterance of 1 Co 14 is disputed. Some believe it is a continuation of the OT prophetic ministry. Others see it as proclamation—as an individual stood to teach some passage of Scripture. It is believed by some that, with the completion of the canon of Scripture, special prophetic messages ceased in the church. The Holy Spirit continues to guide, but not by means of prophets. Yet certainly in the church of the first century the prophet, however his ministry should be understood, did have a significant role (1 Co 12,14; Eph 4:11). Certainly the problem of false prophets (e.g., 2 Pe 2:1; 1 Jn 4:1) testifies to the reliance of early Christians on persons claiming this gift or office.

6. Predictive prophecy in the NT. The Gospels and the Epistles contain portraits of the future. NT predictions about the future bear the general characteristics of OT predictions. They are incomplete, being indefinite concerning times and sequences. Major features of NT predictive prophecy include warnings of a time of tribulation (Mt 24) and promises of Jesus' personal return to earth (1 Th 4), his rule over the earth (Rev 20:1–6), and a new creation (2 Pe 3; Rev 21) after final judgment. There is no essential conflict between NT and OT visions of the future, though how the details fit together is debated by students of prophecy.

7. Conclusions. Prophets, both those of the OT and the NT, were spokesmen for God to their own generation. Today, they minister to us in two ways. First, they call us to that same holy and righteous life to which they called their contemporaries. Second, they portray a fu-

ture determined by God's plans and purposes. We can be sure that history is not careening out of control. History marches toward a divine denouement, an ending that will give all that has happened meaning and purpose.

The question of whether or not there are modern-day prophets is a debatable one. But one thing is sure: God does not leave us without guidance. We have his Word, his Spirit, and his people to show us his way. With or without prophets, God directs us when we commit our lives to him. ♦ *Lead/Guide*

PROSPERITY ♦
Wealth/Riches/Possessions

PROSTITUTION

Normally "prostitution" ("harlotry," NASB) is a translation of *taznût̠*, from the verb *zānâh*, which means "to commit fornication," "to be a prostitute." The word is used in regard to illicit heterosexual intercourse and thus is related to fornication. ♦ *Adultery* The participle of the verb indicates the activity of those who provide sexual services for money (e.g., Ge 34:31; Dt 23:18).

A special type of prostitution is indicated by the word *qādēš*. Its root (*qādaš*) means "holy," "set apart." *Qādēš* referred to a cult or temple prostitute who served in one of the fertility-oriented religions of the Near East. All six OT passages in which this word is used indicate male cult prostitution (Dt 23:17; 1 Ki 14:24; 15:12; 22:46; 2 Ki 23:7; Job 36:14). The presence of female cult prostitution is alluded to in the five OT uses of *qᵉdēšâh* (Ge 38:21–22; Dt 23:17; Hos 4:14).

All such sexual practices were forbidden to God's people. Five of the nine NT references to prostitutes occur in Revelation. The NT adds an especially compelling reason to avoid prostitutes: it is wholly inconsistent and unthinkable that those who are joined to Christ (members of his body) should join themselves to prostitutes (1 Co 6:15–20).

PROVE

The word "prove" is used in a number of senses in the NIV and the NASB. In the NIV, "prove" is often supplied as the translators searched for the best way to express the meaning of a given phrase in the original text (e.g., Jn 2:18; 8:46; Ac 26:20). In Ac 24:13, where Luke speaks of proving the charges against Paul, the text has *paristēmi*, found only here (of its 39 NT occurrences) with the meaning "prove." In Ac 25:7, "prove" is *apodeiknumi* (found 4 times in the NT), meaning "to demonstrate" or "to exhibit." This same idea of demonstration is indicated in two of the sixteen NT occurrences of *synistēmi* (2 Co 7:11; Gal 2:18). The common NASB statement that a person *proved* to be obedient or disobedient (Ac 26:19; Jn 15:8) is a translation of a Greek phrase that includes the common verb *ginomai*, "to be or become."

The most significant notion expressed by "prove" is seen in the NASB rendering of Ro 12:2. The verse speaks of "proving" the will of God. The verb here is *dokimazō*, which suggests putting something to the test in order to approve it or to find it trustworthy. ♦ *Trials*

PROVERB

The meaning of the Hebrew word *māšāl* includes more than the brief capsules of truth we are used to thinking of as proverbs. A *māšāl* can be an extended parable or a vivid illustration, such as was provided in God's punishment of sinning Israel so that she became a *māšāl* ("byword," a public example) to all who saw her degradation. Such vivid presentations of truth are shaped in forms that force the listener or viewer to draw conclusions about his or her own situation. This Hebrew word occurs nearly forty times in the OT (Nu 23:7,18; 24:3,15,20,21,23; Dt 28:37; 1 Sa 10:12; 24:13; 1 Ki 4:32; 9:7; 2 Ch 7:20; Job 13:12; 27:1; 29:1; Ps 44:14; 49:4; 69:11; 78:2; Pr 1:1,6; 10:1; 25:1; 26:7,9; Ecc 12:9; Isa 14:4; Jer 24:9; Eze 12:22,23; 14:8; 17:2; 18:2,3; 20:49; 24:3; Mic 2:4; Hab 2:6. The form *mᵉšōl* occurs only once (Job 17:6). ♦ *Parable*

PROVOKE ♦ *Anger*

PUNISHMENT

We are often confused about the concept of punishment. When and why does God punish? Are believers subject to punishment? What kind of punishment do they suffer? Is punishment of Christians vindictive, or is it intended to bring reform? Or are there other purposes in the punishments about which the Bible speaks? What the Bible teaches about punishment is both reassuring and sobering.

OT 1. Hebrew words for punishment
　　2. The OT idea of punishment
NT 3. Greek words for "punishment"
　　4. Punishment in the NT

OT — 1. Hebrew words for punishment. Several different Hebrew words are translated "punish" and "punishment" in the NIV and the NASB.

Pāqad (verb) and *piquddâh* (noun) are translated in a variety of ways. For example, *pāqad* can be translated "to number," "to reckon," and "to punish." The basic idea in passages in which the word is translated "punish" or "visit" is that of active oversight by a superior. A superior (usually God or a king) inspects the actions of a subordinate and makes a response that powerfully affects the situation or life of the subordinate. Although the subordinate's situation may be improved by the superior's "visitation," in most cases a change for the worse is implied, thus indicating punishment. This root is used about sixty times in the OT in this sense.

Several different Hebrew words speak of specific types of punishment. The word *'ānaš* means "a fine" and is translated "punish" in two of its nine OT occurrences (Pr 17:26; 21:11). *Mûsār* and *yāsar* view punishment as a correction that is intended to educate (as discipline). ♦ *Discipline* *Nāqam* sees punishment as vengeance. ♦ *Vengeance/Revenge*

"Punishment" is often a translation of *'āwōn*. This word means both "iniquity" (or "guilt") and "punishment" (for that iniquity). In OT thought, the act of sin and the punishment of the act are united, for sin inevitably has a tragic impact on the guilty individual or community. A similar concept is expressed where *haṭṭā't*, "sin," is translated "punishment."

2. The OT idea of punishment. The OT views punishment in a personal context. Punishment is the action of someone in a superior and responsible position when that action dramatically affects the situation of a subordinate adversely. God, as the moral judge of the universe, has the right and the responsibility to evaluate and punish humankind. ♦ *Judge/Judging* In the view of the OT, acts that are sinful make the sinner guilty and bring inevitable punishment. No one can sin without a subsequent and necessary change for the worse in his or her situation.

NT — 3. Greek words for "punishment". Several word groups are used to express the idea of punishment.

Dikē ("justice," "punishment"), *ekdikeō* ("to punish," "do justice," "avenge"), and *ekdikēsis* ("vengeance," "punishment") define punishment as a righteous or just response. They may also mean "to avenge." ♦ *Vengeance/Revenge*

Kolazō (verb) and *kolasis* (noun) tend to view punishment from the standpoint of the one being punished, as a painful experience.

The nouns *timōria* and *epitimia* in classic times saw punishment as a vindictive act. In the NT these are closer to the idea of censure or strong rebuke underlined by punishment.

In addition, *paideuō*, "to bring up and direct a child," may also be translated "to punish." ♦ *Discipline*

There are a few instances in which the NT uses words for "punish" in the classical Greek sense of vindictiveness. But in most instances their use reflects the convictions of the OT concerning divine intervention and appropriate action.

4. Punishment in the NT. What do NT passages on punishment teach us?

Eternal punishment is mentioned in two NT passages. One is Mt 25:46, where we find one of the NT's two uses of *kolasis*, and the other is Jude 7, where the Greek word is *dikē*, found three other times in the NT. ◆ *Heaven and Hell* Three other passages are worth consulting, each of which has a different Greek word for the idea of punishment. One of the two NT occurrences of *ekdikos* is in 1 Th 4:6; one of the nine NT occurrences of *ekdikēsis* is found in 2 Th 1:8; and *dikē* is used in 2 Th 1:9.

Mastigoō is used once of God's punishment of his children (Heb 12:6, NIV). The word means "to whip." Whipping was an accepted aspect of the Jewish training of children.

The NT also warns against acts that lead to punishment (Heb 2:2; 10:29). Only by holding fast to Jesus and his word can one escape the punishments that must come because of sin.

The language of punishment is also used with reference to human government, which has been given the task of punishing evildoers (Ro 13:4–5). ◆ *Authorities*

Of particular note is the puzzling passage in 1 John that relates specifically to believers: "Love is made complete among us so that we will have confidence on the day of judgment, because in this world we are like him. There is no fear in love. But perfect love drives out fear, because fear has to do with punishment [*kolasis*]" (1 Jn 4:17–18). Mature love for God dispels fear of punishment.

PURE/IMPURE

Purity and impurity are closely related to associated OT and NT concepts. But in both Testaments, purity has a dimension all its own.

OT 1. Hebrew words and their
       meanings
NT 2. Greek words and their
       meaning

OT — 1. Hebrew words and their meanings. The OT concept of purity has ritual as well as moral aspects. Both aspects are developed and expressed most clearly in the OT teaching on *tāhēr*, "cleanness." ◆ *Clean and Unclean*

Zākak and *zākâh*, along with the adjective *zak* (*zāk*) are the other Hebrew words translated "pure." *Zākâh* is found only in poetry and is used only in a moral sense. *Zāk* (e.g., Ex 30:34) and *zākak* describe unadulterated substances and by extension refer to ways that are not adulterated by sin. These three words are used of moral purity in seventeen of their twenty-three occurrences in the OT (Job 8:6; 9:30; 11:4; 15:14; 16:17; 25:4; 33:9; Ps 51:4; 73:13; 119:9; Pr 16:2; 20:9,11; 21:8; Isa 1:16; La 4:7; Mic 6:11).

The concepts of impurity, cleansing, and purification are also important. ◆ *Clean and Unclean* Bar, from *bārar* ("to purify," "to cleanse or make bright") also may mean "clean" or "pure." The picture is one of brightness undimmed by stain; it is easily extended to the idea of moral purity, untainted by moral fault.

Words for "impure"—especially *niddâh*—speak of such things as menstrual flow, which causes a woman to be ritually unclean. At times, "impure" is used to characterize Israel's grosser sins (e.g., Eze 7:19–20).

NT — 2. Greek words and their meaning. Two families of Greek words are translated "pure" and "impure" in the NIV and the NASB. *Katharismos* is used in the Septuagint to represent cultic or ritual purity, and this general emphasis is retained in this and related words in the NT. ◆ *Clean and Unclean*

The other word group is represented by the adjective *hagnos*, "pure, holy." ◆ *Holy/Holiness* Except at Jn 11:55; Ac 21:24–26; and Ac 24:18, this adjective and its related Greek words are not related to ritual cleanness or dedication. Rather, the idea of purity is clearly one of chastity and moral uprightness.

PURPOSE

God's sovereignty is affirmed in both OT and NT. An important NT aspect of this affirmation is found in the repeated emphasis on that which God has purposed, planned, and decreed.

Two Greek words, *prothesis* and *boulē*, are particularly significant. *Prothesis* means "a plan" or "a resolve," denoting a decision that has been made. The NIV renders this word "purpose" in four of the twelve places where it appears in the NT (Ro 8:28; 9:11; Eph 1:11; 3:11).

Boulē is a strong term, indicating God's fixed intention. That which is his pur-pose stands utterly fixed and cannot be changed by any action of others. Of its twelve occurrences in the NT, seven times *boulē* is used in reference to God's will and purpose (Lk 7:30; Ac 2:23; 4:28; 13:36; 20:27; Eph 1:11; Heb 6:17). When used of human beings, the word has a weaker force, expressing an intention or plan that may or may not be achieved.

Q

QUENCH

Paul warns believers, "Quench not the Spirit" (1 Th 5:19). The Greek word for "quench"in this and other NT passages is *sbennumi* ("to put out or extinguish"). It is used literally of fire (Mt 12:20; 25:8; Mk 9:44,46,48; Heb 11:34) and figurative-ly of extinguishing the "flaming arrows" of Satan (Eph 6:16).

It is difficult to grasp the exact meaning of 1 Th 5:19, as the saying is without specific context. But the imagery itself is helpful. The Spirit's activity in our lives is to be encouraged and not extinguished by ignoring or refusing his promptings.

R

RABBI

"Rabbi" was a title of respect used by ordinary people in NT times when speaking to someone recognized as a teacher or authority in OT law.

RAGE ♦ Anger

RAISE ♦ Resurrection

RANSOM ♦ Redeem/Ransom

REASON

In both Testaments, "reason" is used in the sense of explanation; that is, something happened for a given reason. ♦ Cause But there are also other occasions when the meaning of "reason" is not as clear.

God pleaded with Israel, "Come now, let us reason together" (Isa 1:18). This is not some calm call to sit down and reasonably discuss a matter in dispute. The Hebrew word is yākah, used here in a juridical sense. God through Isaiah had spelled out his charges against an Israelite who had violated the covenant again and again. ♦ Covenant God called the people of Israel to debate the case in court and promised that though they were guilty, if they repented they would be acquitted and cleansed (Isa 1:18–19).

The NT speaks several times of reasoning and reasoning together (as mental or dialogical processes, respectively). The Greek words involved are dialogizomai and logizomai. ♦ Think

REBEL/REBELLION

"Rebellion" is a critical concept in the biblical doctrine of sin. As with other biblical concepts, an understanding of rebellion hinges on core beliefs about the nature of relationships among human beings and between God and man. Key OT terms that give shape to the meaning of rebellion are mārad, mārâh, sārar, and pāša'.

The verb mārad and its cognates are found twenty-six times in the OT. About half of them refer to rebellion against a royal power, and about half refer to rebellion against God. In each case, covenant obligations are implied. Thus mārad indicates the attempt by the vassal to break a covenant relationship. Ancient suzerainty covenants spelled out duties of the superior and of the inferior. Rebellion is the refusal of the inferior to carry out his responsibilities and thus is an attempt to void the relationship.

Rebellion against a human king was sometimes praised (e.g., 2 Ki 18:7,20) and sometimes condemned (e.g., 2 Ki 24:1), depending on God's approval or disapproval of the relationship. But rebellion against God is a great sin, for he was always faithful to his commitments to Israel.

The verb mārâh is found forty-four times in the OT, and the cognate noun is found twenty-three times. Three times the verb is used for rebellion against human beings (Dt 21:18,20; Job 17:2), three times of individuals rebelling against God (1 Ki 13:21,26; Isa 50:5), and the other times of Israel as a people rebelling against God. The rebellion pattern is seen in the events of the Exodus, to which this word often refers. The people were rebellious in attitude, as expressed in their words (e.g., Ex 15:22–24; 16:1–8) and in their actions (e.g., Nu 14). As Isaiah reports in a later day, "Jerusalem staggers, Judah is falling; their words and their deeds are against the Lord, defying [rebelling against] his glorious presence" (3:8).

Sārar has a root meaning of "to be stubborn." The rebellious are hardened, determined not to respond to God.

Pāša' is often translated "transgress" in English versions. It means "to rebel" or "to revolt," indicating a violation of an established relationship by a subordinate. *Pāša'* focuses on those actions that constitute the violation. The sin of rebellion involves a violation of God's laws and covenant requirements, and by it Israel's relationship with God was repeatedly shattered.

At times, "transgress" in the NIV and the NASB is a translation of *'ābar* ("to pass through or over"). Metaphorically, sinning Israel passed outside the boundaries set by the covenant.

Rebellion is one of the most serious concepts associated with sin. It portrays God as ultimate sovereign, who stooped to establish a well-defined relationship with mere human beings. Israel enjoyed many benefits through her unique covenant relationship with God. Yet, though God as the superior in the relationship had been absolutely faithful to his covenant obligations, Israel again and again proved unfaithful. She worshiped other gods, violated the laws and statutes that the Lord established, and stubbornly refused to acknowledge any fault.

How does God react to rebellion? He offers his people two alternatives—turn to him for forgiveness and salvation, or persist in rebellion and be punished. ◆ *Sin* But however terrible the rebellion, there is no possibility that the purposes expressed in God's covenant will be set aside (Isa 46:8–11).

The OT concept of rebellion is carried over into the NT, whether applied to struggles against an established secular authority (Ro 13:2; Mt 10:21) or a spiritual one (Heb 3). Spiritually, rebellion is a violation of the obligations established by the existence of a relationship with God. Thus, rebellion is uniquely a sin of the believing community, though pagan nations can "rebel" against God as the universal sovereign.

What protects the believer today from rebellious attitudes and actions? According to Hebrews, we are to "fix our eyes on Jesus" (Heb 12:2), keep our hearts open to God, and obey his will as revealed in Scripture. ◆ *Voice* The key to responsiveness is a simple but joyful trust in the person of the Lord. As we remain confident of his love and care, we remain open and responsive to him (Heb 3:7–19).

REBUKE ◆ *Convict/Conviction*

RECEIVE

The English verb "to receive" has active and passive aspects. Each is found in a different Greek verb: *lambanō* tended to indicate reaching out to take hold of, and *dechomai* emphasized the passive aspect of receiving.

But *lambanō* in the NT has a wide range of meanings in its over 250 occurrences. It can suggest either active or passive receiving, and so the emphasis must be determined by the context.

In addition, many NT compound words derive from both verbs. These have overlapping meanings, and at times they have specialized meanings.

Also, the NIV translators at times use "receive" to translate the sense of a phrase (e.g., Ro 4:13; 1 Ti 1:16).

Rather than look at every occurrence of this common word with so many shades of meaning, it may be most helpful to consider the uses that have theological significance.

NT 1. Receiving the Word
    2. Receiving Christ
    3. Receiving the Holy Spirit
    4. Receiving God's gifts

NT — 1. Receiving the Word. In the early days of the church, this phrase, using *dechomai*, had a technical theological meaning. It meant to accept by faith the good news about Jesus. The phrase is found seven times in the NT (Lk 8:13; Ac 8:14; 11:1; 17:11; 1 Th 1:6; 2:13; Jas 1:21). *Dechomai* may have a similar meaning when used of accepting the kingdom of God (Mk 10:15) and the gospel (2 Co 11:4).

2. Receiving Christ. The first chapter of John develops this language. John portrays Jesus as the eternal Word, who created this world and came to it in person but was not received by his own (Jn 1:11). The word for "receive" here is *paralambanō*, which means "to welcome and/or offer fellowship." John goes on to state that all who received (*lambanō*) Jesus were given "the right to become children of God" (Jn 1:12). The verse explains the meaning of "receive" in this context by immediately adding the phrase "those who believed in his name." Thus, receiving is equated with believing. Faith is the way in which one lays hold of the gift offered to us in Christ.

3. Receiving the Holy Spirit. The idea of "receiving" (in this usage always *lambanō*) the Holy Spirit is seen several times in Scripture (Jn 20:22; Ac 1:8; 2:38; 8:15,17,19; 10:47; 19:2; Ro 8:15; 2 Co 11:4; Gal 3:2).

It is important to note that Jesus is pictured as the one giving the Spirit (Jn 20:22). Paul argues strongly in Gal 3 that the Spirit was received not through human works but as a gift of God. Christians "received the Spirit" simply because they believed what they heard (v. 2).

Some have taken references in Acts to receiving the Holy Spirit as portraying a separate act of faith, distinct from saving faith. But the Spirit's initial coming was at Pentecost (Ac 1:8; 2:17–18), and later references in Acts to receiving the Spirit involve people who were in a transitional time in God's dealings with believers, especially those who knew only John's message, not the full gospel (Ac 8:15–19; 19:1–7).

Thus, the receiving of the Holy Spirit is firmly within the context of the normal theological use of "receive." It does not stress the human act but God's gift, with

the person receiving simply by believing what is heard.

4. Receiving God's gifts. There are many gifts given by God that believers receive. In Christ we are given—and receive—mercy, grace, honor, glory, reconciliation, and many other rich gifts.

It is important to see receiving as the counterpart of God's act of giving. We do reach out to accept his gifts. But that act of reaching out is no more than believing that we have in our possession what he has promised. ♦ *Belief/Faith*

RECONCILE

The term "reconcile" is found infrequently in the NT. Yet it remains a basic theological term that defines vital aspects of the salvation that God offers us in Christ.

1. **The Greek words**
2. **Reconciliation with God**
3. **Reconciliation between human beings**
4. **The ministry of reconciliation**

1. The Greek words. Various compounds of *allassō* are translated "reconcile." *Allassō* (6 NT occurrences) means "an alteration or change." Words translated "reconcile" or "reconciliation" focus on a change in personal relationships between human beings, or especially between persons and God.

Katalassō is the basic word for "to reconcile" and is found six times in the NT (Ro 5:10; 1 Co 7:11; 2 Co 5:18,19,20). The noun *katallagē* "reconciliation," is found four times (Ro 5:11; 11:15; 2 Co 5:18,19).

Apokatalassō, which stresses the completeness of the restoration effected, occurs four times in the NT (Eph 2:16; Col 1:20,21), and *diallassō* is found only in Mt 5:24.

Synelaunō is found only in Ac 7:26.

2. Reconciliation with God. The Bible pictures sin as an impenetrable barrier to personal relationship. Sin has destroyed our harmony with God, making us hostile toward this one whom we sense must be our judge. Objectively and psychologically we are placed in a position of hostility, at enmity with one whose only desire is to express his love.

Ro 5 calls the death of Jesus for us a demonstration of God's love. By that death, believers are justified (declared legally innocent by God). ♦ *Justify/Justification* But Jesus' death also reconciles, restoring believers to a harmonious relationship with the Lord (5:10–11). Another key NT passage connects the idea of "new creation" with that of reconciliation (2 Co 5:17–19).

Several important truths about reconciliation are expressed in these passages. (1) It is human beings who need reconciliation; their sinful attitude toward God must change. (2) God has acted in Christ to accomplish reconciliation, so that with our sins no longer counted against us, believers no longer have a basis for counting God as an enemy. (3) When we come to believe the gospel, we experience a psychological and spiritual change, as our attitude is brought into harmony with the divine reality. We who once were enemies "rejoice in God through our Lord Jesus Christ" (Ro 5:11).

In pagan religions, human beings might bring offerings designed to win the affection of some wounded deity. Only in Christian faith, however, does God take the initiative to win, at terrible cost, the affection of those who have wounded him by their sins.

3. Reconciliation between human beings. Eph 2:11–21 looks at one special aspect of the work of Jesus at Calvary. Mankind is now a divided race, shattered by hostilities that are precipitated by such distinctions as color, sex, social status, and cultural background. Paul points out that Jew and Gentile, separated by multiplied hostilities and diverse outlooks are now joined "in this one body" (v. 16). In Christ, both are reconciled to God. From being strangers and foreigners, those now united in a common faith have become "fellow citizens" and "members of God's household" (v. 21). All who have been brought into harmony with God are, by that reality, brought into harmony with one another.

Christ provides the basis for loving personal relationships.

The importance of our new unity is seen in the NT's stress on love. ♦ *Love* It is also seen in references to a person-to-person reconciliation in Scripture (e.g., Mt 5:23–24).

4. The ministry of reconciliation. Paul declared that God "has committed to us the message of reconciliation" (2 Co 5:19). The one who wrote that to the Corinthians certainly demonstrated a dedication and determination to communicate the gospel and serve as Christ's ambassador, imploring others on Christ's behalf to be reconciled to God.

Although this ministry no doubt has application to the non-Christian, in context the appeal for a reconciling ministry is directed to believers. Through Jesus, who bore their sin, believers "in him . . . become the righteousness of God" (2 Co 5:21). We experience the fullness of the meaning of our reconciliation to God when our lives are holy and we bear the mark of Jesus' love in all that we do.

REDEEM/RANSOM

Redemption plays a central role in biblical theology. The basic shape of the doctrine is formed in the OT. But the full meaning of all that God has had eternally in mind is unveiled only in the NT. All too often, the wide ranging implications of this biblical concept are missed as we focus on the NT revelation of redemption from sin. The rich texture of the OT reminds us that the God of redemption still stands beside us to meet our every need.

OT 1. The Hebrew words
    2. The OT doctrine of
       redemption
NT 3. The Greek words
    4. The NT doctrine of
       redemption
    5. Conclusions

OT — 1. The Hebrew words. Three different Hebrew words are translated "redeem" or "ransom." Each presents and emphasizes a particular aspect of God's great concern for humanity.

Each word is cast against the background of helplessness. Each finds human beings captured, held captive by the power of forces they cannot overcome. Only by the intervention of a third party can bondage be broken and the person freed.

Pādâh was originally used commercially to indicate a transfer of ownership (e.g., Lev 19:20). The transfer came through payment or some equivalent transaction.

The religious significance of the word was established in the Exodus. The people of Israel were trapped, slaves in Egypt. God acted to bring about their rescue. He intervened with great judgments and finally brought death to the Egyptians when they would not let his people go (Ex 4:23; 12:29). Dt 15:15 looks back on this drama of release and says, "Remember that you were slaves in Egypt and the LORD your God redeemed you."

God's intervention on behalf of Israel is a basis for his claim to this people. He created them. He called Abraham. And he redeemed Israel from servitude. His claim to Israel's allegiance was established in the history of redemption.

Claims of divine ownership are also woven into the Mosaic Law. The firstborn of the people and of every animal belonged to the Lord. Human beings and ritually unclean animals might be purchased back (redeemed) by parents and owners. But the firstborn of each clean animal had to be sacrificed (Ex 13:11–16; 34:19–20; Nu 18:8–32). Thus, each new birth in Israel reminded God's people that they were a people who had been delivered by God and were his unique possession.

The consciousness of redemption is often expressed in Psalms. In present difficulties, the believing nation or individual could look back and find in the Lord a foundation for confidence in history: "Remember his power—the day he redeemed them from the oppressor, the day he displayed his miraculous signs in Egypt" (78:42–43).

The prophets also used the language of redemption as they looked ahead to a day when God would again act to deliver his people from the national bondage that Israel's sin had brought upon them (e.g., Isa 35:10; Jer 15:21; Mic 6:4).

It is striking to note that in all the OT's exploration of the meaning of *pādâh*, only in Ps 130:7–8 is this concept associated with redemption from sin. The proclamation that God acts to deliver believers from sin is found in the NT. The OT believer had the assurance that God had established ownership of this one people through redemption and would continue to act to deliver them as they trusted in him.

The verb *gā'al* means "to play the part of a kinsman," that is, to act on the behalf of a relative in trouble or danger. The verb and its cognate (*ge'ullâh*, "redemption") appear 118 times in the OT. The background to *gā'al* is similar to that of *pādâh*. In each case, persons or objects are in the power of another, and the one whose person or possessions are held is unable to win release. Then a third party appears, and this person is able to effect release.

Gā'al places the emphasis on the relationship between redeemer and redeemed. Because of his close kinship, the redeemer had the privilege and the duty of coming to the relative's aid.

The significance of *gā'al* is illustrated in the OT in several ways. (1) If an Israelite was forced by need to sell some of his property, it could be redeemed for him by a wealthier kinsman (Lev 25:47–55). (2) A person might, by payment of a redemption price, redeem his own property that he had dedicated to the Lord (Lev 27). (3) A near kinsman was to serve as the judicial executioner of the murderer of his relative (Nu 35:12–31). There could be no redemption price paid for the life of a murderer, though money reparation could be set for lesser acts of violence. In carrying out the death sentence that OT law required, there was no initiation of a blood feud, for the killing was judicial and the executioner was held guiltless. (4) The language of redemption often placed God in the role of Israel's near kinsman, who acted to deliver his people from danger. Redemption from Egypt was not only an act of purchase but also the action of a kinsman moved by love. God told the Israelites: "I have remembered my covenant [with Abraham]. . . . I am the LORD and I will bring you out from under the yoke of the Egyptians. I will free you from being slaves to them and will redeem [gā'al] you with an outstretched arm" (Ex 6:5–6). No wonder the psalmists too used this word to celebrate the Lord—"[our] Rock and [our] Redeemer" (Ps 19:14).

Kōper, translated "ransom," comes from kāpar, "to make atonement." It thus means "to atone by making a substitutionary payment." It is used in reference to the money paid to the temple treasury for each Israelite (Ex 30:11–16). The Egyptians who lost their firstborn and those who died in the Red Sea so that Israel might break free of their bondage was the ransom that God gave for Israel's freedom (Isa 43:3). The OT is clear, however, that there was no exchange (kōper) acceptable when murder had been committed (Nu 35:31). This root, unlike the other two, is closely associated with atonement. ◆ **Atonement** However, spiritual redemption should not be read into kōper in the OT.

2. The OT doctrine of redemption. Redemption in the OT involves someone who is in bondage or danger. All of the words for redemption find their source in the common things of daily life, but they all take on great significance as the common meanings are applied to explain God's actions on Israel's behalf.

So interpreted, God's redemption of Israel from Egypt was an intervention that transferred ownership of Israel to the Lord. When Israel became God's by redemption as well as by creation, they could trust him to deliver them in the future. Thus, God's redemption is seen as an affirmation of close kinship with his covenant people. He acted because they were his family. Love and duty combined as God stepped into history to meet the needs of a people who were helpless without him.

Believers today can also count on God. As the Redeemer, he has made them his own, and he will act to deliver.

NT — 3. The Greek words. The conception of redemption is rooted not in Greek culture or in Roman law but in OT revelation. Redemption is a family matter, an expression of the deepest possible relationship. It is never a stranger who has the right to come to the aid of a person who is owned by another or burdened with an unpayable debt. Only the near kinsman, with the resources to rescue, is able to act. Thus, the Greek terms in the NT—lytroō and exagorazō—must be understood within the basic framework provided by the OT.

The verb lytroō means "to redeem or ransom." The verb and other words in the family focus attention on both a release won and the means by which that release is accomplished.

Lytroō is found only three times in the NT (Lk 24:21; Tit 2:14; 1 Pe 1:18), as is lytrōsis, "redemption" (Lk 1:68; 2:38; Heb 9:12). Lytron, "ransom," is found only twice (Mt 20:28; Mk 10:45) and lytrōtēs, "redeemer," or "deliverer," only once (Ac 7:35). These references establish the basic thrust of the NT's teaching on redemption, a teaching reinforced by many parallel concepts, particularly that of salvation. ◆ **Salvation/Save**

These passages make it clear that Jesus' life is the price of redemption (Mt 20:28; Mk 10:45). The redemption price, the "precious blood of Christ, a lamb without blemish or defect," was paid to release people from "the empty way of life" received from the forefathers (1 Pe 1:18–19). Redemption is a release "from all wickedness" (Tit 2:14). The redemption that Jesus accomplished by his blood is an eternal redemption (Heb 9:12), intended to so cleanse us that "we may serve the living God" (v. 14; cf. Tit 2:14). Thus, redemption in the NT focuses on the condition of the believer, who had been locked in a wicked and empty way of life, and on the price of redemption, the blood of Christ. It also focuses on the result of redemption, a commitment by the believer to serve God.

This last aspect of redemption has a parallel in Roman law. A person who had been captured in war and released through the payment of a ransom by another Roman citizen was obligated to his ransomer until the price had been repaid. You and I, ransomed at incalculable cost, are forever in the debt of God and must rightfully surrender ourselves to him (e.g., Ro 6:12–14). But it is in bondage to him that our true freedom lies.

The verb *exagorazō* is found four times in the NT (Gal 3:13; 4:5; Eph 5:16; Col 4:5). The root word, *agorazō*, simply means "to purchase." In the five NT references to God's purchase of believers, *agorazō* is an allusion to the slave market of NT times. ◆ *Serve/Servant/Slave Exagorazō* is an intensive word that could be used to portray the sense of redemption of a slave. In Gal 3 and 4, the believer is pictured as having been redeemed from law's curse and given full rights as a child. ◆ *Adopt/Adoption*

When believers are called on to be "redeeming the time" (KJV—Eph 5:16; Col 4:5), they are to take every opportunity provided to do God's will.

4. The NT doctrine of redemption. The NT applies the concept developed in the OT to the issue of personal salvation. Each person in our world is in the grip of sin. Sin's bondage can be broken only through Christ's blood. Redeemed, the believer is given a place in the family of God and is called to live a life that reflects his new standing.

5. Conclusions. Only the Scriptures, of all the world's great religious writings, so portray the relation between human beings and God in terms of redemption. Redemption reveals a helpless humanity; and redemption affirms a God whose love drives him to take the part of the near kinsman. At his own expense, he paid the price needed to win our release.

REIGN

The Hebrew and Greek words for "reign" mean "to exercise kingly power," or "to have authority as a sovereign." This authority was often absolute in ancient times. ◆ *King* ◆ *Kingdom*

The NT extends the concept to speak of the reign of death (Ro 5:14), of sin (Ro

6:12), and of grace and righteousness (Ro 5:17,21). Because of Jesus, sin has no sovereign power in our lives, but grace and goodness rule there. ◆ *Grace* ◆ *Sin*

REJECT/REJECTION

Two strong words express the OT concept of rejection: *zānah* and *mā'as*. *Zānah* means "to reject" or "to cast off." Its root indicates intense disapproval or dislike of the object rejected. OT psalms show that even believers may, in difficult circumstances, feel that God has turned against them (e.g., Ps 43:1–2; 60:1). But in the believer such feelings stimulate repentance or praise and a deepening trust in God (Ps 43:3–5).

Mā'as means "to reject" or "to despise." It focuses on actions that express a person's attitude. The wicked will reject the knowledge of God (Hos 4:6), turn from his law and his Word (1 Sa 15:23; Isa 5:24; 30:12; Jer 6:19; Am 2:4), and bridle under his discipline (Pr 3:11). But those who reject the Lord will also be rejected by him (Hos 4:6; 9:17). It is important to note that while individuals or particular generations may be rejected by God, the promise to Abraham's family line is never abrogated. By a message from the Lord, Jeremiah comforted a generation that experienced divine rejection: " 'Only if the heavens above can be measured and the foundations of the earth below searched out will I reject all the descendants of Israel because of all they have done,' declares the LORD" (Jer 31:37; cf. 33:25–26).

Three different Greek words express the idea of rejection: *apodokimazō, apōtheō,* and *atheteō.*

Apodokimazō indicates putting something or someone to the test and rejecting that object or person as unfit or not genuine. This word is used in nearly every instance of the Jewish people's examination of Jesus and their rejection of him as the Messiah, the Son of God. *Apodokimazō* is found nine times in the NT (Mt 21:42; Mk 8:31; 12:10; Lk 9:22;

17:25; 20:17; Heb 12:17; 1 Pe 2:4,7). A cognate, *adokimos* ("disapproved"), occurs eight times in the NT and is translated "rejected" by the NIV in 2 Ti 3:8.

Apōtheō means "to thrust away" and thus "to reject." It occurs six times in the NT (Ac 7:27,39; 13:46; Ro 11:1,2; 1 Ti 1:19).

Atheteō is the most common of the words translated "to reject." It can also mean "to despise" and thus "to reject," with the idea of setting aside or ignoring something previously established. This word is found sixteen times in the NT (Mk 6:26; 7:9; Lk 7:30; 10:16; Jn 12:48; 1 Co 1:19; Gal 2:21; 3:15; 1 Th 4:8; 1 Ti 5:12; Heb 10:28; Jude 8).

An important parallel concept, that of abandonment, is covered in another article. ◆ *Abandon/Abandoned*

REJOICE ◆ *Joy*

RELIGION

The words "religion" and "religious" seldom appear in Scripture. This is at least partially because biblical faith is best understood as a relationship and thus stands in distinction from all the religions of the world.

However, where the word "religion" is found in the NT, several different Greek words are used.

In Ac 25:19, Judaism is called by an outsider "their own *deisidaimonia*." The word occurs only here in the NT and may simply mean "religion," or it may carry the connotation of a superstition. A related word, *deisidaimonesteros* ("religious"), is found in Ac 17:22 (its only NT occurrence), where Paul began his sermon in Athens by calling attention to evidence that the Greeks were "very religious."

The more common words in the NT are *thrēskos* ("religious") and *thrēskia* ("religion"). They occur five times in the NT (Ac 26:5; Col 2:18 ["worship"]; Jas 1:26,27). They focus attention on the outward rituals and rites of ceremonial religions.

The third word translated "religion" is *eusebia*, which emphasizes piety in every kind of relationship. It is usually translated "godly" in the NIV and NASB. ◆ *Godly/Godliness*

The NT's view of what some call "religion" is well summed up in two of Paul's letters. In contrast to the trappings of religions, "the reality . . . is found in Christ" (Col 2:17). Moreover, "The kingdom of God is not a matter of eating and drinking, but of righteousness, peace and joy in the Holy Spirit, because anyone who serves Christ in this way is pleasing to God and approved by men" (Ro 14:17–18).

REMEMBER/MEMORY

The past is rightly expected to shape our present. The Scripture suggests little about how human memory works. But it says much about what is to be remembered.

OT 1. The Hebrew words
    2. What we are to remember
    3. Calling on God to remember
    4. Memorials
NT 5. The Greek words
    6. Remembrance in the NT

OT — 1. The Hebrew words

The Hebrew words translated "memory," "remember," "remembrance," etc., are related to *zākar*. *Zākar* has a wide range of meanings, but most of these meanings focus on mental acts and can be grouped into three categories: (1) the mental acts themselves, such as remembering, meditating on, paying attention to, and thinking about; (2) the mental acts and the behavior appropriate to these acts (thus to "remember the covenant" is to act in accordance with covenant stipulations); and (3) speaking to invoke memory or to recite from memory. The first two meanings are the ones that we find in the OT.

2. What we are to remember. The OT call to remember is more than an invitation to think about the past. Instead, it is a call to identify oneself with the past and to let present life be shaped by it. Israel was to remember the Lord and his commands (Nu 15:39–40). Such remembering implies a perspective so shaped by God's words that obedience results. Israel was also to remember their state of slavery in Egypt (Dt 5:15; 15:15; 16:12; 24:18,22) and all that God did to deliver them (Dt 7:18; 8:2; 24:9). Again, remembering suggests identification in such a way that one enters into the historic reality and recognizes oneself as a redeemed person. Failure to remember implies failure to take one's place among God's people and can be equated with disobedience (Eze 16:43–63). ◆ *Hear/Listen*

Thus, the OT stresses that memory should focus on who God is and what he has done for Israel. Memory focuses on the ways that the Lord has marked out and implies obedience to God's will. To fail to remember means abandoning the Lord and his righteous path.

3. Calling on God to remember. The OT contains appeals to God to remember the individual or nation (Ne 13:14). God is asked to remember his "great mercy" (Ps 25:6) and how the enemy has mocked him (Ps 74:18). There is no suggestion that the Lord might have forgotten. Such appeals call on God to act. So when the OT says that God "remembered his covenant" (e.g., Ex 2:24), it means that he acted in covenant faithfulness. To say that God will "now remember their wickedness" (Jer 14:10) is to say that he will now punish them.

4. Memorials. The idea that memory is linked to personal identification with God's historic acts or words is reflected in the Hebrew word *zikkārôn* ("a reminder" or "a remembrance"). It is used of objects or actions designed to help Israel identify with a particular reality or truth. Ex 12:14 calls the annual festival of Passover a "memorial day" (RSV). The ritual of that day reenacted God's great deliverance from Egypt and helped each individual sense his or her identity as one of the redeemed. The pile of stones set beside the river Jordan (Jos 4:7) was to help later generations remember that God acted to part the river for his people.

Such memorial events or objects, which enabled the people to identify with God's historic acts or words, played

a significant role in faith development in Israel. ◆ *Teaching/Learning*

NT — 5. The Greek words. Greek words translated "remember," "recall," and "remind" include *mimnēskō* ("to recall, remember"), *mnēmoneuō* ("to remember," "to mention"), *anamimnēskō* ("to remind"), and *hypomimnēskō* ("to remind"). There are shades of difference, but in general these words should be considered synonyms.

The range of meanings suggested by this word group includes secular and religious meanings from the NT era. In common speech "to remember" may be to recall (Lk 22:61). "To remember" may, as in the OT, mean to help (e.g., Lk 1:54; Gal 2:10). To be mindful of the meaning of some truth or event may indicate that present choices are being shaped by it (e.g., 1 Co 4:17). In addition, there is the act of remembering in prayer (1 Th 1:3; Phm 4) and teaching by reminding (2 Pe 1:12–15).

Most of our NT references are easily understood within the framework of these OT and NT uses. For instance, the covenant promise of full forgiveness reads, "For I will forgive their wickedness and will remember their sins no more" (Heb 8:12). According to the biblical thought, this is best understood as God's promise that forgiven sins are forever beyond punishment (see 1, above). NT admonitions to "remember" are usually calls to consider a truth or event and to so identify with it that our choices are shaped by it.

6. Remembrance in the NT. One of the most significant and debated teachings in the NT relates to the Lord's Supper. When Jesus instituted this sacrament, he said, "Do this in remembrance of me" (Lk 22:19; 1 Co 11:24–25). Catholic and Protestant theologians alike debate the meaning of this "remembrance," which is to be repeated until Jesus comes again. The simplest and perhaps the best way to understand it is as an analogy to the OT *zikkārôn*. The Lord's Supper is a memorial, inviting us to identify ourselves with Jesus' crucifixion. It is repeated, for each new generation of believers must begin their spiritual life in and through the blood shed on Calvary. As a testimony to faith and a call to focus our hope in Jesus, the communion service affirms our identity with Jesus in his death and in his restored life.

REMNANT/SURVIVORS

Several words in the Bible are translated "remnant." They are also sometimes translated "the rest," "remainder," "the survivors," and "those who escaped." Although such words are often applied to mundane objects, such as food (the leftovers), they also have an important theological use.

OT   1. The Hebrew words
     2. The doctrine of the remnant
NT   3. The remnant in the NT

OT — 1. The Hebrew words. Several Hebrew words are translated "rest," "remainder," or "remnant."

The most significant of these words is *šā'ar* (over 130 times in the OT). It means "to remain or survive" and implies some process, catastrophe, or judgment that eliminates many or most of a group. Its related words for "remnant" are *s^e'ār* (26 OT occurrences) and *s^e'ērît* (66 OT occurrences).

The word *šā'ar* is most significant as a technical term used by the prophets. Many prophetic passages that look to the distant future mention a "remnant" made up of those in Israel who will experience conversion and receive the promised covenant blessings. In contemporary settings the remnant is that portion of Israel that remains faithful to God or that God in his love enables to survive a judgment on the nation.

The word *śārîd*, which occurs only about thirty times in the OT, means "those who escape or remain." Joel 2:32 reflects the prophetic doctrine. It looks forward to a "day of the LORD " when "everyone who calls on the name of the LORD will be saved; for on Mount Zion and in Jerusalem there will be deliverance, as the LORD has said, among the survivors [*śārîd*] whom the LORD calls."

P^elêytâh and *pālît* are feminine and masculine nouns respectively, meaning "that which has escaped or has been delivered." The root emphasizes escape, but the term is used in the same ways as other words signifying a remnant. The concept of the remnant applied to a contemporary situation is seen in Eze 6:8–9: "But I will spare some, for some of you will escape the sword when you are scattered among the lands and nations. Then in the nations where they have been carried captive, those who escape will remember me."

Yātar means "to remain," "to leave," "to escape." The verb and cognate noun, *yeter*, which is usually translated "the rest of" or "the remnant," occur over two hundred times in the OT. The concept behind these words is that the remainder or remnant is a (usually a smaller) part of a quantity of persons or objects that has been divided. This too is used in prophetically significant passages (e.g., Zep 2:9; Zec 14:2).

2. The doctrine of the remnant. The theme of "a remnant" runs through the OT. This is an important theme, for it affirms that however great Israel's apostasy and God's judgment, a core of the faithful will still exist (e.g., 1 Ki 19:18; Mal 3:16–18). It is prophetically important, for it pictures the fulfillment of the divine purpose in only a part of the people of Israel. Apostasy, even by the majority of the Jews, could not nullify the divine promise. Over and over the prophets pictured contemporary or coming judgments in which the majority died, and only a believing minority remained. Thus, the doctrine of the remnant underlines the OT teaching on faith. It is not mere physical birth that brought a personal relationship with God. Those who were born within the covenant still needed to respond personally to God and to demonstrate an Abraham-like trust by their response to God's Word.
♦ *Belief/Faith*

NT — 3. The remnant in the NT. Paul picks up the doctrine of the remnant in Romans and uses it in two ways. In Ro 9, he quotes Isaiah to show that Israel's general rejection of Jesus does not indicate God's rejection of his ancient people. God has always worked with a remnant who believe; never in history have the physical descendants of Abraham been identifiable as "Abraham's offspring" (Ro 9:8).

In Ro 11, Paul also uses the doctrine of the remnant to affirm ultimate fulfillment of God's promises: "God's gifts and his call are irrevocable" (v. 29). And so the people's future will still be realized, and "all Israel will be saved, as it is written" (v. 26).

REPENT

Is repentance, as someone has said, "being sorry enough about your sins to stop"? What is true repentance, and how can we know if we have repented?

OT 1. The OT concept of repentance
NT 2. The NT concept of repentance
3. Conclusions

OT — 1. The OT concept of repentance. Two OT words have been translated "repent" in the NIV and NASB. The first, *nāham*, means "to be sorry," "to regret," or "to have pity, compassion." The KJV translated the Niphal stem of this verb by "repent" almost forty times. It is likely that our association of repentance with emotion—with being sorry—is closely linked to this translation. *Nāham* is translated "repent" only once in the NIV (Job 42:6) and only three times in the NASB (Nu 23:19; Job 42:6; Jer 26:3).

The word that expresses the biblical concept of repentance is *šûb*. This verb is found over a thousand times in the OT, with a wide range of meanings. However, in the 164 uses of this word in a covenant context, it indicates turning from evil to God, from evil ways to God's ways, or from God to idols. *Šûb* is that commitment to a faith and way of life that involves turning from a previous way, and this is to "repent."

There is no doubt that at times a change of commitments is preceded by agonizing conviction of sin. But repentance itself, as it is illustrated in the OT, is

essentially the "about-face" of a new commitment.

NT — 2. The NT concept of repentance. The Greek term meaning "to repent" is *metanoeō*, and "repentance" is the NIV and NASB translation of *metanoia*. A number of other words, such as "conversion," are also associated with the new direction for life that repentance implies. But it is *metanoia* that is translated "repentance" in the NIV and the NASB.

In the NT, *metanoeō* and *metanoia* are used in the same way as *šûb* in the OT—to emphasize a change of mind and attitude. To repent is to make a decision that changes the total direction of one's life.

The message of John the Baptist to Israel was that they were to ready themselves for the Messiah by making a decision to turn from their evil ways back to holiness (Mt 3:2; Mk 1:15). In Jesus' early ministry he concentrated on the same theme (Mt 4:17; Mk 6:12). Later, when Jesus himself had become the issue, the call to repentance was a call to change one's mind about him and to make a personal commitment to him (Lk 13:3,5; cf. Ac 2:38; 3:19). In the age of grace it is God's kindness in withholding merited judgment that gives human beings time to repent (Ro 2:4). The significant and controversial mention of repentance in Heb 6:6 is discussed in another article. ♦ *Fall*

3. Conclusions. "Repentance" expresses a basic doctrine, but it does not emphasize emotion or stand beside faith as an added essential for salvation. Repentance in both the OT and the NT provides a perspective on faith. For faith in a biblical sense is commitment, not merely "belief about." One who repents has faith, for it is faith in God that is expressed when we carry out a decision to turn from our old ways and to commit ourselves to God's ways.

REPROACH

The Hebrew word "to reproach" is *harap*. It and the related noun *herpâh* indicate public blame or scorn, to the harm of one's reputation or good name. Israel's sins and God's following judgments exposed her to taunts and jeers of reproach (Ps 44:13–16; Eze 5:14–15).

The NT injunction that a leader of the church must be "above reproach" (1 Ti 3:2) uses the word *anepilēmptos* (found elsewhere only twice in the NT—5:7; 6:14), which indicates he must be a person who deserves his good reputation in the community.

RESCUE

A number of OT words are translated "rescue" in English versions. *Nāṣal* is a word that means "to deliver or save." It is usually used of a literal, personal deliverance from danger. ◗ *Deliver* *Mālaṭ* is also translated "to deliver," "to save," or "to escape." Most often it refers to escape from some threat of death and usually emphasizes the role of the Lord in saving. ◗ *Salvation/Save*

The NIV uses "rescue" in the NT more often than does the NASB. Both versions, however, so translate the Greek *exaireō* and *rhyomai*. *Exaireō* means "to set free or deliver," whereas *rhyomai* means "to deliver or preserve." Each is again linked with the NT doctrine of salvation, which focuses on deliverance from sin and its effects. ◗ *Salvation/Save*

RESPECT

The concept of respect is important in human relationships. In Scripture it is especially important and implies more than it does in common speech.

In the OT where "respect" ("revere," "reverence," NASB) occurs, the term is *yārē'*. ◗ *Fear*

In the NT, the concept of respect has several aspects and is applied in several different contexts. Three different Greek words are consistently translated "respect" in the NIV and the NASB: *entrepō*, *phobos*, and *semnos*.

The NIV renders *entrepō* as "respect(ed)" four times in the NT (Mt 21:37; Mk 12:6; Lk 20:13; Heb 12:9), and it may have that meaning in two other verses as well (Lk 18:2,4). The three NIV Gospel references are in accounts of Jesus' parable of the distant king who sent his son to tenants who had refused to pay rent and had beaten or killed earlier messengers. The thought that they would surely *entrepō* his son is based on the idea that shame would result if such a basic relationship were violated, as well as on fear of the king's authority. But the tenants— that is, Israel's leaders—killed the Son, thinking they would take the place of the true owner and have his vineyard themselves. They were without shame or fear and showed Jesus no respect.

The noun *phobos* is simply "fear." In the OT, fear (*yārē'*) indicates respect as well as terror, as in the "fear of the Lord." ◗ *Fear* *Phobos* is found in six of the verses where the NIV and NASB read "respect" (Ro 13:7; Eph 5:33; 6:5; 1 Pe 2:17,18; 3:15).

As respect, *phobos* implies a moral responsibility to someone in a superior position. It is expressed by responding to that person appropriately. Thus, respect for God is shown in worship and obedience. Respect for government (Ro 13:7) is shown by keeping the laws. Respect for one's master, if a slave, is shown by being submissive and working honestly and wholeheartedly (Eph 6:5–7; 1 Pe 2:18). ◗ *Subject/Submission*

Semnos (found 4 times in the NT) means "worthy of respect." The NIV translates it this way three times (1 Ti 3:8,11; Tit 2:2) and "right" once (Php 4:8). The underlying concept is of a moral and ethical approach to life. The person so described earns respect because his or her life is essentially decent.

The NIV supplies the English word "respect" where there is no specific word for it in the Greek text (1 Th 4:12; 5:12; 1 Ti 6:1–2) and translates *timēn* as "respect" in 1 Pe 3:7. ◗ *Honor/Dishonor*

RESPONSIBLE ◗
Account/Accountable

REST

From the introduction of God's rest after creation to the NT promise of a rest for God's people, "rest" has great theological significance. In this discussion it refers to rest as cessation of labor and enjoyment of quietness.

OT 1. The Hebrew words
      2. The Sabbath
NT 3. The Greek words
      4. Rest in Heb 3–4

OT — 1. The Hebrew words. Many different Hebrew words express various aspects of what the OT suggests by "rest." Three different terms are commonly translated "rest" and express most of these meanings. They are *šābat*, *nûah*, and *šāqat*.

The word *šābat* implies ceasing or coming to an end of activity. Thus, Moses records that God rested when his work of creation was completed (Ge 2:2,3). The impression of peaceful repose is present only in the thirteen instances where this verb is used in a Sabbath context (see 2, below).

Nûah suggests being settled down, an absence of movement. It implies security and a sense of inner ease. In the OT, *nûah* speaks of a psychological release from pressures and tensions (as in Isa 28:12). It is closely associated with the victorious conclusion of conflicts (Jos 21:44; 2 Ch 15:15). The victors enjoy peace as the external threat is removed.

It is very clear from the OT uses of this word that God alone is able to provide such rest (e.g., Ex 33:14; Dt 12:10; Jos 22:4).

The word *šāqat* has the idea of one finding tranquillity. It signifies the absence of external pressures and inner anxiety. This kind of rest comes only through a relationship with the Lord. As Isaiah says, "The wicked are like the tossing sea, which cannot rest. . . . [Thus,] there is no peace . . . for the wicked" (Isa 57:20–21). ♦ *Peace* This Hebrew word too is used of the aftermath of victory and of periods of time in which God's people were faithful to him (e.g., Jdg 3:11; 5:31; 8:28). The prophets looked forward to a promised time of rest, when God would deliver his people from bondage. Despite the agony of preceding judgments, God declared,

"I will surely save you out of a distant place, your descendants from the land of their exile. Jacob will again have peace [*šāqat*] and security, and no one will make him afraid" (Jer 30:10).

In the OT, then, the words that communicate the idea of "rest" imply a wide range of benefits. There is security, an absence of danger and anxiety. There is an ease and confidence that has both outer and inner bases, each of which can be traced directly to one's relationship with the Lord. Only through a relationship with the Lord can we experience the blessing of the rest that God has for those who trust him.

2. The Sabbath. The seventh day of the week, which divided the Hebrew month into four equal parts, was called the Sabbath. ♦ *Month* However, it is the religious significance of the Sabbath that is primarily important in the OT.

First, the Sabbath was a testimony to God the Creator, who rested after his six days of shaping our universe (Ge 2:2–3). The statement about the Sabbath in the Ten Commandments goes like this: "Remember the Sabbath day by keeping it holy. Six days you shall labor and do all your work, but the seventh day is a Sabbath to the LORD your God. On it you shall not do any work, neither you, nor your son or daughter, nor your manservant or maidservant, nor your animals, nor the alien within your gates. For in six days the LORD made the heavens and the earth, the sea, and all that is in them, but he rested on the seventh day. Therefore the LORD blessed the Sabbath day and made it holy" (Ex 20:8–11).

Second, the Sabbath became a symbol of Israel's covenant relationship with the Lord. Ex 31:12–17 identifies it as a lasting sign, celebrating the mutual commitment expressed in the Mosaic covenant. ♦ *Law* Israel's observance of the Sabbath as a day of rest was a clear indication of her spiritual condition, for it showed obedience to the divine law (e.g., Jer 17:19–27; Ne 13:15–22). This relationship of the OT Sabbath to the Mosaic Law is important, for when Jesus instituted the new covenant through his death at Calvary, Sabbath observance, like many other aspects of the old covenant, was done away with. ♦ *Covenant*

Third, the Sabbath is also intimately linked with deliverance from Egypt. God, in repeating the Ten Commandments, says this about the Sabbath: "Remember that you were slaves in Egypt and that the LORD your God brought you out of there with a mighty hand and an outstretched arm. Therefore the LORD your God has commanded you to observe the Sabbath day" (Dt 5:15).

The intimate association of the Sabbath with Creation, redemption, and law gives us insight into how the day was to be used. Each seventh day provided a full-orbed reminder of who God was to his people. He was the source of their life. He was the provider of their freedom. He was the one who ordered their lives and gave them meaning. The Sabbath day provided a rest from the normal activities of life in the world and an opportunity for each believing Israelite to contemplate his roots and his identity.

In addition to these theological aspects of the Sabbath, there was an intensely practical aspect as well. The Sabbath was provided for the benefit of all who lived in the sphere of divine influence. Family members and servants, and even the animals of the land, were to have a time for relaxation and restoration of strength. Even the land was to be given its Sabbath, lest its nutrients be used up. In its rest, the land was to bless the poor and the animals (Ex 23:10–11). As verse 12 goes on to say, "Six days do your work, but on the seventh day do not work, so that your ox and your donkey may rest and the slave born in your household, and the alien as well, may be refreshed."

The humanitarian aspect of Sabbath law was ignored in Jesus' day and gave rise to many of Jesus' conflicts with the Pharisees. These zealous men focused on do's and don'ts that had grown up around and over the basic biblical principles. Again and again they challenged Jesus' right to heal on the Sabbath (e.g., Lk 6:1–11; 13:10–17; 14:1–6; Jn 5:9–18; 7:22–23; 9:14–16). In most of these instances, Jesus, who claimed lordship over the Sabbath (Lk 6:5), pointed out that it had always been right to do good on the Sabbath. Clearly God's humanitarian concern, expressed in Ex 23:12 and other passages, demonstrates that it is not the legalities but the benefits to humankind that the Lord values in this OT holy day.

Theological and humanitarian explanations for the institution of the Sabbath underline a vital truth found often in Scripture. God's demands communicate his concern for the whole person. Both the spiritual and the physical needs of human beings were intended to be met by the Sabbath day of rest.

After the Resurrection, the early church began to meet on the Lord's Day, The first rather than the seventh day become the day of rest. What the believers gathered weekly to remember was the Resurrection. The Lord's Day replaced the Sabbath, but the meaning of the Sabbath as a time for spiritual and physical refreshment remains significant for us today.

NT — 3. The Greek words. The Greek words for "rest" are used in the LXX to translate as many as sixteen different Hebrew words. As they are used in the NT, they often reflect the OT perspective.

Anapauō (used 12 times in the NT) means "to rest" in a physical sense; and, as a transitive verb, it also means "to calm," "to comfort," or "to refresh." Significantly, it is this rest that Jesus promised those who are willing to take his yoke (Mt 11:28–30). The image is of one person in harness with another, the two tied in tandem as two draft animals were tied, in order that they might work together. In the context of Scripture, human beings always find themselves yoked. Most commonly the yoke involves slavery. In Mt 11, as well as Ac 15 and Gal 5:1, the yoke is the law, which humanity experiences as an unbearable burden. Jesus' invitation was for people to commit themselves to him. Paradoxically, when we are bound to Jesus, we can experience rest. ♦ *Yoke*

Anesis indicates a rest that comes from freedom or from the relaxation of a burden. It is found only five times in the

NT (Ac 24:23; 2 Co 2:13; 7:5; 8:13; 2 Th 1:7).

Katapausis (9 times in the NT) is the rest of repose and is found only in Ac 7:49 and Hebrews. As used in Heb 3–4 it has special theological significance (see 4, below).

Just as the OT shared the conviction that human beings can find rest only through a living relationship with the Lord, so the NT expresses the conviction that we can find our rest only in Jesus.

4. Rest in Heb 3–4. The third and fourth chapters of Hebrews explore the significance of God's voice in the believer's experience. ♦ **Voice** The writer argues that only by hearing and responding to the Lord as he speaks to us in our "today" can we find rest. Such rest is not cessation of activity but repose in activity. God's Sabbath rest is defined: God has ceased creating (4:9–11). But the God of the OT is *active*. How then is he at rest? He is at rest from bringing into existence and organizing the basic plan and contents of the universe. He knows the end from the beginning, and his purpose will stand (Isa 46:8–10). Thus, his voice is able to guide us into the paths he intends for us.

The struggle Christians are engaged in is not that of finding their way through life but of entering his rest (4:11). That is, they are to be responsive to the Lord and let his Word and Spirit guide them to the solutions he has already provided for their problems.

In knowing God and responding to him we find true repose.

RESTITUTION

The references in Nu 5:7–8 to restitution represent the Hebrew *šûb*, which means "to turn back or return." One who wronged another had to confess his sin and return to the other full monetary value, plus twenty percent.

Other references to restitution, in Ex 22 and Lev 22, are from *šālam*, "to be complete or sound." The idea is one of restoring a violated relationship by a compensatory payment.

Restitution is one of the most significant concepts in OT criminal law. The person who steals or misappropriates another's property is directly responsible to his victim. OT law directed the criminal to repay double. His own property or labor is demanded as recompense for the harm he did to his neighbor.

This principle is very different from that embedded in our criminal law. In our system of justice a criminal is responsible to society, not to his victim. Society places the criminal in jail as a punishment rather than having him or her make restitution. The OT system is undoubtedly superior, both in its concern for the victim and in its holding the criminal responsible for his or her acts.

RESTORE

In the OT, several Hebrew words are translated "restore." The word *šûb* is one of the most common of the Hebrew verbs and is variously translated. The basic meaning is one of movement, spatially or spiritually. It is sometimes translated "restore" but is also translated in some OT contexts as "return" and "repentance." One of the main themes of the OT is expressed with this verb—the prophets' promise that Israel would one day return from their exile to the Promised Land. In that day they would be restored to relationship with God. But the return was to come only after judgment, and then only a few were to experience deliverance. As Isaiah said, "Though your people, O Israel, be like the sand by the sea, only a remnant will return" (10:22).

Other concepts expressed by "restore" are seen in *hādaš* ("to renew or repair"), *hāyâh* ("to live" or "to make live"—see 2 Ki 8:1–5), and *'āṣam* ("to become strong").

In the NT, several Greek words are translated "restore." Ac 15:16 speaks of restoration of Davidic rule, and uses *anorthoō*, "to set up or erect again" (found only twice elsewhere in the NT— Lk 13:13; Heb 12:12). *Katartizō*, which emphasizes mending or making whole, is rendered "restore" in two of its thirteen occurrences in the NT (Gal 6:1; 1 Pe 5:10).

But the most significant of the Greek words for "restore," and those used most often, are the verbs *apokathistēmi* and *apokathistanō* (which occur a total of 8 times in the NT) and the noun *apokatastasis* (which occurs once in the NT). The root of these words was used in the Greek OT of Jesus' day and by Jewish thinkers in speaking of Israel's hope of a future political restoration. Thus, the political aspect of the Messiah's ministry is clearly reflected in the disciples' question to Jesus after the Resurrection: "Lord, are you at this time going to restore the kingdom to Israel?" (Ac 1:6). Peter's use of this word in one of his sermons in early Acts is a clear indication that he understood that the prophetic vision concerning Israel was yet to be fulfilled. Jesus the Messiah "must remain in heaven until the time comes for God to restore everything, as he promised long ago through his holy prophets" (Ac 3:21).

The same theme is seen in Mt 17:11 and Mk 9:12, though the word is used four times in the ordinary sense of healing (Mt 12:13; Mk 3:5; 8:25; Lk 6:10). The common meaning is also intended in Heb 13:19.

Restoration is something that each of us can identify with. When we are ill, we yearn to be restored to health—when depressed, restored to joy. But only the coming again of Jesus will restore all things and establish the harmony that God intended for his creation.

RESURRECTION

The doctrine of the resurrection is pivotal in the Christian faith. Paul wrote, "If in this life only we hope in Christ, we are to be pitied more than all men" (1 Co 15:19). What, then, is the shape of the believer's hope? The NT speaks decisively. It is not simply the continuation of existence. It is resurrection, with all that resurrection implies!

1. The Greek words
2. Resurrection in the OT
3. Restoration of earthly life
4. The resurrection of Jesus
5. The resurrection of the believer
6. Summary

1. The Greek words. The OT has no special vocabulary of resurrection. In the NT, two families of words are used to express this basic doctrine. The verb *anistēmi* means "to raise" or "to arouse [from sleep]." In this word group are also *anastasis, exanastasis* ("resurrection") and *exanistēmi* ("to raise," "to arouse"). The NT uses all of these words in ordinary senses as well as in the context of resurrection from the dead. These words, almost never used in Greek thought of a recall to life, are used in the NT both of Jesus' resurrection and of the believer's resurrection.

Egeirō is a transitive verb meaning "to wake up," "to rouse." *Egersis* is found only once in the NT (Mt 27:53) and means "an awakening," "a resurrection." Both these groups of words are used when NT writers turn their attention to what happened to Jesus and to what will happen to those who are his.

2. Resurrection in the OT. There is no sharply defined doctrine of resurrection in the OT. At the same time, many believe they can see hints in the OT that God's intention for humanity includes a life that extends beyond the earthly years. Several lines of argument can be developed.

There are passages that can be interpreted to speak of deliverance in this life with a hint at a deliverance that extends beyond this life (e.g., Job 14:14; Ps 17:15; 73:23–26; cf. Ps 49:7–20).

Some passages seem to promise resurrection more specifically. These are found especially in the Prophets. For instance, Isaiah wrote, "He will swallow up death forever" (25:8) and "Your dead will live; their bodies will rise. You who dwell in the dust, wake up and shout for joy" (26:19).

The clearest statement of all is found in this statement: "Multitudes who sleep in the dust of the earth will awake: some to everlasting life, others to shame and everlasting contempt" (Da 12:2).

There are also passages that suggest, rather than explicitly teach, a resurrection. Jesus' interpreted God's claim in Ex 3 (to be the God of Abraham, Isaac, and Jacob) to imply unending existence: "He is not the God of the dead but of the living" (Mt 22:32). The witch of Endor was shocked when the dead Samuel apparently came to give God's message to Saul (1 Sa 28:13–15). Both Enoch and Elijah were taken directly to be with the Lord without passing through death (Ge 5:24; 2 Ki 2:11). Their snatching away suggests the continuation of life beyond our world, though the method by which they left the world is so dramatically different.

While the doctrine of resurrection is not developed in the OT, it is certainly fair to say that the emergence of the NT's clear teaching comes as no surprise. The Pharisees, who held to the doctrine of resurrection, and the Sadducees, who denied it, might argue about the OT's implications for the resurrection, but Jesus justly condemned the denial of the Sadducees, saying, "You are in error because you do not know the Scriptures or the power of God" (Mt 22:29; cf. Mk 12:27; Lk 20:38).

3. Restoration of earthly life. Both OT and NT report incidents in which individuals are restored to earthly life. Among them are the restoration of two women's sons (1 Ki 17:17–24; 2 Ki 4:18–37), Jesus' raising of the daughter of Jairus (Mt 9:18–26; Mk 5:22–43; Lk 8:41–56) and, most spectacularly, the raising of Lazarus three days after his burial (Jn 11). Each of these incidents demonstrates clearly that God has power over death. But none of them involved resurrection. For resurrection, as we discover it in the NT, is to an endless life in a transformed state of being. Each of those restored to earthly life died again, whereas the resurrected pass beyond the power of death and decay.

4. The resurrection of Jesus. The significance of Jesus' resurrection is beyond imagination. Just a few of the NT themes associated with resurrection show the central place that his resurrection must play in our faith.

First, Paul points out that Jesus "through the Spirit of holiness was declared with power to be the Son of God by his resurrection from the dead" (Ro 1:4). The resurrection is proof of all of Christ's claims and a solid foundation for our faith.

It is also true that Jesus is called the "firstfruits of those who have fallen asleep" (1 Co 15:20). His resurrection is the guarantee that the death that grips the human race because of Adam has been conquered and that life is now our destiny.

Next, Jesus' resurrection to endless life guarantees that "because Jesus lives forever, he has a permanent priesthood. Therefore he is able to save completely those who come to God through him, because he always lives to intercede for them" (Heb 7:24–25).

Finally, Jesus' resurrection is the key to fulfillment of all the OT and NT promises about the future. God's purposes will be achieved only when Jesus' returns.

Even this brief survey helps us to understand why the resurrection of Jesus was a keystone in apostolic proclamation of the gospel (Ac 2:24–36; 3:15–26; 4:10; 5:30; 10:40; 13:34,37; 17:18–32).

5. The resurrection of the believer. The NT makes it clear that the dead must appear before God for judgment (Heb 9:27; Rev 20:11–15). But resurrection as transformation to a different state of being is for believers only. We can perhaps best sum up the core of NT teaching on resurrection by answering three questions: What do we know of resurrection as transformation? What do we know about the resurrection state? What is resurrection power?

First, what do we know about resurrection as transformation? John wrote that God has made us his own children (1 Jn 3:1) and then added (v. 2), "What we will be has not yet been made known;" but we do know that when Jesus "appears, we shall be like him." Paul in 1 Th 4 provides the broad outline. When Jesus returns, "those who have fallen asleep" (v. 14) will come with him, and those left alive will meet them in the air. The "dead in Christ" (v. 16) will be raised before the living believers are caught up, and together the whole family will meet Jesus in the air. Paul concludes, "So we will be with the Lord forever" (v. 18).

There are more details in 1 Co 15. To the questions "How are the dead raised?" and "With what kind of body will they come?" (v. 35), Paul simply notes that the resurrection body will correspond to our present body, but in contrast it will be imperishable, glorious, infused with power—spiritual rather than natural (vv. 42–44). ▶ **Soul and Spirit** It will be in "the likeness of the man from heaven" (v. 49), through a transformation that will happen "in the twinkling of an eye, at the last trumpet" (v. 52). Then the "dead will be raised imperishable, and we [who live then] will be changed."

Second, what do we know about the resurrection state? Very little, according to the apostles Paul and John. But many have found it fascinating to observe the capabilities of the resurrected Jesus and speculate what being "like him" might mean. For instance, the resurrected Jesus had "flesh and bones (Lk 24:39). Why not flesh and blood? Is it because "the life of the flesh is in the blood" (Lev 17:11) and a resurrected person is infused with a different kind of life? Others have noted Jesus' sudden appearance among his disciples in a locked room (Jn 20:26). Is this teleportation? Or can a resurrected person move between the atoms of the physical universe?

While such speculation has a fascination, we do best to let the issue rest with God, as John and Paul did. We do not yet know what we will be, but we will be like him. The limitations of our physical nature will be gone, and, whereas we are now perishable, we will then be imperishable. Power will replace weakness; immortality will end mortality. ▶ **Heaven and Hell**

Finally, what is resurrection power? This is one of the most exciting of NT themes. Paul writes that "if the Spirit of him who raised Jesus from the dead is living in you, he who raised Christ from the dead will also give life to your mortal bodies through his Spirit, who lives in you" (Ro 8:11). The point Paul makes is that the Holy Spirit, the agent of Jesus' resurrection, lives within the believer. This means that resurrection power is available to us even in our mortal bodies. Through the Holy Spirit we are raised beyond our human limitations and enabled to live a righteous life.

This doctrine is sometimes overlooked, and certain biblical passages are therefore misinterpreted. For instance, in Php 3, Paul is not expressing uncertainty about his own resurrection when he yearns "somehow, to attain to the resurrection from the dead" (v. 11). The entire sentence reads, "I want to know Christ and the power of his resurrection and the fellowship of sharing in his sufferings, becoming like him in his death, and so, somehow, to attain to the resurrection from the dead" (vv. 10–11). Paul's thought is focused on the present—living a resurrection kind of life now—not on eternity. The "power of his resurrection" at work in our lives today is an exciting prospect for the Christian.

6. Summary. The Greeks thought the soul had permanent existence and even knew renewed life through transmigration (see Plato's *Phaedo* and *Republic*). But the "soul" was not the individual's conscious personality, and the new state was not resurrection. Resurrection was in fact so foreign to Greek thought as to be considered ridiculous.

In the Jewish world of the first century, opinion was divided. The orthodox Pharisees were confident of a resurrection, but the Sadducees denied the doctrine. This division was possible because OT evidence is neither extensive nor certain, with the exception of a single, unequivocal statement (Dan 12:2).

It is the NT that makes God's plan for individual human beings clear. There is an eternal destiny, a life beyond this life. Resurrection lies ahead. Jesus' own appeals to the OT show evidence sometimes overlooked. But it is the resurrection of Jesus that is the final proof. Jesus' resurrection not only declared him to be what he claimed to be, the Son of God, but also provided a guarantee for us who believe. Because Jesus lives, we too will live. And we will share his destiny: "When he appears, we shall be like him, for we shall see him as he is" (1 Jn 3:2).

RETURN ◆ *Appearance of Jesus: the Second Coming* ◆ *Restore*

REVEAL/REVELATION

Christianity is a revealed religion. It rests on the confidence that God has acted to make himself known to human beings and to make known information not available from any other source. Although the Bible texts that use the words "reveal" or "revelation" are relatively few, the doctrine does not rest simply on the use of these terms in the Bible.

OT 1. The Hebrew words
NT 2. The Greek words
    3. God's self-revelation
    4. God's revelation of reality

OT — 1. The Hebrew words. The Hebrew word translated "reveal" is *gālâh*. One of its two main meanings is "to uncover." The other prominent meaning of this word is that of openness and visibility. What is revealed is to be exposed for all. Thus Dt 29:28 says, "The secret things belong to the LORD our God, but the things revealed belong to us and to our children forever, that we may follow all the words of this law." The prophet Amos adds, "Surely the Sovereign LORD does nothing without revealing his plan to his servants the prophets" (Am 3:7).

Gālâh and its cognates are never used in the OT as technical theological terms. But it is clear from their use that the content of revelation includes true information. ◆ *Word* OT saints believed that God revealed himself to Abraham and Moses; and the prophets tell of a coming day of magnificent self-revelation, when "the glory of the LORD will be revealed, and all mankind together will see it" (Isa 40:5). ◆ *Glory*

NT — 2. The Greek words. Two groups of words in the Greek NT are translated "reveal" or "revelation" in the NIV. These words help us develop a NT concept of revelation and are also important for our understanding of the second coming of Christ. ◆ *Appearance of Jesus: the Second Coming*

The first group of words is constructed on a stem that suggests bringing to light, or making manifest. Among the words in this group are *phaneroō* ("to reveal, show, make known"), *epiphainō* ("to show or appear"), *epiphaneia* ("an appearance or revelation"), and *phanerōsis* ("a disclosure or revelation"). In Greek culture these words had an ordinary meaning but also the religious meaning of intervention by, or the personal appearance of, a deity. This word group is found where the NIV reads "reveal" or "revelation" in a number of passages (Lk 2:26; Jn 1:31; 2:11; 17:6; Ro 10:20; 16:26; 1 Co 4:10–11; 2 Ti 1:10; 1 Pe 1:20; Rev 15:4).

The second word group is more significant, for it provides us with the noun *apokalypsis* ("revelation"). *Apokalypsis* is nearly always used with theological significance. The verb *apokalyptō* is also often significant. The verb is found in the following passages: Mt 10:26; 11:25,27; 16:17; Lk 2:35; 10:21,22; 12:2; 17:30; Jn 12:38; Ro 1:17,18; 8:18; 1 Co 2:10; 3:13; 14:30; Gal 1:16; 3:23; Eph 3:5; Php 3:15; 2 Th 2:3,6,8; 1 Pe 1:5,12; 5:1. The noun is found in Lk 2:32; Ro 2:5; 8:19; 16:25; 1 Co 1:7; 14:6,26; 2 Co 12:1,7; Gal 1:12; 2:2; Eph 1:17; 3:3; 2 Th 1:7; 1 Pe 1:7,13; 4:13; Rev 1:1.

Apokalypsis and *apokalyptō* had little religious significance in Greek culture. Thus, the NT was able to take these religiously neutral terms and infuse them with distinctive Christian meaning. That range of meaning is wider than might be expected from a strictly theological definition of "revelation."

Five concepts of revelation appear in the NT—four in the Epistles and one in the Gospels.

First, revelation is a future, visible unveiling at history's end. This will be a revelation of Jesus, of God's attributes and plan, and of believers as God's children (Ro 2:5; 8:18,19; 1 Co 1:7; 3:13; 2 Th 1:7; 1 Pe 1:5,7,13; 4:13; 5:1; cf. Rev 1:1). The word "revealed" is also used of the future appearance of the Antichrist (2 Th 2:3,6,8). ♦ *Antichrist*

Second, revelation is our current knowledge in Christ of God's plans, previously hidden even to OT saints (Ro 1:17,18; 16:26; 1 Co 2:10; 14:6; Gal 1:12; 3:23; Eph 3:3,5). The same term is used of historic knowledge of God unveiled by the OT prophets (1 Pe 1:12). In these uses, the implication is that the new revelation is written in the Scriptures. But "revelation" is also used of fresh, contemporary insights provided to the early church by its own prophets (1 Co 14:26,30; 2 Co 12:1,7; Gal 2:2).

Third, "revelation" is also a term applied to Jesus' expression of himself through the life of a believer (Gal 1:16).

Fourth, revelation is the Holy Spirit's work of shaping the believer's understanding and attitudes to bring them into harmony with truth (Eph 1:17).

Finally, three times the Gospels refer to Jesus' revealing the Father or to Jesus himself being revealed (Mt 11:27; 16:17; Lk 10:22). The sense in each instance is an inner enlightening rather than an objective confrontation.

3. God's self-revelation. The OT declares in many places that God partly showed himself to human beings. The NT era began with God's self-revelation in Jesus. As our Lord himself said, "Anyone who has seen me has seen the Father" (Jn 14:9). But the doctrine of God's self-disclosure is not found in the NT use of *apokalypsis* and *apokalyptō*. Rather, the NT emphasis in these words is on (1) disclosure of information from and about God, (2) the future visible disclosure in history of Jesus and of God's plan, and (3) the outward manifestation of God and truth in the lives of believers.

4. God's revelation of reality. A critical passage for understanding the first meaning of "revelation" is 1 Co 2. Human beings are limited, unable to penetrate by the senses the thoughts of God or the meaning of life on earth. But the

Holy Spirit knows the hidden things, and so God revealed them by his Spirit (v. 10). This revelation is in words given by the Spirit (v. 13).

"Revelation" in the NT primarily applies to the giving and interpretation of information from God.

REVENGE ♦ *Vengeance/Revenge*

REWARD

Equitability, or fairness, is the basic idea expressed in the various Hebrew words the NIV and NASB translate "reward." The idea is sometimes (e.g., Ge 15:1; Pr 11:18; Isa 40:10) expressed by "hire" or "wages" (*śāḵār/śeḵer*). The root *šālam* expresses the idea of balance and harmony, maintained by repayment for doing good (e.g., 1 Sa 24:9; Pr 11:31; 13:13). Ps 19:11 affirms that in keeping God's commands there is great *ʿēqeḇ* ("consequence"). The idea of a return on one's investment of labor is expressed in some passages in Ecclesiastes (e.g., 2:10) by *ḥēleq*, whereas in Ps 18:20 the word expressing the giving of a reward according to one's righteousness is *gāmal* ("to compensate"). Thus, the OT affirms that there is equitability in the moral universe. God is both a rewarder of good and punisher of evil. The person who sows righteousness will surely reap a good reward. ♦ *Wage/Wages*

In the NT, "reward" is almost always a translation of the Greek word *misthos* (used 29 times in the NT), which means "wage." ♦ *Wage/Wages* Its use in Col 3:24 is an exception. There the word is *antapodosis*, which indicates a full return and occurs once in the NT.

RICHES ♦ *Wealth/Riches/Possessions*

RIGHT/LEFT

In Scripture, "right" and "left" sometimes simply indicate directions or alternative choices. But frequently they have symbolic significance; and often where a choice is involved the right is the better alternative or group (e.g., Mt 25:31–46).

The symbolic significance of these words is established in the OT, where the right hand is used in blessing (as in Ge 48:13–20). The right hand is also specifically linked with divine power when God comes to aid his people. So David exults, "Now I know that the LORD saves his anointed; he answers him from his holy heaven with the saving power of his right hand. Some trust in chariots and some in horses, but we trust in the name of the LORD our God" (Ps 20:6–7; cf. Ex 15:6).

The NT continually emphasizes the fact that Jesus has been lifted up and is now at God's right hand (Mt 22:44; 26:64; Mk 12:36; 14:62; 16:19; Lk 20:42; 22:69; Ac 2:33,34; 5:31; Ro 8:34; Eph 1:20; Col 3:1; Heb 1:3,13; 8:1; 10:12; 12:2; 1 Pe 4:19). Today Jesus is in heaven, with all the power of the sovereign God available to him for expression in and through his saints.

RIGHT/RIGHTS

People differ on the subject of personal rights. Are we to insist on our rights? Or must we surrender them? All too often we debate these questions with a misunderstanding of the nature of personal rights.

OT **1. Rights in the OT**
NT **2. Rights in the NT**
    3. Paul's argument in 1 Co 9

OT — 1. Rights in the OT. There are mainly three different Hebrew words that are used in speaking of an individual's "rights": g^e'*ullâh*, *mišpāṭ*, and *dîn*. *G^e'ullâh* is specific. It means "the right to redeem." It refers to an aspect of OT law under which a kinsman could make a payment that would free a relative's person or property. ◆ *Redeem/Ransom*

Mišpāṭ and *dîn* are both legal in character, suggesting a judgment passed down. Behind each is the notion of rights established in law—in the OT these are most often rights established under the rule of God rather than by human custom.

NT — 2. Rights in the NT. When speaking of a person's rights, the Greek word in the NT is *exousia*. This word is often translated "power," and indeed power or authority is one of its basic meanings. But the original thought expressed is one of freedom of action. Thus, a "right" denotes an area in which a person is free to act as he or she chooses.

A believer has no "right" to choose something that God identifies as sin. But the NT makes it clear that in areas of personal conviction, believers are to respect others' freedom and not to judge them (Ro 14). ◆ *Judge/Judging*

3. Paul's argument in 1 Co 9. Paul explores an issue of personal rights in 1 Co 8–10. Some in Corinth argued that the matter of eating meat sacrificed to idols was up to one's own conscience, on the basis "that an idol is nothing at all in the world and that there is no God but one" (1 Co 8:4). Before looking at the specific issue (1 Co 10), Paul dealt with the matter of personal rights (1 Co 9).

In presenting his argument, Paul began by examining his own actions and motives. As an apostle, he had a "right" to be supported by those he served, and he had a "right" to marry and travel with a wife, as the other apostles and Peter did (1 Co 9:3–5). But Paul "did not use this right" (9:12). Rather, he chose to labor to support himself. And there were other rights he chose not to use.

Paul's point is that the existence of a "right"—or an area in which a person has freedom to choose—does not mean that he or she must exercise that right. Paul said, rather, that though he himself was free, he had chosen to make himself "a slave to everyone, to win as many as possible" (9:19). That is, Paul chose to let the convictions of others restrain him in the exercise of his freedom whenever this would help him to influence them and so carry out his ministry.

The application to the situation in Corinth is clear. The debaters each insisted on using their rights, and neither side stopped to consider the impact this use of freedom was having on others.

The Bible does not say that we must surrender our conscience or our rights in order to live in community with other Christians. But it does strongly suggest that the impact a choice will have on others is one factor to consider in using our freedom.

RIGHTEOUS/RIGHTEOUSNESS

Christians are apt to be uncomfortable with the psalmist's claim, "I have done what is righteous and just" (Ps 119:121). From the perspective of the NT, we are likely to think of righteousness as an impossibility. Only God is truly righteous. And only in Jesus can we stand before God as a righteous people. How then can a human being appeal, "Hear, O LORD, my righteous plea" (Ps 17:1)? We feel much more comfortable with Ps 143:2: "No one living is righteous before you."

This sense of discomfort illustrates how important it is for us to understand the biblical concept of righteousness. For righteousness surely is a basic theme in both Testaments and a keystone in Christian theology.

OT 1. **The Hebrew words and their meaning**
    2. **God as righteous**
    3. **The righteous saint**
NT 4. **The Greek words and their meaning**
    5. **Mt 5: the righteousness that surpasses**
    6. **Ro 1: the righteousness in the gospel**
    7. **Ro 2–3: righteousness and the law**
    8. **Ro 3–4: righteousness and faith**
    9. **Ro 6–8: the realization of righteousness**
   10. **Conclusions**

OT — 1. The Hebrew words and their meaning. The Hebrew words translated "righteous" and "righteousness" are constructed on the stem *ṣādaq*. ♦ *Justice/Injustice Saddîq* means "just" or "righteous," *ṣedeq* is "rightness" or "righteousness," and *ṣᵉdāqâh* is "righteousness."

The underlying idea is one of conformity to a norm. People are righteous when their personal and interpersonal behavior accords with an established moral or ethical norm. In the OT there is only one standard by which righteousness can be measured—the revealed will of God, particularly as it is expressed in the law.

Thus, the OT does not deal primarily with abstract or absolute righteousness. When a person is said to be "righteous," no suggestion of sinlessness is implied. Instead, the statement implies actions in harmony with one's obligations in his or her relationship with God.

2. God as righteous. Scripture often speaks of God as righteous. He is the "righteous God" (Ps 4:1; 7:9; Isa 45:21). His acts are "always righteous" (Jer 12:1; cf. Jdg 5:11; Ps 71:24) because all he does is in harmony with his character. As he is the moral judge of the universe, the very character of God is the ultimate standard of righteousness. ♦ *Judge/Judging*

God's righteousness finds expression in the decrees and laws that he gave to govern his people. Moses expressed this when he asked the generation of Israelites about to enter the Promised Land: "What other nation is so great as to have such righteous decrees and laws as this body of laws I am setting before you today?" (Dt 4:8; cf. Ps 119:7,62,75,106, 138,160,164,172).

The OT has two special ways of portraying God as acting righteously. First, "he will judge the world in righteousness" (Ps 9:8; 96:13; 98:9). As moral judge, God hates wickedness (Ps 45:7). His acts of judgment thus are expressions of his intrinsic righteousness. Second, we find in the OT the realization that our righteous God is also a Savior (Isa 45:21). The psalmist cries, "Deliver me in your righteousness" (Ps 31:1; cf. 119:40). God's saving acts are viewed as being in total harmony with his righteousness, something that deeply concerned Paul as he developed his argument in Romans.

3. The righteous saint. The OT speaks freely of righteous people. Despite the psalmist's realization that "no one living is righteous before [God]" (Ps 143:2), the OT does identify individuals as righteous (Ge 6:9; Job 1:1). The reason is found in a certain flexibility implicit in the OT concept of righteousness. Seldom is this word used in any absolute sense. What, then, does the OT say about human righteousness?

First, righteousness can be comparative. Saul, spared by David, was forced to admit, "You are more righteous than I. . . . You have treated me well, but I have treated you badly" (1 Sa 24:17). David's actions were in closer harmony to the divine will than were Saul's. Similarly, Judah said of Tamar, "She is more righteous than I" (Ge 38:26).

Second, righteousness in the OT involves conformity to God's revealed will. Moses, reviewing God's giving the Mosaic Law, told Israel, "If we are careful to obey all this law before the LORD our God, as he has commanded us, that will be to our righteousness" (Dt 6:25). But we must never forget that in both the OT and the NT, obedience flows from a right and loving relationship with the Lord. ◆
Obey/Disobey

Third, righteousness is closely linked with a warm and personal relationship with the Lord. The righteous are "those who serve God" (Mal 3:18). They are glad in the Lord (Ps 33:1; Ps 64:10; 68:3) and will praise his name (Ps 140:13).

Fourth, righteousness brings multiplied blessings. The person who serves God and chooses to live by his standards will be blessed (Ps 5:12) and upheld (Ps 37:17), will flourish (Ps 92:12) and be remembered (Ps 112:6). The righteous may have troubles, but the Lord will help them (Ps 34:19), and they will neither be forsaken nor fall (Ps 37:25; 55:22).

Proverbs adds that their home will be blessed (3:33), they will not go hungry (10:3), and their desires will be granted (10:24). Their prospect is joy (10:28), for God is their refuge (10:29), and they will never be uprooted (10:30). They will thrive (11:28) as they are rescued from trouble (11:8), and they will even have a refuge in death (14:32).

Isaiah, warning of the terrible judgments coming on God's sinning people, can still pause to report this message from the Lord: "Tell the righteous it will be well with them, for they will enjoy the fruit of their deeds" (3:10).

Fifth, righteousness is a basis for confidence in prayer. The person who has lived by God's standards has a better basis for appealing to God. "Hear . . . my righteous plea," says the psalmist (Ps 17:1). Because his request does not "rise from deceitful lips" (v. 1), the psalmist can expect vindication (cf. 2 Sa 22:21,25; Ps 7:8; 18:20,24; 119:121).

Sixth, righteousness is not the ultimate basis of God's favor. While the OT stresses the importance of personal righteousness obtained through committed obedience to the law of the Lord, righteous acts are not the cause of God's choice of Israel. This point is stressed by Moses in Dt 9:4–6. "After the LORD your God has driven them out before you, do not say to yourself, 'The LORD has brought me here because of my righteousness.' . . . It is not because of your righteousness or your integrity that you are going in to take possession of their land. . . . The LORD your God will drive them out before you, to accomplish what he swore to your fathers, to Abraham, Isaac and Jacob. Understand, then, that it is not because of your righteousness that the Lord your God is giving you this good land to possess, for you are a stiffnecked people."

In point of fact it is only the believers' faith response to the Lord that permits God to treat them as though they were righteous. As Scripture says of Abraham, "Abram believed the LORD, and he credited it to him as righteousness" (Ge 15:6).

Finally, righteousness also has an impact on the community. The fruit of righteousness is peace, and its social effect is security (Isa 32:7). When God's kingdom is finally established on earth, righteousness and justice will be the foundation of his throne (Ps 89:14). ◆
Kingdom

NT — 4. The Greek words and their meaning. A single family of words expresses the concept. *Dikaiosynē* means "righteousness," "uprightness." *Dikaios* is "just," "upright," "righteous." And the verb *dikaioō* means "to pronounce or to treat a person as righteous," or "to acquit," "to vindicate."

In the Greek world, this family of words viewed persons within the context of their society. The righteous or upright person was one who met obligations to others in the community and to the gods.

In the Judaism of Jesus' day, righteousness was viewed as behavioral conformity to written or oral law. There was no stress on and little awareness of the relationship with God that generates the righteousness that the law reveals. No wonder Jesus called his listeners to a righteousness that exceeds the righteousness of the scribes and Pharisees of his day (Mt 5:20).

This word group, also translated "just," has a number of important meanings in the NT. ♦ *Justice/Injustice* Let us study key NT passages that explore the theme. Although such passages develop the distinctive contributions of the NT, we should remember that at times "righteous" is clearly used with its OT meaning (e.g., Mt 1:19; 5:45; Mk 6:20). This OT sense is in fact the basic one in most uses in the Gospels.

5. Mt 5: the righteousness that surpasses. In the Beatitudes, Jesus blesses those who hunger for righteousness and those who suffer persecution because of righteousness (Mt 5:6,10). He goes on to explore the relationship between the law and righteousness. Although Jesus' teachings do not abrogate the law, Jesus insists that the righteousness of his followers must exceed "that of the Pharisees and teachers of the law" (5:20). This was a stunning teaching in his day, for those leaders were committed to a life of strict observance of law.

But Jesus continued, giving a series of illustrations. Each illustration begins with "You have heard," referring back to a behavior-regulating command found in the law, and each time Jesus went on to say, "But I tell you. . . ." Each of Jesus' statements focuses, not on the behavior judged by law, but on the inner heart attitude from which the action springs. Thus, law prohibits murder, but Jesus says we must be concerned with the anger that leads to it (5:21–23). Law

prohibits adultery, but Jesus says we must be concerned with the lustful look (5:27–30). The illustrations culminate in a direct confrontation. The OT called on God's people to love their neighbors. Jesus now calls on them to love their enemies. This is necessary because God shows love even to his enemies, and we are to be like our heavenly Father (5:43–48).

Jesus' teaching involved a dramatic shift of focus. Rather than seeing righteousness in terms of behavior, Jesus shifted the issue to within the human personality. It is motives and thoughts and desires that God is concerned with. It is not simply doing what God says, but actually being like him, that is implicit in the divine call to be righteous. Without the inner righteousness that Jesus calls for, one "will certainly not enter the kingdom of heaven" (5:20).

6. Ro 1: the righteousness in the gospel. In Ro 1, Paul introduces the theme of righteousness, on which the entire book focuses. The gospel is about a righteousness that comes from God and is "by faith from first to last" (Ro 1:17). The NT shifts emphasis from a righteousness linked with human behavior to a righteousness that God provides. And the NT emphasizes the theme established in Ge 15:6; that is, that such righteousness is imputed to those who have faith. Thus, the gospel of Jesus is good news, for God through Jesus provides human beings with righteousness as a free gift. All we can do to receive it is to trust the one who promises (see Ro 10:6; Heb 11:7). ♦ *Promise*

7. Ro 2–3: righteousness and the law. Paul moves on in his study of righteousness to demonstrate that Gentile and Jew alike have no righteousness. Each sins, thus falling short of what the law demands. ♦ *Law* Paul proves from the OT that "there is no one righteous, not even one" (Ro 3:10) and that in fact the law silences every human claim to goodness: "No one will be declared righteous in [God's] sight by observing the law; rather, through the law we become conscious of sin" (3:20).

Paul's affirmation is a bold denial of the view of Judaism in his day. Law and righteousness were intimately associated in Jewish thought. Paul's linking law with sin, not righteousness, must have seemed far worse than merely radical!

8. Ro 3–4: righteousness and faith. Paul now rebuilds the structure he had torn down. If righteousness is not linked with law or human behavior, how can human beings obtain it? Paul says that the OT itself testifies to a "righteousness from God, apart from law" (3:21).

Since all have sinned, humanity's only hope is for redemption. Jesus died as a sacrifice of atonement. The sacrifice of Jesus frees God to be just even while he pronounces the sinner guiltless. It is in redemption and atonement that we find the key to righteousness. And it is through faith that this righteousness from God is received by the individual. ♦ *Atonement* ♦ *Belief/Faith* ♦ *Offering and Sacrifice* ♦ *Redeem/Ransom*

Paul then moves on in Romans 4 to show, through what the Scripture says of Abraham and David, that faith has always been the key to righteous standing with God. Paul sums up by saying, "The words 'it was credited to him' were written not for him [Abraham] alone, but also for us, to whom God will credit righteousness—for us who believe in him who raised Jesus our Lord from the dead. He was delivered over to death for our sins and was raised to life for our justification" (4:23–25).

Thus, the "righteousness from God" is, first of all, an imputed righteousness. That is, we are given legal standing before God as righteous persons. We may in fact be sinners, but on the basis of Jesus' death for our sins, God acquits those who believe in him and pronounces them righteous.

9. Ro 6–8: the realization of righteousness. The first part of Romans deals with righteousness in a forensic and judicial sense—human beings are in fact unrighteous, but God through Christ's death has found a legal basis on which to declare the believer righteous anyway. Now Paul turns to another aspect of the

"righteousness from God." He shows that, in Christ, God now acts in our lives to make us righteous persons. As he says elsewhere, we are given a "new self, created to be like God in true righteousness and holiness" (Eph 4:24).

Paul lays the basis for a realized righteousness in the believer's union with Jesus (6:1–14). We died with Jesus and were raised with him. Raised to new life, we are told, "Offer yourselves to God, as those who have been brought from death to life; and offer the parts of your body to him as instruments of righteousness." Experientially, Paul finds this impossible when he struggles in his own strength (Ro 7). But when he accepts his helplessness and applies to his daily life the same principle of faith that brought judicial acquittal, he finds freedom! His trust in the Spirit, expressed by a faith-response of obedience to his promptings (8:9), releases believers so that "the righteous requirements of the law might be fully met in [them], who do not live according to the sinful nature but according to the Spirit" (8:4).

This is the surpassing righteousness of which Jesus spoke. God acts within believers to "give life to [their] mortal bodies through his Spirit" (Ro 8:11) who lives within. Thus, the believer is free to actually live a righteous life, not because of conformity to an outward standard, but because the inner person is shaped by the Spirit to choose spontaneously what God himself chooses.

Many other passages explore the imputed and realized righteousness that Paul describes in this section of Romans (e.g., Ro 9:30–33; Gal 2–3; Php 3:1–11; Jas 2:20–26). ♦ *Belief/Faith* ♦ *Justify/Justification* But this passage remains the key to grasping the NT teaching on righteousness. The emphasis clearly differs from that of the OT, as understood by Judaism in Jesus' day. But there is nothing in the NT doctrine of righteousness that is in conflict with the OT. In fact, from the perspective of the NT, we can see that this view of righteousness infuses the older revelation.

10. Conclusions. In both the OT and the NT, the words translated "righteous" and "righteousness" speak of conformity to a standard or norm. For Israel and the NT church, that norm is the will of God, which is an expression of his nature and character. The OT speaks of God's righteousness, affirming that his acts and his law are in conformity with his character. A "righteous" person in OT parlance is one who fears God and whose relationship with the Lord is expressed in keeping his commandments. There are many blessings promised the righteous, just as the wicked are warned of God's necessary judgment.

The OT references to imputed righteousness and to the fact that God's covenant commitments were not made on account of any human uprightness were ignored in the Judaism of Jesus' day. Righteousness and law were viewed in an integrated way, and the good Jew sought to establish his righteousness by keeping the law.

Jesus, however, challenged this view in bold confrontations. In his Sermon on the Mount, he spoke of a "surpassing" righteousness. He pointed out that in order to win God's approval, the heart and not simply the behavior must be right. True righteousness means being like God, not simply obeying him.

The apostle Paul applied the OT in ways that were totally radical to contemporary Judaism. Human righteousness is impossible, Paul argued. What the law does is condemn. To find a basis for a legal standing as a righteous person, one must look to the OT concepts of redemption and atonement, not to the law. Thus the gospel is good news because it announces that God will declare righteous those who believe in Jesus, whose life was offered in atonement for our sins. Paul also shows that imputation was involved when God "counted" people of the OT righteous, and that this has always come through faith.

But Paul goes on to show that righteousness from God is more than a legal judgment. God acts in Christ to actually make the believer a righteous person. He does this by taking up residence within the believer in the person of the Holy Spirit. The believer now is free to act

righteously by following the promptings of the Spirit, who also enables him to do the actions of faith.

The righteousness that law commanded but could never create now becomes a reality. Through Jesus, God both announced that we have his righteousness and works to make us more and more like him: "God made him who had no sin to be sin for us, so that in him we might become the righteousness of God" (2 Co 5:21).

ROCK

Two Hebrew words, ṣûr and sela', are found where the English versions are likely to read "rock." Ṣûr indicates the massive stone formations that are the building blocks of mountains. These awesome structures are often referred to metaphorically to suggest strength, reliability, and safety. The mountains in ancient religions, as in the religions of many American Indians, were seen as the home of the gods; but in Scripture, mountains remind the believer of the greatness of the one who created them. "There is no Rock [ṣûr] like our God," Hannah affirmed in her prayer (1 Sa 2:2). And the psalmist joins in: "My soul finds rest in God alone; my salvation comes from him. He alone is my rock and my salvation; he is my fortress, I will never be shaken" (Ps 62:1–2; cf. v. 6). "My salvation and my honor depend on God; he is my mighty rock, my refuge" (v. 7).

The other Hebrew term is sela'. It indicates a cliff, or a cleft in a mountain. It too is used metaphorically in the OT. The psalmist expresses its meaning: "Be my rock of refuge, to which I can always go" (Ps 71:3).

In the NT, "rock" is petra. Petra too indicates the mass of rock that can symbolize stability and safety. One of the most debated passages in Scripture is Mt 16:18. It reports Jesus' words to Peter: "You are Peter, and on this rock I will build my church." The play on words is more obvious in Greek. Jesus said, "You are petros, and on this petra I will build my church." Petros indicates, not the mountainous mass, but rather a fragment, a stone, from the larger mass. Most Protestant theologians agree that the foundation of the church is the reality that Peter confessed: "You are the Christ, the Son of the living God" (Mt 16:16). It is Jesus and not Peter on whom the church of God is founded. Christ himself remains our Rock, our source of security and the unshakable foundation for our lives.

ROYAL ♦ King

RULE/DOMINION

In biblical times, authority was viewed as vested in a person rather than in an institution. An understanding of rule and dominion calls for a grasp of this feature of biblical thought. Thus, we need to be alerted to the different terms that are translated "rule."

OT 1. Hebrew words
NT 2. Greek words
    3. The "rule" laid down in the churches

OT — 1. Hebrew words. A number of different Hebrew words are translated "rule" or "dominion," sometimes interchangeably.

Māšal is found over eighty times in the OT. It implies no particular kind of authority but denotes authority in general, with the authority to be defined by the culture or relationship. It is used of an individual's need to master sin (Ge 4:7), a steward's management of property (Ge 24:2), and even of the "rule" of the sun over the day and that of the moon over the night (Ge 1:18). ♦ *Authority*

The words *šāpaṭ* and *mišpāṭ* are translated both "rule" and "judge." These words and their cognates indicate government and may refer to any aspect of government—legislative, executive, or judicial. ♦ *Judge/Judging*

Rāḍâh, translated "to rule," is found twenty-five times in the OT. It indicates the rule of human beings rather than of God, as in Ge 1:28, where humanity is given dominion over animal creation.

NT — 2. Greek words. Passages that speak of rulers and of ruling generally have either *archōn* or *archē* in the Greek. The root idea is one of origin or primacy. This is appropriate to the meaning of ruler in common thought, for the ruler was viewed as the source of those laws and actions that shaped life in his realm. These words are applied in the NT to demonic as well as to human and divine authority. ♦ *Angels* ♦ *Authority*

Dominion is expressed by *kyriotēs,* "lordship," and *kratos,* "strength," "dominion." ♦ *Authority* ♦ *Lord* ♦ *Strength/Might/Power*

3. The "rule" laid down in the churches. The NIV frequently uses the word "rule," as when Paul says, "This is the rule I lay down in all the churches" (1 Co 7:17) and, "Peace and mercy to all who follow this rule" (Gal 6:16). Such passages do not all have the same word in the Greek NT. Gal 6:16 has *kanōn* ("a rod, or standard"), a word that occurs only four other times in the NT (2 Co 10:13,15,16; Php 3:16). The Greek word for "rule" in 1 Co 7:17 is a verb, a military term that suggests issuing "standing orders." In Ro 13:9, the word "rule" is supplied where the Greek simply says that the law is "summed up in this." In each case, however, the Greek has a word or construction that implies the establishment of a recognized standard by which one's actions may be guided.

S

SABBATH ◆ *Rest*

SACRED ◆ *Holy/Holiness*

SACRIFICE ◆ *Offering and Sacrifice*

SADDUCEES

The Sadducees were a religious party in NT times. Unlike the Pharisees, they rejected the idea of an oral law and accepted only the Pentateuch as authoritative. But their orientation was this-worldly. They did not believe in the resurrection, personal existence after death, or divine intervention in history. Thus, they denied the possibility of rewards or punishments after death.

Though naturally hostile to the Pharisees, with whom they differed on nearly every theological issue, they joined with them to resist Jesus and his teaching. This was in part because they were antagonistic to Jesus' supernaturalism. But a more basic reason was that they feared Jesus would upset the accommodation they had made with Rome to preserve their hold on priestly and ritual offices, from which they gained many financial advantages.

SAINT ◆ *Godly/Godliness* ◆ *Holy/Holiness*

SALT

The Hebrew word for "salt" is *melah*. It is referred to in only a few passages, and then without special significance. Salt was used in the making of one kind of OT covenant (e.g., Lev. 2:13; Nu 18:19).
◆ *Covenant* The ability of concentrated salt to kill vegetation made it a symbol of desolation (e.g., Dt 29:23; Jer 17:6).

In the NT salt is *halas*. The salt of NT times was not always the purified sodium chloride we use today. It was often impure salt, bleached from the sea or found in veins in the soil. The saltiness of such salts could be lost in several ways. If a vein of salt was exposed to the sun and other elements, it soon deteriorated to grainy sands. The saltiness of salt could be leached out by dampness or, when placed in a baker's oven to keep bread moist, it would deteriorate from the oven's heat. Thus, Jesus' reference to salt is a reminder to those who have been entrusted with a new way of life: they must live according to that new way and so be an influence in the everyday life of the people around them. Salt from the earth (Mt 5:13) can lose its saltiness, but it is the saltiness that enables it to flavor foods and enrich the lives of those who taste it.

In the context of discipleship (as in Lk 14:34), the imagery is clear. The one who is a committed disciple can, like salt, enrich the lives of many. But one who loses the saltiness of commitment is of no value to anyone.

In Col 4:6 "conversation . . . always full of grace, seasoned with salt," flavors, enriches, and preserves from corruption.

SALVATION/SAVE

"What must I do to be saved?" was the question of the Philippian jailer (Ac 16:30). But perhaps the question we need to ask is, "What does salvation entail?" Both the OT and the NT paint exciting portraits of the meaning of this rich biblical concept.

OT 1. The OT concept
    2. God and humans in salvation
NT 3. The NT concept
    4. Three aspects of salvation
    5. God and humans in salvation
    6. Summary

OT — 1. The OT concept. There are several aspects of "salvation" in OT thought. First, salvation implies that a person or nation is in great distress—perhaps related to danger from enemies or to suffering caused by some disaster. In such situations the sufferers do not have the ability to help themselves.

Second, salvation involves a deliverer (a savior). This is a person who acts on behalf of the sufferers to deliver them from their distress.

Third, the action of the deliverer effects a release from the circumstances that caused the suffering. Thus, salvation portrays movement—from distress to safety.

This overall concept is expressed in a number of Hebrew words. ◗ *Deliver* ◗ *Redeem/Ransom* ◗ *Remnant/Survivors* But the primary word the NIV and NASB translate "save" and "salvation" is *yāša'*. This word, with its many derivatives, occurs 353 times in the OT.

Yāša' and similar terms in the OT deal with primarily concrete, real-life situations. The NT emphasis on salvation from the effects of sin and from evil spiritual powers is not found in the OT, though there may be oblique references to these (e.g., Ps 51:14; 79:9; Eze 37:23). Both Testaments, however, express the conviction that it is God and God only who can save his people. Thus, in the Bible, salvation focuses on the relationships between God and human beings.

2. God and humans in salvation. The OT consistently looks to God as Savior. As Moses said in his final blessing of the people he led from Egypt: "Blessed are you, O Israel! Who is like you, a people saved by the Lord? He is your shield and helper and your glorious sword" (Dt 33:29).

God might choose to work his salvation through a human agency (e.g., Jdg 3:9; 6:14). But the true cause and source of any deliverance the believer might experience is God. "I do not trust in my bow," writes the psalmist, "my sword does not bring me victory; but you give us victory over our enemies, you put our adversaries to shame. In God we make our boast all day long, and we will praise your name forever" (Ps 44:6–8). Again, "No king is saved by the size of his army; no warrior escapes by his great strength" (Ps 33:16).

In view of the fact that salvation must necessarily flow from the Lord, what is the role of the believer? Ps 33 expresses the OT view clearly: "We wait in hope for the Lord; he is our help and our shield. In him our hearts rejoice, for we trust in his holy name" (33:20–21).

The believer can look with trust and confidence to the Lord, expecting that he will act and expressing the joy that comes with the assurance that God is his Savior.

There are other ways of expressing this attitude of trust in the Lord. Each stresses our need to strengthen the bonding relationship that keeps us in tune with God's love.

"My shield is God Most High," David says in Ps 7:10, "who saves the upright in heart." Isaiah reports God's call to a straying Israel: "In repentance and rest is your salvation, in quietness and trust is your strength" (Isa 30:15). Similarly, "Turn to me and be saved, all you ends of the earth; for I am God, and there is no other" (Isa 45:22).

In the OT, it is God who acts to effect salvation. He reaches down to save those who turn to him in trust and rely on him alone to accomplish what they realize they can never do alone.

NT — 3. The NT concept. The core concept established in the OT is carried over into the NT. In fact, the Greek verb *sōzō* ("to save") also implies rescue from some life-threatening danger. In the NT, it is God or Jesus who acts to deliver believers from dangers that threaten not only their physical life but also their prospect of eternal life. ♦ *Life and Death*

Sōzō is found over one hundred times in the NT. In some contexts it refers only to deliverance from some physical threat—e.g., the imminent peril in a storm at sea (Ac 27:20,31) and the danger and suffering Jesus predicted would occur during the future tribulation (Mt 24:13,22; Mk 13:13,20). This same meaning, that of saving one's life, is seen in Christ's prayer (Jn 12:27) and in the people's ridicule of Christ on the cross: "He saved others; he cannot save himself" (KJV, Mt 27:42; Mk 15:31; cf. Mt 27:40,49; Mk 15:30; Lk 23:35,37,39). In contexts related to Jesus' miracles of healing, *sōzō* means "to restore to health and wholeness" (e.g., Mt 9:21–22; Mk 5:23,28,34; 6:56; Lk 7:50; 8:36,48,50). Another use is seen in the passages that mention "saving" and "losing" one's life (Mt 16:25; Mk 8:35; Lk 17:33). ♦ *Life and Death*

In most contexts *sōzō* and *sotēria/sotērios* reveal God's action in Christ to deliver humanity from the powers of sin, death, and Satan, which drain life on earth of its joy and threaten each person with eternal loss. It is to deal with this danger to the human beings whom God loves that he has acted as *sōtēr*, Savior. Of its twenty-four occurrences in the NT, the word *sōtēr* is used sixteen times of Jesus and eight times of God the Father.

4. Three aspects of salvation.

The NT presents three different aspects of the salvation that Jesus has won for us. These may be thought of as the past, present, and future aspects of salvation. First, historically, Jesus died for us and thus accomplished our salvation. Our initial belief in Jesus comes in conjunction with God's application of redemption to us by means of justification and regeneration. Thus, in both the historic and subjective senses it is proper for the NT to speak of our having been saved. "According to his mercy he saved us," Paul writes (Tit 3:5, KJV), and he says to Timothy, "[God] has saved us and called us to a holy life" (2 Ti 1:9).

Second, it is also true that Jesus is saving us. Salvation has an impact on our present experience. Reconciled to God, we are being saved through Jesus' life (Ro 5:10). This aspect of salvation is taught in Ro 6. Released from slavery to sin, we offer ourselves to God, to serve him in righteousness (6:5–14).

Finally, it is true that we will be saved. The ultimate impact of the salvation that Jesus won for us will be known only in the resurrection. Then the last taint of sin will be removed, and we will be perfected at last. The certainty of this future is beautifully expressed in Ro 8:18–39 and 1 Co 15:12–58.

5. God and humans in salvation.

The NT doctrine of salvation stands in perfect parallel to that of the OT. In each, God is the actor. In each, the role of the human being is to trust.

Salvation from sin is something God has accomplished in Jesus. It is only through Jesus that salvation entered our world (Jn 3:17). Through Jesus we are saved from the coming wrath (Ro 5:9). Jesus came into the world to accomplish salvation for us (1 Ti 1:15), and there is no other name under heaven to which we can look for deliverance (Ac 4:12). God's power was exercised to the fullest on our behalf in the death of Jesus for our sins and in the resurrection of Jesus to guarantee what his death won (2 Ti 4:18; Heb 7:25).

What is our part in salvation? Paul's answer to the Philippian jailer expresses the consistent testimony of Scripture: "Believe in the Lord Jesus Christ, and you will be saved" (Ac 16:31). Salvation is a gracious gift of God, received through faith (Eph 2:5–8). The human responsibility now as in OT times is simply to rely completely on the Lord. Thus, salvation today too comes in the context of one's relationship with God and is never based on any human acts.

6. Summary.

Salvation is a basic concept in both Testaments. It clearly defines the human condition, as well as the relationship that must exist between God and human beings.

Salvation implies human helplessness in the face of life-threatening danger. Thus, deliverance must come through the actions of another. Throughout Scripture, the source of salvation is God. He alone can act to deliver his people from the dangers in this present world and from the spiritual, eternal danger. In each Testament, the one in danger may simply turn to the Lord, rely fully on him, and trust him to act.

Also, both the OT and the NT present a basis for confidence in the Lord. The covenant promises that God made to Abraham and his descendants were based on the future coming of Christ as Redeemer, and the promises to NT believers are based on the finished work of Christ Jesus—that is, his death and resurrection. To all believers, faith is an expression of a person's confidence in the trustworthiness of God.

How sure, then, is our salvation! For we rely on a God who has acted for us and whose promise cannot be a lie.

SAMARITANS

The Samaritans were viewed by the Jews as an unclean people. The Jewish view, reflected in the NT, is that these people, who lived on Israel's ancient lands, descended from mongrel races imported by the Assyrians after 722 B.C. The Samaritans adopted the god of the land and offered polluted worship to Yahweh. They even went so far as to build a temple to him on Mount Gerazim in the fourth century B.C.

In NT times the Samaritans were despised by the Jews for these religious reasons and also because they were favorable to Rome. The strong antagonism of the Israelite to the Samaritan makes a number of biblical vignettes more significant. Jesus drank from the vessel of the Samaritan woman (Jn 4), though the rabbis condemned even the dishes of the Samaritans as unclean. Jesus traveled in Samaria, though a pious Jew would add days to his journey rather than pass through Samaritan territory.

Jesus' story of the good Samaritan (Lk 15), casting a Samaritan as one whose actions expressed the spirit of OT law whereas the actions of a Jewish priest and a Pharisee failed to do so, was a stunning affront to his listeners.

It is good that God ignores the biases of humanity, whatever their basis. God offers his saving love to everyone.

SANCTIFY/SANCTIFICATION

"Sanctify" is a significant word in Christian theology. It is also a focus of theological debate. That debate will not be solved by a study of the words in the original language, nor even by a study of the texts in which the words are found. But such studies may help us in evaluating the views of differing Christian traditions.

OT 1. "Sanctify" in the OT
NT 2. The Greek words and their meanings
    3. "Sanctify" in the NT

OT — 1. "Sanctify" in the OT. The NIV does not use the word "sanctify" in the OT. Where the word occurs in the NASB, it is from the Hebrew word *qādaš*, which means "to set apart as holy." In the OT, the context for this use is primarily cultic, relating to persons or objects set apart for use by God and, by this dedication, completely separated from common uses. ◆ *Holy/Holiness*

NT — 2. The Greek words and their meaning. In both the NIV and the NASB, "sanctify" and "sanctification" are translations of the same Greek words—*hagiazō* ("to make holy" or "to sanctify") and *hagiasmos* ("sanctification" or "holiness"). Thus, the concepts of sanctification and holiness are related (sometimes identical) and should be studied in connection with each other. ◆ *Holy/Holiness*

A basic distinction must be made between the OT and the NT doctrines of holiness. In the OT, the holy is that which is set apart from the common so that it is isolated for God's service. In the NT, holiness is a dynamic process. The holy is actually the common, infused now by God's Spirit and transformed for his service. Thus, our sanctification has to do with God's transformation of us into persons whose actions in daily life are expressions of the Lord.

3. "Sanctify" in the NT. What do we learn when we examine the texts where "sanctify" and "sanctification" are found in the NT?

The first such NT text we meet records Jesus' prayer for the sanctification of believers (Jn 17:17,19). The sanctifying agent here is God's Word. The goal of sanctification is that believers will be prepared to be sent into the world as Jesus was sent, to glorify God by doing his work (cf. v. 4).

In other passages, sanctification is spoken of as being part of each believer's experience, an essential part of the past aspect of salvation (Ac 20:32; 26:18; Ro 15:16; 1 Co 1:2; 6:11). In the Romans passage, the Holy Spirit is the agent of sanctification (i.e., salvation).

Only one verse in the NT calls an unbeliever sanctified. That verse, found in Paul's discourse on marriage, states that, in some sense, an unbelieving spouse is sanctified by the believing spouse (1 Co 7:14).

In Paul's desire that God sanctify the believers "through and through" (1 Th 5:23), God is again seen as the agent of sanctification. Paul adds, "May your whole spirit, soul and body be kept blameless at the coming of our Lord Jesus Christ." Here the idea of sanctification is presented as a present and future possibility for believers as God continues to perfect their lives.

Finally, in Heb 10:29, the writer argues that the blood of Jesus sanctifies within, whereas all that the OT's sacrifices could accomplish was an outward, ritual sanctification (Heb 9:13).

From these passages it is clear that God sanctifies believers and that the blood of Christ provides the basis for this. Divine sanctification is effected by the Holy Spirit, and the Word of God is an active agent in the process.

'It is also clear that sanctification, like salvation, has various meanings. "Sanctify" can stand for the accomplished work of God applied to an individual in salvation; in this sense we are sanctified in virtue of our relationship with God. But sanctification also can refer to the working of the Word and the Spirit to equip us to serve God in the world and to be morally blameless until Jesus returns.

Is moral sanctification experienced as a gradual process? Is it a second work of grace? Does it imply sinlessness? To answer questions like these—the issues debated by those with different views of Christian experience—we must look for evidence in some other place than in the texts where we find the word "sanctify."

SANCTUARY

The Hebrew words *qōḏeš* and *miqdāš* are used of the tabernacle and the temple and of the inner rooms of each structure. The common meaning is of a structure or area set apart to the worship of God. ▶ *Holy/Holiness*

In the NT, "sanctuary" is *hagion*. This too is from a root that means "holy." The word is seldom found in the NT, except where used by the writer of Hebrews to contrast the OT structures with the heavenly reality after which they were patterned (Heb 8:2; 9:1,2,3,8,12,24,25; 10:19; 13:11).

SATAN

The Bible presents Satan as a personal being. He was created as Lucifer ("light bearer") and carries a number of names in the OT and the NT. These include the Devil, the serpent, the accuser of the brethren, and the ruler of the kingdom of the air.

The Hebrew word is *śāṭān*, which means "adversary." The Greek *satanas* carries the same meaning. The common name of Satan in the NT is *diabolos*, ("devil"), meaning "one who slanders or accuses."

Both Testaments reveal Satan as God's adversary and the enemy of mankind. Passages taken to refer to Satan (Isa 14:12–15; Eze 28:11–19), with NT references, provide insight into his history and destiny.

Satan was a powerful angel in God's original creation. His pride (Isa 14:12–15; 1 Ti 3:6) and warped desire to take God's place introduced sin into the universe. Satan's initial rebellion included the defection of many angels and led to the expulsion of that host from heaven. ♦ *Angels*

Satan was the power influencing the serpent in Eden, and thus he was an instrument in mankind's fall, by which he introduced sin's corruption into the human race.

Satan still exercises great power in the world. He is called the "ruler of the kingdom of the air" in Eph 2:2 and is at work in all who are disobedient to God. Despite his powers and the devices he uses to deceive humanity, Satan was decisively defeated in every confrontation he had with Jesus (e.g. Mt 4:1–11; Lk 11:14–22; 13:10–16).

The NT foretells a day when Satan will lead another great rebellion, working through individuals he empowers (2 Th 2). But the final destiny of this evil being is fixed. Following yet another final attempt to overthrow the Lord (Rev 20:7–9), Satan will be thrown into the lake of burning sulfur, as Revelation portrays hell, to be "tormented day and night for ever and ever" (v. 10). ♦ *Demons/Evil Spirits*

SAVE ♦ *Salvation/Save*

SCHEME

Twice the NT speaks of the Devil's schemes. In 2 Co 2:11, the word is *noēma*, which means "thoughts and purposes." The emphasis is on Satan's intelligence, devoted to sinister plots designed to entrap human beings. In Eph 6:11, the word is *methodeia*, "craftiness" (its only other NT occurrence being in Eph 4:14). God has equipped us with armor against the methods of Satan (Eph 6:10–18), and we have the mind of Christ to guide us safely past all of Satan's traps (1 Co 2:16).

SCOFF

There is more than mocking derision implied when the NASB speaks of scoffing and the scoffer. There is an unyielding pride, a hardness toward God and others. The scoffer refuses to submit to God's Word and stirs up trouble wherever he goes (e.g., Pr 22:10).

This meaning, expressed in *lāṣôn*, is found in Isa 28:14, where the NIV reads "scoffers" (the Hebrew word occurring twice elsewhere in the OT—Pr 1:22; 29:8). But where the NIV has the verb "scoff," the original usually has *šāraq*. This word (occurring 12 times in the OT) literally means "to whistle." The audible whistle, in context, is interpreted as derisive pleasure or perhaps shock at the results of God's judgments.

SCORN

Various Hebrew words lie behind the few places where the NASB reads "scorn"—*śāhaq* ("to laugh"), *šûṭ* ("to treat with scorn or contempt"), *nābāl* (in a stem that means "to treat as a fool"— i.e., with contempt), and *ḥerpāh* ("to reproach or revile").

The NIV shows many more uses of the word "scorn." The translators focused on other roots, though the tone of mocking and derision remains. Often the Hebrew term translated "scorn" in the NIV is *ḥerpāh*. The root, *ḥārap*, means "to reproach by blaming or scorning." Reproaching shows disrespect and involves a subtle attack on character.

Lā'ag also is translated "scorn" in the NIV. This is a word of derision, in which the object is ridiculed and mocked. Like other words translated "scorn," it involves verbal abuse, here through mockery, designed to diminish its object.

SCRIPTURE

The word for "Scripture" in Greek is *graphē*. It simply means "a writing" or "what has been written." But in the NT this term is used exclusively of Scripture and is used in such a way that quoting Scripture is understood to be the same as quoting God (e.g., Jn 7:38,42; Ro 4:3; 9:17; 10:11; Gal 4:30).

The nature of Scripture is explained by Paul when he writes that "all Scripture is God-breathed and is useful for teaching, rebuking, correcting and training in righteousness" (2 Tim 3:16). Without dictation or blocking out the individuality of the human writers, God the Spirit bore them along as they wrote, so that the product is "the holy Scriptures" (v. 15), the Word of God.

Another important passage is 2 Pe 3:15. In the NT, *graphē* normally refers to the OT revelation or to an OT text. But Peter writes of "our dear brother" Paul's letters and identifies them with "the other Scriptures." This reference and the evidence of church history make it clear that the writings that compose the NT were recognized very early as Scripture.

SEAL

The OT has *hātam* ("to seal") and *hōtām* ("signet" or "seal"). Important documents and, figuratively, revelation (Isa 8:16; Da 12:9) were stamped with a seal. The impression of the engraved ring or tool was a mark of authenticity. The seal also showed ownership and suggests security.

In the NT, "to seal" is *sphragizō*. In Greek culture, the seal had great legal significance. When stamped on possessions, the seal indicated ownership and guarded the possession against theft. On a document the seal authenticated the message and conveyed the authority of the one who stamped it. The seal could serve as a signature, recognized by all. A sealed document was allowed to be opened only by the addressee. For those in power, such as kings or governors, the seal served as the symbol of authority.

In the NT, the various implications of sealing are used to express spiritual truths. Jn 6:27 uses "seal" in the authenticating sense. Jesus speaks with God's own voice and authority. In a sense, Paul wrote, the believing community in Corinth was a seal that authenticated his apostolic legitimacy (1 Co 9:2).

In Ro 4:11, circumcision is called a sign and a seal. Paul's thought is that circumcision was an identifying mark, stamping as God's own people those made righteous by faith. It was never, as Israel thought, a sign that one lives under law.

In 2 Ti 2:19, Paul wrote that "God's solid foundation stands firm, sealed with this inscription: 'The Lord knows those who are his,' and 'Everyone who confesses the name of the Lord must turn away from wickedness.' " Paul's point is that the mark of God's ownership has both invisible and visible aspects. The invisible is the hidden knowledge of God. The visible is the character of those who belong to the Lord. They turn from wickedness and live by God's will.

Three times the Holy Spirit is spoken of as a seal. In Eph 1:13 and 4:30 the image is commercial. The shipment has been accepted, payment has been made, and the owner's seal stamped on the product to secure it. The presence of the Holy Spirit is God's guarantee that he will accept believers, for whom he has paid the price in Christ. The same thought, the seal of ownership, is found in 2 Co 1:22. God the Holy Spirit is God's guarantee that we will be taken into our Father's house, forever his.

The protective aspect of the seal is emphasized in Rev 7, while identification is in view in Rev 22. In other Revelation passages the seal is used to close and keep hidden that which is within.

SEE

The OT and the NT use "see" in the same literal and figurative ways. As in English, words for "see" can encompass perceiving, realizing, and apprehending (i.e., mental acts as well as vision).

SEED ◆ *Offspring*

SEEK

"Seek" is a common word, but it is used in many significant ways. For example, we are to seek God and his kingdom first (Mt 6:33); the one who seeks God finds (Mt 7:8); the Son of Man came to seek and to save the lost (Lk 19:10); believers are not to seek a divorce (1 Co 7:27); and believers are to seek the good of others, not their own good (1 Co 10:24).

In these passages, "seek" is *zēteō*. In classical Greek, "seek" was used of the search for knowledge and came to indicate philosophical investigation. The word was used in the Septuagint in phrases indicating a turning to God. The person seeking the Lord focused his attention on God, on worship, and on obedience. In the NT, "seek" carries a wide range of meanings but most often implies giving attention and priority to, desiring, and deliberately following after.

Except for two verses (Lk 11:50,51), an intensive form, *ekzēteō*, is used with the meaning of a concentrated effort (Ac 15:17; Ro 3:11; Heb 11:6; 12:17; 1 Pe 1:10). When one seeks God, a casual glance in his direction is hardly sufficient. But we can be sure that God "rewards those who earnestly seek him" (Heb 11:6).

SEER

Two Hebrew words are translated "seer." They are *rō'eh* and *hōzeh*. Each is a form of a Hebrew word that means "to see," and each is used as a synonym for prophet (1 Sa 9:9; 1 Ch 29:29). ♦ *Prophecy/Prophet* These words focus on the way in which the one who spoke for God received his revelation, namely, through a vision (i.e., by seeing).

SELAH

Selâh is a Hebrew term, probably from *sālal*, "to lift up." Its use in Psalms and in Hab 3 suggests it is a musical notation, but no one knows its meaning. Perhaps it indicates a pause or a shift from a lower to a higher key.

SELF-CONTROL

The Greek words for "self-control" are *enkrateia* (Ac 24:25; Gal 5:23; 2 Pe 1:6) and *enkratēs* (Tit 1:8). They mean "to have power over oneself" and thus to be able to hold oneself in.

Those without self-control are *akrasia* (Mt 23:25; 1 Co 7:5) or *akratēs* (2 Ti 3:3). They are powerless, overwhelmed by the passions that tug at and control them. ♦ *Serve/Servant/Slave*

SEND ♦ *Apostle/Apostleship*

SENSUAL

The most common NT word for sensuality is *aselgeia*. It appears nine times in the NT (Mk 7:22; Ro 13:13; 2 Co 12:21; Gal 5:19; Eph 4:19; 1 Pe 4:3; 2 Pe 2:7,18; Jude 4). It is a word expressing a shameless self-indulgence, an abandoned commitment to pleasures of the flesh. ♦ *Flesh* There is no sense of restraint or shame.

Katastrēniaō is used only in 1 Ti 5:11. It refers to the sexual impulses felt by young widows. In context, these impulses war against Christ in that they lead the individual to marry, thus necessitating the laying aside of her special commitment to service. It does not imply that sexual desire itself is wrong. ♦ *Sex*

The word for "sensual" in Col 2:23 is *plēsmonē* (found only here in the NT). *Strēnos* is used only in Rev 18:3. This is a strong word and combines impressions of self-indulgence with arrogance and luxury.

God has a remedy when sensual impulses tug at us: "Clothe yourselves with the Lord Jesus Christ, and do not think about how to gratify the desires of the sinful nature" (Ro 13:14).

SEPARATION/SEPARATE

"Separation" is a word used in some Christian communities in ways that may or may not square with its biblical intent. One of our problems in building a contemporary concept of separation is rooted in the fact that different Hebrew and Greek terms are translated by the same English word. Another problem is that factors shaping the life of believers in one era may be dramatically different from those in another.

OT 1. **The Hebrew words**
     2. **The context of separation in the OT**
NT 3. **The Greek words**
     4. **The context of separation in the NT**
     5. **Conclusions**

OT — 1. **The Hebrew words.** A number of different Hebrew words and expressions are translated "separate" and "separation" in a modern version such as the NIV. In some places the verb simply means "to part" (2 Sa 14:6). In 1 Ki 5:9 the thought is one of being discharged, as from a contract or military service. Sometimes the Hebrew word simply means "to be scattered" (e.g., Jer 52:8; Eze 46:18). Two OT passages (2 Ki 15:5; 2 Ch 26:21), speaking of the isolation of a leprous ruler, use *ḥāpšît*, a word found only in these two places in the OT. There are three other Hebrew words that have special significance. They are *bādal*, *pārad*, and *nāzar*.

Bādal means "to separate" (i.e., to remove something from something else and thus to make a distinction between them). This is the word used in Ge 1, as the Creator established order in the universe, dividing day from night, land from sea, the waters on the earth from the waters above. The word is also often used of Israel's separation from other nations (e.g., Ezr 6:21; 9:1; Ne 9:2). In a significant sense, Israel was set apart from all other peoples, the critical distinction being that God had chosen Israel and had entered into covenant relationship with them. ♦ *Covenant*

Separation is also at the root of many of Israel's ritual practices and laws: "I am the LORD your God, who has set you apart from the nations. You must therefore make a distinction between clean and unclean animals and between clean and unclean birds" (Lev 20:24–25). ♦ *Clean and Unclean* In this passage, both "set apart" and "make a distinction" are *bādal*. Thus, the peculiar practices of Israelite religion served to constantly remind God's people that they were different—because of their relationship with him.

The same kind of distinction existed within Israel, as God consecrated the Levites, setting them apart from the other tribes to serve him in worship (e.g., Nu 16:9; Dt 10:8; 1 Ki 8:53; 1 Ch 23:13).

Of the forty-two times that *bādal* is used in the OT, it is translated "separate(d)" or "separation" fifteen times in the NIV (Ge 1:4,6,7,14,18; Ex 26:33; Nu 16:9,21; Ezr 6:21; 9:1; 10:11; Ne 9:2; 10:28; Isa 59:2; Eze 42:20).

Pārad tends toward physical description. It means "to separate" or "to divide," as rivers separate into streams. It is also used in Proverbs to speak of divisive actions that separate friends. Eight of the twenty-six occurrences of *pārad* in the OT are rendered "separate" or "separation" in the NIV (Ge 25:23; 30:40; 2 Ki 2:11; Ru 1:17; Ne 4:19; Est 3:8; Pr 16:28; 17:9).

Nāzar means "to separate" and is often followed by a preposition that gives it the meaning "to abstain from" or "to keep away from." In Lev 15:31, even without this preposition, the meaning is clear: "You must keep the Israelites separate from things that make them unclean, so they will not die in their uncleanness for defiling my dwelling place, which is among them."

This Hebrew word, used in another passage with another preposition, suggests "separation to." This passage (Nu 6:1–21) speaks of consecration to the Lord on the part of those who took the special Nazirite vow. The vow involved refraining from specific things as an act of special devotion to the Lord.

2. The context of separation in the OT. In the OT, the believing community existed as a nation that was socially and geographically separated from its pagan neighbors. The Mosaic Law regulated the total lifestyle of Israel, not simply its religious practices. Many aspects of Israelite life were neither "right" nor "wrong" morally but were still regulated by OT statutes and laws.

As the passages quoted above make clear, the reason for the regulations that served to set Israel apart from other nations was a spiritual one. Israel *was* different. Israel had been called into a relationship with the Lord God, and both Israel and the nations around her had to be constantly reminded of the distinction that God himself had made. ♦ *Clean and Unclean*

NT — 3. The Greek words. Two Greek words are found where the NIV and the NASB read "separate" or "separation": *chōrizō* and *aphorizō*.

Chōrizō means "to separate" or "to divide," and is often used in the sense of separating oneself. When physical separation is in view, the NIV and the NASB may speak of being parted or of departing. But there are a number of figurative uses as well. God's commitment to us is so great that nothing imaginable can separate us from the love of Christ (Ro 8:35,38–39). God's plan for marriage calls for a similar commitment. No one should separate those so joined (Mt 19:6; Mk 10:9). ◗ *Divorce and Remarriage* A related word (*chōris*) is also used in Eph 2:12, which describes the unsaved Gentile as one who is separated from Christ. *Aphorizō* means "to set apart, or separate." It is a strong term, often carrying with it an implication of divine determination. Thus, God will act at history's end to separate the evil and the good (Mt 13:49; 25:32). This is the word Paul used when rebuking Peter for wrongfully separating himself from Gentile believers when Jewish brothers visited Antioch (Gal 2:12).

This is also the word found in 2 Co 6:17. Appealing to the principle of separation from unbelieving nations around Israel, Paul quoted the OT (Isa 52:11), and said, "Come out from them and be separate." The context makes the issue very clear. Paul was writing specifically about yoked relationships with unbelievers. ◗ *Yoke*

4. The context of separation in the NT. The believing community of the NT era exists as clusters of believers within the larger, secular society. It is clear that the separation by total lifestyle appropriate for Israel may not be appropriate for those who must live as members of differing cultures. In fact, separating elements of the law were done away with when the old covenant was superseded by the new covenant at Christ's death. ◗ *Covenant*
What then can we carry over from OT principle into NT practice? Paul said specifically that being yoked with unbelievers is a violation of the ancient separation principle. But in an earlier letter to the Corinthians he clarified the idea of separation: they *were* to associate with

the immoral and ungodly of this world, not to withdraw from them (1 Co 5:9–13). Separation does not imply isolation of the Christian from his or her culture and society, nor from the lost neighbor.

5. Conclusions. Certainly the principle of separation to God has contemporary application to the Christian. But we must apply this principle with great care. As Jesus' representatives in the world, we are called to live within our society and in the company of sinful people. ◗ *World* In its most significant sense, our separation is to God. We are to be different from those around us, not withdrawn from them. The distinction that God seeks to draw in and through our lives is simply that we are to walk as Jesus walked when he was here (1 Jn 2:6). As Jesus sought and helped the lost, so will we. As Jesus suffered the accusations of those who criticized his association with the sinners of his day, so we may suffer the accusations of the religious among us when we reach out to draw others with and to God's love.

SERVE/SERVANT/SLAVE

The relationships implied in the idea of servanthood and slavery, which was prominent in the Bible, are often misunderstood. Yet we believers are called to a life of servanthood. And, like Paul, we are slaves of Christ (Eph 6:6). Only as God's slaves can we find freedom (Ro 6:6–22).

OT 1. The Hebrew words and their meaning
2. Slavery in OT times
3. The Servant of the Lord in Isaiah
NT 4. The Greek words and their meaning
5. Slavery in NT times
6. Spiritual slavery
7. The servanthood of Jesus
8. Servanthood for the believer

OT — 1. The Hebrew words and their meaning. The OT is filled with references to service, serving, servants, and slaves. The significant vocabulary includes the following words: *'ābad, šārat,* and *na'ar.*

The verb *'ābad* means "to work" or "to serve." In intensive stems it means "to enslave" or "to force into service." But more than forced labor can be indicated by this common OT word.

Subjects are said to "serve" a ruler. They perform their tasks according to his will and direction.

The word is also used of the service of God or false gods. The idea of serving God is often translated in the NIV by "worship" (e.g., Ex 3:12; 4:23). In other passages—e.g., Jer 2:20, where the obedience owed to the deity that one worships is involved—"serve" is retained. The context in Jeremiah helps us sense the cluster of ideas summed up in the idea of serving God: " 'Consider then and realize how evil and bitter it is for you when you forsake the LORD your God and have no awe of me,' declares the Lord, the LORD Almighty. 'Long ago you broke off your yoke and tore off your bonds; you said, "I will not serve you!" Indeed, on every high hill and under every spreading tree you lay down as a prostitute' " (vv. 19–20).

This term is also used of the special tasks relating to worship to which God called the Levites: ▶ **Priests and Levites** "They are to perform duties for him [Aaron] and for the whole community at the Tent of Meeting by doing the work of the tabernacle. They are to take care of all the furnishings of the Tent of Meeting, fulfilling the obligations of the Israelites by doing the work of the tabernacle" (Nu 3:7–8).

Thus, *'ābad* covers a wide range of meanings and relationships. The work can be menial, done under threat, or significant, performed as a joyful ministry to the Lord. Where serving God is concerned, the term can encompass all the duties owed the Lord by his people—from worship to the more menial service of maintaining the house of worship to every act of obedience.

This root is significant in another way also. From it comes *'ebed,* a noun that occurs about eight hundred times in the OT with the meaning of "servant" or

"slave." This word too has a range of meanings. It was applied to one who was a slave proper (see 2, below) and to subjects of a king, who are viewed as his servants. It was used to identify a worshiper of a particular god or a worshiper of the Lord. A "servant of Baal" was one who worshiped that pagan deity. It was sometimes used in formal correspondence or speech, much as it is still used by English-speaking people in certain areas of the world ("Your obedient servant").

The term "servant" also has great theological significance when indicating the Messiah, who is cast as the Servant of the Lord in Isaiah especially (see 3, below).

The verb *šārat* also means "to serve," the focus being on ministry. It indicates an important service. The service is important because (1) the person served is of high rank (usually a ruler or some other very important person, or God himself), (2) there is a close relationship with the person being served (the service most likely done in the presence of the other person, rather than in some distant and anonymous post), and (3) it is viewed as important. This servant busies himself with matters of real concern to the person served. For all these reasons, a person identified as a servant or minister by this word is of high status.

This verb (including its participle, which indicates a personal servant or minister) is found in the OT in the following texts among others: Ge 39:4; 40:4; Ex 24:13; 28:35,43; Nu 1:50; 3:6,31; Dt 10:8; 21:5; Jos 1:1; 1 Sa 2:11; 3:1; 2 Sa 13:17,18; 1 Ki 1:4,15; 2 Ki 6:15; 1 Ch 6:32; 15:2; 16:4,37; 2 Ch 5:14; 31:2; Ezr 8:17; Ne 10:36,39; Est 1:10; 6:3; Ps 101:6; 103:21; 104:4; Pr 29:12; Isa 56:6; 60:7,10; 61:6; Jer 33:21,22; Eze 20:32; 43:19; Joel 1:9,13; 2:17.

Some other words, including *na'ar,* which normally refers to a youth but may indicate a personal retainer, are translated "servant." However, *'ābad* and *šārat* are the primary and basic terms.

The roots of these verbs are also used in the nouns "work" and "service." The common noun, indicating any type of labor, including the most menial, is *ᵃḇôḏâh*. ♦ **Work** The noun *šārēṯ*, indicating religious service or ministry, occurs only twice in the OT (Nu 4:12; 2 Ch 24:14).

2. Slavery in OT times. At times, *ʿeḇed* is used in the OT with the specific meaning of "slave"—someone who is owned by another person, or whose personal services were sold to another for a specified length of time. It was not uncommon for a Hebrew with crushing debts to sell himself or his family members into this kind of "voluntary" servitude. ♦ **Poor and Oppressed** A non-Hebrew might be purchased or might be acquired as a spoil of war and would often serve as a slave for life.

The OT carefully regulates the institution of both permanent and temporary servitude (Ex 21:2–11; Lev 25:39–55; Dt 15:1–18). The Hebrew slave enjoyed a special status. He was to be released after six years, unless at that time he chose to remain with his master's family. This same right was extended to women who were not taken as wives or concubines by the master or his sons. ♦ **Concubine** In the Year of Jubilee, the Hebrew slaves in a family were also to be released from any obligation they might have to the owner. ♦ **Redeem/Ransom**

As members of a Hebrew household, even foreign slaves were considered part of the family. They shared in Israel's worship and were protected by Sabbath law, which provided a mandatory day of rest. ♦ **Rest** Even though considered under law to be property, slaves were given significant protection. If a master's beating did so much as cause the slave to lose a tooth, the slave was to be set free.

Slavery in Israel was a household kind of thing. Plantations that used hundreds or thousands of slaves, as in our Old South, were not part of the culture of Israel. It was much less expensive in OT days to hire day labor (*śāḵar*) than to maintain slaves. Thus, the few slaves who might be owned by well-to-do Hebrews were likely to be treated as family members or trusted friends, rather than as beasts or enemies (e.g., Ge 15:1–4; 1 Sa 9:5; 16:22; 1 Ch 2:35).

At times, foreign slaves were owned by the king. Some of them served in the temple. Solomon put slaves to work in his copper mines; he drew levies of workers from peoples his father David had defeated (1 Ki 9:20–21). Ne 7:57–60 mentions that there were 392 hereditary temple slaves.

3. The Servant of the Lord in Isaiah. An important theme in Isaiah is the Servant of the Lord, identified as a person. Servants (pl.) are spoken of in Isa 54–66, servant in Isa 39–53. Even when the reference is in the singular, the people of Israel are often in view (e.g., 41:8–10; 42:18–19; 43:9–10; 44:1–3; 45:4; 48:20). Although chosen and strengthened by the Lord, servant Israel failed to accomplish God's purposes.

So Isaiah introduced another Servant, the Messiah. ♦ **Christ** Four major passages focus on this coming Servant of the Lord.

First, Isa 42:1–9. Filled with God's Spirit (v. 1), the Servant will walk humbly among the bruised and worthless of the earth (vv. 2–3). Taking this unique path, he will in fact establish justice on earth (v. 4). God himself will lead and protect the Servant and make a covenant with him (vv. 5–6). In a stunning, unexpected act, the Servant himself will become the key that releases life's captives (vv. 7–9).

In Isa 49:1–6, the Servant speaks to the nations of the world, announcing his credentials. The Servant has been shaped by God and called to a mission that will display God's splendor (vv. 1–3). Despite what appears to be failure (v. 4), the Servant will call Israel back to the Lord and bring salvation to all mankind (vv. 5–6).

In the next chapter (Isa 50:4–10), God is seen to be constantly speaking to and guiding his Servant (v. 4), who is completely obedient to him (v. 5). Obedience will involve sufferings: "I offered my back to those who beat me, my cheeks to those who pulled out my beard; I did not hide my face from mocking and spitting" (v. 6). But the sovereign God was at work in the Servant's suffering and would fully vindicate him (vv. 7–9). Those who fear the Lord will obey the word of the Servant, trusting in the name of the Lord and relying on him (v. 10).

The next Servant passage is Isa 52:13–53:12. God's Servant was destined to be exalted (52:13), even though at first people turned away from his form, repulsed by his suffering (v. 14). Indeed, the Servant was destined to purify humanity (v. 15).

In Isa 53, the prophet gives us the OT's incredibly graphic portrait of Jesus' sacrificial death. Despised and rejected by sinful people (vv. 1–3), God's Servant was pierced for their transgressions and suffered a punishment that brings them peace (vv. 4–5). All people like sheep have gone astray, but the Lord laid on his Servant the iniquity of them all (v. 6).

His death was for humanity's transgressions (vv. 7–8). He died with thieves and was laid in a rich man's tomb (v. 9). God's eternal intention was to make the Servant's life a guilt offering (v. 10). But the Servant would be restored to life after his suffering and would see the results of his suffering in those he justified (v. 11). He would be exalted, for he poured out his life in death, while bearing our sin, so that he could intercede for us transgressors (v. 12).

In these passages there is a portrait not only of Jesus but also of servanthood. Jesus is a model for us as he demonstrated the servant lifestyle. For Jesus, servanthood meant, and it should mean for us, (1) a desire to serve God, (2) a humble stance before others, (3) a commitment to bring deliverance to others, (4) a willingness to pay the price in personal suffering, and (5) a reliance on the Lord, who alone strengthens and upholds us.

There are a few other references to the Messiah as Servant (e.g., Jer 33:21–22; Eze 34:23–24; 37:24–25).

NT — 4. The Greek words and their meaning.

Four families of Greek words are directly related to this subject. They are represented by four verbs: *douleuō* ("to be subject," "to serve"), *diakoneō* ("to serve," "to aid," "to act as a deacon"), *leitourgeō* ("to serve [as a priest in

worship rituals]"), and *latreuō* ("to serve [in a religious sense]," "to worship").

The first two are the most significant. *Douleuō* means "to serve as a slave." It emphasizes subjection of the will to another. In the NT, the use of this word and its cognates is focused on the Christian's subjection to Jesus as Lord. *Diakoneō* is also connected with service; but here one's attention is focused on meeting the needs of others, especially of brothers and sisters in the church.

In Greek thought, both types of service were shameful. The duty of the Greek person was to himself, to achieve his potential for excellence. To be forced to subject his will or surrender his time and efforts for the sake of others was intensely distasteful, even humiliating. But Jesus came to serve, not to be served. In giving himself for others, Jesus set the pattern for a transformed value system. In Christ, serving is the highway to greatness. In Christ we achieve our full potential by giving, not by grasping.

The following is a survey of the ways in which these words for serving are used in the NT, with listings of key passages.

Words in the *douleuō* group, while often translated "servant" or "serve," designate a relationship of subjection, in which one is subject to another's will as a slave. Words in this group and their appearance in the NT are: (1) *douleia*, "slavery" (Ro 8:15,21; Gal 4:24; 5:1; Heb 2:15); (2) *douleuō*, "to be subject to, to serve" (Mt 6:24; Lk 15:29; 16:13; Jn 8:33; Ac 7:7; 20:19; Ro 6:6; 7:6,25; 9:12; 12:11; 14:18; 16:18; Gal 4:8,9,25; 5:13; Eph 6:7; Php 2:22; Col 3:24; 1 Th 1:9; 1 Ti 6:2; Tit 3:3); (3) *doulē*, "a female slave" (Lk 1:38,48; Ac 2:18); (4) *doulos*, "a slave" (Mt 8:9; 10:24,25; 13:27,28; 18:23,26,27,28,32; 20:27; 21:34,35,36; 22:3,4,6,8,10; 24:45,46, 48,50; 25:14,19,21,23,26,30; 26:51; Mk 10:44; 12:2,4; 13:34; 14:47; Lk 2:29; 7:2,3, 8,10; 12:37,38,43,45,46,47; 14:17,21,22,23; 15:22; 17:7,9,10; 19:13,15,17,22; 20:10,11; 22:50; Jn 4:51; 8:34,35; 13:16; 15:15,20; 18:10,18,26; Ac 2:18; 4:29; 16:17; Ro 1:1; 6:16,17,19,20; 1 Co 7:21,22,23; 12:13; 2 Co 4:5; Gal 1:10; 3:28; 4:1,7; Eph 6:5,6,8; Php 1:1; 2:7; Col 3:11,22; 4:1,12; 1 Ti 6:1; 2 Ti

2:24; Tit 1:1; 2:9; Phm 16; Jas 1:1; 1 Pe 2:16; 2 Pe 1:1; 2:19; Jude 1; Rev 1:1; 2:20; 6:15; 7:3; 10:7; 11:18; 13:16; 15:3; 19:2,5,18; 22:3,6); and (5) *douloō*, "to enslave" (Ac 7:6; Ro 6:18,22; 1 Co 7:15; 9:19; Gal 4:3; Tit 2:3; 2 Pe 2:19).

Two other Greek words suggest the *doulos* relationship: *oiketēs*, "a household servant" (Lk 16:13; Ac 10:7; Ro 14:4; 1 Pe 2:18), and *pais*, "child" or "servant," is translated "servant" several places in the NIV (Mt 8:6,8,13; 12:18; Lk 1:54,69; 7:7; Ac 3:13,26; 4:25,27,30).

Words in the *diakoneō* group denote the giving of personal help to others. A wide range of kinds of help are included, from serving at tables (Lk 10:40) to collecting funds for needy brethren (Ac 11:29; 2 Co 8:4) to sharing Christ's word (2 Ti 4:11; 2 Co 11:8). It is a concept that includes all ministries within the body of Christ—the exercise of all spiritual gifts and all offices (1 Co 12:4–6). The noun "deacon" is applied to men and women holding office in the church (Ro 16:1; Php 1:1; 1 Ti 3:8–13). Of particular importance is the example set by Jesus. *Diakoneō* and cognate words were used by Jesus when he spoke of serving, as when he said, "The Son of Man did not come to be served, but to serve, and give his life as a ransom for many" (Mt 20:28).

Words in this group and their occurrence in the NT are: (1) *diakoneō*, "to serve," "to serve as a deacon," "to minister to" (Mt 4:11; 8:15; 20:28; 25:44; 27:55; Mk 1:13,31; 10:45; 15:41; Lk 4:39; 8:3; 10:40; 12:37; 17:8; 22:26,27; Jn 12:2,26; Ac 6:2; 19:22; Ro 15:25; 2 Co 3:3; 8:19,20; 1 Ti 3:10,13; 2 Ti 1:18; Phm 13; Heb 6:10; 1 Pe 1:12; 4:10,11); (2) *diakonia*, "service," "support," "office of deacon," "ministry" (Lk 10:40; Ac 1:17,25; 6:1,4; 11:29; 12:25; 20:24; 21:19; Ro 11:13; 12:7; 15:31; 1 Co 12:5; 16:15; 2 Co 3:7,8,9; 4:1; 5:18; 6:3; 8:4; 9:1,12,13; 11:8; Eph 4:12; Col 4:17; 1 Ti 1:12; 2 Ti 4:5,11; Heb 1:14; Rev 2:19); and (3) *diakonos*, "servant," "deacon," "minister" (Mt 20:26; 22:13; 23:11; Mk 9:35; 10:43; Jn 2:5,9; 12:26; Ro 13:4; 15:8; 16:1; 1 Co 3:5; 2 Co 3:6; 6:4; 11:15,23; Gal 2:17; Eph 3:7; 6:21; Php 1:1; Col 1:7,23,25; 4:7; 1 Th 3:2; 1 Ti 3:8,12; 4:6).

Two other words share with the *diakoneō* group the sense of a supportive ministry. They are *hypēreteō*, "to serve or render service" (Ac 13:36; 20:34; 24:23), and *hypēretēs*, "a servant, helper, or assistant" (Mt 5:25; 26:58; Mk 14:54,65; Lk 1:2; 4:20; Jn 7:32,45,46; 18:3,12,18,22,36; 19:6; Ac 5:22,26; 13:5; 26:16; 1 Co 4:1).

In Greek culture, the *leitourgeō* word group speaks of community service. In Judaism, it focused specifically on the religious service of priest or Levite. At times in the NT this OT sense is intended; at other times the Greek sense of general service seems to be intended (e.g., Php 2:25,30; Heb 1:7,14). Words in this group and their appearance in the NT are: (1) *leitourgeō*, "to serve," "to minister" (Ac 13:2; Ro 15:27; Heb 10:11); (2) *leitourgia*, "service, help, ministry" (Lk 1:23; 2 Co 9:12; Php 2:17,30; Heb 8:6; 9:21); (3) *leitourgikos*, "serving" (Heb 1:14); and (4) *leitourgos*, "servant" (Ro 13:6; 15:16; Php 2:25; Heb 1:7; 8:2).

Every occurrence of the *latreuō* group in the NT carries the religious sense of worship, or serving God. Words in this group are found in the NT as follows: (1) *latreuō*, "to serve," "to worship" (Mt 4:10; Lk 1:74; 2:37; 4:8; Ac 7:7,42; 24:14; 26:7; 27:23; Ro 1:9,25; Php 3:3; 2 Ti 1:3; Heb 8:5; 9:9,14; 10:2; 12:28; 13:10; Rev 7:15; 22:3); and (2) *latreia*, "service," "worship" (Jn 16:2; Ro 9:4; 12:1; Heb 9:1,6). A totally different word, *thrēskeia*, "the service of God," or "religion," has the same meaning as the words of this group. It is found in Ac 26:5; Col 2:18; Jas 1:26,27.

5. Slavery in NT times. Much is known about slavery in the first century. While the majority of slaves were laborers, among them were educators and physicians, artisans and managers. In general, slaves fared as well as free laborers. They ate as well, were clothed as well, and were sometimes better housed.

The institution of slavery was basic to society in the Roman Empire and is not challenged in the NT. Instead, its existence is assumed, and those Christians who were slaves were called on to serve their masters faithfully (Eph 6:5–8; Col 3:22; 1 Ti 6:1–2; Tit 2:9–10; 1 Pe 2:18).

The machines of their day, slaves were not persons in the legal sense. Yet the laws did provide a certain amount of protection for them. And a slave with higher skills could expect to gain his freedom within a reasonable span of time. Paul mentions this in 1 Co 7, where he says, "Were you a slave when you were called [i.e., when you became a believer]? Don't let it trouble you—although if you can gain your freedom, do so" (v. 21). Freedom might simply be granted by one's master, or a slave could save money from his earnings and purchase his own freedom.

In the first century a person might become a slave in one of three primary ways: (1) by being captured in war, (2) by being born of a slave mother (something Paul builds his analogy on in Gal 4:21–31), and (3) through sale, by another or by himself. It was not unusual for a child to be sold into slavery or for a person to sell himself to satisfy his creditors (Ro 7:14). There was also a stipulation in Roman law that, should a free person act as a slave, he could not claim his freedom. One who acts like a slave is, in fact, a slave. Paul may reflect this principle when he urges the Galatians not to return to law as a way of life, saying, "It is for freedom that Christ has set us free. Stand firm, then, and do not let yourselves be burdened again by a yoke of slavery" (Gal 5:1). ♦ *Law*

However much the bondage of slavery might be mitigated by the comparatively good conditions in which a slave lived, the central fact of slavery remained. A slave was not his own person. He was required to do his master's will, not his own. He was bound to serve, not his own interests, but the interests of his master. This reality underlies many sayings in the Gospels. The Roman soldier said to Jesus, "I say to my servant [*doulos*], 'Do this,' and he does it" (Mt 8:9). Jesus spoke (Lk 17:7–10) of the *doulos* who worked in the fields and then prepared the master's supper: only afterward did he sit down to eat. "Would he thank the servant because he did what he

was told to do?" Jesus asked (v. 9). The answer of course is no. In obeying, the *doulos* only did his duty.

It is true that a slave might be given great responsibility by his master (e.g., Mk 13:34). But the slave remained a slave. When Jesus said, "No one can serve [*douleuō*] two masters" (Mt 6:24; cf. Lk 16:13), he expressed an acknowledged truth. A slave was one who lived without personal will; he existed to do the will of his master. Although the spiritual implications of slavery laws will be discussed later, it is helpful to note Paul's application in Ro 14. Paul made it clear that those believers who sought to impose their personal convictions on others were criticizing someone else's household servants (*oiketēs*). It is, Paul argues, to his own master that he stands or falls. Christ died that he alone might be Lord. Thus, we are all personally responsible to our own Master in such matters—not to critics who claim the right to impose their convictions on other servants. (vv. 1–12).

A life of slavery might end in one of several ways. A slave might be freed by a master. He might die. Or he might be purchased; if so, he remained a slave but had a new master. The NT applies the principles of release in several ways. In dying with Christ, we are released from slavery to the law and from the authority of sin (Ro 6:1–14; 7:1–6). Most significantly, Jesus' death paid the ultimate price for us. Now we are his and his alone, freed to render full obedience to the one master in the universe who is truly loving.

6. Spiritual slavery. We have already seen a number of ways in which slavery provides metaphors in the NT. One of the most significant is found in the repeated reference to human beings as spiritual slaves.

Jesus introduced the analogy of slavery in Jn 8. When the angry Pharisees rejected Jesus' call to follow him and claimed that they were truly free, Jesus answered, "I tell you the truth, everyone who sins is a slave to sin" (8:34). Sin establishes a dominating control over the human personality, and only "if the Son sets . . . free" can one find true freedom (8:36).

Paul reflected established Roman law when he spoke of slavery to sin and said, "Don't you know that when you offer yourselves to someone to obey him as slaves, you are slaves to the one whom you obey?" (Ro 6:16). But Paul went on to say, "Thanks be to God that, though you used to be slaves to sin, you wholeheartedly obeyed the form of teaching to which you were entrusted. You have been set free from sin and have become slaves to righteousness" (vv. 17–18).

This is an important NT concept. The believer finds freedom, not in recovering an independent will, but in submitting his will freely and joyfully to God. Following Jesus, the believer "does not live the rest of his earthly life for evil human desires, but rather for the will of God" (1 Pe 4:2). Paul, who often proudly identifies himself as a slave of Jesus Christ (Ro 1:1; Gal 1:10; Php 1:1; Tit 1:1), argues, "You are not your own; you were bought at a price. Therefore honor God with your body" (1 Co 7:19–20; cf. 7:23). Jesus has paid the purchase price and freed us from the deadly power of sin. He has taken us into his household, and now we find our destiny by accepting his lordship. In becoming slaves, subject to the will of God, we become what God intended us to be.

7. The servanthood of Jesus. In Lk 22:37, Jesus applied Isa 53:12 to himself, thus identifying himself as the Servant of the Lord of OT prophecy. The theme is also seen in other passages, but these passages use *pais* rather than *doulos*. Mt 12:18 is a quotation of Isa 2:1–4 and applies the prophecy to Jesus' ministry. In Acts, several references are made to Jesus as the servant of God (Ac 3:13,26; 4:27,30).

In the Epistles, Paul's great theological statement about Jesus in Philippians uses the word *doulos*. In Christ's self-emptying he "made himself nothing, taking the very nature of a servant, being made in human likeness" (Php 2:7). Here *doulos*, "slave," is properly applied to humanity. Because mankind is subject to sin's domination, we can look at ourselves in no

other light than as slaves. To free us, Jesus, "in very nature God" (v. 6), took on humanity. ♦ *Appear/Appearance*

But generally the NT does not speak of Jesus as a *doulos*. While willingly subjecting himself to the Father's will, Jesus remained free, and he remained Lord. Thus, Jesus said that society should not have "a servant [*doulos*] above his master" (Mt 10:24; cf. Jn 15:20), and the context makes it clear that in every relationship Jesus remains master. It is left for us disciples to be *douloi*.

But Jesus does take on himself *diakoneō*, a ministry of service to others. Never a slave, with a bound will, Jesus freely chose to become a servant dedicated to act for the well-being of others. "The Son of Man did not come to be served, but to serve," Jesus said, "and to give his life as a ransom for many" (Mt 20:28), and "I am among you as one who serves [at tables]" (Lk 22:27). In Jesus' surrender of his life for our sakes we see the ultimate servanthood, that of a free and uncoerced choice in which one places the good of others above oneself.

8. Servanthood for the believer. The NT uses both of these families of words to the describe the servanthood of believers.

The NT stresses the fact that as a *doulos*, the believer is serving the Lord (Ro 12:11; Col 3:24; 1 Th 1:9; Jas 1:1). The believer is to submit his will to the will of God, acknowledging Jesus as Lord. The lordship of Jesus in our lives is worked out as we remain faithful to him, doing the work he has delivered to us (Mt 24:45–48; Lk 12:35–48).

In submission to the will of God, the believer becomes a *diakonos*, a servant of God's people. Indeed, the greatest in the family of God move among the brethren as *douloi* (Mt 20:27). As noted in the previous discussion of *diakoneō* (part 4, above), this word incorporates every kind of ministry to persons. In involves the full exercise of the gifts and abilities each of us has for the benefit of others in Christ's church. In our servanthood, we adopt the selfless attitude of Jesus. As the Scriptures say, "Each one should use whatever gift he has received to serve others, faithfully administering God's grace in its various forms. If anyone speaks, he should do it as one speaking the very words of God. If anyone serves, he should do it with the strength God provides, so that in all things God may be praised through Jesus Christ. To him be the glory and the power for ever and ever. Amen" (1 Pe 4:10–11).

SEVEN

Many have tried to give the numbers found in the Bible symbolic or mystical value. These attempts have never produced significant interpretations, nor do they have a basis in Scripture. The number seven clearly does have significant associations, as with Creation and with the Sabbath. But we would not be wise to attempt numerological interpretations beyond the obvious.

SEX

In other articles, we look at male-female differences and roles. ♦ *Male and Female* ♦ *Women in the Church* In this article we will look specifically at the sexual nature of human beings and how this nature is to find expression.

    1. Indirect references to sex
    2. Sex outside of marriage
    3. Sex within marriage

1. Indirect references to sex. Both Testaments tend to speak indirectly about sex. This does not suggest a negative attitude or an attitude of shame toward sexuality. It simply means that the sexually explicit speech of our day and of other cultures in Bible times was not used in the Scriptures. Sexual matters are dealt with openly but in a vocabulary that honors the privacy of the male and the female. The Bible does not trivialize sex.

One euphemism for having sexual intercourse is "to know" (*yāda'*). Where the NIV reads, "Adam lay with his wife Eve, and she became pregnant" (Ge 4:1), the Hebrew reads, "Adam knew his wife" (cf. Jdg 19:25). The word *šākab*, "to

lie down," is also used to describe sexual intercourse (e.g., Ge 34:7; Nu 31:17–18). References to illicit sexual activity are often expressed as to "uncover [*gālâh*] the nakedness" of someone. This Hebrew expression is found in Lev 18 and 20, where the NIV reads "sexual relations." The phrase "become one flesh" also implies intercourse, though the phrase suggests much more. ♦ *Flesh*

The Bible does not refer directly to genital areas. While specific terms are used in speaking of the female breast (e.g., SS 1:13; 4:5; 7:3,7,8; 8:1,8,10), no specific terms are used for the penis or female sex organs.

The restraint of Scripture is striking in view of the explicit nature of the poetry and religious verse of surrounding pagan nations of Bible times. There is an affirmation in the Bible of the sexual nature of human beings and a deep appreciation for sexuality. But the whole subject is carefully guarded, lest the mystery be lost and the special nature of sexual relationships be made to seem commonplace or unholy.

2. Sex outside of marriage. Sexual expression outside of marriage—both adultery and premarital sex—is forbidden. ♦ *Adultery* Homosexuality and intercourse with animals are strictly proscribed (Lev 18:22–23). Prostitution is also forbidden. ♦ *Prostitution* Although polygamy was practiced in OT times, the divine ideal remained the one provided in the Creation model: a husband joined to one wife for life. ♦ *Marriage* The Bible does not deal with masturbation. But we can say without doubt that sexual intercourse with any living being prior to or outside of marriage is forbidden by Scripture.

3. Sex within marriage. When we turn to questions of sex within marriage, we find, not restriction, but freedom. Sexual activity outside of marriage is tightly regulated. There is no such regulation of sexual practices of married couples. Rather, there is the positive and joyful affirmation of human sexuality. Those who would deny the rightness of marriage are condemned for following "things taught by demons" (1 Ti 4:1), for what God has "created . . . to be received with thanksgiving" (v. 4) is consecrated by the Word of God itself (v. 5). It is clear from the Creation story that God is the one who, when he created human beings, "created them male and female" (Ge 1:27).

The creation of humanity with two sexes is partially explained in the account found in Ge 2. After no other creature was found to be a suitable companion for Adam, God acted, shaping woman from Adam's rib. Adam welcomed her, recognizing at once the fact that Eve was one with him, yet different. The Genesis account immediately announces that "for this reason a man will leave his father and mother and be united to his wife, and they will become one flesh" (Ge 2:24).

The life-long unity of husband and wife in marriage is symbolized by their physical union, and sexual bonding is vital in creating the life-long unity that God intends. It is because of the sacramental impact of sexual bonding that Paul reacted so strongly when asceticism was introduced in Corinth. Some believers there held that believers should not marry, or if they did marry, they were to withdraw from sex to have a pure, "spiritual" union. Paul responds, "The husband should fulfill his marital duty to his wife, and likewise the wife to the husband. The wife's body does not belong to her alone but also to her husband. In the same way, the husband's body does not belong to him alone but also to his wife. Do not deprive each other except by mutual consent and for a time, so that you may devote yourselves to prayer" (1 Co 7:3-5).

Although it is clear that marriage is designed for procreation (Ge 1:28), procreation is not the sole reason for sexual relations. Again, although it is also clear that human beings have sexual drives, and marriage is God's provision for the satisfaction of these drives (1 Co 7:9), these drives should not be the sole reason for engaging in sexual relations. (In fact, it is clear from Paul's exposition in 1 Co 7 that he believes singleness has

many advantages.) Rather, the basic reason for sex within marriage is sacramental; sex is intended to affirm and to express the intimate bonding and unity of the married. Sexual relations are the sign and seal of marital commitment and are vital to maintaining that commitment.

In the context of sacrament, God expects sex to be enjoyed. This is testified to first of all by human nature; all our pleasurable sensations came from God. It is also testified to in the spontaneously joyful Song of Solomon, which celebrates married love. It is further testified to by the separation in Scripture of the concept of shame from married sex; sex outside of marriage is identified as wrong and shameful, but within marriage there is no such shame.

While Scripture may not deal with sex explicitly, the Bible does speak openly about the intimacy of married love. Scripture gives detailed lists of sexually wrong attitudes and acts outside of marriage but frees us within marriage to enjoy his gift to the full. Within the context of marriage, each sensation offered by the couple to one another is a fresh joy, a recognition that it is God who created us male and female, and it is God who blesses our union. Moreover, it is God who frees us to enjoy his gifts to the full.

SHAKE

Five synonymous Hebrew words are translated "shake" or "shaken": môṭ, nûaʿ, nāʿar, rāgaz, and rāʿaš. Such phrases as "nothing will shake me" (Ps 10:6) affirm the stability that comes through one's relationship with God. At the same time, the nations and even heaven and earth themselves are portrayed as things that can be shaken, indeed shattered, by God (Ps 82:5; Isa 2:19,21; Am 9:9; Hag 2:6). In prophecy, shaking is associated with God's coming in judgment (Isa 2:19,21; Hag 2:6-7).

The writer to the Hebrews picks up this imagery in 12:26-27: "At that time his voice shook the earth, but now he has promised, 'Once more I will shake not only the earth but the heavens.' The words 'once more' indicate the removing of what can be shaken—that is, created things—so that what cannot be shaken may remain." And the writer goes on to elicit our response: "Therefore, since we are receiving a kingdom that cannot be shaken, let us be thankful, and so worship God acceptably with reverence and awe" (v. 28).

Because we are living in a universe that can be shaken, only a relationship with God offers us security.

SHAME

In our psychologically oriented age we are likely to think of shame, like guilt, as a feeling. Certainly feelings are involved in shame. But in the Bible shame has greater substance than mere feeling.

OT 1. Shame in the OT
NT 2. Shame in the NT

OT — 1. Shame in the OT. Two Hebrew words are most likely to be translated "shame" or "ashamed" in the NIV and the NASB: *kālam* and *bôš*. *Kālam* and cognate words are used to indicate the disgrace that attends any public humiliation. It portrays some crushing hurt, which may be physical but is more likely to involve destruction of pride and confidence. The prophets often relate such shame to national defeats that were sure to come when Israel trusted foreign alliances rather than God. As Isaiah cried, "Pharaoh's protection will be to your shame, Egypt's shade will bring you disgrace" (30:3).

The most common Hebrew word is *bôš*. This root with its cognates is found 155 times in the OT. Again the underlying thought is one of a failure of some sort that leads to disgrace. This word emphasizes the objective condition that causes the disgrace. The subjective, the shamed state of mind, is also present in shame situations. But the shame itself is the public exposure of the person or group because of the failure.

The most common use of this word group in the OT is to describe the result of defeat by some enemy. The defeated are humiliated and confused. Only by

reliance on God can such defeats be avoided and the Lord's people be guarded against shame. Ps 25 expresses this beautifully: "To you, O Lord, I lift up my soul; in you I trust, O my God. Do not let me be put to shame, nor let my enemies triumph over me. No one whose hope is in you will ever be put to shame, but they will be put to shame who are treacherous without excuse" (vv. 1–3).

The history of Israel shows that God's people all too often failed to trust. They turned to other gods and suffered crushing defeats. They came to know shame only too well. But the prophets continued to express God's commitment to his people. One day God will cause a great turning to him. "Then you will know that I am in Israel, that I am the Lord your God, and that there is no other; never again will my people be shamed" (Joel 2:27).

In some passages, "shame" is used to describe the inner state rather than the objective situation. Ezra was ashamed to ask a pagan king for a military escort to guard him on his return to Jerusalem "because," he said, "we had told the king, 'The good hand of our God is on everyone who looks to him' " (Ezr 8:22). Arriving in Judah, Ezra found that God's people had intermarried with pagans. Crushed, Ezra prayed, "O my God, I am too ashamed and disgraced to lift up my face to you" (9:6). Here a sensitive believer feels shame at the wrong itself, not when the consequences of wrongdoing are experienced. For most people, feelings of shame are associated with the consequences rather than the wrong itself.

Bôš is, by the way, the verb used in Ge 2:25, which says, "The man and his wife were both naked, and they felt no shame." Before the Fall warped humanity there was no humiliation in nakedness, for male and female were guarded by their innocence.

NT — 2. Shame in the NT. Several different Greek words are found where the NIV reads "shame" or "ashamed." The basic words are *aischynō*, *entrepō*, and *atimia*.

Aischynō and its compound forms *kataischynō* and *epaischynomai* are used in the Septuagint as translations of *bôš* and its derivatives. In Greek culture, the focus was not on the objective consequences of actions but on the feeling of shame that might come with exposure of shameful deeds to others. The OT sense of the word is clearly seen in Ro 9:33 and 10:11, each of which quotes from the OT and affirms that anyone "who trusts in him will never be put to shame."

Some other passages, including Mk 8:34–38, raise another issue—that of being ashamed of Christ and his words in an "adulterous and sinful generation." Here is an example of shame in the form of fear of ridicule by others. It is important not only to do right but also to take pride in the right action itself, rather than to rely on the approval of others. Jesus was willing to endure the shame associated with a criminal's death (Heb 12:2). He is not ashamed to call us brothers (Heb 2:11). No wonder Peter wrote, "If you suffer as a Christian, do not be ashamed, but praise God that you bear that name" (1 Pe 4:16).

From this brief survey we can see that the emphasis in this word "shame" is on reaction to public ridicule. It is what others think of us that, in the NT's more subjective sense, is the source of shame.

This word and compounds of it (translated "ashamed" or "shame") are *aischynō* (Lk 16:3; 2 Co 10:8; Php 1:20; 1 Pe 4:16 1 Jn 2:28), *aischynē* (Lk 14:9; 2 Co 4:2; Php 3:19; Heb 12:2; Jude 13; Rev 3:18), *epaischynomai* (Mk 8:38; Lk 9:26; Ro 1:16; 6:21; 2 Ti 1:8,12,16; Heb 2:11; 11:16), and *kataischynō* (Lk 13:17; Ro 5:5; 9:33; 10:11; 1 Co 1:27; 11:4; 2 Co 7:14; 9:4; 1 Pe 2:6; 3:16).

Entrepō is also translated "shame." It does not suggest a reaction to public opinion but a personal shame for unworthy conduct. There is also the suggestion that this shame will lead to a change in behavior. The NIV reads "ashamed" or "shame" in three of the nine NT occurrences of this word (1 Co 4:14; 2 Th 3:14; Tit 2:8) and in both of the NT occurrences of its cognate, *entropē* (1 Co 6:5; 15:34).

Atimia, meaning "dishonor," is translated "shame" by the NIV in one of the seven times it occurs in the NT (2 Co 11:21). ♦ *Honor/Dishonor*

Shame, then, is a complex concept in Scripture. In the OT, shame focuses attention on the objective situation, a personal or national disaster that humbles people before others. In the NT, shame comes with public ridicule and represents a powerful fear that all too often motivates one to conform to the world. God calls on us to follow Jesus, whatever others may think. We are not to be ashamed even if others deride us. But shame in a good person can be a positive force, leading to a change in behavior. Those who are good feel shame when they do a dishonorable act, even though no one may know of that act.

SHARE

The one NT occurrence of the word *koinōnikos* is in a passage that speaks of being generous and willing to share (1 Ti 6:18). A related word, *koinōnos*, is found in Peter's promise that we will share in the glory to be revealed when Jesus returns (1 Pe 5:1). Both words stem from a powerful root, *koinōneō*. ♦ *Fellowship* ♦ *Giving*

The NIV translates two of the six NT occurrences of *metochos* as "share" (Heb 3:1,14) in reference to believers sharing in the heavenly calling and in Christ. This word means "partner," "one who shares."

All such words remind us that we participate in Christ and with Christ. Our participation in Christ means that our destiny is linked forever with the Lord. Our participation with Christ means that we have been given a share in his unveiled glory.

SHEEP/SHEPHERD

Sheep and shepherds provide metaphors for writers in both Testaments. These most commonplace of animals and those who tend them are used to communicate uncommon truths.

OT 1. The Hebrew words and their
      meanings
   2. Images of sheep
   3. Images of shepherds
NT 4. The Greek words
   5. Jesus, the Good Shepherd
   6. Shepherds in the Epistles

**OT — 1. The Hebrew words and their
meanings.** There are three primary
words for "sheep" in the OT. The basic
word is ṣō'n, which means "small cattle." It is used of domesticated flocks and
usually indicates sheep or goats. It is
often used as a symbol for the people of
God (e.g., Ps 100:3; Isa 53:6).

The word śeh is also translated
"sheep." It is used figuratively a few
times, as in Ps 119:176: "I have strayed
like a lost sheep. Seek your servant, for I
have not forgotten your commands."

A third word is keśeḇ, or keḇeś. The
word is usually translated "lamb" and in
the great majority of cases is found in a
context where sacrifices are mentioned.
♦ *Lamb*

In the OT, "shepherd" is rō'eh, from
the word rā'âh, which means "to feed"
or "to pasture." The Hebrew indicates a
herder of domestic animals, one who
pastures and tends them. Rulers in OT
times were often called "shepherds" of
their people. The Bible's best known
psalm announces the conviction of the
believer that the Lord is his shepherd,
and that he has no lack (Ps 23:1).

Sheep and those who cared for them
were significant in OT times. Domesticated animals were often the basis of a
man's wealth; flocks provided food to
eat, wool to be woven to make clothing,
and even shelter as hides were tanned
and sewn together to make tents. It is not
surprising that these animals and the
relationship between them and their
shepherds should be figuratively applied
to illustrate human nature and God's
relationship to the believer.

2. Images of sheep. Sheep are portrayed in the OT as helpless, dependent
animals. Sheep tend to go astray (Isa
53:6). They need to be led (Nu 27:17) and
guided to places where they can pasture
and rest (Ps 23). But sheep were the

wealth of Israel. For all their weaknesses,
they were precious, and shepherds dedicated a lifetime to their care.

3. Images of shepherds. These images are more significant than those of
sheep in the OT. First, God himself is the
shepherd of his people. Israel could call
on him when in need of protection or
guidance, as Ps 80:1 declares: "Hear us,
O Shepherd of Israel, you who lead Jacob
like a flock; you who sit enthroned
between the cherubim, shine forth before
Ephraim, Benjamin and Manasseh.
Awaken in your might; come and save
us." Ezekiel stresses the tenderness of
the shepherd as he uses this image to
express God's love for his people. "I
myself will tend my sheep and have
them lie down, declares the Sovereign
LORD. I will search for the lost and bring
back the strays. I will bind up the injured
and strengthen the weak, but the sleek
and the strong I will destroy. I will
shepherd the flock with justice" (Eze
24:15–16). This passage from Ezekiel and
other OT passages look forward to the
coming of the Messiah, the true shepherd. Jeremiah, after warning false shepherds who do not truly care for God's
flock (Jer 23:1–3), communicates God's
promise: "I myself will gather the remnant of my flock out of all the countries
where they are scattered." All this was to
happen in the days when the Lord raised
up for David "a righteous branch" to rule
the land and save Judah (vv. 4–6). ♦
Branch

The first image, then, is that of God
himself who shepherds his people Israel
and who has sent the Messiah to give
them God's own loving care.

The second image is that of human
leadership. Moses, about to die, said to
the Lord, "May the LORD, the God of the
spirits of all mankind, appoint a man
over this community to go out and come
in before them, one who will lead them
out and bring them in, so the LORD's
people will not be like sheep without a
shepherd" (Nu 27:16–17). Israel's leaders, then, are shepherds, called to provide for the material or spiritual needs of
his people. Even the Persian Cyrus was
called a shepherd by God, because of his

role in providing for the exiles who returned under him to Judah (Isa 44:8).

The prophets strongly condemned leaders of Israel who lacked this caring quality (e.g., Jer 2:8; 3:15; 23:1–4; 25:34–36; 50:6; Eze 34:2–10). Notice one of God's warnings of judgment: "Woe to the shepherds who are destroying and scattering the sheep of my pasture! . . . Because you have . . . not bestowed care on them, I will bestow punishment on you for the evil you have done" (Jer 23:1–2).

NT — 4. The Greek words. The Greek word for "sheep" is *probaton*, and the word for "shepherd" is *poimēn*. The verb *poimainō* means "to act as a shepherd," "to feed and care for the flock." In the Judaism of the first century, the occupation of a shepherd was considered demeaning, and shepherds were generally despised. However, the NT itself reflects the attitude of the OT, and the metaphor continues to be used to represent God's love for his people.

5. Jesus, the Good Shepherd. Jesus often portrayed God and himself as shepherds. The people of Israel were like lost sheep (Mt 10:6). The recovery of an individual sheep who wandered caused the shepherd great joy (Mt 18:12–13). When the day of judgment comes, sheep and goats will be separated, and the sheep—the people of God—will be welcomed into his kingdom (Mt 25:31–46). Jesus' birth in Bethlehem has prophetic significance, for it is from this village that the ruler who was to be the shepherd of God's people Israel (Mt 2:6) would come. Jn 10 develops the identification most clearly. Those who are truly sheep recognize their shepherd's voice (vv. 1–6,16). Jesus himself is the gate as well as the shepherd: "Whoever enters through me will be saved" (v. 9). As a good shepherd, Jesus cares first of all for his sheep. The thief seeks to kill and steal. As the good shepherd, Jesus lay down his life for the sheep (vv. 11,14). There is an intimate relationship between Jesus and his sheep, to whom he gives life to the full (vv. 10,14).

Jesus continues to care for his people as the "great Shepherd of the sheep" (Heb 13:20). One day he will appear as "Chief Shepherd" and distribute rewards (1 Pe 5:4).

6. Shepherds in the Epistles. In view of the imagery in the OT, it is not surprising that leaders are sometimes designated shepherds in the NT. Jesus told a restored Peter, "Feed my lambs," "Take care of my sheep," and "Feed my sheep" (Jn 21:15–17). The Ephesian elders were admonished, "Keep watch over yourselves and all the flock of which the Holy Spirit has made you overseers" (Ac 20:28), and Peter speaks to other elders, charging them, "Be shepherds of God's flock that is under your care, serving as overseers" (1 Pe 5:2). In each passage, the shepherds' attitude of loving concern for the sheep is emphasized. Special note should be taken of Peter's words because he guards us against overextending the image; he says that shepherds are to be "eager to serve, not lording it over those entrusted to [them], but being examples to the flock" (vv. 2–3). ◆ *Serve/Servant/Slave*

SHEKEL

The *šeqel* was a unit of weight, indicating ten to thirteen grams of silver or gold. Usually the silver *šeqel* is the one referred to in the OT. Related terms are the mina (which was worth fifty shekels) and the talent (which was worth three thousand shekels).

During the Exodus period, persons of differing ages and sexes could be dedicated for differing numbers of shekels (Lev 27:2–8), and a firstborn child could be redeemed for five shekels (Nu 3:46). A slave was worth thirty shekels (Ex 21:32), the price that was paid Judas to betray Jesus. ◆ *Serve/Servant/Slave*

In NT times the shekel was equivalent to a day's labor. ◆ *Money*

SHEOL ◆ *Heaven and Hell*

SHOULD

Most occurrences of "should" in the Bible represent the English subjunctive rather than a specific Hebrew or Greek word. A few times words conveying a sense of necessity or moral obligation do occur in the Hebrew or Greek. ♦ *Necessity/Duty*

SICKNESS AND HEALTH

A certain woman's only son was sick (1 Ki 17:7–24). "He grew worse and worse, and finally stopped breathing" (v. 17). In frustration the woman turned to her boarder, the prophet Elijah, and cried out, "What do you have against me, man of God? Did you come to remind me of my sin and kill my son?" (v. 18).

Her reaction is not unusual. Many view sickness as punishment for sin; and there is a basis for that view in the Bible. But can all sickness be so directly linked with God's response to human behavior? And, perhaps more significantly, can believers who walk closely with the Lord expect health and healing? Let us look into some of these questions.

OT 1. **The Hebrew words**
    2. **Sickness and God**
    3. **Sickness and sin**
    4. **Sickness and Isa 53**
NT 5. **The Greek words**
    6. **Sickness and God**
    7. **Sickness and sin**
    8. **Sickness and Jesus' ministry to the whole person**
    9. **Conclusions**

OT — 1. The Hebrew words. The OT vocabulary of sickness includes terms for disease (*mahªlâh*), for ailments (*tahªlu'îm*), and for weakness or illness (*hªlî*). The root word from which most of these are derived is *hālâh*, "to be weak or sick."

The concept includes weakness caused by illness (1 Ki 14:1; 2 Ki 21:1,12) and by wounds (2 Ch 18:33). At times the concept of weakness is extended as a metaphor of national weakness (Hos 5:13–14). Sickness can also be a matter of the heart and portray mental or spiritual anguish (Ps 38:5; Pr 13:12; SS 2:5). The OT has surprisingly few references to illness or sickness in general. Even more surprising, in a language that often multiplies metaphors, sickness and disease are seldom used as symbols of something else.

The vocabulary of health is also limited. *Rāpā'* means "to heal" or "to make healthy." Its cognates and synonyms stand in contrast to the vocabulary of sickness. In contrast to weakness, there is strength; in contrast to debilitating illness, there is health and wholeness. ♦ *Healing* ♦ *Leprosy* ♦ *Pain and Suffering* ♦ *Peace*

2. Sickness and God. The OT unquestionably relates sickness to God. In the OT, all things are oriented to the Lord as their ultimate cause. Moses promised Israel, "If you pay attention to these laws and are careful to follow them . . . you will be blessed more than any other people; none of your men or women will be childless, nor any of your livestock without young. The LORD will keep you free from every disease" (Dt 7:12,14–15; cf. Ex 23:25–26). Likewise, disobedience to God would be punished by sickness. If Israel refused to obey the law and to revere God, there was this dreadful warning: "The LORD will send fearful plagues on you and your descendants, harsh and prolonged disasters, and severe and lingering illnesses" (Dt 28:59).

Solomon's prayer at the dedication of the temple shows the same close relationship between God and illness. He said, "Whatever disaster or disease may come . . . when a prayer or plea is made by any of your people Israel . . . then hear from heaven, your dwelling place. Forgive, and deal with each man according to all he does" (2 Ch 6:28–30).

Although sickness may strike the land or an individual as a direct act of God, it is not always so. Sickness is a reality that affects all humanity, and even a prophet could develop terminal illness (2 Ki 13:14).

3. Sickness and sin. The link between sickness and sin can be seen throughout the OT. One can note the Mosaic Law's clear promise to Israel of divine protection from disease if they were obedient and its warning of illness if they were disobedient.

The link continues to shape the view of later OT writers and is expressed in a number of ways. Ps 103:3 parallels forgiveness and sin, healing and sickness. It is the Lord who "forgives all your sins and heals all your diseases." Isaiah portrays sinful Israel as severely injured by blows from the Lord but unwilling still to turn to him (Isa 1, esp. vv. 5–6).

Hosea speaks of national weakness as illness, illness that has come because of unconfessed guilt. Until Israel admitted guilt and earnestly sought the Lord, there would be no rescue (Hos 5:13–14). The prophet reported the future return: "Come, let us return to the LORD. He has torn us to pieces but he will heal us; he has injured us but he will bind up our wounds. After two days he will revive us; on the third day he will restore us, that we may live in his presence. Let us acknowledge the LORD ; let us press on to acknowledge him" (Hos 6:1–3). Healing is found in a return to the Lord. He who caused the injury is able to restore.

But again, not all sickness is a result of sin. Nor is all healing what is usually thought of when we use the expression "divine healing." Infrequent references to medication and herbal treatment make it clear that the use of remedies was not viewed as a denial of trust in the Lord. God could work through medical treatment and he could work without it. ◢ *Healing* Sickness might come as a result of sin or as a natural consequence of human frailty.

Whatever the nature or cause of sickness, it is appropriate to look to God for help. Prayer and fasting are fitting, and when prayer for healing goes unanswered, mourning for the sick is also fitting (Ps 35:13–14). Sickness, like all suffering and tragedy, cannot automatically be assigned to sin or ascribed to God's judgment on a sinner. ◢ *Pain and Suffering*

4. Sickness and Isa 53. Isaiah uses words for sickness and healing in this great passage that portrays Jesus as the Suffering Servant. Some have taken Isa 53 to teach that physical healing is in the atonement and thus may be appropriated by faith by the believer. Having been healed by Jesus' wounds, so the argument goes, there is no need for the believer to suffer illness.

Both verses 3 and 4 have the word *ḥ°lî* ("weakness" or "sickness"). In the following quotation, the English translations of this word are italicized: "He was despised and rejected by men, a man of sorrows, and familiar with *suffering*. . . . Surely he took up our *infirmities* and carried our sorrows." Isa 53:10 has the Hiphil (causative) stem of *ḥālâh* and reads "Yet it was the LORD's will to crush him and *cause him to suffer*." But Isa 53:5 also describes the bright promise of his suffering: "He was pierced for our transgressions, he was crushed for our iniquities; the punishment that brought us peace was upon him, and by his wounds *we are healed.*"

Because the focus is on transgressions and iniquity, most scholars have taken the verse to promise spiritual restoration. But some have focused on physical healing, especially in view of Mt 8:17, which declares that Jesus' healing ministry in Israel "was to fulfill what was spoken through the prophet Isaiah: 'He took up our infirmities and carried our diseases' " ("diseases" being the word the Septuagint used in Isa 53:4).

However we interpret Mt 8:17, we must first note that the Hebrew verb translated "heal" in Isa 53:5 is *rāpā'*, and it is in the Niphal stem. Other OT uses of the Niphal stem of this verb are not limited to contexts of physical healing. For example, Lev 14:48 refers to the clearing of mildew from the stones of a house, Jer 51:9 points out that the sins of Babylon are beyond healing, and Eze 47:8–11 distinguishes fresh from salt water.

Furthermore, in Jer 17 the word is clearly used to indicate forgiveness of sin and spiritual restoration. The prophet calls the human heart "deceitful above all things and beyond cure" (v. 9). Yet one can still cry to the Lord, "Heal me, O LORD , and I will be healed; save me and I will be saved" (v. 14). Only God can cure the incurable sickness of sin that has infected the center of the human personality. Only he can heal—and save.

So the word "heal" in Isa 53 in a context exploring sin has clear parallel in Jeremiah, and we need not take 53:5 as a promise of physical healing.

But how do we understand Matthew's application of this passage to Jesus' healing ministry? In the same way that we take Jesus' affirmation about John the Baptist, that "this is the one about whom it is written: 'I will send my messenger ahead of you.' . . . if you are willing to accept it, he is the Elijah who was to come" (Mt 11:10,14). The appearance of John did not exhaust the application of Malachi's word of a forerunner, and the healing ministry of Jesus did not exhaust the application of Isaiah's prophecy. Thus, in his death, Jesus would provide for the ultimate release of humanity from every frailty, spiritual and physical. We will experience the fullness of that release in the resurrection—a release experienced in part again and again throughout history. As Jesus acted in Palestine to heal, so God still acts in our world to heal the sick and save the lost.

But never is healing in this life guaranteed to the believer. Even Paul suffered from a weakening illness that God chose not to heal. Yet in his weakness Paul found Christ's strength magnified. And so will we in ours. ◆ *Healing*

NT — 5. The Greek words. The general notion of sickness is expressed in several common NT words, notably *astheneia, nosos,* and *malakia. Astheneia* and its related words mean "weakness," "sickness," "disease." Words in this group are used in the Gospels and Acts in the literal sense of a bodily weakness or sickness. Paul picks up this language and uses it figuratively to explore the meaning of human frailty and weakness in itself. ◆ *Weak/Weakness*

Nosos is used only in the literal sense of illness (the only exception in this word group being the one NT use of the verb *noseō*—1 Ti 6:4). *Malakia* is another general term focusing on bodily weakness and sickness. It occurs only three times in the NT (Mt 4:23; 9:35; 10:1), though it

was often used with *nosos* by the Greeks to signify physical sickness in general. Although other words are translated "illness" or "sickness," etc., these three word groups express the phenomenon of sickness that limits or destroys the powers of once-healthy living beings.

The vocabulary of health also contains general terms, as well as those associated specifically with healing. ◆ *Healing Hygiēs* is the basic term. It means "to be well or healthy." It occurs fourteen times in the NT, and its related word *hygiainō* occurs another twelve times. Of these twenty-six uses, fifteen are in the Gospels, where the literal sense is always intended. These Greek words occur nine times in the Pastoral Epistles, where they are used metaphorically by Paul in reference to "sound" (healthy) faith (Ti 1:13; 2:2), doctrine (1 Ti 1:10; 2 Ti 4:3; Tit 1:9; 2:1), and words (1 Ti 6:3; 2 Ti 1:13; Tit 2:8). In these Epistles, that which is healthy is what conforms to the teachings of the apostles and thus retains its strength and vitality. The concept of health in the NT is something that implies more than physical well-being, though this clearly is central (see 8, below).

Other words for "well" or "healthy" occur less frequently. *Ischys*, "strength, or power," has the sense of "health" at times. The basic meaning of the root is "to be capable," to have the ability to do something according to the unique capacity of living beings. A person with such ability is, by extension, strong and healthy. A limitation of the capacities inherent in living beings is weakness or sickness. Although *ischyō* is found in Mt 9:12 and Mk 2:17 in the sense of "healthy," this word group is more often used in the NT in a spiritual sense, contrasting human weakness with divine strength (e.g., 1 Co 1:25,27; 2 Co 10:10).

Again, it is not so much the meaning of the words themselves, but how they are used in the NT, that draws the biblical portrait of sickness and health.

6. Sickness and God. The OT forges direct links between sickness and God. The NT does not deny such a relationship (e.g., Ac 12:23), but a different emphasis emerges in the Gospels.

By NT times, many of the Jewish rabbis saw sickness as being only divine punishment for sin. Some went so far as to argue that specific illnesses were the result of specific sins, even though there was no direct physical causation. These rabbis were also suspicious of medication; healing could come from God alone, and he needed no intermediate means.

♦ **Healing**

The Gospels, however, tend to link sickness with demonic powers. A typical happening is described in Lk 13:10–16. A woman, crippled for eighteen years, was released from her infirmity on the Sabbath. When attacked for healing on Sabbath, Jesus confronted his critics: "Should not this woman, a daughter of Abraham, whom Satan has kept bound for eighteen long years, be set free on the Sabbath day from what bound her?" (v. 16).

Her identification by Jesus as a "daughter of Abraham" puts her within the family of faith. Even God's people are bound by forces hostile to God. So not all sickness is directly caused by God, though it may be permitted by him (see 2 Co 12:7–10 for a parallel).

This theme is repeated again and again, as in Mt 12. Jesus healed a blind mute whose debility was caused by demons. The frustrated Pharisees tried to start a rumor: Jesus must be in league with Satan to have such power over demons. But Jesus pointed out that no divided kingdom can stand. Satan does not fight against Satan. It is the kingdom of God—the beneficent influence of God at work among humanity—to which Jesus' healings testify.

Throughout the NT, illness and disease are associated with the forces hostile to God and to humanity. Throughout the Gospels, Jesus is always healing, never once causing illness. While the weaknesses of humanity reflect the reality of human alienation from God, Jesus' attitude and actions show that God is and yearns to be man's healer. To see illness only as punishment is to misread the nature of God and to misunderstand the nature of those forces that distort human experience.

7. Sickness and sin. The link the OT forged between sin and illness is not broken by the NT. Sin may bring divine judgment in the form of illness. Luke reports that when Herod "did not give praise to God" when he was honored as a god, "an angel of the Lord struck him down, and he was eaten by worms and died" (Ac 12:23). Paul links the sickness of many in Corinth to their failure to discern the Lord's body when gathered for communion (1 Co 11:27–32); and John speaks of "a sin that leads to [physical] death" (1 Jn 5:16). This may also be true of Jas 5:14–15.

In each of these cases the link between personal sin and sickness is affirmed. But the emphasis in the NT is on other causes of sickness than personal sin. Sickness is an expression of the death that passed on humanity with our original infection by sin. In this broad sense, all sickness is linked with sin; but not every person's sickness is linked with his or her personal sin.

The disciples, like others in their time, assumed that there was a link between sickness and personal sin. One day they pointed out a man who had been born blind and asked Jesus, "Who sinned, this man or his parents, that he was born blind?" (Jn 9:1). Jesus answered, "Neither this man nor his parents sinned" (v. 2). His affliction was not a result of personal sin at all. Rather, "this happened that the work of God might be displayed in his life" (v. 2), and Jesus went on to restore the man's sight (vv. 6–7).

The view that sickness provides an opportunity for the work of God to be displayed in one's life is picked up by Paul, with a very different outcome. Struggling with a sickness that tormented him and affected his appearance (Gal 4:13–16), Paul pleaded with the Lord to remove this "messenger of Satan" (2 Co 12:7). God's answer was no; but at the same time God told Paul, "My grace is sufficient for you, for my power is made perfect in weakness" (v. 9). The physical weakness called Paul to greater dependence on the Lord, whose power was displayed in working mightily despite Paul's disability.

The NT's portrait, then, of individual sickness goes beyond that of the OT. Sickness is imposed on individuals by hostile forces that delight in human suffering. Although God permits suffering, he is capable of redeeming any experience, displaying in the life of ill persons his own wondrous working. Sometimes God's work is displayed in healing, for God is the source of health and wholeness; at other times it is displayed through sickness, 'as he enriches the sufferer and enables him or her to endure in a spirit of praise. Thus, sickness is not necessarily an unmixed evil, nor is it necessarily a result of personal sin.

8. Sickness and Jesus' ministry to the whole person. Special insight into the biblical implication of health is gained when we note that *hygiēs* is used in the Greek version of the OT current in Jesus' day as a translation of *šālôm*. ▶ *Peace* The well-being implied by these words is more than physical.

We sense this in several of Jesus' acts of healing. Often Jesus' healings of physical ailments were associated with the forgiveness of sins (e.g., Mk 2:1–12; Lk 5:17–26). Jn 5 is especially suggestive. Jesus spoke to one who had been an invalid for thirty-eight years. First he asked, "Do you want to get well ["be made whole," *hygiēs*]?" (v. 6). His inner self and his body were both no doubt in some sense crushed by the years of sickness. When Jesus healed him, he warned, "Stop sinning or something worse may happen to you" (v. 14). Restoration thus touched the man physically, mentally, and spiritually. The same thought is conveyed in the restoration of the prodigal son, who came back to his family, once again "safe and sound" (*hygiēs*, Lk 15:27).

There is no clear-cut teaching about the relationship between the spiritual and the physical aspects of a person. But links between forgiveness and healing, and *hygiēs* and *šālôm*, are suggestive. ▶ *Conscience* What is clear is that in Jesus' ministry, body and spirit are not divorced. Jesus sought always to minister to the whole person.

9. Conclusions. The Bible views health as wellness, a condition in which a person fully exercises all his or her capacities as a living being. Sickness is weakness, a diminishing or limiting of these capacities in the individual.

The OT relates sickness in human beings to God and also to sin. God is the source of health for humanity. Right relationship with him means an experience of his healing touch. Sin is the enemy of the body as well as of the spirit. Personal sin may bring sickness as one of many different judgments from God.

The NT accepts the suppositions of the OT but adds details to the picture. While sickness has sin as its original source, an individual's sickness is not necessarily related to his or her personal sin. Mankind is trapped in wreckage scattered across the whole earth by Adam's sin. But man is also vulnerable to the malicious attacks of demons. Even the faithful believer may be victimized by Satan.

Similarly, God's role in sickness is expanded in the NT. He is seen as the cause of some sickness but, more importantly, also as the healer. Jesus gives us a taste of the kingdom in his healing ministry. We see sickness attacked by Jesus as an enemy, not used by him as a scourge. In the NT, we sense the love of a God who yearns to heal and who only reluctantly plays judge before the time for judgment.

Perhaps more importantly, we see that God permits sickness for his own good purposes. Yes, at times sickness comes as discipline or judgment. But more often, perhaps, sickness is permitted so that God may redeem the situation, working in and through the lives of the ill. Paul is an example of this. He prayed for healing, but when healing was refused, he discovered God's power perfected in his weakness. ▶ *Healing*

SIGHT ▶ *See*

SIGN ▶ *Miracle/Sign/Wonder*

SIN

The OT and the NT explain that the tragedy and suffering that mark human experience is the result of sin. The biblical concept of sin has been clouded in modern culture. But the experience of each individual, like the history of every society, provides overwhelming testimony to the existence and the impact of what Scripture calls "sin."

OT 1. The Hebrew words
   2. Psalm 51: a statement of perspective
NT 3. The Greek words
   4. Sin as distortion of human nature
   5. Key NT passages on sin
   6. Summary

OT — 1. The Hebrew words. The OT's principle word for sin is *ḥāṭā'*, which means "to miss" the mark (cf. Jdg 20:16; Pr 19:2). In the OT, this word group, which is used some 580 times, typically speaks of missing the standard that God sets for man. While in much of the OT, "sin" involves a failure to obey the Mosaic Law, we see the concept of sin used prior to the giving of the law. Ge 13:13 identifies the men of Sodom as great sinners. Joseph was repelled when his master's wife tried to seduce him; he refused to "sin against God" (Ge 39:9). Reuben resisted when his brothers wanted "to sin against the boy," that is, to kill the young Joseph (Ge 42:22). In each of these cases there is what may be called a sin against nature. That is, God has expressed his character and standards in the design of human nature, so that certain actions are perceived as violations of right, even though no law has been given (Ro 2:14–15).

Thus, the structure of human nature and the revelation of divine expectations both provide valid standards for humanity. Violation of these standards, by falling short of performing what is expected, is sin.

There are many other OT words in the vocabulary of sin. All of them imply the existence of a divine standard. Most portray human actions in some relationship to that standard. As *ḥāṭā'* indicates

missing the mark, *pešaʿ* ("rebellion," "transgression") indicates a revolt against the standard, and *ʿāwōn* ("iniquity," "guilt") is a deviation from or a twisting of the standard. ◆ **Evil** ◆ **Guilt** ◆ **Rebel/Rebellion**

In Scripture, the language of sin is also the language of redemption. An example of this is the word *ḥaṭṭā'ṯ*. This word means both "sin" and "sin offering." It speaks of both the fact of failure and the wonderful reality of a forgiveness provided by God through the sin offering that removes guilt.

God confronts us in Scripture, calling us to acknowledge our sin. But God also comforts us in Scripture, promising restoration and reassuring us of his love.

2. Ps 51: a statement of perspective. The Hebrew language is not shaped to deal with philosophical issues. It focuses on concrete realities. Yet the OT is filled with hints of the perspective on sin developed fully only in the NT.

The first verses of Ps 51, David's prayer of confession of his sin with Bathsheba, draw together the OT's view of sin in a fascinating way: "Have mercy on me, O God, according to your unfailing love; according to your great compassion blot out my transgressions [*pāšaʿ*]. Wash away all my iniquity [*ʿāwōn*] and cleanse me from my sin [*ḥaṭṭā'ṯ*]. For I know my transgressions [*pāšaʿ*], and my sin [*ḥaṭṭā'ṯ*] is always before me. Against you, you only, have I sinned [*ḥāṭā'*] and done what is evil [*raʿ*] in your sight, so that you are proved right when you speak and justified when you judge. Surely I was sinful [*ʿāwōn*] at birth, sinful [*ḥēṭʾ*] from the time my mother conceived me. Surely you desire truth in the inner parts; you teach me wisdom in the inmost place. Cleanse [*ḥāṭā'*] me with hyssop, and I will be clean; wash me, and I will be whiter than snow. Let me hear joy and gladness; let the bones you have crushed rejoice. Hide your face from my sins [*ḥēṭʾ*] and blot out all my iniquity [*ʿāwōn*]. Create in me a pure heart, O God, and renew a steadfast spirit within me. Do not cast me from your presence or take your Holy Spirit from me. Restore to me the joy of your salvation and grant me a willing spirit, to sustain me. Then I will teach transgressors [pāša'] your ways, and sinners [ḥaṭṭā'] will turn back to you. Save me from bloodguilt [dām], O God, the God who saves me, and my tongue will sing your righteousness." ♦ **Blood**

Looking at the development of the psalm, we note that David identifies his sin by all three major OT terms. In sinning with Bathsheba he rebelled against God's standards, fell short of them, and deviated from the path they marked out (vv. 1–2). Thus, God's mercy and love was the only basis for David's appeal to God for cleansing from sin.

Then (v. 3) David acknowledges his rebellion and failure. Only when sin is acknowledged as such can human beings begin to deal with the misery sin causes. Even more, David confesses to God, "Against you, you only have I sinned" (v. 4). This does not mean his sin did not harm Bathsheba or her husband. Rather, it is an admission that God is the one who establishes the standard of right and wrong. A relativistic morality that measures sin by harm done to others must always fall short of the biblical position. Other people belong to God, and he has established his standards for their protection as well as for our own. So sin is against God, and because it is against God, the Lord is "proved right" and "justified" when he acts in judgment.

Verse 5 has a hint of a doctrine that Paul develops in the NT. From the time of his conception, David had fallen short of the divine standard, and from birth he had deviated from God's norm. There is no rebellion here, because in these premoral stages there is no conscious act implied. But somehow the seeds of sin had taken root deep within David's personality, so deeply that who David is cannot be separated from sin, even if his identity is traced back to conception itself.

Yet it is in the inner person, the core of the human personality, that God desires truth (v. 6). ♦ **Truth** The reference to cleansing with hyssop is a reference to blood sacrifice; the plant was used to sprinkle the cleansing blood of the OT

sacrifices. In view of his own bankruptcy, David then called on God to act—to hide his face from (not look at, not respond in judgment to) David's sins (v. 9). God was asked to do a creative work within David's heart (personality ♦ **Heart**) and empower him by his Spirit. After God answered these pleas, David would be able to move transgressors to follow the path he himself had taken—turning back to God, to rely, not on human righteousness, but on the righteousness of God (vv. 11–14).

Thus, the OT sees sin as involving a person's conscious, responsible choice measured against a known divine standard. But sin is more basic than that; the individual's propensity to react against the divine norm can be traced back to human nature itself. Helpless, people can only recognize their need and appeal to God for forgiveness, inner cleansing, and spiritual power.

NT — 3. The Greek words. Like the OT, the NT is filled with words related to the concept of sin: fault, guilt, injustice, offense, transgression, unrighteousness, and wickedness, to name just a few. And of course there are scores of specific sins mentioned, such as murder, theft, lying, adultery, and idolatry.

There are, however, two major word groups in the Greek language that sum up the concept of sin. One word, *adikia*, means "wrongdoing," "unrighteousness," "injustice." Its focus is on the concept of sin as conscious human action that causes visible harm to other persons in violation of the divine standard. The NIV and NASB translate the words of this group by a variety of English words, showing the flexibility of the concept. The verb *adikeō* is translated "to be unfair," "to harm," "to mistreat," "to hurt," "to wrong," etc. *Adikia* is translated "evildoers," "dishonest," "unjust," "wickedness," "sin," "evil," and "unrighteousness." And *adikos* is translated " unrighteous," "dishonest," "evildoers," "wicked," "unjust," and "ungodly." The Hebrew word to which this Greek concept is most closely related is 'āwōn.

Where the NIV and NASB read "sin," however, the Greek word is almost always *hamartia*. Words in this group incorporate the full range of meaning of all three basic Hebrew words, *ḥāṭā'*, *peša'*, and *'āwōn*. Like them, *hamartia* assumes a divine standard or norm and portrays humanity as missing the mark. Yet sin is also seen in the NT as rebellion and as conscious deviation from known right.

"Sin" is used in a descriptive sense in the Gospels, and there it is almost always associated with forgiveness. The Epistles, especially those of Paul, penetrate beyond observation of human behavior to explore its cause. Paul takes the concept of sin hinted at in Ps 51:5 and implied in the OT doctrine of the new covenant and develops the portrait of a humanity distorted and twisted by the brutal power of sin. Sin is not only missing God's mark; it is an inner reality, a warp in human nature, and a malignant power that holds each individual in an unbreakable grip.

4. Sin as distortion of human nature. In Paul's writings, as in the rest of the NT, "sin" and "sins" often indicate those responsibly committed acts that fall short of the divine standard. The pagans sin without knowledge of the Mosaic Law; but in light of the fact that God has planted in human nature a testimony to moral issues, they are actually sinning against their own standards (Ro 2:12). Wherever a NT writer uses the plural, "sins," we can assume that he has in view those individual choices that issue in actions that violate known and accepted norms.

But the NT clearly shifts much of the focus from sins to sin itself. Paul describes the entry of sin and death into the race by Adam's act (Ro 5:12–13). Sin and death now "dwell" in the human personality; these are twin principles that distort individual personality and society (Ro 7:17–8:2). Eph 2 describes the human condition of those dead in trespasses and sins—a condition believers used to live in and that unbelievers still live in (Eph 2:2–3). ♦ *Life and Death* Thus, acts of sin are portrayed in the NT as an expression of an inner flaw so serious that

humanity is a willing slave to hostile spiritual forces and to the cravings of a warped nature.

This grim view of the human condition drives the NT writers to a reexamination of the OT in search of a solution. The OT sacrificial system did deal with sins—on an individual and piecemeal basis. ♦ *Atonement* As long as action that violates a standard is viewed as the sole issue, such a remedy may be acceptable. And so the Hebrew people of NT times threw their full energy into efforts to live by the standards as they interpreted them, focusing on sins rather than on sin. But if the real issue is understood to be human beings' warped nature and not the actions that express it, then a different remedy must be sought. The solution to sin must involve an inner transformation, so that individuals can be freed from the domination of evil.

Insight into the true nature of sin is a necessary counterpart to what the NT teaches about the meaning of Jesus' death. Only when we sense the full extent of our inner bondage can we appreciate the release that salvation brings.

Perhaps the best way to explore the NT's revelation of the human condition and God's remedy in Christ is to trace through a number of significant NT passages.

5. Key NT passages on sin. Every part of the NT deals with sin, for an understanding of it, with an understanding of Christ, is central to the Christian understanding of reality.

Mt 9:2–6. Jesus announced that a paralytic's sins were forgiven. His pronouncement shocked some observers. To demonstrate his authority to forgive sins, Jesus healed the paralytic. The miracle substantiates his claim to speak with divine authority. Forgiveness of sins is linked forever with the person of Jesus (cf. Mk 2:5–10; Lk 5:20–24).

Mt 15:16–20. Jesus located the source of sin in the human heart. Uncleanness is not a matter of externals. The true issue in relationship with God must focus on the human heart as the source from which all evils spring.

Lk 6:32–34. Despite sin's warp within, and despite some people's choice of a lifestyle of sin, even "sinners" do good to those who are good to them. What some call "total depravity" may well mean that no human act, flowing as it does from a distorted nature, can meet the divine standard. But it surely does not mean that there is no potential in lost humanity for kindness, friendship, loyalty, or love (cf. Ro 5:6–7). Even as sinners, human beings bear the stamp of the eternal and wear the image of God. ▶ *Image and Likeness* But we must not mistake human good as something acceptable to the Lord, for God requires a perfection of motive and action that no person can achieve.

Jn 8:21–42. Without belief in Jesus, people die in their sins. In fact, a person's inner condition is demonstrated by the outward positive or negative response to Jesus. The only freedom from slavery to sin comes from Jesus.

Ro 1–3. Paul demonstrates that all human beings lack righteousness. This is seen by the failure of Gentiles and Jews to live up to the standards they themselves hold. It is proven by Scripture, which charges that all are under sin.

Ro 3:19–20. The law establishes the divine standard against which human actions can be measured. So measured, all people are guilty, and when they compare their own lives to the standard, they become aware of their guilt.

Ro 5:1–11. God's love is demonstrated by the fact that Jesus willingly died for sinners. Words in the passage portray the state of lost humanity. Human beings in the bondage of sin are powerless, ungodly, and enemies of God. Sin's warping influence is expressed in human motives, character, and attitude, as well as in sinful acts.

Ro 5:12–21. Sin's entry into the world through Adam brought death on humanity. ▶ *Life and Death* Even though technically people could not be charged with "sin" (as falling short of a known revealed standard) until Moses, human beings were still in the grip of inner spiritual death. Jesus, Adam's counterpart, brought the countering gifts of grace and righteousness. ▶ *Righteous/Righteousness*

Ro 6. Paul explores the impact that Jesus' death and resurrection have on the believer. Through union with Christ, believers have "died to sin." The point made is that the influence of sin on the human personality is "rendered powerless," so sin and death no longer exert mastery. This frees the believer, through faith expressed in obedience, to live a righteous rather than a sinful life. Paul points out that as creatures, human beings must always surrender their will to some greater power. By surrendering ourselves to God, to obey him, we can be free of sin's domination.

Ro 7. Paul explores the interrelationships between the believer, sin, and the law. Drawing from personal experience, Paul shows that sin is an inner reality for the believer. One who tries to counter its influence by struggle to keep the law must fail. ▶ *Law*

Ro 8. Paul affirms deliverance through the power of the Holy Spirit. Christians rely, not on themselves or their efforts, but completely on the power of God to "give life to [their] mortal bodies" (v. 11). When they rely on the Spirit of God and respond to his promptings, "the righteous requirements of the law" are "fully met" by them (v. 4).

Eph 2:1–4. The impact of sin within is described in these verses. Because human beings by nature are spiritually dead, they are in the grip of the cravings and desires of their warped nature. Only by Christ's gift of new life, accepted by faith, can we be saved.

Heb 10. Jesus died as a sacrifice for sins. ▶ *Offering and Sacrifice* On the basis of his sacrifice, God is able not only to forgive sins but also to renew human beings within, so that the standards expressed in external law become part of their character.

1 Jn 1:5–2:2. John explores the interplay between sin and sins. The sin principle still exists in believers and issues in acts of sin. But confession of sins restores to fellowship with the Lord and opens us to the process of inner cleansing he has begun. Only if we deny the existence of sin within do we lose contact with this reality. The assurance of forgiveness for failures is a motivator of holiness, communicated "so that [we] will not sin" (v. 1).

1 Jn 3:4–9. Acts of sin are violations of the divine standard. Jesus came to earth to remove sin, first legally (by forgiveness) and then experientially (by victory over sin in our daily lives). Believers should be known for their lack of sin; the new birth should make a difference.

6. Summary. The OT views sin in terms of the human response to divine standards. People fall short, deviate, and rebel against the norms that God has established. Such actions result in guilt, but a remedy is implied in the very Hebrew terms themselves. Thus, "sin" and "sin-offering," like "trespass" and "trespass offering," are from the same roots. God calls on human beings to acknowledge their sin, and in that call God invites the believer to look to him for forgiveness.

In the NT, sin is still viewed as deviation from divinely established norms. But sin is more than that. It is deeply rooted in the nature of the fallen race, a reality that holds human beings in slavery to hostile spiritual powers and to baser passions and desires. Because of the corruption of human nature by sin, no person can achieve the standard God must require, and no one, apart from redemption, can please the Lord.

Jesus' entry into the world to deal with sin must be understood on multiple levels. Jesus does forgive sins, and his death on Calvary was a sacrifice that satisfies the demands of justice that sins be punished. But Jesus also is the source of a new life that renews the individual from within. Through Jesus we are provided with the capacity not to sin. But even this is not the full provision. By surrender to God and reliance on the Holy Spirit whom Jesus has sent, the influence of the sin nature in the believer can be dampened, and the Christian can live according to God's will. The promise of resurrection's full release from every taint of sin is tasted here, and at each

moment the possibility of living without sin's corrupting impact does exist.

In 1 John we even have that promise extended. God will not guarantee us sinlessness. But the reality and the power of his life within is a major motivation not to keep on sinning.

SINCERE/SINCERITY

A number of Greek words are translated "sincere" or "sincerity" in the NIV and the NASB.

Anypokritēs means "without hypocrisy." It indicates that a person acts or speaks out of genuine motives, without deceit or wavering. The six NT occurrences of this word are all translated "sincere" by the NIV and the NASB (Ro 12:9; 2 Co 6:6; 1 Ti 1:5; 2 Ti 1:5; Jas 3:17; 1 Pe 1:22).

Haplotēs means "simplicity," "sincerity," or "uprightness." In Col 3:22 it communicates the idea of full commitment to service. *Aplotēs* is found seven other times in the NT (Ro 12:8; 2 Co 1:12; 8:2; 9:11,13; 11:3; Eph 6:5). *Aphelotēs* occurs once in the NT (Ac 2:46).

Eilikrineia also means "simplicity" or "sincerity." It is found three times in the NT (1 Co 5:8; 2 Co 1:12; 2:17).

Gnēsios ("genuine"), used four times in the NT, is the word translated "sincere" in 2 Co 8:8. In its only NT appearance, a fascinating word, *dilogos,* ("not double-tongued") is translated "sincere" in 1 Ti 3:8. It is taken here in the sense of an honest expression of what one really thinks rather than the alternate possibility—that is, gossip. In Heb 10:22, *alēthinos,* "truth," is translated "sincerity." ◆ *Truth*

God places a high value on the undivided heart and on the honest expression of what is in the heart via words and actions.

SLAUGHTER ◆ *Murder/Kill*

SLAVE ◆ *Serve/Servant/Slave*

SLEEP

The words in the original languages that portray sleep have different emphases. There is the sweet rest of natural sleep; but there is also the sleep of death. What are the Hebrew and Greek words and the ideas expressed by them?

OT 1. The Hebrew words
NT 2. The Greek words
    3. "Sleep" as a euphemism for death

OT — 1. The Hebrew words. Several Hebrew words are translated "sleep" in the NIV and the NASB.

Rādam and *tardēmâh* denote a deep sleep, a comalike state often caused by God, making an individual insensible to things around him. This root is found in the following passages: Ge 2:21; 15:12; Jdg 4:21; 1 Sa 26:12; Ps 76:6; Job 4:13; 33:15; Pr 10:5; 19:15; Isa 29:10; Da 8:18; 10:9; Jnh 1:5–6.

The verb *šākab*, "to lie down," is sometimes translated "sleep." It is mainly used in two types of context. One is in connection with illicit sexual relations (e.g., Lev 18:22; 20:13). Licit sexual relations are generally indicated by *yāda'*, "to know" (e.g., Ge 4:1). The other primary use of the root is to indicate lying down in death, or the "sleep of death." Typically, the context of narrative portions will clarify the meaning of "sleep" in the NIV and the NASB. The verb is not translated "sleep" in the Psalms or the Prophets, though it is found in the phrase "to lie down," which may be followed by "sleep."

Yāšēn means "to sleep" or "to be asleep." This word and its cognates, *šēnâh* or *šēnā'* and *š^enāt*, indicate normal, restful sleep. While the image is used at times to suggest laziness (Pr 6:4,9–10; 20:13), it also suggests an inner peace and rest (Ps 127:2). This is especially clear in Ps 3 and 4. When he was fleeing from Absalom and rebellious Israel, despite the pressure of danger and doubt, David remembered that God was his shield and support (3:3). Because he was certain that God would hear his prayers (3:4), David expressed the confidence that released him to rest: "I lie down and sleep; I wake

again, because the LORD sustains me. I will not fear the tens of thousands drawn up against me on every side" (3:5). Ps 4 reviews the same experience, expressing David's thoughts in that situation, and concludes, "I will lie down and sleep in peace, for you alone, O LORD , make me dwell in safety" (4:8).

NT — 2. The Greek words. The Greek words that are translated "sleep" in the NIV and the NASB are *katheudō* ("to sleep"), *koimaomai* ("to sleep" or "to fall asleep"), and *hypnos* ("sleep").

Katheudō is used of normal sleep except in 1 Th 5:10, where it refers to death. In two passages (Eph 5:14; 1 Th 5:6,7) it also implies an unawareness that may be associated with sleep. This word for sleep occurs twenty-two times in the NT (Mt 8:24; 9:24; 13:25; 25:5; 26:40,43,45; Mk 4:27,38; 5:39; 13:36; 14:37,40,41; Lk 8:52; 22:46; Eph 5:14; 1 Th 5:6,7,10).

Except in three passages (Mt 28:13; Lk 22:45; Ac 12:6), *koimaomai* means "to die." The word is used eighteen times in the NT (Mt 27:52; 28:13; Lk 22:45; Jn 11:11,12; Ac 7:60; 12:6; 13:36; 1 Co 7:39; 11:30; 15:6,18,20,51; 1 Th 4:13,14,15; 2 Pe 3:4).

Hypnos indicates a deep sleep and is used metaphorically in Ro 13:11 of insensitivity to the significance of one's present life. It is found five other times in the NT (Mt 1:24; Lk 9:32; Jn 11:13; Ac 20:9).

3. "Sleep" as a euphemism for death. There is an obvious similarity between a person who is asleep and one who is dead. Neither is aware of or responds to what happens around him. But in the NT there is a theological similarity that carries us beyond the obvious. In the two passages in which this word is used several times (1 Th 4; 1 Co 15), the NT speaks of our resurrection. The joyous affirmation of Scripture is that death, like sleep, is followed by a bodily awakening. The sleep of death, which seemed so final to the pagans, takes on a new meaning in Christ. Robbed of its dread, death wears the face of untroubled rest; and so the believer today can say with deeper meaning the ancient words of David: "I lie down and sleep; I wake

again, because the LORD sustains me" (Ps 3:5).

SNAKE/SERPENT/VIPER

A number of names are found in the OT for specific kinds of snakes. The common word for "snake" is *nāḥāš*. Our emotional association of snakes with the dreadful and dangerous may be traced to Ge 3, which pictures the serpent as an agent in the Fall. Some theologians think that "the serpent" in that passage is a name for Satan (which might be suggested by Rev.12:9); others see it as a Satan-inspired creature.

SON

This word occurs thousands of times in the Bible. But it does not necessarily carry the limited meaning of "son" that it does in English.

OT 1. The Hebrew word
      2. "Son of man" in the OT
NT 3. The Greek word
      4. Jesus as Son of Man
      5. Jesus as the Son of God
      6. Our position as sons (children) in God's family

OT — 1. The Hebrew word. The Hebrew word *bēn* occurs nearly five thousand times in the OT. Generally it indicates male offspring, but it often has the sense of descendant rather than immediate offspring.

"Son" is often used idiomatically. The "sons of Israel" are simply the Israelites, members of that group.

"Son" can also imply other things. One is the close relationship of God and Israel is indicated by God's announcement to Pharaoh: "Israel is my firstborn son" (Ex 4:22). ♦ *Firstborn*

Likewise, "son" may indicate membership in a group, as in the phrase "sons of the prophets" (1 Ki 20:35), a phrase that may simply denote prophets or a prophets' guild. The phrase "Sons of God" seldom occurs in the OT (KJV: Ge 6:2,4; Job 1:6; 2:1; 38:7); it usually indicates heavenly beings. ♦ *Angels*

The imprecision of "son" can be illustrated by the fact that to designate a particular king as the "son of" another king may indicate only succession, not family line.

"Son," then, is a flexible term in Hebrew, suggesting but not defining precisely a descendant relationship. It is capable of different idiomatic uses as well.

2. "Son of man" in the OT. This phrase is used often in the OT, being applied to Ezekiel alone almost one hundred times. What is its significance? The phrase probably implies little more than one would mean by addressing a male person as "man."

NT — 3. The Greek word. The Greek word translated "son" is *huios*. While usually designating a male offspring of parents, it also can mean "descendants." Like the Hebrew *bēn*, *huios* is often used in extended or figurative ways. Thus, characteristics of persons or groups, or a spiritual relationship, can be expressed by "son of." For instance, believers are "people of the light" (Lk 16:8), a phrase that literally means "sons of the light," and unbelievers are sons of disobedience (rendered "those who are disobedient" in the NIV, Eph 2:2).

Often the NT's use of "son" has great significance. In the Gospels, Jesus is quite often identified by people who appeal to him as "son of David." This is a confession of faith, for it recognizes Jesus' right of succession to David's throne—i.e., his messiahship (e.g., Mt 9:27; 12:23; 15:22; 20:30,31; 21:9,15; 22:42).

There is little doubt that the three most significant uses of "son" in the NT focus on Jesus' identification as Son of Man and Son of God and on our identification in Christ as sons (children) of God.

4. Jesus as Son of Man. This phrase is the focus of continuing theological debate. It seems clear, however, that the title, which Jesus frequently applied to himself, has more than one implication.

First, it emphasizes Jesus' humanity. In the OT, "son of man" is often used in addressing Ezekiel. In the context of that book it is clear that the title simply means "man" and carries there a special emphasis on the distinction between humanity and God. The NT makes it clear that Jesus took on true human nature, and one implication of the title is to affirm his humanity. ♦ *Appear/Appearance*

Second, it is used in place of "I." There are a number of passages in which it seems best to take the phrase in this way (e.g., Mt 12:8; 17:22; 19:28; 20:18,28).

Third, it identifies Jesus as the focus of OT eschatological prophecy. Daniel reported his vision of history's end, saying, "In my vision at night I looked, and there before me was one like a son of man, coming with the clouds of heaven. He approached the Ancient of Days and was led into his presence. He was given authority, glory and sovereign power; all peoples, nations and men of every language worshiped him. His dominion is an everlasting dominion" (Da 7:13–14). The phrase "like a son of man" undoubtedly means that Daniel saw a being who, in contrast to the exotic figures he had just described (7:1–12), simply looked human. But the phrase is given more meaning in the eschatological passages in the Gospels. Jesus is *the* human being Daniel saw, who will fulfill Daniel's prophecy in times to come (Mt 13,24; Mk 13).

Fourth, it identifies Jesus with humanity in his suffering for us. Often this phrase was chosen by Jesus when he spoke of his coming suffering and death (e.g., Mt 12:40). Jesus the Son of Man did come from heaven (Jn 3:13), but he had to be lifted up in crucifixion, suffering for all so that all who believe in him may have eternal life (Jn 3:14).

It would be difficult to exhaust the significance of the title "Son of Man." But surely it is intended to draw our attention to Jesus as fully human, to make us aware of Jesus' sufferings for us, and to awaken wonder that the eternal Son of God truly entered the world to bring us, victorious, to his eternal glory.

5. Jesus as the Son of God. It is clear from the NT that Jesus is God's Son in a unique sense. This is affirmed by God at Jesus' baptism (Mt 3:17), confirmed by the unwilling testimony of Satan and his demons (Mt 4:3,6; 8:29), and proclaimed by Jesus himself. Later, Paul wrote that Jesus was "declared with power to be the Son of God by his resurrection from the dead" (Ro 1:4). While the full deity of Jesus is taught throughout the NT, a few passages crystallize the evidence.

Mt 21:33–42. Jesus told the story of a landowner who rented out his fields. The tenants refused to pay the rent due and attacked the servants sent to remind them of their obligations. Finally, the owner sent his son to them. But the tenants killed the son. In this story, Jesus is the son, and the religious leaders in Israel are those who rejected every messenger sent from God, the landowner.

Jn 1:1–14. Jesus is identified as God's "one and only Son." His unique position is based on his coexistence with God and as God from the beginning.

Jn 3:16–21; 31–36. Jesus, God's Son, was sent into the world to redeem humanity. Each individual's eternal destiny hinges on his or her response to God's one and only Son. As the one sent by God, Jesus spoke the words of God.

Jn 5:19–27. Jesus and the Father share identity so fully that they speak and act as one. Each is, and together they are, the source of life. Jesus is both human and divine (i.e., "the Son of Man") and has full authority to judge. ♦ *Judge/Judging*

Ro 1:3–4. Jesus is the promised Messiah of the OT, fully human, and demonstrated to be God's Son by his resurrection from the dead.

Heb 1. Jesus is the "exact representation" (v. 3) of God. A Son, he is identified as God by the OT Scriptures.

1 Jn 4:9–15. God's love impelled him to send his Son into the world to be an atoning sacrifice for our sins. One who seeks a relationship with the Father must acknowledge Jesus as the Son of God.

1 Jn 5:11–13. The eternal life that God gives us is in his Son. God has given humanity abundant testimony to Jesus. One who does not accept the testimony that Jesus truly is the Son of God makes God out to be a liar.

There are many other passages that affirm the uniqueness of Jesus' relationship to the Father. Unquestionably, the title "Son of God" affirms the full deity of Jesus, as the title "Son of Man" affirms his true humanity.

6. Our position as sons (children) in God's family.
In significant NT passages, Paul says that believers "receive the full rights of sons" (Gal 4:5). Scripture also speaks of our adoption, *huiothesia*, into God's family, the Greek word occurring five times in the NT (Ro 8:15,23; 9:4; Gal 4:5; Eph 1:5). We become sons and daughters in the family through faith in Christ, receiving the "full rights" of children (Gal 4:5). This phrase reflects Roman law on sonship rather than Jewish tradition. ▶ *Adopt/Adoption*

The writer to the Hebrews emphasizes God's fatherly role in discipline. It is because we are his children now that the Lord works in our experience to correct and punish as part of the process of making us holy (Heb 12:5–13).

Both Paul and John expect that the unveiling of the full meaning of our sonship will occur when Jesus' returns (Ro 8:19,23). According to 1 Jn 3:2, as those who have been born of God (*tekna,* "children," rather than *huioi,* "sons") it is our destiny to be like Jesus. When we see him as he is, then we will at last discover who we truly have become (1 Jn 3:2). ▶ *Born*

SORCERY ▶ *Magic*

SORROW

The ideas of grief, sorrow, and anguish are closely linked in Hebrew. ▶ *Anguish* The NIV tends to focus in its use of "sorrow" on the mental stress and suffering that come with some affliction. The Hebrew word is *yāgôn,* which the NIV translates "sorrow" in all fourteen of its appearances (Ge 42:38; 44:31; Est 9:22; Ps 13:2; 31:10; 107:39; 116:3; Isa 35:10; 51:11; Jer 8:18; 20:18; 31:13; 45:3; Eze 23:33). "Sorrow" (*mak`ôb*) in Isa 53:3–4 emphasizes the physical pain, rather than the mental anguish, that comes with affliction. ▶ *Pain and Suffering*

In the NT, "sorrow" is *lypē,* and "to be sorrowful" is *lypeō.* The Greek terms suggest both physical pain and emotional suffering. In the LXX, this root is a translation of some thirteen different Hebrew roots. The Hebrew terms display subtle shades of meaning; the Greek term and its synonyms do not have the same precision or sensitivity. "Sorrow" in the NT is simply the experience of physical/emotional stress, with consequent pain. The root is also translated "distress" and "grief" in the NIV.

These Greek words are used repeatedly in three NT passages. In Jn 16, Jesus speaks of the *lypē* that the disciples would feel at his departure ("grief," vv. 6,20,22; "grieve," v. 20; "pain," v. 21). Their anguish would turn to joy when they would see the resurrected Jesus again, and they would know the experience of answered prayer when they appealed to the Father in Jesus' name. Thus, here *lypē* stands in contrast with joy. ▶ *Joy*

In 2 Co 2:1–7, the NIV translates *lypeō* (vv. 2,3,5) "grieve" and *lypē* "painful" (v. 1), "distress" (v. 3), and "excessive sorrow" (v. 7). Here Paul uses this word group to discuss the Corinthians' response to Paul's earlier confrontation concerning sin in the community. The Holy Spirit clearly brought conviction here as "sorrow," experienced as inner spiritual pain unassociated with physical harm.

The same words are used in 2 Co 7:8–11. Paul returns to the same incident and concludes that the sorrow has been beneficial in that it produced a change of heart and a fresh sensitivity to God. This seems to be the basic distinction between "godly" and "worldly" sorrow. Godly sorrow "brings repentance that leads to salvation and leaves no regret" (v. 10). Worldly sorrow is resentment and self-pity. A godly response to *lupē* involves acknowledging fault and turning from that which generated conviction's discomfort.

One of the most heart-searching examples of sorrow is Paul's "great sorrow and unceasing anguish" because of Israel's unbelief (Ro 9:2–3).

SOUL AND SPIRIT

Few Bible terms are as difficult to define precisely as "soul" and "spirit." The rather simplistic approach taken by many Christians to these words shows a failure to understand the complexity of each of these concepts in both the OT and the NT.

The confusion may be magnified by the many English words used to translate the original terms for "soul." For instance, the NIV and the NASB (correctly) render *nepeš* (soul) as "life," "person," "self," "being," "I," etc. The multi-term approach adopted by the translators is an attempt to communicate to the English reader a particular shade of meaning that the context seems to imply. But the use of multiple terms in translation may also confuse, as the complexities of the use of the original cannot be easily traced by the English reader.

Because the terms are complex, they can be discussed only in a general way. The reader will have to be alert to determine which of the major shades of meaning seems to best fit a particular context.

OT   1. The human soul: *nepeš*
     2. The human spirit: *rûah*
     3. The divine spirit: *rûah*
NT   4. The soul: *psychē*
     5. The "soulish" person
     6. The spirit: *pneuma*
     7. The "spiritual" person
     8. Conclusions

OT — 1. The human soul: *nepeš*. Most scholars believe that the root of the Hebrew word *nepeš* originally meant "to breathe." In Hebrew and related languages, *nepeš* focuses on life, or the living being (e.g., Ge 1:20,21,24,30; 2:7). But generally "soul" is not life in the abstract.

▶ **Life and Death** Soul is personal existence. It is the life or self of an individual as marked by vital drives and desires. It is the seat of emotion and will. *Nepeš* is the "I" of the individual, and is often used with the sense of a personal pronoun. Thus, while *nepeš* may mean "life," it is the unique personal life, the individual self, that is emphasized.

Nepeš appears over 750 times in the Hebrew Bible. This word is translated "soul" in the NIV only 119 times, and it is the only Hebrew word so translated. The other instances are rendered by English words that the translators believe best express the emphasis in context (e.g., "life," "being," "self," etc.). What, then, about occasions where "soul" is used in English. How are we to understand its meaning?

With heart, soul, and strength. This phrase, shortened at times to heart and soul, occurs in Dt 4:29; 6:5; 10:12; 11:13; 13:3; 26:16; 30:2,6,10; Jos 22:5; 23:14; 1 Sa 14:7; 1 Ki 2:4; 2 Ki 23:3,25; 2 Ch 6:38; 15:12; 34:31; Jer 32:41. What does the repeated phrase suggest? Most Bible scholars agree that no biblical psychology or theological division of the human personality is implied. Rather, the three terms overlap in meaning. They are repeated to communicate the intensity or focused devotion of the individual. Waltke suggests that if the heart and soul were to be taken as different entities, *nepeš* would emphasize the focus of one's personal desires or inclinations on God.

The longing, joyful soul. Often "soul" is used with words that express emotions or state of mind. Here it is a reference to the person, as one whose life consists of his inner experience, his passions, and his emotions. Thus, a soul (i.e., person) can be in anguish (Ps 6:3), hate (11:5), thirst for God (42:2), rest (116:7), long (119:20,81), and be bitter (Job 3:20). It is important to note here not only that the *nepeš* has all these capacities but also that often human longing is focused on God. Thus, the psalmist lifts up his soul (25:1), and the soul rejoices in the Lord (35:9) and praises him (103:1,2,22). We cannot say that the "spirit" is God-conscious and that the "soul" is oriented only to life in the world. The *nepeš* is the entire human being, shaped by God with an inner life that, in the deepest sense, yearns for the Lord.

The redeemed and harmless soul. Often "soul" simply means the person. Finding some "harmless soul" to attack means finding some harmless person (Pr 1:11, though the Hebrew word *nepeš* is not in this verse). The reference in Job 33:28,30 to a soul redeemed from the pit should simply be taken to mean the saving of one's life.

This points up the danger of, without careful study, reading our theological concepts into biblical terms. In Eze 18, which warns that "the soul who sins is the one who will die" (18:4,20), the meaning in context is simply that the individual who sins will suffer physical death in the approaching judgment. In contrast, the person who remains faithful to God will live. Thus, God will show that he makes a distinction between godly and ungodly individuals, even in times of national disaster.

"Soul" in the OT, then, does not indicate some immaterial part of human beings that continues after death. Nepeš essentially means life as it is uniquely experienced by personal beings. Each human being is unique and precious. Nepeš also implies that the meaning of human life cannot be summed up in what happens to the physical body. One can be rich or poor, have success or failure, and live in times of peace or war. But what makes us unique is our rich inner life, vitally interacting with and shaping external circumstances by our drives, will, and emotions.

2. The human spirit: rûaḥ. The word rûaḥ means "wind," "breath," or "spirit." The image is that of breathing, the movement of air that indicates life. Many take the symbolism to suggest that spirit is the vitalizing principle, the unique and immortal personal life that is rooted in God (e.g., Job 12:10; Isa 42:5).

Rûaḥ is used in ways that overlap with nepeš. The spirit of an individual can know anguish (Job 7:11), long for God (Isa 26:9), and be broken (Job 17:1). Yet it is more likely that rûaḥ will be associated with words that emphasize responsible choice or basic personal attitude. God had produced in Sihon a stubborn spirit (Dt 2:30). The psalmist's spirit inquired (Ps 77:6). God honors one whose spirit is humble and contrite (Isa 66:2). He saves the crushed in spirit (Ps 34:18), whereas the haughty in spirit will fall (Pr 16:18). Thus, many conclude that rûaḥ has in view the "immaterial consciousness" of human beings and that it refers to an individual's character and attitude toward God rather than his existence as a living, emotional being.

What is particularly important is to note that rûaḥ is ascribed to God as well as human beings, while nepeš is uniquely human personal existence. Angelic beings are also called "spirits."

3. The divine spirit: rûaḥ. ▶ *Spirit (Holy Spirit)*

NT — 4. The soul: psychē. As with many biblical terms, the basic meaning of psychē is established by its OT counterpart, rather than by its meaning in Greek culture. "Soul" refers to personal life, the inner person. Of its over one hundred NT uses, psychē is rendered by the NIV as "soul(s)" only twenty-five times.

5. The "soulish" person. One distinctive concept introduced in the NT is that of the psychikos. Human beings, our present bodies, earthly wisdom, and false teachers who lack the Spirit are described by this term. This word appears only six times in the NT (1 Co 2:14; 15:44,46; Jas 3:15; Jude 19). It is an adjective that characterizes someone as being dominated by an unredeemed state. The life force is only that which can be provided by one's bodily life.

6. The spirit: pneuma. The word in Greek also means "breath" or "wind." It occurs nearly four hundred times in the NT, but most of the uses refer to God the Holy Spirit. ▶ *Spirit (Holy Spirit).*

Although the NT word pneuma also derives its basic meaning from its OT counterpart, rûaḥ, the NT provides greater definition. The word can be used idiomatically (as "I am with you in spirit"). But it is also used of human interaction with the spiritual realm. It is a person as a being with pneuma who is aware of and responsive to God (e.g., Mt 5:3; Mk 2:8; 8:12; Lk 1:47; Jn 11:33; 13:21; Ac 17:16; Ro 1:9; 8:16; 2 Co 2:13; 7:13; Gal 6:18; Eph 4:23; 2 Ti 4:22; Phm 25; Heb 4:12; Jas 4:5; 1 Pe 3:4).

While there is much overlap in the NT uses of psychē and pneuma, there seems to be some areas of distinction as well. Often the focus of contexts in which these terms appear overlaps. Thus, both are used in speaking of personal existence, of life after death, emotions, purpose, and the self. But *psyche* is also used of one's physical life and of spiritual growth, while *pneuma* is associated distinctively with breath, worship, understanding, one's attitude or disposition, and spiritual power.

7. The "spiritual" person. The adjective *pneumatikos* ("spiritual") is the counterpart of *psychikos* ("soulish"). This significant word is found twenty-six times in the NT (Ro 1:11; 7:14; 15:27; 1 Co 2:13,15; 3:1; 9:11; 10:3; 1 Co 10:4; 12:1; 14:1,37; 15:44,46; Gal 6:1; Eph 1:3; 5:19; 6:12; Col 1:9; 3:16; 1 Pe 2:5).

It is used to describe gifts, the law, persons, the resurrection body, understanding, the community of faith, and even "wickedness" (Eph 6:12, KJV). Its basic function is to identify the thing described as belonging to the realm of the spirit. Spiritual things, such as gifts and the law, are so described because they originate in or are derived from the Holy Spirit. When the adjective is used as a noun, it may be translated "that which is spiritual" or, as in Eph 6:12, it may be understood as referring to that which pertains to the realm of spirits beyond the material world.

Spiritual persons are those who not only possess the Holy Spirit but also live in obedience to the Word that he inspired. His transforming work enables believers to live transformed lives.

8. Conclusions. "Soul" and "spirit" are important biblical concepts that make distinctive statements about humanity. They should not, however, be taken as sharply defined expressions of some tri- or bipartite division of human nature. OT passages that speak of heart and soul and strength use overlapping concepts to emphasize singlehearted devotion to God. NT references such as Heb 4:12 do not teach that soul and spirit can be divided but emphasize the vital power of God's Word, penetrating every depth of the human personality.

What seems most important is that each term treats living beings as sig-

nificant and having a personal existence and life force derived from God. As body, soul, and spirit, human beings have emotions and will and are responsive to experiences in this world and aware of realities beyond it.

No human being should be treated lightly. Each has unique worth and dignity, for human capacities could have been derived only from God.

SOVEREIGN

The NIV translates *'adonay yahweh* as "Sovereign LORD." The first word is an intensive form of "master" or "lord" and is used only of God. The second is the personal name of God, indicated in English versions by LORD. Older versions render the phrase by "LORD God." The NIV translators chose the word "sovereign" to represent in English what Hebrew readers would have understood—that the name acknowledges Israel's God as ultimate Lord.

SPIRIT ▶ *Soul and Spirit*

SPIRIT (HOLY SPIRIT)

Christians confidently affirm the existence of one God, who exists eternally in three persons. The Father and the Son are the most familiar to most Christians. But the Bible's teaching about the Holy Spirit is rich indeed. While the focus of our faith is rightly on Jesus, our Savior, it is freeing to understand the wonderful works of the Spirit, who brings us all the benefits won for us by Christ.

OT 1. The Spirit of God in the OT
NT 2. The Holy Spirit of the NT
3. The Holy Spirit in Christ's life on earth
4. The Holy Spirit in the believer's life
a. His named works
b. His described works
5. Key passages on the Spirit's ministry
6. The believer's response to the Holy Spirit
7. Summary

OT — 1. The Spirit of God in the OT. The Hebrew word *rûaḥ* means "breath," "wind," or "spirit." Applied to human beings, it describes the vital, active principle that vitalizes a living person. ◆ *Soul and Spirit*

In the OT, no clear distinction is made among the persons of the Trinity. Yet, by analogy with the NT (in which *pneuma*, like *rûaḥ*, means "breath" or "wind"), we can see that the Spirit of God is the Holy Spirit in the fullest sense. Looking back with this perspective, we see in the OT close parallels between the Spirit's work in the lives of the ancients and in our own.

As the Holy Spirit is the source of spiritual gifts for the believer today, he was the source of special enablement for God's OT people. The Spirit of God filled with wisdom the skilled craftsmen who made the tabernacle (Ex 35:30–36:1). The Spirit enriched Joshua with the wisdom required for his leadership of God's people (Dt 34:9). The deliverers whom God raised up, emerged when the Spirit "came upon" them (Jdg 3:10; 11:29; 14:6,19; 15:14; 1 Sa 11:6).

The prophets looked forward to the coming of the Messiah. Isaiah especially describes the Messiah as having the fullest possible endowment of God's Spirit (Isa 11:2; 42:1 48:16; 61:1). Through the Messiah, the Spirit was to be "poured upon us from on high" (Isa 32:15). This event was to transform the face of the land and the people in it. In the same vein, Joel announced, "Afterward, I will pour out my Spirit on all people. Your sons and daughters will prophesy, your old men will dream dreams, your young men will see visions. Even on my servants, both men and women, I will pour out my Spirit in those days" (Joel 2:28–29).

When Peter announced on Pentecost that the disciples' speaking in tongues was by the power of the Spirit whom Joel promised, he identified our day as an age in which God's Spirit would work in new and exciting ways in those who believe.

NT — 2. The Holy Spirit in the NT. The Greek word for "spirit," *pneuma*, with the adjective "holy," identifies the Third Person of the Trinity in the NT. The clearest expression of this is found in Mt 28:19, where Jesus gives the Great Commission's baptismal formula. Believers are to be baptized in the name of the Father, the Son, and the Holy Spirit.

Jn 15:26 has been significant in developing a theological understanding of the Holy Spirit. The passage reads, "When the Counselor comes, whom I will send to you from the Father, the Spirit of truth who goes out from the Father, he will testify about me." Here the Spirit is viewed as a person, intimately related to both Father and Son. Jesus sends him, and he "proceeds out from" the Father. He acts as a person would, being the subject of a verb ("testify") that implies personal action. Like a person, he is given a name—Counselor.

Other references to the Spirit permit the same kind of argument. The Spirit can be lied to, the act then being identified as lying to God (Ac 5:3–4). Jesus promises to send "another" Counselor to be with the disciples forever (Jn 14:16–17). The Greek word "another" is not a word meaning "another of a different kind" but "another of the same kind." The Spirit is of the same nature and origin as Jesus, thus one with the Father.

There is a sin against the Holy Spirit that is unforgivable (Mt 12:25–32; Mk 3:29–30; Lk 12:10). ◆ *Forgive* A *thing* cannot be sinned against; and in a technical but important way, only God can be sinned against. ◆ *Sin*

These and other passages of the NT that focus on the Holy Spirit have led believers to the conviction that the Spirit is, like Jesus, a distinct person, one with the Father, and thus God from all eternity.

3. The Holy Spirit in Christ's life on earth. The rabbis of Jesus' day taught that the Spirit, silent in Israel since the time of Malachi some four hundred years earlier, would not be given until the last days. Thus, Jesus' claim to speak and act by the Spirit was a bold announcement of his own messiahship.

The synoptic Gospels have a common emphasis on certain events. The Holy Spirit was the agent in Mary's conception

(Mt 1:18,20; Lk 1:35,41). Thus, Jesus fulfilled the ancient prophecy of Isaiah, that a virgin would bear a child whose name is Emmanuel, "with us is God!" The Holy Spirit came upon Jesus at his baptism in a special way to empower him for ministry (Mt 3:16; Mk 1:10; Lk 3:22). The Holy Spirit led Jesus into the wilderness where, weakened by a forty-day fast, Jesus faced Satan's temptations.

Most important is Jesus' own affirmation of his messiahship, seen in his application of one of Isaiah's Spirit-filled-servant passages to himself (Isa 61:1–2; Lk 4:18) and in his response to those who challenged his acts of healing. Rather than being rooted in the demonic as his enemies charged, Jesus cast out demons by the Spirit of God himself. Referring to the OT's promise of an age of the Spirit, Jesus warned, "If I drive out demons by the Spirit of God, then the kingdom of God has come upon you" (Mt 12:28). Jesus himself was the long-awaited messianic King.

Each of the Synoptics also presents Jesus' promise to the disciples that the Spirit would speak through them (Mt 10:20; Mk 13:11; Lk 12:12).

John's Gospel contains teaching by Jesus concerning the Spirit. Jesus is competent to teach, for "the one whom God has sent speaks the words of God; to him God gives the Spirit without limit" (3:34). Jesus taught that (1) the disciples would later be given the Spirit (7:37–39), (2) the Spirit would remain forever with them as Counselor, through an "in you" relationship different from the "with you" relationship they had enjoyed (14:15–17), (3) the Counselor sent by the Son would "go out from" the Father and would testify concerning the Son (15:26), and (4) the Spirit would not only bring conviction to the world (16:8–11) but also guide the disciples into a fuller understanding of truth (16:13).

The Epistles add an important ministry. The Spirit's dynamic, vivifying power was displayed in Jesus' resurrection from the dead (Ro 1:3–4).

While we cannot grasp the full import of the relationship between Christ as God incarnate and the Spirit as God immanent, we can see that the Spirit's vitalizing power was displayed in Jesus. Also, Jesus' words show how important a role the Spirit is intended to play in our lives.

4. The Holy Spirit in the believer's life. Jesus told his disciples, "It is for your good that I am going away. Unless I go away, the Counselor will not come to you" (Jn 16:7). In a significant sense, Jesus' physical presence with his disciples offered them less benefit than the unseen presence of God's Spirit. As we trace the NT's teaching on the work of the Holy Spirit in the believer's life, we begin to see why Jesus spoke as he did. We see this both in the named works of the Spirit and in the works ascribed to him in description.

His named works. Several specific works of the Holy Spirit linked with the believer's experience are identified. We are told that the Spirit baptizes, fills, seals, and indwells Christians. We are also told that the Holy Spirit gives "gifts" to believers. Most of the named works of the Spirit are discussed elsewhere in this dictionary, so a simple definition is provided here.

(1) Baptism. This is the Spirit's work of uniting all believers with the living body of Christ (1 Co 12:13). ♦ *Baptism*

(2) Filling. This descriptive word portrays the believer in full harmony with the Spirit, vitalized by the divine power.

(3) Sealing. This term is linked with several different important meanings of the Spirit's presence but particularly with the fact that his presence is a guarantee of God's ownership of and commitment to believers. ♦ *Seal*

(4) Indwelling. This refers to the Spirit's permanent presence within the personality of the believer. He has come to be with us and within us, forever.

(5) Gifts. This word represents the working of the Holy Spirit through believers, especially in the ministry of believers to one another in the body of Christ. Scripture emphasizes that each believer is gifted and thus is spiritually significant. ♦ *Gift/Gifts*

These terms are given different shades of meaning in different theological traditions. Our theological definitions should always be checked against the use of a term in the Bible itself; this will help guard against reading into passages a meaning not present in the text.

Perhaps what is most significant in these specified works of the Spirit is the repeated emphasis on the fact that the Holy Spirit maintains a unique relationship with all believers. Gifts are given "to each one" (1 Co 12:7), for "we were all baptized by one Spirit into one body" (v. 13). In Romans, Paul goes so far as to say that "if anyone does not have the Spirit of Christ, he does not belong to Christ" (Ro 8:9). The specific interplay between the Holy Spirit and the believer in these and other areas (as in the need for repeated "fillings") must be explored case by case. But the basic assurance that the Holy Spirit has established a permanent relationship with each Christian is foundational to understanding the Spirit's ministry in our lives. ♦ **Receive**

His described works. In addition to the Spirit's specific works that Scripture identifies, there are other ministries of the Spirit to Christians, and these may be known from various descriptions of the Spirit's activity in the lives of believers.

(1) The Holy Spirit enabled the disciples to speak in tongues (Ac 2:4–13). This is identified as a spiritual gift also in 1 Co 12. ♦ **Tongues**

(2) The Holy Spirit's work of leading is demonstrated in the life of Paul (Ac 11:12,28; 16:6,7; 20:22,23,28; 21:11) and taught in Paul's letters (Ro 8:14). ♦ **Lead/Guide**

(3) The Holy Spirit is the agent in the Christian's inner transformation toward Jesus' likeness (2 Co 3:17–18; Gal 5:22–23). This transformation is one of inner character and not simply of behavior.

(4) The Holy Spirit's active presence gives the believer the freedom to actually produce the righteousness that the OT law required but could never motivate (Ro 8:2–11; Gal 5:5–6).

These and other ministries of the Spirit in our lives deserve careful study as we seek to understand the exciting meaning of his presence within.

5. Key passages on the Spirit's ministry. Several extended passages develop in some detail the meaning of the Spirit's presence and works in the believer.

Ro 8:2–17. The Spirit principle within us releases us from the conflicting "law of sin and death" (v. 2). ♦ *Life and Death* ♦ *Sin* Released, we are enabled to live truly righteous lives. The key is to set our minds on what the Spirit desires rather than on what the sinful nature desires and thus to be controlled by the Spirit's promptings. The Spirit will not only lead us but will also "give life to [our] mortal bodies" (v. 11), just as the Spirit brought the dead body of Jesus back to life.

1 Co 2:6–16. The Holy Spirit, who knows the mind of God, for he is God, is the active agent in revelation. He communicates the thoughts of God in words that have been recorded in the Bible. Thus, the Spirit's ministry enables the believer to have "the mind of Christ."

1 Co 12. God the Spirit gives spiritual gifts to believers "for the common good" (v. 7). He decides what gift(s) will go to each believer in order to enrich the body of Christ.

2 Co 3:1–18. God the Spirit inscribes the law of God on human hearts, a work that can be described as transforming the believer "into his [Jesus'] likeness with ever-increasing glory" (v. 18).

Gal 5:13–25. Those who believe in Christ are free—free to serve one another in love. We experience this freedom when we "live by" the Spirit (vv. 16,25) and "keep in step" with him (v. 25). This means responding to the Spirit's promptings and so letting him produce in us the fruit of love, joy, peace, patience, kindness, goodness, faithfulness, gentleness, and self-control.

6. The believer's response to the Holy Spirit . In every relationship with God, human beings are called on to respond with faith. According to the Bible, such faith is reliance on the Lord expressed in joyful obedience. Thus, in our relationship with the Holy Spirit, the NT also emphasizes a responsive trust.

A number of words and phrases are used to describe the faith response of believers and to describe resistance to the Spirit. Faith in action means that believers "live by" and "keep in step with" the Spirit (Gal 5:16,25). The same idea is conveyed by the terms "believe" and "rely on" (Gal 3:5,10). As in every relationship with God, relationship with the Spirit calls for faith that is obedient, never "human effort" by itself (Gal 3:3). ♦ *Belief/Faith*

In contrast, refusal to respond to the Spirit's promptings or to rely on his presence is in a class with ancient Israel's practice of resistance (Ac 7:51). Such an attitude is also called grieving (Eph 4:30), quenching (1 Th 5:19), and insulting (Heb 10:29). ♦ *Quench* ♦ *Sorrow* In short, we are to develop a sensitivity to and dependence on God the Spirit so that we will be responsive to his promptings, confident that we can trust ourselves to his leading.

7. Summary. Books have been written on the Holy Spirit, as well as on his various ministries. But even a brief survey of the biblical material demonstrates that, together with the Father and the Son, the Spirit is a distinct person of the Trinity. He was active in each aspect of Christ's sojourn on earth, and he is active in the believer's life today. The Holy Spirit baptizes, indwells, fills, seals, and gives gifts to believers; and his presence is expressed not only by leading and empowering Christians but also by his transformation of the believer's character. A number of extended passages explore the many aspects of the Holy Spirit's ministry.

The Christian is to respond to the Spirit as he does to Jesus—that is, with faith. We are to believe God's Word that the Spirit is within us and to rely fully on him for the power we need to be holy.

SPLENDOR ♦ *Glory*

STANDARD ♦ *Banner/Standard*

STONE

The common Hebrew word '*e<u>b</u>en* is used of all types of stone: precious stone, building stone, or hewn stone. It may be used with greater significance than we see at first glance.

OT 1. Law, gods, and the human heart
2. Stoning as a form of execution
3. Cornerstone

OT — 1. Law, gods, and the human heart. While not developed in the OT, it seems significant that '*e<u>b</u>en* is a material on which God's Ten Commandments were inscribed, a material from which human beings shaped idols, and an image of the unresponsive human heart. Dt 4:28 speaks of "man-made gods of wood and stone, which cannot see or hear or eat or smell." ♦ *Idol/Image* This symbolism is maintained in Eze 11:19–20, in which God promises, "I will give them an undivided heart and put a new spirit in them; I will remove from them their heart of stone and give them a heart of flesh. Then they will follow my decrees and be careful to keep my laws."

The chiseling of the Ten Commandments on stone tablets does not suggest so much their permanence as it does the cold, unresponsive, and crushing impact of a law that stands outside the human personality, necessarily judging it (Ro 3:18–19). Picking up this theme in 2 Co 3, Paul contrasts the new and the old covenants, arguing that Christ writes "not with ink but with the Spirit of the living God, not on tablets of stone but on tablets of human hearts" (v. 3). ♦ *Law*

2. Stoning as a form of execution. While the laws of contemporary cultures often called for the death penalty, only in Israel did the law call for stoning as a form of execution. In part, this is because the whole community of Israel was responsible to God for the holiness of the nation. So God commanded Moses, "Take the blasphemer outside the camp. All those who heard him are to lay their hands on his head, and the entire assembly is to stone him" (Lev 24:14). In general, stoning was the penalty for serious spiritual and sexual offenses (e.g., Dt 13:6–10; 17:2–7; 21:18–21; 22:24). Stoning is never prescribed for any offense not directly related to one of the Ten Commandments. This may be partly in Paul's mind when he writes, "I found that the very commandment that was intended to bring life actually brought death" (Ro 7:10). ♦ *Law*

3. Cornerstone. Not stone, but cornerstone, is applied to God and particularly to the coming Messiah. ♦ *Capstone* ♦ *Rock*

STRANGER ♦ *Foreigner*

STRENGTH/MIGHT/POWER

In the Bible, the concepts of strength, might, and power overlap in English as they also do in Hebrew and Greek. But all the different words in the original are used within a common framework: the conviction of Scripture that God's power is supreme, and human strength is insignificant in comparison.

OT 1. The Hebrew words
    2. The testimony of the OT
NT 3. The Greek words
    4. The testimony of the NT
    5. God's application of his power
    6. Conclusion

OT — 1. The Hebrew words. The Hebrew language has numerous words for strength, power, and might. Many are commonly translated by all three English word groups.

There are various sources of strength acknowledged in the OT: physical prowess, numbers, wealth, wisdom, and will. But ultimately, all human powers must be measured, not against other human beings, but against the overwhelming power and strength of God. It is important that no one attempt to test his or her puny strength against the Lord!

2. The testimony of the OT. Again and again the hearts of godly Israelites were drawn to history's record of God's powerful acts. The existence of Israel as a nation and the well-being of the individual depended, not on military might or

physical strength, but on the active power of God, exerted on behalf of his people. As the psalmist cried, "The LORD is my strength and my shield; my heart trusts in him, and I am helped. My heart leaps for joy and I will give thanks to him in song. The LORD is the strength of his people, a fortress of salvation for his anointed one. Save your people and bless your inheritance; be their shepherd and carry them forever" (Ps 28:7–9; cf. Isa 40:10–31).

This confidence was based on God's historic acts for his people. It was because of God's "mighty" hand that Pharaoh let Israel go (Ex 6:1,6) to become his own people (v. 7). Reviewing those events, Moses challenged Israel: "Ask now about the former days, long before your time, from the day God created man on the earth; ask from one end of the heavens to the other. Has anything so great as this ever happened, or has anything like it ever been heard of? Has any other people heard the voice of God speaking out of fire, as you have, and lived? Has any god ever tried to take for himself one nation out of another nation, by testings, by miraculous signs and wonders, by war, by a mighty hand and an outstretched arm, or by great and awesome deeds, like all the things the LORD your God did for you in Egypt before your very eyes?" (Dt 4:32–34).

God, not Israel, was the source not only of deliverance but also of every achievement of his people (Dt 8:17–18). The strength and power of God were available throughout history to protect Israel in their years of obedience. And a return to God brought a promise of power. "Do not fear," God told Israel, "for I am with you; do not be dismayed, for I am your God. I will strengthen you and help you; I will uphold you with my righteous right hand" (Isa 41:10).

Israel did not always trust the Lord. And they knew many defeats. The arm of flesh failed. But when there was a turning to God, when they trusted and were not afraid, when they recognized God as their strength and song, there was renewed victory (e.g., Isa 12:2).

No wonder, then, that Scripture focuses on God's power rather than on human armies. God, with his "great power and outstretched arm," made the earth (Jer 27:5) and then redeemed his people from servitude (Ne 1:10). God's past mighty acts provide the basis on which his people could hope for the future: "Come and see what God has done, how awesome his works in man's behalf! He turned the sea into dry land, they passed through the waters on foot—come, let us rejoice in him. He rules forever by his power, his eyes watch the nations—let not the rebellious rise up against him. Praise our God, O peoples, let the sound of his praise be heard" (Ps 66:5–8).

NT — 3. The Greek words. Several Greek words express varying aspects of power, strength, and might. While other words suggesting great size or a stone-like firmness may appear, the concept of strength and power itself is expressed by *ischys, kratos, exousia,* and *dynamis.*

4. The testimony of the NT. The NT, like the OT, contrasts the innate power of God with the strength of human beings. Paul expresses the conclusion succinctly: Christ is the wisdom of God and the power of God; and "the foolishness of God is wiser than man's wisdom, and the weakness of God is stronger than man's strength" (1 Co 1:25).

5. God's application of his power. The OT celebrates God's power as it is demonstrated in acts of creation and redemption. Because God is all-powerful, he continues to be able to come to the aid of his people. Thus, each fresh deliverance from an enemy or a natural disaster is perceived as God's use of his power to save. ◆ *Salvation/Save*

The NT emphasizes, not (as did the OT) salvation as deliverance from external enemies that threaten, but salvation as deliverance from forces hostile to the inner life of human beings. As we might expect, there is a similar shift in emphasis where the NT draws our attention to God's use of his power. What remains constant is that in both Testaments, God uses his power on behalf of his people.

What shifts is the focal point of that power; in the NT it is released in us as Jesus' people.

Jesus himself becomes the model for God's exercise of his power. Jesus was "declared with power to be the Son of God by his resurrection from the dead" (Ro 1:4). While OT believers constantly returned to Creation and the Exodus as examples of the divine power, the writers of the NT return to the Resurrection (e.g., Eph 1:19–20; 3:16–20; Php 3:10; Col 1:11). The parallelism is striking.

A study of the NT Epistles shows this exciting emphasis again and again. Because "the Spirit of him who raised Jesus from the dead is living in you, he who raised Christ from the dead will also give life to your mortal bodies through his Spirit, who lives in you" (Ro 8:11).

No wonder Paul wrote: "I pray also that the eyes of your heart may be enlightened in order that you may know the hope to which he has called you, the riches of his glorious inheritance in the saints, and his incomparably great power for us who believe. That power is like the working of his mighty strength, which he exerted in Christ when he raised him from the dead and seated him at his right hand" (Eph 1:18–20).

One can also understand how he could exclaim, "Now to him who is able to do immeasurably more than all we ask or imagine, according to his power that is at work within us, to him be glory in the church and in Christ Jesus throughout all generations, for ever and ever! Amen" (Eph 3:20–21).

6. Conclusion. Both Testaments call on us to recognize God as the ultimate power in our universe. The testimony of the OT is that his power is exerted to deliver from danger those who trust and obey him. The testimony of the NT is that God's power is exerted in Christ to bring life to the dead. As we rely on Jesus, we are released from the hostile powers that hold us in their grip, we begin to experience a resurrection kind of life now, and ultimately we will experience a resurrection through which we will be transformed into Jesus' image.

STUBBORN

The two Hebrew roots for "stubborn" are *sārar* and *qāšeh*. The first means "stubbornly rebellious," and the second indicates a hard, obstinate attitude. Both are translated "stubborn" and portray unbelief's antagonistic attitude toward God as a response to his self-revelation.

STUMBLE

The OT meaning of "stumble" is not the same as that of the NT. In the OT, to stumble is to fail or to be ruined. But it may be that Jer 18:15, which pictures people stumbling in the path that God's Word marks out, provides the OT model for the NT use, where "stumble" is associated with falling into sin (as in Ro 14:20; Jas 3:2).

SUBJECT/SUBMISSION

This theme is an extremely sensitive one and much misunderstood. What is the Bible's teaching on submission—in marriage and in other relationships?

1. The Greek words
2. The biblical concept

1. The Greek words. In most occurrences of the words "submit," "subject," and "submission" in the NIV and NASB, the Greek word is *hypotassō* or *hypotagē*. These are words of subjection, implying that one subjects or subordinates himself or herself to someone or something else. They imply a responsive obedience to whoever or whatever one is subject to. Thus, citizens were subject to governing authorities, and slaves to masters.

These two words occur only three times in the Gospels but forty-one times in the Epistles. *Hypotagē* ("subjection") appears only four times in the NT (2 Co 9:13; Gal 2:5; 1 Ti 2:11; 3:4), whereas *hypotassō* ("to subject") appears forty times (Lk 2:51; 10:17,20; Ro 8:7,20; 10:3; 13:1,5; 1 Co 14:32,34; 15:27,28; 16:16; Eph 1:22; 5:21,22,24; Php 3:21; Col 3:18; Tit 2:5,9; 3:1; Heb 2:5,8; 12:9; Jas 4:7; 1 Pe 2:13,18; 3:1,5,22; 5:5).

One other word, *hypeikō* occurs only once in the NT (Heb 13:17). The sense of the main clause of the verse is "Remain open to the persuasion of your leaders and be responsive to them." ◆ **Obey/Disobey** In other passages where the NIV has "submit" or "subject," the concept is supplied by the translators to give English readers the sense of the Greek construction.

2. The biblical concept. The literal meaning of words, even those well defined in their culture, cannot tell us how these words are used to develop or express a biblical perspective. Perhaps this is particularly true with the concept of submission.

A study of the passages dealing with submission show us that it is a complex concept. For instance, submission may be forced ("Even the demons submit to us" [Lk 10:17]) or voluntary ("Submit yourselves, then, to God" [Jas 4:7]). There is no question that the emphasis in the NT is on voluntary submission by believers.

The voluntary submission of believers involves existing social structures. Christians are to "submit . . . to the governing authorities" (Ro 13:1), to "every authority instituted among men" (1 Pe 2:13). The NT applies this specifically to slaves. They are to submit and provide good service, even to harsh masters (Tit 2:9; 1 Pe 2:18). This calls for voluntary submission in roles defined by one's culture and makes no judgment at all on the justice or validity of particular institutions. It simply calls on the believer to live in the world *as it is* and in one's own culture to do what is expected of a good citizen or a good slave. If we wish, we can call this situational submission—a voluntary choice by the believer to do what is deemed right according to the norms of his or her own culture. (Of course, Scripture is not dealing here with the exceptional case in which the culture calls "right" what God calls "wrong.")

Another area in which believers are called on to submit voluntarily is that of Christian interpersonal relationships. In their various roles in the body of Christ, Christians are to "submit to one another out of reverence for Christ" (Eph 5:21). This responsiveness and willingness to yield to one another out of love should be extended not only by younger to older (1 Pe 5:5) but also by everyone to those who devote themselves "to the service of the saints" (1 Co 16:15–16). This is in perfect harmony with the NT portrait of mutual concern among Christians and the surrender of one's own interests to those of others (Ro 12:10; Php 2:3–4). It extends even to Christ's portrait of those who would be great among the disciples; they are to be slaves (*douloi*) to the other believers (Mt 20:27). ◆ *Serve/Servant/ Slave*

One of the critical questions in our day is that of the submission that the NT calls for from the wife to her husband. In the light of the times in which the NT was written, we may take this as situational submission in some contexts and perhaps as an interpersonal submission in others. What is important for us to realize is that however we understand "submission" in such passages, it does not imply an inferiority of person. Submission is not a confession of inferiority but a demonstration of the fact that personal significance does not depend on one's role in society. The Christian is responsive to God, fulfilling his or her highest destiny in choosing to obey the Lord in the matter of submission.

The fact that submission is no admission of inferiority should be established for us by Lk 2:51, the first NT use of *hypotassō*. Luke states that after Jesus' visit to the temple at age twelve, he returned with his parents to Nazareth and was "obedient" to them; literally, and in such other versions as KJV, the Greek word is "subject." God himself entered our world in the person of

Christ, and he himself willingly chose to submit to a parental authority that was appropriate to his condition as a child. Did submission make him inferior? Hardly, for he always remained who he was— God. Nor can submission make us inferior as persons, for we too remain who we are, children of God now, deeply loved and accepted by the Lord.

SUCCESS/SUCCEED

The concept of "success" in the OT, represented by *ṣālaḥ*, focuses on satisfactory accomplishment of an intended task or purpose. The nearest parallel to our concept of "success" is wealth, which is closely linked with the idea of prosperity. ◆ *Wealth/Riches/Possessions*

SUFFER ◆ *Pain and Suffering*

SURVIVE/SURVIVOR ◆ *Remnant/Survivors*

SWEAR ◆ *Oath/Swear*

SYNAGOGUE

The Greek word *synagōgē* comes from a common word meaning "to gather." It was an ordinary term for any religious or secular gathering. By the first century, synagogues were established even in small Jewish communities. On the Sabbath, the people gathered at the synagogue to read and talk about the Scriptures.

T

TABERNACLE AND TEMPLE

The tabernacle and the temple were successive centers of Israel's worship. The design of each, on the same basic pattern, has symbolic as well as contemporary significance. Bible encyclopedias provide detailed background information on each.

OT 1. The Hebrew words
2. Basic Scripture passages
NT 3. The NT treatment of tabernacle and temple

OT — 1. The Hebrew words. The word translated "tabernacle" is *miškān*, which means "a dwelling place" or "tabernacle." Other phrases in the OT also describe the tabernacle as "the tent," "the tent of the Lord," "the house of the Lord" or "the tabernacle of the house of the Lord" as well as "the tent of meeting." This last name occurs some 125 times in the OT, emphasizing that the tabernacle was the place where God and human beings could meet. It was there that people could approach God with sacrifice, and God could communicate his revelations to them.

The tabernacle was constructed during the Exodus, and though it was maintained for some centuries after that era, it was eventually lost to history.

The temple is commonly the "house" of the Lord or *hêkâl*. The history of Israel knows three temples: (1) that of Solomon, (2) a reconstruction in the time of Haggai, and (3) the expanded and beautified temple of Herod. Ezekiel prophesied about another great temple to be constructed on the same Jerusalem site as the others.

2. Basic Scripture passages. Key passages dealing with the tabernacle are limited to the Pentateuch (Ex 25–27; 30–31; 35–40; Nu 3–4,7).

Key passages dealing with the temple are found in the historical and prophetic books (1 Ki 5–9; 2 Ki 22–23; 1 Ch 17, 21–22, 28–29; 2 Ch 2–7; Ezr 1–5; Eze 40–48; Hag).

NT — 3. NT treatment of tabernacle and temple. In the OT system of worship, the tabernacle and the temple were the places of meeting; human beings approached with sacrifice, and God responded with forgiveness, revelation, and answered prayers (e.g., Ex 25:22; 2 Ch 6).

The NT views the tabernacle and the temple as symbolic of realities we now possess in Christ. Jesus entered the true temple in heaven, of which the earthly was merely a shadow, and offered the sacrifice that forever reconciles us to God. Jesus himself thus becomes the place of meeting (Heb 9–10). ♦ *Offering and Sacrifice*

As the dwelling place of God among men, the living personality of the believer replaces the beautiful but cold stone of the temple (1 Co 3:16). Moreover, the church, the body of Christ itself, united by the bond of peace, is growing into a holy temple for the Lord (Eph 2:21).

The tabernacle and the temple did have contemporary significance for God's OT people. They were, each in its turn, the place of meeting, the place where God's presence dwelt. But because of Christ, all is fresh and new now. Today God dwells within us, for Christ has offered the perfect sacrifice and provides perpetual access to the Father. By virtue of God's presence, you and I become the place of meeting Jesus for all who stumble in darkness through our lost world.

TALENT ♦ Money

TASTE

The word "taste" is used in two senses in the OT and the NT. There are both the experience of the taste of a food and, figuratively, the conscious experience of a different reality. The psalmist's call to "taste and see that the Lord is good" (Ps 34:8) is an invitation to turn to God and experience the benefits of a relationship with him. The NT speaks about tasting (experiencing) death (Jn 8:52; Heb 2:9). Also, a much-debated passage speaks about tasting "the heavenly gift" and "the good word of God" (Heb 6:4–5). Based on how this figure is used in Scripture, the phrase cannot indicate "taste" in contrast with "partake." Rather, it seems to suggest a true acceptance of and participation in the reality of the gospel.

TAX

The OT refers to two types of "taxes." The first is a temple tax that was imposed on all males as "a ransom" when the first Exodus census was taken (Ex 30:11–16). That money was used to support services at the tabernacle and later the temple (Mt 17:24). At one time a special tax was levied for the repair of the temple (cf. 2 Ch 24:5–12). The OT also speaks of taxes collected by the pagan kings who ruled Judea as a province (Ezr 4:13,20; 7:24; Ne 5:4). It is in the NT, however, that we learn about taxes in a more modern form.

Taxes and tax collecting in NT times. The practice in NT times was for the government to fix an amount due from a province or area and sell the right to collect the tax. The successful bidder then hired tax collectors (KJV, "publicans," *telōnēs*) from the local population. The original contractor, his agents, and the local collectors all made their profit by collecting more than was due the government. The abuse of this system and the proverbial greed of the tax collectors generated the Jews' hatred of their fellow-citizens, a hatred we see reflected in the Gospels.

The burden of this system was multiplied when we realize that in addition to the basic tax, customs stations (*telōnion*) were established everywhere to collect more tolls and taxes when a person crossed bridges, used roads, came to market to sell, etc. It is no wonder that Jesus' willingness to associate with "tax collectors and sinners" was a cause for intense criticism (Mt 9:9–11; 11:19; Mk 2:15–16; Lk 5:30; 7:34). Yet these outcasts of society were often more ready to respond to Jesus than were the "righteous" (Mt 10:3; Lk 15:1; 18:10–14).

Taxes to Caesar. Many in Judea in Jesus' day resented the fact that they had to pay taxes to their Roman oppressors. Rome brought stability to the ancient world, but the tax burden on its provinces was staggering. Contemporary records indicate a tax rebellion was the root of the revolt of Judea that led to the destruction of Jerusalem in A.D. 70. So the issue was politically explosive when Jesus was asked if it was "right" to pay taxes to Caesar (Mt 22:17; Mk 12:14; Lk 20:22; 23:2). The particular term used in Matthew and Mark, *kēnsos*, indicates the poll tax. Jesus called for a coin, and, pointing out that Caesar's picture was on it, said to render to Caesar what is Ceasar's and to God what is God's. This silenced those who had hoped to trap him.

Jesus' response also sets the tone for the NT's teaching on taxes. It is appropriate for a nation's citizens to support their government, which God has ordained for his own good purposes, with the taxes that are due it (Ro 13:6–7). However, there is also a word for the tax collector. John the Baptist told tax collectors who heard his call to repentance and asked what to do: "Don't collect any more than you are required to" (Lk 3:13). There was no need to resign from the despised profession; but there was a need for God's followers to be honest and fair.

Jesus and the temple tax. According to Mt 17:24–27, tax collectors asked Peter if Jesus paid the annual temple tax. Peter blurted out, "Yes, he does." Then he went into the house where Jesus was, and Jesus asked him, "From whom do the kings of the earth collect duty and taxes—from their own sons or from others?" Peter answered correctly: "from others." Jesus nodded and observed, "Then the sons are exempt."

Often we focus on the fish Peter caught, which had a coin in its mouth large enough to pay Jesus' and Peter's tax. But the real focus is on Jesus' question and his conclusion. As Son of God, Jesus was exempt from the temple tax. But the very fact that God called for such a tax in OT times may have been intended to show that the Israelites, despite their covenant relationship with the Lord, were not yet sons. Throughout the centuries, the existence of the temple tax on all Israelite males could be taken as an indication that each individual must go beyond the rights obtained by birth to find a personal relationship with God through a faith like that of Abraham.

TEACHING/LEARNING

It is never easy for a person to divorce himself from his experiences in his own age and society. We carry into our reading and study of Scripture assumptions that color perceptions of meaning without even being aware of all that we import. This is particularly true in the area of teaching and learning, for assumptions about the nature and goal of education vary dramatically from culture to culture. Thus, one of our major concerns in looking at words associated with education in Scripture, and particularly words translated "teach" and "learn," is to recapture the community and interpersonal context in which they functioned and to understand the goal as well as the process of teaching.

OT 1. The Hebrew words translated "teach" and "learn"
2. The biblical concept of teaching and learning
3. The community context of teaching and learning
4. The interpersonal context of teaching and learning
NT 5. The Greek words translated "teach" and "learn"
6. Teaching and learning in the Gospels
7. Teaching and learning in the Epistles
8. Teachers of Christian faith
9. Summary

OT — 1. The Hebrew words translated "teach" and "learn". A dozen different Hebrew words are associated with teaching in the OT. Some of those translated "teach" and "learn" in the NIV and NASB are worth noting.

Lāmad conveys the sense of training as well as education. Teaching and learning are not academic but are focused on knowing and responding to the will of God. We sense the goal of this teaching and learning in Dt 31:12–13: "Assemble the people . . . so they can listen and learn to fear the Lord your God and follow carefully all the words of this law. Their children, who do not know this law, must hear it and learn to fear the LORD your God as long as you live in the land."

Yārâh in the Hiphil stem means "to teach." It is the root from which *tôrâh*, "law" is drawn. Essentially *tôrâh* means "teaching," or "instruction," focusing on how one should conduct oneself in all of life's situations. The verb is used in Exodus, where God promised Moses, "Now go; I will help you speak and teach you what to say" (Ex 4:1). The practical focus of *tôrâh* is illustrated by Pr 3:1–2, in which a father speaks of his instruction of his son: "My son, do not forget my teaching, but keep my commands in your heart, for they will prolong your life many years and bring you prosperity."

The root *yāda'* means "to know" and often focuses on one's capacity to distinguish. ♦ *Know/Knowledge* We see the implications for teaching and learning in the noun form, *da'at*, "knowledge." In Scripture, such knowledge is personal and experiential. While *da'at* may be used of technical skills, such as those required to build the tabernacle, its normal focus is on one's personal relationship with God and on the moral discernment required to walk in his paths.

Teaching that issues in this kind of knowledge must come from God. As the psalmist cries, "Do good to your servant according to your word, O LORD. Teach me knowledge and good judgment, for I believe in your commands" (Ps 119:66). God gives knowledge, not only through revelation, but, as the psalm goes on to say, through the experiences that God brings into the believer's life: "Before I was afflicted I went astray, but now I obey your word" (Ps 119:65–67).

Yāsar means "to discipline" or "to chastise." It indicates a word or act of correction that results in the education of a learner. The beneficial outcome marks such instruction as loving. So Pr 3:11–12 says, "My son, do not despise the LORD's discipline and do not resent his rebuke, because the LORD disciplines those he loves, as a father the son he delights in."

The meaning of *leqah* is "learning." *Leqah* is derived from a root that means "to receive" or "to acquire." It tends to focus on perception, i.e., acquiring a perspective (e.g., Pr 1:5).

The word *śākal* indicates understanding. When used in a stem that suggests instruction, it focuses on intellectual processes. One thinks through an issue to an understanding that permits successful application and godly living.

2. The biblical concept of teaching and learning. These Hebrew words for teaching and learning give us insight into several aspects of the biblical concept. Teaching and learning involve hearing a word addressed from outside—from the older and wiser person or, most often, from God himself. The word heard is an instruction, designed to shape the learner's moral perceptions and so to lead to godly living. The focus on shaping life's choices is significant. In the OT, the goal of education is a godly life, one that

expresses the believer's loving fear of the Lord. ♦ *Fear*

The famous opening lines of Proverbs explain the purpose not only of those recorded sayings but also of education itself as understood in the OT: "for attaining wisdom and discipline; for understanding words of insight; for acquiring a disciplined and prudent life, doing what is right and just and fair; for giving prudence to the simple, knowledge and discretion to the young—let the wise listen and add to their learning, and let the discerning get guidance" (Pr 1:2–5). Thus, while teaching and learning involve the word coming from outside, that word is sharply focused on the moral life. To learn is to attain wisdom, discipline, and insight and to acquire prudence so that one does what is right and just and fair.

Teaching and learning involve the divine word from "outside" that must be "heard." ♦ *Hear/Listen* So there is unquestionably a "content" in OT education. But because learning is viewed as shaping values, character, and lifestyle itself, the content must be processed in a life-transforming way. It is not enough to gain mental mastery of biblical information. The divine word must be taken into the very heart of the learner and expressed in his every choice and act.

It is important, therefore, to note the context in which the word from outside is heard and processed. Moreover, unlike teaching in our culture, teaching as envisioned in the OT does not presuppose a classroom. Rather, the OT presupposes a distinctive community and a distinctive interpersonal setting for teaching and learning.

3. The community context of teaching and learning. The learner in OT times was viewed as living in a faith community that itself was to be shaped by the words of God. The *tôrâh*, the divine instruction, patterned the society, and the whole community was to be guided by God's Word. Thus, the content to be taught and learned was to be practiced by members of the community with whom the learner lived; modeling was a basic aspect of the process by which the divine Word was taught. ◆ *Example*

OT law established annual worship festivals in which the entire community was to participate. Some of these festivals involved reenactment of the great historic events in which God had acted for the benefit of his people. ◆ *Passover* ◆ *Remember/Memory*

Participation by all members of the family in such events was another vital aspect of OT education. Each celebration was designed to help the learner participate in and identify with God's acts and capture personally the identity shared by all Israel as God's special people.

The sacrificial system symbolically communicated the great themes taught formally in the Scripture. The reality of sin, the necessity of atonement, and the willingness of God to accept the sinner who came to him were constantly acted out as persons brought the required sacrifices to the priests.

These elements are only a few of the aspects of the OT lifestyle through which the community itself provided a unique context for teaching and learning God's Word. But it is important for anyone who thinks seriously about education in faith to consider community relations along with the content to be taught. To teach God's word-from-outside with life-changing impact, modeling and example, participation and identification, and symbolic rehearsal, remain highly important.

4. The interpersonal context of teaching and learning. The lifestyle of the community of faith as laid out in the Mosaic Law is itself a vital context for teaching. But so are the more intimate relationships that the learner has with his teachers. Dt 6:4–9 is the definitive OT passage. Israel is called on to love the Lord wholly. Only by learners who love God can the words of God be truly heard.

The family is envisioned in this passage as the teaching unit, but it is in a broader, extended-family sense that we need to understand the family. ◆ *Family*

The words of God are to be in the heart of those elders of the family who will be the teachers (6:6). The words are to be spoken and impressed on the children. This is done, God told the fathers, by talking "about them when you sit at home and when you walk along the road, when you lie down and when you get up" (6:7). That is, as life is lived by adult and child, the recurrent experiences they share are to be constantly interpreted by the divine Word. Thus, learning does not take place in classrooms but in the cycle of ordinary events. One refers to God's words in order to explain the "why" of life's choices as they are made. In this way, content and practical implication are always linked in the experience of the learner.

This stands in contrast to much modern educational process, which is so designed that the learner is expected to master content apart from his or her present experience.

While we rightly focus on *what* is to be taught to build a biblical understanding of life and to develop Christian character, we all too often miss the process of the teaching that enables us to impress God's Word from "outside." The OT shows us that teaching faith and learning it are intended to take place in the context of a community that lives according to Scripture and in intimate personal relationship with those who share our lives and can help us sense what God's Word means for the reality of daily experience.

NT — 5. The Greek words translated "teach" and "learn". Although the vocabulary of teaching and learning shifts in the NT from Hebrew to Greek, basic assumptions about faith do not change. There is still a word from outside, intended to shape the believer toward holiness; and there is still a necessary process by which that word is to be impressed on the human heart. So while the Greek vocabulary is significant in any study of teaching and learning, we must again be concerned about Scripture's assumptions concerning the context in which they function.

The word *didaskō* ("to teach") has broad application. It suggests a relationship between a teacher and a student or between an instructor and an apprentice. Teaching can involve informing, instructing, and demonstrating. The content may be knowledge or skills. In the Septuagint, this word is commonly chosen to translate the Hebrew *lāmad*.

In the NT, Jesus' teaching as identified by this root included his public preaching and instruction. It involved the use of illustrations and parables as well as a direct statement of concepts. The most impressive aspect of Jesus as a teacher, as far as his hearers were concerned, was apparently the complete authority with which he spoke of God (Mk 1:22). Because this Greek word has so many shades of meaning, the specific meaning must be determined from each context in which it appears.

Katēcheō ("instruction") focuses on giving information or reporting. It is found only eight times in the NT (Lk 1:4; Ac 18:25; 21:21,24; Ro 2:18; 1 Co 14:19; Gal 6:6) and is not used in the Septuagint to translate any Hebrew term.

Paideuō is a broad term meaning "to bring up" (as a child), "to instruct, train, and educate." The Septuagint is most likely to use this word when translating *yāsar*, "to chastise, or correct." *Paideuō* often suggests discipline in the NT, not simply as chastisement but as the whole process by which God trains his people and testifies through a chastening experience to the believer's sonship.

Manthanō means "to learn" but is most recognizable in its noun form, *mathētēs* ("disciple"). Like *didaskō*, it too is often used to translate *lāmad*. ♦ *Disciple*

Other words that are significant in the teaching/learning vocabulary of the NT include *parangellō*, which indicates the instructing or commanding by someone in authority, and *noutheteō*, which involves instructing and warning.

6. Teaching and learning in the Gospels. Jesus was recognized in his society as a teacher, and the NT shows he was often addressed as "Teacher." As other teachers in that day in Judea, Jesus' teaching focused on shaping the hearers' perception of God and God's kingdom, and thus it dealt with the implications of a personal relationship with God. In John's Gospel, much of Jesus' public instruction focused on himself and his own place as Son of God.

Teaching situations are varied and complex. Jesus taught great crowds from a mountain or a boat anchored by the seashore. He dialogued. He illustrated truth by pointing to the commonplace and by telling obscure parables. He answered questions and asked questions. Over and over again, events like the healing of a man with a paralyzed hand led to discussion in which the character and purposes of God were more sharply unveiled.

Jesus maintained an intimate teaching ministry with his disciples. He answered their questions about a day's events and questioned them in turn. The disciples observed Jesus' life while traveling with him, and Jesus gave them life assignments, as when he sent them out two by two. This powerful, intimate form of instruction is best understood as discipling, and it is significant that Jesus' instructions to the disciples after his resurrection were that they should "go and make disciples of all nations," "teaching them to obey everything" he had commanded them (Mt 28:19–20).

Just as in the OT era, the teaching that Scripture finds significant is not that which provides information alone but also the teaching that creates disciples who live in responsive obedience to God's will.

7. Teaching and learning in the Epistles. In the Epistles, the emphasis in contexts where words linked with teaching and learning are found rests squarely on content. The doctrine of Christ is derived from outside of space and time, communicated in words "taught by the Spirit" (1 Co 2:13). ♦ *Reveal/Revelation* Those who are skillful teachers are charged with the task of maintaining the pattern of doctrine delivered them by the apostles (2 Ti 1:13). But in these same contexts we make surprising discoveries. Teaching is not only of "sound doctrine" but of "what is in accord with" sound doctrine (Tit 2:1). Reverence, love for husbands and children, self-control, doing what is good, subjection of slaves to masters, trustworthiness—all these things in Tit 2 are the object of Christian teaching. The pursuit of "righteousness, faith, love and peace" with those who "call on the Lord out of a pure heart" (2 Ti 2:22) is the product of a gentle instruction that relies on God to enlighten and transform (vv. 23–26).

Like the OT, the NT places emphasis on a word from outside; and like the OT, that word from outside is focused on transformation of the believer. So the God-breathed Scripture "is useful for teaching, rebuking, correcting and training in righteousness, so that the man of God may be thoroughly equipped for every good work" (2 Ti 3:16). Although the teaching is not as clearly institutionalized in the NT, the parallelism between the OT and the NT contexts for teaching is also maintained.

Again like the OT, the NT presupposes community as the context for teaching and learning. The church as the body of Christ is an extended family, in which the believer, "rooted and grounded in love" (Eph 3:17, KJV), has the power to grasp the reality of Christ's love and be filled with all the fullness of God (vv. 18–19). ♦ *Body* ♦ *Example* ♦ *Family* ♦ *Gift/Gifts* ♦ *Love* Even Paul, struggling to describe the relationship with others to whom he so successfully taught the Word, could only turn to the image of the family (1 Th 2:7–12). Even the "daily life" emphasis of Dt 6 finds clear expression as Paul reminds Timothy, "You . . . know all about my teaching, my way of life, my purpose, faith, patience, love, endurance, persecutions, sufferings" (2 Ti 3:10–11).

We cannot understand the teaching of faith in the early church simply by studying the Greek vocabulary. Understanding comes only by seeing how teaching actually took place in the context of that first Christ community.

8. Teachers of Christian faith. An understanding of how faith was taught in the early church helps us toward a deeper understanding of the teacher role. There had to be a mastery of the word from outside, committed "to reliable men who [would] also be qualified to teach others" (2 Ti 2:2).

The phrase "qualified to teach" should be understood in the context of qualifications for leadership laid down in the Pastoral Epistles, from which this quote comes. Later in this same chapter, Paul gives specific instructions for Timothy, one of which is that "the Lord's servant . . . must be . . . able to teach" (v. 24). In a previous letter, Paul had said that a bishop had to be "able to teach" (1 Ti 3:2). Both passages use the same Greek word for this English phrase; it is *didaktos*, found only in these two passages in the NT. Thus, skill in teaching is important for church leadership.

As was true in Deuteronomy's early prescription, so it remains true in the church: to be a teacher one must have taken the external Word into the heart, so that it finds expression in a godly life.

9. Summary. Teaching and learning are complex processes, whatever is being taught. The teaching and learning of faith is even more complex.

Both Testaments agree that our teaching is of truth from God, which comes from outside the realm of human experience. Both agree that that truth focuses on a personal relationship with God and on how that relationship is expressed in a godly lifestyle.

To understand the process by which the external Word is translated into personal faith and godliness we need to examine, not just the terms used for teaching and learning in Hebrew and Greek, but also the contexts in which they were expected to function. When we examine contexts, we see that response to the external Word and effective teaching of it calls for participation in a community in which that Word is put into practice, and it calls for intimate, ongoing relationships with those who model and explain the Word in life situations to which it applies.

TEMPLE ♦ *Tabernacle and Temple*

TEMPTATION/TEST/TRIAL

There is some overlapping in the Greek words translated by these English terms. They occur infrequently in the OT, but the NT develops these concepts of temptation, testing, and trials.

OT 1. Testing in the OT
NT 2. Temptation
    3. Testing
    4. Trials
    5. Summary

OT — 1. Testing in the OT. Three Hebrew words are translated "test" in the NIV and NASB: *nāsâh, ṣārap,* and *bāhan.*

Nāsâh occurs thirty-six times in the OT and indicates an attempt to prove the quality of someone or something. Often a time of pressure and difficulty constitutes the test. God tested his people at the time of the Exodus to "see whether" they would follow his instructions (Ex 16:4; cf. 20:20; Dt 8:16; Jdg 2:22).

But human beings have no right to test God (Dt 6:16), unless specifically invited by God to do so (Mal 3:10, the word here being *bāhan*). The historic incident referred to in Dt 6:16 is instructive. God had promised to be with his people and had demonstrated his presence in the fiery cloud that accompanied them. Yet Israel demanded proof, saying, "Is the LORD among us or not?" (Ex 17:7). Because God is totally trustworthy, demanding proof of his power or presence is an insult, demonstrating a failure to walk by faith (cf. Mt 4:5–7).

The word *ṣārap* means "to smelt or refine." It refers to the process by which gold or silver is refined. This process is used to illustrate God's purification of his people, usually through judgment (e.g., Jer 6:27–30; cf. Eze 22:18–22). The NIV translates this word seven times as "test" or "tested" (Ps 17:3; 26:2; 66:10; 119:140; Isa 48:10; Jer 9:7; Zec 13:9).

Bāhan also means "to test," specifically in the spiritual realm, with a focus on some quality, such as integrity. It has the sense of an examination designed to prove the existence of the quality sought. It is found twenty-nine times in the OT (Ge 42:15,16; 1 Ch 29:17; Job 7:18; 12:11; 23:10; 34:3,36; Ps 7:9; 11:4,5; 17:3; 26:2; 66:10; 81:7; 95:9; 139:23; Pr 17:3; Jer 6:27;

9:7; 11:20; 12:3; 17:10; 20:12; Eze 21:13; Zec 13:9; Mal 3:10,15).

While testing may involve the believer in difficult circumstances, God's purpose for us is always good.

NT — 2. Temptation. "To tempt" in the NT is in every instance *peirazō,* and "temptation" is *peirasmos.* The same Greek words are also at times translated "to test" and "trial." In the Septuagint, this family of words is used to translate *nāsâh* and its derivatives. The OT meaning persists in the NT. A temptation is a difficult situation, a pressure that brings a reaction through which the character or commitment of the believer is demonstrated. What does the NT tells us about temptation? A survey of the NIV passages where "tempt" and "temptation" occur is exciting.

First, Jesus himself was tempted by Satan (Mt 4, Lk 4). The three temptations that are recorded parallel pressures under which ancient Israel bridled and turned from God's way. Yet, Jesus trusted God fully for provision, protection, and purpose. Jesus' submission to God's will stands in contrast with Israel's refusal to trust and her resultant disobedience. Thus, Jesus shows himself to be one who has a perfect and whole relationship with the Father, one who thus can lead us to such a relationship.

Second, the Book of Hebrews looks back to Jesus' experience and to all the pressures under which Jesus labored as a human being, and it reassures us. Understanding perfectly the human experience, and "because he himself suffered when he was tempted," Jesus is "able to help those who are being tempted" (Heb 2:18). He who endured the full weight of suffering in testing situations is fully able to understand and sympathize with us.

Third, James points out that God cannot be blamed when someone fails to respond in a godly way under pressure (Jas 1:13–15). The source of human failure is to be found, not in the situation that God permits, but in "his own evil desire" (1:14). The temptation itself is not evil; the evil that emerges comes from within the human personality.

But not every temptation will lead to failure! In fact, we have God's own promise: "No temptation has seized you but such as is common to man. And God is faithful; he will not let you be tempted beyond what you can bear. But when you are tempted, he will also provide a way out so that you can stand up under it" (1 Co 10:13). The victory demonstrated by Jesus is available to us. Like Jesus, we can commit ourselves to obedience, and we will then find God's own way to escape failure.

3. Testing. Most instances of the verb "to test" or the noun "test" in the NIV and the NASB are translations of the Greek verb *peirazō* or the noun *peirasmos* (Mt 19:3; 22:35; Mk 8:11; 10:2; Lk 8:13; Ac 5:9; 15:10; 20:19; 2 Co 13:5; Heb 3:8,9; 11:17; Jas 1:12; Rev 2:2,10; 3:10). *Ekpeirazō*, an intensive form used when speaking of testing God, is found only four times (Mt 4:7; Lk 4:12; 10:25; 1 Co 10:9). Here the emphasis is on the fact that the test itself is an attempt to coerce.

In other passages, the Greek word translated "test" is *dokimazō, dokimē, dokimos,* or *adokimos* (Ro 12:2; 16:10; 1 Co 3:13; 2 Co 2:9; 8:8; 13:6,7; Gal 6:4; 1 Ti 3:10; 1 Jn 4:1). Words in this family emphasize that the test is designed to display the genuineness of that which is tried. In this sense, one who has faith puts God's will to the test, confident that what God wills will prove to be good, pleasing, and perfect (Ro 12:2). The "fire that will test every man's work" (1 Co 3:13) is not intended to display our failures but, by eliminating the worthless, to leave the beautiful uncluttered and on display.

4. Trials. Once again the basic word, except where "trial" is used in a judicial sense, is *peirasmos* (Lk 22:28; Gal 4:14; Jas 1:2,12; 1 Pe 1:6; 4:12; 2 Pe 2:9). Although believers may experience painful trials (1 Pe 4:12), they can live with confidence: "The Lord knows how to rescue godly men from trials" (2 Pe 2:9).

Two other Greek words that the NIV translates as "trial" are *dokimē* (2 Co 8:2) and *thlipsis* (1 Th 3:3; 2 Th 1:4).

5. Summary. "Temptation," "testing," and "trial" are all translations of Greek words that focus our attention on the pressure situations that each of us must experience. When we are under pressure, it is important to realize that God has not permitted the situation in order to entrap us. God does, however, use difficult situations in our lives. As we remain close to him, we find his way of escape, and our godly response to pressure demonstrates the genuineness of our faith.

But we are not to seek pressure in some foolhardy attempt to prove to ourselves that our faith is real. Rather, we should follow Jesus' guidance, and when we pray say, "Lead us not into temptation" (Mt 6:13; Lk 11:4; cf. Mt 26:41; Mk 14:38; Lk 22:40,46). There are tests enough ahead for each of us without our seeking them out. When they come, it is good to know that we can turn to the Lord and expect him to rescue us.

TENT OF MEETING ◆ *Tabernacle and Temple*

TERROR

The NIV and the NASB translate a variety of words for fear by the word "terror." ◆ *Fear*

TEST(ING) ◆ *Temptation/Test/Trial*

TESTIFY/WITNESS/TESTIMONY

Each of these three English words, so close in meaning, is drawn from the same Hebrew and Greek vocabularies.

OT 1. The concept of testimony
NT 2. The concept of witness

OT — 1. The concept of testimony. The Hebrew term from which the variety of words translated "to testify," "to witness," and "to give testimony" are derived is *'ûd*. The basic meaning of this verb is "to repeat, or do again." The witness thus rehearses or repeats his statement concerning what has happened. The word may also be translated "to witness." It suggests a warning. Often it is God who warns his people through the prophets (e.g., Jer 42:19; Am 3:13).

According to the law of the OT, a "witness" (*'ēd*) was someone with firsthand knowledge who could report what he saw or heard (e.g., Lev 5:1). The Ten Commandments speak strongly against bearing false witness (Ex 20:16; Dt 5:20); and one who brings a false charge against any person was to be punished with the penalty for the crime of which he accused the other (Dt 19:15–21). Witnesses were also called for when some commercial transactions were finalized (Jer 32:6–15).

"Testimony" (*'ēdāh, 'ēdût*) often refers to God's testimony to man. "Testimonies" has the sense of "laws" in passages like Ps 19 and 119. The ark, the tabernacle, and the Ten Commandments are often described as God's testimonies—affirmations by him of his promises and purposes.

At times the verb *'ānâh* ("to answer or respond") means "to testify" (as in Ex 20:16).

The underlying concept, then, suggests a strong statement by one with firsthand knowledge of what he or she knows. The testimony may be in a court case, it may be in regard to a business transaction, or it may serve as a warning. It may also be a strong verbal or symbolic statement of assured truth. The OT warns against giving false testimony, and God himself provides the model by remaining ever true to his word.

NT — 2. The concept of witness. The root *martyreō* forms the basis for the Greek words in the NT that are translated by various forms of "witness," "testify," and "testimony." All of the basic terms and the several compounds constructed on them have the same emphatic sense. The witness, who gives testimony, offers evidence of actual events, evidence based on his direct personal knowledge.

This emphasis is maintained throughout the NT. When the disciples met to choose a replacement for Judas, they said, "It is necessary to choose one of the men who have been with us the whole time the Lord Jesus went in and out

among us, beginning from John's baptism to the time when Jesus was taken up from us. For one of these must become a witness with us of his resurrection" (Ac 1:21–22). This same strong sense of objective evidence given by an eyewitness is seen in 1 John. John reports, "That which was from the beginning, which we have heard, which we have seen with our eyes, which we have looked at and our hands have touched—this we proclaim concerning the Word of life. The life appeared; we have seen it and testify to it. . . . We proclaim to you what we have seen and heard" (1 Jn 1:1–3).

The emphasis in Greek culture and in the Bible on one's personal experience of objective reality as a basis for one's witness or testimony, makes an important statement about Christian faith. Our faith is based on historic events. The resurrection of Jesus was not some subjective experience but an objective event that took place in the real world.

THANKS/THANKSGIVING

The OT has no concept parallel to the English word "thanks," that is, simply an expression of appreciation to other persons or to God. What do the words "thanks" and "thanksgiving" mean in the OT? The Hebrew word is *yādāh*, which with its derivative *tôdāh* is often translated "thanks" or "thanksgiving." It means "to declare publicly" or "to acknowledge." It is used of the confession of human sin and also of public confession of God's character and works. ◗ *Confession of Sins* In the latter usage, the Hebrew concept is that of praise, not thanksgiving. ◗ *Praise*

The NT words translated "thank" (*eucharisteō*), "thankful" (*eucharistos*), and "thanksgiving" (*eucharistia*) signify a thankful attitude and a demonstration of gratitude. Only in three passages (Lk 17:16; Ac 24:3; Ro 16:4) are these words used of thanks given to human beings.

In the NT, the swelling sense of gratitude and appreciation expressed in thanksgiving has three primary associations. Thanks is given at the eucharist (communion service) for the broken body and the blood of Jesus (Mt 26; Mk 14; Lk 22; 1 Co 11). Thanks is given for the blessings that have come to us through Christ (1 Co 15:57; 2 Co 2:14; 9:15). Thanks is given for those who come to know Christ and who bring joy to Paul's heart (1 Co 1:4; Eph 1:16; Php 1:3; Col 1:3; 1 Th 1:2; 2:13; Phm 4). Remembering all that Jesus has done for us and in us, it is appropriate to address every prayer with thanksgiving (Php 4:6).

THINK

OT vocabulary makes distinctions between different mental processes. ▶ *Understand/Understanding* One of the key words, *ḥāšab̲,* means "to think" or "to plan." It includes not only the idea of making a judgment but also the faculty of imagination. But that word is translated "think" by the NIV only four times in the OT (Job 35:2; Ps 144:3; Jer 23:27; Zec 7:10). Most often "think" is used in a general sense to translate various OT phrases in English idiom. E.g., where the KJV has "as it pleases you," the NIV has "whatever you think best" (Ge 16:6); instead of "Pharaoh will say of them," the NIV has "Pharaoh will think" (Ex 14:3); and instead of "my father fought for you" the NIV stresses the outraged tone, reading "to think that my father fought for you[!]" (Jdg 9:17).

"Think" and "thoughts" are also supplied at times in the NT (e.g., Lk 1:51; Jn 18:35; Ac 5:4; 11:17; 1 Co 1:26; 2:11; 8:7; 1 Pe 4:4). While there are two Greek word groups that have the primary sense of "to think" or "to consider," there are also a number of other Greek words that are so translated. Because of the wide range of meanings, a complete treatment of all Greek words so translated follows. *Dialogizomai* and *dialogismos* have a negative tone in the NT. They suggest thinking issues through in a calculated, thorough way; but they are closely linked in Greek culture with the teaching of philosophers. In the NT, they suggest the efforts of unaided human beings to arrive at significant truth. These words are translated "thought(s)" in five passages (Mk 7:21; Lk 2:35; 12:17; 1 Co 3:20; Jas 2:4).

Dokeō ("to think, consider, suppose") suggests the acceptance of a point of view, the holding of an opinion. It is translated "think" or "thought" in a number of passages (Mt 3:9; 6:7; 17:25; 18:12; 21:28; 22:42; 26:53,66; Mk 6:49; Lk 10:36; 12:51; 13:2,4; 19:11; Jn 5:39,45; 11:13,56; 13:29; 16:2; Ac 12:9; 25:27; 27:13; 1 Co 7:40; 10:12; 12:23; Heb 10:29; 12:10; Jas 4:5).

Nomizō means "to suppose." It is translated "think" in eight of the fifteen places it appears in the NT (Mt 5:17; Lk 2:44; 3:23; Ac 8:20; 17:29; 1 Co 7:26,36; 1 Ti 6:5).

Another pair of words—*logizomai* and *logismos*—are also translated "think" in the NIV. The root implies concentrated, logical thought. We sense the focused effort in Php 4:8, where believers are encouraged to "think about" the true, noble, right, pure, lovely, and admirable. *Logizomai* is rendered "to think" another four times (Ro 2:3; 2 Co 10:2; 11:5; 12:6), and *logismos* is rendered "thought" once (Ro 2:15).

In many other instances, "think" is a translation of one of many different Greek words that have a variety of shades of meaning.

Axioō, "to consider worthy," is the Greek verb rendered "think" in Ac 15:38.

Dianoēma, used only once in the NT (Lk 11:17), suggests thinking something through in order to arrive at a settled purpose.

Dianoia, in Eph 2:3, indicates one's understanding or disposition.

Dokimazō ("to come to a conclusion after trial") is found in Ro 1:28.

Ennoia includes feelings as well as thoughts and is rendered "attitude(s)" both times it occurs in the NT (Heb 4:12; 1 Pe 4:1).

Epinoia, used only once in the NT (Ac 8:22), has a negative tone; the thoughts are plots or dark intentions.

Eudokeō, "to think well of," is found in 1 Th 3:1.

Gnōmē, in 1 Co 1:10, indicates a considered opinion.

Hēgeomai, "to consider, or think," occurs in two passages (Php 2:25; 2 Pe 1:13).

Hyperphroneō, "to think highly" (i.e., "to be conceited"), is used only once in the NT (Ro 12:3).

Hyponoeō, which occurs three times in the NT and pictures thoughts bubbling up into one's mind, is in Ac 13:25.

Katanoeō, used in Heb 3:1, is a strong word meaning "to fix the mind on" something.

Noēma means "thought," "design," or "purpose" and occurs in 2 Co 10:5.

Oiomai means "to suppose," but this word is used when the supposition is a product of a wrong judgment. One of its three occurrences in the NT is in Jas 1:7.

Phainō, "to appear," is in Mk 14:64, where the high priest asked about Jesus' supposed blasphemy: "What do you think?" (i.e., "How does it appear to you?").

Phroneō, which emphasizes attitude, is found twice (1 Co 13:11; Php 3:15).

Theōreō occurs in Heb 7:4 and stresses active consideration or observation.

THIRST ♦ *Hunger and Thirst*

THRONE

The word "throne" is used in both Testaments, both literally and metaphorically, in reference to the seat of honor and especially of the seat of authority. ♦ *Grace*

TIME

It is difficult to treat "time" philosophically. Scripture does not encourage our speculation. But the Bible does have a viewpoint about the meaning of time.

OT 1. Experienced time
2. Time beyond personal experience
NT 3. *Kairos:* the significant moment
4. Summary

OT — 1. Experienced time. Experienced time is simply that span of time available for an individual or generation to experience. It contrasts with the past

and future that are now outside of that span.

The OT has a number of ways of perceiving experienced time. The word *'ēt* conceives of time as a series of recurring seasons or as a moment that is particularly appropriate or opportune. Often this word is closely linked with meeting the Lord. *Z^emān* occurs four times (Ne 2:6; Est 9:27,31; Ecc 3:1) and means much the same as *'ēt.*

Yôm ("day") divides time into regular units whether of long or short duration, whereas *pa'am* is used flexibly in phrases associated with time.

The OT does see a rhythm to time. It has recurring cycles of days and weeks, of months and seasons and years. Life itself follows the pattern of seasonality, as Solomon points out in Ecc 3, so there is even an appropriate time for dying (Ge 29:21).

But time also flows toward a future determined by God. An individual or nation may find that personal experience intersects with an "appointed time" (*mô'ēd*). This may be a time when God acts in the stream of time to keep history on its appointed course. But *mô'ēd* may also be an appointment with God, such as to keep one of the annual festivals that recalls one of his decisive acts in history.

2. Time beyond personal experience. The OT accepts the reality of past and future time that is beyond the possibility of personal experience by a living generation. This time is real, for it stands within the span of God's own endless "lifetime," and he, the Lord of history, is able to speak about it. The appointed times of history are in his hand and develop according to his purposes.

There are many words in the OT that develop the OT's concept of time and express some aspect of its implications. ♦ *Age* ♦ *Always* ♦ *Ancient* ♦ *Day* ♦ *Eternal* ♦ *Future* ♦ *Today*

NT — 3. *Kairos:* the significant moment. As in the OT, there are a number of terms found in the NT that have temporal significance. ♦ *Hour* ♦ *Imperishable* ♦ *New and Old*

In the NT, *chronos* and *kairos* are the two basic words translated "time." *Chronos* designates a period or space of time. It is very close in meaning to the rather scientific way in which Westerners speak of time. The function of *kairos*, also often translated "time," is to characterize the content and the quality of the time it indicates. *Kairos*, whatever the duration of the *chronos* involved, highlights the significance of that brief or extended moment. It was at the "right time" that Christ died for the ungodly (Ro 5:6; Eph 1:10) and forever changed the character of time. Not only must all of history be reinterpreted by that moment, but time itself has become different too. We live in an "acceptable time," a day of salvation, a day of opportunity (2 Co 6:2).

Kairos—relating to past, present, and future *chronos*—is found eighty-five times in the NT (Mt 8:29; 11:25; 12:1; 13:30; 14:1; 16:3; 21:34,41; 24:45; 26:18; Mk 1:15; 10:30; 11:13; 12:2; 13:33; Lk 1:20; 4:13; 8:13; 12:42,56; 13:1; 18:30; 19:44; 20:10; 21:8,24,36; Jn 5:4; 7:6,8; Ac 1:7; 3:19; 7:20; 12:1; 13:11; 14:17; 17:26; 19:23; 24:25; Ro 3:26; 5:6; 8:18; 9:9; 11:5; 12:11; 13:11; 1 Co 4:5; 7:5,29; 2 Co 6:2; 8:14; Gal 4:10; 6:9,10; Eph 1:10; 2:12; 5:16; 6:18; Col 4:5; 1 Th 2:17; 5:1; 2 Th 2:6; 1 Ti 2:6; 4:1; 6:15; 2 Ti 3:1; 4:3,6; Tit 1:3; Heb 9:9,10; 11:11,15; 1 Pe 1:5,11; 4:17; 5:6; Rev 1:3; 11:18; 12:12,14; 22:10).

4. Summary. Time is significant in the OT and the NT. Scripture locates the significance of time outside the experience of any individual. Time, like the rest of the environment in which human beings move, has been ordered and designed by God. It is marked by cycle and repetition and yet flows from a beginning toward a culmination. Time is also marked by significant moments. The greatest of all significant moments are significant because God sets them aside as times of his own action in history. These moments are also significant because they provide opportunity for each of us to confront the reality of God and to respond to him. Spans of time may be remembered as troubled or peaceful, but the truly significant points in each person's life are those in which he or she

senses the call of God and responds to him—with rejection or with joyful obedience.

The NT focuses on the fact that all time finds its focus and fulfillment in Christ. His coming transforms every moment into opportunity; and when he returns, the fulfillment of every promise God ever made will be achieved.

How important, then, that we use our moments of time wisely, sensing the eternal significance that our relationship with Jesus brings to all time.

TITHE ♦ *Giving*

TODAY

In Hebrew, "today" is usually indicated by using *yôm* ("day"). *Sēmeron* is the Greek word for it. In both Testaments it is often used in the most ordinary sense.

But "today" also may be a theologically significant word that shares in the distinctive way the Bible views time. ♦ *Day* ♦ *Time* We see this particularly in Heb 3–4; there, each use of "today" speaks of a moment of opportunity, marked by hearing God's voice speak a word of guidance and direction. Num 14 records the faithless response of Israel to God's command to go into the Promised Land. As a consequence of their rebellion, that generation could not enter God's rest. The writer of Hebrews tells of a generation that did respond and applies the principle to his readers. In our "today," when we hear God's voice, we are to respond with faith's obedience and thus step into a personal experience of God's rest.

In that personal sense, then, "today" is that moment of personal confrontation when God speaks to an individual or a generation with the unique unveiling of his will for them. It is our moment of personal opportunity to follow in obedience.

Hebrew's sharp redefinition of "today" invites us to look back through the OT and the NT and see how many times "today" is used in this theologically significant way.

TONGUES

The Hebrew word for "tongue" is *lāšôn*. At times it designates the tongue as a physical organ. Most of the 117 OT occurrences, however, have a different meaning. The tongue is an expression of character—an organ that communicates what is in the heart of the speaker. Thus, the OT speaks of deceitful tongues and of tongues that utter praise.

The Greek word is *glōssa*. It is used in five different ways in the NT. First, it is used (as in the OT) to designate the tongue as a physical organ (Mk 7:33,35; Lk 1:64; 16:24).

A second use is found in Ac 2:3, where "tongues of fire" is a description of the visible manifestation of the coming of the Holy Spirit.

Several passages use "tongue" in a distinctively OT way (e.g., Ac 2:26; Ro 3:13; 14:11; Php 2:11; Jas 1:26; 3:5,6,8; 1 Pe 3:10; 1 Jn 3:18).

In other passages "tongue" refers to a foreign language (Ac 2:4,11). This is made clear by the context, which specifically states that at Pentecost the Parthians, the Medes, and the Elamites, and the residents of Phrygia, Pamphylia, Egypt, and other lands heard the apostles speaking in their own native languages (2:7–12). All occurrences of the word "tongues" in Revelation should be understood as referring to foreign languages or national groups.

The greatest number of references, and those that have most fascinated certain segments of Christendom, speak of a spiritual gift of tongues. The references to tongues in this sense are found in 1 Co 12 and 14. Possibly this gift is referred to in Mk 16:17; and some argue that the tongues mentioned in Ac 2:4,11 are the same as those discussed in 1 Corinthians. This seems unlikely because the tongues in Ac 2 clearly involve known contemporary languages. The questions then focus on 1 Corinthians and the nature of the gift of tongues.

Many of the questions raised today are not specifically answered in these passages. But observing several things in the text helps us keep tongues in a biblical perspective.

The historical setting. In the NT era, those with ecstatic experiences were considered especially close to the gods or goddesses. Thus, epilepsy was called "the divine disease." It was assumed that the epileptic seizure and anything that one uttered while in it or recovering from it was inspired.

Paul begins his discussion of gifts, which include speaking in tongues, by saying, "Now about spiritual gifts, brothers" (1 Co 12:1). Here "gifts" is supplied by the translators; it does not occur in the Greek. Literally, it says, "Now about spirituals, brothers," which may very well mean, "Now, brothers, let's examine spirituality." Paul was about to examine very carefully the emphasis that the Corinthians, carrying over their pagan religious notions about the ecstatic, had placed on the gift of tongues.

The biblical argument. Paul first establishes that the Spirit of God expresses himself not only in tongues but in every gift (12:4–11). Each person has a gift, an expression of the Spirit, sovereignly given by the Lord. Thus, those who speak in tongues are not—as the Corinthians had mistakenly assumed—spiritually superior. This point is emphasized as Paul insists that believers are the body of Christ (12:12–30). In a human body, each part is essential, so we must not give some parts greater honor than others. In the same way, every member of Christ's body is significant, whatever one's gifts.

There is much debate about references to tongues in 1 Co 13. Paul clearly is saying that love is more significant than either gifts or bare good works. One who wishes to learn what true spirituality is should not look at what a person's gifts are but at how well he exhibits the quality of love in his interpersonal relationships (13:4–7). The question is, Does the phrase "where there are tongues, they will be stilled" (v. 8) indicate a passing of this spiritual gift from the experience of the church after the apostolic age? Many hold that tongues, along with prophecy and the "word of knowledge," refer to spiritual gifts that had a function before Scripture was completed; with the closing of the canon they were no longer needed in the church. Others argue strongly that these gifts do exist in the modern church and should be recognized.

In 1 Co 14, Paul returns to his correction of the Corinthians' overemphasis on tongues. He argues that the church should focus on gifts that build up the body, especially prophecy. ♦ *Prophecy/Prophet* To edify believers, unless an interpreter of tongues is present, one must speak in intelligible language, for "tongues . . . are a sign, not for believers but for unbelievers" (v. 22).

Paul then turns to the case of the curious outsiders. Nonbelievers may be attracted to a church gathering because of the culture's view of the ecstatic. But if they simply see a group of people speaking some unintelligible words, they will conclude that these people are out of their mind (v. 23) But if someone comes in while the speaker is edifying the body, "he will be convinced . . . that he is a sinner" and realize that "God is really among [them]" (vv. 24–25).

In his summary, Paul does not forbid speaking in tongues in church meetings. Instead, he gives ground rules. Everything done in church must be done to edify the church; so if the gift of tongues is used in a meeting, (1) no more than three persons should speak in tongues, (2) they should speak one at a time, and (3) another with the gift of interpretation must be present (vv. 27–28). It is no excuse for disorder in church meetings to say, "I can't help it, the Spirit made me do it." Why? Because "the spirits of prophets are subject to the control of prophets" (v. 32). That is, God's Spirit does not overwhelm and submerge the human will.

The passage concludes, "Do not forbid speaking in tongues. But everything should be done in a fitting and orderly way" (vv. 39–40).

Conclusions. It is striking that no other references to tongues are made in the Epistles; however, it is clear that we cannot simply dismiss the phenomenon of speaking in tongues. At the same time, we must not overemphasize it. We must neither view it as a touchstone of spirituality nor as one of the more significant spiritual gifts. Moreover, by applying the ground rules laid down by Scripture itself, we should guard our congregations from a wrong view of this gift.

TORMENT

In the NT, "torment" is usually *basanos* or one of its cognates (except in Ac 5:16 and 2 Co 12:7, which use similar terms). *Basanos* originally indicated torture used to elicit information; later it became a general term for torment. The NT uses it to describe the suffering of the sick and demon-possessed. Only in the Book of Revelation is torment spoken of as a result of divine judgment.

TOUCH

The Hebrew word for "touch" is *nāga'*. It indicates physical contact. At times "touch" is used metaphorically, either of sexual relations or of attack. In the NT, the most common word for "touch" is *haptō*; in Jn 20:17 this word probably means "to hold on to." *Thinganō* occurs only three times (Col 2:21; Heb 11:28; 12:20), and *psēlaphaō* occurs four times (Lk 24:39; Ac 17:27; Heb 12:18; 1 Jn 1:1).

There is a striking interplay between the OT and NT in Christ's frequent touching of the sick and sinful. OT law forbade anyone who was ceremonially clean from touching anything unclean. ♦ *Clean and Unclean* One who touched an unclean thing became unclean. But when Jesus touched or was touched by the unclean, as by a woman with a constant menstruous flow (Mt 9; Mk 5), something different happened. According to law, her uncleanness should have been transmitted to Jesus by that touch. Instead, a transforming, healing power flowed from Jesus to her. Jesus remained uncontaminated because of his own dynamic holiness and was even able to channel his inner power through his touch to cleanse and to heal.

TRAIN

A number of significant verses attract our attention to the verb "to train" in the Bible.

In the OT, Pr 22:6 has intrigued many: "Train a child in the way he should go, and when he is old he will not turn from it." The Hebrew verb here is *ḥānak*. It occurs only four other times in the OT (Dt 20:5; 1 Ki 8:63; 2 Ch 7:5). The verb and its cognates are primarily used in connection with some building or construction project. It seems best to translate the verb as "to start" or "to begin." Thus, "train up a child" does not suggest some specific form of child rearing. Rather, it encourages starting religious and moral education in childhood, so that the values taught will be expressed in choices later in life.

Several different Greek words are translated "train" in the NT. *Gymnazō* means "to exercise"; that is, to train and discipline one's body. It is used in Heb 5:14, which teaches that maturity is achieved only when one develops moral potential by making distinctions between good and evil. It is found only three other times in the NT (1 Ti 4:7; Heb 12:11; 2 Pe 2:14).

Paideia is a word linked with the discipline and training of children. ♦ *Discipline* The NIV and the NASB render it "train" twice (Eph 6:4; 2 Ti 3:16) and "discipline" in its other four occurrences (Heb 12:5,6,8,11).

Lk 6:40 is distinctive in that it uses *katartizō*. The word speaks of the full development of one's potential; that is, one's being completely equipped or prepared in the area in question. Jesus' focus in discipleship is on equipping his followers, not with skills, but with character. The person who has been equipped to follow Jesus is the person who has become like him.

Where the NIV has "not a trained speaker" in 2 Co 11:6, the Greek has the deprecating *idiōtēs*—a word used only four other times in the NT (Ac 4:13; 1 Co 14:16,23,24). Paul was saying that he was simply an unskilled lay person as far as oratorical training is concerned.

TRANSGRESSION ♦ *Rebel/Rebellion*

TREASURE

There are a number of words in Hebrew that might be translated "treasure." The word most often so translated is *'ôṣār*, from *'āṣar*, "to store or lay up." The word is used literally of wealth or military equipment and figuratively of divine blessings or resources.

In the NT, "treasure" is *thēsauros* (found 18 times in the NT). When used literally, it too denotes accumulated wealth, but it is also used figuratively in two of its three occurrences in the Epistles (2 Co 4:7; Col 2:3; 1 Ti 6:19).

Jesus' use of *thēsauros* is significant. Earthly treasures are transitory; heavenly treasures, secure. The saying "Where your treasure is, there your heart will be also" (Mt 6:21; Lk 12:34) focuses attention on values. That which is deemed valuable will be the focus of thoughts and efforts and will undoubtedly shape the choices that one makes in life. ♦ *Wealth/Riches/Possessions*

TREATY ♦ *Covenant*

TRIALS ♦ *Temptation/Test/Trial*

TRIBE

Each of the two Hebrew words translated "tribe" in the NIV and the NASB (*maṭṭeh*, *šēbet*) has the literal meaning of "rod" or "staff." Commentators assume that a staff was carried by the tribal leader to denote his authority over his family and that the symbol was extended to indicate the family itself or Israel as a larger family made up of tribes.

The OT makes it clear that Hebrew tribes were the descendants of the children of Israel (Jacob), the tribes of Ephraim and Manasseh being descendants of Joseph's two sons, though at times still reckoned as simply portions of the tribe of Joseph (e.g., Gen 49:22–26; Rev 7:8). When the tribes of Ephraim and Manasseh are counted as two of the tribes, there are thirteen tribal groups composing Israel. But the tribe of Levi was set aside for the service of God and was not reckoned when the land of Canaan was divided into twelve portions. ♦ *Priests and Levites*

In the NT the Greek word for "tribe" is *phylē*. It may designate one of the historic tribes of Israel, but it is also a broad term sweeping together into a single conglomerate all the peoples of the earth.

Another article discusses whether NT references mean literal or spiritual descendants of the OT tribes. ♦ *Israel*

TRIBULATION ♦ *Distress/Trouble*

TROUBLE ♦ *Distress/Trouble*

TRUE ♦ *Truth*

TRUST ♦ *Belief/Faith*

TRUTH

"Truth" is a most significant concept. Our view of truth shapes our societies and our personal lives. It also shapes many aspects of our relationship with God and our view of Scripture.

OT 1. Truth in the OT: *'emet*
NT 2. Truth in the NT: *alētheia*
3. Conclusions

OT — 1. Truth in the OT: *'emet*. This Hebrew word is derived from a verb (*'āman*), which means "to be established, certain, or faithful." There is considerable debate as to whether *'emet* is dual, meaning either "true" or "faithful," or singular, viewing truth as an aspect of divine faithfulness.

In either case, the best English rendering of the Hebrew concept may be "reliable." That which is true is reliable, can be counted on, and thus is trustworthy. As *The New International Dictionary of New Testament Theology*, English edition, ed. Colin Brown, 3 vols. (Grand Rapids: Zondervan, 1975–78), points out, "The Hebrews recognized the *logical* truth that others also recognized, that a true word

can be relied upon because it accords with reality, and that both for a God of truth and for a man of truth, word and deed are one" (3:882).

In the context of reliability, "true" and "faithful" are used to describe God (Ge 24:27; Ps 31:5; Jer 42:5) and God's Word (1 Ki 17:24; Ps 43:3; 119:43,142,151,160). Those who walk in God's truth (Ps 26:3) accept as trustworthy God's view of moral realities and act in harmony with the divine revelation. "Truth in the inner parts" (Ps 51:6) is probably best interpreted by 1 Jn 1. It is living honestly with God and self, confessing failures and yet struggling to choose the path God has laid out in revelation.

NT — 2. Truth in the NT: *alētheia*. Both Paul and John use the concept of truth to make distinct theological affirmations. Other occurrences may contrast truths and falsehoods or serve to underline the reliability of what is about to be said. Distinctive meanings of "truth" are found in the Epistles.

Paul's use of "truth". There are a number of everyday uses of "true" and "truth" in Paul, as in Ro 9:1 ("I speak the truth in Christ—I am not lying"). There are also theologically sensitive uses. Paul spoke of "the truth," meaning all of reality as God has revealed it—in creation (Ro 1:18) and in the gospel (Eph 1:13; Col 1:5; 1 Ti 2:4). Paul's conviction is that God has cleared away humanity's illusory beliefs and notions and in the gospel has provided a clear perspective on reality. Through revelation we at last have reliable knowledge about God, about ourselves, about the nature of the universe, and most importantly about how to live in intimate relationship with the Lord.

Paul wrote the truth (2 Co 12:6) and so described reality, but, beyond that, it is vital that his listeners respond to and obey the truth (Gal 5:7). Paul often referred to his own way of life among those to whom he ministered. He operated with a heart open wide (2 Co 6:3–13), in a relationship so transparent that no one had any reason to suspect his motives (1 Th 2:3–12). He emphasized to

Timothy not only the younger man's full acquaintance with Paul's lifestyle but also the need for Timothy to be a living example of the words Paul spoke (1 Ti 4:12–13; 2 Ti 3:10–11). This aspect of Paul's approach to ministry is reflected in several uses of "truth." The truth is not only reality as God has revealed it. The truth is reality as believers are able to experience it by making choices guided by God's reliable Word. Paul's lifestyle illustrated the reality his words described and to which he called his listeners.

At times where "true" is used in the NT, the *alētheia* root is not found. In 1 Ti 1:2 and Tit 1:4 the "true" son is *gnēsios* ("genuine"), and in Heb 12:8 "true" is supplied. But in 8:2 the writer speaks of the *alēthinos* tabernacle, meaning the "real" tabernacle in heaven, of which the earthly OT tabernacle was merely a shadow or reflection.

John's use of "truth". Over half of the NT's *alētheia* family of words ("truth," "true") appear in John's writings. At times the uses are commonplace, as in contrasting truths and falsehoods (Jn 4:18). But while different shades of emphasis can be distinguished, it is helpful when reading of truth to keep in mind that concept's relationship to reality. What is said in God's Word is reliable, for God's Word is truth, ever in harmony with reality (Jn 17:17). But even more than that, we can be sanctified by the Word; for it strips away our illusions, then takes us by the hand to guide our steps. Jesus is "the truth" (Jn 14:6), for all of reality finds its focus in him. He, who created and sustains the universe, is also man's Redeemer and the goal toward which all history strains (Col 1:15–23).

We can "know the truth" and thus be set free only by keeping Jesus' words (Jn 8:31–32). Only by following his teachings, which unveil reality, can we experience reality and so find the freedom in Christ to be who God knows us to be.

This view of "truth" is important in grasping the teaching of 1 Jn 1 on fellowship with God. We have fellowship when we "live by the truth" (1:6). This is clearly not sinlessness, for the context immediately speaks of Christ's blood purifying us "from all sin" (1:7). The focus of the passage, then, is squarely on reality, and verse 8 deals with the claim of some to be "without sin." Such a claim is self-deceit, and if we hold such a view, "the truth is not in us." The reality is that even though we are redeemed beings, sin finds expression in our lives. We are unable to deal with sin, but God is able. When we confess our sin, God forgives us and continues his purifying work within us. ◗ *Confession of Sins*

In short, John constantly calls us to adopt the divine perspective provided for us in Christ and in God's Word. As we refuse to live self-deceiving and deceitful lives, but rather commit ourselves to act by faith on those things that God says are real, we will personally experience truth and find our heritage of freedom.

3. Conclusions. "Truth" and "true" emphasize reliability in the OT and reality in the NT. However, the two concepts are interwoven in each Testament. God is reliable because his words and works faithfully portray who he is, and they are in full harmony with reality. God's reality can be known and experienced because his reliable words and actions unveil it to a blinded humanity, which must respond to him with faith.

The biblical concept of truth is particularly important in an age in which agreeing with what the Bible teaches is more closely associated with truth than is living out the teachings of Jesus. God's words unveil a reality that we certainly ought to agree with, but that reality can never be experienced until we grasp God's reliable words by faith and put them into practice.

U

UNBELIEF

The Greek word for "unbelief" is *apistia*. Unbelief is a failure to respond to God with trust *(pistis)* and at heart shows, not doubt, but rejection.

"Unbeliever" is a general term that can be applied to anyone who has not yet put his trust in Christ. Such persons are characterized by unbelief, even as Christians are characterized by their believing attitude toward God. We are taught to associate with unbelievers—even with the immoral (1 Co 5:9–13). After all, God may open eyes blinded by Satan through our presentation of the gospel (2 Co 4:4). But we are to remain spiritually sensitive, avoiding compromising situations (1 Co 10:27–33). We are also to avoid entering into "yoked" relationships with unbelievers (2 Co 6:14). ♦ **Yoke**

Whereas "unbeliever" is simply a term that characterizes one who is not yet a Christian, "unbelief" has strong negative overtones. The anxious father can struggle between belief and unbelief (Mk 9:24). Paul can see the relationship between his early unbelief and OT sins of ignorance (1 Ti 1:13). ♦ **Offering and Sacrifice** But at heart, unbelief is staggering back from God's revelation of himself, refusing to respond as Abraham did, with trust (Ro 4:20). Thus, unbelief exhibits a sinful heart "that turns away from the living God" (Heb 3:12).

UNCLEAN ♦ *Clean and Unclean*

UNDERSTAND/UNDERSTANDING

In our day, "understanding" does not mean possession of the facts. A person of understanding is one who can use what he or she knows, wisely, in real-life situations. Is this also what the Bible means by "understanding"?

OT 1. **Hebrew words for "understanding"**
NT 2. **Greek words for "understanding"**
    3. **Conclusions**

OT — 1. Hebrew words for "understanding". Several Hebrew words are translated "understand" and "understanding" in the NIV and the NASB. Sometimes the Hebrew word for understanding is *yāda'*, which generally emphasizes gaining knowledge through personal experience. This Hebrew root is used in referring to a foreign language that Israel would not understand (Dt 28:49) and to the human heart, which is so deceitful that no one but the Lord can evaluate one's hidden motives (Jer 17:9–10).

At other times, *šāma'* ("to hear") and *rā'âh* ("to see") are used in the sense of understanding (Ge 11:7; Eze 12:3). The words *śākal* and *śekel* are also translated "understand" at times. The verb *śākal* suggests a process of reasoning through complex situations to a practical conclusion, enabling one to act wisely. Insight, comprehension, or prudent action that results from the reasoning process may be the intent of the verb in any given situation. When God searched to see if there were any who understood, he looked for one who took the data provided in God's universe and looked beyond material reality for God (Ps 14:2). The Lord found none: "All have turned aside, they have together become corrupt; there is no one who does good, not even one" (v. 3).

Thus, "understanding" has a moral aspect. It is a component of character and is not merely a function of intelligence. The fool (a morally limited person) says in his heart, "There is no God," and then goes on to act wickedly; he has no true understanding (Ps 14:1). ▶ *Fool/Folly*

But the words most often translated "understand" and "understanding" in the NIV and NASB are *bîn* and its cognate *t³bûnâh*. Appearing over two hundred times in the OT, they are often translated "understanding" or "insight." The basic idea presented in *bîn* is one of judgment. The person with understanding can make distinctions between options. Given information, the person who has *bîn* is able to discern the best and right choice.

This quality too is linked to character rather than to IQ. "Fools do not understand," says Ps 92:6. In fact, no one unaided can really understand even his own way (Pr 20:24). But God's understanding has no limit (Ps 147:5). He had given Israel decrees and laws. By observing God's commands carefully, God's people could show his "wisdom and understanding" (Dt 4:6). God's revelation through Moses provided Israel with a basis on which to make distinctions and judgments and thus to know how to conduct their lives. No wonder the psalmist prayed, "Give me understanding, and I will keep your law" (Ps 119:34).

Understanding, then, whatever the root word, is a very practical thing. It expresses the use rather than the possession of knowledge and involves the faculty of judgment. According to the OT, it is only a relationship with God, exhibited in valuing and attempting to live by his revealed will, that can provide human beings with true understanding.

NT — 2. Greek words for "understanding". As with so many biblical concepts, our interpretation of Greek terms must be shaped by the perspective of the OT. Understanding is a moral and spiritual issue, not an intellectual one. Although the mind is involved, to understand spiritual realities one must be open and responsive to God.

Within this frame of reference, many different Greek words are found where the NIV and the NASB, especially the NIV, have "understand."

Synesis, Syniēmi. These words denote insight or comprehension, particularly of spiritual things. Paul prayed for the Colossians, asking that God would fill them "with the knowledge of his will through all spiritual wisdom and understanding [*synesis*]" (Col 1:9). Information is important, but it must be comprehended and applied if it is to lead to a life worthy of the Lord (v. 10). *Synesis* is translated "understanding" in four of its seven NT occurrences (Mk 12:33; Lk 2:47; Col 1:9; 2:2). The negative *asynetos* is translated "understand" in one of the five places it appears in the NT (Ro 10:19). Of the twenty-six times that *syniēmi* is used in the NT, in only three instances (Ac 7:25; 2 Co 10:12) does the NIV not read some form of the word "understand" (Mt 13:13,14,15,19,23,51; 15:10; 16:12; 17:13; Mk 4:12; 6:52; 7:14; 8:17,21; Lk 2:50; 8:10; 18:34; 24:45; Ac 28:26,27; Ro 3:11; 15:21; Eph 5:17).

Noeō, Dianoia. These very common Greek words are not used extensively in the NT. They focus attention on perception, suggesting not so much intellectual capacity as mental orientation. They emphasize an understanding of God's will and a view shaped by that understanding. In eight of its fourteen NT occurrences, the verb *noeō* is translated by some form of the word "understand" (Mt 16:9,11; 24:15; Mk 13:14; Jn 12:40; Ro 1:20; Eph 3:4; Heb 11:3). *Dianoia* is translated "understanding" in two of its thirteen NT occurrences (Eph 4:18; 1 Jn 5:20).

Ginōskō, Epiginōskō, Agnoeō, Oida. Words in this group are generally translated "to know" or "knowledge." Where the translators felt that a context suggests accurate ordering and interpretation of what is known, they were likely to choose "understand" or "understanding." *Oida* is translated several times by one of these words (Mk 4:13a; Jn 16:18; 20:9; Ro 13:11; 1 Co 2:12; 14:16; Jude 10a).

Ginōskō is so translated a number of times (Mt 24:43; Mk 4:13b: Lk 12:39; Jn 3:10; 10:6,38; 12:16; 13:7,12,28; Ac 8:30; Ro 7:15; 10:19; 1 Co 2:8,14; Gal 3:7; 2 Pe 1:20; 3:3). *Epiginōskō* is translated three times by the verb "to understand" (2 Co 1:13,14a; Col 1:6), and *epignōsis* occurs once as "understanding" (Phm 6). *Agnoeō* is translated three times by the verb "to not understand" (Mk 9:32; Lk 9:45; 2 Pe 2:12).

Epistamai, Epistēmōn. The first of these words means "a significant understanding" in three of the fourteen places it appears in the NT (Mk 14:68; 1 Ti 6:4; Jude 10a). The second word is found only once (Jas 3:13).

There are other unique occurrences. *Akouō* ("hear") is translated "understand" twice (Ac 22:9; 1 Co 14:2). *Dysnoētos* ("difficult to grasp") is used only once in the NT (2 Pe 3:16). *Phronēsis* means "wisdom displayed in action," and it occurs twice in the NT; the NIV translates it "wisdom" in Lk 1:17 and "understanding" in Eph 1:8. *Idiōtēs* means "an untrained or unskilled person," and the NIV renders it "understand" in three (1 Co 14:16,23,24) of its five NT occurrences. Of the twenty-eight times that the verb *hēgeomai* ("to think of or to consider") occurs in the NT, the NIV renders it "understand" only once (2 Pe 3:9).

The most controversial word in this category, and the most difficult to translate, is *katalambanō*, which may mean "to overcome" or "to grasp." The translators of Jn 1:5 found here the concept of grasping with one's mind—i.e., understanding. Perhaps the word "master" would fit this context well.

3. Conclusions. Understanding is an important theme in both Testaments. Both say that human beings, apart from God's enlightenment, are not able to distinguish between competing ideas of reality. But God's revelation of himself and his will has provided humanity not only with knowledge but also with understanding. The understanding person is the one who accepts God's revelation by faith and goes on to judge every experience by the standards of revelation. The essence of wisdom and understanding is to grasp spiritual realities and use them in distinguishing how to act in practical life situations.

UNFAITHFUL ♦ *Faithfulness*

UNGODLY ♦ *Godly/Godliness*

UNITY

The theme of Christian unity fascinates many. Yet there is little agreement about the nature of that unity or about the way unity is best expressed.

A literal translation of Jesus' prayer for unity among his followers is "that they may be having been brought to the goal [*teteleiōmenoi*] into one [*eis hen*]" (Jn 17:23). One might argue from context that this is a unity found in a relationship marked by commitment to one another and to common goals; but the Greek wording itself provides no clue.

What of other passages on unity? Ro 15:5 translates *phronein* ("the same mind," i.e., "setting one's mind on") as a "spirit of unity." Again, context is instructive. Unity is seen when "with one heart and mouth you . . . glorify" God (v. 6). *Henotēs* is translated "unity" in both of its NT occurrences (Eph 4:3,13), and in Col 3:14 love is portrayed as bonding other virtues together.

While none of these passages or words does more than give us clues to the nature of Christian unity, there is another Greek word that may help. It is *homothymadon*, sometimes meaning little more than "together," but capable of expressing unanimity and concerted action. It occurs twelve times in the NT (Ac 1:14; 2:1,46; 4:24; 5:12; 7:57; 8:6; 12:20; 15:25; 18:12; 19:29; Ro 15:6). Tracing through these verses, we find additional clues to unity—vital images of the church praying, worshiping, and reaching decisions together. In these activities we have more than togetherness; in *homothymadon* there is an intimation of the harmony of shared lives. A great orchestra gathers. The different instruments express their own individuality. But under the baton of a great conductor, the orchestra is capable of blending different sounds to produce the greatest symphonies.

Perhaps the unity of the church is like that. It is not found in uniformity or in organizations. It is found, however, wherever believers focus together on the Lord, expressing their common commitment in prayer and worship. It is in and through our union with Jesus that unity exists, and it is in our common commitment to Jesus that he shapes us to live in harmony with others in the community of faith.

UNJUST ◆ *Justice/Injustice*

UNLEAVENED

Israel's experience of spectacular deliverance and sudden departure from Egypt—with no time even for bread to rise (Ex 12:8,39)—was to be reenacted annually at the Passover and the following seven-day Feast of Unleavened Bread. ◆ *Feast/Festival* ◆ *Passover* In both Testaments, when unleavened bread is mentioned, it most often refers to this annual time of recalling and rehearsing God's great acts on Israel's behalf. ◆ *Leaven/Yeast* ◆ *Remember/Memory*

UPRIGHT

Uprightness is a characteristic OT concept. The Hebrew word is *yāšar*. Literally it means "straight" or "level." But there is also a moral quality expressed by the verb and the attributive adjective *yōšer*. The upright person remains loyal to his commitments, whether to people (2 Ki 10:15) or to the requirements of the divine covenant (Ps 119:128).

Solomon's complaint about his generation is that while God made people with the moral capacity required for loyalty, they "have gone in search of many schemes" (Ecc 7:29).

In harmony with the theme of covenant, the OT promises many blessings to the person who is upright in heart (e.g., Ps 7:10; 11:7; 49:14; 112:2).

V

VAIN

Two different concepts are reflected in uses of the word "vain" in Scripture. One idea is that of emptiness, of an entity without substance. The other idea is that of uselessness, of being without purpose or reward. We see both of these thoughts in both Testaments.

OT 1. "Vain" in the OT
NT 2. "Vain" in the NT

OT — 1. "Vain" in the OT. Four Hebrew words are translated "vain" in the NIV and the NASB: šāwᵉʾ, rîq, hebel, and hinnām.

The words šāwᵉʾ and rîq both mean "emptiness." The fifty-three times that šāwᵉʾ appears in the OT it is used to designate that which is without substance or worth (Ex 20:7; 23:1; Dt 5:11,20; Job 7:3; 11:11; 15:31; 31:5; 35:13; Ps 12:2; 24:4; 26:4; 31:6; 41:6; 60:11; 89:47; 108:12; 119:37; 127:1,2; 139:20; 144:8,11; Pr 30:8; Isa 1:13; 5:18; 30:28; 59:4; Jer 2:30; 4:30; 6:29; 18:15; 46:11; La 2:14; Eze 12:24; 13:6,7,8,9,23; 21:23,29; Hos 10:4; 12:11; Jnh 2:8; Zec 10:2; Mal 3:14). It describes the unreal. Thus, taking God's name "in vain" (Ex 20:7) is to treat God as unreality, to mention his name without a true awareness of all that his name represents.

Rîq appears only twelve times in the OT (Lev 26:16,20; Job 39:16; Ps 2:1; 4:2; 73:13; Isa 30:7; 49:4; 65:23; Jer 51:34,58; Hab 2:13).

Hebel and hinnām both mean "vain." Hebel literally means "breath" or "vapor" and thus it can also mean "without substance or reality." This word is used again and again in Ecclesiastes to depict the "vanity" or emptiness of a life lived apart from God, with meaning sought only within the confines of the material universe. Hinnām has various meanings, with its "for nothing" emphasis both positive and negative. In Eze 6:10 it is negative: "in vain."

In essence, then, "vain" in English versions of the OT means emptiness—a wandering in shadows without substance, a life lived without the possibility of satisfaction. We may feel at times with the psalmist: "In vain have I kept my heart pure; in vain have I washed my hands in innocence" (Ps 73:13). Yet when life is oriented again to God, we recognize as fantasies those we formerly envied (v. 20), for God himself is "the strength of my heart and my portion forever" (v. 26).

NT — 2. "Vain" in the NT. In Greek as in Hebrew, several words may be translated "vain." But the essential concept remains the same.

Mt 15:9 and Mk 7:7 both quote from Isa 29, repeating God's accusation that his people worship him "in vain." This quoted phrase follows the Septuagint. The Greek word here, matēn (used only in these two passages), indicates that Israel's worship was purposeless. God would not acknowledge those who approached him according to made-up, human rules.

One of the seven NT occurrences of eikē is 1 Co 15:2. This word focuses on result. To believe "in vain" means to believe without the prospect of a reward. But faith in Christ promises the reward of resurrection.

Kenos is rendered "vain" in four of its eighteen NT occurrences (Ac 4:25; 1 Co 15:58; 2 Co 6:1; Gal 2:2). The literal meaning is "empty." Figuratively *kenos* can mean "senseless," "worthless," or "ineffective." In Ac 4:25, Luke stresses with the psalmist the senselessness of plotting something not in accord with God's purposes. The only time *kenodoxia* (a "passion for empty personal glory") appears in the NT is in Php 2:3, used there in sharp contrast with humility. It is good to know as we humble ourselves to follow Jesus that our "labor in the Lord is not in vain" (1 Co 15:58). In Christ there are no empty, meaningless lives.

VALUE

The word "value" appears in a number of theologically significant NT passages. In many of them the Greek word is *ōpheleō, ōpheleia,* or *ōphelimos* (Ro 2:25; 3:1; Gal 5:2; 1 Ti 4:8; Heb 4:2; 13:9). The concept is of something that is beneficial or profitable. A goal that is of value is worth achieving.

Such words are typically used in the NT letters to point up religious notions that are without spiritual benefit. The value in circumcision is not that which was supposed by the Jews (Ro 2:25–3:2). One who relies on his or her own efforts to keep the law is not relying on Christ; in fact, says Paul, Jesus is of no value at all to such a person (Gal 5:2). God's Word itself is without value to the hearer unless it is combined with faith (Heb 4:2). And the external ceremonies of Israel's old way are of no value to those whose hearts are to be strengthened by grace (Heb 13:9).

The same thought and emphasis occurs in the NIV passages where "value" is supplied or is the translation of some other word. Quarreling about words is of no value (*chrēsimos,* "usefulness") to the believer (2 Ti 2:14). "Value" is supplied in Col 2:23, which argues the uselessness of ritual and asceticism to control the old nature.

It is good to know, as Scripture strips away the religious crutches that people depend on, that God has provided all we need for growth and a meaningful life in Jesus Christ (Col 2:9-19).

VEIL

Two "veils" mentioned in Scripture have theological importance. One is the inner veil of the tabernacle or temple— *pārōket* in Hebrew and *katapetasma* in Greek. The other is the veil worn over Moses' face—*masweh* in Hebrew and *kalymma* in Greek. (Women's veils in 1 Co 11 are discussed elsewhere.) ♦ *Head* ♦ *Male and Female*

The tabernacle or temple veil hung between the inner and the outer rooms of the holy structure. In the inner room was the mercy seat, the place where once a year the high priest came to sprinkle the blood of the sacrifice that atoned for all of Israel's sins. ♦ *Atonement* This curtain, as it is called in the NIV, had symbolic significance. Hebrews says that this aspect of OT worship showed "that the way into the Most Holy Place had not yet been disclosed" (Heb 9:9). Thus, the report of the Gospel writers that, at the moment of Jesus' death, "the curtain of the temple was torn in two from top to bottom" (Mt 27:51; Mk 15:38; cf. Lk 23:45) is also significant. With Jesus' death, the way into the holiest—where God himself dwells—was opened for all. Because of Jesus, we can "approach the throne of grace with confidence" (Heb 4:16).

The story of Moses' veil is told in Ex 34. After Moses met with God on Mount Sinai, Moses' face was so radiant that the Israelites were "afraid to come near him" (v. 30). So we are told that, when speaking with the Israelites, Moses covered his face with a veil. But "whenever he entered the LORD's presence," he removed the veil.

Paul applies this incident in 2 Co 3. In a context that stresses the transforming power of God in the life of the believer, Paul first explores Moses' motive in using the veil. It was so that the Israelites might not gaze at his face "while the radiance was fading away" (v. 13). Paul's application of the Exodus incident may indicate that (1) Israel still cannot see

God's glory when they read the Scriptures (vv. 14–15), (2) the veil is removed from the heart and mind of anyone who accepts the gospel (v. 16), and (3) the veil symbolizes hiding our real selves from one another and must be removed in our relationships with other believers. Because Jesus is within believers, affecting their inner transformation, we see his face in one another's lives, for we "are being transformed into his likeness" by the Spirit's work. This attitude of openness is in contrast to the position Moses took, but it is necessary within the church.

VENGEANCE/REVENGE

The words "vengeance" and "revenge" occur only a few times in the Bible. Yet the concept is unmistakably there, boldly affirmed in both the OT and the NT. The idea that God is a "God who avenges" (Ps 94:1) troubles some. Is not vengeance evil? How can a trait that we deplore in human beings be appreciated in God?

OT   1. The OT's teaching on vengeance
      2. Examination of our God-concept
NT   3. The NT's teaching on vengeance
      4. Summary

OT — 1. The OT's teaching on vengeance. In God's revelation of himself to Israel, the Hebrew words *nāqam* and *nāqām* are definitely applied. Moses' early psalm celebrating God focuses several times on vengeance (Dt 32). Speaking of the enemies of Israel, who are devoted to pagan gods, this psalm portrays God crying out, "Have I not kept this in reserve and sealed it in my vaults? It is mine to avenge; I will repay. In due time their foot will slip; their day of disaster is near and their doom rushes upon them" (vv. 34–35).

The Lord then reveals his compassion for those who trust him (32:36–38). After recording God's declaration that he is the one with ultimate power to bring to life and put to death, the psalm returns to the judgment theme: "I will take vengeance on my adversaries and repay those who hate me. . . . Rejoice, O nations, with his people, for he will avenge the blood of his servants; he will take vengeance on his enemies and make atonement for his land and people (vv. 41,43).

At times the OT speaks of God acting in *nāqam* to punish his people when they break the covenant (e.g., Lev 26:24–25). But normally vengeance is focused on those who reject God and actively persecute his people.

Only a few times is vengeance executed through or by human beings (e.g., Nu 31:2–3; Jos 10:13). Even then it is understood that they act as God's agents.
◆ *War* This too is the role of the "avenger of blood" who is to execute the murderer. His act is not personal, but judicial in nature, for he acts as God's agent in bringing the murderer his due.
◆ *Murder/Kill*

The OT makes it clear that individuals are not to act to take vengeance on their own. "Do not seek revenge or bear a grudge against one of your people, but love your neighbor as yourself" is God's word to the individual (Lev 19:18; cf. Dt 32:35). Personal vengeance is ruled out; but judicial vengeance is not.

It is significant that in the prophet's view of the future, vengeance is most often reserved for history's end (esp. Isa 63:1–6; also 34:8; 61:2; Eze 25).

2. Examination of our God-concept. One of the reasons we hesitate to accept the OT's presentation of a God of vengeance is our failure to develop a balanced God-concept. We have tried to measure God by ourselves, and we cannot. Because vengeance is associated with attitudes and emotions that distort the human personality, robbing us of compassion and infusing a bitter vindictiveness, we mistakenly export these human characteristics to God. Yet God is at once and always a God of love and compassion. No emotion or decision can rob any act—even acts of judgment—of those qualities. Only in God is it possible for love, compassion, and vengeance to be exhibited, along with holiness, in the same act.

It is also important to remember that the OT maintains a distinction between personal and judicial acts of vengeance. Infrequently, human beings may be agents of God's vengeance, but taking personal revenge or even bearing a grudge is forbidden in God's law. Thus, it follows that the law, an expression of God's moral standards, unveils an important fact about his vengeance. When God takes vengeance, he does not act merely out of outraged feelings. He acts as the moral judge of the universe, responsible to punish sin as well as to reward righteousness. ♦ *Judge/Judging*

NT — **3. The NT's teaching on vengeance.** The Greek words *dikē* and *ekdikēsis* mean "vengeance" or "punishment," with *dikē* having the primary meaning of "justice." In those passages in which this word group is translated "avenge" or "vengeance" we see a clear expression of the basic position of the OT in regard to justice. Vengeance is God's prerogative alone (Ro 12:19; Heb 10:10). ♦ *Justice/Injustice*

The future perspective is also clear in the NT. The day of vengeance (graphically described in 2 Th 1:5–10) is delayed because in the "riches of his kindness, tolerance and patience" (Ro 2:4) God has chosen to make this present time the day of opportunity and salvation (vv. 1–11).

As the one responsible moral agent in the universe, God can do no less than punish. As the one who truly loves a lost humanity, God chose to delay punishment to provide the human race with an era of opportunity. In reality, God's anger, his vengeance, fell on Christ when he became a sin offering for sinful humanity (see 2 Co 5:17–21).

4. Summary. There is a biblical doctrine of vengeance. We must accept Scripture's testimony to this facet of the divine plan, even as we accept its testimony regarding salvation. Clearly there is no contradiction if our concept of God is adequate and if the necessity for judgment on sin is accepted. As Nahum says, "The LORD is good, a refuge in times of trouble. He cares for those who trust in him" (1:7). He also says, "The LORD is a jealous and avenging God; the LORD takes vengeance and is filled with wrath. The LORD takes vengeance on his foes and maintains his wrath against his enemies. The LORD is slow to anger and great in power; the LORD will not leave the guilty unpunished" (1:2–3). ♦ *Anger* ♦ *Punishment*

VICTORY

In the NASB OT the word translated "victory" is always *tešû'âh*, which means "salvation" or "deliverance." The NIV so translates other words, including *yāša'* ("to save"). The NIV also uses "victory" to translate several other Hebrew words that more literally would be translated "mastery" (Ex 32:18), "slaughter" (Jos 10:10), "smiting" (2 Sa 8:10; 1 Ch 18:10), and "the treading down of [one's enemies]" (Ps 60:12; 108:13). "Victory" is even found on two occasions where the Hebrew is uncertain but is translated in the KJV as "wisdom" (Job 12:16; Pr 2:7).

None of this should obscure the fact that the basic OT concept of victory is an expression of its concept of salvation/deliverance. ♦ *Salvation/Save* It is by God's intervention that his people are saved, and the deliverance he wins for them is the victory.

In the NT, "victory" is the translation of either *nikos* or *nikē*, both related to the verb *nikaō*. *Nikos* occurs four times in the NT (Mt 12:20; 1 Co 15:54,55,57) and *nikē* only once (1 Jn 5:4). ♦ *Overcome* In some of the uses of these words, God's final victory over death is in view. In 1 Co 15:57, that victory is a cause of praise, for through Jesus we experience the victory now. We are no longer captive to the powers Jesus has defeated. As 1 Jn 5:4–5 points out, through faith we participate in Jesus' victory in and over this present world. ♦ *World*

In both Testaments, then, "victory" is deliverance experienced. It is God's salvation worked out in space and time for believers. In the OT, "victory," and indeed salvation, was generally won over physical foes. In the NT, "victory" refers to God's salvation from the very real but immaterial bonds that entangle humanity. God gives us victory today over the world and over sin. He will give us a share in his great victory over death itself at the resurrection.

VINE/VINEYARD

The grapevine (*gepen*) was the source of both raisins and wine for Israel, thus signifying both food and rejoicing. ◗ **Wine** Grapes were cultivated within stone walls in vineyards (*kerem*). The vine is often used as a symbol for Israel in the OT. In the psalmist's appeal to God for help he reminds the Lord, "You brought a vine out of Egypt; you drove out the nations and planted it" (Ps 80:8). And so he appeals, "Watch over this vine, the root your right hand has planted, the son you have raised up for yourself" (vv. 14–15).

Later, Isaiah graphically applied this metaphor. Israel was a vine planted and tended by God in the expectation of a sweet harvest of righteousness. But only the bitter grapes of injustice were found in God's field. So God would tear down the protecting walls and let enemies trample his planting (Isa 5:1–7). Other prophets too applied the image to Israel, both in judgment (Jer 2:21; Hos 10:1) and in promise (Zec 3:10).

In the NT the vine (*ampelos*) and the vineyard (*ampelōn*) again figure prominently. Most significant is Jesus' identification of himself as the "true vine" (Jn 15:1). It is only by being a branch, intimately connected to the vine, that a human being can bring forth God's fruit of righteousness. ◗ *Fruit/Fruitfulness*

VIOLENCE/VIOLENT

In most cases in the OT, the word for "violence" is *ḥāmās*. It is a strong word, not associated with violent upheavals of nature, but with the willfully destructive acts of human beings. The word is first used to describe the "great wickedness" and continually evil acts of the preflood generation in these words: "The earth

was corrupt in God's sight and was full of violence" (Ge 6:11).

Two other words are also translated "violent" or "violence" at times. The word *'ārîṣ* means "a violent or ruthless person," and *pāraṣ* describes one who maliciously tears down rather than builds.

The early Genesis associations of violence with judgment is important. As the Flood came on that violent generation, so will "disaster hunt down men of violence" (Ps 140:11). By contrast, David said, "I know that the LORD secures justice for the poor and upholds the cause of the needy. Surely the righteous will praise your name and the upright will live before you" (vv. 12–13).

Several different terms for "violence" are found in the NT. The demon-possessed men of Mt 8:28 were *chalepos*, "dangerous" or "violent" (found elsewhere only in 2 Ti 3:1). The "violent" earthquakes of Mt 28:2 and Ac 16:26 are literally "great" (*megas*). Ac 2:2 is the only NT occurrence of *biaios* (the "violent" [rushing] wind from heaven), whose root (*biazō*) means "to apply force" or "to use violence." This word does not necessarily imply wicked intention, as do the OT terms translated "violent." The NIV translates *bia* as "violence" in Ac 21:35, one of the four places this Greek word occurs in the NT. A "great" (*polys*) argument is described at Ac 23:10; and Luke records the one NT use of *sphodrōs* ("vehemently") to describe how Paul's foundering ship was being battered (Ac 27:18).

In the Epistles, we return to the OT image of violence as wicked acts directed against others. In 1 Ti 1:13 the word *hybristēs* describes a violent or insolent person (its only other NT occurrence being in Ro 1:30). The two NT uses of another Greek word are found in Paul's lists of attributes of spiritual leaders; "violent" in 1 Ti 3:3 and Tit 1:7 is a translation of the word *plēktēs*, which portrays a bully always willing to impose his will on others by wounding them.

The last NIV occurrence of "violence" is in Rev 18:21. The passage states that a mighty angel hurls a boulder the size of a giant millstone into the sea. It is "with a rushing" (*hormēma*, only here in the NT) that the evil civilization that exists when God's final judgment comes will be devastated.

Violence, then, is a single concept in the OT, portraying willful and sinful acts of aggression by people against people. In the NT, the thought of evil is not dominant, though it is sometimes present. In the Pastoral Epistles, "violent" describes a disposition to inflict harm to gain one's way. But natural phenomena can also be described as violent.

Ultimately, as the OT promises, the violent will be judged. It will be the gentle who are vindicated.

VIRGIN

The word "virgin" has sometimes been a focus of debate because of Isa 7:14: "The virgin will be with child and will give birth to a son, and will call him Immanuel." The Hebrew language has a specific term that emphasizes virginity: *bᵉtûlâh*. It occurs many times in the OT. But Isaiah chose 'almâh to speak of the mother of Immanuel. What does 'almâh mean? The term seems to mean simply "a young woman of marriageable age." It is seldom used in the OT, appearing in only seven passages (Ge 24:43; Ex 2:8; Ps 68:25; Pr 30:19; SS 1:3; 6:8; Isa 7:14). It is clear that the Jewish idea of a marriageable young woman could involve virginity; this can be seen not only in the OT's teaching on adultery but also in the use of 'almâh in Ge 24:43.

The debate is, of course, resolved by the NT. The angel announced to Joseph that Isaiah's prophecy was about to be fulfilled in Mary. The Greek text has the word *parthenos*, which specifically means "virgin." It is God's own divine commentary on Isaiah that settles the question of the implications of 'almâh in the OT.

VISION

Several Hebrew words, most of them from the root *ḥāzâh*, are translated "vision." The words indicate a revelatory vision from God, one of the means by which God communicated his message to his prophets in Bible times. ♦ *Dream* ♦ *Prophecy/Prophet*

VOICE

"Voice" appears often in the OT. It is used primarily in speaking of communication addressed to God or addressed by God to human beings. The word *qôl* probably meant "vocal sound" originally.

Although it is worthwhile to examine the occasions when human beings lifted up their voice to God, examining the occasions when God's voice addressed human beings is especially important. Because "listen to my voice" has the force of "obey," this phrase is often translated "obey" in the NIV (e.g., Ex 19:5; Dt 4:30). But the concept of the voice of God is more significant than this common use might suggest.

We gain insight into the OT significance of God's voice by studying Heb 3–4. The writer isolates a particular "today" in Israel's history in which the people heard God's voice directing them to enter and possess the Promised Land. Israel refused, being unable to respond because of unbelief. The writer of Hebrews goes on to point to other historic "todays" and then warns his readers, "[In your] today, if you should hear his voice, do not harden your hearts" (Heb 3:15).

The point is that God has a contemporary voice, which continues to give guidance and direction to his people. In the OT, this voice was heard through both the written law and the prophets whom God sent to various generations (e.g., Jer 43:1–7, where "obey" and "disobey" are translations of the concepts of listening to God's voice or of not listening to it).

The concept of a contemporary voice of God disturbs some. Yet the NT teaches that God the Holy Spirit is within believers to prompt us toward holiness. ♦ *Spirit (Holy Spirit)* God's contemporary voice may be "heard" by an individual through Scripture (the only wholly reliable source of truth), as well as in other ways (including fellow believers) that are in accord with Scripture.

To explore the subject of God's voice in the OT, a number of passages ought to be examined (Ge 3:8,10; 22:18; 26:5; Ex 15:26; 19:5,19; 23:21,22; Dt 4:30,38; 5:22–28; 26:14,17; 27:10; 28:1,2,15, 45,62; 30:2,8,10,20; Jos 5:6; 24:24; Jdg 2:2,20; 1 Sa 15:19–24; 28:18; Job 37:2–5; Ps 18:13; 29:3–9; 97:5; Isa 6:8; 30:31; Jer 3:25; 7:23,28; 26:13; 42:6,13,14, 21; 44:23; Eze 1:24–28; 10:5; Joel 2:11; 3:16; Mic 6:9; Hag 1:12).

VOW

In the OT and the NT, a "vow" is always a pledge or a promise made to God, never to other persons. A vow was always an expression of unusual devotion or commitment and was usually voluntary. One special vow was that of the Nazirite, described in Nu 6. This was a vow of separation. It involved a span of time during which no product of the vine could be touched, no razor be used on the head, and no dead body touched. When the time period was over, the Nazirite brought prescribed offerings to be sacrificed.

A limitation was placed on women who wished to make a vow (Nu 30:3–9). They could be overruled by a husband or father, who in that age were legally responsible for wives and children. ▶ *Male and Female*

W

WAGE/WAGES

The notion of wages is the same in all cultures. In the transaction involving wages, one exchanges services for money.

The OT has several words for this idea; *śākār* and several similar words are translated "wages." In Isaiah's day, the working class was designated "wage earners" (Isa 19:10). This word is never used to portray a person's relationship with the Lord.

Pᵉˈullâh can mean "wages" or "reward." ▶ **Reward** *Mᵉhîr*, found some fifteen times in the OT, also means "wages." The wages of male (Dt 23:19) and female prostitutes were never acceptable as gifts for the temple of God. In fact, the earnings of a female prostitute were designated by a special term, *ˈetnan*.

The NT plays on the relationship between the wage earner and the employer to demonstrate the nature of a believer's relationship with God. It is sin that pays wages, but the coinage is that of death. ▶ **Life and Death** God relates to us in another way entirely. He gives us, not what our deeds have earned, but a free gift. This gift is eternal life (Ro 4:4; 6:23).

WAIL

Three of the dozen OT words associated with agonized mourning are translated "wail" in the NIV and the NASB: *sāpad* and *nᵉhî* ("to lament" or "to mourn in lamentation"), which are synonyms, and *yālal* ("to howl or wail"). Each expresses the anguished cry of distress caused by death or massive destruction.

WAIT ▶ Hope

WALK

The Hebrew term *hālak* portrays movement. The root is found over fifteen hundred times in the OT. In addition to lateral movement, "walk" can picture the spiritual and moral direction of a person's life. It is especially important that believers "observe the commands of the Lord [their] God, walking in his ways and revering him" (Dt 8:6).

The Greek term *peripateō* is used in the same way. "Walk" may be used in a strictly literal sense (e.g., Mk 1:16; Lk 4:30; Jn 5:9). But it is also used figuratively to indicate one's lifestyle. Believers once walked in the ways of the world (Col 3:7). But now we can walk in the light (1 Jn 1:7), in love and obedience (2 Jn 6), and in the truth (2 Jn 4; 3 Jn 3,4).

WANT

The word "want" is used in two primary senses in the OT. As a desire ("I want to . . .") the concept is expressed in many different ways in the original languages, but not with a specific term parallel to "want." The translators of the NIV have chosen to use "want" in this general and colloquial sense almost entirely (the exception being Job 30:3).

On the other hand, the NASB tends to use "want" in the sense of "lack." The Hebrew root so translated is *hāsar*. Both *hāsēr* and *mahsôr* imply diminished resources. The lack suggested is often that of basic resources, such as bread (e.g., 2 Sa 3:29; Pr 12:9); however, people are in desperate spiritual want as well, trapped

615

by a lack of the wisdom that leads in God's ways (e.g., Pr 6:32; Ecc 6:2).

A living relationship with God is the solution to our every need. As a believer I have the reassuring knowledge that "the LORD is my Shepherd, I shall not be in want" (Ps 23:1).

In the NT, both versions use "want" almost entirely for "desire," or "wish." Here there is a specific Greek word, *thelō*. The sense of *thelō* is usually simply a general desire. ♦ **Desire** ♦ **Will**

WAR

Accounts of war and tragedy abound in the OT. The Bible focuses on the role of God in war and on the attitude of the believer toward war.

It is true that the Bible makes a clear distinction between murder and killing in war. ♦ *Murder/Kill* But surely war is an evil, causing untold suffering. How are we to view war today? How does God view war?

OT 1. Scripture's vision of a world without war
   2. God's involvement in Israel's wars
   3. God's involvement in history's wars: Babylon, a case history
NT 4. God's silence in the NT concerning war
   5. Conclusions

OT — 1. Scripture's vision of a world without war. Perhaps the most famous of Scripture's words of peace are found in Isa 2:3–5: "Many peoples will come and say, 'Come, let us go up to the mountain of the LORD, to the house of the God of Jacob. He will teach us his ways, so that we may walk in his paths.' The law will go out from Zion, the word of the LORD from Jerusalem. He will judge between the nations and will settle disputes for many peoples. They will beat their swords into plowshares and their spears into pruning hooks. Nation will not take up sword against nation, nor will they train for war anymore."

These words do not stand alone in portraying God's promise of international peace (e.g., Mic 4:1–5; Zec 14). But such words offer little support for those who suppose that peace can come to our war-weary world by one nation unilaterally abandoning weapons. For these words, and others like them, appear in a particular context.

That context is first of all temporal. These words of peace are associated with the time of history's end. Peace will be possible then because God will be established in the hearts of redeemed humanity and will be personally present to "judge between many peoples" and to "settle disputes for strong nations" (Mic 4:4). It is on the day that, as Zechariah said, "the LORD my God" will come "and all the holy ones with him" (Zec 14:5) that peace will be imposed on the world. ♦ *Day*

The context is also, surprisingly, one of warfare. Peace will not come by abandoning conflict. Peace in the OT is associated with war waged by God himself against an arrogant, rebellious humanity. Peace will come when it is imposed by the "dread of the LORD and the splendor of his majesty, when he rises to shake the earth" (Isa 2:21).

One of the most striking aspects of Scripture's vision of a final peace is that it is achieved only through the ultimate warfare (Isa 13:4; 24:21–23; 29:5–8). Even in Micah's exalted description, God's promised peace (4:1–5) will come after many nations will have gathered against Israel, and God will cry to her, "Rise and thresh, O Daughter of Zion, for I will give you horns of iron; I will give you hoofs of bronze and you will break to pieces many nations" (4:13).

2. God's involvement in Israel's wars The Hebrew language has two major words that mean "war," "battle," or "fighting": *lāham* and *ṣābā'*. *Lāham* is "to fight or wage war." It occurs 171 times in the OT; and its derivative, *milhāmāh*, is found 319 times. The word *ṣᵉbā'ôt* ("armies"), a derivative of *ṣābā'*, is associated with God's name some 285 times in the OT, as he is called "God of hosts" or "God of armies." This phrase means "almighty," stressing the fact that God is the ultimate ruler of the universe, but it also reflects something basic in the OT's view of God and his relationship to Israel's wars.

We see that view in multiplied passages, such as Ps 44: "With your hand you drove out the nations and planted our fathers; you crushed the peoples and made our fathers flourish. It was not by their sword that they won the land, nor did their arm bring them victory; it was your right hand, your arm, and the light of your face, for you loved them. You are my King and my God, who decrees victories for Jacob. Through you we push back our enemies; through your name we trample our foes. I do not trust in my bow, my sword does not bring me victory; but you give us victory over our enemies, you put our adversaries to shame. In God we make our boast all day long, and we will praise your name forever" (vv. 2–8).

This view is firmly rooted in the Pentateuch and Israel's history. God promised to do battle for Israel when she went to war (e.g., Ex 14:14; Dt 1:30; 3:22; Ne 4:20; Jer 21:5; cf. Ps 124:1–3; 118:10–14). The forces of Israel were the armies of Yahweh. David even identified the Lord as source of his skill in warfare: "Praise be to the LORD, my Rock, who trains my hands for war, my fingers for battle" (Ps 144:1).

This bold identification of God with Israel in warfare has been challenged by commentators on the basis of a supposed inconsistency with the character of God as displayed in Jesus. But we must see war in the OT in the OT's own frame of reference. Two common OT themes are important in understanding the nature and significance of war.

First, Israel existed in covenant relationship with Yahweh. ♦ *Covenant* It is God's obligation to come to the aid of his people, when and if they are faithful to the covenant relationship.

Second, God is the moral judge of the universe. The OT affirms that many of Israel's wars were determined by God, who used his people in a judicial way to punish evildoers (e.g., Dt 7:1–2,16; 20:16–17). This is particularly significant in the wars of "devotion," in which *the enemy* was to be totally destroyed (cf. also

rules for war, Dt 20). The concept is introduced in the time of battle for the Promised Land: "When the LORD your God brings you into the land . . . and . . . has delivered them over to you and you have defeated them, then you must destroy them totally. Make no treaty with them, and show them no mercy" (Dt 7:1–2; cf. Jos 6:17–19,21; 11:11, 12,14,20,21).

The destruction of the people of Canaan was ordered in part because the moral and religious practices of these peoples would surely have drawn Israel's hearts away from God (Dt 7:3–6). But Ge 15:16 gives us another clue. There God told Abraham about the four hundred years that his descendants had to be in Egypt before they would take possession of Canaan. He explained, "For the sin of the Amorites has not yet reached its full measure." God did not act to destroy the peoples of Canaan until that action was demanded by the overflowing flood of matured sin in their society.

God, then, identified himself with Israel in her wars because of the covenant and because he used Israel as an instrument of his judgment on sin.

It is also noteworthy that God used other nations to wage wars of judgment on Israel when his own people sinned (Isa 63:10; Am 3:14–15).

3. God's involvement in history's wars: Babylon, a case history. The OT view of God as judge extends his responsibility for the moral governance of the universe beyond his responsibility for Israel. God is responsible for all the nations of the world. OT wars are often viewed in the framework of judgment. It is sin that moves a people to overstep their boundaries and crush their neighbors. That sin itself leads to further wars, which come as divine judgments. A few extended passages relate war and world politics to God's overarching control (Isa 13–23; Jer 46–51; Eze 25–32; Am 1–2).

Babylon, which emerged as a world power some six hundred years before Christ, provides us with a fascinating case history. Habakkuk cried to the Lord because of the injustices he saw in Israel (Hab 1:1–4). God responded by saying that he would raise up the Babylonians to wage war against multiplied nations and that he would punish Israel for their sin (Hab 1:5–11). Habakkuk realized that the Lord had "appointed them to execute judgment" (1:12). But clearly the Babylonians were less righteous than the nations they destroyed, and their victories led them to view force itself as their god, and thus they failed to acknowledge the universal Lord. The prophet wondered how God could permit that (1:13–17). God answered by displaying some of the principles of judgment that operate within history (2:1–20): "Woe to him who piles up stolen goods and makes himself wealthy by extortion! How long must this go on? Will not your debtors suddenly arise? Will they not wake up and make you tremble? Then you will become their victim. Because you have plundered many nations, the peoples who are left will plunder you. For you have shed man's blood; you have destroyed lands and cities and everyone in them" (Hab 2:6–8).

War establishes a hatred that generates its own judgment. The oppressors themselves are destroyed as the hatred war generates is turned against them. Just as God used Babylon to execute his judgment on Assyria (Isa 10:5–19) and on Israel (Hab 1), so the Lord would use another nation, the Medes, to crush Babylon (Isa 13, esp. v. 17).

The course of history, then, as illustrated in Babylon, is one of successive wars. Each war was an expression of evil and sin (Isa 13:11), and each succeeding war was an expression of the divine judgment that must come when any nation plunders another and sheds human blood.

NT — 4. God's silence in the NT.
The NT is nearly silent on the subject of war. The words of warfare appear, but they are almost always used in a figurative sense. The relevant Greek terms are *strateuō* ("to serve as a soldier"), *polemeō* ("to make war, or fight") and *polemos* ("battle" or "war"), and *machē* ("battle," "fighting," often in the sense of quarrels and disputes).

Because the church is a faith entity, not a national one, there are no guidelines given for waging war, and no prohibitions against war are stated. Yet many in the earliest centuries of the church refused to serve in the military. Many were even executed for their conviction. But there is no direct biblical prohibition against military service. When John the Baptist was asked by soldiers what they should do to demonstrate repentance, he did not tell them to resign from the army. Instead he simply said, "Don't extort money and don't accuse people falsely— be content with your pay" (Lk 3:14).

Many references in Revelation point to the final battle at history's end of which the prophets prophesied. In the Gospels, Jesus warned that until then, history will be filled with wars and rumors of wars (Mt 24:6; Mk 13:7; Lk 21:9).

James wrote of "fights and quarrels" among Christians (Jas 4:1). This passage does not speak directly of war, but it may be relevant as an analysis of the causes of interpersonal and international conflict: "They come from your desires that battle within you. . . . You want something but don't get it. You kill and covet, but you cannot have what you want. You quarrel and fight" (v. 2). The origin of those quarrels that lead to fighting is rooted in man's sinful nature, in covetousness.

Paul's argument that "we do not wage war as the world does" is not an antiwar statement, nor does it imply a rejection of war. It is simply an affirmation that Christians are engaged in spiritual warfare and that it is not appropriate for them to approach that warfare in a worldly way. ♦ *World*

In fact, the NT is silent on the question of war, except to recognize it as a reality that must be confronted.

5. Conclusions. Scripture gives little direct guidance to help us with some of the questions that trouble many Christians. War is unquestionably an evil, and shedding man's blood in war is wrong (Hab 2:8). But living as we do in a world warped by sin and marred by war, we are never told that nations are not to defend themselves.

In the OT we have a model in Israel of a faith community that is also a nation. God's people were actually expected to go to war, and often God identified himself with their cause. God fought for his covenant people and used them as instruments to punish evildoers.

The OT also gives case histories of pagan nations. Some developed into empires by the use of war. Each of them was ultimately destroyed by war. Those who engage in war suffer war's destruction as an appropriate retribution. Here war is a means used by God as moral judge to maintain moral balance in international relations.

But how must we apply these facts? Must we focus on the evil that war is and express our horror in pacifism? Must we focus on war as a moral instrument and commit ourselves to participate only in "just" wars? Must we focus on war as an expression of man's sin nature and maintain the right to defend ourselves when attacked?

Sincere believers have differed in the conclusions they have drawn. There are godly pacifists and godly people in the military. However you or I might come to our personal conclusion as to God's best way for us, we must reach our conclusions only after acknowledging the Bible's teaching that God does not divorce himself from war's tragic reality.

WARN

Many words in Scripture express the idea of warning. In the OT ' *ûd* means "to give testimony," and *zāhar* has the idea of teaching or admonishing or warning.

Similar meanings are found in the NT. A threat, and thus a strong warning, is expressed both times *apeileō* appears in the NT (Ac 4:17; 1 Pe 2:23). *Chrēmatizō* has the sense of admonishing or warning in at least five of the nine times it appears in the NT (Mt 2:12,22; Heb 8:5; 11:7; 12:25).

Earnestly bearing witness, or testifying about a danger and thus warning, is expressed in *diamartyromai*; this is seen in the NIV in four of the fifteen NT passages where this word occurs (Lk 16:28;

Ac 2:40; 1 Th 4:6; 2 Ti 2:14). The Greek word rendered "warn" in Mk 8:15 is *diastellō* ("to charge"). *Embrimaomai* implies an angry warning and is found in only two passages in the NT (Mt 9:30; Mk 1:43).

The idea of a strong reproof or stern warning is seen in *epitimaō*, which occurs twenty-nine times in the NT (Mt 8:26; 12:16; 16:22; 17:18; 19:13; 20:31; Mk 1:25; 3:12; 4:39; 8:30,32,33; 9:25; 10:13,48; Lk 4:35,39,41; 8:24; 9:21,42,55; 17:3; 18:15,39; 19:39; 23:40; 2 Ti 4:2; Jude 9). The word *hypodeiknymi* occurs six times in the NT and means "to show," in the sense of revealing dangers and warning (Mt 3:7; Lk 3:7; 6:47; 12:5; Ac 9:16; 20:35). Once the NIV also translates *martyreō* ("to testify") as "warn" (Rev 22:18).

The idea of admonishing, and thus giving warning, is expressed in *noutheteō*. The NIV conveys this idea in seven of the eight passages where *noutheteō* occurs in the NT (Ac 20:31; 1 Co 4:14; Col 1:28; 3:16; 1 Th 5:12,14; 2 Th 3:15). In at least two of the three NT occurrences of *nouthesia* (1 Co 10:11; Eph 6:4; Tit 3:10), a threat, and thus a strong warning, is expressed.

The NIV renders *prologeō* ("to tell in advance") as "warn" in two places (2 Co 13:2; Gal 5:21). In 1 Ti 5:20 the Greek expression "that they may have fear" is translated "that others may take warning," and the Greek wording of Jn 16:4 ("I warned you") has literally "I said to you."

The picture in both Testaments is of a ministry. Those with knowledge of the implications of an act for the future testify to those in danger, seeking to counsel or teach them God's better way. Warning is a form of confrontation. But it is a confrontation that has a healing purpose.

The Bible's most famous warnings are found in Hebrews, where four digressions from the author's argument confront his readers with implications of the truths he teaches. Heb 2:1–4 warns the reader, in view of Jesus' position as God's Son, to pay strict attention to his message. Heb 3:7–4:13 warns the reader, in view of Jesus' greater revelation, to appropriate his words by faith and to respond with obedience. Heb 6:1–12 warns the readers that unless they press on in building faith they may "fall away" by continually reexamining the foundation. Heb 10:19–39 warns, in view of Jesus perfect sacrifice, to continue unswervingly in the faith by doing God's will.

WASH/BATHE

The two Hebrew words so translated are *kābas* and *rāhas* (cf. *rahṣâh*, "washing"). Each is linked with ceremonial washings that were part of the ritual of Israel. *Kābas*, which occurs fifty-one times, does not refer to the washing of the worshiper's body but to the washing of his clothing. *Rahṣâh* is used when washing the body is involved. Washing is a symbol of cleansing from sin in the OT (e.g., Isa 1:16; 4:4; Eze 16:4,9). ◗ *Clean and Unclean*

The Greek words for "wash" are *louō* and *niptō*. *Louō* means a washing of the entire body; it occurs only six times in the NT (Jn 13:10; Ac 9:37; 16:33; Heb 10:22; 2 Pe 2:22; Rev 1:5). A compound, *apolouō*, is translated "wash" in both the places it appears in the NT (Ac 22:16; 1 Co 6:11). This root speaks symbolically of the total cleansing of the believer's personality that enables him or her to appear before God. In its use concerning the rite of baptism (Ac 22:16), it is the blood of Jesus, not the water of baptism as such, that is God's cleansing agent for his saints (Rev 1:5). ◗ *Baptism*

Niptō is the word that is used when part of the body is washed. It is found seventeen times in the NT (Mt 6:17; 15:2; Mk 7:3; Jn 9:7,11,15; 13:5,6,8,10,12,14; 1 Ti 5:10). Foot-washing (Jn 13) is presented as an example to believers. As Jesus was willing to stoop to wash his disciples' feet, so we must be willing to stoop to serve our brothers and sisters.

WATCH

Two Hebrew words are commonly translated "watch." *Šāmar* means "to guard," "to watch, or observe." It is used

over four hundred times in the OT, with the basic meaning of "take great care [with or of]" (e.g., Ps 17:8; 121:7). ◗ *Guard* *Sāpâh* means "to look about," or "to watch"—i.e., "to keep alert." Its participle is translated "watchman." Eze 33 makes the watchman (that is, spiritual leader) responsible to give warning to God's people, but he is not responsible for the people's response to the warning.

In the NT, "watch" occurs more often in the NIV than in the NASB. The word is used in ways that are familiar to us. A variety of Greek words express our common shades of meaning. *Grēgoreō* ("to keep alert and watchful," is found in a number of passages (e.g., Mt 24:42,43; Mk 13:35; 1 Co 16:13; Rev 3:2). Another verb translated "watch" (e.g., Mt 27:36) is *tēreō* ("to watch over," "to guard"). *Phylakē*, which means "a guard," is used as a temporal term to identify the hour (e.g., the "forth watch of the night" [Mt 14:25]) as well as to indicate watching over (as in Lk 2:8).

There are also unusual or especially focused terms. Gal 6:1 warns those who seek to restore someone caught in a sin: "Watch yourself." The word is *skopeō*, which means "to pay sharp attention to" and is used only six times in the NT. One of the five places where the word *epechō* appears in the NT is when Paul says to "watch your life and doctrine closely" (1 Ti 4:16), its meaning here being "to fix one's attention on." Characterizing leaders as those who "keep watch over" those entrusted to their care (Heb 13:17) pictures a sleepless commitment to standing guard; the Greek word here, *agrypneō*, occurs three other times in the NT (Mk 13:33; Lk 21:36; Eph 6:18).

Where "watch" is literally or figuratively seeing or "seeing to" something— as with five uses of *blepō* (Mt 24:4; Mk 12:38; 13:5; Lk 21:8; Gal 5:15) and one use of *horaō* (Mk 8:15)—the meaning is clear in English.

Essentially, although a number of different Hebrew and Greek words are used, the meaning of "watch" where it appears is easily understood in the NIV and the NASB.

WATER

In the OT, water has two major spiritual associations. The first is with ritual washing, or cleansing from defilement. ♦ **Clean and Unclean.** The rabbis often viewed the Flood as a divine washing of the earth, designed to cleanse it from the defilement of the antediluvians.

The second association of water is with blessing, especially with the day of blessing that God's Spirit will bring to Israel and the world. As Isa 44:3 says, "I will pour water on the thirsty land, and streams on the dry ground; I will pour out my Spirit on your offspring, and my blessing on your descendants."

God's supplying of water for the Israelites in the wilderness is an example of his constant supply of his people's needs: "They did not thirst when he led them through the deserts; he made water flow for them from the rock; he split the rock and water gushed out" (Isa 48:21).

Although most references to water in the NT are literal, some of the symbolism of the OT is retained. Jesus provides the living water that wells up into eternal life (Jn 4). The Holy Spirit is portrayed as producing streams of living water (Jn 7:38). Cleansing from sin is a matter of "washing with water through the word" (Eph 5:26; cf. Heb 10:22). But the water of 1 Pe 3:20–21 is the agent of judgment, as in the ancient Flood. ♦ **Baptism**

The puzzling reference to water in 1 Jn 5:8 fits no established OT symbol.

WAY

The OT establishes the symbolism of this word. "Way" is *derek,* a term that indicates a well-traveled path. Metaphorically, *derek* refers to the actions of human beings who keep or reject the "way of the LORD" (Ge 18:19; cf. Ps 27:11).

In the NT, the sense of "way" is clear. Often it simply means "manner." But often too the OT metaphor of a way of life is retained. When the word refers to following the Lord Jesus Christ, it is often capped (e.g., Ac 9:2: "If he found any there who belonged to the Way, whether men or women, he might take them as prisoners to Jerusalem.").

WEAK/WEAKNESS

"Weak" is a translation of a number of words in the OT. In the NT, "weak" and "weakness" translate the *astheneia* word group. This group of words expresses powerlessness. The weak are without strength, incapacitated in some serious way.

This incapacitation may be physical, as it usually is in the Gospels, where we may translate it correctly by "sick" or "ill." But in the Epistles, the word group is used in a different way. It is a key term in Paul's exploration of the meaning of human frailty.

The flexibility of the concept is seen in its broad application. A believer's faith can be "weak" (Ro 14:1–2), keeping him uncertain about the freedoms won for him by Christ. Such a person is to be accepted by others, and his failings borne with (15:1).

Similarly a weak, frail, or faulty conscience may unnecessarily trouble a believer (1 Co 8:7–13). The conscience is faulty when it either (1) is unable to discern accurately what pleases God or (2) is unable to guard its possessor against making choices God disapproves of.

Paul himself had a physical disability that severely limited him (2 Co 12:1–10). But this weakness was an opportunity for God to demonstrate his power in Paul's ministry. So Paul takes the stunning position that he actually will "delight in weaknesses" (v. 10) on the basis that only in weakness can he find spiritual strength.

The contrast of strength and weakness is found in other critical passages. In one, Paul states that God expresses his power through things that humanity finds of no value (1 Co 1:20–31). Another passage declares that even the law in which Israel boasted had to be set aside "because it was weak and useless" (Heb 7:18). It is also clear that the point of weakness in law as a system linking God and human beings was human nature, which is infected with spiritual weakness (e.g., Ro 7). Law was powerless "in that it was weakened by the sinful nature" (Ro 8:3). ♦ **Law**

In view of the frailty of mankind, human beings must depend completely on the Lord. It is in dependence on God that we find the strength to counter our frailty. ◗ *Strength/Might/Power*

WEALTH/RICHES/POSSESSIONS

How are we to view wealth? As an unmixed good? Or as a dangerous trap to be avoided? Is the possession of riches sinful in itself (e.g., as a practical denial of concern for less-fortunate brothers and sisters)? Whether or not we are comfortable with the idea of riches, we do need to grasp the Bible's viewpoint on wealth.

OT 1. The Hebrew words
    2. The OT attitude toward wealth
NT 3. The Greek words
    4. Jesus' teaching on wealth
    5. The Epistles' teaching on wealth
    6. Key passages on wealth and riches
    7. Conclusions

OT — 1. The Hebrew words. Hebrew has an extensive vocabulary of words linked with wealth. Many are synonymous, with basic meanings overlapping. Some of the major terms are *'ᵃḥuzzâh* ("possession" or "property," usually used of the land promised by God), *'ōšer* ("riches," "treasure"), *gāḏôl* ("rich," indicating one whose possessions have increased in size and importance), *hôn* (a poetic term for wealth, indicating a great enough supply of goods to make life easy), *ḥayîl* ("wealth" in 30 of the approximately 240 OT occurrences but meaning "strength," "might"), *ḥōsen* ("treasure," "wealth," "material prosperity"), *kāḇôḏ* (the riches that make a person weighty or significant in society), *nᵉḵasîm* ("riches"), *yiṯrâh* ("savings"), *yiṯrôn* ("profit," "gain"), *môṯār* ("profit," "gain"), *nᵉḵasîm* ("wealth"), *maṭmôn* ("treasure"), *qinyān* ("property acquired by purchase"), and *kôšārâh* ("estate," the goods owned by an individual).

Clearly the OT is sensitive to the issue, deeply aware of the impact of riches within a society and of the impact on individual members of society. But given this sensitivity, the OT seems to present two radically differing perspectives on wealth.

2. The OT attitude toward wealth. The covenant relationship that God established with Israel provides the framework within which we can understand the OT attitude toward wealth. ◗ *Covenant*

God committed himself to bless Israel if Israel would continue to live by the covenant. The blessings promised seem all-inclusive—an increase in numbers and wealth and freedom from childlessness and disease (Dt 7:12–15). The basic commitment is often repeated, as in Dt 28: "The enemies who rise up against you will be defeated. . . . The LORD will send a blessing on your barns and on everything you put your hand to. . . . The LORD will grant you abundant prosperity—in the fruit of your womb, the young of your livestock and the crops of your ground (vv. 7–8,11).

This commitment to Israel was particularized in the individual, who could expect to be blessed as he or she walked in Yahweh's righteous paths. As the psalmist says in celebration: "Praise the LORD. Blessed is the man who fears the LORD, who finds great delight in his commands. His children will be mighty in the land; each generation of the upright will be blessed. Wealth and riches are in his house, and his righteousness endures forever. Even in darkness light dawns for the upright, for the gracious and compassionate and righteous man. Good will come to him who is generous and lends freely, who conducts his affairs with justice. Surely he will never be shaken; a righteous man will be remembered forever" (Ps 112:1–6). This thread of confidence is often found throughout the OT (e.g., 1 Sa 2:7; 1 Ch 29:28; Pr 10:4,22).

By Jesus' time this theme had been interpreted to imply that riches were a clear sign of God's favor. A person who was rich was *ipso facto* righteous, one of God's blessed ones.

But there is another theme that runs through the OT, along with the riches-are-the-Lord's-blessing-for-the-righteous theme. Deuteronomy warns of a time when Israel's heart might become proud. When the days of riches come, Moses says, "then your heart will become proud and you will forget the LORD your God" (8:14). He goes on to say, "You may say to yourself, 'My power and the strength of my hands have produced this wealth for me.' But remember the LORD your God, for it is he who gives you the ability to produce wealth, and so confirms his covenant" (8:17–18). Wealth is a blessing from God, but wealth is also a danger. It can rob a person of humility and of sensitivity to the Lord!

Wealth also has other drawbacks. A passion for wealth can lead a person into sin (Hos 12:8), but wealth cannot redeem the soul (Ps 49:6–9). Also, wealth is transitory; the psalmist takes this reality to heart and says, "But man, despite his riches, does not endure" (v. 12). So how should one person view another's wealth? "Do not be overawed when a man grows rich, when the splendor of his house increases; for he will take nothing with him when he dies, his splendor will not descend with him. Though while he lived he counted himself blessed—and men praise you when you prosper—he will join the generation of his fathers, who will never see the light of life. A man who has riches without understanding is like the beasts that perish" (vv. 16–20).

Ultimately, it is both the attitude of the believer toward riches and his use of riches that determine whether or not they are a blessing. As for riches without spiritual perceptivity, David sees them only as a disaster: "Surely God will bring you down to everlasting ruin; he will snatch you up and tear you from your tent; he will uproot you from the land of the living. The righteous will see and fear; they will laugh at him, saying, 'Here now is the man who did not make God his stronghold but trusted in his great wealth and grew strong by destroying others!'" (Ps 52:5–7).

It is clear, then, that the OT has no naive view of wealth. Wealth is neither an unmixed blessing nor a guaranteed

prospect for the godly. In the framework of the covenant, God's people can expect blessing, and this will often take the form of riches. But for the believer riches are never to be an end in themselves (cf. Pr 10:2; 15:16; 21:21).

NT — 3. The Greek words. Several Greek words communicate the idea of riches or wealth. *Bios* simply means "life," or one's property as a means of sustaining life. More significant are *thēsauros* and *ploutos*. *Thēsauros* means "treasure." It speaks of that which is stored up and saved by human beings as especially precious. The NT makes it clear that God's value system is different from that of human beings; thus, often what human beings treasure has little value to him. *Ploutos* is "wealth" or "riches." It refers primarily to this world's goods, though "rich" is frequently used in a figurative and spiritual sense (e.g., 2 Co 8:9; Eph 2:4; Jas 2:5). Other words that call for our attention are *mamōnas*, translated "Mammon" in many English versions. It means "wealth" or "property," as does *chrēma*.

From these terms the NT develops aspects of the OT's teaching, refining and defining for us a perspective intended to shape our lives.

4. Jesus' teaching on wealth. Jesus taught about wealth frequently. His primary focus was on attitude. If the believer trusts God as a loving father, he is freed from the pagan's desperate focus on the necessities of life (Mt 6).

The rich man who died found that his wealth had blinded him to spiritual realities. He suffered in torment while a beggar he had scorned was seen in paradise with Abraham (Lk 16:19–31).

The treasures people store up on earth rust and corrode, and they distract us from concentration on God and his righteousness (Lk 12:13–21).

5. The Epistles' teaching on wealth. The Epistles speak less of wealth than do the Gospels. James points out that the rich oppress the poor (Jas 5:1–6). ▶ *Poor and Oppressed* There are some warnings about the love of money (1 Ti 3:3; 2 Ti 3:2; Heb 13:5; 1 Pe 5:2). Included among

Paul's statements on the subject of Christian giving is an exhortation to those who are rich in this world to use their wealth generously to supply the needs of the saints (1 Ti 6:18). ♦ *Giving* Paul reveals his own attitude toward money, reflecting a contentment that can exist whatever one's circumstances (Php 4). The general attitude of the Epistles seems to suggest that riches are irrelevant to the true issues of life but that one who is rich should take advantage of his condition to serve the saints.

6. Key passages on wealth and riches. This brief survey indicates NT passages that one should explore to develop a biblical perspective on wealth.

Mt 6:5–34. Jesus taught his disciples to pray, "Give us today our daily bread" (6:11). The passage develops the thought. Disciples are not to store up treasures on earth, because one's thoughts and motives are focused on his treasures (6:21). Rather, release from anxiety is promised through realization that God is one's loving father, to whom believers are truly important. We can focus on his righteousness and kingdom and leave it to him to supply our needs (6:25–34). Rather than promote laziness, this passage should release us from an anxious preoccupation with material goods. The realities on which we can depend, and on which we should focus our attention, are spiritual and moral.

Mt 13:18–23. The parable of the sower points out that some who hear the word of God have no time for it, being distracted by the "worries of this life and the deceitfulness of wealth" (v. 22).

Mt 19:16–30. The account of the rich young man who asked, "What good thing must I do to get eternal life?" (v. 16) is often misunderstood. The man had kept the commands that dealt with relationships with others. But when Jesus told him what to do ("Sell your possessions and give to the poor. . . . Then come, follow me," v. 21), the young man turned away. When Israel's God called him to make the total heart and soul commitment that the first of the commandments requires, he chose his riches.

The purpose of Jesus was not to make a general statement on wealth, but to confront one individual with reality. The man's heart was focused on his possessions, not on God. When the man left, Jesus warned his disciples, "It is easier for a camel to go through the eye of a needle [possibly Jerusalem's low "needle gate"] than for a rich man to enter the kingdom of God" (v. 24). This statement shocked his disciples, who held the common opinion that a person's wealth indicated that he was close to God.

Lk 12:13–21. The rich fool tore down his barns to build bigger ones, sure that he had "plenty of good things laid up for many years" (v. 19). That night he died, illustrating Jesus' warning against greed. The story also illustrates the vital principle that "a man's life does not consist in the abundance of his possessions" (v. 15).

Lk 16:1–15. Jesus told of a manager who, when he was about to be fired, used his position to revise the records of his master's creditors. He was commended, not for his dishonesty, but because he used wealth to prepare for his future. Jesus urged believers not to be controlled by their possessions but to use their property to prepare for their own welcome "into eternal dwellings" (v. 9). Jesus stressed the fact that no one can be devoted to God and to money at the same time. One or the other will be master. Money is to be used rather than served.

Lk 16:19–31. The story of the rich man and Lazarus makes many points. One's position in this life is no indication of eternal destiny. Those who find money more real than the testimony of Scripture are in great danger.

Acts. Several passages illustrate the impact and use of money. Many in the early church freely gave their possessions to meet others' needs (Ac 2:44–45; 4:32–37). One couple lied to God and the church about a contribution; it was not the withholding of money but the deceit that led to their deaths (Ac 5:1–11). "Wasn't the money at your disposal?" Peter asked (v. 4). Simon the sorcerer's notion that God's gifts and spiritual power could be purchased was scathingly attacked (Ac 8:9–24).

1 Co 8–9. ♦ *Giving*

1 Ti 6:3–10. The desire for riches is a trap, for the love of money is a root from which grows every kind of evil. The believer is to view godliness with contentment as great gain.

1 Ti 6:17–19. The wealthy can "lay up treasure for themselves as a firm foundation for the coming age" (v. 19) by refusing to put their hope in their riches and by being "generous and willing to share" (v. 18).

Jas 2:1–13. Believers are not to show favoritism to the rich. The passage shows a bias against the wealthy, who use their position to exploit the poor. ♦ *Poor and Oppressed*

Jas 5:1–6. Again, wealthy oppressors are warned. The riches for which they have defrauded the innocent not only rot and corrode but also cry out to God against them.

1 Jn 3:16–20. Love calls us to use material possessions for brothers and sisters who are in need.

7. Conclusions. Wealth and riches are blessings from God if they are gained and used in harmony with God's values. But wealth can war against the soul, distracting us from the really significant issues of life and drawing us away from reliance on God alone.

We can thank God if he chooses to give us riches, and then we can use our money in his service. But if he does not choose to enrich us, we need not be concerned. It is godliness with contentment that is the believer's true gain.

WELL ♦ *Healing* ♦ *Sickness and Health*

WEEP

The Hebrew word for "weep" is nearly always *bākāh*, and the Greek, *klaiō*. The NT use is in the framework established in the OT. There weeping, which always expresses strong emotion, has several associations. There is the weeping of sorrow and of joy (but joy only in the narrative about Jacob in Ge 29–46). Weeping is sometimes associated with great distress, especially the distress caused by death. Weeping can also accompany pleading or complaining to God. Infrequently in the OT weeping is an expression of repentance.

WICKED

Wickedness is undoubtedly an aspect of sin. ♦ *Sin* But it has distinctive aspects that set it apart from other words that portray our human condition.

OT 1. Wickedness in the OT
NT 2. Wickedness in the NT

OT — 1. Wickedness in the OT. *Rā'* and *rā'âh* are sometimes translated "wicked." The basic meaning of this word group is "evil," or "bad." ♦ *Evil* When used to describe a person, these words focus on those moral deficiencies that move one to injure others. Such wickedness may be descriptive of the deeds done or of persons who are characterized by wicked attitudes and actions.

The OT word most commonly translated "wickedness" is *rāšā'*. The masculine noun occurs over 250 times in the OT and is found in tandem with the entire Hebrew vocabulary of sin. ♦ *Sin* Wicked acts violate God's standards for life with other people and thus stand in sharp contrast to the divine character. But wickedness is not committed against God (as, for instance, is iniquity). Wickedness is sin against others and one's community. Wicked acts are criminal in character, violating the rights of individuals and threatening the pattern of reciprocity that holds any community together.

Dishonesty, violence, oppression, extortion, fraud, and other sins are the delight of the wicked, who themselves are proud and vicious.

Wickedness, then, looks at those persons and acts that damage other persons and twist the pattern of society away from righteousness.

NT — 2. Wickedness in the NT. Several different Greek words are translated "wicked" and "wickedness" in the NIV, while the NASB tends to rely on two Greek roots to express this idea.

Both versions translate *ponēria* and *ponēros* as "wicked." The concept is a strong one, focusing on actions that are dangerous because they are destructive to others. These Greek words are found most often in the Gospels, where the OT sense dominates, and are translated "wicked" or "wickedness" in the NIV in a number of passages (Mt 12:39,45; 13:49; 16:4; 18:32; Lk 6:35; 11:26,29,39; 19:22; Ro 1:29; 1 Co 5:8,13; 2 Th 3:2; 2 Jn 11).

Adikia and *adikos* are also translated "wicked" and "wickedness" in both versions. The words indicate the idea of committing an injustice and thus are also clearly in the OT tradition. They are found in several NT passages (Ac 1:18; 24:15; Ro 1:18; 6:13; 2 Th 2:12; 2 Ti 2:19; 2 Pe 2:15).

Other words are translated "wicked" in the NIV NT. One of them is *anomia*, which indicates one's contempt for the law by acting contrary to it. This word occurs fifteen times in the NT (Mt 7:23; 13:41; 23:28; 24:12; Ro 4:7; 6:19; 2 Co 6:14; 2 Th 2:7; Tit 2:14; Heb 1:9; 8:12; 10:17; 1 Jn 3:4); its related word *anomos* occurs ten times (Mk 15:28; Lk 22:37; Ac 2:23; 1 Co 9:21; 2 Th 2:8; 1 Ti 1:9; 2 Pe 2:8). The NIV translates *kakos* ("evil") as "wicked" in two of its fifty-one NT occurrences (Mt 24:48; Rev 2:2) and *kakia* ("malice," "wickedness") in one of its eleven occurrences (Ac 8:22). ♦ *Evil* The Greek word that the NIV renders "wicked" in Ro 4:5 is *asebēs* ("ungodly"). ♦ *Godly/Godliness* In all instances of the use of this word, the image is of a destructive and malicious person.

WIDOW

The OT views widows, with the fatherless, as vulnerable members of society. Thus, OT law singles them out for special consideration. No one is to take advantage of a widow (Ex 22:22) but must defend "the cause of the fatherless and the widow" (Dt 10:18). The special institutions established in law for the poor mention widows as beneficiaries (Dt 24:19–21; 26:12–13). ♦ *Poor and Op-*

pressed Thus, OT psalms celebrate God by saying that he "watches over the alien and sustains the fatherless and the widow, but he frustrates the ways of the wicked" (146:9).

Widows are mentioned also in the NT. In Ac 6 we see that the Jerusalem church established a system to provide for the needs of those widows who had no other support. In later decades a widows' corps was apparently established in many churches. While younger widows were to remarry (1 Ti 5:11–14), and those with families were to be cared for by their relatives (vv. 3–8), a special group of older widows was formed. These women, noted for good deeds, were supported by the church. It is probable that they served the body not only by the acts of caring described in 1 Ti 5 but also by training the younger wives (Tit 2:3–5).

WIFE ♦ Marriage

WILL

In most cases where the verb "will" is found in the Bible, no single corresponding Greek or Hebrew term is in the text. The verb construction itself communicates what we communicate when expressing intention by "will" ("I will appear before the Lord").

At times both Testaments speak of the "will of God." The phrase is commonly used by Christians today. But few are certain just what is intended by "God's will" as it is used in the Bible, or when it is related to an individual's Christian experience.

OT **1. Words expressing action of the will**
NT **2. The Greek words**
    3. Significant NT passages
    4. Conclusions

OT — 1. Words expressing action of the will. A number of Hebrew words imply the motion or action of a person's will. They are seldom found where the NIV and the NASB speak of "will" or "willing," except as noted below.

The word *'āḇâh* means "to be willing" or "to consent to," and is usually linked with a request. Except in Isa 1:19 and Job 39:9, it is always in the negative: "not willing." The NIV renders *'āḇâh* as "willing" in a number of places (Ex 10:27; Dt 29:20; 1 Sa 22:17; 2 Sa 6:10; 2 Ki 8:19; 24:4; 1 Ch 19:19; 2 Ch 21:7; Isa 1:19; Eze 3:7).

Nāḏaḇ indicates a voluntary movement of the will and is often linked with offerings gladly given to the Lord. This word or a derivative of it is found in seven passages where the NIV has "willing" (Ex 35:21,29; Jdg 5:9; 1 Ch 29:5,9; Ps 110:3; 119:108).

Rāṣôn speaks of a willing that brings the doer pleasure. The verb *rāṣâh* is often translated "to be pleased." A word in this Hebrew word group occurs in five of the passages where the NIV has "will," in reference to God's good and pleasing will (Ezr 10:11; Ps 40:8; 143:10; Pr 11:27; 14:9).

Ḥāp̄ēṣ ("to delight in or take pleasure in") is translated by the NIV twice as "will" (1 Sa 2:25; Isa 53:10) and once as "willing" (Ru 3:13).

Yā'al indicates the exercise of one's will, the exerting of oneself to do something. It is not found where the NIV has "will" or "willing."

In addition, translators often use "will" or "willing" to communicate some colloquial expression in the original, even when no such specific term is found in the text.

The delicate shades of meanings indicate the interplay of motives linked with divine and human choices. There can be a willingness based on obligation or on pleasure, as a response to a request, or simply as a voluntary, spontaneous act.

All of these words and phrases show that the OT believer was sure that God had expressed his will, as the divine expectation for human behavior, in the law that he had given through Moses. ▶ *Law* ▶ *Word*

NT — 2. The Greek words. Two different families of Greek words express the idea of "will" or "willing." *Boulomai* and *thelō* function in the NT in a synonymous way. While many scholars have struggled to make distinctions between

them, they do not agree about the distinctive stress of each of these words. Each can represent choice and inclination; each can represent intention and fixed purpose. The NT displays about the same ratio of the use of *boulomai* to *thelō* as does the common Greek of NT times (about 1 to 6); so no conclusions can be drawn from frequency of use. But where *boulomai* and *boulē* do indicate the purpose of God, they always are used in the sense of an absolute determination (e.g., Lk 7:30; Ac 2:23; 4:28; Eph 1:11; Heb 6:17).

3. Significant NT passages. Observation of a number of NT passages and their use of "will" helps us to understand the significance of the concept of the will of God.

Mt 7:21 (cf. 12:50); Mk 3:35. A person can "do the will" of the Father. This simply means that the individual is responsive to God's revealed standards and desires.

Mt 26:39; Mk 14:36; Lk 22:42. Jesus prayed that "if possible" the cup of suffering he was about to drink be taken from him. But he concluded, "Yet not as I will, but as you will" (Mt 26:39). The human will is to be subject to the purpose and intentions of the Father; as it was in Jesus, so it must surely be in us.

Jn 1:13; 1 Pe 1:23. The new birth does not have its source in man's will but in the divine will. The NIV translation indicates that the analogy is between types of birth; it does not make any statement about the role of the individual's personal exercise of will in choosing to follow Jesus.

Jn 6:38–40. God has determined that everyone who looks to the Son and believes in him will have eternal life. This set purpose assures us that Jesus will "lose none" (v. 39) of all those whom God has given him.

Jn 7:17. Choosing to do God's will is basic if an individual is to discover that Jesus' teaching is from God (cf. Jn 8:31–32).

Ac 4:28. Jesus' death was according to the fixed purpose and determined will of God (cf. Ac 2:23).

Ac 18:21 (cf. Ro 1:10). Paul's use of the expression "if it is God's will" indicates Paul's own uncertainty about the future and his confidence that God in fact controlled his personal destiny on earth.

Ac 20:27. The "whole will of God" is an expression indicating all that God has revealed to us in Scripture (cf. Ro 2:18; 1 Pe 2:15).

Ro 12:2. God's will, as the perspective on life unveiled in revelation, is to be done so that by practicing it we will experience the fact that his will for us is good and pleasing and perfect.

Gal 1:4. God's purpose, to rescue us from this present evil age through Jesus, is according "to the will of our God and Father."

Eph 1:5–11. God's fixed purpose and conscious choices made concerning salvation's plan are described in these verses.

Col 1:9–14. A practical and applied knowledge of that which God has willed is vital for growth in goodness. This is again a reference to revelation.

Heb 9:16–17. Here the reference is to what in our day is known as a "last will and testament."

Jas 4:15. Plans that are made without awareness of dependence on God show an evil attitude. We are to plan, but we are also to be aware that what we plan will happen only "if it is the Lord's will."

1 Pe 4:2. The believer, rescued from sin, is to live according to God's will rather than according to inner passions.

1 Jn 5:14. Believers can pray according to God's will. When they offer such prayers, they have a basis on which to expect a positive answer.

4. Conclusions. The "will of God" is used in a number of senses. It expresses the divine purpose, fixed and unalterable. It expresses God's general and revealed standards for human behavior. It expresses God's current involvement in human life, ranging from his call to perform a specific action to his shaping of our personal future.

The NT also deals with human response to God's will. Believers are to submit to God's will, to determine to do it, and in doing it to discover how good God's way is.

The very fact that God has a will for an individual's life indicates that it is possible to discover it. But passages dealing with the will of God do not focus on this personal aspect. ◗ *Lead/Guide*

WINE

There are two Hebrew words translated "wine" in the NIV and the NASB: *tîrôš* and *yayin. Tîrôš* is "new wine," the unfermented product of grape vines. It is associated in the OT with blessing (e.g., Dt 7:13; 11:14; 2 Ki 18:32) and was an important product for the agricultural economy. *Yayin* is fermented wine, which in Bible times contained about seven to ten percent alcohol. In the NT era the rabbis called for dilution of this wine when it was used at the Passover. But fermented wines were drunk at feasts, given as gifts (1 Sa 25:18; 2 Sa 16:1), and used in offerings to God (Ex 29:40; Lev 23:13; Nu 15:7). Yet the OT calls for moderation and rejects both drunkenness and a love for drink (Pr 20:1; 21:17; 23:20). The two sides of the use of wine—abuse and proper use—are both seen in Amos: God's people were condemned for sins associated with wine (Am 2:8,12; 5:11; 6:6) and, in the later chapters, which are filled with promise of restoration, they were promised that wine would "drip from the mountains" (Am 9:13) and that they would "plant vineyards and drink their wine" (v. 14).

The Greek word for wine is *oinos.* References in the NT show the same appreciation of wine and the same condemnation of its abuse as the OT. Wine is associated with the joy of the marriage feast at Cana (Jn 2), but drunkenness is condemned as characteristic of a pagan lifestyle (1 Pe 4:3; Eph 5:18). Wine was also recommended by Paul to Timothy for medicinal use (1 Ti 5:23). Probably Eph 5:18, which calls on believers not to "get drunk on wine, which leads to debauchery," but rather to "be filled with the Spirit," puts the issue in perspective. The Christians' bubbling joy is produced by the Spirit of God, who lifts all of life beyond the ordinary. If we are filled with the Spirit, there is little need for wine's artificial stimulation.

WISDOM

The concept of wisdom is an important one. It may be particularly important for us in our technological society, where we place a strong emphasis on knowledge. The Scriptures do not make the mistake of confusing wisdom with other mental capacities or of giving wisdom less than its central place.

OT 1. The Hebrew words
    2. OT wisdom literature
    3. Wisdom personified in Proverbs
NT 4. The Greek words
    5. Wisdom in 1 Co 1–3
    6. Wisdom in practice in the NT

OT — 1. The Hebrew words. The basic word group expressing the idea of wisdom includes *ḥākam* and its cognates *ḥokmâh* and *ḥākām*. Together they occur in the OT over three hundred times. The closest other words in meaning to this group are cognates of *bîn*, which means "understanding."

The *ḥākam* stem expresses a person's approach to life. Wisdom to master life's challenges can be found only in one's relationship with God. The Hebrew view is practical in focus. Wisdom is expressed in godly living, "for the LORD gives wisdom, and from his mouth come knowledge and understanding. . . . You will understand what is right and just and fair—every good path. For wisdom will enter your heart, and knowledge will be pleasant to your soul. Wisdom will save you from the ways of wicked men, from men whose words are perverse" (Pr 2:6,9–10,12).

The wise person, then, is one who is sensitive to God and who willingly subjects himself to him. The wise person is one who goes on to apply divine guidelines in everyday situations and, guided by God's will, makes daily choices. It is only in wedding the Lord's words to experience that wisdom can be found or demonstrated.

The wedding of knowledge and experience so that one gains skill and becomes wise is seen in other uses of *ḥākam*. A person can be wise (skilled) in arts (Ex 36:1–4), in government (Pr 8:15), in making money (v. 18). Combining knowledge and experience to successfully meet moral or other challenges in daily life is what demonstrates the possession of wisdom.

While "wisdom" and "wise" are usually expressed by *ḥākam* or its cognates in the Hebrew text, we infrequently find other words so translated in the NIV and the NASB. *Tûšîyâh* is a term meaning "sound judgment" that leads to success. It occurs only twelve times in the OT (Job 5:12; 6:13; 11:6; 12:16; 26:3; 30:22; Pr 2:7; 3:21; 8:14; 18:1; Isa 28:29; Mic 6:9). At times *śekel*, "understanding," is also translated "wisdom." This word also focuses on the success that comes through the application of wisdom.

2. OT wisdom literature. Wisdom literature in the OT includes Proverbs, Ecclesiastes, Job, and several psalms (19, 37, 104, 107, 147, 148). Wisdom literature does not express itself in terms of prescriptive law, nor even in exposition of the Mosaic Law. Rather, wisdom literature describes a lifestyle, contrasting the wise and foolish choices that individuals make. Only one who approaches life with a deep awe and fear of the Lord will discover and apply wisdom. ▶ *Fear*

3. Wisdom personified in Proverbs. One section of the Book of Proverbs uses a distinctive literary device; it presents wisdom as a woman. The use of this device in Pr 1–9 is partly explained by the fact that the noun "wisdom" is feminine. Yet the image is powerful, leading some scholars to speculate that the wisdom mentioned in Proverbs is the Logos of the NT. Most, however, doubt such an identification.

NT — 4. The Greek word. The concept of wisdom is expressed in the Greek NT by *sophia*. In Greek culture, "wisdom" represents an unusual ability, an attribute. By NT times the subject of "wisdom" was philosophic or speculative knowledge.

Words in this group appear seldom in the Gospels, but when they do appear, they are used in the OT sense. The greatest number of uses of "wise" and "wisdom" are clustered in 1 Cor 1–3 (see below). In the rest of the NT, "wisdom" focuses on that same practice of the godly life that is the concern of the OT.

5. Wisdom in 1 Co 1–3. First Corinthians is a book of problems. Paul focuses on issue after issue that tore at the unity of the church in Corinth. Again and again he guided his readers to an understanding of how to deal effectively with each.

The first problem Paul touched in this Epistle was the divisions that developed at Corinth as little groups formed, claiming allegiance to this or that leader. Paul invited the Corinthians to think about the nature of wisdom, for he believed their division was caused by the application of a merely human wisdom to spiritual issues.

In 1:18–31, Paul notes that the world's *sophia* did not bring it to a knowledge of God. This is because the Jews (who demanded miracles) and the Greeks (who look for "wisdom" in the sense of a philosophical system) approached God on their own terms. Their basic orientation to life left no room to recognize Christ as the power and wisdom of God (1 Co 1:24). Here Christ is presented as God's practical solution to the problem of man's alienation from God—the one who himself is "our righteousness, holiness and redemption" (v. 30).

Human wisdom—i.e, man's approach to the problem of relationship with God—is thus demonstrated to be foolishness, though God's approach is viewed as foolishness by the world. Paul shows that for a correct perspective, one must gain access to the very thought processes of God (1 Co 2). These thought processes have been revealed to us in words taught by the Holy Spirit (vv. 13–16; cf. 2 Ti 3:15; 2 Pe 3:15).

In 1 Cor 3, Paul returns to the problem of divisions. The Corinthians had been acting and thinking as mere human beings, not applying the revealed words of God nor seeking to discern their implications.

Paul then applies several basic truths to show the error in the debate over leaders (1 Co 4).

In this extended passage "wisdom" represents the perspective or orientation that one brings to dealing with the issues of life. Human beings are foolish, because they fail to recognize the fact that their notions must be subject to divine evaluation. Only when one abandons what seems wise by human standards to accept without hesitation the divine viewpoint as revealed in Scripture can he claim true wisdom.

6. Wisdom in practice in the NT. This theme—that Christ is God's wisdom, applied to resolve the problems caused by human sin (1 Co 1–3)—is picked up in Eph 3:10, which expresses God's intention to make known to spiritual (angelic) powers "the manifold wisdom of God" as his purpose is worked out in history "through the church."

In most places, however, "wisdom" is the divine perspective available to and applied by believers to the issues of their lives. Thus, Paul prayed that God would fill the Ephesians with "the Spirit of wisdom and revelation" so they might grasp and experience the power available in Christ (Eph 1:17). The same theme is addressed in a prayer in Col 1. Paul yearned for these believers to be filled with a knowledge of "what God has willed" (*tou thelēmatos autou*, v. 9). He qualified his prayer by adding that the knowledge must be treated with spiritual wisdom and insight, so that the believers might "live a life worthy of the Lord and . . . please him in every way" (v. 10). It is wisdom that guides the application of what is known.

Paul turned again to human notions in Col 2:23, speaking of religious approaches that "have an appearance of wisdom," that is, approaches that seem to be practical, effective ways to spiritual growth. But again Paul turned his readers to Jesus. The word of Christ, dwelling in us, alone enables us to teach and admonish each other in wisdom (3:16).

James, reflecting the OT's convictions, said that one who lacks wisdom should appeal to God and expect God to provide it (1:5–7). Later (3:13–18) he carefully defined the characteristics of the wisdom that comes from above. It is "pure, . . . peace-loving, considerate, submissive, full of mercy and good fruit, impartial and sincere" (v. 18). A character that displays envy, selfish ambition, and similar destructive traits is not from God.

Wisdom, then, is a critical concept in both Testaments: wisdom is concerned with how one lives his or her life. Both the OT and the NT make it clear that only when our life is oriented to God and his revealed viewpoint is applied to our daily experience can we become wise.

WITCHCRAFT ♦ Divination

WITNESS ♦ Testify/Witness/Testimony

WOE

In both the OT and the NT "woe!" is an interjection, an exclamation of grief or a denouncement. The Greek is *ouai*. There are a number of short Hebrew exclamations that may be so translated (*'ôy, 'ôyâh, 'î, 'allay, hôy,* and *rāzî*). The last word occurs only two times in the OT and means "wasting," or "leanness" (both in Isa 24:16).

WONDERS ♦ Miracle/Sign/Wonder

WOMEN ♦ Male and Female

WOMEN IN THE CHURCH

In other articles we have explored women as persons and women as wives. **♦ Male and Female ♦ Marriage** In this article we look specifically at the question of women's roles in the NT church. This is not an issue that can be resolved by a study of words alone. In fact, no certain conclusions can be drawn, however we approach the issues. But the issues involved and a number of facts that are important in reaching our own conclusions can be explored.

1. **Evidence of the significance of women**
2. **Women in church office**
3. **Women in the worship service**
4. **Implications for today**

1. **Evidence of the significance of women.** Despite the reality of life in a male-dominated culture, women played a surprisingly significant role in the early church. The reason is undoubtedly that, in Christ, women as well as men are the recipients of spiritual gifts for ministry. **♦ Gift/Gifts** Thus, the contribution of women to the total ministry of the body of Christ is basic to the health and growth of the whole congregation.

Specific lines of NT evidence show that an important place was given to women in the life of the church. A few facts are worth noting.

First, women played a critical role in the establishment of several NT congregations (e.g., Ac 16:13–15,40; 17:4,12).

Second, women are identified by name and called "fellow workers" by Paul (esp. Ro 16, where seven women are identified by name). This inclusion of women in a ministry team is a significant departure from Jewish practice. The naming of Priscilla before her husband Aquila is also extremely significant (Ro 16:3).

Third, women are seen participating through prayer and prophecy in church meetings (1 Co 11:5). Although the OT foretold a day when sons and daughters would prophesy as the Spirit was poured out on "both men and women" (Joel 2:28–32; Ac 2:17–18), the participation of women in church gatherings again violates OT tradition.

Fourth, Phoebe is identified in Ro 16:1 as a deaconess, and other evidence suggests that women may have participated with men in the diaconate.

Despite the clarity of evidence in each of these areas, suggesting that women participated freely in the life of the early church and were recognized as significant contributors of ministry, there are problem passages that are difficult to interpret.

2. Women in church office. The offices mentioned in the NT were ordinarily filled by males. This seems true whether one speaks of apostles, elders, or overseers (bishops). This is not true, however, of the office of deacons. Phoebe is identified in Ro 16:1 as a deaconess of the church in Cenchrea. The word means "servant" and is so rendered in most English versions, but it is the same word used in 1 Ti 3, where deacons are supposed to be (among other things) "men worthy of respect, sincere, not indulging in much wine." Then verse 11 says, "In the same way, women [*gynē*] are to be worthy of respect, not malicious talkers . . . " (3:11). The NIV and some other versions interpret this as "their wives," but the NIV adds a footnote: "Or . . . *deaconesses.*" The lack in the original of a possessive ("their") suggests that the best translation is "women," not "wives." The passage may well be speaking of those women who, like the men Paul referred to, were deacons and bore the responsibility of that office.

While there is evidence that women served as deacons in the early church, there is a lack of evidence concerning their serving in any other office. We should be careful how we argue from silence. But whatever role deacons had in the church, we have positive indications that women served among them. ▶ *Serve/Servant/Slave*

3. Women in the worship service. The most controversial NT passages regarding women have a common context; they deal with issues related to worship. However we understand these passages, we need to interpret them in the total context of a gathering in which women *did* (at least in the church at Corinth) take part, for Paul wrote about women praying and prophesying when the congregation gathered (1 Co 11:5). Within this framework of participation, the passages and the most likely interpretations follow.

According to 1 Co 14:34–36, women are to "remain silent in the churches" to the extent that they "are not allowed to speak." Any questions should be held till they are at home and can "ask their own husbands." This very blunt instruction has been interpreted in several ways: (1) It decisively rules out female participation. (2) It was added by someone other than Paul. (3) It is an example of Paul's inconsistency and reflects his culture-bound, antifeminine view. (4) Paul's statements in 1 Co 11 are misunderstood, and women are not to speak in church. (5) The prohibition in 1 Co 14 must be seen in a narrow view, as dealing with some specific problem rather than reflecting a pattern in church meetings as a whole.

This last option is most in keeping with a high view of Scripture and with careful attention to the text. In 1 Co 14:26–40, Paul is dealing not only with disorderly meetings but also with the question of prophetic revelation (v. 30). Paul has indicated that "two or three prophets should speak, and the others should weigh carefully what is said" (v. 29). The Greek verb rendered "weigh" is *diakrinō* ("judge," "discern"). ▶ *Judge/Judging* It is in this immediate context that Paul gives his instructions about the silence of women. Thus, it is best to take the passage to mean that in the process of weighing prophets, women are to remain silent and not participate.

This interpretation is in harmony with an understanding of the other critical passage, 1 Ti 2. In writing to Timothy, Paul again turns to the congregational meeting. Here he says of women, "A woman should learn in quietness and full submission. I do not permit a woman to teach or to have authority over a man; she must be silent" (2:11). Paul then goes on to give a theological argument from Creation and the Fall as basis for his ruling (vv. 13–14).

There is a difference between this and the 1 Co 14 passage. Here "quietness" and "silent" are both translations of *hēsychia*, whereas in 1 Co 14 the word is *sigaō*. This latter word is used nine times in the NT (Lk 9:36; 20:26; Ac 12:17;

15:12,13; Ro 16:25; 1 Co 14:28,30,34) and means "be silent," with the force of "shut up." But *hēsychia* is used only four times in the NT (Ac 22:2; 2 Th 3:12; 1 Ti 2:11,12) and indicates a restful but attentive receptiveness. That attitude, which promotes learning, is further set in contrast with "teaching" or "having authority" over a man. It is best not to separate the concepts of teaching and authority, though this is possible grammatically. Rather, we need to see in the whole discussion the issue of "authoritative teaching." Authoritative teaching in the church is thus viewed as incompatible with the woman's appropriate role of *hēsychia* and submission. ◗ *Subject/Submission*

The parallelism between the two passages is thus made clear. Women did participate to some extent in the gatherings of the church at Corinth in the form of prayer and prophesying. But any prominent or dominant role was specifically forbidden, especially the judging of prophets and the uttering of authoritative teaching for the church body.

4. Implications for today. The two limitations on women's ministry that the Epistles specify are part of the role that most believe was filled by elders or bishops (overseers) in the early church. ◗ *Elders* ◗ *Overseer*

Essentially, these offices seem directly linked with guarding the health of the local body by protecting those processes that make for spiritual healthiness in a church. Included might well be the judging of the message of a contemporary prophet and the giving of an authoritative teaching (interpretation of the Scripture) intended to guide the local body.

If this view is correct, it seems clear that the early church did not include women among its elders or overseers. It seems possible that, since Paul's arguments for his position are rooted in theology rather than in contemporary custom, this limitation is intended for the church today as well.

But we must remember that much debate continues to go on over these passages. Certainly whatever conviction one develops must be held humbly and balanced by a strong affirmation of the significance of women as persons in the church of Jesus Christ.

WORD

"Word" occurs often in the OT and the NT. Many times it has special theological implications. From the OT's "word of the LORD " to the NT's unveiling of Jesus as the eternal Word, this common term makes vital statements about God and his commitment to reveal himself to humanity.

OT 1. The Hebrew words
    2. The Word of the Lord
NT 3. The Greek words
    4. Jesus as the Word
    5. Summary

OT — 1. The Hebrew words. The Hebrew word most often translated "word" in the NIV and the NASB is *dābār*. It occurs over fourteen hundred times in the OT. The verb *dābar*, "to speak or talk," occurs over eleven hundred times. Thus, this is a very common root in the OT. Also it is translated in many different ways—as many as seventy in the KJV!

There are other Hebrew words that are synonymous to these. In the NIV and the NASB *'ēmer* and *'imrâh*, which mean "utterance" or "speech," are infrequently translated "word" or "words." At times also the colloquial expression "mouth of" (*peh*) may be rendered "word."

2. The Word of the Lord. The most significant use of "word" is in contexts in which God's revelatory word to man is clearly in view. Literally hundreds of times the phrase "the word of Yahweh" is found in the OT, and there are hundreds more that speak of God's sending his word to his people or that identify a particular message as a word from God.

The OT shines with the confidence that every word from God is both reliable and relevant. "As for God," the psalmist says, "his way is perfect; the word of the LORD is flawless" (Ps 18:30). God's Word is reliable because he is faithful, and it is relevant because his expressed power and purpose shape the universe. "For the word of the LORD is right and true; he is faithful in all he does. . . . By the word of the LORD were the heavens made, their starry host by the breath of his mouth. He gathers the waters of the sea into jars; he puts the deep into storehouses. Let all the earth fear the LORD ; let all the people of the world revere him. For he spoke, and it came to be; he commanded, and it stood firm. The LORD foils the plans of the nations; he thwarts the purposes of the peoples. But the plans of the LORD stand firm forever, the purposes of his heart through all generations" (Ps 33:4–11).

The Word of God functions through the OT as the vital expression of his active presence. It is by God's word that the universe itself flared into existence (e.g., Ps 33:6,9; 148:5; Isa 40:26). It is by God's "ten words" (Dt 4:13) that the moral order is established, and it is by his words of covenantal promise that Israel's existence was ordered (Ex 20:22–23:19; Dt 32:47; Ps 147:15). God's words expressed through the prophets promised judgment and salvation, and gave shape to the future before it happened. God's word fixes the future, for he says, "I make known the end from the beginning, from ancient times, what is still to come. I say: My purpose will stand, and I will do all I please" (Isa 46:10).

The OT believer, coming to the Word of God, met God in his fullness. He came to know the plans and power and purposes of God. He came to understand God's ways and to sense his love and holiness. In the Word the believer found both guidance for daily living and joy. By living in harmony with the spoken words of God, the believer could find great peace and the confident expectation of salvation (Ps 119:165–66).

For insight into the way the revealed Word of God is to enrich life, we can study and meditate on Ps 119.

NT — 3. The Greek words. Two words are commonly found where the NIV and the NASB read "word." One is *rhēma*, which typically focuses attention on a specific word or utterance. In contrast, *logos* is a broad term, sometimes including the entire Christian message

and often used in technical theological senses.

Rhēma occurs seventy times in the NT (Mt 4:4; 5:11; 12:36; 18:16; 26:75; 27:14; Mk 9:32; 14:72; Lk 1:37,38,65; 2:15,17,19,29, 50,51; 3:2; 4:4; 5:5; 7:1; 9:45; 18:34; 20:26; 24:8,11; Jn 3:34; 5:47; 6:63,68; 8:20,47; 10:21; 12:47,48; 14:10; 15:7; 17:8; Ac 2:14; 5:20,32; 6:11,13; 10:22,37,44; 11:14,16; 13:42; 16:38; 26:25; 28:25; Ro 10:8,17,18; 2 Co 12:4; 13:1; Eph 5:26; 6:17; Heb 1:3; 6:5; 11:3; 12:19; 1 Pe 1:25; 2 Pe 3:2; Jude 17; Rev 17:17).

The significance of *rhēma* can be illustrated by its first occurrence. Challenged by Satan in the wilderness, Jesus responded that man is to live by "every *rhēma* that comes from the mouth of God" (Mt 4:4). In the context he then proceeds to counter Satan's temptations by applying very specific words from Scripture to each situation that Satan creates.

The theologically critical term, however, is *logos*. *Logos* has a long tradition in Greek philosophy, in which it developed a variety of complex meanings. In the eastern world, words were believed to have magical powers. The NT uses *logos* to speak to both Greek and oriental worlds and in the process infuses "word" with a significance even greater than that found in the OT.

Logos occurs over three hundred times in the NT and is often used in commonplace ways, with meanings such as "speech," "report," "discourse," "subject matter." But often the use of *logos* has great theological significance. The "word" is the active, powerful presence of God, through which he works his will in history.

The word that "came to John" (Lk 3:2) was the revelatory word of the OT, calling him to his ministry as herald of the kingdom and the King of Kings.

The word that Jesus spoke was the word of transforming power. By his word the sick were made whole (Mt 8:8; Lk 7:7) and demons driven out (Mt 8:16).

The word that Jesus spoke was the word of salvation that was able to bring life to the dead and transform the spiritually decayed (Jn 5:24; 17:17; cf. Jas 1:18; 1 Pe 1:23).

Because of the authority and efficacy of Jesus' words, human beings are to respond to them appropriately. Jesus' words are to be heard and planted deep within one's life, as seed is planted in prepared ground (Mt 13:18–23 and parallels). We are to let Jesus' word dwell in us (Jn 5:38), to have room for it (Jn 8:37), and to keep it (v. 51), even as Jesus knows the Father intimately and keeps his word (Jn 8:55). It is in the Word that we meet God, and our response to the Word is our response to him. Thus, we should never build mere human traditions as a hedge around the Word, so nullifying its impact in our lives (Mt 15:6; Mk 7:13).

In Acts and the Epistles, *logos* is used in other ways. Its primary meaning in Acts is "gospel." All that Christ is and offers to mankind is summed up in the "the word of God" or the "word of Christ" (e.g., Ac 4:29,31; 6:7; 8:4; cf. Eph 1:13; Php 2:16). In Ro 9:6, *logos* again reflects an OT meaning; the word is God's expressed purpose, which shapes history and cannot be changed, however human beings may respond.

In the Epistles we see again the OT's affirmation that God's spoken word brought the universe into existence (2 Pe 3:5) and that his word is what keeps it going till God's appointed time and means of future destruction (2 Pe 3:7). We also learn that the Holy Spirit has communicated God's truth to the human race through Scripture's words, but only those who believe on Christ can receive and understand God's truth (1 Co 2:6–16).

The "word of God" thus is far more than a record of human experience or a report of spiritual realities by long-dead men. The Word of God is a living and active power, a timeless moment at which, in our own time and space, we can meet the living God. God expresses himself in his revealed Word and continues to act through it. The Word is both recorded truth and our moment of truth—both truth about God and the place where we meet God personally.

We remain deaf to God's voice until we recognize both aspects of the divine Word. It is content, giving shape and form to reality, and it is confrontation, the moment of meeting God that calls for our personal response of faith.

4. Jesus as the Word. John's Gospel opens with the affirmation that Jesus is the preexistent *logos*, who was with God and was God from eternity (Jn 1:1). This person, the agent of creation and source of life in the universe, became flesh and lived among humanity. Although he was unrecognized by his own generation, John claimed that he and others had "seen his glory" (v. 14), and all who receive him are given "the right to become children of God" (v. 12). John concluded, "No one has ever seen God, but God the One and Only, who is at the Father's side, has made him known" (v. 18).

The use of *logos* here has many levels of significance. It roots the logical ordering of the universe, grasped by the Greeks, in the existence of a personal God. It also takes the OT's concept of the Word of God and personalizes it, showing how fully God expresses himself in revelation. The use of *logos* bonds not only the being of the God-man Jesus into one fused personality, but also bonds the natural and supernatural aspects of the written *logos*. Jesus the living Word, like the written Word, becomes the place of meeting, where God's hidden glory is unveiled and the Father becomes known.

The introduction to 1 John completes the picture. John wrote about that Word of Life: "The life . . . which we have looked at and our hands have touched—this . . . we proclaim to you" (1:1–2). The Word that is and brings life, Jesus himself, is expressed in the message about Jesus. As we respond to the message, we experience the reality that it both expresses and contains.

5. Summary. The biblical word cannot be separated from God's personal presence and power. In both Testaments, "word" is that through which God expresses himself. God's creative word brought our universe into existence. His prophetic word unveils the future. His "ten words" outlined his plan for moral order. He was ultimately revealed in Jesus, eternal *logos* and flesh united in one. He was in the message about Jesus. God as a living person and as divine power finds expression in every word he utters.

It is because God can never be isolated from his utterances that Scripture calls out to us: "Today, if you hear his voice, do not harden your hearts" (Heb 3:15). Rather, we are to combine the message with faith, and by so discovering both God and his power, enter his rest (Heb 4:2–3).

WORK/LABOR

One of Adam's responsibilities in the Garden of Eden was "to work it and take care of it" (Ge 2:15) And Paul bluntly informed the Thessalonians that the idle must be put to work. "If a man will not work, he shall not eat" (2 Th 3:10) was the apostle's rule.

While the Bible surely does present a work ethic, not every aspect of human toil is pleasing.

OT   **1. The Hebrew words**
     2. The OT attitude toward work
NT   **3. The Greek words**
     4. The NT attitude toward work

OT — 1. The Hebrew words. The OT displays an extensive vocabulary of work. The words express awareness that work is undoubtedly a mixed blessing.

While God set Adam to work in the Garden of Eden as a way to participate and find satisfaction in the Lord's own meaningful labor, the Fall introduced a dark aspect to work. Adam and later generations were to wrest their living from the ground only by "painful toil" (Ge 3:17).

The dark side of toil is revealed in several Hebrew words translated "work" or "labor." The word '*āmāl* means "labor," "toil," "trouble." It recognizes the fact that work can be unpleasant and frustrating, plunging human beings into a round of drudgery that never yields satisfaction or profit. This word is chosen by Solomon to describe the labor he engaged in in his search for life's meaning apart from God. Solomon reported, "My heart took delight in all my work, and this was the reward for all my labor. Yet when I surveyed all that my hands had done and what I had toiled to achieve, everything was meaningless, a chasing after the wind; nothing was gained under the sun" (Ecc 2:10–11).

Yāga' means "to toil" or "to labor" but emphasizes the exhaustion that hard work entails. There may be a product from toil, but there is a great price to pay. This is the word where the NIV says, "Do not wear yourself out to get rich; have the wisdom to show restraint" (Pr 23:4). God reassures his people in Isaiah's famous passage of comfort that although even youths faint and "grow weary," God does not tire. Always God is present to strengthen and to carry his own (Isa 40:28–31).

Two words indicate compulsory or forced labor. Neither *mas* nor *s^ebālāh* is likely to bring joy to one's heart. Not only is such labor forced by oppression, but the profit of it is gained by someone other than the worker (e.g., Ex 1:11).

There is also in the Hebrew vocabulary a recognition that work can bring great satisfaction and have real significance. The word '*ābad* means "to work" or "to serve." A derivative noun, '*bôdâh* ("labor," "service") is found about 150 times in the OT. The word has religious significance, for it is often used of service to God. ♦ *Serve/Servant/Slave* But it can also be used of forced service or of the bondage experienced by a captive. This work may well find its significance in the person for whom it is done and thus bring joy or frustration.

The verb '*āśāh* means to "to do, make, accomplish." Its derivative noun, *ma'^aśeh*, indicates what is done or made and is often used in the sense of "work." Thus, both the process and the product can be in view in the use of this word. This is a theologically significant term, for God's acts in history are often called his wonderful works. ♦ *Miracle/Sign/Wonder* The heavens are the "work of [God's] fingers" (Ps 8:3); the product proclaims the "work of his hands" (Ps 19:1). Release from Egypt came through God's great acts or works (Dt 11:3,7).

Ma'aśeh is applied to human labor in a number of senses. It is the work and toil itself (Ge 5:29; Ex 23:12) and the product and outcome of our labor (Dt 15:10; 16:15; 2 Ch 32:30).

Pā'al also means "work" or "do." One cognate, *pō'al*, means "work" or "recompense." The works of God's hands are explored with the latter word (Dt 32:4; Isa 5:12). The Lord will also act in response to human works, to reward (as Ru 2:12) and to punish (as Pr 24:12; Jer 25:14). This is because a person's moral character is displayed in his deeds (Pr 20:11). This aspect of work, as deeds that call for an appropriate return, is expressed also in another derived noun, *pe'ullâh.* ♦ *Reward*

2. The OT attitude toward work.
Human beings live in a world in which work has meaning. Sin has affected the universe to the extent that work has become a struggle with an unresponsive earth rather than the simple and creative joy intended in the original creation.

Work can be done voluntarily, as an offering to God, or involuntarily, as forced labor for others. Work can be productive and satisfying or fruitless and frustrating. Work can exhaust us with its drudgery or exalt us with a sense of accomplishment.

But whatever we may say about work as it is portrayed in the OT, we can never say that work is meaningless.

Work takes its meaning first of all from the example of God, who acted and by his action brought the universe into being. God continues to work, and his work has affected human history. His powerful and wonderful deeds provided Israel with her identity and her hope.

Human work is patterned on God's in several senses. Like the work performed by God, human work affects the worker and others. More than the satisfaction of physical needs is involved in work. The product of our labors can glorify God, or it can witness against us, just as the idols

shaped by God's rebellious people testified against them.

NT — 3. The Greek words.
A number of Greek words explore the different aspects of "work" seen in the OT. Among the most common are *ergazomai* and *ergon*. Words in this group speak of such things as labor, activity, achievement, and business. God is particularly at work in the deeds and actions of Jesus (e.g., Jn 4:34; 17:4). *Poieō* also means "to do" or "to make," and *poiēma* means "work" and can refer to what is made. Creation is the result of God's activity (Ac 4:24; Ro 1:20), as is salvation (Eph 2:10;14; Heb 7:27). *Prassō* and *praxis* represent another group of words having to do with acts and accomplishments. It is seldom found in the NT and never relates to a divine activity.

Another set of words focuses on work as labor or toil. *Kopos* emphasizes the wearying aspect of hard work and is often used in a general sense to represent everyday employment. *Kopos* is used in the phrase "labor of love" (1 Th 1:3), the kind of labor that faith in Christ motivated in the Thessalonians. Paul often uses it to describe his own ministry (e.g., Gal 4:11; Php 2:16; 1 Ti 4:10) It is also used of work, as of Paul's tentmaking, to earn a living (1 Co 4:12). It is the honest toil that former thieves are called on to undertake; such "must work, doing something useful with his own hands, that he may have something to share with those in need" (Eph 4:28).

Ergazomai is also used often in the sense of everyday labor or occupation (e.g., Mt 21:28; Jn 6:27; 1 Co 4:12; 9:6; 1 Th 2:9; 4:11; 2 Th 3:10,11,12).

A stronger word is *mochthos*, which moves beyond toil to hardship or extreme exertion. *Mochthos* appears only three times in the NT (2 Co 11:27; 1 Th 2:9; 2 Th 3:8).

4. The NT attitude toward work.
Paul's writings lift work to an even greater significance than was seen in the OT. The apostle himself did not accept support from those to whom he ministered, though that would have been an acceptable option (1 Co 9:7–15). Paul

worked so that all might see that his ministry was voluntary and that the gospel he preached was offered free of charge to all (9:15–18). Paul also worked to set an example in the churches. Idleness, or dependence on others, is not a godly trait for the able-bodied. Believers are to remain busy, to take responsibility for themselves, and not to be a burden on others (2 Th 3:6–15).

But work has even more positive aspects. It provides an honest way to do something useful (*agathos*, "good") and also produces "something to share with those in need" (Eph 4:28). The thought here may be first that work is service, enabling the individual to contribute to the well-being of others and the community. The second thought is clear; work produces income that enables the believer to share with "those in need." Thus, the value of work is not to be measured by the wealth it produces for us but by the opportunities it provides for ministry. ♦ *Giving*

It remains true that work may involve toil and drudgery. But as long as we retain the perspective of the NT, work will be satisfying. Work enables us to care for our own needs, to promote the general good of others in our community, and to share and so meet the needs of others whom God loves.

WORKS

Within the vocabulary of "work" emerges the concept of "works." ♦ *Work/Labor* This takes on special focus in the NT, where Paul and others explore the relationship of human efforts and accomplishments to faith in God. In the Judaism of Jesus' day, such works were called for by the law and were thought to establish a person as righteous, not only in his own and the community's eyes but also in the eyes of God. The NT, with its understanding of Jesus as the One through whom God offers a righteousness that is apart from law, reevaluates and clarifies the relationship of good works to one's relationship with God.

The NT's conclusion can be summed up in two statements: (1) salvation is not by one's own works, and (2) those who are God's must be careful to maintain good works. This balanced position is expressed clearly in Eph 2:8–10: "It is by grace you have been saved, through faith—and this not from yourselves, it is the gift of God—not by works, so that no one can boast. For we are God's workmanship, created in Christ Jesus to do good works, which God prepared in advance for us to do." The balance is maintained when we affirm both that no human effort or accomplishment can merit God's acceptance and that "those who have trusted in God" are to be "careful to devote themselves to doing what is good" (Tit 3:8). These two facets of grace and works are seen also in 2 Ti 2:19: "God's solid foundation stands firm, sealed with this inscription: 'The Lord knows those who are his,' and, 'Everyone who confesses the name of the Lord must turn away from wickedness.' "

Other articles discuss related issues, including human effort, the relationship between faith and works (especially what James teaches on it), and goodness. ♦ *Belief/Faith* ♦ *Good* ♦ *Law* ♦ *Righteous/Righteousness*

WORLD

"World" is another of the common English words that has distinctive meanings in NT Greek. The world we live in may very well not be the "world" we live in.

OT 1. The Hebrew words
NT 2. The Greek words
    3. The Christian's relationship to the "world"

OT — 1. The Hebrew words. The words most often translated "world" in English are *'eres,* which means "land" except in its broadest sense, and *tēḇēl.* ♦ *Land* *Tēḇēl* can mean the whole earth, the inhabited earth, or the inhabitants of the earth. It occurs without the theological overtones of the Greek *kosmos.*

NT — 2. The Greek words. Various Greek words are translated "world" in the NIV and the NASB. *Aiōn,* which means "age," is translated "world" in several verses. The word may simply mean "the world" or it may focus on characteristics by which a particular time is categorized. Of the over a hundred times that *aiōn* appears in the NT, the NIV translates it "world" eight times (Lk 16:8; Ro 12:2; 1 Co 1:20; Eph 2:2; 6:12; 1 Ti 6:17; 2 Ti 4:10; Heb 9:26).

Gē is the earth—that is, the ground, in contrast to water and sky. Of its approximately 250 occurrences in the NT, it is translated "world" only six times (Mk 9:3; Ac 17:24; Rev 3:10; 13:3; 16:14; 17:8).

Oikoumenē is found fifteen times in the NT, probably to be taken in a popular sense, as "inhabited earth," rather than in a political, imperial sense. *Oikoumenē* is translated "world" in all of its occurrences (Mt 24:14; Lk 2:1; 4:5; 21:26; Ac 17:6,31; 19:27; 24:5; Ro 10:18; Heb 1:6; 2:5; Rev 3:10; 12:9; 16:14).

The most significant word for "world" is *kosmos*. Its original and basic meaning is "order" or "arrangement." The OT has no word corresponding to this one, which is found nearly two hundred times in the NT. It has a very flexible meaning, indicating, for example, (1) the world (i.e., all created things), (2) the arena where human life and experience occur, or (3) humanity itself. As a theological term, *kosmos* portrays human society as a system warped by sin, tormented by beliefs and desires and emotions that surge blindly and uncontrollably. The world system is a dark system (Eph 6:12), operating on basic principles that are not of God (Col 2:20; 1 Jn 2:16). The entire system lies under the power of Satan (1 Jn 5:19) and constitutes the kingdom from which believers are delivered by Christ (Col 1:13–14). Its basic hostility to God is often displayed (1 Co 2:12; 3:19; 11:32; Eph 2:2 Jas 1:27; 4:4; 1 Jn 2:15–17; cf. Jn 12:31; 15:19; 16:33; 17:14; 1 Jn 3:1,13; 5:4–5,19).

3. The Christian's relationship to the "world". Christians live on planet Earth, scattered in every society. Thus, believers are, in each generation's space and time, members of their culture's own unique expression of the *kosmos*.

The Bible's teaching is that every human culture is warped and twisted by the impact of sin. The perceptions of each generation, the basic desires that move human beings, the injustices institutionalized in every society, testify to sin's warping power.

The Christian church is a gathering of believers called to display on earth a completely different set of values, not based on the cravings, the lusts, or the boastings of sinful humanity. Rather than being squeezed into the world's mold, we are to be "transformed by the renewing of [our minds]" (Ro 12:2). ◆ **Mind** Bluntly put, the believer is one who "does not live the rest of his earthly life for evil human desires, but rather for the will of God" (1 Pe 4:2).

If we remember that the world represents the systematic expression of human sin in human cultures, we understand why the believer is not to be of the world, though he is in it (Jn 17:14–18). We are members of our society, yet the values we display and the structures we create in church and home and occupation are to be distinctively Christian.

This understanding helps us sense the deadliness of worldliness. Worldliness is not a matter of engaging in those practices that some question. It is unthinkingly adopting the perspectives, values, and attitudes of our culture, without bringing them under the judgment of God's Word. It is carrying on our lives as if we did not know Jesus (see esp. Mt 16:26; Mk 8:36; Lk 9:25; 1 Cor 5:10; 7:31,33–34; 2 Cor 7:10; 1 Jn 2:15–16; 4:17).

WORRY ◆ *Anxiety/Worry*

WORSHIP

In the OT, "worship" is usually *šāḥâh* or *šāḥâh,* meaning "to bow down," or "to prostrate oneself out of respect." At times *'āṣab,* "to serve," is also translated "worship." ◆ *Serve/Servant/Slave*

Several words are translated "worship" in the NT. One is *latreuō,* which occurs twenty-one times in the NT. The Septuagint uses this verb to translate *'āṣab,* which in the OT is linked specifically with cultic aspects of worship (i.e., service in the tabernacle or temple). This sense is retained in Hebrews (8:5; 9:9; 10:2; 13:10), but Luke uses this word to indicate Christian worship as well (Ac 24:14). Thus, *latreuō* is a Christian's worshipful serving of God in heart and by life (Php 3:3; Ro 1:9).

Sebomai and other words in its group mean "to show reverence for." ♦ *Godly/Godliness* These words are rare in the NT but generally can be understood to mean "worship" as the showing of respect and reverence to a deity. The pagan world showed such reverence for creatures rather than the Creator (Ro 1:25). The Jewish people showed outward reverence for God, but in vain, because their hearts were distant from him (Mt 15:9; Mk 7:7). *Sebomai* is expressed "to worship" in a few other of its ten NT occurrences (Ac 16:14; 18:7,13; 19:27). The word "worshiped" in 2 Th 2:4 is *sebasma* (its only other NT occurrence being in Ac 17:23).

The most used NT word for "worship" is *proskyneō*, "to worship," "to bow down to." It occurs sixty times in the NT, twenty-four in Revelation. *Proskyneō* is used in the Septuagint for the Hebrew word *šāḥâh*. In the NT, *proskyneō* indicates worship that is directed or should be directed to God. Although worship is a matter of the heart and an expression of one's inner relationship with God, it may also be a public expression of a corporate relationship with God (Jn 12:20; Ac 8:27; 24:11). In Revelation, worship clearly has the sense of praise and adoration.

Another article discusses the subject of how to worship God. ♦ *Praise*

WORTHY

Axios and *kataxioō* express the idea of worthiness. In the Gospels, the original sense—of weight or value—predominates (as in Jesus' directive to his disciples to "search for some worthy person" [Mt 10:11]). Compared to the Messiah, who was about to appear, even the prophet John the Baptist viewed himself as of little weight (Mk 1:7).

In the Epistles, *axios* is often used in the sense of appropriateness. Christians are to live "worthy of the calling" (Eph 4:1; cf. Col 1:10) they have received in Christ, in harmony with his person and teaching. The phrase "worthy of respect" (1 Ti 3:8,11; Tit 2:2) is a translation of the word *semnos*. A believer is considered "worthy," not on the basis of talent or position, but by how well his or her actions display Christian character. ♦ *Respect* Our goal as Christians should be to "live lives worthy of God, who calls you into his kingdom and glory" (1 Th 2:12).

WRATH ♦ *Anger*

WRONG

Hebrew and Greek have a number of words that the NIV and the NASB translate as "wrong." ♦ *Sin* In the NT, the NIV renders *adikeō* as "wrong(ed)" in eight of its twenty-seven occurrences (Ac 25:10; 1 Co 6:7,8; 2 Co 7:2,12; Gal 4:12; Col 3:25; Rev 22:11) and *adikia* as "wrongdoing" in one of its twenty-five occurrences (1 Jn 5:17). *Adikōs*, "unjustly," is found only in 1 Pe 2:19, where the NIV renders it "unjust." ♦ *Justice/Injustice*

Kakos is an evil that damages or harms. It is translated "wrong(s)" in the NIV in Jn 18:23; Ac 23:9; Ro 13:3,4; 14:20; 1 Co 13:5; 2 Co 13:7; 1 Th 5:15. A compound, *kakopoios* ("evildoer") is found five times in the NT (Jn 18:30; 1 Pe 2:12,14; 3:16; 4:15), and "wrongly" in Jas 4:3 is *kakōs*.

The Greek word for "wrong" in Lk 23:41 is *atopos*, denoting something that is wrong because it is out of line or out of place. It is found only twice elsewhere (Ac 28:6; 2 Th 3:2).

Gal 2:11, which speaks of Peter's being "in the wrong," has *kataginōskō* (its other two NT occurrences being in 1 Jn 3:20,21). His conduct in refusing to eat with Gentile believers condemned him. *Hyperbainō* occurs only once in the NT (1 Th 4:6) and means "to sin by overstepping the limits." *Paranomia* indicates a specific breach of the law and occurs only in 2 Pe 2:16. In one other place where the NIV uses "wrong" (Heb 8:7), the idea is that the covenant of the law was not faultless, the Greek word being *amemptos* ("blameless," "faultless"). ♦ *Sin*

Y

YEAST ♦ *Leaven/Yeast*

YOKE

The yoke is a powerful symbol in the Bible. It refers to a cattle yoke, which bound animals to a plow, often together so they could work in tandem.

In the OT the yoke is often used figuratively of bondage and of the burden borne by slaves (Ex 6:6–7; cf. 1 Ti 6:1). The image is used powerfully by the prophets to portray the fate of disobedient generations (Isa 10:27; Jer 27:11; Eze 34:27).

This same image is used in unique ways in the NT. For example, Jesus' invitation attracts us: "Come to me, all you who are weary and burdened, and I will give you rest. Take my yoke upon you and learn from me, for I am gentle and humble in heart, and you will find rest for your souls. For my yoke is easy and my burden is light" (Mt 22:28–30). Is this a reference to the cattle yoke, a symbolic invitation to join Jesus and find in his strength release from our own unbearable burden? Or is this Jesus' call to people to become his slaves and find in their new master release from the crushing weight they experienced when law was their master? In either case, the theme and the invitation are central. Jesus calls, "Come," and he promises us rest for our souls.

The rabbis did not feel that being under the yoke of the law was burdensome. But with Christ came a fresh perspective. When some in the early church demanded that the Mosaic Law be imposed on Gentile converts, a council at Jerusalem refused to comply. Law had been a burden "that neither we nor our fathers have been able to bear," Peter told the council (Ac 15:10).

In Galatians, Paul develops his own distinctive grasp of the nature of law. ♦ *Law* Because of the weakness in human nature, law could neither justify a person nor provide power for a righteous life. All who try to live under law do by that choice turn their backs on the principle of grace, which alone brings "the righteousness for which we hope" (Gal 5:5). No wonder that law offers no one freedom but instead is a "yoke of slavery" (Gal 5:1).

The yoke of slavery is mentioned again in 1 Ti 6:1, but here it is the yoke of literal slavery to a human master. And here, as in some other passages, the NT supports the existing social order without making judgments as to its rightness. ♦ *Serve/Servant/Slave*

In 2 Co 6:14, Paul speaks of being "yoked together with unbelievers." In such a relationship there can be no agreement or harmony, and it is to be avoided. The verdict is prefigured in OT law, which forbids mating different kinds of animals (Lev 19:19) and even plowing with an ox and a donkey together (Dt 22:10). Paul called his colaborers in the gospel "true yokefellows" (Php 4:3), but it is inconceivable that any enterprise calling for total unity of heart and purpose can mix believers and unbelievers. The extent to which this principle is to be applied may be discovered by studying the issues Paul explores in his correspondence to the believers in Corinth, especially in discussing lawsuits and marriage (1 Co 6:1–6; 7:12–39).

YOUNG/YOUTH

Several Hebrew words are translated "young person" or "youth." *Bēn*, which means "son" or "grandson," is translated "young man" a few times. The more specific terms are *na'ar*, *bāḥûr*, and *bᵉhûrîm*, with their many cognates. *Na'ar* is a flexible term that can be used to refer to a child between the time of weaning and marriageable age. *Bāḥûr* seems to indicate a person of military age. Each of these terms expresses the idea of vigor. But "even youths grow tired and weary, and young men stumble and fall; but those who hope in the LORD will renew their strength" (Isa 40:30–31).

In the NT, "young" and "youth" are from the word *neos*. In the basic temporal sense, the new is freshly on the scene. ▶ *New and Old* The specific terms for younger person (*neotēs*, *neōteros*) are not linked with any specific age. Rather, they are essentially comparative. Thus, the word of Paul to Timothy in 1 Ti 4:12 simply indicates that he was considered young for the role he filled in the church. ▶ *Age/Ages*

Indexes

Index of
Hebrew Words

'āb 39
'āḇ 266,267
'āḇaḏ 483
'āḇâh 627
'āḇal 446
'āḏām 426,430
'āḏôn 313,416,438
'aḏōnāy 416,577
'āhēḇ 297,418,419
'āḥ 142
'aḥar 285
'aḥᵃrît 300
'ᵃḥuzzâh 622
'āḵal 188,225,241
'ālâh 207,460
'allay 631
'āman 114,115,259, 602
'āmar 173
'ap 46
'ārar 207,208
'ārôn 72
'āsar 125
'āṣar 601
'āšam 182,322
'āššāp 81
'aššāp 81
'āwâh 221
'āyab 247
'êḇâh 247
'eḇeḏ 549
'eḇen 581
'eḇyôn 488
'ēl 33,312,313
'ᵉlōhîm 312,313

'ᵉlôah 312,313
'elep 168
'ēmer 633
'ᵉmet 602
'ᵉmûnâh 259,260
'ᵉnôš 431
'ereṣ 240,241,388,638
'ēš 280
'eṯnan 615
'î 631
'imrâh 633
'îš 426,430,433
'išāh 433
'išeh 280
'iššâh 427
'iwwelet 286
'ôṣār 601
'ôt 444
'ôy 631
'ôyâh 631

'abad 636
'āḇaḏ 549
'āḇar 513
'ᵃḇôḏâh 550,636
'āḵar 231
'al 19
'ālal 18
'ālâh 77
'lmâh 613
'am 481
'āmaḏ 470
'āmāl 231,636
'ammî 481

'ānâh 26,346,488, 497,595
'ānaš 509
'ānî 488
'āpār 238
'ārab 30
'ᵃrāḇâh 221
'ārâh 453
'āraṣ 96
'ārîṣ 612
'ārôm 453
'aṣaḇ 639
'āṣam 526
'āṣaḇ 472
'aṣṣeḇet 473
'aśâh 154,179
'āśâh 18,636
'āšaq 489
'āṯar 497
'attîq 42
'ᵃṭārâh 204,205
'āwal 370
'āwōn 509,566,567, 568
'ayin 62,257
'āzaḇ 1,293
'ebrâh 46
'ēḏ 595
'ēḏâh 78,595
'ēḏûṯ 595
'ēmû 259
'ēqeḇ 531
'eṣâh 191,192
'eṣeḇ 472,473,474
'ēṯ 37,597
'ezrâh 30

'ēzer 433
'iṣṣāḇôn 473,474
'iwwēr 132
'ōlâh 465,468
'ōlām 28,37,42
'ōṣeḇ 472
'ōšeq 489
'ōšer 622
'ûḏ 148,594,619
'ûl 156
'ûr 96,453

ba'al 433
bā'ar 146
bāḏal 230,547
bāḡaḏ 124
bahan 593
bāhar 159
bāḥîr 159
bāḥûr 642
bāḵâh 625
bāḵar 281
bānâh 144
bāqaš 10
bar 510
bar mitzvah 158,196
bārā' 200,202
bāraḥ 282
bārak 130,131,132,207
bārar 510
bāśār 134,135,282, 283,431
bāṭaḥ 114
bayiṯ 263
bāzâh 223

INDEX OF HEBREW WORDS

bᵉʾîr 52
bᵉhēmâh 51,52
bᵉhûrîm 642
bᵉkôrâh 126
bēn 157,572,642
bᵉrîaḥ 104
bᵉrîṯ 29,194,195
bᵉṯûlâh 613
beṭen 135,138
bikkûr 282
bîn 188,226,605,629
bōhû 245
bôš 557,558
brākāh 130
brekāh 130

da'aṯ 589
dābar 173
dābār 18,191,230
dābar 633
dābār 441,633
dak 489
dal 488
dallâh 488
dām 132,567
dārak 399
dāraš 10,400
degel 99
dᵉmûṯ 350,351
derek 621
dîn 189,363,532
dôd 419
dôr 302
dûn 189

g'ullâh 516
gā'âh 75
gā'al (1) 169; (2) 516
gā'al 4
ga'ᵃwâh 75
gā'ôn 75
gābah 75
gādap 129
gādôl 622
gālâh 256,530
gālal 179
gāmal 531

gāraš 233
gē 75
gē'âh 75
gē'eh 75
gᵉ'ullâh 532
gepen 612
gēr 31
gib'âh 338
gîl 361
gôy 303,454
gôyim 303
gûr 96,272

hālak 285,615
hālal 134,424,495
har 338
hārag 448,449
hebel 141,608
hêkâl 586
hillûl 495
hôlēlâh 424
hôlēlûṯ 424
hôn 622
hôy 631

ḥābaš 125
ḥādaš 526
ḥag 275
ḥāgag 154,275
ḥākam 629
ḥālâh 561,562
ḥālāl 487
ḥᵃlôm 237
ḥāmās 612
ḥāmad 200,221
ḥāmal 179,180
ḥānak 214,601
ḥānan 271,317,439, 497
ḥānēp 315,487
ḥᵃnukâh 214
ḥāpār 347
ḥāpēṣ 215,486,627
ḥāpśî 293
ḥāpśîṯ 547
ḥārâh 46
ḥāram 225

ḥarap 522
ḥārap 355,544
ḥarôn 46
ḥārôn 276
ḥāsar 615
ḥāsēr 615
ḥāsîd 315
ḥāšab 188,596
ḥāṭam 545
ḥāṭa' 566,568
ḥaṭṭā' 567
ḥaṭṭā'ṯ 509,566
ḥay 203,406
ḥāyâh 406,526
ḥayil 4,5,622
ḥayyâh 51
ḥāzâh 613
ḥēbel 473
ḥēleq 531
ḥēmâh 46
ḥēn 271,317
ḥerpâh 230,522,544
ḥesed 195,375
ḥēṭᵉ' 566
ḥîl 473
ḥinnām 608
ḥōdeš 446
ḥokmâh 629
ḥᵒlî 561,562
ḥôq 501
ḥōsen 622
ḥôṭām 545
ḥōzeh 505,546

kā'ab 472
kā'as 46
kābas 620
kābôd 310,311,342, 622
kāhan 443
kāhaš 213
kālâh 181,188,246,279
kālam 342,355,557
kālîl 482
kāna' 346
kāpar 39,82,288,517
kappōreṯ 439

kᵉ'ēb 472
kēbeś 559
kehaš 213
kᵉlimmâh 229
kēn 341
kerem 612
kesep 445
kᵉsîl 286
keśeb 559
kilyâh 441
kippur 82,83
kōhēn 502
kōper 517
kôšārâh 622

lā'ag 544
lāḥam 616
lāḥaṣ 489
lāmad 588,591
lāṣôn 544
lāšôn 599
lāyil 459
lēb 283,334,441
lēbāb 441
lehem 140
leqaḥ 589

mā'as 518
ma'ᵃśeh 18,636,637
mabbûl 285
mahᵃlāl 495
mahᵃlâh 561
mahseh 113,114
mahsôr 615
mak'ôb 472,574
mal'āk 43,505
mālaṭ 523
mālē' 181,277,470
malᵉkû 377
malᵉkûṯ 377
mamlākâh 377
maqhēl 78
mar'eh 62
mārad 512
mārâh 127,512
mārar 127
marpē' 329

mas 636
māṣā' 279
maṣṣâh 140
maśśâ' 470
māśah 54
māšal 92,538
māšāl 147,508
māšîah 54
matmôn 622
matteh 601
mᵉ'râh 207
mᵉgôrâh 272
mᵉḥîr 615
melah 539
melek 376,377,401
mᵉnôrâh 388
mᵉšōl 147,509
mᵉšûbâh 98
midbār 221
milḥāmâh 616
mîn 52,375
minhâh 304
miqdāš 543
miqneh 51
miqweh 343
miṣwâh 174,175,176
miš'ālâh 221
miškan 586
mišmeret 239
mišpāḥâh 263
mišpāṭ 363,368,501,
    532,538
mišteh 100,275
mizbēah 34
mizmôr 495
mô'ēd 275,597
môledet 40
môpēt 444
mōṣ 155
môtār 622
mōṭ 556
mûsār 228,509
mût 406,448

nᵉ'um 470
nā' 497
nā'ap 21,22,23

nā'aṣ 129,223
na'ar 157,549,642
nā'ar 556
nābāl 286,544
nābî' 505,507
nādab 627
nādad 282
nādah 99
nāga' 600
nāgad 214
nāgaś 489
nāgaš 69
nāhag 399
nāhal 399
nāhâh 399
nāhal 353
naḥᵃlâh 353
nāham 173,441,522
nāhaš 232
nāhāš 572
nākâh 448
nākar 15
nāpal 260
nāqab 129
nāqâh 293
nāqam 509,610
nāqām 610
nāqî 169,293,354
nāsâh 593
nāṣal 216,523
nāśā' 288,289
nāśî 403
nāšā' 213
nātan 78,216,304
nātaš 2
nāzar 547
nᵉ'āṣâh 129
nᵉ'um 214
nᵉbālâh 230,286
nᵉbû'lâh 505
nᵉdābâh 297,308
nᵉhî 615
nēkār 288
nᵉkasîm 622
nepeš 203,283,406,
    407,441,575,576
nᵉqēbâh 427
nēs 99

nesek 468
neṣah 37
nēṣer 139
nēzer 204,205
niddâh 510
nō'am 109
nokrâh 288
nûa' 556
nûah 524
nûs 282

pā'al 637
pa'am 597
pādâh 516
pāga' 355,497
pāhad 96,272
pālā' 444
pālâh 230
pālal 355,497
pālaṭ 216
pālîṭ 521
pānîm 258,502
pāqad 30,509
pārad 547
pārâh 298
pārar 141
pāraṣ 612
pārōket 609
pāsah 478
pāša' 512,513
pātâh 213
pᵉ'ullâh 615,637
peh 174,191,447,633
pᵉlêyṭâh 521
pᵉri 298
peša' 566,567,568
pinnâh 151
piqqûdîm 501
piquddâh 509
pō'al 637

qābab 207
qādal 320
qādar 446
qādaš 214,339,340,
    508,542
qādēš 508

qāhâl 78
qālâh 342,555
qālal 207,208,223
qālôn 230,342
qānā' 358
qārā' 148,149
qārab 69
qāsam 232
qāṣâh 246
qaṣap 46
qāšar 125
qāšeh 584
qātar 146
qaw 471
qāwâh 343
qeber 336
qedem 42
qedem 457
qᵉdēšâh 508
qᵉhillâh 78
qᵉlālâh 207
qeren 345
qesem 232
qeṣep 46
qinyān 622
qōdeš 543
qôl 613
qûṣ 96

rā'âh 604
ra' 226,231,251,252,
    253,566
rā'a' 231,251
rā'ab 265
rā'âh 62,188,251,456,
    559,625
rāš 556
rābab 320
rābâh 320
rādâh 538
rādam 571
rāham 179,180,419,
    439
rāhaṣ 620
rahṣâh 620
rāmâh 124,212
rānan 361
rāpā' 329,561,562

rāqaz 556
rāṣaḥ 448,449,450
rāṣâh 8,215,486,627
rāṣaṣ 489
rāṣôn 8,221,271,486, 627
rāšā' 182,251,625
rāz 451
rāzî 631
rē'šît 110,111
rēa' 297,456
rᵉpu'âh 329
reša' 251
rêqām 245
rîḇ 14,230,188
ripûṭ 329
rîq 608
rō'eh 505,546
rᵛ'î 62
rō'š 327
rō'eh 559
rōa' 251
rûaḥ 441,576,578
rûq 245
rûš 488

sālaḥ 289
sālal 546
sāmar 620
sammâh 223
sāpaḏ 446,615
sārar 512,513,584
sᵉḇālâh 636
sela' 537
selâh 546
sēper 138

ṣāḇā 33,346,616
ṣāḏaq 17,368,371,372, 533
ṣaddîq 533
ṣāḥaq 389
ṣālaḥ 585
ṣapâh 620
ṣār 232,247
ṣāra'at 405
ṣārâh 231

ṣārap 593
ṣārar 231,232,247
ṣaw 471
ṣāwâh 174,470
ṣᵉḇā'ôṭ 346,616
ṣᵉḇî 108,109
ṣᵉḏāqâh 533
ṣedeq 533
ṣelem 350,351
ṣemaḥ 139
ṣî 203
ṣō'n 559
ṣôm 265
ṣōneh 51
ṣᵒrî 99
ṣûm 265
ṣûr 537

śāḇēa' 277
śāḥaq 544
śākal 589,604
śākar 550
śākār 531,615
śāmah 361
śānē' 325
śar 403
śārap 146
śārîḏ 521
śāṭâh 81
śāṭān 14,543
śeh 559
śekel 604,629
śeker 531
śîm 188
śimḥâh 485
śoba' 277
śûś 361

š'ôl 335,336,337
ša'al 400,497
ša'ar 521
šā'a' 216
ša'ᵃsu'îm 216
šāḇa' 460
šāḇaḥ 495
šāḇaṭ 524
šadday 33

šāga' 424
šāgag 81
šāgâh 81
šāhâh 139,639,640
šāḥaḥ 347,639
šāḥaṭ 190
šāḥaṭ 448
šākaḇ 555,571
šākan 239
šākar 238
šākēn 456
šālaḥ 233,293
šālam 526,531
šālôm 479,480,481, 565
šām'a 331,332,333, 461,497,604
šāmar 125,239
šāmayim 335
šāmēm 61,222
šānē' 247
šāpaṭ 363,368,401,538
šāpēl 347
šāqâh 237
šāqar 212
šāraq 544
šāraṭ 443,549
šārēt 550
šāṭâh 237
šāw' 213
šāwᵛ' 608
šᵉ'ār 521
šᵉ'ēr 282
šᵉ'ērîṭ 521
šēḇeṭ 601
šᵉḇû'âh 460
šēḏ 217
šēḏu 217
šēkār 110,238
šelem 275,480
šēm 453
šemen 469
šᵉmû'âh 441
šēnā' 571
šēnâh 571
šᵉnāṭ 571
šᵉnînâh 147
šeper 108

šāqaṭ 524
šeqel 560
šeqer 212
šiqqûṣ 6
šôḇāḇ 98
šôḇēḇ 98
šôpār 345
šúḇ 522,526
šûṭ 544

ta'ᵃlâh 460
tā'aḇ 4
tā'âh 81,213
taḇnîṭ 478
taḥᵃlu'îm 561
tām 128,482
tāmam 128,279
tāmîḏ 37
tāmîm 128,215,482
tarbîṭ 370
tardēmâh 571
taznûṭ 508
tēḇēl 638
tᵉḇûnâh 605
tᵉhillâh 495
tᵉhillâh 111
tᵉhôm 214
tᵉpillâh 439,497
tᵉšû'âh 611
tᵉšûqâh 24,434
tip'arâh 310
tiqwâh 343
tîrôš 628
tô'ēḇâh 6
tôḏâh 495,595
tōhû 245
tôlḏôṭ 302
tôrâh 389,390,392, 398,588,589
tûšîyâh 629

ṭāhēr 169
ṭāmē' 169,170
ṭap 156
ṭôḇ 108,109,124,252, 315,316,485

yā'al 627
yā'aṣ 191,192
yād 92
yāda' 16,188,382,383,
555,571,588,604
yādâh 495,595
yāga' 636
yāgôn 574
yâh 416
yāhab 78
yâhweh 416,417,577
yāhal 343,344
yākâh 71
yākah 512
yâkōl 5
yālad 40,138,266
yālal 615
yānag 156

yāpeh 108
yārâh 588
yāraš 338,353
yārē' 96,272,523
yāšab 239
yāsad 292
yāsar 228,589
yāša' 540
yāša' 216,611
yāšar 509,607
yāšēn 571
yâtar 521
yātôm 271
yâtab 124
yayin 628
yeled 156
yeqār 310
yešîmôn 221

yeter 521
yišhār 469
yitrâh 622
yitrôn 622
yôm 37,210,597,598
yōšer 607

zābah 34
zādôn 75
zāhar 619
zak 510
zāk 510
zākâh 510
zākak 169,510
zākar 519
zākār 426,427
zākēn 457

zāmar 495
zānâh 21,22,23,508
zānah 518
zāqēn 243
zār 31
zēd 75
zemān 597
zera' 469
zerôa' 73
zîd 75
zikkārôn 520
zûd 75

Index of
Greek Words

abba 4,267
abyssos 7
achyron 155
adelphos 143,144
adikēma 204
adikeō 567,640
adikia 567,626,640
adikos 568,626,640
adokimos 239,259,518, 594
adynateō 352
adynatos 352
aer 30
agapaō 420
agapē 212,297,298, 420,422
agapētos 298
agalliaō 362
agathos 109,316, 375, 638
agnoēma 350
agnoeō 350,605,606
agnoia 350
agnōsia 350
agōnizomai 242
agorazō 518
agrypneō 620
aichmalōtizō 152
aineō 496
ainesis 496
ainos 496
aiōn 27,28,638,639
aiōnas 28
aiōnios 250
aiōnōn 250
aischynē 558

aischynō 557,558
aisthēsis 383
aitēma 499,500
aitia 204,323
aitima 323
aition 323
akakos 355
akatharos 170
akeraios 354
akouō 332,462,606
akoloutheō 285,286
akrasia 546
akratēs 546
akrogōniaios 151
akyroō 459
alazōn 134
alazoneia 134
aleiphō 55
alētheia 602,603
alēthinos 570,602
alisgēma 487
allassō 514
allotrios 288
alypoteros 57
amemptos 127,640
amnos 388
amōmos 128
amōmētos 128
ampelōn 612
ampelos 612
anabainō 77
anaireō 450
anaitios 354
anakrinō 364,365,366
anamimnēskō 520

anankaios 456
anankazō 181,456
anangelei 163
anankē 456
anapauō 525
anapologētos 256
anastasis 527
anastrophē 113
anathema 208
anathematizō 126,461
anatrepō 224
anechomai 107
anenklētos 128
anepilēmptos 128,523
anēr 428,435
anesis 525
angelos 45
anistēmi 527
anoētos 287
anomia 399,626
anomos 399,626
anomōs 399
anorthoō 526
antapodosis 531
anthistēmi 470
anthropos 428,431
antichristos 56
antilegō 470
antitassō 470
anypokritēs 570
apagō 81
apallotrioō 32
apangellō 504
aparneomai 219
apataō 213

apatē 193,213
apechomai 7
apeileō 619
apeithei 462
apeitheō 462
apeithēs 462
aphanismos 225
aphanizō 224,483
aphelotēs 570
aphesis 290
aphiēmi 289
aphilargyros 446
aphistēmi 3
aphorizō 547,548
aphrōn 287
aphtharsia 352
aphthartos 352
apistia 604
aplotēs 570
apochrēsis 483
apodeiknumi 508
apodeixis 219
apodektos 9
apodokimazō 145,518
apokalypsis 67,530, 531
apokalyptō 530,531
apokatalassō 514
apokatastasis 527
apokathistanō 527
apokathistēmi 527
apokteinō 450,451
apollymi 224,483
apolouō 620
apostellō 59

apostolos 58
apōtheō 518,519
apothnēskō 408
aproskopos 128
archaios 42,43,457
archē 111,112,538
archēgos 86
archōn 538
arēn 388
areskō 486
arestos 486
argyrion 445
arkeō 189
arneomai 219
arnion 388
arrabōn 220,322
arsēn 428
asebeia 315
asebēs 315,626
aselgeia 212,546
asōtia 212
astheneia 563,621
asynetos 605
atheteō 518,519
athōos 354
atimaō 342
atimazō 355
atimia 557,558
atopos 640
authadēs 76
authenteō 95
auxanō 321
auxō 321
axioō 596
axios 640

baptizō 101
baptō 100,101
baros 107
basanismos 29
basanos 475,600
basileia 378
bastazō 107
bdelygma 6
bdelyktos 6
bdelyssomai 6
bebaioō 332

bebaios 184,322
bebaiōsis 322
bebēlos 315
bēma 368
bia 612
biaios 612
biazō 612
biblos 137
bioō 410
bios 410,623
biōsis 410
biōtikos 410
blasphēmeō 129,355
blasphēmia 129,430
blasphēmos 129
blepō 125,620
boulē 511,627
bouleuō 192
boulomai 627

chairō 362
chalepos 612
chalkos 446
charaktēr 351
charis 317,318
charisma 305,306,307
charizomai 289,317
cheirotoneō 68
chōreō 8
chōris 548
chōrizō 547,548
chrēma 623
chrēmatizō 619
chrēsimos 609
chrēstos 375,376
chrēstotēs 375,376
chriō 54
chrisma 55
christianos 163
christos 162
chronos 597,598

daimonion 217
dechomai 7,9,513
deēsis 499
dei 455
deilos 273

deipnon 100
deisidaimonesteros 519
deisidaimonia 519
dektos 9
deleazō 61
dēnarion 446
deō 125,126
deomai 499
deos 96
desmos 137
despotēs 438
dia 117
diabolos 430,543
diadēma 204
diakoneō 20,443,551,
  552,554
diakonia 443,552
diakonos 443,552,554
diakrinō 236
dialassō 514
dialogismos 71,596
dialogizomai 71,512,
  596
diamartyromai 619
diamonizomai 494
dianoēma 596
dianoia 442,596,605
diapragmatyomai 147
didaskaleia 235
diasōzō 330
diastellō 619
diathēkē 195
didōmi 304
diermēneuō 356
didaktos 592
didaskō 590
dikaioō 354,373,534
dikaios 354,355,371,
  534
dikaiosynē 534
dikē 509,510,611
dilogos 570
diōkō 243,483
dipsychos 236
distazō 236
dokeō 383,596
dokimazō 70,259,508,
  594,596

dokimē 155,594
dokimos 70,594
dilioō 213
doloō 213
dolos 213
dōran 305
dōrea 304
dōrean 304,305
dōron 304
doulē 551
douleia 551
douleuō 551,553
douloi 554,585
douloō 552
doulos 443,551,552,
  553,554
doxa 331
doxazō 496
drakōn 237
dynamai 5
dynamis 5,444,483
dysnoētos 606

echthra 248,249
echthros 248
egeirō 64,527
egersis 527
eikē 608
eikōn 351,352
eilikrineia 570
eirēnē 480
eis 117
ek 105
ekakouloutheō 286
ekaleiphō 151
ekapataō 210
ekdikeō 509
ekdikēsis 509,510,611
ekdikos 510
ekkaiomai 146
ekkleiō 32
ekklēsia 79,164,165,
  166,167
eklanthanomai 288
eklegomai 160,161
eklektos 160
eklogē 160

ekpeirazō 594
ekpiptō 32,259,261, 262
ekplessō 38
ekzēteō 546
elaion 55
eleeō 439
elegmos 190
elenchō 190
eleos 179,180,439
eleutheria 294
eleutheroō 294
eleutheros 294
elpis 344
elpizō 344
embrimaomai 619
emphanizō 63
empimplēmi 277
empiptō 261
emporeuomai 147
emporia 147
en 117
enantios 470
endeiknymi 219
endeixis 219
engyos 322
enkaleō 15
enkataleipō 3
enkauchaomai 134
enkrateia 546
enkratēs 546
ennoia 86,596
enochleō 232
enochos 323
enoikeō 239
entellomai 176
enteuxis 499
enthymeomai 188
entolē 176,177,178
entrepō 523,557,558
entropē 558
entynchanō 61,355, 499
enybrizō 355
epaineō 496
epainos 496
epaischynomai 558
epangelia 504

epangelma 504
epangelomai 504
epanorthōsis 190
epechō 620
epi 105
epibareō 146
epiblepō 86
epieikēs 303
epieikia 303
epigeios 241
epignōsis 606
epiginōskō 605,606
epikaleomai 61
epilanthanomai 288
epinoia 596
ēpios 375
epiphainō 63,530
epiphaneia 64,66,67, 530
episkopos 244,471
epistamai 606
epistatēs 438
epistēmōn 606
epitassō 176
epithymeō 200,222, 415
epithymia 222,423,477
epitimaō 619
epitimia 509
ergasia 147
ergazomai 19,637
ergon 19,113,445,637
eritheia 38,259
eros 420
erōtaō 499
esthiō 242
ethnos 303,454
ēttaomai 471
euangelion 316
euangelistēs 251
euangelizō 316,501
euaresteō 486
euarestos 9,486
euarestōs 486
eucharisteō 595
eucharistia 595
eucharistos 595
euchē 499

euchomai 499
eudokeia 486
eudokeō 486,596
eudokia 222
eugenēs 459
eulogeō 496
eulogētos 496
eulogia 131,496
euōdia 75
euphrainō 362
euprosdektos 9
eusebeia 315
eusebēs 315
eusebia 519
eusebōs 315
euthymeō 193
euthymos 246
exagorazō 517,518
exaireō 523
exaleiphō 150
exanastasis 527
exanistēmi 527
exapataō 213
exapostellō 59
exesti 399
existēmi 38
exomologeomai 496
exousia 87,92,93,94, 95,532,583
exouthenēmenous 13
exoutheneō 223

gameō 435
gamiskō 435
gamizō 430
gamos 100,275,435
gē 240,639
geenna 337
genea 302
gennaō 138
genos 469
ginomai 280,508
ginōskō 383,605,606
glōssa 599
gnēsios 570,603
gnōmē 596
gnōsis 383

gramma 405
graphē 544,545
grēgoreō 31,620
gymnazō 601
gymnos 453
gynē 428,435,632

hades 337
hagiasmos 542
hagiazō 542
hagion 543
hagios 340
hagnos 354,510
haima 133
haireomai 160
halas 539
hamartia 568
haplotēs 570
haptō 600
hēdonē 486
hēgeomai 188,596,606
hēmera 211
henotēs 606
heortazō 275
heortē 275
hēsychia 632,633
hetairos 143
heuriskō 279
hieros 340
hilaros 156
hilaskomai 83
hilasmos 83
hilastērion 83
histēmi 250
homoioō 351
homoios 352
homoiōsis 351
homologeō 17,183,220, 447
homothymadon 606
hoplon 74
hōra 346
hōraios 109
horaō 620
horkomōsia 461
horkos 461
hormēma 613

hosios 340
hosiotēs 340
huioi 574
huios 572
huiothesia 20,574
hybris 76,355
hybristēs 355,612
hybrizō 355
hygiaino 563
hygiēs 563,565
hymneō 496
hymnos 496
hypakouō 462
hypeikō 584
hyper 475
hyperbainō 640
hyperentynchanō 356
hyperēphania 76
hyperēphanos 76
hypēreteō 552
hypēretēs 552
hyperphroneō 597
hypnos 571
hypodeigma 256
hypodeiknymi 619
hypodikos 12,323
hypokrinomai
hypokrisis 348
hypokritēs 348
hypomenō 484
hypomimnēskō 86,520
hyponoeō 597
hypostasis 80
hypotagē 584
hypotassō 137,584,585
hypotypōsis 478
hypsēlphroneō 76

iama 330
iaomai 330
iasis 303
idiōtēs 601,606
ischyō 5,563
ischys 563,583
isos 249
isotēs 249

kainos 458
kairos 597,598
kakia 232,254,626
kakoētheia 430
kakoō 254,483
kakopatheō 475
kakopoieō 254
kakopoios 254,640
kakos 204,251,253,
  254,255,626
kaleō 149
kalos 109,124,316
kalymma 609
kanōn 538
kardia 334
kata 105
katabolē 201,293
katabrabeuō 230
katadikazō 182
kataginōskō 182,640
kataischynō 558
katakaiō 146
kataklysmos 285
katakrinō 182,364
katalambanō 606
katalassō 514
kataleipō 3
katallagē 514
katalyō 224
katalysai 6
katanarkeō 146
katangellō 504
katanoeō 188,442,597
katapausis 526
katapetasma 609
kataphroneō 223
katapinō 225
katapiptō 261
katara 208
kataraomai 208
katargeō 32,224,225,
  459
katargēsas 6
katartizō 526,601
kataskeuazō 144
katastrēniaō 546
katazioō 640
katēcheō 591

katēgoreō 14,15
katēgoria 14
katesthiō 225
katexousiazō 93
katharismos 510
katharizō 171
katharos 171,354
katheudō 571
katoikeō 239
kauchaomai 134
kauchēma 76,134
kauchēsis 76,134
keimai 501
keleuō 176
kenodoxia 609
kenos 246,609
kephalē 327
kephalēn gōnias 151
kēryssō 501,504
kitēnos 51
klados 140
klaiō 625
klēma 139
klēronomos 338
klēsis 149
klētos 148
kodrantēs 446
koimaomai 571
koinōneō 309,558
koinōnia 276,309,476
koinōnikos 558
kionōnos 558
kolasis 509,510
kolazō 509
kōlyō 470
kopos 232,637
koptō 446
kosmos 241,638,639
kratos 34,583
kreissōn 124,125
krima 182,364
krinō 182,364
krisis 15,364
kritēs 364
ktēnos 51
ktizō 201,202
kybernēsis 20

kyrios 416,417,418,
  438
kyriotēs 538

lambanō 7,513,514
lampas 388
laos 481
latreia 552
latreuō 551,552,639,
  640
leitourgeō 551,552
leitourgia 443,552
leitourgikos 443,552
leitourgos 443,552
lepton 446
lepra 405
logismos 596
logizomai 188,203,
  512,596
logomacheō 72
logomachia 72
logos 441,634,635,636
loidoreō 355
loidoros 355
louō 620
lychnia 388
lychnos 388
lyō 224
lypē 475,574
lypeō 446,574
lytron 517
lytroō 517
lytrōsis 517
lytrōtēs 517

machē 618
mageia 425
mageuō 425
magos 425
makairos 131,132
makrothymeō 478
makrothymia 478
malakia 563
mamōnas 623
manthanō 226,591
martyreō 595,619
masaomai 29

mastigoō 510
matēn 608
mathētēs 226,227,591
megalynō 496
megas 320,612
melei 181
melos 439
merimna 57,182
merimnaō 57
merizō 79
metanoeō 522
metanoia 522
meteōrizomai 57
methodeia 544
metochos 558
miainō 215,487
mimeomai 286,352
mimētēs 352
mimnēskō 520
miseō 325
misthos 531
mnēmoneuō 520
mochthos 637
moicheia 23,24,25
molynō 215
mōria 287
mōros 287
mystērion 452

nekros 408
neos 458,642
neōteros 458,642
neotēs 642
nēpios 156,157
nikaō 471,611
nikē 611
nikos 611
niptō 620
noēma 442,544,597
noeō 188,442,605
nomizō 596
nomos 392,394,395,
    398
noseō 563
nosos 563
nous 350,442
nouthesia 20,619

noutheteō 20,591,619
nyx 459

ōdin 475
ōdinō 475
oida 383,605
oikeios 263
oiketēs 552,553
oikodomē 145
oikodomei 188
oikodomeō 145
oikonomia 20
oikonomos 20
oikos 263
oikoumenē 639
oiktirmos 179,180
oinos 628
oiomai 597
olethras 224
omnyō 461
oneidismos 355
oneidizō 355
onoma 453
ōpheleia 609
ōpheleō 609
opheilē 456
opheilēma 456
opheiletēs 455
opheilō 455,456
ōphelimos 609
ophthalmos 257
optomai 64
orexis 423
orgē 49
orgilos 49
orgizomai 49
orkos 195
osmē 75,340
ouai 631
ouranos 336

paideia 228,601
paideuō 190,228,509,
    591
paidion 157
pais 156,157,158,522,
    554

palaioō 458
palaios 457,458
palaiotēs 458
pan 34
panoplia 74
pantokratōr 34
pantote 37
paradidōmai 124,216
parakaleō 61,173,246
parakatathēkē 220
paraklēsis 61,173,246
paraklētos 192
paralambanō 514
paramytheomai 246
parangellō 591
paranomia 640
parapiptō 261
paratithēmi 179
parepidēmos 31
parerchomai 225
paristēmi 508
paroikeō 31
paroikia 31
paroikos 31
parousia 65,66
paroxynomai 232
parrēsia 70,80,137,
    184,193
parthenos 613
pas 326
paschō 475
patēr 4,41,267,268,
    270
pathēma 475,477
pathos 423, 477
patria 263
peirasmos 593,594
peirazō 593,594
peitharcheō 462
peithō 184,462,484
pempō 59
penēs 492
penichros 492
pentheō 447
periergazomai 147
periergos 147,426
peripateō 615
peripiptō 261

perisseō 124
perisseuō 6
petra 537
petros 537
phainō 63,597
phaneroō 63
phanerōsis 530
pheugō 282
philadelphia 420
philargyria 446
philargyros 445
philēdonos 486
phileō 420
philia 420
philos 297,420
philotimeomai 38
phobeomai 273
phobos 96,273,523
phoneuō 450,451
phonos 450
phortion 107
phragmos 104
phronein 606
phroneō 86,441,597
phronēma 441
phronēsis 355,441,606
phronimos 441
phronimōs 441
phthanō 85
phtheirō 190,224
phthoneō 249
phthonos 249
phylakē 620
phylē 602
phyrama 105
physikos 454
physioō 76
physiōsis 75
physis 454,455
pikrainō 127
pikria 126
pikros 127
pimplēmi 277
piptō 261
pisteuō 117
pistis 115,117,122,604
pistos 260

pithanologia 71
planaō 81,213
planē 213,250
planos 213
pleion 124
plēktēs 612
pleonazō 321
pleonektēs 199
pleonexia 423
plērēs 277,278
plērōma 277,278,279
plēroō 181,277,278
plērophoreō 80,277, 484
plērophoria 80,277
plēsion 456
plēsmonē 546
plēthō 278
plēthos 79
plēthynō 321
ploutos 622
pneuma 576,577,578
pneumatikos 577
poiēma 637
poieō 19,179,637
poimainō 560
poimen 471
poimēn 560
polemeō 618
polemos 618
polis 162,293
polys 320,612
ponēria 254,626
ponēros 251,253,254, 255,626
ponos 475
porneia 23,24,25
pornos 23
pragmateuomai 147
praos 303
praotēs 303
prassō 637
praus 303,304,439
prautēs 303,439
praxis 637
prepō 456
presbyteros 43,244,471
probaton 560

proechomai 123
prokaleō 148
prologeō 619
promerimnaō 57
proorizō 501,502
prophasis 256
prophēteia 507
prophētēs 507
prophētis 507
prosagōgē 10
prosechō 125
proserchomai 79
proseuchē 499
proseuchomai 499
proskoptō 261
proskyneō 139,640
proslambanō 7
prosōpon 64
protassō 176
prothesis 511
prōtos 281
prōtotokos 282
psallō 496
psēlaphaō 600
pseudochristos 56
pseudomai 214
pseudos 193
psychē 410,411,576, 577
psychikos 454,576,577
ptōcheia 492
ptōcheuō 492
ptōchos 495
ptōma 134
pyroō 477
pyroomai 146

rhēma 441,634
rhyomai 217,523

sarkikos 283,284
sarkinos 283,284
sarx 282,283,284,431
satanas 543
sbennumi 511
schēma 65
sebomai 640

sēmeion 444
semnos 459,523,640
sigaō 632
skandalizō 260,464
skandalon 464
skopeō 620
sōma 135
somatos 65
sophia 629,630
sōtēr 541
sotēria 541
sotērios 541
sōzō 217,330,540,541
spatalaō 487
sperma 469
sphodrōs 612
sphragizō 70,545
spiloō 487
splanchna 25
splanchnizomai 25, 179,180,181
spoudazō 243
spoudē 243
stauron 204
stauros 204
stephanos 204
stērizō 250
stoma 447
strateuō 618
strēnos 546
sylagōgeō 152
symballō 470
symbouleuō 192
symboulion 190
symmorphoomai 185
symmorphos 185
symparakaleomai 246
sympaschō 475
sympherō 124
symphōneō 29
symphōnēsis 29
symphōnos 29
synagōgē 164,585
synapagō 81
synanamignymi 80
synchraomai 79
syndesmos 137
synechō 181

synēdomai 216
synedrion 190,191
syneidēsis 185
synelaunō 514
synesis 355,605
syneudokeō 70
syniēmi 605
synistēmi 219,508
synkatathesis 29
synthēkē 195
syschēmatizō 185
syzēteō 71

tapeinos 347
tarassō 232
tartaroō 337
tassō 256
taxis 470
tekmērion 484
tekna 574
teknion 156,157,158, 159
teknon 156,157,158, 159
teleios 438,482
teleiotēs 438
teleioō 482
teleō 181,247,280
telōnēs 587
telōnion 587
telos 247
teleotēs 482
teras 445
tēreō 620
thambeō 38
thanatoō 408
thanatos 408
tharreō 137
tharseō 193
thaumazō 37
thelō 222,486,616,627
thēlys 428
themelioō 250
themelios 293
theōreō 597
theotēs 454
thēsauros 601,623

therapeia 330

therapeuō 330

thērion 51,203

theos 314

thinganō 600

thlibō 483

thlipsis 26,231,483, 594

thnētos 50

thrēskeia 552

thrēskia 519

threskos 519

thymos 50

thysiastērion 36

timaō 342

timēn 459

timōria 509

tithēmi 79,179,501

tolmaō 137,193

tolmētēs 137

tropos 155

typhlos 132

typos 256,478

xenos 31

xylon 204

zēloō 222,358,359

zēteō 545

zētēsis 71

zōē 410,411

zōgreō 152

zōon 203

zophos 414

zymē 404

Index of Subjects

(chief references in **bold figures**)

Abandonment   1–4,288,518–19
Abba   4
Ability   4–6,18,114
Abomination   6
Abortion   429
Abounding   6
Abraham   159
  and faith   114,115,120
  family of   264
Abstinence   7,547
Abundance   7
Abuse   355
Abyss   7. See also Hell
Acceptance   7,8–9,143,221,440,638
Access   10,270
Accountability   **10–13**,18,162,322,334,385,
  432
  age of   27
  of the church   367
  day of   12
  of families   626
  to God   10,12,87,160
  of human government   90
  individual   12,252,266,275,366,386,489,491
  and the law   12
  of leaders   403,620
  legal   323
  for others   10,11,12,81,87,88,144,153,231
  of parents   474
  social   489–90
  of society   11,96,448,449,581–82
Accursed   13. See also Curse
Accusation   13–15,323
Acknowledgment   **15–17**,20,383
  of God   16,17,20,236,454,495
  of guilt   16,98
  of Jesus   16,17,20,220,447
  of sin   101,567
  of truth   17
Acquittal   17,293,323,354,371,373
Actions   17–19,121,374
  and attitude   86
  and faith   114,115
Adam   148,408,410
Adam and Eve   87,111,112,202,257,260,272,
  274,331,407,448,465,474,556,636
Administration   19–20

Admission   20
Adoption   **20–21**,268,502,518,574
Adult   26,157,159
Adultery   **21–25**,175,233–35,415,435,508,
  555
Advent, Second. See Second Coming
Adversary   25,543. See also Enemies
Advice   191–93
Advocate   14
Affection   25
Affliction   26,440
Age   **27–29**,56,578. See also World
Age (old age)   **26–27**,56,578,641. See also
  World
Agony   4,29
Agreement   29
Air   30
Alarm   31
Alcohol   100,110,237–38,628
Alert   31
Aliens   **31–32**,142,168,288,314,419
Alive. See Life
Alliance   33
Almighty   33–34
Alms   110
Altar   34–36,502
Always   36–37
Amazement   37–38
Ambassador   515
Ambition. See Desires, Motivation
Amen   38–39
Ancestors   39–41,327. See also Father
Anchor   41
Ancients   43
Angels   15,34,**43–46**,44,62,90,125,219,237,
  281,313,335,346,356,360,414,417,505,543–
  44,564,576
Anger
  of God   7,46,**48–51**,84,85,88,98,161,183,
    206,211,358,364,409
  of humans   7,46–51,71,84,85,98,127,161,
    206,208,211,232,286,358,364,409,419,464
Anguish   51
Animals   **51–53**,148,
  clean and unclean   169,171,242
  and human beings   351
  and sacrifice   130,215

and sex   555
Animal sacrifice   83
Annihilationism. *See* Immortality
Anointing   **54–55**,162,470
Anselm of Canterbury   84
Antichrist   6,**56–57**,66,531
Antichrists   220
Anxiety   **57–58**,182,232,270,286,524,624
Apocalyptic writing   56
Apostasy   97,98,152,521
Apostles   330,595,632
Apostleship   59–60
Appeal   61
Appearance   61–65. *See also* Image
Appetite   68
Appointing   68,244
Apprenticeship   490
Approaching
    God   10,35,77,171,440,465,504
    Others   68–70
Approval   70–71,155,558
Argument   71–72
Ark   72–73,83
Arm   73
Armageddon   73,74
Armies   346
Armor   74
Aroma   74–75
Arrogance   75–77,137,470,546. *See also*
    Pride
Ascension   59,77–78,173
Asceticism   105,107
Ashamed. *See* Shame
Asleep. *See* Sleep
Assembly   78–79,164. *See also* Community
Association   79–80,587
Assurance   80–81,113
Astonishment   80,81
Astray   81
Astrology   81–82,425
Athletics   107,173,230,242
Atonement   35,39,73,**82–84**,120,132,133,
    170,172,175,199,219,274,288,289,290,319,
    329–30,338,371,407,421,439,468,476,536,
    573,609
Attention   85–86
Attitude   **86**,544,584,595,623,633. *See also*
    Heart
Attributes of God   123,460,494,496
Authentication   545
Author   86–87
Authorities   87–91,250
Authority   68,87,90,91–96,111,157,174,175,
    205,267,270,321,347,363,401,402,435,447,
    470,532,538,545
    of Jesus   90,91,92,220,417,418,445,568,
        591,635
    and leaders   93,259
    spiritual   146
    and women   633
Avenging. *See* Vengeance

Avenger of Blood   96
Award. *See* Rewards
Awe   96,273,274,275,280

Baal   97
Babylon   88,89,90,**97**,170,617
Backsliding   97–98
Bad. *See* Evil
Balaam   98–99
Balm   99
Banishment   99
Banner   99
Banquet   100
Baptism
    and fire   281
    of the Holy Spirit   102–3,579
    of Jesus   30
    water   **100–102,103–4**,173,324,454
Bar (crossbar)   104
Barrenness   104
Barrier   104–5
Basis   105
Batch   105–6
Battle. *See* War
Beasts. *See* Animals
Beatitudes   131,380,447,492,535
Beauty   **107–10**,316,482
Beer   110
Beggar   110,492
Beginning   110–13,327
Behavior   113
Belief   113–23,541
Belonging   123
Benevolence. *See* Blessing, Grace
Betrayal   124,216
Better   124–25
Bible   190,544–45
Binding   125–26,207
Birth   138–39,170. *See also* Born again
Birthright   126
Bishop   471
Bitterness   126–27,215
Blame   128–29,182,523
Blamelessness   128,482
Blasphemy   129–30,597
Blemish   130
Blessing   2,7,26,104,122,**130–32**,156,174,179,
    195,205,230,289,308,324,333,346,395,419,
    447,473,496,502,521,532,596,607,622–23
    and the law   131,154,391
    and obedience   2,7,39,104,131,175,462
    and righteousness   534
    withdrawal of   208
Blindness, spiritual   132,388
Blood   30,82,120,**132–33**,172,407,448,478
    and cleansing   170
    and forgiveness   205
    of Jesus   30,50,73,83,129,**133**,161,187,195,
        198,276,290,316,371,388,503,517,543,620
    and sacrifice   35,465

Boasting   133–34,540
Body   24,134–35,556
Body of Christ   57,93,102,105,135,136–37,
    165,166,227,245,279,303,305–7,321,327,
    328,336,347,367,403,439,471,515,552,580,
    585,586,599
Boldness   137,184,193
Bond   137
Bondage. *See also* Slavery
    physical   294,412,516,517,518,641
    spiritual   152,179,295,319,395,518,553–54,
        568,569
Bones   138
Book   138
Born again   119,138,161,165,178,225,354,
    381,574,627. *See also* Birth
Borrowing   143,308,**404–5**
Branch   139–40
Bread   140,141,607
Breath   141
Bribe   370
Bride   **142**,166,437
Brother   142–44,166
Brute. *See* Animals
Building   144–46,195
Burden   107,146,179
Business   6,**147**,427,637
Busybody   147
Byword   147

Calamity. *See* Disaster
Call   **148–50**,502
    of Abraham   195
    efficacious   150,505
    to repentance   522
Canaanites   97,150,153,349,359,424,466,617
Capital punishment   10,11,96,132,407,425,
    431,516,581–82,610. *See also* Murder
Capstone   145,151
Captivity   152
Cares. *See* Anxiety
Causation   152–54,216,334,335,512
Celebration   154,590
Celibacy   8
Certainty   80,113,116,155,259
Chaff   155
Change   155,184
Character   155,298,299,342,345,447,476,593,
    599,601,605,631,640
Chastening. *See* Discipline
Chastisement. *See* Discipline
Cherubim   43
Childbirth   434,473–74
Childlikeness   158,320,347
Children   4,9,27,**156–59**,175,208,214,229,
    262,266,286,474,588,601
    of Abraham   469
    of believers   437
    of God   4,94,123,158,166,178,269,274,295,
        338,340,354,356,469,483,514,574

and leaders   14,263
and parents   228,343
punishment of   510
teaching of   157
Choice   149,153,**159–62**,174,180,222,252,
    284,286,288,321,323,334,407,438,456,486,
    489,502,522,532,536,544,567,568,584,589,
    601,626–29. *See also* Election, Judg-
    ment, Predestination
accountability for   18
God's   **160–62**,326,327,419,421,440
Christ   55,162–63. *See also* Jesus
Christian   163
Christian living   32,38,48,61,71,72,76,80,85,
    86,90,131,134,142,152,179,224,228,229,
    231,261,281,284,320,340,380,384,386,396,
    421,463,536,581,591,603,615,629,630,640
Christlikeness   146,185,220,227,244,258,312,
    321,341,352,422,463,502,529,535,580
Church   12,13,19,20,28,32,71,76,79,80,88,93,
    102,123,126,137,142,157,161,**164–67**,171,
    190,205,236,242,279,281,284,321,359,372,
    538,586,618,630,632,641
and community   458,492
discipline   23,224,229,366,367,404,458
divisions. *See* Divisions in the church
as family   227,263,264,276,298,309,387,
    422,436,437,592
and headship   327
and Israel   166,357
leaders   20,27,60,68,94,243–45,270,304,
    308,402–3,471,523,560
meetings   167,600
offices   59,60,160,306,632
organization   328
and the poor   492–93
prophets in   507
rich and poor in   493
and society   451
unity of   515,606
and widows   626
and women   95,199,245,328,430,**631–33**
Circumcision   100,**167–68**,195,545,609
Citizenship   31,**168**,288,584,587
and believers   31,32,88,90,168,249,288,
    336
in God's kingdom   31
Roman   31,61,168,191,204
Class distinctions   488–93
Class system   488
Clean and unclean   52,**168–72**,242,286,340,
    405,547,568,600. *See also* Defilement,
    Holy, Pollution
Cleansing   103,170,186,290,510,570,603,620
Clouds   173
Cloudy-fiery pillar   173
Collections. *See* Giving
Comfort   26,61,173,246
Commandments   9,32,152–53,168,**173–78**,
    187,286,342,358,365,390,393,420
and holiness   339

of Jesus 184,299,362,462
and love 397
Commendation 496
Commitment 16,22,41,70,80,98,101,118,120, 144,158,160,**179**,227,236,240,242,285,322, 326,340,341,361,419,450,454,460,484,488, 522,539,570,593,606,607,614
Common grace. *See* Grace
Communion 141,198,206
Community **78–79**,80,98,144,162,164,167, 242,362,385,422,458,492,589,592
and the church 144,164,276,321
of Israel 361
Companionship 143
Compassion 25,173,**179–81**,238,267,317, 325,341,439,457,492,610
Compensation 203,531
Competence. *See* Ability
Complaining. *See* Contentment, Peace
Completeness 181,482
Compulsion 181,456. *See also* Force
Conceit 347. *See also* Pride
Concern 181–82
Concubine 182,434,550
Condemnation 15,119,**182–83**,319,364,365, 372,560
Confession 182,290,415. *See also* Acknowledgment
of God 595
of Jesus 417
as praise 496
of sin 17,84,101,128,**183–84**,223,290,324, 346,366,567,569,595,603
Confidence 69,70,75,80,168,**184–85**,236, 320,322,440,461,484,499,540,571,582. *See also* Boldness, Hope
Confirming 185
Conformity 28,**185**,273
Confrontation 619
Congregation. *See* Assembly, Church
Conscience 5,14,70,83,172,183,**185–88**,215, 236,261,468,476,503,532,621
Consciousness 576
Consecration 341. *See also* Holy
Consequences 298,322,323
Consideration 188
Consistency. *See* Hypocrisy
Contempt 223,544
Contending 188–89
Contentment 189,625
Contribution. *See* Giving
Control 189
Conversion 100,487,522
Conviction 189–90,224
Convictions 153,186,187,261,417,484,532
Convincing. *See* Persuasion
Corban 271,305,343
Cornerstone. *See* Capstone
Correction 86,189,190,589. *See also* Discipline, Punishment
Corruption 190

Council 190–91
Council of Jerusalem 172,395
Counsel 191–93,578
Counterfeit 193,445
Courage 193
Court 193
Covenant 193–99. *See also* Agreement
Abrahamic 2,126,195,208,211,264,326, 353,389,390,431,469,521
Ark of 72,83
Davidic 2,54,139,197,267,376,526,572
eschatological 2,391
existential 2,41,196
and law 391
Mosaic 2,7,131,172,178,196–97,356,397, 406,458,502,524,581
new 2,3,119,133,172,177,179,197,322,344, 393,397,442,458,468,,548,581
of peace 480
relationship 22,33,39,42,46,49,78,98,114, 116,125,126,129,141,153,160,166,167, 174,207,223,233,235,248,270,272,274, 279,288,303,308,314,332,343,353,358, 372,375,418–19,421,444,456,460–61, 498,512–13,517,518,520,522,568,588, 607,610,617,622–623,634
renewal 196
and salt 539
unconditional 2
as a will 195
Cover 199–200
Coveteousness 177,200,221,358,394,618
Creation 19,42,43,111,112,131,154,161, 174,**200–202**,210,233,241,245,267,280,293, 316,328,335,406,407,411,413,415,427,435, 442,444,448,469,498,524–25,547,556,583, 634,637
of the ages 28
and animals 52
of man 351,431
new 202,336,337,412,432,458
order in 429
order of 454
Credit 203
Creeds 220
Crime 88,**203–4**,370,407,450,464,526,625
Criminal justice system, OT 236,595
Criticism. *See* Judgment
Cross 204,287,411,421
and believers 206,220
of believers 411
Crown 204–5
Crucifixion
of Jesus 4,30,117,**205–6**,216,377,397,520
with Jesus 103,121,411,457
Cruelty. *See* Persecution, Suffering
Cry. *See* Prayer
Cubit 206
Cup 103,206–7
Cure. *See* Healing
Curse 129,**207–9**,434. *See also* Oath

Darkness   257,274,276,**413–15**
Day   210–12
  of Atonement   73,83,468,503
  of the Lord   211,521,616
Deacon   68,430,552,632
Deaconness   631
Death   95,117,120,125,**405–12**
  abolition of   224
  eternal   569
  fear of   408
  and inheritance   354
  of Jesus   3,6,15,30,32,36,69,75,78,84,87,
    102,103,104,105,119,125,126,129,133,
    195,209,216–17,219,248,250,290,371,
    373,397,409,410,417,418,450,468,502,
    515,541,551,553,569,573
  physical   127,169,170,204,224,238,336,412,
    425,431,446,448,483,564,576,582,624
  of sacrifices   82
  second   409
  and sin   408
  as sleep   571–72
  spiritual   29,106,118,119,134,190,224,294,
    295,318,319,392,407,408,409,421,434,
    448,564,569,580
  versus life   159,364,406
  victory over   611
Debauchery   212
Debt   142,455,491,550
Deceit   123,212–14. See also Falsehood, Lie
Decision   191,219
Declaration   214
Decree   214
Dedication   214
Deep, the   214–15
Defeat   557
Defect   215
Defilement   169,215
Deity. See God, Jesus, Holy Spirit
Delight   215–16. See also Pleasure
Deliverance   **216–17**,523,525,527,533,540,
  583,611. See also Salvation
Demon possession   147,424,494,600,612.
  See also Demons
Demons   7,45,93,171,**217–19**,237,349,425–
  26,538,556,564,579,584
Demonstration   219
Denarius   446
Denial   219–20
Dependability. See Faithfulness
Dependence   492,497,498,499,559,622,628
Deposit   220
Depravity   221,254,567
Descendant   469,572–74,641
Desert   221
Desires   61,86,108,152,200,212,**221–22**,358,
  410,415,423,434,477,486,556,569,593,616
Desolation   222–23
Despair   126
Destiny. See Eternity, Predestination
Destruction   223–25

Devil. See Satan
Devotion   225
Disappearance   225
Disaster   226,252
Discernment   226,231
Disciple   59,60,190,220,**226–27**,270,285,286,
  298,315,411,591,624
Discipleship   539,591
Discipline   12,23,126,190,224,226,**228–29**,
  261,265,266,286,367,404,458,591,601. See
  also Punishment
  church   12,23,126,190,224,366,367,404,458
  by God   3,26,48,50,99,127,180,194,248,
    267,269,366,419,462,518,589
  and grace   128
  self-   107
Discontent. See Contentment
Discouragement. See Desolation, Despair,
  Encouragement
Disease. See Health, Sickness
Disgrace   229–30,557
Dishonesty   6. See also Honesty
Dishonor   355. See also Honor, Shame
Disobedience   48,75,85,116,151,152,175,207,
  223,264,265,286,288,389,390,**461–64**,500,
  520,561
Disowning   219–20
Disputes   13,71,153,**230**
Disqualification   230
Distinction   230–31
Distress   231–32,625. See also Evil, Sorrow
Divination   232,465
Divisions in the church   76,157,284,630
Divorce   8,24,70,112,124,126,202,**232–35**,
  393,435,437,548. See also Remarriage
Doctrine   218,**235–36**,367,386,591,620
Dominion   52,53,91,342,431,**538**. See also
  Authority, Ruling
Doubt   236
Dragon   237
Dreams   89,123,237
Drinking   237–38
Drunkenness   110,237,**238**,628
Dust   238–39
Duty   239,561. See also Obligation

Ear   240
Earth   146,155,202,225,**240–41**,277,335,337,
  344. See also Land, World
Eating   225,237,**241–42**. See also Food
Ecumenicity. See Apostasy, Church, Unity
Edification   145,188,600
Education   588–92. See also Teaching
Effort   242–43
Elders   128,**243–45**,427,632
  church   19,27,68,164,167,236
  Israel's   13,26,88,301,370,401
Election   160,161,195. See also Choice, Pre-
  destination
Emotions   575. See also Heart

Empty 245–46. *See also* Vanity
Enablement 278,392
Encouragement 173,246
End 246–47
Endurance 247,345,484
Enemies 147,155,231,**247–49**,326,348,375, 419,484
Envy 249
Ephod 249
Equality 249–50,428
Error 250
Escape 521–22
Eschatology. *See* Future, Prophecy
Establishment 250
Eternity 37,111,155,161,**250–51**,335,378,431
Evaluation 86,182,316,325,326,347,375. *See also* Judgment
Evangelism. *See* Witness
Evangelist 251
Everlasting 36–37
Evil 28,32,87,89,90,96,106,125,144,152,158, 174,177,187,213,216,217,226,231,232, 237,**251–55**,274,316,324,325,326,340,382, 384,404,414,442,447,450,565,593,601,613, 625. *See also* Sin, Wickedness
Evil spirits 180,255,425,540. *See also* Demons
Exaltation 255–56
Example 27,113,**256**,286,441. *See also* Imitation
 of Abraham 114
 of God 107,249,270,314,483,637
 of Jesus 86,256,309,310,321,347,476,552, 583
 of leaders 113,244,256,403,404,478,560, 603
 of others 86,590
 of parents 157,266
 of Paul 146,638
Excuse 256
Exercise 601
Exhortation 246
Exile 256,356
Existence of God 416
Exodus 19,42,116,134,216,219,416,516
Exorcism 218,426
Expectation. *See* Hope
Exposure of infants 429
Eye 256–57,414

Face 258–59
Factions 259,284
Failure 259,557
Faith 6,8,41,80,83,92,**113–23**,161,162,168, 199,203,240,242,251,260,269,281,285,287, 307,309,311,335,361,371,384,387,395,421, 440,441,469,471,474,476,480,484,514,534, 541,569,594,603,638
 and the armor of God 74
 and Christian growth 32,85

communication of 157,262,266,520,588–92
counterfeit 10,19,118,119,121
defective 236
and healing 330
and the Holy Spirit 219
and justification 33,121,373,459,505
and the law 105,250,262,394,396
nature of 374
and obedience 115,116,122,333
and promise 105
and repentance 522
and righteousness 77,78,114,120,122,184, 270,505,535,536
and salvation 134,262,394
superficial 118
and trials 593
weak 621
and works 10
Faithfulness 113,116,117,233,**259–60**,343, 358,435,460,520. *See also* Loyalty, Truth
 of God 2,153,160,220,239
 and marriage 22
Faithlessness 98
Fall 260–62
 of angels 43,45
 from grace 32,33,261,320
 of man 149,222,334,**433–34**,544,636
 of Satan 76
False Christs 56
Falsehood 603. *See also* Deceit, Lie
False prophets 507
False teachers 13,32,53,61,98,137,213,224, 262,296,404
Family 6,123,142,158,**262–65**,585,590
 of Abraham 39,41,119,159,167,267,318, 356,357,518,522,564
 accountability of 626
 of believers 156
 church as 143,163,165,227,298,309,387, 422,436,437,592
 of God 6,8,20,119,123,159,387,574,588
 in Israel 434,550
 of Jesus 143
 relationships 87,157,228,229,354,517
 of Satan 143,270,333
Famine 265,493
Fasting **265**,348,369,562
Fate 265,455
Father 58,265–71,435. *See also* Ancestors
 authority of 266,435
 God as 4,21,58,123,158,166,180,229,266, 266,**268–70**,314,354,483,492,499,593, 623,624
 obligations to 147,266
Faultless 128
Favor 271,348. *See also* Acceptance, Grace
Favoritism 493
Fear 38,47,96,111,169,220,**271–75**,286,315, 414,558,588. *See also* Respect
 of death 408

of God 111,160,176,231,**272–75**,286,315, 588,589
Feast l00,275
Feelings. *See* Heart
Fellowship 275–76
  with God 86,121,183,219,220,237,367, 412,415,432,463,481,500,603
  with humans 8,72,123,242,309,363,385, 422,455,476,558
Female 426–30
Festivals 154,**275**,325,590
Fetus 138
Fierce 276. *See also* Anger
Fighting 230,618. *See also* War
Filling 277–79,579
Fire 103,280–81
First 111,281
Firstborn 123,126,223,236,**281–82**,516,517
Firstfruits 106,154,275,282,528
Flesh 168,189,259,**282–85**,326,384,433,546, 555,581. *See also* Body
Flood 19,87,104,112,202,215,**285**,431,612
Folly. *See* Fool, Foolishness
Food 171,172,224,242,265,**286**,365,386. *See also* Eating
Fool 286–87,605
Foolishness 630
Footstool 287
Footwashing 620
Force 181,**287–88**,455,456,584
Forefathers. *See* Ancestors
Foreigner 31,142,288
Foreknowledge 161,476
Foretelling. *See* Prophecy
Forgetfulness 288
Forgiveness 233–34,**288–92**,338,365,367, 387,415,419,432,435,455,469,482,483,499, 503,513,568,586
  and adultery 23,25
  and approach to God 69
  and blood 205
  by God 3,14,36,49,82,83,84,120,128,133, 151,171,183,198,199,205,219,316,319, 321,322,323,329,371,393
  and healing 565
  by Jesus 92
  of others 39,50,107,143,290–91,321,341
  and sacrifice 35,36
  of sin 3,12,14,36,133,219,289,290,316,468
Fornication 21,508
Forsaken 3,410. *See also* Abandonment
Fortress 292
Fortunate. *See* Blessing
Forty 292
Foundation 292–93
Founder 270
Freedom 70,103,143,149,152,153,168,172, 188,261,273,**293–97**,334,385,417,436,518, 532,553,554,568,603
  and authority 91,92
  and believers 399

and choice 91,94
of Christians 365
and the church 93
from fear 273
of God 85,91,92,160,326
and the Holy Spirit 580
of Jesus 92
and law 395–97
limitations on 126
in relationships 184
from sin 133,294,295,516
surrender of 95
of women 328
Free will 61,149,161,175,334
Freewill offering 297
Friend 143,297–98,456
Friendship 142,241,242,**297–98**
Fruit 101,123,127,161,387,396,412,415
  and believers 139
  good and bad 106
  of the Holy Spirit 107,398,580
  and morality 2
Fruitfulness 140,298–99
Fulfillment 299–300
Fullness. *See* Filling
Funeral customs 446
Fury. *See* Anger
Future 28,34,49,50,51,56,58,63,66,67,68,73, 74,89,106,107,111,139,139,140,144,155, 163,171,180,210,211,213,225,241,246,247, 248,249,277,**300**,303,311,335,336,**343–45**, 356,360,377,378,379,382,413,419,445,447, 458,466,506,507,521,526–27,544,548,556– 57,573,597,616,634

Gabriel 43
Gain. *See* Success, Wealth
Gate 301
Gatherings. *See* Assembly
Genealogies 41,302. *See also* Ancestors
Generation 302–3
Generosity 405,558
Gentiles 303
  and Israel 248,356
  and Jews 31,39,60,80,93,104,129,139,171, 248,454,481,515
Gentleness **303–4**,341,375
Gethsemane 4
Gifts 78,108,120,174,**304–7**,353
  of God 78,108,120,162,235,278,310,316, 318,319,357,389,390,456,514,615
  to God 308,353
  of the Holy Spirit 579–80
Giving 9,110,143,146,156,276,**307–10**,405, 443,457,467,486,491,493,624,625,638
Gladness 485
Glorification. *See* Glory
Glory 108,258,280,281,**310–12**,496,502,558, 610. *See also* Honor
Gnosticism 384

God   7,28,33,34,37,42,48–49,68,114,200,
    201–2,250,253,258,260,268,283,289,293,
    305,310,**312–15**,317,320,321,325–26,335,
    349,352,361,364,369,371,376,383,394,400,
    413,444–45,453–54,473,486,498,533,559–
    60,597,610–11,616–19
God as Father. *See* Father
Godlessness   315
Godliness   96,**315**,625
Gods   5
Good   9,26,80,90,106,107,108,109,124,125,
    158,174,187,202,252,254,296,299,**315–16**,
    341,369,375,382,384,387,395,447,467,476,
    477,569,601,638. *See also* Better
Good news. *See* Gospel
Good Samaritan   297,457,542
Gospel   8,9,32,74,80,109,120,122,150,151,
    152,153,161,172,206,219,251,314,**316**,371,
    374,379,458,501,515,535,602
Gossip   316–17
Government. *See* Human Government
Grace   7,49,67,128,143,161,184,195,215,220,
    229,246,248,307,315,**317–20**,393,439,497,
    565,609. *See also* Favor
  fall from   32,33,261,262,320
  and law   317,505
  second work of   543
  and sin   317
Gratitude   317,595
Grave   336,337
Greatness   158,551,**320–21**,495
Greed   7
Grief   265,472. *See also* Mourning, Sorrow,
    Suffering
Grieving the Holy Spirit   581
Groom   142
Growth   32,85,123,136,262,263,279,306,**321–
    22**,325,387,403,418,438,600
  and faith   32
  and spiritual gifts   136
Guarantee   322,545
Guarding   322. *See also* Watching
Guidance   81,178,191,192,232,366,388,**399–
    401**,497,503,505,507,526,613. *See also*
    Lead
  and dreams   237
  by God   237,419
  and the Holy Spirit   580
Guilt   14,35,82,84,98,128,151,182,186,256,
    292,**322–23**,371,372,391,450,453,509,557–
    58,562,567,569
  acknowledgment of   16,39
  and forgiveness   289
  release from   504
Guiltlessness. *See* Innocence

Hades. *See* Hell
Hand   324,532
Happiness   361. *See also* Blessing, Joy
Hardness of heart   115,,233,235,**334**

Harm   324,483. *See also* Evil
Harvest   325
Hatred   248,270,**325–27**,415,430,450,533,
    618. *See also* Enemies
Haughtiness. *See* Arrogance, Pride
Head   327–28,**429**
Headship   45,87,165,279,**436–37**
  of husbands   327,328
  of Jesus   90,94,**136–37**,327,403,418,429
  of men   429,436–37
Healing   55,92,93,98,99,117,127,171,180,
    324,**329–31**,399,470,525,541,565,579,600.
    See also Health, Sickness
Health   406,504,561. *See also* Sickness
Hearing   240,331–33. *See also* Obedience,
    Prayer
Heart   69,77,81,87,103,115,168,170,171,172,
    175,176,177,178,184,254,257,283,299,
    308,**334–35**,348,393,397,420,447,450,463,
    498,567,568,570,580,581,590,599,601,640.
    See also Conscience, Hardness of Heart
Heaven   124,335–38
Hebrew   338
Heir   158,236,**338**,354,380
Hell   29,124,146,219,255,**336,337**. *See also*
    Abyss, Perishing, Punishment
Help   520,552
High priest   503–4
Hills   338
History   42,111
  biblical view of   28,34,42,66,111,153,194–
    98,210,228,275,300,344,413,419,431,444,
    475,502,530,541,595,597,618,635
  and God   28,42,189,210,318,361
  God's acts in   18,154,311,383,384,457,
    495,582
Holiness   88,274,275,307,319,**339–41**,476,
    482,502,504,510–11,515,522,542,570,581–
    82,590,600,613
  and believers   9,66,73,83,86,90,106,113,
    127,129,135,150,161,166,170,172,190,
    229,266,273,290,295,296,314,326,328,
    339,384,397,410
  and commands   339
  cultic   339,341
  and the fear of God   273
  of God   8,69,73,96,169,174,280,311,314,
    394
  and law   396
  and morality   339
  ritual   339–40
  and worship   69,467
Holy   239,464,524,542,543. *See also* Clean
    and Unclean
Holy Spirit   30,54,74,81,105,112,121,130,
    135,164,165,166,178,189,200,238,258,274,
    341,344,352,366,388,441,454,459,507,511,
    519,526,529,536,545,560,567,569,574,
    576,**577–81**,613,629,630,635
  and anointing   55,193
  baptism of   101,102,579

and believers   219,220,222,254,255,295,
    296,304,310,312,322,335,340,348,355,
    362,363,385,398,401,410,412,579–81
and the body   24
and the body of Christ   136–37
as Counselor   192
and faith   219
filling by   102,278,579
and fire   281
and flesh   284
and freedom   580
and fruit   107,398,580
and fruitfulness   299
gifts of   579–80
grieving   581
and guidance   401
indwelling of   579
and Jesus   578–79
and the law   397
and the Messiah   139
and the new birth   381
and prayer   356,500–501
quenching   511,581
receiving   514
and revelation   215,531,580
and righteousness   397,580
and sanctification   543
and Scripture   544
and the sin nature   295
and spiritual gifts   305–7
and tongues   580,599–600
and transformation   580
and unity   103
Home. *See* Family, Marriage
Homosexuality   6,230,286,428,454,555
Honesty   214,341,370,570
Honor   342–43. *See also* Glory
Hope   66,67,114,141,247,**343–45**,361,387,
    421,455,474,476,540. *See also* Anchor
Hopelessness. *See* Desolation, Despair,
    Hope
Horn   345
Horror   223
Host   346
Hostility   104,127,129,205,248,249,303,409,
    450,479,515. *See also* Enemies
Hour   346
Household salvation   264. *See also* Family
Human beings   87,337,**350–52**,,469
    and angels   46
    and anger   47–51
    and animals   52,53,83,351
    and created order   52
    destiny of   46,53,241,336,352,431,527,529
    and dominion   342
    and God's image   316
    and weakness   317
Human government   11,**87–91**,92,204,243,
    254,255,342,363,366,367,368,450–51,510,
    538,584. *See also* Authorities, Leader-
    ship

Human nature   4,28,108,177,186,222,238,
    241,253,254,282,283,284,294,296,316,319,
    334,350–51,364,394,407,409,427,430–32,
    441,454–55,525,556,566,567,568,621,630
Humility   147,158,239,291,341,**346–48**,402,
    439,488,497,609,623
Hunger   265,348
Husband
    headship of   327,328
    and wife   262,266,358
Hymns   496
Hypocrisy   79,129,257,348,485,570

I AM   416
Ideal   235,435,448
Idolatry   3,36,48,88,98,152,170,175,242,277,
    303,326,340,**349–50**,358,386,435,449,482,
    581. *See also* Image
    and demons   217
    and immorality   6,7,97
    and spiritual adultery   23
Ignorance   287,350,386
Illness. *See* Sickness
Image
    of God   52,87,316,**350–52**,406,407,427,
    431,448–49,569
    of human beings   351
Imitation   352
Immanuel   453
Immaturity   157
Immorality   18,22,80,99,170,190,220,230,238,
    284,286,299,340,349,367,450,456
    and idolatry   6,7,21,22,97
    and judgment   24
Immortality   352,529
Impossibility. *See* Inability
Impurity   510–11
Imputation   535–36
Inability   5
    of human beings   5,352,540
    of the law   177
    of pagan gods   5
Incarnation   258,269,311,312,315,336,351,
    432,579
Incense   35,352–53,502
Increase. *See* Growth
Independence   294,295
Indwelling   239,259,312,579
Inferiority   585
Inheritance   15,126,322,338,353–54,380
Iniquity. *See* Sin
Injustice   294,428,474,**488–90**,500,612. *See
    also* Justice, Sin, Wickedness
Innocence   169,187,**354–55**,372
Insight   355
Inspiration   190
Instinct   454
Instruction   20,389,390. *See also* Discipline,
    Teaching
Insult   355

Intelligence 286,443
Intercession 162,355–56. *See also* Prayer
Interest 491
Intermediate state. *See* Immortality, Life, Resurrection
Interpretation
of dreams 123,237
of the law 140,484
of prophecy 506
rabbinic 271,327
of Scripture 192,232,563
of tongues 356
Intimacy 165
Invitation 96,100,149,173
Irrationality 424
Irreligious 315
Israel 2,4,13,26,31,33;54,79,85,88,97,98,99, 106,115,139–40,142,143,144,148,151,152, 160,162,166,174,175,226,243,259,263,264, 266,267,281,298,302,308,310,314,332,339, 340,348,353,**356–57**,376,401,481,491–92, 494,523,547,550
and the church 357
restoration of 348,356,377,389

Jahweh. *See* Yahweh
Jealousy 47,76,127,**358–59**
Jerusalem 359–60
Jesus 247,360
abandoned by Father 4
as advocate 183
and the Angel of the Lord 44
and angels 125
as the Anointed One 55
ascension of 59,77,173
authority of. *See* Authority
baptism of 30,101
birth of 560
blood of. *See* Blood
as capstone 145
and the church 165,329
commandments of 178,184,299,362,463
compassion of 180
as Creator 45,202,328
crucifixion. *See* Crucifixion
death of. *See* Death
deity of 77,112,148,163,249–50,268,269, 278,290,328,338,351,384,417,528,573–74
and demons 218,219
exaltation of 324
as example. *See* Example
family of 144
as first and last 281
as firstborn 282
forty-day fast of 265
and God the Father 138,258,268,269, 282,328,351,364,385,402,410,486,531, 573–74
as God's wisdom 630
headship of. *See* Headship

healing ministry of 324,330,600
and the Holy Spirit 578–79
humanity of 41,83,128,135,265,351,384, 410,417,463,476,503,554,573
humility of 347
incarnation of 258,269,311,336,351,421, 432,579
indwelling of 239
intercession of 503
as judge 364
as king 377
kingdom of. *See* Kingdom
and the law 247,392
and life 411
as Lord 187,240,327,335,365,417,476,525, 551,553–54
as Lord of Sabbath 417,525,550
love of. *See* Love
as Mediator 504
miracles of. *See* Miracles
name of 500
obedience of 463
as object of faith 117
perfection of 482
physical body of 135
power of 94,119,600
and prayer 499–500
preexistence of 112
preincarnate appearance 44
priesthood of. *See* Priesthood
prophecies about 506,551
rejection of 518
resurrection of. *See* Resurrection
and revelation. *See* Revelation
at the right hand of God 324,532
sacrifice of. *See* Sacrifice
and Satan 265
second coming of. *See* Second Coming
as servant 474,480,554
and shame 558
as shepherd 560
as Son of God 573
as Son of Man 572–73
spiritual rock 10
and suffering. *See* Suffering
as teacher 270,591
temptation of 90,141,593
union with. *See* Union with Jesus
as vine 140,299,612
as the Word 635
words of 333,635
yoked with 525,641
Jews 360–61. *See also* Gentiles, Judaism
Joint-heirs 354
Joy 66,142,156,181,216,237,345,**361–63**,389, 494–95,556. *See also* Pleasure
Judaism 30,42,45,59,79,100,191,217,226,318, 337,361,429,519,529,535
Judas 124
Judges 363,376,428

Judgment   24,44,93,96,97,132,182,216,
    238,**363–68**,372,386,432,442,470,492,502,
    509,533,556,560,567,593,605,611,612,634
  by believers   143,153,183,186,187,224,230,
    257,291,364,**365–68**,532
  final   12,36,45,50–51,67,79,280–81,325,
    337,414
  by God   14,48,49,50,61,76,87,105,112,133,
    147,151,187,189,208,211,222,248,255,
    280,284,294,332,350,358,**364**,371,378,
    409,413,424,431,444,451,453,617–18
Just. *See* Righteous
Justice   9,11,83,154,248,271,287,340,**368–72**,
    383,467,485,489,500,550,589
Justification   49,50,120,133,168,304,354,
    371,**372–74**,409,464,468,480,502,515,541.
    See also Righteousness
  and faith   32,121,373,459,505
  and the law   32,320,373,   459
  and righteousness   505
  and works   373

Keys of the kingdom   126
Keystone   145,151
Killing.   132. *See also* Murder, War
Kindness   317,341,364,**375–76**,522. *See also*
    Love
King   34,54,162,310,**376–77**. *See also* Lead-
    ership
Kingdom   31,251,377–82
  coming   34,67,88,163,196,321,378,380,382,
    419,480,507,560
  of darkness   90
  Davidic   55,139
  of God   24,31,97,132,156,158,265,321,325,
    354,378,384,411,492,499,501,514,557,
    564,579,624
  gospel of   378–79
  of heaven   126,176,320,336,347,351,378,
    379,392,492
  of Israel   356
  of Jesus   217,268,269,316,336,**377–80**,404,
    456
  parables of   452
  of Satan   218,238,318,544,564,639
Kinsman redeemer   516–17,532
Knowledge   105,181,192,**382–87**. *See also*
    Understanding
  of God   16,111,134,314,349,364,383,386,
    442,519,531,534,545
  of God's will   627
  human   42,72
  and morality   16
  religious   384
  of truth   589
  and wisdom   629

Labor   531,637. *See also* Work
Lake of Fire. *See* Heaven, Hell

Lamb of God   60,84,**388**,467,478
Lament   615
Lamp   388
Land   **388–89**,490,494,638. *See also* Earth
Last Supper   158
Laughter   389
Law   12,82,140,141,158,173,186,196–98,235,
    261,287,294,319,338,344,356,358,365,368,
    369,370,371,386,387,**389–99**,405,409,410,
    428,432,458,464,498,503,504,516,533,534,
    550,569,581,595,609,638,641
  abolished   6,32,151,178,209,393,396,459
  and believers   85,172,216,284,296,391–92,
    395
  binding on aliens   31
  and blessings   39,122,131,154,391
  ceremonial and ritual   4,35,390,547
  and Christian growth   85
  civil   390,487–92
  as a curse   208
  and the death of Jesus   32
  failures of   88
  and faith   105,115–16,121,250,262,394,
    396
  and freedom   395–97
  fulfillment of   6,178,392
  and grace   317,505
  and health   561
  and holiness   396
  and hostility   105
  human   32,87,88,89,168,392,451
  imperfection of   482
  interpretation of   484
  and Israel   4
  and Jesus   247,392
  and justification   32,320,373,459
  and love   143,422
  and marriage   434
  moral   4,35,390
  and moral standards   18
  Mosaic   209,326
  natural   246,444
  nature of   177,208
  and the New Covenant   3
  and obedience   41,104,116,420
  oral   535
  powerlessness of   621
  and revelation   174,175,369
  and righteousness. *See* Righteousness
  and the Sabbath   524
  and salvation   134,296,318,394
  and self-righteousness   77,78
  and sickness   561
  and sin   35,318,399,536,566
  and social order   88,204
  and understanding   605
  weakness of   394,395
  as yoke   5,525,641
Lawfulness   399
Lawlessness   399
Lawsuits   153

Leaders, church   14,20,27,59,60,68,76,79,
    93,94,95,128,137,145,149,164,167,243,
    244–45,264,270,304,308,328,471,560.
    See also Leadership
  accountability of   620
  and alcohol   238
  and authority   93,259
  and children   14,263
  condemned   560
  enablement of   278
  as examples. *See* Example
  family of   263
  obedience to   404,584
  ordination of   470
  qualifications of   523,612
  respect for   404
  responsibility of   403
  and teaching   592
Leadership   327,352,376,**401–4**,471,559–60
  by elders   243–44
  by women   428,430,632
Leading   81,173,**399–401**
Learning   226,227,**588–92**. *See also* Teach-
    ing
Leaven   106,125,381,**404**,457
Left. *See* Right
Legal justice system, OT   10,11,12,13,14,
    88,96,142,153,203,230,243,301,370,371,
    449–50,490,526
Legal terminology, NT
  accountable   12
  accuse   14,15
  acknowledge   17
  acquit   17
  adoption   21
  alien   31
  appeal   61
  blameless   128
  cancel   150,151
  citizen   31,168
  condemn   182
  confession   183
  confirm   185
  crime   204
  deposit   220
  excuse   256
  free   295
  guarantee   322
  guilt   323
  heir   354,380
  inheritance   353
  innocent   354
  judge   364
  judgment seat   368
  justice. *See* Justice
  justify. *See* Justification
  nullify   459
  pardon. *See* Forgiveness
  ransom   517–18
  seal   545
  slave   295,552–53

Legalism   7,24,43,235,287,399
Lending   143,308,**404–5**
Leprosy   171,405
Letter   405
Levirate marriage   435
Levites   307,**502–4**,547,549. *See also* Priest-
    hood
Liberality   459
Liberty. *See* Freedom
Lie   90,461. *See also* Deceit, Falsehood
Life   117,130,**405–13**
  beginning of fetal   138
  and death   95,159,364,405–13
  earthly   36,58,87,130,132,135
  eternal   93,118,119,122,141,238,251,319,
    337,344,345,385,392,406–7,411,412,415,
    528,541,573,627
  physical   87,169,174,238,541,575
  respect for   132
  sanctity of   448
  spiritual   42,86,102,103,120,134,135,139,
    224,319,352,396,397,410,635
Lifetime   302
Light   257,274,276,326,**413–15**
Likeness. *See* Appearance, Image
Limitations, human   5
Lion   415
Loose   125–26,207
Lord   33–34,44,67,94,163,165,187,240,313,
    327,335,365,**415–18**,551,553–54,577
Lord of Sabbath   417,525,550
Lord's Day   525
Lord's Prayer   141,380,499,624
Lord's Supper   102,195,242,520–21,595
Lost   418
Love   180,259,275,**418–23**,439
  for brothers   491
  and the commandments   397
  command to   462–63
  for enemies   249,270,326,348,421,484,535
  and fear   274
  and forgiveness   291
  for God   143,168,175,177,255,273,291,307,
    407,467,496,510,534
  God's   7,25,49,96,160,161,173,174,219,228,
    241,246,249,269,274,291,299,314,317,
    319,325,326,330,344,345,358,375,385,
    387,393,399,414,440,540,559,567,569,
    573,589
  husbands'   328,437
  for Jesus   184,220
  Jesus'   61,279,328,437,484
  and labor   637
  and law   143,422
  of money   446,623–24
  for neighbor   249,297,325,326,369,456–
    57,535
  and obedience   275,462–63
  for others   72,136,139,143,146,167,176,
    177,184,212,228,233,250,263,296,309,

328,341,367,387,397,399,415,443,450, 585,592
parents' 156
and the poor 491
and righteousness 422
and spirituality 599
and the Ten Commandments 142
and unity 515,606
Loyalty 460,607. *See also* Faithfulness
Lucifer 543. *See also* Satan
Lust 423
Luxury 487,546

Madness 424
Magic 207,217,**424–26**
Male 426–30
Malice 430
Mammon 623
Mankind 430–32. *See also* Human beings
Marriage 7,8,21,23,24,112,124,125,126,142, 202,206,233,239,262,264,283,328,358,393, 423,**432–38**,453,543,546,548,555–56
and faithfulness 22
headship in. *See* Headship
and law 434
with pagans 557
and submission 585
to unbelievers 70
Mary 41,144
Master 416,433,438
Materialism 58,90,126,270,287,310,362,363, 608. *See also* Wealth
Maturity 27,85,137,158,181,187,188,192,244, 247,261,278,279,304,321,422,**438**,482–83
Meals, ritual 242
Measure 438
Mediator 502,504
Medication 329,470. *See also* Healing
Meekness 439
Melchizedek 41,271,394,504
Member 439
Memorial 36,54,520. *See also* Memory
Memory 86,288,361,**519–21**
Mercy 7,14,98,140,161,233,269,287,372,**439–41**,467,485,499,567. *See also* Compassion, Grace
Mercy seat 439,609
Message 441
Messiah 54,99,101,125,139,162,196,324,330, 347,360,377,378,480,518,522,527,550,559, 573,578,579
Michael 44
Might 582–84. *See also* Power
Military service. *See* War
Mind 28,53,86,190,215,248,286,350,441–43, 605. *See also* Reason, Thinking
Mind of Christ 366,580
Minister 443–44,552. *See also* Servant
Ministry 165,168,278,309,**443–44**,515,544, 552,631,637,638

Miracles 10,92,114–19,130,425–26,**444–45**, 582
counterfeit 193,445
and faith 116,117
of Jesus 37,92,117,118,249,269,273,330, 379,425,568
and Moses 115
reaction to 37,38,114–15,273,385,444
and unbelief 115
Missions 60,244,251,362. *See also* Apostles
Mockery 389,544
Model. *See* Example, Imitation, Pattern
Money 155,180,309,341,403,**445–46**,625. *See also* Possessions, Wealth
Monogamy 434
Month 446
Moral influence theory 84
Morality 4,11,16,18,48,88,129,139,154,160, 169,170,171,172,174,176,178,184,186,189, 226,238,246,254,282,283,284,286,288,293, 294,316,341,349,364,365,368,375,386,394, 395,409,431,455,482,507,509,510,523,531, 533,568,589,602,605,607,611,615,617,634
and elders 244
and evil 251
and the fear of God 273
and holiness 339
and results 2
and revelation 252
and worship 9,325,466–67
Mortality 135,141,155,412
Motivation 61,184,365,422,535,569,570,627
Mountain 338
Mourning 265,**446–47**,615
Mouth 447
Murder 11,24,50,87,96,132,175,204,370,406, 407,431,434,**447–51**,610
Music 496,504
Mustard seed 381
Mystery 452

Nakedness 453,555,557
Name 148,317,**453–54**,500
Names of God 208,317,494,608
Banner 99
God Almighty 33,34
Healer 329
Lord Almighty 33
Lord of Armies 33,34
Lord of Hosts 346
Yahweh 33,34,44,166,313,416
Nation 454
Nature 454–55
Nazirite 547,614
Necessity **455–56**,457,491,615–16,624
Neighbor 249,297,325,326,369,371,393, 404,**456–57**,535
New 42,457–59
birth 139,412
commandment 458

covenant and law 3
person 432
Nicodemus 118,138
Night 459. *See also* Darkness
North 459
Nullification 459–60
Nurture 157,214,228,229,263,266

Oath 125,185,195,293,322,327,**460–61**
Obedience 41,85,86,107,124,152,178,215,
220,227,236,240,248,261,264,265,273,280,
285,299,331,342,361,362,380,384,390,406,
407,422,**461–64**,476,484,500,520,523,524,
534,546,549,550,551,553,569,584,594,613
and blessing 2,7,39,104,131,175,462
and faith 115,116,122,333
and fear 275
and fruitfulness 140
to human government 90
and law 41,104,116,420
to leaders 404
and love 275,**462–63**
of Jesus 463
Obligation 455. *See also* Duty
Occult 6,81,232,424–26,465,505
Ocean. *See* Deep, the
Offense 464,584
Offering 275,282,297,304308,353,**464–69**,
502–4
Offspring 469
Oil 55,469–70
Old 42,432,457–59. *See also* Ancient
Omnipresence 277
Openness 184. *See also* Boldness
Opinion 86,596
Opposition 470
Oppression 26,30,66,110,152,231,370,**487–
94**
Oracle 470
Order 470–71
Ordinance 100. *See also* Commandments
Ordination 324,470
Origin 455,538
Orphan 271,307,489
Overcoming 471
Overseer **471**,560,632
Ownership 516,517,545

Pacifism. *See* War
Paganism 5,33,35,36,58,97,217,265,303,313,
315,338,349,350,362,363,424,449,455,508,
515,555,557,623
Pain 229,231,**472–77**,574
Palestine 353
Parables 147,380,452,**477**,508
Pardon. *See* Forgiveness
Parents 156,157,158,175,208,228,229,266,
271,305,343,474,556,585

Participation 238,241,519–29,558,590,631.
See also Fellowship
Partnership 558
Passion 477,546
Passions 628
Passover 106,154,170,241,275,388,426,478,
520,607. *See also* Bread
Past, the
biblical view of 42,216,246,284
and God 300
Pastors 167. *See also* Shepherd
Patience 48,107,121,219,247,341,439,**478**
Pattern 478
Peace 471,**479–81**,551,571. *See also* War
with God 129,133,205,373,480
and healing 565
inner 30,58,98,127,479,480,481,524
international 107,479
interpersonal 146,303,479,481,534
offering 480
universal 378
Penalty. *See* Guilt
Pentecost 102,166,514,599
Perception 86,115,230,257,332,333,350,382,
383,442,443,453,589,605,630
Perfection 86,247,469,**482–83**
Perishing 483
Persecution 3,359,362,**483–84**,493,535
Perseverance 484. *See also* Endurance
Persuasion 484
Petition. *See* Prayer
Pharisees 24,42,43,101,109,125,140,143,158,
170,171,176,223,227,233,235,237,271,287,
291,318,392,393,397,399,421,435,445,**484–
85**,525,528,535,539,542,564
Philosophy 152
Piety 519
Pilate 94,95,124,204,377
Pilgrimage 154
Pity 173. *See also* Compassion
Plan of God 84,111,112,247,343,344
Pleasure 216,**485–87**,627
Pollution 487
Polygamy 434,555
Poor 26,77,86,110,143,239,271,308,369,404,
419,453,**487–94**,550,623–24,625,626. *See
also* Humility
Possession 276,494
Possessions 7,132,176,249,270,493. *See also*
Money, Wealth
Posterity 469
Poverty 88,132
Power 5,33,34,54,73,77,85,88,90,91,94,97,
103,114,115,117,119,120,123,201,202,219,
236,262,284,311,320,324,330,338,339,341,
345,346,380,403,409,411,426,488–90,495,
502,516,528,529,532,541,565,569,579,582–
84,600,621,630,641. *See also* Authority
and believers 54,85,103,117,236,262,284,
320,341,409,411,482,529,565,569,583–
84,621,630,641

of death   541
of God   5,33,73,77,90,114,115,117,120,
   123,201,202,219,236,311,324,330,339,
   346,380,411,426,444–45,482,495,516,
   528,532,541,565,579,582–84,621
of government   88
human   97
of Jesus   94,119,600
and leaders   403
of Satan   541
of sin   222,541
social   488–90
Powerlessness   488–90
Praise   43,49,78,123,131,309,310,311,
   312,**494–96**,534,565,575,595,611
Prayer   44,58,85,90,110,121,128,148,149,168,
   217,236,240,258,265,269,279,291,309,328,
   332,352,355,362,380,387,419,439,442,454,
   474,**496–501**,520,556,562,571,574,586,606,
   607,613,624,631,632
and agreement   29
conditions for answered   500–501
and God's will   628
and the Holy Spirit   356
as intercession   162,355,356
the Lord's   141,380,499,624
and righteousness   534
and ritual   498
and sacrifice   497
for the sick   330
Preaching   501,591
Precepts   501
Predestination   79,112,153,161,214,268,334,
   432,476,**501–2**. See also Choice, Election, Sovereignty
Prejudice. See Judgment, Opinion
Presence   416,502
Pressure   231,456,524,593
Pride   75,76,256,291,304,386,543,557,623,
   625. See also Arrogance, Boasting
Priesthood   502–4,551
of believers   9,166,168,308,340,503
of Jesus   36,41,77,83,162,182,185,471,
   478,**503–4**,528
Levitical   26,36,41,54,69,82,88,171,275,
   281,339,353,394,400,405,427,443,466,
   471,502,503,504,552
of Melchizedek   271,394
Priority   281,546
Prison   370
Profit   147
Prohibitions. See Commandments
Promises of God   2,3,41,58,65,85,105,114,
   120,121,122,125,126,131,133,141,184,187,
   192,194,195,198,203,223,230,247,248,260,
   269,283,299,300,319,326,327,356,357,389,
   395,408,412,444,460,469,481,500,504–5,
   520,521,522,528,535,559,593,607,629,634
Proof   219,484,508
Prophecy   174,300,328,345,372,441,466,**505–
   8**,556,573,579,600,631,632

fulfillment of   181,277,506
interpretation of   506
concerning Jerusalem   360
Prophet   62,63,81,192,214,237,400,401,428,
   489,**505–8**,531,546,572,613
Propitiation   83
Prosperity   97,174,288
Prostitution   21,22,23,97,288,**508**,555,615
Proverb   147,508
Providence   34,53,91,154,253,336,348,400
Punishment   26,30,84,203,293,295,322,323,
   325,366,367,368,**509–10**,551. See also Discipline, Judgment
by church   366,367
eternal   337,510
and fear   274
and forgiveness   289
by God   99,174,207,225,226,229,237,358,
   371,432,473,486,508,513,520,561,637
by government   89,90,526
and guilt   322
of nations   99,226
Purchase   518
Purification   100,178,280,281,510,593
Purity   169,215,**510**
Purposes of God   36,111,123,141,162,191,
   195,205,210,247,299,422,476,506,**510–11**,
   595,627,628

Qualifications of church leaders   533,612
Quarreling   71,248,618
Quenching   511,581

Rabbi   226,270,512
Rabbinic interpretation   271,327
Race. See Generation
Ransom   450,**517–18**,587. See also Redemp-
   tion
Rape   230,286
Rapture   529
Reality   66,171,236,246,250,286,295,350,383,
   386,394,442,468,531,595,602–3,608,635
and deceit   213
and revelation   67
and symbol   36,73,168
Reason   71,162,**512**. See also Knowledge,
   Mind, Thinking, Understanding
Rebellion   75,98,144,171,254,432,**512–13**
Rebelliousness   3,83,286,385,584
Rebuke   189
Receiving   7–8,513–14
Reconciliation   82,179,248,384,409,421,
   414–15
Redemption   34,66,106,133,149,163,174,220,
   255,269,281,282,290,311,318,322,344,371,
   395,419,432,468,478,498,**502,515–18**,525,
   532,536,541,566,573,575,583,616. See also
   Deliverance
Regeneration. See Conversion

Reign   518. *See also* King
Rejection   2,230,325,**518–19**,604
Rejoicing. *See* Joy
Relationship
    with enemies   348
    with God   3,4,7,9,10,16,17,23,34,35,41,50,
        58,67,69,75,76,79,80,83,105,107,113,114,
        120–22,129,133,134,142,144,159,162,
        174,177,182,207,220,222,236,251,257,
        258,264,267,268,269,270,274,275,278,
        281,284,286,298,305,318,320,325,329,
        332,335,343,344,347,358,361,363,369,
        385,387,392,394,396,400,406,407,409,
        412,416,418,421,425,435,463,474,479,
        480,486,498,500,505,512–13,514,521,
        524–25,534,549,556,557,559,560,572,
        584,588,589,593,603,605,615,630,640
    with the Holy Spirit   341,500,**577–81**
    with Jesus   117,123,129,136–37,185,219,
        255,258,261,276,279,299,305,312,341,
        362,365,385,500
    in marriage   221,233,235,429,436,555–56,
        585
    with other Christians   8,20,47,50,57,72,
        80,81,85,93,94,95,107,131,134,137,139,
        143,165,175,188,189,215,223,224,227,
        245,261,263,270,276,279,284,287,289–
        91,305–7,309,321,328,342,347,362,364,
        365,366,380,386,387,397,403,415,422,
        436,437,443,455,481,515,585,590,602,610
    with others   221,247,248,251,325,369,370,
        375,420,431481,515,523,625,639
    between teacher and learner   590–91
    in the Trinity   138
    with unbelievers   30,33,70,80,131,235,
        237,255,298,365,366,437,548,587,600,
        604,639,641
Reliability. *See* Faithfulness
Religion   440,**519**,630
Remarriage   24,125,126,**234–35**
Remembrance. *See* Memory
Remnant   356,521–22
Renewal   96,202,206,351,443,526
Repentance   50,101,155,190,220,298,349,364,
    467,**522**,540. *See also* Restoration
Reproach   230,522–23
Reputation   523
Request. *See* Prayer
Rescue   523,540. *See also* Deliverance
Resentment   127
Respect   132,342,404,416,437,457,**523**,640.
    See also Fear, Reverence
Response   387
Responsibility. *See* Accountability
Rest   261,280,344,**523–26**,598
Restitution   39,123,203,204,236,370,**526**
Restoration   526–27
    of health   527
    of Israel   99,104,106,139–40,142,180,211,
        419,521–22,526–27,550,559
    of sinning saints   367

Resurrection   224,484,**527–30**
    of all human beings   53,337,338,344
    of believers   28,45,65–66,68,135,136,155,
        185,227,337,344,352,408,410,412,432,
        454,463,**528–29**,530,541
    of Jesus   42,45,59,60,64,92,93,102,103,
        104,117,120,121,126,135,163,227,282,
        290,335,337,344,408,410,412,417,432,
        454,484,525,**528**,541,569,573,574,579,583
    in the Old Testament   96,335,336
        527–28
    power   85,103,583
Revelation   195,214,303,344,390,432,
    452,**530–31**,533,602,628,634
    and angels   44,46
    and dreams   237,452,613
    God's self-revelation   16,17,62,68,115,
        215,256,272,280,310–11,338,384,385,
        386,443,444,473–74,531,604,630,635
    of God's will   533,628,630
    and the Holy Spirit   580
    and Jesus   46,117,161,163,237,258,269,
        270,387,531,635
    and the law   174,175,369
    and morality   252
    and the prophets   62–63
    and reality   67
    and righteousness   178,253,627
    and the Second Coming   68
Revenge   47,50,248. *See also* Vengeance
Reverence   273,274,640. *See also* Respect
Revival   359
Rewards   12,67,145,205,336,418,**531**,608,637.
    See also Wages
Riches   77,86,110,624,625. *See also* Wealth
Ridicule   558
Right, the   531–33
    hand of God   532
    side   531–32
Righteousness   9,49,83,90,101,119,121,127,
    139,152,154,176,178,198,203,216,223,228,
    241,254,256,295,314,319,325,344,348,354,
    355,373,380,392,393,394,395,396,398,399,
    405,419,421,428,439,482,485,492,499,509,
    519,**533–37**,541,567,569,612,622,623,641.
    See also Justice, Justification
    and anger   47
    and armor of God   74
    and believers   86,261,284,299,320
    and blessing   534
    and faith   77,78,114,120,122,184,270,505,
        535,536
    of God   219
    and the Holy Spirit   580
    human   534
    imputation of   535–36
    and justification   505
    and the law   6,105,120,233,397,422,535
    and love   422
    and prayer   534
    and resurrection   85

and revelation 253
and works 85,120,184,638
Rights 532-33
of aliens in Israel 31
of aliens in Roman Empire 31
of animals 53
of believers 303
of Christian leaders 95
of citizens 293
of firstborn 126,223,236,281
of heirs 338
of individuals 92
of inheritance 15,126
of noncitizens in Rome 31
of the poor 489
of slaves 295
of slaves in Israel 550
of sons 574
of women in the Old Testament 428, 435
Ritual 69,465,498
Rock 10,537-38
Ruling 87,91,111,427,431,434,**538**. *See also* Authority, Judgment
Rumor. *See* Accusation, Gossip

Sabbath 140,175,249,339,344,399,417,**524-25**. *See also* Rest
Sabbatical year 240,308,404,490,550
Sacrament 100,556
Sacred 315,339,340. *See also* Holy
Sacrifice 35,73,82-84,124,128,130,132,133, 169,170,172,199,215,241,275,280,289,290, 324,339,353,391,407,486,502,503,504,543, 559,567,569,586,590. *See also* Offering
acceptable 9,74-75
and blood 465
first recorded 34
inadequacy of 186
of Jesus 29,36,50,56,83,122,125,126,134, 184,198,219,261,274,292,319,372,373, 388,421,468,536,573
limitations of 5
meaning of 36
and mercy 467
and prayer 497
of self to God 9,71,75,135,440,468
for sin 388,465
spiritual 9,166,503-4
unacceptable 9
Sadducees 539
Sadness 472
Saints 340,341,483,533-34
Salt 539
Salvation 10,32,50,80,102,103,112,117,120, 122,123,145,150,161,182,216,217,220,242, 268,304,314,316,320,335,341,354,360,362, 363,364,371,372,374,396,418,432,463,502, 513,522,523,**539-42**,550,583,598,611,634, 637. *See also* Redemption

and armor of God 74
and faith 6,262,394
of household 264
and the law 296,318,394
and repentance 540
and works 134
Samaritans 41,163,**542**,547
Sanctification 172,264,341,344,**542-43**
Sanctuary 543
Sanhedrin 191,193
Satan 13,14,28,30,42,43,44,45,56,76,89,90, 123,130,143,152,158,213,218,219,224,237, 238,254-255,265,270,282,294,311,318,333, 366,379,385,408,409,415,471,511,**543-44**, 564,634,639
as accuser 13,14
and angels 44,45
and believers 282
fall of 76
and final rebellion 56
as the god of this age 28
and human government 90
and Jesus 265
kingdom of 218,238
oppressive influence of 30
and the world 89
Satisfaction 277
Savior. *See* Deliverance, Salvation
Scheme 544
Scoffing 544
Scorning 523,544
Scripture 190,544-45
Sea. *See* Deep, the
Seal 545,579
Second Coming 28,38,63,**65-68**,163,173, 247,248,268,311,337,338,344-45,352,357, 417,446,476,528,530,560
Security 28,41,113,114,292,524,534
Seed 381. *See also* Offspring
Seeing 415,545
Seek 279,545-46
Seer 546
Selah 546
Self 410,411
Self-confidence 75,320
Self-control 121,212,478,**546**
Self-denial 220
Self-discipline 601
Self-evaluation 70,187,366
Self-examination 257,259,346
Self-indulgence 546
Selfishness 38,248,304
Self-justification 456
Self-righteousness 77,78,318,485
Sensuality 546. *See also* Desires
Separation 33,54,79,80,97,169,230,233,235, 242,340,341,435,437,542,**546-48**
Septuagint 59,83,164,189,195,217,241,314, 315,316,362,417,496,510,545,591,639
Serpent 572

Servant   145,260,321,363,365,474–75,
    480,**548–55**
    Jesus as   480,554
    leadership   94
    of the Lord   554
Servanthood   79,94,402,443,490,548–55
Service
    to God   9,54,79,150,179,187,225,227,273,
        420,443,517,534,549,602,636
    to others   260,281,296,305–7,321,402,443,
        544,551,620,624,637
Servitude   490
Seven   555
Sex   23,24,69,97,108,146,169,282,284,286,
    297,340,415,420,453,508,546,**555–56**,571,
    600
    and animals   52
    and marriage   7,22,125,283,423,433,435,
        437,455–56
    outside of marriage   21,555
Sexuality   22
Shame   229,342,346–47,355,453,556,**557–58**.
    See also Disgrace
Shamelessness   546
Sharing   173,309,493,**558**. See also Fellow-
    ship
Sheep   558–60
Shekel   560
Sheol. See Hell
Shepherd   164,399,412,471,**558–60**
Sickness   98,117,217,406,470,494,**561–65**,
    621. See also Healing
    and anointing   55
    and believers   330–31
    and sin   329,405,561–63
Sign. See Miracles
Sin   46,76,84,89,99,124,128,135,153,170,171,
    172,173,175,179,194,230,254,261,294,320,
    321,323,338,349,352,365,368,371,373,383,
    385,386,387,391,396,398,406,409,410,412,
    415,425,432,450,464,480,503–4,512–13,
    532,540,543,544,551,553–54,**566–70**,584,
    612,640. See also Evil, Wickedness
    and anger   47,50
    and approach to God   69
    and atonement   35,82
    and baptism   103
    and believers   178,225,253,284,295,342,
        366
    bondage to. See Bondage
    cause of   335
    cleansing from   139,178,504,603
    confession of. See Confession
    consciousness of   394,395
    consequences of   2,11,36,49,85,87,92,149,
        182,186,202,207,221,233,235,248,272,
        274,367,407,428,430,433–34,442,448,
        473,483,637,639,641
    conviction of   189,522
    covering of   199
    and crime   203

    and darkness   414
    and death   408,576
    and deceit   213
    as distortion   568
    and fellowship with God   183
    forgiveness of. See Forgiveness
    freedom from   133,294,295,516
    and God's image   351
    and grace   317
    and guilt   322
    and human government   87,88
    intentional   81,82,83
    and jealousy   358
    and judgment   36,48,144,567
    and the law   35,318,399,536,566
    and marriage   433–34
    nature of   39
    and new birth   139
    origin of   224
    and pleasure   485
    and poverty   489–90
    power of   222,541,569
    punishment of   30,82,424,509
    religious   6
    results of. See Death, Guilt, Judgment,
        Punishment
    revelation of   256
    and sacrifice   83,388,465
    and salvation   541
    sex   21–24,555–56
    and sickness   329,405,561–63
    and society   639
    and suffering   2,473–74
    and unbelief   119
    unintentional   81,82,83,250,503
    unpardonable   130,578
    and wealth   623
    and world system   66
    willful   503
Sin nature   88,123,135,177,253,278,**282–84**,
    294–96,326,334,335,359,364,386,392,393,
    396,398,409,414,421,423,432,439,442,450,
    454,477,487,536,546,567,568,593,618
    and the body of sin   134
    and desires   61,86,152,212,222
    expression of   87
    and fruitfulness   299
    and the Holy Spirit   295
    and hostility   249
    and the mind   32,248
    and values   222
Sinai   173,339
Sincerity   570
Singing   496
Singleness   235,436,556
Sinlessness   483,533,543,603
Slander   129,355,365
Slavery   4,9,107,143,150,152,157,293,436,
    443,518,**548–55**,584,641. See also Bond-
    age
    and fear   274

and the law   294
and sin   294,295–96,569
as yoke   525
Sleep   571–72
Snake   572
Social justice   368–72
Social justice system, OT   88,110,142,271,
  307,308,371,404,488–92
Society   11,96,241,435,474,488,639
Son   572–74,641
  of the covenant   158
  of David   572
  of God   46,55,56,117,118,119,130,138,163,
    220,247,385,573
  of man   572–73
Sons
  of God   43,157
  of the prophets   572
Sorcery   81,232,425
Sorrow   472,574
Soul   135,529,**575–77**. See also Death, Life
Sovereignty   577
  of God   5,30,31,34,48,85,111,150,154,160,
    161,175,180,195,201,217,241,253,265,
    269,272,300,326,335,346,348,363,377–
    78,426,451,455,476,496,501,550
  and government   89,90
  of Jesus   417
Spirit. See Holy Spirit, Soul
Spiritism   217,425
Spiritual authority   93,94,146,270
Spiritual gifts   136,165,167,168,244,260,
    279,**305–7**,544,578,579631
  administration   19
  encouragement   246
  healing   330
  interpretation of tongues   30,356
  prophecy   507
  teaching. See Teaching
  tongues   30,356,580,**599–600**
Spiritual growth   287
Spirituality   85,105,136,152,230,340,366,418,
    485,576,577,599
Spiritual warfare   30,43,44,89
Standard. See Banner
Standards   70,105,178,186,349,368,369,370,
    371,372,533,538,566,568,569,625,627
Stars   335,346
Stealing   175,526
Stewardship. See Giving, Ministry, Tithe
Stone   145,151,**581–82**
Stranger   31
Strength   34,247,338,563,**582–84**. See also
    Power
Stress   232
Strife   479
Strong drink   110
Stronghold   292
Stubbornness   513,584
Subjection   551,584–85

Submission   175,229,248,296,304,328,346,
    417,426,427,436,437,443,476,523,**584–85**,
    627,633. See also Obedience
Subordination   328
Substitutionary death   36,84
Success   585,629
Suffering   2,26,67,86,90,103,121,125,127,163,
    173,185,188,206,207,229,344,362,419,
    440,**472–77**,540,550,551,558,562,573,593,
    600. See also Agony, Anguish, Bitter-
    ness, Pain
  and character   476
  of Jesus   26,86,163,207,475–76,562,573,
    593
  with Jesus   26,67,103,185,476
  results of   476
  and sin   2,473–74
  unjustly   90
Sunday   525
Superiority   327
Superstition   519
Supper   100
Supplication. See Prayer
Survivor   521–22
Swearing   208. See also Oath
Sword of the Spirit   74
Symbol   73,83,84,97,168,170,172,388
  altar as   36
  animal sacrifice   130
  and apocalyptic material   56
  ark of the covenant   73
  Babylon as   88,89,97
  baptism   100–104
  bride   142
  claws   345
  dreams   237
  drinking   237,238
  eating (food)   241–42
  fire   280–81
  fullness   277
  generation   302
  harvest   325
  hearing (ear)   240
  horn   345
  incense   352
  lamp   388
  marriage   435
  mountain   338
  mourning   446
  nakedness   453
  oil   469–70
  and Old Testament sacrifices   83,84
  and reality   36,73,168
  right and left   532–33
  and ritual cleanness   170,171
  and sacrifice   172
  sheep   558–59
  shepherd   559–60
  sickness   562
  sleep   571
  stone   581

tabernacle as   36,586
teeth   345
vine   612
walk   615
washing   620
yoke   641
Sympathy. *See* Compassion, Love, Pity
Synagogue   164,585

Tabernacle   35,36,69,82,83,140,154,162,239,
   258,275,361,388,443,465,468,478,502,504,
   543,**586–87**,609
Talent   446. *See also* Money
Tartaros   337
Taste   587
Tax   90,587–88
Teaching   226,227,228,235,270,352,389,403,
   502–3,520,**588–92**,632–33. *See also*
   Warnings
Temper   286
Temple   6,35,69,73,140,148,151,166,224,227,
   239,258,321,338,359,388,443,466,504,
   543,**586–87**,609
 believers as   145,151,**166**,224,227,321
 of the Holy Spirit   24,166
 tabernacle and   586–87
 tax   588
Temptation   90,141,222,261,**592–94**,634
Ten Commandments   21,88,142,175,349,
   390,581,582,634
 adultery. *See* Adultery
 coveting   200
 false witness   595
 God's name   129,454
 idolatry   349
 and love   142
 murder   449
 Sabbath   524–25
 Stealing   175,526
 Swearing   208
Terror. *See* Fear
Testimony   594–95
Testing   70,155,259,**592–94**
Thanksgiving   495,595–96
Theocracy   88
Thinking   441,596–97. *See also* Knowledge,
   Mind, Reason, Understanding
Thirst   348
Throne   320,499,597
Time   28,37,42,155,181,210–12,246–47,
   458,**597–98**,641
Tithe   41,307,308,309,491,504. *See also*
   Giving
Today   598,613
Toil. *See* Work
Toleration   107
Tongue   121,483
Tongues   599–600
 of fire   102,599
 gift of   599–600

and the Holy Spirit   580
 interpretation of   30,356
Torah. *See* Law
Torment   600
Touch   600
Tradition   43,64,80,92,125,152,171,177,278,
   485,535
Training   20,228,229,588,**601**
Transfiguration   66,173
Transformation   19,26,28,42,48,107,109,121,
   133,139,155,184,185,198,220,227,258,290,
   312,344,345,350,352,422,432,442,458,468,
   502,529,568,580,592,634
 and believers   121,220
 and the Holy Spirit   580
Transgression. *See* Rebellion
Treachery   123
Treasure   335,381,**601**. *See also* Wealth
Trials   476,484,**593–94**
Tribe   601–2
Tribulation, the Great   161,231–32,413,507,
   541
Trichotomy   283
Trinity   268,269,313,314,501,578
Trouble   252. *See also* Distress
Trust   33,47,48,81,114,117,122,179,232,236,
   272,283,307,314,320,343,362,363,450,484,
   513,540,557,604. *See also* Belief, Faith
Trustworthiness. *See also* Faithfulness
Truth   71,72,105,113,178,213,218,250,259,
   270,296,355,384,385,393,403,567,570,
   589,**602–3**. *See also* Faithfulness
 acknowledgment of   17,20
 and armor of God   74
 and falsehood   214
 and freedom   295
Types   478

Unanimity   606
Unbelief   5,36,37,50,51,115,116,119,162,220,
   286,302,333,463,**604**. *See also* Belief,
   Faith
Unbelievers   70,79,190
Uncircumcision   168
Unclean. *See* Clean and Unclean
Understanding   604–6. *See also* Knowledge, Mind, Thinking, Wisdom
Uniformitarianism   112,202
Union with Jesus   23,55,102,103,104,106,
   121,125,133,136,206,220,238,276,395,397,
   410,437,536,569
Unity   20,30,**606–7**
 and the church   103,104,136,146,167,180,
   365,422,481,606,641
 of the church   6,104,164205,303,306,515
 and the Holy Spirit   103
 and Israel   79
 and prayer   29,500
Universe   58,66,141,201,202,225,241,245,
   246,311,321,352,384,386,557

moral nature of 154,531
order of 635
physical 28,112,174,283,293,335,529
spiritual 43,45,46,87,122,141,250,294,335,
384,424–26,442,529,540,568,604,605
supernatural 217–19
Unjust governments 90
Unleavened bread 140,607
Unpardonable sin 130,578
Unrighteousness. See Sin
Uprightness 607
Urim and Thummim 249,400,503

Values 287,326,380,**609**. See also Heart
Vanity 608–9
Vegetarianism 286
Veil 328,609–10
Vengeance 67,449,**610–11**. See also Punishment, Revenge
Vicarious atonement. See Atonement
Victory 471,524,**611–12**
Vine 299,500,**612**
and believers 106
and Israel 2
Jesus as 140,299,612
Vineyard 612
Violence 132,324,325,345,430,448,**612–13**
Viper. See Serpent
Virgin 613
Virtue 459
Vision 613
Voice of God 280,333,526,560,598,**613–14**
Vows 427,460–61,547,**614**

Wages 531,**615**,637
Wailing 615
Waiting. See Hope
Walking 615
Wants 615–16
War 30,43,72,85,90,107,132,248,287,294,
550,553,557,610,**616–19**
Warnings 20,31,48,67,69,70,86,116,142,155,
175,207,288,320,326,365,462,591,594,**619–
20**
Washing 100,620
Watching 65,125,**620**. See also Guarding
Watchman 620
Water 103,621
and baptism 30,101,102,103,104
and cleansing 170
Way 621
Weakness 238,559,**621–22**,641
Wealth 90,98,124,131,141,312,342,343,410,
488,**622–25**. See also Money
Wedding 100
Weeping 625
Welcome 8
Wheat and tares 381
Wholeness 480–81,482

Wickedness 18,182,203,430,431,479,518,
524,612,**625–26**. See also Evil, Sin
Widow 271,307,435,489,**626**
Wife 166,182
Will 189,502,553,569,600,**626–28**
Will of God 9,70,71,86,152,161,184,186,
187,192,193,206,220,336,340,350,354,426,
455,456,499,501,502,503,511,513,533,545,
594,605,620,626–28. See also Ordain
Wine 110,458–59,**628–29**
Wineskins 458–59
Wisdom 111,145,228,355,606,616,**629–31**
and believers 121
of God 123,287,630
human 28,287,630
and knowledge 629
of the world 121
Wisdom literature 629
Witchcraft 81,232,425
Witness 13,14,88,148,173,259,449,**594–95**.
See also Warning
Woes 631
Women 585. See also Male
and authority 95,633
and beauty 108,109
in the church 199,245,328,430,**631–33**
and head coverings 199
and leadership 428,430,632
rights of 428,435
silence of 632
and teaching 632–33
and vows 614
and worship 632
Wonders. See Miracles
Word 633–36
Word of God 7,59,71,74,77,81,86,96,107,
112,116,128,143,157,185,187,190,198,214,
215,225,229,236,237,240,245–46,251,252,
259,261,272,274,315,321,331,332–33,347,
350,361,387,388,406,412,438,445,447,459,
462,463,471,505,513–14,526,543,544,545,
589,603,609,634–36
Work 95,147,231,434,459,473,531,549–50,
636–38
Works 10,85,114,115,120,121,134,146,184,
202,315,316,319,326,337,364,368,373,387,
394,418,487,505,514,**638**. See also Effort
and believers 146,202
and faith 10,114,115,121
and justification 373
and righteousness 85,120,184
World 67,89,90,121,123,152,326,340,447,
471,487,543,548,611,**638–39**
Worldliness 315,639
Worldly concerns 57,58
Worry. See Anxiety
Worship 36,54,62,78,82,167,170,171,258,
265,269,275,308,311,312,314,315,324,328,
339,342,348,349,353,361,362,419,443,466,
471,478,494,504,523,543,546,549,551,552,
590,607,608,**638–40**

acceptable 8,9
and the commandments 9
first recorded instance of 34
and the heart 69
and holiness 69
hypocritical 325
and justice 467
and morality 9,325,466–67
pagan 33,35,97,338,350,508
ritual and ceremonial 8,9,69,140,169,
    503,519,586,639
and ritual meals 242
and sacrifice 464–65
self-sacrifice as 468
and women 632

Worthiness 640
Wrath. *See* Anger
Wrong 640. *See also* Sin

Yahweh 33,34,44,166,313,416
Year of Jubilee 490,491,550
Yeast. *See* Leaven
Yoke 525,548,**641**
  the law as 5
  with unbelievers 30,604
Youth 642

Zeal 358–59
Zion 338

Index of
Scripture
References

(chief references in **bold figures**)

Genesis

1 — 112,148,316,430,
    448,547
1:1 — 200,313
1:2 — 214,245,313
1:4 — 413,547
1:5 — 148,413
1:6 — 547
1:7 — 547
1:8 — 148
1:9 — 112
1:10 — 112,148
1:11 — 106,111
1:14 — 547
1:15 — 413
1:18 — 413,547,538
1:20 — 575
1:21 — 200,407,575
1:24 — 52,**375**,575
1:25 — 52
1:26 — 53,238,313,
    350,**351**,427,
    431,**433**
1:27 — 53,200,350,407,
    427,431,**433**,
    556
1:28 — 433,556
1:30 — 575
2 — 262,430,448
2:1 — 346
2:2 — 524
2:3 — 200,339,524
2:4 — 10
2:7 — 238,322,406,**407**,
    431,575
2:9 — 107
2:15 — 636
2:15-17 — 431
2:17 — **407**
2:18-25 — 431
2:19 — 148
2:20 — 433
2:21 — 571
2:23 — 138,282,**427**,433

2:24 — 282,**283**,556
2:25 — 453,557
3 — 407,438,448,572
3:4 — 76
3:5 — 76,257,**382**
3:6 — 407
3:7 — 257,407,453
3:8 — 331,614
3:8-13 — 434
3:10 — 272,453,614
3:11-13 — 87
3:13 — 213
3:14 — **238**
3:15 — 327
3:16 — **221**,**427**,434,
    473,474
3:17 — 331,473,474,636
3:17-19 — 433,434
3:19 — 238
3:20 — 148
3:21 — 34,413,465
3:22 — 382
3:24 — 43
4 — 87,149,407,448,
    465
4:1 — 555,571
4:1-18 — 434
4:2 — 207
4:3 — 207,373
4:4 — 126
4:7 — 221,434,448,538
4:8-16 — 440
4:11-12 — 207
4:13 — 106
4:15 — 448
4:18 — 138
4:19-22 — 434
4:19-24 — 87
4:21 — 266
4:23-24 — 434
4:25 — 448
4:26 — 149
5 — 26,40
5:1 — 200,302
5:1-3 — 350,**351**

5:2 — 200
5:22 — 397
5:24 — 528
5:29 — 473,637
6 — 72,375,431
6-8 — 431
6:1-4 — 217
6:2-4 — 43
6:2 — 109,572
6:3 — 72,189
6:4 — 572
6:5 — 87,189
6:6 — 189
6:7 — 200
6:9 — 302,533
6:11 — 190,241,277,612
6:11-14 — 189
6:12 — 190,282
6:17 — 285
6:18 — 250
6:19 — 282
7 — 72,375,431
7:2 — 169
7:4 — 292
7:6-7 — 285
7:10 — 285
7:11 — 214
7:12 — 292
7:17 — 285,292
8 — 72,431
8:6 — 292
8:20 — 34,169,465
8:21 — 465
9 — 88
9:2 — 324
9:3 — 286
9:4 — 133
9:4-6 — 132
9:5-6 — **11**,87,89,**351**,
    406,407,448
9:6 — 132,350,431
9:9 — 250
9:11 — 250,285
9:15 — 285
9:28 — 285

10:1 — 285
10:8 — 138
10:15-18 — 150
10:32 — 285
11 — 26,40
11:7 — 331,604
11:10 — 285
12 — 115,131,431
12-22 — 115
12:1 — 195,389
12:2 — 114,195,196
12:3 — 195,196
12:7 — 62,196,469
12:8 — 465
12:11 — 108
12:13 — 497
12:14 — 108
13:4 — 465
13:15 — 469
13:16 — 469
14 — 40
14:13 — 194,338
14:18 — 271,313
14:19 — 313
14:20 — 308
15 — 114,194
15:1 — 531
15:1-4 — 550
15:1-21 — 195
15:2 — 92
15:3 — 469
15:5 — 114,469
15:6 — 113,114,168,
    397,534,535
15:7 — 389
15:7-21 — 196
15:8-21 — 133
15:9 — 426
15:12 — 571
15:16 — 97,151,617
15:18 — 469
16:2 — 144
16:4-5 — 223
16:6 — 596

681

16:9 — 92
16:9-13 — 44
16:13 — 313
17 — 131
17:1 — 33
17:1-22 — 195
17:5 — 453
17:7 — 250,469
17:9 — 469
17:10 — 469
17:10-27 — 168
17:11 — 469
17:14 — 167,195
17:15 — 148
17:17 — 106,389
17:19 — 469
18:1 — 62
18:12 — 389,416
18:15 — 213
18:16-33 — 355,498
18:19 — 160,397,621
19:1 — 44
19:2 — 416,438
19:3 — 100
19:19 — 252
19:24 — 280
20:3-7 — 237
20:11 — 273
20:17 — 329
21:22-39 — 460
21:23 — 213
21:33 — 313
22 — 465
22:2 — 156,418
22:11 — 44
22:15-18 — 44
22:18 — 614
24 — 62,400,416,419,
435
24:3 — 241,313
24:7 — 44
24:8 — 293,461
24:16 — 109
24:27 — 602
24:40 — 44
24:41 — 460
24:43 — 613
24:57 — 148
24:58 — 149
24:63 — 68
25 — 126
25:8 — 141
25:19-23 — 326
25:23 — 547
25:31-34 — 126
25:34 — 223
26:2 — 62
26:5 — 614
26:7 — 109,272
26:9 — 10
26:24 — 314
26:25 — 35,465
26:28 — 460
26:29 — 252

26:31 — 474
27:4 — 418
27:9 — 418
27:12 — 63
27:14 — 418
27:36 — 126
28:3-4 — 33
28:12 — 77
28:17 — 301
28:18 — 54
28:22 — 308
29-46 — 625
29:4 — 142
29:14 — 282
29:17 — 108
29:21 — 597
29:21-30 — 434
29:22 — 435
29:27 — 435
30:1 — 156,358
30:23 — 230
30:27 — 232
30:40 — 547
31:11 — 45
31:29 — 252
31:44-55 — 194
31:48-49 — 148
31:52 — 252
32:22-31 — 258
32:28 — 356
33:10 — 279
34 — 47
34:7 — 230,555
34:13 — 212
34:14 — 230
34:15 — 426
34:19 — 215
34:22 — 426
34:24 — 301,426
34:25 — 426,472
34:30 — 231
34:31 — 508
35:1 — 62
35:2 — 170
35:3 — 35,231
35:7 — 35
35:9 — 62
35:10 — 356
35:11 — 33
37:11 — 358
38:21-22 — 508
38:26 — 534
39:4 — 549
39:6 — 108
39:9 — 566
39:14 — 338
39:19 — 47
39:20 — 47,370
39:20-22 — 370
40-41 — 237
40:3 — 370
40:4 — 549
40:5 — 370
40:8 — 123

40:14 — 370
40:19 — 282
40:23 — 288
41:19 — 488
41:35 — 92
41:51 — 231
42:11 — 341
42:15 — 593
42:16 — 370,593
42:19 — 341,370
42:21 — 231
42:22 — 566
42:31 — 341
42:33 — 341
42:34 — 341
42:38 — 574
43:1 — 148
43:9 — 106
43:33 — 126
43:34 — 110,238
44:20 — 418
44:31 — 574
45:8 — 267
45:26 — 113
46:6 — 231
47:6 — 50
47:9 — 252
48:3 — 62
48:13-20 — 532
48:18 — 324
49 — 130
49:6 — 47,221
49:7 — 47
49:21 — 108
49:22-26 — 601
49:26 — 42
50:15 — 252
50:17 — 252
50:20 — 252
50:24-25 — 30

Exodus

1:1 — 636
1:11 — 636
1:14 — 127
1:18 — 149
1:26 — 346
2:1 — 263
2:2 — 108
2:6 — 180
2:13 — 456
2:14 — 448
2:24 — 520
3 — 44,528
3:2 — 44,62,280
3:5 — 69
3:6 — 62,314
3:7 — 489
3:8 — 216
3:12 — 416,549
3:13-15 — 416
3:14 — 416

3:15 — 302,314
3:16 — 62,243,356
3:19-20 — 324
4 — 115
4:1 — 62,113,115,588
4:1-8 — 115
4:5 — 62,113,314
4:8 — 113,115
4:9 — 113
4:14 — 48
4:21 — 293,334,444
4:22 — 572
4:23 — 516,549
4:31 — 113
5:2 — 332,383
5:9 — 213
5:19 — 231,252
5:22 — 231
5:23 — 231
6:1 — 582
6:3 — 33,62,416
6:5 — 517
6:6 — 34,73,517,582,
641
6:7 — 444,582,641
6:16-20 — 41
7:1-2 — 505
7:3 — 334,444
7:5 — 444
7:9 — 444
7:11 — 424
7:13 — 334
7:14 — 334
7:22 — 334,424
8:7 — 424
8:15 — 334
8:19 — 334,425
8:23 — 230
8:29 — 18
8:30-31 — 497
8:32 — 334
9:7 — 334
9:11 — 5
9:12 — 334
9:18 — 292
9:35 — 334
10:1 — 334
10:2 — 16
10:14 — 49
10:20 — 334
10:21 — 413
10:27 — 334,627
11:1 — 49
11:2 — 456
11:7 — 230
11:10 — 334
12 — 106,478
12:3 — 356
12:3-28 — 266
12:5 — 159,426
12:8 — 140,607
12:12 — 444
12:14 — 302,520
12:21 — 149

12:29 — 516
12:31 — 445
12:39 — 140,607
12:43-44 — 242
13:2-15 — 280
13:3 — 389
13:3-10 — 154,275
13:5 — 389
13:11-16 — 516
13:12 — 426
13:14-16 — 266
13:15 — 426,448
13:19 — 30
13:21 — 173,399
13:22 — 173
14:3 — 596
14:4 — 311,334
14:8 — 334,**383**
14:12 — 124
14:14 — 617
14:19-20 — 173
14:31 — 113,115
15 — 428
15:15-17 — 196
15:6 — 532
15:7 — 49
15:13 — 419
15:20 — 428,505
15:22-24 — 513
15:23 — 148
15:26 — 329,614
16:1-8 — 513
16:4 — 593
16:10 — 311
16:29 — 106
16:33-34 — 73
17:1 — 174,447
17:7 — **593**
17:9 — 327
17:15 — 99
18:4 — 433
18:25 — 327
19-24 — 82
19:4 — 196
19:5 — 196,332,613,614
19:9 — 113,173
19:15 — 7
19:16-25 — 69
19:18 — 280
19:19 — 280,614
19:23 — 339
20 — 175
20:1 — 196
20:2-7 — 196
20:3 — 175
20:4 — 175,349
20:5 — 313,358
20:6 — 358
20:7 — 129,175,608
20:8-11 — 175,339,524
20:12 — 175,266
20:13 — 175,449
20:14 — 21,175
20:15 — 175

20:16 — 175,176,213, 595
20:17 — 175,313,358
20:20 — 593
20:21 — 413
20:22-23:19 — 634
20:24-26 — 36
21-24 — 176
21:1-23:19 — 196
21:2 — 293
21:2-11 — 88,550
21:5 — 293,418
21:6 — 240
21:10 — 282
21:12-36 — 88
21:15 — 266
21:17 — 266
21:19 — 52
21:22 — 52,433
21:23 — 406,407
21:32 — 560
22 — 526
22:1-15 — 88,370
22:4 — 203
22:4-9 — 236
22:7 — 203
22:9 — 203
22:11 — 324,460
22:16-31 — 88
22:18 — 425
22:21 — 31
22:22 — 626
22:22-24 — 48
22:25 — 488
22:25-27 — 404
23:1 — 213,608
23:1-9 — 88
23:3 — 488,490
23:6 — 488,490
23:7 — 213
23:9 — 31
23:10-11 — 491,525
23:10-19 — 88
23:11 — 2,488
23:12 — 525,637
23:16 — 154
23:17 — 62
23:20 — 43
23:20-33 — 198
23:21 — 614
23:22 — 614
23:25-26 — 561
23:32 — 33
23:33 — 104,153
24 — 196
24:1-8 — 196
24:7 — 138
24:12 — 175
24:13 — 549
24:14 — 243,275
24:15-18 — 280
24:16 — 173,275
24:18 — 292
25-26 — 82,478

25-27 — 586
25:8 — 239
25:9 — 478
25:10-20 — 73
25:11 — 169
25:17 — 169
25:22 — 586
25:40 — 478
26:33 — 547
27 — 82
28-29 — 82,470
28:1-3 — 427
28:16 — 400
28:20 — 503
28:30 — 400,502
28:35 — 549
28:38 — 8,464
28:41 — 54
28:43 — 549
29:1 — 130
29:35 — 82
29:36 — 54,82
29:37 — 82
29:38-41 — 465
29:40 — 628
29:45-46 — 239
30 — 82
30-31 — 586
30:6 — 35
30:11-16 — 517,587
30:15 — 488
30:16 — 82
30:30 — 54
30:34 — 510
30:35-37 — 353
31:12-17 — 524
31:17 — 7
32:7-12 — 48
32:11-14 — 498
32:12 — 226
32:13 — 353
32:18 — 611
32:19 — 47
32:22 — 252
32:34 — 30
33:12-23 — 258
33:14 — 524
33:19 — 180,311
33:20 — 258,311
34:6 — 7,49,419
34:7 — 49,289,419
34:19-20 — 516
34:23-24 — 62
34:26 — 339
34:28 — 265
34:30 — 609
34:34 — 502
35-40 — 586
35:8 — 54
35:21 — 627
35:28 — 54
35:29 — 627
35:30-36:1 — 578
36 — 297,308

36:1-4 — 629
38:21 — 174
40:5 — 35
40:10 — 54
40:34 — 311
40:35 — 311

Leviticus

1-4 — 502
1:3 — 8,221,426
2:1-2 — 353
2:1-16 — 304
2:13 — 539
2:14 — 282
3:1 — 426
4:2 — 467
4:3 — 54
4:3-12 — 82
4:4 — 85
4:5 — 54
4:13-21 — 82
4:15 — 24,243
4:20 — 289
4:22-26 — 82
4:24 — 85
4:26 — 82,289
4:27-35 — 82
4:29 — 85
4:31 — 289
4:35 — 289
5:1 — 460,595
5:10 — 289
5:12 — 289
5:13 — 304
5:16 — 289
5:18 — 289
5:26 — 289
6:2 — 213
6:3 — 213
6:5 — 213
6:7 — 289
6:14-23 — 304
6:15 — 353
7-8 — 470
8:8 — 400
8:10 — 54
8:12 — 54
9:4 — 62
9:6 — 62
9:23 — 62
10:1-3 — 69
10:1-4 — 503
10:3 — 339
10:10 — 339
10:11 — 339,502,504
10:16 — 503
11 — 169,375
11:43-44 — 170
12:1-5 — 427
12:13-14 — 169
13 — 405
13-15 — 504

13:42-53 — 405
13:45-46 — 169
14 — 82,405
14:10 — 130
14:19 — 69
14:21 — 488
14:47-52 — 405
14:48 — 562
15 — 169
15:31 — 547
16 — 69,83
16:2 — 173
16:12 — 35
16:15 — 83
16:16 — 83
16:21 — 83
16:29 — 265
16:30 — 83
16:31 — 265
16:34 — 83
17:7 — 22
17:11 — 35,82,132,**407,
465,529**
18 — 176,453,555
18:5 — 375
18:6 — 69,282
18:6-10 — 435
18:12 — 282
18:13 — 282
18:22 — 6,555,571
18:23 — 52,555
18:25 — 30
19 — 176,502
19:1 — 394
19:2 — 339
19:5 — 221
19:10 — 488,491
19:11 — 176,212,213
19:12 — 213
19:13 — 176
19:14 — 96,132,176
19:15 — 176,370,488,
490
19:17 — 325
19:18 — 106,176,**297,**
325,418,610
19:18-32 — 456
19:19 — 641
19:20 — 516
19:26 — 232,425
19:29 — 21
19:31 — 425
19:32 — 26
19:33-34 — 31
20 — 204,453,502,555
20:6 — 425
20:6-8 — 208
20:9 — 208
20:10 — 21
20:13 — 6,571
20:19 — 282
20:21 — 18
20:24-25 — 547
20:26 — 314,339

20:27 — 425
21:2 — 282
21:7 — 339
21:10 — 470
21:14 — 234
22 — 526
22:1-33 — 8
22:19 — 221
22:20-21 — 8
22:22 — 221
22:31 — 8,9
22:32 — 8,9,16
23:4 — 37,68
23:4-8 — 154,275
23:5-8 — 478
23:9-21 — 154,275
23:13 — 628
23:14 — 302
23:22 — 491
23:26-32 — 265
23:33-43 — 154,275
23:37 — 68
24:7 — 353
24:10-23 — 11
24:11 — 129,208
24:12 — 447
24:13-16 — 11
24:14 — 581
24:16 — 129
24:17 — 431
24:17-21 — 11
24:22 — 31
25:17 — 96
25:18-19 — 462
25:23-24 — 490
25:35 — 31
25:35-37 — 491
25:39-54 — 490
25:39-55 — 550
25:47-55 — 516
25:49 — 282
26 — 40
26:7-17 — 248
26:15 — 259
26:16 — 608
26:18 — 228
26:19 — 76
26:20 — 608
26:24-25 — 610
26:28 — 228
26:30 — 4
26:42 — 40
26:45 — 40
27 — 52,516
27:1-8 — 26,427
27:2-8 — 560
27:26 — 123
27:30-33 — 307

Numbers

1 — 504
1:4 — 327

1:16 — 149
1:18 — 40
1:20 — 427
1:22 — 427
1:50 — 549
3 — 504
3-4 — 586
3:1-45 — 281
3:3 — 470
3:6 — 549
3:7-8 — 549
3:12-15 — 427
3:31 — 549
3:39 — 41,174
3:46 — 560
4:3 — 26
4:12 — 550
4:15 — 146
4:19 — 146
4:23 — 26
4:30 — 26
4:35 — 26
4:39 — 26
5 — 358
5:1-4 — 169
5:7-8 — 526
5:8 — 123,526
5:19 — 81
5:20 — 81
5:21 — 460
5:23 — 460
5:27 — 460
5:31 — 106,293
6 — 614
6:1-21 — 547
6:3 — 7
7 — 586
7:10-11 — 214
7:84 — 214
7:88 — 214
8 — 504
9:1-14 — 478
9:2 — 68
9:6 — 10
9:6-12 — 169
9:7 — 68
10:2 — 79
10:9 — 248
11:1 — 48
11:1-3 — 280
11:6 — 68
11:11 — 231
11:15 — 252
11:33 — 48
12:1-8 — 505
12:3 — 347
12:6 — 237
12:9 — 48
13:27 — 10
14 — 115,474,513,598
14:3 — 124
14:10 — 62
14:10-19 — 355
14:11 — 113,115

14:11-19 — 498
14:18 — 49,289,474
14:19 — 289
14:22 — 311
14:29 — 27
14:33 — 292
14:34-35 — 474
15:7 — 628
15:18 — 106
15:22 — 259
15:30 — 129
15:39-40 — 519
16 — 504
16:3 — 427
16:9 — 547
16:16 — 62
16:19 — 62
16:21 — 547
16:30 — 115,200
17:10 — 73
18 — 504
18:1-7 — 69
18:8-32 — 516
18:12-14 — 282
18:19 — 539
18:21-32 — 516
19 — 169
19:7 — 282
20:12 — 113
20:14 — 142
21:7 — 497
22:4-6 — 207
22:22-25 — 98
23:7 — 508
23:18 — 508
23:19 — 522
23:23 — 232
24:3 — 508
24:15 — 508
24:20 — 508
24:21 — 508
24:23 — 508
25 — 99
25:3 — 48
26 — 168
27:11 — 282
27:12-23 — 324
27:16-17 — 559
27:17 — 559
27:21 — 400
28:7 — 110
28:16-25 — 478
30 — 460
30:3-9 — 614
30:3-11 — 125
31 — 504
31:2-3 — 610
31:16 — 191
31:17-18 — 555
32:10 — 48
32:13 — 252,292
32:15 — 153
33:55 — 231
35 — 96

35:12-31 — 516
35:22-25 — 449
35:23 — 252
35:27 — 449
35:30 — 449
35:31 — 449,517
35:33 — 487

Deuteronomy

1:8 — 389
1:12 — 106
1:13 — 159
1:16 — 142
1:17 — 123,142
1:26 — 174
1:30 — 617
1:31 — 266,267
1:32 — 113
1:38 — 356
1:39 — 382
1:42 — 75,248
1:43 — 76,174
1:43-45 — 500
2:30 — 576
3:22 — 617
4:1 — 175
4:4 — 77,88
4:5-9 — 252
4:6 — 605
4:9-10 — 156
4:11 — 413
4:13 — 634
4:15-19 — 349
4:16-17 — 52
4:23-26 — 48
4:24 — 280,313
4:25 — 49,252
4:28 — 581
4:29 — 279,575
4:30 — 442,613,614
4:32 — 200
4:32-34 — 582
4:34 — 18,444
4:37 — 174,419
4:38 — 419,533,614
4:39 — 15,16,252,383
4:40 — 174,175,252
5 — 175
5:5 — 272
5:11 — 129,454,608
5:12 — 339
5:15 — 520,525
5:16 — 266
5:17 — 449
5:18 — 21
5:20 — 213,595,608
5:22-28 — 614
5:23-27 — 280
5:29 — 37
5:32-33 — 174
6 — 592
6:2 — 175

6:3 — 462
6:4-6 — 157,175
6:4-9 — 157,590
6:5 — 420,575
6:6 — 420,590
6:7 — 157,590
6:7-9 — 157
6:8 — 125
6:13 — 273,460
6:16 — 593
6:22 — 444
6:25 — 534
7 — 160,161
7:1-2 — 617
7:3-4 — 435
7:3-6 — 617
7:6 — 160,339,502
7:7-9 — 160
7:9 — 175,313,419
7:10 — 175
7:9-11 — 325
7:12 — 375,419,561,628
7:12-15 — 252,622
7:12-24 — 33
7:13-15 — 419
7:14 — 104,561
7:15 — 252,561
7:16 — 617
7:18 — 520
7:19-24 — 444
7:25 — 200
7:28 — 622
8 — 229
8:1 — 175
8:1-5 — 228
8:2 — 520
8:3 — 141,228,348
8:5 — 228,267,314
8:6 — 615
8:11 — 125
8:11-19 — 288
8:14 — 623
8:16 — 593
8:17-18 — 582,623
8:18 — 134
9:1-8 — 49
9:4-6 — 534
9:5 — 10
9:5-8 — 390
9:23 — 113,115
9:28 — 5
10:8 — 547,549
10:12 — 175,273,420,
        575
10:13 — 173,175,420
10:16 — 168
10:17-18 — 314
10:18 — 31,152,271,626
10:19 — 31,314,418
11:1 — 37,175
11:1-7 — 228
11:3 — 637
11:7 — 637
11:9 — 175

11:13 — 575
11:14 — 628
11:16 — 125
11:16-17 — 48
11:26-28 — 131,462
11:29 — 338
12 — 131
12:1-7 — 35
12:5 — 160,466
12:5-14 — 307
12:6 — 126,466
12:7 — 62
12:10 — 175,524
12:11 — 160
12:13-14 — 466
12:17 — 126
12:18 — 160
12:21 — 160
12:23 — 133
13:1-5 — 505
13:3 — 575
13:6-10 — 582
13:6-11 — 449
13:8-9 — 449
13:17 — 180
14 — 375
14:2 — 160,339
14:3-21 — 169
14:12-15 — 308
14:23 — 37,126
14:21 — 339
14:22-26 — 307
14:23-25 — 160
14:26 — 110
14:27-29 — 307
14:28-29 — 491
14:29 — 31
15 — 131
15:1-3 — 491
15:1-4 — 488
15:1-11 — 488
15:1-18 — 550
15:2 — 160
15:3 — 143
15:4 — 488
15:6 — 160
15:7 — 143,160,488
15:8 — 143
15:7-10 — 405
15:7-11 — 491
15:9 — 125,488
15:10 — 637
15:11 — 160
15:12-15 — 143
15:12-18 — 240,490
15:13-14 — 490
15:15 — 516,520
15:15-16 — 160
15:20 — 160
16:1-8 — 154,275,478
16:5 — 637
16:9-11 — 154,275
16:12 — 520
16:13 — 154,275

16:15 — 361
16:18-20 — 370
16:20 — 175
17:1 — 130
17:1-7 — 370
17:2-7 — 582
17:2-20 — 1
17:8 — 160
17:9 — 504
17:10 — 160
17:14-20 — 376
17:17 — 434
17:19 — 96
18 — 81
18:2 — 353
18:5 — 37,160
18:6 — 160
18:9-12 — 217,425
18:9-13 — 400,505
18:9-14 — 6
18:10 — 232
18:10-11 — 81
18:14 — 232
18:14-20 — 82
18:14-21 — 192
18:15 — 393,505
18:16 — 175
18:18 — 400
18:20 — 505
18:21 — 505
18:22 — 505
19 — 96
19:1-20 — 11
19:9 — 37
19:12 — 243
19:15 — 13,14,270
19:15-21 — 595
19:18 — 213
19:18-19 — 13
19:21 — 407
20 — 617
20:3-4 — 272
20:5 — 214,601
20:16-17 — 617
20:16-18 — 435
21:1-9 — 243
21:5 — 160,549
21:17 — 15,126,236,281
21:18 — 512
21:18-21 — 582
21:19 — 243,301
21:20 — 238,512
21:21 — 301
22:7 — 175
22:10 — 641
22:13-30 — 435
22:15 — 243
22:24 — 582
22:29 — 234
23:14 — 216
23:17 — 508
23:18 — 508
23:19 — 615
23:19-20 — 143,491

23:21 — 230
24:1-4 — 233
24:2-9 — 234
24:4 — 433
24:5 — 293
24:9 — 520
24:10-13 — 143,404
24:12 — 488
24:14 — 31,488
24:15 — 488
24:17 — 31,271
24:18 — 31,520
24:19 — 31
24:19-21 — 626
24:22 — 520
25:7 — 301
25:13-16 — 6
25:15 — 175
26:2 — 160
26:11-15 — 31
26:12-13 — 626
26:12-15 — 308
26:14 — 614
26:16 — 575
26:17 — 614
27:10 — 614
27:15-16 — 207
27:15-26 — 39
27:18 — 132
27:19 — 271
28 — 131,462
28:1 — 614
28:2 — 614
28:7 — 32,622
28:8 — 174,622
28:11 — 622
28:13 — 327
28:15 — 614
28:15-68 — 391
28:16-18 — 207
28:25 — 154
28:28 — 424
28:37 — 147,223,508
28:41 — 152
28:45 — 614
28:47 — 348
28:48 — 348,490
28:49 — 604
28:52 — 114
28:59 — 561
28:62 — 614
28:66 — 113
29 — 196
29:12 — 207,460
29:14-21 — 207,460
29:16-18 — 128
29:19 — 460
29:21 — 252,460
29:23 — 539
29:23-28 — 48
29:26 — 460,627
29:28 — 530
29:29 — 123
30 — 77,462

30:2 — 575,614
30:3 — 180
30:4 — 99
30:6 — 168,575
30:7 — 460
30:8 — 614
30:9-10 — 265,391
30:10 — 575,614
30:12 — 77
30:14 — 77
30:15 — 252
30:15-20 — 406
30:16-20 — 420
30:18 — 175
30:19 — 159,174,407
30:20 — 614
31:5 — 216
31:8 — 2
31:11 — 62,160
31:12-13 — 588
31:16 — 1
31:17 — 252
31:21 — 252
31:29 — 190,252
32 — 610
32:4 — 260,369,482,637
32:6 — 267
32:15 — 313
32:17 — 217
32:18 — 138
32:20 — 259
32:23 — 252
32:24 — 265
32:34 — 610
32:35 — 610
32:36 — 293
32:36-38 — 610
32:41 — 610
32:43 — 610
32:47 — 175,634
33:7 — 433
33:8 — 315,400
33:8-10 — 502
33:9 — 15
33:15 — 42
33:17 — 246
33:29 — 213,433,540
34:9 — 324,578

Joshua

1 — 88
1:1 — 549
1:7-8 — 391
1:11 — 213
1:15 — 286
1:21 — 109
1:25 — 231
2:11 — 193
2:17 — 293,460,461
2:19 — 293
2:20 — 293,460,461
3:10 — 313

3:12 — 159
3:15 — 285
4:7 — 520
4:18 — 285
4:24 — 37
5:6 — 614
5:10-12 — 478
5:13-14 — 34
5:14 — 346
6 — 225
6:17-19 — 617
6:18 — 231
6:21 — 617
6:26 — 292
7 — 225
8:33 — 243,338
9:14 — 191,400,497
9:19 — 460
9:27 — 160
10:10-19 — 34
11:11 — 617
11:12 — 617
11:14 — 617
11:20 — 617
11:21 — 617
15:63 — 5
17:12 — 5
20 — 96
20:4 — 243
21:13-38 — 14
21:44 — 524
22 — 35
22:4 — 524
22:5 — 420,575
23:3 — 34
23:6-13 — 97
23:7 — 79
23:12 — 33,79
23:14 — 575
23:15 — 252
23:16 — 48
24 — 196
24:15 — 266
24:19 — 339
24:24 — 614
24:31 — 78,88

Judges

1:27-2:3 — 97
2:1-4 — 44
2:2 — 614
2:7 — 78
2:11 — 252
2:15 — 252
2:17 — 97
2:22 — 614
2:26 — 614
3:9 — 540
3:10 — 578
3:11 — 524
4:4 — 428,505
4:5 — 428

4:6-10 — 428
4:21 — 571
5:9 — 627
5:11 — 533
5:31 — 524
6:9 — 216
6:12 — 62
6:13 — 2
6:14 — 540
6:15 — 488
6:24 — 36
6:34 — 278
7:7 — 466
8:28 — 524
9:8 — 54
9:8-15 — 477
9:15 — 54
9:16 — 18
9:17 — 596
9:19 — 18
9:23 — 18
9:29 — 92
10:14 — 160
11:7 — 231
11:20 — 113
11:24 — 278,578
11:29-40 — 465
11:31 — 465
11:35 — 231
13 — 44
13:3 — 62
13:10 — 62
13:20 — 77
13:20-22 — 44
14:1-2 — 435
14:4 — 92
14:6 — 578
14:10 — 435
14:10-17 — 100
14:19 — 278,578
15:2 — 109
15:14 — 578
15:15-16 — 125
16:21 — 370
16:25 — 370
17:2 — 460
17:10 — 267
18:19 — 267
18:25 — 71
19:1 — 356
19:23 — 230,286
19:24 — 230,286
19:25 — 555
20:6 — 230
20:10 — 230
20:16 — 566
20:34 — 252
20:41 — 252
21:10 — 79

Ruth

1:6 — 29

1:17 — 547
1:20 — 127
2:12 — 637
3:11 — 459
3:13 — 627
4:1 — 301
4:2 — 243
4:9 — 243
4:11 — 243,301

1 Samuel

1:3-17 — 156
2:1 — 497
2:1-10 — 498
2:2 — 537
2:3 — 313
2:7 — 622
2:8 — 239,488
2:9 — 315,413
2:11 — 549
2:24 — 441
2:25 — 627
2:35 — 37
3:1 — 549
3:21 — 62
4 — 73
4:19 — 434,441
5 — 73
6 — 73
6:7 — 125
6:20 — 313
7:7 — 78
7:7-17 — 35
8 — 376
8:4 — 243
8:10-20 — 376
9:5 — 550
9:6-10 — 506
9:9 — 546
9:16 — 54
10:1 — 54
10:6-8 — 54
10:12 — 508
10:19 — 231,252
10:22 — 497
11:2 — 230
12:7 — 18
12:22 — 2
12:12 — **376**
13 — 466
13:13 — 466
14:6 — 18
14:7 — 575
14:9-10 — 400
14:13 — 18
14:24 — 191,460
14:27 — 191
14:29 — 231
15:1 — 54
15:19-24 — 614
15:22 — 124,215
15:23 — 518

15:29 — 212
16 — 63
16:2-5 — 465
16:3 — 54
16:6 — 63
16:7 — 63
16:9-10 — 160
16:12 — 54
16:13 — 54
16:16 — 416
16:22 — 550
17:20 — 2
17:25 — 293
17:26 — 230
17:28 — 2,47
17:45 — 314
17:47 — 34
18-20 — 297
18:8 — 47
18:23 — 488
19:24 — 453
20:6 — 29
20:7 — 552
20:9 — 552
20:13 — 552
20:29 — 465
20:34 — 47
21 — 140
21:14 — 424
22:17 — 627
22:21 — 448
24:6 — 400
24:9 — 252,531
24:13 — 508
24:17 — 252,534
25 — 428
25:3 — 108
25:17 — 252
25:18 — 628
25:21 — 252
25:25 — 230,453
25:28 — 47
25:31 — 47
25:43 — 434
26:9-23 — 54
26:12 — 571
26:23 — 260
26:24 — 231
27:3 — 434
27:8 — 42
27:12 — 113
28:5 — 272
28:6 — 400,401
28:13-15 — 528
28:15 — 231
28:18 — 614
30:5 — 434
30:6-8 — 400
30:18 — 434
30:21-25 — 78
31:13 — 265

2 Samuel

1:10 — 205
1:12 — 356
1:26 — 142
2:2 — 434
3:1 — 488
3:21 — 78,194
3:29 — 615
3:39 — 252
4:1 — 193
4:4 — 441
4:9 — 231
4:11-12 — 449
5:3 — 194
5:13 — 434
6 — 73
6:7 — 18
6:10 — 627
7 — 197
7:14 — 267
7:16 — 197
7:18-29 — 498
7:28 — 197
8:10 — 611
9:7 — 37
9:10 — 37
9:13 — 37
11 — 183
11:2 — 102
11:26 — 433
12:1 — 488
12:1-7 — 477
12:3 — 488
12:4 — 488
12:7 — 54
12:10 — 223
12:11 — 252,434
12:13-23 — 498
12:14-25 — 156
12:16-22 — 265
12:18 — 252
13:3 — 488
13:12 — 230,286
13:13 — 230
13:17 — 549
13:18 — 549
13:30 — 441
14:6 — 547
15:12 — 465
15:24 — 465
15:25 — 279
16:1 — 628
17 — 191
17:14 — 252
18:32 — 252
19:5 — 434
19:7 — 252
19:11 — 243
19:26 — 124
21:1 — 258,263
21:3 — 39
21:6 — 159,160
22:2 — 313

22:3 — 313
22:20 — 215
22:21 — 534
22:25 — 534
22:26 — 315
22:31 — 482
22:33 — 482
23:1-16 — 376
24:14 — 231
24:15 — 505
24:16 — 252
24:17 — 44
24:25 — 497

1 Kings

1:4 — 549
1:15 — 549
1:17 — 460
1:29 — 231
1:34 — 54
2:3 — 391
2:4 — 259,575
2:28 — 441
2:36 — 370
3:21 — 106
4:24 — 479
4:25 — 479
4:26 — 479
4:32 — 508
5-9 — 586
5:1 — 37,297
5:4 — 252
5:9 — 547
5:17 — 292
6:9 — 181
7:10 — 292
8:16 — 160
8:22-53 — 498
8:23 — 419
8:27 — 239
8:30-50 — 289
8:31 — 460
8:53 — 547
8:57 — 2
8:63 — 214,601
9:3 — 37
9:5 — 356
9:7 — 147,508
9:9 — 252
9:13 — 142
9:20-21 — 550
20:7 — 441
20:9 — 215
11 — 33
11:1-11 — 434
11:8 — 353
11:25 — 231,252
11:36 — 37
11:38 — 144
12 — 191
12:7 — 37
12:20 — 79

13:18 — 213
13:21 — 512
13:26 — 512
14:1 — 561
14:10 — 252,293
14:24 — 508
15:12 — 252
15:26 — 508
16:34 — 292
17-18 — 265
17:7-24 — 561
17:14 — 113
17:17 — 561
17:18 — 561
17:24 — 602
18:13 — 448
18:16-40 — 35
18:18 — 231
18:24 — 149
19 — 44
19:1 — 448
19:8 — 265
19:10 — 1
19:14 — 1
19:14-18 — 356
19:16 — 54
19:18 — 521
20:3 — 109
20:7 — 231,252
20:11 — 134
20:33 — 232
20:35 — **372**
21:8 — 243
21:21 — 252,293
21:27 — 265,282
21:29 — 252
22:8 — 252
22:18 — 252
22:19 — 346
22:27 — 370
22:46 — 508

2 Kings

1:10-14 — 280
2:9 — **236**
2:11 — 528,547
2:12 — 267
2:21 — 153
2:23-24 — 157
4:27 — 127
6 — 44
6:15 — 549
6:17 — 44
6:21 — 267
6:32 — 449
6:33 — 226
8:1-5 — 526
8:12 — 252
8:19 — 627
9:8 — 293
9:11 — 424
9:20 — 424

9:36 — 282
10:15 — 607
11:12 — 205
12:15 — 10,18
13:4 — 271
13:14 — 561
13:23 — 180
14:10 — 153,231,252
14:26 — 293
15:5 — 25,547
17:4 — 370
17:14-15 — 116
17:17 — 232
17:34 — 96
17:37 — 37
18:4-6 — 97
18:7 — 512
18:20 — 512
18:29 — 213
18:32 — 628
19:3 — 231
19:6 — 129
19:7 — 441
19:10 — 213
19:14-19 — 498
19:22 — 129,339
19:23 — 77
20:9 — 444
21:1 — 561
21:1-26 — 49
21:6 — 232
21:12 — 252,561
21:14 — 2,216
22-23 — 586
22:11-13 — 428
22:14 — 428,505
22:16 — 252
22:19 — 223,347
23:3 — 575
23:4-15 — 97
23:7 — 508
23:21-23 — 478
23:25 — 575
24:4 — 627
24:14 — 488
25:12 — 488
25:19-23 — 326
25:27 — 370
25:29 — 370

1 Chronicles

2:7 — 231
2:35 — 550
4:22 — 42
6:32 — 549
7:9 — 302
9:13 — 5
11:3 — 194
12:17 — 124
13 — 73
13:1 — 191
15 — 73

15:2 — 549
16 — 73
16:4 — 549
16:9 — 19,444
16:10 — 311
16:11 — 37
16:12 — 444
16:13 — 159
16:23-31 — 361
16:24 — 444
16:28 — 311,312
16:34 — 419
16:35 — 314
16:37 — 549
16:41 — 419
17 — 586
17:9 — 370
17:10 — 248
17:12 — 250
17:13 — 267
17:16-27 — 498
18:10 — 611
18:19 — 627
21-22 — 586
21:13 — 231
21:15 — 44
21:26 — 35
22 — 466
22:10 — 267
22:19 — 123
23 — 466,504
23:13 — 547
23:28 — 239
26 — 504
26:7 — 5
26:9 — 5
26:30 — 5
26:32 — 5
28-29 — 586
28:4 — 160
28:6 — 267
29:5 — 627
29:9 — 627
29:17 — 593
29:28 — 622
29:29 — 546

2 Chronicles

1:7 — 62
2-7 — 586
2:4 — 68
3:1 — 62
3:3 — 292
5:1-2 — 126
5:10 — 175
5:14 — 549
6 — 586
6:1 — 239
6:6 — 160
6:12-42 — 498
6:14 — 419
6:21 — 332

6:22 — 460
6:23 — 17,332
6:25 — 332
6:27 — 332
6:28-30 — 561
6:30 — 332
6:33 — 332
6:34 — 160
6:35 — 332
6:37 — 18
6:38 — 160,575
6:39 — 332
6:41 — 315
7:1 — 311
7:2 — 311
7:5 — 214,601
7:9 — 214
7:12 — 62
7:14-16 — 329
7:16 — 37
7:20 — 147,508
7:22 — 252
7:30 — 147
8 — 504
9:6 — 113,441
9:8 — 215
9:18 — 287
10:7 — 37
10:19 — 263
12:5 — 1,369
12:6 — 369
13:3 — 5
13:8 — 378
15:2 — 2,279
15:6 — 231
15:12 — 575
15:15 — 221,524
16:10 — 370
16:12 — 329
16:14 — 353
17:9 — 502,504
18:7 — 252
18:17 — 252
18:22 — 252
18:23 — 561
18:26 — 370
19:2 — 326
20:1-29 — 265
20:5-12 — 498
20:7 — 297
20:9 — 231,252
20:20 — 113,116
20:35-37 — 33
20:37 — 33
21:7 — 627
21:19 — 252
23:11 — 205
23:18 — 92
24:5-12 — 587
24:14 — 550
24:20-26 — **11**
25:4 — 18
25:7 — 191
25:19 — 231,252

26:16-17 — 76
26:21 — 547
28:15 — 329
28:22 — 231
29:8 — 223
30:1 — 478
30:7 — 223
30:14 — 353
30:18-19 — 170
31:2 — 549
31:13 — 92
31:15 — 92
32:6 — 68
32:13-15 — 5
32:15 — 113,213
32:20 — 498
32:21 — 5,44
32:30 — 637
33:6 — 232
33:18-19 — 497
34:22 — 428,505
34:24 — 460
34:31 — 575

Ezra

1-5 — 586
1:4 — 308
2 — 39
2:62 — 40
2:63 — 400
3:10-12 — 292
4:2 — 40
4:13 — 587
4:20 — 587
6:16-17 — 214
6:19-22 — 478
6:21 — 547
7:10 — 225
7:24 — 587
8 — 502
8:3-14 — 427
8:17 — 549
8:21 — 497
8:22 — 557
9:1 — 547
9:5-15 — 498
9:6 — 557
10:8 — 243
10:11 — 221,547,627

Nehemiah

1:3 — 230,231
1:4 — 265
1:10 — 583
2:6 — 597
2:17 — 230,231
4:18 — 125
4:19 — 547
4:20 — 617
5 — 143

5:4 — 587
5:7 — 14,160
5:16 — 225
6:14 — 505
6:18 — 460
7:56 — 400
7:57-60 — 550
7:64 — 169
8 — 504
9:2 — 547
9:13 — 369
9:17 — 7,49,289
9:24 — 221
9:26 — 20
9:30 — 20,106
9:32 — 419
9:33 — 369
9:37 — 221
10:28 — 547
10:29 — 460
10:31 — 2
10:36 — 126,549
10:39 — 549
11:17 — 497
12:27 — 214
13:14 — 520
13:15-22 — 524

Esther

1:10 — 549
1:11 — 109
1:17 — 433
1:20 — 433
2:2-3 — 109
2:12 — 181
2:19 — 301
2:21 — 301
3:2-3 — 301
3:8 — 547
4:2 — 301
4:6 — 301
5:9 — 301
5:10 — 297
5:13 — 301
5:14 — 297
6:3 — 549
6:6-9 — 215
6:10 — 301
6:11 — 215
6:12 — 301
6:13 — 297
9:5 — 221
9:6 — 448
9:10 — 448
9:12 — 448
9:22 — 574
9:27 — 597
9:31 — 597

Job

1:1 — 223,482,533
1:5 — 465
1:6 — 43,572
1:8 — 473
1:16 — 280
2:1 — 43,572
2:10 — 231
2:11 — 29,252
3:3-11 — 138
3:10 — 231
3:20 — 127,575
4:6 — 343
4:8 — 231
4:13 — 571
4:18 — 113
5:6 — 231
5:7 — 231
5:12 — 629
5:16 — 488
6:2 — 252
6:10 — 339
6:13 — 629
7:3 — 608
7:11 — 576
7:14 — 237
7:18 — 593
8:6 — 510
8:13 — 315
9:16 — 113
9:28 — 482
9:30 — 510
9:31 — 4
9:32 — 193
11:4 — 510
11:6 — 629
11:11 — 213,608
12:10 — 431,576
12:11 — 593
12:13 — 123
12:16 — 123,611,629
12:22 — 214
13:12 — 508
13:16 — 315
13:18 — 252
13:27 — 252
14:12 — 96
14:14 — 527
14:16-17 — 482
14:22 — 472
15:14 — 510
15:15 — 113,169
15:22 — 113
15:31 — 113,608
15:34 — 315
16:11 — 252
16:17 — 510
17:1 — 576
17:2 — 512
17:6 — 147,508
17:8 — 315
17:13 — 343
17:13-16 — 336

17:15 — 343
17:16 — 301
19:19 — 4
20:5 — 315
20:10 — 39,488
20:19 — 488
23 — 139
23:5-6 — 139
23:10 — 281,593
24:9 — 147,488
24:19-20 — 336
24:22 — 113
25:2 — 123
25:4 — 510
26:3 — 629
26:7 — 459
27:1 — 508
27:5 — 20
27:8 — 315
29:1 — 508
29:11-17 — 492
29:12 — 488
29:16 — 267,488
29:24 — 113
30:3 — 615
30:10 — 4
30:22 — 629
30:25 — 492
31:5 — 213,608
31:16 — 488
31:16-21 — 492
31:17 — 271
31:18 — 138
31:29 — 231
31:30 — 460
31:35 — 14
33 — 139
33:9 — 510
33:12 — 431
33:15 — 139,571
33:15-22 — 139
33:19 — 138,472
33:28 — 575
33:30 — 575
34:3 — 593
34:10 — 253
34:19 — 488
34:28 — 488
34:30 — 315
34:36 — 593
35 — 5
35:2 — 596
35:33 — 608
36:3 — 78
36:4 — 213
36:13 — 315
36:14 — 508
38:4 — 292
38:7 — 43,45,572
38:17 — 301
39 — 5
39:3 — 434
39:5 — 293
39:9 — 627

39:12 — 113
39:16 — 608
39:24 — 113
40:2 — 14
40:14 — 20
41:11 — 123
42:6 — 482,522
42:7-9 — 465
42:8 — 230

Psalms

1:1 — 131
1:2 — 215
2:1 — 608
2:2 — 54
2:7 — 138,267
3 — 571
3:3 — 312,571
3:4 — 571
3:5 — 571,572
4 — 571
4:1 — 317,479,497,533
4:2 — 310,479,608
4:3 — 149,315
4:4 — 47
4:8 — 479,571
5:4 — 253,486
5:4-6 — 325
5:5 — 424
5:7 — 419
5:12 — 131
6:1 — 48
6:2 — 138,317
6:3 — 575
6:4 — 419
6:6 — 285
6:9 — 439
7:6 — 49,96
7:8 — 534
7:9 — 533,593
7:10 — 540,607
7:14 — 213,231
7:16 — 231
8 — 431
8:3 — 636
8:4-6 — 351
8:5-6 — 342
9:7 — 250
9:8 — 533
9:9 — 231
9:10 — 1
9:11 — 495,511
9:13 — 301,317
9:18 — 37
9:19-20 — 431
10:1 — 231
10:2 — 76
10:4 — 76
10:6 — 231,252,556
10:7 — 212,231,460
10:11 — 288
10:12 — 488

10:14 — 231
10:15 — 11,252
10:37 — 267
11:4 — 593
11:5 — 575,593
11:7 — 258,607
12:1 — 315
12:2 — 213,608
12:5 — 488
12:7 — 375
13:2 — 574
14:1 — 18,190,286,605
14:2 — 604
14:3 — 605
14:6 — 114,488
15:3 — 252
15:3-9 — 267
16:1 — 375
16:5 — 79
16:7 — 192
16:8 — 37
16:9-10 — 282
16:10 — 315,339
16:11 — 277,361,407
16:13 — 215
17:1 — 533,534
17:3 — 593
17:7 — 419
17:8 — 620
17:14 — 348
17:15 — 96,258,527
18 — 151
18:3 — 149
18:10 — 43
18:11 — 413
18:13 — 614
18:19 — 215
18:20 — 531,534
18:23 — 128
18:24 — 534
18:25 — 315
18:27 — 346
18:28 — 413
18:30 — 630
18:46 — 314
18:50 — 54
19 — 595,629
19:1 — 311,637
19:1-4 — 203
19:7-11 — 392
19:8 — 174,361,501
19:11 — 531
19:14 — 517
20:1 — 231
20:2 — 433
20:5 — 221
20:6-7 — 532
20:20-22 — 131
21:4-6 — 407
21:7 — 419
21:11 — 252
22:1 — 1,506
22:3 — 339
22:8 — 179

22:9 — 138
22:15 — 238
22:18 — 506
22:24 — 1,488
22:28 — 123
23 — 559
23:1 — 559,616
23:4 — 173
23:5 — 54
24:1 — 241
24:3 — 77
24:4 — 169,213,608
24:6 — 258
24:7 — 42
24:9 — 42
25:1 — 575
25:1-3 — 557
25:4-5 — 400
25:6 — 520
25:7 — 419
25:9 — 400
25:16 — 317
25:18 — 231
26:1 — 128
26:2 — 593
26:3 — 419,602
26:4 — 213,608
26:7 — 18
27:1 — 413
27:4 — 108,109
27:5 — 231,252
27:8 — 258
27:11 — 621
27:12 — 141,213
27:13 — 113
28:3 — 282
28:7-9 — 582
29:1 — 43,311
29:3 — 313
29:3-9 — 614
29:10 — 285
29:11 — 479
30 — 214
30:4 — 315
30:5 — 49,407
30:9 — 238
30:21 — 106
31:1 — 533
31:5 — 313,506,602
31:6 — 608
31:7 — 419
31:9 — 231,317
31:10 — 574
31:19 — 273
31:23 — 315,343
31:24 — 343
32 — 184
32:1 — 131,199
32:1-5 — 289
32:5 — 16
32:6 — 315
32:8 — 192
32:10 — 419
33:1 — 534

33:4 — 260
33:4-11 — 634
33:5 — 241
33:6 — 634
33:8-11 — 273
33:9 — 174,634
33:10-11 — 192
33:12 — 160
33:16 — 540
33:16-22 — 361
33:17 — 213
33:18-19 — 273
33:20 — 433
33:20-21 — 540
33:20-22 — 273
34:1 — 37
34:3 — 312
34:7 — 44
34:8 — 131,587
34:9 — 273
34:18 — 576
34:19 — 534
34:19-21 — 252
34:20 — 506
35:1 — 189
35:2 — 30
35:5 — 44,155
35:6 — 44
35:9 — 575
35:10 — 489
35:13-14 — 562
35:16 — 315
35:20 — 14
35:23 — 96,189
35:26 — 229,231,252
35:27 — 37,215
36:1-4 — 273
36:5 — 260,419
36:6 — 53
36:8 — 237
36:9 — 413
37 — 629
37:4 — 221
37:5 — 179
37:6 — 179
37:7 — 48
37:8 — 48
37:9 — 48
37:11 — 353
37:16 — 124
37:17 — 534
37:19 — 252
37:25 — 1,110,534
37:26 — 37
37:28 — 315
37:33 — 1
37:37 — 48,300
37:39 — 231
38:1 — 48
38:5 — 561
38:12 — 252
39:2 — 231
39:4 — 246
39:5-6 — 141

39:7 — 141,142,343
39:8 — 216
40:4 — 131
40:8 — 221,627
40:10 — 260
40:11 — 37
40:12 — 252
40:16 — 37
40:17 — 488
41:1 — 131,231,252, 317,488
41:6 — 213,608
41:7 — 252
42:1-2 — 348
42:2 — 313,575
42:9 — 288,313
42:10 — 29,138
43:1 — 315
43:1-2 — 518
43:3 — 413,602
43:3-5 — 518
44:2-8 — 617
44:6 — 114
44:6-8 — 540
44:13-16 — 523
44:14 — 147,508
44:15 — 229
44:16 — 129
44:17 — 212
44:23 — 96
44:26 — 419
45:7 — 533
45:9 — 142
45:17 — 302
46:1 — 114,231,292
46:7 — 292
46:8 — 223
47:5 — 77
47:7 — 241
47:9 — 123
49:4 — 508
49:5 — 252
49:6 — 114
49:6-9 — 623
49:7-20 — 527
49:12 — 623
49:14 — 607
49:16-20 — 623
49:19 — 413
50:5 — 315
50:6 — 313
50:8-15 — 465
50:15 — 149,231
50:22 — 313
51 — 183,566
51:1 — 317,419
51:1-2 — 183,372,567
51:3 — 37,183
51:4 — 372,510
51:4-6 — 183
51:5 — 372,568
51:6 — 602
51:7-9 — 183
51:7-14 — 372

51:8 — 138
51:10 — 200
51:10-12 — 183
51:14 — 216
51:15 — 138
51:16 — 215,486
51:17 — 223
51:18 — 221
51:19 — 215,486
52:1 — 134
52:3 — 213
52:5-7 — 623
52:7 — 114
52:9 — 315
53:1 — 286
53:4 — 149
54:5 — 252
55:22 — 534
55:23 — 114
56:1 — 317
56:3-4 — 272
56:4 — 283
56:5 — 37
56:13 — 413
57:1 — 317
57:3 — 567
57:4 — 567
57:5 — 567
57:6 — 567
57:9 — 567
57:11-14 — 567
58:11 — 241,313
59:12 — 460
59:17 — 314
60:1 — 518,608
60:11 — 30
60:12 — 611
62:1 — 279,537
62:2 — 537
62:4 — 215
62:5 — 279,344
62:6 — 344,537
62:7 — 537
62:8 — 114
62:10 — 114
63:3 — 124
64:10 — 534
65:1-2 — 495
65:5 — 18
65:5-8 — 495
66:3 — 18
66:5 — 18
66:5-8 — 583
66:10 — 593
66:20 — 419
68:3 — 534
68:5 — 267,271
68:9 — 297,308
68:10 — 488
68:18 — 77,78,152
68:19 — 146
68:25 — 613
68:33 — 42
69:11 — 147,508

69:12 — 301
69:14 — 216
69:16 — 419
69:16 — 497
69:17 — 231,497
69:19 — 229,230
69:21 — 506
69:33 — 488
70:2 — 252
70:4 — 37
70:5 — 433
71:3 — 37,537
71:6 — 138
71:7 — 114
71:13 — 229,252
71:14 — 37,343
71:16 — 18
71:17 — 18
71:20 — 127,252
71:21 — 173
71:22 — 339
71:24 — 18,252,533
72:2 — 488
72:18 — 18
73:3 — 424
73:13 — 510,608
73:15 — 124
73:17 — 53
73:19 — 223
73:20 — 608
73:22 — 53
73:23 — 37
73:23-26 — 527
73:26 — 259,282,608
74:18 — 520
74:21 — 488,489
75:4 — 424
76:6 — 571
76:10 — 49
77:2 — 231
77:6 — 576
77:14 — 313
78 — 115
78:2 — 508
78:4 — 18
78:4-6 — 156
78:20 — 282
78:22 — 113,115
78:27 — 282
78:31-38 — 48
78:32 — 113,115
78:38 — 49
78:39 — 283
78:41 — 339
78:42-43 — 516
78:69 — 250
78:70 — 160
79:2 — 315
79:9 — 216,540
79:13 — 302
80:1 — 559
80:5 — 237
80:8 — 612
80:14-15 — 612

81:1 — 313
81:7 — 231,593
81:12 — 293
82 — 492
82:3 — 152,271,488
82:4 — 488
82:5 — 556
84:5 — 131
84:9 — 54
84:12 — 131
85:2 — 199
85:2-3 — 49
85:8 — 315
86:2 — 225,315
86:5 — 7,289
86:6 — 439
86:7 — 231
86:10 — 18
86:15 — 7,49,419
86:16 — 317
88:3 — 231,252,277
88:5 — 293
88:11 — 260
89:1 — 260
89:2 — 250,260
89:2-4 — 197
89:3 — 159,376
89:5 — 43,260
89:5-13 — 201
89:6 — 43
89:7 — 43
89:8 — 260
89:10 — 92
89:12 — 200
89:14 — 534
89:15 — 131,413
89:18 — 339
89:19 — 315,433
89:24 — 260
89:26 — 267,313
89:28 — 419
89:29 — 250
89:30-37 — 2
89:32 — 30
89:33 — 2
89:35 — 460
89:38 — 54
89:39 — 205
89:47 — 200,608
89:48 — 336
89:49 — 260
89:51 — 54
90:8 — 413
90:10 — 25,231
90:15 — 231,252
90:17 — 108,109
91:1 — 459
91:4-6 — 459
91:6 — 413
91:9 — 114
91:10 — 252
91:15 — 231
92:2 — 260
92:6 — 605

92:12 — 534
93:1 — 250
93:2 — 250
94:1 — 610
94:6 — 271
94:9 — 240,332
94:12 — 131
94:13 — 231,252
94:14 — 2
94:19 — 215
95:4 — 123
95:9 — 593
95:10 — 302
96:10 — 250
96:10-13 — 363
96:13 — 533
97:2 — 173
97:5 — 614
97:7 — 134
97:10 — 315
98:3 — 260
98:9 — 533
99:8 — 289
99:9 — 339
100:3 — 559
100:5 — 260
101:6 — 549
102 — 488
102:7 — 213
102:13 — 180
102:25 — 111,292
102:26-27 — 155
103:1 — 131,575
103:2 — 131,575
103:3 — 562
103:8 — 7,49,419
103:9 — 14,37
103:9-10 — 14
103:13 — 180,267
103:14 — 238
103:17 — 419
103:19 — 250,377
103:20-21 — 43
103:21 — 549
103:22 — 575
104 — 629
104:2 — 203
104:4 — 281,549
104:5 — 292
104:10-30 — 203
104:18 — 123
105:1 — 18
105:2 — 18
105:4 — 37
105:6 — 159
105:8 — 174
105:8-11 — 197
105:43 — 159
106:2 — 18
106:3 — 131
106:4 — 30
106:5 — 159
106:12 — 113
106:23 — 159,160

106:24 — 113
106:29 — 49
106:36-37 — 217
106:39 — 170
107 — 629
107:9 — 277
107:11 — 223
107:18 — 301
107:26 — 252
107:27 — 238
107:28 — 242
107:39 — 252,574
107:41 — 488
108:12 — 30,608
108:13 — 611
109:10 — 110
109:31 — 488
110:3 — 627
110:4 — 41
110:75 — 260
110:86 — 260
110:90 — 260
110:138 — 260
111:9 — 174
111:10 — 111,123
112:1 — 131,215,279
112:1-6 — 622
112:2 — 607
112:5 — 405
112:6 — 534
112:7 — 441
112:7-8 — 272
113:7 — 239,488
113:9 — 156
115:6 — 240
115:9 — 433
115:10 — 433
115:11 — 433
115:16 — 123
115:17 — 407
116:3 — 231,574
116:5 — 179,180,314
116:7 — 575
116:10 — 113
116:15 — 315
118:8 — 114,124
118:9 — 124
118:10-14 — 617
118:15-21 — 495
118:17 — 18
118:20 — 301
118:21 — 145
118:22 — 145,151
118:23 — 145
118:25 — 497
118:27 — 125
119 — 595
119:1 — 131
119:2 — 131
119:7 — 533
119:8 — 257
119:9 — 510
119:12-16 — 392
119:14 — 361

119:16 — 216
119:20 — 575
119:24 — 216
119:25 — 239
119:29 — 213
119:30 — 160
119:34 — 605
119:35 — 215,279
119:37 — 608
119:39 — 230
119:40 — 533
119:43 — 602
119:47 — 174,216,418
119:48 — 174,418
119:49-50 — 344
119:52 — 174
119:62 — 533
119:64 — 419
119:65 — 589
119:65-68 — 462
119:66 — 113,589
119:67 — 589
119:68 — 174
119:70 — 216
119:71 — 25
119:72 — 124,462
119:73 — 160
119:75 — 533
119:76 — 160
119:77 — 216
119:81 — 575
119:82 — 173
119:86 — 174
119:90 — 250
119:92 — 216
119:97 — 389
119:104 — 213
119:105 — 388
119:106 — 460,533
119:108 — 297,308,627
119:113 — 420
119:117 — 37
119:119 — 420
119:121 — 533,534
119:124 — 419
119:126 — 141
119:127 — 418,420
119:128 — 213,325,607
119:130 — 413
119:132 — 317
119:138 — 533
119:140 — 593
119:142 — 602
119:143 — 174,216
119:151 — 602
119:159 — 420
119:160 — 533,602
119:161 — 96
119:162 — 361
119:163 — 4,213,325,
        420
119:164 — 533
119:165 — 420,479
119:165-166 — 634

119:167 — 420
119:172 — 533
119:174 — 216
119:176 — 559
121:1 — 433
121:2 — 433
121:7 — 252,620
124:1-3 — 617
124:8 — 433
127:1 — 608
127:2 — 571,608
127:3-4 — 156
128:1 — 131,271
128:2 — 242
128:3 — 156
128:4 — 156
128:6 — 156
130:3-4 — 289
130:7 — 344,419,516
130:8 — 516
132:9 — 315
132:10 — 54
132:15 — 488
132:16 — 315
132:17 — 54
132:18 — 205
133:3 — 174
135:17 — 240
136:26 — 313
138:7 — 231
138:8 — 419
139:11-12 — 413
139:13 — 138
139:20 — 608
139:21 — 325
139:23 — 593
140:9 — 231
140:11 — 252,612
140:12 — 152,612
140:13 — 534,612
141:2 — 352
141:8 — 257
142:2 — 231
143:1 — 260,439
143:2 — 533
143:10 — 221,627
143:11 — 231
144:1 — 617
144:3 — 596
144:8 — 213,608
144:10 — 252
144:11 — 213,608
145:3-7 — 495
145:4 — 18
145:8 — 49,419
145:10 — 315
145:11-13 — 378
145:12 — 18
145:16 — 221
145:17 — 315
145:19 — 221
146:3 — 114
146:5 — 131,433
146:7 — 152

146:8-9 — 419
146:9 — 626
147 — 629
147:5 — 605
147:6 — 346
147:10-11 — 215
147:15 — 634
148 — 629
148:2 — 43
148:5 — 634
148:14 — 315
149:1 — 315
149:4 — 215
149:5 — 315
149:9 — 315
150:2 — 18

Proverbs

1:1 — 508
1:2-3 — 228
1:2-5 — 589
1:3 — 273
1:5 — 589
1:6 — 508
1:7 — 111,272
1:22 — 544
1:27 — 231
1:29 — 160
1:31 — 242
1:32 — 98
2:2 — 230
2:6 — 629
2:7 — 629
2:8 — 315
2:9-10 — 629
2:12 — 629
2:13 — 1
2:16 — 288
2:17 — 611
3:1 — 389
3:1-2 — 589
3:5 — 16
3:6 — 16
3:9 — 343
3:11 — 228,518,589
3:12 — 215,228,267,
419,589
3:14 — 124
3:19 — 292
3:21 — 629
3:30 — 14,252
3:31 — 358
3:33 — 207,534
4:2 — 1
4:3-4 — 156
4:6 — 1
4:9 — 205
4:17 — 242
4:20 — 85
5 — 45
5:10 — 288
5:11 — 282

5:19 — 37
5:20 — 81,288
5:23 — 81
6:4 — 571
6:9-10 — 571
6:16-19 — 6
6:19 — 213
6:20 — 156
6:21 — 125
6:23-26 — 25
6:24 — 288
6:25 — 108,200
6:32 — 616
6:33 — 230
7:5 — 288
7:25 — 81
8 — 45
8:11 — 124
8:13 — 76
8:14 — 629
8:15 — 629
8:18 — 629
8:19 — 124
8:23 — 111
8:29 — 292
8:30 — 216
9:10 — 111,339
9:11 — 26
9:21 — 105
10:1 — 266,508
10:2 — 105,623
10:3 — 534
10:4 — 488,489,622
10:5 — 571
10:5-6 — 105
10:12 — 199,325
10:15 — 488
10:17 — 1
10:18 — 325
10:22 — 622
10:24 — 534
10:28 — 534
10:29 — 534
10:30 — 534
11 — 105
11:1 — 215
11:2 — 76
11:6 — 105
11:8 — 231,534
11:9 — 124,315
11:14 — 191
11:16 — 105
11:17 — 231,282
11:18 — 531
11:20 — 215
11:22 — 108
11:27 — 627
11:28 — 534
11:29 — 231
11:31 — 531
12:4 — 459
12:8 — 231
12:9 — 615
12:17 — 213

12:21 — 252
12:22 — 215
12:28 — 407
13:1 — 156
13:5 — 213,325
13:7 — 488
13:8 — 488
13:10 — 76
13:12 — 561
13:13 — 531
13:14 — 389
13:16 — 18
13:17 — 259
13:18 — 488
13:21 — 252
13:23 — 488,489
14:5 — 213,259
14:9 — 39,627
14:12 — 251
14:15 — 113
14:20 — 488
14:21 — 488
14:24 — 205
14:29 — 286
14:31 — 488,489
14:32 — 534
14:35 — 215
15:1 — 48
15:6 — 231
15:10 — 1
15:15 — 252
15:16 — 623
15:16-17 — 124
15:20 — 266
15:22 — 191
15:24 — 407
15:26 — 108
15:27 — 231
15:30 — 441
16:2 — 510
16:3 — 179
16:4 — 252
16:8 — 124
16:10 — 232
16:16 — 124
16:18 — 76,576
16:19 — 124
16:23 — 447
16:24 — 108
16:26 — 68
16:28 — 547
16:30 — 252
16:31 — 205
16:32 — 92,124
17:1 — 124
17:3 — 593
17:5 — 488
17:6 — 310
17:9 — 547
17:21 — 266
17:26 — 509
18:1-9 — 629
18:3 — 229,230
18:7 — 447

18:23 — 488
18:24 — 297
19:1 — 124,488
19:2 — 566
19:4 — 488
19:7 — 488
19:15 — 571
19:17 — 488
19:22 — 124,488
19:23 — 231,252
19:59 — 213
20:1 — 81,110,628
20:6 — 259
20:9 — 510
20:11 — 18,510,637
20:13 — 489,571
20:16 — 288
20:17 — 213
20:18 — 191
20:24 — 605
21:8 — 510
21:9 — 124
21:11 — 509
21:13 — 488
21:17 — 489,628
21:19 — 124
21:21 — 623
22:1 — 124
22:2 — 488
22:3 — 252
22:6 — **214,601**
22:7 — 405,,488
22:9 — 488
22:10 — 544
22:15 — 228,**286**
22:16 — 488
22:22 — 267,488
22:23 — 267
22:28 — 42
23:4 — 636
23:10 — 42
23:17 — 358
23:18 — 300
23:19 — 266
23:20 — 628
23:21 — 238,489
23:22 — 138,266
23:24 — 266
23:27 — 288
24:2 — 231
24:6 — 191
24:10 — 231
24:12 — 637
24:14 — 300
24:17 — 249
24:20 — 300
24:34 — 488,489
25:1 — 508
25:7 — 124
25:14 — 213
25:18 — 213
25:19 — 231
25:21 — 348
25:24 — 124

25:25 — 441
26:1 — 342
26:7 — 508
26:9 — 508
26:25 — 113
27:2 — 288
27:3 — 288
27:4 — 48
27:5 — 124
27:10 — 124
27:12 — 252
27:24 — 205
28:3 — 488
28:6 — 124,488
28:8 — 370,488
28:11 — 488
28:12 — 310
28:14 — 231,252
28:15 — 488
28:19 — 488
28:27 — 207,488
29:7 — 488
29:8 — 48,544
29:10 — 325
29:12 — 213,549
29:13 — 488
29:14 — 488
29:15 — 228
29:17 — 228
29:22 — 48
29:23 — 76
29:24 — 460
30:3 — 339
30:5 — 313
30:8 — 608
30:19 — 613
30:33 — 48

Ecclesiastes

1:17 — 424
2:1-10 — 486
2:1-11 — 485
2:8 — 485
2:10 — 531
2:10-11 — 636
2:12 — 424
3:1 — 597
3:18-21 — 52
4:14 — 488
5:3 — 237
5:8 — 488
5:9 — 418
6:1 — 252
6:2 — 616
6:8 — 488
7:14 — 252
7:25 — 424
7:29 — 607
8:6 — 252
8:7 — 300
8:9 — 252
9:3 — 252,424

10:5 — 252
10:13 — 424
11:2 — 252
11:9 — 294
12:1 — 200,231,252
12:9 — 508

Song of Songs

1:3 — 613
1:13 — 555
2:4 — 99,100
2:5 — 561
4:5 — 555
6:8 — 613
7:3 — 555
7:5 — 448
7:7 — 555
7:8 — 555
7:10 — 221,434
8:1 — 555
8:8 — 555
8:10 — 555

Isaiah

1 — 562
1:4 — 329,339
1:5-6 — 329,562
1:13 — 608
1:13-15 — 325
1:13-17 — 467
1:15 — 257
1:15-17 — 498,500
1:16 — 510,620
1:17 — 152,271
1:18 — 329,512
1:19 — 329,512,627
1:23 — 271
2:1-4 — 554
2:2 — 107,338
2:3 — 107,338
2:3-5 — 616
2:4 — 107
2:5 — 413
2:6 — 2
2:8-22 — 349
2:10-17 — 9
2:11 — 76
2:17 — 76,211,256
2:19 — 556
2:21 — 556,616
3:8 — 513
3:9 — 252
3:10 — 534
3:11 — 252
3:13-14 — 14
3:14-15 — 488
4 — 139
4:1 — 230
4:2 — 108,109,139
4:2-6 — 139

4:4 — 620
4:5 — 200
5:1 — 419
5:1-7 — 2,477,612
5:7 — 216
5:9 — 223
5:12 — 637
5:14 — 68
5:16 — 313,340
5:18 — 213,608
5:19 — 339
5:20 — 252
5:24 — 339,518
5:25 — 324
6:1-8 — 149
6:2-4 — 43
6:6 — 280
6:7 — 280
6:8 — 614
7:9 — 113
7:14 — 506,613
7:15 — 160,230
7:16 — 160
7:18-25 — 211
8:7 — 285
8:11 — 228
8:16 — 545
8:17 — 344
8:18 — 156
8:19 — 217
8:22 — 231
9:1 — 506
9:2 — 413,506
9:6 — 266,480,506
9:7 — 54,480,506
9:9 — 280
9:14 — 327
9:15 — 213
9:17 — 180,230,315
9:19 — 144
10:2 — 488
10:5 — 34,49
10:5-19 — 618
10:6 — 34,315
10:13 — 618
10:17 — 339
10:20 — 339
10:23 — 181
10:27 — 211,641
11 — 139
11:1 — 139,506
11:1-5 — 54
11:2 — 139,578
11:3-9 — 139
11:4 — 488,492
11:5 — 260
11:6 — 578
11:8 — 216
11:10 — 99
11:11-16 — 99
11:22 — 526
12:2 — 313,582
12:6 — 339
13-23 — 617

13 — 618
13:4 — 616
13:9 — 223
13:11 — 253,618
13:17 — 618
13:18 — 180
14:1 — 31,160,180
14:3 — 474
14:4 — 508
14:12-15 — 543
14:13 — 76,77,338
14:14 — 76,77
14:24 — 192
14:27 — 192
14:30 — 488
16:5 — 419
17:7 — 339
18:3 — 194
19:4 — 92
19:10 — 615
19:11 — 412
19:13 — 213
19:14 — 238
19:18 — 460
20:2-4 — 453
20:8 — 194
22 — 211
22:13 — 237
22:18 — 230
22:21 — 267
23:5 — 473
23:9 — 108
23:18 — 194
24:6 — 207,460
24:12 — 223
24:16 — 124,631
24:18 — 292
24:21-23 — 616
25:1 — 260
25:4 — 488
25:8 — 230,527
26:2 — 259
26:6 — 488
26:9 — 576
26:11 — 280
26:19 — 527
27:11 — 180
28:1-4 — 108
28:5 — 108,109,205
28:7 — 81
28:9 — 441
28:10 — 471
28:10-13 — 470
28:12 — 524
28:13 — 217,471
28:16 — 113,151
28:19 — 441
28:29 — 629
29 — 608
29:5-8 — 34,616
29:9 — 132,216
29:10 — 132,571
29:13 — 69,342,467,498
29:18 — 132

29:19 — 132,488
29:23 — 16,96,339
30:1-2 — 400,497
30:3 — 229,557
30:5 — 230
30:6 — 231
30:7 — 608
30:11 — 339
30:12 — 339,818
30:15 — 339,540
30:18 — 180,313
30:28 — 608
30:31 — 614
31:1 — 339
32:5 — 459
32:6 — 230
32:7 — 534
32:8 — 459
32:15 — 578
32:16-17 — 480
33:1 — 124
33:2 231
33:11 — 280
33:14 — 280,315
34:1-12 — 34
34:8 — 610
34:11 — 244
35:10 — 516,574
36:14 — 213
37:4 — 313
37:6 — 129
37:10 — 213
37:14-20 — 498
37:16 — 313
37:23 — 129,339
37:24 — 77
37:36 — 44
38:4-8 — 506
38:7 — 444
38:10 — 301
38:12 — 488
38:14 — 30
38:18 — 407
38:19 — 266
38:21 — 329
39-53 — 550
40:1 — 173
40:5 — 174,530
40:10-31 — 335,582
40:11 — 399
40:18 — 350
40:21 — 111
40:25 — 339
40:26 — 200,634
40:28-31 — 200,636
40:29-31 — 26
40:30-31 — 642
40:41 — 111
41 — 5
41:1 — 54,172
41:4 — 111
41:8 — 160,297,550
41:9 — 160,550
41:10 — 582,550

41:14 — 339
41:15 — 338
41:16 — 339
41:17 — 1
41:20 — 111,200,339
41:26 — 111
42 — 85
42:1 — 159,215,550,578
42:1-9 — 550
42:2-3 — 550
42:4 — 241,550
42:5 — 200,576
42:5-6 — 550
42:7-9 — 550
42:18-19 — 550
42:20-25 — 85
43:1 — 200
43:1-7 — 419
43:3 — 339,517
43:6 — 459
43:7 — 200
43:9-10 — 550
43:12 — 113
43:14 — 339
43:15 — 200,339,376
43:20 — 159
44:1 — 160
44:1-3 — 550
44:3 — 324,621
44:5 — 123
44:6 — 376
44:6-23 — 349
44:7 — 42
44:8 — 560
44:21-23 — 356
44:28 — 292
45:4 — 16,160,550
45:7 — 226,252,253
45:7-8 — 200
45:11 — 339
45:12 — 174,200
45:13 — 293
45:15 — 313
45:16 — 229
45:17 — 356
45:18 — 200
45:21 — 313,533
45:22 — 540
45:23 — 460
46:3 — 138
46:8 — 526
46:8-11 — 513
46:9 — 506,526
46:10 — 42,505,526,634
46:11 — 506
46:13 — 310
47:3 — 497
47:4 — 339
47:11 — 252
47:13 — 81
48:10 — 593
48:13 — 292
48:16 — 578
48:17 — 339

48:20 — 550
48:21 — 621
49:1 — 138
49:1-3 — 550
49:1-6 — 550
49:4 — 550,608
49:5-6 — 550
49:7 — 4,339
49:10 — 180,348
49:13 — 25,173,180
49:18 — 142
49:22 — 99
50:4-10 — 550
50:5 — 512
50:8 — 14
50:10 — 551
51:6 — 335
51:11 — 574
51:13 — 292
51:16 — 292
52:11 — 548
52:13 — 551
52:14 — 551
52:15 — 551
53 — 388,472,561,562,
563
53:1 — 113,441
53:1-3 — 551
53:3 — 474,562
53:3-9 — 574
53:4 — 25,289,329,551,
562
53:4-6 — 475
53:5 — 329,330,480,
551,562,563
53:6 — 81,373,551,559
53:7 — 25
53:7-8 — 551
53:9 — 79,506,551
53:10 — 474,551,562,
627
53:11 — 106,373,475,
551
53:12 — 373,497,506,
551,554
54-66 — 550
54:1 — 222
54:1-8 — 104
54:4 — 230
54:5 — 241,313,339,
434,435
54:6 — 434
54:7 — 3,180
54:8 — 180
54:10 — 180
54:16 — 200
55:3 — 419
55:5 — 339
55:6-7 — 279,289
55:8-9 — 335
55:10 — 246
55:11 — 244
55:12 — 246
56:4 — 160

56:6 — 549
56:7 — 8
57:4 — 213
57:15 — 239
57:16 — 14,37
57:17 — 98
57:18 — 329
57:19 — 200,329
57:20-21 — 479,524
58:2-10 — 369
58:6 — 293,348,489
58:7 — 348,488,489
58:7-9 — 500
58:11 — 37
58:12 — 42
58:13 — 215
59:1 — 500
59:2 — 500,547
59:3 — 169,213
59:9 — 500
59:12 — 16
60 — 63
60:7 — 549
60:9 — 339
60:10 — 180,549
60:11 — 37
60:14 — 223,339
60:19-20 — 414
61:1 — 125,578,579
61:2 — 579,610
61:4 — 42
61:5 — 31
61:6 — 549
61:7 — 229
61:8 — 325
61:9 — 15
61:10 — 142
62:2 — 174
62:3 — 310
62:4 — 215
62:5 — 142
62:8 — 460
62:10-12 — 99
63 — 49
63:1-6 — 610
63:3 — 169
63:8 — 212
63:9 — 231
63:10 — 617
63:16 — 15,267
64:4 — 42,386
64:8 — 267
65:9 — 159
65:12 — 160
65:15 — 159
65:16 — 313
65:17 — 200,241,336
65:17-25 — 202
65:18 — 200
65:20 — 26
65:22 — 159
65:23 — 608
65:25 — 433
66:3 — 215

66:4 — 160
66:6 — 248
66:7 — 434
66:12 — 216
66:13 — 173
66:15 — 280
66:22 — 241,336
66:23 — 241,431
66:24 — 431

Jeremiah

1:5 — 138
1:14 — 252
1:16 — 1
2:2 — 142,419
2:3 — 252
2:8 — 560
2:15 — 223
2:19 — 98,252,549
2:20 — 549
2:21 — 612
2:23 — 170
2:27 — 231,252
2:28 — 231,252
2:30 — 608
2:34 — 488
3:1-9 — 23
3:5 — 37
3:6 — 98
3:8 — 98
3:9 — 435
3:11 — 98
3:12 — 98,315
3:13 — 16,98
3:14 — 98,434
3:15 — 560
3:19-20 — 267
3:22 — 98
3:25 — 229,614
4:4 — 168,280
4:6 — 252
4:7 — 223
4:10 — 213
4:18 — 18,127
4:19 — 29,127
4:23-26 — 245
4:30 — 608
5:4 — 488
5:5 — 98
5:6 — 98
5:12 — 252
5:15 — 41
5:17 — 114,292
5:21 — 257
5:28 — 488
5:30 — 223
5:31 — 92
6:10 — 240
6:16 — 41
6:19 — 252,518
6:20 — 8
6:24 — 473

6:27-30 — 593
6:29 — 608
7:3 — 18
7:5 — 18
7:6 — 31
7:9 — 97
7:15 — 502
7:20-23 — 467
7:23 — 614
7:28 — 614
7:29 — 2
7:34 — 142
8:3 — 99
8:5 — 98
8:14 — 237
8:18 — 574
8:21 — 223
9:3 — 16
9:4 — 144
9:6 — 16
9:7 — 593
9:15 — 242
9:23 — 134
9:24 — 134,215
10:10 — 313
10:18 — 231
10:22 — 441
11:11 — 252
11:12 — 252
11:14 — 252
11:15 — 252
11:17 — 252
11:20 — 593
11:23 — 252
12:1 — 533
12:2 — 69
12:3 — 593
12:6 — 113,124
12:7 — 1,2
12:15 — 180
13:14 — 180
13:16 — 312
13:25 — 213
14:7 — 98
14:8 — 231,344
14:10 — 520
14:14 — 213
14:20 — 16
15:1 — 502
15:4 — 4
15:11 — 231
15:14 — 280
15:21 — 516,223
16:9 — 142
16:10 — 252
16:15 — 99
16:18 — 277
16:19 — 231
17:5 — 114
17:6 — 539
17:9 — 334,562,604
17:10 — 593,604
17:13 — 344
17:14 — 562

17:17 — 252
17:18 — 252,375
17:19 — 301
17:19-27 — 524
18:1 — 252
18:8 — 252
18:9-10 — 144
18:11 — 18,253
18:15 — 42,584,608
18:16 — 223
19:3 — 252
19:8 — 223
19:15 — 252
20:2 — 370
20:4 — 297
20:6 — 213,297
20:9 — 138
20:11 — 229
20:12 — 593
20:13 — 488
20:18 — 231,574
21:5 — 617
21:7 — 180
21:10 — 252
21:12 — 19
22:3 — 31,369
22:5 — 460
22:15 — **16**,383
22:15-17 — 369
22:16 — **16**,152,383
23:1-3 — 559
23:1-4 — 560
23:4-6 — 559
23:8 — 99
23:10 — 207,460
23:14 — 213
23:15 — 242
23:17 — 252,223
23:23 — 314
23:24 — 277
23:25-26 — 213
23:27 — 596
23:32 — 213
23:33 — 2
23:39 — 2
23:40 — 230
24:9 — 4,252,508
25:7 — 252
25:9 — 223
25:11 — 223
25:14 — 637
25:18 — 223
25:32 — 252
25:34-36 — 560
25:38 — 223
26:3 — 252,522
26:13 — 18,252,614
26:19 — 252
27:5 — 583
27:10 — 99
27:11 — 641
27:15 — 99,213
27:18 — 497
28:1-17 — 506

28:8 — 252
29:1 — 243
29:2 — 193
29:8 — 213
29:9 — 213
29:10 — 181
29:11 — 252,300,345
29:12 — 498
29:13 — 279,498
29:14 — 99,498
29:18 — 4,223,460
29:21 — 213
30-33 — 198
30:1-17 — 211
30:7 — 197,231
30:10 — 524
30:19-31 — 211
30:40 — 211
31 — 119,393
31:3 — 197,418,419
31:4 — 197
31:9-10 — 267
31:13 — 574
31:16-17 — 344
31:19 — 230
31:20 — 180,216
31:21-37 — 356
31:22 — 98,200
31:31 — 198
31:31-32 — 197
31:31-34 — 166,178
31:33 — 391,397
31:33-34 — 133,198
31:37 — 198,518
32-33 — 389
32:2 — 370
32:6-15 — 595
32:17 — 73
32:23 — 252,332
32:37 — 99
32:39 — 37
32:41 — 575
32:42 — 252
33:6 — 329
33:7-9 — 144
33:8 — 171
33:9 — 310
33:21 — 549,551
33:22 — 549,551
33:25-26 — 518
34:5 — 353
34:17 — 4
35:15 — 18
35:17 — 252
36:1-10 — 265
36:3 — 252
36:31 — 252
37:4 — 370
37:9 — 213
37:15 — 370
37:18 — 370
37:21 — 370
38:4 — 252
38:6 — 370

39:10 — 92,488
38:11 — 92
39:12 — 252
39:16 — 252
40:2 — 252
40:7 — 488
40:14 — 113
42:5 — 602
42:6 — 614
42:10 — 252
42:13 — 614
42:14 — 614
42:17 — 252
42:18 — 223,460
42:19 — 595
42:21 — 614
43:1-7 — 613
44:2 — 252
44:4-6 — 326
44:11 — 252
44:12 — 223,460
44:22 — 223
44:23 — 252
44:26 — 460
44:27 — 252
44:29 — 252
45:3 — 574
45:5 — 252
46-51 — 617
46:10 — 123
46:11 — 608
46:19 — 223
48:2 — 252
48:9 — 223
48:16 — 252
49:4 — 98
49:13 — 223,460
49:14 — 441
49:16 — 213
49:17 — 223
49:23 — 441
49:30 — 192
49:37 — 252
50:3 — 223
50:6 — 98,560
50:23 — 223
50:29 — 339
50:42 — 180
51:2 — 252
51:5 — 339
51:8 — 329
51:9 — 562
51:17 — 562
51:25 — 338
51:27 — 99
51:29 — 223
51:33 — 325
51:34 — 608
51:35 — 282
51:37 — 223
51:41 — 223
51:43 — 223
51:46 — 441
51:51 — 229

51:58 — 608
51:60 — 252
51:64 — 252
52:8 — 547
52:11 — 370
52:15 — 488
52:16 — 488
52:31 — 370
52:33 — 370

Lamentations

1:2 — 124
1:21 — 231,252
2:2 — 180
2:14 — 213,608
3:23 — 260
3:30 — 230
3:32 — 180
3:38 — 252
3:43 — 180
3:65 — 460
4:7 — 510
4:12 — 113
4:14 — 169
5:1 — 230
5:19 — 302
5:20 — 37

Ezekiel

1 — 280
1:5 — 62
1:5-14 — 43
1:13 — 62
1:24-28 — 614
2:62 — 169
3:7 — 627
5:14-15 — 523
5:16 — 252
6:8-9 — 521
6:10 — 252,608
7:5 — 252
7:19-20 — 510
7:26 — 441
8 — 466,562
10:5 — 614
10:19-22 — 43
11 — 562
11:9 — 216
11:19-20 — 581
12:3 — 604
12:16 — 15
12:22 — 508
12:23 — 508
12:24 — 213,608
13:6 — 608
13:6-9 — 213
13:7 — 608
13:8 — 608
13:9 — 608
13:22 — 213

13:23 — 213,608
14:8 — 147,508
14:22 — 18,252
14:23 — 18
15:7 — 280
16:3 — 39
16:4 — 620
16:9 — 620
16:14 — 482
16:15 — 108
16:43-63 — 520
16:49 — 488
16:52 — 106,229
16:54 — 229
16:56 — 441
16:59 — 460
16:60-63 — 250
17 — 76
17:2 — 508
17:5 — 283
17:7 — 283
17:13 — 460
17:16 — 460
17:18 — 460
17:19 — 460
18 — 11,13,182
18:2 — 508
18:3 — 508
18:4 — 11,123,**576**
18:5-9 — 11
18:10-13 — 11
18:14-20 — 11,266
18:17 — 488
18:20 — 576
18:21-29 — 12
18:23 — 486
19:9 — 370
19:14 — 280
20:5 — 129
20:7 — 170
20:18 — 170
20:26 — 277
20:27 — 129
20:30-31 — 170
20:32 — 599
20:49 — 508
21:7 — 441
21:13 — 593
21:23 — 213,608
21:29 — 213,608
22:7 — 31
22:9 — 18
22:18-22 — 593
22:28 — 213
22:29 — 31
23:1-45 — 23
23:25 — 11
23:33 — 223,574
23:37 — 435
23:41 — 353
23:49 — 11
24:3 — 508
24:14 — 18

24:15-16 — 559
25 — 610
25-32 — 617
25:15 — 42
26:20 — 42
28:11-19 — 76,543
28:12 — 482
28:24 — 472
32:12 — 154
32:19-29 — 144
32:24 — 106
32:30 — 229
33:6 — **12**
33:8 — 12
33:13 — 114
34:2-10 — 560
34:20-31 — 480
34:23 — 551
34:24 — 480,551
34:25 — 180,480
34:2: — 641
35:5 — 42
36:2 — 42
36:17 — 18
36:19 — 18
36:25 — 171
36:26 — 171,283
36:30 — 230
37:23 — 540
37:24-25 — 551
38 — 211
38:21 — 144
39 — 211
39:7 — 339
39:25 — 180
40-48 — 466,586
41:7 — 77
42:20 — 547
43:4-5 — 311
43:19 — 549
43:22 — 130
46:18 — 547
47 — 562

Daniel

1:8 — 169
1:9 — 154
1:20 — 425
2 — 89,237
2:2 — 425
2:18 — 452
2:19 — 452
2:20 — 425
2:27 — 452
2:28 — 452
2:29 — 452
2:30 — 452
2:35 — 155
2:37-38 — 89
2:44 — 378
2:47 — 452
3:2-3 — 214

3:28 — 43
4 — 89
4:3 — 378
4:7 — 425
4:9 — 425,452
4:13 — 43
4:16 — 53
4:17 — 43,89,378
4:23 — 43
4:25-36 — 16
4:30 — 310
4:32 — 16
4:34 — 53
4:35 — 89
4:36 — 310
5 — 89
5:20 — 76
5:21 — 16,53,378
5:26-28 — 89
6:2-3 — 19
6:22 — 44
6:26-27 — 378
7 — 89,237,378
7:1-12 — 573
7:13-14 — 573
7:18 — 89
7:23 — 63
8:4 — 221
8:13 — 6,43
8:16 — 43
8:18 — 571
8:19 — 68
8:20-21 — 345
9:3-19 — 265
9:9 — 289
9:11 — 207,460
9:12 — 252
9:13 — 252
9:14 — 252
9:19 — 18
9:21 — 43
9:27 — 6
10 — 44,90
10:9 — 571
10:12-15 — 16
11 — 56
11:2-4 — 63
11:3 — 221
11:10 — 285
11:16 — 221
11:23 — 29
11:27 — 68
11:29 — 68
11:31 — 6
11:35 — 68
11:36 — 221,313
11:40 — 285
11:44 — 441
12 — 56
12:1 — 231
12:2 — 95,407,527,529
12:9 — 545
12:11 — 6

Hosea

1:2 — 23
1:4 — 263
1:6-7 — 180
2:20 — 260
2:23 — 180
3:1 — 23
4 — 23
4:1 — 16,383
4:2 — 16,213,383,460
4:4 — 14
4:6 — 518
4:7 — 230
4:14 — 508
5:2 — 228
5:9 — 223
5:13-14 — 561,562
5:15 — 20,23
6 — 63
6:1 — 329
6:1-3 — 562
6:11 — 325
7:12 — 228
9:7 — 424
9:10 — 350
9:17 — 518
10:1 — 612
10:4 — 213,460,608
10:13 — 114
11:1 — 419
11:7 — 98
11:9 — 339
11:12 — 339
12:8 — 623
12:11 — 608
13:9 — 433
13:13 — 434
14:2 — 23
14:3 — 180
14:4 — 23,98,297,308,
         419
14:5-8 — 23

Joel

1:1 — 211
1:2 — 211
1:7 — 223
1:9 — 549
1:13 — 549
1:19 — 280
1:20 — 280
2:2 — 413
2:4 — 62
2:11 — 614
2:12-15 — 265
2:13 — 7,49,419
2:17 — 549
2:18 — 358
2:27 — 557
2:28 — 431,578
2:29 — 578

2:31 — 413
2:32 — 521
3:10 — 107
3:13 — 325
3:16 — 614

Amos

1 — 617
1:4 — 280
1:7 — 280
1:10 — 280
1:12 — 280
1:14 — 280
2 — 617
2:4 — 518
2:6 — 488
2:7 — 97,488
2:8 — 628
2:12 — 628
3:6 — 152,252,253
3:7 — 530
3:13 — 595
3:14-15 — 617
4:1 — 488
4:2 — 460
4:4 — 466
4:13 — 200,413
5 — 211
5:11 — 488,628
5:12 — 474,488
5:13 — 252
5:18 — 211,418
5:20 — 418
5:21 — 325
5:21-27 — 467
5:23-24 — 498
6:3 — 252
6:6 — 628
6:8 — 460
8:5 — 212
8:6 — 488
8:7 — 460
9:4 — 252
9:7-15 — 355
9:9 — 556
9:10 — 252
9:13 — 626
9:14 — 626
9:15 — 389

Obadiah

1 — 441
3 — 213
7 — 213
12 — 231
13 — 252
14 — 231
21 — 378

Jonah

1:5-6 — 571
2:8 — 608
3:4 — 292
3:5-10 — 265
3:10 — 252
4:2 — 49,252,419
4:6 — 252
4:11 — 53

Micah

1:12 — 252
2:1-10 — 170
2:3 — 252
2:4 — 508
2:6 — 229
2:11 — 213
3:1-4 — 500
3:2-3 — 283
4 — 211
4:1-2 — 338
4:1-5 — 616
4:3 — 107
4:9 — 473
4:10 — 473
4:13 — 616
5:2 — 42
6:2 — 14
6:4 — 516
6:6-8 — 467
6:8 — 18
6:9 — 614,629
6:11 — 510
6:16 — 223
7:2 — 315
7:5 — 113
7:13 — 305
7:18 — 215
7:19 — 180
7:20 — 419

Nahum

1:2 — 611
1:3 — 49,611
1:7 — 231,611
1:9 — 231

Habakkuk

1 — 618
1:1-4 — 617
1:4 — 11,88,370
1:5 — 113
1:5-11 — 618
1:12 — 339,618
1:13 — 253
1:13-17 — 618
2:1-20 — 618

2:4 — 121
2:6 — 508
2:6-8 — 618
2:9-10 — 342
2:12 — 370
2:13 — 608
2:14 — 277
2:16 — 230
2:18 — 213
3 — 546
3:2 — 19
3:3 — 339
3:6 — 42,338

Zephaniah

1 — 211
1:14 — 211
1:15 — 211,231,413
2 — 49,68
2:9 — 521
2:15 — 223
3:1 — 169
3:7 — 18
3:8 — 280
3:12 — 488
3:13 — 212,356
3:15 — 252,376

Haggai

1:12 — 614
2:3 — 311
2:6-7 — 556
2:8 — 292
2:13-14 — 170

Zechariah

1 — 44
1:12 — 180
1:14 — 358
1:15 — 252
1:16 — 180
1:18-21 — 345
3:1 — 14
3:8 — 139
3:9 — 139
3:10 — 612
4:9 — 292
5:3 — 460
5:4 — 213
6:12 — 139
7:9-10 — 489
7:10 — 252,271,488,596
7:11-12 — 489
7:14 — 223
8:9 — 292
8:19 — 265
9 — 63
9:11 — 293

9:14-16 — 34
9:16 — 205
9:17 — 108
10:2 — 213,608
10:6 — 180
10:11 — 231
12-14 — 360
12:1 — 292
12:4 — 424
12:10 — 506
13:3 — 213
13:6 — 297
13:9 — 593
14 — 211,616
14:2 — 521
14:2-21 — 34
14:5 — 616
14:9 — 377
14:10 — 389
14:16 — 377

Malachi

1:2 — 326,419
1:3 — **326**,419
1:6 — 267
1:7 — 169
1:10 — 8
1:12 — 169
1:14 — 376
2:1 — 20
2:1-4 — 63
2:2 — 207
2:4 — 20
2:5 — 96
2:6 — 96,155
2:10 — 200,267
2:14 — 233
2:15 — 233
2:16 — 233
3:2-4 — 280
3:5 — 31,213,271
3:9 — 207
3:10 — 308,593
3:12 — 215
3:14 — 608
3:15 — 593
3:16 — 521
3:17 — 180,521
3:18 — 230,521,534

Matthew

1 — 40
1-2 — 45
1:1-26 — 377
1:18 — 579
1:19 — 371,535
1:20 — 63,237,401,579
1:21 — 360,453
1:22 — 93
1:23 — 360

1:24 — 571
1:27 — 93
2:1 — 425
2:6 — 560
2:7 — 425
2:11 — 304
2:12 — 401,619
2:12-23 — 237
2:13 — 401
2:16 — 158,425,450
2:19 — 401
2:22 — 401,619
2:23 — 239
3 — 101
3:2 — 379,522
3:7 — 49,50,619
3:9 — 270,596
3:10 — 280
3:11 — 102,281
3:12 — 146,280
3:13 — 552
3:15 — 102,456
3:16 — 574
3:17 — 336,486,573
3:26 — 552
4 — 593
4:1-2 — 265
4:1-11 — 544
4:2 — 292
4:3 — 573
4:4 — 141,634
4:5 — 593
4:6 — 573,593
4:7 — 593,594
4:8 — 311,338
4:10 — 552
4:11 — 552
4:17 — 379,522
4:18-22 — 492
4:20-22 — 285
4:23 — 379,563
4:24 — 475
4:25 — 552
4:27 — 552
4:30 — 552
5 — 124
5:3 — 492,576
5:3-10 — 131
5:3-11 — 131
5:3-12 — 380
5:4 — 447
5:5 — 132,303,304,439
5:6 — 277,535
5:7 — 440
5:10 — 535
5:11 — 15,254,335,483,
634
5:12 — 336
5:13 — 539
5:14-16 — 414
5:15-16 — 388
5:16 — 336,496
5:17 — 6,24,392,396
5:17-42 — 380

5:18 — 225,392
5:18-48 — 392
5:19 — 176,392
5:20 — 392,535
5:21 — 150,193,241,
415,428,450,
457
5:21-23 — 535
5:21-24 — 176
5:21-43 — 428
5:22 — 49,150,193,241,
287,323,337,
415
5:23-24 — 304,467,515
5:24 — 514
5:25 — 193,552
5:27 — 457
5:27-28 — 24,415
5:27-30 — 535
5:28 — 415
5:29 — 124,257
5:29-30 — 124,337
5:31 — 234
5:32 — 24,234
5:33 — 428,457,461
5:34 — 336
5:35 — 336
5:36 — 327
5:37 — 254,461
5:39 — 254
5:42 — 405
5:43 — 249,423,456
5:43-48 — 27,326,535
5:44 — 249,484
5:45 — 249,254,336,
371,535
5:48 — 483
6 — 623
6:1 — 86,269
6:1-3 — 348
6:1-4 — 110
6:1-9 — 336
6:1-18 — 380
6:5 — 420,499
6:6 — 269,270,499
6:7 — 499,596
6:8 — 269,499
6:9-13 — 499
6:10 — 336,380
6:11 — 141,624
6:12 — 455,456
6:13 — 55,217,254,594
6:14-15 — 291
6:15-33 — 286
6:16 — 224,483
6:16-18 — 265
6:17 — 620
6:19 — 224,241,483
6:19-33 — 380
6:20 — 224,336,483
6:21 — 355,601,624
6:22-23 — 257,388
6:23 — 254,414
6:24 — 223,551,553

6:25-26 — 53
6:25-33 — 492
6:25-34 — 57,270,624
6:28 — 321
6:32 — 499
6:33 — 281,381,499,545
6:34 — 232,254
6:51 — 141
7:1 — 365
7:1-14 — 380
7:2 — 365,439
7:3 — 442
7:3-5 — 257
7:7-11 — 499,500
7:8 — 545
7:9-11 — 254
7:11 — 254,269,336
7:12 — 393
7:13-14 — 301
7:15 — 86,125
7:15-20 — 106
7:15-27 — 380
7:17 — 254
7:18 — 254
7:19 — 280
7:21 — 268,336,627
7:22 — 211
7:23 — 626
7:24 — 441
7:24-26 — 145
7:24-27 — 333
7:26 — 287
7:28 — 38
8:1-3 — 330
8:2 — 171,417
8:3 — 171
8:4 — 304,467
8:6 — 158
8:8 — 158,634
8:9 — 92,551,553
8:10 — 37
8:11-12 — 382
8:13 — 158
8:15 — 552
8:16 — 282,634
8:17 — 329,562
8:19 — 285
8:20 — 492
8:21 — 147,417
8:22 — 147,285
8:24 — 571
8:26 — 211,619
8:27 — 37
8:28 — 218,494,612
8:29 — 573,598
8:31 — 218
8:33 — 218
9 — 600
9:2 — 117,193
9:2-6 — 568
9:4 — 254
9:6-8 — 93
9:8 — 37,496
9:9 — 287

9:9-11 — 587
9:9-13 — 440
9:12 — 563
9:13 — 221,467
9:15 — 447
9:16 — 457,**458**
9:17 — 457,**458**
9:18 — 324
9:18-26 — 528
9:21-22 — 330,541
9:22 — 117,193
9:23-26 — 330
9:24 — 571
9:27 — 572
9:28 — 5
9:29 — 117
9:30 — 619
9:32 — 218
9:33 — 37,218
9:33-38 — 180
9:35 — 379,563
9:36 — 25,180
9:37-38 — 325
10:1 — 330,563
10:1-16 — 492
10:1-42 — 180
10:2 — 59
10:3 — 587
10:6 — 354,560
10:7 — 379
10:8 — 305,330
10:11 — 640
10:14 — **239**
10:16 — 441
10:17 — 86
10:20 — 579
10:21 — 144,513
10:24 — 226,551,554
10:25 — 551
10:26 — 274,530
10:28 — 135,274,337,
      451
10:29-30 — 269
10:31 — 274
10:32 — 16,268,336
10:33 — 219,**220**,268,
      336
10:34 — 481
10:37 — 270,420
10:38 — 206,285
10:39 — **411**,418
11 — 227
11:2 — 59
11:10 — 563
11:13 — 393
11:14 — 563
11:15-22 — 524
11:16 — 143
11:17 — 446
11:19 — 297,298,420,
      587
11:20 — 355
11:23 — 337

11:25 — 157,268,336,
      496,530,598
11:26 — 268,486
11:27 — 161,179,269,
      530,531
11:28-12:13 — 317
11:29 — 303,347
12 — 564
12:1 — 598
12:1-7 — 440
12:1-14 — 399
12:3-7 — **234**
12:3-8 — 141
12:5 — **354**
12:7 — 221,**354**,467
12:8 — 417,573
12:13 — 527
12:16 — 619
12:18 — 554
12:20 — 511,611
12:22-28 — 218
12:23 — 38,572
12:24 — 445
12:25-28 — 578
12:28 — 579
12:31 — 130
12:33-37 — 19
12:34 — 254,335,447
12:34-45 — 254
12:35 — 254,447
12:36 — 12,17,**447**,634
12:37 — 17
12:39 — 254
12:40 — 573
12:41-42 — 182
12:44 — 410
12:45 — 254
12:46-50 — 143
12:50 — 268,336,627
13 — 573
13:1-23 — 332
13:3-9 — 381
13:11 — 379,452
13:13 — 45,605
13:14 — 605
13:15 — 332,605
13:18-23 — 381,624,635
13:19 — 254,333,605
13:20-21 — 332-33
13:22 — 57,213,333
13:23 — 333,605
13:24-30 — 381
13:25 — 32,571
13:26 — 63
13:27 — 551
13:28 — 551
13:30 — 146,325,598
13:31 — 381
13:32 — 321,381
13:33 — 381,404
13:34-43 — 381
13:35 — 201,379
13:36-42 — 325
13:38 — 254

13:39 — 28
13:40 — 146
13:40-43 — 28
13:41 — 626
13:44 — 381
13:45-46 — 381
13:47-50 — 381
13:49 — 254,548,626
13:51 — 605
13:52 — 457
13:54 — 38
13:55-56 — 144
14:1 — 598
14:2 — 158
14:7 — 461
14:9 — 461
14:14 — 25,180
14:15 — 271
14:20 — 278
14:22 — 181,456
14:25 — 620
14:27 — 193
14:31 — 236
15:1-9 — 177
15:1-21 — 348
15:2 — 43,620
15:3-6 — 271
15:4-6 — 343
15:5 — 225,304,305
15:6 — 459,635
15:8 — 485
15:9 — 399,485,608,640
15:10 — 605
15:10-20 — 170
15:13 — 268
15:14 — 132,485
15:16-20 — 568
15:17 — 442
15:18-19 — 254,335
15:19 — 71,254,450
15:21-28 — 31
15:22 — 440,572
15:28 — 330
15:31 — 37,496
15:32 — 25,180
15:37 — 278
16 — 126
16:1 — 336
16:3 — 64,598
16:4 — 254,626
16:5 — 288
16:6 — 86,404
16:7 — 71
16:8 — 71
16:9 — 442,605
16:11 — 86,125,404,
      442,605
16:12 — 404,605
16:16 — **538**
16:17 — 268,336,530,
      531
16:18 — 164,301,337
16:19 — 126
16:21 — 455,475

16:22 — 619
16:23 — 441
16:24 — 206,220,285
    411
16:25 — **411,418,511**
16:26 — **411,639**
16:27 — 311
16:28 — 382
17 — 66
17:1 — 338
17:2 — 258
17:3 — 64
17:5 — 173,486
17:10 — 445
17:11 — 527
17:13 — 605
17:14-18 — 494
17:15 — 440
17:18 — 158,164,218,
    619
17:20 — 117,352
17:22 — 573
17:24 — 587
17:24-27 — **588**
17:25 — 596
18 — 124,126,181,478
18:1-4 — 347
18:1-5 — 158
18:1-20 — 158
18:2 — 158
18:2-5 — 156,320
18:3-4 — 158
18:6 — 124
18:7 — 124,152,456
18:8 — 124
18:9 — 124,337
18:10 — 45,268,336
18:10-15 — 290
18:12 — 213,321,560,
    596
18:13 — 213,321,560
18:14 — 321,336
18:15-17 — 189,367
18:15-18 — 126,321
18:15-35 — 143
18:16 — 634
18:18 — 126
18:19 — 268,269,336,
    499,500
18:21-33 — 440
18:21-34 — 317
18:21-35 — 321
18:22 — 291
18:23-35 — 455
18:23 — 551
18:24 — 455
18:26 — 551
18:27 — 25,180,551
18:28 — 158,456,551
18:30 — 456
18:32 — 254,455,551,
    626
18:33 — 455
18:34 — 49,456

18:35 — 268
18:39-45 — 626
19 — 112
19:1-9 — 435
19:1-12 — 158
19:3 — 158,233,594
19:3-9 — 393
19:3-12 — 234
19:4 — 158,201,233,428
19:5 — 233
19:6 — 233,548
19:7 — 233,393
19:8 — 201,233,393
19:9 — 24,234
19:10 — 8,124,234,235
19:11-12 — 8,234,235
19:12 — 234,235,436
19:13 — 324,619
19:13-15 — 157,159
19:15 — 324
19:16-30 — 624
19:17 — 316
19:18 — 450
19:19 — 456
19:21 — 285,436,624
19:24 — 624
19:25 — 38
19:26 — 352
19:27 — 285
19:28 — 285,573
19:29 — 144
20 — 403
20:1-16 — 317
20:13 — 143
20:15 — 254
20:18 — 573
20:20 — 573
20:21 — 378,382
20:22 — 206,378
20:23 — 206,378
20:25 — 93,94
20:25-28 — 321,328,402
20:26 — 552
20:27 — 551,554,585
20:28 — **410**,443,467,
    517,552,554
20:29-34 — 321
20:30 — 572
20:31 — 572,619
20:34 — 25,180
21:5 — 303,304,439
21:8 — 447
21:9 — 572
21:12-13 — 467
21:15 — 158,572
21:16 — 157,496
21:20 — 37
21:21 — 117,236
21:22 — 117,499
21:23-29 — 93
21:25 — 71
21:28 — 596,637
21:33-42 — 573
21:34-36 — 551

21:34-41 — 598
21:37 — 523
21:41 — 254
21:42 — 145,151,518
21:46 — 274
22 — 100
22:1-10 — 435
22:2-10 — 149
22:3 — 551
22:4 — 551
22:5 — 85,86,147
22:6 — 355,551
22:7 — 49,450
22:8 — 551
22:9 — 100
22:10 — 254,278,551
22:12 — 143
22:13 — 552
22:14 — 149
22:16 — 227
22:17 — 587
22:18 — 254
22:18-22 — 348
22:22 — 37
22:28-30 — 641
22:29 — 213,528
22:30 — 45
22:32 — 528
22:33 — 38
22:35 — 393,594
22:36-40 — 177,393
22:37 — 393,420,442
22:38 — 393,420
22:39 — 393,420,456
22:40 — 393,397
22:42 — 572,596
22:44 — 532
23 — 485
23:1 — 402
23:6 — 100,420
23:8-11 — 270
23:8-12 — 328,402
23:9 — 336
23:11 — 552
23:13 — 348
23:15 — 337,348
23:16 — 132,348,
        456,**461**,485
23:17 — 132,287,485
23:18 — 304,456
23:19 — 132,287,304,
        485
23:23 — 287,301,348,
        440,455,485
23:24 — 132,485
23:25 — 348,546
23:25-28 — 170,171
23:26 — 132,485
23:27 — 64,109,348
23:28 — 64,626
23:29 — 348
23:33 — 337
23:37 — 450
24 — 507,573

24:3 — 65,338
24:4 — 620
24:6 — 31,455,618
24:8 — 434,475
24:9 — 483
24:11 — 64,65
24:12 — 321,626
24:13 — 541
24:14 — 379,639
24:15 — 56,442,605
24:21 — 201,231
24:22 — 161,541
24:24 — 56,64
24:25 — 65,441
24:27 — 65
24:28 — 135
24:29 — 231
24:30 — 311,446
24:31 — 161
24:34 — 302
24:35 — 336
24:36 — 268
24:37 — 65
24:38 — 72,285
24:39 — 65,285
24:42 — 31,65,620
24:43 — 606,620
24:45 — 260,551,598
24:45-48 — 554
24:46 — 65,551
24:48 — 254,551,626
24:50 — 551
24:51 — 79
25 — 45
25:1 — 382
25:2 — 287,441
25:3 — 287
25:4 — 441
25:5 — 571
25:8 — 287,441,511
25:9 — 441
25:13 — 31
25:14 — 551
25:15 — 446
25:19 — 551
25:21 — 260,551
25:22 — 260
25:23 — 260,551
25:26 — 254,485,551
25:27 — 455
25:30 — 551
25:31 — 311
25:31-34 — 28
25:31-46 — 531
25:32 — 548
25:34 — 201,354,382
25:35 — 31
25:36-44 — 453
25:38 — 31
25:41 — 45,219,251,337
25:43-44 — 31
25:44 — 443,552
25:46 — 251,510
26 — 220,596

26:3 — 193
26:4 — 213,450
26:10 — 109
26:17-30 — 177
26:18 — 598
26:26-27 — 124
26:28 — 133,198,290,
467
26:29 — 382
26:30 — 496
26:31 — 260
26:31-46 — 560
26:33 — 10,220,260
26:34 — 220
26:35 — 220,455
26:39 — 206,268,627
26:39-42 — 269
26:40 — 571
26:41 — 594
26:42 — 268
26:43 — 571
26:45 — 571
26:48 — 420
26:50 — 143
26:51 — 551
26:53 — 596
26:54 — 455
26:58 — 552
26:64 — 532
26:65 — 130
26:66 — 596
26:72 — 461
26:75 — 634
27 — 205
27:1 — 377
27:4 — 354
27:7 — 31
27:14 — 37,634
27:18 — 249
27:19 — 368
27:23 — 204,254
27:24 — 354
27:29 — 205
27:33 — 338
27:36 — 620
27:37 — 323,377
27:39 — 355
27:40 — 541
27:42 — 541
27:43 — 217
27:46 — 410
27:48 — 278
27:49 — 541
27:51 — 70,609
27:52 — 571
27:53 — 527
27:55 — 552
27:63 — 213
27:64 — 213
28 — 117
28:2 — 612
28:11-15 — 117
28:13 — 571
28:16 — 338

28:17 — 93,236
28:19 — 227,578,591
28:20 — 28,93,591

Mark

1 — 40,101,316
1:4 — 290
1:7 — 640
1:8 — 102
1:10 — 579
1:11 — 486
1:13 — 552
1:15 — 379,522,598
1:16 — 615
1:16-20 — 492
1:18 — 285
1:22 — 38,591
1:25 — 619
1:27 — 38
1:31 — 552
1:32 — 218
1:40 — 171
1:40-42 — 180
1:41 — 24,25,180
1:43 — 619
1:44 — 467
2:1-12 — 565
2:5 — 117,289
2:5-10 — 568
2:6 — 71
2:7 — 130,289
2:8 — 71,576
2:10 — 93,290
2:12 — 38,496
2:14 — 285
2:15 — 587
2:16 — 237,587
2:17 — 563
2:18 — 227
2:21 — 457,458
2:22 — 457,458
3:4 — 254
3:5 — 527
3:12 — 619
3:14 — 59,68,226,227
3:15 — 93
3:20 — 5
3:21 — 38
3:28 — 130
3:29 — 130,290,323
3:29-30 — 578
3:32-34 — 143
3:35 — 627
4:1-20 — 332
4:8 — 321
4:10-13 — 379
4:11 — 452
4:12 — 605
4:13 — 605,606
4:19 — 57,213,222
4:24 — 439
4:27 — 571

4:28 — 278
4:38 — 571
4:39 — 619
5 — 600
5:1-15 — 424
5:3 — 49
5:15 — 273
5:16-18 — 218
5:20 — 38
5:22-43 — 528
5:23 — 541
5:28 — 541
5:34 — 117,541
5:39 — 571
5:42 — 38
6:2 — 38
6:5 — 324,330
6:13 — 330
6:6 — 37,38
6:7 — 93
6:11 — 93,239
6:12 — 522
6:13 — 330
6:17 — 55
6:20 — 535
6:21 — 100
6:26 — 461,519
6:29 — 135
6:34 — 25,180
6:43 — 278
6:45 — 181,456
6:49 — 596
6:50 — 193
6:51 — 38
6:52 — 605
6:56 — 541
7:1-23 — 171
7:3 — 43,620
7:4 — 101
7:5 — 43
7:7 — 608,640
7:9 — 519
7:10 — 343
7:10-12 — 267
7:11 — 225,304,305
7:13 — 459,635
7:14 — 605
7:14-23 — 170
7:18 — 442
7:18-23 — 172
7:19 — 171,335
7:21 — 71,254,450,596
7:22 — 76,212,213,254,
546
7:23 — 254,255
7:24 — 30-31
7:26 — 218
7:29-30 — 218
7:33 — 599
7:35 — 599
7:37 — 38
8:2 — 25-180
8:12 — 576
8:14 — 288

8:15 — 404,619,620
8:16 — 71
8:17 — 71,442
8:19 — 278
8:23 — 324
8:25 — 527
8:31 — 455,475,518
8:33 — 441
8:34 — 149,206,220,285
8:34-38 — 558
8:35 — 411,418,541
8:36 — 411
8:38 — 311
9 — 66,124
9:3 — 639
9:4 — 64
9:7 — 173
9:11 — 455
9:12 — 475,527
9:14 — 71
9:16 — 71
9:22 — 180
9:22-27 — 25
9:24 — 604
9:25 — 619
9:32 — 350,606,634
9:33 — 71
9:33-37 — 156
9:42 — 124
9:43 — 281,337
9:43-47 — 124
9:44 — 511
9:45 — 337
9:46 — 511
9:47 — 257,337
9:48 — 337,511
10 — 93,112,235
10:6 — 201,428
10:9 — 548
10:13-16 — 156,158
10:15 — 514
10:17-18 — 316
10:19 — 270,343,450
10:21 — 285
10:24 — 38
10:26 — 38
10:27 — 352
10:28 — 285
10:29-30 — 28,267,270
10:32 — 38
10:37 — 311
10:38 — 206
10:42 — 93,94
10:44 — 281,551
10:45 — 467,517,552
10:49 — 193
11:8 — 447
11:10 — 382
11:13 — 598
11:15-17 — 467
11:17 — 148
11:18 — 38
11:23 — 236
11:25 — 291

11:28-33 — 93
12:2 — 551,598
12:4 — 551
12:6 — 523
12:10 — 145,151,518
12:12 — 273
12:14 — 587
12:17 — 38
12:24 — 213
12:25 — 45
12:27 — 213,528
12:30 — 442
12:31 — 456
12:33 — 355,456,605
12:33-34 — 467
12:36 — 532
12:38 — 620
12:39 — 100
12:40 — 225
12:41-42 — 446
12:44 — 446
13 — 28
13:5-6 — 213
13:7 — 31,455
13:8 — 112,434,475
13:9 — 201
13:9-13 — 270
13:10 — 455
13:11 — 57,579
13:13 — 541
13:14 — 455
13:16 — 311
13:19 — 232
13:20 — 161,541
13:22 — 56,64,65
13:24 — 232
13:26 — 173
13:30 — 302
13:32 — 211,268
13:33 — 598,620
13:34 — 551,553
13:35 — 31
13:36 — 571
13:37 — 31
14 — 124,596
14:1 — 213
14:6 — 109
14:22-25 — 177
14:24 — 133,198
14:25 — 382
14:27 — 260
14:29 — 260
14:31 — 455
14:36 — 4,206,268,627
14:38 — 31
14:44 — 420
14:61 — 55,496
14:61-64 — 163
14:64 — 130
14:71 — 126,461
15 — 205
15:2 — 337
15:5 — 38
15:10 — 249

15:14 — 204,254
15:17 — 205
15:26 — 322,377
15:28 — 626
15:30 — 541
15:31 — 541
15:32 — 117,355
15:36 — 4
15:38 — 609
15:40 — 429
15:41 — 429,552
15:43 — 193,135,382
15:44 — 38
16 — 117
16:1 — 55
16:9 — 63
16:9-11 — 429
16:9-20 — 10
16:10 — 532
16:14 — 355
16:16 — 103
16:17 — 10,599
16:19 — 532
16:20 — 10,322

Luke

1 — 45
1:1 — 10,484,352
1:2 — 552
1:3 — 112
1:4 — 591
1:8 — 471
1:11 — 64
1:15 — 278
1:17 — 278,355,441,606
1:19 — 43
1:20 — 5,598
1:21 — 38
1:23 — 278,443,552
1:24 — 156
1:25 — 156,355
1:26 — 43
1:29 — 71
1:30 — 279
1:31 — 360,453
1:32 — 148,360
1:33 — 263,360
1:35 — 341,579
1:36 — 102
1:37 — 352,634
1:38 — 551,634
1:41 — 278,579
1:46 — 496
1:47 — 576
1:48 — 86,551
1:50 — 302
1:51 — 76,442,596
1:54 — 158
1:57 — 278
1:63 — 38
1:64 — 496,599
1:65 — 634

1:67 — 278
1:68 — 496,517
1:69 — 158,346
1:73 — 461
1:74 — 217,552
1:75 — 340
1:77 — 290
1:78 — 180
1:80 — 321
2 — 45
2:1 — 639
2:4 — 263
2:6 — 278
2:7 — 282
2:8 — 620
2:13 — 496
2:15 — 634
2:17 — 634
2:18 — 38
2:19 — 634
2:20 — 496
2:21 — 278
2:22 — 278
2:26 — 530
2:29 — 551,634
2:32 — 530
2:33 — 38
2:35 — 71,530,596
2:37 — 265,552
2:38 — 517
2:40 — 321
2:43 — 158
2:44 — 596
2:47 — 38,355,605
2:48 — 38
2:49 — 455
2:50 — 605,634
2:51 — 584,585,634
3 — 37,40,101
3:2 — 634
3:3 — 290
3:7 — 49,50,619
3:8 — 101,270
3:13 — 587
3:14 — 618
3:15 — 71
3:16 — 102,281
3:17 — 146,280
3:18 — 246
3:19 — 254
3:21 — 37
3:22 — 486,579
3:23 — 26,444,596
4 — 593
4:1 — 278,401
4:1-3 — 265
4:4 — 141,634
4:5 — 90,639
4:8 — 552
4:12 — 594
4:13 — 598
4:15 — 496
4:16-21 — 125
4:18 — 9,55,290,579

4:20 — 552
4:22 — 38
4:24 — 9
4:28 — 150,278
4:30 — 615
4:32 — 38
4:33-35 — 218
4:35 — 619
4:36 — 38
4:39 — 552,619
4:41 — 619
4:43 — 379,455
5:1-11 — 492
5:5 — 438,634
5:7 — 98
5:9 — 38
5:11 — 285
5:12 — 171,278
5:14 — 467
5:17-26 — 565
5:20-24 — 568
5:21 — 71,130
5:22 — 71
5:24 — 93
5:25 — 496
5:26 — 273,278,496
5:27-29 — 492
5:28 — 285
5:30 — 587
5:30-33 — 237
5:33 — 227
5:36 — 29
5:36-39 — 457,**458**
6:1-11 — 525
6:5 — 525
6:8 — 71
6:10 — 527
6:11 — 278
6:13 — 59,161
6:20-22 — 131,492
6:22 — 254,355
6:23 — 336
6:28 — 131
6:32-34 — 569
6:35 — 254,255,405
6:36 — 180,269,**365**,440
6:37 — 365
6:38 — 365,439
6:39 — 485
6:40 — 226,227
6:41 — 257,442
6:42 — 257
6:43-45 — 106
6:45 — 254,299,316,335
6:48-49 — 145
7:1 — 634
7:2 — 551
7:3 — 551
7:5 — 303
7:6 — 297
7:7 — 158,634
7:8 — **92**,551
7:9 — 38,117
7:10 — 117,551

7:11-14 — 171
7:13 — 25,180
7:15 — 317
7:16 — 64,496
7:21 — 254
7:23 — 260
7:30 — 511,519,627
7:34 — 297,587
7:36-50 — 317
7:38 — 55
7:39 — 291
7:42 — 289
7:43 — 289,291
7:46 — 55
8:1 — 379
8:2 — 254
8:3 — 430,552
8:4-15 — 322
8:10 — 452,605
8:13 — 514,598,599
8:14 — 57,410,486
8:16-18 — 388
8:21 — 143
8:24 — 438,619
8:25 — 37,38
8:27-29 — 218
8:36 — 218,541
8:36 — 218,541
8:41-56 — 578
8:43 — 410
8:45 — 438
8:48 — 193,541
8:50 — 541
8:51 — 158
8:52 — 446,571
8:54 — 158
8:56 — 38
9 — 66
9:1 — 93,330
9:2 — 379
9:5 — 235
9:6 — 330
9:8 — 342,457
9:11 — 379
9:19 — 342,457
9:21 — 619
9:22 — 455,518
9:23 — 206,220,285
9:24 — **411**,418
9:25 — **411**,418,639
9:26 — 331,558
9:29 — 258
9:31 — 64
9:32 — 571
9:33 — 438
9:34-35 — 173
9:36 — 632
9:38 — 86
9:42 — 158,218,619
9:43 — 38
9:45 — 350,606,634
9:46 — 71
9:47 — 71,156
9:48 — 156

9:49 — 438
9:55 — 619
9:57 — 285
9:58 — 492
9:59 — 147,285,417
9:60 — 147,379
9:61 — 285
10:1-17 — 492
10:2 — 325
10:3 — 388
10:8-12 — 93
10:9 — 379
10:11 — 379
10:12 — 130
10:15 — 337
10:16 — 519
10:17 — 584
10:19 — 93
10:20 — 336,584
10:21 — 157,268,269,
        362,486,496
10:22 — 161,179,269,
        530,531
10:25 — 594
10:25-37 — 297,457
10:27 — 442,456
10:27-37 — 477
10:29 — 456
10:33 — 75,180
10:36 — 596
10:38-42 — 298,429
10:40 — 552
10:41 — 57
11:2 — 268
11:3 — 101
11:4 — 217,254,594
11:5 — 297
11:5-8 — 298
11:6 — 297
11:8 — 297
11:12-13 — 254
11:13 — 254,269,336
11:14 — 38,218
11:14-22 — 218,544
11:17 — 596
11:18 — 279
11:20 — 379
11:21-22 — 218
11:22 — 74
11:26 — 254,626
11:29 — 254,626
11:33-36 — 388
11:34 — 254,257,**388**
11:34-35 — **414**
11:38 — 38,101
11:39 — 254,626
11:39-41 — 171
11:40 — 287
11:42 — 455
11:45 — 355
11:48 — 70
11:49 — 483
11:50 — 201,546
12:1 — 86,404

12:2 — 530
12:4 — 135,273,297
12:5 — 337,619
12:6 — 288
12:7 — 273,327
12:9 — 219,**220**
12:10 — 578
12:11 — 57
12:12 — 455,579
12:13-21 — 623,624
12:17 — 71,596
12:19 — 624
12:20 — 287
12:22 — 57
12:22-23 — 411
12:22-31 — 270
12:22-34 — 57
12:24 — 188,442
12:25 — 57
12:26 — 57
12:27 — 321,442
12:29 — 57
12:30 — 269
12:31 — 411
12:32 — 269,270,486
12:33 — 270,488
12:34 — 270,335,601
12:35-48 — 554
12:37 — 551,552
12:39 — 606
12:42 — 20,411,598
12:45 — 158,551
12:46 — 79,551
12:49-53 — 270
12:51 — 481,596
12:56 — 64,598
12:58 — 147
13:1 — 598
13:2 — 596
13:4 — 239,596
13:10-16 — 544,564
13:10-17 — 525
13:13 — 324,496,526
13:14 — 455
13:16 — 294,455,564
13:17 — 558
13:19 — 321
13:21 — 404
13:24 — 5,242
13:26-27 — 237,242
13:28-29 — 382
13:33 — 455
14 — 100
14:1-6 — 525
14:9 — 558
14:10 — 297
14:11 — 347
14:12 — 297
14:15 — 382
14:16-24 — 149
14:18 — 456
14:21 — 49,551
14:23 — 181,456,551

14:26 — 227,267,270,
        326
14:27 — 206
14:29 — 5
14:30 — 5
15 — 181,542
15:1 — 587
15:6 — 297,420
15:6-9 — 298
15:9 — 297,420
15:10 — 46
15:11-32 — 477
15:12 — 410
15:16 — 222
15:20 — 180
15:22 — 551
15:26 — 158
15:27 — 565
15:28 — 49
15:29 — 297,420,551
15:30 — 410
15:32 — 455
16 — 235
16:1 — 20
16:1-15 — 624
16:2 — 10,20
16:3 — 20,558
16:4 — 20
16:8 — 20,441,496,572,
        639
16:9 — 420,624
16:13 — 223,551,552,
        553
16:14 — 446
16:15 — 6
16:16 — 379,393
16:17 — 393
16:19-31 — 623,624
16:20 — 110
16:23 — 337,475
16:24 — 29,101,281,
        337,599
16:25 — 29,254
16:26 — 337
16:28 — 337,475,619
17:1 — 153
17:2 — 153
17:3 — 86,143,619
17:7-10 — 553
17:8 — 552
17:15 — 496
17:16 — 595
17:18 — 496
17:19 — 117
17:20 — 382
17:22-35 — 67
17:25 — 455,475,519
17:27 — 72,285
17:30 — 530
17:31 — 211
17:33 — 418,541
17:37 — 135
18:1 — 455
18:2 — 523

18:4 — 523
18:9 — 223
18:10-14 — 587
18:12 — 265
18:14 — 347
18:15 — 619
18:15-17 — 158
18:17 — 158
18:20 — 343,450
18:22 — 285
18:27 — 352
18:28 — 285
18:30 — 28,598
18:32 — 355
18:33 — 450
18:34 — 605,634
18:39 — 619
18:42 — 117
18:43 — 496
19 — 147
19:5 — 455
19:8 — 438
19:10 — 545
19:11 — 382,596
19:11-27 — 477
19:13 — 147
19:15 — 147
19:16 — 438
19:17 — 92,316
19:18 — 438
19:20 — 438
19:22 — 254,626
19:25 — 438
19:37 — 496
19:39 — 619
19:44 — 598
19:45 — 467
20:2-8 — 93
20:6 — 484
20:10 — 598
20:13 — 523
20:14 — 71
20:17 — 145,151,519
20:20 — 92
20:22 — 587
20:23 — 442
20:26 — 38,632,634
20:36 — 45
20:38 — 528
20:40 — 193
20:41 — 55
20:42 — 532
20:42-44 — 417
20:46 — 86,100,420
21:1 — 304
21:2 — 492
21:4 — 304,410
21:8 — 213,598,620
21:9 — 455,618
21:12 — 483
21:16 — 297,420
21:23 — 49,50
21:24 — 598
21:26 — 639

21:27 — 173,311
21:31 — 382
21:32 — **302**
21:33 — 336
21:34 — 57,86,410
21:36 — 598,620
22 — 93,124,220,596
22:2 — 450
22:17-20 — 177
22:19 — 520
22:20 — 133,198,458,
467
22:26 — 552
22:27 — 552,554
22:28 — 594
22:40 — 594
22:42 — 206,268,627
22:43 — 64
22:45 — 475,571
22:46 — 521,594
22:47 — 420
22:61 — 520
22:69 — 532
23 — 205
23:2 — 377,587
23:4 — 323
23:8 — 343
23:11 — 223
23:12 — 297,420
23:14 — 323
23:16 — 228
23:17 — 456
23:22 — 204,254,323
23:23 — 228
23:25 — 124
23:27 — 446
23:34 — 268
23:35 — 161,541
23:27 — 541
23:38 — 377
23:39 — 355,541
23:40 — 619
23:41 — 640
23:43 — 382
23:45 — 609
23:46 — 179
23:47 — **354**
23:51 — 382
24 — 117
24:7 — 124,455
24:8 — 634
24:11 — 634
24:12 — 38
24:18 — 31
24:21 — 163,517
24:22 — 38
24:25 — 287
24:26 — 455,475
24:27 — 356
24:34 — 64
24:38 — 71
24:39 — 529,600
24:41 — 38
24:44 — 455

24:45 — 442,605
24:46 — 455
24:47 — 290,496
24:53 — 496

John

1 — 101
1:1 — 351,635
1:5 — 202,269
1:1-14 — 573
1:3 — 411
1:4 — 411,414
1:4-9 — 414
1:5 — 414
1:7 — 117
1:11 — 302,514
1:12 — 94,119,139,514,
635
1:13 — 139,627
1:14 — 258,278,311,
351,635
1:17 — 202,393
1:18 — 635
1:19 — 361
1:29 — 467
1:31 — 530
1:32-34 — 30
1:35-37 — 227
1:36 — 467
1:41 — 55
1:43 — 285
1:47 — 213
2 — 628
2:2 — 435
2:4 — 212
2:5 — 552
2:6 — 361
2:9 — 552
2:11 — 118,311,445,530
2:13 — 361
2:13-17 — 467
2:18 — 361,508
2:20 — 361
2:22-23 — 118
3 — 118,119,138
3:1 — 361
3:2 — 118,241,445,459
3:3 — 381
3:5 — 113,381
3:6 — 139
3:7 — 38,455
3:8 — 487
3:10 — 606
3:13 — 77,573
3:15-36 — 412
3:16 — 119,415
3:16-21 — 573
3:17 — 182,364,415,541
3:18 — 182,415
3:19 — 254,274,414
3:19-21 — 364,415
3:20 — 274,326,414

3:21 — 414
3:25 — 72,361
3:29 — 297,420
3:30 — 321,455
3:31-36 — 573
3:34 — 579,634
3:35 — 227
3:36 — 49,50,182
4 — 542
4:2 — 7
4:4 — 455
4:4-26 — 31
4:7-27 — 429
4:9 — 79,361
4:10 — 304
4:18 — 603
4:20 — 455
4:22 — 361
4:23 — 314
4:24 — 314,349,455
4:25 — 55,162
4:27 — 38
4:34 — 637
4:51 — 158,551
5 — 118,119,565
5:1 — 361
5:4 — 598
5:6 — 565
5:9 — 615
5:9-18 — 525
5:10 — 361
5:15 — 361
5:16 — 361
5:17-23 — 269
5:18 — 249,269,361,450
5:19-27 — 573
5:19-30 — 364
5:20 — 37,38,420
5:21 — 269
5:21-26 — 412
5:22 — 269,364
5:24 — 119,182,635
5:24-26 — 411
5:26 — 411
5:27 — 93
5:28 — 38
5:29 — 182
5:36 — 269,369
5:37 — 369,635
5:38 — 635
5:39 — 596
5:41 — 496
5:44 — 496
5:45 — 14,596
5:47 — 634
5:51 — 635
5:55 — 635
6 — 118
6:4 — 361
6:25-58 — 348
6:27 — 70,545,637
6:27-68 — 412
6:35 — 119
6:37 — 268

6:38-40 — 627
6:41 — 361
6:42 — 336
6:44 — 268
6:52 — 361
6:53-55 — 238
6:53-56 — 133
6:57 — 269
6:60 — 118
6:62 — 77
6:63 — 634
6:65 — 268
6:66 — 118,227
6:68 — 634
7:1 — 361
7:2 — 361
7:3 — 445
7:5 — 177
7:7 — 254
7:8 — 598
7:8-11 — 177
7:11 — 361
7:12 — 213
7:13 — 273,361
7:15 — 38,226,361
7:16 — 118
7:17 — 118,627
7:20 — 218
7:21 — 38
7:22-23 — 525
7:31 — 118
7:35 — 361
7:37 — 238
7:39 — 7
7:37-39 — 348,379
7:38 — 544,621
7:41 — 162
7:42 — 544
7:45-47 — 118
7:47 — 213
8 — 118,119
8:1-11 — 23
8:12 — 285,414,415
8:15 — 364
8:16 — 269,364
8:18 — 269
8:19 — **384**
8:20 — 634
8:21-42 — 569
8:22 — 361
8:24 — 119
8:28 — 269
8:29 — 486
8:31 — 119,227,603,627
8:31-32 — 119,603,627
8:31-47 — **384**
8:32 — 119,385,603,627
8:33 — 551
8:34 — 551,553
8:35 — 551
8:36 — 554
8:39-41 — 159,270
8:42 — 269,270,420
8:43 — 333

8:43-47 — 270
8:44 — 90,123,143,201,
        221-22
8:46 — 508
8:47 — 124,333,634
8:48 — 361
8:48-52 — 218
8:48-59 — 249
8:49-51 — 342
8:50-54 — 311
8:52 — 361,587
8:54-55 — 269
8:56-58 — 269
8:57 — 361
9 — 132
9:1 — 564
9:2 — 564
9:4 — 455
9:6 — 564
9:7 — 564,620
9:8 — 110
9:11 — 620
9:13 — 620
9:14-16 — 525
9:15 — 620
9:18 — 361
9:22 — 361
9:24 — 312
9:28 — 355
9:29 — 42
9:32 — 28
9:33 — 445
9:34 — 445
9:39 — 485
9:40 — 485
10:1-6 — 560
10:4 — 285,385
10:5 — 285
10:6 — 606
10:9 — 301,560
10:10 — 560
10:10-28 — 412
10:11 — 560
10:14 — 560
10:14-15 — 385
10:16 — 455
10:17-18 — 93
10:19 — 361
10:20 — 218
10:21 — 218,634
10:24 — 361
10:25 — 445
10:27 — 285,385
10:31 — 361
10:32 — 445
10:33 — 130,269,361
10:38 — 118,269,606
11 — 118,119,528
11:1-44 — 412
11:2 — 54,55
11:3 — 420
11:8 — 361
11:11 — 297,420,571
11:12 — 571

11:13 — 571,596
11:19 — 246,361
11:24 — 119
11:27 — 119
11:31 — 246,361
11:33 — 361,576
11:36 — 361,420
11:41 — 268
11:45 — 118,361
11:50 — 71
11:54 — 361
11:55 — 361,510
11:56 — 596
12:1-8 — 298
12:2 — 552
12:3 — 55
12:9 — 361
12:11 — 118,361
12:16 — 606
12:18 — 153
12:20 — 640
12:23 — 346
12:25 — **411**,418,420
12:26 — 285,552
12:27 — 268,346,541
12:27 — 268
12:31 — 639
12:34 — 455
12:38 — 530
12:40 — 442
12:42 — 273
12:43 — 496
12:44 — 117
12:47 — 375,634
12:47-49 — 364
12:48 — 182,519,634
12:49 — 269
13-15 — 298
13:1-17 — 256
13:5 — 620
13:7 — 606
13:8 — 620
13:10 — 620
13:12 — 606,620
13:14 — 456,620
13:15 — 256
13:16 — 551
13:18 — 161
13:21 — 576
13:26 — 101
13:28 — 606
13:29 — 596
13:30 — 459
13:33 — 159,178,361
13:34 — 177,178,422,
        458
13:34-35 — 144
13:35 — 227
14 — 565
14-17 — 463
14:1 — 117,232,414
14:1-3 — 65
14:1-13 — 269
14:6 — 117,499,603

14:9 — 258,269,351,531
14:10 — 269,634
14:10-17 — 268
14:11 — 118,269
14:13 — 312,**454**,499,
        500
14:14 — **454**,499,500
14:15-17 — 579
14:16-17 — 578
14:21 — 422,463
14:21-23 — 269
14:23 — 422,463
14:24 — 463
14:26 — 192
14:27 — 481
14:28 — 268,269
15 — 139
15:1 — 612
15:1-8 — 106
15:1-16 — **299**
15:2 — 140,269
15:4 — 140
15:6 — 147,280
15:7 — 499,634
15:8 — 227,312,508
15:10 — 463
15:10-11 — 362
15:13 — 140,297,420
15:14 — 297,420
15:15 — 123,297,420,
        551
15:16 — 161,**454**,499,
        500
15:18 — 32
15:18-25 — 326
15:19 — 32,123,161,
        420,639
15:20 — 483,551,554
15:22 — **256**
15:25 — 305,326
15:26 — 192,578,579
15:27 — 112,140
16:2 — 451,552,596
16:4 — 619
16:6 — 475,574
16:8 — 189
16:8-11 — 579
16:12-15 — 55,192
16:13 — 55,579
16:14 — 192
16:15 — 500
16:18 — 605
16:20 — 475,574
16:21 — 475,574
16:22 — 475,574
16:23 — 454,499,500
16:24 — 362,454,500
16:26 — 454
16:27 — 270,420
16:33 — 193,471,481,
        639
17:2 — 93
17:4 — 312,543,637
17:6 — 530

17:6-18 — 32
17:8 — 634
17:10 — 312
17:11 — 341
17:13 — 362
17:14-18 — 639
17:15 — 255
17:17 — 543,603,635
17:19 — 543
17:24 — 201
18 — 124,220
18:3 — 74,552
18:10 — 551
18:11 — 206
18:12 — 361,552
18:14 — 361
18:15 — 193
18:18 — 551,552
18:20 — 361
18:22 — 552
18:23 — 254,646
18:26 — 551
18:30 — 254
18:31 — 361
18:33 — 377
18:35 — 361,596
18:36 — 361,377,382,
          552
18:38 — 204,323,361
18:38-19:16 — 377
19 — 205
19:2 — 205
19:4 — 204,323
19:5 — 205
19:6 — 204,323,552
19:8-13 — 94
19:10-11 — 94
19:12 — 94,297,361,
          377,420
19:12-15 — 204
19:13 — 368
19:14 — 361
19:16 — 124
19:19 — 377
19:20 — 361
19:21 — 361,377
19:26 — 212
19:29 — 278
19:31 — 361
19:38 — 361
19:40 — 361
19:42 — 361
20:1-18 — 429
20:2 — 420
20:9 — 455,605
20:17 — 77,600
20:19 — 361
20:22 — 514
20:26 — 529
20:28 — 417
20:31 — 55,118
21:3 — 459
21:15 — 388,420,560
21:15-19 — 420

21:16 — 420,560
21:17 — 420,560
21:19 — 285
21:22 — 285
21:25 — 8

Acts

1:1-11 — 77
1:3 — 484
1:6 — 357,378,382,527
1:7 — 268,357,378,
          382598
1:8 — 514
1:9 — 172
1:11 — 336,337
1:14 — 500,606
1:16 — 455
1:17 — 552
1:18 — 180,626
1:21 — 59,595
1:22 — 59,455,595
1:25 — 552
2 — 59,102
2:1 — 606
2:1-4 — 101,166
2:2 — 612
2:3 — 280,281,599
2:4 — 278,599
2:4-13 — 580
2:7 — 38
2:7-12 — 599
2:11 — 599
2:12 — 38
2:14-41 — 501
2:17-18 — 211,514,631
2:18 — 551
2:23 — 205,476,511,
          626,627,450
2:24 — 29,475
2:24-36 — 528
2:26 — 344,599
2:27 — 3,337,340
2:30 — 461
2:31 — 3,337
2:33 — 324,532
2:34 — 77,324,532
2:38 — 102,205,290,
          522,304,514
2:39 — 205
2:40 — 619
2:41 — 102
2:42 — 59,141,276
2:42-47 — 276
2:43 — 59
2:44 — 624
2:45 — 493,624
2:46 — 141,242,263,
          570,606
2:47 — 496
3:1-10 — 10,330
3:2 — 109
3:2-11 — 110

3:5 — 85,86
3:8-9 — 496
3:10 — 38,109,278
3:11-26 — 501
3:12 — 38
3:13 — 158,552
3:15 — 87,450
3:15-26 — 528
3:16 — 105,330
3:17 — 350
3:18 — 163,475,476
3:19 — 151,163,522,598
3:19-21 — 65
3:20 — 68,163
3:21 — 28,455,526
3:24 — 211
3:25 — 263
3:26 — 158,254,552
4:8 — 278
4:9-30 — 33
4:10 — 528
4:10-12 — 205
4:11 — 145,151,223
4:12 — 279,455,541
4:13 — 38,193,601
4:16 — 445
4:17 — 619
4:22 — 445
4:24 — 606,637
4:25 — 158,609
4:27 — 55,158,552
4:29 — 551,635
4:30 — 10,158,552
4:31 — 278,635
4:32-37 — 309,624
4:34-35 — 309
5 — 218
5:1-11 — 624
5:3-4 — 578
5:4 — 596
5:9 — 29,594
5:11 — 274
5:12 — 59,606
5:12-16 — 274
5:16 — 330,600
5:17 — 278,358
5:19-23 — 278
5:20 — 634
5:22 — 552
5:27 — 63
5:29 — 455,462
5:30 — 528
5:31 — 290,324,532
5:32 — 462,634
5:35 — 86
5:37 — 3
5:38 — 192
5:39 — 5,192
6 — 626
6:1 — 321,552
6:1-4 — 59
6:1-6 — 278,471
6:1-7 — 493
6:2 — 443,486,552

6:3 — 68,278
6:4 — 443,552
6:5 — 160,278
6:6 — 68,324
6:7 — 321,635
6:8 — 10,278
6:9 — 71
6:11 — 634
6:13 — 634
7:2 — 64
7:5 — 368
7:6 — 31,254,554
7:7 — 551,552
7:9 — 358
7:10 — 25
7:17 — 321
7:19 — 254
7:20 — 598
7:21 — 450
7:22 — 228
7:25 — 605
7:26 — 514
7:27 — 519
7:29 — 31
7:30 — 64,280
7:31 — 38,442
7:35 — 64,517
7:38 — 79
7:39 — 519
7:42 — 263,552
7:49 — 526
7:51 — 581
7:52 — 450,483
7:55 — 278,324
7:56 — 324
7:57 — 606
7:60 — 571
8 — 218
8:1 — 70
8:3 — 621
8:4 — 635
8:6 — 85,606
8:7 — 330
8:8 — 362
8:9 — 38,425
8:9-24 — 625
8:10 — 85
8:11 — 38,425
8:12 — 102
8:13 — 38,102
8:14 — 8,511
8:15-19 — 514
8:16 — 102
8:17 — 324,514
8:19 — 514
8:20 — 304,596
8:21 — 444
8:22 — 254,596,626
8:23 — 127,137,152,567
8:24 — 499
8:27 — 640
8:30 — 606
8:32 — 388
8:36 — 102

8:38 — 102
9:1-2 — 191
9:1-6 — 60
9:2 — 621
9:6 — 38,455
9:13 — 254
9:14 — 92
9:16 — 455,476,616
9:17 — 64,278,324
9:18 — 102
9:21 — 38
9:23 — 450
9:31 — 145,321
9:34 — 330
9:37 — 620
10 — 45
10:6 — 455
10:7 — 552
10:9-28 — 172
10:20 — 236
10:22 — 298,420,456
10:28 — 31,79
10:31 — 297
10:35 — 9
10:37 — 101,634
10:38 — 55
10:40 — 528
10:43 — 290
10:44 — 634
10:45 — 38,102,304
10:46 — 102,496
10:47 — 102,514
10:48 — 102
11 — 45
11:1 — 8,514
11:1-18 — 59
11:2 — 31
11:3 — 31,242
11:6 — 442
11:12 — 236,580
11:13 — 63
11:14 — 634
11:15 — 102
11:16 — 634
11:17 — 304,596
11:18 — 496
11:22 — 164
11:24 — 278
11:26 — 163,227
11:27-30 — 507
11:28 — 580
11:29 — 552
12 — 45
12:1 — 254,483,596
12:3 — 486
12:6 — 571
12:7 — 32
12:9 — 596
12:10 — 3
12:16 — 38
12:17 — 632
12:20 — 606
12:21 — 368
12:23 — 496,564

12:24 — 321
12:25 — 552
13:1 — 164
13:1-3 — 470,507
13:2 — 552,264,401,443
13:3 — 324,401
13:5 — 552
13:6 — 425
13:8 — 425,470
13:9 — 278
13:10 — 213,278
13:11 — 598
13:12 — 38
13:16-43 — 501
13:17 — 31
13:25 — 597
13:27 — 350
13:30 — 408
13:34 — 340,528
13:35 — 340
13:36 — 302,511,552,
        571
13:37 — 528
13:38 — 290
13:39 — 373
13:41 — 38,224,483
13:42 — 634
13:45 — 278,358
13:46 — 456,519
13:48 — 68
13:51 — 239
13:52 — 362
14:1 — 621
14:2 — 254,621
14:5 — 355
14:8 — 352
14:9 — 330
14:14 — 60,634
14:16 — 303
14:17 — 362,598
14:21-23 — 244
14:22 — 455
14:23 — 68,244,265,470
14:26 — 179
15 — 172,525
15:1 — 168,621
15:1-29 — 168
15:1-35 — 59
15:2-23 — 244
15:3 — 303
15:5 — 455
15:7 — 457,621
15:9 — 236
15:10 — 5,395,594,641
15:12 — 633
15:13 — 633
15:14 — 481
15:15 — 29
15:16 — 526
15:17 — 546
15:18 — 28
15:20 — 487
15:21 — 457
15:22 — 59,160

15:23 — 303
15:25 — 606
15:38 — 3,596
15:40 — 160
16 — 147
16:6 — 580
16:7 — 580
16:9-10 — 401
16:13 — 631
16:14 — 631,640
16:15 — 102,263,631
16:16 — 147,264
16:16-18 — 218
16:16-40 — 168
16:17 — 551
16:19 — 147
16:25 — 496
16:26 — 612
16:28 — 254
16:30 — 455,539
16:31 — 541
16:32 — 264
16:33 — 102,264,620
16:34 — 117,264,362
16:35-39 — 91
16:38 — 634
16:40 — 631
17:3 — 455,475
17:4 — 631
17:5 — 254,358
17:6 — 639
17:11 — 8,514
17:16 — 232,576
17:18 — 31
17:18-32 — 528
17:21 — 31
17:22 — 519
17:22-31 — 501
17:23 — 350,640
17:24 — 639
17:26 — 469,598
17:27 — 600
17:28 — **469**
17:29 — 455,469,596
17:30 — 350
17:31 — 68,639
18:4 — 484
18:6 — 470
18:7 — 640
18:8 — 102
18:10 — 254
18:12 — 193,368,606
18:13 — 640
18:14 — 204,254
18:16-17 — 368
18:21 — 455,628
18:25 — 101,591
19 — 147,218
19:1-7 — 94
19:2 — 514
19:3-4 — 101
19:5 — 102
19:6 — 324
19:8 — 379,484,501

19:9 — 3
19:12 — 254
19:13 — 254
19:13-16 — 218,494
19:15 — 254
19:16 — 254
19:20 — 321
19:21 — 455
19:22 — 552
19:23 — 598
19:24-25 — 147
19:27 — 639,640
19:28 — 50,278
19:29 — 278,606
19:30 — 63
19:31 — 420
19:32 — 79
19;36 — 455
19:41 — 79
20 — 164
20:7 — 141
20:9 — 571
20:11 — 141
20:12 — 158
20:19 — 551,594
20:22 — 181,401,580
20:23 — 25,580
20:24 — 552
20:25 — 379
20:26 — 354
20:27 — 354,511,628
20:28 — 86,471,560,580
20:31 — 20,31,619
20:32 — 543
20:34 — 552
20:35 — 455,619
21:8 — 251
21:10 — 507
21:11 — 507,580
21:15 — 77
21:16 — 457
21:19 — 552
21:21 — 591
21:22 — 455
21:24 — 591
21:24-26 — 510
21:35 — 612
22:1 — 143
22:2 — 633
22:3 — 228
22:4 — 483
22:9 — 606
22:16 — 103,620
22:20 — 70
22:22-29 — 91,168
22:23 — 29,30
22:24 — 323
23:4 — 355
23:6 — 344
23:9 — 254,640
23:10 — 612
23:11 — 19,455
23:12 — 126,461
23:14 — 126,461

23:21 — 126,461
23:28 — 323
25:1-12 — 91
25:6 — 193,368
25:7 — 323,508
25:10 — 368,455,640
25:11 — 61
25:12 — 61,190
25:17 — 368
25:18 — 323
25:19 — 519
25:21 — 61
25:24 — 355,455
25:25 — 61
25:27 — 323,596
26:4 — 112,410
26:5 — 519,552
26:6 — 344
26:7 — 344,552
26:8 — 408
26:9 — 455
26:10 — 92
26:11 — 181,456,552
26:12 — 92
26:15-18 — 60
26:16 — 64
26:18 — 290,543
26:19 — 508
26:20 — 508
26:25 — 634
26:28 — 163
26:32 — 61
27:3 — 297,420
27:10 — 355
27:13 — 596
27:18 — 612
27:20 — 541
27:21 — 455,462
27:22 — 193
27:23 — 552
27:24 — 455
27:25 — 193
27:26 — 455
27:31 — 541
27:35 — 141
27:36 — 246
27:39 — 442
28:5 — 254
28:6 — 640
28:8 — 324,330
28:15 — 193
28:18 — 323
28:19 — 181,456
28:21 — 254
28:22 — 441
28:23 — 379
28:25 — 634
28:26 — 605
28:27 — 605
28:31 — 379

Romans

1:1 — 149,295,316,551,
      554,577
1:3 — 573
1:4 — 412,528,573,583
1:5 — 7
1:6 — 123,148,149,150
1:7 — 123,149,150
1:9 — 552,576,640
1:10 — 499,628
1:11 — 305
1:12 — 246
1:13 — 350
1:14 — 287,456
1:16 — 120,558
1:17 — 120,281,530,
       531,535
1:18 — 49,50,530,531,
       602,626
1:18-21 — 409
1:18-32 — 302,349,385,
          432
1:20 — 202,
            250,**256**,385,
            442,605,627
1:21 — 71,256,386,442
1:21-32 — 335,409
1:23 — 352
1:25 — 28,496,552,640
1:26 — 423,428,454,
       455,477
1:27 — 3,146,213,423,
       428,455
1:28 — 442,596
1:29 — 213,249,254,
       430,450
1:32 — 70,386
2 — 535
2:1 — 186,256
2:1-3 — **365**
2:1-4 — 350
2:1-11 — 611
2:3 — 596
2:4 — 50,350,364,375,
      376,522,611
2:5 — 49,50,211,530,
      531
2:6 — 364
2:7 — 352
2:8 — 38,49,50,259,
      364,462
2:9 — 254
2:10 — 312
2:12 — 568
2:14 — 303,454,455,
       566,596
2:15 — 14,186,566,596
2:17-29 — 70
2:18 — 186,591,628
2:20 — 157,287
2:22 — 6
2:23 — 342
2:24 — 129

2:25 — 609
2:25-3:2 — 609
2:27 — 454
2:29 — 496
3 — 120,535
3:1 — 609
3:3 — 459
3:5 — 49,219,371
3:6 — 371
3:7 — 312
3:8 — 254
3:9 — 124
3:10 — 535
3:11 — 546,605
3:12 — 376
3:13 — 213,599
3:14 — 127
3:18 — 581
3:19 — 12,318,323,394,
       569,581
3:20 — 120,283,318,
       394,535,569
3:21 — 318,395,536
3:21 — 318
3:21-26 — 314
3:21-31 — 373
3:23-26 — 318
3:24 — 305
3:24-26 — 371
3:25 — 83,133,219,290,
       468
3:26 — 290,598
3:27 — 32,395
3:31 — 394,459
4 — 120,198,270,504,
    536
4:1 — 267,283
4:1-8 — 120
4:2 — 134
4:3 — 117,505,544
4:4 — 455,615
4:5 — 117,199,505,626
4:7 — 199,289,626
4:8-9 — 123
4:9-17 — 166
4:11 — 168,545
4:13 — 194,**395**,469,513
4:14 — 194,**395**,396
4:15 — 49,194,**395**
4:16 — 194,318,
       322,**395**,469,
       505
4:17 — 117,120,194
4:18-21 — 114
4:18-25 — 120
4:19 — 236,442
4:20 — 236,604
4:21 — 80,198,236
4:23-25 — 536
4:24 — 117
4:25 — 120,216,409
5 — 195
5:1 — 373,480
5:1-11 — 569

5:2 — 10,312
5:2-5 — 344
5:3 — 476,484
5:4 — 155,345,476,484
5:5 — 335,345,558
5:6 — 421,569,598
5:7 — 569
5:8 — 219,248,421,468
5:9 — 49,50,133,248,
      413,468,541
5:10 — 248,409,413,
       421,514,515,
       541
5:11 — 514,515
5:12 — 408,568
5:13 — 568
5:12-21 — 569
5:14 — 408,478,518
5:15 — 6,304,305
5:15-16 — 182,305
5:15-21 — 318
5:17 — 304,518
5:20 — 321
5:21 — 518
6 — 103,439,563
6:1 — 321
6:1-10 — 84,397,410
6:1-14 — 206,536
6:2-23 — 294
6:3-8 — 103
6:3 — 350
6:5-14 — 541
6:6 — 135,206,294,457,
      551
6:6-22 — 548
6:8 — 85
6:12 — 135,222
6:12-14 — 152,518
6:13 — 74,85,626
6:14 — 317,395
6:15-23 — **295**
6:16 — **554**
6:16-20 — 551
6:17-18 — 554
6:18 — 552
6:18-22 — 294
6:19 — 284,626
6:21 — 558
6:22 — 305,408,552,615
7 — 126,177,200,439,
    569
7:1 — 94,350
7:1-6 — 395,397,553
7:1-8 — 126
7:2 — 32,235,397
7:3 — 235
7:3-6 — 294
7:4 — 107,412
7:4-6 — 396
7:4-25 — 284
7:5 — 123,189,396,477
7:6 — 32,107,551
7:7 — 394
7:7-11 — 284

7:7-13 — 83
7:15-20 — 284
7:8 — 200
7:9-19 — 394
7:10 — 582
7:11 — 213,450
7:12 — 394,396
7:14 — 177,283,553,577
7:15 — 283,606
7:17-8:2 — 563
7:18 — 222
7:19 — 253
7:21 — 253,395
7:21-25 — **396**
7:22 — **216,396**
7:23 — **396**,442
7:24 — 135,217,**396**,409
7:25 — **396**,442,551
8 — 536,569
8:1 — 182
8:1-4 — 206
8:1-11 — 254,255,410,
413
8:1-14 — 397
8:2 — 392,407,442
8:2-3 — 177,294
8:2-11 — **295**,580
8:2-17 — 580
8:3 — 89,182,284,294,
351,352,
394,**396**,410,
621
8:3-14 — 284
8:4 — 398,410,536,569
8:4-9 — 178
8:4-13 — 284
8:5 — 222,441
8:6 — 189,441,443
8:7 — 248,312,432,441,
584
8:8 — 486
8:9 — 222,536,580
8:10 — 135
8:11 — 135,239,409,
412,529,536,
569,583
8:12 — 455
8:14 — 401,580
8:14-25 — 432
8:15 — 4,21,274,514,
551
8:15-23 — 574
8:16 — 159,576
8:17 — 159,**354**
8:18 — 188,232,530,
531,598
8:18-23 — 202
8:18-25 — 474
8:18-39 — 541
8:19 — 530,531,574
8:19-22 — 407,408
8:20 — 344,433,584
8:20 — 433

8:21 — 137,158,159,
202,293,294,
433,551
8:22 — 433,434
8:23 — 21
8:24 — 344
8:26 — 356,455,500
8:27 — 335,441,500
8:28 — 150,511
8:29 — 150,185,227,
282,312,352,
501
8:30 — 150,312,501
8:31-39 — 30
8:32 — 305,421
8:33 — 15,323
8:34 — 15,182,324,355
8:35 — 548
8:38 — 218,548
8:39 — 421,484,548
9 — 160,440,521
9-11 — 267
9:1 — 208,602
9:2 — 208,475,574
9:3 — 143,208,283,574
9:4 — 552,574
9:5 — 40,496
9:6 — 32,**259**,354,635
9:6-9 — 160
9:7 — 159,354
9:8 — 159,354,522
9:9 — 598
9:10-13 — 161
9:11 — 254
9:12 — 551
9:13 — **326**
9:14 — 317
9:15 — 180
9:16 — 161,222,242
9:17 — 219,544
9:22 — 49,50,161,219,
320
9:30-32 — 85
9:30-33 — 536
9:33 — 558
10 — 120
10:1 — 222
10:2 — 359
10:3 — 350,584
10:4 — **247**,395
10:5-8 — 120
10:6 — 535
10:7 — 7
10:8 — 634
10:8-13 — 335,447
10:9-13 — 121
10:11 — 544,558
10:15 — 109
10:17 — 121,634
10:18 — 634,639
10:19 — 605,606
10:20 — 530
11 — 440
11:1 — 519

11:1-5 — 106
11:1-6 — 318
11:1-40 — 140
11:2 — 61,356,519
11:5 — 598
11:6 — 317
11:11 — 260
11:11-24 — 106
11:13 — 552
11:15 — 514
11:20 — 76
11:21 — 455
11:22 — 375
11:24 — 455
11:25 — 350,441,452
11:26 — 140,217,315
11:26 — 522
11:28 — 195
11:29 — 140,195,305,
357,552
11:34 — 442
12 — 165,267,306,439
12:1 — 75,135,180,441,
468,552
12:1-2 — 9,71,305,486
12:2 — 28,71,185,
442,**508**,594,
628
12:3 — 441,455,597
12:3-8 — 305,328
12:3-16 — 347
12:4 — 165
12:5 — 136,165
12:6 — 305
12:6-8 — 165
12:8 — 246,570
12:9 — 254,326,422,570
12:9-16 — 263
12:9-18 — 305
12:9-21 — 165
12:10 — 225,342,422,
585
12:11 — 359,551,554,
598
12:12 — 345,493
12:13 — 309,493
12:14 — 131,208,484
12:16 — 441
12:17 — 254
12:19 — 49,50,611
12:20 — 146,348
12:21 — 254,471
13 — 89,91,255,367
13:1 — 89,250,584
13:1 — 584
13:1-7 — 168,342,**366**
13:1-13 — 305
13:2 — 470,513
13:3 — 254,496,640
13:3-7 — 204
13:3-10 — 254
13:4 — 89,254,451,552,
640
13:4-5 — 49,50,510

13:5 — 456,584
13:6 — 91,443,552,587
13:7 — 91,456,523,587
13:8 — 455,456
13:8-10 — 142,177,397,
415
13:8-14 — 74
13:9 — 450,456,538
13:10 — 178,254,421
13:11 — 346,598,605
13:12 — 74,414,459
13:13 — 213,238,358,
546
13:14 — 546
14 — 153,172,187,532
14:1 — 71,621
14:2 — 621
14:1-6 — 186
14:1-10 — 187
14:1-12 — 553
14:1-18 — **365**
14:3 — 183,223
14:4 — 552
14:5 — 417,442
14:9 — 186,403,417
14:10 — 186,223,368
14:10-13 — 143
14:11 — 599
14:13-16 — 187
14:14 — 153
14:14-23 — 172
14:15 — 80,**223**,422
14:16 — 441
14:17 — 362,380,519
14:18 — 71,486,519,551
14:19 — 223,145,146,
187,242,243
14:20 — 223,254,584,
640
14:21 — **261**
14:22 — 71,182,187,236
14:23 — 236
15:1 — 107,352,455,
456,621
15:1-3 — 486
15:2 — 145,146
15:3 — 355
15:5 — 247,441,606
15:6 — 552,606
15:7 — 8,496,621
15:8 — 322,552
15:9 — 440,496
15:11 — 496
15:13 — 362
15:14 — 20,181
15:16 — 9,316,443,543
15:18 — 462
15:20 — 38
15:21 — 605
15:25 — 552
15:25-28 — 493
15:26 — 276,309,486
15:26-27 — 486

15:27 — 283,443,455,,
          486,552,577
15:31 — 9,217,552
15:33 — 480
16 — 430,631
16:1 — 430,552,631,632
16:3 — 430,631
16:4 — 595
16:5 — 164,263
16:7 — 60
16:9 — 354
16:10 — 70,594
16:12 — 430
16:18 — 68,213,551
16:19 — 254,362
16:20 — 480
16:25 — 29,451,530,633
16:26 — 462,530,531

1 Corinthians

1 — 128
1:1 — 149
1:1-3 — 629,630
1:1-24 — 630
1:2 — 150,164,165,543
1:3 — 480
1:4 — 596
1:6 — 322
1:7 — 247,530,531
1:8 — 128,247,322
1:9 — 260,276,309
1:10 — 61,442,596
1:10-17 — 167
1:14-17 — 102
1:17 — 206
1:18 — 206,287
1:18-31 — 630
1:19 — 355,519
1:20 — 639
1:20-25 — 27
1:20-30 — 493
1:20-31 — 621
1:21 — 287
1:22 — 445
1:23 — 287
1:25 — 287,563,583
1:26 — 459,493,596
1:27 — 287,558,563
1:27 — 287,558,563
1:27-28 — 161
1:29 — 283
1:30 — 134,630
1:31 — 134
2:4 — **219**
2:6 — 438
2:6-16 — 580,635
2:7 — 452,501,502
2:8 — 386,606
2:9 — **386**
2:10 — 67,215,386,530,
          531
2:10-13 — 215

2:11 — 596
2:12 — 605,639
2:13 — 531,591
2:13-16 — 630
2:14 — 287,454,576
2:15 — **366**
2:16 — 366,442,544
3 — 145
3:1 — 157,283
3:1-4 — **284**
3:1-9 — 403
3:3 — 283,358
3:4 — 283
3:5 — 552
3:5-8 — 145
3:6-7 — 321
3:9-15 — 145
3:10-15 — 12,368
3:13 — 530,531,594
3:13-15 — 280
3:16 — 341,586
3:17 — **223**
3:18 — 213,287
3:18-24 — 263
3:19 — 27
3:20 — 71,596
4:1 — 20,452,552
4:1-3 — 630
4:2 — 20,260
4:3-5 — 70,**365**
4:4 — 187,354
4:5 — 187,496,598
4:6 — 76,441
4:7 — 236
4:10 — 287,342,441
4:10-11 — 530
4:12 — 131,355,484,637
4:14 — 20,159,558,619
4:14-17 — 267
4:17 — 159,260,520
4:18-19 — 76
4:20 — 380
4:21 — 303
5:1-9 — 80
5:1-12 — 23
5:2 — 76,447
5:3 — 366
5:4 — 366,367
5:5 — **223**,366
5:6-7 — 106,404
5:7 — 457,468,478
5:8 — 254,275,457,570,
          626
5:9 — 80,340
5:9-13 — 548,604
5:10 — 23,80,200,340,
          456,639
5:11 — 80,200,238,
          242,355,366
5:12 — 164,**365,366**
5:13 — 254,**366**,626
5:19 — 527
6:1-6 — 641
6:2 — 193,386,387

6:2-5 — 366
6:3 — 46,410
6:4 — 12,164,193,223,
          410
6:5 — 144,558
6:7 — 640
6:8 — 640
6:9 — 213,354,380,386,
          464
6:9-11 — 365
6:10 — 200,238,354,
          355,380
6:11 — 543,620
6:12 — 399
6:12-20 — 23
6:15-20 — 508
6:16-20 — 135
6:19-20 — 295
6:20 — 342
7 — 57,126
7:3 — 437,456
7:3-4 — 437
7:3-5 — 556
7:5 — 29,500,546,598
7:7 — 234,235
7:9 — 146,477,556
7:10-14 — 235
7:11 — 514
7:12 — 70,437
7:12-39 — 641
7:13 — 70,235
7:14 — 159,172,**264**,543
7:15 — 437,552
7:16 — 437
7:17 — 150,538
7:17-23 — 79
7:17-24 — 150
7:18-19 — 168
7:19-20 — 554
7:20 — 150
7:21 — 150,551,553
7:22 — 295,551
7:23 — 551,554
7:24 — 150
7:25-35 — 8
7:25-38 — 436
7:26 — 596
7:27 — 545
7:28 — 283
7:29 — 598
7:31 — 639
7:32 — 57
7:32-34 — 57,182,486
7:33-34 — 57,639
7:36 — 456,596
7:37 — 189,456
7:38 — 125
7:39 — 126,294,437,571
7:40 — 596
8 — 386,487
8:1 — 76,145,422
8:1-3 — 72
8:2 — 386,455
8:4 — 532

8:7 — 186,215,596
8:7-13 — 621
8:8 — 124,286
8:8-13 — 95
8:9-13 — 144
8:13 — 260
9 — 60
9:1 — 294
9:2 — 545
9:3-5 — 532
9:4-18 — 95
9:6 — 637
9:7-15 — 403,637
9:10 — 456
9:11 — 283
9:12 — 316,532
9:13 — 36,340
9:15-18 — 638
9:16 — 456
9:19 — 294,532,552
9:21 — 626
9:25 — 205,352
9:26 — 30
9:27 — 107,**230**
10:1 — 267,350
10:1-10 — 261
10:2 — 103,173
10:3 — 10,173
10:4 — 10,286
10:5 — 486
10:6 — 254
10:6-13 — 349
10:9 — 594
10:10 — 487
10:11 — 28,619
10:12 — **261**,596
10:13 — 260,261,594
10:14 — 349
10:14-22 — 242
10:15 — 366,441
10:16 — 133,135,206,
            238,276
10:17 — 135,238
10:18 — 36,283
10:19 — 349
10:20 — 217,218
10:21 — 218
10:20-22 — 349
10:22 — 358
10:23 — 146,188
10:23-25 — 145
10:24 — 146,545
10:27-33 — 604
10:31 — 312
10:32 — 128,165
11 — 199,**328**,436,596,
        609
11:1 — 256
11:2 — 496
11:2-16 — 328,429
11:3-9 — 95
11:4 — 342,558
11:5 — 342,631,632
11:6 — 199,456

11:7 — 199
11:9 — 201
11:10 — 46,95,456
11:11-12 — 95,199
11:13 — 366
11:14 — 454
11:16 — 165
11:17 — 496
11:19 — 70,455
11:22 — 165,496
11:23 — 459
11:23-26 — 238
11:23-28 — 141
11:24 — 520
11:25 — 133,198,458,
520
11:27 — 133,135,323
11:27-32 — 564
11:29 — 135,236
11:30 — 571
11:31 — 366
11:32 — 366,639
11:33 — 242
12:1 — 350,577,599
12:2 — 81,303,349,350
12:4 — 165,305
12:5 — 165,552
12:4-6 — 552
12:4-11 — 599
12:4-26 — 249
12:7 — 199,305,306,580
12:7-11 — 165
12:9 — 305,330,482
12:12 — 306
12:12-30 — 599
12:13 — 102,136,166,
281,295,551,
579
12:14-26 — 165,305
12:15 — 443
12:22 — 456
12:23 — 596
12:25 — 57,58
12:26-28 — 57,136
12:28 — 60,305,330
12:30 — 305,330
12:31 — 222,305
13 — 165,422
13:1 — 441
13:1-7 — 422
13:2 — 452
13:4 — 76,478
13:4-7 — 599
13:5 — 232,254,640
13:8 — 32,259,599
13:10 — 225
13:11 — 157,597
13:14 — 309
14 — 507,599,632
14:1 — 577
14:1-19 — 30
14:2 — 452
14:3 — 145
14:3-18 — 146

14:4-5 — 145
14:6 — 530,531
14:9 — 30
14:12 — 145
14:13-15 — 500
14:14 — 442
14:15 — 442,496
14:16 — 496,601,605,
606
14:17 — 145
14:18 — 306
14:19 — 442,591
14:20 — 158,254,430
14:22 — 600
14:23 — 600,601,606
14:24 — 600,601,606
14:25 — 600
14:26 — 145,167,530,
531
14:26-40 — 632
14:27 — 600
14:28 — 600,633
14:29 — 167,236,632
14:30 — 530,531,632,
633
14:31 — 167
14:32 — 189,584,600
14:33 — 480
14:34 — 584,633
14:34-36 — 632
14:37 — 17
14:38 — 350
14:39 — 600
14:40 — 471,600
15 — 65,571
15:2 — 608
15:3-7 — 60
15:5-8 — 64
15:6 — 571
15:9 — 165
15:12-52 — 408
15:12-57 — 410
15:12-58 — 541
15:18 — 571
15:20 — 528
15:23 — 65,455
15:24-28 — 93
15:26 — 224
15:27 — 584
15:28 — 584
15:29 — 102,103
15:31 — 134
15:32 — 237
15:33 — 190,213,254
15:33-44 — 135
15:34 — 350,558
15:35 — 529
15:39 — 53,283
15:40 — 241
15:42 — 352
15:42-44 — 529
15:42-49 — 53
15:44 — 454,576,577
15:45-59 — 33

15:46 — 454,576,577
15:49 — 529
15:49-54 — 352
15:50 — 352,354,380
15:51 — 155,452,571
15:52 — 155,352,412,
529
15:53 — 352,455
15:54 — 352,412,611
15:55 — 337,412,611
15:56 — 287,396
15:57 — 611
16:1 — 164
16:1-4 — 493
16:2 — 309
16:11 — 223
16:13 — 31,122,620
16:15 — 552,585
16:16 — 585
16:17 — 65
16:19 — 164,429
16:22 — 420

2 Corinthians

1:1 — 165
1:2 — 480
1:3 — 132,180,496
1:3-7 — 173
1:4 — 132,173
1:5 — 6,132
1:6 — 132,247
1:8 — 350
1:8-10 — 173
1:10 — 217
1:11 — 305,499
1:12 — 187,283,570
1:13 — 606
1:14 — 606
1:18 — 260
1:20 — 312
1:21 — 55
1:22 — 220,322,335,545
1:24 — 122,362
2:1 — 475
2:1-7 — 574
2:2 — 594
2:3 — 184,455,475
2:6 — 367
2:7 — 475
2:7-10 — 289
2:8 — 367
2:8-11 — 574
2:9 — 155,462,594
2:11 — 350,442,544
2:12 — 316
2:13 — 526,576
2:14 — 596
2:14-17 — 353
2:15 — 75
2:17 — 570
3 — 258
3:3 — 552,581

3:6 — 405,450,458,552
3:7 — 405,552
3:8 — 552
3:9 — 552
3:12-18 — 413
3:13 — 609
3:14 — 442,458,610
3:15 — 610
3:16 — 610
3:17 — 295,580
3:18 — 25,26,27,155,
220,227,259,
312,352,580
4:1 — 440,552
4:1-12 — 413
4:2 — 213,558
4:4 — 28,351,414,442,
604
4:4-6 — 415
4:5 — 251
4:7 — 601
4:9 — 3
4:11 — 135
4:15 — 6,321
4:17 — 312
4:18 — 155,184,250
5:1 — 145,241,337
5:2 — 570
5:4 — 412,552
5:5 — 220,322
5:6 — 193
5:7 — 122
5:8 — 193
5:9 — 9,12,38,486
5:10 — 12,254,368
5:12 — 6,77
5:12-15 — 184
5:13 — 38,526
5:14 — 181,422
5:17 — 42,184,202,412,
457,458,515
5:18 — 496,515
5:19 — 179,514
5:20 — 61,514,515
5:21 — 383,515,537
6:1 — 609
6:2 — 9,598
6:3 — 552
6:3-13 — 602
6:4 — 25,27,552
6:6 — 376,570
6:7 — 74
6:8 — 213,342
6:12 — 180
6:13 — 159
6:14 — 276,437,604,
626,641
6:14-18 — 33
6:15 — 29
6:16 — 29,239
6:17 — 548
7:2 — 8,640
7:4 — 76,134,184,362
7:5 — 526

7:6 — 362
7:7 — 362
7:10 — 475,639
7:11 — 354,508
7:12 — 640
7:13 — 576
7:14 — 134,558
7:15 — 25,26,180
7:16 — 184
8 — 309,493
8:1 — 165
8:1-7 — 493
8:2 — 6,165,570
8:4 — 276,309,552
8:8 — 309,570,594
8:9 — 493
8:9 — 310,492,628
8:10 — 192,222
8:12 — 8,309
8:13 — 309,493,526
8:14 — 309,493,598
8:15 — 309,321
8:17 — 61
8:18 — 496
8:19 — 20
8:24 — 76,134,422
9 — 309,493
9:1 — 443,552
9:4 — 558
9:5 — 456
9:6-11 — 321
9:7 — 156,456,475
9:7-12 — 308
9:8 — 5
9:8-11 — 493
9:9 — 492
9:10 — 325
9:11 — 309,570
9:12 — 6,309,443,552
9:13 — 155,309
9:14 — 276,309,496,
        552,570,584
9:15 — 304,310,596
10 — 94
10:1 — 61,303,304,347
10:1-7 — 64
10:2 — 596
10:4 — 74,283
10:5 — 442,597
10:6 — 601
10:8 — 94,146,403,558
10:10 — 65,223,563
10:12 — 605
10:13 — 79,538
10:14 — 316
10:15 — 122,538
10:18 — 70
11 — 60
11:2 — 142,358
11:3 — 213,442,570
11:4 — 514
11:5 — 596
11:7 — 305,316
11:8 — 552

11:9 — 146
11:15 — 552
11:16 — 287
11:19 — 287,441,552
11:20 — 552
11:21 — 20,558
11:22 — 338
11:23 — 552
11:25 — 459
11:27 — 637
11:28 — 57,60
11:30 — 455
11:31 — 496
12:1 — 531
12:1-10 — 621
12:4 — 634
12:6 — 287,596,602
12:7 — 531,564,600
12:8 — 330,564
12:9 — 564
12:10 — 216,355,564
12:11 — 181,212,287,
        306,456
12:12 — 306
12:13 — 146,289,471
12:14 — 146,156,159,
        456
12:16 — 213
12:19 — 145
12:20 — 50,76,259,273,
        358
12:21 — 447,546
13 — 60,94
13:1 — 634
13:2 — 619
13:3 — 94
13:5 — 594
13:5-7 — 259
13:6 — 594
13:7 — 70,254,594,640
13:10 — 94,146
13:11 — 61,441
13:14 — 276

Galatians

1:3 — 480
1:4 — 27,255,628
1:5 — 39
1:6 — 38
1:7 — 316
1:10 — 70,551,554
1:12 — 530,531
1:13 — 112,165
1:15 — 486
1:16 — 530,531
1:22 — 350
1:24 — 496
2 — 60,536
2:2 — 530,531,609
2:3 — 456
2:4 — 294
2:5 — 584

2:6 — 64
2:8 — 60,444
2:9 — 276
2:10 — 493,520
2:11 — 31,470,640
2:12 — 31,273,303,548
2:13 — 31,81
2:14 — 31,181,303,456
2:15 — 454,455
2:16 — 373,464
2:17 — 552
2:18 — 508
2:19 — 395
2:20 — 121,135,206,
        216,411
2:21 — 216,305,396,519
3 — 85,121,195,198,
        504,518,536
3:1 — 262,287
3:1-14 — 85
3:2 — 262,396,514
3:3 — 242,262,287,393,
        581
3:5 — 581
3:6 — 354
3:6-9 — 166
3:7 — 354,606
3:8 — 303
3:10 — 373,581
3:10-14 — 208,**396**
3:11 — 121,373,396
3:12 — 105,396
3:13 — 518
3:15 — 141,519
3:15-18 — 194
3:15-22 — 505
3:15-25 — 194,197
3:16 — 141,469
3:17 — 141,459
3:18 — 105
3:21 — 105,396
3:22 — 396
3:23 — 530,531
3:26 — 21,166,328
3:27 — 103,328,428
3:28 — 295,328,354,
        428,430,493,
        551
3:29 — 354
4 — 578
4:1 — 157,557
4:2 — 20,157
4:3 — 157,552
4:5 — 20,395,574
4:6 — 4,335
4:7 — 21,338,551
4:8 — 349,454,551
4:9 — 551
4:10 — 598
4:11 — 637
4:12 — 640
4:13 — 283
4:13-16 — 564
4:14 — 223,594

4:17 — 32
4:18 — 359
4:19 — 159,434,475
4:21-31 — 294,360,553
4:22-23 — 295
4:24 — 551
4:25 — 159,551
4:26 — 159,295,337
4:27 — 159,475
4:28 — 159
4:30 — 295,544
4:31 — 159,295
4:47 — 434
5 — 32
5-6 — 580
5:1 — 295,525,
        551,**553**,641
5:1-6 — **396**
5:1-13 — 294
5:1-26 — **295**
5:3 — 455
5:4 — 32,260,**261**,262,
        320,396
5:5 — 344,641
5:7 — 602
5:8 — 484
5:9 — 106,404
5:10 — 441
5:11 — 206
5:13 — 295,296,422,551
5:13-25 — 580
5:13-26 — 397
5:14 — 422,456
5:15 — 581,620
5:16 — 222,581
5:16-25 — 398
5:16-26 — **284,299**
5:17 — 222
5:18 — 398
5:19 — 546
5:19-21 — 19,249,398
5:20 — 38,50,259,326,
        358
5:21 — 238,249,354,
        380,450,619
5:22 — 107,249,362,
        376,398,580
5:23 — 249,398,580
5:24 — 206,477
5:25 — 296
5:26 — 249
6:1 — 527,577,**620**
6:2 — 146,609
6:2 — 107
6:4 — 77,594
6:5 — 107
6:6 — 309,591
6:7 — 12,213
6:9 — 325,598
6:10 — 123,493,598
6:12 — 181,206,456
6:14 — 206
6:15 — 202,458
6:17 — 232

6:18 — 576

Ephesians

1:1 — 260
1:2 — 480
1:3 — 132,496
1:4 — 128,160,202,268
1:5 — 20,268,486,501,
502,574
1:6 — 311,496
1:7 — 133,290
1:8 — 355,441,606
1:9 — 452,486
1:10 — 598
1:11 — 160,501,502,
511,627
1:12 — 312,496
1:13 — 316,545,602,635
1:14 — 220,312,322,
354,496
1:15 — 117,122
1:15-22 — 77
1:15-23 — 279
1:16 — 596
1:17 — 530,531,630
1:17-23 — 387
1:18 — 150,257,387,
443,583
1:18-23 — 344
1:19 — 320,583
1:19-21 — 34
1:20 — 45,324,532,583
1:21 — 45,91,218,219,
324,417,583
1:21-23 — 93
1:22 — 45,68,91,137,
165,327,584
1:23 — 137
2 — 104
2:1 — 94
2:1-3 — 421
2:1-4 — 569
2:1-6 — 90,408
2:1-10 — 410
2:1-11 — 318
2:2 — 30,94,544,568,
572
2:3 — 49,50,133,159,
322,409,442,
454,455,568,
596
2:4 — 320,440,623
2:5 — 19,317,440
2:5-8 — 541
2:7 — 375
2:8 — 122,134,304,638
2:9 — 134,638
2:10 — 19,202,637,638
2:11 — 303
2:11-21 — 575
2:11-22 — 303

2:12 — 32,40,104,421,
548,598
2:13 — 32,421
2:14 — 104,480,637
2:14-17 — 480
2:15 — **6**,178,202,458
2:16 — 135,450,514
2:17-19 — 205
2:18 — 10
2:19 — 31,168,263
2:20 — 151,263,293
2:21 — 51,145,165,321,
586
2:22 — 165
3 — 70
3:1 — 303,577
3:2 — 20
3:3 — 452,530,531
3:4 — 355,442,452,605
3:5 — 530,531
3:6 — 74,354,357
3:7 — 304,552
3:9 — 20,28,276,452
3:10 — 90,630
3:11 — 250,511
3:12 — 10,69,122,185
3:14 — 166,268
3:14-16 — 248
3:14-19 — 387
3:15 — **263**
3:16 — 205,311
3:16-19 — 263
3:16-20 — 583
3:17 — 122,165,239,
250,442,592
3:17-19 — 205,321,422
3:18 — 10,165
3:19 — 279
3:20 — 5,74,442
3:21 — 312
3:23 — 442
4 — 78,165
4:1 — 150,640
4:1-6 — 167
4:2 — 107,303,347
4:3 — 74,138,242,430,
480,606
4:4 — 136,150
4:5 — 103
4:7 — 78,304
4:7-16 — 78
4:8 — 152
4:8-10 — 77
4:11 — 36,165,507
4:11-16 — 227
4:12 — 36,279,306,403,
438,443,552
4:12-16 — 145,146,263
4:13 — 84,122,279,306,
438,606
4:13-16 — 85,321
4:14 — 157,213,544
4:14-16 — 158,165

4:15 — 36,137,279,321,
327
4:16 — 36,306,321
4:17 — 303
4:18 — 32,350,442,605
4:19 — 212,423,546
4:22 — 113,190,213,
222,294,457
4:23 — 86,190,576
4:24 — 86,190,202,340,
442,458,536
4:25 — 74,214
4:25-32 — 165
4:26 — 49,50
4:28 — 637,638
4:30 — 201,545,581
4:31 — 49,50,127,254
4:32 — 50,289,291,376
5 — 328,437
5:1 — 159,328,352,468
5:1-21 — 263
5:2 — 75,421,422,468
5:3 — 74,456
5:5 — 200,354
5:6 — 49,213,246
5:8 — 159,414,415
5:9 — 414,415
5:10 — 9,486
5:11 — 414
5:14 — 571
5:15-21 — 328
5:16 — 255,578,598
5:17 — 287,605
5:18 — 212,238,278,628
5:19 — 496,577
5:21 — 437,584
5:21-33 — 142
5:22 — 584
5:22-33 — 137,**328**
5:22-6:9 — 263
5:23 — 165,327
5:24 — 165,437,584
5:25 — **328**,437
5:25-30 — 437
5:26 — 172,328,621,634
5:27 — 128,**328**
5:28 — 437,456
5:29 — **329**
5:29-33 — 438
5:32 — 452
5:33 — 437,523
6:1 — 459
6:1-4 — 267
6:2 — 343
6:4 — 20,156,159,601,
619
6:5 — 523,551,553,570
6:6 — 523,548,551,553
6:7 — 523,551,553
6:8 — 295,551,553
6:9 — 295
6:10-18 — 544
6:11 — 74,**544**

6:12 — 27,74,90,219,
254,255,287,
294,577,639
6:13 — 5,74,255
6:16 — 255,511
6:17 — 634
6:18 — 499,598,620
6:19 — 452
6:20 — 455
6:21 — 260,552
6:24 — 352

Philippians

1:1 — 295,471,551,552,
554
1:2 — 480
1:3 — 596
1:4 — 362
1:5 — 276,309
1:6 — 184,211
1:7 — 185,441
1:8 — 25,180
1:9 — 7
1:10 — 128,211
1:11 — 312,496
1:14 — 19,246
1:15 — 249
1:16 — 38,259
1:17 — 38
1:19 — 499
1:20 — 135,193,558
1:21 — 411
1:22 — 160
1:23 — 222
1:24 — 456
1:25 — 122,362
1:26 — 6,362
1:29 — 476
2 — 86
2:1 — 25,180,276
2:1-11 — 86
2:2 — 105,181,362,422,
441
2:3 — 38,188,259,347,
441,585,609
2:4 — 347,585
2:5 — 86,441,442
2:5-8 — 347
2:5-11 — 77
2:6 — 45,188,249,554
2:6-11 — 417
2:7 — 351,551,554
2:8 — 64,65,463
2:9-11 — 45,418
2:10 — 241
2:10-11 — 67,312
2:12 — 65,86,462,463
2:13 — 19,86,463
2:14 — 71,86
2:15 — 86,128,159,302
2:16 — 86,211,635

2:17 — 86,122,443,468, 552
2:20 — 57,58
2:22 — 155,159,551
2:25 — 443,456,552,597
2:27 — 331,475
2:28 — 57
2:29 — 362
2:30 — 443,552
3 — 86
3:1-11 — 536
3:2 — 125,254
3:3 — 168,552,640
3:3-6 — 184
3:5 — 338
3:6 — 359
3:8 — 387
3:9 — 85,105,122
3:10 — 185,276, 476,**529**,583
3:11 — 84,**529**
3:11-16 — 85
3:13 — 188,288
3:15 — 86,438,441,442, 530,597
3:16 — 84,441,538
3:17 — 478
3:18 — 206
3:19 — 68,241,441,558
3:20 — 32,168
3:21 — 136,185,312,584
4 — 624
4:1 — 362
4:2 — 441
4:3 — 641
4:5 — 303
4:6 — 57,58,596
4:7 — 442
4:8 — 496,523,596
4:9 — 58,256,480
4:10 — 441
4:12 — 200
4:14-19 — 353
4:15 — 309
4:17 — 10,321
4:18 — 8,9,75,468,486

Colossians

1 — 630
1:2 — 480
1:3 — 596
1:4 — 117,122
1:5 — 345,602,631
1:6 — 606,631
1:7 — 260,552,631
1:9 — 63,107,355,605
1:9-12 — 387
1:9-14 — 628
1:10 — 106,107,324, 605,630,640
1:11 — 311,583
1:12 — 268,380,414

1:13 — 90,217,268,380, 414,639
1:13-17 — 205
1:14 — 290,639
1:15 — 282,351
1:15-20 — 137,163,278
1:15-23 — 603
1:16 — 90,202
1:18 — 112,282,327
1:19 — 278,486
1:20 — 133,205,514
1:21 — 32,112,248,255, 421,442,514
1:22 — 14,128,129,135, 384,410
1:23 — 122,250,552
1:24 — **25**
1:25 — 552
1:26 — 26,302,452
1:27 — 312,344,452
1:28 — 20,619
2 — 45
2:2 — 181,355,422,452, 605
2:3 — 601
2:4 — 72
2:5 — 122,471
2:7 — 6,122
2:8 — 152,213
2:9 — 239,278,384
2:9-19 — 608
2:9-23 — 384
2:10 — 45,93,239,278, 327
2:11 — 45
2:12 — 103,122
2:13 — 289
2:14 — 151
2:15 — 84,90
2:16 — 275,365
2:16-19 — 167
2:16-23 — 278
2:17 — 519
2:18 — 76,230,347,442, 519,552
2:19 — 137,138,327,418
2:20 — 639
2:20-23 — 152,340
2:21 — 600
2:22 — 64,105,483
2:23 — 64,80,347,546, 609,630
3:1 — 324,532
3:1-4 — 45
3:1-4:1 — 384
3:2 — 441,442
3:4 — 65,311,312
3:5 — 254,423,477
3:5-11 — 341
3:6 — 49
3:7 — 615
3:8 — 49,50,254,430
3:9 — 214,294,457,517

3:10 — 202,214,352, 412,432,458
3:10-12 — 293
3:11 — 293,295,551
3:12 — 25,180,267,303, 376
3:12-14 — 341
3:12-15 — 263,481
3:12-17 — 422
3:13 — 107,289
3:13-18 — 631
3:14 — 137,606
3:15 — 150
3:16 — 20,239,496,577
3:18 — 584,631
3:19 — 127,287
3:20 — 9,159,486
3:21 — 159
3:22 — 551,553,554
3:25 — 640
4:1 — 295,336,551
4:3 — 452
4:4 — 455
4:5 — 518,598
4:6 — 455,539
4:7 — 260,552
4:11 — 251,380
4:12 — 438,551
4:17 — 552

1 Thessalonians

1 — 45
1:2 — 596
1:3 — 122,247,345,520, 637,422
1:4 — 160
1:5 — 80
1:6 — 7,8,352,362,514
1:8 — 117,122
1:9 — 349,551,554
1:10 — 49,50,217,337
1:13 — 335
1:19 — 66
2:2 — 355
2:3 — 61,213
2:3-12 — 602
2:6 — 94
2:7 — 159,375
2:7-12 — 592
2:8 — 316
2:9 — 316,637
2:10 — 340
2:11 — 159,243
2:12 — 246,311,312, 380,640
2:13 — 514,596
2:14 — 165,352
2:15 — 450
2:16 — 49,50
2:17 — 222,243,598
2:19 — 362
2:20 — 362

3:1 — 596
3:2 — 122,552
3:3 — 25,316,594
3:4 — 483,484
3:5-7 — 122
3:9 — 362
3:10 — 122
3:12 — 6,321
3:13 — 66
4 — 507,571
4:1 — 455
4:3 — 7
4:5 — 477,422
4:6 — 143,510,619,640
4:8 — 519
4:9 — 166,422
4:10 — 422
4:11 — 38,637
4:12 — 523
4:13 — 344,350,447
4:13-15 — 571
4:13-18 — 66
4:14 — 337,528
4:16 — 337,529
4:17 — 30,173
4:18 — 529
5:1 — 598
5:2 — 211
5:3 — 434
5:5 — 414,459
5:6 — 571
5:7 — 238,459,571
5:9 — 49,50,68
5:10 — 571
5:11 — 145
5:12-13 — 404
5:12-14 — 20,619
5:14 — 246
5:15 — 254,640
5:17 — 500
5:19 — 281,511,581
5:20 — 223
5:22 — 7,255
5:23 — 480,543
5:24 — 260

2 Thessalonians

1:2 — 480
1:3 — 122,321,456
1:4 — 122,134,165,594
1:5 — 380,476
1:5-10 — 611
1:6 — 248,371
1:6-10 — 50,51
1:7 — 248,280,337,371, 526,530,531
1:8 — 280,316,371,385, 462,510
1:9 — 112,311,510
1:10 — 38,67
1:11 — 122,150,500
2 — 56,544

2:1-2 — 66
2:1-12 — 56
2:3 — 56,213,399,530,
531
2:3-12 — 66
2:4 — 56,640
2:6 — 530,531,598
2:7 — 452,626
2:7-8 — 399
2:8 — 66,530,531,626
2:9-10 — 445
2:10 — 193
2:11 — 213
2:12 — 626
2:13 — 112,160,213,456
2:14 — 150,312
2:17 — 246
2:19 — 205
3:2 — 217,255,626,640
3:3 — 255,260
3:5 — 422
3:6 — 143
3:6-15 — 638
3:7 — 286,352,455
3:8 — 305,459,637
3:9 — 286,352
3:10 — 636,637
3:11 — 147,637
3:12 — 633,637
3:14 — 80,558
3:15 — 20,143

1 Timothy

1:2 — 159,268,440,480,
603
1:2 — 159
1:4 — 71
1:5 — 187,570
1:7 — 442
1:8 — 398
1:9 — 315,395,398,626
1:10 — 23,563
1:11 — 316
1:12 — 552
1:13 — 350,563,604,612
1:15 — 541
1:16 — 219,440,478,513
1:17 — 28,352,440
1:18 — 159,268,440
1:19 — 187,519
2 — 632
2:1 — 91
2:2 — 91,94,410,563
2:3 — 9
2:4 — 602
2:6 — 455,598
2:7 — 60,122,303
2:8 — 71,340
2:10 — 19,315,456
2:11 — 584,632,633
2:12 — 94,563
2:13 — 632

2:14 — 213,632
2:15 — 122
2:24 — 455
3 — 244,632
3:1 — 222
3:1-7 — 403
3:1-12 — 26
3:2 — 127,455,459,523,
592
3:3 — 303,304,
446,**612**,623
3:4 — 156,159,263,584
3:5 — 165,263
3:6 — 260,543
3:7 — 355,455
3:8 — 404,523
3:8-13 — 430,552
3:9 — 122,187,452
3:10 — 127,552,594
3:11 — 404,523,632,640
3:12 — 159,263,552
3:13 — 80,552
3:15 — 165,263,455
3:16 — 452
4:1 — 122,213,218,556,
598
4:1-5 — 7
4:3 — 7
4:3-4 — 202
4:4-5 — 556
4:6 — 122,552
4:7 — 315
4:8 — 552,570,609,640
4:10 — 355,637
4:11-16 — 403
4:12 — 27,113,256,603,
642
4:13 — 603
4:14 — 305,324
4:16 — 620
5 — 263,500,626
5:1 — 166,246
5:1-16 — 493
5:2 — 166
5:4 — 9,159,315
5:6 — 487
5:7 — 127,523
5:8 — 122,343
5:9 — 26
5:10 — 19,26,620
5:11 — 222,546,626
5:12 — 519,626
5:13 — 147,426,455,626
5:14 — 355,626
5:16 — 309
5:17 — 236,309
5:18 — 309
5:19 — 14,105
5:20 — 189,619
5:23 — 331,628
6:1 — 523,551,553,641
6:2 — 523,551,553
6:3 — 563
6:3-10 — 625

6:4 — 71,72,249,255,
568,606
6:5 — 190,442,596
6:6-8 — 189
6:9 — 287
6:10 — 122,254,422,446
6:11 — 122,247,303
6:12 — 122,150
6:14 — 127,523
6:15 — 598
6:17 — 76,625,639
6:18 — 19,558,624,625
6:19 — 28,601,625
6:20 — 220,315

2 Timothy

1:2 — 159,268,440,480
1:3 — 187,552
1:4 — 362
1:5 — 484,570
1:5 — 122
1:6 — 305,324
1:7 — 455
1:8 — 558
1:9 — 64,112,541
1:10 — 64,66,224,352,
530
1:11 — 68,303,455
1:12 — 68,558
1:13 — 122,478,563,591
1:14 — 220,239
1:16 — 558
1:18 — 552
2:1 — 159,268
2:2 — 523,592
2:3 — 247
2:4 — 410
2:5 — 205
2:6 — 455
2:7 — 442
2:10 — 160,312
2:11-13 — 220
2:13 — 260
2:14 — 72,403,609,619
2:14-19 — 71
2:15 — 70
2:16 — 315
2:18 — 122,224
2:19 — 3,545,626,638
2:19-21 — 224
2:21 — 438
2:22 — 282,480,592
2:23 — 287
2:24 — 375,455,552
2:25 — 190,303,304
2:26 — 152,294
2:33 — 72
3:1 — 598
3:1-13 — 211
3:2 — 76,134,446,462,
623
3:3 — 317

3:4 — 486
3:7 — 17
3:8 — 122,442,470,519
3:10 — 247,403,592,603
3:11 — 217,592,603
3:12 — 484
3:13 — 213,255
3:15 — 26,117,122,340,
545,619,630
3:16 — 190,229,544,
592,601
4:1 — 67,364
4:2 — 190,619
4:3 — 190,563,598
4:5 — 190,251,484,552
4:6 — 598
4:7 — 121,122
4:8 — 205,364
4:10 — 3,639
4:16 — 3
4:11 — 552
4:14 — 254
4:15 — 470
4:16 — 3
4:17 — 217,484
4:18 — 217,541,255
4:19 — 429
4:22 — 576

Titus

1 — 244
1:1 — 160,552
1:2 — 112,344,345
1:3 — 112,598
1:4 — 122,159,268,480,
603
1:5 — 69,244
1:5-9 — 403
1:6 — 14,127,159,264
1:7 — 20,49,76,127,**612**
1:8 — 340,546
1:9 — 189,470,563
1:11 — 224
1:13 — 122,189
1:15 — 186,190,215,442
1:16 — 6
2:1 — 456,554,591
2:2 — 247,404,640
2:3 — 317,552,626
2:4 — 156,437,626
2:5 — 584,626
2:7 — 352
2:8 — 563,558
2:9 — 9,486,552,553,
584
2:10 — 553
2:11 — 64,66
2:11-13 — 229
2:11-14 — 66
2:12 — 27,477
2:13 — 66,311,320,344
2:14 — 517,626

2:15 — 189
3:1 — 462,584
3:2 — 303,304
3:3 — 213,249,254,287,
326,430,477,
486,551
3:4 — 64,66,375
3:5 — 105,440,541
3:7 — 344
3:8 — 117,638
3:9 — 72,287
3:10 — 20,619
3:14 — 456
3:15 — 122,420
3:16 — 64

Philemon

2 — 263
3 — 480
4 — 520,596
5-6 — 122
6 — 276,309,606
7 — 25,362
7-12 — 180
8 — 61
9 — 61
10 — 61,159,268
12 — 8,25
13 — 552
14 — 288,456
16 — 552
17 — 8
18 — 456
20 — 25,180
25 — 576

Hebrews

1-2 — 351
1:1 — 237,267
1:2 — 28,68,211,237
1:3 — 45,138,311,324,
336,351,532,
573,634
1:4 — 125,138
1:4-14 — 45
1:5 — 45,138
1:6 — 45,282,639
1:7 — 45,281,443,552
1:8 — 45
1:9 — 55,626
1:10 — 112
1:10-12 — 46
1:11 — 458
1:13 — 46,324,532
1:14 — 46,354,552
2:1 — 86,455
2:1-4 — 619
2:2 — 46,322,510,371
2:2-4 — 86
2:3 — 185,320,322

2:5 — 46,584
2:8 — 584
2:9 — 78,410,587
2:9-16 — 410
2:10 — 87,312,456,482
2:11 — 558
2:12 — 86,496
2:13 — 158
2:14 — 158,224
2:14-18 — 432
2:15 — 408
2:16 — 46,431
2:17 — 83,260,456
2:18 — 5,593
3 — 513,526
3-4 — 598,613
3:1 — 60,442,558,597
3:1-6 — 145
3:3-4 — 144
3:6 — 193,145,322,345
3:7-11 — 463
3:7-19 — 513
3:7-4:13 — 619
3:8 — 594
3:9 — 594
3:10 — 81,213,302
3:10-19 — 81,302
3:11 — 49,50,461
3:12 — 3,115,255,463
3:13 — 213
3:14 — 322,558
3:15 — 613,636
3:19 — 5,333,463
4 — 70,256,526
4:1-11 — 463
4:2 — 122,333,609,636
4:3 — 49,50,202,**280**,
461,636
4:9-11 — 526
4:11 — 243,**261**,242
4:12 — 86,576,577,596
4:12-13 — 86
4:13 — 12,453
4:14 — 122,320
4:14-5:10 — 503
4:15 — 440
4:16 — 7,69,128,184,
270,279,320,
439,440,499,
609
5:1 — 304
5:1-10 — 184
5:2 — 81,213,350
5:3 — 456
5:6 — 471
5:7-10 — 463
5:9 — 463,482
5:10 — 471
5:11-14 — 286,321
5:12 — 456
5:13 — 157,158
5:14 — 254,438,601
6:1 — 117
6:1-3 — 261

6:1-8 — 10
6:1-12 — 620
6:2 — 102
6:4 — 261,304,352,587
6:5 — 28,261,587,634
6:6 — 206,**261**,522
6:8 — 208
6:9 — **10**,261
6:10 — 288,552
6:11 — 80,222,345
6:12 — 122,352
6:13-20 — 185
6:14 — 321
6:16 — 71,461
6:17 — 195,322,461,
511,627
6:18 — 322,352,461
6:19 — 41,321,461
6:20 — 471
7 — 503
7:3 — **271**
7:4 — 597
7:10 — 41
7:11 — 105,394,471
7:11-28 — 36
7:12 — 394,456
7:16 — 41,105,283
7:17 — 471
7:18 — 178,621
7:19 — 125,482
7:20 — 461
7:21 — 461,471
7:22 — 125,322,461
7:23-8:2 — 77
7:24 — 528
7:25 — 5,355,503,528,
541
7:26 — 340,355,456
7:26-8:2 — 503
7:27 — 456,637
7:28 — 461,482
8-10 — 468
8:1 — 324,336,532
8:1-13 — 357
8:2 — 443,543,552,603
8:3 — 304,456
8:4 — 304
8:5 — 336,468,478,619,
640
8:6 ← 125,443,552
8:7 — 640
8:8 — 458
8:10 — 178,394,442,503
8:12 — 468,520
8:13 — 225,458
9 — 73,83
9:1 — 543,552
9:1-14 — 73
9:1-24 — 36
9:1-10:18 — 290
9:2 — 145,543
9:3 — 543
9:4 — 175
9:5 — 73,83

9:6 — 552
9:7 — 350
9:8 — 69,543
9:9 — 5,83,186,304,
394,468,552,
598,609,640
9:9-14 — 36
9:10 — 172,468,598
9:12 — 133,251,468,
517,543,626
9:13 — 468,543
9:13-22 — 195
9:14 — 128,133,172,
187,468,504,
552
9:15 — 195,504
9:15-22 — 468
9:15-28 — 133
9:16 — 198,456,628
9:17 — 198,287,351,628
9:21 — 443,552
9:22 — 290
9:23 — 125,456
9:23-10:14 — 83
9:24 — 133,336,543
9:25 — 133,543
9:26 — 28,29,133,455,
468,504,639
9:27 — 29,409,528
9:28 — 29,68,290,468
10 — 569
10:1 — 394,468,482
10:2 — 187
10:2-14 — 394
10:3 — 186
10:4 — 352
10:5 — 222
10:6 — 486
10:8 — 222,486
10:9 — 450
10:10 — 135,187,469,
504,611
10:11 — 443,552
10:11-18 — 469
10:12 — 324,532
10:14 — 187,290,469,
482
10:15-18 — 394
10:16 — 198,442
10:17 — 187,198,290,
292,626
10:18 — 290,504
10:19 — 70,184,543
10:19-22 — 70
10:19-39 — 620
10:22 — 80,122,172,
323,570,620,
621,255
10:23 — 80,260,345
10:24 — 19,80,167,188,
422,442
10:25 — 167
10:28 — 180,519

10:29 — **355**,510,543,
        581,596
10:30 — 364
10:31 — 260
10:33 — 355
10:35 — 80,184,187,484
10:36 — 184,187,484
10:38 — 122,486
11 — 122
11:1 — 80,122,173
11:2 — 43
11:3 — 28,29,122,442,
        605,634,
11:4 — 124,304
11:4-40 — 122
11:5 — 486
11:6 — 122,455,486,546
11:7 — 72,145,535,619
11:8-12 — 114
11:8-16 — 32
11:9 — 31
11:11 — 260,598
11:13 — 20,31
11:15 — 598
11:16 — 558
11:17 — 594
11:23 — 158
11:25 — 160
11:25-29 — 155
11:26 — 355
11:27 — 150
11:28 — 96,282,600
11:34 — 511
11:37 — 483
11:38 — 213
11:40 — 125
12 — 127,129
12:2 — 206,324,513,
        532,538
12:4-13 — 228
12:5 — 288,601
12:7-10 — 127
12:7-11 — 269
12:8 — 601,603
12:9 — 268,523,584
12:10 — 229,596
12:11 — 127,229,475,
        601,325
12:12 — 127,229,526
12:13 — 127,330
12:14 — 215,242,243,
        480
12:15 — 127,128,
        215,**232**
12:16 — 315
12:17 — 519,546
12:18 — 280,600
12:19 — 634
12:20 — 600
12:22 — 337,360
12:23 — 282,336,364
12:24 — 458
12:25 — 619
12:26 — 275,556

12:27 — 275,556
12:28 — 275,379,486,
        552,557
12:29 — 275,280
13 — 404
13:1 — 143
13:2 — 288
13:4 — 24,364
13:5 — 3,446,496
13:6 — 137
13:7 — 113,122,286,
        352,404
13:8 — 28
13:9 — 31,322,609
13:10 — 36,552,640
13:11 — 36,135,146,543
13:12 — 36,476
13:13 — 36,355
13:16 — 276,288,309,
        486
13:17 — 12,94,362,462,
        584
13:18 — 222
13:19 — 527
13:20 — 320,480,560,
        617
13:21 — 9,486
13:22 — 246

James

1:1 — 552,554
1:2 — 121,362,594
1:3 — 121,484
1:4 — 121,438,484
1:5 — 121,355,499,500
1:6 — 121,236
1:7 — 121,236,597
1:8 — **236**
1:9 — 77
1:9-11 — 155
1:10 — 77
1:11 — 32
1:12 — 70,205,594
1:13 — 254,593
1:14 — 222,423,593
1:15 — 222,593
1:16 — 81,213
1:17 — 268,307
1:18 — 161,635
1:19 — 49,50
1:19-25 — 121
1:20 — 49,50,222
1:21 — 254,303,430,
        439,574
1:23 — 442
1:24 — 288,442
1:25 — 333
1:26 — 121,213,519,552
1:27 — 121,487,519,
        552,639
2:1 — 311
2:1-7 — 493

2:1-13 — 625
2:3 — 86
2:4 — 71,236,596
2:5 — 354,380,623
2:6 — 193,355
2:8 — 456
2:10 — 323
2:11 — 450
2:14 — 19,121,374
2:14-16 — 493
2:14-19 — 374
2:14-26 — 121
2:15 — 144,453
2:16 — 144
2:17 — 10
2:19 — 121
2:20-26 — 19,374,536
2:22 — 121
2:23 — 297,420
2:24 — **373**
3:1-12 — 121
3:2 — 483,584
3:3 — 462
3:5 — 599
3:6 — 337,487,599
3:7 — 454,455
3:8 — 254,599
3:9 — 496
3:10 — 496
3:11 — 127
3:13 — 113,303,439,606
3:13-18 — 121
3:14 — 38,127,259
3:15 — 241,454,576
3:16 — 38,259
3:17 — 188,303,570
3:18 — 325
4:1 — 248,486,618
4:1-6 — 121
4:2 — 248,618
4:3 — 248,486,640
4:4 — 297,420,639
4:5 — 239,249,576,596
4:6 — 76,249,470
4:7 — 282,584
4:8 — 236
4:9 — 447
4:11 — 144,**365**
4:12 — 364,**365**
4:13 — 147
4:13-17 — 147
4:14 — 63,224,483
4:15 — 628
4:16 — 134
5:1-6 — 623,625
5:5 — 487
5:6 — 355,470
5:7-8 — 66
5:7-11 — 121
5:11 — 180
5:12 — 461
5:13 — 193,496
5:13-18 — 121
5:14 — 55,470,564

5:15 — 564
5:14-16 — 330
5:15 — 55
5:19 — 81,189,250
5:20 — 189,199,213,250

1 Peter

1:1 — 30,97,160
1:2 — 160,321
1:3 — 344,440,496
1:3-9 — 476
1:4 — 352,354
1:5 — 122,530,531,598
1:6 — 66,455,476,594
1:6-9 — 362
1:7 — 67,281,312,476,
        496,530,531
1:8 — 67
1:10 — 546
1:11 — 475,598
1:12 — 530,531,552
1:13 — 67,442,530,531
1:13-25 — 476
1:14 — 159,185,350
1:15 — 113,150,340
1:16 — 340
1:17 — 31,294
1:18 — 113,517
1:19 — 128,133,388,517
1:20 — 160,202,530
1:21 — 117,122
1:22 — 143,166,570
1:23 — 139,352,412,
        627,635
1:25 — 634
1:29 — 388
1:36 — 388
2-3 — 437
2:1 — 213,249,254,430,
        476,507
2:1-11 — 32
2:2 — 321
2:3 — 376
2:4 — 519
2:5 — 9,145,503,577
2:6 — 151,558
2:7 — 145,519
2:9 — 123,340,414,441,
        503
2:10 — 441
2:11 — 31,283,340
2:12 — 15,113,211,254,
        340,640
2:13 — 91,92,94,402,
        436,476,584
2:13-15 — 91,476
2:13-23 — 91
2:14 — 91,254,402,496,
        640
2:15 — 287,350,628
2:16 — 254,295,296,
        430,552

2:16-18 — 91
2:17 — 274,342,436,523
2:18 — 303,523,552,
    553,584
2:19 — 475,476,640
2:21 — 150,476
2:21-23 — 439
2:21-3:6 — 328
2:22 — 213
2:23 — 355,619
2:24 — 135
2:25 — 81,213,244,471
3:1 — 113,436,437
3:1-7 — 263
3:2 — 113
3:3-5 — 109
3:4 — 303,304,352,436,
    439,576
3:6 — 159,437
3:7 — 188,437,523
3:8-13 — 476
3:9 — 150,355
3:9-12 — 254
3:10 — 213,599
3:12 — 417
3:13 — 254,352
3:13-17 — 345
3:14 — 476
3:15 — 303,345,417,
    439,523
3:16 — 113,187,254,
    558,640
3:17 — 125,254
3:18 — 135,475,476,477
3:20 — 72,145,477,621
3:21 — 104,187,621
3:22 — 324,417
4 — 86
4:1 — 86,135,596
4:2 — 86,104,410,477,
    554,628,639
4:3 — 213,238,410,546,
    628
4:4 — 596
4:5 — 12,364
4:8 — 199,422
4:10 — 19,20,305,306,
    552,555
4:11 — 496,552,555
4:12 — 31,594
4:13 — 67,311,530,531
4:14 — 355,476
4:15 — 254,476,640
4:16 — 163,476,477,558
4:17 — 263,598
4:19 — 260,476,532
5:1 — 61,67,311,530,
    531,558
5:2 — 560,623
5:3 — 256,560
5:4 — 205,506
5:5 — 76,470
5:6 — 598
5:7 — 57,58

5:8 — 31,225,415
5:9 — 122
5:10 — 150,477,527
5:12 — 404
5:13 — 97,268,404
5:22-23 — 328
5:25-27 — 328
5:29 — 329

2 Peter

1:1 — 552
1:2 — 321
1:4 — 190,454,455
1:5 — 242,243
1:5-8 — 261
1:6 — 546
1:8 — 321
1:9 — 172
1:10 — 261,322
1:11 — 251
1:12 — 250
1:12-15 — 520
1:13 — 597
1:15 — 243
1:16 — 286
1:17 — 311,486
1:19 — 322
1:20 — 606
2:1 — 438
2:2 — 286
2:3 — 147
2:4 — 45,337,414
2:5 — 42,285,457
2:7 — 113,213,217,546
2:8 — 213,256,626
2:9 — 211,217,496,594
2:10 — 76,94,137
2:11 — 14
2:12 — 53,350,454,606
2:13 — 213,486
2:14 — 13,24,159,601
2:15 — 98,213,286,626
2:16 — 640
2:17 — 414
2:18 — 61,213,246,296,
    546
2:19 — 294,296,471,552
2:20 — 471
2:22 — 620
3:1 — 442
3:2 — 634
3:3 — 211,606
3:4 — 66,112,202,571
3:5-7 — 66,635
3:6 — 202,285
3:7 — 202,211,375
3:9 — 606
3:10 — 146,211,225
3:11 — 113,129,455
3:11-13 — 66,212
3:13 — 458
3:14 — 128,129,242,243

3:14-16 — 60
3:15 — 545,630
3:16 — 606
3:17 — 32,213,262
3:18 — 262,321

1 John

1 — 602
1:1 — 112,411,600,635
1:1-3 — 595
1:2 — 63,411,635
1:3 — 87,276,309
1:4 — 87,181,362
1:5 — 414
1:5-2:2 — 178,183,569
1:5-7 — 183,415
1:6 — 276,367,603
1:7 — 133,276,290,603
1:8 — 83,183,213,290,
    483,603
1:9 — 83,183,260,290,
    371,415,483
1:10 — 183
1:18 — 56
2-3 — 412
2:1 — 84,159,183,290,
    570
2:2 — 83,84,183,290
2:3 — 463
2:3-8 — 178
2:6 — 455,456,548
2:7 — 458
2:8 — 458
2:8-10 — 415
2:9-11 — 143,178,326
2:12 — 159
2:13 — 112,158,255,471
2:14 — 112,158,255,471
2:15 — 422
2:15-17 — 639
2:16 — 134,222,410,
    423,639
2:18 — 56,158,211
2:20 — 55
2:20-23 — 385
2:20-27 — 178
2:22 — 56,220
2:23 — 17,220
2:25 — 55
2:26 — 81,213
2:27 — 55,193
2:28 — 66,159,558
3:1 — 136,159,269,312,
    320,528,639
3:1-10 — 178
3:2 — 27,136,159,227,
    312,344,352,
    528,530,574
3:3 — 27,344,345
3:4 — 178,399,626
3:4-9 — 570
3:6 — 139

3:7 — 81,159,213
3:8 — **224**
3:9 — 139,224
3:10 — 159
3:11-15 — 165
3:12 — 254,255
3:13 — 38,639
3:14-15 — 326
3:16 — 456
3:16-18 — 422,493
3:16-20 — 625
3:17 — 25,144,180
3:18 — 159,599
3:20 — 182,183,640
3:21 — 182,183,184,640
3:22 — 463,486,500,501
3:24 — 385,463
4:1 — 507,594
4:3 — 56
4:4 — 159,219
4:6 — 213
4:7 — 139,274,385
4:7-15 — 56
4:7-21 — 165
4:8 — 274
4:9 — 274,421
4:9-15 — 573
4:10 — 83,84,274,421
4:11 — 466
4:13 — 385
4:15 — 17,274,385
4:16 — 184,274,385,421
4:17 — 184,510,639
4:18 — 274,482,510
4:19 — 119,421
5 — 70
5:1 — 139,421
5:2 — 139,159
5:3 — 442,463
5:4 — 122,139,471,611,
    639
5:5 — 611,639
5:8 — **30**,621
5:10-12 — 412
5:11-12 — 80
5:11-13 — 573
5:14 — 69,80,499,500,
    628
5:15 — 500
5:16 — 499,564
5:17 — 640
5:18 — 139,255,385
5:19 — 90,255,385,639
5:20 — 385,442,605

2 John

1 — 159
2 — 440
3 — 480
4 — 159,362
5 — 458
6 — 615

7 — 16,56,213
8 — 278
11 — 255,626
12 — 362
13 — 159,362,615

3 John

3 — 362,615
4 — 159,362,615
5 — 31
8 — 456
10 — 86,255
11 — 254,286,352
14 — 297,420

Jude

1 — 269,552
2 — 321,440
3 — 122,456
4 — 212,221,438,546
6 — 45,414
7 — 281
8 — 94,487,519
9 — 14,619
10 — 53,454,605,606
11 — 98,213
12 — 173
13 — 414,558
15 — 189
16 — 38
17 — 634
19 — 454,576
22 — 236
23 — 487
24 — 5,128,375

Revelation

1:1 — 455,530,531
1:3 — 598
1:5 — 133,260,282,503,
        620
1:6 — 380
1:7 — 446
1:14 — 280
1:16 — 258
1:17 — 281
1:20 — 452
2 — 44
2:2 — 254,594,626
2:7 — 240
2:8 — 281
2:10 — 205,594

2:11 — 240
2:14 — 98,99
2:17 — 240
2:19 — 552
2:20 — 213
2:20-22 — 23
2:23 — 159
2:29 — 240
3 — 44
3:2 — 31,620
3:5 — 151
3:9 — 17
3:10 — 594,639
3:12 — 360
3:14 — 202
3:18 — 281,558
3:19 — 420
4:1 — 455
4:4 — 245
4:9-11 — 312
4:10 — 245
4:14 — 260
5:5 — 415
5:8 — 245
5:10 — 380,503
5:12-13 — 312,496
6:8 — 286,451
6:15 — 295,552
6:16 — 49
6:17 — 49,211
7 — 545
7:3 — 552
7:8 — 601
7:10 — 123
7:12 — 496
7:15 — 552
7:17 — 151
8:3 — 35
8:5 — 36
8:7-10 — 146
8:11 — 127
9:5 — 29,451
9:11 — 338
9:15 — 451
9:18 — 451
9:20 — 451
10:7 — 452,552
10:9-10 — 127
10:11 — 455
11:2 — 193
11:5 — 451,455
11:8 — 135
11:9 — 97,135
11:10 — 304
11:13 — 451
11:16 — 245
11:18 — 49,552,598
11:19 — 73
12:1 — 64,65

12:2 — 29,65,475
12:3 — 205
12:4-5 — 159
12:9 — 42,81,213,457,
        572,639
12:11 — 14
12:12 — 50
12:12-14 — 598
12:17 — 50
13 — 56
13:1 — 205
13:3 — 38,639
13:9 — 240
13:10 — 451,455
13:14 — 213
13:15 — 451
13:16 — 295,552
13:18 — 442
14:4 — 285,286
14:5 — 128,213
14:7 — 312
14:8 — 50,97,286
14:9 — 286
14:10 — 50,206
14:11 — 29
14:13 — 286
14:15 — 325
14:17-19 — 97
14:19 — 50
15-16 — 371
15-18 — 97
15:3 — 552
15:4 — 340
15:8 — 311
15:14 — 530
15:17 — 50
16:1 — 50
16:2 — 254,255
16:5 — 340
16:10 — 29,475
16:11 — 475
16:14 — 211,639
16:15 — 453
16:16 — 73,338
16:17 — 30
16:19 — 50
17:1 — 97
17:1-16 — 23
17:4-5 — 6
17:5-7 — 97,452
17:6-8 — 38
17:8 — 639
17:9 — 442
17:10 — 455
17:16 — 146,453
17:17 — 634
18 — 88
18:3 — 50,97,546
18:5 — 286

18:7 — 29
18:8 — 146
18:9 — 146,446
18:10 — 29
18:11 — 447
18:15 — 29,204,447
18:18 — 146
18:19 — 447
18:21 — 612
18:23 — 81,213
19:1 — 123
19:2 — 552
19:4 — 245
19:5 — 496,552
19:6-9 — 438
19:7-9 — 142
19:11 — 260
19:12 — 205
19:13 — 101
19:14 — 286
19:15 — 150
19:18 — 295,552
19:20 — 147,213,337
19:21 — 451
20:1-6 — 507
20:2 — 42,438,457
20:3 — 213,455
20:6 — 503
20:7-10 — 544
20:8 — 213
20:9 — 438
20:10 — 147,213
20:10-15 — 337
20:11-15 — 528
20:12 — 364
20:13 — 337
20:14 — 281,337,409
21 — 507
21-22 — 337
21:1 — 241,336,458
21:2 — 337,360,458
21:4 — 151,446,475
21:5 — 458
21:6 — 112,305
21:8 — 6,24
21:10 — 360
21:11 — 311
21:14 — 60
21:23 — 311
21:27 — 6
22 — 545
22:3 — 552
22:6 — 455,552
22:10 — 598
22:11 — 640
22:13 — 112,281
22:15 — 24,420
22:17 — 305
22:18 — 619